ROYAL NAVY ROLL OF HONOUR

Between the Wars

1918-1939

Part 1 - by Name, Part 2 - by Date and Ship

by

Don Kindell

including Dominion Navies, Royal Naval Division and Royal Marines

taken from Admiralty Death Ledgers, Admiralty Communiqués and other Official sources

Foreword by

Captain Christopher Page, Royal Navy Rtd
Head of the Naval Historical Branch of the Naval Staff

edited by Gordon Smith

Naval-History.Net

"To all those who have gone before, in war and peace,

protecting our homelands, heroes all."

First published 2009

© Don Kindell 2009

ISBN 978-0-578-02790-6

Published by Naval-History.Net, Penarth, UK
www.naval-history.net – available as searchable download

Main cover photographs:
Leading Seaman John Turner, lost in Thetis, only photograph extant, courtesy Joyce Bentley
HMS Thetis, rescue and salvage attempts, courtesy CyberHeritage
Background - Bristol Channel in a near gale

FOREWORD

by

Christopher Page, Naval Historical Branch, Portsmouth

When I took over as Head of the Naval Historical Branch of the Royal Navy nearly ten years ago, I was very surprised to learn that RN casualties for both World Wars had not been fully documented. Every casualty search entailed a look through some or all of the documents in the National Archive; casualty lists of the time, some of which were still retained under the Data Protection Act; a trawl through the data base of the Commonwealth War Graves Commission; or research into the various War Memorial books. Even then, a researcher could not be sure that he had covered every source.

I quickly discovered, however, that a US researcher was some way down the track in listing all RN casualties, staring with World Wars One and Two, but moving on to cover all RN dead from 1914 virtually up to the present. In this task he was assisted principally by the indefatigable, greatly missed, Arnold Hague, and my staff, particularly Mike McAloon. The painstaking work and attention to detail of Don and Arnold have been absolutely crucial to the eventual fruition of this major and invaluable record.

Don Kindell's contribution to Royal Navy history has been enormous over a very long period. An American, he became fascinated by the RN over 40 years ago and has devoted a large part of his life to this work. All has been done with meticulous attention to detail and accuracy. This labour of love had daunted all others by its sheer scale. The task involved the detailed investigation of the records of more than 120,000 individuals, and has formed an authoritative data base that is daily of invaluable use by the Naval Historical Branch, the Casualty Section, and Veterans' Departments of the Ministry of Defence. It also provides a priceless permanent record for all naval researchers, and is often used by the Imperial War Museum and the Commonwealth War Graves Commission.

Some of this information has already been made available on Gordon Smith's web site Naval-History.Net, and I pay a special tribute to Gordon for his efforts in publicising Don's work and making it available.

I would add that Don Kindell's huge achievement is, however, only part of a much wider contribution to British maritime history that includes a comprehensive catalogue of naval events and actions up to the middle of the Second World War. Work is continuing to complete this huge undertaking. In addition, he is in the process of compiling a complete list of RN prisoners of war for World War Two.

This astonishing corpus of work had been achieved over decades and is material that will have lasting benefits. All of this was undertaken with absolutely no thought of personal gain, or expectation of recognition. Indeed most of the substantial financial costs have been borne by himself. For all his self-effacement and reticence, he is known and highly respected around the world for his knowledge and application. I am delighted and honoured to have been asked to write this short Foreword to an invaluable source of reference.

May 2009

INTRODUCTION

by

Don Kindell

My work on the Royal Navy and Royal Marine casualty lists started in the mid 1990s with an interest in Fleet Air Arm officers. Then, while studying the Norwegian campaign of April to June 1940, I came across lists of men killed in ships sunk and damaged, that were not covered by the specific Admiralty Communiqués released when a ship was sunk. From that point, the project grew in all directions to where, today, I am involved in all RN and Dominion (later Commonwealth) casualties from the late nineteenth century to the present. I have extensively used original Admiralty Death Ledgers, Admiralty Communiqués, and numerous official documents held at The National Archives (previously the Public Records Office – PRO) and the Naval Historical Branch (NHB) of the Ministry of Defence. After retirement in 1990 and through to 2006, I made about 25 trips to the UK to research at the NHB and the then PRO, where I made a good many British friends. I have also coordinated my research with the Commonwealth War Graves Commission and Canadian Archives.

Now online, the casualty lists are referred to by naval and family historians and next of kin worldwide. They have also been used to ensure the accuracy of the plaque listing those lost, which was placed on the wreck of battlecruiser HMS Hood, and are now helping the Royal Marine Museum draw up their own lists of RM casualties over the years.

Thanks must go the David Brown, and later Chris Page of the Naval Historical Branch and their staffs, and most of all, to naval historian and author Arnold Hague who was a tremendous help and inspiration.

by

Gordon Smith, Naval-History.Net

The website, www.naval-history.net has been considerably enriched in recent years by the original researches of Don Kindell and it is a particular pleasure to join him in making his casualty lists available as books and downloads. This is the second of a number of volumes covering the period 1914 to the present, and perhaps later going back to the 19th Century, arranged both by Name (Part 1) and by Date/Ship or Unit (Part 2). The Name Lists, in effect, provide the index for the Date Lists – find a name and date of death in Part 1, and then more information on the background to the death in Part 2. This includes type of ship or location of base, whether the ship was lost or damaged, the casualty killed, died of wounds, injuries, illness, or was drowned.

My own father was killed in action with the Royal Navy in 1943. Finding out about him, his ship, the circumstances of his death and his shipmates was a real challenge in the 1980's. Now, through the Internet, and the work of researchers like Don Kindell, it is becoming increasingly easy. Many of us owe him a great debt of gratitude.

Unless otherwise stated all photographs are courtesy of David Page of Navy Photos (NP). Our grateful thanks to all contributors.

Note to readers: Corrections and additions will be gratefully received and incorporated in the main database for later editions. You can email naval-history@ntlworld.com

ABBREVIATIONS

1c – First Class
2c – Second Class
3c – Third Class
Act/ - Acting
Bantie – locally engaged rating
CMB – coastal motor boat
CWO – Commissioned Warrant Officer
(E) - Engineer
FAA – Fleet Air Arm
Krooman - locally engaged rating
ML – motor launch
MMR - Mercantile Marine Reserve
O/P – on passage
PC – Patrol Craft
Py/ - Probationary
Pens – Pensions or Pensioner
QARNNS - Queen Alexander's Royal Naval Nursing Service
RAF – Royal Air Force
RAN – Royal Australian Navy
RFA – Royal Fleet Auxiliary
RFR – Royal Fleet Reserve
RFR A, B, C, IC - RFR A, men in receipt of a life pension from RN; RFR B, men who served in RN but were not in receipt of a pension; RFR C, artisan ratings who have passed through the dockyards as boy apprentices for the RN; RFR IC, Immediate Class, similar to B, but could be called up for service without a Royal Proclamation.
RIM - Royal Indian Marine
RM - Royal Marines
RMA - Royal Marine Artillery
RMB – Royal Marine Band
RME - Royal Marine Engineers
RMLI - Royal Marine Light Infantry
RMP – Royal Marine Police
RN – Royal Navy or Royal Naval
RNAS - Royal Naval Air Service
RND – Royal Naval Division
RNH – Royal Naval Hospital
RNR - Royal Naval Reserve
Rtd – Retired
Seedie - locally engaged rating
Sqn - Squadron
TB – Torpedo Boat
Ty/ - Temporary
Tindal – locally engaged rating
WRNS – Women's Royal Naval service

SUMMARY OF SELECTED CASUALTIES

Every life lost is a tragedy, for those who died and those left behind. Without underestimating the impact of each and every death, these are some of the losses suffered by the Royal Navy in the years between World War 1 and World War 2. All ships listed were lost unless otherwise stated; some of the submarines were salvaged.

1918

THE SPANISH INFLUENZA
The pandemic lasted from approximately July 1918 to April 1919 with a major peak in the UK between September 1918 and January 1919. It can be assumed that the vast majority of illness deaths in these periods were due to the Spanish flu.

* Russian Intervention, 1918-1919

14 October, Cochrane, armoured cruiser (0)
22 November, G.11, submarine (2)
5 December, *Cassandra, light cruiser (11)

1919

1 January, Iolaire, Admiralty yacht (203)
4 February, Penarth, minesweeper (37)
7 February, Erin's Isle, paddle minesweeper (23)
26 April, Hughli, RFA tug (18)
29 April, Frostaxe, Admiralty trawler (9)
4 May, Tryphon, destroyer (0)
5 May, Cupar, minesweeper (0)
21 May, *Emile Nobel, gunboat, damaged in action (5)
4 June, *L.55, submarine (42)
16 June, Kinross, minesweeper (11)
24 June, *Sword Dance, minesweeper (1)
3 July, *Fandango, minesweeper (8)
16 July, *Gentian (6) and *Myrtle (6), fleet sweeping sloops
2 August, Princess Mary II, patrol paddle vessel (0)
18 August, attack on Kronstadt, *3 CMB's lost (8)
27 August, 8, 9 Sept, *Royal Marines (13)
1 September, *Vittoria, destroyer (8)
4 September, *Verulam, destroyer (16)
17 October, *Dragon, light cruiser, damaged by gunfire (9)
18 October, H.41, submarine (0)
31 December, *Catspaw, Admiralty drifter (14)

1920

25 July, IRA attack on Ballygrovane Coastguard Station (2)

1921

20 January, K.5, submarine (57)

1922

23 March, H.42, submarine (26)
12 June, Blue Sky, Admiralty drifter (15)
8 August, Raleigh, cruiser (12)
24 September, Speedy, destroyer (10)

1924

10 January, L.24, submarine (44)

1925

12 November, M.1, submarine monitor (69)

1926

9 August, H.29, submarine (1 and 5 civilians)
5 September, "Wahnsien Incident", Yangste River, men from light cruiser Despatch, river gunboats Cockchafer, Scarab (7)
22 October, Valerian (85)

1929

9 July, H.47 (21) and L.21 (3), submarines
26 July, Devonshire, heavy cruiser, damaged by turret explosion (17)

1930

12 January, St Genny, Admiralty rescue tug (23)
8 April, Sepoy, destroyer, damaged by depth charge explosion (6)

1931

9 June, Poseidon, submarine (20)
11 November, Peterfield, minesweeper (0)

1932

26 January, M.2, seaplane-carrying submarine (60)
17 February, Suffolk, heavy cruiser, damaged by Japanese shellfire (2)

1937

13 May, Hunter, destroyer, mined and damaged during Spanish Civil War (8)

1939

1 June, Thetis, submarine (99)

ROYAL NAVY ROLL OF HONOUR

Between the Wars

1918-1939

Part 1 - by NAME

A

ABBAS, Habid B, Seedie Stoker, Aden 401, Triad, 8 April 1924
ABBAS, Sulman, Lascar Stoker 1c, Bramble, 4 September 1919
ABBILL, Rowland G, Able Seaman, J 34950, Argus, 9 May 1927
ABBOT, Reginald F V, Able Seaman, J 31489, Centaur, 18 July 1919
ABBOTT, Edgar G, Petty Officer, J 108344, Medway, 5 March 1938
ABBOTT, Harry, Officer's Steward 3c, LX 20348, Pembroke, 31 October 1929
ABBOTT, Henry N, Lieutenant, RNR, Singleton Abbey, Swansea, Wales, 9 July 1931
ABBOTT, William F C, Deck Hand, MMR, North Star II, 6 February 1919
ABDI, Ahmed, Seedie, Cornflower, 21 February 1925
ABDILLA, Paul, Petty Officer Steward, E/LX 20219, Duncan, 31 May 1934
ABDULLAH, Ahmed, Seedie Stoker, Crocus, 25 January 1928
ABDULLAH, Zariut, Seedie, Britomart, 11 September 1919
ABLETT, John G, Sick Berth Attendant, P/M 38616, RN Hospital, Haslar, 9 January 1934
ABLETT, Joseph H, Sick Berth Steward, 351615, Undaunted, 21 November 1918
ABRAHAM, Arthur, Petty Officer, C/J 18810, Valiant, 20 February 1935
ABURROW, Cecil F J, Able Seaman, J 4284 (Po), K.5, 20 January 1921

ACHESON, Lon S, Commander, Royal Navy (ex-Godetia), 28 June 1934
ACOURT, John J, Leading Signalman, P/J 26116, Hawkins, 17 August 1933
ACTON, Fitzmaurice, Commander, HM Coast Guard, 7 August 1920
ACWORTH, Richard F, Act/Sub Lieutenant, Course at Portsmouth, 27 June 1930

ADAM, Herbert A, Captain, Pembroke, 27 September 1920
ADAM, William, Gunner, RMA, RMA 13580, Hercules, 6 May 1920
ADAMS, Albert A B, Boy 2c, J 96948, Ganges, 23 July 1920
ADAMS, Albert E, Engine Room Artificer 2c, M 122, Hollyhock, 1 June 1921
ADAMS, Alfred H, Stoker 1c, C/K 62450, York, 7 March 1932
ADAMS, Cecil F W, Private, RMLI, 20068 (Ch), Gibraltar, 26 May 1921
ADAMS, Cecil P, Leading Seaman, J 52992, M.1, 12 November 1925
ADAMS, Charles R, Deck Hand, RNR, D S 2867, Island Prince, 10 February 1919
ADAMS, Clifford, Telegraphist, P/JX 136214, Cormorant, 4 July 1937
ADAMS, E (initial only) T, Honorary Lieutenant, RNVR, Ulster Division, RNVR, 28 July 1926
ADAMS, Frank D, Midshipman, York, 21 April 1939
ADAMS, Henry C, Petty Officer, 213543, Victory, 10 October 1922
ADAMS, Herbert A O, Engine Room Artificer Apprentice, M 37911, Pembroke, 18 September 1926
ADAMS, Herbert J, Stoker 1c, K 24581 (Ch), L.55, 4 June 1919
ADAMS, John J, Able Seaman, J 52524, Pembroke (ex-Superb), 16 February 1920
ADAMS, John T, Seaman, Newfoundland RNR, X 1516, Ganges, 30 November 1918
ADAMS, Percy, Gunner, Cordelia, 1 March 1920
ADAMS, Randal J F, Deck Hand, RNR, SD 2629, Halcyon, 7 December 1918
ADAMS, Richard C H, Boy 2c, JX 148273, Royal Navy, 9 July 1936
ADAMS, Vincent, Band Corporal, RMLI, 13528 (Ch), RM Headquarters, 19 June 1920
ADAMS, Vincent, Corporal, RMLI, 13518 (Ch), Chatham Division, RMLI, 19 June 1920
ADAMS, William E, Engine Room Artificer Apprentice, MX 45990, Pembroke, 29 March 1930
ADAMS, William G A, Stoker 1c, K 25237, Implacable, 25 March 1919
ADAMS, William J, Able Seaman, J 107355, Benbow, 21 September 1927
ADAN, Suleman, Somali Stoker, 2/259, Bideford, 22 April 1935
ADDE, John W, Writer, D/MX 48532, Drake, 26 January 1934
ADDIS, Philip, Ordinary Seaman, J 89049, Carnarvon, 30 January 1919
ADKINS, Douglas C, 2nd Writer, M 15535, Crescent, 17 February 1919
ADLAM, Charles F, Able Seaman, P/JX 126050, Dauntless, 21 March 1932
ADSHEAD, Alfred E, Commissioned Gunner, Cornwall, 20 November 1933
ADSLEY, George W, Mechanician, 308309, Glowworm, 25 June 1920

AFFON, Arthur Mc K, Petty Officer, D/J 62910, Neptune, 24 March 1939

AGGETT, William H, Shipwright 3c, D/M 8077, Drake, 7 August 1935
AGIUS, Dominick, Leading Steward, E/L 4478, Warspite, 10 May 1938

AH, Chong, Officer's Cook 1c, Adventure, 7 February 1934
AH, Gon, Officer's Cook 1c, Tamar, 2 February 1930
AH, Kay, Officer's Steward 3c, Titania, 18 November 1926
AH, Lum, Officer's Steward 3c, Tamar, 31 October 1928
AH, Ming, Officer's Steward 3c, Hawkins, 23 August 1927
AH, Mohamed, Seedie Seaman, Aden 2/386, Hastings, 3 March 1932
AH, Nam, Officer's Steward 2c, Hawkins, 10 February 1921
AH, Po, Leading Steward, Kent, 16 August 1935
AH, Pong, Sailmaker, Tamar, 5 September 1926
AH, Soo, Steward 2c, Royal Navy, 6 February 1938
AH, Wing, Stoker, Tarantula, 19 August 1925
AH, Yow, Leading Seaman, Tamar, 27 February 1925
AHMED, Gafar A S, Seedie Stoker 1c, 56258, Britomart, 10 February 1919

AITKEN, Mark J, Surgeon Commander, Victory, 29 June 1932
AITKEN, Richard, Private, RMLI, 9868 (Ply), RMLI, Plymouth Division, 24 August 1919
AITKEN, William, Fireman, MMR, Eaglet, 8 January 1920

AKASSA, Emir, Krooman, W 250, Delphinium, 7 July 1930
AKED, George W, Able Seaman, RNVR, R 1308, 150th (RN) Field Ambulance, RM Medical Unit, RND, assigned Hood Battalion, 5 December 1918
AKERS, Henry C, Petty Officer, 206030, London, 12 November 1918

ALBERT, Lancelot G A, Able Seaman, J 27242, Victory, 6 August 1919
ALBOROUGH, Sidney A, Boy 1c, J 57072, Victory, 23 April 1919
ALCORN, Charles F S, Able Seaman, D/J 23415, Rodney, 5 September 1933
ALDIS, Charles W, Electrical Artificer 1c, M 9367, Sandhurst, 2 January 1928
ALDRED, James, Stoker 1c, K 18460, Valerian, 22 October 1926
ALDRIDGE, Archibald P, Officer's Steward 2c, L 7061, Caterham, 1 February 1920
ALDRIDGE, Raymond A, Lieutenant, FAA, 403 Flight, Hermes,

20 June 1928
ALESSANDRO, Antonio, Officer's Steward 1c, L 4825, Tobago, 4 December 1920
ALEXANDER, Arthur H, Petty Officer, J 14439, M.1, 12 November 1925
ALEXANDER, Charles E, Private, RMLI, S 5717 (Ply), RMLI, Plymouth Division, 9 March 1919
ALEXANDER, Frederick, Engineer Commander, Cleopatra, 2 July 1920
ALEXANDER, Frederick W, Stoker 1c, K 41772, Sapphire, 18 December 1918
ALEXANDER, Henry, Able Seaman, SS 2011, TB.82, torpedo boat, 8 December 1918
ALEXANDER, Walter, Stoker 1c, 311118 (Ch), Fandango, 3 July 1919
ALFORD, Richard C, Petty Officer, D/J 21044, Defiance, 4 December 1930
ALFORD, Robert F, Able Seaman, 194808, ML.473, 27 February 1924
ALFORD, William H P, Stoker 1c, K 63582, Steadfast, 16 March 1930
ALI BIN ISSA, Ailee, Seedie, X 118, Flora, 13 October 1927
ALI, Ahmed, Seedie Stoker, Aden 460, Triad, 23 January 1924
ALI, Ahmet, Seedie Stoker, Hannibal, 19 May 1919
ALI, Yusef, Tindal, 130, Odin, 16 November 1919
ALLAM, Frank J, Ordinary Seaman, C/SSX 15858, Royal Navy, 14 December 1935
ALLAN, Alexander, Officer's Cook 2c, L 14118, Valerian, 22 October 1926
ALLAN, James L, Boy 2c, J 103807, Ganges, 21 April 1922
ALLAN, John, Ordinary Seaman, J 52387 (Ch), Erin's Isle, 7 February 1919
ALLCOM, Eli F J, Boy 2c, JX 132417, St Vincent, 7 January 1929
ALLEN, Alexander, Supply Chief Petty Officer, M 1029, Pembroke, 25 February 1929
ALLEN, Edward C, Stoker 2c, K 53025, Glenboyne, 4 January 1919
ALLEN, George, Able Seaman, RNVR, Bristol Z 5190, Princess Thyra, steamship, 16 November 1918
ALLEN, George, Private, RMLI, 14462 (Ply), RMLI, Plymouth Division, 25 November 1918
ALLEN, Harold V, Supply Assistant, P/MX 45900, Victory, 28 March 1932
ALLEN, Harry A, Warrant Engineer, Enterprise, 11 December 1931
ALLEN, Henry J, Petty Officer, 187212, Wireless Telegraph Station, Coulmer, 7 July 1929
ALLEN, Henry W, Officer's Steward 2c, 366101, Vivid, 21 January 1919
ALLEN, Herbert, Sick Berth Petty Officer, D/M 39287, Cardiff, 20 August 1938
ALLEN, Herbert A, Yeoman of Signals, 221355, Iron Duke, 15 February 1922
ALLEN, James A, Chief Petty Officer, J 1811, Vivid, 22 March 1929
ALLEN, James H, Stoker 1c, K 29689, Kildorrey, 6 December 1918
ALLEN, John T, Warrant Engineer, Repulse, 14 May 1921
ALLEN, Percival W, Engineer Commander, Calcutta, 17 January 1934
ALLEN, Richard J, Boy 2c, J 94070, Impregnable, 25 February 1919
ALLEN, Robert, Stoker 1c, K 17094, Calypso, 10 November 1921
ALLEN, Robert, Ty/Lieutenant, RNVR, Actaeon, 29 November 1918
ALLEN, Sam O, Private, RMLI, 21338 (Ch), Repulse, 5 November 1925
ALLEN, Thomas C, Stoker 1c, K 24703, Rodney, 31 December 1927
ALLEN, Walter, Able Seaman, RNVR, Tyneside Z 5681, 253rd Divisional Employment Company, RND, 23 December 1918
ALLEN, William, Private, RMLI, 15419 (Po), RM HQ Portsmouth, 16 April 1920
ALLEN, William, Private, RMLI, 4347 (Po), RM HQ Portsmouth, 26 February 1919
ALLEN, William C, Able Seaman, J 51425, M.1, 12 November 1925
ALLEN, William E, Leading Telegraphist, D/JX 135513, Thetis, 3 June 1939
ALLEN, William E, Stoker 1c, D/K 65334, Renown, 8 May 1932
ALLEN, William T, Chief Sick Berth Steward, 150307, Victory, 30 November 1918
ALLEY, Cyril C, Petty Officer, D/J 62087, Vivid, 14 October 1931
ALLIN, Leslie J W, Lieutenant, President, 6 March 1919
ALLISON, Eric W, Able Seaman, J 66121, Dunedin, 24 November 1920
ALLISON, Kenneth, Boy 1c, J 103169, Pembroke, 13 June 1923
ALLOTT, Charles, Deck Hand, MMR, 975096, Wallington, 26 February 1919
ALLSOP, Frederick W, Signalman, RNVR, London Z 5997, Boadicea II, 10 December 1918
ALLSOP, William B, Sub Lieutenant, RNR, Pembroke, 6 March 1919
ALLUM, Eric A F, Petty Officer Cook, C/M 10323, Malabar, 31 March 1935
ALMOND, Amos, Engine Room Artificer 1c, C/M 2922, Vindictive, 23 April 1932
ALMOND, Joseph A, Electrical Artificer 5c, M 33797, Emperor of India, 28 December 1920
ALMOND, Percy J, Able Seaman, J 22758 (Ch), Dragon, 17 October 1919
ALMOND, William W, Stoker 1c, K 44070, Vivid, 21 December 1918
ALTON, Barclay S F, Py/Lieutenant, RM, Exeter, 24 March 1933
ALUM, George, Stoker 1c, 98665, President VI, 5 May 1919

AMEY, John E H, Stoker 1c, MC 360 (Po), Myrtle, 15 July 1919
AMEY, William H, Stoker 1c, P/K 21194, Cormorant, 31 May 1933
AMOS, Edward W, Stoker 1c, C/K 66576, Pembroke, 26 June 1932

AN, Yow, Leading Stoker, Tamar, 21 February 1924
ANDERSON, Charles H, Leading Fireman, MMR, 787481, Eaglet, 28 February 1919
ANDERSON, Edward A, Lieutenant, Philomel, 6 January 1924
ANDERSON, Frederick C, Stoker 1c, K 19512, Castor, 3 March 1929
ANDERSON, Gustave A M, Surgeon Lieutenant Commander, Impregnable, 26 July 1924
ANDERSON, Herbert C, Leading Stoker, K 24252, H.42, 23 March 1922
ANDERSON, James, Leading Stoker, K 9274, Dublin, 12 August 1922
ANDERSON, James, Quartermaster, MMR, 643978, Eagle, 19 February 1919
ANDERSON, John A, Signalman, J 11253, Victory, 3 August 1920
ANDERSON, John L, Petty Officer Telegraphist, 239158, Vivid, 15 July 1919
ANDERSON, Joseph E S, Lieutenant, Coventry, 21 October 1926
ANDERSON, Toby, Krooman, W 7, Afrikander, 13 August 1921
ANDERSON, William O, Able Seaman, J 25289, Theseus II, 28 August 1919
ANDERSON-STUART, Archibald P, Surgeon Lieutenant Commander, Royal Navy, 16 February 1930
ANDREWS, Albert, Able Seaman, J 7918, Boadicea, 20 February 1919
ANDREWS, Albert D, Private, RMLI, 14925 (Ply), Valiant, 28 April 1921
ANDREWS, Benjamin H, Petty Officer, C/J 6697, Duchess, 9

August 1933
ANDREWS, Clifford, Engine Room Artificer 3c, D/MX 50319, Speedwell, 26 January 1937
ANDREWS, Edward W T, Leading Seaman, J 41479, Sutton, 24 September 1927
ANDREWS, Enoch J, Able Seaman, J 39562, M.1, 12 November 1925
ANDREWS, Henry G, Ty/Lieutenant Commander, RNVR, 2nd Reserve Battalion, RND, 22 November 1918
ANDREWS, Herbert G, Petty Officer, J 5147 (Po), K.5, 20 January 1921
ANDREWS, Leslie S, Leading Stoker, C/KX 76787, Royal Oak, 24 January 1934
ANDREWS, Robert J, Leading Cook, M 3690, Dunedin, 5 April 1921
ANGUS, Donald M, Engine Room Artificer 3c, 272470 (Ch), L.55, 4 June 1919
ANKERS, Thomas, Civilian Contractor, Thetis, 3 June 1939
ANNETTS, Ivy, Private, RMLI, 8750 (Po), Victoria & Albert, 11 December 1920
ANNING, John H, Private, RMLI, 20683 (Ply), RM Deal, 3 September 1920
ANSELL, Alfred, Petty Officer 2c, 125583, HM Coastguard Station Sutton, 17 May 1919
ANSELL, Frederick L, Private, RMLI, 16646 (Po), President III, 8 March 1919
ANSELL, George, Commissioned Gunner (T), Victoria & Albert, Royal Yacht, 10 July 1933
ANSELL, Jesse, Stoker 1c, K 55316, Cleopatra, 27 November 1919
ANSELL, John A, Stoker 1c, KX 75156, Birmingham, 29 August 1927
ANSELL, Walter, Boy Servant, L 14039, President, 25 January 1922
ANSTREE, Edward C, Stoker 1c, K 10164, Tyrian, 23 May 1921
ANTHONY, George M, Sub Lieutenant, Course at Portsmouth, 18 August 1935

APPLEBY, James G, Marine, 211570 (Po), Royal Marines HQ, 26 January 1926
APPLEBY, John R, Able Seaman, D/JX 152168, Drake, 11 September 1937
APPLETON, Ernest, Able Seaman, C/SSX 18858, Pembroke, 30 July 1939
APPLETON, George W, 2nd Officer, MMR, Susetta, 14 December 1918
APPLETON, Wilfred G, Telegraphist, P/J 72284, Courageous, 28 August 1931
APPLEYARD, Harold P L L, Paymaster Lieutenant, Royal Navy, 1 March 1937

ARBERRY, John, Private, RMLI, 19517 (Ply), 3rd Battalion, RM, 17 December 1918
ARBUTHNOT, Crofton K, Lieutenant Commander, M.2, 29 January 1932
ARCHER, Richard, Able Seaman, D/JX 136245, Norfolk, 28 August 1936
ARGENT, William E, Chief Petty Officer, 212349, Shakespeare, 5 December 1921
ARIS, Frederick J, Able Seaman, J 98858, Valerian, 22 October 1926
ARLAND, Gerald A T, Able Seaman, C/JX 145158, Camber, 15 December 1938
ARMISON, James R, Telegraphist, J 111484, Victory, 10 April 1930
ARMITAGE, Stanley E, Leading Seaman, C/J 71497, Pembroke, 4 May 1931
ARMSTRONG, Francis C, Cook, MMR, 846770, Ophir, 8 February 1919
ARMSTRONG, Isaac, Regulating Petty Officer, 221060, Ajax, 15 June 1920
ARMSTRONG, James I, Civilian Contractor, Thetis, 3 June 1939
ARMSTRONG, William L O, Sub Lieutenant, RNR, Royal Naval Reserve, 15 February 1920
ARNOLD, Charles H, Petty Officer, 236201, Excellent, 2 April 1923
ARNOLD, Frederick, Leading Telegraphist, J 34941, Vortigern, 27 November 1918
ARNOLD, George, Trimmer, MMR, 971592, Morea, 1 March 1919
ARNOLD, Norman M, Boy 1c, C/JX 141016, Malabar, 17 February 1935
ARNOLD, Robert A, Boy 2c, JX 139161, St Vincent, 19 September 1933
ARNOT, David, Chief Yeoman of Signals, 233591, Columbine, 18 February 1928
ARNOTT, George, Stoker 1c, K 60731, Hood, 10 November 1924
ARROW, George, Stoker 1c, K 60201, Fisgard, 26 March 1926
ARSCOTT, Thomas H, Stoker Petty Officer, 310264, Vivid, 4 February 1926
ARUNDELL, George, Telegraphist, C/J 102463, Elfin (Alecto), 17 July 1936

ASH, Charlie, Private, RMLI, 14771 (Po), Kent, 25 May 1919
ASH, Edward G, Chief Stoker, 294823, Marlborough, 5 February 1920
ASHDOWN, Harold H, Shipwright, C/M 19187, Sheffield, 1 January 1938
ASHDOWN, Henry, Ordinary Seaman, J 92539 (Ch), Yarmouth, 23 August 1919
ASHE, Harry, Private, RMLI, 20227 (Ch), Hawkins, 15 July 1925
ASHEWANDEN, Cecil K, Lieutenant, Pilot's Course No.17, 15 December 1930
ASHFORD, Thomas S, Shipwright 1c, P/M 33941, Victory, 7 April 1937
ASHFORD, William J S, Boatswain, Repulse, 16 April 1919
ASHLEY, Alexis W, Midshipman, Verulam, 4 September 1919
ASHLEY, Robert C, Leading Stoker, 297291, Vivid, 22 May 1921
ASHMORE, Eric H, Able Seaman, C/J 126869, Royal Oak, 17 May 1931
ASHTON, Reginald W A, Paymaster Lieutenant Commander, Medway, 19 February 1930
ASKEW, George S, Stoker 1c, K 52144, Scarab, 6 August 1925
ASLETT, William H, Admiralty Civilian, Thetis, 3 June 1939
ASMUSSON, William M, Leading Seaman, J 11351, Rosalind, 7 August 1919
ASPINALL, Samuel, Leading Deck Hand, RNR, SD 1377, Persian Empire, 21 February 1919
ASQUITH, James W, Gunner, Valerian, 22 October 1926
ASTLEFORD, Samuel, Stoker 1c, SS 119889, Cairo, 15 April 1922
ASTLEY, Harold R, Ordinary Seaman, J 109902, Eagle, 2 June 1927
ASTLEY-RUSHTON, Edward A, Vice Admiral, Effingham, Vice Admiral Reserve Fleet, 18 July 1935
ASTON, Samuel, Leading Stoker, KX 75995, Marshal Soult, 17 April 1928

ATCHESON, Robert Mc L, Fireman, MMR, 914382, Pembroke, 26 March 1920
ATHROLL, Francis H, Boy 1c, J 101827, Ganges, 5 May 1922
ATKINS, Ernest F, Petty Officer, D/J 55586, Drake, 16 February 1939
ATKINS, James S, Marine, X 392 (Ch), RM Barracks Chatham, 13 December 1936
ATKINS, John, Stoker Petty Officer, K 7375, Pembroke, 21 February 1919
ATKINS, Thomas E, Engineman, RNR, ES 3859, Fair Isle, 5 March 1919
ATKINS, Tom, Petty Officer, 217729 (Po), Bee, 1 April 1921
ATKINS, Walter J, Able Seaman, J 114309, Enterprise, 29 April 1930

ATKINSON, Charles H F, Surgeon Lieutenant, RNVR, Royal Naval Volunteer Reserve, 14 January 1920
ATKINSON, Charles H, Stoker Petty Officer, 308044, Iridescence, 31 January 1921
ATKINSON, Eric, Able Seaman, D/J 97757, Gannet, 22 July 1932
ATKINSON, George, Officer's Steward 1c, L 8058 (Po), Talbot, 1 April 1919
ATKINSON, Horace W, Boy 2c, JX 152770, Ganges, 15 January 1938
ATKINSON, Stephen B, Marine, X 1356 (Ply), RM Plymouth Division, 6 April 1936
ATTARD, Joseph, Petty Officer Steward, E/L 7214, Resolution, 23 February 1932
ATTERBY, William, Able Seaman, 235767, Colombo, 25 August 1925
ATTWOOD, Douglas R, Lieutenant, RNR, G.5, 24 November 1918

AUBREY, George, Surgeon Lieutenant Commander, Tamar, 9 May 1927
AUSTEN, Frederick T L, Chief Engine Room Artificer 2c, C/M 31522, Cochrane, 18 November 1938
AUSTEN, Henry T, Petty Officer, 233645, Dolphin, 17 November 1926
AUSTIN, Arthur G, Boy 2c, J 93548, Powerful, 18 January 1919
AUSTIN, Ronald N, Able Seaman, J 109535, Valentine, 13 January 1930
AUSTIN, Thomas, Chief Petty Officer Telegraphist, J 2072, Ganges, 16 March 1932
AUSTIN, William R, Leading Stoker, K 19479, Senator, 23 February 1924

AVANT, John H, Stoker Petty Officer, P/K 63397, Cameronia, steamship, 18 December 1935
AVES, Thomas, Leading Stoker, K 1919, Turbulent, 28 February 1920
AVIS, Alfred E, Stoker Petty Officer, K 18121, Victory, 13 March 1929
AVIS, William B, Private, RMLI, 19136 (Ch), Ceres, 6 February 1924
AVIS, William T, Sick Berth Chief Petty Officer, M 1717, Suffolk, 25 June 1930

AYERS, Fred, Lieutenant Commander, Blake, 12 December 1921
AYERS, Harold, Master at Arms, 202816, Vivid, 12 April 1921
AYLING, Harry T, Leading Stoker, K 17614 (Po), Vampire, 28 July 1920
AYLWARD, Albert, Gunner, RMA, RMA 3358, RMA Eastney, 8 March 1919
AYLWIN, Charlie, Chief Petty Officer Cook, 358237, Caroline, 21 October 1919
AYNSLEY, Thomas, Chief Engine Room Artificer 1c, 271623, Fisgard, 2 April 1924
AYRES, Albert A, Ordinary Seaman, J 96319, Pembroke, 12 September 1922
AYRES, Arthur W, Leading Stoker, K 13360, Prince Eugene, 20 November 1918
AYRES, James F, Private, RMLI, 18488 (Po), St Vincent, 21 January 1919
AYRES, Joseph, Officer's Steward 2c, L 6251, Glowworm, 25 August 1919
AYTON, Alfred, Petty Officer, J 4029, Renown, 17 July 1922

AZZOPARDI, Eugenio, Officer's Cook 2c, 365058, Europa, 26 January 1919
AZZOPARDI, Giuseppe, Officer's Cook 2c, LX 20223, Vimiera (on books of Egmont II), 10 September 1931

B

BABBAGE, George, Stoker Petty Officer, K 6682, Chrysanthemum, 4 April 1927
BABBAGE, Sidney J, Lieutenant, President, 15 May 1919
BABBINGTON, Hugh, Lieutenant, Fox, 27 November 1919
BABY, Ernest A, Able Seaman, J 71374, M.1, 12 November 1925
BACK, Charles, Stoker Petty Officer, K 6263, Vivid, 7 January 1920
BACK, George P, Telegraphist, J 40179 (Ch), G.11, 22 November 1918
BACK, Leonard S, Electrical Artificer 3c, D/M 37056, M.2, 29 January 1932
BACKHOUSE, Albert E, Stoker 1c, K 21000 (Ch), K.5, 20 January 1921
BACKHOUSE, John R, Engine Room Artificer 4c, M 33124, Tiger, 18 February 1919
BACKLEY, John F, Telegraphist, J 48931, Carysfort, 20 April 1925
BACKWELL, George, Petty Officer 1c, 136192, Eaglet, 11 January 1919
BACON, Edgar J, Petty Officer, J 23487, Tasmania (RAN), 3 July 1924
BACON, Edward, Corporal, RM, 19230 (Po), Devonshire, 26 July 1929
BACON, Thomas S, Able Seaman, J 97017, Titania, 24 April 1927
BACON, William, Petty Officer, 219887, Victoria & Albert, Royal Yacht, 14 September 1922
BADCOCK, Frank, Seaman, RNR, C 3374, President III, 1 January 1919
BADHAM, Seymour W, Ordinary Seaman, P/JX 137592, Suffolk, 19 January 1935
BAGDEN, Herbert T, Boy 1c, J 113865, Ajax, 28 February 1926
BAGGLEY, Henry S, Leading Telegraphist, J 41284 (Po), Birmingham, 19 November 1920
BAGGS, Albert G, Chief Gunner, Excellent, 5 June 1919
BAGLEY, Arthur J, Stoker 1c, C/KX 75549, Poseidon, 9 June 1931
BAGULEY, Joseph W, Engineer Commander, Victory XI, 9 November 1929
BAILEY, Arthur J, Private, RMLI, 11767 (Ch), Pembroke, 3 December 1920
BAILEY, Charles E, Ordnance Artificer 3c, M 37513, Walpole, 8 December 1929
BAILEY, Charles E, Stoker 1c, SS 116957, Assistance, 18 May 1919
BAILEY, Francis H, Able Seaman, J 99122, Hawkins, 28 June 1927
BAILEY, Frank, Admiralty Civilian, Thetis, 3 June 1939
BAILEY, John, Able Seaman, RNVR, Z 3513 (Palace), President III, 4 February 1919
BAILEY, John, Leading Stoker, D/KX 76248, Furious, 14 September 1933
BAILEY, Joseph A, Engineman, RNR, TS 832, Thistle III, 20 September 1919
BAILEY, Newman J, Engine Room Artificer 4c, M 14638, Blake, 23 November 1918
BAILEY, Reginald C, Stoker 1c, P/KX 91419, Kempenfelt, 11 July 1939
BAILEY, Samuel G W, Leading Stoker, C/KX 75436, Warspite, 15 August 1939
BAILEY, Walter S, Honorary Lieutenant, RNR, Royal Naval Reserve, 1 February 1928
BAIN, Alexander, Able Seaman, MMR, 973883, Lavatera, 2 September 1919
BAIN, David, Able Seaman, J 70878, H.47, 9 July 1929
BAIN, Edward H, Able Seaman, P/J 80602, Whitshed, 18 February 1934
BAIN, James, Honorary Engineer Commander, RNR, Royal Naval Reserve, 8 June 1922
BAIN, Ronald C, Engineer Lieutenant Commander, RNR, Royal Naval Reserve, 3 June 1936
BAIN, William, Seaman, RNR, A 9221, Fanad Head, steamship, 27 December 1918
BAIN, William A, Chief Petty Officer, D/M 3045, Queen Elizabeth, 6 January 1932
BAINES, John, Petty Officer, 239220, Vernon, 16 April 1924
BAINES, Michael H, Midshipman, Malaya, 4 April 1938
BAIRD, Alexander, Able Seaman, RNVR, Clyde Z 4043, Drake Battalion, RND, 10 July 1919
BAIRD, Sir George H, Rear Admiral, Coventry (Rear Admiral Destroyers), 22 October 1924
BAIRD, James (real name, but served as James Manson), Sergeant, RMLI, 12258 (Ch), RMLI Headquarters, Chatham Division, 3 February 1921
BAKER, Alfred J, Chief Stoker, 281693, Victor, 12 November 1918
BAKER, Alfred R, Stoker 1c, KX 79349, Titania, 6 July 1929
BAKER, Alfred W, Telegraphist, C/JX 133942, Folkestone, 27 August 1938
BAKER, Arthur J, Able Seaman, J 96315, Caradoc, 23 March 1929
BAKER, Arthur J, Chief Stoker, D/K 11977, Cornwall, 10 September 1930
BAKER, Bertie N, Ty/Sub Lieutenant, RNVR, President, 21 December 1918
BAKER, Charles F, Able Seaman, J 48065, H.50, 16 July 1928
BAKER, Cyril H G, Able Seaman, C/JX 132107, Shropshire, 29 December 1938
BAKER, Edward C G, Stoker Petty Officer, K 12959, M.1, 12 November 1925
BAKER, Frederick, Stoker 1c, K 22941, Valerian, 22 October 1926
BAKER, George C, Warrant Supply Officer, Pembroke, 18 September 1928
BAKER, George T H, Chief Engine Room Artificer 1c, M 695, M.29, 9 February 1925
BAKER, George W, Engineer Lieutenant, K.5, 20 January 1921
BAKER, George W, Leading Seaman, 217831, Ursa, 29 November 1918
BAKER, Harry, Leading Seaman, J 20682, Tigress, 8 December 1918
BAKER, Harry E, Engine Room Artificer Apprentice, M 35663, Fisgard, 2 May 1921
BAKER, Henry, Petty Officer, J 2045, Triad, 6 February 1920
BAKER, Henry, Stoker 1c, K 14458, Woolwich, 1 June 1921
BAKER, Henry J, Supply Petty Officer, M 35120, Royal Navy, 26 April 1928
BAKER, Henry W, Petty Officer Telegraphist, P/J 5700, L.23, 13 July 1933
BAKER, Hugh S, Lieutenant, RM, Chatham, 9 October 1932
BAKER, Norman S, Engine Room Artificer 3c, D/M 87009, Caradoc, 25 October 1933
BAKER, Percy H, Able Seaman, D/J 81794, Furious, 16 August 1932
BAKER, Reginald H, Marine, CH/X 1549, Cardiff, 3 May 1937
BAKER, Robert, Stoker 1c, 297161 (Po), Penarth, 4 February 1919
BAKER, Robert, Stoker 1c, K 6474, Pembroke, 27 May 1919
BAKER, Sidney C A, Able Seaman, J 102919, Dunedin, 4 January 1927
BAKER, Sydney C, Able Seaman, J 21831 (Ch), K.10, 12 February 1919
BAKER, Sydney W, Boy 2c, JX 128200, Renown, 2 January 1929
BAKER, William H, Marine, 20808 (Ply), Philomel, 28 June 1929
BAKER, William J L, Able Seaman, J 109467, Victory, 14 April 1929
BAKER, William W J, Deck Hand, RNR, DA 3575, Western Queen, 17 November 1918

BALDOCK, Thomas, Able Seaman, C/J 105047, Ramillies, 11 November 1935
BALDWIN, Albert J, Able Seaman, J 55663, Valentine, 27 June 1921
BALDWIN, Bertram W T, Petty Officer, P/JX 131302, Excellent, 20 June 1938
BALDWIN, John R, Boy 1c, J 104052, Vivid, 17 January 1922
BALFOUR, Robert S, Engine Room Artificer 3c, M 16479, Gloucester, 9 April 1919
BALL, Daniel, Private, RM, RMES 5670, RM Engineers, 20 December 1918
BALL, George B, Wireless Operator, RNCVR, VR 545, Seagull (RCN), 14 November 1918
BALL, Harold, Able Seaman, J 39475, M.1, 12 November 1925
BALL, John S, Leading Stoker, K 35944, M.1, 12 November 1925
BALLARD, George H, Able Seaman, J 68625, Speedy, 23 September 1922
BALLARD, Sidney R, Stoker 1c, J 22780, L.24, 10 January 1924
BALLS, George W, Motor Driver, MMR, Ivanhoe, 9 January 1919
BALSHAW, Robert, Stoker 1c, K 78864, Poseidon, 9 June 1931
BALZAN, Frank, Officer's Steward 2c, 361116, Egmont, 14 April 1929
BAMBA, Abdia B, Seedie, X 146, Flora, 20 September 1929
BAMBRIDGE, Herbert K, Able Seaman, J 3947 (Ch), Vittoria, 31 August 1919
BAMFORD, Edward, Major, RM, Tamar, 30 September 1928
BAMFORD, Herbert E, Boy 2c, RAN, 11130, Tingira (RAN), 16 March 1919
BAMPTON, Arthur, Able Seaman, J 108390, Vivid, 8 July 1928
BAMSEY, Richard, Leading Stoker, K 1944, Wolverine, 3 July 1923
BANBURY, Harry, Shipwright 1c, D/M 10283, Vivid, 24 August 1932
BANCONE, Francesco C, Deck Hand, RNR, DA 18798, George Aunger, 19 February 1919
BANFIELD, George A V, Officer's Steward 1c, L 1033, Sea Bear, 17 February 1919
BANHAM, Karl F, Able Seaman, J 18609, Pembroke, 19 February 1919
BANISTER, Charles, Supply Petty Officer, P/K 55412, Royal Sovereign, 4 June 1934
BANISTER, George, Officer's Steward 3c, L 12419, Queen Elizabeth, 5 May 1924
BANKS, Ernest A, Able Seaman, C/JX 135601, Pembroke, 17 March 1937
BANKS, Harold, Able Seaman, J 32459, St Genny, 12 January 1930
BANKS, Herbert L, Stoker 1c, SS 123889, Pembroke, 28 September 1919
BANKS, Jack S, Lieutenant, Dwarf, 20 April 1939
BANKS, John R, Shipwright 3c, M 11859, Vivid, 14 April 1924
BANKS, Sydney W, Petty Officer, C/J 48971, M.2, 29 January 1932
BANNISTER, Frank D, Able Seaman, J 61094, Vivid, 14 April 1922
BARBER, Albert V, Deck Hand, RNR, DA 15004, Girl May, 12 November 1918
BARBER, Arthur, Deck Hand, RNR, DA 8163, Ceto, 16 November 1918
BARBER, Joseph, Marine, RM, 15639 (Ply), Devonshire, 27 July 1929
BARBER, William H, Chief Engine Room Artificer 1c, M 1545, Vivid, 25 October 1924
BARBER, William H, Chief Skipper, RNR, Royal Naval Reserve, 31 March 1937
BAREHAM, Francis A, Ordinary Seaman, RNVR, London Z 9868, RN Depot, Crystal Palace, 24 November 1918
BARFF, Edward M, Lieutenant (E), Penelope, 28 January 1939
BARGERY, David C, Commissioned Gunner, Jumna, 10 August 1920

BARHAM, William, Leading Stoker, SS 114275, Kildimo, 21 February 1919
BARKER, Albert H, Boy 1c, JX 125176, Ramillies, 15 July 1927
BARKER, Alfred, Stoker 1c, K 13516, Victory, 18 March 1920
BARKER, Allan, Able Seaman, D/J 98120, Revenge, 23 March 1938
BARKER, Edward G, Leading Aircraftsman, RAF, 364505, Glorious, 15 October 1930
BARKER, George H, Able Seaman, 239724, Revenge, 14 January 1925
BARKER, William, Chief Petty Officer, 209391, Victory, 21 February 1922
BARKER, William A H, Commissioned Gunner, Vernon, 26 September 1923
BARLEY, Hubert, Private, RM, RME 3152, RM Engineers, 6 February 1919
BARLEY, Ronald L, Able Seaman, P/J 98175, St Angelo, 9 September 1936
BARLING, Charles F, Engine Room Artificer 3c, M 27333, Pembroke, 20 June 1928
BARLOW, Charles E, Engine Room Artificer 3c, M 4609, Truculent, 17 November 1918
BARLOW, Frederick W, Stoker Petty Officer, K 62738, Windsor, 15 March 1928
BARLOW, John R, Able Seaman, J 75456, Cinceria, 15 February 1919
BARLOW, William, Plumber 1c, 345350, Malaya, 9 June 1922
BARNARD, George L, Stoker 1c, K 29260, H.42, 23 March 1922
BARNARD, Walter F, Stoker 1c, 295020, Espiegle, 3 September 1919
BARNES, Frank V, Stoker 1c, K 5666, Barham, 21 November 1918
BARNES, Fred, Stoker 1c, K 7861 (Po), Renown, 9 September 1920
BARNES, Frederick L – see HASARL, Frederick L, Chief Stoker
BARNES, Jack N, Chief Petty Officer Writer, M 8494, Valerian, 22 October 1926
BARNES, John T, Private, RM, S 11945 (Deal), RM Labour Corps, 8 April 1919
BARNES, William, Commissioned Engineer, Cyclamen, 28 June 1928
BARNES, William J, Chief Petty Officer Writer, 345816, Danae, 5 October 1927
BARNETT, Fred, Marine, Ply X 515, Exeter, 15 October 1931
BARNETT, Harry P, Paymaster Lieutenant Commander, Pekin, 6 February 1919
BARNETT, William H, Marine, 13826 (Ply), Frobisher, 27 November 1924
BARNFATHER, Norman, Able Seaman, 228236, Zetland, 11 July 1919
BARNFIELD, Frederick J, Signalman, P/J 113377, Fowey, 13 December 1932
BARNSHAW, Sidney F, Boy 1c, JX 133237, Ganges, 4 April 1930
BARR, Lewis W, Stoker 1c, K 13350, Actaeon, 17 April 1921
BARR, Samuel A J, Boy 1c, J 97828, Barham, 31 October 1921
BARR, Walter, Cook, MMR, 821587, Cymric, 1 January 1919
BARRABLE, Harry G, Boy 2c, J 93977, Impregnable, 3 June 1919
BARRACK, Horace H, Able Seaman, 175021, Indus, 14 August 1919
BARRATT, Walter, Deck Hand, RNR, DA 20489, Wallington, 8 December 1918
BARRETT, Augustine, Stoker 1c, K 43568, Eaglet III, 28 April 1920
BARRETT, Charles A, Petty Officer Telegraphist, J 20177, Victory I, 24 December 1929
BARRETT, Edward G, Boy 1c, JX 141391, Ganges, 4 January 1935
BARRETT, Ernest, Leading Seaman, J 8093 (Dev), Lucia, 19 June 1920

BARRON, John L, Chief Stoker, 310664, Repulse, 17 October 1925
BARROW, Alfred O, Marine, 22953 (Ch), Royal Marines HQ, 16 July 1926
BARROW, Dick, Sick Berth Steward, 351003, RN Hospital Capetown, 13 August 1919
BARTER, Adrian E, Leading Seaman, RNVR, London 6/3568, Collingwood Battalion, RND, 1 December 1918
BARTER, Albert E (real name, but served as Frederick Brown), Stoker 1c, SS 117137, Calypso, 19 October 1919
BARTER, Arthur T, Able Seaman, J 103212, Eagle, 27 May 1929
BARTER, Frederick, Engineer Captain, Gibraltar Dockyard, 25 May 1923
BARTER, Reginald W, Boy 1c, J 90112 (Dev), Malaya, 8 June 1920
BARTLETT, Charles W E, Sick Berth Attendant, C/MX 48842, Woolwich, 11 May 1936
BARTLETT, Harry L, Telegraphist, J 108182, Berwick, 16 July 1928
BARTLETT, Leonard G, Able Seaman, J 10066, Tiger, 22 November 1918
BARTLETT, Leslie, Able Seaman, C/J 107136, Wolfhound, 8 February 1936
BARTLETT, William H, Stoker 1c, K 19642, Vivid, 9 February 1923
BARTLETT, William H, Supply Chief Petty Officer, D/M 1996, Glorious, 8 June 1933
BARTOLO, Andrea, Officer's Cook 3c, L 8048, Ajax, 22 October 1919
BARTON, Albert, Able Seaman, J 104976, Tamar, 14 June 1925
BARTON, Donald H, Lieutenant, L.24, 10 January 1924
BARTON, Ernest W, Able Seaman, J 16667, Victory, 21 January 1926
BARTON, Robert, Leading Seaman, 238187, Stuart, 12 December 1919
BARTON, William E, Leading Seaman, J 7512 (Dev), L.55, 4 June 1919
BARTRAM, John E, Ordinary Seaman, J 78133, Kilkeel, 6 February 1919
BARTRAM, Stanley T, Stoker 1c, K 35202, TB.30, torpedo boat, 11 January 1919
BASHFORD, Charles, Deck Hand, RNR, DA 12313, Victory, 11 February 1919
BASHFORD, Herbert, Stoker 1c, SS 123275, Raleigh, 8 August 1922
BASHFORD, William H, Stoker 1c, 312508, Bacchante, 20 February 1919
BASKERFIELD, Albert, Leading Seaman, J 22193, Carysfort, 30 April 1924
BASS, Charles, Stoker Petty Officer, 298365, Attentive II, 19 September 1919
BASSETT, Thomas, Petty Officer, J 4877, Sterling, 29 April 1927
BASSINDALE, William H, Able Seaman, RNVR, Tyneside Z 4991, Eaglet, 9 February 1919
BATCHELOR, Edward E, Able Seaman, J 36735, Hawkins, 2 January 1926
BATCHELOR, Frederick G H, Mechanician, K 1533, Pembroke, 11 October 1928
BATCHELOR, Leonard J, Signalman, C/J 109536, Thames, 30 November 1932
BATCHELOR, Thomas A, Paymaster Lieutenant, Royal Air Force, 22 April 1919
BATCOCK, Frederick G, Boy 2c, J 96140, Impregnable, 14 February 1920
BATE, John M I, Shipwright 3c, M 34326, Fitzroy, 11 November 1928
BATEMAN, Frederick C, Stoker 1c, C/K 64805, Pembroke, 12 October 1938
BATEMAN, Herbert I, Able Seaman, J 22494, Serene, on books of Columbine, 17 May 1920
BATES, Arthur E, Supply Chief Petty Officer, M 37484, Iron Duke, 22 July 1930
BATES, Arthur R, Stoker 1c, C/K 63362, Valiant, 27 August 1932
BATES, George, Chief Officer, HM Coast Guard, HM Coastguard Station Par Cornwall, 4 May 1919
BATES, John E, Stoker 1c, SS 125141, Victory, 3 October 1922
BATES, John T G, Ty/Sub Lieutenant, RNVR, Norsholt, 17 November 1918
BATES, Percival F, Leading Sick Berth Attendant, M 5509, Pembroke, 17 December 1920
BATH, John A, Captain, RM, Devonshire, 26 July 1929
BATH, William G, Civilian Contractor, Thetis, 3 June 1939
BATTEN, Francis B, Leading Signalman, D/JX 129058, Thetis, 3 June 1939
BATTEN, Henry C, Private, RMLI, 14067 (Ch), Chatham Division, RMLI, 10 February 1920
BAULSON, George, Chief Stoker, 304992, Hyacinth, 24 November 1918
BAUM, Charles, Leading Seaman, RNVR, Bristol Z 5775, President III, 1 December 1918
BAVERIDGE, Albert C, Able Seaman, P/J 111587, Hood, 12 April 1931
BAVERSTOCK, Cecil G, Able Seaman, J 97768, Vernon, 13 April 1926
BAXTER, Frederick G, Telegraphist, D/JX 125974, FAA, 821 Sqn, Courageous, 11 May 1937
BAXTER, Frederick J, Stoker 1c, C/KX 77499, Colombo, 28 January 1935
BAXTER, George, Deck Hand, RNR, DA 1538, Classin, 13 December 1918
BAXTER, George R, Deck Hand, RNR, DA 15977, Halcyon, 18 November 1918
BAXTER, Gordon W, Engineman, RNR, TS 4759, Halcyon II, 18 February 1919
BAXTER, Joseph E, Leading Stoker, K 20414, Petunia, 14 November 1918
BAYLIS, Frederick W, Able Seaman, J 5450, Renown, 6 October 1921
BAYLY, Richard W U, Lieutenant Commander, Comus II, 16 October 1921
BAYNE, John, Stoker 1c, KX 7858, Victory, 13 July 1920

BEADELL, Cecil L G, Chief Electrical Artificer, C/M 35415, Woolwich, 20 October 1936
BEAGARIE, Frederick B, 2nd Hand, RNR, DA 2197, Dove II, 3 April 1919
BEAK, George H, Cadet Paymaster, Iron Duke, 4 November 1921
BEAL, Charles, Leading Stoker, C/KX 80601, Vesper, 29 January 1935
BEAL, Frederick, Petty Officer, 178228, Castor, 24 February 1919
BEAL, George W (real name, but served as George W Brown), Leading Stoker, K 18357, L.11, 5 December 1923
BEALE, Harvey M, Ordinary Seaman, J 70671, Resolution, 13 March 1919
BEALE, Joseph, Officer's Chief Cook, L 743, Conqueror, 13 January 1922
BEALES, Henry A, Chief Petty Officer, 233857, Pembroke, 7 May 1928
BEAMES, John, Cook, M 7573, Kinross, 16 June 1919
BEAMS, Percy T, Private, RMLI, 15826 (Ch), Lowestoft, 15 May 1923
BEAN, George B, Seaman, RNR, A 7007, Cufie, steamship, 15 November 1918
BEARD, Eva G (sometimes listed as Gladys Eva), Nursing Sister, QARNNS, Queen Alexander's Royal Naval Nursing Service, 14 March 1920
BEARD, Francis J, Stoker 1c, K 10768, Emperor of India, 3 August 1921
BEARD, George A, Petty Officer, P/JX 127198, Somali, 20 April 1939
BEARD, Gladys Eva – see BEARD, Eva G, Nursing Sister, QARNNS

BEARD, Sidney J, Leading Stoker, C/K 63616, Pembroke, 25 May 1937
BEARDSALL, Elizabeth, Section Leader Steward, WRNS, G 3243, Women's Royal Naval Service, 18 December 1918
BEARER, James H, Stoker 1c, K 26421, Eagle, 4 February 1926
BEARN, Reginald Y R, Petty Officer, J 16630, Maidstone, 20 May 1921
BEATON, Alex, Able Seaman, MMR, 968068, Iolaire (Rose II, O/P), 1 January 1919
BEATON, George, Leading Deck Hand, RNR, DA 5012, Pembroke, 31 January 1919
BEATTIE, Peter, Deck Hand, RNR, DA 6432, Satellite, 18 November 1918
BEATTY, William B, Civilian Contractor, Thetis, 3 June 1939
BEAUMONT, Charles J, Stoker 1c, D/KX 79220, Poseidon, 9 June 1931
BEAUMONT, George L, Chief Engine Room Artificer 2c, 272157 (Po), K.5, 20 January 1921
BEAUMONT, Harry, Able Seaman, C/JX 129191, Titania, 11 July 1932
BEAUMONT, Owen D, Boy 2c, JX 128867, Ganges, 5 February 1927
BEAVIS, James T, Stoker 1c, K 19172, Vivid, 11 December 1922
BECHETT, Charlie, Stoker 1c, K 57475, Victory II, 21 October 1922
BECK, James M, Sergeant, RM, RM Police, RN Hospital, Chatham, 6 July 1939
BECK, Robert H, Stoker 1c, K 12758, Neptune, 26 January 1919
BECK, Sydney, Deck Hand, RNR, SD 2496, Pembroke, 12 November 1918
BECKETT, Albert E, Leading Deck Hand, RNR, DA 7172, Pekin, 10 December 1918
BECKETT, John F, Deck Hand, RNR, DA 12692, Soar, 7 February 1919
BECKINGHAM, Frank W L, Ordinary Seaman, P/JX 133992, Cornwall, 1 May 1932
BECKINGTON, Ernest A, Officer's Steward 2c, L 3458, Stag, 17 January 1919
BECKMAN, Sidney C, Deck Hand, RNR, DA 4627, Halcyon II, 6 December 1918
BECKWITH, Alfred, Chief Stoker, 281274, Victory II, 27 August 1919
BEDDOW, Enoch, Able Seaman, RNVR, Bristol Z 3659, Drake Battalion, RND, 28 January 1919
BEDFORD, Arthur W F, Boy 1c, C/JX 144182, Orion, 1 February 1937
BEDFORD, Frederick C, Leading Seaman, D/J 77984, Vivid, 3 October 1931
BEDWELL, William B, Able Seaman, J 34857, Sandhurst, 22 April 1927
BEE, Robert W, Lieutenant Commander, RNR, Royal Naval Reserve, 16 May 1933
BEECH, George H, Able Seaman, J 104450, Wild Swan, 3 October 1926
BEECH, Victor G, Officer's Steward 3c, L 12113, Pembroke, 3 March 1919
BEECH, Walter H, Officer's Steward 2c, L 9859, Commonwealth, 2 March 1919
BEECHAM, Gilbert H, Stoker 1c, K 16245, Valerian, 22 October 1926
BEER, Frank E, Able Seaman, D/JX 129720, Vivid, 23 July 1931
BEER, Reginald J, Chief Petty Officer Writer, D/M 6960, Vivid, 29 December 1930
BEER, William A, Petty Officer, 208197, Vivid, 26 April 1922
BEESON, Albert H, Able Seaman, C/J 107425, Pembroke, 6 July 1935
BELA, Husif, Stoker Seedie, Cyclamen, 9 February 1928
BELCHER, Arthur, Able Seaman, 197362, Victory, 1 November 1920
BELCHER, Frederick E, Gunner, RMA, RMA S 2354, Crescent, 2 March 1919

BELDERSON, William, Petty Officer, J 29333, Sepoy, 8 April 1930
BELDHAM, Allen E, Assistant Steward, MMR, Wahine, 24 March 1919
BELFIELD, James S, Engineer Sub Lieutenant, RIM, Lewis Pelley, launch, attached Inland Water Transport, 24 April 1919
BELL, Charles S, Engineer Commander, Royal Navy, 9 June 1926
BELL, Edwin J, Telegraphist, RNVR, London Z 7057, Daniel Henly, 3 December 1918
BELL, George, Stoker 1c, SS 120609, Canada, 17 July 1919
BELL, Harper, Boy 2c, JX 158259, Caledonia, 29 January 1939
BELL, John H, Warrant Victualling Officer, Queen Elizabeth, 18 January 1921
BELL, Raymond T, Leading Telegraphist, P/J 37637, Malabar, 15 July 1932
BELL, Robert Mc C, Able Seaman, D/JX 128282, Watchman, 15 July 1933
BELL, Sidney E, Signal Boy, D/JX 148885, Revenge, 4 March 1938
BELL, William MacD, Engine Room Artificer 3c, M 7020, M.1, 12 November 1925
BELLAIRS, George, Deck Hand, RNR, Theban, 15 November 1919
BELLINGHAM, Cecil P, Telegraphist, P/J 110190, Emperor of India, 5 October 1930
BELLIS, Thomas, Stoker 1c, K 33651 (Po), Penarth, 4 February 1919
BELLIS, William H, Commissioned Engineer, Valerian, 22 October 1926
BELSEY, Clifford N, Boy 2c, JX 137631, Ganges, 15 March 1933
BELSEY, Percy T, Petty Officer, 207845, Victory, 7 January 1922
BELTON, James, Stoker Petty Officer, 154822, Sandringham, 3 March 1919
BENCH, William J, Petty Officer, 192728, Cormorant, 24 February 1920
BENCKE, John A, Engineer Sub Lieutenant, RNR, John Pender, 14 February 1919
BENDELL, Albert, Lieutenant (ret), Royal Navy, 26 April 1920
BENDELOW, James, Plumber 1c, M 622, Queen Elizabeth, 13 December 1919
BENGER, Walter F, Able Seaman, J 17941, Hood, 5 February 1924
BENHAM, Arthur J A, Able Seaman, J 43246, Repulse, 24 November 1921
BENHAM, Edwin, Stoker 1c, K 39501, Suffolk, 19 June 1919
BENNETT, Arthur, Ordinary Seaman, RNVR, Tyneside Z 12834, RN Depot, Crystal Palace, 16 November 1918
BENNETT, Charles C, Leading Sick Berth Attendant, D/M 24673, RN Hospital, Plymouth, 22 October 1930
BENNETT, Charles P, Gunner, Furious, 26 December 1919
BENNETT, Clifton, Electrical Artificer 5c, M 30467, Vernon, 14 November 1918
BENNETT, Edward, Marine, 19821 (Ch), RM Barracks Chatham, 5 April 1937
BENNETT, Edwin, Regulating Petty Officer, M 38034, Dolphin, 12 August 1924
BENNETT, Francis E, Able Seaman, D/JX 127229, Cygnet, 20 July 1934
BENNETT, Francis T, Stoker 2c, K 59110, Raleigh, 9 September 1921
BENNETT, George H, Petty Officer, 191017, Catspaw, 31 December 1919
BENNETT, James, Leading Stoker, RAN, 8835, Australia (RAN), 15 June 1919
BENNETT, John H, Stoker 1c, K 64918, Pembroke, 2 September 1926
BENNETT, Robert W, Petty Officer, D/JX 135100, Eagle, 7 September 1937
BENNETT, Sidney F, Petty Officer, J 15947, L.24, 10 January 1924

BENNETT, Thomas E, Marine, 21491 (Po), St Angelo, 5 April 1936
BENNETT, William, Chief Stoker, 287559, Mallard, 14 February 1919
BENNEY, Frederick S, Lieutenant Commander, FAA, 461 Flight, Glorious, 2 October 1931
BENNIE, James, Chief Engine Room Artificer 1c, 269188, Pembroke, 2 October 1919
BENNING, Charles S, Captain, Dolphin, 7 March 1924
BENTHAM, James T, Able Seaman, CH/X 126569, Cambrian, 29 February 1932
BENTLEY, Joseph H, 2nd Hand, RNR, SA 2047, Attentive II, 21 November 1918
BENZIE, William R, Fireman, MMR, 897261, Taliesin, 26 January 1919
BERESFORD, Douglas R, Mechanician, 308090, Repulse, 8 February 1921
BERESFORD, James H, Stoker 2c, K 66152, Revenge, 26 October 1925
BERESFORD, William C, Able Seaman, J 41740, Thanet, 27 May 1925
BERLYN, Arthur C, Lieutenant (E), Rainbow, 4 February 1937
BERNARD, William J, Signalman, J 76283, Cormorant, 19 April 1924
BERRIDGE, William L, Lieutenant, L.15, 10 April 1926
BERRIMAN, George, Chief Petty Officer, 231083, Coventry, 21 August 1925
BERRIMAN, Wiiliam, Gunner, RMA, RMA 10689, Lion, 1 May 1919
BERRY, Arthur C, Able Seaman, J 45637, Victory, 7 December 1922
BERRY, Percival A, Stoker 2c, SS 119509, Vivid, 26 February 1919
BERRY, Richard, Leading Stoker, D/K 20193, Dunoon, 20 December 1933
BERRY, Robert E, Telegraphist, J 89337, Benbow, 30 August 1922
BERRY, Samuel, Able Seaman, RNVR, R 1921, Drake Battalion, RND, 15 November 1918
BERRY, Thomas C J, Stoker 2c, RAN, 11260, Sydney (RAN), 6 December 1919
BERRY, William F, Engine Room Artificer 1c, 270639, Renown, 27 February 1919
BESSANT, Frederick A, Stoker 1c, K 35840 (Po), Emile Nobel, 21 May 1919
BEST, Frederick G, Able Seaman, J 17362, Acacia, 14 April 1919
BEST, George, Supply Petty Officer, M 10303, Mantis, 13 May 1927
BESTLEY, Oliver C, Marine, A 24365 (Ch), Royal Marines HQ, 5 January 1929
BESTOW, Leslie W, Able Seaman, RNVR, London Z 4773, President III, 9 February 1919
BESWICK, Harry, Stoker 1c, C/K 65244, Scimitar, 28 June 1932
BETTRIDGE, Arthur, Leading Seaman, D/JX 135096, Hunter, 13 May 1937
BEVAN, George P, Captain, Triad, 14 January 1920
BEVAN, Louis H B, Captain, Dragon, 5 September 1930
BEVAN, Winston, Marine, 22690 (Ply), Royal Marines HQ, 27 December 1926
BEVEL, Ernest H, Stoker Petty Officer, 293392, Larkspur, 9 June 1919
BEVIS, Albert J, Gunner, RMA, RMA 13514, King George V, 1 January 1919
BEVIS, Restal R, Honorary Lieutenant, RNVR, Royal Naval Volunteer Reserve, 1 April 1932
BEWS, Samuel T, Commissioned Engineer, Royal Navy, 23 May 1926
BEYER, Albert F, Petty Officer, P/J 15292, Fisgard, 6 August 1931

BIBBY, John, Able Seaman, J 50577 (Dev), Cordelia, 20 November 1918
BICKER, Ernest J, Ordinary Seaman, P/JX 132011, Glorious, 1 April 1931
BICKER, Roland, Chief Petty Officer, 224812, M.1, 12 November 1925
BICKLEY, Frederick H, Engine Room Artificer 3c, M 15652, Vivid, 16 March 1922
BICKMORE, Noel A, Lieutenant, H.47, 9 July 1929
BIDWELL, Norman R, Petty Officer, J 13512, Ambrose, 26 August 1928
BIGGS, Archibald A G, Able Seaman, J 43366, Veronica, 8 June 1928
BIGGS, William, Stoker 1c, SS 111180, Anzac, 4 March 1919
BIGNELL, Alfred J, Able Seaman, J 27918, Victory, 30 May 1922
BIGWOOD, George R, Stoker 1c, SS 112779, Tyrant, 24 December 1918
BILBIE, William, Leading Stoker, K 6939, Velox, 16 February 1919
BILLINGHURST, Arthur, Stoker 1c, K 57348, Curacoa, 24 September 1921
BILTON, Matthew W, Marine, 20945 (Ch), York, 8 September 1930
BILTON, Reginald E, Regulating Petty Officer, 224787, Eaglet, 5 December 1919
BINGHAM, John, Private, RMLI, 7622 (Ply), RMLI, Plymouth Division, 20 December 1918
BINNS, Alfred, Chief Motor Mechanic, RNVR, MB 918, Hermione, 15 December 1918
BINSTEAD, Charles E, Ordinary Telegraphist, P/JX 137172, Hood, 5 November 1934
BIRCH, Alexander, Stoker 1c, MC 375 (Po), Myrtle, 15 July 1919
BIRCH, Augustus H, Steward, MMR, 998218, Marchioness of Bute, 25 October 1919
BIRCH, Fred, Leading Signalman, 236774, Vivid, 18 November 1918
BIRCH, Henry J M, Stoker 1c, P/K 57831, Iron Duke, 23 October 1933
BIRCH, Steuart C, Ordinary Seaman, J 93587 (Dev), Cairo, 26 November 1920
BIRD, Albert E, Sick Berth Attendant, M 33621, Pembroke, 22 October 1923
BIRD, Alfred L, Engine Room Artificer 3c, RAN, 3542, Encounter (RAN), 7 May 1919
BIRD, Edward F, Boy 2c, JX 156251, Ganges, 2 October 1938
BIRD, Edward G, Rev, Chaplain, Portsmouth Dockyard, 28 October 1928
BIRD, John O, Leading Seaman, J 34198, Stonehenge, 18 April 1920
BIRD, Stanley, Able Seaman, J 58513, Lord Nelson, 7 May 1919
BIRD, William, Ordinary Seaman, J 72647 (Ch), Sentinel, 15 April 1919
BIRMINGHAM, William, Supply Petty Officer, M 37350, Eagle, 23 May 1925
BIRRELL, John, Stoker 1c, K 60709, Sussex, 21 May 1929
BISH, Harold T, Able Seaman, J 104725, Pandora, 2 February 1922
BISHOP, Albert H, Leading Telegraphist, RNVR, London Z 2253, Wireless Telegraph Station Ipswich, 18 December 1918
BISHOP, Alfred J, Gunner, Viscount, 26 August 1925
BISHOP, Frederick W J, Ordnance Artificer 2c, M 8918, Excellent, 4 December 1929
BISHOP, John H, Boy 2c, JX 125927, Ganges, 21 February 1926
BISHOP, John R, Deck Hand, RNR, DA 493, Europa, 19 January 1919
BISHOP, William W, Able Seaman, C/J 109403, Tarantula, 2 September 1932
BISS, Frederick J, Able Seaman, D/JX 125338, Vivid (ex-Malaya), 19 November 1930

BISSET, John D, Engineman, RNR, ES 2308, Glenboyne, 4 January 1919
BISSON, John, Private, RMLI, 17006 (Po), 3rd Battalion, RM, 18 December 1918

BLABEY, Robinette, Act/Officer's Chief Steward, 364034, Inflexible, 24 November 1919
BLACK, Benjamin, Stoker 1c, K 31201, Botha, 8 December 1918
BLACK, James, Chief Petty Officer, 191084, Excellent, 14 August 1921
BLACK, Thomas, Private, RM, S 13809 (Deal), RM Labour Corps, 1 February 1919
BLACK-BARNES, Charles T, Lieutenant, Royal Oak, 21 February 1919
BLACKBURN, Ernest B, Gunner, RMA, RMA 13311, Crescent, 5 May 1920
BLACKBURN, John, Stoker 1c, P/KX 79634, Despatch, 2 November 1933
BLACKFORD, George D, Private, RMLI, S 2411 (Ply), 1st RM Battalion, RND, 19 June 1919
BLACKFORD, William J, Ty/Engineer Commander, Engadine, 1 January 1920
BLACKHAND, Alfred, Ordinary Seaman, SSX 12573, Vivid, 8 March 1927
BLACKLER, George F, Leading Boatsman, 215761, Belfast Coast Guard, 17 February 1923
BLACKLOCK, Percy R, Chief Engine Room Artificer 1c, M 1355, Royal Sovereign, 21 March 1929
BLACKMAN, James W R T, Marine, RM, 22306 (Ply), Devonshire, 26 July 1929
BLACKMORE, Alfred E, Able Seaman, D/JX 126146, Westcott, 18 March 1936
BLACKMORE, Arthur E C, Supply Chief Petty Officer, M 4550, Frobisher, 26 October 1926
BLACKMORE, Charles, Able Seaman, 185210, London, 9 December 1918
BLACKMORE, Joseph C, Mechanician, D/K 57495, Norfolk, 21 October 1936
BLACKMORE, Vernon J, Ordinary Seaman, P/JX 132096, Coventry, 27 April 1931
BLACKWELL, Arthur W, Chief Engine Room Artificer, 272345, H.42, 23 March 1922
BLAGG, George, Stoker 1c, K 61495, Effingham, 4 May 1928
BLAIR, Thomas M, Able Seaman, J 113613, Ambuscade, 26 August 1929
BLAKE, Frank M, Coastguardsman 3c, 178535, Pembroke, 11 April 1922
BLAKE, Frederick J, Petty Officer, P/J 46983, M.2, 29 January 1932
BLAKE, Marcus, Paymaster Commander, Norfolk, 22 August 1933
BLAKE, Noah A G, Able Seaman, P/J 98067, Iron Duke, 5 December 1930
BLAKE, William H, Py/Schoolmaster, Impregnable, 18 April 1921
BLAKE, William K, Able Seaman, MMR, Liberty, 30 November 1918
BLAKE, William R, Able Seaman, J 3711, Musketeer, 6 January 1919
BLAKELEY, Frederick J, Able Seaman, J 37779 (Ch), Dunedin, 20 January 1921
BLAKELEY, Thomas, Paymaster Lieutenant, RNR, Royal Naval Reserve, 13 April 1922
BLAKEMAN, Alexander J, Sergeant, RMA, RMA 11551, RMA Eastney, 24 November 1919
BLAKEMAN, George E, Officer's Steward 3c, L 13338, Thunderer, 13 September 1924
BLAKEMORE, John A, Leading Seaman, J 9300 (Ch), Dolphin, 12 June 1919
BLAKEY, Andrew H, Lieutenant, RNR, Mastiff, 19 February 1919

BLAKEY, John, Private, RMLI, S 1049 (Po), Renown, 26 February 1919
BLANN, Frank A, Master at Arms, M 6580, Dublin, 18 May 1925
BLATCHFORD, Albert, Petty Officer, 220400, Tay, 27 May 1920
BLEEK, John F, Able Seaman, J 75386, Nelson, 4 July 1930
BLESSINGTON, Thomas, Private, RMLI, 8085 (Ply), Hyacinth, 22 March 1919
BLEWETT, Bertie, Able Seaman, RNVR, Bristol Z 1246, Antilochus, steamship, 29 November 1918
BLEWITT, Albert P, Ordinary Seaman, J 54766 (Dev), Temeraire, 3 January 1919
BLIGH, William V, Stoker 1c, K 3614, Wallington, 24 February 1919
BLINCH, John R, Chief Petty Officer, 187787, Botha, 16 January 1920
BLISS, Montagu H, Lieutenant, Royal Navy, 27 October 1936
BLOOM, Reginald W, Boy 2c, J 105271, Ganges, 7 June 1922
BLOOR, Edward W, Telegraphist, J 57992, Victory, 16 April 1919
BLOW, Charles H, Stoker 1c, P/K 22161, Victory, 28 September 1933
BLOWFIELD, Robert, Telegraphist, C/UDX/604, Bulldog, 17 March 1937
BLUNDY, Frank S, Leading Stoker, K 50717, Tetrarch, 9 August 1927
BLYTH, Joseph, Engine Room Artificer 3c, M 27519, Spiraea, 20 January 1919
BLYTHE, Claude R, Private, RMLI, 16620 (Ch), Northumbria, steamship, 9 January 1919

BOAL, James, Stoker Petty Officer, 287397, Pembroke, 17 May 1919
BOARD, Thomas W, Able Seaman, D/J 115271, Basilisk, 17 March 1932
BOARDMAN, Richard H, Leading Seaman, 217196, Cordelia, 30 July 1922
BOCKING, Andrew R, Able Seaman, P/JX 127652, Resource, 9 January 1937
BODDY, Robert H G, Engineer Commander, Engineer In Chief Division, 6 October 1930
BODDY, Walter M, Private, RMLI, 18767 (Po), Iron Duke, 21 July 1921
BODY, William J, Chief Petty Officer Writer, M 7649, Warspite, 22 May 1926
BOHO, Mordhammen, Seedie, Crocus, 24 October 1923
BOLAM, Thomas, Warrant Engineer, Hermes, 23 May 1928
BOLT, John G, Chief Engine Room Artificer 2c, M 1002, Defiance, 24 November 1923
BOLTON, Cyril, Stoker 1c, K 19211, Vivid, 30 July 1924
BOLTON, Joseph E, Stoker Petty Officer, 278551, Victoria & Albert, 14 May 1921
BOLUS, Guy H, Lieutenant Commander, Thetis, 3 June 1939
BOND, Alfred, Able Seaman, D/J 55438, Capetown, 21 June 1937
BOND, John D, Able Seaman, C/JX 128633, Pembroke, 13 September 1932
BOND, John, Chief Warrant Engineer, RNR, Minotaur, 24 February 1920
BOND, Walter C R, Able Seaman, P/J 11313, Courageous, 5 February 1933
BOND, Wilfred C, Leading Seaman, J 10428, Barham, 4 January 1923
BONE, Samuel T, Engine Room Artificer 5c, M 21995, Tiger, 2 August 1921
BONHAM, William, Stoker 2c, K 54778, Pembroke, 12 December 1918
BONHAM-CARTER, Philip H, Lieutenant Commander, Royal Navy, 7 January 1934
BONSOR, George, Chief Petty Officer, 200028, Vernon, 1 February 1922
BOOKER, Edward, Stoker Petty Officer, K 8774, Barham, 17 June 1926

BOOT, William, Engine Room Artificer 2c, M 12731, Blake, 5 February 1919
BOOTH, Charles, Honorary Captain, RNR, Royal Naval Reserve, 9 December 1938
BOOTH, Charles, Ty/Lieutenant, RNR, Hazel, 13 December 1918
BOOTH, Charles S, Lieutenant, FAA, 422 Sqn, Argus, 6 September 1928
BOOTH, Edwin W, Ordinary Seaman, MMR, 998910, Lobster, 26 August 1919
BOOTH, Harry, Ordinary Seaman, D/JX 138752, Royal Sovereign, 14 February 1936
BOOTH, Henry L, Leading Signalman, 231204, Pembroke (ex-Commonwealth), 16 March 1919
BOOTH, Major H, Able Seaman, J 26633, Wanderer, 21 April 1921
BOOTH, Patrick A, Lieutenant, FAA, 711 Sqn, London, 30 November 1937
BOOTH, Sidney G, Leading Stoker, K 22689, Restless, 13 November 1927
BOOTHROYD, Richard, Private, RMLI, 18942 (Po), RM, 6th Battalion, 27 August 1919
BOREHAM, Wilfred M, Able Seaman, C/J 112917, Calypso, 13 January 1931
BORG, John, Officer's Steward 1c, LX 20438, Frobisher, 22 September 1928
BORGNET, Eric C J, Boy 2c, J 107596, Impregnable, 29 August 1923
BORNE, John, Stoker Petty Officer, 288252, Dolphin, 24 January 1919
BORTHWICK, William J, Able Seaman, J 40070, Malaya, 16 February 1927
BOSLEY, Luther, Telegraphist, J 35185 (Po), Speedy, 11 May 1919
BOSWELL, James, Boy Servant, L 11998, Victory, 30 March 1919
BOSWELL, Walter O, Lieutenant, RNVR, ML.240, motor launch, 3 March 1919
BOTHERAS, William R, Lieutenant, RNR, Royal Naval Reserve, 6 April 1932
BOTTOMLEY, Frederick C, Lieutenant Commander, Victory, 19 July 1921
BOTTOMLEY, Joseph H, Stoker Petty Officer, K 22901, Conquest, 17 April 1925
BOTTOMLEY, William E, Petty Officer, J 41477, Enterprise, 2 December 1929
BOTTOMS, Arthur, Able Seaman, RNVR, KP 556, Anson Battalion, RND, 28 February 1919
BOTWRIGHT, Tom W, Gunner, Excellent, 22 February 1922
BOULT, George W, Officer's Cook 1c, L 5921, Ramillies, 6 March 1919
BOULTON, John, Able Seaman, J 45039 (Ch), Verulam, 4 September 1919
BOULTON, Robert, Lieutenant (ret), Royal Navy, 3 April 1919
BOULTON, Robert W, Boy 2c, J 94034, Impregnable, 24 February 1919
BOUNDS, Francis C, Officer's Steward 1c, 357382, Royal Oak, 13 January 1922
BOURDEN, Harry H, Seaman, Newfoundland RNR, X 2793, Vivid, 11 December 1918
BOW, Robert W, Ordinary Seaman, J 101624, Emperor of India, 19 May 1924
BOWDEN, Albert H, Able Seaman, J 103863, Vivid, 25 April 1930
BOWDEN, Sidney N, Leading Supply Assistant, C/MX 45468, Pembroke, 13 March 1936
BOWELL, Ernest W, Leading Seaman, J 30334, Danae, 24 August 1922
BOWEN, Morris, Stoker 1c, K 11695, Tiger, 25 May 1920
BOWEN, Thomas, Leading Stoker, 116939 (Dev), Cairo, 14 April 1921
BOWEN, Thomas, Leading Stoker, K 11639, Tamar, 15 April 1921
BOWER, Ivor, Chief Engine Room Artificer 2c, D/M 33637, Exeter, 14 January 1934
BOWER, James, Petty Officer, J 572, Barham, 2 October 1925
BOWER, Reginald T, Signalman, J 72840, Cardiff, 27 January 1921
BOWERMAN, Thomas J, Engine Room Artificer 5c, M 14502, Catspaw, 31 December 1919
BOWERS, Robert C, Able Seaman, C/J 104875, Poseidon, 9 June 1931
BOWIE, George N, Able Seaman, Dockyard Employee, Zest, water carrier, 12 March 1932
BOWLER, Henry E, Leading Seaman, RNVR, Sussex 3/334, President III, 17 February 1919
BOWLES, Edward J, Engineer Lieutenant, K.5, 20 January 1921
BOWLES, Gordon G, Private, RMLI, 16757 (Po), M.22, monitor, 20 February 1919
BOWLES, John T, Engineman, RNR, DA 6507, John Robert, 1 February 1919
BOWMAN, Alfred, Stoker, RNR, U 1597, Challenger, 21 February 1919
BOWMAN, Henry, Chief Skipper, RNR, Royal Naval Reserve, 19 November 1928
BOXALL, Cyril H, Able Seaman, P/JX 135148, Birmingham, 3 April 1939
BOXALL, Frederick A B, Sick Berth Attendant, M 30697, Pembroke, 22 July 1923
BOXALL, Henry R, Engine Room Artificer 2c, M 12568, Crocus, 22 November 1922
BOXER, Peter N, Sub Lieutenant, FAA, 714 Flight, Manchester, 23 December 1938
BOYD, Alfred, Engine Room Artificer 2c, M 18099, P.47, 24 September 1923
BOYD, Kenneth Mac C, Petty Officer, 217767, Pembroke, 17 April 1921
BOYD, Leonard F, Able Seaman, P/J 109533, Ladybird, 9 May 1932
BOYD, William, Stoker Petty Officer, 297448 (Po), Gentian, 15 July 1919
BOYD, William, Supply Petty Officer, M 3879, Sandhurst, 9 May 1928
BOYD, William A, Musician, RMB, RMB 1059, Commonwealth, 19 February 1919
BOYES, Jack, Stoker 1c, K 63216, Valerian, 22 October 1926
BOYLE, James C C, Surgeon Lieutenant, Egmont (ex-Wolsey), 29 August 1927
BOYLE, William, Able Seaman, RNVR, Tyneside Z 4517, 2nd Reserve Battalion, RND, 5 February 1919
BOYNE, John, Seaman, RNR, A 7628, President III, 19 December 1918
BOZMAN, David, Stoker Petty Officer, D/K 64310, RN Hospital, Plymouth, 11 December 1938

BRACE, Benjamin, Chief Engine Room Artificer 1c, D/M 1987, Lucia, 19 April 1931
BRACE, Edward C, Leading Seaman, P/J 31814, Pembroke, 12 May 1935
BRACE, George W, Stoker Petty Officer, K 7108, Egmont (Wolsey), 3 January 1929
BRACEGIRDLE, James E, Ordinary Seaman, J 76736, Resolution, 30 December 1918
BRACEWELL, Frank, Senior Reserve Attendant, M 10546, Classic, hospital ship, 13 February 1919
BRACEWELL, Robinson, Chief Engine Room Artificer 1c, 270477, Kinross, 16 June 1919
BRACKENBURY, Albert V, Deck Hand, RNR, DA 6940, Principal, 25 November 1918
BRADBURY, Arthur E, Leading Seaman, J 21068, King George V, 4 March 1921

BRADBURY, Henry A, Officer's Steward 2c, L 6249, Victory, 24 May 1919
BRADDICK, James W, Able Seaman, J 87229, H.44, 28 February 1925
BRADE, Frank T, Act/Lieutenant Commander, RNR, CMB.67A, coastal motor boat, 18 August 1919
BRADFORD, Samuel A, Gunner, RMA, RMA 10424, Emperor of India, 7 February 1921
BRADLEY, Arthur R, Surgeon Captain, RNVR, Royal Naval Volunteer Reserve, 20 August 1930
BRADLEY, Charles A B, Chief Ordnance Artificer 1c, D/M 7379, Drake, 30 May 1934
BRADLEY, George F, Petty Officer, C/J 28505, Pembroke, 12 February 1937
BRADLEY, Henry G N, Telegraphist, C/J 32678, Wolfhound, 10 October 1937
BRADLEY, James G, Chief Engine Room Artificer 2c, D/M 10895, Drake, 12 March 1936
BRADLEY, Joseph A, Chief Stoker, P/K 55729, Drake, 18 March 1936
BRADLEY, Robert G, Stoker 1c, K 21424, Cyclamen, 3 August 1928
BRADLEY, Samuel S, Gunner, RMA, RMA 15500, RMA Eastney, 6 February 1919
BRADLEY, Thomas H J, Private, RMLI, 18070 (Po), Portsmouth Division, RMLI, 11 November 1920
BRADLEY, William J, Able Seaman, J 78842, Victory, 18 March 1919
BRADSHAW, Robert H, Lieutenant, RM, P R /T Course, 6 March 1935
BRADY, Arthur C, Able Seaman, P/JX 141066, Royal Navy, 14 March 1938
BRADY, Daniel, Quartermaster, MMR, 997437, Eaglet, 1 February 1920
BRAGG, Edward C, Sick Berth Attendant, M 35459, Pembroke, 9 June 1922
BRAGG, Frederick E, Leading Seaman, J 98090, Vivid, 10 June 1927
BRAGG, Leslie P, Stoker 1c, D/KX 83226, Drake, 12 November 1936
BRAHAM, Harry G, Petty Officer, J 31109, Valerian, 22 October 1926
BRAID, Alexander C, Petty Officer, J 7272, Ramillies, 15 July 1927
BRAIN, Frederick J, Stoker Petty Officer, K 21058, Pembroke, 25 July 1927
BRAITHWAITE, Charles, Stoker 1c, K 50409, Vivid, 17 December 1919
BRAMBRICK, Thomas, Stoker 1c, D/KX 86324, Thetis, 3 June 1939
BRANAGH, Henry, Master at Arms, M 7886, Vivid, 15 August 1923
BRAND, Frank H, Petty Officer, 239324, Pembroke, 5 September 1921
BRAND, Frederick A, Stoker Petty Officer, 307776, Gilia, 26 March 1919
BRAND, James H, Leading Seaman, RNR, A 5859, Merlin II, 26 November 1918
BRANDON, Edwin S, Petty Officer, 238874, Victory, 22 March 1920
BRANFILL, Richard B, Private, RMLI, 14189 (Ch), Chatham Division, RMLI, 14 March 1919
BRANSBY, Arthur, Able Seaman, 238417, Pembroke, 13 December 1920
BRANSFIELD, Michael J, Shipwright 1c, 346265, Tarantula, 11 July 1926
BRASNETT, Archibald H, Stoker Petty Officer, K 5384 (Po), Mallow, 22 February 1919
BRATBY, Kenneth K, Able Seaman, RNVR, R 6054, Drake Battalion, RND, 3 April 1919
BRAY, Albert E, Chaplain, Victory, 29 April 1924
BRAY, George B, Lieutenant Commander, RNR, Royal Naval Reserve, 26 March 1930
BRAY, John, Chief Petty Officer Cook, 347534, Vivid, 25 July 1928
BRAY, William C, Boy 2c, J 87718, Powerful, 25 November 1918
BRAY, William J, Boy 2c, J 103439, Impregnable, 10 January 1922
BRAY, William J, Chief Stoker, 163063, Pomone, 14 December 1919
BRAY, William J, Stoker Petty Officer, K 11968, Silvio, 30 November 1919
BRAYBROOKE, Charles W, Major, RM, Royal Marines, 24 March 1920
BRAZELL, William, Private, RM, S 14208 (Deal), RM Labour Corps, 27 February 1919
BRAZIER, Robert, Trimmer, MMR, 864773, Eaglet, 15 February 1919
BREACH, Mark E, Officer's Steward 1c, L 3459, Wessex, 11 April 1927
BREDDY, Gilbert, Stoker Petty Officer, K 11187, Vixen, 21 November 1918
BREHANT, John T, Able Seaman, MMR, 954203, Seadog, 22 February 1919
BREINGAN, Henry H, Stoker 1c, SS 116567 (Po), Penarth, 4 February 1919
BREMNER, John, Leading Stoker, SS 101525, Economy, 25 November 1918
BREMRIDGE, James P A, Lieutenant Commander, Delhi, 21 September 1926
BRENNAN, Albert, Stoker 1c, C/KX 80311, Valiant, 24 April 1931
BRENNAN, Arthur P, Paymaster Lieutenant, RNR, Royal Naval Reserve, 24 August 1932
BRENNAN, Joseph, Able Seaman, SS 5442, Raleigh, 11 November 1921
BRENTON, Alfred, Chief Painter, 346970, Vivid, 1 August 1925
BRESNER, Frank R, Civilian Contractor, Thetis, 3 June 1939
BRETT, Bertram H, Gunner, Leith, 1 December 1935
BRETT, George F, Officer's Steward 3c, L 10024, Hermione, 24 February 1919
BREWER, Albert E J, Able Seaman, J 51017 (Dev), Suffolk, 5 December 1918
BREWER, Arthur B, Mechanician, 310926, Catspaw, 31 December 1919
BREWER, Arthur H, Able Seaman, J 36739, Tiger, 27 August 1919
BREWER, Herbert W, Regulating Petty Officer, D/M 38607, Carysfort, 27 November 1930
BREWER, William E, Telegraphist, J 41903, Blue Sky, tender to Queen Elizabeth, 12 June 1922
BREWETON, Charles T, Stoker 1c, SS 124245, Emperor of India, 25 February 1922
BRICKNELL, Victor J, Able Seaman, P/J 86829, Royal Navy, 23 April 1939
BRIDGER, Arthur, Stoker Petty Officer, K 21764, Valerian, 22 October 1926
BRIDGEWATER, Harold E, Paymaster, RNCVR, Rainbow (RCN), 22 October 1919
BRIDLE, Sidney J, Telegraphist, J 32026, Mersey, 1 January 1919
BRIEN, Peter J, Stoker 1c, K 57245, Valerian, 22 October 1926
BRIFFA, Carmelo, Officer's Cook 3c, L 11138, Egmont, 10 July 1919
BRIGGS, Ernest F, Paymaster Sub Lieutenant, RNR, Teutonic, 20 December 1918
BRIGGS, Harry, Telegraphist, J 52442, Victory, 26 February 1919
BRIGGS, James F, Stoker 1c, K 42368, Lake Tanganyika Flotilla, 6 January 1919
BRIGGS, Oscar C, 2nd Hand, RNR, DA 2576, Pekin, 28 November 1918
BRIGHT, George H, Engine Room Artificer 2c, M 1671, Pembroke, 2 September 1920

BRINCAT, Carmelo, Officer's Cook 2c, L 10884, Berberis, 16 December 1918
BRINDLE, Harold, Able Seaman, J 15930, Victory, 26 May 1919
BRINDLE, Joseph S, Marine, RM, 222157 (Ply), Devonshire, 26 July 1929
BRINDLEY, Thomas, Boy 1c, D/JX 148446, Devonshire, 21 June 1937
BRINSON, Alfred S, Coastguardsman 3c, 9763 (Ch), Colleen, 27 April 1921
BRINTON, Gerald L, Lieutenant, RAF service, 18 August 1931
BRISCOE, George, Stoker 1c, P/KX 78217, Champion, 31 January 1931
BRISCOE, Robert F, Honorary Lieutenant, RNR, Royal Naval Reserve, 28 October 1920
BRISK, William, Stoker Petty Officer, 304964, Pembroke, 16 April 1924
BRISTOW, Clifford L, Engine Room Artificer 4c, M 39528, Birmingham, 22 March 1928
BRISTOW, Geoffrey L, Lieutenant, RNVR, London Division, RNVR, 24 November 1932
BRISTOW, John G, Plumber 2c, M 34887, Vernon, 21 December 1927
BRISTOW, Reginald, Stoker 1c, K 47221, Pembroke, 21 February 1919
BRITTAIN, Harold J, Chief Shipwright 2c, C/M 2447, Pembroke, 28 August 1933
BROAD, Charles W, Able Seaman, J 20915 (Ch), Dragon, 17 October 1919
BROAD, John R, Electrical Artificer 1c, 347604, Caradoc, 10 December 1926
BROAD, Samuel, Civilian Contractor, Thetis, 3 June 1939
BROAD, Thomas M (real name, but served as Thomas Coombes), Petty Officer, 229152, Hood, 31 January 1923
BROADRIBB, Walter F, Able Seaman, D/JX 127701, Drake, 4 October 1935
BROCK, Edwin F, Boy 2c, J 104079, Colossus, 7 November 1921
BROCKBANK, Harold G, Petty Officer, 234681, ML.389, motor launch (also shown as ML.365), 20 September 1919
BROCKHURST, Archibald, Leading Stoker, K 6755, Valerian, 22 October 1926
BROCKS, Leslie B, Officer's Steward 3c, L 8946, Superb, 12 December 1918
BROMLEY, James A E, Able Seaman, J 113690, Sheffield, 24 February 1939
BROOKE, Edward E, Lieutenant Commander, President (ex-Strongbow), 10 February 1919
BROOKE, Robert S, Leading Stoker, D/KX 81583, Thetis, 3 June 1939
BROOKER, Alfred A, Supply Petty Officer, D/M 37366, Laburnum, 7 September 1934
BROOKER, Alfred W, Stoker 1c, K 37828, Bacchante, 16 February 1919
BROOKES, Frederick R, Stoker 1c, K 43616, Rocket, 5 January 1924
BROOKES, Reginald, Private, RMLI, 17630 (Ply), London, 31 July 1919
BROOKE-SHORT, Cecil, Major, RM, Cumberland, 28 June 1937
BROOKS, Albert H, Stoker 1c, K 23341 (Dev), Kinross, 16 June 1919
BROOKS, Albert W, Stoker 1c, K 12890, Hecla, 5 March 1920
BROOKS, Albert, Petty Officer 1c, 174789, Agamemnon, 31 March 1919
BROOKS, Ernest E, Stoker 1c, K 49403, London, 4 December 1918
BROOKS, George, Stoker 2c, K 48680, Albatross, 12 January 1919
BROOKS, Henry T, Petty Officer, D/J 33798, Adventure, 3 July 1933
BROOKS, William R, Petty Officer, P/J 23358, Royal Navy, 31 October 1935
BROOKSMITH, Eldred S, Captain, Iron Duke, 3 December 1931

BROOKWAY, Henry T, Leading Signalman, J 19058, Hawkins, 12 June 1921
BROOMHAM, Charles, Chief Stoker, KX 75990, Cardiff, 18 December 1937
BROTHERHOOD, Richard H, Sapper, RM, S 845 (Deal), 2nd Field Company, Divisional Engineers, RND, 23 February 1919
BROUGH, George T, Boy 2c, JX 150358, Ganges, 2 March 1937
BROUGHTON, Frederick G, Stoker 1c, K 35876, Thisbe, 19 March 1919
BROWN, Albert G T, Lieutenant Commander, Rtd, Royal Navy, 7 December 1934
BROWN, Albert H, Able Seaman, J 76555, Ben Alder, 12 March 1919
BROWN, Alfred H, Leading Stoker, K 9126, Argus, 17 November 1924
BROWN, Annesley G L, Surgeon Lieutenant Commander, Medical Officer's Promotion Course, 8 April 1934
BROWN, Archibald Mc I, Stoker 1c, K 45315, Dianthus, 3 December 1918
BROWN, Arthur, Marine, X 1283 (Ch), RM Deal, 31 December 1935
BROWN, Arthur H, Painter 3c, M 13869, Fisgard, 18 March 1919
BROWN, Brian M, Sub Lieutenant, RNR, Royal Naval Reserve, 1 November 1931
BROWN, Charles, Coastguardsman, 166914, HM Coastguard Station Ballygrovane, 25 July 1920
BROWN, Dougal Mc P, Leading Steward, C/L 12605, M.2, 29 January 1932
BROWN, Eric G, Able Seaman, J 45321, Sunflower, 1 February 1919
BROWN, Ernest A, Trimmer Cook, RNR, TC 902, Iolaire, 1 January 1919
BROWN, Ernest E G, Able Seaman, D/JX 135452, Grimsby, 29 May 1936
BROWN, Eustace W, Engine Room Artificer 3c, M 34385, Castor, 28 August 1923
BROWN, Francis, Leading Sick Berth Attendant, M 21645, Pembroke, 28 July 1927
BROWN, Frederick - see BARTER, Albert E, Stoker 1c
BROWN, George, Deck Hand, MMR, Ivanhoe, 9 January 1919
BROWN, George J, Leading Stoker, D/KX 76521, Hastings, 16 January 1933
BROWN, George V, Trimmer, RNR, TS 3905, Rene, 25 February 1919
BROWN, George W - see BEAL, George W, Leading Stoker,
BROWN, Harry G, Stoker 1c, K 8124, Furious, 4 February 1929
BROWN, Jack R, Deck Hand, RNR, DA 10376, Pembroke, 1 January 1919
BROWN, James, Stoker Petty Officer, 288047, Sapphire, 13 December 1918
BROWN, James M, Boy 1c, P/JX 141271, Hood, 19 January 1935
BROWN, John, Able Seaman, RNCVR, VR 3184, Niobe (RCN), 22 November 1918
BROWN, John R S, Able Seaman, SS 7409, Marlborough, 26 June 1920
BROWN, John W, Private, RMLI, S 236 (Ch), 3rd Battalion, RM, 6 December 1918
BROWN, Joseph, Able Seaman, J 15869, Tenedos, 1 April 1921
BROWN, Leslie C F, Boy 2, SX 122166, Ganges, 31 December 1928
BROWN, Ralph, Signal Boy, J 89978, Ganges, 28 November 1918
BROWN, Richard J, Engineer Commander, Pembroke, 11 November 1928
BROWN, Robert A, Ordinary Seaman, P/JX 136366, Nelson, 10 October 1935
BROWN, Sidney A, Shipwright 2c, P/M 33945, Nelson, 19 November 1932
BROWN, Thomas W, Salvage Boatswain, MMR, Hughli, Royal Fleet Auxiliary, 26 April 1919
BROWN, Walter M, Private, RMLI, 15988 (Ch), RM Siege

Battery, 29 November 1918
BROWN, William, Chief Stoker, 154094, Pembroke, 15 November 1918
BROWN, William, Civilian Contractor, Thetis, 3 June 1939
BROWN, William G, Lieutenant, RNR, Duchess of Rothesay, 8 March 1919
BROWNE, Charles A, Captain, Glasgow, 30 June 1937
BROWNE, Ernest R, Skipper, RNR, Cromorna, 7 April 1919
BROWNE, Louis C, Stoker 1c, SS 23159, Titania, 7 October 1920
BROWNLOW, Frederick, Able Seaman, C/SSX 17721, Diana, 8 May 1938
BROWNLOW, John H, Gunner, RMA, RMA S 2055, 3rd Battalion, RM, 2 February 1919
BRUCE, Alfred N, Leading Seaman, P/J 104004, H.24, 17 June 1932
BRUCE, George, Leading Seaman, RNVR, London Z 2817, Hood Battalion, RND, 28 March 1920
BRUCE, Henry, Trimmer, RNR, TS 5423, Leonard, 8 January 1920
BRUCE, James A, Leading Seaman, 193410, Poppy, on books of Colleen, 11 March 1920
BRUCE, John, Able Seaman, RNVR, Tyneside 2/169, Collingwood Battalion, RND, 14 November 1918
BRUEN, Charles J, Private, RMLI, 18554 (Po), RMLI, 1st Reserve Battalion, 21 April 1919
BRUNDLE, Archie L, Able Seaman, C/JX 131734, Medway, 26 July 1939
BRUNNING, David, Naval Cadet, Sea Cadet Corps, 12 July 1929
BRUNNING, David J, Joiner 1c, C/M 4523, Hermes, 22 April 1932
BRUNO, Oltemus, Wardroom Steward, L 390 (Maltese), Comet, 12 January 1937
BRUNSDON, Richard T, Marine, 20456 (Po), Egmont, 31 December 1930
BRURTON, Harold, Leading Stoker, D/JX 77767, Selkirk, 21 December 1935
BRYAN, Francis, Stoker 1c, K 37201, Pembroke, 24 June 1922
BRYAN, Thomas L G, Lieutenant, RM, Egmont, 30 March 1926
BRYAN, William C, Boy 1c, J 103997, Ganges, 14 July 1922
BRYANT, Edward, Deck Hand, RNR, SD 3121, Victory, 22 February 1919
BRYANT, Frederick A, Leading Seaman, J 11302, Defiance, 30 May 1924
BRYANT, George, Engineman, RNR, ES 3152, Wallington, 10 December 1918
BRYANT, William C, Engine Room Artificer 4c, C/MX 48241, Hussar, 8 December 1938
BRYANT, William W, Ordinary Seaman, RAN, 6171, Australia (RAN), 16 March 1920
BRYCE, Hugh, Stoker 1c, K 61869, Effingham, 28 June 1929
BRYDON, William E, Signalman, RAN, 4562, Huon (RAN), 29 September 1919
BRYMNER, John, Linesman, MMR, Mollusc, Royal Fleet Auxiliary, 10 December 1918

BUCHAN, Charles, Marine, RM, Ply/18555, Hood, 12 March 1930
BUCHAN, James, Stoker 1c, K 33821, Rob Roy, 16 February 1919
BUCHANAN, Peter, Seaman, RNR, A 7700, Iolaire (Pembroke, O/P), 1 January 1919
BUCHANAN, William M, Lieutenant, RNR, President, 19 February 1919
BUCK, Elijah F, Chief Petty Officer, 224883, L.24, 10 January 1924
BUCK, Jack L W, Engine Room Artificer 5c, D/MX 47650, Glorious, 15 October 1933
BUCK, James W, Deck Hand, RNR, DA 15469, Petrel, 10 March 1919
BUCKIE, Barry, Yeoman of Signals, 212183, Victory, 2 March 1921
BUCKIE, Herbert, Stoker 1c, 291863, Pembroke, 10 December 1918
BUCKINGHAM, John, Petty Officer, J 395, Benbow, 12 May 1927
BUCKLAND, Herbert, Chief Stoker, 308049, Victory, 5 March 1919
BUCKLE, Harry J, Engineer Lieutenant, Excellent, 17 August 1919
BUCKLE, Hugh C, Captain, RN War College, Greenwich, 21 May 1924
BUCKLEE, Fred, Stoker Petty Officer, 297696, Pembroke, 18 April 1919
BUCKLER, George A, Gunner, RMA, RMA 9792, RMA Eastney, 17 February 1919
BUCKLEY, John H, Lieutenant, Otway, 9 February 1932
BUCKLEY, Patrick J, Donkeyman, MMR, 600804, Almanzora, 29 November 1918
BUDGE, John S, Engineer Commander, Devonport Dockyard, 25 March 1924
BUDGEON, James, Stoker 1c, K 23665, Victory, 26 December 1921
BUGG, Rupert W, Leading Deck Hand, RNR, SD 5046, Victory, 22 March 1919
BUGG, William H, Able Seaman, J 6759, Valerian, 22 October 1926
BUGGS, Harry, Stoker Petty Officer, K 4487, Dunedin, 13 October 1920
BUGLER, Albert E, Ordinary Seaman, J 77855, Paxton, 20 December 1918
BULBECK, Harold J, Leading Seaman, J 27703, L.24, 10 January 1924
BULL, Charles E, Leading Signalman, J 40968, L.12, 9 July 1929
BULL, Donald S, Boy 1c, C/J 156960, Curlew, 13 March 1939
BULL, Edward G, Leading Seaman, J 82644, Pembroke, 1 February 1930
BULL, William M, Surgeon Commander (D), RNVR, London Division, RNVR, 15 December 1938
BULLAMORE, Arthur, Deck Hand, RNR, SD 3177, Lively II, 2 February 1919
BULLEN, Albert T W, Electrical Artificer 5c, M 30451, Vernon, 27 December 1918
BULLEN, Ernest, Petty Officer, 236107, Mersey, 2 January 1919
BULLEN, Henry C, Stoker 1c, 302962, Antrim, 7 March 1920
BULLEN, John F, Engine Room Artificer Apprentice, M 26915, Indus, 18 October 1921
BULLEN, John J, Marine, P/X 1484, Orion, 10 February 1937
BULLER, Gordon, Able Seaman, C/J 111766, Mantis, 16 February 1931
BULLOCK, Harry, Stoker 1c, K 32792, Heather, on books of Colleen, 17 November 1918
BULLOCK, James W, Able Seaman, J 21915, Phaeton, 27 September 1919
BULLOCK, Osmund F L, Lieutenant, FAA, 811 Sqn, Furious, 2 October 1933
BUMFORD, John R, Boy 2c, J 91937, Ganges, 15 November 1918
BUNDEY, Walter R T, Able Seaman, P/J 36942, Vernon, 3 September 1934
BUNDY, Walter W, Stoker 1c, K 10451, Victoria & Albert, Royal Yacht, 27 July 1924
BUNGEY, Stewart A, Boy 2c, J 103932, Impregnable, 19 March 1922
BUNKER, Ronald O, Able Seaman, J 19911, Westcott, 21 July 1921
BUNT, Frederick N, Leading Cook, D/M 39109, Caradoc, 8 June 1933
BUNTING, Francis, Engineman, MMR, Basuto, mercantile fleet auxiliary, 9 December 1918
BUNTING, Henry J, Colour Sergeant, RMLI, 22760, RM Headquarters, 19 June 1920

BURBERRY, Bert, Leading Stoker, K 22945, Valerian, 22 October 1926
BURBRIDGE, Stanley H G, Boy 2c, J 112093, Ganges, 28 November 1924
BURCH, Ronald E, Leading Seaman, D/JX 130255, Matabele, 19 July 1939
BURDEN, Edward P, Private, RMLI, S 2503 (Po), 1st RM Battalion, RND, 24 November 1918
BURDEN, Norman W, Private, RMLI, 18317 (Ch), Chatham Division, RMLI, 8 February 1919
BURDEN, Walter, Chief Mechanician 2c, 358236, Victory, 20 November 1921
BURDON, John E, Engine Room Artificer 2c, M 11023, Tartar, 18 November 1918
BURDY, Wallace J, Leading Signalman, J 37130, Royal Oak, 23 March 1928
BURFORD, Frederick W, Able Seaman, MMR, 100302, Walton Belle, 3 August 1919
BURGE, Samuel, Able Seaman, J 12020, Vivid, 14 April 1922
BURGESS, Ewart, Stoker, D/KX 90840, Furious, 20 April 1938
BURGESS, Gilbert M, Able Seaman, J 40911, Cleopatra, 3 November 1920
BURGESS, Harold, Mate, Furious, 27 January 1919
BURGESS, Robert O, Officer's Steward 2c, L 6606, Vivid, 12 April 1920
BURGESS, William, Stoker 1c, K 47262, Valerian, 22 October 1926
BURKE, James A, Stoker 1c, 296276, Devonshire, 10 February 1919
BURKE, Richard S, Chief Yeoman of Signals, 209562, Vivid, 27 February 1922
BURN, Allen J, Able Seaman, J 49807, Vernon, 14 May 1924
BURN, John, Commander, RNR, Victory, 18 May 1920
BURNBY, Henry J, Chief Petty Officer, P/J 6397, Victory, 13 January 1931
BURNELL, Arthur E, Private, RMLI, 19174 (Po), Caledon, 31 August 1920
BURNETT, John, Leading Telegraphist, P/J 26636, Vernon, 4 March 1932
BURNETT, John E, Bandmaster 1c, RMB 1467, Renown, 13 February 1927
BURNETT, Oliver D, Stoker Petty Officer, 309917 (Ch), Emile Nobel, 21 May 1919
BURNETT, Reginald J, Ordinary Seaman, J 113249, Concord, 9 May 1927
BURNEY, James, Marine, 22256 (Po), Cornwall, 22 March 1933
BURNS, Allan R, Able Seaman, J 24920, Excellent, 17 September 1923
BURNS, Erasmus J, Gunner, Archer, 22 February 1919
BURNS, Frederick G, Ty/Lieutenant, RNVR, President, 23 November 1918
BURNS, John, Stoker 1c, K 17609 (Po), K.5, 20 January 1921
BURNS, Norman S, Leading Aircraftsman, RAF, 590712, FAA, 711 Sqn, London, 30 November 1937
BURNS, Richard, Ordinary Seaman, C/SSX 18996, Pembroke, 10 October 1936
BURRAGE, John, Seaman, Newfoundland RNR, Z 1789, Hyndford, steamship, 19 November 1918
BURREL, Thomas H, Chief Stoker, 307218, Waterhen, 24 February 1925
BURRELL, Sykes S, Able Seaman, P/JX 132937, Victory, 27 April 1933
BURREN, Charles H B, Boatswain, St Genny, 12 January 1930
BURRIDGE, Jack, Leading Telegraphist, P/J 60943, M.2, 29 January 1932
BURROWS, Alfred H S, Stoker 1c, K 57934, Valerian, 22 October 1926
BURROWS, Edmund G, Lieutenant, Constance, 16 September 1924
BURROWS, William R, Able Seaman, P/J 113797, Challenger, 15 August 1933

BURT, Fred H J, Chief Stoker, K 10238, Coventry, 8 March 1923
BURTON, George W, Leading Telegraphist, J 39729, FAA, 423 Sqn, Eagle, 18 January 1927
BURTON, James, Engine Room Artificer 4c, M 28432, Centaur, 20 March 1919
BURTON, Richard, Captain, RMLI, RM, 6th Battalion, 8 September 1919
BURTON, Victor L, Seaman, RNR, A 8845, Penarth, 4 February 1919
BURY, George W, Lieutenant, RNVR, Egmont, 23 September 1920
BUSBY, Victor A H, Private, RMLI, 21231 (Ch), Chatham Division, RMLI, 13 April 1920
BUSH, Joseph, Corporal, RMLI, 5112 (Po)(RFR A 833), Portsmouth Battalion, RND, 13 March 1919
BUSH, Nathaniel, Able Seaman, D/JX 146057, Defiance, 26 February 1936
BUSHE, Thomas, Boy 2c, JX 142505, Ganges, 16 January 1935
BUSHELL, Sidney, Stoker Petty Officer, K 22803, Cumberland, 15 May 1930
BUSHELL, William J, Petty Officer, P/JX 126659, Frobisher, 27 January 1932
BUSS, John W, Able Seaman, J 2144 (Ch), Fandango, 3 July 1919
BUSTARD, Albert E, Able Seaman, MMR, 986733, Peter Pan, 9 July 1919
BUSUTTIL, Guiseppe, Bandsman, E/M 4664, St Angelo, 15 June 1935
BUSWELL, Leonard W, Able Seaman, D/J 109194, Exeter, 21 January 1933
BUTCHER, Edward M, Stoker 1c, 158337, Blenheim, 20 July 1923
BUTCHER, Harold F, Able Seaman, C/J 91916, M.2, 29 January 1932
BUTCHER, Henry J, Boy 2c, J 103454, Impregnable, 12 June 1922
BUTCHER, William, Deck Hand, RNR, DA 19656, Newbury, 2 March 1919
BUTLAND, Richard W H, Officer's Steward, L 9741 (Po), K.5, 20 January 1921
BUTLER, Cecil, Telegraphist, J 89971, Rodney, 27 April 1930
BUTLER, Charles W, Petty Officer Steward, P/L 4258, Victory, 15 October 1934
BUTLER, Frank V, Able Seaman, J 31120, Tiger, 4 January 1922
BUTLER, Henry C, Petty Officer, 228827, Barham, 14 August 1927
BUTLER, Henry, Stoker 1c, K 15724 (Po), L.55, 4 June 1919
BUTLER, James, Ordinary Seaman, RNVR, MC 922, Larkspur, 9 June 1919
BUTLER, John, Stoker 1c, K 61542, Tenacious, 25 June 1927
BUTLER, Sidney A, Marine, 18375 (Po), Portsmouth Division, RM, 15 August 1925
BUTLER-COLE, Thomas B, Lieutenant (E), Britannia, RN College, Dartmouth, 27 July 1930
BUTLIN, Edward S R, Lieutenant, Queen Elizabeth, 10 June 1922
BUTT, Ronald A F, Signal Boy, J 112249, Revenge, 30 September 1926
BUTTERWORTH, Arthur, Able Seaman, RNVR, S 1992 (Palace), Ganges II, 16 November 1918
BUTTIGIEG, Giovanni, Able Seaman, 228300, Egmont, 17 December 1918
BUTTLE, James F, Able Seaman, J 22045, M.1, 12 November 1925
BUTTLER, Sidney A, Marine, 18375 (Po), Centurion, 15 August 1925
BUXTON, Bernard, Commander, Birmingham, 29 December 1923
BUXTON, James F, Able Seaman, J 78202, TB.18, torpedo boat, 31 December 1918

BYCROFT, George E, Stoker Petty Officer, 310823, Victory, 25 December 1918

BYGRAVE, William, Able Seaman, J 22823, M.25, monitor, 4 December 1918
BYRNE, Alan W, Electrical Artificer 2c, P/MX 47269, Thetis, 3 June 1939
BYRNE, John, Able Seaman, RNVR, R 3758, 1st RM Battalion, RND, attached Howe Battalion, 15 April 1919
BYRNE, John, Boy 2c, JX 149054, Royal Navy, 27 March 1937
BYRON, Charles G, Ty/Lieutenant, RNR, Earl of Peterborough, 10 December 1918
BYRON, John, Warrant Engineer, L.24, 10 January 1924

C

CADAGAN, Albert, Able Seaman, J 55263, ML.291, motor launch, 26 December 1921

CADD, William, Boy 1c, J 89738, Ramillies, 27 April 1919

CADELL, Alexander R, Lieutenant, Victory, 14 May 1928

CAFFERY, William H, Stoker 1c, 283835, Collingwood Battalion, RND, 22 February 1919

CAHALANE, Daniel, Seaman, RNR, A 5310, Anson Battalion, RND, 2 May 1919

CAHILL, Joseph, Able Seaman, J 12725, Warspite, 6 October 1923

CAIN, James, Ordinary Seaman, P/SSX 14980, Victory I, 2 May 1935

CAIN, John T, Able Seaman, RNVR, Clyde Z 7679, President, 14 February 1919

CAIN, John, Assistant Cook, MMR, 898718, Hughli, Royal Fleet Auxiliary, 26 April 1919

CAIN, Percy E, Act/Lieutenant Commander, RNVR, Royal Naval Volunteer Reserve, 23 March 1921

CAIRNS, David C, Able Seaman, C/SSX 16483, Caledonia, 3 March 1939

CAITHNESS, William, Surgeon Lieutenant Commander, RNVR, Royal Naval Volunteer Reserve, 28 March 1931

CAKE, Percy L, Boy 2c, J 112646, Ganges, 1 June 1925

CAKEBREAD, Arthur, Lieutenant, RNVR, Juno, 7 July 1919

CALDER, Robert, Telegraphist, J 82617, Vivid, 25 September 1925

CALDICOTT, Alfred G, Stoker Petty Officer, C/K 58055, Pembroke, 26 October 1931

CALEY, William, Able Seaman, J 83751, Ladybird, 22 August 1921

CALLAGHAN, James, Coastguardsman 3c, 177301, Vivid, 13 October 1921

CALLAGHAN, James, Stoker 1c, K 30260, Kilfinny, 26 February 1919

CALLAGHAN, Sir George A, Admiral of the Fleet, Royal Navy, 23 November 1920

CALLAN, William D, Chief Gunner, Ark Royal, 8 March 1920

CALLARD, William G, Leading Cook, M 5663, Glorious, 17 March 1930

CALLAWAY, Albert A W, Leading Seaman, J 16817, Excellent, 22 June 1923

CALLAWAY, Frank Le M, Paymaster Lieutenant, Egmont, 3 March 1919

CALLEJA, Carmelo, Officer's Cook 1c, 167026, Victory, 14 January 1920

CALLINGHAM, Harry V, Able Seaman, P/JX 132669, Excellent, 9 June 1933

CALLISTER, George, Sergeant, RMA, RMA 10298, Royal Marines HQ, 20 February 1923

CALLOW, Cecil C, Musician, RMB X 259, Excellent, 18 August 1935

CALLOW, William, Private, RMLI, 16679 (Po), Leviathan, 20 January 1919

CALLUS, Angelo, Petty Officer 1c, 235504, Egmont, 7 February 1921

CALVERT, John J, Skipper, RNR, Royal Naval Reserve, 19 December 1931

CALVERT, Thomas F P, Rear Admiral, Royal Navy, 1 July 1938

CAME, John, Leading Telegraphist, J 808, Calypso, 20 July 1920

CAMERON, George W L, Chief Petty Officer, D/J 5457, Mersey Division, RNVR, 28 June 1934

CAMERON, John, Gunner, RMA, RMA 8752, RM Headquarters, 3 July 1921

CAMERON, Robert F, Seaman, RNR, X 18393 A, Blanche, 15 July 1939

CAMERON, Robert, Engineman, RNR, ES 2970, White Lilac, 30 October 1919

CAMERON, Simon, Salvage Shipwright, MMR, Hughli, Royal Fleet Auxiliary, 26 April 1919

CAMERON, Stanley R, Ordinary Seaman, P/JX 140622, Dorsetshire, 27 June 1937

CAMM, Thomson, Ordinary Seaman, J 85434, Marlborough, 12 April 1919

CAMPBELL, Alexander, Deck Hand, RNR, DA 11999, Iolaire (Venerable, O/P), 1 January 1919

CAMPBELL, Alexander, Deck Hand, RNR, DA 13353, Iolaire (Venerable, O/P), 1 January 1919

CAMPBELL, Alexander, Leading Seaman, RNR, C 2999, Iolaire (Victory, O/P), 1 January 1919

CAMPBELL, Alexander, Stoker 1c, C/K 63149, Pembroke, 21 September 1930

CAMPBELL, Angus, Seaman, RNR, C 3590, Iolaire (Excellent, O/P), 1 January 1919

CAMPBELL, Donald, Deck Hand, MMR, 973810, Ugie Bank, 10 December 1918

CAMPBELL, Donald, Leading Seaman, RNR, C 2058, Iolaire (Pembroke, O/P), 1 January 1919

CAMPBELL, Donald, Seaman, RNR, B 3356, Iolaire (Victory, O/P), 1 January 1919

CAMPBELL, George H, Supply Petty Officer, 306297, Caroline, 7 May 1922

CAMPBELL, George, Chief Officer, HM Coast Guard, HM Coastguard Station Craster, 3 March 1920

CAMPBELL, Gunning M, Major General, RM, RMLI, Adjutant General, 29 November 1920

CAMPBELL, Guy, Act/Paymaster Lieutenant Commander, Venerable, 25 November 1918

CAMPBELL, James, Able Seaman, J 20620 (Ch), Francol, Royal Fleet Auxiliary, 27 December 1919

CAMPBELL, James, Skipper, RNR, Royal Naval Reserve, 15 April 1936

CAMPBELL, John, Stoker 1c, P/K 58712, Stuart, 4 October 1930

CAMPBELL, Kenneth, Seaman, RNR, A 4804, Iolaire (Galatea, O/P), 1 January 1919

CAMPBELL, Lawrence, Able Seaman, J 28822, Victory, 24 February 1919

CAMPBELL, Murdo, Deck Hand, RNR, DA 20536, Iolaire (Matthew Flynn, O/P), 1 January 1919

CAMPBELL, O (initial only) M, Construction Worker, Construction Inspector (ion) R (abbreviation only partly known), 28 August 1921

CAMPBELL, Patrick M, Boy 1c, JX 148593, Royal Oak, 27 April 1937

CAMPBELL, William, Able Seaman, RAN, 9073 (RN J 7936), Australia (RAN), 1 June 1920

CAMPKIN, Herbert C, Stoker 2c, K 53408, Vivid, 26 November 1918

CANN, Headley, Leading Stoker, K 16998, L.24, 10 January 1924

CANNEL, James, Deck Hand, RNR, DA 18512, Vivid, 18 March 1919

CANNIFFE, James, Able Seaman, 229493, Hood, 22 May 1927

CANNON, Andrew J, Chief Stoker, 294688, Gardenia, 10 February 1920

CANNON, Sidney R F C, Marine, 22080 (Po), Dryad, 4 July 1934

CANT, Athol H, Leading Telegraphist, J 34995, H.42, 23 March 1922

CARBERY, Patrick, Marine, 17700 (Ch), Tamar III, 9 April 1933

CARD, Ernest, Boy 2c, J 109656, Impregnable, 30 November 1924

CARD, Frederick J, Stoker 2c, K 47579, Calliope, 27 January 1925

CARDY, William H, Greaser, MMR, 915126, Eaglet, 2 March 1919

CAREY, Alfred, Able Seaman, J 9112, Vivid (ex-Somme), 10 September 1920

CAREY, Michael (real name, but served as William Carter), Stoker 1c, 292476, Prince Eugene, 15 November 1918

CAREY, Thomas G, Lieutenant, Exeter, 24 March 1933
CAREY, William F H, Sergeant, RMA, RMA 7425, Iliona, hired yacht, 13 December 1918
CARISS, Philip H, Victualling Chief Petty Officer, M 2636, Vivid, 28 May 1919
CARLINE, Leonard, Leading Telegraphist, J 6437, L.7, 20 August 1926
CARN, Francis C, Stoker 1c, K 58953, Pembroke, 17 March 1929
CARN-DUFF, Herbert J, Lieutenant, Valiant, 13 February 1922
CARNE, Robert R B, Stoker 2c, K 49920, Bacchante, 10 February 1919
CARNE, Thomas W, Stoker Petty Officer, 312380, Woolwich (ex-Garland), 18 March 1920
CARNEIRO, Victor C, Officer's Steward 2c, L 8960, Crocus, 9 January 1925
CARNEY, Edward, Ordinary Seaman, J 65549, Moorsom, 11 February 1919
CARNOCHAN, Andrew, Able Seaman, J 32306, Marlborough, 3 March 1919
CARPENTER, Allan B, Deck Hand, RNR, DA 3818, Mitres, 9 January 1919
CARPENTER, Henry L, Schoolmaster, Delhi (ex-Curlew), 13 February 1928
CARR, Arthur C, Leading Telegraphist, J 90634, Wallflower, 22 June 1930
CARR, George A, Boy 2c, JX 130747, Impregnable, 11 March 1928
CARR, John G O, Telegraphist, J 51463, Diomede, 14 February 1928
CARR, Robert W, Able Seaman, C/SSX 14782, Ivanhoe, 2 July 1939
CARRICK, James A, Seaman, RNR, B 3519, Alston, steamship, 15 December 1918
CARRIE, Alec M, Lieutenant Commander, M.1, 12 November 1925
CARROLL, Albert E W, Fireman, MMR, 525049, Avoca, 20 November 1918
CARROLL, George, Lieutenant Commander, RNR, Royal Naval Reserve, 21 July 1928
CARROLL, Henry, Stoker Petty Officer, 152362, Wildfire, 29 November 1919
CARROLL, John J, Surgeon Lieutenant Commander, Hong Kong Dockyard, 14 December 1927
CARSLAKE, Henry L, Lieutenant, Egmont I, 21 October 1926
CARSTAIRS, Cyril R J, Lieutenant, Torpedo Course, 27 January 1931
CARTER, Alfred E, Chief Skipper, RNR, Boscawen, 23 May 1938
CARTER, Charles E, Stoker 1c, K 56694, Vivid, 29 April 1929
CARTER, Edward W, Officer's Steward 2c, L 7528, Dido, 23 June 1920
CARTER, Francis A W, Able Seaman, D/J 100637, Cygnet, 1 May 1936
CARTER, Frank, Chief Electrical Artificer 1c, M 201, Diomede, 21 June 1928
CARTER, Frederick A, Leading Telegraphist, C/J 39482, Wireless Telegraph Station, Matara, Ceylon (Sri Lanka), 21 October 1934
CARTER, Frederick H, Marine, 24423 (Ch), RM Barracks Eastney, 10 August 1935
CARTER, George A, Petty Officer, 218672, Excellent, 21 July 1927
CARTER, George H, Stoker 1c, K 56465, Despatch, 26 May 1923
CARTER, Horace W H, Signalman, 236058, Vivid, 30 April 1930
CARTER, Joseph E, Stoker 1c, P/KX 82927, Aurora, 24 February 1939
CARTER, P (initial only) W, Paymaster Lieutenant (Registrar Clerk), RNR, Royal Naval Reserve, June 1938
CARTER, Percival R, Telegraphist, J 70337, FAA, 446 Flight, Courageous, 12 May 1928
CARTER, Richard K D H, Lieutenant (E), Malta Dockyard, 3 April 1936
CARTER, Walter W, Stoker 1c, D/KX 81328, Barham, 2 May 1935
CARTER, William - see CAREY, Michael, Stoker 1c,
CARTER, William E, Engineer Commander, Royal Navy, 18 March 1928
CARTWRIGHT, Harry, Able Seaman, RNVR, Mersey Z 296, President III, 8 March 1919
CARTWRIGHT-TAYLOR, John W D, Paymaster Sub Lieutenant, RNVR, Royal Naval Volunteer Reserve, 4 April 1935
CARUANA, Salvatore, Able Seaman, JX 125615, Egmont, 1 July 1930
CARVER, Eric A J, Boy 2c, JX 145536, Ganges, 14 June 1936
CASELEY, Gordon T, Marine, 24303 (Ch), RM Chatham Division, 21 June 1931
CASEY, Patrick, Yeoman of Signals, 227466, Glowworm, 25 August 1919
CASEY, Robert C, Lieutenant, RAN, M.1, 12 November 1925
CASPALL, William C, Junior Reserve Attendant, M 19971, Crescent, 30 November 1918
CASS, Arthur, Ordinary Seaman, P/SSX 14881, Courageous, 6 April 1935
CAST, William J, Engine Room Artificer Apprentice, MX 47799, Pembroke, 7 April 1932
CASTER, William, Trimmer, RNR, TS 6708, Aiglon, 18 February 1919
CATELINET, John A, Private, RMLI, 19184 (Po), 3rd Battalion, RM, 4 December 1918
CATHIE, Archibald, Boy Artisan, M 33270, Fisgard, 5 November 1919
CATOR, Richard B, Midshipman, Blue Sky, tender to Queen Elizabeth, 12 June 1922
CATTELL, Charles V, Gunner, RMA, RMA 3102, RMA Eastney, 21 December 1918
CAUSER, Bert H, Leading Signalman, J 38389, Vivid, 10 July 1927
CAVE, Percy H E, Leading Seaman, 182484, Ganges, 14 November 1918
CAVINEY, Martin, Stoker 1c, K 13925, Ranger, 16 March 1919
CAWKWELL, George W, Able Seaman, J 36153, Caledon, 2 February 1922
CAWTE, Cecil F, Boy 2c, J 102033, Impregnable, 30 May 1921
CAZENAVE, Robert J, Petty Officer, J 936, Pembroke, 6 July 1926

CECIL, Richard F B, Lieutenant, FAA, 441 Flight, Argus, 6 February 1929

CHADDOCK, Richard, Chief Steward, MMR, 724836, Greyhound II, 24 November 1918
CHADWICK, Charles H, Marine, X 480 (Po), Royal Marines HQ Portsmouth, 24 February 1933
CHAFE, Edwin, Lieutenant, FAA, 423 Sqn, Eagle, 18 January 1927
CHALCROFT, Ernest F, Leading Stoker, P/K 21165, Searcher, 4 April 1932
CHALLEN, Charlie W, Musician, RMB, RMB X 13, Sussex, 3 January 1937
CHALLIS, Charles E, Deck Hand, RNR, DA 10501, Silver King, 21 January 1919
CHALMERS, Andrew W, Seaman, RNR, A 8873, Freesia, 5 December 1918
CHAMBERLAIN, Frederick C S, Musician, RMB, RMB X 153, Glorious, 27 November 1933
CHAMBERLAIN, Henry, Able Seaman, J 7481, Ormonde, 20 June 1928
CHAMBERLAYNE, Tankerville, Honorary Lieutenant, RNR, Royal Naval Reserve, May 1924
CHAMBERS, Alfred C, Able Seaman, D/JX 131754, St Angelo (Fame), 22 July 1936
CHAMBERS, Reuben H, Able Seaman, RAN, 9656 (former RN, J 17841), Royal Australian Navy, 13 January 1924

CHAMBERS, William F H, Boy 1c, J 94935, Impregnable, 22 December 1919
CHAMPNESS, Richard A B, Shipwright 3c, P/M 39532, Royal Sovereign, 25 June 1935
CHANCE, Gilbert H T, Able Seaman, J 43099, Benbow, 20 October 1921
CHANDLER, Henry, Private, RMLI, 19831 (Ch), RM, 8th Battalion, 21 May 1921
CHANDLER, John M, Lieutenant, Pilot's Course, No.1, 10 November 1924
CHANDLER, Samuel, Stoker Petty Officer, 292046, Pembroke, 3 April 1919
CHANNER, Frank, Stoker 1c, K 21141 (Ch), Frostaxe, 29 April 1919
CHAPLIN, William, Stoker 1c, K 266900, Clonmel, 27 November 1918
CHAPMAN, Albert E, Able Seaman, D/J 29850, Drake, 21 October 1935
CHAPMAN, Cecil, Able Seaman, C/JX 126505, M.2, 29 January 1932
CHAPMAN, Charles M S, Lieutenant, L.55, 4 June 1919
CHAPMAN, Charles W, Boy 1c, J 102166, Vivid, 30 May 1921
CHAPMAN, Charles W, Leading Seaman, 236737, Victory, 4 February 1922
CHAPMAN, Edward M H, Ty/Midshipman, RNR, Royal Naval Reserve, 28 November 1919
CHAPMAN, Ernest, Engine Room Artificer 2c, M 7355, Repulse, 26 July 1922
CHAPMAN, Ernest F, Engine Room Artificer 2c, M 7579, Curlew, 5 January 1922
CHAPMAN, George W, Able Seaman, J 22107, Victory, 6 December 1918
CHAPMAN, Harold, Lieutenant, Thetis, 3 June 1939
CHAPMAN, Richard H, Stoker Petty Officer, 299203, Vivid, 10 January 1923
CHAPMAN, Samuel C, Commissioned Gunner, Royal Navy, 1 June 1935
CHAPMAN, Sydney, Lieutenant, RNR, Royal Naval Reserve, 19 April 1931
CHAPMAN, William H, Able Seaman, J 22830, Royal Sovereign, 14 March 1924
CHAPMAN, William J, Deck Hand, RNR, DA 4071, Attentive II, 23 August 1919
CHAPPELL, Alfred L, Private, RME, RME 7895, RM Engineers, 11 January 1919
CHAPPELL, Frederick J T, Leading Signalman, J 23743, Benbow, 6 December 1924
CHARLES, Harold, Chief Sick Berth Attendant, M 359, Valerian, 22 October 1926
CHARLESWORTH, Herbert, Boy 2c, J 115226, Impregnable, 2 March 1926
CHARLWOOD, Frederick E, Master at Arms, 203311, Victory, 26 October 1922
CHARMAN, William H, Leading Telegraphist, J 31517 (Po), K.5, 20 January 1921
CHARNOCK, Robert, Cook, MMR, 756501, St Aubin, 15 May 1919
CHARTERIS, Hugh L, Midshipman (A), Peregrine, 2 June 1939
CHASE, Frederick W, Able Seaman, J 101278, M.2, 2 January 1930
CHASE, Frederick W, Leading Stoker, K 3799 (Po), K.5, 20 January 1921
CHAUB, Edgar C, Leading Signalman, J 15794, Kent, 22 December 1928
CHAWNER, James, Able Seaman, RNVR, Bristol Z 4441, Victory, 17 February 1919
CHEAL, Frederick J, Stoker Petty Officer, 286273, Bacchante, 22 February 1919
CHEESEBROUGH, Thomas M, Ordinary Seaman, J 85493, Fox, 2 July 1919
CHEESMAN, Donald A, Boy 2c, J 93372, Powerful, 21 November 1918
CHEESMAN, Eric, Naval Cadet, Sea Cadet Corps, 12 July 1929
CHEETHAM, Sydney W, Able Seaman, J 69217 (Ch), Astraea, 13 January 1919
CHENERY, Rowland W, Leading Sick Berth Attendant, M 5510, RN Hospital Bermuda, 1 February 1925
CHENG, Chew, Able Seaman, Cicala, 5 October 1929
CHERRY, George H, Able Seaman, P/J 49823, Excellent, 2 July 1932
CHEVES, Henry E, Able Seaman, J 78832, Wessex, 2 July 1926
CHEVIS, Harry F, Leading Signalman, J 13882, L.24, 10 January 1924
CHEW, Henry, Able Seaman, J 62026, Vivid, 21 February 1919
CHILCRAFT, Albert, Leading Deck Hand, DA 12331, Victory, 3 April 1919
CHILD, Archibald E, Able Seaman, J 31371, M.24, monitor, 2 July 1919
CHILDS, William H, Private, RMLI, 19612 (Pensioner), RM Headquarters, 2 July 1921
CHILTON, Harry, Corporal, RM, E 17893, Royal Marines HQ, 27 March 1930
CHILTON, Thomas E, Stoker 1c, K 58237, Victory, 14 May 1922
CHILVERS, George L, Boy 1c, J 113528, Ajax, 12 March 1926
CHINN, Cyril, Able Seaman, RFA, Bacchus, RFA, 14 April 1925
CHINN, Arnold G, Civilian Contractor, Thetis, 3 June 1939
CHINNERY, Arthur, Mechanician, K 57977, Revenge, 15 June 1930
CHINNERY, Herbert C, Officer's Cook 1c, 363502, Chatham, 23 February 1923
CHIPPENDALE, Albert H, Leading Seaman, J 2645, Victory, 2 January 1920
CHISHOLM, James, Engineer Commander, Armadale Castle, 27 April 1919
CHISHOLM, Joseph, Deck Hand, RNR, DA 10910, Victory, 16 May 1919
CHISMAN, Stanley, Able Seaman, J 20791, Fox, 18 August 1919
CHITTENDEN, Arthur H J, Stoker 1c, K 5910, Endeavour, 3 May 1926
CHITTS, Thomas J, Able Seaman, RAN, 2047, Brisbane (RAN), 2 December 1918
CHIVERS, Edward G, Officer's Steward 2c, L 3555, Queen Elizabeth, 8 March 1924
CHIVERS, Horace W, Stoker 1c, K 14297, Agamemnon, 17 September 1923
CHONG, Ah, Cook, Adventure, 7 February 1934
CHONG, Ah, Officer's Steward 1c, Castor, 25 January 1929
CHRISTIAN, Arthur H, Admiral, Rtd, Royal Navy, 20 August 1926
CHRISTIAN, Harold, Captain, President, 15 November 1918
CHRISTIE, Charles P, Lieutenant Commander, Courageous, 7 February 1929
CHRISTIE, James, Able Seaman, RNVR, Clyde Z 7153, Hawke Battalion, RND, 3 March 1919
CHRISTIE, Thomas, Leading Trimmer, RNR, ST 693, Hannibal, 15 January 1919
CHU, Tsing, Officer's Steward 1c, Tamar, 31 August 1926
CHUNG (no first name listed), Plumber's Mate (Chinese), Tamar, 16 September 1927
CHURCH, Colin J, Py/Midshipman, RNR, Port Jackson, 7 August 1938
CHURCHER, Francis W G, Stoker 1c, K 5891, Iron Duke, 20 November 1920
CHURCHER, Lionel S, Able Seaman, 200540, Victory, 17 January 1930
CHURCHMAN, Henry E E, Petty Officer, J 12266, Ramillies, 29 October 1923

CIVIL, Herbert G, Chief Engine Room Artificer 1c, M 804, St Genny, 12 January 1930

CLACKETT, William, Stoker 1c, 175961 (Ch), Frostaxe, 29 April 1919
CLAIF, Frank G, Able Seaman, D/J 93773, Queen Elizabeth, 16 December 1932
CLAPTON, Thomas, Lieutenant, RNR, President, 14 January 1919
CLAREY, Albert W, Petty Officer, J 7631 (Ch), Vittoria, 31 August 1919
CLARK, Charles L, Stoker 2c, C/KX 84988, Titania, 7 September 1935
CLARK, Daniel, Private, RME, RME 8179, RM Engineers, 18 November 1918
CLARK, Duncan, Able Seaman, J 95446, Walker, 30 October 1923
CLARK, Ernest A, Officer's Steward 4c, L 14378, Victory, 6 January 1924
CLARK, Ernest W, Chief Petty Officer Telegraphist, C/J 39039, Pembroke, 29 October 1935
CLARK, Frederick C, Able Seaman, J 96779, Excellent, 17 March 1930

CLARK, George, Engineman, RNR, TS 6440, Ottelie, 9 December 1918
CLARK, Gilbert J, Stoker Petty Officer, 307291, Bacchante, 13 February 1919
CLARK, Harold J, Able Seaman, J 22370 (Ch), Erin's Isle, 7 February 1919
CLARK, Harry R, Corporal, RMA, RMA 9842, Emperor of India, 22 August 1919
CLARK, James C, Stoker 1c, K 43186, Pembroke, 14 February 1919
CLARK, James W S, Boy 2c, C/SSX 23928, Wildfire, 11 May 1938
CLARK, Joseph, 2nd Hand, RNR, SA 346, Alert, 12 November 1918
CLARK, Malcolm G, Stoker Petty Officer, K 3401, Diomede, 20 September 1924
CLARK, Percy E, Boy 2c, J 92931, Ganges, 6 December 1918
CLARK, Percy H, Boy 1c, J 112873, Ajax, 16 December 1925
CLARK, Reginald H, Stoker 1c, K 30262, Pomone, 4 November 1921
CLARK, Robert, Able Seaman, D/J 50353, Vivid, 7 December 1933
CLARK, Robert E, Master at Arms, 195657, Marlborough, 28 August 1923
CLARK, Roland A, Commander, Pembroke, 1 February 1926
CLARK, Thomas J, Stoker 1c, SS 117078 (Ch), Verulam, 4 September 1919
CLARK, Walter T, Able Seaman, J 98456, M.1, 12 November 1925
CLARK, Wilfred T De L, Major, RMLI, 3rd Battalion, RM, 22 February 1919
CLARK, William, Seaman, RNR, A 2682, Clan Menzies, steamship, 16 November 1918
CLARK, William H, Shipwright 1c, M 10278, Greenwich, 25 April 1930
CLARKE, Allan, Petty Officer, D/J 43273, M.2, 29 January 1932
CLARKE, Benjamin J, Lieutenant, K.5, 20 January 1921
CLARKE, Cecil F, Able Seaman, J 32900 (Ch), K.5, 20 January 1921
CLARKE, Christopher G, Lieutenant, Royal Navy, 7 April 1925
CLARKE, Digby A P, Surgeon Lieutenant, Hercules, 23 July 1921
CLARKE, Ernest D, Able Seaman, J 443113, Kinsha, 10 January 1921
CLARKE, Ernest E, Stoker 1c, K 29851, Valerian, 22 October 1926
CLARKE, Frank, Lance Corporal, RMLI, S 1993 (Ch), Chatham Division, RMLI, 1 December 1918
CLARKE, Frederick, Deck Hand, RNR, DA 15332, Egmont, 29 March 1919
CLARKE, George A, Ordinary Seaman, D/JX 135585, Shropshire, 26 November 1933
CLARKE, Hugh D, Able Seaman, RNVR, Bristol Z 9166, Spider, 23 November 1918
CLARKE, James C, Seaman, Newfoundland RNR, X 2327, Duchess of Fife, 13 November 1918
CLARKE, Lucie E, Clerk, WRNS, G 6087, Women's Royal Naval Service, 24 November 1918
CLARKE, Nelson, Stoker 2c, C/KX 9543, Royal Navy, 27 January 1939
CLARKE, Wilbert, Able Seaman, P/J 80329, Medea, 7 January 1936
CLARKE, Wilfred W, Boy 1c, JX 136868, Ganges, 24 January 1933
CLARKE, William D, Able Seaman, J 45514 (Ch), Erin's Isle, 7 February 1919
CLARKE, William F, Officer's Cook 2c, P/L 14027, Nelson, 1 November 1937
CLARKE, William H, Engineer Lieutenant Commander, Vivid, 23 October 1924
CLARKE, William R, Skipper, RNR, Annford Melville, 3 March 1919
CLARKSON, Albert, Leading Seaman, J 28603, L.55, 4 June 1919
CLARKSON, Sydney W W, Able Seaman, J 58122, Pembroke, 12 June 1929
CLAY, Harold V, Able Seaman, J 92692, Victory, 3 May 1925
CLAY, William, Chief Plumber, 344151, Cambrian, 10 November 1920
CLAYDON, Walter, Chief Petty Officer, 222485, Marlborough, 27 February 1923
CLAYTON, Edward W, Signalman, RNVR, London Z 3371, Glen Usk, 2 April 1919
CLAYTON, Harold E, Able Seaman, J 36354, Shikari, 31 March 1926
CLAYTON, James, Reserve Wardmaster, M 9413, Pembroke, 3 December 1918
CLEAR, John, Able Seaman, J 41724, Emperor of India, 6 January 1925
CLEAVE, Robert H, Engine Room Artificer 1c, D/M 8936, Vivid, 13 June 1933
CLEAVER, Arthur, Petty Officer, J 10356, Victory, 24 March 1920
CLEAVER, Edward G, Stoker 1c, K 58802, M.1, 12 November 1925
CLEMENT, Sydney W, Sick Berth Steward, 351228, Inflexible, 16 October 1919
CLEMENTS, Edward F, Stoker 1c, K 16147, Vivid II, 2 November 1919
CLEMENTS, Harry, Stoker 1c, SS 104283, Penarth, 4 February 1919
CLEMENTS, Harry M, Petty Officer, RNVR, Wales Z 373, Hawke Battalion, RND, 18 February 1919
CLEMENTS, Nat F J, Able Seaman, J 39755, Courageous, 26 February 1919
CLEMENTSON, William E, Marine, X 1632 (Ply), Dorsetshire, 10 March 1939
CLEMOTT, Thomas, Shipwright 1c, M 8518, Comus, 8 August 1927
CLERRY, Cornelius, Stoker Petty Officer, D/K 55392, Vivid, 26 May 1931
CLEVELAND, Robert G, Leading Seaman, J 16266, Glowworm, 25 August 1919
CLEVERTON, Stanley, Stoker Petty Officer, D/K 5216, Cornwall, 1 November 1930
CLEWORTH, William A, Stoker 1c, C/K 64940, Scout, 8 September 1932
CLIFF, Harold, Leading Stoker, D/K 56978, Poseidon, 9 June 1931
CLIFFE, Wilfred C, Ordinary Seaman, J 83784, Emperor of India, 25 February 1919
CLIFTON, Frederick, Stoker 1c, K 18374 (Po), L.55, 4 June 1919

CLIFTON, George E, Signalman, J 44897, Lupin, 12 June 1927
CLINCH, Arthur, Able Seaman, SS 4778, Chrysanthemum, 7 December 1921
CLOUGH, Nelson O, Signalman, J 39848, M.1, 12 November 1925
CLOVER, William G, Leading Signalman, C/J 77754, Pembroke, 24 March 1938
CLOWES, John H T, Able Seaman, J 25669 (Po), K.5, 20 January 1921
CLUBB, Ernest C, Able Seaman, J 54346 (Ch), Myosotis, 6 January 1919

COASE, Edward H, Able Seaman, J 16309, Glowworm, 25 August 1919
COATES, Arthur, Able Seaman, P/J 108548, Courageous, 21 June 1934
COATES, Edward, Petty Officer, 239255, Waterhen, 21 February 1919
COATES, Edwin J, Able Seaman, 232473, Excellent, 11 June 1927
COATES, Fred, Trimmer, RNR, ST 1310, Totnes, 27 January 1919
COATES, Samuel, Ordinary Seaman, J 84904, Victory, 24 November 1918
COATES, Thomas P, Leading Telegraphist, D/J 39362, Drake, 18 October 1937
COBB, William, Chief Stoker, 296193, Victory II, 1 October 1921
COBBETT, William, Marine, 20288 (Ch), Kent, 8 November 1935
COCHRANE, Basil R, Lieutenant, President, 14 March 1919
COCK, William C, Coastguardsman 3c, 158101, Victory, 9 October 1921
COCKING, John, Deck Hand, RNR, DA 15882, Pearl III, 18 May 1919
COCKRILL, Francis T, Chief Petty Officer Telegraphist, 240069, Birmingham, 17 November 1924
COCKS, George, Engineer Commander, York, 8 December 1929
CODROY, Harry, Able Seaman, D/J 111912, Gipsy, 24 September 1936
COELLO, Vincent C, Officer's Steward 1c, L 11945, Enterprise, 10 March 1929
COGGIN, Michael, Leading Stoker, MMR, 884479, Philol, Royal Fleet Auxiliary, 14 November 1918
COGHILL, Thomas, Stoker 1c, 304353, Craigie, 21 February 1919
COLBURN, Henry N, Marine, X 2068 (Ply), Pembroke, 4 April 1938
COLBY, Charles R, Trimmer, RNR, TS 7240, Leonard, 8 January 1920
COLCLOUGH, George, Able Seaman, C/SSX 12913, Moth, 24 September 1930
COLE, Albert H, Leading Telegraphist, P/J 45179, Victory, 7 August 1934
COLE, Charlie E, Victualling Chief Petty Officer, 361337 (Dev), Concord, 6 June 1920
COLE, Cyril J, Private, RMLI, 14909 (Po), 11th Battalion, RM, 21 May 1923
COLE, Ernest, Petty Officer, J 7325, Defiance, 11 February 1929
COLE, Ernest D, Stoker 1c, K 61253, Victory, 10 April 1929
COLE, Ernest G, Able Seaman, J 37271, Victory, 10 April 1922
COLE, Francis G, Chief Petty Officer, P/J 6566, Excellent, 8 May 1933
COLE, George V A, Able Seaman, J 112966, Lucia, 5 March 1930
COLE, George, Private, RM, S 2621 (Deal), 63rd Divisional Train, RND, 25 November 1918
COLE, James, Leading Deck Hand, RNR, SD 4665, ML.457, motor launch, 25 February 1919
COLE, James J, Petty Officer, 236546, Ramillies, 2 January 1925
COLE, Leonard W, Able Seaman, J 89323, Benbow, 27 March 1924
COLE, Walter, Marine, 21783 (Ply), Emperor of India (ex-Hood), 4 August 1927
COLEMAN, Herbert, Petty Officer, 222544, Vivid, 22 February 1920
COLEMAN, James, Deck Hand, RNR, DA 16307, Caesar, 24 December 1918
COLEMAN, Thomas, Stoker 1c, SS 119415 (Po), Haldon, 27 July 1919
COLES, Arthur S, Stoker 1c, SS 124891, Senator, 11 February 1920
COLES, Edwin G, Warrant Writer, President, 29 December 1926
COLESHILL, Charles J, Able Seaman, P/J 102918, M.2, 29 January 1932
COLLARD, William A, Able Seaman, J 36559 (Ch), Emile Nobel, 21 May 1919
COLLETT, Leonard S, Marine, 21700 (Ply), Emperor of India, 17 September 1928
COLLEY, William T, Sick Berth Attendant, M 18537, Laburnum, 24 January 1924
COLLIER, Augustus H N, Leading Seaman, J 26855, Concord, 23 September 1922
COLLIN, James, Deck Hand, RNR, DA 10993, T W Mould, trawler LH.82 (10 crew died), 1 December 1918
COLLINGS, Amos D, Able Seaman, D/J 105478, Poseidon, 9 June 1931
COLLINGWOOD, Joseph W, Petty Officer Telegraphist, P/J 8578, Victory, 30 January 1933
COLLINS, Albert A, Musician, RMLI, 21296 (Po), Royal Marines HQ, 12 December 1922
COLLINS, Alfred G, Ordinary Telegraphist, J 49051 (Ch), Erin's Isle, 7 February 1919
COLLINS, Alfred H, Yeoman of Signals, 225337, King George V, 14 February 1919
COLLINS, Arthur H, Warrant Electrician, Resource, 15 December 1934
COLLINS, Arthur L, Officer's Cook 2c, L 4293, Impregnable, 23 November 1918
COLLINS, Cornelius R, Private, RMLI, 12030 (Po), RM Headquarters, 11 September 1920
COLLINS, Daniel, Able Seaman, J 26937, Ark Royal, 9 May 1926
COLLINS, Edgar G, Leading Stoker, K 23859, Kent, 9 November 1928
COLLINS, Edward, Honorary Captain, RNR, Royal Naval Reserve, 23 March 1928
COLLINS, Edwin T, Petty Officer, D/J 12991, Vivid, 3 July 1932
COLLINS, Francis J, Able Seaman, P/J 111235, Cormorant, 8 March 1935
COLLINS, Frank, Joiner 3c, M 8097, Pembroke, 14 February 1919
COLLINS, Fred, Yeoman of Signals, 210007, Vivid, 2 April 1919
COLLINS, Frederick S, Ordinary Seaman, J 82741, Barham, 12 November 1918
COLLINS, Gilbert P, Petty Officer, 223640, Royal Arthur, 25 July 1920
COLLINS, Henry, Private, RMLI (no service number listed, possibly pensioner), RN Hospital, Great Yarmouth, 26 October 1936
COLLINS, Herbert P, Stoker Petty Officer, K 3290, Wanderer, 3 May 1925
COLLINS, James, Leading Seaman, J 24829, Lord Nelson, 16 December 1918
COLLINS, John, Stoker 1c, D/K 26399, Drake, 4 November 1936
COLLINS, Reginald C, Ty/Engineer Lieutenant, RNR, Quadrille, 26 November 1918
COLLINS, Richard H, Able Seaman, J 91136, Walpole, 28 January 1922
COLLINS, Thomas S, Act/Warrant Engineer, Exeter, 11 March 1932
COLLINS, Vincent H, Sergeant, 10298 (Ply), Cairo, 10 August 1921
COLLINS, William, Fireman, MMR, 862678, Sonia, 30 January 1919

COLLINS, Walter J, Able Seaman, D/J 31104, Drake, 4 October 1936
COLLINS, William J, Able Seaman, J 85585, Pembroke, 2 December 1929
COLLINSON, Darlof J H, Stoker 2c, KX 79828, Vivid, 21 December 1929
COLLIS, John F R, Sub Lieutenant (A), FAA, 714 Flight, Manchester, 23 December 1938
COLLYER, Albert, Stoker Petty Officer, 311651, Dublin, 15 November 1922
COLLYER, Henry G, Leading Seaman, J 58, Pembroke, 26 December 1918
COLLYER, William A, Able Seaman, P/J 13580, Shamrock, 2 December 1931
COLMAN, George, Leading Seaman, J 91594, X.1, 5 July 1930
COLQUHOUN, James A S, Lieutenant, FAA, 446 Flight, Courageous, 19 May 1931
COLRIDGE, Bernard, Officer's Steward 3c, l 13377, Hood, 22 January 1925
COLSTON, Charles S, Captain, Royal Navy, 25 November 1918
COLTHERUP, Frederick C, Joiner 1c, M 8132, Valerian, 22 October 1926
COMBEN, Horace S, Stoker 2c, K 59125, Iron Duke, 12 September 1921
COMBES, Harry, Able Seaman, J 28776, Vernon, 9 December 1918
COMPTON, Alexander F, Able Seaman, J 43708, Comus, 26 December 1921
COMPTON, Charles L, Honorary Paymaster Commander, RNR, Royal Naval Reserve, 15 June 1925
COMSTOCK, William T, Corporal, RM, 21387 (Ply), Renown, 27 January 1931
CONBOY, Alexander, Private, RMLI, S 749 (Ply), 3rd Battalion, RM, 27 November 1918
COND, Frederick T P, Ty/Lieutenant, RNVR, Royal Naval Volunteer Reserve, 17 April 1919
CONDLIFFE, William F G, Electrical Artificer 2c, P/M 35270, Vernon, 5 May 1932
CONDON, Thomas J, Leading Deck Hand, RNR, SD 234, Victory, 12 July 1919
CONDON, William J, Leading Seaman, J 17366, Ramillies, 27 October 1922
CONDY, Arthur, Boatswain, Fisgard, 1 October 1921
CONDY, Edward J, Leading Boatman, HM Coast Guard, 205835, HM Coastguard Station Charlestown, 24 April 1919
CONLIN, James, Able Seaman, J 96196, Defiance, 18 April 1924
CONLON, Eugene, Stoker Petty Officer, D/K 22980, Emerald, 9 January 1932
CONN, David, Able Seaman, RNVR, Clyde Z 6845, RMLI, 2nd Reserve Battalion, 26 February 1919
CONNEELY, James, Stoker 1c, 300248, Valorous, 1 September 1920
CONNELL, Ernest W, Lieutenant, RNR, Laconia, 12 February 1937
CONNELL, James J, Stoker Petty Officer, K 63236, Javelin, 8 July 1939
CONNELL, Thomas J, Supply Petty Officer, 310418, Durban, 22 April 1922
CONNETT, Archibald, Engine Room Artificer 1c, 272114, Ramillies, 18 May 1920
CONNOLLEY, Peter, Stoker, RNR, T 2709, Tyne, 1 February 1919
CONNOLLY, Gerald S, Officer's Steward 3c, L 8710, Pembroke, 26 February 1919
CONNOLLY, Joseph P, Ordinary Seaman, MMR, 907559, Stobo Castle, 26 February 1919
CONNOLLY, William H, Able Seaman, C/JX 139213, Wishart, 5 August 1937
CONNOR, Albert W, Cook, MMR, 521605, Flying Fish, 10 February 1919
CONNOR, John, Able Seaman, 203843, Vivid, 13 March 1920
CONNOR, John, Able Seaman, D/SSX 16501, Diamond, 18 November 1938
CONNOR, John, Deck Hand, RNR, SD 2647, Vivid, 16 November 1918
CONNOR, John, Fireman, RNR, War Pathan, RFA, 11 April 1939
CONNOR, John, Warrant Electrician, Tiger, 31 May 1930
CONROY, Walter, Stoker 1c, K 6865, Tribune, 17 August 1920
CONSTABLE, Frederick H, Stoker 1c, K 12620, Colleen, 4 June 1920
CONYBEARE, Charles B, Captain, RM, RM Deal, Kent, 21 January 1926
COOK, Albert E, Able Seaman, RNVR, London Z 4590, Phaeton, 7 March 1919
COOK, Alfred C, Chief Officer, HMCG, HMCG Dungeness, Kent, 1 January 1924
COOK, Alfred W J, Stoker Petty Officer, K 15869, Pembroke, 4 July 1923
COOK, Archibald, Private, RM, S 14426 (Deal), RM Labour Corps, 22 December 1918
COOK, Charles E C, Petty Officer, D/J 18194, Capetown, 8 April 1935
COOK, Edward, Signalman, J 107346, Pembroke, 10 April 1928
COOK, Fred, Marine, 15265 (Po), Queen Elizabeth, 8 January 1924
COOK, Frederick T, Assistant Cook, MX 48016, Pembroke, 28 July 1930
COOK, George P, Leading Stoker, K 27636, Resolution, 26 August 1928
COOK, Harry G, Stoker Petty Officer, P/K 58697, Vimy, 16 February 1934
COOK, Harry S, Deck Hand, RNR, SD 4402, Hermione, 14 March 1919
COOK, Ivan, 1st Writer, M 5295, Pembroke, 19 April 1919
COOK, John W, Sergeant, RMLI, 7259 (Ply), 2nd RM Battalion, RND, 2 June 1919
COOK, Percy S, Skipper, RNR, Offa II, 19 April 1919
COOK, Robert, Able Seaman, J 103562, Cyclops, 2 February 1928
COOK, Robert, Able Seaman, RNVR, Tyneside Z 5377, Pembroke I, 14 February 1919
COOK, Thomas W, Seaman, RNR, A 3740, Gitano, steamship, 20 December 1918
COOK, W (initial only), Paymaster Sub Lieutenant, RNR, Royal Naval Reserve, 25 May 1925
COOK, William C, Stoker 1c, K 35042, Bee, 12 March 1919
COOK, William H G, Officer's Steward 2c, L 5301, Vivid, 4 February 1919
COOK, William H, Petty Officer, 220522, Impregnable, 6 February 1925
COOK, William H, Stoker Petty Officer, K 27073, Collingwood, 30 December 1921
COOK, William J W, Signalman, 111469, Cuckoo, 2 July 1919
COOK, William R, Chief Petty Officer, 206122, Widgeon, 8 August 1920
COOKE, Cecil H, Able Seaman, P/SSX 14152, Royal Navy, 2 July 1938
COOKE, Reginald, Stoker 1c, K 5547, Cornflower, 1 October 1928
COOKE, Sidney E, Signalman, J 77474, Courageous, 9 December 1922
COOKE, Walter C, Senior Master, Vernon, 3 November 1937
COOKE, William C, Able Seaman, P/J 101384, Courageous, 31 December 1930
COOKE-HURLE, William A, Captain (Rtd), Royal Navy, 1 May 1920
COOKMAN, Sidney G, Private, RME, RME 1168, RM Engineers, 31 March 1919
COOKSON, Edgar C, Sub Lieutenant, Verulam, 4 September 1919
COOKSON, James W, Able Seaman, P/J 86453, Victory, 19 September 1932

COOKSON, Joseph, Able Seaman, J 62848, Ambrose, 18 July 1920

COOMBE, Frederick H, Able Seaman, J 52858 (Dev), Crescent, 18 November 1920

COOMBER, Ernest, Stoker 1c, K 55250, Caterham, 23 April 1929

COOMBES, Alfred E L, Stoker 1c, KX 76581, St Genny, 12 January 1930

COOMBES, Alfred L, Boy 2c, J 94057, Impregnable, 5 April 1919

COOMBES, Thomas - see BROAD, Thomas M, Petty Officer

COONEY, Joseph A, Stoker, P/KX 91806, Medway, 1 April 1939

COOPER, Albion, 2nd Hand, RNR, SA 1225, Vigorous, 24 March 1919

COOPER, Charles, Shipwright 3c, 346965, Leamington, 13 September 1921

COOPER, Gilbert W, Stoker 1c, K 18140, Victory, 14 March 1920

COOPER, Harold A, Stoker 1c, K 60045, Valerian, 22 October 1926

COOPER, Henry, Bandmaster 1c, RMB 1073, RM School of Music, 24 November 1918

COOPER, Herbert A S, Leading Seaman, J 2054, Valerian, 3 January 1922

COOPER, Russell, Ordinary Seaman, J 58364, Cleopatra, 3 November 1920

COOPER, Sidney F, Stoker 1c, KX 77402, Verity, 25 January 1928

COOPER, Stanley G, Engine Room Artificer 4c, RNR, E B X 891, Nelson, 1 October 1934

COOPER, Thomas W, Able Seaman, C/JX 129289, Emerald, 23 July 1934

COOPER, William G, Able Seaman, J 52280, Ramillies, 17 November 1926

COOTE, John H, Private, RM, S 14085 (Deal), RM Labour Corps, 18 February 1919

COPELAND, Alfred G, Engine Room Artificer 5c, M 37093, Furious, 22 August 1927

COPELAND, Robert, Able Seaman, RNVR, Tyneside Z 718, Collingwood Battalion, RND, 2 March 1919

COPKING, Frederick T, Engine Room Artificer 3c, M 32342, Westcott, 6 April 1922

COPP, Ambrose, Stoker 1c, K 11976, King George V, 4 August 1923

COPP, Richard H, Stoker Petty Officer, 295964, Lively, 7 December 1918

CORBEN, Percy M, Commissioned Gunner, Greenwich, 23 January 1938

CORBETT, George E, Ordinary Seaman, SS 9760, Ivy, 20 January 1920

CORBITT, Albert M, Seaman, RNR, C 3458, Pembroke, 13 August 1919

CORCORAN, John, Stoker 1c, 165758, Colleen, 28 February 1919

CORDELL, James H, Petty Officer, C/J 52070, Brilliant, 13 July 1934

CORDELL, Walter C E, Petty Officer, C/J 25139, Sussex, 12 May 1932

CORDIER, Albert R, Able Seaman, 190947, Victory, 13 December 1918

CORDING, Edward, Boy 1c, J 101694, Ceres, 29 August 1923

CORK, Frederick T, Boatswain, MMR, 998921, Lobster, 26 August 1919

CORKE, Bernard A, Able Seaman, MMR, J 747559, Vereker, 18 December 1918

CORLETT, Douglas, Ordinary Seaman, J 113269, Eagle, 1 March 1929

CORNELIOUS, William F, Able Seaman, P/J 27450, Victory I, 10 November 1936

CORNER, John, Stoker 1c, K 31731, Cambrian, 15 May 1921

CORNES, William H, Able Seaman, J 94454, Emperor of India, 31 October 1919

CORNFORD, John E, Private, RM, S 8086 (Deal), RM Labour Corps, 18 January 1919

CORNICK, Percy J, Leading Boatman, HM Coast Guard, 202822, HM Coastguard Station Cahore, 26 November 1918

CORNISH, George P, Chief Petty Officer, C/J 71379, Thetis, 3 June 1939

CORNISH, John A, Able Seaman, C/J 17871, Scarborough, 16 August 1931

CORNISH, Percy W, Able Seaman, J 11540 (Ch), K.5, 20 January 1921

CORNOCK, William C, Constable, RM Police, R M P X 355 (Ply), Devonport Dockyard, 12 May 1939

CORNWELL, Arthur J, Supply Petty Officer, C/M 38229, Folkestone, 24 December 1937

CORNWELL, George F, Stoker 1c, KX 77887, Tarantula, 28 October 1929

CORRIGAN, Patrick, Private, RMLI, S 673 (Po), 2nd RM Battalion, RND, 17 November 1918

CORSTORPHINE, James W, Deck Hand, RNR, DA 10919, Hecla II, 23 November 1918

COSTELLO, Thomas, Able Seaman, D/SSX 17624, Drake, 2 December 1938

COSTLEY, James, Able Seaman, P/J 64330, Thetis, 3 June 1939

COTGROVE, Arthur T, Stoker 2c, K 50103, Pembroke, 26 February 1919

COTTAM, Charles H, Leading Stoker, K 9856, Tiger, 5 October 1920

COTTEN, Richard R, Stoker 1c, K 62115, St Genny, 12 January 1930

COTTER, Leonard E, Lieutenant, RNR, Iolaire, 1 January 1919

COTTON, Albert J A, Boy 2c, JX 144440, Ganges, 4 August 1935

COTTON, Alfred E, Stoker 1c, SS 120397, Silvio, 30 November 1919

COUCH, Fred T, Shipwright 2c, M 7734, Resolution, 12 December 1921

COUGHLAN, William H, Petty Officer, J 4691, Pembroke, 26 July 1921

COUGHLIN, Bernard A, Leading Seaman, D/JX 137538, Glorious, 30 January 1939

COULL, Andrew, 2nd Hand, RNR, SD 757, Sir John French, 21 November 1918

COULL, William, Deck Hand, RNR, DA 11369, Attentive, 29 November 1918

COULTER, Charles, Leading Signalman, J 12893, Pembroke (ex-Prince George), 24 September 1919

COUNIHAN, William J, Officer's Cook 1c, L 2813, Warspite, 4 January 1919

COUPE, Frederick C, Boy 1c, J 99262, Vivid, 11 February 1921

COURCEY, James, Ordinary Seaman, D/JX 135584, Watchman, 17 January 1934

COURT, Helen I, Steward, WRNS, G 2405, Women's Royal Naval Service, 15 November 1918

COUSINS, Charles T, Able Seaman, J 96963, Malcolm, 5 March 1930

COUSINS, Frederick W, Gunner, RMA, RMA 10757, RM Headquarters, 24 May 1921

COUSINS, William L, Able Seaman, J 43266, Gibraltar, 30 August 1920

COVE, James P, Engine Room Artificer 1c, 268543, Elf, 4 September 1919

COVENTRY, John H, Able Seaman, J 5773 (Ch), Vulcan II, 2 April 1920

COVERDALE, Arthur M J, Engine Room Artificer 3c, P/M 38400, Dolphin, 25 April 1934

COWAP, Charles R, Captain, RNR, Royal Naval Reserve, July 1939

COWAP, John G, Trimmer, RNR, TS 4642, White Hill, 7 March 1919

COWDREY, William J, Musician, RMB, RMB 2559, Ganges, 31 December 1924

COWE, Thomas W, Stoker 1c, SS 119925, Sirdar, 8 July 1923
COWELL, Edward W, Able Seaman, P/J 98346, Royal Navy, 31 January 1935
COWELL, John R, Leading Seaman, RNR, B 4733, Sentinel, steamship, 26 March 1919
COWIE, Thomas, Fireman, MMR, 976119, Victory, 26 January 1919
COWIN, Maurice T, Lieutenant, Glorious, 15 October 1930
COWL, Edwin R, Marine, A 21171 (Ply), Dorsetshire, 31 December 1934
COWLES, Edward J, Leading Signalman, J 12334, Abdiel, 2 October 1919
COWLEY, Alfred J, Able Seaman, J 30149, Canterbury, 4 May 1920
COWLING, Albert G, Act/Leading Stoker, K 18120, M.1, 12 November 1925
COWLING, James F, Stoker 1c, K 23934, Laburnum, 18 February 1922
COWLING, John W, Midshipman, RNR, Teutonic, 22 December 1918
COWPER, William P, Surgeon, Valiant, 1 February 1919
COWSILL, Richard, Stoker 1c, C/K 60651, Hermes, 22 November 1931
COX, Albert C M, Engine Room Artificer 3c, P/MX 45610, Enterprise, 21 June 1938
COX, Albert, Stoker Petty Officer, K 5970, Fisgard, 4 October 1924
COX, Frank, Leading Seaman, SS 5817, Gainsborough, 23 October 1919
COX, Frank, Leading Stoker, K 1162, St Vincent, 25 February 1928
COX, John, Petty Officer, J 14302, Scarab, 2 April 1921
COX, John, Stoker 1c, 303808, Dido, 20 April 1925
COX, John E, Petty Officer Writer, P/M 34948, Victory, 17 May 1930
COX, John S, Telegraphist, J 49821 (Po), K.5, 20 January 1921
COX, Joseph, Chief Stoker, 308749, Pembroke, 18 February 1923
COX, Joseph, Private, RMLI, 12939 (Deal), RM Deal, 12 March 1919
COX, Lionel W, Cook's Mate, M 20988, Egmont, 3 December 1918
COX, Thomas, Private, RMLI, 14931 (Po), Portsmouth Division, RMLI, 19 March 1919
COX, Thomas H, Stoker 1c, K 58473, Centurion, 17 June 1923
COX, Walter J, Ordinary Seaman, J 44853, Pembroke (ex-Tamatrix), 4 March 1920
COYLE, Henry, Able Seaman, J 49359, Glowworm, 3 September 1920

CRABTREE, George A, Able Seaman, RNVR, Tyneside Z 3348, Anson Battalion, RND, 15 November 1918
CRACKNELL, George N, Paymaster Lieutenant, Iron Duke, 12 August 1921
CRADDICK, Frederick B, Deck Hand, RNR, DA 18779, Victory, 23 February 1919
CRADDOCK, William H, Commissioned Engineer, Ambrose, 23 June 1930
CRAGG, Harold, Stoker 1c, K 58062, Valerian, 22 October 1926
CRAGG, Horace T, Civilian Contractor, Thetis, 3 June 1939
CRAIG, George A, Cook's Mate, M 7668 (Po), Erin's Isle, 7 February 1919
CRAIG, James, Stoker 1c, D/KX 77855, Thetis, 3 June 1939
CRAIG, Thomas, Deck Hand, RNR, SD 2968, Halcyon, 15 February 1919
CRAIG, Thomas E, Able Seaman, J 46678 (Po), Maidstone, 22 November 1918
CRAIGIE, Gideon, Petty Officer, C/J 17079, Diomede, 31 March 1934
CRAIGIE, James W, Deck Hand, MMR, Loch Rannoch, 4 March 1919

CRAINES, Frederick C, Able Seaman, J 90335, Douglas, 3 February 1926
CRANE, Clarence C, Chief Yeoman of Signals, 223279, Vivid, 28 March 1924
CRANER, Victor, Cook's Mate, M 10421 (Po), Bristol, 13 May 1919
CRAVEN, Archibald, Civilian Contractor, Thetis, 3 June 1939
CRAVEN, George J, Stoker, P/KX 75188, Bee, 27 July 1934
CRAWFORD, George H, Ordinary Seaman, D/SSX 17152, Hunter, 13 May 1937
CRAWFORD, James A, Able Seaman, 213515, Victory, 27 May 1920
CRAWFORD, James F, Deck Hand, RNR, DA 8002, Bloemfontein, 21 February 1919
CRAWFORD, John, Stoker 1c, K 63473, Effingham, 2 September 1929
CRAWFORD, Robert E, Electrical Artificer 1c, M 616, Vernon, 17 September 1927
CRAWFORD, Sidney E J, Ordinary Seaman, J 48129 (Ch), Erin's Isle, 7 February 1919
CRAWFORD, Thomas J, Able Seaman, MMR, 933204, Victory, 14 June 1919
CRAWFORD, William R, Engineer Captain, Gunnery Course, 3 October 1924
CREASEY, Jack C, Engine Room Artificer, D/MX 47691, Thetis, 3 June 1939
CREASY, Sydney E, Warrant Engineer, Effingham, 18 June 1929
CREBBIN, George, Private, RMLI, 13568 (Ply), Cormorant, 27 December 1918
CREED, Beauford H, Able Seaman, RNVR, R 4944, Drake Battalion, RND, 24 December 1918
CREED, Ernest J, Able Seaman, D/J 113017, Drake, 5 September 1934
CREETON, Cornelius, Leading Stoker, 291785, Tarlair, 24 February 1919
CRESSWELL, Ernest, Leading Seaman, RNVR, Tyneside Z 7182, Gitano, steamship, 20 December 1918
CRESSWELL, John, Act/Lieutenant, Excellent, 16 October 1920
CRESSY, Alexander R, Stoker 1c, C/KX 81535, Royal Oak, 17 July 1933
CREW, Albert H, Able Seaman, J 74774, Calypso, 15 March 1921
CREW, John, Stoker 1c, K 60475, H.47, 9 July 1929
CRIBB, Sidney G, Able Seaman, J 91145, Curacoa, 3 January 1923
CRIBBEN, William S, Petty Officer, 191518, Castor, 10 August 1920
CRICHTON, Angus, Seaman, RNR, B 2687, Iolaire (Ganges II, O/P), 1 January 1919
CRICHTON, D (initial only), Engineer Lieutenant, RNR, Princess Margaret, 21 January 1920
CRICHTON, Donald, Seaman, RNR, A 9066, Iolaire (Pembroke, O/P), 1 January 1919
CRICHTON, Thomas L, Able Seaman, J 31570, Blake, 19 February 1919
CRICK, Alfred R, Chief Petty Officer Writer, P/M 35004, Victory, 19 March 1938
CRIDLAND, Henry J, Stoker 1c, KX 76592, Queen Elizabeth, 18 April 1928
CRIMMINS, Benjamin J, Stoker 1c, K 60910, H.47, 9 July 1929
CRIMMINS, Daniel, Ordinary Seaman, SS 9473 (Dev), Vivid, 21 May 1920
CRIPPS, Charles T, Ordinary Seaman, J 7827, Assistance, 20 June 1919
CRISPIN, Grenville, Boy 2c, J 105978, Ganges, 20 March 1923
CRITCHELL, Arthur W J, Stoker 1c, K 46631, Vancouver, 14 January 1924
CRITCHLEY, David, Able Seaman, J 17823, Vivid, 7 July 1920
CRITTALL, Henry, Leading Seaman, J 48747, Coventry, 28 February 1927
CROCKER, Albert, Leading Stoker, D/K 23313, Cyclops, 22 December 1930

CROCKER, Frederick, Stoker 1c, K 66563, Victory, 10 May 1927
CROCKER, Philip J B, Able Seaman, JX 127008, Resolution, 23 July 1930
CROCKFORD, George, Ordinary Seaman, J 493499, Comus, 14 December 1921
CROCKFORD, Henry G, Stoker 1c, P/K 10170, Victory, 31 May 1932
CROCKFORD, William, Able Seaman, J 104387, Impregnable, 18 May 1925
CROFTON, Harold M M, Act/Paymaster Sub Lieutenant, Curacoa, 29 November 1918
CROMBLEHOME, Stanley, Able Seaman, D/SSX 14810, Thetis, 3 June 1939
CROMER, Ernest, Deck Hand, RNR, DA 11688, Red Rose, 6 December 1918
CRONIN, Christopher, Stoker 1c, SS 122727, Swindon, 30 November 1919
CRONIN, Michael, Stoker 1c, K 18115, Philomel, 21 February 1921
CRONSHAW, James W, Trimmer, RNR, TS 4838, Balmoral, 14 February 1919
CROOK, Arthur C, Officer's Steward 3c, L 12003, Columbine, 15 February 1927
CROOK, Frank W, Engine Room Artificer 2c, M 4908, Victory, 20 June 1921
CROOK, Herbert, Petty Officer, J 4894 (Ch), L.55, 4 June 1919
CROOKSHANK, Godfrey C C, Captain, Royal Navy, 30 December 1933
CROSBIE, Walter, Stoker 1c, K 28791, Bryony, 23 December 1918
CROSS, Herbert, Yeoman of Signals, 232863, Columbine, 3 October 1922
CROSS, Stanley E, Private, RMLI, 19816 (Po), Furious, 9 February 1919
CROSS, William G N, Boy Shipwright, M 14328, Vivid, 3 November 1919
CROSSLEY, George, Leading Victualling Assistant, 101470, Pembroke, 20 December 1918
CROSSLEY, James W, Able Seaman, J 53036 (Dev), Sceptre, 4 December 1918
CROUCH, Ernest J, Stoker 1c, SS 122351, Speedy, 23 September 1922
CROUCH, Horace, Able Seaman, RNVR, Bristol Z 4098, Hood Battalion, RND, 22 February 1919
CROUCH, William H, Leading Seaman, C/J 33828, Illness, 11 February 1936
CROUT, Robert W, Civilian Contractor, Thetis, 3 June 1939
CROW, Andrew A, Electrical Artificer 4c, MX 46100, Repulse, 21 October 1929
CROW, David, Stoker 1c, K 56426, Valerian, 22 October 1926
CROW, John W, Leading Stoker, K 18378, Victory, 1 February 1921
CROWDER, Robert J, Leading Telegraphist, J 40580, Dolphin, 14 August 1920
CROWLEY, Albert, Stoker 1c, K 6200, Vivid, 24 February 1920
CROWLEY, Cornelius P, Telegraphist, J 46514, Afrikander, 23 August 1921
CROWLEY, John M, Ordinary Telegraphist, J 25366, Pembroke, 2 April 1919
CROWSON, George E, Ordinary Seaman, J 77145, Ophir, 24 February 1919
CROWTHER, George W, Petty Officer, C/J 39552, Kent, 27 June 1936
CROWTHER, James R, Stoker 1c, K 16109, St Genny, 12 January 1930
CROZIER, William E, Telegraphist, J 57974, Ambrose, 8 December 1920
CRUICKSHANK, David A, Boy 2c, JX 129600, Ganges, 3 June 1927
CRUIKSHANK, George G, Surgeon Lieutenant Commander (D), Royal Navy, 28 March 1931
CRUMBIE, David W, Stoker 1c, K 55839, L.24, 10 January 1924
CRUMP, William G, Yeoman of Signals, 220097, Revenge, 16 March 1919
CRUSH, Edmond V, Signalman, J 87122, Repulse, 18 July 1929
CRUST, Harold S, Sick Berth Attendant, M 39264, RN Hospital, Chatham, 15 September 1926
CRYSELL, Albert W, Able Seaman, J 15756 (Ch), L.55, 4 June 1919
CUBBY, John, Signalman, J 3685, Taurus, 14 March 1919
CUDBY, Frederick, Chief Stoker, 288464, Victory II, 9 April 1920
CUDDEFORD, Frederick W F, Lieutenant, K.5, 20 January 1921
CULLIMORE, Henry J, Able Seaman, J 28699, ML.434, motor launch, 24 November 1919
CULME-SEYMOUR, Sir Michael, Vice Admiral, Royal Navy, 2 April 1925
CULVER, Ivor R, Ordinary Signalman, C/JX 141755, Cairo, 16 February 1936
CUMING-GIBSON-CRAIG, Robert J A, Lieutenant, H.43, 19 February 1930
CUMMINGS, Charles W, Ordinary Seaman, D/SSX 28928, Drake, 21 March 1939
CUMPSTEY, Harold, Gunner, RMA, RMA 16072, Emperor of India, 3 August 1920
CUNDY, Thomas, Trimmer, RNR, ST 237, Pekin, 24 November 1918
CUNNINGHAM, David, Act/Leading Stoker, C/KX 80547, Thetis, 3 June 1939
CUNNINGHAM, Joseph, Petty Officer, 187326, President III, 14 February 1919
CUNNINGTON, George E W, Telegraphist, C/JX 132330, Cumberland, 12 March 1932
CURETON, Herbert R, Able Seaman, RNVR, Bristol Z 9862, President III, 15 December 1919
CURLING, John E, Musician, RMB X 478, RM Plymouth Division, 25 December 1935
CURRAN, James J, Able Seaman, J 11215, Veteran, 13 January 1922
CURRIE, William H, Telegraphist, C/JX 133704, FAA, 821 Sqn, Courageous, 15 February 1937
CURRY, Hugh F, Commander, Royal Australian Navy, 17 March 1932
CURRY, John H, Chief Engine Room Artificer, MX 46717, Forth, 31 October 1938
CURRYER, Henry, Private, RMLI, 17016 (Ch), Lowestoft, 19 March 1920
CURSENS, Alfred H, Stoker 1c, K 63460, Cockchafer, 18 October 1928
CURTAIN, Edgar C, Commissioned Gunner, Gloucester, 15 May 1938
CURTHOYS, Frederick A, Stoker Petty Officer, K 12943, Clematis, 4 November 1922
CURTHOYS, George J, Quartermaster Sergeant, RM, 21804 (Ply), Royal Marines HQ, 22 July 1925
CURTHOYS, Herbert W J, Able Seaman, D/JX 126453, Herald, 15 December 1933
CURTIN, Cornelius, Engine Room Artificer 1c, M 624, Eagle, 2 May 1927
CURTIS, Arthur, Petty Officer, 230628, Doris, 25 December 1918
CURTIS, Charles, Leading Seaman, P/J 15863, Greenwich, 19 August 1934
CURTIS, Charles E, Canteen Manager, Admiralty civilian, St Vincent, 13 May 1919
CURTIS, George, Supply Chief Petty Officer, M 1459, Titania, 14 July 1927
CURTIS, Harold W, Engineman, RNR, ES 1999, Halcyon II, 20 February 1919
CURTIS, Henry J, Cooper 1c, 343597, Pembroke, 24 February 1919
CURTIS, James, Stoker 1c, 291836, Hecla II, 26 July 1919

CURTIS, Owen S C, Leading Telegraphist, J 8621, Victory, 4 June 1920
CURTIS, Percy J, Leading Stoker, K 13430, P.33, patrol boat, 16 March 1919
CURTIS, Walter W, Leading Signalman, J 14483, P.62, patrol boat, 23 February 1919
CURTISS, Ernest F, Petty Officer, D/JX 143378, Drake, 10 November 1936
CUSICK, John, Able Seaman, RNVR, Clyde Z 4373, Anson Battalion, RND, 16 January 1919
CUSSE, Francis N W, Chief Engine Room Artificer 2c, 271233, TB.63, torpedo boat, 31 March 1919
CUSWORTH, William R, Lance Sergeant, RM, 185644, Royal Marines HQ, 30 December 1926
CUTAJAR, Giovanni, Stoker 1c, K 55154, Caesar, 16 April 1919
CUTHBERTSON, William, Deck Hand, RNR, DA 20407, Emmanuel Camelaire, 10 March 1919
CUTMORE, William A, Gunner, RMA, RMA 13536, Marlborough, 4 February 1923
CUTSFORTH, Charles L, Commander, RNR, Royal Naval Reserve, 18 April 1933
CUTTER, Frederick J, Engine Room Artificer Apprentice, MX 49499, Pembroke, 11 June 1933
CUTTER, William H, Engine Room Artificer 4c, D/MX 46008, Diomede, 19 May 1935

D

DABNOR, Frederick H, Boy 2c, JX 159907, Ganges, 6 February 1939

DAE, Min C, Officer's Steward 3c, Gannet, 11 September 1932

DAGG, Charles F, Petty Officer Telegraphist, J 3758 (Po), L.55, 4 June 1919

DAGGER, William F, Stoker 2c, K 63988, Windsor, 21 March 1925

DAGLEISH, David, Able Seaman, J 41983, Hood, 16 November 1924

DAGNELL, Arthur A, Stoker 1c, P/KX 80689, Warspite, 10 May 1932

DALBY, Amos W, Telegraphist, P/JX 125356, Victory, 9 September 1933

DALE, Ernest, Able Seaman, J 29304, Cockchafer, 20 March 1926

DALE, Frederick, Able Seaman, P/J 30004, Pandora, 4 December 1937

DALE, Samuel G, Boy 1c, J 98338, H.42, 23 March 1922

DALE, William E, Petty Officer, 231041, Royal Sovereign, 4 August 1919

DALES, William, Seaman, RNR, A 8406, Pembroke, 30 January 1919

DALEY, Ernest, Stoker 1c, K 59298, Tiger, 25 May 1924

DALEY, John, Coastguardsman 2c, 147025, Colleen, 16 April 1922

DALGLISH, Robin C, Rear Admiral, Royal Navy, 17 December 1934

DALLIMORE, Arthur, Petty Officer, 236802, Excellent, 16 January 1920

DALLIMORE, Kenneth J, Boy 2c, JX 140169, Ganges, 8 March 1934

DALLISON, Stanley F, Able Seaman, C/J 115336, Cumberland, 16 August 1930

DALTON, Alexander, Fireman, MMR, 865477, Eaglet, 2 March 1919

DALTON, James, Able Seaman, RNVR, London Z 3857, Egmont, 18 August 1919

DALTON, Robert W, Chief Engine Room Artificer, 272358, H.29, 9 August 1926

DALY, Edward, Stoker 1c, K 54873, Vivid, 16 November 1918

DALZIEL, William, Sub Lieutenant, RNR, Sunhill (Heroic, O/P), 2 May 1919

DAMEN, Arthur C, Able Seaman, SS 8331, Victory, 11 March 1922

DAMMS, George L, Stoker, RNR, S 2046, Western Queen, 17 November 1918

DANAFORD, Harold W, Chief Petty Officer, RAN, 8295, Cerberus, 7 December 1919

DAND, William, Petty Officer, J 5946, Lucia, 19 June 1920

DANDO, Wyndham G, Able Seaman, J 44115 (Dev), Erin, 2 October 1919

DANEO, Santo, Officer's Cook 2c, L 11102, Curacoa, 15 December 1929

DANIEL, Charles T, Lieutenant, RNR, President, 19 February 1919

DANIEL, Horace S, Lieutenant, RNR, Dido, 11 March 1919

DANIELS, John K, Commissioned Gunner, P.52, patrol boat, 4 November 1919

DANIELS, Thomas W, Stoker 1c, KX 77287, Delphinium, 27 April 1929

DANN, Arthur C, Seaman, RNR, A 16114, Orion, 27 February 1936

DANN, William S, Able Seaman, J 43883, Marlborough, 21 November 1924

DANNAN, Kenneth P, Paymaster Midshipman, Shropshire, 13 April 1939

DANVERS, Herbert, Surgeon, Royal Navy, 18 March 1920

DARCH, George, Leading Steward, D/L 9398, Drake, 17 March 1938

DARCH, Herbert S, Chief Sick Berth Steward, 150397, Vivid, 28 February 1919

D'ARCY, Richard J, Paymaster Lieutenant, RNR, Royal Naval Reserve, 8 September 1926

DARGE, John, Engine Room Artificer 2c, 272208, Lydiard, 16 January 1919

DARKE, Herbert R, Chief Engine Room Artificer 2c, M 1 (Dev), Emile Nobel, 22 May 1919

DARKLEY, Albert E, Stoker 1c, K 60632, Veronica, 1 June 1929

DARLEY, Frederick C, Commander, Despatch, 5 September 1926

DARMANIN, Carmelo, Leading Steward, E/LX 21227, St Angelo, 17 January 1935

DARNELL, George E, Engineman, RNR, ES 3694, J H F, drifter, 21 November 1918

DARRACOTT, Harold T, Signalman, J 13633 (Dev), Erin's Isle, 7 February 1919

DASH, Percy D T, Chief Petty Officer Cook, 351548, Centurion, 12 August 1922

DAVENPORT, George, Corporal, RM, S 3749 (Deal), Hood Battalion, RND, attached RM Medical Unit, 21 January 1919

DAVENPORT, Harry, Boy Telegraphist, D/JX 149205, Ganges, 2 July 1937

DAVEY, Alfred, Assistant Cook, MMR, 851395, Iolanda, 12 February 1919

DAVEY, Frederick S, Stoker Petty Officer, D/K 59067, Devonshire, 3 August 1932

DAVEY, Herbert, Private, RMLI, 17711 (Ch), RM, 6th Battalion, 8 September 1919

DAVEY, Joseph S, Boy 2c, J 93961, Impregnable, 3 March 1919

DAVEY, Mark H, Private, RM, S 9613 (Ply), RM Engineers, Chatham, 5 April 1919

DAVEY, Martin J, Leading Stoker, P/K 60311, Courageous, 27 February 1930

DAVEY, Sidney J, Boy 1c, J 98664, Ganges, 22 December 1921

DAVEY, Thomas G, Stoker Petty Officer, 302099, Victory, 22 August 1922

DAVEY, William J, Petty Officer, 193429, Lucia, 3 July 1920

DAVIDSON, Adair, Deck Hand, RNR, SD 1601, Northolt, 11 May 1919

DAVIDSON, Alexander, Chief Shipwright 2c, 343859, Victory, 24 December 1918

DAVIDSON, Frank, Steward, 91507, Royal Scot, 19 February 1919

DAVIDSON, James, Chief Artificer Engineer, Gunner, 23 January 1919

DAVIDSON, John D, Engineer T, RNR (T abbreviation not known), Lady Moyra, 15 May 1919

DAVIDSON, John H, Able Seaman, J 75864, Strathlethen, 11 February 1919

DAVIDSON, Robert G, Petty Officer, C/J 8339, Malabar, 22 May 1932

DAVIDSON, William, Engineman, RNR, ES 2419, Nairn, 12 December 1918

DAVIES, Albert G, Able Seaman, J 11457, Tenacious, 9 March 1920

DAVIES, Arthur H, Private, RM, S 2180 (Deal), 63rd Divisional Train, RND, 3 December 1918

DAVIES, David, Able Seaman, J 96644, Pembroke, 18 April 1928

DAVIES, David J, Officer's Cook 1c, L 9680, Vivid, 26 March 1919

DAVIES, David J, Stoker 1c, K 19673, Rodney, 22 March 1929

DAVIES, Edwin G, 1st Writer, M 4566, Pembroke, 16 January 1919

DAVIES, Ernest, Engine Room Artificer, RNR, EA 1792, Kingfisher, 23 February 1919

DAVIES, George S, Stoker Petty Officer, RNR, ES 1669, Peter Lovett, 20 April 1919

DAVIES, Harry, Marine, 17756 (Ch), Repulse, 23 April 1931

DAVIES, Harry R B, Commander, RNR, Rtd, Royal Naval Reserve, 5 September 1936
DAVIES, Herbert E, Lieutenant, RNR, Hughli, Royal Fleet Auxiliary, 26 April 1919
DAVIES, James, Lance Corporal, RM, S 3477 (Deal), 150th RN Field Ambulance, RM Medical Unit, RND, 20 November 1918
DAVIES, John, Yeoman of Signals, 198789, Comus, 24 February 1919
DAVIES, John H, Petty Officer, 200545, Hawkins, March 1921
DAVIES, Leonard F, Leading Signalman, J 7627 (Po), L.55, 4 June 1919
DAVIES, Morris, Stoker 1c, 234928, Vivid, 1 March 1924
DAVIES, Richard F, Able Seaman, D/J 63005, Drake, 31 July 1935
DAVIES, Samuel W, Stoker 1c, K 10515, Kildysart, 19 November 1918
DAVIES, Sydney, Chief Stoker, P/K 60052, Victory, 30 April 1937
DAVIES, Thomas, Boy 1c, J 48302, Victory, 28 December 1919
DAVIES, William H, Shipwright 2c, 346304, Pembroke, 17 February 1919
DAVIES, William J, Colour Sergeant, RMLI, 9303 (Ply), Caesar, 23 March 1919
DAVIES, William J, Shipwright 2c, 344865, Pembroke, 26 February 1919
DAVIS, Charles A, Engine Room Artificer 3c, M 6102, Pembroke, 10 February 1919
DAVIS, Charles A, Leading Signalman, C/J 73968, Keith, 3 January 1935
DAVIS, David K, Stoker 1c, SS 120441, Silvio, 30 November 1919
DAVIS, Edward C, Leading Seaman, J 10556, Badminton, 24 October 1924
DAVIS, Franklin H, Chief Engine Room Artificer, P/M 6236, Royal Navy, 28 January 1938
DAVIS, Frederick J, Lieutenant Commander, RNR (Rtd), President, 13 May 1919
DAVIS, George E, Marine, 16163 (Ply), Queen Elizabeth, 9 November 1927
DAVIS, James, Able Seaman, J 12861 (Dev), Ambuscade, 1 December 1918
DAVIS, John G, Stoker 2c, C/KX 85637, Pembroke, 19 April 1935
DAVIS, Montague E, Leading Telegraphist, J 85592, H.42, 23 March 1922
DAVIS, Reginald W, Cook's Mate, M 25166 (Po), Penarth, 4 February 1919
DAVIS, Walter, Private, RM, S 12416 (Deal), RM Labour Corps, 28 January 1919
DAVIS, William, Stoker 1c, C/KX 76800, Royal Navy, 2 October 1936
DAVIS, William F, Stoker Petty Officer, K 11817, Sutton, 5 April 1928
DAVIS, William J, Stoker 2c, K 49520, Pembroke, 20 December 1918
DAVISON, Anthony J, Honorary Engineer Commander, RNR, Royal Naval Reserve, 24 January 1932
DAVISON, James R, Stoker 1c, K 56119, Centaur, 28 October 1928
DAVISON, William J, Paymaster Lieutenant Commander, Warspite, 27 February 1920
DAW, Walter E, Boy 1c, D/SSX 19193, Rodney, 19 August 1937
DAWE, Reginald, Warrant Master at Arms, Royal Navy, 30 September 1931
DAWE, Samuel H, Painter 1c, 344039, Dolphin, 20 August 1921
DAWE, William J T, Stoker Petty Officer, D/K 20268, Danae, 19 February 1932
DAWES, Arthur D, Electrical Artificer 5c, P/MX 58426, Royal Navy, 15 January 1939
DAWES, George, Able Seaman (RFR B 1973), 166211 (Po), Penarth, 4 February 1919

DAWES, George, Leading Seaman, J 12434, Glowworm, 25 August 1919
DAWSON, Alfred C, Officer's Cook 1c, 361164, Victory, 21 March 1920
DAWSON, John H, Able Seaman, J 35065, Hyacinth II, 11 October 1919
DAWSON, Leslie T, Ordinary Seaman, J 112750, Pembroke, 15 July 1928
DAWSON, William, Engine Room Artificer 1c, M 4302, Dolphin, 15 April 1929
DAY, Albert, Able Seaman, C/J 33641, Victory, 4 October 1930
DAY, Charles S, Able Seaman, J 37762, Vivid, 4 February 1920
DAY, Ernest F, Honorary Lieutenant Commander, RNVR, Royal Naval Volunteer Reserve, 15 December 1926
DAY, James J, Stoker 1c, K 43638 (Po), Southampton, 13 June 1919
DAY, John T, Stoker 1c, 312283, Saxifrage, 1 February 1919
DAY, Peter, Stoker Petty Officer, K 6063, Nelson, 27 February 1930
DAY, Sydney G, 3rd Writer, M 18560, President, 24 November 1918
DAY, Thomas E, Private, RMLI, 16844 (Ch), Cormorant, 5 January 1919
DAY, Thomas M, Lieutenant, RNR, President, 7 August 1921
DAYKIN, John R, Stoker 2c, SS 119164, Victory, 21 February 1919
DAYRELL-REED, Archibald, Lieutenant, CMB.88BD, coastal motor boat, 18 August 1919

DE BONO, Emanuele, Officer's Cook 1c, 360394, Egmont, 22 March 1926
DE BURGH, Francis V, Commander, RIM, Aden Command, attached to, 7 December 1918
DE CAEN, Raymond G F H, Lieutenant Commander, Eagle, 12 April 1922
DE CARTERET, Harold R, Able Seaman, RNVR, AA 2787, President, 26 January 1919
DE JERSEY, Norman S, Right Rev, Honorary Chaplain, RNVR, Royal Naval Volunteer Reserve, 28 November 1934
DE ROBECK, Sir John M, Admiral of the Fleet, Royal Navy, 20 January 1928
DE SOUZA, Gaetano A, Officer's Steward 1c, 157258, Crocus, 25 July 1922
DE SOUZA, Joao V, Cook 2c, 356465, Lupin, 14 November 1928
DE SOUZA, Pedro C, Officer's Cook 1c, 355326, Highflyer, 5 November 1920
DE VOIL, Eric J, Gunner, St Vincent, 29 March 1931
DEACON, Charles J R, Engine Room Artificer Apprentice, M 36122, Fisgard, 14 February 1921
DEACON, Donald C, Lieutenant, K.26, 14 November 1925
DEACON, Henry S, Chief Stoker, 296535, Diligence, on books of Blenheim, 5 September 1921
DEACON, William, Able Seaman, SS 9734, Benbow, 4 August 1922
DEACON, William H, Able Seaman, P/JX 149948, Esk, 4 March 1937
DEADMAN, Arthur, Able Seaman, RNVR, London Z 2788, Howe Battalion, RND, 6 December 1918
DEADMAN, William D, Stoker 1c, C/K 60990, Gallant, 28 December 1936
DEAKIN, James, Greaser, MMR, 496680, Vivid, 22 November 1918
DEAN, Arthur G, Ordnance Artificer Apprentice, C/MX 46517, Pembroke, 12 November 1931
DEAN, Charles L, Leading Sick Berth Attendant, M 37776, Triad, 28 June 1930
DEAN, Edmund A, Stoker 1c, K 38050, Victory, 21 June 1919
DEAN, Ernest J D, Able Seaman, J 3955, Velox, 12 February 1919
DEAN, George, Engine Room Artificer 4c, M 11786, Victory, 15 March 1919

DEAN, Lionel S K, Ordinary Seaman, P/SSX 14268, Victory, 6 November 1933
DEAN, Norman E, Paymaster Lieutenant, Southampton, 30 June 1924
DEANE, Patrick, Regulating Petty Officer, 228541, Vivid, 27 April 1920
DEAR, Ivo L, Able Seaman, J 94740, Ursula, 18 December 1927
DEARING, Leonard A P, Able Seaman, J 48620, M.1, 12 November 1925
DEARLING, Robert G, Leading Seaman, J 10528, Victory, 11 March 1920
DEARLOVE, Reginald A, Private, RMLI, 17106 (Ply), Glory, 12 November 1918
DEARNELEY, Thomas, Boy 1c, J 82849, Thunderer, 5 April 1919
DEARNS, Edmund, Able Seaman, J 60545, Cleopatra, 24 October 1920
DEATON, John, Stoker, RNR, S 2220, Pembroke, 12 February 1919
DEDMAN, James V, Electrical Artificer Apprentice, MX 58809, Pembroke, 11 May 1936
DEE, Paul, Able Seaman, D/JX 128356, Malaya, 9 September 1932
DEGGAN, Hubert S, Chief Petty Officer, C/J 28977, Marshall Soult, 19 January 1935
DEGNIN, Francis, Stoker 1c, 282529, Kildangan, 20 February 1919
DEIGHTON, Henry, Leading Stoker, 299695, Vivien, 28 January 1922
DELEMARE, Herbert A, Petty Officer, J 16376, Revenge, 4 September 1925
DELHI, Alfred J, Able Seaman, J 16934, Fantome, 5 June 1921
DELL, Henry J, Gunner, RMA, RMA 1848, RMA, Portsmouth, 13 February 1919
DELL, Reginald W, Chief Petty Officer, P/J 2002, Excellent, 5 October 1930
DELLBRIDGE, Arthur F, Engineer Lieutenant Commander, Arrow, 19 February 1934
DELLOW, Alfred J, Stoker Petty Officer, D/K 20937, Drake, 20 May 1935
DEMELLWEEK, Joseph M, Seaman, RNR, B 3302, Colleen, 24 March 1919
DEMPSEY, William G, Leading Seaman, 215684, L.24, 10 January 1924
DENCH, Munro R, Leading Stoker, K 15254 (Po), Penarth, 4 February 1919
DENHAM, Ernest, Petty Officer, J 13071, Vivid, 19 December 1926
DENHAM, William H, Regulating Petty Officer, D/M 39140, Queen Elizabeth, 18 October 1931
DENISON, Christopher, Pilot Officer, RAF, 440 Flight, Hermes, 30 April 1925
DENNER, Frederick, Petty Officer Telegraphist, RAN, 10827 (RN 236025), Royal Australian Navy, 21 October 1924
DENNETT, Aubrey J D, Ordnance Artificer 2c, C/M 38740, Marshall Soult, 6 August 1934
DENNINGTON, James R, Able Seaman, 227476 (Po), Penarth, 4 February 1919
DENNIS, Edward A, Leading Stoker, K 35336, Fisgard, 5 April 1924
DENNIS, Gerald W, Lieutenant, FAA, 405 Flight, Glorious, 18 November 1932
DENNIS, John S C, Deck Hand, MMR, Mollusc, 16 November 1918
DENNIS, John, Petty Officer 1c, 175529, Excellent, 4 January 1919
DENNIS, William, Electrical Artificer 2c, M 12651, M.1, 12 November 1925
DENNIS, William F, Petty Officer, 190208, Daisy, 17 February 1919
DENNISON, William W, Engine Room Artificer 2c, 271982 (Ch), Fandango, 3 July 1919
DENT, Edward S, Able Seaman, J 34711, Vernon, 5 June 1929
DENYER, Leonard G, Officer's Steward 2c, L 8260, Victory III, 12 May 1922
DERBYSHIRE, William A, Signalman, J 19095 (Dev), Vivid, 11 July 1920
DERIA, Yusuf, Seedie, Lupin, January 1927
DERRICK, David, Officer's Cook 1c, C/L 14247, Renown, 7 March 1933
DERRICK, John H, Stoker 1c, KX 76591, Adamant, 17 May 1930
DES ROCHES, Philfras E, Ordinary Seaman, RNCVR, VR 3219, Gannet, 20 September 1919
DEUCHAR, William J, Gunner, Excellent, 13 October 1937
DEVEY, John, Able Seaman, J 110792, Vivid, 10 May 1929
DEW, George, Stoker 1c, K 12398, Valerian, 22 October 1926
DEWEY, Guy F J, Leading Cook, M 38718, Pandora, 5 July 1930
DEWING, Alfred P, Lieutenant, Dauntless, 11 May 1926
DEWSBURY, Charles, Leading Deck Hand, MMR, Iolaire, 1 January 1919
DEXETER, Ernest, Ordinary Seaman, SS 8694, Splendid, 20 November 1919

DIBLEY, Samuel F, Stoker 1c, SS 120419, Tiger, 29 November 1921
DICK, Andrew S, Assistant Steward, MMR, 943289, St Elvies, 5 February 1919
DICKASON, Alfred C, Able Seaman, SS 849, Vivid, 21 February 1919
DICKENS, Gerald H C, Lieutenant, Codrington, 15 October 1936
DICKENS, Leslie A, Able Seaman, J 100803, Castor, 19 July 1930
DICKENS, Walter, Stoker 1c, K 56538, Senator, 23 February 1924
DICKENSON, James W E, Ordinary Seaman, J 112240, Royal Sovereign, 11 January 1927
DICKESON, Arthur E, Signal Boy, RNR, SB 1555, Erin's Isle, 7 February 1919
DICKINSON, Arthur, Lieutenant, RNR, Victory, 7 July 1919
DICKINSON, Cecil C, Lieutenant Commander, Vivid, 2 February 1928
DICKINSON, Jesse, Chief Engine Room Artificer 1c, M 452, Valerian, 22 October 1926
DICKINSON, William A C, Leading Stoker, D/KX 78081, Royal Navy, 12 June 1938
DICKSON, Frederick, Engine Room Artificer 3c, M 549, Victory, 5 March 1920
DICKSON, John H, Warrant Engineer, Royal Navy, 22 June 1923
DICKSON, Robert D L, Lieutenant, Pilot's Course, 1 October 1932
DICKSON, Thomas H, Lieutenant Commander, Merchant Navy Defence Instructional Officer, Cardiff, 28 April 1939
DIGGLE, Edward, Quartermaster Sergeant, RMLI, 770 (Po), 1st RM Battalion, RND, 6 February 1919
DIKE, Frederick J, Boatswain, 56437, Ceto, 20 November 1918
DILBY, Robert J, Cook (S), D/MX 49645, Drake, 5 June 1935
DILLON, Joseph, Stoker 1c, K 15795, Centurion, 17 June 1923
DILLON-SHALLAND, Harold J, Chief Stoker, P/K 58669, Thetis, 3 June 1939
DIMENT, Percy J, Able Seaman, J 23290, Colleen, 3 June 1921
DINAN, Edward, Able Seaman, J 47798, Whirlwind, 9 January 1919
DINES, William S, Stoker Petty Officer, 306682, Vivid, 22 July 1919
DINGLE, Edward H, Stoker 1c, K 24623, Catspaw, 31 December 1919
DINMORE, Sidney A, Able Seaman, J 3412, Thisbe, 31 May 1920
DIPLOCK, Harry, Signalman Petty Officer, 311859, Revenge, 27 December 1923
DISTIN, Alfred, Shipwright 2c, M 6749, Botha, 13 December 1918

DITCHER, John A, Engine Room Artificer 4c, M 37028, H.47, 9 July 1929
DITES, Samuel, Leading Stoker, D/K 66002, Glorious, 14 August 1936
DITTON, Hugh, Lieutenant Commander, FAA, 401 Flight, Courageous, 25 February 1932
DIXIE, Albert E, Lieutenant Commander, Crescent, 16 May 1920
DIXON, Albert W, Stoker Petty Officer, D/K 61059, Norfolk, 25 January 1934
DIXON, George E, Boy 2c, JX 150012, Ganges, 16 February 1937
DIXON, Herbert, Able Seaman, J 11166, Abeille, 1 January 1919
DIXON, Joseph, Leading Telegraphist, J 22450, Curlew, 23 March 1922
DIXON, Reginald C, Petty Officer, 231628, M.1, 12 November 1925
DIXON, Thomas, Leading Stoker, K 8572, Ship or unit not listed, 29 November 1921
DIXON, William, Stoker Petty Officer, 298628 (Ch), Blake, 16 January 1920
DIXON, William H, Stoker Petty Officer, K 1625, Vivien, 23 November 1918

D'LOYDE, Phillip J, Marine, 18709 (Po), Queen Elizabeth, 19 February 1926

DOALEH, Ali, Seedie Stoker, 402, Comus, 13 July 1921
DOBELL, John W, Lieutenant, President, 1 March 1919
DOBELLS, Gilbert H, Civilian Contractor, Thetis, 3 June 1939
DOBSON, Ernest, Stoker 1c, K 66560, Argus, 21 February 1927
DOBSON, Frederick H J, Ordinary Seaman, J 93563, Julius (ex-Caradoc), 27 June 1920
DOBSON, Herbert, Able Seaman, 223645, Clinit, 28 December 1918
DOBSON, John, Fireman, MMR, 918552, Hughli, Royal Fleet Auxiliary, 26 April 1919
DOBSON, Vernon W, Sub Lieutenant, Pilot's Course, 1 October 1932
DODD, Charles, Petty Officer, 198415, Vivid IV, 21 April 1922
DODD, James P, Paymaster Lieutenant Commander, RNR, Royal Naval Reserve, 8 January 1934
DODDRIDGE, Arthur H G, Stoker Petty Officer, D/K 33246, Thanet, 3 February 1934
DODNEY, William E F, Private, RMLI, 19817 (Po), Curacoa, 6 June 1923
DODRIDGE, Arthur C, Musician, RMB, RMB 2051, Renown, 21 June 1929
DODSON, Alfred W, Able Seaman, P/J 104696, Milford, 6 January 1937
DOEL, Joseph, Officer's Steward 1c, 364987, Victory, 15 March 1919
DOHERTY, Henry E, Petty Officer, D/J 90806, Galatea, 1 February 1939
DOMVILLE, Sir James H, Lieutenant, P.19, patrol boat, 13 September 1919
DONALD, Edgar J, Officer's Cook 3c, L 14164, Pembroke, 24 August 1926
DONALD, Hugh J, Able Seaman, 228142, L.24, 10 January 1924
DONALDSON, Robert H, Lieutenant, RM, Portsmouth, 30 April 1925
DONALDSON, William, Fireman, MMR, Goissa, 15 November 1918
DONEGAN, Ernest G, Able Seaman, 223779, Valerian, 22 October 1926
DONNELLY, Thomas, Commissioned Gunner, Pembroke, 8 December 1923
DONOHUE, James, Fireman, MMR, 891620, Richard Welford, 16 February 1919
DONOVAN, Alexander M, Lieutenant Commander, Royal Navy, 20 April 1932
DONOVAN, Cornelius, Leading Seaman, RNR, A 5639, President III, 2 March 1919

DONOVAN, Edward, Leading Stores Assistant, M 11680, Vivid, 29 June 1930
DONOVAN, John J, Ordinary Seaman, J 102224, Vivid, 10 April 1922
DONOVAN, Michael, Able Seaman, J 18322 (Po), K.5, 20 January 1921
DONOVAN, Richard C, Stoker Petty Officer, K 12426, Restless, 14 November 1922
DONOVAN, Walter H, Boy 1c, JX 131171, Ramillies, 16 March 1930
DOPSON, Thomas, Able Seaman, J 23419, Caledon, 10 October 1919
DORAN, Hugh, Stoker 1c, K 57884, Chatham, 1 December 1922
DORMER, Archibald P, Engineer Lieutenant Commander, Excellent, 10 December 1927
DORRELL, Alfred E, Ordinary Seaman, J 71751, Reclaim, 31 December 1918
DOUGHTY, Henry M, Rear Admiral, Rear Admiral 1st Battle Squadron, 1 May 1921
DOUGLAS, Archibald R, Sub Lieutenant, President, 17 February 1919
DOUGLAS, Arthur J, Boy Servant, L 13021, Vivid, 4 March 1920
DOUGLAS, Edward, Coastguardsman 3c, 181487, Vivid, 4 August 1922
DOUGLAS, Frederick T, Sub Lieutenant, RNR, Teakol, 14 March 1919
DOUGLAS, Gordon, Boy 2c, JX 154758, Caledonia, 7 December 1937
DOUGLAS, Robert, Signalman, P/JX 125837, Royal Navy, 22 June 1938
DOVE, Victor A, Able Seaman, P/J 104847, Dolphin, 29 January 1935
DOWDE, Thomas, Stoker Petty Officer, C/K 3294, Pembroke, 29 August 1939
DOWDING, Norman P O, Sergeant, RMLI, 17082 (Ch), 1st RM Battalion, RND, 8 February 1919
DOWELL, William E, Gunner, RMA, RMA 11871, Konakry, steamship, 1 December 1918
DOWLER, Bertie E, Cook's Mate 2c, M 34574, Victory, 1 May 1919
DOWLING, Frank, Leading Seaman, C/J 106162, Poseidon, 9 June 1931
DOWLING, Frank, Shipwright 1c, 168832, Dolphin, 22 July 1919
DOWLING, Frederick V, Able Seaman, J 11944, Crocus, 29 January 1924
DOWN, Eric F, Leading Stoker, D/KX 79932, Berwick, 6 June 1937
DOWN, John, Private, RMLI, 20694 (Ply), RM Deal, 11 March 1920
DOWNER, Albert E, Stoker 1c, P/KX 77672, Centaur, 7 October 1930
DOWNES, Joseph L, Commissioned Engineer, RNR, British Mariner, 5 December 1932
DOWNEY, Cyril F, Officer's Cook 1c, L 7085, Excellent, 7 May 1928
DOWNIE, David, Lieutenant, RNR, President, 1 February 1919
DOWNINE, Alexander P, Paymaster Commander, RNR, Royal Naval Reserve, 23 January 1929
DOWNING, Edward E G, Boy 1c, JX 125064, Emperor of India, 27 January 1927
DOWNS, George, Stoker 1c, SS 125714, Blue Sky, tender to Queen Elizabeth, 12 June 1922
DOWNS, John M, Stoker 1c, K 56695, Europa, 26 January 1920
DOWNS, John P, Lieutenant, RNR, Gosforth, 29 March 1919
DOWSON, John, Stoker 1c, K 32400, Leviathan, 27 January 1919
DOXSLEY, Richard J, Boy 1c, C/JX 142674, Pembroke, 17 March 1936
DOYLE, Christopher, Stoker 1c, D/K 65333, Defiance, 10 December 1930
DOYLE, John, Ordinary Seaman, RNVR, Tyneside Z 12801, John Cooper, 19 January 1919

DOYLE, John, Seaman, RNR, B 5322, Trebiskin, 12 November 1918
DOYLE, Leslie R, Boy, SS 3007, Royal Navy, 4 August 1939
DOYLE, Martin, Leading Seaman, J 15434, Vivid, 17 October 1926
DOYLE, Matthew, Trimmer, RNR, TS 8185, Eaglet III, 11 March 1920

DRAKE, William P, Stoker 1C, SS 125649, Truant, 12 March 1924
DRAKE-BROCKHAM, Lewis, Major, RMLI, Glory, 10 May 1919
DRANSFIELD, Herbert, Able Seaman, D/JX 137532, Dolphin, 3 July 1939
DRAPER, William J A, Able Seaman, J 111460, Sepoy, 8 April 1930
DREDGE, Felix A St G, Lieutenant, Pilot's Course, 29 April 1925
DREW, Benjamin, Leading Stoker, 300885, Ramilles, 2 December 1920
DREW, Herbert G, Warrant Engineer, Cumberland, 4 August 1931
DREW, John A V, Senior Reserve Attendant, M 10514, Victory, 15 February 1919
DREW, Stanley W, Marine, G/X 318, Royal Marines HQ, 29 April 1928
DREWERY, James E, Stoker 1c, C/KX 87003, Woolwich, 28 March 1939
DREWRY, Dorothy M, Telephonist, WRNS, G 2091, Women's Royal Naval Service, 25 February 1920
DRIEU, Emile, Officer's Steward 3c, L 7071, Victory, 18 February 1919
DRING, Jack E, Gunner, Whitley, 31 January 1922
DRISCOLL, Denis, Leading Stoker, 283113, Venerable, 3 May 1919
DRISCOLL, James, Seaman, RNR, A 9300, Fylde, 18 December 1918
DRISCOLL, Walter J, Commissioned Gunner, Ark Royal, 13 May 1927
DRIVER, Henry W, Leading Seaman, C/J 111730, Cardiff, 15 January 1938
DRUETT, Eldred W, Cook, M 36480, Ross, 22 February 1925
DRUGGAN, Thomas, Stoker 1c, KX 76889, Ramillies, 16 January 1928
DRUITT, Robert, Able Seaman, D/JX 143457, Furious, 4 September 1938
DRUMMOND, James, Stoker 1c, P/K 62886, M.2, 29 January 1932
DRUMMOND-HAY, Edward de V, Lieutenant, Emperor of India, 12 May 1920
DRYDEN, Kenneth E, Engine Room Artificer 4c, D/MX 47900, Delhi, 20 September 1936
DRYSDALE, Georgina, Telephonist, WRNS, G 668, Women's Royal Naval Service, 23 November 1918

D'SOUZA, Raimundo C, Officer's Steward 1c, L 9101, Hyacinth, 15 June 1919

DUCKWORTH, Thomas W, Engine Room Artificer 3c, M 34520, H.43, 23 December 1929
DUFF, William, Stoker 1c, SS 125019, Hawkins, 8 November 1921
DUFFERIN and AVA, MARQUESS of, Captain, RNVR, Ulster Division, RNVR, 21 July 1930
DUFTON, Henry H, Stoker 1c, K 54540, Wessex, 11 April 1924
DUGGAN, Albert F H, Leading Seaman, J 62085, M.1, 12 November 1925
DUGGAN, Frederick C, Stoker Petty Officer, 233709, Valerian, 22 October 1926
DUGGAN, Patrick, Stoker 1c, D/K 65829, Drake, 26 February 1934
DUMARESQ, John S, Rear Admiral, Royal Navy, 22 July 1922

DUMINGHAM, James, Able Seaman, D/SSX 15375, Drake, 11 January 1939
DUMMER, John W, Able Seaman, P/JX 149704, Courageous, 22 June 1938
DUNBAR, Bernard C, Able Seaman, J 18422, Caradoc, 4 December 1921
DUNCAN, David N, Civilian Contractor, Thetis, 3 June 1939
DUNCAN, George W D, Lieutenant Commander, Dryad, 20 July 1935
DUNCAN, Henry, Telegraphist, J 93280, Greenwich, 14 January 1929
DUNCAN, James C, Ty/Sub Lieutenant, RNVR, George Robinson, 25 November 1918
DUNCAN, William, Corporal, RM, S 10560 (Deal), RM Labour Corps, 16 February 1919
DUNDAS, David, Midshipman, Blue Sky, tender to Queen Elizabeth, 12 June 1922
DUNHAM, Bernard W C, Boy 2c, JX 153295, Ganges, 28 November 1937
DUNKLING, George W, Private, RMLI, 21068 (Ch), Vulcan, 10 February 1920
DUNKS, Frederick, Able Seaman, J 53176 (Po), Erin's Isle, 7 February 1919
DUNLOP, Frederick J, Corporal, RM, X 449 (Ch), Drake, 27 May 1935
DUNN, Alfred G, Stoker Petty Officer, 306007, Rocket, 27 January 1926
DUNN, Alfred H, Stoker 1c, D/KX 86322, Thetis, 3 June 1939
DUNN, Anthony, Petty Officer, D/J 20868, Osiris, 12 January 1934
DUNN, Arthur, Sub Lieutenant, RNR, Kilcock, 8 March 1919
DUNN, Arthur E, Captain, RNR, Royal Naval Reserve, 6 January 1927
DUNN, Charles W, Able Seaman, C/J 96476, Pembroke, 2 May 1935
DUNN, Edward P, Gunner, Queen Elizabeth, 1 December 1920
DUNN, Herbert O, Air Mechanic 1c, F 1231, RNAS, 20th Armoured Car Squadron, 18 November 1918
DUNN, Joseph C J, Chief Engine Room Artificer 2c, C/M 2194, Pembroke, 27 November 1931
DUNN, William C, Stoker Petty Officer, 304436, Hawkins, 16 March 1921
DUNN, William H, Able Seaman, J 94919, Defiance, 31 August 1925
DUNNE, Denis, Ship's Cook, MMR, 998261, Hughli, Royal Fleet Auxiliary, 26 April 1919
DUNNETT, Herbert C, Stoker 1c, SS 124104, Marlborough, 1 December 1922
DUNRAVEN, Earl of, Honorary Captain, RNR, Royal Naval Reserve, 14 June 1926
DUNROE, John, Able Seaman, 203394, Violent, 17 April 1923
DUNSTAN, George A F, Private, RMLI, S 2745 (Ch), Chatham Division, RMLI, 16 November 1918
DUNSTAN, William J, Chief Ordnance Artificer, D/M 34953, Newcastle, 17 October 1938
DUPEN, Arthur P L, Engineer Captain, Egmont, 25 December 1918
DURANT, Arthur M, Stoker 1c, K 64431, Dolphin, 2 June 1930
DURCAN, James, Stoker Petty Officer, K 2237, Adventure, 9 March 1929
DURDLE, Reginald H, Corporal, RMLI, 15940 (Po), Portsmouth Division, RMLI, 13 April 1921
DURHAM, Ernest R, Able Seaman, RNVR, London Z 198, Nelson Battalion, RND, 27 March 1919
DURKIN, Frederick C - see PALMER, Charles, Stoker Petty Officer,
DURR, Henry, Trimmer, MMR, 863285, Macedonia, 4 January 1919
DURRAN, James E, Stoker 1c, C/K 65768, Pembroke, 22 November 1931
DURRANT, Arthur G, Deck Hand, RNR, DA 7872, Strathgeldie,

4 January 1919

DURRANT, Stanley R, Ordinary Seaman, C/JX 153427, Eskimo, 18 June 1939

DURRELL, Jack, Able Seaman, JX 126734, Wakeful, 2 July 1930

DUVEY, Archibald F, Officer's Steward 2c, L 7203, Undine, 13 March 1919

DUXFIELD, John, Private, RM, S 515 (Deal), RM Labour Corps, 15 June 1919

DWYER, Robert M, Paymaster Lieutenant Commander, RNR, Royal Naval Reserve, 22 October 1930

DYE, Edgar E, Able Seaman, RNVR, R 744, Anson Battalion, RND, 28 May 1919

DYER, Albert E, Able Seaman, J 103385, Enterprise, 9 February 1928

DYER, George, Ordinary Seaman, J 95962, Diomede, 18 June 1923

DYER, William H, Stoker Petty Officer, K 18819, Restless, 27 November 1918

DYMOND, Hubert, Lance Corporal, RMLI, 15297 (Ch), President III, 27 February 1919

DYSON, Alan W, Able Seaman, SS 9575, Veteran, 30 September 1921

DYSON, Henry R, Ty/Sub Lieutenant, RNVR, Regimental HQ, RND, attached to RAF, 25 November 1918

DYSON, Sidney H, Electrical Artificer 4c, P/MX 46285, Revenge, 2 August 1930

E

EADES, Thomas E, Engine Room Artificer 4c, D/MX 53904, Royal Oak, 9 October 1937

EAGER, Albert J, Telegraphist, J 44662, Tartar, 29 November 1918

EAGLES, George C, Leading Telegraphist, C/JX 130135, Ramillies, 20 September 1936

EALES, Archibald I, Able Seaman, J 115552, Pembroke, 2 April 1929

EALES, Joseph S, Supply Petty Officer, D/M 34126, Rodney, 12 September 1932

EALES, Thomas B, Leading Signalman, J 25873, Enterprise, 12 May 1926

EARL, Ernest, Able Seaman, J 29063, Pembroke, 2 January 1923

EARL, Leslie W H, Boy 2c, RAN, 6902, Tingira (RAN), 16 March 1919

EARLE, John C M, Cadet, Royal Navy, 22 February 1937

EARWICKER, Henry, Stoker Petty Officer, 119546, Victory, 19 March 1919

EARWICKER, William A, Telegraphist, P/JX 127484, Revenge, 3 January 1934

EASEN, Henry J, Stoker 1c, K 60457, Curlew, 18 November 1924

EASEY, John S, 2nd Hand, RNR, DA 3433, Crescent, 2 November 1919

EASON, Jesse, Stoker 2c, SS 119490, Victory, 25 February 1919

EASON, William H W, Leading Seaman, J 14154, Syringa, 17 November 1918

EASTLEY, John, Mechanician, 358829, Concord, 13 May 1921

EASTMENT, Walter J, Able Seaman, SS 5934, Victory, 3 November 1923

EASTON, Alfred, Able Seaman, J 35475, Vanity, 26 May 1920

EASTON, Arthur R, Ordnance Artificer 4c, P/MX 54557, Excellent, 5 August 1937

EASTON, Sidney T, Able Seaman, P/J 18183, Courageous, 19 July 1932

EASTON, William S, Able Seaman, J 84915, Venomous, 9 December 1921

EASTWOOD, Frank, Boy 2c, J 92268, Powerful, 28 December 1918

EASTWOOD, Fred, Able Seaman, J 69111, Bacchante, 14 February 1919

EATON, George A, Chief Engine Room Artificer 2c, P/M 2114, Constance, 28 January 1932

EATON, Joseph S, Stoker Petty Officer, K 395, Pembroke, 9 March 1929

EATON, William, Joiner 1c, 301045, Philomel, 10 May 1921

EBBS, Sidney C, Able Seaman, J 39043, Endeavour, 23 April 1919

EBLING, Francis J, Engine Room Artificer 3c, M 2182 (Ch), L.55, 4 June 1919

EBSWORTH, William F, Stoker 1c, K 41588 (Ch), Kildysart, 27 November 1918

ECCLES, John, Able Seaman, RNVR, Mersey Z 1031, Chama, steamship, 9 February 1919

ECCLESTON, Harold, Civilian Contractor, Thetis, 3 June 1939

ECKETT, Urbain T M, Lieutenant, RNVR, Research, 21 February 1919

EDDEN, Thomas H, Engine Room Artificer 3c, M 14514, M.1, 12 November 1925

EDDIS, Paul L, Lieutenant Commander, L.24, 10 January 1924

EDE, Sidney W G, Telegraphist, J 77429, Diligence, 17 February 1924

EDEY, George E, Leading Seaman, J 5173, Vansittart, 21 October 1921

EDGAR, Frederick W, Stoker 1c, 160092, Pembroke, 27 December 1918

EDGE, Charles H, Marine, X 278 (Ch), Colombo, 27 July 1934

EDGECOMBE, Arthur W, Midshipman, Verulam, 4 September 1919

EDGECOMBE, Arthur, Leading Stoker, K 18083, Resolution, 30 December 1919

EDGECOMBE, Sydney W V, Able Seaman, J 5382, Defiance, 29 July 1922

EDGINGTON, Frederick J, Ordnance Artificer Apprentice, M 35360, Indus, 14 February 1922

EDMONDS, Charles, Leading Seaman, J 2996 (Ch), K.5, 20 January 1921

EDMONDS, Frederick W J, Leading Signalman, J 5921, Victor, 13 November 1918

EDMONDS, Henry A, Able Seaman, J 46839, Royal Sovereign, 8 September 1925

EDWARDES, George M, Stoker, RAN, 5324, Australia (RAN), 21 August 1919

EDWARDS, Albert, Able Seaman, RFA, Bacchus, RFA, 14 April 1925

EDWARDS, Albert E, Able Seaman, J 32905, Daffodil, 10 January 1929

EDWARDS, Albert E, Leading Signalman, 225965, Espiegle, 19 March 1920

EDWARDS, Alfred, Able Seaman, J 102259, Emperor of India, 6 March 1925

EDWARDS, Arthur C, Ordnance Artificer 2c, M 6589, Devonshire, 27 July 1929

EDWARDS, Arthur W, Stoker Petty Officer, K 370, Pembroke, 23 April 1919

EDWARDS, Frederick R, Ordinary Seaman, SS 9684 (Ch), Tempest, 20 July 1920

EDWARDS, Garnet, Officer's Steward 1c, 360453, Lucia, 13 December 1923

EDWARDS, George A, Stoker Petty Officer, C/K 23225, Ark Royal, 25 April 1934

EDWARDS, Henry F, Lieutenant, Victory, 10 February 1933

EDWARDS, James, Stoker Petty Officer, 305412, Defiance, 12 March 1923

EDWARDS, John, Marine, 22605 (Ply), Royal Marines HQ, 22 June 1926

EDWARDS, John H, Able Seaman, D/J 106978, M.2, 29 January 1932

EDWARDS, John W, Chief Stoker, 277719, Vivid II, 20 November 1919

EDWARDS, Leonard, Leading Signalman, J 41856, Valerian, 22 October 1926

EDWARDS, Leonard T, Officer's Steward 2c, L 10673, Hood, 25 March 1921

EDWARDS, Walter W, Ordinary Seaman, J 22025, Pembroke (ex-Powerful), 2 November 1919

EDWARDS, William, Stoker 1c, K 65969, Hermes, 7 May 1929

EDWARDS, William, Stoker Petty Officer, K 15468, Wistaria, 2 March 1921

EELS, Alfred H, Stoker 1c, K 4447 (Ch), Fandango, 3 July 1919

EFFARD, Edward P, Stoker Petty Officer, 303078, Raleigh, 8 August 1922

EGERTON, Wilfred A, Rear Admiral, Tactical Course, 18 July 1931

EGGLESTON, Charles H, Stoker 1c, K 31712 (Dev), Cassandra, 5 December 1918

EGGLETON, John H G, Able Seaman, C/JX 126702, Valiant, 29 May 1931

EGGLETON, William G, Stoker 1c, K 61596, Blenheim, 16 May 1925

ELBOURNE, Henry J L, Gunner, Greenwich, 24 November 1927

ELDERTON, Charles, Able Seaman, J 43592, Witherington, 12 October 1927

ELDERTON, Henry E, Stoker 1c, K 12072, Coventry, 11 March 1919

ELDRED, Leslie N, Boy 1c, J 96872, Ganges, 7 January 1921

ELEMENT, William H, Able Seaman, P/J 112399, Blanche, 23 November 1933

ELLEN, Ernest G, Stoker 1c, K 4481, P.23, patrol boat, 25 November 1918

ELLERBECK, George W, Boy 1c, J 79594, Curacoa, 21 November 1918

ELLERY, Thomas, Stoker Petty Officer, 276591, Jupiter, 16 July 1919

ELLIOTT, Archibald G, Lieutenant Commander, FAA, 461 Flight, Glorious, 2 October 1931

ELLIOTT, Edmund L V, Petty Officer, J 22587, H.47, 9 July 1929

ELLIOTT, Edward P R, Marine, 16223 (Ply), Hermes, 4 September 1929

ELLIOTT, George, Dockyard Fitter, civilian, H.29, 9 August 1926, accidentally killed

ELLIOTT, George H, Shipwright 2c, D/M 7213, Snapdragon, 17 November 1931

ELLIOTT, John, Ordinary Seaman, J 78058, Glasgow, 4 December 1918

ELLIOTT, John, Stoker 1c, K 13388, Verulam, 4 September 1919

ELLIOTT, John C, Able Seaman, J 2534, Titania, 10 April 1922

ELLIOTT, John G, Private, RMLI, 16932 (Po), Portsmouth Division, RMLI, 2 April 1919

ELLIOTT, Stanley, Private, RM, S 2540 (Deal), Divisional Train Reserves, RND, 26 March 1919

ELLIOTT, William B, Private, RMLI, 20278 (Po), RM, 6th Battalion, 27 August 1919

ELLIS, Albert G, Petty Officer Cook, P/M 7670, Whitshed, 15 April 1935

ELLIS, Albert H, Engine Room Artificer 1c, P/M 5868, Dolphin, 15 March 1931

ELLIS, Charles A, Stoker 1c, SS 124701 (Ch), K.5, 20 January 1921

ELLIS, Charles W, Marine, 17747 (Ch), Kent, 22 September 1930

ELLIS, John A E, Marine, X 263 (Po), Revenge, 18 April 1930

ELLIS, Percival S, Engine Room Artificer 2c, 271960, P.16, patrol boat, 19 February 1919

ELLIS, Stanley G, Petty Officer Telegraphist, P/J 29040, M.2, 29 January 1932

ELLUL, Carmelo, Officer's Cook 2c, L 3784, Waterhen, 24 January 1920

ELLUL, Emmanuel, Able Seaman, E/JX 145940, St Angelo, 27 April 1939

ELLUL, Lorenzo, Steward, E/LX 21107, Brazen, 11 January 1935

ELSDON, Albert J, Musician, RMB, RMB 2802, Effingham, 19 June 1926

ELSEY, Edwin, Able Seaman, J 109529, Emerald, 16 October 1929

ELSON, Alfred, Stoker 1c, K 24549, Colossus, 28 February 1919

ELSON, Dennis A R, Leading Seaman, D/JX 138407, Royal Sovereign, 1 May 1937

ELSWORTHY, Frederick J, Officer's Steward 3c, L 9242, Venturous, 3 November 1922

ELY, Charles, Stoker 1c, 291586, Royal Arthur, 14 November 1918

EMERY, Bertie G, Able Seaman, D/J 107505, Vidette, 19 October 1931

EMERY, Charles J, Able Seaman, SS 6565, Venomous, 20 October 1920

EMMERSON, John, Bugler, RMLI, 21014 (Po), Assistance, 27 December 1920

EMMERSON, William G, Armourer, 342312, Malabar, 6 March 1920

EMMS, Frederick G, Boy 1c, C/SSX 19089, Pembroke, 30 November 1936

EMSLIE, Alexander, Engine Room Artificer 3c, RAN, 2016, Brisbane (RAN), 25 September 1920

ENDACOTT, Ernest H, Able Seaman, J 44817, Vivid, 23 January 1927

ENDERBY, Frederick, Ordinary Seaman, J 112342, Cumberland, 23 June 1928

ENGLAND, George, Able Seaman, C/J 58560, M.2, 29 January 1932

ENGLAND, Maurice C, Sick Berth Attendant, M 27761, Tamar, 18 June 1929

ENNION, Peter, Leading Seaman, D/J 39263, Queen Elizabeth, 26 December 1936

ENTWHISLTE, William, Private, RMLI, 18059 (Ply), RMLI, Plymouth Division, 1 July 1920

ENTWISTLE, Harold, Stoker 1c, K 9848, Cockchafer, 8 May 1921

ENTWISTLE, John G, Victualling Petty Officer, 341795, Scarab, 14 March 1922

ENTWISTLE, William, Private, RMLI, 18459 (Ply), RM Headquarters, 1 July 1920

ERSKINE, Ralph J, Lieutenant, Basilisk, 1 December 1937

ERSKINE, William, Act/Leading Stoker, K 63811, M.1, 12 November 1925

ESPOSITO, Joseph, Officer's Steward 2c, 360075, Egmont, 15 March 1923

ESSAM, Charles A W, Gunner, Wishart, 7 June 1928

ESTCOURT, George, Act/Stoker Petty Officer, C/K 65495, M.2, 29 January 1932

ETHERINGTON, Harry T, Leading Stoker, K 12739, Victory, 11 January 1929

ETHERINGTON, John A G, Officer's Cook 1c, 366011, Victory, 23 October 1922

EVANS, Albert, Able Seaman, J 96694, M.1, 12 November 1925

EVANS, Arthur W, Telegraphist, J 52560 (Po), St Mallows, 19 June 1919

EVANS, Bertram S, Captain, Europa, 2 March 1919

EVANS, Charles, Chief Engine Room Artificer 2c, D/MX 52413, Dorsetshire, 24 March 1938

EVANS, David, Steward, MMR, 785375, Sonia, 24 February 1919

EVANS, Evan, Lieutenant, RNVR, Royal Naval Volunteer Reserve, 24 December 1919

EVANS, Fred, Coastguardsman, 282409, HM Coastguard Station Inch, 22 July 1919

EVANS, Frederick, Chief Petty Officer, 238216, Curlew, 10 July 1929

EVANS, Frederick R, Private, RMLI, 21797 (Ch), Chatham Division, RMLI, 6 February 1919

EVANS, Geraint M, Ordinary Telegraphist, J 45719, Victory, 24 August 1919

EVANS, Harry, Sick Berth Petty Officer, M 3178, Vivid, 4 December 1923

EVANS, John, Chief Stoker, 147793, Vivid, 17 January 1919

EVANS, John H, Able Seaman, J 14734 (Dev), K.5, 20 January 1921

EVANS, Leslie, Stoker 2c, K 65088, Vivid, 8 January 1925

EVANS, Reginald A, Petty Officer, C/J 6504, Pembroke, 29 January 1933

EVANS, Richard, Stoker 1c, K 56091, King George V, 21 April 1924

EVANS, Richard W, Telegraphist, RNVR, Mersey Z 4039, Heugh, 17 November 1918

EVANS, Robert, Able Seaman, J 28518, Woolwich, 13 November 1918

EVANS, Robert P, Leading Seaman, RAN, 2138, Australia (RAN), 20 January 1919

EVANS, Robert W, Stoker Petty Officer, D/K 65280, Brazen, 27 January 1937

EVANS, Theophilus, Signalman, D/JX 128708, Vesper, 13 September 1931

EVANS, William E (no rank listed), C/MX 389, Pembroke, 3 August 1938

EVANS, William J, Stoker Petty Officer, RAN, 8478 (RN K 8858), Australia (RAN), 26 September 1919

EVANS, William T G, Boy 2c, J 92152, Ganges II, 28 January 1919

EVEA, Ronald, Engine Room Artificer 2c, 271890, Vivid, 11 November 1920

EVERETT, George A, Petty Officer, J 21596, TB.29, torpedo boat, 20 December 1918

EVERETT, Walter H, Private, RM, S 2534 (Deal), 63rd Divisional Train, RND, 30 December 1918

EVERETT, William B, Paymaster Commander, RNR, Royal Naval Reserve, 4 March 1925

EVERITT, Bertram A, Chief Petty Officer Writer, P/M 35463, Victory, 10 January 1937

EVERSHED, Frederick W, Able Seaman, P/J 15722, Stuart, 19 June 1931

EVERY, George E, Commissioned Engineer, Royal Navy, 15 April 1924

EVES, Arthur, Commissioned Gunner, Cornwall, 14 June 1935

EVES, William H, Paymaster Captain, RN Hospital, Plymouth, 22 November 1928

EVISON, Alfred W, Ordinary Seaman, D/SSX 30581, Drake, 17 August 1939

EWENS, Arthur G, Electrical Artificer 2c, P/MX 4751, Barham, 27 June 1938

EYEIONS, Jack, Skipper, RNR, Royal Naval Reserve, 9 October 1934

EYRE, Harry, Stoker Petty Officer, K 23807, Verdun, 17 December 1925

EYRES, Frederick C, Stoker 1c, K 61309, Marshal Soult, 5 February 1939

F

FAHEY, Michael T, Supply Chief Petty Officer, M 4604, Durban, 16 July 1926
FAIRBANKS, James, Able Seaman, J 39862, Victory, 14 January 1927
FAIRBRASS, Percy J, Stoker 1c, C/KX 77149, Kent, 1 December 1936
FAIRBURN, Arthur R, Leading Seaman, P/J 104894, Dauntless, 6 November 1933
FAIRCHILD, Harry J, Chief Petty Officer, 157878, Vivid, 22 November 1918
FAIRCLOUGH, Michael, Leading Seaman, 188414, Vivid, 13 April 1928
FAIRLEY, Albert V, Stoker Petty Officer, K 17442, Pembroke, 29 October 1925
FAIRMAN, Richard M, (also known as Richard Morgan), Leading Stoker, K 48653, Hawkins, 12 July 1927
FAIRWEATHER, Frederick A, Able Seaman, J 7766, Queen Elizabeth, 30 October 1923
FAIRWEATHER, Henry J, Stoker 1c, K 3600, Constance, 20 January 1924
FAKELEY, Sidney J, Chief Stoker, C/K 56436, Medway, 6 January 1939
FALKNER, Hubert E S, Act/Sub Lieutenant, Royal Navy, 18 March 1939
FARAH, Awali, Seaman Seedie, 2/360, Ormonde, 20 February 1931
FARAH, Yoosef, 2nd Seedie, Bramble, 4 February 1919
FARMER, Alfred A L, Marine, 21630 (Po), Courageous, 25 March 1937
FARMER, Dennis, Signalman, J 94295, M.3, 24 July 1925
FARMER, George, Able Seaman, RNVR, Bristol Z 5630, President, 3 February 1919
FARMER, Stanley J, Ordinary Seaman, J 105755, Calliope, 12 October 1924
FARMER, Thomas W, Signalman, J 33401, Glowworm, 25 August 1919
FARMINER, Norman J, Able Seaman, J 108648, Despatch, 5 September 1926
FARR, Derrick W, Able Seaman, P/JX 141054, Dainty, 26 December 1938
FARRANT, William H, Able Seaman, C/JX 134749, MTB.6, 27 September 1937
FARRELL, Alfred M, Lieutenant, RNVR, Royal Naval Volunteer Reserve, 30 September 1934
FARRELL, James N, Stoker Petty Officer, C/K 65172, Hastings, 7 April 1938
FARRELL, Joseph A, Commissioned Boatswain, St Angelo, 15 August 1935
FARRELL, Michael L, Storekeeper, MMR, 603603, Eaglet, 28 November 1918
FARREN, Daniel, Chief Stoker, 172103, Vivid, 17 August 1919
FARREN, Ernest R, Shipwright 3c, P/MX 45699, Glasgow, 7 October 1938
FARRER, Wilfred L, Ordinary Seaman, J 91781, Egmont, 10 March 1920
FARRIMOND, Joseph, Senior Reserve Attendant, M 9918, Pembroke, 25 November 1918
FARRINGTON, George, Able Seaman, J 25501 (Dev), Resolution, 2 February 1919
FARROW, Frederick J, Able Seaman, J 91863, Scarab, 5 September 1926
FARRUGIA, Giuseppe, Officer's Cook 2c, 365483, Blenheim (ex-Tobago), 30 December 1919
FARTHING, Frank C, Able Seaman, J 20334, Resolution, 7 February 1920
FARWELL, Frederick B, Stoker Petty Officer, P/K 60857, Repulse, 6 June 1938
FAST, Frank, Deck Hand, RNR, SD 3246, Actaeon, 26 February 1919
FAUX, James, Able Seaman, J 103187, Curlew, 1 September 1924
FAWCET, George H, Stoker 1c, K 38574, Vivid, 13 November 1918
FAWCETT, Albert, Stoker 1c, KX 76083, Dolphin, 4 June 1929
FAWCETT, Harry W, Marine, 21934 (Ch), Carlisle, 9 July 1928
FAWCETT, Henry, Major, RMLI, Glory, 29 December 1918
FAWCKNER, William F S, Captain, RM, RM Barracks, 23 July 1926
FAWCUS, Victor C B, Midshipman, New Zealand, 5 April 1919
FAWDEN, William H, Officer's Steward 3c, L 10619, Pegasus, 1 August 1919
FAYER, Edward F, Leading Stoker, K 52364, Pembroke, 17 July 1928
FAZAKERLEY, Walter E, Private, RMLI, 19580 (Ch), RM, 6th Battalion, 9 August 1919

FEARNE, Sidney F, Stoker 1c, K 42233, Octavia, 27 April 1919
FEATHERSTONE, Henry V, Chief Engine Room Artificer 2c, 271283, Starfish, 13 April 1920
FEBEN, Herbert E, Able Seaman, SS 7007, Vernon, 5 November 1920
FEDARB, Frederick, Surgeon Commander, Vernon, 25 May 1919
FEENSTRA, William M, Petty Officer, 237498, Resolution, 31 July 1929
FEGAN, James, Sick Berth Attendant, C/MX 45757, RN Hospital, Chatham, 14 November 1932
FEGAN, Joseph, Commissioned Engineer, Royal Navy, 4 February 1922
FELLOWS, Charles W, Boy 2c, RAN, 6802, Tingira (RAN), 16 March 1919
FELLOWS, John, Petty Officer, D/J 23876, Medway, 13 February 1932
FELTHAM, Frank, Stoker 1c, K 54863, M.1, 12 November 1925
FENN, Cecil H, Lieutenant, RNR, Thistle, 9 April 1919
FENN, Cyril D, Lieutenant Commander, Royal Navy, 9 August 1921
FENN, Sidney, Chief Petty Officer Cook, P/M 38642, Victory, 9 April 1939
FENN, William, Able Seaman, J 18493 (Po), L.55, 4 June 1919
FENNELL, Alfred E W, Officer's Cook 2c, D/L 9663, Royal Sovereign, 7 October 1937
FENNELL, Walter J, Sick Berth Attendant, D/M 37262, RN Hospital, Plymouth, 29 February 1924
FENNEY, James S, Leading Stoker, C/KX 81255, Thetis, 3 June 1939
FENTON, Samuel, Able Seaman, RNVR, KW 884, Collingwood Battalion, RND, 10 December 1918
FENTON, William, Able Seaman, D/J 28811, Drake, 1 November 1934
FERDIS, William H, Able Seaman, J 108534, Walpole, 8 December 1929
FERGUSON, Alexander B, Sub Lieutenant, Veronica, 14 July 1920
FERGUSON, Douglas, Stoker 1c, P/KX 79049, M.2, 29 January 1932
FERGUSON, James, Able Seaman, D/JX 126620, L.56, 31 October 1933
FERGUSON, John W, Private, RMLI, 20051 (Po), Barham, 18 September 1919
FERGUSON, Murdo, Deck Hand, RNR, SD 258, Iolaire (Morgan Jones, O/P), 1 January 1919
FERGUSON, Peter, Able Seaman, J 7715, Pembroke, 24 July 1921
FERGUSON, Robert E, Telegraphist, P/JX 134393, Royal Navy, 24 March 1939
FERGUSON, William J, Trimmer, RNR, TS 7543, Pekin, 13 December 1918

FERHAN, Hassan, 2nd Tindal, Aden 503, Effingham, 28 July 1926
FERNANDES, Domingo A, Officer's Cook 1c, G/LX 20874, Colombo, 8 March 1934
FERNANDES, Louis C, Officer's Cook 2c, L 11047, Southampton, 29 July 1924
FERRIS, Ernest J, Officer's Cook 1c, 365682, Munster, 4 December 1918
FERRIS, William H, Able Seaman, J 8534, Walpole, 8 December 1920
FETHERSTON, John Mc D, Sub Lieutenant, RNVR, ML.218, motor launch, 6 December 1918

FICKLING, Henry P, Boy 2c, J 93378, Powerful, 22 November 1918
FIDLER, Archibald F, Able Seaman, J 60983, Courageous, 18 July 1928
FIDLER, Fred, Stoker 1c, D/K 46727, Dunoon, 8 June 1933
FIDLER, Richard, Ordinary Seaman, C/SSX 23693, Pembroke, 23 June 1938
FIELD, Alfred, Commissioned Gunner, Calypso, 2 August 1932
FIELD, Alfred G, Boy 1c, J 96703, Hood, 22 August 1922
FIELD, Harry W, Private, RMLI, 15429 (Ply), Tamar, 8 December 1922
FIELD, Percival C T, Petty Officer, P/J 22592, Duncan, 11 September 1933
FIELD, Robert L E, Sub Lieutenant, Valkyrie, 10 June 1927
FIELD, Silas, Stoker 1c, K 59500, Raleigh, 8 August 1922
FIELD, Staunton A, Major, RM, Portsmouth, 29 January 1938
FIELD, William C, Able Seaman, P/J 24499, Nelson, 13 October 1933
FIELD, William J, Chief Petty Officer Telegraphist, 213956, Pembroke, 13 March 1919
FIELDER, Ernest B, Boy 1c, J 94861, Impregnable, 25 February 1920
FIELDING, Thomas L, Able Seaman, D/JX 136957, Kempenfelt, 19 January 1936
FIGG, Bertram G E, Chief Engine Room Artificer 1c, P/M 559, Greenwich, 5 February 1932
FIGGETT, Arthur P, Able Seaman, J 102645, Malabar, 26 November 1928
FILER, Ernest W, Able Seaman, RNVR, Bristol Z 1269, Drake Battalion, RND, 3 April 1919
FILLERY, Stanley E, Able Seaman, P/JX 140643, Nightingale, 24 January 1938
FILMER, William E, Signalman, C/J 84441, Crescent, 20 April 1936
FINAMORE, John S, Stoker Petty Officer, 308467, Impregnable, 4 February 1923
FINCH, Francis A, Stoker 1c, K 50279, Foxglove, 12 May 1926
FINCHAM, Alfred S, Able Seaman, J 85499, Royal Sovereign, 20 April 1924
FINDLAY, Charles, Able Seaman, RNVR, Clyde Z 6589, Pembroke, 24 November 1918
FINDLAY, James, Engine Room Artificer 3c, M 6587, Vivid, 5 April 1920
FINDLAY, Wallace, Private, RMLI, 17626 (Ply), RMLI, Plymouth Division, 16 March 1919
FINLAY, Thomas A, Lieutenant, RNR, Royal Naval Reserve, 11 March 1919
FINNEMORE, George H, Private, RM, S 10853 (Deal), RM Labour Corps, 18 November 1918
FINNEY, David, Warrant Mechanician, Royal Navy, 6 June 1924
FINNIS, Frank, Admiral (Rtd), Royal Navy, 17 November 1918
FINNIS, Jack F, Stoker 1c, K 16255 (Po), L.55, 4 June 1919
FIRTH, Cyril J, Commander, Westcott, 8 August 1938
FIRTH, Edward, Skipper, RNR, Northumbria, 5 October 1920
FISHENDEN, James W, Gunner (Rtd), Pekin, 20 September 1919
FISHER, Charles R, Officer's Steward 1c, 362953, Lucia, 1 March 1919

FISHER, D'Arcy G, Ty/Sub Lieutenant, RNVR, President, 30 November 1918
FISHER, Edward G, Surgeon Lieutenant, Vigorous, 12 May 1919
FISHER, Ernest E, Gunner, Turbulent, 6 February 1921
FISHER, George, Stoker 1c, SS 120369, Raleigh, 8 August 1922
FISHER, James L, Yeoman of Signals, J 4601, Revenge, 24 May 1925
FISHER, Robert, Engineman, RNR, ES 4335, Leonard, 8 January 1920
FISHER, Sir William, Admiral, Victory, 24 June 1937
FIST, Thomas, Able Seaman, D/JX 135210, Escapade, 14 April 1936
FITZGERALD, John, Able Seaman, 184643, Vivid, 31 January 1920
FITZGERALD, John, Stoker 2c, D/KX 86011, Drake, 29 January 1936
FITZGERALD, Michael, Able Seaman, D/JX 110635, Rodney, 1 August 1937
FITZGIBBONS, Frederick T, Able Seaman, MMR, 998936, Lobster, 22 July 1919
FITZHERBERT-BROCKHOLES, Roger H, Lieutenant, Glory, 2 July 1919
FITZJOHN, George, Leading Seaman, 231743, Commonwealth, 18 February 1919
FITZMAURICE, John, Marine, 24691 (Ch), Ganges, 3 December 1936
FITZPATRICK, Charles A, Chief Stoker, K 15291, Pembroke, 14 January 1929
FITZPATRICK, Robert, Stoker, RNR, V 760, Wireless Telegraph Station Falkland Islands, 26 August 1919
FITZSIMONS, Charles T, Marine, 21921 (Po), Cardiff, light cruiser, 5 August 1925
FITZSIMONS, William, Able Seaman, 195687, Excellent, 9 November 1919

FLAKE, Frederick C, Cook, M 7107, Valerian, 22 October 1926
FLAMARK, Joseph S, Able Seaman, J 8498, Montrose, 17 February 1926
FLANAGAN, Bertie W, Stoker 1c, K 61053, L.24, 10 January 1924
FLANAGAN, William J, Assistant Cook, MMR, 881022, Epic, 20 November 1918
FLANNERY, Patrick, Skipper, RNR, Strathalva, 12 December 1919
FLATMAN, Alfred J, Stoker Petty Officer, 291902 (Ch), Royal Oak, 25 November 1919
FLEMING, Ernest K, Engineer Lieutenant, Glorious, 20 March 1919
FLEMING, Patrick, Ordinary Seaman, J 107373, Comus, 10 December 1926
FLEMING, William J, Able Seaman, J 80923, Victory, 11 March 1930
FLETCHER, David K, Engine Room Artificer 4c, M 21883, L.24, 10 January 1924
FLETCHER, Ernest E, Leading Cook, M 5864, Revenge, 27 September 1929
FLETCHER, Henry A, Able Seaman, J 41003 (Ch), Archer, 22 February 1919
FLETCHER, John, Labourer, civilian, H.29, 9 August 1926, accidentally killed
FLETCHER, Thomas D, Engineman, RNR, ES 2932, Sea Sweeper, 29 November 1918
FLETT, John R, Commissioned Engineer, RNR, Royal Naval Reserve, 7 July 1932
FLICKER, John, Able Seaman, P/J 107300, Victory I, 11 June 1937
FLINTHAM, Arthur E, Stoker 1c, K 52538, Emperor of India, 10 April 1919
FLOCKHART, William, Engine Room Artificer 4c, RNVR, MC 400, Gentian, 15 July 1919

FLODIN, Robert, Leading Stoker, K 8277 (Ch), L.55, 4 June 1919
FLOOD, Arthur, Stoker Petty Officer, 292870 (Ch), Kinross, 16 June 1919
FLOOK, Harry, Signalman, RNVR, Wales Z 41, Attentive, 23 November 1918
FLORENCE, George W, Leading Cook, M 4585 (former L 45188), Royal Arthur, 26 July 1920
FLORY, John, Lance Corporal, RMLI, S 2260 (Po), Portsmouth Division, RMLI, 14 February 1919
FLOWER, William A, Blacksmith 3c, P/MX 46419, Vivid, 30 June 1933
FLUSKEY, Harry T, Signalman, J 33304, Diomede, 20 July 1927
FLYNN, Declan, Petty Officer, 198423, Salmon, 18 September 1919
FLYNN, James, Stoker 1c, K 34462, Dianthus, 23 November 1918

FODEN, James, Able Seaman, 215875, Victory, 19 March 1919
FOGERTY, Harold E, Gunner, RMA, RMA 1756, ex-RMA, 28 September 1919
FOGERTY, James, Able Seaman, J 91673, Thunderer, 19 March 1924
FOLEY, John F, Able Seaman, J 48199, M.1, 12 November 1925
FOOKES, William, Stoker 1c, K 21909, H.42, 23 March 1922
FOORD, Harold R, Ty/Sub Lieutenant, RNVR, 2nd Reserve Battalion, RND, 4 April 1919
FORBES, Haydon M S, Lieutenant Commander, FAA, 402 Flight, Eagle, 9 June 1927
FORBES, William, Leading Seaman, D/JX 132031, Leander, 30 September 1937
FORD, Arthur J, Leading Stoker, K 973, Espiegle, 25 July 1922
FORD, Ernest L, Stoker 1c, K 65176, Pembroke, 14 October 1929
FORD, Frederick A, Stoker 1c, K 55403, Pembroke, 21 March 1919
FORD, Frederick W, Petty Officer, D/J 110354, Drake, 10 September 1937
FORD, Henry E, Stoker 1c, 310426, Burslem, 28 August 1923
FORD, Peter H W, Captain, RM, RM Plymouth Barracks, 8 May 1938
FORD, Samuel H, Chief Engine Room Artificer 2c, M 2648, Vernon, 27 February 1925
FORD, Victor, Boatswain, Blake, 25 March 1920
FOREMAN, Esau, Ordinary Seaman, SS 8362, Iron Duke, 19 October 1919
FOREMAN, Roland J, 2nd Writer, M 10383, Phaeton, 9 February 1919
FOREMAN, Ronald J, Leading Stoker, P/K 61778, Victory, 6 July 1933
FORMBY, Henry J C, Ordinary Seaman, J 75191, Honeysuckle, 11 December 1918
FORMOSA, Vincenzo, Officer's Chief Cook, 359813, Caledon, 22 March 1919
FORSHAW, Joseph A, Stoker Petty Officer, 311358, Wallington, 30 January 1919
FORTIER, Richard L, Act/Commander, RNR, Royal Navy, 7 March 1921
FORTLEY, William G, Able Seaman, J 36611, Seraph, 26 December 1921
FOSTER, Charles W, Stoker 1c, K 58245, Iron Duke, 19 August 1923
FOSTER, Edward, Private, RM, S 14979 (Deal), RM Labour Corps, 2 December 1918
FOSTER, Edwin J, Lance Corporal, RMLI, S 1582 (Ply), 2nd RM Battalion, RND, 9 January 1919
FOSTER, Ernest C, Able Seaman, J 48676, Delhi, 30 July 1922
FOSTER, Frederick, Petty Officer, 219244, Scimitar, 16 January 1924
FOSTER, Harry E, Painter 4c, M 30107, Rodney, 30 August 1929
FOSTER, Herbert C, Corporal, RMLI, 14061 (Ch), 3rd Battalion, RM, 6 January 1919
FOSTER, Joseph, Private, RM, S 3491 (Deal), Hawke Battalion, RND, attached RM Medical Unit, 31 January 1919

FOSTER, Pliny, Stoker 1c, SS 110928 (Dev), G.11, 22 November 1918
FOSTER, Victor F, Signalman, J 71403, Iron Duke, 24 June 1922
FOSTER, Walter, Able Seaman, J 105336, Verity, 7 January 1928
FOWKES, Charles W, Stoker 1c, K 12738, Conflict, 29 November 1918
FOWLER, Alick E, Signal Boy, J 67552, Tomahawk, 30 July 1919
FOWLER, Charles L, Able Seaman, J 21027, Queen Elizabeth, 3 June 1922
FOWLER, Lawrence P, Engineer Commander, Royal Navy, 10 January 1933
FOWLER, Richard, Engine Room Artificer 2c, M 4712, H.42, 23 March 1922
FOWLER, Sidney F, Private, RMLI, S 1604 (Po), 1st RM Battalion, RND, 30 November 1918
FOWLER, William, Stoker Petty Officer, D/K 18396, Hermes, 5 November 1932
FOWLOW, John, Seaman, Newfoundland RNR, X 688, Erin's Isle, 7 February 1919
FOX, Alfred F, Boatswain, Tiger, 12 February 1921
FOX, Frederick C, Officer's Cook 2c, L 12270, Vectis, 25 March 1925
FOX, Frederick W R, Boy 2c, JX 129344, Ganges, 2 October 1927
FOX, Harold, Leading Stoker, D/K 21273, Lucia, 21 May 1932
FOX, Reginald W, Ty/Paymaster Sub Lieutenant, RNVR, Royal Naval Volunteer Reserve, 7 January 1919
FOX, Samuel A, Petty Officer, J 8603, Hood, 14 June 1927
FOYLE, Frederick W, Telegraphist, J 87114, Vendetta, 28 July 1926

FRANCE, Alfred J M, Able Seaman, J 20742, L.24, 10 January 1924
FRANCIS, Arthur W, Ordinary Seaman, JX 126147, Warspite, 1 February 1929
FRANCIS, Bernard, Gunner, RMA, RMA 14710, RM Headquarters, 14 May 1921
FRANCIS, Hubert A, Able Seaman, C/JX 132017, Suffolk, 17 February 1932
FRANCIS, William, Stoker 1c, K 11660, Pembroke, 16 June 1928
FRANCIS, William G, Bugler, RMLI, 21338 (Po), Argus, 23 July 1923
FRANK, Harry, Chief Petty Officer, 199039, President, 12 May 1925
FRANKLIN, Charles, Major, RMLI, Royal Marine Light Infantry, 5 September 1919
FRANKLIN, Charles E, Signalman, J 52260, Hannibal, 29 August 1919
FRANKLIN, Herbert, Able Seaman, C/SSX 12843, Winchester, 9 November 1935
FRANKLIN, Percy, Stoker 1c, SS 112819, Boadicea, 4 March 1919
FRANKLIN, Richard G, Leading Seaman, J 10734 (Po), Renown, 10 November 1919
FRANKS, Alfred G, Stoker 1c, K 55851, Glorious, 23 February 1924
FRANKS, George F, Telegraphist, J 100304, Furious, 12 December 1928
FRASER, Donald R H, Paymaster Cadet, Barham, 5 June 1927
FRASER, Gideon, Deck Hand, RNR, DA 19951, William Biggs, 8 July 1919
FRASER, Henry J W, Officer's Steward 1c, L 4549, Ursa, 29 November 1918
FRASER, James, Stoker Petty Officer, K 4534, Vivid, 29 March 1927
FRASER, James F, Warrant Engineer, Titania, 5 August 1924
FRASER, John, Able Seaman, SS 5470, Veteran, 14 March 1920
FRASER, Leonard J, Leading Signalman, 235685, Europa, 23 December 1918
FRASER, William, Able Seaman, P/JX 151460, Weston, 30 September 1937

FRATER, Thomas F, Stoker 1c, 303083, Actaeon, 25 September 1919
FRAY, Thomas, Engine Room Artificer 2c, M 34649, St Genny, 12 January 1930
FRAZER, John, Chief Engine Room Artificer 2c, 269600, Victory, 3 November 1919
FREDERICKS, Arthur H, Ordinary Telegraphist, J 54669, Myosotis, 6 January 1919
FREEBORN, Richard, Stoker 1c, K 62300, Vindictive, 6 January 1927
FREEMAN, Ernest W, Petty Officer, M 6981, Tarantula, 8 June 1921
FREEMAN, Henry G, Telegraphist, P/J 105551, Cormorant, 27 October 1931
FREER, Henry, Seaman Rigger, 227022, Victoria & Albert, Royal Yacht, 4 June 1924
FREESTONE, Albert E, Able Seaman, J 2534, Wild Swan, 27 April 1920
FRENCH, Alfred F, Petty Officer, 214229 (Po), K.5, 20 January 1921
FRENCH, George, Electrical Artificer 2c, M 6171, Calcutta, 2 November 1924
FRENCH, Henry G H, Boy Telegraphist, J 79157 (Dev), L.55, 4 June 1919
FRENCH, Howard W E, Engine Room Artificer, D/MX 49582, Thetis, 3 June 1939
FRENCH, Percy, Deck Hand, MMR, Medusa II, 14 December 1918
FRENCH, Wilfred E, Engineer Commander, Engineer In Chief Department, 1 October 1933
FRENCH, William E A, Sergeant, RMLI, 15863 (Ply), 3rd Battalion, RM, 11 December 1918
FREWEN-LATON, Ivo W L, Commander, Bryony, 7 March 1933
FRIBBANCE, George, Leading Stoker, K 43955, Victory, 9 August 1927
FRIDAY, Tom, Krooman, Ascension Island, 7 July 1921
FRIEND, Frederick J, Private, RMLI, 14014 (Ch), Abercrombie, 20 March 1919
FRIEND, George J, Able Seaman, J 87667, Pembroke, 10 April 1928
FRIEND, Norman E, Leading Cook, C/MX 49165, Ganges, 25 June 1936
FRIMSTON, George F, Able Seaman, D/JX 134542, Hermes, 6 January 1936
FRIZZELL, Samuel, Able Seaman, J 55335, Emerald, 16 February 1926
FROST, Bert, Trimmer, RNR, TS 3908, Caesar, 22 March 1919
FROST, Frank R, Boy Servant, L 13010, Vivid, 27 February 1920
FROST, John E, Ordinary Seaman, J 110205, Effingham, December 1925
FROST, Robert G, Able Seaman, D/J 30105, Defiance, 6 November 1937
FROW, William, Trimmer, RNR, TS 524, David Ogilvie, 26 November 1918
FRY, Claude F, Stoker 1c, K 18575 (Ch), M.1, 24 January 1919
FRY, Harold J, Sailmaker, D/J 28639, Greenwich, 7 March 1937
FRY, Harry, Stoker Petty Officer, K 16115, Vivid, 7 February 1929
FRY, James, Chief Petty Officer, 215283, Vigorous, 7 January 1924
FRYATT, Frederick T, Leading Seaman, J 15046, Thanet, 27 May 1925
FRYER, Percy S, Leading Seaman, J 11258, Pembroke, 23 July 1927

FUDGE, George, Commissioned Gunner, Vernon, 11 January 1928
FUDGE, John E, Stoker Petty Officer, P/KX 64958, Victory II, 24 July 1936
FUDGE, John W, Stoker 1c, 308262, P.23, patrol boat, 27 November 1918

FUGE, James S, Mechanician, 297278, Vivid II, 6 August 1921
FULBROOK, Frank, Shipwright 1c, 347150, Valerian, 22 October 1926
FULCHER, Frederick E, Stoker 1c, K 38413, Pembroke, 22 February 1919
FULCHER, Herbert T, Stoker 1c, K 23502, Pembroke, 26 February 1920
FULLARTON, Kenneth, Ty/Lieutenant, RNVR, ML.43, motor launch, 17 November 1918
FULLER, Arthur J, Leading Stoker, 307571, Wolfhound, 22 May 1923
FULLER, Frank, Leading Telegraphist, C/J 108308, Wireless Telegraph Station, Matara, Ceylon (Sri Lanka), 10 January 1933
FULLER, George B, Leading Telegraphist, J 48642, Cornflower, 7 November 1928
FULLER, Henry R, Stoker 1c, SS 111647, Galatea, 2 March 1919
FULLER, Walter T, Able Seaman, J 46176 (Ch), Bluebell, 24 January 1921
FULLSTONE, Frederick, Leading Telegraphist, P/J 27717, Wireless Telegraph Station, Flowerdown, near Winchester, 16 August 1934
FUNNELL, Denis H, Stoker 2c, KX 79703, Victory, 15 March 1929
FUNNELL, Henry G, Private, RMLI, 22734 (Ch), Gibraltar, 8 October 1921
FUNNELL, Thomas R, Chief Yeoman of Signals, 208436, Greenwich, 20 January 1921
FUNNELL, Victor A, Boy 2c, J 93768, Ganges, 9 March 1919
FURBER, Arthur J, Supply Chief Petty Officer, P/M 30215, Cornflower, 2 November 1933
FURLONG, Allan H, Lieutenant, RNR, Carol, 14 March 1920
FURNEAUX, Otto – see OSBORNE, Otto V, Musician, RMB
FUSSELL, Bertram R, Chief Writer, 347127, Egmont, 23 June 1919
FUTCHER, William, Able Seaman, J 32378, Warspite, 10 January 1919

FYSH, Alfred J, Gunner, Diligence, 18 July 1922

G

GABRIEL, Charley, Marine, 23167 (Ch), Sussex, 9 October 1931
GADD, James, Able Seaman, 211709, Glowworm, 17 October 1920
GAGE, Walter, Leading Stoker, K 10712, Blue Sky, tender to Queen Elizabeth, 12 June 1922
GAGO, John, Officer's Cook, L 33, Barham, 2 June 1927
GAIMES, John A, Lieutenant Commander, K.5, 20 January 1921
GAINES, Ernest G, Leading Stoker, P/K 26669, Poseidon, 9 June 1931
GALE, Leonard F, Able Seaman, J 8830, L.11, 3 January 1919
GALE, William I, Stoker 1c, K 30752 (Po), P.46, patrol boat, 12 September 1920
GALLAGHER, Christopher, Deck Hand, RNR, SD 2591, Vernon, 22 February 1919
GALLAGHER, John - see McCANN, John, Stoker 2c
GALLIGHAN, Alfred J, Private, RMLI, 10475 (Po), Agincourt, 28 February 1919
GALLOP, Edward H, Stoker Petty Officer, 308006, Sherborne, 21 August 1925
GALLOWAY, Trevor A, Boy 2c, JX 138934, Ganges, 15 October 1933
GALYER, James M, Able Seaman, 187621, Crescent, 20 April 1919
GAMBLE, John W, Ordinary Seaman, SS 8499, Victory, 11 March 1919
GAMBLE, Robert L, Able Seaman, J 30047, Munster, 5 December 1918
GAMBLEN, Cyril, Leading Seaman, J 15398, H.42, 23 March 1922
GAMBLIN, Reginald, Marine, X 1942 (Po), Malaya, 10 September 1938
GAMBRILL, Frank, Leading Seaman, J 101320, Pembroke, 30 August 1926
GAME, George F, Regulating Petty Officer, M 36835, Vivid, 22 January 1922
GAME, Neville L, Able Seaman, J 104373, Pembroke, 30 June 1926
GANDER, Albert J, Leading Seaman, C/J 108661, Cardiff/Calcutta, light cruisers, 6 January 1937
GANDER, Harry, Supply Chief Petty Officer, 229146, Victory, 16 April 1927
GANDERTON, Charles F, Stoker 2c, D/KX 80593, Vivid, 3 February 1931
GARDINER, Bernard C, Colonel, RM, Portsmouth, 6 January 1932
GARDINER, William H, Chief Skipper, RNR, Royal Naval Reserve, 5 January 1936
GARDNER, Albert J, Commissioned Gunner, Terror, 7 April 1930
GARDNER, Alfred, Private, RMLI, 12268 (Po), RM Headquarters, 6 June 1921
GARDNER, Charles, Chief Stoker, 233422, M.1, 12 November 1925
GARDNER, Frederick E W, Stoker 1c, K 42033, Radstock, 30 November 1918
GARDNER, Henry R, Surgeon Commander, Royal Navy, 31 October 1921
GARDNER, Herbert S, Able Seaman, C/J 109202, Rochester, 9 November 1933
GARDNER, Hugh, Officer's Steward 3c, L 13534, Champion, 16 November 1928
GARDNER, Walter G, Electrical Artificer 4c, M 27779, Victory, 26 March 1919
GARFORTH, Holland, Stoker 1c, 307334, Dublin, 22 July 1925
GARLAND, Daniel, Stoker 1c, D/K 57373, Vivid, 3 January 1931
GARLINGE, Frederick J, Leading Stoker, K 21049, Pembroke, 26 November 1927
GARNER, William, Stoker Petty Officer, K 5490, Birmingham, 17 November 1924
GARNETT, Richard N, Lieutenant Commander, Thetis (Taku), 3 June 1939
GARRAWAY, Francis, Able Seaman, P/J 29054, Repulse, 17 February 1937
GARRETT, Albert E, Private, RMLI, 11656 (Po), Patuca, 21 November 1918
GARRETT, Alfred L, Stoker 1c, KX 75052, Birmingham, 1 June 1927
GARRETT, Ernest W, Chief Engine Room Artificer 1c, M 3192, Titania, 5 March 1928
GARRINGTON, Alfred E, Signalman, RNVR, Bristol Z 4122, Erin's Isle, 7 February 1919
GARRIOCK, Andrew, Boatswain, MMR, 502401, Verdun II, 5 December 1918
GARRISH, William J, Able Seaman, J 16122, L.24, 10 January 1924
GARTLAND, Henry, Gunner, RMA, RMA 11590, RMA Eastney, 14 February 1919
GARTON, Bert, Petty Officer, J 24317, Ceres, 24 September 1922
GARTRELL, Arthur E, Seaman Rigger, 219941, Victoria & Albert, Royal Yacht, 16 December 1925
GARWOOD, Richard H, Paymaster Lieutenant, Penelope, 16 June 1939
GASCOYNE, Alfred H R, Boy 2c, JX 133447, St Vincent, 16 December 1929
GASCOYNE, Archibald T, Able Seaman, J 11344 (Po), L.55, 4 June 1919
GASK, Vivian D, Lieutenant, Cornwall, 16 December 1935
GASKIN, Percy G, Petty Officer, 166544, Bacchante, 20 February 1919
GASSTOWN, Ernest W, Stoker Petty Officer, K 17657, Iron Duke, 22 May 1929
GATES, William G, Leading Stoker, K 19883, Pembroke, 20 May 1930
GAUNT, George, Leading Stoker, K 18101, Oracle (ex-Dido), 26 December 1919
GAVAN, William O, Petty Officer, J 4930, Vivid, 15 May 1923
GAVIN, Charles M, Paymaster Commander, Victoria & Albert, Royal Yacht, 14 April 1933
GAVIN, James J, Able Seaman, J 37572, Tamar, 27 August 1925
GAY, Albert A, Telegraphist, J 62961, M.1, 12 November 1925

GEACH, William D, Leading Cook, D/M 8597, Resolution, 3 May 1931
GEALER, Reginald W, Act/Warrant Engineer, Furious, 22 August 1927
GEAR, Bert J J, Ordinary Seaman, J 77919, Cleopatra, 3 November 1920
GEAREY, William G, Chief Petty Officer, 200304, Birmingham, 13 February 1920
GEARY, Maurice, Leading Seaman, J 17915, Vivid, 2 February 1924
GEARY, William, Stoker Petty Officer, K 165, Cairo, 20 December 1926
GEDDES, Alexander, Deck Hand, RNR, DA 4857, Zaria, mercantile fleet auxiliary, 19 February 1919
GEDDES, James, Deck Hand, RNR, DA 5019, Nairn, 9 December 1918
GEE, Cecil G, Able Seaman, D/J 27481, Vivid, 28 January 1931
GEE, John C, Colour Sergeant, RM, 17337 (Ch), RN Hospital, Chatham, 6 September 1932
GEEVES, William C J, Leading Seaman, RNR, A 8052, Waltonhall, steamship, 17 January 1919
GELL, William G, Deck Hand, RNR, DA 16266, Satellite, 16 November 1918
GENGE, Reginald G R, Leading Telegraphist, D/J 43631, Renown, 13 September 1930
GENTRY, Frederick, Stoker 1c, K 46224, Victory II, 11 March 1920

GEORGE, Edgar R, Officer's Cook 1c, L 2734, Victory, 27 January 1926
GEORGE, Frank, Signalman, SX 49, RN Signal Shore Station, Needles, Isle of Wight, 17 April 1934
GEORGE, Joseph W, Fireman, MMR, Iolaire, 1 January 1919
GEORGE, Walter, Able Seaman, J 17015 (Po), K.5, 20 January 1921
GERAGHTY, John P, Boy 1c, JX 126712, Ganges, 5 February 1927
GERRARD, John W, Officer's Steward 3c, LX 20571, Vivid, 7 April 1930

GIAMBELLI, John E, Leading Seaman, P/J 93139, Dolphin, 1 January 1931
GIBBONS, Thomas, Stoker, RNR, S 4936, St Vincent, 14 February 1919
GIBBS, Charles H, Stoker 1c, P/KX 80427, RN Hospital, Haslar, 17 November 1938
GIBBS, Henry P, Chief Petty Officer, MMR, 571460, Limol, Royal Fleet Auxiliary, 20 February 1919
GIBBS, James W, Leading Seaman, 234449 (Ch), Astraea, 1 April 1919
GIBBS, Robert W, Telegraphist, J 81144, Egmont, 21 October 1926
GIBSON, Albert, Able Seaman, J 9285, Wryneck, 3 July 1930
GIBSON, Walter P, Boy 2c, J 101348, Impregnable, 12 May 1921
GIBSON, William, Boy 1c, J 100938, Vivid, 30 March 1921
GIBSON, William Mc L, Sick Berth Petty Officer, M 4131, Greenwich, 26 March 1928
GIDDY, Joseph, Stoker Petty Officer, 279642 (Dev), Cassandra, 5 December 1918
GIDLEY, Arthur T, Ordinary Seaman, J 89907, Warspite, 17 July 1921
GIDLEY, Reginald, Stoker Petty Officer, D/K 17999, Berwick, 22 April 1934
GIDNEY, Francis W, Chief Stoker, 310023, Pembroke, 19 November 1921
GILBERT, Edwin, Stoker Petty Officer, SS 109330, Marlborough, 23 February 1919
GILBERT, Frederick J, Stoker Petty Officer, 305652, Excellent, 1 May 1922
GILBERT, George E, Stoker 1c, K 55719, H.34, 9 May 1927
GILBERT, George W H, Leading Seaman, J 42464, Royal Oak, 17 September 1928
GILBERT, Reginald R, Paymaster Lieutenant Commander, York, 13 February 1938
GILBERT, William A, Sick Berth Attendant, M 38156, Egmont, 18 May 1930
GILCREST, John, Stoker 1c, K 58766, Blue Sky, tender to Queen Elizabeth, 12 June 1922
GILES, Frederick, Boy 1c, J 100463, Impregnable, 14 November 1921
GILES, Thomas H, Stoker 1c, K 57320, Whitehall, 25 April 1925
GILFILLAIN, Joseph E, Stoker 1c, D/KX 87920, Victory, 19 December 1937
GILFOY, Albert H, Private, RMLI, 16706 (Po), 2nd RM Battalion, RND, 11 July 1919
GILHOOLY, John J, Stoker Petty Officer, 305788 (Dev), Cassandra, 5 December 1918
GILL, Sydney M, Able Seaman, J 162149, Columbine, 26 May 1926
GILL, Thomas, Engine Room Artificer 1c, C/M 27234, Pembroke, 13 February 1933
GILL, Thomas A, Engineer Lieutenant, RNR, Hughli, Royal Fleet Auxiliary, 26 April 1919
GILL, William, Musician, RMB, RMB X 146, Victory, 27 November 1935
GILLEN, Bernard, Able Seaman, C/SSX 15861, Emerald, 15 November 1936
GILLES, Walter A, Able Seaman, J 26257, Pembroke (ex-Whitshed), 27 January 1920

GILLESPIE, Douglas E, Lieutenant, Verity, 24 January 1934
GILLESPIE, Robert J, Engineer Lieutenant, Royal Navy, 4 January 1921
GILLETT, Victor A, Able Seaman, J 24980 (Po), K.5, 20 January 1921
GILLHAM, Alfred, Able Seaman, 195805, Satyr, 14 December 1918
GILLHAM, Wilfred F, Electrical Artificer 5c, C/MX 54472, Vernon, 20 September 1937
GILLIES, Angus, Seaman, RNR, A 4502, Iolaire (Seahorse, O/P), 1 January 1919
GILLIES, Archie, Able Seaman, RNVR, R 855, Anson Battalion, RND, 20 January 1919
GILLIES, Donald W, Seaman, RNR, A 3309, Iolaire (Pembroke, O/P), 1 January 1919
GILLIES, Henry N, Chief Engineman, RNR, ES 4606, Wallington, 3 February 1919
GILLIES, James C, Engine Room Artificer 4c, MC 410 (Po), Myrtle, 15 July 1919
GILLIES, Roderick, Deck Hand, RNR, DA 20647, Leonard, 8 January 1920
GILLIES, Wilfred W, Stoker 1c, P/K 60825, Victory II, 25 July 1939
GILLINGHAM, William H, Marine, 23040 (Ch), Enterprise, 12 September 1931
GILLINGWATER, Lewis T E, Able Seaman, J 34181 (Ch), Dragon, 17 October 1919
GILLMORE, Charles R, Ordinary Seaman, J 112780, Yarmouth, 14 June 1928
GILLOW, Walter F P, Cook, C/M 36446, Ganges, 22 September 1935
GILMAN, Francis E J, Sub Lieutenant, Teal, 18 May 1926
GILPIN, Frederick, Leading Stoker, K 9480, Vivid, 8 December 1927
GILROY, James, Stoker 1c, K 55462, Caesar, 29 August 1919
GIMBLET, William J H, Chief Stoker, 305267, Highflyer, 24 February 1921
GISBORNE, Edward, Admiralty Civilian, Thetis, 3 June 1939
GISSING, Joseph, Able Seaman, J 8374 (Po), L.55, 4 June 1919
GITTINGS, Arthur E, Stoker Petty Officer, 307391, Victory, 19 March 1922
GITTINS, George W, Coastguardsman 2c, 157060, Berwick Wireless Station, 23 December 1921

GLADDIS, Albert O, Assistant Cook, P/MX 52136, Victory, 23 February 1937
GLADWIN, Frank H, Marine, 18254, Valiant, 11 September 1935
GLANVILLE, Auston H, Able Seaman, J 105569, Barham, 4 July 1927
GLANVILLE, John H, Chief Engine Room Artificer 1c, 269246, Pegasus, 24 November 1920
GLANVILLE, John J, Able Seaman, 222971, Collingwood, 24 November 1920
GLANVILLE, John W V, Chief Stoker, 293909, President, 24 July 1927
GLANVILLE, Leonard, Able Seaman, J 90427, Glowworm, 25 August 1919
GLANVILLE, Patrick, Able Seaman, MMR, 500659, Mollusc, Royal Fleet Auxiliary, 30 November 1918
GLASHEEN, Patrick J, Able Seaman, 197086, Vivid, 20 September 1919
GLAZEBROOK, Alfred, Leading Signalman, J 23547, Heather, 25 December 1920
GLEESON, John W, Deck Hand, RNR, DA 12512, Ipswich, 3 December 1918
GLEN, George R, Signalman, J 48580 (Ch), Erebus, 29 December 1919
GLEN, Roy D, Commissioned Engineer, Thetis, 3 June 1939
GLENDAY, Jan, Chief Engine Room Artificer 2c, 272152, Tribune, 26 August 1919

GLENISTER, Henry, Officer's Cook 1c, 166000, Superb, 6 March 1919
GLINN, John H, Shipwright 2c, M 17053, Sandhurst, 5 July 1924
GLINN, Ronald E, Able Seaman, D/J 110049, Waterhen, 22 April 1932
GLINN, Samuel, Boy 2c, J 103059, Ganges, 28 September 1921
GLOVER, George E, Stoker 1c, SS 118734, Egmont, 5 October 1919
GLOVER, Percy, Chief Stoker, P/K 59714, Victory, 31 March 1937
GLOVER, Samuel J, Mate, Mersey, 6 January 1919

GOAD, Thomas T, Petty Officer, C/J 108935, Thetis, 3 June 1939
GOCHER, Arthur W, Able Seaman, RNVR, R 1614, Hood Battalion, RND, 2 December 1918
GODBOLD, James, Able Seaman, C/JX 13236, Sussex, 10 October 1932
GODDARD, Colin F, Leading Seaman, J 10907, Weymouth, 10 March 1927
GODDARD, Raymond H, Able Seaman, J 102209, Calypso, 7 February 1924
GODDEN, William, Coastguardsman, 149623, Victory (HM Coast Guard), 14 December 1920
GODDING, Alexander, Musician, RMB, RMA X 151, Kent, 19 September 1934
GODFREY, Benjamin E, Marine, X 515 (Ch), RM Chatham Division, 5 May 1938
GODFREY, Charles J, Able Seaman, RNVR (Bugler), Bristol Z 474, Nelson Battalion, RND, 5 April 1919
GODFREY, Joseph, Leading Seaman, J 646, Pembroke, 1 April 1927
GODIER, John F, Stoker 2c, RAN, 6546, Brisbane (RAN), 2 December 1918
GODLEY, William, Private, RMLI, S 2313 (Po), Portsmouth Division, RMLI, 1 May 1919
GODLONTON, William C, Ordinary Seaman, J 58614 (Ch), Erin's Isle, 7 February 1919
GODWIN, James, Chief Stoker, 292626, (ship or unit not listed), 27 February 1920
GOLDFINCH, James R, Chief Officer, HM Coast Guard, HM Coast Guard, 21 January 1919
GOLDING, Richard F, Stoker 1c, K 61836, Revenge, 30 December 1924
GOLDRING, Henry B, 3rd Hand, MMR, Ivanhoe, 9 January 1919
GOLDSMITH, Charles C, Able Seaman, J 20910, Pembroke, 20 April 1924
GOLDSMITH, Edward P, Paymaster Commander, Hawkins, 10 February 1935
GOLDSMITH, Frederick W, Shipwright 1c, 91771, Wildfire, 28 May 1920
GOLDSMITH, John A, Lieutenant, FAA, 810 Sqn, Courageous, 17 August 1937
GOLDSMITH, Samuel, Marine, 23034 (Ch), Devonshire, 26 July 1929
GOLDSTRAW, Ralph, Corporal, RMLI, 16513 (Po), 2nd RM Battalion, RND, 23 December 1918
GOLDSWORTH, Albert E, Sergeant, RMA, RMA 12665, Crescent, 12 January 1920
GOLDSWORTHY, Oliver W, Engine Room Artificer Apprentice, MX 47959, Pembroke, 18 February 1932
GOLEBY, Leonard E, Able Seaman, J 104429, Pembroke, 17 January 1928
GOOCH, Frederick W, Able Seaman, J 65665, Hecla, 9 July 1921
GOOCH, Thomas S, Commander, Admiralty, Ty/Assistant Inspector of Steel, 11 December 1918
GOOD, Cyril S, Warrant Engineer, M.1, 12 November 1925
GOODALL, Arthur E, Band Boy, RMB, RMB X 395, Durban, 30 April 1934
GOODBAND, Charles W, Leading Seaman, P/J 81759, Curacoa, 1 August 1931
GOODCHILD, Alfred E, Private, RMLI, 21889 (Ch), Chatham Division, RMLI, 28 December 1918
GOODEY, Walter E, Leading Cook, M 5855, Victory, 26 November 1928
GOODFIELD, James, Able Seaman, J 8320, Cricket, 30 September 1920
GOODIER, George, Private, RM, S 11272 (Deal), RM Labour Corps, 12 January 1919
GOODLET, Robert J N, Chief Engine Room Artificer 2c, 272329, H.47, 9 July 1929
GOODMAN, William L, Chief Stoker, 292767, Warspite, 5 February 1919
GORDON, Alan, Leading Seaman, J 3435, Vivid, 30 January 1919
GORDON, John A, Able Seaman, J 42767, Victory, 20 October 1924
GORDON, Joseph T, Stoker 1c, P/K 62182, Delphinium, 16 December 1930
GORDON, Robert W, Lieutenant, RM, Furious, 8 November 1928
GORDON, Thomas, Sub Lieutenant, RNR, Hughli, Royal Fleet Auxiliary, 26 April 1919
GORDON, William E, Ordinary Seaman, MMR, Crescent, 26 February 1919
GORDON, Willie, Chief Petty Officer, D/J 12581, Rodney, 3 April 1935
GORE, Sidney J E, Engine Room Artificer 1c, M 4730, M.1, 12 November 1925
GORING, William H, Stoker 1c, K 25380, Wallace, 28 May 1921
GORMAN, James, Stoker, RNR, S 3410, Maidstone, 2 March 1919
GORRING, Thomas W, Stoker 1c, C/KX 82296, Renown, 8 December 1933
GORRY, Angus H, 2nd Hand, RNR, DA 12434, Ebenezer, 25 November 1918
GOSLIN, Joseph W, Deck Hand, RNR, DA 15349, George Borthwick, 24 December 1918
GOSS, Herbert H, Leading Seaman, J 11484, Defiance, 12 April 1922
GOSS, Sydney L, Signalman, D/JX 130532, Watchman, 5 November 1933
GOSWELL, Arthur F, Leading Seaman, J 31277, H.24, 22 May 1928
GOTT, Francis S, Sub Lieutenant, Badminton, 2 October 1920
GOUGE, William A, Sergeant Major, 21832 (Deal), Royal Marines HQ, 26 October 1928
GOUGH, Charles H, Able Seaman, J 21314, Vivid, 29 September 1920
GOUGH, Ernest E, Commissioned Signal Boatswain, Royal Navy, 24 August 1934
GOULD, Alfred G, Petty Officer, 208490, Victory, 25 February 1919
GOULD, Harold P A, Officer's Steward 1c, L 6443, Caledon, 23 February 1920
GOULD, William R, Ordinary Seaman, J 100332, Victory, 19 February 1925
GOULDING, Albert, Able Seaman, RNVR, Sussex 1/228, DEMS Gunner, on books of President III, Themistocles, steamship, 22 November 1918
GOULDING, Michael J, Able Seaman, RNVR, London Z 7014, Pembroke, 22 February 1919
GOURD, William A, Leading Stoker, K 23868, Vivid, 15 June 1922
GOURLAY, Frank L, Petty Officer, 234705, Pembroke, 11 September 1919
GOURLAY, James, Deck Hand, RNR, DA 10283, Western Queen, 15 November 1918
GOWER, Frederick J B, Stoker 1c, K 62483, Valerian, 22 October 1926
GOWER, John J, Commissioned Signal Boatswain, Pembroke, 27 February 1924
GOY, Leslie N, Able Seaman, C/JX 138693, Glasgow, 20 May 1939

GOYNS, William F, Leading Telegraphist, P/J 41465, FAA, 811 Sqn, Furious, 2 October 1933

GRAHAM, Albert E, Chief Engineer 1c, MMR, Tiflis, 20 January 1919

GRAHAM, Christopher P, Stoker 1c, K 28796 (Po), Erin's Isle, 7 February 1919

GRAHAM, Edward E, Ordinary Seaman, J 98979, Vivid, 3 March 1923

GRAHAM, Francis C, Warrant Ordnance Officer, Royal Navy, 29 October 1926

GRAHAM, George R, Stoker 1c, 144440, Argo, 21 July 1919

GRAHAM, Graham T W, Telegraphist, P/J 112924, Thetis, 3 June 1939

GRAHAM, John H P, Lieutenant, FAA, 440 Flight, Hermes, 3 April 1928

GRAHAM, John, Engine Room Artificer 1c, 270411, Tamar, 21 August 1919

GRAHAM, Roderick, Seaman, RNR, C 1815, Pembroke, 30 December 1918

GRAHAM, Samuel R, Stoker 1c, K 20381, Woolwich, 1 December 1918

GRAINGER, Alfred A, Paymaster Commander, RNR, Royal Naval Reserve, 30 April 1932

GRAINGER, Frederick S, Stoker 1c, K 39910, Vivid, 14 January 1919

GRANT, Ernest H, Marine, X 140 (Po), Durban, 14 November 1931

GRANT, Heathcote A J, Lieutenant, FAA, 441 Flight, Argus, 6 February 1929

GRANT, John F H, Ty/Sub Lieutenant, RNVR, Royal Naval Volunteer Reserve, 10 December 1919

GRANT, Peter, Able Seaman, SSX 15583, Grafton, 8 September 1937

GRANT, Thomas F, Chief Engine Room Artificer 2c, M 17547, Conqueror, 20 November 1918

GRANT, Walter, Able Seaman, J 25919, Speedy, 23 September 1922

GRANT, William J, Chief Stoker, 290035, Gilia, 19 March 1919

GRAVER, William F, Boy 1c, J 91997, Pembroke, 17 May 1920

GRAVES, Clarence C, Able Seaman, D/J 6308, Vivid, 24 January 1933

GRAVES, George A, Leading Stoker, K 10914, Lion, 31 March 1919

GRAVESTOCK, Louis B, Stoker 1c, K 56743, Valerian, 22 October 1926

GRAY, Alexander, Gunner, RMA, RMA 13122, New Zealand, 29 March 1920

GRAY, Allan, Stoker 1c, P/K 76663, Poseidon, 9 June 1931

GRAY, Donald N, Lieutenant, L.24, 10 January 1924

GRAY, Ernest C, Boy 2c, J 100801, Impregnable, 27 March 1921

GRAY, Ernest H, Private, RMLI, S 2547 (Ch), Glory, 23 November 1918

GRAY, George, Lieutenant Commander, RNVR, Royal Naval Volunteer Reserve, 25 April 1937

GRAY, John J, Leading Cook, P/M 1242, Sandwich, 22 February 1931

GRAY, Robert E, Paymaster Commander, RNR, Royal Naval Reserve, 20 January 1923

GREEN, Alfred J, Able Seaman, J 38148, Viceroy, 20 March 1925

GREEN, Charles W, Stoker 2c, K 61453, Pembroke, 8 July 1923

GREEN, Charles, Leading Stoker, K 14964 (Po), Penarth, 4 February 1919

GREEN, Eric, Engine Room Artificer 3c, M 11777, Anzac (RAN), 25 May 1920

GREEN, Ernest, Private, RMLI, 20866 (Ch), Ganges, 8 February 1922

GREEN, Frank, Commissioned Engineer, Egmont, 5 January 1928

GREEN, George F, Paymaster Sub Lieutenant, RNR, President V, 25 April 1919

GREEN, George R, Deck Hand, RNR, DA 967, Ocean Retriever, 28 February 1919

GREEN, George W F, Stoker 1c, J 59790, L.24, 10 January 1924

GREEN, George W, Able Seaman, J 20759, Wolfhound, 27 August 1924

GREEN, James S, Petty Officer, 239935 (Ch), Tintagel, 26 January 1919

GREEN, James, Leading Stoker, P/KX 87359, Nelson, 14 February 1937

GREEN, John, Musician, RMB, RMB 2076, Pembroke, 27 September 1923

GREEN, Joseph H, Signal Boy, J 81609, Bellerophon, 9 April 1919

GREEN, Lawrence, Stoker 1c, K 48925, Victory, 27 December 1918

GREEN, Leonard C, Stoker 1c, K 62435, St Genny, 12 January 1930

GREEN, Louis E, Stoker 1c, P/KX 80815, Thetis, 3 June 1939

GREEN, Samuel J, Stoker 1c, P/KX 81131, Victory, 23 January 1937

GREEN, Sebald W B, Commander, Glowworm, 26 August 1919

GREEN, Thomas F, Paymaster Lieutenant, RNR, Royal Naval Reserve, 30 January 1923

GREEN, Victor J, Leading Signalman, J 21033, Vivid, 12 January 1919

GREEN, William C, Able Seaman, J 38408, Vivid, 5 March 1920

GREEN, William S A, Private, RMLI, 19654 (Ch), RM, 6th Battalion, 9 September 1919

GREENE, William J, Engine Room Artificer 2c, C/M 38816, Vindictive, 19 September 1931

GREENLEES, Ean C C, Lieutenant, Lucia, 20 June 1925

GREENWAY, William, Officer's Steward 2c, L 7403, Warspite, 8 June 1924

GREENWELL, Evelyn E, Ty/Lieutenant, RNVR, Research, 23 February 1919

GREENWELL, Peter, Stoker 2c, D/KX 80514, Vivid, 18 June 1931

GREENWOOD, Arthur G, Stoker 1c, K 59964, Valerian, 22 October 1926

GREENWOOD, Charles, Paymaster Lieutenant Commander, RNVR, Royal Naval Volunteer Reserve, 2 December 1920

GREENWOOD, Edward R, Ordinary Seaman, J 57143, Ramillies, 4 December 1918

GREENWOOD, Samuel, Private, RM, S 1550 (Deal), 149th RN Field Ambulance, RM Medical Unit, RND, 17 November 1918

GREENWOOD, William J, Stoker 1c, P/KX 76929, Dauntless, 27 August 1930

GREET, William C, Paymaster Lieutenant, RN Hospital, Plymouth, 21 June 1932

GREGG, Claude J M, Sub Lieutenant, Venomous, 9 September 1928

GREGG, Horace C, Leading Seaman, J 17905, Actaeon, 19 May 1919

GREGORY, Arthur W, Corporal, RMLI, 16107 (Po), Queen Elizabeth, 1 August 1919

GREGORY, Charles F, Stoker 1c, C/K 60527, Pembroke, 13 October 1932

GREGORY, Edward, Private, RM, S 9447 (Deal), RM Labour Corps, 31 December 1918

GREGORY, Leslie, Leading Aircraftman, RAF, 364018, M.2, 29 January 1932

GREGORY, Reginald, Lieutenant Commander, Hong Kong Dockyard, 21 June 1922

GREGSON, Frank, Sergeant, RMLI, 15775 (Po), Egmont, 11 December 1918

GREGSON, John R, Assistant Mechanician, K 31502, Blue Sky, tender to Queen Elizabeth, 12 June 1922

GREIG, Alexander S, Able Seaman, J 95524, Caradoc, 12 July 1929

GREIG, Donald, Commander (Rtd), Royal Navy, 27 July 1921

GRENYER, Alfred J, Engineman, RNR, ES 5076, Bombardier, 27 March 1919

GREY, Arthur T, Ty/Skipper, RNR, R R S, Admiralty hired trawler, 16 November 1918
GREY, John, Stoker, RNR, S 3001, Medway, 5 September 1919
GRIBBIN, John, Able Seaman, RNVR, Tyneside Z 11042, Westgate, steamship, 8 January 1919
GRIFFIN, Arthur W B, Boy 2c, J 93638, Impregnable, 30 March 1919
GRIFFIN, Edward, Deck Hand, RNR, DA 13903, Leyland, 7 December 1918
GRIFFIN, Harold E M, Electrical Artificer Apprentice, M 37697, Fisgard, 7 August 1924
GRIFFIN, John J, Gunner, Colleen, 15 January 1921
GRIFFIN, Leonard D, Stoker 1c, K 59339, Valerian, 22 October 1926
GRIFFIN, Stephen, Stoker 1c, D/K 64428, Walrus, 4 October 1931
GRIFFITH, George, Able Seaman, D/JX 125757, Bridgewater, 14 July 1934
GRIFFITHS, Albert J, Commissioned Shipwright, President, 16 April 1922
GRIFFITHS, Arthur L, Officer's Steward 1c, 361492, Caesar, 11 June 1919
GRIFFITHS, Clifford, Leading Stoker, K 12449, L.55, 4 June 1919
GRIFFITHS, Ernest, Chief Petty Officer Cook, 347943, Barham, 8 October 1926
GRIFFITHS, Frederick C E, Able Seaman, J 27007, Pembroke, 5 February 1922
GRIFFITHS, Frederick J, Deck Hand, RNR, DA 19120, Lavatera, 9 December 1918
GRIFFITHS, Harold W J S, Electrical Artificer 5c, M 30408, Vernon, 24 December 1918
GRIFFITHS, John, Civilian Contractor, Thetis, 3 June 1939
GRIFFITHS, John H, Petty Officer Cook, D/MX 48073, Hunter, 13 May 1937
GRIFFITHS, Philip G L, Boy 1c, JX 130149, Caradoc, 3 July 1929
GRIFFITHS, Raymond O J, Marine, X 2215 (Ply), RM Plymouth Division, 26 May 1938
GRIFFITHS, Willie, Able Seaman, J 47924, Walrus, 19 March 1919
GRIGG, Alfred J, Stoker 1c, J 60726, L.24, 10 January 1924
GRIGSON, Edmond G B, Telegraphist, J 77760, FAA, 422 Sqn, Argus, 6 September 1928
GRIGSON, Frederick W, Leading Seaman, 240073, Marlborough, 11 March 1928
GRILLS, Thomas V, Petty Officer, P/J 23507, Poseidon, 9 June 1931
GRIMA, Paolo, Officer's Cook 3c, E/LX 20939, Glorious, 6 May 1934
GRIMMA, Guiseppe, Able Seaman, E/J 54000, St Angelo, 14 February 1936
GRIMSHAW, Francis J, Able Seaman, J 6522, Petunia, 15 November 1918
GRINDLE, Frank, Marine, 22763 (Ply), Devonshire, 26 July 1929
GRINDROD, John W, Private, RM, S 11717 (Deal), RM Labour Corps, 11 February 1919
GROCUTT, Richard, Able Seaman, D/J 14906, Vivid, 25 November 1932
GROSE, Arthur E D, Stoker 2c, P/KX 87879, Victory, 30 April 1936
GROSSMITH, George H, Stoker 1c, K 3775, Victory, 11 April 1921
GROUND, Brian K U, Py/Sub Lieutenant, RNR, Royal Naval Reserve, 10 March 1939
GROUT, Egbert W J, Petty Officer, 193771, Queen Elizabeth, 1 December 1920
GROVES, Albert E, Officer's Steward 3c, F 37525, Pembroke, 23 November 1918
GRUBB, Ernest G, Leading Seaman, 234683, Argus, 22 August 1922
GRUBB, George H, Warrant Engineer, RNR, Royal Naval Reserve, 6 February 1921
GRUNDY, John W, Leading Stoker, K 17771 (Po), Penarth, 4 February 1919

GUEST, Frank, Able Seaman, RNVR, Tyneside Z 4756, Hood Battalion, RND, 5 December 1918
GUEST, George H, Leading Signalman, C/J 29344, Esk, 27 January 1935
GUEST, John D, Chief Petty Officer, 221761, Lupin, 11 December 1925
GUILLARD, Fred Mc L, Joiner 4c, M 18574 (Po), Penarth, 4 February 1919
GULLIFORD, Leonard H, Leading Seaman, K 18802, Silvio, 30 November 1919
GULLIS, George, Stoker 1c, K 56738, Antrim, 26 October 1921
GULLIS, Harold V P, Ordinary Seaman, P/JX 133175, Victory, 3 February 1932
GUNDRY, George G, Engine Room Artificer 4c, M 30849 (Po), Penarth, 6 February 1919
GUNFIELD, Ernest A, Ordinary Seaman, J 53761, TB.35, torpedo boat, 16 March 1919
GUNN, Edwin H, Engine Room Artificer 1c, M 1547, Ambrose, 11 December 1922
GUNNINGHAM, Frank, Stoker Petty Officer, 287128, Challenger, 13 December 1918
GURNEY, Harold C, Sick Berth Attendant, MX 45765, Pembroke, 13 February 1927
GURR, Hubert W J, Lance Corporal, RM, A 24453 (Ch), RM Barracks Chatham, 26 January 1935
GUTTERIDGE, Sydney G W, Leading Seaman, J 32179, Victory, 12 October 1926
GUY, Arthur T H, Able Seaman, P/J 113125, Warspite, 20 June 1932
GUY, Francis, Officer's Steward 3c, L 11870 (Dev), Dauntless, 27 July 1920
GUY, James, Chief Petty Officer, 226859, L.55, 4 June 1919

H

HABENS, Eric C, Able Seaman, P/J 115394, Courageous, 23 January 1931

HACKING, Harry V, Able Seaman, RNVR, Mersey Z 1786, Ganges, 14 November 1918

HACKWORTH, John, 4th Engineer, MMR, Goissa, 15 November 1918

HADDAWAY, Herbert, Quartermaster, MMR, 566173, Richard Welford, 28 February 1919

HADDOW, James W, Leading Telegraphist, J 48913, FAA, 421 Sqn, Furious, 6 September 1926

HADWICK, Frederick G, Stoker 1c, K 10413, Victory, 23 January 1919

HAGGIS, Henry G, Stoker, RAN, 9536, Platypus, 7 July 1919

HAGON, Selonso, Stoker 1c, K 38860, Bacchante, 13 February 1919

HAIGH, Ernest, Able Seaman, J 44770 (Ch), Gentian, 15 July 1919

HAINES, Neville E, Midshipman, RNR, Housatonic, 30 July 1931

HAIZELDEN, Alfred G, Colour Sergeant, 10591 (Ch), Pens No. 19937, Chatham Division, RM, 1 April 1937

HAKE, George, Able Seaman, D/J 16213, Chrysanthemum, 30 August 1931

HALE, Alfred G, Able Seaman, RNVR, Wales Z 1481, Nelson Battalion, RND, 8 February 1919

HALE, Alfred J, Able Seaman, J 34121, Maidstone, 6 July 1924

HALE, Alfred, Private, RMLI, 6935 (Ch), Wisby, steamship, 10 February 1919

HALE, Hubert, Engine Room Artificer 1c, 270376, Vivid, 3 March 1922

HALE, John W, Lieutenant Commander, FAA, 447 Flight, London, 31 May 1936

HALES, Ernest E, Ordinary Seaman, RNVR, London Z 7424, Egmont, 17 November 1918

HALES, Victor R, Musician, RMB, RMB 1485, St Vincent, 3 December 1930

HALEY, James, Leading Stoker, P KX 79017, Berwick, 18 May 1939

HALEY, Thomas J, Petty Officer 1c, 163619, President VI, 15 January 1919

HALFPENNY, John, Greaser, MMR, 587394, Marchioness of Bute, 27 February 1919

HALL, Albert E, Able Seaman, C/J 102984, Wanderer, 10 May 1937

HALL, Albert E, Able Seaman, D/J 38950, Laburnum, 9 November 1933

HALL, Archie, Able Seaman, D/J 114285, Seraph, 7 September 1931

HALL, Bertie S, Able Seaman, C/J 115638, Diomede, 14 November 1936

HALL, Cecil, Chief Motor Mechanic, RNVR, MB 1307, ML.205, motor launch, 3 March 1919

HALL, Charles F, Stoker 1c, K 55015, Dolphin, 2 May 1922

HALL, Charles F, Stoker 2c, D/KX 80523, Adventure, 6 May 1931

HALL, Edward H, Stoker Petty Officer, K 55279, Victory, 10 July 1919

HALL, Ewart E, Stoker Petty Officer, D/KX 79481, Drake, 1 June 1936

HALL, Frank, Stoker 2c, P/KX 87709, Cormorant, 7 January 1937

HALL, Frank E, Leading Seaman, 214858, Victory, 28 March 1919

HALL, Frederick J, Able Seaman, C/J 87024, Whirlwind, 19 August 1930

HALL, Henry J, Able Seaman, P/J 115344, Whitshed, 21 August 1932

HALL, John R, Boy 2c, J 105097, Ganges, 27 December 1921

HALL, John W, Lieutenant Commander, RAF service, 31 May 1936

HALL, Matthew, Chief Yeoman of Signals, C/227218, Glasgow Recruiting Office, 1 April 1936

HALL, Sarah A, Cook, WRNS, G 2676, Women's Royal Naval Service, 14 December 1918

HALL, Sidney R, Able Seaman, J 14076, Benbow, 11 June 1922

HALL, Stanley P G, Petty Officer, D/J 64483, Rodney, 19 October 1936

HALL, Thomas, Stoker 1c, C/KX 86083, Victory, 4 March 1938

HALL, Thomas J, Stoker 2c, P/KX 80392, Victory, 4 February 1934

HALL, Walter R, Trimmer, MMR, 867606, Eaglet, 30 January 1919

HALL, Wilfred E, Petty Officer, D/J 23775, Danae, 18 April 1935

HALL, William, Stoker 1c, D/KX 86583, Furious, 22 September 1937

HALLAM, Thomas - see WOOD, Thomas, Able Seaman

HALLAM, William, Chief Stoker, 284942, Pembroke, 5 December 1918

HALLCHURCH, Frank D, Boy 1c, J 103137, Valiant, 18 October 1922

HALLETT, Edward J, Engine Room Artificer Apprentice, MX 49508, Pembroke, 14 June 1936

HALLETT, Fred, Leading Stoker, MMR, 589058, Belgol, Royal Fleet Auxiliary, 27 November 1918

HALLETT, Robert, Corporal, RM, 18527 (Ply), Curlew, 27 August 1928

HALLIDAY, Albert J W, Leading Signalman, J 63052, Dunedin, 3 May 1930

HALLIGAN, Alexander, Leading Stoker, 288982, Pansy, 16 December 1918

HALLIMAN, Stanley H, Stoker 2c, C/KX 80885, York, 30 January 1932

HALLIWELL, Jack, Able Seaman, RNVR, Tyneside Z 8924, President III, 24 February 1919

HALLS, Francis W G, Yeoman of Signals, 239838, K.26 (Cyclops), 12 March 1927

HALLS, Frank, Leading Stoker, C/K 24861, Sutton, 21 February 1934

HALSALL, Frederick N, Act/Warrant Engineer, Dorsetshire, 27 April 1938

HALSTONE, Emly J, Ordinary Signalman, J 49378, Vivid, 4 March 1919

HALTON, Samuel, Pilot Officer RAF, 422 Sqn, Argus, 6 September 1928

HALY, Charles V, Boy Artisan, M 33210, Fisgard, 15 August 1919

HAM, George, Private, RMLI, 3707 (Ply), Wheatear, steamship, 2 December 1918

HAM, John B, Chief Gunner, Excellent, 31 March 1921

HAMBLY, John R, Chief Gunner, Excellent, 5 March 1919

HAMBLY, Richard B, Stoker Petty Officer, 172334, Westcott, 9 January 1919

HAMBROOK, Walter L, Act/Leading Seaman, P/J 115289, Thetis, 3 June 1939

HAMER, Fred, Boy 1c, J 89948, Delhi, 24 May 1920

HAMER, Harry, Able Seaman, RNVR, Mersey Z 607, Hawke Battalion, RND, 18 May 1919

HAMILL, Henry P, Able Seaman, SS 5674, Revenge, 30 November 1919

HAMILTON, Archibald, Midshipman, Resolution, in Glorious aircraft, 25 April 1932

HAMILTON, Clifford J S, Civilian Contractor,, Thetis, 3 June 1939

HAMILTON, James, Corporal, RMLI, 12453 (Ply), Cornwall, 9 December 1918

HAMILTON, Rowan T, Lieutenant Commander, Royal Navy, 11 August 1931

HAMILTON, Shaun R, Boy 2c, JX 158409, Caledonia, 30 November 1937

HAMMELL, Joseph, Petty Officer, 204818, Blenheim, 16 July 1922

HAMMERSLEY, Rupert L, Leading Seaman, J 5015 (Ch), L.55, 4 June 1919
HAMMETT, Leonard, Able Seaman, D/J 54919, Emerald, 2 May 1931
HAMMETT, William A, Shipwright 1c, D/M 3415, Defiance, 8 June 1935
HAMMOND, Albert V, Able Seaman, P/JX 126023, Egmont I, 20 January 1931
HAMMOND, Edward, Stoker 2c, K 66893, Pembroke, 16 January 1926
HAMMOND, George R, Stoker 1c, SS 119282 (Dev), Glowworm, 9 July 1919
HAMMOND, James, Leading Stoker, 300492, Danae, 27 January 1923
HAMMOND, Leslie V, Able Seaman, P/J 113195, FAA, 716 Flight, Amphion, 20 January 1938
HAMMOND, Percy R, Deck Hand, RNR, DA 8759, Pembroke, 5 February 1919
HAMMOND, Samuel M, Keeper & Steward of Royal Cabins, Victoria & Albert, Royal Yacht, 24 November 1932
HAMMOND, Thomas S, Coastguardsman 2c, 172058, Pembroke, 16 February 1923
HAMMOND, Thomas V, Signalman, C/J 87102, Pembroke, 19 November 1930
HAMPER, William, Chief Blacksmith, P/M 27874, Royal Navy, 14 April 1938
HANCOCK, Thomas G, Petty Officer 1c, 132137, Cuckoo, 23 December 1918
HANCOCK, William G, Stoker Petty Officer, P/K 7725, Pangbourne, 4 November 1931
HANCOX, Henry R, Lieutenant, FAA, 405 Flight, Eagle, 10 February 1926
HANDEL, Thomas H, Sick Berth Attendant, M 7794, Berbice, hospital ship, 4 October 1919
HANDFORD, Isaac J, Chief Stoker, C/K 2154, Cairo, 22 February 1931
HANDLEY, George, Telegraphist, J 56327, Inconstant, 14 February 1919
HANDLEY, Herbert P, Sick Bay Berth Petty Officer, M 294, Pembroke, 25 January 1930
HANKS, Cecil J, Able Seaman, J 61034, Pembroke, 12 May 1919
HANLON, John, Leading Seaman, C 3177, Victory, 20 December 1918
HANNAFORD, Alfred E, Chief Shipwright 2c, D/M 13711, Vivid, 14 August 1931
HANNAFORD, William G, Stoker 1c, K 1234, Vivid, 20 February 1921
HANNAM, Bertram W, Chief Yeoman of Signals, J 6510, Vivid, 23 May 1929
HANNAN, Michael, Petty Officer, 217443 (Ch), Danae, 9 November 1919
HANSFORD, Archibald R, Leading Seaman, J 18293 (Po), Sword Dance, 24 June 1919
HANSFORD, James G, Stoker Petty Officer, 308223, H.42, 23 March 1922
HANSON, Albert H, Able Seaman, J 64229, Clan Graham, mercantile fleet auxiliary, 22 June 1919
HARBER, Rowland G, Able Seaman, SS 10831, Victory, 4 February 1926
HARBIN, George E, Chief Engine Room Artificer 2c, P/M 27315, Victory, 1 February 1936
HARBOARD, Ernest G, Engineman, RNR, ES 5151, Eaglet, 8 February 1920
HARBOTT, Charles, Leading Stoker, K 13639, Lilac, 18 November 1918
HARD, William, Krooman, Ascension Island, 3 April 1920
HARDEN, Frederick S, Ordnance Artificer 2c, C/M 35988, Pembroke, 14 February 1921
HARDIE, Cyril N, Steward, D/LX 20573, Vivid, 27 January 1933
HARDING, Albert E, Ty/Paymaster Sub Lieutenant, RNR, Colleen, 10 December 1918
HARDING, Sir Charles O' B, Honorary Lieutenant Commander, RNVR, Royal Naval Volunteer Reserve, 7 June 1929
HARDING, Dennis, Chief Petty Officer, D/JX 146583, Cockchafer, 18 October 1937
HARDING, Fred A, Leading Stoker, RAN, 8476, Sydney (RAN), 28 February 1919
HARDING, Frederick G, Stoker 1c, 304429, Peterel, 13 November 1918
HARDING, Gordon G, Engine Room Artificer 2c, M 10953, M.1, 12 November 1925
HARDING, Kenneth G, Private, RMLI, 16409 (Ply), Plymouth Battalion, RND, 29 December 1918
HARDING, Thomas H, Able Seaman, P/J 12004, Cornwall, 4 January 1933
HARDING, Thomas, Quartermaster Sergeant, 4300 (Po), Portsmouth Division, RMLI, 12 January 1919
HARDING, Thomas, Yeoman of Signals, 234639, Lion, 6 January 1920
HARDY, Charles A, Stoker Petty Officer, 309983, TB.63, torpedo boat, 16 March 1919
HARDY, Charles P, Engine Room Artificer 1c, P/M 31105, M.2, 29 January 1932
HARDY, George, Greaser, MMR, King Edward, 14 December 1918
HARDY, Henry, Ordinary Seaman, RNVR, MDX 1683, Valiant, 24 March 1935
HARDY, Hercules, Seaman, RNR, B 2981, Gitano, steamship, 20 December 1918
HARDY, Joseph, Able Seaman, J 41148, Caesar, 18 October 1919
HARDY, Richard, Able Seaman, 228588, Queen Elizabeth, 9 May 1924
HARDY, William H, Lieutenant, Badger, 24 December 1918
HARE, Percy A, Leading Seaman, 213902, Caroline, 2 January 1920
HARE, William G, Stoker Petty Officer, K 11033, Valentine, 2 September 1924
HARFIELD, William L, Shipwright Lieutenant, St Vincent, 5 March 1929
HARFIELD, William S B, Boy 2c, JX 141612, St Vincent, 24 November 1934
HARGREAVES, David, Senior Reserve Attendant, M 9843, Agadir, hospital ship, 24 December 1918
HARLAND, Sydney, Officer's Steward 3c, L 2612, Active, 28 February 1919
HARLEY, William R, Lieutenant, FAA, 801 Sqn, Furious, 11 October 1937
HARMAN, Charles G, Lieutenant, RNR, Royal Naval Reserve, 19 April 1931
HARMAN, Frank J, Leading Aircraftsman, RAF, 364868, M.2, 29 January 1932
HARMAN, George E, Engineer Lieutenant, Indus, 23 September 1922
HARMAN, Robert C, Petty Officer, 238099, Larkspur, 9 June 1919
HARMAN, Robert, Able Seaman, MMR, 912591, St Aubin, 15 May 1919
HARMER, Jack, Stoker 2c, C/KX 92050, Pembroke, 4 February 1938
HARMON, George E, Engineer Lieutenant, Speedy, 23 September 1922
HARMS, Edward F, Able Seaman, 228812, Victory, 21 June 1920
HARN, Cedric W, Able Seaman, J 98752, Pembroke, 3 July 1925
HARNESS, John D, Able Seaman, J 31257 (Ch), Vittoria, 31 August 1919
HARNOTT, Joseph T, Able Seaman, 225207, Danae, 25 April 1919
HARPER, Arthur G, Able Seaman, J 28006, Pembroke, 12 March 1919
HARPER, Edward J, Boy 1c, J 80072, Curacoa, 3 December 1918
HARPER, Francis B, Deck Hand, RNR, DA 3925, Ocean Angler, 8 February 1919

HARPER, James H, Officer's Steward 2c, L 7144, Racehorse, 15 November 1918
HARPER, Kenneth, Able Seaman, J 92090, Vivid, 14 November 1925
HARPER, William, Stoker 1c, SS 123134, Pembroke, 17 August 1919
HARPHAM, Cecil R, Gunner 2c, RMA, RMA 16286, RMA Eastney, 5 February 1919
HARRHY, William J, Able Seaman, J 1625, Dauntless, April 1924
HARRIES, William, Stoker 1c, K 35797, Devonshire, 22 April 1919
HARRIS, Arthur, Leading Stoker, K 15653, Vivid, 13 July 1922
HARRIS, Charles, Stoker Petty Officer, D/K 59550, Drake, 19 May 1936
HARRIS, Charlie, Petty Officer, P/J 7492, Fisgard, 4 January 1932
HARRIS, Dermot, Boy 2c, J 101204, Impregnable, 9 June 1921
HARRIS, Edward C, Marine, X 315 (Ply), Devonshire, 26 July 1929
HARRIS, Francis R, Able Seaman, J 80263 (Dev), Crescent, 18 November 1920
HARRIS, James A, Warrant Shipwright, Caledon, 2 July 1920
HARRIS, Joseph E, Able Seaman, P/JX 132423, Suffolk, 28 May 1935
HARRIS, Richard C, Stoker 1c, C/KX 85030, Pembroke, 15 February 1939
HARRIS, Sidney R, Chief Petty Officer, 216991, Vernon, 21 February 1926
HARRIS, Stanley F, Chief Petty Officer Cook, 347299, Pembroke, 10 March 1923
HARRIS, Thomas E H, Greaser, MMR, Iolaire, 1 January 1919
HARRIS, Tom H, Leading Seaman, J 33023, H.47, 9 July 1929
HARRIS, Walter G, Stoker 1c, J 18681, H.42, 23 March 1922
HARRIS, William P, Boy 1c, JX 130253, Vivid, 13 January 1930
HARRIS, William T, Corporal, RM, 21436 (Ply), Delhi, 13 October 1930
HARRISON, Albert E, Signalman, RNVR, Mersey Z 3453, Vivid, 6 December 1918
HARRISON, Edward H, Leading Seaman, 239613, Victory, 25 February 1929
HARRISON, George, Leading Seaman, J 19548, Wivern, 11 January 1922
HARRISON, John A, Ordinary Seaman, RNVR, Mersey Z 4687, Penarth, 4 February 1919
HARRISON, John, Boy 1c, J 102159, Vivid, 29 May 1921
HARRISON, Lawrence R, Petty Officer, D/J 32191, Shoreham, 7 January 1933
HARRISON, Robert, Stoker Petty Officer, C/K 20727, Pembroke, 29 June 1934
HARRISON, Thomas, Fireman, MMR, 620629, Hughli, Royal Fleet Auxiliary, 26 April 1919
HARRISON, Walter, Skipper (Warrant Officer), RNR, Vasco Da Gama, 19 February 1919
HARRISON, William, Private, RME, RME 2048, RM Engineers, 16 March 1919
HARROLD, Arthur S C, Able Seaman, J 65203, Blue Sky, tender to Queen Elizabeth, 12 June 1922
HARROWER, James, Ordinary Seaman, J 80387, Vivid, 1 December 1919
HART, Charles, Petty Officer, 218441 (Dev), Lucia, 19 June 1920
HART, George (real name, but served as George Routley), Private, RMLI, S 7304 (Ch), RMLI, HQ Chatham, 18 February 1919
HART, Percy, Deck Hand, RNR, DA 16352, Kenilworth, 22 February 1919
HART, Thomas J, Petty Officer, C/JX 127585, Keppel, 16 June 1938
HART, William H, Stoker 1c, C/KX 77685, H.43, 15 December 1932
HARTLAND, Edward G, Boy 2c, JX 127194, Ganges, 4 November 1926
HARTLAND, Frederick G, Leading Seaman, C/JX 134825, Pembroke, 10 March 1939
HARTLAND, Sydney, Able Seaman, J 95907, H.47, 9 July 1929
HARTLESS, Herbert W, Able Seaman, J 19492, Tumult, 14 November 1921
HARTLEY, Horace B, Chief Engine Room Artificer 1c, 270515, Vivid, 27 June 1923
HARTNELL, Frank C, Gunner, RMA, RMA S 1827, Cyclops II, 12 March 1919
HARTWILL, William, Marine, E 16529, Royal Marines HQ, 6 February 1929
HARVEY, Charles, Chief Armourer (Pens), 159077 (Dev), Spear, 20 December 1918
HARVEY, Charles W, Able Seaman, RNVR, AA 2345, President V, 23 November 1918
HARVEY, Desmond, Act/Sub Lieutenant (E), Engineer Course, 9 February 1932
HARVEY, Edward J, Leading Signalman, J 10580, H.42, 23 March 1922
HARVEY, Harold E, Bugler, RMLI, 12169 (Ch), Malabar, 12 February 1923
HARVEY, Henry, Coastguardsman 2c, 157954, Vivid, 23 April 1922
HARVEY, Leonard, Sergeant, RMA, RMA 5973, RMA Battalion, South African Heavy Artillery, 11 March 1919
HARVEY, Philip H, Stoker 1c, K 15306, Vivid, 8 February 1919
HARVEY, Thomas, Joiner 1c, M 14661, Vivid, 3 July 1927
HARVEY, William, Chief Officer, HM Coast Guard, HM Coast Guard Wireless Telegraph Station Rame Head, 15 March 1920
HARVEY, William C, Ordinary Seaman, J 99015, Wolsey, 20 February 1924
HARVEY, William C, Ordinary Seaman, MMR, 927496, Woonda, 10 December 1918
HARVEY, William E, Leading Seaman, RNR, B 5151, Oak, steamship, 28 November 1918
HARVEY, William G A, Able Seaman, J 34108, Superb, 2 November 1919
HARVEY, William J, Leading Seaman, RNR, A 4702, Everilda, steamship, 17 November 1918
HARWOOD, Archibald, Leading Stoker, P/KX 84801, Victoria & Albert, Royal Yacht, 10 September 1936
HARWOOD, Ernest R, Leading Seaman, J 90941, Vivid, 1 November 1928
HARWOOD, George A, Act/Petty Officer, C/JX 134789, Thetis, 3 June 1939
HARWOOD, William T, Corporal, RMLI, 1300 (Ply), RM Headquarters, 17 August 1919
HASARL, Frederick L (served as Frederick L Barnes), Chief Stoker, K 16139, Vampire, 24 December 1927
HASKELL, Thomas R H, Able Seaman, J 73419, Warspite, 16 August 1920
HASKELL, Thomas W R H, Able Seaman, J 73410, Warspite, 10 August 1920
HASLAM, Herbert, Leading Seaman, J 102105, Scarab, 5 September 1926
HASLAND, Francis H, Able Seaman, J 9622, Vivid, 25 September 1929
HASSAM, Suleiman B, Seedie, X 230, Flora, 7 August 1928
HASSETT, Blenner C, Petty Officer, P/J 17282, Victory, 16 September 1933
HASSLIN, Elmi, Seedie Stoker, 2/123, Colombo, 19 May 1925
HASTIE, Robert, Stoker 1c, SS 110259, Vivid, 17 January 1919
HATHERLY, Sidney W B, Able Seaman, J 49371, Watchman, 11 September 1920
HATTON, Alfred, Chief Stoker, 309247, Venomous, 22 March 1926
HATTON, Ronald F, Supply Petty Officer, M 32054, Centurion, 5 July 1928
HAVARD, William D, Able Seaman, RNVR, R 4209, Army, Command Depot, Aldershot, 13 November 1918
HAVERSON, Frank, Leading Telegraphist, RNVR, London Z 6091, President IV, 29 November 1918

HAVILL, Harold E, Able Seaman, J 15241, Victory, 6 April 1920
HAWES, Cyril G, Private, RMLI, S 1619 (Po), 1st RM Battalion, RND, 13 November 1918
HAWES, Thomas W, Private, RMLI, 22061 (Ch), RM, 6th Battalion, 8 September 1919
HAWKEN, Alfred G, Leading Seaman, 238809, Royal Indian Marine, 8 November 1920
HAWKESWORTH, Cyril E, Cook, M 38529, St Vincent, 1 August 1929
HAWKEY, Joseph, Able Seaman, J 25896, Vivid, 22 May 1921
HAWKINS, Alfred J G, Boy 2c, JX 31987, St Vincent, 6 August 1928
HAWKINS, Arthur W, Leading Seaman, J 16167, Effingham, 13 June 1926
HAWKINS, Astley R, Lieutenant, RNR, Attentive, 16 February 1919
HAWKINS, George, Leading Stoker, P/K 47313, Iroquois, 1 December 1930
HAWKINS, Henry W, Able Seaman, 225264, Warwick, 24 December 1920
HAWKINS, James, Chief Skipper, RNR, Warland, 30 March 1930
HAWKINS, Veines J, Leading Seaman, J 15592 (Po), Vindictive, 2 May 1919
HAWLEY, Frederick, Able Seaman, J 105790, H.47, 9 July 1929
HAWORTH, Albert, Stoker 2c, K 26437, Vivid, 11 February 1919
HAWTHORN, George E, Leading Stoker, K 60245, Viscount, 2 July 1928
HAY, Charles P, Midshipman, Royal Sovereign, 31 May 1936
HAY, William H, Leading Seaman, 208122, Ceres, 4 March 1920
HAY, William J, Leading Cook, M 4687, Valerian, 22 October 1926
HAYCOCK, Albert, Able Seaman, J 100477, Pembroke, 20 March 1929
HAYDEN, Thomas (real name, but served as Thomas Helton), Chief Shipwright 2c, 343328, Bryony, 9 October 1920
HAYES, Alfred G, Private, RM, S 8818 (Deal), RM Labour Corps, 30 April 1920
HAYES, Daniel J, Boy 2c, JX 150083, Ganges, 12 October 1936
HAYES, Edwin, Leading Seaman, RNVR, KP 204, Hawke Battalion, RND, 12 June 1919
HAYES, John F, Stoker Petty Officer, 303978, Colossus, 20 November 1918
HAYES, William A, Warrant Engineer, M.2, 29 January 1932
HAYNES, Clarence F, Boy Artisan, M 22614, Fisgard, 18 February 1919
HAYNES, Edwin A, Able Seaman, J 105458, Pembroke, 16 April 1929
HAYNES, Henry C, Able Seaman, J 95694, Valerian, 22 October 1926
HAYNES, Henry S J, Corporal, RM, 22744 (Po), RM Portsmouth Division, 14 June 1937
HAYNES, Hubert H, Cook, P/MX 48449, Nelson, 25 July 1934
HAYNES, John F, Surgeon Commander, Royal Navy, 16 July 1935
HAYNES, William G, Able Seaman, P/J 103857, MTB.7, 26 April 1939
HAYTER, Reginald G B, Commander, Naval Engineering Department, Thetis, 3 June 1939
HAYWARD, Ernest J, Officer's Chief Cook, C/L 3664, Pembroke, 4 October 1930
HAYWARD, Frank, Chief Officer, HM Coast Guard, HM Coast Guard Harwich, 31 July 1919
HAYWARD, Walter J, Corporal, RMLI, 217037 (Po), Hood, 8 March 1937
HAYWARD, William, Chief Engine Room Artificer 2c, 271630 (Dev), Moorhen, 2 August 1919
HAYWOOD, Arthur R, Warrant Shipwright, Yarmouth, 20 July 1921
HAZELL, Charles E, Able Seaman, J 32084, Pembroke, 18 March 1919
HAZELL, William J, Able Seaman, J 11956, H.42, 23 March 1922

HEAD, Albert H, Canteen Assistant, Admiralty civilian, Yarmouth, 18 March 1919
HEAD, Hamilton C W, Lieutenant, M.2, 29 January 1932
HEAD, Herbert W, Private, RMLI, 11997 (Po), Iolaire, 1 January 1919
HEAD, Walter, Stoker Petty Officer, K 11511, Montrose, 31 May 1921
HEAD, William A J, Private, RME, RME 859, RM Engineers, 14 March 1919
HEAD, William R, Boatswain, Exe, 13 December 1922
HEADLAND, Ernest H, Stoker 1c, K 38404, Pembroke, 28 February 1919
HEADLY, William, Petty Officer, 233067, Glowworm, 13 January 1922
HEALEY, Norton G, Marine, 22408 (Po), Royal Marines HQ, 25 February 1926
HEALEY, Patrick, Stoker Petty Officer, 297395, TB.55, torpedo boat, 28 February 1919
HEALEY, Timothy, Deck Hand, RNR, DA 18829, Bird, 21 May 1919
HEALING, John W M, Lieutenant Commander, Royal Sovereign, 11 May 1932
HEANEY, John, Private, RMLI, 11460 (Ply), Cambrian, 16 April 1921
HEARN, Francis M, Able Seaman, J 109767, Egmont, 12 February 1929
HEARN, John, Coastguardsman 3c, 186260, HM Coast Guard Station St Agnes, 4 July 1921
HEARNE, Charles W, Able Seaman, 238051, PC.61, patrol boat, 4 May 1919
HEARNE, Joseph, Regulating Petty Officer, D/M 39809, Royal Navy, 23 December 1938
HEARNE, William R, Corporal, RMA, RMA 5030 (RFR B 220), RMA Battalion, 15 November 1918
HEATH, Ernest S, Petty Officer, 239570, Victory, 9 June 1922
HEATH, Maurice, Able Seaman, J 24409, Argus, 11 December 1924
HEATH, William H K, Leading Seaman, D/J 100045, Renown, 28 January 1932
HEATHCOTE, Charles F, Stoker 1c, P/K 57710, Victory, 9 April 1933
HEATHCOTE, Thomas, Able Seaman, D/J 106481, Osprey, 1 March 1935
HEATHER, Charles, Petty Officer, J 12617, Colombo, 15 September 1921
HEATHER, Thomas, Petty Officer Rigger, 169382, Victoria & Albert, 7 January 1920
HEATHERINGTON, Alexander, Chief Cook, MMR, 839736, Stobo Castle, mercantile fleet auxiliary, 13 February 1919
HEATON, James, Chief Engine Room Artificer 1c, 269745, Iron Duke, 2 March 1920
HEATON-ELLIS, Michael, Sub Lieutenant, Queen Elizabeth, 24 January 1919
HEBEL, Frederick J B, Leading Stoker, K 59712, St Genny, 12 January 1930
HEINEMANN, Peter D, Lieutenant, FAA, 406 Flight, Emerald, 21 December 1931
HEINSEN, Alfred W, Able Seaman, J 109121, Pembroke, 7 April 1928
HEITZMAN, Arthur J, Leading Telegraphist, D/J 111899, Furious, 24 September 1936
HELLIER, Frederick J J, Officer's Steward 1c, L 4490, Delphinium, 27 April 1929
HELLIN, Hubert W, Stoker 2c, P/KX 84105, Victory II, 20 September 1934
HELLYER, William E, Marine, 2125 (Ply), Devonshire, 27 July 1929
HELPS, Walter J, Stoker 1c, K 3186, Champion, 8 April 1919
HELTON, Thomas - see HAYDEN, Thomas, Chief Shipwright 2c
HEMMETT, Albert G, Able Seaman, D/J 103913, Venetia, 19 July 1936

HEMMING, Charles, Petty Officer, 217661, Victory, 16 December 1918
HEMP, Bertie G T, Able Seaman, J 30557, Royal Sovereign, 25 September 1922
HEMPENSTALL, Daniel, Boatswain, MMR, 854217, Day Star, 2 December 1918
HEMSTED, James E, Paymaster Commander, Barham, 14 May 1936
HENDERSON, Algernon C F, Honorary Captain, RNR, Royal Naval Reserve, 14 February 1934
HENDERSON, Andrew, Chief Skipper, RNR, Braemar, 22 April 1938
HENDERSON, Clifford, Leading Stoker, J 44507, H.47, 9 July 1929
HENDERSON, Colin M H, Lieutenant (E), Thetis (Dolphin), 3 June 1939
HENDERSON, James T, Chief Stoker, 303510, Columbine, 18 December 1924
HENDERSON, Sir Reginald G H, Admiral, Royal Navy, 2 May 1939
HENDERSON, William C, Chief Yeoman of Signals, 197526, Vivid, 24 October 1921
HENDLEY, Cyril, Able Seaman, P/J 98737, Boreas, 17 August 1934
HENDRY, James S, Gunner, RMA, 9777, Barham, 15 October 1920
HENDRY, John, Sergeant, RMLI, 15078 (Ch), Chatham Division, RMLI, 5 April 1919
HENLEY, Alfred, Cook, MMR, Iolaire, 1 January 1919
HENNESSY, John J, Able Seaman, J 23710, Julius, 24 September 1921
HENNESSY, Joseph, Lieutenant Commander, Royal Navy, 23 February 1930
HENRY, Donald Mc I, Able Seaman, J 55290, Carlisle, 10 November 1925
HENRY, James A, Honorary Lieutenant, RNVR, Clyde Division RNVR, 25 November 1928
HENRY, John T, Able Seaman, MMR, 586207, Duke of Cornwall, 13 October 1919
HENRY, Robert, Private, RMLI, S 588 (Po), King George V, 26 December 1918
HENWOOD, Benjamin T, Chief Engine Room Artificer 1c, 271162, Lowestoft, 12 November 1922
HEPWORTH, Campbell M W, Captain, RNR, Royal Naval Reserve, 25 February 1919
HERBERT, George A, Coastguardsman 2c, 155129, HM Coast Guard Station Tollesbury, 5 January 1920
HERBERT, Harry, Able Seaman, J 18644, Ramillies, 16 November 1922
HERBERT, Herbert N F, Petty Officer, 158045, Vivid, 13 February 1919
HERBERTSON, James D, Lieutenant, RNVR, ML.378, motor launch, 30 November 1919
HERITAGE, William H, Cook, M 11180, Victory III, 1 September 1921
HEROD, Adrian C, Petty Officer, D/J 111751, Capetown, 9 October 1936
HERON, Michael, Able Seaman, MMR, Eaglet, 2 February 1920
HERRIDGE, William H P, Leading Seaman, P/J 99618, L.23, 2 August 1931
HERRING, Arthur V, Able Seaman, J 34273, Egmont, 1 July 1919
HERRING, George, Marine, X 2103 (Po), RM Portsmouth Division, 29 April 1938
HERRINGTON, Frederick A, Stoker 2c, K 62089, Royal Sovereign, 15 April 1924
HERSEY, Leslie E, Cook 1c, M 36876, Danae, 22 October 1924
HESELTINE, John R, Able Seaman, J 39607, Defiance, 31 January 1919
HESTER, William J, Engine Room Artificer 3c, M 1516 (Po), K.5, 20 January 1921

HEWES, Albert, Deck Hand, RNR, DA 13146, ML.440, motor launch, 31 December 1918
HEWETSON, John C C, Act/Sub Lieutenant, Royal Sovereign, 23 August 1919
HEWETT, George R, Deck Hand, RNR, DA 3556, Aspasia, 7 March 1919
HEWETT, Joseph H, Lieutenant, RNVR, Arrogant, 26 February 1919
HEWINS, William, Stoker 1c, K 5131, Cornwall, 4 March 1930
HEWITSON, Bertie, Able Seaman, J 6905 (Po), Queen Elizabeth, 1 December 1920
HEWITT, Richard C, Able Seaman, J 99374, Teal, 5 August 1924
HEWITT, William J, Boy 2c, J 93486, Powerful, 16 November 1918
HEWS, George C, Able Seaman, D/J 93255, Poseidon, 9 June 1931
HEWSON, Philip, Ordnance Artificer 3c, M 8641, M.1, 12 November 1925
HEYWOOD, Ernest E, Able Seaman, J 42399, Valerian, 22 October 1926
HEYWOOD, Robert W, Able Seaman, J 110561, Sepoy, 8 April 1930

HIBBERD, James H, Cook, M 38486, Defiance, 22 October 1927
HIBBERD, Lewis R, Private, RMLI, 21083 (Po), RM Deal, 7 December 1918
HICKEY, Henry, Boy 2c, J 93862, Powerful, 26 February 1919
HICKEY, Thomas E, Ordinary Telegraphist, P/JX 140554, Royal Navy, 8 June 1936
HICKLIN, Leslie J, Ordinary Signalman, J 106757, Queen Elizabeth, 18 June 1925
HICKLIN, William O, Leading Stoker, K 12306 (Ch), K.5, 20 January 1921
HICKMAN, Alfred H J, Boy 2c, JX 132367, Ganges, 6 October 1928
HICKMAN, Leonard R, Chief Electrical Artificer 2c, M 2469, Repulse, 10 August 1924
HICKS, Albert E, Leading Seaman, J 18063, Emperor of India, 9 November 1919
HICKSON, James, Engine Room Artificer 1c, D/MX 52498, Caledon, 24 July 1936
HIGGINS, Alfred G, Act/Cook, C/MX 57607, Pembroke, 31 March 1939
HIGGINS, Alfred R, Lieutenant, Despatch, 5 September 1926
HIGGINS, Arthur W, Stoker 1c, D/K 58913, Vivid, 1 November 1932
HIGGINS, Denis, Able Seaman, D/J 44452, Royal Navy, 1 May 1938
HIGGINS, Wilfred A, Lieutenant Commander, Teal, 12 August 1926
HIGGINS, William, Marine, 15909 (Po), Resolution, 18 October 1926
HIGGINSON, Charles W, Leading Telegraphist, D/J 16611, Beaufort, 30 June 1935
HIGGINSON, Edgar, Constable, RM Police, RMP X 266 (Ply), Devonport Dockyard, 6 February 1937
HIGGINSON, Nelson, Able Seaman, J 17064, E.42, 1 September 1919
HIGGIS, Harry C, Petty Officer, 238503, Ramillies, 28 October 1925
HIGGS, Jack D, Ordnance Artificer Apprentice, MX 47665, Pembroke, 24 January 1933
HIGGS, Joseph, Gunner, RMA, RMA 2165, 3rd Battalion, RM, 27 November 1918
HIGH, Claude H, Able Seaman, J 18554, Humber, 13 March 1919
HIGHAM, Robert, Stoker Petty Officer, C/KX 87773, Topaze, 17 June 1936
HIGNETT, Samuel M, Paymaster Lieutenant Commander, RNR, Royal Naval Reserve, 4 March 1929
HILDICK, James, Commissioned Gunner, Douglas, 28 December 1928

HILDRETH, Edward J, Petty Officer, P/J 21797, Excellent, 26 February 1936
HILL, Albert A F, Admiralty Civilian, Thetis, 3 June 1939
HILL, Albert H, Leading Seaman, J 91934, Repulse, 8 November 1925
HILL, Charles H, Marine, 23280 (Ch), Danae, 7 August 1927
HILL, Charles T, Stoker 1c, SS 109647, Victory, 3 December 1918
HILL, Douglas, Engineer Commander, Cleopatra, 10 January 1925
HILL, Edward, Leading Stoker, K 3475, Assistance, 11 March 1920
HILL, Ernest, Able Seaman, 148261, Liverpool, 25 December 1918
HILL, Frederick C, Ty/Lieutenant, RNVR, Excellent, 2 August 1919
HILL, Geoffrey F K, Lieutenant, X.1, 14 July 1924
HILL, George H, Boy 2c, JX 132042, St Vincent, 11 April 1929
HILL, Harold M, Surgeon Lieutenant (D), Greenwich, 15 June 1929
HILL, Henry, Dockyard Fitter, civilian, H.29, 9 August 1926, accidentally killed
HILL, Henry C, Midshipman, Effingham, 2 July 1927
HILL, Henry T, Leading Seaman, J 58022, Defiance, 29 January 1921
HILL, Herbert, Ordinary Seaman, RNVR, Tyneside Z 11526, Thomas Booth, 10 January 1919
HILL, Hubert, Stoker 1c, K 44813, Challenger, 14 December 1918
HILL, John H, Stoker Petty Officer, K 5328, Dolphin, 18 February 1924
HILL, Leonard T, Sailmaker, 190552, Victory, 22 January 1927
HILL, Sidney, Able Seaman, SS 8798, Glowworm, 25 August 1919
HILL, Thomas J E, Marine, 22672 (Ply), Delhi, 19 June 1935
HILL, Victor A, Petty Officer Telegraphist, 223042, Ganges, 26 March 1919
HILLIARD, Harold, Stoker Petty Officer, C/K 21428, Cyclamen, 28 December 1931
HILLIARD, William G, Chief Stoker, 299354, Sorceress, 25 July 1922
HILLIER, Horace J, Stoker 1c, K 55832, H.42, 1 February 1922
HILLMAN, Edward J, Stoker Petty Officer, K 15258, L.24, 10 January 1924
HILLMAN, Fred, 2nd Writer, M 25676, Pembroke, 4 December 1922
HILLS, Albert G, Stoker 1c, C/K 63453, Pembroke, 6 June 1932
HILLS, Albert G, Stoker 1c, P/K 61207, Thetis, 3 June 1939
HILLS, Charles Frederick - see KILLHAM, Frederick, Steward 1c
HINDE, Joseph, Chief Petty Officer, J 1611, Defiance, 17 May 1925
HINDLEY, James T, Petty Officer, J 22852, Vivid, 14 April 1927
HINE, William F, Leading Seaman, J 98680, ML.291, 25 February 1923
HINE, William J, Marine, 19699 (Ply), Royal Marines HQ, 12 May 1926
HINES, Thomas H, Leading Stoker, K 30224, Neptune, 2 February 1919
HINGSTON, Arthur E, Stoker, Drake, 9 December 1938
HINGSTON, Edwin H, Chief Engine Room Artificer 2c, D/M 2662, Drake, 24 June 1934
HINGSTON, John, Able Seaman, 118541, Vivid, 21 January 1922
HINGSTON, Sydney, Chief Stoker, 306670, Hood, 15 June 1920
HINSELWOOD, George, Chief Petty Officer, 198586, Pembroke, 6 January 1921
HINTON, Alfred E, Able Seaman, D/JX 129414, Osprey, 16 September 1932
HINTON, Harry, Stoker Petty Officer, K 9766, Indus, 21 May 1921
HIRE, Ashton H, Major, RM, Rtd, Baronet, Royal Marines, 3 September 1936
HIRE, Thomas J, Stoker 1c, 292159, Valiant, 23 November 1918
HIRST, John, Able Seaman, RNVR, Tyneside Z 9031, Gentian, 12 July 1919
HISCOCK, Reginald J, Able Seaman, J 93946, Fisgard, 19 February 1924
HISCOCK, William G, Telegraphist, D/J 41575, Vivid, 9 June 1932
HISLOP, Alexander, Able Seaman, P/JX 131909, Medway, 3 December 1936
HITCHIN, Bertie T, Private, RMLI, 18521 (Ch), Glory III, 3 May 1919
HOBBS, John B, Boy 1c, C/JX 154987, Barham, 17 June 1939
HOBBS, Roland A, Surgeon Lieutenant, RAN, Melbourne (RAN), 13 February 1919
HOBBS, Wilfred J, Stoker, RAN, 8566 (RN - K 19874), Marguerite (RAN), 9 February 1920
HOBBS, William R, Blacksmith 4c, M 32223, Assistance, 8 July 1921
HOBDAY, Albert E, Petty Officer, 236378, M.1, 12 November 1925
HOBMAN, Jack W, Master at Arms, C/M 35729, Pembroke, 18 January 1932
HOBSON, William, Stoker 1c, 310797, TB.70, torpedo boat, 21 November 1918
HOCKLEY, Charles C, Leading Seaman, D/J 105705, Defiance, 15 November 1933
HODDER, Henry, Stoker Petty Officer, 293754, Oriana, 6 March 1919
HODDS, Thomas H, Shipwright 2c, M 13355, Hecla, 16 February 1919
HODGE, Alfred L, Stoker Petty Officer, MC 1187, Victory (ex-Eaglet), 16 December 1919
HODGE, Harold, Petty Officer, J 1248, Conqueror, 30 December 1918
HODGE, Harold R, Sick Berth Attendant, M 4418, Vivid, 25 February 1919
HODGE, Samuel C, Chief Engine Room Artificer 2c, M 1647, Vivid, 9 February 1927
HODGES, Albert A, Schoolmaster, New Zealand Division of Royal Navy, 10 January 1930
HODGES, George H, Stoker 2c, K 49505, Bacchante, 19 February 1919
HODGMAN, Edward J, Skipper, RNR, Royal Naval Reserve, 26 August 1927
HODGSON, George C R, Able Seaman, J 115510, Marlborough, 29 January 1930
HODGSON, Harold, Ordinary Seaman, SSX 13351, Vivid, 18 May 1929
HODKINSON, Enoch D, Ty/Warrant Telegraphist, RNR, Tarlair, 14 November 1918
HODKINSON, Frederick C, Able Seaman, J 99607, Carlisle, 18 August 1923
HODNETT, Herbert, Able Seaman, 218089, Mantis, 24 January 1922
HODSON, Ernest, Private, RM, S 14332 (Deal), RM Labour Corps, 18 April 1919
HODSON, George H, Deck Hand, RNR, DA 12217, Victory, 18 March 1919
HOGG, Audley A, Lieutenant Commander (E), Ramillies, 20 February 1936
HOKINS, Llewellyn J, Stoker 2c, D/KX 95205, Devonshire, 24 May 1939
HOLDEN, Ernest, Able Seaman, J 40164, Valerian, 22 October 1926
HOLDEN, Thomas, Ordinary Signalman, J 85519, Scimitar, 3 December 1919
HOLE, Wilfred T, Stoker 1c, D/KX 80876, Thetis, 3 June 1939
HOLE, William G, Marine, X 310 (Ply), Devonshire, 26 July 1929
HOLGATE, Harold R, Telegraphist, J 42659, Clematis, 6 November 1922
HOLLAND, Frederick R, Stoker 1c, D/KX 80584, Bideford, 1 April 1936

HOLLAND, Stanley L, Musician, RMLI, 16035 (Po), RM Headquarters, 16 May 1920

HOLLANDS, Arthur J, Boy Artisan, M 35327, Fisgard, 4 May 1920

HOLLIDAY, Percy W, Stoker 1c, K 19040, Pembroke, 30 October 1921

HOLLINGTON, Vernon, Ty/Lieutenant, RNVR, ML.284, motor launch, 25 February 1919

HOLLOWAY, Frederick E, Leading Seaman, P/J 94303, Peterel, 9 December 1937

HOLLOWAY, Harold L, Petty Officer, J 3262, Moth, 23 September 1926

HOLLOWAY, Henry E, Sick Berth Chief Petty Officer, M 1413, Kent, 1 September 1929

HOLLOWAY, John W B, Marine, 19800 (Po), Queen Elizabeth, 2 September 1923

HOLLOWAY, Sidney C, Able Seaman, J 18737, Dolphin, 8 November 1919

HOLMES, Alfred J, Boy 1c, JX 136069, Ganges, 31 January 1932

HOLMES, Bernard F, Chief Petty Officer Cook, RAN, 5054, Fantome, 21 September 1919

HOLMES, Francis R, Petty Officer, J 16086, Victory, 4 June 1921

HOLMES, Harold, Engine Room Artificer 1c, 270288, Blenheim, 18 February 1922

HOLMES, James, Warrant Engineer, Titania, 21 July 1920

HOLMES, Sidney D, Leading Seaman, J 15841 (Po), CMB.62BD, coastal motor boat, 18 August 1919

HOLMES, Thomas W, Chief Electrical Artificer 1c, 345111, Hecla, 26 April 1921

HOLMES, Walter, Boy 1c, J 100094, Ganges, 28 October 1921

HOLNESS, Ernest R, Warrant Officer 2c, Royal Marines HQ, 12 April 1923

HOLNESS, Thomas H, 2nd Hand, RNR, DA 16328, Robert Barton, 29 December 1918

HOLSAN, William J, Leading Stoker, K 15620, Burslem, 7 February 1926

HOLT, Alfred, Private, RMLI, S 602 (Ply), 1st RM Battalion, RND, 30 March 1919

HOLT, Benjamin, Able Seaman, J 50716, Crescent, 8 December 1918

HOLT, Ronald J, Marine, X 1440 (Ply), RM Plymouth Division, 16 June 1937

HOLT, William E, Private, RM, S 15739 (Deal), RM Labour Corps, 31 January 1919

HOLTON, Alfred E, Lieutenant, RMA, Howitzer Brigade, RMA, 22 February 1919

HOLTON, Cecil, Stoker 1c, K 57457, Lowestoft, 17 December 1927

HOLTON, William, Able Seaman, MMR, 810230, Gosforth, 11 December 1918

HOME, Ian H, Marine, X 1655 (Ply), RM Barracks Chatham, 14 April 1937

HOMER, Richard, Civilian Contractor, Thetis, 3 June 1939

HOMERSHAM, Cecil, Ordinary Seaman, RNVR, London Z 8019, Penarth, 4 February 1919

HONEYBUN, Francis C, Warrant Telegraphist, Victory, 27 September 1933

HONEYWELL, Albert E, Engine Room Artificer 2c, M 7062, Curlew, 27 October 1927

HONEYWELL, John H, Petty Officer, 218927, Tomahawk, 5 March 1919

HOOD, George C, Engine Room Artificer 3c, M 37005, Victory, 11 August 1927

HOOD, Martin A F, Lieutenant Commander, Royal Navy, 14 May 1919

HOOKER, David, Able Seaman, J 2030, Pembroke, 11 February 1919

HOOKEY, Samuel W, Stoker Petty Officer, 161337, Venerable, 30 November 1918

HOOKINGS, James G, Leading Steward, D/L 14645, Carlisle, 3 April 1936

HOOLIHAN, Thomas, Stoker 1c, SS 115558, Lilac, 21 November 1918

HOOPER, Albert E, Leading Cook's Mate, M 3531, Pembroke, 17 December 1918

HOOPER, Alwin S, Able Seaman, J 14872, H.42, 23 March 1922

HOOPER, Eric C W, Supply Assistant, C/MX 47883, Colombo, 28 April 1935

HOOPER, Geoffrey W W, Lieutenant Commander, Hawkins, 2 January 1923

HOOPER, George, Able Seaman, 219911, Sturgeon, 6 July 1924

HOOPER, Harold W, Leading Stoker, C/K 64549, Scarab, 28 August 1931

HOOPER, Harry J, Chief Petty Officer Writer, P/M 7108, Courageous, 23 January 1935

HOOPER, Reginald J, Leading Seaman, 229738, Vivid, 27 January 1919

HOOPER, Robert, Stoker Petty Officer, 288183, Vivid, 16 January 1919

HOOPER, Samuel, Cook, M 34989, King George V, 15 April 1922

HOOPER, William, Stoker 1c, K 22357, Assistance, 21 October 1925

HOPE, John A, Act/Petty Officer, D/J 81414, Thetis, 3 June 1939

HOPE, John, Able Seaman, P/JX 130644, Greenwich, 7 July 1933

HOPKINS, Alec A, Private, RMLI, S 1853 (Ch), Chatham Division, RMLI, 14 January 1919

HOPKINS, Alex T, Colour Sergeant, RM, 214967 (Po), Victoria & Albert, Royal Yacht, 13 February 1937

HOPKINS, Herbert A, Leading Seaman, C/JX 136803, Folkestone, 9 February 1939

HOPKINS, James H, Telegraphist, D/JX 138891, Drake, 23 February 1937

HOPKINSON, James A, RM Band, RMB 1103, RM Headquarters, 16 October 1921

HOPLEY, Ernest, Stoker 1c, K 7532, Lowestoft, 6 August 1928

HOPPER, Edwin J, Able Seaman, 228745, Vivid, 8 December 1919

HOPTON, Albert W, Stoker Petty Officer, 294505, Victory, 17 December 1921

HOPWOOD, John, Stoker 1c, K 19441, Agincourt, 17 September 1919

HORBURY, Norman, Engine Room Artificer 1c, D/M 14530, Caradoc, 5 September 1933

HORGAN, William H, Chief Stoker, 308642, Weymouth, 16 August 1924

HORN, John E, Stoker Petty Officer, C/KX 88273, Sheldrake, 3 February 1939

HORN, Stanley C A, Engine Room Artificer 1c, D/M 21453, M.2, 29 January 1932

HORNE, Charles H, Leading Stoker, K 29221, Vivid, 23 June 1919

HORNE, Charles W, Admiralty Civilian, Thetis, 3 June 1939

HORNE, John G, Lieutenant Colonel, RM, Chatham, 10 August 1929

HORNE, Reginald J, Leading Sick Berth Attendant, D/M 19542, RN Hospital, Plymouth, 22 October 1928

HORNE, William J D, Painter 1c, D/M 5158, Vivid, 2 April 1933

HORNER, Frederick W, Chief Petty Officer, 199744, Carlisle, 10 November 1920

HORNSBY, Stanley H, Warrant Shipwright, Theseus, 23 November 1918

HORNSSY, Frederick, Petty Officer, 116222, Vivid, 18 April 1923

HORROCKS, Arthur R, Engine Room Artificer Apprentice, M 34515, Fisgard, 9 November 1921

HORSHAM, Sidney, Able Seaman, J 13230, Veteran, 19 January 1922

HORSLER, Cyril G, Boy Servant, L 12399, President, 15 December 1919

HORSLEY, Ernest W, Leading Cook's Mate, M 7602, Pembroke, 14 March 1919

HORSMAN, Harry R, Admiralty Civilian, Thetis, 3 June 1939
HORSPOLE, John H, Able Seaman, J 108949, Pembroke, 9 September 1929
HORSPOOL, Leslie G, Chief Engine Room Artificer 2c, M 6613, Pembroke, 29 March 1927
HORSWELL, Alfred R, Petty Officer, J 16410, Vernon, 5 June 1928
HORTON, Bertie W J, Leading Victualling Assistant, M 4640, Caroline, 10 June 1920
HORTON, Edwin, Chief Stoker, 299022 (Dev), Hydrangea, 22 May 1919
HORTON, Horace W, Marine, X 560 (Ply), Queen Elizabeth, 8 April 1935
HORTON, James, Able Seaman, J 102952, Hood, 25 November 1923
HORTON, James A, Private, RMLI, 17932 (Ply), 3rd Battalion, RM, 1 December 1918
HOSEY, Edward, Stoker 1c, K 64954, Repulse, 11 July 1925
HOSKIN, Albert L, Boy 2c, JX 126819, Impregnable, 1 January 1927
HILL, Henry, Dockyard Fitter, civilian, H.29, 9 August 1926, accidentally killed
HOSKING, Norman V, Marine, X 1743 (Ply), RM Plymouth Division, 6 January 1938
HOSKINS, Alfred, Seaman, RNR, X 17783 A, St Delphine (Boscawen), 9 March 1939
HOSSEU, Said M, Officer's Cook 1c, Afrikander, 5 July 1920
HOSTLER, Thomas W, Officer's Steward 2c, L 3592, Victory, 10 March 1920
HOTHAM, Robert, Boy 2c, JX 153869, St Vincent, 23 January 1938
HOTSTON, Albert, Stoker Petty Officer, P/K 57765, Victory, 22 April 1933
HOUFE, William L, Signalman, J 50197, Dolphin, 28 November 1922
HOUGH, Harold J, Ordinary Seaman, J 115155, Benbow, 25 May 1927
HOUGHTON, Charles A H, Able Seaman, D/J 51607, Vivid, 1 February 1931
HOUGHTON, James E, Deck Hand, RNR, SD 5090, Colleen, 8 March 1919
HOUGHTON, Reginald R R, Engineer Lieutenant, RNR, Camito, 27 February 1919
HOUGHTON, Walter C, Engine Room Artificer 2c, M 14971, Philomel, 23 December 1927
HOULDSWORTH, Harold J, Sub Lieutenant, President, 23 February 1919
HOULIHAN, James, Private, RM, S 14804 (Deal), RM Labour Corps, 14 November 1918
HOUNSEL, Stephen J P, Able Seaman, P/JX 139937, Royal Navy, 20 March 1938
HOURIHANE, Daniel, Stoker 1c, K 56500, Thunderer, 23 March 1926
HOURIHANE, Patrick, Leading Stoker, D/K 22319, Berwick, 2 April 1933
HOUSE, Joseph, Engineer Lieutenant, Verulam, 4 September 1919
HOUSE, Leslie V, Able Seaman, D/JX 135005, Hunter, 13 May 1937
HOUSE, Samuel J, Shipwright 2c, 344854, Auricula, 24 February 1919
HOUSE, Samuel R, Chief Stoker, P/KX 88125, Royal Navy, 8 May 1936
HOW, Alfred, Stoker Petty Officer, K 3435, Wistaria, 27 December 1919
HOW, Frank B, Private, RMLI, 9953 (Ch), Agincourt, 21 January 1919
HOWARD, Albert J, Marine, 14972 (Po), Furious, 23 May 1926
HOWARD, Alfred J, Able Seaman, C/JX 126592, Cardiff, 5 July 1937
HOWARD, Andrew, Captain, RAF (ex-Assistant Paymaster, RNVR), RAF (ex-Caribbean), 28 October 1919
HOWARD, Atholl C, Schoolmaster (CWO), Excellent, 28 February 1936
HOWARD, Ernest, Deck Hand, RNR, SD 2125, Halcyon, 1 March 1919
HOWARD, John, Greaser, MMR, 927433, Eaglet, 20 November 1918
HOWARD, Ronald, Ordinary Seaman, C/SSX 18584, Pembroke, 10 January 1937
HOWARD-CROCKETT, Edward W, Lieutenant, Wallflower, 13 December 1929
HOWARTH, Edward R A, Cook, MMR, 803012, Redoubtable, 18 February 1919
HOWE, Arthur G, Petty Officer, 209255, Gibraltar (ex-PC.72), 25 June 1921
HOWE, Desmond J, Able Seaman, J 72191, Seawolf, 15 September 1921
HOWE, Edward, Engine Room Artificer 3c, M 13672, Speedy, 19 April 1921
HOWE, Ernest S R, Boy 1c, J 101273, Weymouth, 1 June 1922
HOWE, James W, Marine, 215519 (Po), RM Portsmouth Division, 8 September 1937
HOWE, Thomas, Private, RMLI, S 6950 (Ch), President III, 4 December 1918
HOWELL, Aubrey W J, Stoker Petty Officer, P/K 58588, Barham, 9 March 1939
HOWELL, David, Petty Officer Mechanic, F 2722, Armoured Car Division, Russia, 20 November 1918
HOWELL, George, Boy 1c, J 99576, Marlborough, 24 April 1922
HOWELL, George H, Able Seaman, J 11297, Centurion, 31 July 1922
HOWELL, Harold G, Engine Room Artificer, D/MX 50785, Thetis, 3 June 1939
HOWELL, Harry, Able Seaman, J 92392, Vega, 14 November 1928
HOWELL, Reginald, Stoker Petty Officer, K 18653, Ladybird, 8 October 1927
HOWELL, Thomas C S, Trimmer, RNR, TS 6651, Eaglet, 28 February 1920
HOWELL, William J, Chief Engine Room Artificer 1c, 269099, Seabear, 21 June 1919
HOWELLS, Charles W, Seaman, RNR, A 2444, Trewta Y Tres, steamship, 4 January 1919
HOWES, George A, Able Seaman, J 105307, St Genny, 12 January 1930
HOWES, James, Stoker 1c, K 23105 (Ch), L.55, 4 June 1919
HOWLETT, Harold, Boy 2c, JX 145007, Ganges, 31 January 1936
HOWLETT, Walter G, Boy 2c, J 113957, Ganges, 13 January 1926
HOY, Alfred J, Officer's Cook 1c, 363365, Sarepta, 2 September 1919
HOYE, Albert C, Stoker 1c, SS 125865, Victory, 27 November 1921
HOYLAND, Frederick A, Leading Seaman, P/J 108745, Excellent, 26 November 1931
HOYLE, William, Shipwright 2c, M 7409, Marlborough, 12 August 1920

HUBBARD, Frederick, Deck Hand, RNR, DA 3032, Vintage, 23 November 1918
HUBBARD, John E, Ordinary Seaman, MMR, 909321, Eaglet, 19 April 1919
HUBBER, Frederick G, Electrical Artificer 3c, D/M 46203, Defiance, 29 March 1931
HUBBLE, Walter J H, Able Seaman, C/J 62699, Pembroke, 2 February 1938
HUCKIN, Reginald A, Able Seaman, J 9676, M.1, 2 June 1921
HUDSON, Dudley J T, Leading Steward, C/LX 20555, Jervis, 29 August 1939
HUDSON, Herbert, Stoker Petty Officer, P/K 55909, Stronghold,

23 August 1934

HUDSON, John A, Engineer Commander, Vindictive, 1 August 1922

HUDSON, John F, Leading Telegraphist, D/J 75323, Queen Elizabeth, 28 October 1933

HUDSON, John S, Ordinary Seaman, P/JX 141980, Barham, 9 December 1937

HUDSON, Joseph, Ordinary Seaman, J 111510, Valerian, 22 October 1926

HUDSON, Nathaniel, Private, RM, S 2344 (Deal), 149th RN Field Ambulance, RM Medical Unit, RND, 27 November 1918

HUGGETT, William H, Stoker Petty Officer, P/K 62459, Delphinium, 10 January 1931

HUGHES, Alfred S, Chief Engine Room Artificer 2c, D/M 12699, Danae, 31 May 1933

HUGHES, Arthur F, Stoker 1c, K 56690, Durban, 28 August 1922

HUGHES, Cecil H, Stoker 1c, P/KX 79864, Iron Duke, 5 November 1930

HUGHES, Dick A, Petty Officer, J 11582, Impregnable, 28 September 1922

HUGHES, Ifor L, Lieutenant, RNR, Ramillies, 26 July 1926

HUGHES, John F, Ordinary Seaman, P/SSX 23092, RN Barracks Portsmouth, 14 November 1937

HUGHES, Joseph C, Petty Officer Cook, P/MX 48198, Thetis, 3 June 1939

HUGHES, Robert, Ordinary Seaman, J 99237, Ambrose, 11 June 1922

HUGHES, Robert S P, Able Seaman, 216567, Cricket, 28 July 1920

HUGHES, Trevor H, Able Seaman, D/JX 130400, Adventure, 22 January 1935

HUGHES, William, Trimmer, MMR, 934705, Vindex, 19 March 1919

HUGHES, William H, Corporal, RM, 17759 (Ply), Diligence, 14 December 1925

HUGHES, William, Able Seaman, SS 3214, Norseman, 22 February 1919

HUGHES, Wilson, Marine, 17810 (Ply), Emperor of India, 20 February 1928

HUGHSON, William, Seaman, RNR, B 4848, Valverda, steamship, 22 December 1918

HULL, Herbert O, Leading Stoker, P/K 21458, Victory, 26 March 1931

HULSE, George T, Able Seaman, J 98409, Marlborough, 23 October 1926

HULSE, William, Boilermaker, MMR, 89596, Teutonic, 23 December 1918

HUME, Frank, Telegraphist, J 28980, Pembroke, 23 October 1921

HUME, John H D, Able Seaman, J 16805, Marlborough, 4 February 1929

HUME, Walter J, Seaman, RNR, B 4017, Hawaker, steamship, 19 November 1918

HUME, Wellington B, Engineer Commander, Carysfort, 17 January 1925

HUME-GOODIER, Robert S, Commander, RNR, Royal Naval Reserve, 6 November 1930

HUMM, William, Leading Stoker, 303310, Victory II, 5 December 1919

HUMPAGE, William T, Officer's Cook 1c, L 6176, New Zealand, 29 December 1918

HUMPHREY, Frank, Steward, MMR, Iolaire, 1 January 1919

HUMPHREY, Frank A, Leading Stoker, P/K 65561, Osiris, 10 February 1931

HUMPHREY, Fred, Able Seaman, J 23348 (Po), Royal Sovereign, 6 July 1920

HUMPHREY, George, Petty Officer, J 7069, Victory, 15 December 1925

HUMPHREY, Wallace E, Telegraphist, J 60949, Victory, 27 October 1927

HUMPHREYS, Arthur F, Paymaster Commander, Curacoa, 6 August 1935

HUMPHREYS, Ernest E, Lieutenant, RNVR, Tarlair, 14 January 1919

HUMPHREYS, James W, Marine, 22085 (Ch), Royal Sovereign, 2 July 1930

HUMPHREYS, Thomas H, Signalman, 221190, Cambrian, 16 February 1919

HUMPHREYS, William G, Leading Seaman, J 53757, Ramillies, 9 June 1928

HUMPHRIES, Morgan, Able Seaman, 204595, Seabear, 5 June 1926

HUMPHRYES, John, Able Seaman, J 25494, Hawkins, 20 September 1920

HUNN, Leslie W, Admiralty Civilian, Thetis, 3 June 1939

HUNT, Edward W C, Ordinary Seaman, J 48744 (Po), Ladybird, 2 October 1919

HUNT, Francis, Marine, 15139 (Ply), Erebus, 6 February 1930

HUNT, Frederick, Able Seaman, RNVR, Bristol Z 74, Indus, 3 February 1919

HUNT, Frederick A, Chief Petty Officer, P/J 10673, Ladybird, 4 November 1932

HUNT, Herbert, Leading Seaman, J 79164, Pembroke, 31 December 1926

HUNT, James, Seaman, Newfoundland RNR, X 1986, Vivid, 3 December 1918

HUNT, John T, Warrant Engineer, Rugby, 22 September 1920

HUNT, Percy S, Private, RMLI, 18181 (Ch), 188th Brigade Machine Gun Company, RND, 2 July 1919

HUNT, Richard H H, Officer's Steward 2c, L 5615, Oakley, 11 September 1919

HUNTER, Bessie S, Steward, WRNS, G 2066, Women's Royal Naval Service, 15 March 1919

HUNTER, George C, Leading Trimmer, RNR, ST 2555, Beluga, 15 February 1919

HUNTER, Gordon, Leading Telegraphist, J 35039, Shikari, 18 June 1924

HUNTER, John A, Telegraphist, P/J 112421, FAA, 822 Sqn, aircraft No.918, Furious, 7 January 1936

HUNTER, Joseph, Stoker 1c, K 6497, Pembroke, 14 March 1919

HUNTER, Lucy A, Steward, WRNS, G 2508, Women's Royal Naval Service, RAF Eastbourne, 18 November 1918

HUNTER, William F, Supply Assistant, P/MX 46492, Victory, 2 June 1933

HUNTINGFORD, George T, Able Seaman, J 13272, Barham, 16 October 1923

HUNTINGFORD, Walter L, Lieutenant Colonel, RM, RM Deal, 17 March 1933

HURD, Edwin G, Officer's Cook 1c, L 411, Dolphin, 29 April 1928

HURLEY, Joseph, Able Seaman, J 12837, Pembroke, 2 July 1928

HURN, Henry T, Engine Room Artificer 4c, M 11515 (Po), Carlisle, 28 January 1921

HURR, James D, Deck Hand, RNR, DA 11974, Comrade, 14 November 1918

HURST, Cecil C, Able Seaman, RNVR, Bristol Z 4594, Hood Battalion, RND, 22 February 1919

HURST, George G, Stoker 2c, MC 956, Duchess of Richmond, 28 June 1919

HUSKINSON, Herbert, Leading Stoker, C/KX 78924, Cairo, 5 November 1936

HUSSEY, Percy, Boy Telegraphist, J 83490, King George V, 13 September 1919

HUTCHENCE, Harry, Stoker 1c, K 22154 (Po), K.5, 20 January 1921

HUTCHIESON, George P, Sub Lieutenant, RNVR, Pactolus, 14 December 1920

HUTCHINGS, Ernest, Able Seaman, J 41101 (Ch), Vittoria, 31 August 1919

HUTCHINGS, Richard H, Chief Stoker, 302620, Birmingham, 10 March 1923

HUTCHINSON, Ernest H, Lieutenant, RNR, Royal Naval Reserve, 10 January 1920

HUTCHINSON, George M, Able Seaman, D/SSX 16796, Hasty, 20 May 1939
HUTCHINSON, Henry, Captain, RNR, Royal Naval Reserve, 9 October 1920
HUTCHINSON, Thomas, Private, RMLI, 21149 (Po), RM HQ, 8 April 1920
HUTCHISON, George S H, Lieutenant Commander, RNR, Royal Naval Reserve, 21 January 1936
HUTT, Ralph, Able Seaman, J 15181, Crocus, 15 August 1925
HUTT, Reuben J, Chief Yeoman of Signals, P/J 51430, Royal Navy, 26 August 1939
HUTT, Victor S, Marine, X 1142 (Po), St Vincent, 7 January 1937
HUTTON, Illtyd A R, Commander, Tamar, 2 April 1921
HUTTON, James, Able Seaman, P/JX 139667, Resource, 21 November 1937
HUTTON, John, Leading Stoker, 286939, Kildorrey, 14 January 1919
HUXFORD, Edward, Leading Boatman, 204643, HM Coastguard Station Cleggan, 12 February 1919
HUXLEY, Arthur G, Engine Room Artificer 1c, 271303, Renown, 9 March 1922
HUXLEY, Robert, Chief Petty Officer, P/J 14199, Vernon, 15 December 1932
HUXTABLE, William, Stoker Petty Officer, 217062, Cambrian, 16 August 1921
HUZZEY, Herbert C, Engine Room Artificer 2c, M 36944, Vindictive, 23 July 1929

HYAMS, Philip, Stoker 1c, SS 117451, Chester, 17 December 1919
HYATT, Archibald A, Cook, P/M 38493, Dunedin, 3 February 1939
HYDE, Patrick, Stoker 1c, 300251, Spear, 25 September 1919
HYNE, Bernard S F, Marine, X 1498 (Po), RM Deal, 11 January 1935
HYNES, James F, Leading Seaman, J 26607, New Zealand, 5 December 1919

I

IDDON, Austin N, Telegraphist, J 112380, Pembroke, 6 December 1929
IDE, Frederick, Chief Stoker, 276281, Victory, 17 May 1919
IDLE, Richard, Stoker Petty Officer, K 59696, Revenge, 13 July 1927

IGUANEY, Antonio, Officer's Cook 1c, 363966, Warspite, 22 December 1929

ILES, Alexander J E, Boy Servant, L 12074, Agamemnon, 19 August 1919
ILIFF, Edward, Engineer Commander, Concord, 29 September 1932

IMMS, David H, Commissioned Boatswain, Portsmouth Dockyard, 2 June 1927

INCHCAPE, the Earl of, Honorary Captain, RNR, Royal Naval Reserve, 23 May 1932
INGLIS, William H, Officer's Cook, C/MX 59002, Pembroke II, 4 April 1939
INGOLDSBY, George, Able Seaman, J 100648, Rodney, 29 May 1928
INGRAM, Arthur J, Private, RMLI, 11964 (Po), Portsmouth Division, RMLI, 20 January 1919
INGRAM, Frederick, Stoker Petty Officer, C/K 59866, Skipjack, 21 May 1937
INIGHT, Walter, Leading Seaman, J 10959 (Po), K.5, 20 January 1921

IRLAM, Wilfred, Able Seaman, SS 2770, Leander, 1 March 1919
IRONS, Harold R, Able Seaman, J 114442, Marshall Soult, 4 August 1929
IRVEN, Herbert, Chief Stoker, 308877, Tomahawk, 5 August 1922
IRVEN, Paul L H D, Lieutenant, FAA, 462 Sqn, Glorious, 25 April 1932
IRVINE, James, Greaser, MMR, 886886, Ireland, 7 January 1919
IRVINE, Walter R, Engine Room Artificer 4c, M 31608, Ramillies, 9 March 1919
IRWIN, Hugh, Able Seaman, 229237, Afrikander, 9 November 1921

ISAAC, David, Stoker, RNR, S 4910, Attentive III, 28 November 1918
ISAAC, Frederick W, Chief Gunner, Changuinola, 30 January 1919
ISAACS, George J, Officer's Cook 2c, L 5485, Pembroke, 15 August 1922
ISAACSON, Egerton W, Captain, Victory, 31 August 1929
ISMAIL, Abubakar, Seedie, 2/354, Folkestone, 18 March 1931
ISOM, Arthur W, Leading Seaman, J 8084, Ramillies, 1 October 1920

IVEAGH, Earl, Honorary Lieutenant, RNR, Royal Naval Reserve, 7 October 1927
IVES, Sydney J, Leading Seaman, J 24083, Diomede, 4 March 1923

IZZARD, Cyril R, Telegraphist, J 44080, Pembroke, 14 October 1922
IZZARD, Henry W, Engineman, RNR, TS 623, Pavlova, 17 December 1918
IZZARD, Thomas, Private, RMLI, 15267 (Ch), Sapphire, 12 December 1918

J

JACKETT, Albert E, Stoker 2c, K 63160, Vivid, 26 August 1924
JACKMAN, Maurice S, Shipwright Apprentice, MX 53959, RN Barracks Portsmouth, 9 July 1939
JACKSON, Arthur F, Able Seaman, J 41800 (Ch), Verulam, 4 September 1919
JACKSON, Arthur T, Able Seaman, 230276, Vivid (ex-Lord Nelson), 21 August 1919
JACKSON, Cyrus E T, Leading Seaman, J 19496, Vernon, 12 January 1926
JACKSON, Edward V, Engine Room Artificer 4c, C/M 39396, M.2, 29 January 1932
JACKSON, Ernest W, Leading Signalman, J 30788, Dwarf, 14 September 1924
JACKSON, Garibaldi, Engine Room Artificer 3c, M 33565, Coventry, 8 March 1923
JACKSON, George, Engineman, RNR, ES 2287, Halcyon, 17 April 1919
JACKSON, John, Able Seaman, RNVR, Mersey Z 1564, Victory, 17 February 1919
JACKSON, Joseph W, Leading Signalman, J 5922, Tiger, 30 March 1930
JACKSON, Peter F O, Act/Chief Engine Room Artificer, C/MX 46112, Thetis, 3 June 1939
JACKSON, Stanley, Engineer Captain, Thetis (Dolphin), 3 June 1939
JACKSON, Stanley, Telegraphist, J 77956, FAA, 440 Flight, Hermes, 3 April 1928
JACKSON, William S, Lieutenant Commander, RNR, Orcades, steamship, 24 March 1924
JACOBS, Albert E, Leading Seaman, C/J 96297, M.2, 29 January 1932
JACOBS, Edward R, Stoker Petty Officer, P/K 63515, Victory, 24 February 1934
JACOBS, Thomas E G, Petty Officer, 205244, Victory, 10 November 1920
JACQUES, Frederick, Stoker 1c, 295765, New Zealand, 10 May 1919
JACQUES, James A, Leading Telegraphist, P/J 40558, President II, 5 August 1936
JAGGER, Norman V, Engine Room Artificer 4c, M 7104, Theseus II, 15 December 1919
JAGO, Frank, Supply Chief Petty Officer, M 4557, Vivid, 14 July 1927
JAKEMAN, Edward V, Petty Officer, J 26111, Active, 5 April 1930
JAKEMAN, George A, Chief Engine Room Artificer 2c, C/M 28793, Pembroke, 20 February 1936
JAMA, Mohamed, Seedie, Aden 411, Southampton, 15 November 1921
JAMES, Albert, Armourers Crew, M 12815, Bacchante, 23 March 1919
JAMES, Arthur G, Leading Stoker, K 14152, Valerian, 22 October 1926
JAMES, Arthur G, Stoker 1c, K 58470, ML.249, 25 December 1922
JAMES, Frederick D, Headmaster, Victory, 17 February 1927
JAMES, Harold, Petty Officer Steward, D/L 10647, Drake, 7 January 1934
JAMES, Henry, Stoker 1c, K 44628, Prince Eugene, 18 November 1918
JAMES, John R, Chief Engine Room Artificer 1c, 272512, Fisgard, 31 March 1925
JAMES, Richard B, Petty Officer, D/J 20826, Codrington, 6 August 1934
JAMES, Robert P, Officer's Steward 4c, L 13416, Ramillies, 23 June 1922
JAMES, Robert, Able Seaman, P/JX 131872, Effingham, 25 December 1933
JAMES, Sidney F, Act/Warrant Cook, Drake, 15 March 1939
JAMES, Thomas D, Able Seaman, P/JX 132157, Adventure, 7 June 1933
JAMES, Walter, Able Seaman, J 27900, Vivid, 31 March 1920
JAMIE, Donald F, Able Seaman, J 52449, Valerian, 22 October 1926
JAMIESON, Andrew, Lieutenant, Chatham Division, RMLI, RMLI, 13 August 1919
JAMIESON, John, Able Seaman, J 24771, Vivid, 27 February 1919
JAMIESON, John, Stoker Petty Officer, 298536, Brisk, 25 November 1918
JAMIESON, Robert, Able Seaman, P/J 102721, Cornwall, 13 September 1931
JAMIESON, William J M, Ordinary Seaman, P/SSX 15525, Courageous, 8 May 1935
JAMISON, Antony G, Lieutenant (E), Thetis, 3 June 1939
JANE, James H, Stoker 1c, K 56194, Warspite, 4 March 1923
JANES, Frederick, Ordinary Seaman, J 89461, Achilles, 24 December 1918
JANION, Arthur C A, Paymaster Lieutenant Commander, Southampton II, RN Base, Ceylon (Sri Lanka), 14 November 1922
JAQUES, Frank, Engineer Commander, Royal Navy, 26 July 1933
JARDINE, Peter G, Chief Motor Mechanic, RNVR, MB 1721, Egmont, 6 May 1919
JARMAN, Frederick J, Mechanician, 221248, Coventry, 8 August 1919
JARMAN, Thomas W H, Company Sergeant Major, RMLI, 5372 (Ply), Ambitious, 10 February 1919
JARRETT, Sidney R W, Able Seaman, C/J 100140, M.2, 29 January 1932
JARVIS, Clifford, Able Seaman, J 61069, Pembroke, 16 January 1923
JARVIS, Francis H, Officer's Cook, 360324, Excellent, 26 February 1929
JARVIS, Harold W, Leading Stoker, K 488 (Ch), Verulam, 4 September 1919
JARVIS, James H, Able Seaman, RNVR, London Z 3110, Hawke Battalion, RND, 30 November 1918
JARVIS, Thomas A, Boy 2c, JX 159123, St Vincent, 6 August 1938
JAY, George H, Trimmer, RNR, TS 7386, Idaho, 10 May 1919

JEANS, George, Able Seaman, J 110233, Resource, 18 February 1930
JEEMS, Herbert, Stoker 1c, K 57433, Chatham, 7 December 1924
JEFFERIES, Archibald J, Boy 1c, P /JX 150264, Glasgow, 12 October 1937
JEFFERS, James, Stoker 1c, 295885, Woolwich, 31 January 1933
JEFFERSON, Ronald G, Engineering Commander, Royal Navy, 4 November 1938
JEFFERSON, Sydney, Private, RMLI, 16706 (Ch), Chatham Division, RMLI, 9 February 1919
JEFFERSON, Thomas, Deck Hand, RNR, DA 11417, Ethelwulf, 1 December 1918
JEFFERY, Arthur S, Stoker Petty Officer, D/K 18457, Drake, 13 February 1935
JEFFERY, Bertie, Able Seaman, J 11870, Valkyrie, 26 April 1921
JEFFERY, Ernest H, Private, RMLI, 7074, RM Headquarters, 5 June 1921
JEFFERY, George H, Able Seaman, J 179, Vivid, 26 February 1926
JEFFES, Charles B, Sick Berth Attendant, M 36035, Witherington, 3 January 1927
JEFFREY, Archibald, Able Seaman, J 89758, Kiawo, 29 August 1927
JEFFREY, Robert, Deck Hand, RNR, DA 5024, Jaboo II, 4 March 1919
JEFFRY, Leonard N, Shipwright 3c, M 22076, Emerald, 10 October 1927

JELF, Christopher B, Lieutenant, FAA, 800 Sqn, Courageous, 22 March 1937
JENKINS, Albert J, Engineman, RNR, ES 2715, Pactolus, 25 November 1918
JENKINS, Arthur, Private, RMLI, 17498 (Ch), RM, 6th Battalion, 8 September 1919
JENKINS, David J, Stoker 1c, SS 120469, Catspaw, 31 December 1919
JENKINS, Herbert, Private, RMLI, 14914 (Ply), Warspite, 24 August 1919
JENKINS, John H, Stoker Petty Officer, 310627, Vivid, 2 July 1920
JENKINS, John J, Stoker Petty Officer, U 898, Victory, 4 July 1919
JENKINS, Mortimer A, Ordinary Seaman, J 79190, Saltburn, 4 August 1919
JENKINS, William H, Engineman, RNR, E V 158, Vivid, 14 January 1933
JENKINS, William J, Stoker 1c, D/K 64793, Centurion, 15 May 1938
JENKINSON, George W, Deck Hand, RNR, DA 16193, Falstaff, 16 December 1918
JENKINSON, Harry, Gunner, RMA, RMA S 2216, RMA Eastney, 26 February 1919
JENKINSON, James H, Stoker 1c, SS 120091, Pembroke, 19 November 1919
JENNER, Harold J, Able Seaman, J 8826, Afrikander, 27 December 1921
JENNER, Harry D, Commissioned Gunner, Delight, 28 August 1935
JENNINGS, Francis C H, Lieutenant, Blue Sky, tender to Queen Elizabeth, 12 June 1922
JENNINGS, Frederick H, Boy 2c, J 113579, Ganges, 25 June 1925
JENNINGS, Harold, Electrical Artificer 2c, M 4843, Southampton, 6 August 1921
JENNINGS, Harry C, Lieutenant, L.55, 4 June 1919
JENNINGS, Henry, Stoker, RNR, U 1672, Arrogant, 26 February 1919
JENNINGS, Rodney P, Py/Midshipman, RNR, Peshawur, liner, 28 October 1936
JENNINGS, Thomas J, Stoker 1c, P/KX 77678, Whitley, 21 August 1939
JEPSON, Charles F, Commander, Admiralty, Plans Division, 4 January 1931
JERMY, John T, Signalman, J 111554, Durban, 22 August 1930
JERRARD, James A, Leading Steward, P/L 8226, Curacoa, 25 January 1936
JERVIS, Geoffrey, Boy 1c, JX 129450, Danae, 11 January 1929
JERVIS, William, Chief Petty Officer, 115760, HM Coast Guard Station Par, 28 January 1919
JESSOP, Charles J, Boy 2c, J 111087, Impregnable, 15 May 1925
JEWELL, Courtney, Officer's Cook 2c, D/L 14669, Vivid, 1 May 1932
JEWELL, Henry G, Able Seaman, J 48749, M.1, 12 November 1925

JOHN, Edwin, Stoker 1c, K 35290, Liverpool, 7 March 1919
JOHNS, Edward, Stoker 1c, K 56073, Constance, 26 March 1922
JOHNS, Richard, Leading Stoker, 305812, Pomone, 12 September 1920
JOHNS, William J V, Boatman, J 43841, Wireless Telegraph Station Kingstown, 20 December 1920
JOHNSON, Albert J, Stoker 1C, K 8490, Tiger, 26 August 1929
JOHNSON, Arthur, Shipwright 1c, D/M 34810, Drake, 24 March 1934
JOHNSON, Arthur G, Shipwright 4c, M 31798, Colossus, 20 November 1918
JOHNSON, Charles F, Chief Engine Room Artificer 2c, 270756, Dolphin, 14 February 1919
JOHNSON, Edwin G, Act/Leading Stoker, K 20107, L.24, 10 January 1924
JOHNSON, Ernest E, Telegraphist, RNVR, Palace Z 1647, Hughli, Royal Fleet Auxiliary, 26 April 1919
JOHNSON, Ernest H, Leading Seaman, J 97617, Pembroke, 20 February 1927
JOHNSON, Ethelburt A, Chief Wardmaster, 346516, Ganges, 16 February 1922
JOHNSON, Frank P, Telegraphist, J 50081, Spear, 4 September 1920
JOHNSON, Fred A, Skipper, RNR, Vambery, 22 January 1935
JOHNSON, Frederick R M, Captain, Caledon, 18 June 1939
JOHNSON, George E, Ordinary Seaman, RAN, 6418, Australia (RAN), 7 April 1920
JOHNSON, George F, Private, RMLI, 19362 (Ch), Sapphire, 11 December 1918
JOHNSON, James, Ty/Skipper, RNR, John Corwarder, 28 November 1918
JOHNSON, John, Stoker 1c, KX 78536, Centaur, 12 July 1930
JOHNSON, John E, Ordinary Seaman, MMR, 977324, Crescent, 30 December 1918
JOHNSON, John N, Stoker Petty Officer, K 927, Durban, 4 January 1924
JOHNSON, John S, Leading Supply Assistant, P/MX 47183, RN Hospital, Haslar, 28 August 1938
JOHNSON, John W, Shipwright 3c, 343852 (Ch), Cicala, 4 September 1920
JOHNSON, Josephus, Boy Servant, L 13750, President, 3 June 1922
JOHNSON, Leslie T, Telegraphist, J 94125, Victory, 28 January 1928
JOHNSON, Oliver W, Stoker 1c, C/KX 85597, Valiant, 28 August 1936
JOHNSON, Robert, Shipwright 3c, M 13305 (Ch), Myrtle, 15 July 1919
JOHNSON, Sidney, Able Seaman, P/SSX 12444, Dauntless, 27 August 1930
JOHNSON, William, Leading Seaman, J 63059, Columbine, 15 August 1928
JOHNSON, William, Stoker 1c, D/KX 81784, Hermes, 10 February 1935
JOHNSON, William, Stoker 1c, SS 123848, Mutine, 7 September 1921
JOHNSON, William, Supply Petty Officer, P/M 38276, Durban, 1 April 1933
JOHNSON, William H, Chief Skipper, RNR, Royal Naval Reserve, 15 January 1938
JOHNSON, William H, Stoker 1c, K 57511 (Po), Hood, 22 May 1935
JOHNSON, William W, Marine, 18124 (Po), RM Portsmouth Division, 8 October 1935
JOHNSTON, Andrew, Able Seaman, RNVR, Tyneside Z 6830, Drake Battalion, RND, 10 March 1919
JOHNSTON, Harry, Stoker, RNR, S 5741, Pembroke, 26 February 1919
JOHNSTON, James, Gunner, RMA, RMA 7527 (RFR B), RNAS Armoured Cars, 11 December 1918
JOHNSTON, John, Chief Engine Room Artificer 2c, 271071, Glasgow, 19 December 1918
JOHNSTON, John J, Deck Hand, RNR (Shetland Section), L 362, Balmoral, 5 December 1918
JOHNSTON, Joseph M, Able Seaman, J 2196 (Ch), Fame, 10 October 1919
JOHNSTON, Stewart R, Surgeon Commander, Medical Officer's Post Graduate Course, 13 December 1934
JOHNSTON, William, Commissioned Gunner, Carysfort, 4 November 1930
JOHNSTON, William, Ty/Sub Lieutenant, RNVR, Anson Battalion, RND, 17 November 1918
JOHNSTONE, Edward J, Stoker 1c, D/K 17268, Rodney, 22 May 1931
JOHNSTONE, Edwin G, Leading Stoker, K 20107, L.24, 10 January 1924

JOHNSTONE, Hope, Telegraphist Lieutenant, Victory, 19 April 1932
JOHNSTONE, John, Petty Officer, 200342, Victory, 26 October 1921
JOINER, Colin, Surgeon Lieutenant, Valerian, 22 October 1926
JOLLEY, John, Stoker Petty Officer, 126381, Vivid, 12 March 1919
JOLLEY, Leslie A, Writer, C/MX 30221, Achilles, 4 February 1935
JOLLY, Frederick, Able Seaman, J 83696, Victory, 9 November 1920
JONES, Albert, Private, RMLI, 14534 (Ply), 3rd Battalion, RM, 17 December 1918
JONES, Albert E, Able Seaman, D/J 98728, L.53, 14 October 1931
JONES, Arthur, Able Seaman, J 30864, Vernon, 31 May 1925
JONES, Arthur E, Deck Hand, RNR, SD 5097, Destiny, 7 February 1919
JONES, Benjamin J, Able Seaman, RNVR (Bugler), London Z 471, Anson Battalion, RND, 13 February 1919
JONES, Bertie, Petty Officer, J 20035, M.1, 12 November 1925
JONES, David A, Able Seaman, RNVR, Mersey 4/57, Vivid III, 10 February 1919
JONES, David R, Lieutenant, Vernon, 28 November 1921
JONES, David, Petty Officer, J 31300, Malaya, 26 February 1929
JONES, Denis J, Corporal, RM, X 765 (Ch), RM HQ Chatham, 25 April 1939
JONES, Derek H A, Py/Midshipman, RNR, Woodarra, steamship, 22 June 1928
JONES, Edward L, Ty/Lieutenant, RNR, Queen Victoria, 1 December 1918
JONES, Edward, Telegraphist, J 40462, Victory, 26 March 1919
JONES, Elias, Leading Seaman, RNVR, Wales Z 250, Corfe Castle, steamship, 19 November 1918
JONES, Elisha, Ordinary Seaman, J 78578 (Dev), Penarth, 4 February 1919
JONES, Ernest J, Able Seaman, J 105207, Queen Elizabeth, 24 February 1930
JONES, Francis J, Lieutenant (E), Excellent, Course, 30 November 1935
JONES, Francis P, Stoker 1c, K 23368, Vivid, 28 October 1923
JONES, Frank J, Private, RMLI, 16467 (Ply), 3rd Battalion, RM, 17 November 1920
JONES, Frederick J, Officer's Steward 4c, L 13948, Pembroke, 2 May 1923
JONES, George C, Able Seaman, RNVR, London Z 1211, Collingwood Battalion, RND, 5 March 1919
JONES, George S, Marine, X 93 (Po), RN Hospital, Haslar, 26 December 1934
JONES, George W, Leading Seaman, 206942, Pembroke I, 25 December 1919
JONES, Harold G, Petty Officer, J 7994, Dolphin, 13 October 1923
JONES, Harold, Signalman, RNVR, Mersey Z 3527, Vivid, 30 November 1918
JONES, Harry, Private, RMLI, S 74 (Ply), 2nd RM Battalion, RND, 25 June 1919
JONES, Henry, Commissioned Gunner, Adventure, 27 October 1930
JONES, Herbert F, Petty Officer, J 36662, Defiance, 24 December 1928
JONES, James A, Chief Stoker, 300369, Vivid, 15 November 1918
JONES, James, Leading Sick Berth Attendant, D/M 35544, RN Hospital, Plymouth, 14 August 1932
JONES, John, Cook, MMR, 898630, Limpet, Royal Fleet Auxiliary, 18 November 1918
JONES, John, Stoker 1c, K 40258, Hercules, 30 November 1918
JONES, John L, Chief Engine Room Artificer, D/MX 28769, Diomede, 1 September 1938
JONES, Leo F F, Able Seaman, J 17672, Iron Duke, 27 January 1922
JONES, Leonard T, Leading Cook, C/M 38155, Sandhurst, 2 December 1931
JONES, Myrddin E, Surgeon Lieutenant, Indomitable, 4 December 1918
JONES, Norman W B, Ordinary Seaman, SS 11859, Victory, 28 December 1921
JONES, Oswald O, Midshipman, Engineering Course, 17 August 1924
JONES, Richard, Engineman, RNR, ES 1696, Eaglet, 27 January 1919
JONES, Robert, Leading Stoker, C/KX 76100, Dolphin, 16 May 1935
JONES, Robert H, Able Seaman, C/JX 130702, Curlew, 5 July 1936
JONES, Samuel R, Able Seaman, J 24585, TB.34, torpedo boat, 4 February 1919
JONES, Sidney, Able Seaman, J 653, Vivid, 6 September 1919
JONES, Thomas C, Boy 2c, J 92056, Ganges II, 23 November 1918
JONES, Thomas H, Stoker 1c, K 7491, Vivid, 21 February 1919
JONES, Thomas I, Able Seaman, 237257, TB.36, torpedo boat, 13 April 1919
JONES, Thomas O, Private, RM, S 10412 (Deal), RM Labour Corps, 29 January 1919
JONES, Walter T C, Lieutenant Colonel, RM, Royal Marines, 16 August 1923
JONES, William F, Stoker Petty Officer, K 3646, Pembroke, 18 February 1919
JONES, William H, Stoker 1c, K 6202, Cornwall, 4 July 1930
JONES, William J, Commissioned Engineer, ex-Marlborough, 8 October 1922
JONES, William T, Stoker 1c, SS 111269 (Po), Penarth, 4 February 1919
JORDAN, Albert C, Able Seaman, P/JX 126823, Victory, 30 October 1933
JORDAN, Frederick L A, Able Seaman, J 36608, Speedy, 23 September 1922
JORDAN, John A, Private, RMLI, 18411 (Po), St Vincent, 19 December 1918
JORDAN, Richard, Stoker, RNR, S 4347, Magpie, 12 November 1918
JORDAN, Victor, Leading Stoker, K 22513, Victory, 8 December 1918
JOSSER, Sydney N, Boy 1c, J 112168, Malaya, 4 December 1926
JOURDAIN, David C, Paymaster Midshipman, Norfolk, 11 April 1939
JOWETT, Arthur R, Engine Room Artificer 1c, M 3910, Fisgard, 10 October 1925
JOYCE, Ralph, Stoker 1c, SS 118607 (Po), Kinross, 16 June 1919

JUDD, Alfred J, Stoker Petty Officer, K 1833, Speedy, 23 September 1922
JUDGE, Harry W F, Able Seaman, C/J 107145, Brilliant, 22 December 1933
JUDGE, William J, Corporal, RMLI, 17318 (Ch), Royal Marines HQ (ex-Vulcan), 9 October 1922
JUSTIN, Thomas H, Able Seaman, J 20176, Catspaw, 31 December 1919

K

KAN, Dow, Officer's Steward 3c, Tamar, 11 November 1924
KAY, Andrew B, Lieutenant, Pilot's Course, 16 August 1932
KAY, William, Engineman, RNR, ES 2222, Morning Star, 21 February 1919
KAYLL, Hugh O, Ty/Lieutenant, RNVR, Colleen, 11 December 1918

KEAN, Cuthbert, Trimmer, RNR, TS 946, Firefly, 4 March 1919
KEANS, Ernest H, Boy 1c, P/JX 143177, Victory, 4 May 1936
KEARN, George J, Able Seaman, J 15564, H.42, 23 March 1922
KEARNEY, Thomas E, Leading Boatman, 218553, HM Coast Guard Station Raffnay Head, 1 January 1921
KEAST, Daniel C, Officer's Steward 3c, L 10802, Vivid, 29 December 1923
KEATE, Harry A D, Lieutenant Commander, Vivid, 26 April 1925
KEEBLE, John E, Leading Supply Assistant, M 37378, Pembroke, 9 November 1928
KEEGAN, Denis L, Stoker 1c, P/K 66573, Hood, 15 October 1933
KEEHNEMUND, Edward (real name, but served as Edward Jarvis), Stoker 2c, SS 125807, Lowestoft, 30 September 1921
KEELING, Thomas, Gunner, RMA, RMA 15740, Minotaur, 21 November 1918
KEEN, William G, Leading Seaman, J 18263, Cleopatra, 3 November 1920
KEENAN, Daniel, Able Seaman, 230581, Ship or unit not listed, 5 August 1919
KEENAN, Louis Mc N, Supply Petty Officer, M 7655, Cicala, 4 September 1929
KEIGHLEY, Harold S, Sub Lieutenant, Julius, 8 January 1921
KEITH, Alexander, Leading Seaman, 195605, Glowworm, 25 August 1919
KEITH, John, Private, RM, S 1116 (Deal), RM Labour Corps, 28 June 1919
KEITH, William, Stoker 1c, K 54636, Lavatera, 27 February 1919
KELD, John R, Boy 1c, P/JX 140814, Barham, 16 March 1936
KELLAND, Harold V, Electrical Artificer 1c, P/M 8185, Victory, 25 August 1933
KELLAND, William, Able Seaman, 214072, Theseus, 5 December 1918
KELLAWAY, Frederick C, Signalman, J 24505 (Po), Penarth, 4 February 1919
KELLINGTON, Sydney R, Able Seaman, J 92220, St Genny, 12 January 1930
KELLY, Charles E, Marine, 18486 (Po), RN Hospital, Haslar, 1 April 1939
KELLY, Ernest, Able Seaman, D/J 109116, Londonderry, 17 July 1939
KELLY, Francis G, Deck Hand, RNR, DA 10799, Nairn, 10 January 1919
KELLY, Hugh, Marine, 18851 (Ply), Delhi, 17 October 1932
KELLY, James, Private, RM, S 15905 (Deal), RM Labour Corps, 7 February 1919
KELLY, John, Able Seaman, J 41061, Sir John Moore, 6 January 1919
KELLY, John, Trimmer, RNR, ST 609, Hecla II, 17 November 1918
KELLY, Sir John D, Admiral of the Fleet, Royal Navy, 4 November 1936
KELLY, John J, Able Seaman, MMR, 928448, Transfer, 9 January 1919
KELLY, John W, Marine, 24393 (Ch), Enterprise, 3 October 1928
KELLY, Lionel M, Lieutenant, RNR, Royal Naval Reserve, May 1922
KELLY, Phillip, Able Seaman, C/JX 134903, Tamar II, 9 December 1938
KELLY, Richard R E U, Py/Lieutenant, RM, Malaya, 27 August 1939

KEMBLE, George, Leading Stoker, K 10184, M.1, 12 November 1925
KEMP, Claud W N, Officer's Steward 2c, L 12749, St Genny, 12 January 1930
KEMP, John F, Corporal, RMLI, 13262 (Ch), 3rd Battalion, RM, 27 January 1919
KEMP, William C, 2nd Hand, RNR, DA 7474, Zaria, mercantile fleet auxiliary, 17 February 1919
KEMPSHALL, William A, Engine Room Artificer 2c, M 28880, Berwick, 16 February 1929
KENCHINGTON, Frederick W, Able Seaman, P/J 40267, Excellent, 24 March 1936
KENDALL, Alfred P, Painter 1c, C/MX 46708, Curlew, 5 July 1938
KENDALL, Frederick G H, Ordinary Seaman, J 103519, Birmingham, 25 January 1924
KENDALL, John G, Stoker 1c, K 24052 (Po), K.5, 20 January 1921
KENDRICK, Edward A, Able Seaman, D/JX 157904, Thetis, 3 June 1939
KENEFICK, Edward, Chief Stoker, K 190, Vivid, 31 December 1926
KENNA, John, Stoker 1c, C/K 65940, Cormorant, 13 April 1932
KENNARD, Alfred E, Stoker 1c, C/KX 78034, Anthony, 4 June 1938
KENNARD, Michael S, Able Seaman, J 10427, Wivern, 21 February 1928
KENNEDY, Alfred M, Able Seaman, J 10439, Vanessa, 9 September 1923
KENNEDY, Angus, Seaman, RNR, A 10014, Hecla, 12 March 1924
KENNEDY, Arthur F, Able Seaman, J 24122, Blenheim, 1 June 1921
KENNEDY, Michael, Private, RM, S 12959 (Deal), RM Labour Corps, 19 February 1919
KENNEDY, Thomas, Stoker 2c, KX 79070, Pembroke, 14 April 1928
KENNEDY, William O, Chief Engine Room Artificer 1c, 271897, Benbow, 9 September 1924
KENNETT, John G, Petty Officer, J 13074, King George V, 11 February 1919
KENNEY, Thomas W, Leading Stoker, C/KX 82462, Thetis, 3 June 1939
KENNINGTON, William J, Coastguardsman 3c, 185133, Colleen, 12 June 1921
KENNY, Michael, Stoker 1c, 175623, Indus, 18 March 1919
KENNY, Thomas M, Ordinary Seaman, J 86589, Canada, 1 December 1918
KENT, Arthur W, Leading Seaman, J 15182, M.1, 12 November 1925
KENT, Edward, Private, RMLI, S 1540 (Po), Portsmouth Division, RMLI, 2 February 1919
KENT, Henry E, Warrant Engineer, Royal Navy, 24 March 1928
KENT, William J, Ordinary Telegraphist, J 75161 (Ch), Penarth, 4 February 1919
KENYON, Herbert L D, Petty Officer, D/J 89788, Montrose, 22 November 1932
KENYON, Walter, Stoker 1c, SS 117527, Antrim, 8 November 1920
KEOGH, John A, Surgeon Commander, Pembroke, 5 February 1919
KEOHANE, Daniel, Petty Officer, 211781, Vivid, 9 February 1920
KERR, George, Marine, RM Chatham Division, 28 November 1935
KERR, Thomas, Boatman, 294815, HM Coast Guard Station Skibbereen, 17 November 1918
KERR, William, Engine Room Artificer 2c, M 9383, Pembroke, 21 October 1923

KERSHAW, Cecil, Able Seaman, J 83717, Malaya, 24 January 1922

KETCHLEY, Reginald E, Warrant Wardmaster, Royal Navy, 7 November 1921

KETT, Harry, Deck Hand, RNR, DA 8085, Qui Saits, 3 December 1918

KETTLE, Alfred, Shipwright 2c, 345932, Lucia, 10 March 1919

KETTLEY, Victor, Able Seaman, J 95438, Victory, 16 December 1926

KEY, Frederick G, Officer's Steward 2c, L 3217, Vulcan, 8 March 1919

KEYES, Arthur W, Officer's Cook 1c, L 10311, Fantome, 19 November 1920

KIDD, Frederick J, Leading Steward, D/LX 21491, Seal, 25 June 1939

KIDNEY, James, Leading Seaman, J 53085, M.1, 12 November 1925

KIDSTON, James, Able Seaman, D/JX 130799, Capetown, 3 September 1935

KILBURN, William A, Leading Stoker, P/KX 80210, Cornwall, 2 September 1934

KILLHAM, Frederick (served as Charles Frederick Hills), Steward 1c, L 3205, Capetown, 6 December 1926

KILLIAN, Albert E, Shipwright 2c, 346954, Gibraltar, 13 June 1919

KILMARTIN, James, Stoker 1c, K 32248, Pembroke, 24 February 1919

KILVERT, Robert E, Major, RM, Barham, 28 March 1923

KING, Albert, Marine, 16262 (Ch), 11th RM Battalion, 29 October 1922

KING, Albert E, Leading Stoker, K 60859, Royal Navy, 11 March 1929

KING, Arthur J, Stoker Petty Officer, K 19344, Sutton, 5 April 1928

KING, Edgar W, Leading Seaman, 233441, St Vincent, 20 December 1918

KING, Edward, Stoker 1c, 281599, Wildfire, 13 February 1919

KING, Ernest, Engineman, RNR, ES 341, P Fannon, Admiralty hired trawler, 26 January 1919

KING, Frederick, Greaser, MMR, Goissa, 15 November 1918

KING, Frederick W, Commissioned Supply Officer, Victory, 15 August 1931

KING, George E, Boy 1c, J 109168, Iron Duke, 15 October 1925

KING, Henry D, The Right Hon, Captain (Commodore 2c), RNVR, Royal Naval Volunteer Reserve, 20 August 1930

KING, Henry M, Lieutenant, FAA, 401 Flight, Courageous, 26 September 1932

KING, Howard J, Chief Motor Mechanic, RNVR, MB 3058, Fresh Hope, 5 February 1919

KING, James, Act/Chief Petty Officer, C/J 18133, M.2, 29 January 1932

KING, John L, Able Seaman, J 49364, Vanity, 8 April 1920

KING, Joseph W, Stoker, C/K 50749, Pembroke, 1 October 1938

KING, Lexie W, Chief Stoker, 308406, Vimiera, 23 January 1923

KING, Norman W, Electrical Artificer 3c, D/MX 46544, Rodney, 13 September 1936

KING, Percival, Engineer Lieutenant Commander, Winchester, 23 October 1919

KING, Samuel G, Chief Skipper, RNR, Royal Naval Reserve, 23 September 1928

KING, Thomas D, Leading Stoker, P/K 21104, London, 31 March 1931

KING, Valentine E, Ordinary Seaman, J 68337, Furious, 9 February 1919

KING, Walter E, Able Seaman, D/JX 127981, Drake, 28 August 1937

KING, William, Chief Stoker, 286715 (Ch), Verulam, 4 September 1919

KING, William, Petty Officer, 240039, Pembroke, 1 March 1927

KING, William F, Petty Officer, 185277, Vernon, 13 February 1920

KING, William J, Able Seaman, J 81400, Verity, 5 March 1922

KINGCROSS, George, Trimmer, RNR, TS 7876, Crescent, 28 November 1919

KINGSBURY, Walter S, Stoker 2c, K 52659 (Dev), Cassandra, 5 December 1918

KINLEY, James, Seaman, RNR, C 2366, Orcoma, 21 January 1919

KIPLING, Robert, Civilian Contractor, Thetis, 3 June 1939

KIRBY, Francis H, Petty Officer, D/J 54543, Vivid, 8 June 1931

KIRBY, Frank, Supply Chief Petty Officer, C/M 11104, Hermes, 9 November 1931

KIRBY, George R S, Stoker 1c, K 2995 (Po), Penarth, 4 February 1919

KIRBY, George W, Leading Seaman, P/J 58367, Cornwall, 1 March 1932

KIRBY, John L, Ordinary Seaman, P/JX 148912, Victory, 14 November 1938

KIRK, Henry, Able Seaman, J 16149, Blue Sky, tender to Queen Elizabeth, 12 June 1922

KIRK, Herbert, Able Seaman, P/J 25950, Acheron, 24 September 1933

KIRKHAM, Alfred J, Corporal, RM, 21082 (Ch), RM Barracks Chatham, 7 November 1937

KITCHEN, Henry, Able Seaman, 222959, Vivid, 11 May 1921

KITCHEN, William H, Petty Officer 1c, 97163, Thalia, 18 March 1919

KITCHENER, Walter, Able Seaman, 190701, Centurion, 15 July 1924

KITCHIN, Reginald H, Paymaster Commander, Cornwall, 6 July 1936

KITCHING, Cecil, Stoker 2c, K 54025 (Dev), Berwick, 19 January 1919

KITLEY, John, Chief Stoker, 298539, Vivid, 5 April 1922

KITSON, Roger W B, Midshipman, RNR, Royal Naval Reserve, 14 January 1922

KITSON, William T O, Boy Telegraphist, P/JX 133604, Marlborough, 10 February 1931

KITT, Herbert F, Able Seaman, J 106736, Curlew, 2 July 1926

KITT, Reginald S, Private, RMLI, 17996 (Ply), Lucia, 18 September 1920

KITT, Walter J S, Chief Petty Officer Cook, 347577, Vivid, 31 March 1926

KNAGGS, Herbert, Deck Hand, RNR, DA 15743, Principal, 1 December 1918

KNAPP, Christopher R, Warrant Mechanician, Royal Navy, 3 November 1923

KNIGHT, Albert W, Engine Room Artificer 5c, C/MX 46545, Pembroke, 13 January 1932

KNIGHT, Charles A, Private, RMLI, 21881 (Ch), Chatham Division, RMLI, 10 February 1919

KNIGHT, Christopher H, Able Seaman, P/J 74225, Dainty, 10 August 1936

KNIGHT, Frederick A, Stoker 1c, K 65419, St Genny, 12 January 1930

KNIGHT, George, Private, RM, S 9492 (Deal), RM Labour Corps, 25 March 1919

KNIGHT, John A, Leading Stoker, K 20738, Foxglove, 5 July 1922

KNIGHT, Leonard J, Able Seaman, C/J 103068, Pembroke I, 9 September 1930

KNIGHT, Sidney H, Able Seaman, P/JX 140965, Express, 20 July 1938

KNIGHT, Sidney J, Musician, RMB, RMB 2457, Sussex, 31 December 1932

KNIGHT, William, Able Seaman, 222481, Vimiera, 18 November 1924

KNIGHTLEY, Frederick J, Stoker Petty Officer, K 23803, Arrow, 28 July 1930

KNIGHTS, Edward, Petty Officer, P/J 69388, Orpheus, 8 September 1934
KNOCKER, Charles A, Sub Lieutenant, FAA, 801 Sqn, Furious, 3 September 1937
KNOWLES, Alice, Telephonist, WRNS, G 6330, Women's Royal Naval Service, 29 November 1918
KNOX, John, Able Seaman, J 98171, Emerald, 24 March 1927
KNOX, Thomas E N, Lieutenant, RM, Portsmouth, 28 September 1929

KOHLER, Julius, Able Seaman, J 5647, Pembroke, 25 February 1919

KREIS, Percy H, Paymaster Lieutenant, Broke, 15 October 1926

KUM, You, Able Seaman (Chinese), Tamar, 27 September 1925

KWASNIEWSKI, Francis J, Gunner, RMA, RMA 8946, RMA Eastney, 16 March 1920
KWOK, Chun, Able Seaman, Alacrity, 10 February 1921
KWOK, Kam, Able Seaman (Chinese), Tamar, 12 January 1923

KYNVIN, Thomas C, Act/Gunner, Marlborough, 9 July 1924

L

LA TROBE, Ronald, Petty Officer, D/JX 25586, On loan to RAN, 9 July 1937

LACEY, Leonard, Leading Seaman, P/JX 128212, Neptune, 22 January 1937

LADD, William, Able Seaman, J 96479, Vernon, 22 September 1925

LAI, Ying K, Stoker 2c, Petersfield, 12 April 1928

LAIDLAW, Henry M S, Captain, RNR, Royal Naval Reserve, 16 April 1939

LAIDLAW, Robert S, Lieutenant (on loan to RAN), Melbourne (RAN), 23 April 1919

LAILLEY, Frank, Officer's Steward 2c, L 4930, Glasgow, 16 February 1919

LAING, George A T, Lieutenant Commander, FAA, 822 Sqn, Furious, 5 March 1936

LAING, William, Stoker 1c, 298328, Implacable, 12 February 1919

LAIRD, John K, Captain, Senior Naval Officer Aberdeen, 21 December 1920

LAKE, Charles, Stoker Petty Officer, 310710, Pembroke, 28 June 1919

LAKE, George E, Sub Lieutenant, FAA, 821 Sqn, Courageous, 15 February 1937

LAKE, James C, Chief Petty Officer Telegraphist, 309546, Glorious, 30 December 1921

LAKE, James H, Chief Officer, HM Coast Guard, HM Coastguard Station Sunderland, 12 September 1919

LAKE, Percival G, Leading Signalman, D/J 48740, Devonshire, 4 October 1932

LAKE, William T, Engine Room Artificer 4c, M 8379, E.11, 8 March 1919

LAKIN, John W, Leading Stoker, P/K 59059, M.2, 29 January 1932

LAMB, Albert C, Master at Arms, C/M 35500, Pembroke, 19 February 1932

LAMB, Albert J, Chief Petty Officer, 139171, Vivid, 24 September 1919

LAMB, Charles W, Petty Officer Mechanic, F 2406, Pembroke, 5 December 1918

LAMB, Clement J, Petty Officer, J 12104, Amazon, 1 September 1927

LAMB, Edward J, Stoker 1c, K 59104, Ramillies, 28 February 1922

LAMB, James G (rank not listed) New Zealand Division, 1430, Achilles, 19 April 1939

LAMB, Robert M, Ty/Lieutenant, RNVR, (The) King's Lancashire Military Convalescent Hospital, Blackpool, Assistant Instructor, 16 July 1919

LAMB, Samuel G, Officer's Steward 2c, L 9093, Parker, 30 November 1918

LAMBERT, Arthur, Ordnance Artificer 2c, M 11751, Excellent, 16 November 1928

LAMBERT, Harry E, Warrant Wardmaster, RN Hospital Pembroke, 17 December 1919

LAMBERT, James, Stoker 2c, K 53096, Blackburn, 9 January 1919

LAMBERTH, Charles W, Stoker 1c, D/K 59731, Hermes, 19 March 1939

LAMBIRTH, Horace, Able Seaman, J 30941, Paladin, 27 July 1919

LAMERTON, James H G, Master at Arms, 117580, Impregnable, 1 February 1919

LAMKIN, John, Stoker 1c, K 31865, Sligo, 5 December 1918

LAMONT, Archibald, Lieutenant, RNR, Asteria, 21 September 1919

LAMPARD, Thomas F, Leading Seaman, J 12698 (Po), K.5, 20 January 1921

LAMPKIN, Harry, Able Seaman, SS 2423, President III, 20 February 1919

LAMPORT, Albert J, Leading Seaman, J 6059 (Po), K.5, 20 January 1921

LAMPORT, James E, Leading Stoker, SS 112469, Pembroke, 11 May 1919

LAMPSHIRE, James H, Coastguardsman 3c, 182845, Charlestown Coast Guard Station, Cornwall, 27 January 1923

LANDLER, Charles H R, Boy 2c, J 102255, Impregnable, 14 July 1921

LANDON, Arthur J, Captain, Greenwich, 17 April 1931

LANE, David H, Boy 2c, JX 149128, St Vincent, 2 January 1937

LANE, George H, Able Seaman, P/J 27327, Sandwich, 11 February 1933

LANE, Harry, Warrant Shipwright, Canterbury, 18 September 1921

LANE, Henry J, Chief Stoker, 298042, Pembroke, 17 February 1923

LANE, Herbert G, Able Seaman, J 6139, Caledon, 11 October 1921

LANE, Jeremiah, Boatswain, Marlborough, 12 February 1919

LANE, John, Private, RM, S 10971 (Deal), RM Labour Corps, 10 April 1919

LANE, Maurice, Chief Stoker, 139625, Colleen, 7 September 1919

LANE, Percy, Engine Room Artificer 1c, M 3721, L.24, 10 January 1924

LANE, William H, Officer's Steward 3c, L 8197 (Po), Erin's Isle, 7 February 1919

LANG, Arthur, Stoker Petty Officer, P/K 10159, Victory, 13 June 1931

LANG, Ernest G, Leading Seaman, P/J 22361, Waterhen, 9 September 1931

LANG, James A, Cook, M 6160, Castor, 22 April 1930

LANG, William H, Leading Seaman, 220690, Watchman, 10 July 1919

LANGDON, Fernley J, Stoker 1c, D/K 66004, Drake, 1 January 1936

LANGDON, Reginald, Stoker 1c, SS 124415, Resolution, 17 November 1919

LANGFORD, Alfred A, Able Seaman, 204179, Comus, 27 July 1921

LANGFORD, George E S, Chief Petty Officer Writer, C/M 37559, Dunedin, 9 January 1934

LANGFORD, Martyn H, Surgeon Lieutenant Commander, Challenger, 15 December 1918

LANGMAN, Harold, Petty Officer, D/J 13665, Danae, 2 December 1934

LANGSTAFF, Edward G, Lieutenant, Wolfhound, 13 January 1926

LANGWORTHY, Charles H, Engine Room Artificer 4c, M 19324, Pembroke, 24 March 1919

LANGWORTHY, William H, Leading Stoker, K 6228, Vivid, 14 November 1925

LANSDELL, William J, Stoker 1c, K 58445, Peterel, 25 November 1928

LAPPIN, Albert, Leading Stoker, SS 109827, Pembroke, 16 February 1919

LARAMAN, Garfield H K, Boy 2c, JX 137684, Ganges, 5 December 1932

LARCOMBE, Matthew F, Sick Berth Attendant, M 36018, Hood, 24 February 1925

LARDNER, Joseph J H, Chief Petty Officer, 169994, Dolphin, 14 March 1919

LARDNER, William G, Stoker Petty Officer, 312176, Inflexible, 18 March 1919

LARGE, Charles A E, Leading Seaman, J 3485, Niobe (RCN), 24 December 1919

LARGE, Edwin R, Captain, RNR, City of Harvard, 1 November 1928

LARGE, Ted S, Stoker 1c, C/KX 75999, Cambrian, 23 July 1933

LARKIN, Arthur, Leading Seaman, RNVR, Sussex 6/55, Victory X, 1 February 1919

LARKINS, Arthur T, Leading Seaman, J 14227 (Ch), Tempest, 20 July 1920

LARKINS, Frank L, Sub Lieutenant, RAN, J.2 (Platypus, O/P), 20 June 1919

LARN, William, Ordinary Seaman, J 84897 (Ch), Dragon, 17 October 1919

LARNDER, Frederick J, Able Seaman, J 12675, Canada, 12 January 1919

LARNER, Henry, Able Seaman, J 34741, Voyager, 30 July 1920

LASHMAR, Bertram A, Engine Room Artificer 2c, M 4306 (Po), K.5, 20 January 1921

LASHMAR, John M, Petty Officer, C/J 109212, Greenwich, 28 December 1936

LATHAM, Arthur H, Stoker 1c, K 66009, Vivid, 23 June 1930

LATHAM, William G, Boy 1c, P/JX 141609, Barham, 17 May 1936

LATTER, Leonard H, Petty Officer, C/J 32329, Pembroke, 24 September 1934

LAUGHTON, Reginald W, Lieutenant (E), Britannia, RN College, Dartmouth, 11 May 1929

LAURENCE, William G, Able Seaman, D/J 101904, Royal Navy, 4 March 1933

LAW, John W, Able Seaman, J 65730, M.1, 12 November 1925

LAWDAY, William R, Able Seaman, MMR, 837044, Frisky, 9 November 1919

LAWES, Thomas N E, Yeoman of Signals, 222699, Vivid, 13 April 1919

LAWLER, Edward A, Gunner, Strenuous, 30 March 1920

LAWLEY, Arthur R, Able Seaman, J 76961, L.24, 10 January 1924

LAWLOR, Leslie, Lieutenant Commander, RNR, Registan, 8 June 1924

LAWRENCE, Benjamin, Stoker, RNR, S 4627, Whitby Abbey, 24 April 1919

LAWRENCE, Edwin T, Petty Officer, J 15888, Blenheim, 11 January 1922

LAWRENCE, Ernest S, Ordinary Seaman, J 53916, ML.368, motor launch, 29 July 1919

LAWRENCE, Frederick G, Stoker Petty Officer, K 4758, Pembroke, 14 March 1919

LAWRENCE, Frederick T, Boy 2c, J 95478, Ganges, 26 March 1920

LAWRENCE, James G, Leading Seaman, J 26878 (Ch), K.5, 20 January 1921

LAWRENCE, Robert R, Ty/Lieutenant, RNVR, ML.506, motor launch, 31 January 1919

LAWRENCE, Samuel L, Warrant Ordnance Officer, Vivid, 2 April 1920

LAWRENCE, Stanfield, Stoker 1c, K 24155 (Po), K.5, 20 January 1921

LAWRENCE, Victor A, Victualling Chief Petty Officer, 342141, Comus, 28 November 1919

LAWRENCE, Walter T, Able Seaman, C/JX 139708, Cardiff, 18 March 1934

LAWRENCE, William H, Writer, P/MX 46828, Dolphin, 1 January 1931

LAWRIE, Edward Mc C W, Captain, Hong Kong Dockyard, 29 June 1933

LAWRIE, Simon, Trimmer, RNR, TS 2252, Sabrina, 10 September 1919

LAWRY, Edwin S J, Sick Berth Attendant, M 38148, Vivid, 8 February 1926

LAWS, Gilbert U, Lieutenant, RNVR, Catania, 3 December 1919

LAWS, John, Trimmer, RNR, TS 7610, Pembroke, 27 December 1919

LAWSON, Thomas, Mate, MMR, Leonard, 8 January 1920

LAWSON, William, Chief Stoker, K 618, Marlborough, 12 November 1927

LAXTON, Percy A, Chief Petty Officer, 211099, Maidstone, 2 October 1924

LAY, Harold A, Leading Signalman, C/JX 130491, Vindictive, 21 October 1937

LAY, Hugh N, Lieutenant, Hermes, 21 October 1926

LAYFIELD, Henry, Marine, 18892 (Ply), Delhi, 17 February 1924

LAYTON, Albert G, Able Seaman, SS 9191, Vernon, 10 September 1921

LAYZELL, Edward F, Stoker 1c, C/KX 85270, Arethusa, 15 December 1936

LE HURAY, Donald L, Able Seaman, P/J 51936, Greenwich, 12 March 1937

LE LION, Philip F, Stoker 1c, K 22356, Conflict, 28 November 1918

LEA, Frederick, Stoker 1c, K 23535, Lowestoft, 25 August 1920

LEA, Harold, Able Seaman, 170584, Actaeon, 27 February 1919

LEACH, Albert G, Shipwright 1c, P/M 6688, Champion, 27 June 1931

LEACH, Ernest, Cook, P/MX 48050, Cornwall, 6 August 1932

LEACH, Frederick S, Petty Officer, 208350 (Ch), Lapwing, 17 December 1919

LEACH, Harry, Stoker 1, K 3202, Victory, 10 February 1919

LEACH, James, Stoker Petty Officer, K 11874, Rocket, 2 April 1921

LEACH, John E, Able Seaman, D/J 106865, Resolution, 21 January 1932

LEADBETTER, William G, Able Seaman, J 20444, Glowworm, 25 August 1919

LEADON, John, Able Seaman, SS 6815, Catspaw, 31 December 1919

LEAF, Alfred W, Warrant Shipwright, Fox, 26 March 1919

LEAH, George, Able Seaman, SS 8177, Ambrose, 23 August 1922

LEAHY, Herbert T, Supply Assistant, D/MX 52765, Drake, 10 May 1937

LEAN, Philip S, Commissioned Gunner, St Genny, 12 January 1930

LEAR, Alfred J, Petty Officer, 239379, Devonshire, 6 February 1919

LEARLY, Lionel F, Stoker 2c, KX 76175, Victory, 7 September 1926

LEARY, John H, Act/Cook, MX 56971, Royal Navy, January 1938

LEARY, Timothy, Telegraphist, J 42012, Defiance, 26 May 1919

LEATHES, John D De M, Lieutenant Commander, M.2, 29 January 1932

LEAVY, Frederick W, Signalman, D/J 94973, M.2, 29 January 1932

LECKY, Arthur M, Captain, Portland, RN Base, Captain In Charge, 2 April 1933

LEDWORD, Charles H, Marine, 215079 (Po), Barham, 12 June 1928

LEE, Douglas W, Stoker Petty Officer, K 19549, Blake, 19 May 1920

LEE, Douglas, Boy 2c, JX 140841, Ganges, 26 July 1934

LEE, Frank, Able Seaman, J 103081, Witch, 20 December 1928

LEE, Godfrey B, Stoker, RNR, S 2326, Wildfire, 17 November 1918

LEE, John J, Engine Room Artificer 2c, M 3270, Bee, 26 August 1925

LEE, Leonard, Ordinary Seaman, D/JX 153690, Glorious, 25 July 1939

LEE, Pierce, Deck Hand, RNR, DA 1420, Pembroke, 14 November 1918

LEE, Thomas A, Stoker 1c, K 32961, Penarth, 4 February 1919

LEE, Thomas F, Sick Berth Steward, 133683, Imperieuse, 13 September 1919

LEECH, Charles W, Chief Steward, 307850, Pembroke, 13 June 1925

LEECH, William D, Able Seaman, J 5899, Blue Sky, tender to Queen Elizabeth, 12 June 1922

LEEDS, Roland, Lieutenant Commander, Durban, 28 March 1933

LEEDS, The Duke of, Honorary Captain, RNVR, Tyne Division RNVR, 10 May 1927
LEE-DUNCAN, Harry, Surgeon Lieutenant, Mantis, 1 September 1931
LEEHANE, Charles, Leading Seaman, 193534, Vivid, 5 February 1921
LEEMING, William L, 2nd Hand, RNR, DA 17145, John Robert, 1 February 1919
LEES, Andrew, Stoker 2c, SS 118635 (Po), Penarth, 4 February 1919
LEES, Arthur, Stoker 1c, K 55385, Catspaw, 31 December 1919
LEES, Charles C D, Lieutenant, Verulam, 4 September 1919
LEES, John R, Ordinary Seaman, J 85413, Benbow, 20 February 1919
LEE-WHITE, Ronald, Paymaster Midshipman, Cormorant, 6 November 1938
LEFEAUX, Joseph H, Stoker 1c, K 31507 (Po), Blenheim, 15 January 1919
LEGG, Alfred A, Engine Room Artificer 4c, MX 46179, H.47, 9 July 1929
LEGG, Arthur F, Boy 1c, J 111100, Effingham, 28 July 1925
LEGG, Edward, Commissioned Gunner, Victory, 25 December 1930
LEGG, John T, Boy 1c, J 78784 (Dev), Ramillies, 19 May 1919
LEGG, Reginald G, Able Seaman, J 99300, Calcutta, 6 July 1923
LEGG, Walter J, Stoker 1c, P/KX 91808, Suffolk, 9 January 1939
LEGGETT, Ernest, Deck Hand, MMR, Iolaire, 1 January 1919
LEGGETT, Frederick T, Leading Stoker, K 5166, Vanquisher, 25 October 1925
LEGGETT, Russell, Petty Officer, C/J 56608, Fortune, 12 November 1937
LEICESTER, Ian E, FAA Apprentice, FX 75561, Caledonia, 22 April 1939
LEIGH, Alfred, Able Seaman, J 12317, Pembroke, 14 May 1925
LEIGH, William R, Stoker Petty Officer, K 7600, Pembroke, 14 August 1919
LEMARCHARD, Francis W, Surgeon Sub Lieutenant, RNVR, Phoebe, 12 February 1919
LEMMEY, Harry, Able Seaman, RNVR, London Z 3010, Sunland, steamship, 20 November 1918
LEMMON, Frank E, Paymaster Lieutenant, RNR, Royal Naval Reserve, 26 July 1930
LEMON, David, Leading Boatman, 168749, HM Coast Guard Rosmoney, 11 March 1919
LENNOX, William B, Able Seaman, SS 9172, Pembroke, 29 December 1919
LENTHALL, Frederick W, Stoker, RAN, 11026, Geranium (RAN), 1 July 1921
LEONARD, Emmanuel, Chief Engine Room Artificer 1c, M 2238, Laburnum, 26 March 1930
LEONARD, Hubert, Signalman, D/JX 134796, Drake, 15 February 1937
LEONARD, Thomas, Chief Carpenter, MMR, Mantua, 10 March 1919
LEPPER, Edgar W, Master at Arms, M 35792, Revenge, 28 October 1929
LESLIE, Maurice B, Lieutenant Commander, Royal Navy, 11 March 1925
LESLIE, Norman, Lieutenant Commander, RNR, Royal Naval Reserve, 24 January 1932
LESLIE, William D, Signalman, J 53447, Voyager, 19 April 1925
LESSLIE, David G, Leading Telegraphist, J 21679, Vivid, 25 January 1922
LETHBRIDGE, James A, Stoker 1c, K 14459 (Dev), Kinross, 16 June 1919
LETHERBY, Arthur H, Stoker Petty Officer, D/KX 76197, Drake, 4 October 1936
LETLEY, Leonard W, Midshipman, RNR, Excellent, 27 April 1919
LEUNG, Sui, Leading Stoker (Chinese), Tamar, 7 November 1938

LEVEN, Bernard, Leading Stoker, K 11579 (Po), L.55, 4 June 1919
LEVERETT, William, Engineman, RNR, ES 1505, Ceto, 29 March 1919
LEVERSIDGE, Harry T, Leading Telegraphist, J 30404, Victory, 25 April 1920
LEVINS, James, Corporal, RM, 19038 (Ply), Devonshire, 26 July 1929
LEVITT, Arthur, Leading Seaman, L 17145, Valerian, 22 October 1926
LEWER, Ernest, Stoker 1c, K 38640, Tiger, 18 March 1919
LEWIN, William P, Stoker 1c, K 56891, Southampton, 26 April 1923
LEWINGTON, Leonard F, Officer's Steward 1c, 364140, Centaur, 25 November 1926
LEWIS, Benjamin, Commissioned Engineer, RNR, Royal Naval Reserve, 12 May 1921
LEWIS, Charles A, Ty/Lieutenant, RNVR, Egmont, 17 December 1918
LEWIS, David L, Surgeon Lieutenant, Pembroke, 2 March 1919
LEWIS, Edward H, Civilian Contractor, Thetis, 3 June 1939
LEWIS, George, Private, RM, S 13220 (Deal), RM Labour Corps, RM Depot Deal, 25 April 1919
LEWIS, George, Trimmer Cook, RNR, TC 458, Emmanuel Camelaire, 10 March 1919
LEWIS, Harold, Able Seaman, D/J 108180, Comus, 8 May 1931
LEWIS, Harry I, Able Seaman, J 79546, Vivid, 18 January 1922
LEWIS, Hugh, Ty/Engineer Sub Lieutenant, RNR, Kildonan Castle, 4 December 1918
LEWIS, John W J, Stoker 1c, D/K 63662, M.2, 29 January 1932
LEWIS, Sidney J, Engine Room Artificer 3c, 272320, Blake, 1 February 1919
LEWTHWAITE, Cecil T M, Sick Berth Attendant, P/MX 47906, RN Hospital, Haslar, 7 February 1931
LEY, Ernest A, Able Seaman, 221764, Kilfullert, 21 November 1918
LEYSHON, Edward G, Paymaster Commander, Constance, 10 February 1923
LEYSHON, Gomer T, Leading Telegraphist, RNVR, Wales Z 257, Thomas Robins, 13 April 1919

LIBBY, John F, Stoker 1c, K 46174, Tenacious, 11 May 1922
LIDDELL, Buchan M, Lieutenant, RNR, Royal Naval Reserve, 29 October 1919
LIDSTONE, Frederick T, Able Seaman, 209638, Pembroke, 15 October 1919
LIFTON, Gilbert D, Boy 2c, JX 127352, Impregnable, 14 January 1927
LIGHT, Reginald, Able Seaman, 236934 (Po), Renown, 10 November 1919
LIGHT, Robert, Leading Stoker, K 2544, Mistley, 4 October 1920
LIGHT, Walter J, Stoker Petty Officer, 306662, Centurion, 4 April 1923
LILL, Joseph, Stoker 1c, K 30408, Victory, 26 January 1923
LILLEY, Austen G, Captain, Personnel Services Department, Admiralty, 29 March 1937
LILLEY, George H, Leading Stoker, K 17175, Valerian, 22 October 1926
LILLEY, James, Stoker 1c, K 11769, Phaeton, 29 January 1920
LILLEY, Roger A, Electrical Artificer 4c, M 29898, L.55, 4 June 1919
LILLY, Reginald F, Able Seaman, J 35357, Victory, August 1921
LILLY, Robert, 2nd Hand, RNR, SA 279, Astral, 28 February 1919
LILLYSTONE, Charles T, Able Seaman, J 37020, Danae, 20 April 1926
LILLYWHITE, Charles H, Petty Officer, C/J 105965, Marshal Soult, 21 February 1935

LIMBRICK, Harold N, Stoker Petty Officer, 303473, Medina, 17

November 1918
LINCOLN, Edward A, Stoker 1c, 174298, Europa, 12 December 1918
LINDEMANN, Frederick, Engine Room Artificer 2c, M 10835, Excellent, 17 April 1925
LINDLEY, Leslie F, Ordnance Artificer, C/M 39470, Tarantula, 8 October 1936
LINDSAY, William T, Able Seaman, J 7462, Vivid, 1 May 1920
LINEHAM, John J, Stoker 1c, K 20284, Capetown, 21 September 1922
LINEY, James F T, Able Seaman, J 25576, Marlborough, 14 June 1924
LINFORD, Thomas, Leading Boatman, 174122, HM Coastguard Station Whitburn, 12 December 1918
LING, Cheung, Officer's Steward 3c, Ambrose, 20 June 1926
LINGARD, Edward V, Leading Stoker, K 23637, Marazion, 9 December 1923
LINGWOOD, George, Sapper, RME, RME 1874332, RM Engineers, 3 November 1937
LINK, William, Petty Officer, 211675 (Dev), Abingdon, 31 October 1919
LINKHORN, Walter R, Deck Hand, RNR, DA 5073, Attentive III, 14 March 1919
LINNINGTON, Albert E, Chief Engine Room Artificer 2c, M 1336, L.17, 6 September 1920
LINTONBON, Henry J, Able Seaman, J 45654, Actaeon, 26 September 1920
LIPPIETT, Alfred H, Engine Room Artificer 1c, 271673, Loyal, 28 November 1918
LIST, John, Honorary Engineer Commander, RNR, Royal Naval Reserve, 1 October 1926
LISTER, Herbert, Ordinary Seaman, J 103458, Centurion, 24 June 1924
LISTER, William, Able Seaman, RNVR, Tyneside Z 1032, Anson Battalion, RND, 6 January 1919
LISTER, William H, Petty Officer, J 24936, Victory, 27 January 1930
LITHERLAND, Harold, Able Seaman, J 37340, Resolution, 6 July 1924
LITTELL, Robert C, Ordnance Artificer 3c, M 35596, M.1, 12 November 1925
LITTLE, Dugald C, Armourer's Crew, M 6574, Barham, 19 November 1918
LITTLE, William H, Leading Victualling Assistant, M 14267, Julius, 28 August 1921
LITTLEDALE, Bernard J, Commander (E), Bee, 15 January 1929
LITTLEFIELD, Albert F, Canteen Manager, Admiralty civilian, Valerian, 22 October 1926
LITTLETON, Hugh, Paymaster Commander, Titania, 27 September 1929
LIVESAY, James T, Gunner, Fandango, 3 July 1919
LIVETT, Sidney G, Telegraphist, C/SSX 13943, Norfolk III, RN Base, Aden, 20 September 1936
LIVINGSTON, Charles, Honorary Commander, RNVR, Royal Naval Volunteer Reserve, 2 May 1937
LIVINGSTONE, Campbell W, Paymaster Lieutenant, ex-Southampton, 18 November 1922
LIVINGSTONE, John A, Lieutenant, RNR, Hero, 23 February 1919

LLEWELLYN, Griffith D, Schoolmaster, Pembroke, 29 November 1935
LLEWELLYN, John W, Chief Petty Officer, 163981, Vivid, 10 February 1919
LLOYD, Charles E, Stoker, K 57322, Victory, 15 August 1929
LLOYD, Daniel, Able Seaman, RNVR, Wales Z 693, RMLI, 2nd Reserve Battalion, 22 November 1918
LLOYD, David M, Lieutenant, Colombo, 21 July 1939
LLOYD, George D, Commissioned Gunner, Constance, 19 June 1932

LLOYD, George V, Able Seaman, J 112402, Cornflower, 15 November 1928
LLOYD, Harry, Regulating Petty Officer, M 36479, Titania, 8 October 1925
LLOYD, John E, Stoker Petty Officer, 306551, Raleigh, 8 August 1922
LLOYD, John W, Corporal, RM, S 8245 (Deal), RM Labour Corps, 27 November 1918
LLOYD, Joseph A, Leading Seaman, J 01118, Barham, 6 July 1928
LLOYD, Stanley P, Act/Sub Lieutenant, RNR, Royal Naval Reserve, 3 June 1938
LLOYD, Thomas C C, Lieutenant Commander, Thetis (Trident), 3 June 1939
LLOYD, Thomas J, Surgeon Lieutenant, RNVR, Royal Naval Volunteer Reserve, 5 November 1930

LO, Leung, Able Seaman (Chinese), Tamar, 13 August 1938
LOADER, Arthur E, Deck Hand, RNR, DA 10563, Ben Glas, 21 November 1918
LOADER, Claude A E, Able Seaman, 238326, Challenger, 12 December 1918
LOAN, Reginald C, Able Seaman, P/J 64648, Nelson, 19 August 1934
LOCK, Alfred S, Victualling Chief Petty Officer, 341256, Vivid, 4 April 1921
LOCK, Arnold V, Stoker 1c, 295899, Caesar, 8 March 1919
LOCK, Christopher, Carpenter, MMR, 981391, Victorious, 23 December 1919
LOCK, Frederick, Chief Motor Mechanic, RNVR, MB 761, ML.229, motor launch, 15 September 1919
LOCK, Walter W, Engineer Commander, Royal Navy, 3 September 1924
LOCKER, Philip C, Able Seaman, J 36999, Vansittart, 23 March 1920
LOCKERBIE, Bruce, Boy 2c, JX 158771, Caledonia, 24 July 1938
LOCKETT, Herbert A, Paymaster Commander, RNVR, London Division, RNVR, 31 January 1929
LOCKWOOD, John G, Chief Petty Officer Writer, M 7785, Pembroke, 17 December 1929
LOCOCK, Victor G, Able Seaman, J 58584, Queen Elizabeth, 8 November 1923
LODDER, Sydney N, Telegraphist, J 90181, Valerian, 22 October 1926
LODER, Hubert G, Act/Chief Engine Room Artificer 2c, P/M 6253, L.71, 12 September 1935
LODGE, Edgar, Boy 2c, J 106632, Ganges, 22 January 1924
LONERGAN, Terrance N, Sick Berth Attendant, C/MX 50739, Ladybird, 12 December 1937
LONEY, Edwin T, Petty Officer, D/J 92359, Defiance, 20 June 1938
LONG, Alexander A, Leading Seaman, J 9853, Royal Oak, 16 April 1922
LONG, Frederick, Stoker Petty Officer, 301101, Pembroke, 24 November 1919
LONG, George G, Able Seaman, P/JX 129165, Boreas, 6 March 1938
LONG, Harold R, Leading Seaman, J 80028, Vidette, 16 April 1928
LONG, Henry G, Stoker 2c, K 52822, Vivid, 29 December 1918
LONG, Mok K, Stoker (Chinese), Tamar, 22 January 1920
LONGHURST, Gerald F, Commander, Carnarvon, 8 January 1921
LONGSTAFF, Norman, Able Seaman, P/JX 132478, Thetis, 3 June 1939
LONGTHORPE, Percy, Able Seaman, J 10308, Adventure, 14 December 1918
LORAINE, Henry, Stoker 1c, 300767, Vivid, 23 January 1924
LORAINE, John C, Private, RMLI, 19949 (Po), St Vincent, 11 December 1918

LORENZ, Charles, Private, RMLI, S 354 (Ch), 3rd Battalion, RM, 5 December 1918
LOUGH, Frederick C I, Able Seaman, J 11342, L.24, 10 January 1924
LOVE, Herbert, Officer's Steward 4c, L 14804, Pembroke, 9 January 1924
LOVE, James, Stoker 1c, K 26166, Victory, 17 December 1921
LOVE, Robert, Chief Gunner, President, 5 January 1919
LOVE, William, Stoker 1c, K 57930, Vivid, 6 March 1920
LOVEDAY, George F, Shipwright, C/MX 47403, York, 27 November 1937
LOVEGROVE, John W, Mechanician, K 16698, Enterprise, 16 June 1928
LOVEJOY, Arthur T, Stoker 2c, K 65041, Victory, 18 January 1925
LOVELESS, Albert E, Engine Room Artificer 4c, C/M 38821, Sussex, 2 October 1931
LOVELL, Albert, Chief Petty Officer, 108631, Vivid, 18 April 1919
LOVELL, Edgar W, Private, RMLI, S 1989 (Po), 2nd RM Battalion, RND, 17 November 1918
LOVELL, Frederick B R, Stoker 2c, KX 75657, Victory, 22 May 1926
LOVELY, Ernest C, Ordinary Seaman, MMR, 938211, Victory, 15 July 1919
LOVERIDGE, Walter, Ordinary Seaman, J 43419, Vivid, 16 November 1918
LOVERING, Ernest T, Able Seaman, J 24879, M.1, 12 November 1925
LOVETT, Charles H, Private, RMLI, 9046 (Po), Tamar, 25 September 1919
LOVETT, Ernest J, Officer's Steward 3c, L 5980, Pembroke, 9 December 1919
LOVOCK, Arthur H J, Able Seaman, C/J 100346, Poseidon, 9 June 1931
LOWCOCK, Alfred W B, Ty/Lieutenant, RNVR, ML.367, motor launch, 12 November 1918
LOWDON, Sidney, Able Seaman, J 40777, Wallace, 27 February 1919
LOWE, Frederick W, Able Seaman, RNVR, R 5539, Hawke Battalion, RND, 4 April 1919
LOWE, George W, Able Seaman, J 38578 (Ch), Dragon, 17 October 1919
LOWE, Ronald W, Steward, D/LX 21116, Vivid, 24 November 1933
LOWER, James D, Petty Officer, J 6677, Vanoc, 30 July 1927
LOWER, Lewis C, Chief Petty Officer Writer, 347962, Wallflower, 25 October 1926
LOWMAN, Edgar M, Able Seaman, P/JX 128978, Victory I, 18 May 1937
LOWNDES, Alexander, Captain, Impregnable, 20 March 1921

LUARD, Herbert Du C, Commander, HM Coast Guard Plymouth, 21 February 1919
LUBBOCK, Albert W, Able Seaman, J 109370, Whirlwind, 30 August 1927
LUCAS, John, Private, RMLI, S 1190 (Po), 2nd RM Battalion, RND, 26 November 1918
LUCAS, John J, Marine, RMLI, 14122 (Ch), Royal Marines HQ, 9 November 1923
LUCAS, Joseph A, Officer's Steward 2c, L 7454, Effingham, 14 August 1925
LUCK, Walter A, Leading Seaman, C/JX 134188, Thetis, 3 June 1939
LUCKHURST, Henry W, Stoker 1c, C/K 48734, Vivien, 22 August 1932
LUCY, Richard H, Lieutenant, Flinders, 11 June 1925
LUMSDEN, James, Shipwright 2c, 345616, Malaya, 4 July 1921
LUPTON, Richard, Able Seaman, J 59349, Severn, 27 April 1919
LUSCOMBE, James F, Coastguardsman 3c, 180480, Pembroke, 17 August 1922
LUSCOMBE, John A G, Stoker 2c, D/KX 93424, Drake, 3 June 1938
LUSH, William J, Gunner, RMA, RMA 15739, Renown, 24 March 1920
LUXTON, George J, Able Seaman, J 39970, Victory I, 20 November 1919

LYCETT, Harold, Chief Ordnance Artificer 2c, P/M 35424, Hood, 3 May 1936
LYNCH, Herbert R, Chief Engine Room Artificer 2c, P M 347783, Suffolk, 18 June 1938
LYNCH, James P, Leading Stoker, K 45626, Frobisher, 9 November 1929
LYNCH, John P, Leading Seaman, J 94301, Resolution, 17 January 1926
LYNCH, Michael J, 1st Writer, M 1928, Eaglet, 22 February 1920
LYNCH, Philip, Leading Trimmer, RNR, ST 1573, Shincliffe, 4 May 1919
LYNCH, William, Able Seaman, J 44937, Vivid, 6 February 1919
LYON, Herbert, Admiral (Rtd), Royal Navy, 15 March 1919
LYONS, Edmond, Stoker 1c, K 17360, L.24, 10 January 1924
LYONS, Edward J, Chief Stoker, 304685, Ajax, 24 November 1923

M

MABBITT, Thomas H W, Blacksmith 1c, M 5712, Europa, 19 December 1918

MACARTHUR, Donald, Deck Hand, RNR, SD 4443, Iolaire (Implacable, O/P), 1 January 1919

MACASKILL, John, Deck Hand, RNR, 14567, Iolaire (Sir John Fitzgerald, O/P), 1 January 1919

MACASKILL, John, Leading Deck Hand, RNR, DA 9635, Iolaire, 1 January 1919

MACASKILL, John, Seaman, RNR, A 3397, Iolaire (Redoubtable, O/P), 1 January 1919

MACASKILL, John A, Signaller, RNVR, Clyde Z 8453, Iolaire (Vivid, O/P), 1 January 1919

MACAULAY, Donald, Deck Hand, RNR, A 2576, Iolaire (Gunner, O/P), 1 January 1919

MACAULAY, Donald, Deck Hand, RNR, SD 2658, Iolaire (Max Pemberton, O/P), 1 January 1919

MACAULAY, John, Deck Hand, RNR, DA 19586, Joseph Burgin, 14 November 1918

MACAULAY, John, Leading Boatman, 198280, Wireless Signal Station Butt of Lewis, 27 January 1919

MACAULAY, John, Seaman, RNR, C 1567, Iolaire (Imperieuse, O/P), 1 January 1919

MACAULAY, Murdo, Deck Hand, RNR, SD 4004, Iolaire, 1 January 1919

MACCABEE, Cyril T, Leading Stoker, K 62991, H.47, 9 July 1929

MACCUISH, Roderick, Deck Hand, RNR, DA 18329, John Corwarder, 17 December 1918

MACDONALD, Alexander, 2nd Hand, RNR, DA 11708, Iolaire (Pembroke, O/P, 1 January 1919

MACDONALD, Angus, Deck Hand, RNR, SD 2597, Iolaire (Primrose, O/P), 1 January 1919

MACDONALD, Angus, Seaman, RNR, A 4554, Iolaire (Kent, O/P), 1 January 1919

MACDONALD, Angus, Seaman, RNR, D 1830, Iolaire (Imperieuse, O/P), 1 January 1919

MACDONALD, Donald, Leading Deck Hand, RNR, DA 12453, Iolaire (Pembroke, O/P), 1 January 1919

MACDONALD, Donald, Seaman, RNR, A 3947, Mars, 25 February 1919

MACDONALD, Donald, Seaman, RNR, A 5296, Iolaire (Vernon, O/P), 1 January 1919

MACDONALD, Donald, Seaman, RNR, C 2373, Iolaire, 1 January 1919

MACDONALD, Ewen, Deck Hand, RNR, DA 19896, Iolaire (John Gray, O/P), 1 January 1919

MACDONALD, George, Engineman, RNR, ES 1442, John Robert, 1 February 1919

MACDONALD, Harry, Deck Hand, RNR, A 12209, Europa, 6 December 1918

MACDONALD, James W, Officer's Steward 2c, L 9730, Nerissa, 1 March 1919

MACDONALD, John, Deck Hand, RNR, DA 19654, Iolaire (Boy George III, O/P), 1 January 1919

MACDONALD, John, Deck Hand, RNR, DA 21078, Iolaire (Genia, O/P), 1 January 1919

MACDONALD, John, Leading Seaman, RNR, C 2443, Iolaire (Arrogant, O/P), 1 January 1919

MACDONALD, John, Leading Seaman, RNR, C 2554, Iolaire (Arrogant, O/P), 1 January 1919

MACDONALD, John, Seaman, RNR, A 5812, Drake Battalion, RND, 14 June 1919

MACDONALD, John, Seaman, RNR, B 3339, Iolaire (Emperor of India, O/P), 1 January 1919

MACDONALD, Louis P, Stoker Petty Officer, P/K 16558, M.2, 29 January 1932

MACDONALD, Malcolm, Seaman, RNR, C 1874, Iolaire (Victory, O/P), 1 January 1919

MACDONALD, Murdo, Deck Hand, RNR, DA 11997, Iolaire (Aspire, O/P), 1 January 1919

MACDONALD, Murdo, Deck Hand, RNR, DA 20516, Iolaire (Venerable, O/P), 1 January 1919

MACDONALD, Murdo, Seaman, RNR, A 9534, Iolaire (Pembroke, O/P 1 January 1919

MACDONALD, Murdo, Seaman, RNR, A 9905, Ajax, 12 January 1926

MACDONALD, Roderick W, Lieutenant, FAA, 821 Sqn, Courageous, 15 February 1937

MACDONALD, Somerled, Lieutenant, M.2, 29 January 1932

MACDONALD, William, Deck Hand, RNR, DA 1436, Iolaire (Surf, O/P), 1 January 1919

MACE, George W, Ordinary Seaman, P/SSX 17573, Enterprise, 16 April 1937

MACE, Sidney E, Painter 3c, M 13549, Colossus, 29 November 1918

MACFARLANE, Donald, Deck Hand, RNR, SD 4113, Boadicea II, 20 January 1919

MACFARLANE, Thomas L, Lieutenant, RNVR, Glowworm, 25 August 1919

MACGREGOR, Robert S R, Stoker 1c, K 19376 (Po), K.5, 20 January 1921

MACINNES, David, Deck Hand, RNR, DA 19531, Iolaire (Daniel Henry, O/P), 1 January 1919

MACINTOSH, Evelyn M, Assistant Principal, WRNS, Women's Royal Naval Service, 18 December 1918

MACINTYRE, John, Honorary Surgeon Commander, RNVR, Royal Naval Volunteer Reserve, 29 October 1928

MACIVER, Charles, Honorary Captain, RNR, Royal Naval Reserve, 28 August 1926

MACIVER, Henry, Honorary Captain, RNR, Royal Naval Reserve, 5 April 1921

MACIVER, Kenneth, Leading Seaman, A 5561, Sagua, steamship, 26 February 1919

MACIVER, Malcolm, Deck Hand, RNR, DA 10235, Iolaire, 1 January 1919

MACIVER, Malcolm, Seaman, RNR, A 2778, Iolaire (Victory, O/P), 1 January 1919

MACKAY, Angus, 2nd Hand, RNR, D 2258, Iolaire, 1 January 1919

MACKAY, Donald, Deck Hand, RNR, DA 12090, Iolaire, 1 January 1919

MACKAY, George W, Seaman, RNR, A 5533, Trewellard, steamship, 3 January 1919

MACKAY, Malcolm, Seaman, RNR, A 7699, Iolaire (Pembroke, O/P), 1 January 1919

MACKAY, Murdo, Deck Hand, RNR, DA 16652, Iolaire (Shikari II, O/P), 1 January 1919

MACKAY, Murdo, Seaman, RNR, B 4511, Iolaire, 1 January 1919

MACKAY, Norman, Seaman, RNR, A 9494, Iolaire (Pembroke, O/P), 1 January 1919

MACKAY, William, Signalman, RNVR, Clyde Z 8218, Iolaire (Vivid, O/P), 1 January 1919

MACKENZIE, Alexander, Deck Hand, RNR, DA 12080, Iolaire (Mary, O/P), 1 January 1919

MACKENZIE, Alexander, Seaman, RNR, C 3360, Iolaire, 1 January 1919

MACKENZIE, Alexander S, Private, RMLI, S 2180 (Ply), 3rd Battalion, RM, 19 December 1918

MACKENZIE, Allan A, Captain, Royal Engineers (ex-Sub Lieutenant, RNR), Inland Water Transport, 3 November 1919

MACKENZIE, Donald, Deck Hand, MMR, 967820, Iolaire (Wickstead, O/P), 1 January 1919

MACKENZIE, Donald, Stoker 1c, K 107944, Heather, 21 September 1919

MACKENZIE, John, Engineman, RNR, ES 3071, Victory, 9 February 1919

MACKENZIE, John, Seaman, RNR, A 5937, Iolaire (Vivid III, ex-Albemarle, O/P), 1 January 1919

MACKENZIE, John, Seaman, RNR, C 2038, Iolaire (Victory, O/P), 1 January 1919
MACKENZIE, Kenneth, Seaman, RNR, A 3046, Iolaire, 1 January 1919
MACKENZIE, Murdo, Seaman, RNR, C 2793, Iolaire (President, O/P), 1 January 1919
MACKENZIE, Norman, Deck Hand, RNR, DA 20072, Iolaire (Victory, O/P), 1 January 1919
MACKERSY, William A N, Able Seaman, P/J 110194, Cormorant, 11 May 1936
MACKEY, Michael, Officer's Steward 1c, L 6031, Hood, 16 November 1924
MACKIE, Andrew, Leading Seaman, J 4237, Verdun, 6 April 1919
MACKILLOP, Norman, Seaman, RNR, A 9522, Iolaire (Pembroke, O/P), 1 January 1919
MACKIN, Laurence, Leading Seaman, RNR, B 4800, Highland Glen, steamship, 14 December 1918
MACKINNION, Murdo, Deck Hand, RNR, DA 21209, Iolaire (Eddy, O/P), 1 January 1919
MACKINNON, John, 2nd Hand, RNR, DA 10750, Balmoral Castle, 25 December 1918
MACKINNON, John, Able Seaman, RNVR, R 1187, Army, Command Depot, Aldershot, 22 November 1918
MACKINTOSH, Donald, Boy 2c, J 98326, Ganges, 4 March 1921
MACLEAN, Donald, Seaman, RNR, B 2820, Iolaire (Colleen, O/P), 1 January 1919
MACLEAN, Hector F, Sub Lieutenant, CMB.62BD, coastal motor boat, 18 August 1919
MACLEAN, Kenneth, Deck Hand, RNR, DA 20994, Iolaire (Venerable, O/P), 1 January 1919
MACLEAN, Malcolm, Seaman, RNR, B 4280, Iolaire, 1 January 1919
MACLEAN, Murdo, Deck Hand, MMR, 947252, Iolaire (Snipe, O/P), 1 January 1919
MACLENNAN, John, Deck Hand, RNR, DA 19878, Ruby Gem, Admiralty hired drifter, 16 January 1919
MACLEOD, Alexander, Deck Hand, RNR, DA 17041, Iolaire (Vivid, O/P), 1 January 1919
MACLEOD, Alexander J, Deck Hand, RNR, DA 20422, Iolaire, 1 January 1919
MACLEOD, Allan, Seaman, RNR, A 4661, Iolaire (President III, O/P), 1 January 1919
MACLEOD, Donald A, Stoker 1c, K 6317, Pytchley, 28 November 1918
MACLEOD, Donald, Deck Hand, RNR, DA 4944, Iolaire, 1 January 1919
MACLEOD, Donald, Deck Hand, RNR, DA 6665, Iolaire, 1 January 1919
MACLEOD, Donald, Deck Hand, RNR, SD 3968, Iolaire (Victory, O/P), 1 January 1919
MACLEOD, Donald, Deck Hand, RNR, SD 4125, Iolaire (Beatrice, O/P, 1 January 1919
MACLEOD, Donald, Leading Seaman, A 6994, Ardgarvez, steamship, 30 December 1918
MACLEOD, Donald, Ordinary Seaman, RNVR, Clyde Z 9964, Iolaire (Crystal Palace, O/P), 1 January 1919
MACLEOD, Donald, Seaman, RNR, A 3329, Iolaire (Victory, O/P), 1 January 1919
MACLEOD, Finlay, Deck Hand, RNR, SD 1449, Pembroke, 25 September 1919
MACLEOD, John, Deck Hand, RNR, DA 19890, Iolaire (Implacable, O/P), 1 January 1919
MACLEOD, John, Deck Hand, RNR, SD 4435, Iolaire (ML.502, O/P), 1 January 1919
MACLEOD, John, Mate, MMR, Iolaire (Cornrig, O/P), 1 January 1919
MACLEOD, John, Seaman, RNR, A 5415, Oak Branch, steamship, 1 February 1919
MACLEOD, John, Seaman, RNR, B 2736, Iolaire (Excellent, O/P), 1 January 1919

MACLEOD, Kenneth, Captain, Royal Navy, 23 February 1927
MACLEOD, M (initial only), Leading Seaman, RNR, A 5478, Iolaire, 1 January 1919
MACLEOD, Malcolm, Able Seaman, MMR, 973832, Iolaire (Agnes Nutten, O/P), 1 January 1919
MACLEOD, Malcolm, Deck Hand, RNR, DA 20774, Iolaire (Sabreur, O/P), 1 January 1919
MACLEOD, Malcolm, Deck Hand, RNR, SD 4234, ML.368, motor launch, 9 July 1919
MACLEOD, Malcolm, Leading Deck Hand, RNR, SD 4793, Iolaire (ML.485, O/P), 1 January 1919
MACLEOD, Malcolm, Ordinary Seaman, J 65506 (Dev), Iolaire (Maidstone, O/P), 1 January 1919
MACLEOD, Murdo, Able Seaman, J 76479 (Dev), Iolaire (Revenge, O/P), 1 January 1919
MACLEOD, Murdo, Deck Hand, RNR, DA 12034, Pansy III, Admiralty hired drifter, 14 November 1918
MACLEOD, Norman, Deck Hand, RNR, A 7242, Eslem, 12 November 1918
MACLEOD, Norman, Leading Seaman, RNR, A 4803, Iolaire, 1 January 1919
MACLEOD, Norman, Seaman, RNR, C 3343, Iolaire, 1 January 1919
MACLEOD, Norman, Trimmer Cook, RNR, TC 1186, Iolaire (Venerable, O/P), 1 January 1919
MACLEOD, William, Deck Hand, RNR, DA 14603, Iolaire (Dreel Castle, O/P), 1 January 1919
MACMAHON, Joseph, Commander, RNR, Rtd, Royal Naval Reserve, 1 September 1936
MACPHAIL, Kenneth, Seaman, RNR, A 3320, Iolaire (Pembroke, O/P), 1 January 1919
MACPHAIL, Norman, Deck Hand, RNR, DA 14663, Iolaire (Venerable, O/P), 1 January 1919
MACPHERSON, Alan, 2nd Writer, M 15860, Diligence, 17 February 1919
MACRITCHIE, Donald, Cooper 4c, M 23885 (Ch), Iolaire (Pembroke, O/P), 1 January 1919
MACRITCHIE, Donald, Deck Hand, RNR, DA 13258, Iolaire (Scarboro, O/P), 1 January 1919
MADDEFORD, Frederick R, Engine Room Artificer 5c, M 35404, Resolution, 4 September 1924
MADDEN, Edward, Leading Stoker, MC 688, Hexham, 12 June 1919
MADDEN, Frank H, Leading Cook's Mate, M 3053, TB.17, torpedo boat, 26 December 1918
MADDISON, Ernest, Leading Stoker, K 4355, Birmingham, 24 December 1919
MADDISON, Robert, Able Seaman, RNVR, Tyneside Z 3456, Hood Battalion, RND, 19 January 1919
MAGEE, Richard D M, Act/Sub Lieutenant, Anthony, 20 January 1937
MAGEE, William, Greaser, MMR, 960901, Hazel, 29 December 1918
MAGGINNIS, Richard E, Gunner, RMA, S 2208, 3rd Battalion, RM, 20 December 1918
MAGOWAN, Richard, Paymaster, Lieutenant Commander, RNR, Royal Naval Reserve, 18 March 1925
MAGRI, Emmanuelle, Petty Officer, 236002, Egmont, 9 February 1926
MAGUIRE, Edward, Chief Stoker, 297375, Clematis, 3 September 1921
MAGUIRE, Thomas, Able Seaman, MMR, Vivid, 3 July 1919
MAGUIRE, William, Able Seaman, J 15873, Curacoa, 22 September 1924
MAHMOOD, Isman, Seedie Stoker, 140 (Aden), Odin, 9 August 1920
MAHONEY, Arthur M, Paymaster Sub Lieutenant, RNR, Royal Naval Reserve, 24 June 1937
MAHONEY, Francis J, Chief Petty Officer Cook, 347582, Vivid, 24 July 1926

MAHONEY, Henry C J, Cooper 1c, 344158, Ambrose, 12 August 1920
MAHONEY, Michael, Able Seaman, MMR, 997972, St Aubin, 15 May 1919
MAHONY, George H, Private, RMLI, 19167 (Po), 3rd Battalion, RM, 16 December 1918
MAHONY, John, Blacksmith, 340008, Pembroke, 2 May 1922
MAHONY, Thomas S, Stoker 1c, K 22564, Cairo, 22 May 1922
MAIN, Frank M, Commander, RNR, Royal Naval Reserve, 21 October 1924
MAIN, Frederick A, 2nd Hand, RNR, DA 15511, Loch Wasdale, 5 February 1919
MAIN, Isaac, Engineman, RNR, ES 3260, Zaria, mercantile fleet auxiliary, 29 November 1918
MAIN, James Mc C, Lieutenant Commander, RNR, Royal Naval Reserve, 27 August 1924
MAIN, Sampson, Able Seaman, RNVR, Tyneside Z 9065, Wessex, 6 March 1919
MAINWARING, Sir Harry S, Honorary Commander, RNR, Royal Naval Reserve, 30 December 1934
MAITLAND, Paul, Able Seaman, J 100943, St Genny, 12 January 1930
MAITLAND, Robert G, Able Seaman, J 70442, Marjoram, 30 November 1918
MAKIN, Herbert, Petty Officer, D/J 46697, Berwick, 3 February 1935
MALAFANE, Joseph, Bantie, Cape Station B 10, Afrikander, 9 July 1939
MALE, Bert E, Chief Stoker, 302183 (Po), K.5, 20 January 1921
MALES, William, Able Seaman, J 29834, Vivid, 3 March 1920
MALIA, Carmelo, Leading Steward, E/LX 20877, Devonshire, 11 April 1937
MALLIA, Guiseppe, Able Seaman, J 81541, Egmont, 1 June 1922
MALONEY, James A, Leading Telegraphist, C/J 100558, Hussar, 15 January 1939
MALONEY, John J, Stoker 1c, RNR, S 9288, Cottesmore, 12 October 1919
MALTBY, Charles W, Able Seaman, 226206, Penelope, 18 February 1919
MANCTON, Harry G, Stoker 2c, K 62882, Victory, 18 January 1925
MANKELTOW, Joseph, Chief Shipwright, K 4494, Enterprise, 6 July 1929
MANKEY, John, Engineer Lieutenant, Spindrift, 8 August 1921
MANN, Adam, Ordinary Seaman, J 79193, Ivy, 20 January 1920
MANN, Cyril S, Leading Signalman, J 64425, H.47, 9 July 1929
MANN, Frank H, Able Seaman, J 29403, Royal Oak, 23 November 1929
MANN, Frederick A, Sick Berth Petty Officer, D/M 15592, Drake, 20 October 1936
MANN, John, Sub Lieutenant, RNVR, Sanfoin, 17 February 1919
MANN, William G, Coastguardsman 3c, 9085 (Po), Vivid, 14 October 1922
MANN, William H, Private, RMLI, 17185 (Ply), RMLI, Plymouth Division, 19 February 1919
MANNING, Alfred E, Leading Seaman, P/J 98935, London, 27 April 1931
MANNING, Frederick J, Able Seaman, MMR, 507186, Crescent, 9 December 1918
MANNING, John, Able Seaman, J 103109, M.1, 12 November 1925
MANNING, Robert, Petty Officer, 229246, Pembroke, 28 February 1920
MANNS, Albert A B, Leading Steward, P/LX 20008, Halcyon, 24 September 1937
MANSELL, Cecil G C, Stoker 1c, K 60530, M.1, 12 November 1925
MANSELL, Robert, Leading Stoker, D/KX 56422, RN Hospital, Malta, 27 May 1935
MANSFIELD, Francis D, Stoker 1c, SS 122132, Caledon, 4 February 1920
MANSFIELD, Richard A, Able Seaman, J 2617 (Ch), K.5, 20 January 1921
MANSON, David, Deck Hand, RNR, DA 12388, Victory X, 3 March 1919
MANSON, James – see BAIRD, James, Sergeant, RMLI,
MANSON, Samuel, Stoker, RNR, S 3567, Kent, 18 February 1919
MANTON, Walter H, Marine, 22513 (Ply), Vindictive, 9 January 1928
MAPLESDEN, William J, Chief Stoker, 286221, Fisgard, 21 March 1919
MARCHANT, Thomas, Signal Boy, J 60737, Emperor of India, 21 February 1919
MARDON, Arthur G, Able Seaman, J 41617, Clematis, 17 January 1923
MARECAUX, Gerald C A, Vice Admiral, Royal Navy, 3 September 1920
MAREHANT, Reginald W, Able Seaman, J 12395, Victory, 24 October 1922
MARGETTS, Dennis J, Lieutenant, FAA, 466 Flight, Furious, 8 June 1932
MARINER, Henry O, Deck Hand, MMR, 821982, Iolaire, 1 January 1919
MARKEY, Charles A, Ty/Sub Lieutenant, RNVR, Hood Battalion, RND, 23 January 1920
MARKS, Albert E, Chief Stoker, P/K 28977, Cardiff, 23 August 1937
MARKS, Alfred E, Wireless Telegraph Operator, RNR, WTS 375, Europa, 14 November 1918
MARKS, Nathan, Able Seaman, RNVR, London Z 5421, Linmere, steamship, 27 December 1918
MARNOCK, William, Leading Deck Hand, RNR, SD 1563, ML.72, motor launch, 4 February 1919
MARR, Henry G, Paymaster Lieutenant Commander, RNVR, London Division, RNVR, 11 May 1931
MARR, William, Engineman, RNR, ES 1290, Thalia, 21 November 1918
MARRAY, William, Yeoman of Signals, 207266, Tiger, 8 January 1919
MARRINER, Harold, Butcher 3c, RAN, 4908, Australia (RAN), 8 January 1920
MARRIOTT, Edward, Able Seaman, P J 41822, Nelson, 2 February 1936
MARROTTE, William, Able Seaman, J 46224, Scarab, 5 September 1926
MARS, Walter P, Shipwright 1c, 345979, Vindictive, 24 August 1925
MARSH, Alex B, Surgeon Commander, RN Hospital, Haslar, 7 September 1923
MARSH, Arthur E S, Able Seaman, P/J 90381, Victory, 28 January 1931
MARSH, Eugene, Able Seaman, J 42309, Emperor of India, 17 July 1921
MARSH, Henry, Stoker Petty Officer, K 14716, Carlisle, 22 October 1919
MARSH, Sydney H B, Stoker Petty Officer, C/K 61916, Ceres, 25 June 1934
MARSH, Thomas, Shipwright 1c, P/M 26662, Excellent, 13 March 1936
MARSH, William A, Stoker 1c, C/K 63651, Kent, 26 July 1938
MARSHALL, Albert H, Leading Stoker, K 10007, K.15, 29 August 1919
MARSHALL, Albert, Able Seaman, 208743, Landrail, 1 January 1919
MARSHALL, Charles A, Leading Stoker, 305171, Centurion, 14 September 1923
MARSHALL, Edwin J A, Ordinary Seaman, JX 130182, Nelson, 29 March 1930
MARSHALL, George E, Able Seaman, J 99203, Brisbane (RAN), 9 May 1923
MARSHALL, Harry H, Lieutenant (E), Dolphin, 10 June 1935
MARSHALL, Henry G, Leading Seaman, J 23995, Victory, 14

July 1923
MARSHALL, James, Fireman, MMR, 956807, Eaglet, 18 November 1919
MARSHALL, John J, Stoker 2c, P/KX 85612, Royal Navy, 13 April 1935
MARSHALL, Robert, Able Seaman, RNVR, Mersey Z 1 149, Hood Battalion, RND, 9 April 1919
MARSHALL, Robert N, Lieutenant, RNR, Royal Naval Reserve, 23 January 1920
MARSHALL, Stanley, Able Seaman, RNVR, Tyneside Z 3/144, Collingwood Battalion, RND, 28 March 1919
MARSHALL, Thomas W, Ordinary Seaman, J 58619, Pembroke, 12 March 1919
MARSHALL, William, Officer's Chief Cook, 364083, Victory III, 29 October 1919
MARSHALSEA, Percy G, Lieutenant, Naval Ordnance Department, Admiralty, 11 March 1937
MARSHMAN, Kenneth, Stoker 1c, P/KX 80136, Effingham, 17 January 1931
MARTIN, Alexander, Seaman, RNR, A 3059, Rugby, 27 November 1918
MARTIN, Aubrey L, Telegraphist, RNVR, Bristol Z 6631, Vaunter, 15 November 1918
MARTIN, Charles J, Able Seaman, J 90561, M.1, 12 November 1925
MARTIN, Daniel C, Deck Hand, RNR, DA 18370, John Robert, 1 February 1919
MARTIN, Edward W, Private, RM, S 14015 (Deal), RM Labour Corps, 11 April 1919
MARTIN, Ernest A, Chief Petty Officer, 211200, Caroline, 7 June 1926
MARTIN, George E, Boy 2c, J 97437, Ganges, 11 July 1920
MARTIN, Gilbert, Leading Seaman, RNVR, Clyde Z 6503, Mandala, steamship, 18 April 1919
MARTIN, Harold E, Able Seaman, SS 10737, Dragon, 14 September 1924
MARTIN, Henry T, Able Seaman, C/J 106200, Pembroke, 18 December 1931
MARTIN, James F, 2nd Hand, RNR, SA 1122, Boadicea II, 6 March 1919
MARTIN, John, Deck Hand, MMR, 933879, Frank, 14 October 1919
MARTIN, John, Leading Seaman, 230259, Blenheim, 1 July 1921
MARTIN, John A, Lieutenant, RNR, Lobster, 6 October 1919
MARTIN, Lawrence M, Cadet, Revenge, 30 July 1927
MARTIN, Malcolm, Deck Hand, RNR, DA 12067, Iolaire (Pembroke, O/P), 1 January 1919
MARTIN, Norman, Seaman, RNR, C 3397, Iolaire (Victory, O/P), 1 January 1919
MARTIN, Percy, Able Seaman, J 18000, Snowdrop, 22 February 1919
MARTIN, Percy, Shipwright 1c, 345735, Cyclops, 17 December 1925
MARTIN, Reginald T, Officer's Steward 1c, L 3191, Hermes, 18 May 1924
MARTIN, Richard, Ty/Surgeon Lieutenant, Grenville, 25 December 1919
MARTIN, Ronald H, Marine, 23006 (Ch), Enterprise, 31 October 1929
MARTIN, Samuel A, Ordinary Seaman, MMR, 930305, Prestol, mercantile fleet auxiliary, 1 April 1919
MARTIN, Thomas W, Private, RMLI, 12898 (Ch), Dragon, 17 December 1920
MARTIN, Wilfrid W G G, Musician, RMB, RMB X 532, Hermes, 21 March 1935
MARTIN, William E, Chief Stoker, 276984, Comus, 22 February 1919
MARTIN, William G, Able Seaman, J 103840, Diomede, 3 July 1925
MARTINS, Reginald C K, Leading Seaman, 202519, Wallington, 20 February 1919

MARTYN, John L, Ty/Lieutenant, RNR, Vivid, 25 October 1919
MASON, Arthur J, Stoker 1C, KX 78370, Cairo, 5 January 1930
MASON, Francis R, Able Seaman, RNVR, Clyde Z 4732, Drake Battalion, RND, 7 March 1919
MASON, Henry G, Private, RMLI, 20517 (Po), RM Headquarters, 31 July 1921
MASON, Joseph H, Chief Petty Officer, D/JX 160909, Codrington, 1 July 1939
MASON, Marcus B (real name, but served as James Biggs), Leading Seaman, 226435, Collingwood Battalion, RND, 28 November 1918
MASON, Peter, Stoker 1c, K 26961, Lilac, 12 November 1918
MASON, Reginald G W, Commander, RNR, Iolaire, 1 January 1919
MASON, Reginald, Marine, X 1685 (Po), RM Deal, 10 June 1935
MASON, Walter J, Chief Petty Officer Cook, 346978 (Po), Malaya, 17 February 1921
MASSIE, Thomas, Deck Hand, RNR, DA 2549, Thalia, 16 May 1919
MASSON, James, Chief Petty Officer, 147752, Greta, 11 February 1919
MASTERS, Charles J, Chief Petty Officer, J 2296, Royal Navy, 2 October 1928
MASTERS, George A, Leading Stoker, 312517, Diligence, 15 February 1919
MATHER, Charles W, Boy 2c, J 101646, Ganges, 12 May 1921
MATHER, George, Stoker, RNR, S 5251, Astraea, 24 April 1919
MATHESON, Angus, Deck Hand, RNR, DA 18694, Iolaire (Winner, O/P), 1 January 1919
MATHESON, Angus, Seaman, RNR, X 7434, St Delphine (Boscawen), 9 March 1939
MATHESON, Donald, Trimmer, RNR, TS 2637, George Fenwick, 16 February 1919
MATHESON, George Mc I, Stoker Petty Officer, D/K 60027, Gannet, 25 January 1934
MATHESON, Malcolm, Deck Hand, RNR, DA 11907, Iolaire (Iceland, O/P), 1 January 1919
MATSON, Charles L, Able Seaman, J 32394, Prince Eugene, 15 November 1918
MATTHEWS, Albert R, Leading Victualling Assistant, M 15986, Iolaire, 1 January 1919
MATTHEWS, Alfred W, Warrant Master at Arms, Tamar, 22 May 1939
MATTHEWS, Arthur, Leading Cook, M 1634, Vivid, 21 April 1923
MATTHEWS, Charles, Engine Room Artificer 2c, M 6689, L.24, 10 January 1924
MATTHEWS, David O, Petty Officer Cook, M 97, King George V, 15 April 1922
MATTHEWS, Edward, Signalman, RNVR, Bristol Z 1576, Hazel, 3 December 1918
MATTHEWS, Edward, Stoker 1c, P/K 64672, M.2, 29 January 1932
MATTHEWS, Ernest E, Stoker 1c, K 37610, Fox, 1 January 1919
MATTHEWS, Francis V, Boy 2c, JX 144760, Pembroke, 5 November 1935
MATTHEWS, Frederick W T, Regulating Petty Officer, 300592, Tiger, 17 December 1919
MATTHEWS, Henry J, Able Seaman, J 21664, Fisgard, 14 November 1927
MATTHEWS, Leslie N, Ordnance Artificer 1c, M 5197, Revenge, 1 September 1929
MATTHEWS, Patrick, Private, RM, S 14588 (Deal), RM Labour Corps, 18 February 1919
MATTHEWS, Sydney H, Boy 1c, JX 137694, Ganges, 13 September 1933
MATTHEWS, William A, Stoker 1c, C/KX 87674, Thetis, 3 June 1939
MATTHEWS, William B, Boy 1c, J 106576, Ganges, 16 March 1924
MATTHIAS, Joseph, Stoker Petty Officer, 306237, Vivid, 18

February 1921
MATTIN, Nigel, Ordinary Seaman, J 106965, Hood, 26 November 1925
MATTINGLEY, William J, Able Seaman, SSX 18955, Repulse, 17 June 1938
MATTISON, Cuthbert W, Chief Shipwright 2c, 343935, Ark Royal, 19 May 1920
MATTISON, Sidney, Stoker Petty Officer, K 375, Merlin, 7 July 1921
MAUDE, Maurice A, Lieutenant, FAA, 401 Flight, Vindictive, 12 December 1926
MAULKIN, William H, Leading Seaman, J 7706, Calypso, 24 November 1918
MAUNDER, Cecil E, Leading Telegraphist, RNVR, ZP 1028, President IV, 8 December 1918
MAUNDERS, Harry L T, Stoker Petty Officer, K 58502, Vivid, 29 December 1926
MAUNSELL-SMYTH, George H, Commander (E), Frobisher, 28 February 1932
MAXEY, Lawrence S, Leading Seaman, J 12586, Royal Oak, 31 January 1922
MAXTED, Albert V, Petty Officer, 211613, Colombo, 28 October 1921
MAXWELL, George E, Stoker 1c, C/KX 75548, Cyclops, 25 December 1932
MAXWELL, Henry S, Chief Petty Officer Writer, M 7313, Vivid, 22 January 1929
MAXWELL, James, Lieutenant, RNR, Macedonia, 15 October 1924
MAXWELL, John G, Leading Stoker, P/K 60408, Pangbourne, 10 May 1931
MAY, Charles H, Chief Petty Officer, 186585 (Ch), Kent, 7 August 1919
MAY, Charles, Leading Stoker, K 23562, Savage, 20 February 1919
MAY, Cyril, Stoker 1c, C/K 62438, Valiant, 22 December 1930
MAY, Fredrick J, Gunner, RMA, RMA S 1042, Howitzer Brigade, RMA, 12 February 1919
MAY, George, Stoker Petty Officer, K 1615, Carlisle, 20 August 1925
MAY, Harry, Stoker Petty Officer, 305369, Magnolia, 17 April 1920
MAY, James, Deck Hand, RNR, SD 4299, Essex II, 7 March 1919
MAY, Percival C, Able Seaman, P/J 100631, Royal Sovereign, 3 March 1932
MAY, Walter, Corporal, RM, S 11334 (Deal), RM Labour Corps, 13 December 1918
MAY, William, Chief Writer, 345195, Impregnable, 11 October 1921
MAY, William C A, Chief Shipwright 2c, 342960, Tamar, 6 September 1922
MAY, William H, Lieutenant Commander, Pembroke, 23 March 1919
MAY, William P, Able Seaman, J 29283 (Po), Erin's Isle, 7 February 1919
MAY, William T J, Boatswain, Blenheim, 11 June 1921
MAYDELL, Stanley A, Stoker Petty Officer, C/KX 77914, Pandora, 6 March 1939
MAYHEW, Bertie, Chief Stoker, 308183, Pembroke, 18 April 1925
MAYLE, George W H, Leading Seaman, 202701, Pembroke, 15 December 1918
MAYNARD, Gilbert J, Able Seaman, J 52901, Iron Duke, 23 July 1922
MAYNARD, Sidney, Stoker 1c, K 57904, Cricket, 5 July 1925

McA'LEARY, Peter, Stoker 2c, K 66154, Curlew, 23 August 1926
McALISTER, Donald, Lieutenant, RNR, Mikasa, 12 February 1919
McALLISTER, George H, Lieutenant, RNR, Pontypool, 23 May 1919

McARA, William J, Electrical Artificer 3c, M 8402, Victory, 20 February 1919
McARTHUR, Archibald, Deck Hand, RNR, DA 13257, Wallington, 11 December 1918
McASKILL, Donald, Deck Hand, RNR, DA 21143, Iolaire (Gunner, O/P), 1 January 1919
McASKILL, Donald, Seaman, RNR, A 7041, Iolaire (Sigismund, O/P), 1 January 1919
McASKILL, John, Deck Hand, RNR, SD 4519, Plumpton, 12 November 1918
McASKILL, Malcolm, Leading Seaman, RNR, A 2338, Vesta, 12 November 1918
McAULAY, Donald, Seaman, RNR, C 2065, Iolaire (Emperor of India, O/P), 1 January 1919
McAULAY, Donald M, Deck Hand, RNR, SD 4363, Iolaire (ML.372, O/P), 1 January 1919
McBEARTY, Henry, Petty Officer, D/J 25675, Terror, 31 August 1934
McBRIDE, John L, Engine Room Artificer 4c, RNVR, Mersey 5/102, Repulse, 10 June 1923
McBURNEY, David, Trimmer, RNR, ST 3082, Duchess of Kent, 7 December 1918
McCABE, William J, Private, RMLI, 15918 (Ply), Foresight, 23 March 1919
McCALL, Robert, Stoker 1c, K 61736, Fisgard, 3 February 1930
McCALMONT, Andrew, Ordinary Seaman, J 69697, Hannibal, 21 March 1919
McCANN, John (real name, but served as John Gallagher), Stoker 2c, K 54407 (Ch), Erin's Isle, 7 February 1919
McCARRY, Daniel B, Blacksmith 3c, C/MX 51606, Sheffield, 9 October 1938
McCARTHY, Charles J, Signalman, D/SX 86, Royal Navy, 9 January 1939
McCARTHY, Frank L, Colour Sergeant, RMLI, 11191 (Ch), Chatham Division, RMLI, 8 February 1919
McCARTHY, Fred C, Carpenter, MMR, Iolaire, 1 January 1919
McCARTHY, Horace G, Leading Seaman, J 38359, Pembroke, 3 November 1929
McCARTHY, James R, Telegraphist, RNVR, London Z 5486, Goissa, 15 November 1918
McCARTHY, Patrick, Leading Stoker, 304730, Bellerophon, 19 January 1919
McCARTHY, William G, Commissioned Supply Officer, Drake, 26 August 1939
McCLINTOCK, John W L, Vice Admiral, President, RN College, Greenwich, 23 March 1929
McCLURE, John S, Electrical Artificer 3c, M 30409, Victory, 28 September 1925
McCLURE, John, Warrant Mechanician, RAN, Sydney (RAN), 1 February 1919
McCLYMONT, John, Deck Hand, RNR, SD 3856, Victory, 10 December 1918
McCOMB, David, Chief Stoker, 299381, Vivid, 12 March 1919
McCORMACK, Frederick S, Able Seaman, C/J 97004, Pembroke, 9 August 1933
McCORMACK, William G, Able Seaman, MMR, 600928, Revenger, 29 November 1918
McCORMICK, Robert W J, Stoker 1c, KX 76884, Pembroke, 8 August 1929
McCORQUODALE, Duncan, Engine Room Artificer 4c, M 33412, Kinross, 17 June 1919
McCOY, Harold J, Able Seaman, J 23268, Argus, 11 November 1919
McCOY, John R, Able Seaman, SS 7701, Glowworm, 26 August 1919
McCRAE, John, Stoker 1c, K 22922, Glowworm, 25 August 1919
McCREA, Robert L, Stoker Petty Officer, MC 49 (Ch), Gentian, 15 July 1919
McCULLOCH, John, Py/Midshipman, RNVR, Mersey Division, RNVR, 7 May 1939

McCULLOCH, John D, Able Seaman, 216573, Pembroke, 8 April 1919
McCULLOCH, Robert, Telegraphist, J 90378, Curacoa, 23 November 1922
McCUTCHEON, Richard, Boy 2c, J 113441, Ganges, 31 January 1926
McDERMOTT, Edward, Leading Seaman, 208984, Aphis, 2 January 1921
McDERMOTT, James, Coastguardsman, 283038, HM Coast Guard Station Sandgate, 28 November 1920
McDIARMID, Peter C, Chief Engine Room Artificer 2c, M 17438, Pembroke, 11 January 1919
McDONAGH, John J, Stoker 1c, K 14409, Victory, 4 April 1921
McDONAGH, William, Stoker 1c, P/KX 78559, Delphinium, 16 December 1930
McDONALD, Alexander, Leading Seaman, C 2046, Iolaire (Nairn, O/P), 1 January 1919
McDONALD, Angus, Leading Seaman, RNR, A 3091, Bronwen, steamship, 27 November 1918
McDONALD, Angus, Seaman, RNR, A 4433, Themistocles, steamship, 13 December 1918
McDONALD, Augustus A, Marine, 19389 (Ply), Devonshire, 26 July 1929
McDONALD, David, Signal Boy, RNR, SB 1265, Iolaire, 1 January 1919
McDONALD, Donald, Deck Hand, RNR, DA 17809, Iolaire (Santora, O/P), 1 January 1919
McDONALD, Donald, Engine Room Artificer 4c, M 7995, H.42, 23 March 1922
McDONALD, Donald, Leading Deck Hand, RNR, SD 3516, Iolaire (Dreel Castle, O/P), 1 January 1919
McDONALD, Donald, Leading Seaman, RNR, B 2688, Iolaire (Ganges, O/P), 1 January 1919
McDONALD, Donald, Seaman, RNR, A 5351, Iolaire (SS Mandala, O/P), 1 January 1919
McDONALD, Donald G L L, Petty Officer Telegraphist, J 67471, Adventure, 31 January 1930
McDONALD, Edward S, Private, RM, S 2518 (Deal), 63rd Divisional Train, RND, 13 November 1918
McDONALD, Edward V J, Private, RMLI, 18042 (Ch), Royal Oak, 14 March 1922
McDONALD, Francis, Junior Reserve Attendant, M 34146, Victory, 29 November 1918
McDONALD, James, Able Seaman, J 36476, Vivid, 29 March 1920
McDONALD, John, Seaman, RNR, A 2558, Iolaire (Venerable, O/P), 1 January 1919
McDONALD, John, Seaman, RNR, A 3074, Iolaire (Emperor of India, O/P), 1 January 1919
McDONALD, John, Seaman, RNR, A 4490, Iolaire (Seahorse, O/P), 1 January 1919
McDONALD, Lionel E, Engineer Lieutenant, Lucia, 1 November 1924
McDONALD, Roderick J, Seaman, RNR, A 2966, Iolaire (Wallington, O/P), 1 January 1919
McDONALD, William G, Engineer Lieutenant Commander, Bruce, 31 May 1932
McDONALD, William H, Marine, 18423 (Ch), Hermes, 26 March 1929
McDONNELL, John, Stoker Petty Officer, K 9465, Torch, 6 July 1923
McDOUGAL, William J, Able Seaman, 233413, Fantome, 6 October 1923
McDOWALL, Thomas, Able Seaman, J 18352, PC.61, patrol boat, 4 May 1919
McDOWELL, Alexander M, Lieutenant, Pilot's Course, 23 March 1931
McELHERAN, George F, Boy 1c, J 100410, Erin, 9 March 1922
McELHINNEY, Richard J, Writer, D/MX 56415, Drake, 17 May 1938
McEMERY, Henry W, Regulating Petty Officer, C/M 39907, Pembroke, 8 October 1935
McEVELY, David A, Petty Officer 1c, 196906, Caledon, 4 November 1919
McFADYEN, John, Engineman, RNR, ES 2563, Lily & Maggie, 25 November 1918
McFARLANE, Francis, Fireman, MMR, 904813, Eaglet, 7 April 1919
McFARLANE, Henry, Chief Stoker, 292760, Fisgard, 22 May 1921
McFETRIDGE, Robert, Trimmer, RNR, TS 8708, Satellite, 19 September 1919
McGARRY, John L, Able Seaman, J 97436, Danae, 13 August 1927
McGEORGE, Reginald H, Able Seaman, J 101426, Valerian, 22 October 1926
McGILL, William A, Petty Officer, 217484, Victory, 17 November 1919
McGILLVRAY, William, Stoker 1c, 309172 (Dev), Cassandra, 5 December 1918
McGLADDERY, William, Sub Lieutenant, RNVR, Hughli, Royal Fleet Auxiliary, 26 April 1919
McGOWAN, Donald O, Leading Telegraphist, RAN, 13919, FAA, 440 Flight, Adelaide (RAN), 19 March 1930
McGOWAN, Joseph, Able Seaman, J 114296, Mantis, 3 October 1927
McGOWAN, Patrick, Leading Stoker, K 60604, Conquest, 10 July 1927
McGOWN, James, Seaman, RNR, A 6345, Goeland II, 27 March 1919
McGRATH, Matthew, Stoker 2c, K 63398, Victory, 22 March 1924
McGREGOR, James, civilian engineer, Hood, battlecruiser, 19 May 1919, ship building, explosion on board, killed
McGUINNESS, Richard A, Stoker Petty Officer, K 12851, Ormonde, 30 March 1924
McGUIRE, William, Private, RMLI, 7315 (Ch)(RFR B 1213), Deal Battalion, RND, 16 April 1919
McHUGH, James, Engineman, RNR, ES 1133, Rigoletto, 11 January 1920
McHUGH, Niel, Stoker, RNR, V 310, Maidstone, 25 March 1919
McHUGO, Henry E, Private, RMLI, 12125 (Ch), Saranac, steamship, 26 December 1918
McILKENNON, Patrick, Deck Hand, RNR, DA 22775, Victory, 19 December 1919
McINNES, Gilbert, Leading Seaman, 234343, Matador, steamship, 21 February 1919
McINNES, Malcolm, Seaman, RNR, A 8896, Iolaire (Dublin, O/P), 1 January 1919
McINTOSH, Harold, Stoker 1c, K 59805, Bryony, 1 August 1923
McINTOSH, James, Skipper, MMR, Cinceria, 10 December 1918
McINTOSH, Ronald C G, Ordinary Seaman, D/SSX 22241, Rodney, 16 June 1938
McIVER, Alexander, Leading Seaman, C 1691, Iolaire, 1 January 1919
McIVER, Angus, Seaman, RNR, C 1855, Iolaire, 1 January 1919
McIVER, Donald, Deck Hand, RNR, DA 18720, Iolaire, 1 January 1919
McIVER, George A, Leading Stoker, C/K 58124, L.26, 17 January 1933
McIVER, John, Mate, MMR, Iolaire, 1 January 1919
McIVER, John, Seaman, RNR, A 2496, Iolaire (Letterflourie, O/P) 1 January 1919
McIVER, John, Seaman, RNR, C 2619, Iolaire (Victory, O/P), 1 January 1919
McIVER, Murdo, Deck Hand, RNR, SD 775, Iolaire (Zena Dare, O/P), 1 January 1919
McIVOR, Louis, Seaman, MMR, 669951, Gosforth, 17 January 1919
McKAY, David, Colour Sergeant, RMLI, 8618 (Ply), Colleen, 3 February 1919
McKAY, John, Seaman, RNR, B 7239, Nelson, 7 September 1931

McKAY, Malcolm, Seaman, RNR, C 2613, Iolaire, 1 January 1919

McKENNA, John, Aircraftsman 1c, F 36250, RNAS Oldbury, 12 November 1918

McKENNAN, William D, Engine Room Artificer 4c, P/MX 52949, Glasgow, 4 January 1938

McKENZIE, Alexander, Seaman, RNR, B 3892, Iolaire, 1 January 1919

McKENZIE, Alexander, Seaman, RNR, C 1663, Iolaire (Roman Empire, O/P), 1 January 1919

McKENZIE, John, Seaman, RNR, A 3274, Iolaire (Emperor of India, O/P), 1 January 1919

McKENZIE, Malcolm A, Lieutenant, Department Naval Ordnance, Admiralty, 2 April 1922

McKENZIE, Maurice, Leading Signalman, 233095, Red Gauntlet, 6 December 1918

McKENZIE, Murdo, Seaman, RNR, B 3122, Iolaire (Pembroke, O/P), 1 January 1919

McKENZIE, Murdo, Trimmer, RNR, TS 6842, Silanion, 24 February 1919

McKENZIE, Roderick, 2nd Hand, RNR, DA 7246, Iolaire (Romilly, O/P), 1 January 1919

McKEON, John T, Leading Stoker, K 3417, Assistance, 19 May 1920

McKIE, William, Able Seaman, RNVR, Clyde Z 5128, Orcoma, 29 November 1918

McKINNION, Niel, Deck Hand, RNR, DA 14734, Nairn, 8 May 1919

McKINNON, Angus, Deck Hand, RNR, SD 2615, Iolaire (Attentive III, O/P), 1 January 1919

McKNIGHT, William, Petty Officer Recruiter, C/188612, Royal Navy, 13 November 1938

McLAIN, John W, Private, RM, S 2086 (Deal), 149th RN Field Ambulance, RM Medical Unit, RND, attached 63rd Divisional Train, RND, 12 December 1918

McLAUGHLIN, Charles, Plumber 1c, 344307, Lion, 8 October 1920

McLAUGHLIN, Cyril E, Lieutenant, Humber, 11 August 1919

McLEAN, James, Leading Seaman, 237977, Mersey, 3 January 1919

McLEAN, Malcolm, Seaman, RNR, C 2679, Iolaire (Vernon, O/P), 1 January 1919

McLEAN, Murdo, Deck Hand, MMR, 974252, Iolaire (Snipe, O/P), 1 January 1919

McLEAN, Murdo, Seaman, RNR, D 1903, Iolaire (Victory, O/P), 1 January 1919

McLEAY, Angus, Seaman, RNR, B 3689, Iolaire (Emperor of India, O/P), 1 January 1919

McLELLAN, Duncan, Deck Hand, RNR, SD 4759, ML.161, motor launch, 8 December 1918

McLENNAN, Finlay, Deck Hand, RNR, DA 18771, Iolaire, 1 January 1919

McLENNAN, Murdo, Deck Hand, RNR, DA 18784, Queen, 24 December 1918

McLEOD, Alexander, Deck Hand, RNR, DA 12625, Pekin, 2 December 1918

McLEOD, Alexander, Seaman, RNR, A 2745, Iolaire (Imperieuse, O/P), 1 January 1919

McLEOD, Alexander A, Deck Hand, RNR, SD 3455, Iolaire (Idaho, O/P), 1 January 1919

McLEOD, Angus, Deck Hand, MMR, 973997, Iolaire (Snipe, O/P), 1 January 1919

McLEOD, Angus, Deck Hand, RNR, DA 19972, Iolaire (Resmilo, O/P), 1 January 1919

McLEOD, Angus, Deck Hand, RNR, SD 4548, Iolaire (Pembroke, O/P), 1 January 1919

McLEOD, Angus, Seaman, RNR, C 2808, Iolaire, 1 January 1919

McLEOD, Angus, Seaman, RNR, D 1920, Iolaire (Vernon, O/P), 1 January 1919

McLEOD, Donald, Deck Hand, RNR, DA 10941, Iolaire (Quercia, O/P), 1 January 1919

McLEOD, Donald, Deck Hand, RNR, SD 1427, Iolaire (Dreel Castle, O/P), 1 January 1919

McLEOD, Donald, Seaman, RNR, B 3553, Iolaire (SS Saxonia, O/P), 1 January 1919

McLEOD, John, Able Seaman, MMR, 109650, Eaglet, 22 March 1920

McLEOD, John, Able Seaman, MMR, 974908, Iolaire (Rose, O/P), 1 January 1919

McLEOD, John, Deck Hand, MMR, 968097, Iolaire (Victor, O/P), 1 January 1919

McLEOD, John, Deck Hand, RNR, DA 15739, Iolaire (Attentive III, O/P), 1 January 1919

McLEOD, John, Deck Hand, RNR, DA 3691, Blue Sky, 8 December 1918

McLEOD, John, Deck Hand, RNR, SD 3607, Iolaire (ML.411, O/P), 1 January 1919

McLEOD, John, Seaman, RNR, C 4847, Blenheim, 8 April 1923

McLEOD, John, Seaman, RNR, D 2261, Flexin, steamship, 13 November 1918

McLEOD, John K, Lieutenant Commander, Victory, 26 September 1920

McLEOD, Malcolm, Deck Hand, RNR, DA 12081, Iolaire (Wallington, O/P), 1 January 1919

McLEOD, Malcolm, Deck Hand, RNR, DA 14384, Iolaire (Idaho, O/P), 1 January 1919

McLEOD, Murdo, Seaman, RNR, B 4219, Iolaire, 1 January 1919

McLEOD, Murdo, Seaman, RNR, X 18132 A, Royal Naval Reserve, 11 April 1935

McLUCKIE, John, Warrant Engineer, Mackay, 28 May 1926

McMAHON, Maurice, Lieutenant Commander, President, 25 October 1919

McMAHON, Patrick, Leading Signalman, D/JX 133965, Drake, 13 February 1937

McMANUS, Thomas M, Private, RM, S 310 (Deal), RM Deal, 25 May 1919

McMANUS, William, Trimmer, MMR, Crescent, 24 March 1919

McMILLAN, Allan Mc R, Shipwright 2c, RNVR, CD/X 1275, Pembroke, 27 April 1936

McMILLAN, John, Able Seaman, J 91891, Cornwall, 15 March 1930

McMILLAN, John, Deck Hand, RNR, SD 4589, Mazurka, 9 July 1919

McMILLAN, John, Stoker, RNR, S 2753, Grafton, 21 May 1919

McMILLAN, Malcolm, Seaman, RNR, D 1848, Iolaire (Imperieuse, O/P), 1 January 1919

McMORRIS, Robert W, Stoker, RNR, V 1736, Victory, 13 November 1932

McMURRAY, Frederick L, Able Seaman, J 105537, Vivid, 29 August 1927

McNAB, John, Honorary Captain, RNR, Royal Naval Reserve, 12 February 1925

McNAIR, George Mc F, Lieutenant, RNR, Europa, 6 January 1919

McNAUGHT, Alexander, Able Seaman, J 104206, Vernon, 17 February 1930

McNEAL, John, Stoker 1c, C/KX 75275, Emerald, 11 March 1938

McNEIL, Allan, Ty/2nd Lieutenant, RMLI, 1st RM Battalion, RND, 24 February 1919

McPHAIL, Donald, Seaman, RNR, D 2222, Iolaire (Pembroke, O/P), 1 January 1919

McPHEE, Neil, Deck Hand, RNR, SD 1715, Europa, 15 December 1918

McPHERSON, David R, Engineman, RNR, S 2477, J A C, Admiralty hired drifter, 5 February 1919

McPHERSON, John E, Boy 2c, RAN, 11126, Tingira (RAN), 16 March 1919

McQUADE, William, Marine, 17376 (Ply), Queen Elizabeth, 18 January 1933

McQUEEN, Andrew, Paymaster, RNR, Hughli, Royal Fleet Auxiliary, 26 April 1919

McQUILLAN, James, Seaman, RNR, A 7602, John Robert, 1

February 1919
McRAE, Alexander, Seaman, RNR, X 6106 C, Vivid, 20 December 1932
McRITCHIE, Angus, Deck Hand, RNR, DA 16522, Iolaire (Hero, O/P), 1 January 1919
McSHANE, James, Stoker 1c, K 55302, Pembroke, 13 August 1922
McSHANE, Jeremiah, Leading Stoker, RNR, U 1510, Pembroke, 29 November 1918
McSWEENEY, John, Stoker 1c, K 24837, Bootle, 26 January 1919
McSWEENEY, John P, Leading Stoker, K 40797, H.47, 9 July 1929
McVEIGH, John M, Stoker 1c, Mc 433 (Ch), Gentian, 15 July 1919
McWATTIE, John J H, Lieutenant, RNR, Aspasia, 2 January 1919

MEACHIN, Arthur, Stoker Petty Officer, 297045, Cerberus, 15 March 1923
MEAD, Albert J, Able Seaman, C/J 97731, Pembroke, 3 October 1933
MEAD, Edward M L, Private, RMLI, S 2569 (Ch), Glory, 13 February 1919
MEAD, Frank, Chief Engine Room Artificer 1c, 268938, Vivid, 4 April 1919
MEAD, George W, Officer's Steward 2c, L 6193, TB.36, torpedo boat, 22 January 1919
MEAD, John D, Leading Cook, M 2042, Dido, 17 March 1920
MEADOWCROFT, Allan, Able Seaman, J 94841, Valerian, 22 October 1926
MEAKER, Leonard S, Able Seaman, J 108162, Valerian, 22 October 1926
MEAKIN, William, Ty/Gunner, Peregrine, 9 December 1918
MEARS, Arthur F, Act/Warrant Officer, Royal Navy, 6 February 1920
MEARS, Ivor W J, Boy 2c, J 94269, Impregnable, 28 February 1919
MEASOM, Ernest, Able Seaman, JX 125478, Campbell, 11 January 1930
MEATON, Charles H, Leading Stoker, K 21965, Victory, 16 January 1927
MEDWAY, Samuel W, Able Seaman, D/J 109647, Vivid, 19 September 1931
MEECH, Stanley E, Able Seaman, P/J 98805, Victory, 30 January 1931
MEEHAN, Michael A, Surgeon Lieutenant, Earl of Peterborough, 13 December 1918
MEEK, Leslie, Chief Warrant Engineer, RNR, Royal Naval Reserve, 1 December 1919
MEEK, Thomas, Foreman Rigger, MMR, 777136, Hughli, Royal Fleet Auxiliary, 26 April 1919
MEEKER, Stanley W, Stoker 1c, KX 91301, Penelope, 16 June 1939
MEHIGAN, Sidney L, Sick Berth Attendant, P/M 39307, RN Hospital, Malta, 13 October 1931
MELDRUM, John, Ordinary Seaman, MC 574, Larkspur, 9 June 1919
MELDRUM, Robert, Ordinary Seaman, RNVR, 14**66 (only partly decipherable), Royal Sovereign, 22 March 1924
MELVILL, James C D, Ty/Lieutenant, RNVR, Royal Naval Volunteer Reserve, 30 January 1920
MELVIN, John, Engine Room Artificer 3c, M 35372, Curlew, 17 July 1929
MEMORY, Stanley T, Electrical Artificer Apprentice, M 54069, Pembroke, 23 February 1937
MEN, Chuen, Officer's Steward 1c, Tamar, 1 September 1927
MENDHAM, Edward, Private, RMLI, 12147 (Po), Mersey, 31 December 1918
MENEREAU, Cecil D, Gunner, Voyager, 31 August 1939
MENHENITT, Arthur, Leading Cook's Mate, M 2827, Concord, 11 March 1919

MERCER, David, Major General, RM, RM, Adjutant General, 1 July 1920
MERCER, Stuart W A, Stoker 2c, K 54268, Dominion, 28 November 1918
MERCHANT, Henry P, Engineer Lieutenant, Whitley, 21 April 1926
MEREFIELD, William V, Able Seaman, 226574, Espiegle, 12 June 1922
MERLE, Harold E, Leading Stoker, P/K 7140, Excellent, 19 December 1931
MERRYWEATHER, John C, Petty Officer, J 8602, Victory, 18 February 1929
MERSH, Frederick A, Stoker 1c, K 14089, Goshawk, 22 January 1919
MESSENGER, William G, Lieutenant, RNR, Kunishi, 30 December 1918
METCALF, Walter, Chief Petty Officer, 154022, Courageous, 15 February 1919
METCALFE, Fred, Able Seaman, SS 8401 (Po), K.5, 20 January 1921
METCALFE, John F, Midshipman (E), Engineering Course, 11 October 1926

MICKLEBOROUGH, William L, Ty/Skipper, RNR, Quintia, 26 November 1918
MIDDLEDITCH, Frederick J, Able Seaman, J 98494, Columbine, 26 February 1928
MIDDLEMIST, Robert J M, Lieutenant, K.5, 20 January 1921
MIDDLETON, Allan G T, Able Seaman, P/J 105859, Victory, 12 November 1930
MIFSUD, James, Petty Officer Steward, 362346, St Angelo, 26 July 1936
MIHELL, George V, Chief Engine Room Artificer 2c, M 1960, Victory, 17 February 1919
MILES, Albert E, Stoker Petty Officer, K 17884, Pembroke, 8 June 1921
MILES, Archie S, Regulating Petty Officer, K 14922, Ramillies, 16 May 1920
MILES, Claude L, Stoker 1c, P/K 59275, Royal Sovereign, 23 July 1932
MILES, Ernest A, Leading Seaman, J 8763 (Ch), Vittoria, 31 August 1919
MILES, Harold A, Sick Berth Steward, 350984, Fox, 8 March 1919
MILES, John G, Engine Room Artificer Apprentice, C/MX 46948, Pembroke, 6 September 1931
MILES, William G, Corporal, RME, RME S 1277, RM Engineers, 30 January 1919
MILES, William H, Junior Reserve Attendant, M 19708, Victory, 15 February 1919
MILES, William S, Stoker Petty Officer, 307232, Columbine, 2 August 1920
MILFORD, Albert J, Commissioned Gunner, Clematis, 17 July 1926
MILLAIS, Sir John E, John, Lieutenant Commander (Rtd), Royal Navy, 30 September 1920
MILLAR, Hugh, Petty Officer, P/J 15505, Effingham, 11 January 1933
MILLAR, Thomas, Deck Hand, RNR, SD 3520, Victory, 9 March 1919
MILLARD, Harold, Stoker 1c, K 62220, M.1, 12 November 1925
MILLARD, Thomas Mc G, Able Seaman, J 95327, Merazion, 30 April 1929
MILLER, Alexander, Chief Skipper, RNR, Royal Naval Reserve, 15 March 1936
MILLER, Alexander S, Chief Petty Officer, 171848, Victory, 17 December 1919
MILLER, Allan W, Able Seaman, J 51831, Dunedin, 26 September 1926
MILLER, Arthur J, Leading Stoker, D/KX 75520, Ormonde, 29 October 1933

MILLER, Arthur S, Private, RM, 15924 (Po), President III, 22 March 1919
MILLER, Charles F, Chief Engine Room Artificer 2c, 271248, Ganges, 9 February 1920
MILLER, Francis L, Stoker 2c, K 59873, Victory, 21 November 1922
MILLER, George W G, Deck Hand, RNR, DA 19340, Pekin, 25 January 1919
MILLER, George W, Leading Seaman, J 11912, Jed, 1 March 1919
MILLER, Herbert, Act/Ty/Paymaster, RNR, Halcyon, 6 December 1918
MILLER, Herbert, Leading Seaman, J 13236, Hawkins, 2 May 1921
MILLER, John, Leading Seaman, J 13442, Vernon, 1 May 1922
MILLER, John J, Musician, RMB, RMB 809, RM Eastney, 15 December 1920
MILLER, Lawrence W, Leading Seaman, J 20680, Grenville (ex-Skate), 19 October 1919
MILLER, Major H Mac D, Colour Sergeant, RM, 215819 (Po), RM Depot Portsmouth, 3 February 1937
MILLER, Robert, Master at Arms, 233010, Benbow, 17 August 1925
MILLER, Robert O, Engine Room Artificer 1c, 272509, Cyclops, 27 April 1924
MILLER, Roy L, Corporal, RM, 213488 (Po), Royal Marines HQ, 1 June 1924
MILLER, William J, Engineman, RNR, ES 5280, Marconi III, 10 January 1919
MILLER, William O, Stoker Petty Officer, D/K 65711, Drake, 4 December 1934
MILLETT, Edward G, Artificer Engineer, Titania, 16 January 1919
MILLETT, Thompson H, Paymaster Captain, Victory, 10 April 1920
MILLIGAN, John D, Surgeon Lieutenant, Blake, 7 January 1920
MILLINER, Sydney S, Leading Seaman, RNR, C 1708, Batsford, steamship, 11 January 1919
MILLS, Alfred J, Boy 2c, J 91628, Impregnable, 11 February 1919
MILLS, Arthur J, Ordnance Artificer Apprentice, M 38432, Fisgard, 19 August 1926
MILLS, Edward M (served as Edward Haddock), Telegraphist, P/J 101509, Cormorant, 6 July 1932
MILLS, Frederick W, Mechanician, 309822, Queen Elizabeth, 8 October 1920
MILLS, Harry H, Leading Seaman, C/JX 132693, Ramillies, 1 November 1936
MILLS, Herbert G, Private, RMLI, 14270 (Ch), Europa, 29 November 1918
MILLS, Herbert J, Able Seaman, J 33787, Argus, 9 October 1929
MILLS, John Y, Lieutenant, FAA, 402 Flight, Eagle, 1 February 1927
MILLS, Samuel R, Chief Stoker, 145479, Vivid, 3 February 1919
MILLS, Walter, Able Seaman, J 60799, Arrogant, 27 November 1918
MILLS, William H, Warrant Shipwright, Pandora, 17 January 1923
MILLSON, Henry B, Stoker 1c, SS 119660, Victory, 9 April 1919
MILLWARD, Edgar F, Electrical Artificer 3c, M 25784, Valiant, 5 July 1925
MILNER, Dermod R, Chaplain, Garth Castle, hospital ship, 17 September 1919
MILNER, Frank, Able Seaman, RNVR, Tyneside Z 7991, Egmont, 6 December 1918
MILVERTON, Frederick W, Gunner, RMA, RMA 1859, RM Eastney, 6 February 1919
MINETT, Desmond R, Midshipman, RNVR, Royal Naval Volunteer Reserve, 15 May 1936
MINIHANE, Thomas, Coastguardsman 3c, 182289, Colleen, 27 July 1921
MINTER, Alfred E, Stoker 1c, 303046, Galatea, 21 March 1919

MITCHELL, Albert E, Chief Mechanician 2c, 289904, Pembroke, 24 September 1920
MITCHELL, Alfred D, Petty Officer, J 24827, Pembroke, 11 July 1928
MITCHELL, Benjamin, Stoker 1c, KX 75243, Revenge, 1 May 1927
MITCHELL, Cecil C, Deck Hand, RNR, DA 21024, Tea Rose, 8 December 1918
MITCHELL, Charles A, Ordinary Seaman, SS 8741 (Ch), Erin's Isle, 7 February 1919
MITCHELL, David C, Chief Petty Officer Cook, 347257, Southampton, 31 March 1923
MITCHELL, Dennis E, Able Seaman Air Mechanic, P/JX 154173, RN Hospital, Haslar, 4 February 1939
MITCHELL, Ernest, Petty Officer, P/J 102658, Thetis, 3 June 1939
MITCHELL, Frederick C, Officer's Cook 1c, L 4508, Curacoa, 17 September 1921
MITCHELL, George C, Marine, 19924 (Ply), Drake, 22 December 1937
MITCHELL, Harold, Petty Officer, 216864, Lucia, 28 February 1919
MITCHELL, Henry H, Stoker 1c, K 21403, Royal Sovereign, 12 January 1927
MITCHELL, James, Telegraphist, J 92053, L.24, 10 January 1924
MITCHELL, Percy, Able Seaman, RNVR, ZW 752, Drake Battalion, RND, 10 April 1919
MITCHELL, Richard C, Stoker 1c, D/K 64155, Vivid, 26 May 1932
MITCHELL, Robert M, Ordinary Seaman, D/JX 146035, Devonshire, 11 August 1938
MITCHELL, Sam W, Electrical Artificer 4c, M 31010, Iron Duke, 20 December 1922
MITCHELL, Thomas P, Engine Room Artificer 4c, M 7080, Columbine, 24 January 1921
MITCHELL, Thomas, Able Seaman, JX 126137, Glorious, 14 January 1930
MITCHELL, Tom, Engine Room Artificer 4c, M 25028 (Po), Penarth, 4 February 1919
MITCHELL, William, Able Seaman, RNVR, R 2702, Regimental Depot, RND, Aldershot, 18 November 1918

MOBBS, William E, Ordinary Seaman, J 91196, Benbow, 12 June 1919
MOCKRIDGE, Frederick J, Leading Cook, D/MX 50531, Rodney, 28 August 1938
MOFFAATT, Alfred, Able Seaman, C/JX 126876, Cumberland, 17 July 1933
MOFFATT, Alaister S, Stoker 1c, P/KX 84091, Proteus, 5 May 1938
MOFFATT, John, Colour Sergeant, RMLI, 12336 (Ply), Impregnable, 7 August 1919
MOHAMED, Ismail, 2nd Tindal, 357, Stork, 22 August 1938
MOIST, Leslie, Able Seaman, D/J 81175, Norfolk, 22 December 1938
MOLES, Frank G F, Yeoman of Signals, 230523, Victory, 30 May 1921
MOLONEY, Stephen, Seaman, RNR, B 4558, Anson Battalion, RND, 23 March 1919
MONAGHAN, Edward, Private, RM, S 15116 (Deal), RM Labour Corps, 6 December 1918
MONAGHAN, Joseph, Able Seaman, JX 126384, Queen Elizabeth, 19 February 1930
MONEY, John P, Lieutenant Commander, Royal Navy, 10 October 1933
MONGER, William, Private, RMLI, 14136 (Ply), RMLI, Plymouth Division, 27 February 1919
MONK, William J, Able Seaman, D/J 113852, Malaya, 4 January 1932
MONKCOM, George W L, Commissioned Writer, Victory, 16 January 1922

MONKS, Henry G, Stoker 1c, K 16124, Benbow, 22 June 1920
MONTE, Emilio, Officer's Steward 2c, 122493, Kinross, 16 June 1919
MONTGOMERY, Angus, Deck Hand, RNR, SD 1445, Iolaire (Unity, O/P), 1 January 1919
MONTGOMERY, Hugh F, Major & Brevet Lieutenant Colonel, RM, on loan to Army, 9 December 1920
MONTGOMERY, Norman, Seaman, RNR, C 3391, Iolaire (Ariel II, O/P), 1 January 1919
MOODY, Charles J, Able Seaman, J 7839 (Dev), Vesper, 24 June 1919
MOODY, George C, Stoker Petty Officer, P/K 59431, Royal Navy, 20 March 1937
MOONEY, James G N P, Chief Stoker, C/K 11764, Vivid, 6 October 1931
MOONEY, John, 2nd Hand, RNR, A 6297, Dreel Castle, 26 April 1919
MOORE, Alfred, Petty Officer 1c, 144186 (Ch), Chelmsford, 16 October 1919
MOORE, Arthur H, Able Seaman, J 38131, Velox, 18 February 1919
MOORE, Bertie M, Able Seaman, J 30231, M.27, monitor, 28 November 1918
MOORE, Charles A, Ordinary Seaman, SS 8551, Simpson, 13 April 1919
MOORE, Edmund L D, Lieutenant, Furious, 3 August 1928
MOORE, Frank, Gunner, RMA, RMA 14288, 3rd Battalion, RM, 9 June 1919
MOORE, Frederick F, Painter 1c, M 2593, Challenger, 14 December 1918
MOORE, George P, Blacksmith 2c, M 12644, Victory, 21 April 1922
MOORE, Harold, Deck Hand, MMR, Iolaire, 1 January 1919
MOORE, Henry, Chief Officer, HM Coast Guard, HM Coast Guard Cornwall, 7 September 1919
MOORE, Joseph G, Cooper 1c, 341717, Ajax, 2 June 1919
MOORE, Reginald, Able Seaman, J 34369, Verdun, 24 May 1921
MOORE, Reginald, Marine Tailor, 22988 (Ch), RM Barracks Chatham, 25 June 1938
MOORE, Ronald W, Stoker 1c, K 57902, Chelmsford, 7 December 1922
MOORE, Thomas W, Honorary Lieutenant, RNR, Royal Naval Reserve, 7 April 1937
MOORE, Walter, Chief Stoker, P/K 28982, Royal Navy, 3 January 1938
MOORE, Walter E, Able Seaman, RNVR, R 6241, Anson Battalion, RND, 16 February 1919
MOORE, William E, Gunner, RMA, RMA 15359, RMA Eastney, 10 February 1919
MOORE, William E, Leading Seaman, 235944 (Po), Julius, 13 February 1920
MOORE, Willilam P, Bandsman, 14997 (Po), Royal Marines HQ, 29 May 1924
MOOREY, Charles F, Stoker 1c, C/KX 77630, Cumberland, 11 April 1933
MOOSSA, Almas, 2nd Seedie, Britomart, 21 April 1919
MORAM, James M, Stoker 1c, SS 121536, Tring, 17 May 1920
MORCEL, Headby A, Ordinary Seaman, J 91014, Catspaw, 31 December 1919
MORCOM, John E, Sub Lieutenant (E), RN Engineering College, Keyham, 26 November 1938
MORETON, John A, Captain, Erebus, 19 March 1920
MOREY, Reginald G, Petty Officer, P/J 113934, Widgeon, 22 May 1939
MORGAN, David B, Lieutenant, Pilot's Course, 15 May 1925
MORGAN, Frederick, Petty Officer 1c, 139526, Vivid, 27 March 1919
MORGAN, George, Able Seaman, RNVR, Bristol Z 322, Howe Battalion, RND, 9 January 1919
MORGAN, George P, Petty Officer, 239799, M.1, 12 November 1925
MORGAN, Harold H, Engine Room Artificer Apprentice, MX 46033, Fisgard, 8 November 1929
MORGAN, Harry, Leading Stoker, K 17310, Titania, 23 March 1922
MORGAN, John, Greaser, MMR, 997498, St Fagan, 25 July 1919
MORGAN, John C V, Commander, RNR, Royal Naval Reserve, 26 April 1937
MORGAN, John E, Skipper, RNR, Royal Naval Reserve, 12 February 1937
MORGAN, Richard - see FAIRMAN, Richard M, Leading Stoker
MORGAN, Richard, Able Seaman, MMR, 757076, Fylde, 19 November 1918
MORGAN, Thomas D, Stoker 1c, D/KX 78737, Stormcloud, 18 May 1931
MORGANS, James A, Able Seaman, P/JX 132797, Thetis, 3 June 1939
MORLEY, James W, Officer's Steward 2c, L 7828, Alecto, 14 July 1919
MORLEY, Rowland C, Able Seaman, J 86911, Durban, 22 August 1922
MORRELL, George J, Midshipman (E), RN College Keyham, 21 June 1936
MORRELL, Philip H, Leading Seaman, J 47854, Victory, 23 October 1926
MORRIS, Arthur S H, Commander, Nelson, 28 March 1937
MORRIS, Ernest J, Able Seaman, 202794, Victory, 19 May 1921
MORRIS, Frank, Electrical Artificer 4c, MX 47096, Victory, 9 September 1928
MORRIS, George, Able Seaman, J 50369, Benbow, 19 January 1919
MORRIS, James F, Act/Lieutenant, Julius, 2 February 1921
MORRIS, Nelson V, Petty Officer, P/216174, RN Hospital, Haslar, 29 October 1938
MORRIS, Percy F, Petty Officer 1c, Wales Z 1891, President, 19 November 1918
MORRIS, Sidney, Coastguardsman 2c, 154368, Pembroke, 28 November 1922
MORRIS, Thomas, Able Seaman, C/J 96156, M.2, 29 January 1932
MORRIS, Thomas, Engineman, RNR, TS 1205, Eaglet, 27 April 1920
MORRIS, Thomas H, Ordinary Telegraphist, J 40837, Cyclops, 21 February 1919
MORRIS, William J, Able Seaman, P/J 113074, Shamrock, 19 January 1933
MORRISEY, James, Stoker 1c, K 62854, M.1, 12 November 1925
MORRISON, Angus, Deck Hand, RNR, DA 12126, Iolaire (St Ayles, O/P), 1 January 1919
MORRISON, Angus, Leading Deck Hand, RNR, DA 14310, Iolaire (Implacable, O/P), 1 January 1919
MORRISON, Daniel J, Shipwright 1c, 342391, Challenger, 16 December 1918
MORRISON, Donald, Deck Hand, RNR, DA 11859, Iolaire (Sir Mark Sykes, O/P), 1 January 1919
MORRISON, Donald, Deck Hand, RNR, DA 14665, Pontefract, 26 October 1919
MORRISON, Douglas, Deck Hand, RNR, DA 16315, Excel, 10 January 1919
MORRISON, Farquhar, Seaman, RNR, B 3161, Iolaire (Pembroke, O/P), 1 January 1919
MORRISON, Finlay, Deck Hand, RNR, SD 4515, Iolaire (ML.560, O/P), 1 January 1919
MORRISON, George, Deck Hand, RNR, SD 3499, Iolaire (ML.307, O/P), 1 January 1919
MORRISON, John, Deck Hand, RNR, DA 21746, Iolaire (David Conn, O/P), 1 January 1919
MORRISON, John, Leading Seaman, RNR, C 3026, Iolaire (SS Norwood, O/P), 1 January 1919
MORRISON, John, Petty Officer, A 5306, Iolaire (Vivid, O/P), 1 January 1919

MORRISON, John, Seaman, RNR, A 4645, Iolaire (Venerable, O/P), 1 January 1919
MORRISON, Norman, Deck Hand, RNR, DA 12088, Iolaire (Urka, O/P), 1 January 1919
MORRISON, Roderick, Honorary Engineer Commander, RNR, Royal Naval Reserve, 6 September 1931
MORRISON, Roderick, Seaman, RNR, C 1750, Iolaire (Ganges II, O/P), 1 January 1919
MORROW, Carlton H, Chief Petty Officer, 215589, Abdiel, 21 February 1924
MORSE, William C, Corporal, RM, G 17740 (Ply), RN Hospital, Plymouth, 3 September 1937
MORTEMORE, James A, Private, RMLI, 12302 (Po), Portsmouth Division, RMLI, 25 January 1920
MORTIMER, Thomas W, Telegraphist, D/JX 138326, Thetis, 3 June 1939
MORTON, John, civilian engineer, Hood, battlecruiser, 19 May 1919, ship building, explosion on board, killed
MORTON, John A, Captain, Royal Navy, 19 March 1920
MORTON, William J R, Boy 2c, J 108571, Ganges, 27 January 1924
MORTON, William M, Engineer Lieutenant, Ark Royal, 28 December 1918
MOSS, George T, Chief Stoker, 306064, Raider, 23 June 1920
MOSS, Herbert, Ordinary Seaman, J 89339, Pembroke, 11 December 1919
MOSS, James G, Engineer Lieutenant Commander, President, 12 November 1918
MOTT, Alan B, Lieutenant, Conqueror, 13 February 1919
MOTTERAM, Roy, Leading Seaman, P/J 10964, Victory, 4 February 1934
MOUGHTON, Arthur W, Deck Hand, RNR, DA 5260, Crescent Moon, 8 March 1919
MOULD, Arthur L, Petty Officer 2c, 177745, Vernon, 11 November 1919
MOULD, William, Petty Officer, J 7392 (Po), K.5, 20 January 1921
MOULDEN, Robert B, Private, RMLI, 9312 (Ch), Chatham Division, RMLI, 27 February 1919
MOULTON, Arthur W, Leading Signalman, C/J 113007, Medway, 13 May 1936
MOULTRIE, Lionel G F, Midshipman, Valiant, 23 April 1919
MOUNCE, Harold, Engine Room Artificer 4c, M 6280, Ramillies, 24 January 1920
MOUNTJOY, Robert E, Seaman, RNR, A 5650, Vivid, 14 December 1918
MOXHAM, Henry C, Able Seaman, D/JX 130512, Vivid, 25 January 1933
MOYES, Arthur J, Signal Lieutenant, Vivid, 22 November 1920
MOYLAN, Thomas J, Yeoman of Signals, RAN, 7619, Australia (RAN), 16 February 1919
MOYSE, Albert, Engineman, RNR, ES 3862, Dorothy Rose, 7 December 1918
MOYSE, Victor C, Able Seaman, J 23751, M.1, 12 November 1925

MUDFORD, Edward S, Leading Seaman, J 26706, P.54, patrol boat, 18 March 1920
MUGGLETON, Leonard H J, Chief Petty Officer, 224713, Valerian, 22 October 1926
MUIR, George, Leading Stoker, D/KX 78208, Diamond, 18 November 1938
MUIR, Robert J, Corporal, RMLI, 11359 (Ply), RM, 8th Battalion, 10 November 1920
MUIR, Robert W R, Chief Ordnance Artificer, C/MX 58260, Pembroke, 11 April 1939
MULFORD, Alfred, Stoker 1c, C/K 61933, Pembroke, 27 December 1932
MULLANEY, Frank, Trimmer, MMR, 949505, Britisher, 18 September 1919
MULLEN, John, Private, RM, S 14610 (Deal), RM Labour Corps, 27 May 1919
MULLETT, Loftus, Stoker 2c, D/KX 83457, Drake, 17 February 1934
MULLIGAN, Patrick, Stoker 1c, D/KX 89328, Diamond, 18 November 1938
MULLINS, Edward F, Deck Hand, RNR, DA 13045, ML.73, motor launch, 15 November 1918
MULLROY, Christopher, Petty Officer, 196715, Cleethorpes, 10 September 1919
MUNDAY, John W, Leading Boatman, 232149, Pembroke, 10 October 1922
MUNDY, Thomas C G, Leading Seaman, C/J 41099, Wessex, 19 August 1930
MUNN, James T, Stoker Petty Officer, K 2715, Godetia, 22 April 1920
MUNNO, Charles J, Yeoman of Signals, 239367, Ramillies, 3 January 1928
MUNRO, Alexander, Stoker 1c, 300999, Victory, 23 July 1921
MUNRO, Henry, Stoker Petty Officer, C/308914, Pembroke, 9 October 1938
MUNRO, Torquil, Seaman, RNR, A 4517, President III, 31 January 1919
MUNROE, Thomas D, Able Seaman, J 114228, Delphinium, 18 April 1929
MUNSON, Cecil J, Able Seaman, C/J 110993, Medway, 23 January 1932
MUNT, James, Stoker 2c, SS 125724, Victory II, 13 March 1921
MURCH, John, Chief Officer, HM Coast Guard, HM Coast Guard, 2 September 1920
MURDOCH, Peter, Able Seaman, J 50732, Crescent, 22 December 1918
MURLEY, Edward J, Leading Stoker, K 12273, Cardiff, 24 August 1927
MURPHY, Alexander, Schoolmaster (CWO), Ganges, 7 March 1927
MURPHY, Christopher, Stoker 1c, K 26523, Chelmer, 22 November 1918
MURPHY, David, Commissioned Gunner, Royal Navy, 25 May 1925
MURPHY, Frederick L, Boy 2c, J 97898, Impregnable, 6 October 1920
MURPHY, Robert J, Stoker Petty Officer, P/K 63070, Dainty, 21 October 1934
MURPHY, Sidney G, Able Seaman, P/JX 128569, Barham, 30 March 1939
MURPHY, William D R, Lieutenant, RNR, Lobelia, 1 January 1919
MURRAY, Albert, Able Seaman, C/JX 148718, Hostile, 7 November 1937
MURRAY, Alexander, Deck Hand, RNR, DA 6787, Bon Accord, 25 February 1919
MURRAY, Archibald, Ordinary Seaman, J 82097 (Dev), New Zealand, 24 October 1919
MURRAY, David, Midshipman, Royal Navy, 10 September 1935
MURRAY, David, Telegraphist, P/JX 138913, Victory, 28 November 1936
MURRAY, Donald, Deck Hand, RNR, DA 19804, Iolaire (Joseph Burgen, O/P), 1 January 1919
MURRAY, Donald, Petty Officer, RNR, B 2811, Iolaire (Imperiuese, O/P), 1 January 1919
MURRAY, Edward G, Paymaster Rear Admiral, Admiralty Paymaster Director General, 3 July 1933
MURRAY, Evander, Seaman, RNR, DA 1829, Iolaire (Thames, O/P), 1 January 1919
MURRAY, Frederick, Able Seaman, J 44493 (Ch), Glowworm, 25 August 1919
MURRAY, John A, Telegraphist, J 54248, Birmingham, 2 April 1921
MURRAY, John, Deck Hand, RNR, DA 22055, Leonard, 8

January 1920
MURRAY, John, Deck Hand, RNR, SD 4689, Iolaire (ML.461, O/P), 1 January 1919
MURRAY, John, Seaman, RNR, C 2061, Iolaire (Pembroke, O/P), 1 January 1919
MURRAY, Lindley A, Petty Officer, J 57, Argus, 4 January 1925
MURRAY, Roderick, Ordinary Seaman, J 86329, Iolaire (Roxburgh, O/P), 1 January 1919
MURRAY, Wallace, Private, RMLI, 20779 (Po), RM, 6th Battalion, 27 August 1919
MURRAY, William, Seaman, RNR, A 6772, Iolaire (Pembroke, O/P), 1 January 1919
MURRAY, William J, Deck Hand, RNR, DA 11925, Iolaire (Pactolus, O/P), 1 January 1919
MURRELL, Charles E, Petty Officer, C/J 57064, Royal Oak, 28 August 1930
MURRIE, James, Stoker 1c, D/KX 80608, Berwick, 4 September 1935
MURTON, James J, Able Seaman, C/JX 126051, Whirlwind, 6 January 1932
MURTON, Willis, Boy 2c, JX 158216, Royal Navy, 6 June 1938
MUSKETT, Ernest W, Stoker Petty Officer, K 111, Pembroke, 23 February 1920
MUSSELL, Walter F, Steward, P/L 14878, Challenger, 24 August 1932
MUSSETT, Leslie A, Seaman, RNR, X 8198 B, Victory XI, 11 February 1932
MUSTOE, Andrew, Able Seaman, 166669, Victory, 3 April 1919
MUTTER, Ernest W, Able Seaman, SS 6441, Delphinium, 12 July 1919

MWINGE, Bin A, Seedie, X 222, Flora, 10 February 1930

MYATT, George, Stoker, D/K 20522, Terror, 15 February 1935
MYERS, Charles, Able Seaman, C/JX 128824, RN Barracks Portsmouth, 30 October 1937

N

NANCARROW, Alfred G, Commissioned Engineer, Blenheim, 18 March 1924

NANGLE, Henry N M, Lieutenant, FAA, 446 Flight, Courageous, 19 May 1931

NANGLE, James J, Able Seaman, D/J 27816, Dunoon, 28 September 1933

NAPIER, Sir Trevylyan W, Admiral, Commander in Chief North America Station, 30 July 1920

NAPP, Ernest J, Able Seaman, J 30765, Pembroke, 2 February 1919

NARAN, Tomas, Officer's Steward 3c, LX 20237, Dauntless, 4 December 1926

NASH, Albert, Telegraphist, RNVR, London Z 6563, P.40, patrol boat, 13 November 1918

NASH, Arthur J, Stoker 1c, K 25515, Hawkins, 5 October 1924

NASH, Arthur P, Stoker Petty Officer, K 7380, Pembroke, 8 December 1918

NASH, Charles A, Ordinary Seaman, J 89843, Warspite, 25 May 1921

NASH, Jack, Stoker Petty Officer, P/K 17438, Royal Navy, 27 December 1934

NASON, George W P, Sergeant, RM, 15738 (Po), Egmont, 26 December 1932

NAUDE, Reginald C, Sick Berth Attendant, D/MX 47018, RN Hospital, Plymouth, 2 July 1929

NAUGHTON, Daniel, Stoker Petty Officer, 289258, Despatch, 14 September 1924

NAYLOR, Charles G, Commander, Admiralty, Plans Division, 27 January 1924

NAZARETH, John B, Officer's Chief Cook, G/LX 10888, Emerald, 12 February 1935

NEAL, Henry, Trimmer, RNR, TS 2240, Zaria, mercantile fleet auxiliary, 24 December 1918

NEALE, Arthur A, Sergeant, RMLI, 16383 (Ch), RM, 6th Battalion, 9 September 1919

NEALE, George, Able Seaman, J 99423, Tiger, 7 May 1928

NEARY, Lawrence, Stoker 1c, K 33841, Speedy, 23 September 1922

NEATE, John H D, Victualling Chief Petty Officer, 347341, Cormorant, 13 March 1919

NEEDHAM, Louis, Lieutenant Paymaster, RNR, Godetia, 20 December 1918

NEEDHAM, Tom, Leading Seaman, J 7891, Vivid, 21 January 1929

NEIGHBOUR, Herbert E, Able Seaman, J 89919, M.1, 12 November 1925

NEIL, Arthur C, Able Seaman, J 110537, Defiance, 30 March 1929

NEILD, James H, Lieutenant Commander, President IV, 6 July 1919

NEILSON, Stanley, Leading Stoker, K 6673, Lucia, 26 August 1928

NELSON, Charles W, Officer's Steward 2c, L 4055 (Ch), Fandango, 3 July 1919

NELSON, Henry, Leading Stoker, RNR, V 466, Marlow, 11 December 1918

NELSON, John L, Shipwright 1c, P/M 17302, Hood, 1 January 1934

NELSON, Walter J, Engineman, RNR, ST 1220, Ganges, 3 January 1919

NESBITT, Samuel, Stoker 1c, C/K 65899, Pembroke, 15 December 1932

NETHERWAY, William P J, Private, RMLI, 11323 (Ch) (RFR B 1755), 1st RM Battalion, RND, 25 February 1919

NETTALL, Fred, Chief Engine Room Artificer 2c, M 7307, H.33, 21 January 1929

NETTLETON, George E H, Sergeant, RMLI, 15241 (Ch), 3rd Battalion, RM, 23 November 1918

NETTLETON, James W, Able Seaman, 215030, Pembroke, 10 December 1918

NEVIN, John T, Regulating Petty Officer, M 36359, Pembroke, 3 September 1923

NEW, Herbert, Boy 2c, J 99722, Ganges, 12 December 1920

NEW, John E, Able Seaman, C/J 92566, Boadicea, 14 August 1939

NEWBOLD, Aubrey C, Lieutenant Commander, Titania, 14 September 1924

NEWBY, Alfred, Leading Boatman, 308779, Victory, 8 December 1921

NEWCOMBE, William, Stoker 3c, K 59393, Vivid, 2 June 1921

NEWELL, Alfred, Able Seaman, 198325, Fisgard, 5 February 1925

NEWHAM, Jesse, Armourers Crew, M 4485, Victory, 7 February 1919

NEWING, Edward, Stoker 1c, K 22771, L.24, 10 January 1924

NEWING, William, Stoker Petty Officer, 280636, Prince Eugene, 17 November 1918

NEWINGTON, James P, Stoker Petty Officer, 307026, Harrow, 22 February 1919

NEWLAM, Frank, Petty Officer, C/J 5034, Calcutta, 23 September 1931

NEWLAND, Frederick J, Leading Seaman, J 49071, Hood, 12 June 1921

NEWLAND, Harold E, Stoker 1c, C/K 67153, Cambrian, 16 January 1932

NEWLAND, William, Officer's Cook 2c, P/L 7505, Victory, 20 April 1934

NEWMAN, Albert A, Private, RMLI, 7825 (Ch) (RFR B 800), Chatham Battalion, RND, 5 December 1918

NEWMAN, George, Stoker 1c, 295503, Bullfinch, 9 June 1919

NEWMAN, Henry, Seaman, RNR, C 1744, Harden, mercantile fleet auxiliary, 22 February 1919

NEWMAN, James V, Able Seaman, J 43827, Eagle, 27 December 1929

NEWMAN, John W, Able Seaman, D/J 105864, Norfolk, 18 April 1935

NEWMAN, Percival G, Chief Engine Room Artificer 2c, M 785, Valerian, 22 October 1926

NEWPORT, John, Stoker 1c, K 1189, Terror, 5 November 1928

NEWSHAM, James, Lieutenant, FAA, 466 Flight, Furious, 8 June 1932

NEWTON, Alfred N, Regulating Petty Officer, C/M 37819, Pembroke, 11 December 1934

NEWTON, Charles W, Able Seaman, P/J 91324, Victory, 20 September 1932

NEWTON, George W, Boy 2c, J 102912, Ganges, 27 October 1921

NEWTON, Isaac, Armourer, 342179, Titania, 19 November 1918

NEWTON, William H, Petty Officer, J 30575, Vivid, 22 February 1922

NG, Fook, Officer's Cook 3c, Herald, 6 January 1929

NICHOLAS, Adolphus C J, Able Seaman, J 33795, Blue Sky, tender to Queen Elizabeth, 12 June 1922

NICHOLAS, Eric, Able Seaman, D/JX 146070, Pearl, 22 June 1936

NICHOLAS, Henry S, Musician, RMB, RMB 736, Eagle, 9 January 1925

NICHOLAS, Reginald D, Marine, 21667 (Ply), Queen Elizabeth, 15 August 1935

NICHOLAS, Richard, Leading Seaman, J 94358, Victory, 22 July 1927

NICHOLL, Horace R, Cook, D/MX 51489, Capetown, 18 December 1937

NICHOLLS, Albert, Petty Officer 1c, 137402, Vivid, 23 November 1918

NICHOLLS, David, Stoker 1c, K 57984, M.1, 12 November 1925
NICHOLLS, Douglas J, Boy 1c, J 103993, Iron Duke, 4 August 1923
NICHOLLS, Thomas A, Gunner, RMA, RMA 16203, Revenge, 9 March 1921
NICHOLS, Christopher H, Commissioned Engineer, Veronica, 31 August 1928
NICHOLS, Edgar, Marine, Ply/21303, Hood, 18 August 1923
NICHOLS, William R, Ty/Skipper, RNR, Bombardier, 27 March 1919
NICHOLSON, Basil E E, Petty Officer, C/J 90818, Pembroke, 27 February 1935
NICHOLSON, Donald, Deck Hand, RNR, DA 8955, Iolaire (Calera, O/P), 1 January 1919
NICHOLSON, George A, Engine Room Artificer, RNR, EA 1923, Satellite, 26 January 1919
NICHOLSON, John, Lieutenant, FAA, 463 Sqn, Courageous, 25 June 1928
NICHOLSON, Roland, Able Seaman, J 108665, Vivid, 23 February 1928
NICHOLSON, Stanley G, Act/Leading Seaman, P/J 107109, Hood, 10 May 1936
NICHOLSON, William F, Leading Seaman, J 19840, M.1, 12 November 1925
NICKELS, Denis W G, Able Seaman, J 97780, Vivid, 15 August 1927
NICKLEN, Reginald J, Able Seaman, J 45235 (Po), Caradoc, 22 September 1919
NICKLEN, Thomas A, Able Seaman, RNVR, Bristol Z 1916, Doric, steamship, 10 August 1919
NICOLAIDI, Leonard F, Stoker 1c, SS 123040 (Ch), Empress, 14 August 1919
NICOLL, David I, Py/2nd Lieutenant, RM, RM Deal, Kent, 12 January 1933
NICOLL, Kenneth C, Sergeant, RMLI, 11676 (Po), Portsmouth Division, RMLI, 19 December 1918
NICOLSON, Malcolm, Seaman, RNR, A 5396, Iolaire (Magpie, O/P), 1 January 1919
NICOLSON, Murdo, Deck Hand, RNR, SD 4258, Iolaire (ML.10, O/P), 1 January 1919
NIGHTINGALE, Albert H, Able Seaman, J 93827, Pembroke, 15 December 1922
NIGHTINGALE, Stanley J, Able Seaman, RNVR, Bristol Z 11066, Duchess of Devonshire, 19 March 1919
NIXON, Ernest G, Lieutenant (E), Excellent, Course, 30 November 1935
NIXON, John, Gunner, RMA, RMA 9841, Tamar, 24 April 1922

NOAD, Augustus J, Leading Signalman, J 26921, Vivid, 27 February 1919
NOAD, William S, Chief Stoker, 306741, Lowestoft, 20 May 1925
NOAKES, Ernest S, Stoker 1c, K 18600, Jumna, 9 December 1920
NOBES, Arthur J R, Leading Seaman, J 26386, Excellent, 19 February 1921
NOBES, George F, Able Seaman, J 27933, Tomahawk, 12 June 1921
NOBLE, Alexander, Leading Trimmer, RNR, TS 1513, Vivid, 12 May 1919
NOBLE, Alexander, Trimmer, RNR, TS 1476, William Bond, 1 January 1919
NOBLE, George H, Private, RMLI, S 476 (Po), Portsmouth Battalion, RND, 25 June 1919
NOBLE, James, Deck Hand, RNR, DA 19967, Satellite, 21 March 1919
NOBLE, William, Stoker 1c, K 41261, Cumberland, 14 December 1918
NOONAN, John, Stoker 2c, P/KX 8456, Royal Navy, 14 February 1935
NORLEY, Percy G, Petty Officer, J 6568, Impregnable, 1 November 1927
NORLON, William G, Able Seaman, J 102840, Diomede, 3 July 1925
NORMAN, George T, Colour Sergeant, RM, B 15674, Royal Marines HQ, June 1928
NORMAN, Horace O D, Lieutenant Commander, RNR (Rtd), Royal Naval Reserve, 18 June 1919
NORMAN, William, Leading Stoker, 308772, Titania, 23 November 1921
NORMAN, William, Stoker 1c, K 1223, Wireless Telegraph Station Seychelles, 6 May 1919
NORMAN, William H, Act/Leading Airman, FX 76326, FAA, 800 Sqn, Ark Royal, 2 August 1939
NORMAN, William H, Chief Engine Room Artificer 2c, M 2535, Centaur, 23 February 1920
NORMANTON, Joe, Leading Seaman, J 78462, Diomede, 20 May 1925
NORMINGTON, Herbert H, Able Seaman, J 45712 (Dev), K.10, 12 February 1919
NORRIS, Allan V, Able Seaman, J 88069, Iroquois, 14 February 1923
NORRIS, Edward J, Private, RMLI, S 1048 (Ch), Cyclops II, 12 January 1919
NORRIS, Leslie C, Leading Telegraphist, C/J 101627, Moth, 3 February 1932
NORRIS, Walter, Petty Officer, RNR, C 3585, Satellite, 20 February 1919
NORRIS, William C, Commissioned Boatswain, Fisgard, 21 September 1920
NORTH, Percy B, Ordinary Seaman, JX 125329, Cardiff, 19 June 1928
NORTH, William, Able Seaman, MMR, 614548, Viscol, Royal Fleet Auxiliary, 17 February 1919
NORTHCOTT, George T, Able Seaman, J 29731, Teal, 18 February 1924
NORTON, Charles, Leading Seaman, 171791 (Ch), Douglas, 10 February 1919
NORTON, Frank, Officer's Steward 1c, L 4709, Valerian, 22 October 1926
NORTON, Reginald J, Stoker Petty Officer, D/K 23339, Calcutta, 18 May 1935
NOSWORTHY, Ernest P, Lieutenant Commander, RNR, Royal Naval Reserve, 18 January 1925
NOYCE, Alfred G, Act/Yeoman of Signals, J 22520, Valerian, 22 October 1926

NUGENT, Charles R, Leading Telegraphist, J 35887, Duke, 15 December 1918
NUTTALL, Fred, Act/Chief Engine Room Artificer 2c, M 7304, H.33, 21 September 1929
NUTTON, John T, Officer's Steward 1c, L 3351, Shakespeare, 12 July 1929

O

OADES, Arthur, Stoker 1c, K 9154, Pembroke, 21 February 1930

OAKES, George, Artificer Engineer, TB.36, torpedo boat, 28 November 1919

OAKLEY, Alfred E, Engineer Sub Lieutenant, RNR, Sunhill, 2 June 1919

OAKLEY, William T, Stoker 1c, K 3331, Emperor of India, 23 February 1919

OATES, George, Marine, X 218 (Ch), Valiant, 13 April 1931

OATES, Thomas, Leading Seaman, RNVR, Clyde Z 6365, President III, 18 February 1919

O'BRIEN, Cornelius, Stoker 1c, K 29524, Vixen, 21 November 1918

O'BRIEN, Daniel, Mechanician, 304458 (Dev), Cassandra, 5 December 1918

O'BRIEN, Dermod D, Lieutenant, RAF Station Gosport, 21 March 1939

O'BRIEN, Joseph, Stoker 1c, K 14645, Dolphin, 29 December 1923

O'BRIEN, Terence R, Able Seaman, J 100437, Ramillies, 8 November 1929

O'BRIEN, Wilfred, Stoker 1c, P/K 66554, Peterel, 13 August 1930

O'BRIEN, William, Chief Stoker, P/K 12324, Courageous, 12 June 1932

O'CALLAGHAN, Denys P, Lieutenant Commander, Constance, 16 September 1924

O'CALLAGHAN, Frederick G, Supply Chief Petty Officer, M 2767, Caradoc, 9 August 1925

O'CARROLL, Kevin, Fireman, MMR, 898499, Eaglet, 22 November 1918

O'CONNELL, Denis, Leading Stoker, K 9557 (Dev), L.55, 4 June 1919

O'CONNELL, George, Engineman, RNR, TS 5876, Warland, 6 January 1919

O'CONNELL, Richard P, Fireman, MMR, Victory, 30 March 1919

O'CONNELL, Thomas F, Petty Officer, 89851, Indus, 15 July 1919

O'CONNOR, Denis, Trimmer, RNR, TS 7697, Goissa, 15 November 1918

O'DRISCOLL, Denis, Stoker 1c, D/K 46480, Bryony, 12 June 1933

O'DRISCOLL, James A, Ordinary Seaman, D/SSX 17998, Capetown, 15 September 1937

O'DRISCOLL, Michael D, Ty/Lieutenant, RNR, Western Queen, 6 December 1918

O'DWYER, Albert A E, Able Seaman, C/J 102310, M.2, 29 January 1932

O'DWYER, Arthur, Lieutenant, RM, Royal Marines, 13 March 1920

O'FEE, Stewart, Naval Schoolmaster, Vivid, 13 March 1920

O'FLYNN, William, Leading Stoker, K 21706, Vivid, 12 May 1926

OGBORNE, Charles S, Stoker 1c, K 58212, Vivid, 4 May 1920

OGSTON, Alexander L, Captain, RM, Royal Marine Light Infantry, 8 February 1919

O'HARA, Bernard P, Paymaster, Espiegle, 11 October 1919

O'HARA, Robert, Able Seaman, J 12732, Cornflower, 15 November 1928

OKE, Thomas W H, Boy 2c, JX 158150, Impregnable, 10 September 1938

O'KEEFE, Daniel, Stoker Petty Officer, 305268, Vivid II, 17 January 1920

O'KEEFE, Sara, Steward, WRNS, G 4649, Crescent, 18 February 1919

OLD, Ernest W, Leading Seaman, D/J 7357, Royal Navy, 10 July 1930

OLD, John J, Marine, 14735 (Ply), Devonshire, 26 July 1929

OLDERSHAW, Charles W, Boy 1c, J 97546, Victory, 18 July 1921

O'LEARY, Patrick B, Able Seaman, P/J 87296, Boreas, 12 October 1931

OLIVER, Carl L D, Telegraphist, J 48587, FAA, 440 Flight, Hermes, 6 May 1925

OLIVER, Charles W, Armourer, 342977, Collingwood, 31 March 1920

OLIVER, Frank H J, Leading Steward, C/L 12825, M.2, 29 January 1932

OLIVER, William F, Engine Room Artificer, M 34041, Repulse, 17 August 1925

OLIVER, William S, Able Seaman, J 11034 (Ch), Kinross, 16 June 1919

O'MAHONEY, Patrick, Chief Stoker, 288189, Vivid II, 26 March 1920

O'NEILL, Daniel, Stoker Petty Officer, 294586, Colleen, 5 February 1920

O'NIELL, Arthur J, Private, RMLI, 13755 (Ply), Revenge, 25 July 1920

ONIONS, Horace F, Able Seaman, J 3176, Pembroke, 1 December 1918

ORBELL, Charles T, Regulating Petty Officer, P/M 39588, Vernon, 3 April 1932

ORE, James, Commissioned Gunner, Actaeon, 5 December 1921

O'RIORDON, Timothy, Private, RM, S 12860 (Deal), RM Labour Corps, 10 April 1919

ORME, Joseph, Assistant Steward, MMR, 575280, Eaglet, 15 November 1918

ORME, Louis, Able Seaman, J 22122 (Dev), L.55, 4 June 1919

ORMES, William C, Chief Engine Room Artificer, C/M 14525, Thetis, 3 June 1939

ORRIN, Percival J, Ordinary Seaman, J 112929, Pembroke, 9 August 1926

ORROCK, William, Stoker 1c, D/KX 85664, Thetis, 3 June 1939

OSBORN, George F, Yeoman of Signals, 224043, Capetown, 17 December 1922

OSBORNE, Arthur G, Engine Room Artificer Apprentice, MX 46037, Fisgard, 18 May 1929

OSBORNE, Charles W, Officer's Cook 2c, L 12612, Pembroke, 27 April 1926

OSBORNE, George, Able Seaman, RNVR, Bristol Z 3912, President III, 1 March 1919

OSBORNE, George R, Engineer Lieutenant, Whitley, 14 February 1921

OSBORNE, Otto V (served as Otto Furneaux), Musician, RMB, RMB 1273, Berwick, 25 July 1928

O'SHEA, Maurice M, Stoker 2c, C/KX 84431, Pembroke II, 13 November 1934

O'SHEA, William H, Leading Sick Berth Attendant, P/MX 47445, RN Hospital, Haslar, 21 August 1937

OSMAN, Arthur T, Stoker 2c, K 46992 (Po), Erin's Isle, 7 February 1919

OSMAN, Charles E, Able Seaman, J 41711, Sportive, 31 July 1921

OSMOND, Charles W, Able Seaman, 226286, Victory, 8 November 1919

O'SULLIVAN, Frederic D, Assistant Steward, P/LX 22363, Victory, 10 March 1938

O'SULLIVAN, John J, Stoker Petty Officer, K 62603, Pangbourne, 13 January 1928

OSWALD, Donald J S, Lieutenant Commander, Gloucester, 6 January 1919

OSWELL, Thomas M, Lieutenant, H.42, 23 March 1922

OSWICK, Harold G, Stoker 1c, C/KX 79898, Pembroke, 16 December 1936

OTHER, George W, Able Seaman, J 103925, Tamar, 25 April 1925

OUGH, George H, Able Seaman, 234417, Widgeon, 7 July 1922

OULD, John H, Paymaster Lieutenant, RNR, Royal Naval Reserve, 26 August 1934

OUSLEY, Sydney J, Chief Joiner, M 2594, Ganges, 19 December 1925

OUTHOUSE, Ernest A, Deck Hand, RNR, DA 16561, Vernon, 16 February 1919

OVERAL, Bert, Telegraphist, P/JX 129984, FAA, 825 Sqn, Glorious, 5 February 1937

OWEN, Alec, Stoker 2c, K 62705, Pembroke, 10 February 1924

OWEN, Fred, Stoker Petty Officer, 293326, Monarch, 8 September 1919

OWEN, Harold W S, Paymaster Lieutenant, RNR, Julius, 15 February 1920

OWEN, James E, Petty Officer, C/J 25504, Frobisher, 15 February 1936

OWEN, Samuel D, Officer's Steward 4c, LX 20778, Victory, 27 August 1929

OWEN, Walter, Civilian Contractor, Thetis, 3 June 1939

OWENS, Harold T, Leading Seaman, P/J 110411, Gnat, 27 November 1936

OWENS, Henry J, Stoker 1c, C/KX 78437, Pembroke, 17 February 1934

OWENS-JONES, Guy O, Lieutenant, FAA, 423 Sqn, Eagle, 18 January 1927

OWERS, Leonard G, Able Seaman, J 36904 (Ch), Vittoria, 31 August 1919

P

PACE, Edward W, Boy 1c, J 108006, Royal Sovereign, 9 November 1925

PACEY, James T, Skipper, MMR, Cawdor Castle, steamship, 30 March 1919

PACKARD, Max W, Petty Officer, 173121, President II, 21 September 1927

PACKER, James A, Chief Engine Room Artificer 2c, C/M 4779, Pembroke, 9 January 1934

PACKER, Thomas W, Chief Engine Room Artificer 1c, 270828, Fisgard, 2 July 1924

PACKHAM, Charles R, Able Seaman, J 14619, Velox, 10 August 1923

PACKMAN, Thomas R, Chief Engine Room Artificer 2c, M 23475 (Po), Myrtle, 15 July 1919

PACKWOOD, William J, Stoker 1c, D/KX 80371, Vivid, 27 October 1932

PAFFEY, Rowland J, Stoker Petty Officer, K 10862, Usk, 1 December 1918

PAFFORD, Gordon J, Electrical Artificer 1c, P/M 34357, Victory, 22 December 1933

PAGE, Alfred G, Stoker Petty Officer, 229695 (Po), K.5, 20 January 1921

PAGE, George F L L, Commander, HM Dockyard Pembroke, 27 October 1920

PAGE, George J, Able Seaman, J 105046, Ajax, 26 January 1926

PAGE, Geo W, Boy 2c, RAN, 6790, Tingira (RAN), 16 Mar 1919

PAGE, James A, Civilian Contractor, Thetis, 3 June 1939

PAGE, Mark W, Telegraphist, J 113114, Marlborough, 16 December 1929

PAGE, William J, Stoker 2c, D/KX 90844, Drake, 4 April 1937

PAGET, Alfred L, Lieutenant, ML.358, motor launch, 9 December 1921

PAIGE, Henry P, Leading Seaman, RAN, 9340 (former J 9760), Platypus (RAN), 30 September 1919

PAIN, Philip T, Petty Officer, 233073, Iron Duke, 28 December 1921

PAINE, Albert V, Engine Room Artificer 2c, P/M 15007, Poseidon, 9 June 1931

PAINE, Alfred E, Able Seaman, 214039, Valerian, 22 October 1926

PAINE, Arthur F, Engine Room Artificer Apprentice, M 36100, Fisgard, 22 September 1924

PAINE, Horace S, Officer's Steward 3c, L 13079, Valerian, 22 October 1926

PAINE, William C, Engine Room Artificer 2c, M 6252, Valerian, 22 October 1926

PAINTER, William B, Boy 1c, JX 127608, Benbow, 19 May 1927

PAINTIN, Leslie A C, Able Seaman, P/JX 133896, Douglas, 29 June 1937

PALLETT, Frederick C, Sick Berth Attendant, M 4453, Egmont, 14 December 1918

PALMER, Arthur S, Signalman, J 35450 (Ch), Tenedos, 16 December 1919

PALMER, Charles (real name, but served as Frederick C Durkin), Stoker Petty Officer, 308482, Caroline, 4 February 1920

PALMER, Charles E, Private, RMLI, S 2690 (Ch), 1st RM Battalion, RND, 20 November 1918

PALMER, Ernest S, Leading Stoker, K 3790, Sarepta, 18 October 1919

PALMER, George F, Stoker Petty Officer, K 6993, Pembroke, 24 July 1925

PALMER, George L, Leading Seaman, J 27459, President, 21 November 1927

PALMER, Henry, Skipper, RNR, Jamaica, 25 January 1930

PALMER, Philip N, Leading Seaman, C/JX 133774, Pembroke, 1 July 1939

PALMER, Reginald J, Able Seaman, J 64437, Shikari, 13 February 1926

PALMER, Victor M, Able Seaman, J 93436, Emperor of India, 10 May 1924

PAMMENT, William F, Stoker 1c, K 41353, Scarab, 11 October 1925

PAMPLIN, Arthur J, Corporal, RMLI, 17060 (Ch), RM Headquarters, 4 January 1920

PANG, Ping, Able Seaman, Tamar, 27 January 1939

PANNETT, Hudson, Able Seaman, RNVR, KP 840, Anson Battalion, RND, 21 April 1919

PANNETT, William J T, Able Seaman, J 69170, Pembroke, 25 February 1919

PANTLING, Henry, Able Seaman, J 105596, Hollyhock, 4 April 1926

PARADISE, Harris, Signalman, J 25052, Pembroke, 23 December 1919

PARFITT, Bob, Private, RMLI, 8576 (Po), Patuca, 25 November 1918

PARFITT, Cyril N, Chief Engine Room Artificer 2c, P/MX 52062, Enterprise, 6 October 1936

PARFITT, George V, Able Seaman, D/J 110652, Carlisle, 9 August 1936

PARFITT, James H, Engine Room Artificer 2c, M 24132, Vivid, 2 May 1928

PARK, John R, Deck Hand, RNR, DA 5522, Satellite, 21 January 1919

PARKER, Albert T, Stoker 1c, K 48040, Temeraire, 23 July 1920

PARKER, Edward C, Chief Officer, HM Coast Guard, 6 December 1919

PARKER, Edward, Able Seaman, J 36614, Vortigern, 29 November 1918

PARKER, Frederick W, Able Seaman, 217317, Vivid, 4 September 1923

PARKER, George E, Able Seaman, SS 10980, Victory, 1 April 1923

PARKER, Henry, Stoker 1c, K 10078, Neptune, 24 November 1918

PARKER, James E, Stoker 1c, K 55691, Victory, 25 March 1920

PARKER, James H, Trimmer Cook, RNR, TC 603, Research, 19 February 1919

PARKER, Reginald H, Deck Hand, RNR, DA 16937, Hopeful, 16 December 1918

PARKER, Reginald H, Midshipman, Marlborough, 25 June 1920

PARKER, Richard, Leading Seaman, D/J 103850, Harebell, 19 August 1934

PARKER, Tom, Sub Lieutenant, RNR, Sir John Moore, 26 November 1918

PARKER, William, Gunner, RMA, RMA 14560, RM Headquarters, 14 May 1921

PARKER, William, Stoker 1c, K 63846, Ramillies, 5 May 1924

PARKER, William F, Able Seaman, J 254, Coronado, 12 November 1918

PARKES, Henry W, Engine Room Artificer 4c, M 6248 (Po), Penarth, 6 February 1919

PARKHURST, Thomas M J, Petty Officer Telegraphist, J 8157, L.24, 10 January 1924

PARKINSON, James F, Air Mechanic 1c, F 27459, President, 24 November 1918

PARNELL, Urban O, Able Seaman, J 27739, P.66, patrol boat, 22 December 1918

PARNELL, William, Act/Stoker Petty Officer, K 5042 (Ch), L.55, 4 June 1919

PARNIS, Charles, Engineer Lieutenant, Theseus, 4 June 1919

PARR, Frederick, Stoker 1c, K 20815 (Po), K.5, 20 January 1921

PARRATT, Leonard W, Chief Stoker, P/K 58935, Hawkins, 6 April 1934

PARRIS, Arthur C, Petty Officer Telegraphist, P/J 45264, Royal Navy, 26 June 1936

PARROTT, Albert D, Boy 1c, JX 127320, Benbow, 15 May 1927

PARRY, James F, Stoker 1c, K 17768 (Po), K.5, 20 January 1921

PARRY, John, Private, RMLI, S 2368 (Ply), RMLI, Plymouth Division, 9 March 1919

PARRY, John L, Act/Sub Lieutenant, Course at Portsmouth, 12 October 1927
PARSLEY, Ernest R, Officer's Steward 2c, C/L 14115, Ganges, 8 March 1931
PARSON, Guy F, Lieutenant Commander, Nigella, 6 March 1919
PARSONS, Cunliffe Mc N, Major General, RM, Royal Marines, 21 January 1923
PARSONS, George W, Able Seaman, J 1878, H.42, 23 March 1922
PARSONS, Randall R, Leading Seaman, 238893 (Ch), Verulam, 4 September 1919
PARSONS, William, Private, RM, S 11118 (Deal), RM Labour Corps, 24 December 1918
PARSONS, William R, Private, RMLI, 16296 (Po), Portsmouth Division, RMLI, 30 January 1919
PARTRIDGE, Frederick, Stoker 1c, D/KX 60320, Malabar, 29 June 1934
PARTRIDGE, John R, Ordinary Seaman, SS 7160 (Ch), Frostaxe, 29 April 1919
PARTRIDGE, Richard H, Stoker 2c, K 43684 (Ch), Cassandra, 5 December 1918
PARTRIDGE, Sydney G, Petty Officer, D/J 25481, President II, 2 August 1935
PARTRIDGE, Thomas J, Able Seaman, P/JX 132377, Victory, 27 September 1936
PARVEN, Walter J, Able Seaman, P/JX 138466, Boadicea, 24 February 1937
PASCOE, Archibald J, Act/Cook, D/MX 55869, Rodney, 13 April 1939
PASCOE, John, Stoker Petty Officer, K 18892, Emerald, 5 April 1928
PASCOE, Nicholas, Deck Hand, RNR, DA 6592, Egmont, 19 March 1919
PASH, Sidney E, Petty Officer, J 99424, PC.74, 26 November 1928
PASS, Charles F, Telegraphist, RNVR, Bristol Z 10317, Favorita, 12 November 1918
PATCHETT, John E, Leading Trimmer, RNR, TS 1312, Pekin, 8 December 1918
PATERSON, Alexander M, Able Seaman, D/JX 142115, Leander, 30 September 1937
PATERSON, Donald, Seaman, RNR, A 9521, Iolaire (Pembroke, O/P), 1 January 1919
PATERSON, John, Trimmer, RNR, TS 3667, William Bond, 30 December 1918
PATERSON, William, Deck Hand, RNR, DA 538, John Robert, 1 February 1919
PATEY, William P, Petty Officer 1c, 169866, Bootle, 12 February 1919
PATIENCE, Charles G, Chief Petty Officer, 167749, Victory, 11 May 1920
PATON, John, Trimmer, RNR, TS 2378, Duthies, 15 February 1919
PATRICK, Fred, Able Seaman, RNVR, Tyneside Z 9780, President III, 8 February 1919
PATRICK, Fred, Telegraphist, RNVR, Tyneside Z 11598, Alaburn, 24 November 1918
PATRICK, Kenneth C, Boy 2c, JX 150327, Ganges, 17 January 1937
PATRICK, Ronald S, Ordinary Seaman, D/JX 139167, Capetown, 6 December 1934
PATTENDEN, Reginald E, Able Seaman, D/J 103017, Drake, 17 July 1936
PATTERSON, Francis W J, Artificer Engineer, Indomitable, 27 December 1919
PATTERSON, John, Private, RM, S 14684 (Deal), RM Labour Corps, 8 June 1919
PATTERSON, John, Trimmer, RNR, TS 5167, Gunner, 25 December 1918
PATTERSON, William, Rigger, MMR, Hughli, Royal Fleet Auxiliary, 26 April 1919
PATTERSON, William G, Able Seaman, 228491, Victory, 4 August 1919
PATTERSON, William F, Supply Petty Officer, M 31842, Valerian, 22 October 1926
PATTINSON, William, Petty Officer, J 11184 (Dev), Lucia, 19 June 1920
PAUL, Charles F, Lieutenant, St Genny, 12 January 1930
PAWSEY, Henry, Fireman, MMR, Mollusc, Royal Fleet Auxiliary, 7 December 1918
PAXMAN, Percy, Chief Stoker, 293753, Victory, 13 February 1921
PAY, George E, Private, RMLI, S 1181 (Po), Dryad, 21 February 1919
PAY, James A J, Leading Boatman, 202680, Pembroke, 26 April 1922
PAYNE, Albert, Able Seaman, 223540, Victory, 10 July 1923
PAYNE, Alfred J, Boy 1c, J 90873 (Ch), Dragon, 17 October 1919
PAYNE, James H, Able Seaman, 229737, Egmont, 13 November 1919
PAYNE, Thomas A, Warrant Telegraphist, RNR, Macedonia, 28 February 1919
PAYNE, Tom G C, Signalman, RNVR, Palace Z 1312, HM Coast Guard Station Swanage, 29 November 1918
PAYNE, Walter A, Stoker Petty Officer, 291029, Tumult, 19 July 1919
PAYNE, Wilfred H, Officer's Steward 2c, P/L 12177, Constance, 17 October 1930

PEACH, Reginald H, Act/Ty/Paymaster Lieutenant, RNR, Kingfisher, 26 November 1918
PEACOCK, Augustine P, Petty Officer, J 9709, Vivid, 9 May 1930
PEACOCK, George B, Able Seaman, 215778, Vivien, 2 February 1922
PEACOCK, Hubert W, Able Seaman, P/J 49260, Bee, 18 April 1938
PEARCE, Charles H, Stoker Petty Officer, 308604, Vivid, 21 November 1918
PEARCE, Ernest A, Chief Engine Room Artificer, 12235, Royal Navy, 8 September 1935
PEARCE, Henry W G, Act/Sub Lieutenant (A), FAA, 758 Sqn, Raven, 26 August 1939
PEARCE, Henry W, Chief Shipwright 2c, D/M 7407, Vivid, 2 November 1932
PEARCE, William A, Able Seaman, J 17236, H.42, 23 March 1922
PEARCE, William F, Commander, RNR, Royal Naval Reserve, 17 July 1925
PEARKS, Donald W, Shipwright 4c, M 19193, Pembroke, 11 December 1921
PEARMAIN, Charles, Able Seaman, RNVR, London Z 1281, Vivid, 22 December 1918
PEARN, Joseph, Chief Petty Officer (Pensioner), 118408, Royal Navy, 10 March 1938
PEARSE, Clarence E, Able Seaman, J 105084, Harebell, 30 November 1925
PEARSE, Cyril A, Lieutenant, RNR, Royal Naval Reserve, 2 November 1925
PEARSE, Hugh C B, Midshipman, Cumberland, 9 March 1934
PEARSON, Herbert W, Engineman, RNR, ES 1166, Conway Castle, 17 November 1918
PEARSON, James, Chief Petty Officer, P/J 22430, Speedwell, 12 February 1936
PEARSON, Mabel C, Steward, WRNS, G 4229, WRNS, London Division, 4 December 1918
PEARSON, Magnus S, Seaman, RNR, A 9990, Victory, 26 January 1922
PEARSON, Sidney J, Able Seaman, J 47400 (Ch), Frostaxe, 29 April 1919
PEARSON, William, Able Seaman, J 91664, Walker, 19 November 1929

PEARSON, William, Stoker 1c, K 16318, Bonaventure, 29 March 1919
PEARSON, William A, Able Seaman, J 42464, M.1, 12 November 1925
PEARSON, William B, Able Seaman, J 78869, Vivid, 12 February 1926
PEART, J R G, Private, RMLI, S 2037 (Ch), 3rd Battalion, RM, 8 December 1918
PEAT, Arnold, Ordinary Seaman, SS 11386, Centurion, 14 April 1923
PEATY, William H, Boy 2c, J 93811, Impregnable, 3 March 1919
PECK, Francis W, Shipwright 1c, M 215827, Victory, 13 December 1925
PECK, Humphrey, Captain, RMA, Emperor of India, 9 February 1922
PEDDLE, Percy, Chief Mechanician 2c, D/K 55163, Norfolk, 28 September 1935
PEDLEY, William, Ordinary Seaman, J 85356, Benbow, 25 February 1919
PEEK, Albert E, Yeoman of Signals, 230972, Anemone, 23 December 1918
PEEK, Albert G, Able Seaman, 237697, Dartmouth, 6 September 1920
PEEL, James, Marine, 211377 (Po), Portsmouth Division, RM, 23 August 1935
PEEL, John W, Chief Engine Room Artificer 1c, 271103, Barham, 16 March 1924
PEEL, John, Midshipman (E), Engineering Course, 30 April 1929
PEERMAN, Robert H, Leading Signalman, D/JX 135816, Glorious, 30 January 1939
PEET, Frederick H, Gunner, Excellent, 18 August 1923
PEGGS, James, Private, RME, RME 5043, RM Engineers, 31 January 1919
PELLET, Frank E, Ordinary Seaman, J 94860, Caroline, 26 April 1921
PENDLEBURY, Herbert, Petty Officer, 239381, Victory, 5 March 1919
PENDRILL, Reginald J, Able Seaman, J 38465 (Dev), Verulam, 4 September 1919
PENGELLY, Silvanus, Leading Stoker, K 55939, Laburnum, 31 January 1930
PENGILLEY, Edward G, Able Seaman, J 105021, Adventure, 27 March 1929
PENMAN, Andrew, Able Seaman, RNVR, Palace Z 2468, Crescent, 12 November 1918
PENNA, Richard J, Stoker 1c, K 56973, Vivid, 25 January 1921
PENNINGTON, Archibald, Able Seaman, J 35931, Sabre, 9 March 1919
PENNINGTON, Lionel G, Commander (E) Thetis (Engineer in Chief's Department), 3 June 1939
PENNY, Ernest, Petty Officer, J 9617, H.42, 23 March 1922
PENWILL, William T, Gunner, RMA, RMA 2428 (RFR A), RMA Battalion, 5 January 1919
PEPLAR, William H, Engine Room Artificer 1c, M 14878, St Genny, 12 January 1930
PEPLOE, Charles R, Captain, Victory, 8 February 1933
PEPLOE, Norman B F, Lieutenant, Assistant Naval Attache, Italy, Greece, Rumania, Serb-Croatia-Slovenia, 5 February 1922
PEPLOW, William, Able Seaman, D/J 101056, M.2, 29 January 1932
PEPPER, Alexander J, Chief Engine Room Artificer 2c, 271368, Vivid, 11 November 1921
PEPPER, Frank V, Supply Chief Petty Officer, C/MX 53383, Resource, 27 February 1937
PERDUE, Henry O, Petty Officer, P/J 104459, Tedworth, 23 August 1939
PERING, Arthur W, Ordinary Seaman, P/JX 134915, London, 21 November 1933
PERKINS, Alan H, Marine, A 18530 (Ch), Renown, 3 April 1935
PERKINS, Arthur, Senior Reserve Attendant, M 10090, Actaeon, 8 May 1919

PERKINS, Cyril E, Stoker 1c, K 41030 (Dev), Cassandra, 5 December 1918
PERKINS, James H, Chief Petty Officer, J 403, Vindictive, 22 December 1927
PERKINS, Norman G, Ordinary Telegraphist, RNVR, Bristol Z 7455, Wireless Telegraph Station Aberdeen, 23 June 1919
PERRETT, Warren, Chief Shipwright 2c, 346856, Greenwich, 21 November 1920
PERRING, William, Chief Stoker, 306472, Vivid, 26 March 1919
PERRING, William, Supply Chief Petty Officer, D/MX 52336, Drake, 16 May 1935
PERRY, Arthur W, Leading Stoker, K 21312, Vivid, 26 December 1918
PERRY, Cecil J, Marine, 216432 (Po), Barham, 24 October 1926
PERRY, Frank W F, Seaman, RNR, A 8572, Abinsi, steamship, 23 November 1918
PERRY, John F S, Deck Hand, RNR, DA 17585, Goissa, 13 December 1918
PERRY, Kenneth T, Armourers Crew, M 20684, Excellent, 25 February 1919
PERRY, Laylard G, Engine Room Artificer 5c, M 34931, Verity, 18 September 1924
PERRY, Percy W, Petty Officer, D/JX 147102, Enterprise, 22 October 1937
PERRY, Sidney W, Able Seaman, J 70254, Pembroke, 11 March 1922
PERRY, Walter F, Officer's Cook 2c, P/LX 20111, Dunedin, 13 December 1932
PERRYMAN, Dennis, Stoker Petty Officer, D/K 56057, Drake, 11 May 1937
PESTELL, William C A, Petty Officer Steward, P/LX 21914, Victory, 9 April 1938
PETERS, Frederick W, Ordinary Seaman, J 80625, Galatea, 1 December 1919
PETERS, John, Gunner, RMA, RMA S 2477, RMA Eastney, 10 February 1919
PETERS, Vicary, Lieutenant Commander, RNR, Laconia, steamship, 12 May 1924
PETERS, William, Petty Officer, 188315, Vivid, 29 January 1919
PETERSEN, Sir William, Honorary Commander, RNR, Royal Naval Reserve, 12 June 1925
PETFORD, Ernest, Cook, M 10275, Maidstone, 2 November 1919
PETO, Frederick, Private, RMLI, 7940 (Po), Portsmouth Division, RMLI, 7 September 1919
PETRIE, George, Officer's Steward 1c, L 8115 (Po), Penarth, 4 February 1919
PETT, Ernest E, Stoker 1c, C/KX 79348, Parthian, 23 May 1932
PETTET, Pat, Able Seaman, J 42323, Raleigh, 8 August 1922
PETTETT, John T, Deck Hand, RNR, SD 3858, Aiglon, 20 February 1919
PETTIGREW, James R H, Able Seaman, J 21842, Westcott, 23 April 1919
PETTIT, Peter F, Chief Skipper, RNR, Royal Naval Reserve, 5 February 1937
PETTITT, John E, Able Seaman, J 48470 (Ch), Vittoria, 31 August 1919
PETTMAN, Herbert H, Stoker 1c, K 65730, Pembroke, 10 April 1928
PEYTON (Pexton in Admiralty List), Dennis G W, Able Seaman, J 89272, Valerian, 22 October 1926
PEYTON, Edward L, Lieutenant Commander, Devonport Dockyard, 21 November 1936

PHALP, Arthur S, Leading Signalman, P/JX 127503, Victory, 9 April 1935
PHEASANT, Martin A, Able Seaman, RNVR, R 991, Drake Battalion, RND, 24 November 1918
PHILIP, Francis, Able Seaman, J 28184, Pembroke, 27 March 1919
PHILIPS, Thomas C R, Midshipman, Royal Sovereign, 31 July 1927

PHILLIPS, Bert G, Stoker 1c, K 18519, Glorious, 14 February 1922
PHILLIPS, Charles F, Commissioned Gunner, St Just, 24 July 1931
PHILLIPS, Charles J, Able Seaman, J 34124, Sylph, 19 October 1920
PHILLIPS, Frank, Stoker 1c, K 57617, Valerian, 22 October 1926
PHILLIPS, Frederick A, Chief Engine Room Artificer 1c, M 2019, Tara, 5 May 1930
PHILLIPS, George, Able Seaman, RNVR, R 1814, Hood Battalion, RND, 16 November 1918
PHILLIPS, Iver J, Stoker 1c, SS 118035, Yarmouth, 24 February 1923
PHILLIPS, John M, Stoker 2c, KX 80386, Pembroke, 29 July 1935
PHILLIPS, Joseph L, Armourer, 295133, Actaeon, 31 December 1920
PHILLIPS, Richard R, Able Seaman, RNVR, Mersey Z 2508, Jabirn, steamship, 5 December 1918
PHILLIPS, Sydney F, Stoker 1c, K 60396, L.24, 10 January 1924
PHILLIPS, Walter, Chief Officer, HM Coast Guard, HMCG Southend, Essex, 14 July 1937
PHILLIPS, William, Private, RMLI, 13247 (Po), Venus, 15 June 1919
PHILLIPS, William G, Able Seaman, J 81964, Theseus, 25 January 1919
PHILLIPS, William H, Lieutenant, Drake, 5 October 1937
PHILLIPS, William L, Able Seaman, J 96198, Valhalla, 17 September 1929
PHILLIPS, William T, Rev, Honorary Chaplain, RNVR, Severn Division, RNVR, 1937
PHILLIPS, William T E, Mechanician, D/K 58418, Malaya, 5 August 1930
PHILP, Stephen R, Able Seaman, D/J 107388, Furious, 4 September 1937
PHILPIN, Thomas W, Able Seaman, J 30152, Calliope, 12 October 1924
PHILPOTT, James T, Petty Officer, 234270, Pembroke, 1 October 1922
PHILPOTT, Leonard G, Leading Steward, C/L 13487, Skipjack, 26 August 1937
PHILPOTT, Thomas W, Lieutenant, M.1, 12 November 1925
PHIMINTER, Alexander, Able Seaman, C/SSX 10873, Eskimo, 17 May 1939
PHIPPARD, Albert E, Stoker, P/K 56837, Royal Navy, 23 June 1936
PHIPPS, Ronald, Boy 2c, JX 141713, Ganges, 24 August 1934
PHIPPS, Sydney G, Leading Seaman, C/J 102377, Colombo, 24 March 1935
PHYTHIAN, Richard, Stoker 1c, P/KX 76632, Victory, 14 December 1938

PICK, Henry T, Painter 1c, 145746, Vivid, 17 January 1920
PICKETT, Edward H, Leading Stoker, K 12218, Hibiscus, 11 January 1921
PICKFORD, Harry, Stoker 1c, SS 112746, Vivid, 7 May 1921
PICKLES, Albert E, Senior Reserve Attendant, M 15705, Victory, 9 March 1919
PICKUP, William H, Surgeon Lieutenant, Prince Rupert, 27 November 1918
PICKWORTH, Alfred N, Private, RMLI, S 2805 (Ch), RM Submarine Miners, 2 December 1918
PIDGEON, William J, Petty Officer, J 11337, Comus, 16 October 1923
PIGEON, Harold L, Boy 2c, J 93259, Ganges, 12 November 1918
PIGGOTT, Harold F F, Private, RMLI, 21096 (Ch), Crescent, 11 April 1920
PIGGOTT, William C, Private, RMLI, 19459 (Ch), RM, 6th Battalion, 9 September 1919
PIKE, Charles A, Telegraphist, J 49161, Pembroke, 13 February 1919
PIKE, Edward L, Engine Room Artificer 1c, M 2667, H.47, 9 July 1929
PIKE, Ernest C, Able Seaman, J 8633, Valerian, 22 October 1926
PIKE, Stanley J, Painter 4c, M 7895, Columbine, 8 June 1926
PIKE, William H H, Engine Room Artificer 3c, C/M 34932, Poseidon, 9 June 1931
PILCHER, Richard L, Able Seaman, J 91388, Moth, 25 December 1926
PILE, Harry H, Leading Seaman, 235972, Hawkins, 31 August 1923
PILLAR, Langmead C, Chief Engine Room Artificer 1c, 347832, Defiance, 8 March 1926
PINDER, Charles, Able Seaman, J 39932, Pembroke, 29 January 1919
PINDER, Thomas H, Leading Seaman, J 25342, Tourmaline, 15 February 1923
PINE, Henry C, Chief Yeoman of Signals, P/JX 149535, RN Hospital, Haslar, 11 February 1939
PINHORNE, Alfred S G, Able Seaman, P/J 113463, Centurion, 15 November 1930
PINK, Frederick G, Leading Stoker, K 59106, St Genny, 12 January 1930
PINK, William G, Stoker 1c, K 23787, Valerian, 22 October 1926
PINN, William H, Leading Seaman, 188778, Vivid, 9 April 1919
PIPE, William T, Skipper, RNR, Blanche, 17 March 1928
PIPER, Alfred T, Private, RMLI, 19218 (Po), 3rd Battalion, RM, 7 January 1919
PIPER, Frederick, Able Seaman, J 27625, Dido, 22 July 1922
PIPON, John R, Lieutenant, RNR, Victory, 4 February 1919
PIRIE, George, Engineman, RNR, TS 3259, Nairn, 26 March 1919
PITCHER, Charles O, Chief Officer, HMCG, HMCG, 16 January 1922
PITCHER, James R, Chief Engine Room Artificer, 116531, Vernon, 10 November 1919
PITCHERS, Benjamin R, Engineman, RNR, TS 3444, Falstaff, 18 December 1918
PITHER, Henry, Able Seaman, J 34433, Victory, 13 November 1921
PITMAN, Frederick G, Chief Petty Officer, P/J 76252, Birmingham, 16 October 1938
PITT, Arthur, Petty Officer, J 838, Pembroke, 16 December 1918
PITT, Charles H, Leading Stoker, K 22939, Victory, 23 September 1925
PITT, George E, Stoker Petty Officer, 119896, Vernon, 8 February 1919
PITT, Herbert C, Stoker 1c, K 63750, Magnolia, 12 April 1929
PITTMAN, Francis R, Stoker 2c, D/KX 94065, RN Hospital, Plymouth, 6 December 1938
PITTS, Thomas E, Commander, RNR, Rawalpindi, 22 July 1930

PLANT, Lewis N W, Stoker 1c, K 55480, Pembroke, 14 April 1920
PLATT, James, Stoker 1c, K 64537, Cumberland, 10 July 1930
PLATT, Joseph, Greaser, MMR, 897131, Hazel, 29 November 1918
PLATT, Leonard, Able Seaman, P/SSX 1557, Exmouth, 13 August 1936
PLATT, Maurice C, Ty/Sub Lieutenant, RNVR, Hawke Battalion, RND, 26 November 1918
PLATTS, Leonard H, Stoker 1c, P/KX 92289, Maidstone, 10 January 1939
PLATTS, William, Chief Skipper, RNR, Royal Naval Reserve, 2 June 1937
PLEASANTS, Andrew D, Private, RMLI, 14646 (Ch), Chatham Division, RMLI, 1 May 1920
PLEASANTS, Andrew D, Private, RMLI, E 14646 (Ch), RM Headquarters, 1 May 1920
PLESTED, William J, Private, RMLI, 8631 (Po), Portsmouth Division, RMLI, 18 June 1920
PLOWRIGHT, Edward, Able Seaman, J 27751, Wryneck, 27 April 1921

PLUCK, Thomas L, Ordinary Seaman, J 109702, Royal Sovereign, 16 September 1925
PLUMMER, John R, Private, RMLI, S 1508 (Ply), 3rd Battalion, RM, 3 December 1918
PLUMMER, William J, Engineman, RNR, TS 6592, County of Nairn, 4 December 1918
PLUMTRE, Montague W, Lieutenant, Valiant, 20 August 1927
PLUNKITT, George H, Ordinary Seaman, SS 9150 (Ch), Curacoa, 13 May 1919

POINTER, Frederick T A, Stoker 1c, C/K 48329, Poseidon, 9 June 1931
POINTER, George H, Engineer Sub Lieutenant, RNR, Hermione, 22 February 1919
POLAND, William A W, Lieutenant, Thetis, 3 June 1939
POLE, Magnus, Seaman, RNR, B 3043, Arrogant, 28 March 1919
POLING, Edward J, Leading Stoker, K 62218, Tiger, 4 October 1924
POLING, Raymond G, Stoker 1c, K 60480, Valerian, 22 October 1926
POLKINGHORNE, James, Stoker Petty Officer, K 1494, P.42, patrol boat, 12 December 1918
POLLARD, George, Engine Room Artificer 3c, M 10901 (Dev), K.5, 20 January 1921
POLLARD, Henry W, Signalman, J 90130, Victory, 9 November 1928
POLLARD, James W, Stoker 2c, D/KX 82183, Vivid, 11 May 1933
POLLARD, John, Able Seaman, 229756 (Po), Erin's Isle, 7 February 1919
POLLEY, Frank A R, Able Seaman, J 32369 (Ch), Verulam, 4 September 1919
POLLINGTON, Arthur B, Stoker 1c, SS 116444, Glory, 2 July 1919
POLMEAR, Harold A, Officer's Cook 3c, L 13090, Vivid, 9 March 1920
POMEROY, Arthur E, Shipwright 2c, 346236, Despatch, 1 June 1927
POND, Herbert G, Petty Officer, 201045, Penarth, 4 February 1919
PONSONBY, Patrick S J, Lieutenant, L.8, 11 July 1922
PONTING, Percy R, Lance Corporal, RMLI, 13786 (Ch), Queen, 19 March 1919
POOLE, Albert E, Blacksmith 1c, 345362 (Po), Caroline, 11 August 1920
POOLE, Arthur, Stoker Petty Officer, C/K 63929, Pembroke, 4 August 1934
POOLE, Jack, Marine, 24629 (Ch), Royal Marines HQ, 28 November 1925
POOLE, Percy W, Petty Officer, C/J 46187, Pembroke, 26 November 1934
POOLE, Thomas, Private, RMLI, 12274 (Ch), Northumbria, steamship, 9 January 1919
POOLE, Walter J, Able Seaman, J 66240, Benbow, 16 January 1919
POOLE, William W, Chief Stoker, K 309575, Vivid, 1 October 1925
POOLER, Cyril, Gunner, RMA, RMA 16754, RMA Eastney, 5 February 1919
POOTS, Albert, Able Seaman, J 9595, Teazer, 22 May 1925
POPE, Archibald F C, Marine, 22602 (Po), Courageous, 20 January 1930
POPE, Ernest W, Petty Officer Steward, D/L 12262, Leander, 27 April 1935
POPE, James, Seaman, RNR, A 4949, Maori, 24 November 1918
POPE, William C, Petty Officer, 236687, Vivid, 11 June 1927
POPLE, Frederick R, Stoker 2c, K 48782, Attentive III, 11 February 1919
POPPELSTONE, William H, Able Seaman, D/J 25014, Westcott, 8 February 1935

POPPLESTONE, Horace, Chief Stoker, D/K 28493, Devonshire, 18 February 1934
PORCH, George F, Yeoman of Signals, 226476, Pembroke, 29 January 1925
PORCH, Robert E, Petty Officer, J 12072, H.42, 23 March 1922
PORT, Philip, Chief Engine Room Artificer 2c, 270423, President, 14 March 1919
PORTAL, Nigel H, Lieutenant, Pilot's Course, 30 April 1926
PORTER, Albert E, Ordinary Seaman, J 98344, H.42, 23 March 1922
PORTER, Alfred A, Commissioned Boatswain, Portsmouth Dockyard, 15 November 1932
PORTER, Charles H, Trimmer Cook, RNR, TC 585, Bombardier, 27 March 1919
PORTER, Thomas A, Commissioned Gunner, Belfast, 18 April 1939
POSSEE, William C N, Corporal, RMLI, 13149 (Ch), Royal Marines HQ, on board Argus, 23 January 1923
POSTLETHWAITE, John, Leading Stoker, D/KX 78237, Carlisle, 1 March 1935
POTTER, Albert A, Stoker 1c, K 21548, Badminton, 23 April 1920
POTTER, Cyril C N, Engine Room Artificer 2c, M 2722 (Ch), L.55, 4 June 1919
POTTER, Douglas P, Electrical Artificer 4c, M 8032, Vivid, 14 March 1929
POTTER, Maurice W, Stoker 1c, K 38152, Pembroke, 8 March 1919
POTTER, Samuel, Private, RMLI, 10904 (Ply), RMLI, Plymouth Division, 5 March 1919
POTTER, William J, Petty Officer, RNR, C 3395, Daybreak, 23 September 1919
POTTO, John E, Chief Petty Officer, P/J 27056, Victory, 8 February 1936
POTTS, Bertram D, Able Seaman, C/JX 141042, Hotspur, 12 December 1937
POTTS, Bertram E, Able Seaman, J 1511 (Ch), L.55, 4 June 1919
POTTS, John E, Able Seaman, J 27413, Dauntless, 19 May 1928
POULTER, William C, Act/Cook, C/MX 59324, Pembroke, 31 July 1939
POULTNEY, Albert D, Leading Telegraphist, C/82640, Wireless Telegraph Station, Aden, 27 December 1931
POUND, Ernest P V, Stoker 1c, K 24137, L.24, 10 January 1924
POUNDS, Henry O J, Engine Room Artificer 4c, M 23085, Victory, 10 March 1919
POVALL, William, Stoker 1c, K 14974, Speedy, 23 September 1922
POVEY, Charles A, Able Seaman, J 39684, Victory, 27 November 1927
POWELL, Arthur F, Lieutenant Commander, Argus, 19 June 1919
POWELL, Bernard, Electrical Artificer 3c, M 33891, Centaur, 23 September 1923
POWELL, Cecil J, Boy 2c, J 98975, Impregnable, 24 April 1921
POWELL, Gilbert G, Driver, RMA, RMA S 1272, Howitzer Brigade, RMA, 22 February 1919
POWELL, Henry, Act/Leading Stoker, P/K 60855, M.2, 29 January 1932
POWELL, Herbert, Stoker 1c, K 66627, Repulse, 29 December 1928
POWELL, John, Stoker Petty Officer, K 3347, Colleen, 24 August 1921
POWELL, Joseph, Engine Room Artificer, P/MX 54699, Suffolk, 21 December 1938
POWELL, Owen P, Sub Lieutenant, Verulam, 4 September 1919
POWELL, Thomas, Engine Room Artificer 1c, 271798, Dolphin, 16 September 1921
POWELL, Warrington B, Honorary Lieutenant, RNR, Royal Naval Reserve, 24 April 1921
POWELL, William F, Chief Petty Officer, 239372, Spear, 12 October 1921

PRATT, Arthur C, Musician, RMB, RMB 1172, Pembroke, 17 March 1922
PRATT, Arthur W J, Boy 2c, JX 153704, Ganges, 27 July 1937
PRATT, Daniel J, Signalman, J 19619 (Ch), Frostaxe, 29 April 1919
PRATT, Frederick G, Able Seaman, RNVR, R 459, Hawke Battalion, RND, 9 July 1919
PRATT, George A M, Petty Officer, J 12015, Victory, 30 April 1920
PRATT, John E, Ship's Steward, Petrobus, RFA, 6 June 1939
PRATT, Stephen J, Stoker Petty Officer, 230458, Colombo, light cruiser, 24 October 1922
PRATT, Thomas, Stoker 1c, K 19474, Warwick, 12 August 1923
PREECE, Bernard A, Ordinary Seaman, RNVR, Bristol Z 11927, RN Depot, Crystal Palace, 10 December 1918
PREECE, Richard P, Engine Room Artificer 2c, M 135, Tamar, 11 September 1922
PRENTICE, Charles L, Shipwright 4c, M 23950, Theseus II, 5 January 1919
PRESTON, Alec, Boy 2c, J 94569, Ganges, 8 March 1919
PRESTON, James, Stoker Petty Officer, 311643, Valerian, 22 October 1926
PRESTON, James A, Stoker 1c, K 23631, Comus, 30 June 1923
PRESTON, James S, Ordinary Seaman, SSX 12239, Argus, 13 April 1927
PRETTY, Gerald H A, Gunner, King George V, 10 February 1919
PREVOST, Annette M, Nursing Sister, QARNNS, RN Hospital Chatham, 19 November 1918
PRICE, Albert H, Stoker (no service number listed), ex-New Zealand, 21 July 1921
PRICE, Albert V, Able Seaman, J 110281, Royal Sovereign, 22 June 1929
PRICE, Alfred J, Leading Stoker, K 14102, Venomous, 11 December 1920
PRICE, Frederick J, Seaman, Newfoundland RNR, X 1408, Gainsborough, 10 August 1919
PRICE, Horace H, Ordinary Seaman, SS 10376, Resolution, 15 February 1922
PRICE, James C W, Lieutenant, H.42, 23 March 1922
PRICE, John C H, Lieutenant, FAA, 716 Flight, Amphion, 20 January 1938
PRICE, John E, Petty Officer, P/J 109494, Excellent, 24 May 1938
PRICE, Philip E, Able Seaman, D/JX 126797, Devonshire, 26 June 1933
PRICE, William F, Leading Seaman, J 25784, M.1, 12 November 1925
PRIDMORE, William R, Signalman, C/J 112576, Pigmy, 17 December 1931
PRIEST, Albert J, Officer's Steward 3c, L 14694, St Genny, 12 January 1930
PRIESTLEY, William B, Marine, 11970 (Ply), Royal Marines HQ, 17 February 1925
PRIMMETT, Arthur, Leading Stoker, K 2814 (Po), Myrtle, 15 July 1919
PRINCE, Herbert, Lieutenant, RNR, President, 21 February 1919
PRINCE, William A, Stoker 1c, D/KX 76072, Lucia, 22 September 1934
PRINGLE, Robert G, Able Seaman, J 71837, Bacchante, 18 February 1919
PRINGLE, Thomas E, Stoker 1c, SS 110615, Marlborough, 3 March 1919
PRIOR, Alfred, Leading Stoker, P/KX 78832, Effingham, 20 December 1935
PRIOR, George H, Leading Stoker, K 16131 (Dev), Bombardier, 27 March 1919
PRIOR, Herbert G, Leading Seaman, P/J 96430, Suffolk, 17 February 1932
PRISCOTT, Arthur, Colour Sergeant, RMLI, S 6711 (Po), 3rd Battalion, RM, 27 November 1918
PRISCOTT, Robert T, Stoker 1c, 116608, Fisgard, 22 March 1919
PRISTON, Julian L, Surgeon Commander, RN Hospital, Chatham, 7 March 1936
PRITCHARD, Henry G, Sergeant, RM Police, RMP X 98, Plymouth Dockyard, 21 October 1936
PRITCHARD, Thomas A, Petty Officer, P/J 32637, Vernon, 22 December 1931
PRITCHARD, Tom, Officer's Steward 1c, 363129, Excellent, 28 December 1926
PROBERT, Thomas G, Leading Seaman, C/J 96331, Royal Navy, 10 June 1938
PROBIN, David H, Able Seaman, P/J 113537, Achilles, 6 April 1936
PROCTOR, Donald C, Ordinary Signalman, P/JX 156557, Hood, 21 August 1939
PROCTOR, John H, Stoker 1c, D/KX 83046, Lucia, 13 February 1937
PROOM, Joseph, Stoker 1c, C/KX 76957, Rochester, 25 September 1935
PROWSE, Joseph, Deck Hand, MMR, Warrior, 5 January 1919
PROWSE, Thomas C, Leading Signalman, J 6330, Cleopatra, 12 March 1919
PRYNN, Samuel H G, Able Seaman, 224200, Indus, 2 July 1921
PRYOR, Charles J, Private, RM, S 11645 (Deal), RM Labour Corps, 2 December 1918
PUDDICK, Frank, Act/Engine Room Artificer 4c, P/MX 47971, Hood, 24 April 1936
PULLEN, George E W, Ordinary Seaman, C/JX 151891, Resolution, 27 August 1939
PULLING, William J, Chief Petty Officer, 206709, Laburnum, 9 January 1921
PULMAN, Arthur, Leading Seaman, RNVR, London Z 2865, Courtfield, steamship, 24 December 1918
PUNNETT, George W, Petty Officer, P/238386, Victory, 17 September 1930
PUNSHON, Alfred D, Commissioned Signal Boatswain, Hood, 25 March 1924
PUPLET, Joseph R, Gunner, RMA, RMA S 1973, 3rd Battery, RMA, 29 December 1918
PURDON, Alexander, Private, RME, RME 1899, RM Engineers, 16 February 1919
PURKINS, John H, Able Seaman, J 102141, Rorqual, 1 March 1939
PURKIS, Frederick W, Stoker 1c, K 19579 (Ch), K.5, 20 January 1921
PURSE, Horace F, Officer's Steward 1c, L 4362, Hermione, 28 February 1920
PURSER, Arthur A, Able Seaman, J 96521, Endeavour, 2 September 1926
PURTON, Leslie F, Boy 1c, P/JX 136155, St Vincent, 31 October 1932
PURVIS, Thomas, Engineman, RNR, ES 824, Pembroke, 27 January 1919
PUTNAM, Pelham W, Boy 2c, J 102647, Ganges, 23 December 1921
PUTT, Walter, Stoker 1c, D/K 28508, Royal Sovereign, 5 March 1936
PUTTOCK, Denys E, Sub Lieutenant, Valorous, 20 March 1919

PYCROFT, Cecil C, Petty Officer, J 535, Vernon, 29 August 1925
PYGRAM, Thomas, Leading Signalman, J 16583, Vivid, 4 October 1919
PYM, Frederick G, Telegraphist, RNVR, Bristol 1/1247, Cyclops, 12 February 1919
PYNE, William R, Stoker 1c, C/K 61364, Poseidon, 9 June 1931
PYRKE, William H, Stoker 1c, 291189, Pembroke, 29 January 1921

Q

QUAINTON, Reginald J, Able Seaman, J 55896, Pembroke, 27 January 1919

QUANTOCK, Thomas H, Able Seaman, J 42358, L.24, 10 January 1924

QUAYLE, Harold D, Able Seaman, J 83810, Pembroke, 27 March 1922

QUICK, Richard H, Gunner, Defiance, Torpedo School, with monitor M.31 for minelaying instruction, 8 March 1921

QUICK, Richard L, Shipwright 4c, D/MX 45721, Adventure, 1 January 1933

QUICK, Ronald A, Telegraphist, J 87884, Furious, 12 August 1929

QUIGGAN, Edmund C, Ty/Lieutenant, RNVR, Royal Naval Volunteer Reserve, 15 January 1920

QUIN, Augustine W, Marine, 215839 (Po), Warspite, 5 January 1929

QUINE, William J A, Surgeon Lieutenant Commander, Royal Navy, 16 February 1923

QUINN, Philip L, Civilian Contractor, Thetis, 3 June 1939

QUINN, William, Boy 1c, D/JX 148364, Devonshire, 27 September 1937

R

RACE, George L, Stoker 1c, SS 122289, Centurion, 18 June 1923
RACKSTRAW, Frank, Blacksmith 2c, C/M 3669, Canterbury, 2 August 1931
RADCLIFFE, John W, Leading Stoker, P/KX 54557, Royal Navy, 10 May 1938
RADFORD, Victor G H, Sergeant, RM, 23203 (Ch), Frobisher, 20 July 1936
RADMORE, Edwin C, Engine Room Artificer 2c, D/M 36704, Huntley, 2 June 1936
RADWELL, Reginald L, Leading Stoker, C/K 63393, Sussex, 18 July 1934
RAE, John, Able Seaman, RNVR, R 1247, Hawke Battalion, RND, 28 November 1918
RAGGETT, Alfred D, Stoker 1c, K 26671 (Po), K.5, 20 January 1921
RAINBIRD, Frank L, Signal Boy, J 103500, Constance, 18 March 1924
RAINES, Alec W, Shipwright 1c, P/M 19782, Victory, 4 October 1938
RAINEY, Michael, Stoker 1c, D/K 6603, Vivid, 3 April 1932
RAISTRICK, Charles, Private, RMLI, 17633 (Ch), 6th Battalion, RM, 9 September 1919
RALPH, George W, Able Seaman, RNVR, London Z 4410, Caldy, 13 December 1918
RALPH, Harry, Stoker Petty Officer, C/K 58194, Pembroke, 22 January 1932
RAMAGE, Arthur, Able Seaman, J 32546, Pembroke, 27 August 1921
RAMPTON, Frederick G, Chief Petty Officer, 183835, Princess Margaret, 30 July 1919
RAMSAY, Charles T, Honorary Engineer Commander, RNR, Royal Naval Reserve, 12 July 1935
RAMSAY, David, Seaman, RNR, D 1350, Iolaire, 1 January 1919
RAMSAY, Hubert L, Private, RMLI, 20471 (Ch), Caradoc, 17 July 1920
RAMSEY, Kenneth G, Lieutenant Commander, Columbine, 10 November 1923
RANALOW, William H, Paymaster Lieutenant Commander, RNR, Royal Naval Reserve, 17 September 1929
RANCE, Harry T, Chief Stoker, P/K 63059, Royal Navy, 1 March 1939
RANDALL, Albert, Stoker 1c, K 28336, Gazelle, 28 November 1918
RANDALL, Ernest J, Ordinary Seaman, C/JX 144652, Royal Navy, January 1939
RANDALL, John M, Stoker 1c, K 55547, Greenwich, 29 January 1929
RANDALL, Norman L W, Marine, 21942 (Po), Barham, 27 August 1926
RANDALL, William H, Leading Supply Assistant, M 38226, Kiawo, 4 July 1928
RANDELL, Alfred, Stoker Petty Officer, P/K 29660, Campbell, 5 August 1931
RANKIN, Charles, Engineer Sub Lieutenant, RNR, Iolaire, 1 January 1919
RANKIN, Edward H, Lieutenant, RNVR, ML.407, motor launch, 6 February 1919
RANKIN, John, Leading Signalman, RNVR, Clyde Z 10, TB.18, torpedo boat, 26 December 1918
RANN, Charles, Officer's Steward 2c, L 6011, Columbine, 30 March 1922
RANSOME, Harry, Boy 2c, J 94107, Impregnable, 1 May 1919
RANSOME, Philip C, Lieutenant Commander, Gipsy, 12 June 1937
RANSON, George A, Lieutenant, RNR, Leda, 11 January 1919
RAPLEY, Horace, Stoker 1c, 223291, Partridge, 22 November 1918

RAPPE, Charles E, Colour Sergeant, RM, 14854 (Po), Repulse, 10 July 1938
RATE, William R, Able Seaman, 196037, Spey, 11 April 1919
RAVEN, Frederick W, Leading Signalman, 225331, Sabre, 2 November 1920
RAVEN, Henry A, Stoker 1c, K 58432, St Genny, 12 January 1930
RAVEN, John I, Stoker Petty Officer, C/K 60365, Medway, 12 January 1939
RAVENSCROFT, Joseph W, Boy 2c, JX 129157, Ganges, 21 May 1927
RAWLINGS, Albert J B, Petty Officer, J 20014, Greenwich, 28 July 1929
RAWLINGS, Ernest W, Able Seaman, J 16094, Vivid, 22 May 1923
RAWLINGS, Percy, Able Seaman, RNVR, Bristol Z 9906, Victory, 16 February 1919
RAWLINGS, William H, Able Seaman, C/J 108253, M.2, 29 January 1932
RAXWORTHY, Henry F W, Able Seaman, J 34915, Dragon, 11 December 1919
RAXWORTHY, Willie, Able Seaman, 211094, Vivid, 22 May 1925
RAY, Bertram J, Ordinary Seaman, J 96458, Centurion, 30 April 1923
RAY, Francis E, Boy Servant, L 12053, Victory, 22 February 1919
RAY, Samuel H, Stoker Petty Officer, D/KX 86816, Hastings, 19 April 1938
RAYFIELD, Alfred A, Able Seaman, J 101799, Royal Sovereign, 8 April 1924
RAYHILL, Frank, Sick Berth Chief Petty Officer, P/M 28992, RN Hospital, Haslar, 3 July 1937
RAYNER, Frederick W, Able Seaman, J 104392, Royal Navy, 30 May 1930

READ, Cecil W, Petty Officer, 227245, Chatham, 23 August 1923
READ, Edward P, Able Seaman, J 79595, Victory, 19 August 1925
READ, Edward, Stoker Petty Officer, K 11509, Valerian, 22 October 1926
READ, Harry C, Engineer Commander, Vivid, 26 December 1920
READ, John A, Leading Seaman, C/J 107220, Thetis, 3 June 1939
READ, Thomas E, Stoker Petty Officer, P/K 57548, Victory, 8 April 1936
READER, Ernest W, Able Seaman, J 103275, Woodcock, 6 April 1925
READY, Frank, Able Seaman, P/J 25478, M.2, 29 January 1932
REBBECK, Thomas, Stoker 2c, C/KX 87887, Pembroke, 12 February 1936
REDDY, Nicholas L, Engineman, RNR, ES 924, Satellite, 12 February 1919
REDE, Roger L' E M, Captain, Senior Officers' War Course, 3 March 1930
REDFERN, James, Stoker 2c, P/KX 89427, Suffolk, 25 June 1937
REDFERN, Richard J, Able Seaman, J 99353, Royal Sovereign, 25 July 1925
REDGWELL, Harry, Stoker Petty Officer, K 13586, Titania, 6 July 1922
REDMAN, Douglas F, Chief Mechanician, C/K 58892, Pembroke, 29 April 1938
REDMAN, George L, Leading Seaman, 231081, Undine, 9 March 1919
REDMOND-COOPER, James N, Able Seaman, J 109926, Sepoy, 8 April 1930
REDPATH, James F, Able Seaman, J 34210, Whirlwind, 30 March 1928
REDSHAW, George W, Sergeant, RM, 24483 (Ch), RM Chatham Division, 25 August 1936
REDWOOD, Arthur J, Gunner, RMA, RMA S 1645, Howitzer Brigade, RMA, 11 January 1919

REED, George H, Leading Seaman, J 2608, Rodney, 30 June 1928
REED, Henry J, Chief Engine Room Artificer 1c, 269195, Ambuscade, 1 March 1919
REED, James V, Midshipman (A), Naval Pilot's Course No.3, 15 June 1939
REED, John L, Ordinary Seaman, J 89773, Victory, 13 July 1921
REED, John L, Stoker 1c, K 33083, Bacchante, 14 February 1919
REED, Leslie G, Gunner, Sepoy, 8 April 1930
REED, William, Fireman, MMR, 917350, President VI, 9 March 1920
REED, William, Petty Officer, 235966, Concord, 23 February 1919
REED, William, Stoker 1c, P/K 27125, Tamar, 30 May 1931
REED, William H, Private, RMLI, 20028 (Po), Carlisle, 9 September 1919
REED, William J S, Able Seaman, J 62895, Thruster, 17 September 1928
REEMAN, Lancelot E, Stoker 1c, P/K 58359, L.56, 7 December 1932
REES, Cedric W, Petty Officer, J 469, Colleen, 21 March 1920
REES, Elias, Stoker 1c, KX 76195, Lowestoft, 18 November 1927
REES, Frederick J, Act/Warrant Supply Officer, Short Course, 16 October 1927
REES, John L L, Lieutenant, RM, Royal Marines, RAF Base Gosport, 17 August 1926
REES, John, Warrant Schoolmaster, Cornwall, 25 July 1932
REES, Samuel G, Boy 1c, P/JX 142385, Despatch, 16 September 1936
REES, Thomas E, Marine, 22314 (Po), Nelson, 19 June 1931
REEVE, Frederick C, Stoker 1c, K 39160, Maidstone, 24 July 1919
REEVE, Stanley E, Able Seaman, P/JX 128669, Durban, 15 March 1933
REEVE, Tom, Chief Stoker, 222003, Pembroke, 19 March 1922
REEVES, Ernest A, Stoker 1c, K 22764, Pembroke, 19 December 1921
REEVES, Henry A, Musician, RMB, RMB 2037, King George V, 27 March 1919
REEVES, Sidney G A, Officer's Steward 1c, 360506, Crocus, 1 August 1921
REGAN, Daniel, Chief Gunner, Dreadnought, 6 July 1919
REID, Herbert G, Shipwright 1c, 345752, Sandhurst, 15 April 1921
REID, Horatius, Stoker 1c, 276385, Dolphin, 17 February 1919
REID, John S G, Lieutenant, RNR, L.55, 4 June 1919
REID, William B F, Ordinary Seaman, P/SSX 14407, Victory, 2 March 1924
REID, William J, Seaman, RNR, A 7833, Cresco, steamship, 30 November 1918
REILLY, Peter, Able Seaman, 231076, Marlborough, 12 February 1919
REILLY, Trevor B, Ty/Lieutenant, RNR, Topaze, 28 November 1918
RELF, Benjamin O, Able Seaman, J 37822, Thruster, 1 August 1921
REMFRY, Charles J, Commissioned Gunner, Pegasus, 11 May 1921
RENDALL, William G, Private, RMLI, 18931 (Ch), 6th Battalion, RM, 27 August 1919
RENDELL, Walter J, Petty Officer, D/J 18076, Norfolk, 7 May 1936
RENDELL, William J, Petty Officer, 233572, Benbow, 9 January 1925
RENNIE, Andrew, Able Seaman, J 13182, New Zealand, 1 April 1919
RENNIE, Robert D, Able Seaman, M/C 518, Larkspur, 9 June 1919
RENNIE, Thomas C, Lieutenant, RNR, Passing, 13 February 1919
REVANS, John C, Able Seaman, P/JX 126782, Effingham, 19 November 1932
REVELL, George W, Stoker 1c, P/K 61173, Coventry, 30 September 1934
REVELL, William, Stoker Petty Officer, K 15419, Victory, 30 March 1924
REYNARD, Joseph, Trimmer, MMR, 947298, Hecla II, 30 November 1918
REYNER, James F, Gunner, RMA, RMA S 2598, Hyacinth, 10 February 1919
REYNOLDS, Arthur G, Private, RMLI, 16799 (Po), 526 Siege Battery, RMA, attached, 22 November 1918
REYNOLDS, Ernest, Leading Stoker, K 14221, Fisgard, 11 July 1926
REYNOLDS, Ernest J, Ordinary Seaman, J 34880, Greenwich, 6 March 1919
REYNOLDS, Francis C, Boy Artisan, M 35356, Indus, 9 March 1920
REYNOLDS, Hubert H, Signalman, RNVR, Bristol Z 6879, Duke, 17 December 1918
REYNOLDS, James A, Commissioned Gunner, Revenge, 1 July 1930
REYNOLDS, John A, Able Seaman, C/J 103403, Pembroke, 28 April 1934
REYNOLDS, Leonard F, Stoker 1c, D/KX 82363, Drake, 23 March 1936
REYNOLDS, Patrick, Stoker Petty Officer, 287229 (Dev), Cassandra, 5 December 1918
REYNOLDS, Rowland, Act/Lieutenant, Catspaw, 31 December 1919
REYNOLDS, William H, Marine, X 2076 (Po), RM Portsmouth Division, 14 February 1937

RHODES, Harry, Deck Hand, RNR, DA 12439, Anthony Aslett, 7 December 1918
RHODES, Leonard, Able Seaman, D/J 107566, L.26, 8 October 1933
RHODES, Robert W, Boy 2c, J 93453, Ganges, 28 November 1918

RIBBINS, Charles J (real name, served as Charles J Rivvins), Able Seaman, C/J 30155, Diomede, 23 March 1932
RICE, Frank C, Victualling Petty Officer, 342743, Dianthus, 30 March 1920
RICE, John, Private, RMLI, 19099 (Ply), King George V, 25 May 1921
RICE, William V, Commander, Endeavor, 8 June 1932
RICHARDS, Edward A, Stoker 1c, K 14474 (Dev), Kinross, 16 June 1919
RICHARDS, Ernest, Petty Officer, 237418, Vivid, 6 December 1921
RICHARDS, Guy W, Lieutenant, RNR, Royal Naval Reserve, 18 July 1921
RICHARDS, Hugh le F, Lieutenant, Neptune, 18 May 1936
RICHARDS, William, Deck Hand, RNR, Motor Lighter C.224, 9 June 1925
RICHARDS, William A, Electrical Artificer 2c, M 26877, Despatch, 4 September 1928
RICHARDS, William H, Boy 1c, J 96325, Impregnable, 10 July 1921
RICHARDSON, Bertie, Petty Officer, 237493, Attentive III (ex-Gainsborough), 28 November 1919
RICHARDSON, Dudley J, Leading Stoker, K 21018, Tamar, 4 November 1923
RICHARDSON, John J W, Stoker 1c, P/KX 80336, Porpoise, 30 March 1938
RICHARDSON, Quinton H, Surgeon Lieutenant Commander, Dragon, 23 June 1919
RICHARDSON, Raymond De D., Lieutenant, President, 21 March 1919
RICHARDSON, Thomas, Telegraphist, J 160468, Effingham, August 1929
RICHARDSON, William J M, Engineer Lieutenant, RNR,

Kurambra (RAN), 15 February 1919

RICHER, Douglas E, Able Seaman, 210449, Thisbe, 14 March 1919

RICHES, George H, Musician, RMB, RMB 1187, Monarch, 19 February 1919

RICHINGS, Reginald S, Private, RMLI, 19336 (Po), Caledon, 27 March 1920

RICKARD, George H, Able Seaman, J 13668, H.42, 23 March 1922

RICKARD, Thomas G, Marine, 16252 (Ply), RM Deal, 14 January 1938

RICKETT, Reuben R, Able Seaman, 181006, Gainsborough, 28 November 1918

RICKWOOD, Alfred H, Telegraphist, J 47053, Charm, 28 June 1919

RIDDELL, Francis R C, Lieutenant, Chrysanthemum, 30 August 1923

RIDDELL, Frederick, Able Seaman, P/JX (number not listed), Royal Navy, 2 March 1935

RIDDELL, Percivial B, Telegraphist, J 46220, Vivid, 12 March 1920

RIDDLE, Frederick C, Band Sergeant, RM, G 17069, Royal Marines HQ, 27 July 1929

RIDDLE, John, Stoker, RFA, Bacchus, RFA, 14 April 1925

RIDEOUT, Reginald J, Private, RMLI, S 1520 (Po), 3rd Battalion, RM, 1 December 1918

RIDGE, Christopher F, Sub Lieutenant, Cockchafer, 5 September 1926

RIDGE, Samuel J, Boatman, J 42243, Pembroke, 30 July 1922

RIDHOLLS, Percy, Engine Room Artificer 1c, D/M 3860, Comus, 1 September 1930

RIDOUT, George W, Gunner, RMA, RMA 10438, Konakry, steamship, 1 December 1918

RIED, Frederick T, Stoker Petty Officer, K 18667, Gnat, 25 December 1928

RIGBY, Bertie, Able Seaman, J 12654, Vivid, 10 February 1924

RIGELSFORD, Joseph J, Stoker 1c, P/K 19044, Ross, 1 July 1933

RIGGS, Reginald O, Able Seaman, J 22629, P.59, 14 September 1923

RIGGS, Sidney G, Leading Stoker, K 11704 (Dev), Dauntless, 30 September 1919

RILEY, Herbert, Engine Room Artificer 2c, M 4194 (Ch), K.5, 20 January 1921

RILEY, John, Able Seaman, D/J 110869, Drake, 28 February 1936

RILEY, Wilfred, Boy 2c, J 104129, Ganges, 5 February 1922

RILEY, William C, Fireman, MMR, 864152, Alsatian, 26 February 1919

RIMINGTON, Percy W, Commander, Cormorant, 12 June 1919

RINGSHAW, William, Electrical Artificer 1c, M 6026, Effingham, 16 February 1929

RINTOUL, John G E, Corporal, RM, 19851 (Ch), Kent, 12 March 1932

RIPLEY, John C C, Engine Room Artificer 3c, M 16984, Curacoa, 27 November 1918

RIPON, Lord Bishop of, Honorary Chaplain, RNVR, Royal Naval Volunteer Reserve, 23 August 1934

RITCHIE, Alexander, Deck Hand, RNR, DA 21749, Scour, 27 January 1919

RITCHIE, Cyril H, Cadet, RN Engineering College Keyham, 14 December 1918

RITCHIE, James, Private, RMLI, S 3310 (Ch), Chatham Division, RMLI, 4 January 1919

RIVVINS, Charles J - see RIBBINS, Charles J, Able Seaman

ROBBINS, Arthur J, Stoker Petty Officer, 311639, Penarth, 4 February 1919

ROBBINS, George A, Able Seaman, J 105630, Effingham, 24 October 1928

ROBBINS, Percival H, Petty Officer, J 33626, H.47, 9 July 1929

ROBERTS, Albert S, Able Seaman, J 44650 (Ch), Bristol, 12 May 1919

ROBERTS, Arthur C, Ordinary Seaman, JX 127593, Barham, 18 October 1928

ROBERTS, Bertie, Leading Stoker, SS 114049, Suffolk, 7 February 1919

ROBERTS, Charles F, Deck Hand, RNR, DA 14448, ML.486, motor launch, 18 December 1918

ROBERTS, David, Able Seaman, J 41628, Aracari, 25 March 1919

ROBERTS, Ernest W, Engineer Rear Admiral, Admiralty, 2nd Sea Lord's Office, 19 November 1933

ROBERTS, Henry C, Boy 2c, J 89707, Impregnable, 13 November 1918

ROBERTS, Henry D, Chief Stoker, D/K 15040, Hastings, 30 September 1931

ROBERTS, Ivor E S, Engineer Captain, Admiralty Dockyard Department, 31 October 1926

ROBERTS, James W, Sergeant, RM, 24471 (Ch), RM Barracks Chatham, 22 January 1937

ROBERTS, John D, Able Seaman, P/J 113282, Campbell, 14 January 1932

ROBERTS, Michael, Commissioned Mechanician, Magnolia, 27 April 1924

ROBERTS, Peter H H, Lieutenant Commander, Royal Sovereign, 1 March 1933

ROBERTS, Richard S, Leading Seaman, J 26461, Lucia, 14 May 1920

ROBERTS, Robert W, Able Seaman, RNVR, R 3417, Hawke Battalion, RND, 29 November 1918

ROBERTS, Roy M, Seaman, Newfoundland RNR, X 2538, Roxburgh, 8 December 1918

ROBERTS, Thomas R, Stoker, Tiger, 10 June 1927

ROBERTS, W (initial only) C, Honorary Engineer Commander, RNR, Royal Naval Reserve, 25 July 1919

ROBERTSON, Alexander, Engine Room Artificer 1c, D/M 6286, Medway, 2 September 1931

ROBERTSON, David J, Mechanician, P/K 59052, Excellent, 11 August 1930

ROBERTSON, Frederick L, Engineer Commander, Royal Navy, December 1923

ROBERTSON, Gerald W T, Captain, Penelope, 12 August 1936

ROBERTSON, Jack, Act/Sub Lieutenant (A), 751 Sqn, 2 June 1939

ROBERTSON, John A, Private, RMLI, 16607 (Ply), 2nd RM Battalion, RND, 1 January 1919

ROBERTSON, John, Seaman, RNR, B 4083, President III, 8 April 1919

ROBERTSON, Stewart, Painter 1c, 344870, Doris, 2 May 1919

ROBERTSON, Sydney L, Leading Seaman, J 21332, Emperor of India, 31 December 1926

ROBILLIARD, Albert F, Leading Telegraphist, J 38478, Valerian, 22 October 1926

ROBINS, Henry, Able Seaman, P/J 31591, Blackwater, 3 August 1936

ROBINS, James A, Stoker 1c, K 50283, Pembroke (ex-Euryalus), 30 December 1919

ROBINS, Leo V W, Ordinary Seaman, J 104408, Carysfort, 11 June 1922

ROBINSON, Alfred W C, Lieutenant Commander, RNR, Royal Naval Reserve, 13 November 1930

ROBINSON, Arthur B, Civilian Contractor, Thetis, 3 June 1939

ROBINSON, Benjamin J, Mate, MMR, Ivanhoe, 9 January 1919

ROBINSON, Edward J, Electrical Artificer 4c, M 35224, Vernon, 19 February 1923

ROBINSON, Frederick, Gunner, Tyrian, 10 April 1921

ROBINSON, Frederick S, Sergeant, RM, 21853 (Ply), Durban, 10 January 1926

ROBINSON, George, Stoker Petty Officer, 216001, Hawkins, 17 June 1925

ROBINSON, Henry, Stoker 1c, K 60966, Queen Elizabeth, 18 October 1924

ROBINSON, Hubert C, Able Seaman, J 32860, Vortigern, 19 July 1922
ROBINSON, Hugh F R, Ordinary Seaman, P/JX 13354, Vivid, 17 June 1929
ROBINSON, Jack, Petty Officer, 230068, Valiant, 26 April 1921
ROBINSON, James, Officer's Steward 2c, MC 1923, Duchess of Richmond, 6 July 1919
ROBINSON, James, Stoker 1c, P/KX 75510, Hawkins, 25 January 1933
ROBINSON, John, Petty Officer, J 925, Cuckoo, 27 May 1919
ROBINSON, John S, Ty/Instructor Lieutenant, Royal Oak, 13 November 1918
ROBINSON, John W, Surgeon Lieutenant (D), Devonshire, 16 July 1934
ROBINSON, Leonard, Ordinary Seaman, SS 10758, Marlborough, 12 May 1922
ROBINSON, Robert H, Signal Boy, D/JX 134184, Malaya, 26 March 1932
ROBINSON, Robert, Deck Hand, RNR, SD 3036, Shepherd Boy, 23 November 1918
ROBINSON, Thomas W, Stoker 1c, K 58687, Venomous, 9 October 1925
ROBINSON, Wilfred J, Marine, 20953 (Ply), Danae, 15 April 1932
ROBINSON, William G, Leading Telegraphist, J 27404, Calliope, 30 August 1925
ROBINSON, William H, Able Seaman, 218742, RN Hospital, Plymouth, 31 August 1939
ROBISON, Thomas I C, Ty/Sub Lieutenant, RNVR, 2nd Reserve Battalion, RND, 28 February 1919
ROBSON, George, Petty Officer, RNVR, KX 459, Hood Battalion, RND, 6 December 1918
ROBSON, Stephen L, Private, RMLI, 12113 (Ply), RM Headquarters, 5 July 1920
ROCHE, Michael H, Stoker 1c, K 6343, Botha, 14 December 1918
ROCHESTER, James L, Engine Room Artificer 3c, M 14974, Valerian, 22 October 1926
ROCHFORD, John, Ordnance Artificer 4c, MX 45752, Renown, 21 November 1927
RODEN, Walter, Able Seaman, 218464, Vivid, 13 June 1924
RODGER, James W, 2nd Hand, RNR, DA 11432, Coronatia, 18 July 1919
RODGERS, William J, Able Seaman, 186873, Holderness, 16 August 1919
RODHAM, Thomas, Stoker 1c, K 22037, Titania, 22 July 1921
ROE, Thomas F, Able Seaman, D/JX 125986, Apollo, 23 September 1937
ROEBUCK, George A, Ordinary Seaman, D/SSX 18227, Neptune, 24 October 1937
ROGERS, Arthur R, Officer's Steward 4c, LX 20362, Rodney, 19 June 1928
ROGERS, Edward E, Ty/Skipper, RNR, Ranmanika, 7 January 1919
ROGERS, Frank, Able Seaman, D/JX 135735, Thetis, 3 June 1939
ROGERS, Frederick, Able Seaman, 226638, Vivid, 11 March 1919
ROGERS, Harry E, Able Seaman, J 13661, Australia (RAN), 13 February 1930
ROGERS, Harry L G, Petty Officer, 230176, Vernon, 22 March 1920
ROGERS, Robert, Telegraphist, J 87856, Egmont, 6 December 1924
ROGERS, Thomas G, Painter 1c, 341097, Fisgard, 2 February 1919
ROGERSON, John B, Able Seaman, J 11103, Carlisle, 27 November 1929
ROGERSON, Richard, Civilian Contractor, Thetis, 3 June 1939
ROLFE, Percy H, Honorary Commander, RNR, Royal Naval Reserve, 10 May 1935
ROLLE, Absolom R, Engineer Captain, RAN, Franklin (RAN), 19 September 1919
ROLLIN, Herbert, Private, RMLI, S 1332 (Po), 1st RM Battalion, RND, 20 November 1918
ROLLINGS, Frederick G, Chief Mechanician 2c, P/K 13206, Nelson, 18 May 1933
ROMERIL, Philip E, Able Seaman, J 62692, Valerian, 22 October 1926
RONAYNE, Patrick, Able Seaman, 101251, Francol, Royal Fleet Auxiliary, 27 December 1919
ROOKE, Robert L, Warrant Engineer, Royal Navy, 29 May 1932
ROOKELL, George, Ordinary Seaman, D/SSX 21559, Furious, 4 November 1938
ROOS, Henry, Lance Corporal, RMLI, D 312, RM Headquarters, 25 December 1919
ROOTS, James, Able Seaman, RAN, 8510, Australia (RAN), 8 January 1920
ROSE, Charles W, Petty Officer, J 531, Vivid, 12 December 1919
ROSE, Robert G, Able Seaman, MMR, 877446, St Just, 17 February 1919
ROSE, William, Assistant Steward, MMR, 981310, Hughli, Royal Fleet Auxiliary, 26 April 1919
ROSER, Herbert, Marine, 21-61 (Ch), Ganges, 8 September 1937
ROSEVAERE, Harry L, Lieutenant, Pilot's Course, 1 May 1925
ROSIE, Alexander, Seaman, RNR, A 5290, Penarth, 4 February 1919
ROSS, Alexander, Stoker 1c, P/K 62944, Barham, 31 October 1936
ROSS, Alexander W, Surgeon Lieutenant, Valerian, 28 March 1924
ROSS, Andrew, Able Seaman, C/J 115702, Pembroke, 3 June 1939
ROSS, David D, Lieutenant Commander, RANR, Penguin (RAN), 24 June 1919
ROSS, John F, Ordinary Seaman, MC 1644, Larkspur, 9 June 1919
ROSS, John Mc S, Trimmer, RNR, ST 2022, Victory, 13 January 1919
ROSS, Reginald W G, Able Seaman, J 16762, Wryneck, 22 July 1929
ROSS, William, Cook, MMR, Bendigo, 10 February 1919
ROSS, William, Leading Stoker, D/K 10811, Flora, 4 June 1931
ROSS, William D, Able Seaman, D/J 104953, Norfolk, 16 July 1936
ROSSITER, John, Commissioned Signal Boatswain, Carysfort, 5 November 1928
ROUGH, Ronald M, Able Seaman, J 103030, Tamar, 9 March 1928
ROUQUETTE, Arthur P H, Act/Paymaster Lieutenant Commander, Grafton, 15 November 1918
ROURKE, John F, Chief Petty Officer Writer, D/M 5265, Tamar, 5 November 1930
ROUSE, Eric J, Ordinary Seaman, JX 129090, Nelson, 6 July 1930
ROUTLEDGE, Richard F, Engine Room Artificer 3c, D/M 38825, Furious, 29 June 1935
ROUTLEY, George - see HART, George, Private, RMLI
ROWBOTHAM, Cyril S, Signalman, RNVR, Mersey Z 1403, Victory, 31 January 1919
ROWBOTHAM, Reginald, Private, RMLI, 17804 (Ch), Dwarf, 19 February 1922
ROWE, Ernest T, Chief Engine Room Artificer 1c, P/M 2254, Revenge, 17 October 1931
ROWE, George M A, Commander, Conqueror, 30 April 1920
ROWE, George, Able Seaman, P/J 105935, Excellent, 7 March 1932
ROWE, George, Petty Officer, 212126, Lucia, 7 August 1920
ROWE, Thomas, Stoker 1c, D/K 75974, Comus, 10 June 1931
ROWELL, Alfred C, Petty Officer, J 15045, Tern, 4 February 1928
ROWELL, Leonard H, Stoker 1c, SS 124939, Shakespeare, 14 January 1922
ROWLAND, John W, Able Seaman, P/JX 132292, Raven, 7

August 1939
ROWLANDS, Arthur, Private, RMLI, 19823 (Po), Portsmouth Division, RMLI, 21 April 1921
ROWLEY, Arthur, Engine Room Artificer, RNR, EA 1271, Halcyon, 30 November 1918
ROWNTREE, James D, Able Seaman, J 43089, Scarab, 6 August 1923
ROWSE, Aaron C, Stoker 1c, 296287, New Zealand, 30 December 1918
ROWSELL, Raymond R, Boy 1c, J 107722, Barham, 2 January 1925
ROY, Peter A, Engineer Sub Lieutenant, RNR, Sobo, 23 February 1919
ROYSE, William J, Marine, 23164 (Ch), Malaya, 4 January 1939

RUCK-KEENE, Ernest L, Lieutenant, Egmont, 24 December 1918
RUDDOCK, William T, Stoker 1c, K 5670, Maori, 4 December 1918
RUDGE, Anthony M, Stoker 1c, K 61362, Pembroke, 1 December 1928
RUFFELL, William F, Ordinary Telegraphist, J 84918 (Ch), Verulam, 4 September 1919
RULE, Samuel J, Leading Stoker, K 24541, Adventure, 6 April 1928
RUMBELOW, Robert H, Stoker 1c, P/KX 83740, RN Barracks Portsmouth, 23 February 1937
RUNDLE, Ernest, Chief Petty Officer, 217987, Stormcloud, 16 June 1925
RUNDLE, Joseph A M, Leading Seaman, RNR, B 4225, Westgate, steamship, 8 January 1919
RUNICLES, Charles N, Chief Petty Officer Writer, P/M 34998, Victory, 20 November 1933
RUNNICLERS, Frederick J, Able Seaman, SS 5256 (Ch), Superb, 23 November 1918
RUSBRIDGE, Percy M, Able Seaman, J 18638, Colombo, 4 May 1920
RUSE, George E, Gunner, RMA, RMA 14218, RMA Eastney, 19 February 1919
RUSH, John, Stoker, RNR, V 457, Tiger, 23 December 1918
RUSSELL, Edward G, Able Seaman, P/JX 126916, Eagle, 18 October 1934
RUSSELL, Edward, Lieutenant, Fisgard, 1 September 1924
RUSSELL, George E L, Leading Seaman, J 40716, Vivid, 23 September 1924
RUSSELL, James W, Stoker 1c, D/KX 87097, Centurion, 25 June 1938
RUSSELL, John R, Petty Officer 1c, 120983 (Po) (RFR A 1308), Drake Battalion, RND, 5 June 1919
RUSSELL, Leslie S, Commander (E), Admiralty Engineer in Chief's Department, 19 July 1929
RUSSELL, Thomas, Blacksmith 1c, 341077, Bacchante, 16 February 1919
RUSSELL, William H, Petty Officer, J 21098, Dee, 12 August 1921
RUSSUM, Sidney W, Engineer Sub Lieutenant, RNR, Viscol, 11 February 1919
RUST, Henry T, Lieutenant, FAA, 440 Flight, Hermes, 6 May 1925
RUSTON, James W F, Private, RMLI, 19243 (Ch), Diana, 25 December 1918
RUTHERFORD, Robert, Private, RMLI, 17872 (Ply), Fantome, 8 October 1921
RUTTER, John T, Leading Telegraphist, C/J 45926, Albury, 9 February 1934

RYAN, Albert J, Victualling Assistant, M 33103, Crescent, 3 March 1919
RYAN, Jack, Able Seaman, D/JX 134116, Osprey, 21 October 1934
RYAN, John, Mate, Pilot's Course, No.2, 14 July 1925
RYAN, Michael J, Stoker 1c, K 64655, Emerald, 18 August 1927
RYAN, Patrick E J, Lieutenant, Thetis (Trident), 3 June 1939
RYAN, Patrick, 2nd Writer, M 7677, President VI, 25 April 1919
RYCE, Robert W, Stoker 1c, 221494, Walpole, 5 February 1919
RYDER, Henry C, Electrical Artificer 3c, C/MX 48522, Cyclops, 3 June 1934
RYDER, Thomas, Stoker Petty Officer, K 9251 (Dev), Cassandra, 5 December 1918

S

SABISTON, James, Trimmer, RNR, TS 6291, Victorious, 24 November 1919

SACKREE, Albert, Blacksmith 1c, 304140, Pembroke, 7 March 1920

SADD, Charles W J, Commissioned Gunner, Harebell, 15 September 1935

SADLE, Reginald C, Leading Seaman, J 29087, Ramillies, 24 November 1925

SADLER, Frederick, Able Seaman, RNVR, KP 874, Anson Battalion, RND, 15 November 1918

SAFE (second name not listed), Seedie, X 53, Birmingham, 30 October 1924

SAID, Mohammed B, Steward, L 15173, Flora, 25 January 1933

SAINSBURY, Leonard J, Supply Assistant, M 38220, Victory, 12 August 1927

SAINSBURY, Walter H, Chief Officer, HMCG, HM Coast Guard, 2 November 1922

SALAH, Abdullah B, Seedie, Flora, 1 November 1923

SALES, Arthur J, Petty Officer, J 13923, Hood, 19 November 1928

SALIBA, Carmelo, Able Seaman, J 95744, Europa, 19 December 1919

SALISBURY, James, Gunner, Vivid, 11 March 1920

SALISBURY, William W, Able Seaman, J 97120, Curlew, 1 June 1926

SALLEY, Cyril J, Private, RMLI, 16659 (Ply), RM Headquarters, 22 April 1920,

SALMOND, Rawdon F G, Lieutenant, RAF Training Base Leuchars, Scotland, 22 June 1927

SALMOND, William A C, Lieutenant Commander, Whirlwind, 20 March 1921

SALTER, Ernest J, Stoker 1c, K 24355, Vivid, 30 August 1926

SAMMONS, Frank, Petty Officer, 218503, Pembroke, 24 January 1924

SAMMUT, Constantino, Officer's Steward 2c, L 14987, Adamant, 7 October 1925

SAMPHIER, Frank, Private, RMLI, 20648 (Po), RM Headquarters, 2 October 1921

SAMPSHIRE, Thomas C, Stoker 1c, K 58448, Marlborough, 7 March 1926

SAMPSON, Archibald C, Officer's Steward 1c, 361436, Vivid (ex-Valorous), 25 March 1921

SAMPSON, Arthur E R, Able Seaman, J 46212, L.12, 9 July 1929

SAMPSON, James, Boy 2c, JX 158483, Caledonia, 22 June 1938

SAMUEL, Jack, Assistant Cook, MMR, Langton, 1 January 1919

SAMUEL, John, Chief Petty Officer, J 4791, Voyager, 30 October 1928

SAMUELS, Arthur, Able Seaman, 362723, Mollusc, Royal Fleet Auxiliary, 21 November 1918

SANDEL, George W, Boy 2c, J 94638, Ganges II, 10 March 1919

SANDEMAN, John G, Honorary Lieutenant, RNR, Royal Naval Reserve, 1 December 1921

SANDERS, Arnold E, Cook, MMR, 550781, Elmol, Royal Fleet Auxiliary, 13 May 1919

SANDERS, Frederick J, Able Seaman, J 56750, Fantome, 12 August 1921

SANDERS, Herbert, Engine Room Artificer, D/MX 49136, Regent, 18 October 1938

SANDERS, James, Private, RMLI, 14064 (Ply), Plymouth Division, RMLI, 1 April 1921

SANDERS, Thomas, Stoker Petty Officer, 300974, Vivid, 16 September 1919

SANDERSON, David, Able Seaman, C/JX 148081, RN Hospital, Capetown, 18 February 1939

SANDERSON, Harold A, Honorary Captain, RNR, Royal Naval Reserve, 26 February 1932

SANDFORD, Francis H, Captain, Admiralty, Plans Division, 15 February 1926

SANDFORD, Richard D, Lieutenant, G.11, 23 November 1918

SANDS, William, Able Seaman, RNVR, Tyneside Z 4145, Hood Battalion, RND, 13 November 1918

SANDY, Walter E, Stoker 1c, K 24214, Ganges, 8 March 1920

SANKEY, Edward F, Telegraphist, RNVR, Mersey Z 1965, Ethelwulf, 1 December 1918

SANSOM, Harry, Able Seaman, 203674, TB.98, torpedo boat, 13 September 1919

SARGENT, John, Stoker 2c, D/KX 90084, Drake, 14 January 1937

SATCHELL, George E, Leading Cook's Mate, M 8061, Lord Nelson, 9 December 1918

SATTERFORD, Richard D, Chief Petty Officer Writer, D/M 19148, Queen Elizabeth, 4 August 1930

SAUER, Frederick J, Leading Seaman, SS 1647, President III, 20 February 1919

SAUNDERS, Albert E, Petty Officer, 149374, Vivid, 13 June 1919

SAUNDERS, Alexander F, Telegraphist, J 96342, Vulcan, 6 February 1924

SAUNDERS, Alfred E, Trimmer Cook, RNR, TE 725, Raymont, 22 November 1918

SAUNDERS, Alfred J, Shipwright 3c, 345351, Assistance, 31 July 1919

SAUNDERS, Algernon H, Leading Sick Berth Attendant, M 2473, RN Hospital, Bermuda, 8 July 1930

SAUNDERS, Arthur, Stoker, P/KX 76060, Royal Fleet Wing, Plymouth, 22 August 1937

SAUNDERS, Charles, Chief Petty Officer Telegraphist, 201032, President, 27 June 1923

SAUNDERS, Ernest J, Stoker Petty Officer, K 11571, St Vincent, 24 December 1918

SAUNDERS, George H, Able Seaman, P/JX 126228, Nelson, 12 February 1931

SAUNDERS, George W, Leading Seaman, 210574, Highflyer, 11 February 1921

SAUNDERS, Henry, Yeoman of Signals, P/J 13571, Dolphin, 21 August 1931

SAUNDERS, James, Able Seaman, J 34737, Columbine, 27 March 1919

SAUNDERS, John H, Private, RMLI, 12164 (Po), Portsmouth Division, RMLI, 24 November 1918

SAUNDERS, Leonard, Able Seaman, J 37056, Pontefract, 18 January 1919

SAUNDERS, Robert, Master at Arms, 196653, Egmont, 3 November 1919

SAUNDERS, Sidney S, Officer's Chief Cook, L 686, Cyclops, 13 February 1919

SAUNDERS, Sydney, Marine, 13829 (Ch), Constance, 14 September 1923

SAUNDERS, William, Mechanician, K 426, Ceres, 8 May 1925

SAVAGE, Arthur, Able Seaman, C/J 100974, Royal Navy, 9 December 1934

SAVAGE, Arthur W, Engine Room Artificer 3c, M 3487, (ship or unit not listed), 16 May 1921

SAVAGE, James T, Able Seaman, J 44609, Hope, 27 June 1919

SAVAGE, Robert, Leading Seaman, J 30724, Queen Elizabeth, 28 April 1929

SAVILL, Jack H, Able Seaman, SS 9463, Valerian, 4 January 1922

SAVILLE, Ernest R B, Chief Writer, 345591, Victory, 20 August 1920

SAVILLE, Percy S, Stoker 1c, K 10730, Impregnable, 27 June 1926

SAVILLE, Samuel J, Able Seaman, SS 7258, Vivacious, 24 January 1921

SAVORY, Ernest, Able Seaman, 213258, Valerian, 20 November 1918

SAWLE, Walter, Boy 2c, J 93962, Impregnable, 25 February 1919

SAWNEY, Ronald, Ordinary Seaman, JX 129209, Nelson, 9 October 1929

SAWYER, Herbert J, Chief Petty Officer, C/JX 152928, Dolphin, 22 May 1937
SAWYER, Lewis C, Able Seaman, J 8399, Pembroke, 1 November 1919
SAWYER, Reginald S, Able Seaman, P/JX 137877, Victory, 27 December 1936
SAXBY, Douglas A E, Boy 2c, J 94174, Powerful, 4 March 1919
SAYER, George S, Deck Hand, RNR, DA 18561, Queen, 18 December 1918
SAYERS, Charles A, Able Seaman, J 31401, M.1, 12 November 1925
SAYLE, James, Seaman, RNR, A 10182, Britannia, RN College, Dartmouth, 11 April 1924

SCAIFE, Irving, Stoker 1c, SS 120477, Columbine, 17 April 1922
SCAIFE, John D, Stoker, RNR, T 2431, Ocean Hope, 25 January 1919
SCANLON, John, Able Seaman, SSX 17110, Royal Navy, 17 October 1938
SCANTLEBURY, Robert A, Leading Stoker, D/K 62794, Caledon, 6 November 1933
SCARLETT, Bernard R, Able Seaman, J 104660, Eagle, 24 May 1929
SCARLETT, George J H, Corporal, RM, 16605 (Po), Iron Duke, 23 January 1930
SCARTH, George L, Civilian Contractor, Thetis, 3 June 1939
SCHEPENS, Ferdinand, Private, RMLI, 12825 (Po), Barham, 18 August 1920
SCHJONEMAN, Laurtiz P, Chief Skipper, RNR, Royal Naval Reserve, 11 May 1932
SCHLOSSER, Robert E, Lieutenant Commander, RNR, Royal Naval Reserve, 22 February 1925
SCHOFIELD, James, Private, RMLI, 11561 (Po), Warrior, 23 December 1918
SCHOFIELD, Wilfred, Able Seaman, SS 9727, Vivid, 26 June 1920
SCHOLES, Henry P, Lieutenant, Diomede, 7 February 1923
SCHUBERT, Frederick W H, Private, RM, S 337 (Deal), RM Deal, 18 March 1920
SCOREY, Ernest J, Able Seaman, 231624, Barham, 24 February 1926
SCOREY, Percival L, Warrant Shipwright, Curacoa, 1 December 1918
SCOTCHER, Cyril G, Sub Lieutenant, RNR, Welland, 16 March 1919
SCOTCHER, Percy E, Gunner, RMA, RMA S 1967, 3rd Battalion, RM, 27 November 1918
SCOTT, Alfred W, Marine, 22359 (Ch), Valiant, 23 January 1933
SCOTT, Arthur, Able Seaman, J 78912, Renown, 30 January 1919
SCOTT, Charles, Stoker 1c, K 15386, Espiegle, 9 May 1923
SCOTT, Edgar J, Leading Stoker, K 5724, Lilac, 15 November 1918
SCOTT, George E D, Petty Officer, J 9020, Velox, 15 February 1919
SCOTT, George H, Marine, 22916 (Ch), RM Barracks Chatham, 31 August 1937
SCOTT, George W, Ordinary Seaman, RNVR, London Z 6108, Pembroke, 25 February 1919
SCOTT, Henry J, Surgeon Lieutenant, Cricket, 14 December 1928
SCOTT, Henry T, Chief Petty Officer, 212649, Excellent, 11 January 1920
SCOTT, Percival G, Senior Reserve Attendant, M 10047, Ganges, 31 March 1919
SCOTT, S (initial only) A, Major, RM, Royal Marines, 29 January 1938
SCOTT, Samuel, Warrant Engineer, Ark Royal, 5 June 1920
SCOTT, Thomas L, Engineer Commander, Rochester, 30 September 1933
SCOTT, Victor G, Lieutenant (E), Antelope, 16 February 1938
SCOTT, William H, Engine Room Artificer 1c, M 1655, Royal Sovereign, 14 April 1928
SCOTT, William J, Sub Lieutenant, RNVR, ML.364, motor launch, 23 April 1919
SCOVELL, Albert C, Stoker 1c, P/K 65231, Curacoa, 26 September 1932
SCRACE, Harold W, Able Seaman, J 97275, Calcutta, 15 September 1929
SCRAGG, William A, Regulating Petty Officer, M 37148, Pembroke, 2 November 1923
SCREECH, William, Able Seaman, J 66673, Pegasus, 12 November 1918
SCRIBBENS, Cecil W T, Leading Stoker, 304677, Concord, 24 June 1919
SCRIVNER, Harold, Able Seaman, J 20222 (Dev), Lucia, 19 June 1920
SCULLIN, John, Signalman, RNVR, Clyde 1/199, Vivid III, 24 February 1919
SCULLY, James, Stoker, RAN, 5738, Australia (RAN), 7 September 1920

SEABROOK, Archibald W, Commissioned Gunner, Royal Navy, 14 May 1938
SEAGRAVE, Percy G, Painter 1c, M 5138, Repulse, 27 April 1927
SEAL, Jack, Ordinary Seaman, J 74031, Pembroke, 24 March 1919
SEALE, Henry, Officer's Steward 2c, South African, Y 5, Birmingham, 6 February 1921
SEALY, Douglas C, Lieutenant, H.42, 23 March 1922
SEAMAN, Ernest, Artificer Engineer, Britannia, 15 December 1918
SEAR, William R T, Scullion, MMR, 877632, Serbol, Royal Fleet Auxiliary, 24 November 1918
SEARLE, Frederick, Able Seaman, J 91327, Excellent, 6 December 1925
SEARLES, Leonard, Naval Cadet, Sea Cadet Corps, 12 July 1929
SEARLES, Walter, Able Seaman, J 25694 (Ch), Vittoria, 31 August 1919
SECKER, Thomas J, Able Seaman, C/J 114050, Pembroke, 3 July 1933
SEDDALL, Harry V, Commander, RNR, Royal Naval Reserve, 4 July 1930
SELBY, George L, Leading Seaman, J 90116, Teazer, 21 August 1929
SELFE, Alfred T, Ordinary Seaman, P/SSX 16449, Fury, 12 August 1936
SELLEY, Samuel G, Sailmaker's Mate, 149321, Glorious, 18 January 1924
SELLICK, Leslie J, Able Seaman, J 49989, Liverpool, 7 December 1918
SELLS, Charles H, Petty Officer, D/J 21262, Proteus, 18 September 1933
SELMAN, George J, Leading Seaman, C/J 114881, Curlew, 6 March 1936
SELWAY, Henry J, Chief Electrical Artificer 1c, 344628, Sarepta, 25 August 1919
SELWAY, Upton, Petty Officer, 227897, Neptune, 30 November 1918
SENNETT, George H C, Chief Engine Room Artificer 2c, 270992, Titania, 10 April 1923
SEPHTON, George, Telegraphist, RNVR, Mersey Z 3633, President IV, 24 November 1918
SERCOMBE, William H, Able Seaman, J 1271, Vanquisher, 5 September 1922
SERVANT, Harold D, Private, RMLI, S 458 (Ch), 1st RM Battalion, RND, 3 January 1919
SERVICE, John G, Ordinary Seaman, P/JX 132024, Queen Elizabeth, 15 December 1931
SESSFORD, James H, Engineer Lieutenant, Royal Navy, 15 September 1927
SEVERS, Fred, Signalman, P/JX 133233, Sandwich, 19 July 1935

SEWARD, Ernest J, Able Seaman, RNVR, London Z 4121, Sunflower, 6 February 1919
SEWARD, Reginald W J, Able Seaman, D/J 88015, Cricket, 24 September 1932
SEXTON, John, Leading Seaman, J 24832 (Dev), Fox, 2 July 1919
SEXTON, Sidney W, Engine Room Artificer 3c, M 11523, Ajax, 11 May 1925
SEYBURN, David, Telegraphist, J 27892, Marlborough, 23 November 1922
SEYMOUR, George, Stoker 1c, K 24204 (Ch), K.5, 20 January 1921
SEYMOUR, Joseph C, Private, RM, S 12473 (Deal), RM Labour Corps, 16 February 1919
SEYMOUR, Ralph F, Commander, Victoria & Albert, Royal Yacht, 4 October 1922

SHACKLEFORD, Harry E, Stoker 1c, P/K 63177, Vindictive, 19 September 1932
SHAMGAMA, Abuda, Seedie, X 252, Flora, 29 July 1929
SHANKLEY, Richard, Leading Seaman, J 7876, Marlborough, 30 December 1921
SHANNON, William, Leading Seaman, RNR, B 5107, Nero, steamship, 6 December 1918
SHARKEY, Walter, Signalman, J 39913, Victory, 8 October 1919
SHARMAN, George H, Signalman, SX 61, RN Shore Signal Station, Spurn Point, 8 January 1934
SHARMAN, Herbert V, Deck Hand, RNR, DA 18372, Halcyon II, 5 December 1918
SHARMAN, John A, Telegraphist, J 38974 (Ch), Frostaxe, 29 April 1919
SHARMAN, John R, Stoker 1c, C/K 65522, Pembroke, 12 June 1935
SHARMAN, Laurence C, Commander, Admiralty Torpedo Depot, 31 December 1932
SHARP, Alfred E, Officer's Steward 1c, 359227 (Ch), Starfish, 29 October 1919
SHARP, Francis R G, Leading Seaman, RNVR, London Z 2833, Hawke Battalion, RND, 1 December 1918
SHARP, James, Able Seaman, RNVR, Clyde Z 8330, Westgate, steamship, 8 January 1919
SHARP, William, Chief Stoker, 291284, Royal Oak, 26 July 1920
SHARPE, George, Leading Stoker, P/K 59370, M.2, 29 January 1932
SHARPE, George E, Stoker 2c, KX 79754, Victory, 27 April 1929
SHARPLIN, George W, Warrant Engineer, Royal Navy, 27 September 1934
SHAW, Fred, Stoker Petty Officer, K 7917, Sirdar, 10 February 1928
SHAW, George W, Coastguardsman 3c, 278674, Victory, 10 August 1922
SHAW, Harold J, Paymaster Commander, RNR, Royal Naval Reserve, 12 February 1931
SHAW, Norman, Stoker 1c, C/K 64933, Shropshire, 23 July 1931
SHAW, Robert J, Able Seaman, 217865, Vivid, 1 February 1925
SHAW, William, Stoker 1c, K 18174, Dolphin, 30 April 1928
SHAW, William F, Engine Room Artificer 2c, 271948 (Po), L.55, 4 June 1919
SHAWYER, Frederick W, Marine, 18993 (Po), Victoria & Albert, 6 March 1930
SHEARER, Frederick, Able Seaman, J 30199 (Po), Torch, 25 December 1918
SHEARS, Reuben G, Commissioned Supply Officer, Vivid, 23 December 1932
SHEATH, Ernest K, Petty Officer, J 1828, Victory, 10 June 1926
SHEEHAN, Edric W, Stoker Petty Officer, D/KX 79775, Drake, 23 February 1939
SHEEHAN, Francis P O, Able Seaman, D/J 36681, Royal Navy, 17 August 1935
SHEEHAN, Henry J, Stoker Petty Officer, K 13726, Protea, 2 April 1926

SHEEN, Harold, Marine, 22355 (Ply), Cormorant, 19 September 1936
SHEERAN, Charles, Greaser, MMR, 713819, Francol, Royal Fleet Auxiliary, 27 December 1919
SHEPHARD, Frederick E, Petty Officer Cook, 347798, Barham, 28 July 1923
SHEPHARD, Reginald S, Able Seaman, J 99766, Diomede, 20 May 1925
SHEPHEARD, William F H, Chief Petty Officer, D/JX 148414, Drake, 15 March 1936
SHEPHERD, Edward N S, Deck Hand, RNR, DA 13423, Colleen, 25 November 1918
SHEPHERD, Moses, Leading Seaman, J 44339, Whitley, 13 July 1924
SHEPHERD, William K, Boy 2c, J 155466, Caledonia, 30 November 1937
SHEPPARD, John W, Able Seaman, 179962 (Po), Royal Sovereign, 22 November 1919
SHEPPARD, Stanley H, 2nd Writer, M 27905, Victory, 22 July 1922
SHEPPARD, William C, Petty Officer, J 5572 (Po), K.5, 20 January 1921
SHERIDAY, John E, Chief Petty Officer Telegraphist, D/J 33153, Montrose, 3 October 1935
SHERRIFF, John W, Able Seaman, RNVR, Bristol Z 5254, President III, 1 March 1919
SHERROCKS, Sydney, Leading Stoker, P/K 59646, Poseidon, 9 June 1931
SHERRY, Francis J, Boy 1c, J 100577, Erin, 24 April 1922
SHERRY, William, Private, RM, S 11677 (Deal), RM Labour Corps, 11 December 1918
SHIELDS, John E, Stoker 1c, SS 118468, Marlborough, 23 January 1923
SHIELDS, Robert, Petty Officer 1c, 137680, Pembroke VII, 21 December 1919
SHIELS, George, Stoker 1c, P/KX 76611, Victory, 15 September 1937
SHIMMIN, Robert F, Deck Hand, RNR, DA 11025, Fifinella, hired trawler, 26 November 1918
SHIPLEY, Alexander W, Sergeant, RMLI, 9115 (Ply), Plymouth Division, RMLI, 23 March 1919
SHIRES, John E, Engine Room Artificer Apprentice, MX 45253, Fisgard, 28 March 1928
SHIRLEY, Donald M E, Ordinary Seaman, J 70973, Marlborough, 2 September 1919
SHIRLEY, Gerald A, Stoker 1c, K 19504, Clematis, 15 April 1928
SHIRLEY, Henry C, Boy 2c, J 93559, Powerful, 28 December 1918
SHOEBRIDGE, Henry F, Engine Room Artificer 1c, 269037, Platypus, 12 September 1920
SHOOBRIDGE, Ernest A, Signalman, J 51841, Pembroke I, 3 January 1927
SHORE, William E, Leading Stoker, K 62747, Benbow, 23 September 1927
SHORTER, Leonard F T, Supply Chief Petty Officer, P/M 37639, RN Hospital, Haslar, 19 October 1938
SHORTER, Leonard W, Boy 2c, J 93796, Ganges, 4 March 1919
SHORTER, Robert F, Able Seaman, RNVR, R 6001, Anson Battalion, RND, 12 November 1918
SHORTMAN, James H, Ordinary Seaman, J 77887, Challenger, 10 December 1918
SHRAPNELL, Arthur F, Able Seaman, J 26736 (Dev), Cassandra, 5 December 1918
SHRUBSALL, William W M, Chief Sick Berth Steward, 140885, Pembroke, 7 February 1919
SHUE, Wah, Officer's Steward 3c, Tamar, 23 February 1924
SHUTE, William H, Deck Hand, RNR, DA 6805, Europa, 27 November 1918
SHUTT, Edward P, Able Seaman, D/J 98403, Adventure, 5 August 1931
SHUTTLEWORTH, Stanley, Able Seaman, D/SSX 15187,

Diamond, 18 November 1938

SIBLEY, Cyril V W, Able Seaman, P/J 19127, Resolution, 13 January 1934
SIBLEY, Eric R, Signalman, RAN, 460, Ascania, 23 February 1919
SIBLEY, John R, Fireman, MMR, Liberty IV, 24 November 1918
SIBLEY, Walter, Marine, 124709, Royal Marines, 10 February 1936
SIDEN, Ivor, Naval Cadet, Sea Cadet Corps, 12 July 1929
SIDLEY, William, Able Seaman, J 10846, Wivern, 19 January 1922
SILCOCK, Frederick W S, Able Seaman, J 16490, Benbow, 3 January 1926
SILCOCK, Thomas R, Leading Signalman, RNVR, Wales Z 668, President IV, 25 March 1919
SILLAR, David A C, Lieutenant, Courageous, 27 October 1930
SILLENCE, Ernest, Bugler, 15575 (Ch), Royal Marines HQ, 10 December 1924
SIM, Ah, Stoker, Woodlark, 30 September 1919
SIM, James, Stoker 1c, D/KX 80799, Caledonia, 3 February 1938
SIMKINS, Albert T, Stoker 1c, KX 76998, Vivid, 2 October 1927
SIMM, Moses, Able Seaman, D/SSX 13487, Adventure, 14 April 1936
SIMMONDS, Albert, Boy 2c, JX 141179, Ganges, 28 March 1934
SIMMONDS, Arthur H, Trimmer, RNR, TS 1966, Pembroke, 9 December 1918
SIMMONDS, Samuel, Officer's Steward 2c, L 2083, Kempenfelt, 13 May 1920
SIMMONDS, William L, Stoker 1c, K 44781, Roxburgh, 11 December 1918
SIMMONS, Ernest F, Able Seaman, J 27761, Dolphin (ex-Arethusa), 10 February 1919
SIMMONS, Joseph, Private, RM, S 8820 (Deal), RM Labour Corps, 25 March 1919
SIMMONS, Leonard, Stoker 1c, K 66047, Hawkins, 10 August 1926
SIMONS, James, Leading Stoker, D/K 21515, Resolution, 6 January 1933
SIMONS, William, Stoker Petty Officer, 302622, Westcott, 15 February 1921
SIMPKIN, Joseph A, Sergeant, RMLI, 12439 (Ch), 3rd Battalion, RM, 16 December 1918
SIMPKINS, Leslie C, Ordinary Seaman, J 74969, Victory, 18 May 1922
SIMPSON, Alfred, Blacksmith 4c, M 37793, Queen Elizabeth, 17 May 1926
SIMPSON, Charles E, Regulating Petty Officer, 237028, Magnolia, 7 January 1924
SIMPSON, Charles H, Gunner, RMA, RMA 15954, RM Eastney, 23 December 1919
SIMPSON, Gibson W, Lieutenant, Medusa, 26 March 1926
SIMPSON, James, Engineman, RNR, TS 3336, Pembroke, 26 February 1919
SIMPSON, John, Able Seaman, J 2683, Pembroke, 27 February 1919
SIMPSON, Peter, Colour Sergeant, RMA, RMA 1985 (RFR A), RMA Battalion, 17 April 1919
SIMPSON, Walter, Able Seaman, J 51382, Collingwood, 24 November 1918
SIMS, Cecil F, Private, RMLI, S 2205 (Po), 1st RM Battalion, RND, 11 February 1919
SIMS, Edward E, Gunner, RMA (RMR B 1259), RMA 9544, DEMS Gunner, Konakry, steamship, on books of President III, 1 December 1918
SIMS, Edward T, Electrical Artificer 3c, M 36225, Hood, 16 June 1926
SIMS, Edward, Stoker 1c, C/K 66438, Scarborough, 12 April 1935
SIMS, Frank, Telegraphist, J 34970, Foresight, 5 January 1919
SIMS, Henry T, Stoker 1c, K 22447 (Ch), Moorhen, 15 August 1920
SIMS, John H, Engine Room Artificer 3c, P/M 35324, M.2, 29 January 1932
SIMS, Thomas J, Able Seaman, J 61241, Kruger, 27 July 1919
SINCLAIR, Robert J, Gunner, Conqueror, 18 February 1919
SING, Yes H, Able Seaman, Tamar, 11 October 1930
SINKINS, James, Chief Skipper, RNR, Royal Naval Reserve, 14 January 1932
SINNOT, William, Trimmer, RNR, TS 7316, Caldy, 10 December 1918
SISK, Richard, Boy 2c, JX 129690, Impregnable, 16 March 1928
SITWELL, Peter S L, Paymaster Midshipman, Ramilles, 6 August 1937
SIVITER, George, Stoker 1c, K 11842, Valerian, 22 October 1926

SKEA, Patrick, Stoker 1c, K 754, Maidstone, 19 June 1922
SKEET, Henry T, Stoker Petty Officer, P/K 59513, Cornwall, 11 February 1932
SKELT, William P, Engine Room Artificer 4c, M 34508, Pembroke, 4 September 1925
SKELTON, Charles T W, Able Seaman, J 12923, Gnat, 1 September 1926
SKEWS, Nathaniel R H, Leading Seaman, J 93752, Marlborough, 4 November 1926
SKILLERN, Reginald R, Engine Room Artificer 4c, M 35040, Dolphin, 1 November 1926
SKINGSLEY, Ronald S, Marine, X 899 (Ply), Royal Oak, 15 December 1937
SKINNER, Arthur, Stoker Petty Officer, C/K 18614, Ganges, 6 November 1932
SKINNER, Benjamin, 1st Writer, 347122, Attentive II, 7 December 1918
SKINNER, Frederick, Signalman, J 68143, Capetown, 5 September 1924
SKINNER, George, Assistant Cook, MMR, 926367, Princess Ena, 13 December 1918
SKINNER, Harry C, Ordinary Seaman, P/SSX 23413, Victory, 25 January 1938
SKINNER, John G, Armourer, M 5198, Crocus, 31 October 1924
SKINNER, John J, Marine, 216487 (Po), Tiger, 14 March 1924
SKINNER, Robert R, Private, RMLI, 21403 (Ch), 3rd Battalion, RM, 3 December 1918
SKINNER, William, Boy 2c, J 101626, Impregnable, 5 May 1921
SKITTLE, William F, Chief Stoker, 312059, Hermes, 17 March 1926

SLACK, Frederick C, Chief Petty Officer, P/J 14245, Dundee, 22 June 1933
SLACK, John, Private, RMLI, 10043 (Ch), Chatham Division, RMLI, 17 January 1919
SLADE, Clifford S, Boy 1c, J 96081, Resolution, 28 January 1921
SLADE, Harry, Able Seaman, 167464 (Dev), Valiant, 19 February 1920
SLADE, John H, Stoker 1c, K 6773 (Po), Penarth, 4 February 1919
SLASOR, Edward, Stoker 1c, P/K 66205, Folkestone, 7 July 1931
SLATER, Guy B S, Lieutenant, Ganges, 7 December 1938
SLATER, Matthew W, Engineman, RNR, TS 2157, Coningsby, 13 November 1918
SLATER, Reginald G, Boy 1c, J 93226, Malaya, 7 October 1919
SLATTER, John I, Able Seaman, SS 4314, Tintagel, 26 January 1919
SLATTERY, Ernest J, Stoker 1c, C/K 9976, Pembroke, 24 June 1932
SLAUGHTER, Harry G, Stoker 1c, SS 124145, Endeavour, 28 June 1921
SLAYFORD, Ernest, Able Seaman, C/J 90496, Medway, 20 April 1935
SLAYMAKER, William T, Signalman, J 12533, Lucia, 26 March 1920
SLEATH, James W, Ordinary Seaman, SS 8121 (Ch), Dragon, 17 October 1919

SLEE, Frederick, Stoker Petty Officer, K 157, Vesper, 2 December 1918

SLOAN, Hugh, Leading Stoker, K 24060, Greenwich, 2 November 1929

SMALE, Andrew C, Engine Room Artificer 2c, M 3152, Vivid, 16 November 1920

SMALE, Reginald F, Leading Seaman, J 43418, Caradoc, 19 March 1927

SMALE, Richard G A, Boatswain, King George V, 10 November 1921

SMALE, Sydney C, Ordnance Artificer 4c, D/M 37937, Vivid, 25 August 1932

SMALES, Joseph F, Yeoman of Signals, D/J 22885, M.2, 29 January 1932

SMALL, Ernest E, Petty Officer, 238010, Victory, 10 January 1926

SMALL, John E, Gunner, RMA, RMA 14079, Renown, 24 September 1921

SMALLBONE, Alfred, Stoker 1c, K 39531 (Po), Nugent, 27 November 1918

SMART, Frederick T, Chief Petty Officer, 234844, Dolphin, 13 June 1929

SMART, Henry J, Stoker 1c, K 18164, H.42, 23 March 1922

SMART, Percy, Private, RMLI, S 1946 (Po), 3rd Battalion, RM, 16 December 1918

SMART, Thomas W L, Able Seaman, JX 127578, Shakespeare, 7 July 1929

SMEE, Frederick J, Stoker 1c, D/KX 85130, Rodney, 19 November 1935

SMITH, Albert, Able Seaman, RNVR, Mersey Z 1325, Plasma, steamship, 22 November 1918

SMITH, Albert, Stoker 1c, K 67118, Alresford, 1 June 1927

SMITH, Albert, Stoker Petty Officer, K 331, Vivid, 17 March 1923

SMITH, Albert G, Able Seaman, RNVR, R 5695, 1st RM Battalion, RND, attached Nelson Battalion, 22 November 1918

SMITH, Albert H, Able Seaman, J 22170, Dwarf, 2 December 1924

SMITH, Alec, Musician, RMB, RMB 1910, Royal Oak, 4 September 1920

SMITH, Alfred H, Leading Seaman, D/J 80062, Thetis, 3 June 1939

SMITH, Alfred V, Writer, P/MX 47197, Excellent, 29 October 1933

SMITH, Algie A, Stoker Petty Officer, 308836, Cleopatra, 26 August 1920

SMITH, Allan, Signalman, J 86413, L.24, 10 January 1924

SMITH, Arnold, Private, RMLI, S 40 (Ply), 2nd RM Battalion, RND, 11 January 1919

SMITH, Arthur, Skipper, RNR, John Cope, 27 January 1919

SMITH, Arthur A, Deck Hand, RNR, DA 5058, Ganges, 13 November 1918

SMITH, Arthur H, Boy 2c, J 100100, Ganges, 9 August 1921

SMITH, Benjamin, Able Seaman, J 109501, Garland, 29 July 1939

SMITH, Bertie E, Officer's Steward 1c, 363090, Iron Duke, 24 February 1926

SMITH, Charles, Mechanician, 303360, Victory, 20 July 1922

SMITH, Charles, Stoker 1c, SS 124290, Wryneck, 16 April 1921

SMITH, Charles, Stoker Petty Officer, 309543, Vivid II, 13 March 1920

SMITH, Charles E, Lieutenant, Crescent, 28 July 1920

SMITH, Charles H H, Able Seaman, D/J 110664, Snapdragon, 25 September 1932

SMITH, Charles H, Marine, X 3652 (Po), RM Portsmouth Division, 3 February 1939

SMITH, Charles H, Officer's Steward 2c, L 3554, Valerian, 22 October 1926

SMITH, Charles W, Coastguardsman 3c, 279999, Victory, 8 March 1922

SMITH, Cornelius, Civilian Contractor, Thetis, 3 June 1939

SMITH, D (initial only) J, Gunner, RMA, RMA S 2588, RMA Eastney, 31 July 1919

SMITH, David, Fireman, MMR, North Star, steamship, 14 February 1919

SMITH, David, Petty Officer, J 10781, Heliotrope, 8 August 1919

SMITH, David J, Leading Stoker, 297225, Carlisle, 24 September 1919

SMITH, Dennis L, Leading Signalman, C/JX 137083, Pembroke, 30 June 1938

SMITH, Donald, Leading Seaman, RNR, A 4173, Iolaire, 1 January 1919

SMITH, Donald, Seaman, RNR, A 2971, Iolaire, 1 January 1919

SMITH, Douglas D, Ordinary Seaman, C/JX 141775, Hood, 6 March 1937

SMITH, Duncan S, Sick Berth Attendant, D/M 36565, RN Hospital, Plymouth, 24 March 1933

SMITH, Edgar H, Leading Seaman, Newfoundland RNR, X 1204, Trebiskin, steamship, 12 November 1918

SMITH, Edgar J, Leading Seaman, P/J 109628, Victory, 12 March 1935

SMITH, Ernest S, Stoker 1c, K 25583, Pembroke, 19 March 1919

SMITH, Frederick C, Petty Officer, 227488, Mantua, 18 February 1919

SMITH, Frederick G, Able Seaman, D/J 79452, Dorsetshire, 22 December 1936

SMITH, Frederick J, Stoker Petty Officer, 299134 (Po), K.5, 20 January 1921

SMITH, Frederick W G, Engineer Captain, Engineer In Chief Department, 11 October 1935

SMITH, Frederick W, Petty Officer Telegraphist, J 9944, M.1, 12 November 1925

SMITH, Frederick W, Stoker 1c, P/KX 64748, Ladybird, 8 August 1938

SMITH, George, Quartermaster, MMR, 588305, Handy, 8 January 1920

SMITH, George B, Trimmer, RNR, TS 5477, Ganges II, 30 November 1918

SMITH, George H, Able Seaman, J 100920, Victory, 1 October 1926

SMITH, George J, Cook, M 36574, Pembroke, 26 January 1929

SMITH, Harold F, Armourer's Crew, D/M 10801, Drake, 2 April 1936

SMITH, Harry, Yeoman of Signals, 226225, Danae, 24 November 1919

SMITH, Harry B, Private, RME, RME 5261, RM Engineers, Bedenham, 21 January 1919

SMITH, Henry R J, Ordinary Seaman, P/JX 145036, Protector, 9 May 1939

SMITH, Herbert W, Stoker 1c, K 63117, Triad, 17 July 1927

SMITH, Horace L, Stoker 1c, K 57944, Conquest, 28 September 1922

SMITH, Hugh C, Engine Room Artificer 2c, M 7333, Pembroke, 4 June 1924

SMITH, James, Able Seaman, J 86785, Endeavour, 4 September 1929

SMITH, James E, Engine Room Artificer 3c, M 14558, Delhi, 27 October 1923

SMITH, James H, Able Seaman, RNVR, Tyneside 6131, Drake Battalion, RND, 24 March 1919

SMITH, James R, Deck Hand, RNR, DA 6730, Maggies, 19 November 1918

SMITH, James W, Marine, 19397 (Ply), Royal Marines HQ, 24 November 1926

SMITH, John, Leading Bombardier, RMA, RMA 9643, RMA Eastney, 15 February 1919

SMITH, John, Mechanician, K 757, Dolphin, 5 May 1925

SMITH, John, Seaman, RNR, A 8055, Iolaire (Pembroke, O/P), 1 January 1919

SMITH, John, Seaman, RNR, B 3516, Iolaire (Duchess of Devonshire, O/P), 1 January 1919

SMITH, John A, Commissioned Shipwright, Greenwich, 13 February 1930
SMITH, John A, Petty Officer Cook, M 18, Pembroke, 23 November 1919
SMITH, John C, Able Seaman, J 107989, Pembroke, 16 March 1929
SMITH, John E S, Midshipman, Royal Oak, 26 July 1919
SMITH, John P de B, Lieutenant Commander, Warspite, 6 October 1929
SMITH, Joseph, Greaser, MMR, 410591, Rollicker, 5 June 1919
SMITH, Kenneth, Seaman, RNR, C 1620, Iolaire (Cove, O/P), 1 January 1919
SMITH, Kenneth, Seaman, RNR, D 1958, Iolaire (Pembroke, O/P), 1 January 1919
SMITH, Lancelot W H, Able Seaman, J 14515, Glowworm, 25 August 1919
SMITH, Lester H, Able Seaman, RNVR, AA 2752, Naval Anti Aircraft Corps, London, 27 November 1918
SMITH, Louis A, Supply Petty Officer, D/M 37351, Danae, 24 February 1932
SMITH, Oliver, Leading Boatman, 290949, Pembroke, 3 March 1919
SMITH, Patrick C, Lieutenant, Tarantula, 22 November 1923
SMITH, Percy E, Able Seaman, J 18802, Renown, 24 January 1919
SMITH, Peter G, Lieutenant, Royal Navy, 21 May 1926
SMITH, Reginald, Able Seaman, C/J 99442, M.2, 29 January 1932
SMITH, Reginald, Able Seaman, J 105873, Revenge, 23 December 1922
SMITH, Rodney B F, Lieutenant, RM, RM Plymouth Barracks, 1 June 1937
SMITH, Ronald J, Ordinary Seaman, JX 131188, Cumberland, 5 May 1930
SMITH, Samuel E, Bandmaster 2c, RMB 1311, Conqueror, 21 November 1918
SMITH, Sidney G, Able Seaman, J 23246, Veteran, 16 February 1920
SMITH, Sidney I, Stoker 1c, K 62449, Waterhen, 11 April 1928
SMITH, Sidney N, Telegraphist, D/J 106613, L.27, 12 August 1932
SMITH, Sydney J, Sick Berth Attendant, C/M 38532, RN Hospital, Chatham, 10 November 1928
SMITH, Thomas, Able Seaman, SS 7705, Actaeon, 6 November 1919
SMITH, Thomas B, Stoker Petty Officer, K 22271, Pembroke, 10 March 1919
SMITH, Thomas E, Able Seaman, JX 125791, Sepoy, 8 April 1930
SMITH, Walter D, Painter, D/MX 50250, Rodney, 16 March 1937
SMITH, Waugh, Leading Signalman, 223412, Larkspur, 25 December 1919
SMITH, William, Able Seaman, RNVR, Tyneside 5/216, Macoris, steamship, 23 February 1919
SMITH, William, Chief Motor Mechanic, RNVR, MB 1383, ML.62, motor launch, 12 February 1919
SMITH, William, Private, RMLI, 19614 (Po), St Vincent, 12 December 1918
SMITH, William, Stoker 1c, SS 125760, Blue Sky, tender to Queen Elizabeth, 12 June 1922
SMITH, William B, Stoker 1c, K 19915 (Po), K.5, 20 January 1921
SMITH, William C A, Chief Petty Officer, J 8688, Excellent, 4 December 1929
SMITH, William C, Able Seaman, J 34717, Vivid, 12 January 1930
SMITH, William C, Able Seaman, J 6219 (Ch), K.5, 20 January 1921
SMITH, William F, Leading Seaman, 211985, Pembroke, 3 December 1918
SMITH, William G, Able Seaman, J 18754 (Ch), CMB.79A, coastal motor boat, 18 August 1919
SMITH, William G, Officer's Steward 2c, L 12593, Valerian, 22 October 1926
SMITH, William H, Civilian Contractor, Thetis, 3 June 1939
SMITH, William J, Stoker 1c, SS 121644, Iron Duke, 24 October 1921
SMITH, William S, Leading Stoker, 238460, Valerian, 22 October 1926
SMITH, William T, Ordnance Artificer, P M 35984, Nelson, 28 January 1934
SMITHERS, Adrian H, Able Seaman, SSX 12728, Fisgard, 28 November 1929
SMITHERS, Cecil E, Act/Petty Officer, C/JX 129326, Thetis, 3 June 1939
SMITHERS, William A, Leading Seaman, J 31011, Victory, 31 March 1929
SMOOTHY, Harold T, Ordinary Seaman, J 73560, Pembroke, 3 March 1919
SMYTH, Arthur W, Marine, A 21265 (Ch), RM Chatham Division, 4 April 1939
SMYTH, Sidney R, Shipwright 2c, 347216, Argus, 3 December 1923

SNAGG, Bertram C K, Captain, RM, RM Headquarters, 27 February 1919
SNAITH, Frederick, Stoker 1c, K 23857 (Ch), Pembroke, 13 May 1919
SNAPE, Edward, Private, RMLI, S 2258 (Ch), Chatham Division, RMLI, 16 November 1918
SNEDDON, John, Able Seaman, J 43079, Witherington, 30 January 1927
SNELL, Horace S, Colour Sergeant Major, 7121 (Po), Portsmouth Division, RMLI, 22 October 1919
SNELL, Horace S, Warrant Officer 2c, RM Headquarters, 22 October 1919
SNELL, Stanley W, Stoker 1c, 311447, Vivid, 3 June 1926
SNELL, Walter E, Sergeant, RM, 21394 (Ply), Devonshire, 26 July 1929
SNELL, William E, Shipwright 1c, 104092, Impregnable, 9 March 1919
SNELLGROVE, Ernest, Able Seaman, J 43244, Glowworm, 25 August 1919
SNELLING, Edward L, Stoker 1c, K 16304, Pembroke, 14 March 1919
SNEWIN, Phillip W, Chief Officer, HM Coast Guard, 132104, HM Coastguard Station Ballygrovane, 25 July 1920
SNOOK, Alfred J, Ordinary Seaman, J 55388, Constance, 5 July 1919
SNOW, John N, Lieutenant, RM, FAA, 801 Sqn, Furious, 12 October 1938
SNOW, Joseph B, Telegraphist, J 78013, Tern, 5 May 1929
SNOWDEN, George I, Deck Hand, RNR, DA 12757, Sarpedon, 12 November 1918
SNOWDEON, Leonard, Able Seaman, C/JX 125048, Valiant, 4 December 1931
SNOWLING, Bert, Corporal, RMLI, Royal Marines HQ, 1 April 1923

SOANES, Frederick G, Able Seaman, J 97395, Tiger, 23 October 1927
SOANES, William F, Stoker 1c, SS 123994, Cardiff, 24 November 1919
SOLKHON, William G, Engine Room Artificer 1c, 268462, Pembroke, 3 January 1919
SOLLARS, Claude E, Ordinary Seaman, D/SSX 15764, RN Hospital, Malta, 29 August 1935
SOLLITT, Daniel K, Signalman, P/JX 128638, Salmon, 23 January 1938
SOLOMON, Walter H, Chief Petty Officer, 200412, Vivid, 14 February 1922
SOLWAY, William E, Chief Petty Officer, 234593, Vivid, 28 September 1929

SOMERSET, John B, Sub Lieutenant, Short Course, 26 September 1921
SOMNER, Arthur C, Armourer Quartermaster Sergeant, RM, S 351 (Deal), RM Deal, 11 August 1920
SONE, John D, Commissioned Engineer, Royal Naval Reserve, 10 October 1921
SOPER, Sydney A, Stoker 1c, K 22972, Tiger, 13 June 1920
SOPP, Wilfred H, Marine, X 1136 (Po), Penelope, 19 March 1939
SORE, Charles E, Stoker Petty Officer, K 13050, Victory, 23 March 1920
SOUTER, John, Leading Deck Hand, RNR, DA 6963, Grecian Prince, 15 December 1918
SOUTHALL, Lawrence E, Able Seaman, J 34682, Revenge, 12 October 1922
SOUTHWELL, Henry K M, Lieutenant, L.55, 4 June 1919
SOUTHWICK, John H, Engineman, RNR, ES 3236, Implacable, 29 April 1919
SOWDEN, William J, Leading Stoker, K 20564, Raleigh, 8 August 1922

SPALDING, Leonard C, Boy 1c, J 101839, Barham, 13 September 1922
SPARGO, William H, Chief Engine Room Artificer 1c, M 1057, Petersfield, 12 March 1927
SPARKS, John B, Captain, Royal Navy, 29 March 1920
SPARKS, William T, Warrant Engineer, L.20, 8 June 1934
SPARLING, John, Petty Officer, 138852, HM Coastguard Station Ballycotten, 12 February 1919
SPARROW, Edwin W, Telegraphist, J 94124, Kiawo, 25 November 1927
SPARROW, George E, 2nd Hand, RNR, DA 17406, Victory, 21 November 1918
SPARROW, George R S, Chief Sick Berth Steward, 137897, Victory, 27 December 1918
SPEARING, John, Able Seaman, P J 6262, Egmont, 27 August 1932
SPEARS, Thomas, Leading Stoker, P/KX 7893, Iron Duke, 15 August 1938
SPEDDING, Edgar C, Leading Signalman, D/J 110206, Rodney, 15 November 1936
SPEED, Harry, Gunner, RMA, RMA 10004, RMA Eastney, 9 February 1919
SPELMAN, John B, Private, RMLI, 15805 (Po), King George V, 26 November 1918
SPENCE, Archibald W, Stoker 1c, SS 122692, Merlin, 17 December 1921
SPENCER, Cecil E R, The Hon, Lieutenant Commander, Renown, 14 February 1928
SPENCER, Gerald, Able Seaman, J 69706, Wivern, 14 March 1923
SPENCER, Leonard D, Able Seaman, C/J 113345, Sussex, 1 January 1935
SPENCER, Nathaniel, Leading Seaman, J 20156, H.47, 9 July 1929
SPENCER, Samuel E H, Lieutenant, M.3, 20 July 1930
SPENCER, Thomas H, Officer's Steward 3c, L 9309, Peyton, 27 August 1919
SPENCER, William, Stoker Petty Officer, 290271, Victory, 8 March 1919
SPENDER, Joseph G, Greaser, MMR, 601925, Richard Welford, 20 February 1919
SPENDER, Stanley G, Stoker 1c, K 57853, Victory, 28 February 1927
SPENDLOVE, Charles E, Engine Room Artificer 3c, M 2809, Vivid, 4 March 1920
SPERRING, Charles H, Lieutenant (E), Active, 13 November 1937
SPICER, Frank A, Boy 2c, JX 28249, Ganges, 22 November 1926
SPICER, Hector C, Stoker Petty Officer, D/K 58974, Apollo, 2 November 1937
SPICER-SIMSON, Geoffrey E F, Lieutenant, Anthony, 11 May 1930
SPILLER, George C, Leading Signalman, J 5727, Pembroke, 7 March 1919
SPILSTED, William T, Engine Room Artificer, C/M 39546, Campbell, 26 January 1937
SPINDLEY, Alfred E, Engineman, MMR, Eaglet, 15 March 1919
SPINKS, Ernest, Engineman, RNR, TS 240, William Carr, 4 December 1918
SPINKS, Thomas, Stoker Petty Officer, K 772, Wren, 15 November 1924
SPINNER, James D, Engine Room Artificer Apprentice, MX 14605, Pembroke, 20 January 1930
SPITERI, Angelo, Carpenters Mate, 343832, Blenheim, 2 October 1920
SPITERI, Paolo, Officer's Cook 3c, 359710, Pembroke, 5 April 1921
SPOONER, William H, Leading Signalman, D/J 25439, Olympus, 18 March 1932
SPRATLEY, Percival, Telegraphist, J 69385, M.1, 12 November 1925
SPRAY, William, Stoker 1c, 235034, Mersey, 3 January 1919
SPRIDDELL, Nicholas J, Shipwright 1c, 347387, Vivid, 28 October 1927
SPRINGETT, George W, Leading Cook, M 5990, Hawkins, 25 October 1922
SPRINGETT, James E, Able Seaman, J 4305, Pembroke, 1 March 1928
SPRINGETT, Percy, Assistant Steward, MMR, Rosabelle, 25 February 1919
SPURDEN, Charles, Leading Stoker, K 15501, Repulse, 22 January 1922
SPURGEON, Clement E, Stoker 1c, SS 112997, Kilfullert, 17 November 1918
SPURR, David, Able Seaman, SS 4971, Charon, 13 November 1918

SQUIRE, William, Chief Stoker, K 10540, Valerian, 22 October 1926

ST JOHN, Ralph G J, Act/Sub Lieutenant, Queen Elizabeth, 31 May 1937
STACEY, George, Stoker Petty Officer, K 3037, Warspite, 10 June 1923
STAFFORD, George, Petty Officer, C/JX 127679, Vernon, 17 July 1937
STAFFORD, Herbert C C, Boy 2c, J 93277, Ganges, 4 December 1918
STAFFORD, John J, Stoker 1c, K 21726, Gnat, 18 April 1925
STAGG, Sidney H, Boy 2c, J 94424, Powerful, 27 February 1919
STAINES, John P, Stoker 1c, K 15531 (Ch), L.55, 4 June 1919
STAMPF, Charles W, Plumber, M 805, Diligence, 12 June 1923
STANDING, Thomas W, Able Seaman, RNVR, Palace Z 1772, Wildfire, 27 February 1919
STANFORD, Ernest E, Commissioned Gunner, Renown, 8 January 1929
STANFORD, Ernest J, Boy 2c, J 93420, Impregnable, 2 March 1919
STANIFORD, George F, Able Seaman, D/J 109508, Impregnable, 20 April 1937
STANLEY, Frank A, Ordinary Seaman, RNVR, Sussex 6/47, Vortigern, 18 March 1925
STANLEY, George T, Signalman, J 9099, Geranium, 30 June 1919
STANLEY, Harry E, Able Seaman, J 102399, Pembroke, 13 March 1929
STANLEY, James, Able Seaman, P/SSX 12188, Courageous, 17 February 1932
STANLEY, Watson N, Signalman, J 87460, Wolsey, 4 February 1927

STANLEY, William J J, Deck Hand, MMR, Iolaire, 1 January 1919
STANNARD, Richard G, Stoker Petty Officer, K 29220, Ceres, 5 June 1929
STANSBURY, William T, Chief Engine Room Artificer, D/M 7954, Drake, 22 September 1937
STANSFIELD, Frederick, Trimmer Cook, RNR, TC 1123, Eaglet, 18 December 1918
STANSFIELD, George S E, Able Seaman, J 93754, Vivid I, 21 April 1921
STANTON, Richard H, Able Seaman, RNVR, London Z 6022, President III, 30 November 1918
STAPLES, Henry B G, Stoker 1c, K 13048 (Po), Penarth, 4 February 1919
STAPLETON, Joseph B, Leading Seaman, J 7681, L.24, 10 January 1924
STARES, James T, Private, RMLI, S 3122 (Po), Portsmouth Division, RMLI, 10 January 1919
STARES, John T, Private, RMLI, 16058 (Po), Royal Sovereign, 26 September 1920
STARK, Albert E, Stoker 1c, K 37438, Lion, 9 June 1919
STARK, Maurice E, Sick Berth Attendant, M 38686, Victory, 15 May 1925
STARKEY, Arthur E J, Able Seaman, 231624, Barham, 24 February 1926
STARKEY, Frank A, Able Seaman, J 87050, Vivid, 25 January 1924
STARKEY, Sydney W, Corporal, RM, X 537 (Ch), RM Chatham Division, 30 April 1938
STARKIE, Henry, Private, RM, S 11625 (Deal), RM Labour Corps, 28 December 1918
STARKS, Alfred, Stoker Petty Officer, K 11445, Sturdy, 27 February 1920
STARLING, Percy V, Gunner, RMA, RMA 13560, RM Headquarters, 8 November 1920
STATTERS, Harold, Signalman, RNVR, Tyneside Z 8699, Duchess of Kent, 7 December 1918
STAYTE, Joseph J, Able Seaman, D/J 114260, Impregnable, 21 March 1937
STEAD, Christopher D, Stoker 1c, KX 83701, Resource, 7 July 1938
STEADMAN, Gilbert, Officer's Cook 2c, MC 1654, Pekin (ex-Cotswold), 1 October 1919
STEADMAN, Joseph G, Marine, 17067 (Ch), Royal Marines HQ, 1 December 1924
STEADMAN, Lester, Ty/Lieutenant, RNVR, Royal Naval Volunteer Reserve, 30 January 1920
STEBBING, William F, Stoker 1c, K 61886, Vulcan, 4 February 1928
STEDALL, Eric A, Sub Lieutenant, L.24, 10 January 1924
STEEDMAN, Robert, Ty/Skipper, RNR, Ethelwulf, 1 December 1918
STEEGMAN, Edward J, Surgeon Commander, RNVR, Royal Naval Volunteer Reserve, 8 June 1923
STEEL, John, Leading Fireman, MMR, 838261, Retort, 11 December 1919
STEEL, Richard W, Warrant Engineer, Spey, 18 July 1932
STEELE, Frank C, Warrant Shipwright, Cleopatra, 3 November 1920
STEELE, Reginald J, Chief Stoker, P/K 64220, Victory, 3 February 1936
STEELE, William R, Lieutenant, Vancouver, 6 October 1921
STEEN, Joseph E, Able Seaman, J 100794, Vivid I, 1 August 1929
STEER, Eli, Able Seaman, J 38492, King George V, 5 June 1921
STEER, William, Leading Cook's Mate, M 1850, Vivid, 25 February 1919
STEER, William J, Leading Seaman, 215835, Vivid, 14 May 1921
STENNING, Frederick G, Musician, RMB, RMB 2185, Royal Sovereign, 5 December 1920
STEPHEN, Alexander, Deck Hand, RNR, DA 7386, John Robert, 1 February 1919
STEPHEN, William C, Engine Room Artificer, RNR, EA 1810, Cupar, 17 May 1919
STEPHENS, Alec J F, Able Seaman, J 111312, Vidette, 14 May 1929
STEPHENS, Alfred G, Sailmaker, D/J 21722, Resolution, 2 September 1933
STEPHENS, Archibald A, Shipwright 4c, M 35260, Carlisle, 5 March 1927
STEPHENS, Francis E, Chief Motor Mechanic, RNVR, MB 3005 (Po), CMB.79A, coastal motor boat, 18 August 1919
STEPHENS, Frank H, Surgeon Commander, Victory, 26 March 1924
STEPHENS, Reginald A, Lieutenant Commander, Ormonde, 14 April 1931
STEPHENS, Richard, Stoker Petty Officer, 174246, Vivid, 9 April 1920
STEPHENS, Richard, Sub Lieutenant, RNR, Terrible, 7 February 1919
STEPHENS, Wilfred, Sick Berth Petty Officer, D/M 39527, RN Hospital, Capetown, 4 May 1938
STEPHENS, William, Petty Officer, 120024, Vernon, 26 January 1919
STEPHENSON, Gerald, Chief Skipper, RNR, Syringa, 18 July 1936
STEPHENSON, Joseph H, Stoker 1c, K 59895, Dragon, 21 January 1926
STEPHENSON, Robert W, Leading Stoker, K 1561, Assistance, 3 March 1920
STEVENS, Albert E, Leading Stoker, 201785 (Po), Bristol, 30 April 1919
STEVENS, Albert W, Stoker 1c, K 62923, Repulse, 3 March 1925
STEVENS, Alfred S, Ordinary Seaman, J 64364 (Dev), Tiger, 9 March 1920
STEVENS, Alfred W, Boy 2c, J 94136, Impregnable, 19 April 1919
STEVENS, Edmund, Chief Stoker, 299118, Hecla, 25 March 1919
STEVENS, Ernest, Stoker 1c, K 19466, Vivid, 17 February 1930
STEVENS, Frank R, Signalman, J 88422, Blue Sky, tender to Queen Elizabeth, 12 June 1922
STEVENS, George H, Leading Stoker, K 19708, ML.291 (Rhine Patrol Flotilla), 4 July 1922
STEVENS, Harry G, Ordinary Seaman, J 99539, Royal Sovereign, 26 April 1924
STEVENS, John M D, Leading Telegraphist, P/J 32661, Dauntless, 2 February 1935
STEVENS, Richard, Private, RM, S 8440 (Deal), RM Labour Corps, 4 February 1919
STEVENS, Robert J, Leading Stoker, C/K 26078, Hussar, 22 January 1937
STEVENS, Roland, Supply Assistant, M 37956, Pembroke, 20 September 1926
STEVENS, Stanley W G, Leading Seaman, P/JX 135921, Thetis, 3 June 1939
STEVENS, Stanley, Leading Supply Assistant, M 35208, Calliope, 23 February 1926
STEVENS, Thomas H, Chief Petty Officer, 212326, Excellent, 18 July 1921
STEVENS, Walter, Stoker Petty Officer, K 7821, Lupin, 7 January 1928
STEVENSON, Harry B P, Marine, 18767 (Ch), Ganges, 29 November 1931
STEVENSON, James, Leading Signalman, RNVR, Clyde Z 3173, HM Coast Guard Station Staithes, 19 February 1919
STEWARD, William F V, Corporal, RM, 213977 (Po), Iron Duke, 3 August 1924
STEWART, Charles J, Stoker 1c, P/KX 77023, Victory, 26 July 1937
STEWART, Charles, Deck Hand, RNR, DA 18072, Pride of Buckie, 27 November 1918

STEWART, Donald, Deck Hand, RNR, DA 21701, Victory, 29 January 1919
STEWART, George W, Stoker 1c, K 56820, L.24, 10 January 1924
STEWART, John, Ty/Skipper, RNR, John Robert, 1 February 1919
STEWART, William, Leading Seaman, 233149, St George, 7 December 1918
STEWART, William J, Engineman, RNR, TS 1376, Egmont, 31 March 1919
STICKELLS, Harry J, Able Seaman, C/J 90095, Medway, 1 July 1938
STICKLY, Frederick, Petty Officer, 233420, C.30, 28 November 1918
STILL, Jasper, Stoker 1c, K 39625, Europa, 24 November 1918
STILLMAN, Alfred H, Able Seaman, P/JX 128809, M.2, 22 December 1931
STIRLING, Norman R, Petty Officer, C/J 22976, Veteran, 27 December 1932
STIRLING, William, Gunner, RMA, RMA 15137, Barham, 14 November 1918
STOBBS, John Y, Able Seaman, RNVR, Tyneside Z 2619, Howe Battalion, RND, 6 December 1918
STOCK, Francis H, Leading Steward, C/LX 21640, Thetis, 3 June 1939
STOCKMAN, Frederick, Able Seaman, 203678, Seawolf, 9 October 1923
STOCKS, Frederick A, Act/Cook, MX 46255, Victory, 24 July 1927
STOKES, John, Seaman, RNR, C 2602, Penarth, 4 February 1919
STOKOE, Frederick, Engine Room Artificer 3c, M 15821, Victory, 20 April 1920
STONE, Alec C, Able Seaman, P/J 96241, Winchester, 27 February 1936
STONE, Arthur C, Able Seaman, J 80084, H.47, 9 July 1929
STONE, Ernest A, Able Seaman, J 36196, Pembroke, 6 November 1922
STONE, Henry T, Stoker 1c, K 17232 (Dev), Kinross, 16 June 1919
STONE, Horace G, Ty/Lieutenant, RNVR, Hermione, 15 December 1918
STONE, John E, Stoker 1c, K 18080, Blake, 15 November 1918
STONE, Michael, Ordinary Seaman, MMR, 968726, Eaglet, 14 July 1919
STONE, Percy C, Marine, 23281 (Ch), Frobisher, 25 September 1936
STONE, Sydney H, Victualling Chief Petty Officer, M 3052, Kellett, 26 March 1921
STONE, Walter, Able Seaman, 183434, Lion, 24 January 1922
STONE, William H T, Able Seaman, SS 8782, Vortigern, 9 November 1921
STONEHOUSE, Cyril, Radio Officer, RFA, Bacchus, RFA, 14 April 1925
STONEHOUSE, William, Stoker 1c, K 56308, Centurion, 26 August 1930
STONEMAN, Christopher J, Leading Stoker, K 11962, K.2, 20 May 1924
STONER, Archibald M, Petty Officer, J 14922, Excellent, 9 July 1922
STONHAM, John G, Petty Officer, RNVR, Sussex 4/78, Victory II, 2 August 1919
STOPFORD, Frederick L, Private, RMLI, 19449 (Po), 6th Battalion, RM, 27 August 1919
STOREY, Charles C, Stoker 1c, K 58415, M.1, 12 November 1925
STOREY, Edward C, Ordinary Seaman, SSX 13238, Pembroke, 11 February 1929
STORIE, James, Stoker 2c, P/KX 84722, Victory, 19 July 1935
STORIER, Arthur, Able Seaman, 239943, Victory I, 17 August 1927
STOTT, Fred, Ty/Engineer Sub Lieutenant, RNR, Styx, 10 December 1918
STOUT, Ernest C, Leading Stoker, C/K 11512, Valiant, 22 January 1933
STOWELL, Ernest F, Leading Stoker, P/K 62320, Courageous, 17 March 1931
STOY, Albert F, Paymaster Commander, RNR, Royal Naval Reserve, 25 June 1929
STRANGE, Philip A, Boy 2c, JX 157782, Ganges, 26 May 1938
STRATFORD, Henry B, Private, RMLI, 13180 (Ply), Plymouth Division, RMLI, 31 March 1919
STRATH, Harold E, Chief Electrical Artificer, D/M 10050, Eagle, 28 April 1933
STREAMER, George W, Able Seaman, P/J 114782, Excellent, 11 December 1930
STREET, Edward W L, Paymaster Captain, Pembroke, 4 June 1919
STREET, Reginald C, Able Seaman, J 17962, Iron Duke, 5 September 1925
STREET, Stanley, Officer's Cook 2c, D/L 13200, Drake, 19 March 1936
STRETTON, Albert E, Signalman, C/J 110814, Marshal Soult, 2 August 1931
STRETTON, Thomas J, Able Seaman, P/J 34209, Vernon, 6 February 1933
STREVENS, Charles E, Boatswain, Superb, 8 December 1918
STRICK, James K, Honorary Major, RM, Unattached List, 13 January 1919
STRICKLAND, John, Private, RM, S 4101 (Deal), 150th (RN) Field Ambulance, RM Medical Unit, RND, 5 January 1919
STRINGER, Frederick T, Lieutenant, Redpole, 26 March 1919
STRINGLER, Albert, Chief Motor Mechanic, RNVR, MB 1316, Iolaire, 28 November 1918
STRODE, John H, Supply Chief Petty Officer, D/M 985, Vivid, 30 June 1932
STROUD, John S, Petty Officer, 204391 (Ch), Dragon, 17 October 1919
STRUGNELL, Harold F H, Major, Portsmouth Division, RMLI, RMLI, 21 March 1919
STRUTTON, William F, Private, RM, S 1795 (Deal), RND, 63rd Divisional Train, 20 November 1918
STUART, Alfred, Chief Stoker, P/K 11554, Cormorant, 8 October 1932
STUART, Colin S, Instructor Lieutenant, Hawkins, 4 October 1921
STUART, Robert, Marine, 23587 (Ch), Royal Marines HQ, 27 May 1924
STUART, Robert J, Warrant Writer, Impregnable, 4 July 1928
STUBBINGS, Frederick E, Able Seaman, C/J 113783, Pegasus, 31 May 1936
STUBBINS, Herbert H, Ordinary Seaman, J 112647, Columbine, 30 April 1926
STUDDY, Francis R B, Lieutenant, Vulcan, 24 February 1921
STUNDEN, George, Able Seaman, P/JX 126669, Effingham, 27 April 1933
STUNNELL, Henry E, Able Seaman, J 95644, Thames, 30 November 1932
STURDEE, Sir Frederick C D, Admiral of the Fleet, Royal Navy, 7 May 1925
STURROCK, Peter A C, Lieutenant, Penarth, 4 February 1919
STUTCHBURY, Frederick N, Telegraphist, J 70431, Victory, 21 September 1923
STUTTER, Alex F, Stoker 1c, K 27428, Lowestoft, 5 November 1919
STYLES, Reginald P, Able Seaman, J 28159, M.1, 12 November 1925

SUDELL, John W, Able Seaman, J 61819, Rob Roy, 27 November 1918
SULIMAN, Ali, Seedie, Lupin, 4 April 1925
SULLEY, Richard, Able Seaman, J 43778 (Ch), Frostaxe, 29 April 1919

SULLIVAN, Albert, Coastguardsman 2c, 142339, HM Coast Guard Station Pentewan, 25 December 1919
SULLIVAN, David F, Boy 2c, JX 126379, Impregnable, 6 December 1926
SULLIVAN, Harold L, Leading Seaman, MC 1846, Victory, 10 March 1920
SULLIVAN, John, Leading Stoker, 306251, Clematis, 12 August 1925
SULLIVAN, John A, Signalman, D/J 30235, Tamar, 26 December 1933
SULTANA, Joseph, Officer's Steward 3c, LX 20270, Stuart, 27 November 1928
SUMMERFORD, Ronald B, Sub Lieutenant, Valerian, 22 October 1926
SUMMERS, George A, Civilian Contractor, Thetis, 3 June 1939
SUMMERS, Harry L, Able Seaman, D/SSX 12228, Vivid, 5 January 1931
SUMNER, John A, Engine Room Artificer 3C, M 26727, Capetown, 25 February 1923
SUPPLE, George, Able Seaman, J 26315, Gnat, 15 October 1921
SUTCLIFFE, Charles G, Stoker Petty Officer, K 29511, Witherington, 30 August 1929
SUTHERLAND, Bertram R U, Lieutenant Commander, RNR, Royal Naval Reserve, 16 August 1926
SUTHERLAND, David L, Able Seaman, RNVR, Clyde 1/2611, Anson Battalion, RND, 19 January 1919
SUTHERLAND, James H, Seaman, RNR, B 3207, W S Bailey, 6 February 1919
SUTHERLAND, Thomas, Engineman, RNR, S 2789, Thalia, 28 April 1919
SUTTERS, Henry J, Sick Berth Steward, 351434 (Po), Tamar, 10 August 1920
SUTTON, Charles, Armourers Mate, M 4207, Pembroke, 10 February 1920
SUTTON, Edward T, Supply Chief Petty Officer, P/M 37209, Victory, December 1936
SUTTON, Harold, Able Seaman, J 16325, Lucia, October 1922
SUTTON, Herbert, Ordinary Seaman, SS 9330 (Po), Erin's Isle, 7 February 1919
SUTTON, John, Stoker 1c, SS 112473, P.67, patrol boat, 27 November 1918
SUTTON, John W E, Signalman, J 69324, Mackay, 21 April 1925
SUTTON, Leonard L, Engine Room Artificer 3c, M 8850 (Ch), Frostaxe, 29 April 1919
SUTTON, Sidney L, Leading Stoker, K 5326 (Po), Penarth, 4 February 1919
SUTTON, Wilfrid J, Act/Paymaster Sub Lieutenant, Queen Elizabeth, 9 December 1918
SUTTON, William S, Petty Officer, 213903, Victory, 16 March 1920

SWAIN, Cecil E, Able Seaman, J 99183, Victory, 9 April 1924
SWALLOW, Reginald F, Corporal, RM, 21782 (Ply), Berwick, 2 December 1929
SWANKIE, Robert, Deck Hand, RNR, SD 4601, Fifinella, hired trawler, 5 April 1919
SWANSON, Angus S, Deck Hand, RNR, DA 19161, Pembroke, 11 December 1918
SWANSON, Thomas N, Leading Deck Hand, RNR, DA 9751, Victory, 15 February 1919
SWANSTON, John, Trimmer, RNR, TS 2918, Idaho, 22 April 1919
SWANTON, Francis J Y, Private, RMLI, 16677 (Ply), President III, 2 December 1918
SWANTON, Herbert F, Blacksmith, 346627, Carlisle, 27 August 1923
SWATHERIDGE, Leonard F, Joiner 4c, P/MX 54253, Victory, 5 May 1937
SWATRIDGE, Leslie W, Leading Signalman, J 23733, Carysfort, 10 March 1920
SWAYNE, Henry J, Warrant Writer, Centurion, 13 April 1926
SWAYNE, Philip M, Cadet, Royal Navy, 23 February 1937
SWEENEY, John, Petty Officer, RNVR, Clyde 3 509, Anson Battalion, RND, 2 June 1919
SWEENEY, William H, Officer's Steward 1, 363033, Veronica, 22 September 1926
SWEETLAND, Cecil S, Stoker 1c, D/KX 75588, M.2, 29 January 1932
SWEETLOVE, Lancelot D, Engineer Commander, Bee, 11 August 1926
SWIFT, Albert E, Stoker 1c, D/K 29607, Centurion, 12 November 1936
SWIFT, Lionel W, Engineer Commander, Nairn, 24 August 1919
SWIFT, Stanley, Ordinary Seaman, C/SSX 21825, Malaya, 16 August 1939
SWIGGS, Wilfrid R, Stoker Petty Officer, D/K 56346, Hunter, 13 May 1937
SWINDLE, Robert, Ordinary Seaman, J 76031 (Dev), Shincliffe, 15 May 1919
SWINHOE, Thomas W, Stoker 2c, K 50362, Monarch, 1 January 1919

SYDENHAM, Ernest W, Boy 1c, J 104367, Ganges, 27 July 1922
SYKES, George H, Able Seaman, J 80580, Valerian, 22 October 1926
SYKES, Harold, Armourers Crew, J 55280, Glowworm, 25 August 1919
SYKES, John, Able Seaman, RNVR, Tyneside Z 10849, President III, 12 February 1919
SYKES, William A, Sub Lieutenant (A), FAA, 802 Sqn, Glorious, 19 May 1939
SYLVESTER, Sidney, Chief Artificer Engineer, Victory, 18 March 1920
SYMES, Walter C, Ordinary Seaman, P/JX 136030, Wild Swan, 15 October 1935
SYMES, William C, Leading Seaman, J 8036, Tiger, 23 February 1925
SYMMS, Harry G, Petty Officer, 220122, Victory, 23 February 1919
SYMONS, Albert, Colour Sergeant, RM, 16662 (Ply), Plymouth Division, RM, 10 June 1937
SYMONS, Herbert, Able Seaman, 214508, Vivid, 15 April 1921
SYMONS, Samuel E, Stoker 1c, D/K 59472, Vivid, 28 June 1931
SYMONS, Thomas H, 3rd Writer, M 18229, Warrior, 21 December 1918

T

TAAFE, William H, Chief Petty Officer, 227963, Cricket, 7 October 1922

TABONE, Guiseppe, Officer's Steward 2c, L 5320, Torch, 23 March 1920

TACK, John P, Commissioned Gunner, Royal Navy, 21 October 1924

TADD, Charles W, Stoker 2c, KX 78062, Victory, 7 February 1928

TAIT, Henry, Petty Officer, J 1555, Pembroke, 25 August 1929

TALBOT, Alfred R, Boy 2c, D/JX 141440, St Vincent, 9 June 1934

TALBOT, Ernest T S, Stoker 1c, SS 102740, Mimosa, 1 June 1919

TALBOT, Henry F G, Captain, Osborne, 4 July 1920

TALBOT, William F, Able Seaman, P/J 69605, Titania, 1 March 1933

TALL, John W H, Officer's Steward 2c, L 10807, Rigorous, 11 July 1919

TAMBLIN, Frederick T, Ordinary Seaman, J 53828, Vivid, 23 December 1918

TAMBLIN, William, Leading Seaman, J 94557, M.1, 12 November 1925

TAMBLING, Leonard J, Able Seaman, J 35268, Chatham, 6 May 1921

TANDY, Frederick, Stoker 1c, 294401, Pembroke, 7 December 1918

TANNER, Frank S, Able Seaman, P/J 95659, Lupin, 30 June 1935

TANNER, Thomas, Leading Stoker, K 7540, Sylph, 6 May 1921

TANNER, William H E, Able Seaman, 206524, P.40, 23 May 1922

TANNER, William T, Signalman, J 21454 (Po), K.5, 20 January 1921

TANQUERAY-WILLAUME, Frederick G, Major, RMA, RMA Eastney (ex-Princess Royal), 11 February 1919

TARDREW, Paul W, Lieutenant, RNVR, Royal Naval Volunteer Reserve, 12 October 1929

TARRANT, Edward C, Stoker Petty Officer, 295348 (Po), Foxglove, 29 January 1921

TATE, Thomas, Staff Sergeant, RM, S 3023 (Deal), 63rd Sanitary Section, RM Medical Unit, RND, 15 November 1918

TATHAM, Percival E, Officer's Steward 1c, L 6647, Leonidas, 22 November 1918

TATTON, Archibald, Engineman, RNR, ES 3728, Attentive III, 27 December 1918

TATTON, Tom, Private, RMLI, S 1408 (Po), 1st RM Battalion, RND, 10 March 1919

TAVINOR, Harold L, Stoker 2c, D/KX 85466, Drake, 19 November 1935

TAYLOR, Albert W, Seaman, RNR, A 7279, Research, 19 February 1919

TAYLOR, Alexander, Engineer Sub Lieutenant, RNR, Ophir, 9 February 1919

TAYLOR, Alexander G, Surgeon Commander, RN Hospital, Plymouth, 21 October 1937

TAYLOR, Alfred, Stoker Petty Officer, D/K 18808, Sturdy, 22 August 1931

TAYLOR, Alfred G, Leading Stoker, K 18022, Valiant, 16 March 1920

TAYLOR, Alfred J H, Telegraphist, J 101888, H.47, 9 July 1929

TAYLOR, Alfred S, Assistant Steward, MMR, Iolaire, 1 January 1919

TAYLOR, Anthony, Able Seaman, D/JX 138966, Wolsey, 21 January 1938

TAYLOR, Arthur, Petty Officer, 218813, Venus, 8 March 1919

TAYLOR, Cecil C, Boy Telegraphist, J 86916, Renown, 22 September 1919

TAYLOR, Charles R R, Lieutenant Commander, RNVR, Royal Naval Volunteer Reserve, 30 December 1929

TAYLOR, Charles W, Able Seaman, RNVR, Tyneside Z 8097, President III, 27 November 1918

TAYLOR, Claude C R, Leading Stoker, P/KX 81948, Royal Navy, 12 July 1938

TAYLOR, David, Engine Room Artificer 3c, M 5369, J.5, 29 November 1918

TAYLOR, Edgar H J, Marine, 23649 (Ch), Royal Sovereign, 29 April 1925

TAYLOR, Edwin, Ordinary Seaman, J 50439, Pasley, 21 December 1918

TAYLOR, Frank, Musician, RMB X 257 (Ch), RM Barracks Chatham, 31 July 1937

TAYLOR, George A, Signalman, RNVR, Tyneside Z 12241, Almanzora, 26 November 1918

TAYLOR, George R, Ordinary Seaman, C/JX 132968, Dragon, 10 April 1932

TAYLOR, Harold, Regulating Petty Officer, M 35731, Valerian, 22 October 1926

TAYLOR, Hector R, Ordinary Seaman, J 46659, Dragon, 17 September 1919

TAYLOR, Henry F C, Private, RME, RME S 4885, RM Engineers, 18 December 1918

TAYLOR, Herbert C, Telegraphist, J 101213, Victory, 23 January 1926

TAYLOR, Herbert S, Stoker, RAN, 335, Sydney (RAN), 9 May 1919

TAYLOR, Ivor E, Able Seaman, RNVR, Wales Z 634, Hawke Battalion, RND, 22 December 1918

TAYLOR, James, Private, RM, S 14166 (Deal), RM Labour Corps, 4 December 1918

TAYLOR, James, Able Seaman, RNVR, Clyde Z 5898, Oanfa, steamship, 23 November 1918

TAYLOR, James P, Private, RMLI, 21551 (Ch), Glory, 7 January 1919

TAYLOR, John, Leading Signalman, RNVR, Bristol Z 748, Richard Welford, 25 February 1919

TAYLOR, John W, Act/Petty Officer, RAN, 7738, Warrego (RAN), 14 February 1919

TAYLOR, John W, Boy 2c, J 94284, Impregnable, 13 March 1919

TAYLOR, Lionel R, Marine, 22343 (Ply), Devonshire, 26 July 1929

TAYLOR, Martin H, Leading Seaman, J 11405, Pembroke, 28 February 1919

TAYLOR, Robert, Able Seaman, J 41914, M.1, 12 November 1925

TAYLOR, Robert J R, Ordinary Seaman, SSX 12204, Argus, 25 October 1927

TAYLOR, Stephen, Mechanician, 307681, Vivid, 17 November 1924

TAYLOR, Thomas, Boy 2c, JX 140922, St Vincent, 18 June 1934

TAYLOR, Thomas, Ordinary Seaman, J 86534 (Dev), Resolution, 11 March 1920

TAYLOR, Thomas G, Officer's Steward 3c, L 8185, Penarth, 4 February 1919

TAYLOR, Thomas J C, Petty Officer, J 13653 (Po), L.55, 4 June 1919

TAYLOR, Thomas T, Chief Shipwright 2c, M 6594, Vivid, 20 July 1930

TAYLOR, Thomas V, Skipper, RNR, Stelma, 3 February 1919

TAYLOR, Thomas W, Stoker 1c, K 63776, Hollyhock, 24 May 1925

TAYLOR, Thomas W, Stoker 2c, SS 119041, Osea, 30 December 1918

TAYLOR, Walter J C, Stoker Petty Officer, C/K 34349, Pembroke, 2 January 1932

TAYLOR, William, Driver, RMA, RMA S 828, RMA Eastney, 1 June 1919

TAYLOR, William, Private, RMLI, 19297 (Ply), Teutonic, 19 November 1918

TAYLOR, William, Stoker 1c, 286537, Victory, 5 November 1919

TAYLOR, William H, Petty Officer, RNVR, Bristol Z 754, Pembroke, 8 April 1919
TAYLOR, William O' F, Boy 1c, JX 140419, Marlborough, 14 July 1928
TAYLOR, William S, Stoker 1c, P/KX 84825, Hawkins, 11 August 1938
TAYLOR, William T, Leading Stoker, K 12468, Victory, 18 July 1924

TEAHEN, Henry, Private, RMLI, 22323 (Ch), Chatham Division, RMLI, 1 March 1919
TEBBETT, Thomas R C, Signalman, MMR, 977439, Hughli, Royal Fleet Auxiliary, 26 April 1919
TEE, Alfred T, Chief Writer, 347262, Victory, 16 January 1921
TEE, Thomas G, Able Seaman, J 29582, Southampton II, RN Base, Ceylon (Sri Lanka), 25 April 1922
TELFER, John R, Able Seaman, J 91303, Dunedin, 18 January 1924
TELFORD, William, Leading Stoker, K 10747, Vivid, 4 October 1923
TEMME, Francis B, Chief Petty Officer, C/JX 146573, Robin, 12 May 1938
TEMP, George, Chief Petty Officer, D/J 20729, Delhi, 21 August 1932
TEMPLE, Harry P, Able Seaman, J 93647, Pembroke, 20 January 1929
TENNANT, Sidney, Able Seaman, J 37079, Diana, 17 April 1919
TENSON, Walter, Cook, MMR, 837360, Belgol, Royal Fleet Auxiliary, 4 May 1919
TERNDRUP, John H, Lieutenant Commander, RNR, Royal Naval Reserve, 30 May 1926
TERREY, Henry C, Able Seaman, J 24742 (Ch), Erin's Isle, 7 February 1919
TERRY, Albert E, Deck Hand, RNR, DA 14301, Miura, 4 December 1918
TEUMA, Albert, Officer's Steward 3c, 358428, Ajax, 11 July 1923

THAIN, Alfred, Chief Shipwright 2c, 344427, Vivid (ex-Malaya), 8 November 1920
THAIN, Charles, Shipwright 2c, 346319, Pelargonium, 28 November 1918
THATCHER, Francis L H, Chief Motor Mechanic, RNVR, MB 1974 (Po), CMB.62BD, coastal motor boat, 18 August 1919
THIRSK, Harold, Chief Engine Room Artificer 1c, M 1590, Pembroke, 8 August 1927
THOM, Frederick C W, Chief Electrical Artificer 1c, M 1007, Vulcan, 24 August 1926
THOM, James M W, Midshipman (A), Naval Pilot's Course No.3, 3 June 1939
THOM, William S, Ordinary Seaman, J 81793, Queen Elizabeth, 16 April 1921
THOMAS, Albert H, Private, RMLI, 19176 (Po), 3rd Battalion, RM, 17 December 1918
THOMAS, Charles E, Gunner, RMA, RMA 9404, Crescent, 8 January 1921
THOMAS, Charles F, Leading Cook, M 1724, Victory, 9 February 1920
THOMAS, Charles G, Leading Seaman, 188000, Cumberland, 26 April 1919
THOMAS, Charles H, Stoker 1c, K 58945, Calcutta, 5 November 1924
THOMAS, Clifford B, Stoker 1c, SS 16491, Erin, 24 February 1919
THOMAS, David H, Shipwright Apprentice, M 35267, Pembroke, 13 April 1924
THOMAS, Denis H, Leading Seaman, J 73983, Valerian, 22 October 1926
THOMAS, Edward A, Petty Officer, D/J 13291, Vivid, 22 July 1931
THOMAS, Ernest J, Telegraphist, P/J 76817, M.2, 29 January 1932

THOMAS, Evan, Paymaster Lieutenant Commander, RNR, Royal Naval Reserve, 9 September 1926
THOMAS, George E, Private, RM, S 14875 (Deal), RM Labour Corps, 22 February 1919
THOMAS, George H B, Able Seaman, D/J 108505, Drake, 19 October 1937
THOMAS, Henry J, Able Seaman, J 40178, Pembroke, 13 February 1919
THOMAS, Hugh, Stoker 2c, K 61997, Resolution, 17 February 1924
THOMAS, John E, Private, RMLI, 20396 (Ply), Colleen, 20 March 1922
THOMAS, John F, Petty Officer, 197274, Vivid, 14 April 1919
THOMAS, John J W, Able Seaman, J 64690, Nerissa, 1 January 1919
THOMAS, Kenneth W, Engine Room Artificer 2c, D/M 34509, Drake, 12 February 1937
THOMAS, Lancelot J, Able Seaman, J 45533, Emerald, 14 September 1926
THOMAS, Leon A M, Stoker 2c, K 63496, Victory, 22 March 1924
THOMAS, Louis A, Commissioned Shipwright, Royal Oak, 17 March 1934
THOMAS, Moses, Stoker 1c, P/KX 76319, Victory, 21 May 1934
THOMAS, Phillip, Marine, 21653 (Ply), Royal Marines HQ, 3 April 1929
THOMAS, William H, Able Seaman, 129962, Victory, 14 April 1919
THOMAS, William J, Station Officer, HMCG, HM Coast Guard, 20 October 1924
THOMPSON, Albert H, Deck Hand, RNR, DA 6839, Lavatera, 4 December 1918
THOMPSON, Arthur, Signalman, RNVR, Tyneside Z 6967, Vulcan, 17 December 1918
THOMPSON, Douglas P, Able Seaman, C/JX 141095, Kent, 3 October 1938
THOMPSON, Edwin, Private, RMLI, 16580 (Ply), 3rd Battalion, RM, 25 November 1918
THOMPSON, George (real name, but served as James Casey), Trimmer, RNR, TS 5369, Romilly, 27 November 1918
THOMPSON, Harold A, Paymaster Commander, Boscawen, 13 September 1936
THOMPSON, Hubert H, Chief Petty Officer (Quartermaster Sergeant), RNVR, London Z 485, Benbow Battalion, RND, 20 February 1919
THOMPSON, John, Chief Petty Officer, 214105, Pembroke, 20 August 1923
THOMPSON, John, Private, RMLI, 15927 (Ply), RND, 2nd RM Battalion, 18 November 1918
THOMPSON, John, Stoker 1c, K 40926, Victory, 2 December 1918
THOMPSON, John E, Able Seaman, MMR, 934374, Strachmaree, 7 December 1918
THOMPSON, John J H, Stoker 2c, C/KX 91463, Pembroke, 24 July 1937
THOMPSON, John M, Able Seaman, J 100923, Wolverine, 22 May 1924
THOMPSON, Joseph H, Able Seaman, J 46436, Tyrant, 27 December 1918
THOMPSON, Stanley E, Engine Room Artificer 2c, M 4718, Endeavour, 15 February 1922
THOMPSON, Victor E, Boy 1c, D/JX 143708, Delhi, 31 May 1936
THOMPSON, Walter J, Able Seaman, C/J 110745, Escort, 12 November 1934
THOMPSON, William, Private, RM, S 11012 (Deal), RM Labour Corps, 11 February 1919
THOMPSON, William G, Able Seaman, J 25667, Dolphin, 4 December 1922
THOMPSON, William H, Stoker Petty Officer, K 13914, Valerian, 22 October 1926

THOMSON, Alexander P, Petty Officer, C/J 113357, Calcutta, 16 August 1938

THOMSON, Frederick W, Able Seaman, J 44418, Bruce, 21 February 1920

THOMSON, George, Engineman, RNR, ES 3036, Cheery, 9 February 1919

THOMSON, James R, Leading Seaman, RNR, A 2202, President III, 19 December 1918

THOMSON, James R, Stoker Petty Officer, RNR, TS 561, Pekin, 23 October 1919

THOMSON, Malcolm, Seaman, RNR, A 4557, Iolaire (Redoubtable, O/P), 1 January 1919

THOMSON, Michael W, Act/Warrant Schoolmaster, Hecla, 12 February 1919

THOMSON, Peter, Engineer Sub Lieutenant, RNR, Duke of Cornwall, 20 February 1919

THOMSON, Robert B, Commander, RNR, Royal Naval Reserve, 9 September 1924

THORNBACK, James J O, Officer's Steward 1c, L 3246, Valerian, 22 October 1926

THORNE, Sydney R, Regulating Petty Officer, 216932, New Zealand, 19 January 1920

THORNHILL, George M, Stoker 1c, SS 122759, Raleigh, 8 August 1922

THORNTON, Arthur B, Stoker 1c, SS 122115, Crocus, 5 April 1922

THORNTON, John, Chief Engine Room Artificer, RNR, EA 1025, Acacia, 7 April 1919

THORNTON, Thomas, Able Seaman, C/JX 128413, M.2, 29 January 1932

THORNTON-JONES, Horatio, Lieutenant Commander, Royal Sovereign, 1 March 1934

THORPE, Charles A R, Lieutenant, M.1, 12 November 1925

THORPE, Clement G, Officer's Steward 3c, L 11661, Silvio, 30 November 1919

THORPE, George, Stoker 1c, K 64074, Valerian, 22 October 1926

THORPE, William, Skipper, RNR, James & Walter, steamship, 7 March 1919

THRELFALL, Charles H, Stoker 1c, P/KX 75873, M.2, 29 January 1932

THRING, Harry L, Chief Engine Room Artificer 2c, M 849, Victory, 16 May 1922

THROWER, John E, Leading Seaman, C/J 113794, Veteran, 15 April 1935

THURNALL, William E V, 2nd Lieutenant, RMLI, Commonwealth, 1 February 1921

THURSFIELD, Richard M R, Surgeon Lieutenant, Glowworm, 25 August 1919

THURSTAN, Denzil R, Paymaster Lieutenant Commander, Royal Air Force, 24 February 1919

THURTIE, Herbert R, Engineman, RNR, DA 2994, Kingfisher, 18 June 1919

TICKELL, William G, Stoker Chief Petty Officer, M 618, Philomel, 20 October 1923

TICKNER, Stephen, Stoker 1c, K 35723, Radstock, 27 November 1918

TIDDY, Richard J, Cook, M 7507, Clematis, 2 October 1920

TIDMAN, Robert H, Signal Boy, RNR, SB 2477, Ganges, 13 November 1918

TILLETT, William, Stoker 1c, K 65323, Barham, 8 November 1927

TILLING, John, Petty Officer, 202967, Abercrombie, 8 May 1919

TILSON, Bertie W, Able Seaman, J 90737, Malaya, 15 February 1921

TIMMS, Arthur F, Leading Seaman, 228889, Beacon Grange, steamship, 23 January 1919

TIMMS, Reginald A, Petty Officer, J 25827, Gnat, 2 February 1929

TINDAL-CARILL-WORSLEY, Charles N, Captain, Royal Navy, 21 September 1921

TINDALL, Noel S, Commander, Egmont, transferred from Clematis to hospital, 2 October 1920

TINGEY, Edward, Stoker 1c, SS 120405, Pembroke, 13 October 1921

TINKER, Henry W C, Ty/Honorary Lieutenant Commander, RNVR, Royal Naval Volunteer Reserve, 7 February 1928

TINKLER, Basil I, Stoker 2c, D/KX 87942, Amphion, 6 August 1936

TINLEY, Walter J, Chief Petty Officer, 155526, Attentive II, 10 May 1919

TIPPEN, George J N, Leading Stoker, K 16549, L.24, 10 January 1924

TITBALL, John, Stoker Petty Officer, K 5300, Revenge, 20 September 1924

TITE, Luther V, Commissioned Gunner, Royal Navy, 24 June 1937

TITE, William E, Private, RMLI, 15412 (Ply), Powerful, 4 March 1919

TITMUS, Sidney S, Able Seaman, J 106605, St Genny, 12 January 1930

TOBIN, John F A, Trimmer, RNR, TS 8790, Vivid, 18 November 1918

TODD, William, Able Seaman, D/JX 131618, Laburnum, 8 October 1934

TOFTS, John R, Chief Writer, 347287, Vivid III, 2 March 1920

TOLHURST, Frank, Leading Cook, M 7796, Pembroke (ex-Carnarvon), 6 January 1921

TOLLIDAY, Frederick C H, Able Seaman, C/J 93958, Poseidon, 9 June 1931

TOLMIE, A. (initial only), Private, RM, S 12516 (Deal), RM Labour Corps, 7 November 1919

TOLSON, Albert E S, Boy 2c, JX 138327, St Vincent, 10 October 1933

TOMLIN, Edwin, Ordinary Seaman, RNVR, Bristol Z 7436, Pembroke, 20 July 1919

TOMLINSON, Thomas H, Seaman, RNR, A 7506, Pembroke, 16 February 1919

TOMLINSON, William J, Trimmer, RNR, TS 5493, Raven III, 19 November 1918

TOMLINSON, William W, Stoker Petty Officer, K 485, Vivid, 20 March 1928

TOMPKINS, Albert J, Stoker 1c, P/KX 76068, Effingham, 17 January 1933

TOMPKINS, Joseph G, Petty Officer, J 6002, Victory, 16 April 1928

TOMS, Ernest, Able Seaman, J 20076, Vivid, 9 October 1924

TONG, Cyril F P, Writer, C/MX 46352, Kent, 10 July 1931

TONKIN, Frederick, Electrical Artificer Apprentice, MX 45299, Fisgard, 7 August 1927

TONNER, Charles, Chief Stoker, 302413 (Ch), Dwarf, 5 November 1920

TOOTELL, Edward, Major, RM, Royal Marines, 11 January 1920

TOOZE, Percy D, Leading Seaman, J 86905, Greenwich, 2 August 1929

TOPP, John H, Lieutenant, Tamar, 20 December 1926

TOPPIN, Henry C, Lieutenant (Pilot), M.2, 29 January 1932

TOPPING, William J M, Leading Seaman, C/J 24196, Dolphin, 21 September 1931

TORR, John, Private, RM, S 11616 (Deal), RM Labour Corps, 8 December 1918

TOSH, James C, Boy 1c, J 104186, Vivid, 28 January 1922

TOTHILL, Edwin J, Leading Stoker, K 22986 (Dev), Resolution, 15 May 1920

TOTTENHAM, Charles L, Ty/Lieutenant, RNR, Lorna, 27 November 1918

TOTTERDELL, Arthur E N, Boy 2c, J 94032, Impregnable, 11 April 1919

TOTTERDELL, James H F, Act/Leading Stoker, D/K 61154, M.2, 29 January 1932

TOTTMAN, Alfred G, Stoker 1c, C/K 59486, Cumberland, 11 January 1932
TOTTMAN, William, Able Seaman, 221957, Pembroke, 1 April 1919
TOURLE, Cecil T, Leading Seaman, C/J 100904, Pembroke, 23 November 1933
TOWELL, Thomas, Marine, 216788 (Po), RN Hospital, Haslar, 4 July 1939
TOWER, Ernest C, Sub Lieutenant, Engineering Course, 22 August 1924
TOWERS, Charles, Marine, X 210 (Ch), Centurion (ex-Hawkins), 16 September 1930
TOWNER, Arthur L A, Able Seaman, J 99640, Wrestler, 22 October 1925
TOWNSEND, Albert V, Boy 1c, J 70937, Hawkins, 17 October 1919
TOWNSEND, Claud R, Lieutenant (Observer), M.2, 29 January 1932
TOWNSEND, John, Chief Stoker, 296026, Pembroke, 13 March 1919
TOWNSLEY, William E, Stoker Petty Officer, K 1855, Pembroke, 26 September 1929

TRANTER, John J S, Able Seaman, P/JX 127271, Warspite, 15 August 1933
TRANTER, Thomas, Petty Officer, 220796, Vivid (ex-Revenge), 5 February 1921
TRAVERS, Leonard G, Signalman, C/J 107114, Anthony, 20 July 1931
TRAVERS, William A, Stoker 1c, SS 116368, Thunderer, 8 October 1919
TRAVERSE, Stephen, Private, RMLI, 17697 (Ch), 3rd Battalion, RM, 18 November 1918
TRAVIS, Albert, Signalman, J 22463, Valiant, 14 October 1921
TREACY, Philip, Leading Seaman, C/J 105646, M.2, 29 January 1932
TREADWELL, Albert W, Chief Engine Room Artificer 1c, M 714, Woodcock, 13 January 1927
TREADWELL, Joseph T, Able Seaman, J 27654, Malaya, 10 January 1922
TREAGUS, James G, Leading Stoker, K 13717, L.33, 11 May 1924
TREASURE, Douglas G, Lieutenant, RNVR, Kylemore, 10 March 1919
TREJIDJO, Frederick T, Leading Seaman, D/JX 126449, Herald, 22 October 1937
TRELEASE, Ernest, Stoker 1c, P/K 58558, Dolphin, 13 November 1937
TREMAYNE, John W L, Act/Sub Lieutenant, Tarantula, 15 February 1923
TREMERE, Albert, Petty Officer, 192669, Pembroke, 2 April 1920
TREMLETT, Francis F, Petty Officer, 212980 (Dev), Benbow, 5 May 1920
TREMLETT, Sidney W, Officer's Chief Steward, 359608, Malabar, 23 July 1920
TRESCOTHIE, Henry, Greaser, MMR, 960802, Hazel, 8 December 1918
TRETHEWEY, Walter A, Able Seaman, J 51871 (Po), Resolution, 28 May 1920
TRETT, William R H, Boy 1c, J 86811 (Ch), Dragon, 17 October 1919
TREVARTHEN, William H, Stoker 1c, K 60501, Pembroke, 31 August 1929
TREVELYAN, Percy, Sub Lieutenant, Sable, 10 March 1919
TREVELYN, Roger de T, Lieutenant, Pembroke, 17 December 1928
TREVETT, Arthur W, Master at Arms, 218878, Danae, 26 November 1924
TRIBBLE, Sidney L, Regulating Petty Officer, D/M 39274, Cumberland, 27 November 1932

TRICE, William J, Shipwright 2c, 342862, Calcutta, 26 December 1921
TRICKETT, Charles, Stoker 1c, K 14239 (Po), L.55, 4 June 1919
TRIGGS, Harry F, Able Seaman, P/JX 132275, Victory, 20 August 1932
TRILL, Charles F, Officer's Steward 3c, L 12662, Nelson, 11 May 1929
TRIPP, Sydney G, Leading Stoker, K 14053, Raleigh, 8 August 1922
TROLLOPE, Douglas K, Lieutenant, Tobago, 11 December 1918
TROLLOPE, Frank E, Private, RMLI, 19239 (Ch), Chatham Division RMLI, (ex-Superb), 8 September 1919
TROTTER, Alfred, Artificer Engineer, Penarth, 4 February 1919
TROTTER, Robert C W, Sub Lieutenant, Course at Portsmouth, 8 May 1932
TROUPIS, Demetrius, Donkeyman, MMR, Billbrough, 14 June 1919
TROUT, Alfred E, Master at Arms, D/M 37395, Drake, 6 April 1934
TRUDGEON, Frederick, Stoker Petty Officer, RAN, 9431, Platypus, 23 November 1919
TRUE, Henry L, Ordinary Seaman, J 102934, Curlew, 16 February 1924
TRUMBLY, Benjamin, Able Seaman, J 2192, Pembroke, 8 December 1928
TRUSCOTT, Arthur, Dockyard Fitter, civilian, H.29, 9 August 1926, accidentally killed
TRY, Leonard C A, Able Seaman, J 94777, Dublin, 5 February 1923

TUCK, Arthur A, Petty Officer, 225535, Victory, 28 June 1927
TUCK, Arthur F, Able Seaman, C/JX 140107, Moth, 20 June 1938
TUCKER, Alfred, Stoker Petty Officer, 302038, Comus, 28 July 1920
TUCKER, Charles R, Chief Stoker, 305252 (Dev), Crescent, 14 February 1920
TUCKER, Edward, Stoker, RFA, Bacchus, RFA, 14 April 1925
TUCKER, Frank P, Petty Officer, D/J 120, Vivid, 5 June 1931
TUCKER, Frederick J, Officer's Steward 3c, 363935, Alecto, 21 December 1923
TUCKER, George W, Able Seaman, J 15265, Ladybird, 31 March 1929
TUCKER, Hector J, Marine, 22594 (Ply), Queen Elizabeth, 25 July 1929
TUCKER, Hubert F, Able Seaman, J 50198 (Po), Nairana, 4 August 1919
TUCKER, John W J, Skipper, MMR, Ivanhoe, 9 January 1919
TUCKER, Leslie J, Leading Seaman, D/J 95992, Drake, 23 January 1937
TUCKER, Oliver G, Skipper, RNR, St Delphine (Boscawen), 9 March 1939
TUCKER, Robert H, Stoker 1c, K 47056, Pembroke, 14 September 1923
TUCKER, Victor E, Petty Officer, D/J 19624, Vivid, 2 June 1932
TUKE, Samuel F G, Lieutenant, L.7, 5 May 1925
TULBY, Victor E, Able Seaman, J 104682, Shropshire, 25 June 1930
TULL, Alfred H, Corporal, RM, 14447 (Ply), Delhi, 17 August 1927
TULLETT, James A, Leading Seaman, J 41685 (Po), Caledon, 17 October 1920
TULLY, Ernest, Engine Room Artificer 4c, M 18353, Dolphin, 24 September 1921
TUMBER, John W, Engine Room Artificer 2c, M 7094, Cambrian, 23 August 1928
TUNBRIDGE, Harold W, Petty Officer, 209951, Vivid, 2 March 1923
TUNDERVARY, John H, Act/Leading Stoker, K 10680 (Po), L.55, 4 June 1919
TUNNICLIFF, Herbert, Able Seaman, J 32051, Marlborough, 13 August 1922

TURK, Albert G, Able Seaman, D/JX 133320, Decoy, 1 January 1939
TURNBULL, Claude S B, Lieutenant, Scarab, 10 June 1932
TURNBULL, Walter, Telegraphist Lieutenant, Effingham, 4 June 1929
TURNER, Albert A C, Able Seaman, J 114047, Marlborough, 25 August 1929
TURNER, Albert E, Able Seaman, SS 6856, Superb, 7 February 1919
TURNER, Albert G, Able Seaman, J 83715, Pembroke, 13 September 1923
TURNER, Alec T, Lieutenant, RM, RM Plymouth Barracks, 2 March 1939
TURNER, Archer, Rev, Chaplain, Royal Navy, 18 July 1932
TURNER, Bertie C, Petty Officer, D/J 72652, Hunter, 13 May 1937
TURNER, Edwin S, Lieutenant, RNVR, ML.360, motor launch, 6 March 1919
TURNER, Ernest G, Signalman, J 64645, Resolution, 26 November 1926
TURNER, Fred, Ordinary Seaman, RNVR, Tyneside Z 13092, Victory, 29 November 1918
TURNER, George D W, Lieutenant, Tamar, 1 July 1920
TURNER, Harry W J, Stoker Petty Officer, 296381, Karavnos, 24 April 1919
TURNER, Henry W, Chief Petty Officer, 164104, Commonwealth, 13 February 1919
TURNER, John, Chief Skipper, RNR, Royal Naval Reserve, 6 May 1932
TURNER, John F, Able Seaman, P/J 92408, Cairo, 13 February 1937
TURNER, John G, 2nd Hand, RNR, SD 945, Rainstorm, 19 March 1919
TURNER, John H, Act/Leading Seaman, D/JX 134566, Thetis, 3 June 1939
TURNER, Percy, Commissioned Shipwright, Enterprise, 23 November 1923
TURNER, Robert C, Stoker 1c, K 21158, Victory, 14 November 1918
TURNER, Stephen L, Warrant Engineer, on loan to New Zealand Division of Royal Navy, 2 November 1928
TURNER, Timothy, Lieutenant, Tumult, 27 November 1922
TURNER, Walter, Stoker Petty Officer, 158282, Attentive III, 26 August 1919
TURNER, Walter I, Leading Signalman, J 36092, M.1, 12 November 1925
TURRELL, Arthur T, Able Seaman, J 106497, Cardiff, 15 May 1927
TURTLE, Arthur V, Stoker 1c, K 61242, Fisgard, 2 January 1929
TUSLER, Thomas, Petty Officer, J 24729, Columbine, 5 July 1922
TUSSLER, Henry, Able Seaman, 238070, Kent, 6 June 1930
TUTT, Frederick E, Electrical Artificer Apprentice, C/MX 45652, Pembroke, 21 April 1931
TUTT, William C E, Petty Officer, 155763, Challenger, 13 December 1918

TWIDDY, Ernest F C, Stoker Petty Officer, C/K 65944, Valiant, 22 April 1931
TWIGG, Charles, Stoker 1c, K 7163, Mistley, 16 April 1920
TWITCHETT, Frederick G, Stoker 1c, K 31335, Lucia, 14 February 1920

TYLEE, Errol T, Engineer Sub Lieutenant, RNR, Nairana, 26 January 1919
TYLER, Donald V, Civilian Contractor, Thetis, 3 June 1939
TYLER, Frederick P, Electrical Artificer 1c, 345114, Superb, 12 September 1919
TYLER, John, Ordinary Seaman, MMR, 883964, Francol, Royal Fleet Auxiliary, 27 December 1919
TYLER, Reuben, Leading Stoker, K 18030, Raleigh, 8 August 1922
TYLER, William T R, Stoker 1c, KX 78336, Victory, 7 February 1930
TYNAN, Patrick, Stoker 1c, SS 121079, Pembroke, 1 October 1919
TYRWHITT, Robert, Sub Lieutenant, Orpheus, 3 May 1932
TYSON, Thomas J, Chief Engine Room Artificer 1c, 269749, Jumna, 11 May 1920
TYTE, Frederick C, Motor Mechanic, RNVR, MB 2586, CMB.52, coastal motor boat, 3 December 1918

U

UDEN, Albert E, Able Seaman, J 81315, Royal Oak, 7 October 1926

UNWIN, William H, Stoker 1c, MC 1672, Hannibal, 19 June 1919

UPTON, Kenneth P, Stoker 1C, P/KX 91207, Aurora, 14 October 1938

URQUHART, Kenneth W, Engine Room Artificer 2c, M 3156, Vivid, 10 March 1920

USBORNE, Thomas R G, Sub Lieutenant, CMB.79A, coastal motor boat, 18 August 1919

USHER, Charles J, Able Seaman, J 93569, Valerian, 22 October 1926

USHER, David E, Ordinary Seaman, J 104705, Vimiera, 4 December 1924

USHER, Robert, Seaman, RNR, A 5331, Vivid, 17 February 1919

UTTING, Fredeick J, Stoker 1c, SS 124832, Calypso, 4 February 1921

V

VAIARELLA, Antonio, Steward, E/LX 21002, Hood, 12 September 1938
VALENTINE, Victor E D, Paymaster Lieutenant Commander, Victory, 21 May 1922
VALLANCE, William R, Cadet, RN Engineering College Keyham, 13 December 1918
VALLINGS, Frederick F O, Sub Lieutenant, Catspaw, 31 December 1919
VALLIS, William G, Able Seaman, J 12116, Britomart, 5 August 1919
VAN DER VORD, Richard F, Paymaster Lieutenant Commander, RNR, Royal Naval Reserve, 28 June 1936
VANCE, William, Private, RM, S 8469 (Deal), RM Labour Corps, 14 February 1919
VANHORN, Frederick, Constable, Malta Dockyard, 15 December 1935
VANNER, Eric G, Engine Room Artificer 1c, D/M 11315, Devonshire, 10 March 1933
VANSTONE, Jim, Commissioned Supply Officer, Revenge, 20 December 1927
VANSTONE, Wilfred J, Leading Seaman, 232533 (Dev), Bombardier, 27 March 1919
VARCOE, Alfred, Stoker 1c, K 18051, Vivid, 28 September 1929
VARDON, Gerald A, Lieutenant, FAA, 825 Sqn, Glorious, 5 February 1937
VASS, David A, Seaman, RNR, A 5309, Victory, 14 December 1918
VASS, Jack, Able Seaman, 204902, Tryphon, 3 July 1919
VASS, Reginald, Chief Petty Officer, 223858, Excellent, 7 September 1926
VATTER, George S W, Petty Officer Telegraphist, J 6164, Victory, 17 March 1919
VAUDIN, George C, Ordnance Artificer Apprentice, C/MX 58919, Pembroke, 26 March 1939
VAUGHAN, William C A, Leading Seaman, J 32281, M.1, 12 November 1925

VEAL, Frederick, Able Seaman, J 17299, Attentive III, 26 August 1919
VEAL, John B G, Private, RMLI, S 1704 (Ch), Ambitious, 18 February 1919
VEALE, Frederick L, Able Seaman, J 50203, Vivid, 12 April 1930
VELLA, Guiseppe, Officer's Cook 1c, E/LX 20649, Curlew, 5 June 1931
VELLA, Joseph, Petty Officer Steward, E/LX 20354, Cyclops, 16 October 1932
VELLA, Raphaell, Officer's Steward 2c, 358722, Ceres, 19 September 1923
VENABLES, George, Yeoman of Signals, 203160, Victory, 24 February 1919
VENING, George, Signalman, J 21276, RN Shore Signal Station, Beachy Head, 6 October 1931
VENN, Samuel G, Able Seaman, J 45892, Champion, 30 January 1919
VEREKER, Foley G P, Lieutenant, Venturous, 14 February 1921
VERNON, John D, Petty Officer Steward, C/LX 20513, Sutton, 28 April 1938
VESEY, Blakeman, Lieutenant, Danae, 14 November 1933
VESEY-FITZGERALD, William P D, Lieutenant, Carlisle, 14 February 1923

VIALES, Ernest J, Assistant Steward, MMR, 702625, Eaglet, 17 February 1919
VICE, Wilfred, Able Seaman, C/J 13006, Kent, 19 December 1930
VICKERY, Richard H, Supply Chief Petty Officer, P/M 5347, Dryad, 14 September 1930
VICKERY, Samuel H, Surgeon Commander, Thalia, 25 July 1919
VICKERY, William J, Able Seaman, 210467, Seraph, 26 December 1921
VIGOUR, Cyril, Stoker 1c, P/KX 78095, Victory, 21 August 1933
VINCENT, Arthur J, Able Seaman, C/J 24276, M.2, 29 January 1932
VINCENT, John, Gunner, RMA, RMA 14332, Eileen, 13 February 1919
VINCENT, Reginald G, Able Seaman, J 29249, Victory, 16 March 1920
VINCENT, William C, Leading Seaman, 219905, Ajax, 2 October 1922
VINES, Alfred E, Commissioned Gunner, Royal Navy, 17 June 1921
VINEY, Frederick C, Officer's Steward 1c, 365890, Minerva, 19 November 1918
VINEY, Rolf, Commander, Fitzroy, 20 April 1922
VINSON, Arthur W, Leading Cook, P/M 15326, Nelson, 21 September 1935
VIVIAN, Golfred R, Petty Officer, P/J 92875, Victory, 21 August 1933
VIVIAN, Leslie T, Able Seaman, J 62748, Speedy, 23 September 1922

VOAK, William J, Able Seaman, P/J 109338, H.24, 16 June 1932
VOSS, Ernest E, Private, RME, RME 346, RM Engineers, 10 January 1919

W

WACE, Stephen C, Lieutenant Colonel, RMA, RM Artillery, 21 May 1920
WADDLE, David, Boy 2c, JX 151631, Ganges, 11 January 1937
WADE, Joseph J, Chief Officer, HM Coast Guard, HM Coastguard Station Withernsea, 30 November 1919
WAGANOFF, Walter G, Lieutenant (Russian Interpreter), Fox, 25 August 1919
WAITE, James H, Marine, 24396 (Ch), Enterprise, 10 May 1926
WAITES, Alfred, Stoker 1c, D/KX 86525, Hunter, 13 May 1937
WAKE, William G, Chief Stoker, K 16568, Warspite, 23 May 1928
WAKEHAM, John, Private, RM, S 13624 (Deal), RM Labour Corps, 27 December 1918
WAKEHAM, Robert, Chief Petty Officer, 163258, Vivid, 23 February 1919
WAKELEY, Victor Mortimer, 3rd Officer, RFA, Bacchus, RFA, 14 April 1925
WAKELY, Alfred H, Artificer Engineer, L.55, 4 June 1919
WALDRON, Albury A, Officer's Steward 2c, L 5528, Vivid, 21 March 1919
WALDRON, Edward L, Ordinary Seaman, J 103545, Emperor of India, 11 October 1924
WALDRON, John, Midshipman, Ramillies, 13 June 1926
WALE, William L K, Leading Stoker, K 59814, Pembroke, 9 April 1926
WALES, Michael, Leading Stoker, 303910, Hecla, 2 June 1920
WALKER, Alexander, Engineman, RNR, ES 1292, Boy Bob, 23 March 1919
WALKER, Alfred J, Stoker Petty Officer, D/K 55148, Dorsetshire, 2 May 1937
WALKER, Archibald R H, Lieutenant, Whitshed, 4 September 1934
WALKER, Charles G, Stoker 1c, C/KX 75281, Wolsey, 8 December 1934
WALKER, Edward C, Able Seaman, J 101332, Pembroke, 19 May 1929
WALKER, Ernest, Able Seaman, J 90331, Whirlwind, 3 January 1926
WALKER, Francis H G, Captain, Greenwich, 11 January 1937
WALKER, Frederick G, Able Seaman, RNVR, Bristol Z 3644, Vivid, 23 January 1919
WALKER, Frederick M, Captain (Rtd), President, 7 February 1919
WALKER, George H, Signal Boy, RNR, SB 1944, Idaho, 12 February 1919
WALKER, James H, Sub Lieutenant, Douglas, 5 May 1932
WALKER, John, Able Seaman, RNVR, Clyde Z 6921, Ceto, 12 November 1918
WALKER, John H, Private, RMLI, 20036 (Ch), Chatham Division, RMLI, 17 March 1919
WALKER, Ralph, Stoker 1c, P/KX 78023, M.2, 29 January 1932
WALKER, Robert H, Leading Seaman, 238522, Blue Sky, tender to Queen Elizabeth, 12 June 1922
WALKER, Robert R, Able Seaman, C/JX 138078, Kent, 25 July 1939
WALKER, Thomas, Chief Engine Room Artificer 1c, 269982 (Ch), Peregrine, 19 November 1918
WALKER, William, Stoker 1c, K 22942, L.24, 10 January 1924
WALKER, William E, Leading Boatman, 204453, HM Coastguard Station Deal, 28 November 1920
WALL, Arthur W, Able Seaman, J 6916, Emerald, 30 November 1927
WALL, Francis B, Petty Officer Cook, P/M 34657, Victory, 28 February 1938
WALL, Horace, Leading Signalman, 220825, Blake, 24 November 1918
WALL, John T, 2nd Hand, RNR, DA 12571, Morning Star, 29 July 1919
WALL, Leslie A, Cook, P/M 38483, Boscawen, 5 July 1935
WALL, William J, Stoker 1c, C/KX 75909, Frobisher, 9 August 1933
WALLACE, Andrew C, Chief Engine Room Artificer 2c, M 1390, L.24, 10 January 1924
WALLACE, Donald C, Able Seaman, J 69473, Revenge, 19 July 1920
WALLACE, Malcolm A, Sub Lieutenant, RNR, Alice, 7 May 1919
WALLACE, William, Leading Seaman, RNVR, Clyde Z 8667, President III, 1 April 1919
WALLER, Richard H, Stoker 1c, C/K 62005, Shoreham, 1 May 1933
WALLIS, Henry (real name, but served as Henry Schwartz), Stoker 1c, K 6949, Pembroke, 20 February 1920
WALLIS, James G, Surgeon Commander, Impregnable, 19 July 1922
WALLWORK, James, Stoker 2c, C/KX 89886, Pembroke, 13 January 1937
WALNE, Archibald F D, Signalman, RAN, 10030, Royal Australian Navy, 12 January 1924
WALSH, John, Private, RM, S 13001 (Deal), RM Labour Corps, 24 November 1918
WALSH, Joseph A, Leading Telegraphist, J 41572, Victory I, 29 February 1920
WALSH, Michael, Stoker 1c, K 31017, Lobelia, 18 January 1919
WALSH, William, Stoker 1c, K 21647, Sterling, 9 August 1928
WALSWORTH, Arthur N, Able Seaman, J 99609, Iroquois, 4 May 1930
WALTER, Arthur, Petty Officer, J 22770, Cricket, 24 September 1925
WALTER, Charles A, Petty Officer, J 1304, Pembroke, 15 October 1924
WALTERS, Alfred C, Able Seaman, RNVR, Bristol Z 1811, Tanfield, steamship, 20 February 1919
WALTERS, Harold G, Stoker Petty Officer, K 30, Egmont, 3 July 1919
WALTERS, Maurice H, Midshipman, Devonshire, in RN Hospital, Malta, 28 January 1934
WALTON, Albert, Able Seaman, J 29140, Victory, 12 November 1918
WALTON, Alfred R, Able Seaman, C/J 100300, Pembroke, 9 August 1931
WALTON, Laverick, Trimmer, RNR, TS 788, John Bradford, 28 November 1918
WALTON, Reginald F, Sick Berth Attendant, P/MX 49299, RN Hospital, Haslar, 24 February 1934
WALTON, William D, Stoker 1c, K 24565, Constance, 12 September 1925
WARBURTON, Herbert J, Engine Room Artificer 4c, M 13378, Carnarvon, 17 October 1919
WARBURTON, Llewellyn R, Surgeon Commander, RN Hospital, Haslar, 5 March 1932
WARBY, Joseph P, Able Seaman, RNVR, London Z 6251, President III, 15 March 1919
WARD, Alfred E, Chief Artificer Engineer, Magic, 12 February 1919
WARD, Arthur J, Stoker 1c, SS 122597, Ajax, 10 April 1922
WARD, Arthur R, Engine Room Artificer 3c, M 11360, Marlborough, 5 July 1924
WARD, Cecil C, Signalman, RNVR, Bristol Z 10792, Gibraltar, 15 November 1918
WARD, Charles E, Able Seaman, J 1286, Pembroke, 31 March 1920
WARD, Charles H V, Chief Petty Officer, D/239383, Caroline, 16 September 1937
WARD, Charles W, Stoker 1c, P/KX 79238, Grimsby, 20 May 1935
WARD, Edward, Ordinary Seaman, J 73811, Savage, 10 December 1918

WARD, Edward, Petty Officer, 154371, HM Coastguard Station Coverack, 13 February 1919
WARD, Edward G, Shipwright 2c, M 6763, Titania, 20 October 1924
WARD, Frederick G, Able Seaman, J 4150, Vampire, 2 November 1920
WARD, Frederick J, Able Seaman, 181956, Vivid, 9 April 1919
WARD, Horace W, Able Seaman, SS 8464 (Ch), K.5, 20 January 1921
WARD, Lawrence, Stoker 1c, SS 121004, Vivid, 6 June 1919
WARD, Patrick, Able Seaman, C/JX 131085, Cumberland, 9 January 1932
WARD, Thomas, Able Seaman, RNVR, Mersey Z 3368, Hebburn, steamship, 5 December 1918
WARD, Thomas H, Ordinary Seaman, J 113840, Warspite, 5 April 1927
WARD, Thomas W, Officer's Cook 2c, C/LX 20162, Sabre, 20 December 1938
WARD, William R, Musician, RMB, RMB 2263, Highflyer, 8 January 1921
WARDER, Richard B G, Major, RMA, Resolution, 22 January 1921
WARDLEY, Edward, Armourers Mate, M 2872, Pembroke, 25 February 1919
WARE, John T, Gunner, Glorious, 15 June 1923
WAREHAM, Edward J, Boy 2c, J 94474, Impregnable, 28 February 1919
WAREHAM, Leslie, Leading Telegraphist, P/JX 134173, Deptford, 24 September 1938
WAREING, Percy, Stoker 2c, K 63504, Vivid, 28 February 1924
WARING, George H, Petty Officer, J 1411, Thanet, 27 May 1925
WARMAN, Edmund, Chief Skipper, RNR, Royal Naval Reserve, 26 October 1937
WARNES, William H, Able Seaman, C/J 108521, Pembroke, 4 September 1931
WARREN, Christopher F, Mechanician, 308634 (Ch), Fandango, 3 July 1919
WARREN, Edwin N, Able Seaman, J 95403, Emerald, 28 December 1926
WARREN, Ernest P, Able Seaman, J 44287, Mutine, 30 May 1921
WARREN, Frederick C, Able Seaman, P/J 48212, Hawkins, 22 April 1938
WARREN, George A, Chief Yeoman of Signals, 160645, Crescent, 28 December 1918
WARREN, Harold W, Leading Stoker, K 18826, Ajax, 25 February 1919
WARREN, James W, Sergeant, RMA, RMA 10751, Ramillies, 8 April 1919
WARREN, John T, Skipper, RNR, Arctic Whale, 23 November 1919
WARREN, Thomas S, Stoker Petty Officer, K 4688, Tiverton, 16 April 1919
WARREN, Thomas, Marine, 5994 (Ch), Cleopatra, 20 June 1929
WARREN, William, Stoker Petty Officer, K 3363, Pembroke, 24 May 1919
WARRINGTON, Harry, Able Seaman, RNVR, Tyneside Z 9687, HM Coast Guard Inchkeith, 11 March 1919
WARWICK, Ralph D, Able Seaman, J 28845, Colombo, 13 January 1926
WASH, Walter H, Able Seaman, J 12352 (Po), L.55, 4 June 1919
WASHINGTON, Harry G, Able Seaman, RNVR, R 2683, Hood Battalion, RND, 3 April 1919
WASHINGTON, Sidney W, Leading Seaman, J 24140, M.1, 12 November 1925
WASS, Leonard, Signalman, RNVR, Tyneside Z 8792, Ocean Roamer, 16 December 1918
WATERFIELD, George H, Able Seaman, J 32831, L.24, 10 January 1924
WATERMAN, William, Chief Yeoman of Signals, C/J 13749, Pembroke, 9 September 1935
WATERS, Frederick W A, Stoker 1c, K 60872, Britannia, RN College, Dartmouth, 7 October 1926
WATERS, Thomas J, Able Seaman, J 35067, Vivid, 22 May 1923
WATERWORTH, Frank R, Petty Officer, J 41623, Tamar, 5 June 1924
WATKIN, William R, Ordinary Seaman, J 94909, Ajax, 9 October 1920
WATKINS, Albert E, Able Seaman, J 101435, Pembroke, 27 May 1926
WATKINS, Charles J, Able Seaman, J 98026, Excellent, 25 October 1927
WATKINS, James G, Warrant Engineer, Iron Duke, 25 April 1928
WATKINSON, Arthur S, Civilian Contractor, Thetis, 3 June 1939
WATKINSON, Donald J G, Lieutenant, L.24, 10 January 1924
WATLING, Victor G, Able Seaman, J 47170, Royal Sovereign, 9 December 1918
WATNEY, Basil G, Lieutenant, RNVR, ML.236, motor launch, 28 October 1919
WATSON, Albert E, Private, RMLI, 19810 (Ch), RM Headquarters, 26 April 1921
WATSON, Alexander, Skipper, RNR, Vivid, 30 May 1919
WATSON, Bernard C, Gunner, Lucia, 13 February 1924
WATSON, Charles E, Sub Lieutenant (A), FAA, 800 Sqn, Ark Royal, 2 August 1939
WATSON, Charles J T, Surgeon Lieutenant, RNVR, London Division, RNVR, 25 December 1938
WATSON, George, Engine Room Artificer 1c, C/MX 52472, Woolston, 12 January 1937
WATSON, Henry C, Able Seaman, D/J 104432, Drake, 27 October 1936
WATSON, James, Marine, 18380 (Ch), Royal Oak, 6 March 1926
WATSON, John A, Stoker 1c, SS 125895, Lowestoft, 1 March 1926
WATSON, Robert, Engineman, RNR, ES 651, Implacable, 2 December 1918
WATSON, Robert, Ty/Lieutenant, RNVR, Royal Naval Volunteer Reserve, 11 September 1919
WATSON, Robert D, Able Seaman, J 28030, Valerian, 22 October 1926
WATSON, Thomas B, Able Seaman, J 31885, Dunedin, 17 July 1929
WATSON, Thomas T, Able Seaman, RNVR, Tyneside Z 6537, Caledonian, steamship, 4 December 1918
WATSON, William, Petty Officer, J 7759, Pembroke, 22 November 1918
WATSON, William A, Stoker 1c, C/KX 67092, M.2, 29 January 1932
WATSON-PAUL, Guy V, Lieutenant, RNR, Egmont, 19 August 1919
WATT, David, Seaman, RNR, C 1721, Avoca, 17 November 1918
WATTERS, William, Leading Seaman, D/JX 130358, Hunter, 13 May 1937
WATTERSON, William, Civilian Contractor, Thetis, 3 June 1939
WATTS, Albert E, Stoker 1c, K 65436, Effingham, 9 June 1927
WATTS, Albert W L, Leading Stoker, P/KX 83422, Dainty, 27 July 1939
WATTS, Alexander W, Stoker 1c, K 11139, Tamar, 10 September 1926
WATTS, Allan J N, Leading Seaman, J 10560, Vivid, 5 July 1924
WATTS, Cecil G E, Able Seaman, SSX 12937, Courageous, 13 July 1930
WATTS, Edward, Coastguardsman 3c, 285179, HM Coast Guard Station Southsea, 24 November 1919
WATTS, John C, Able Seaman, P/J 86158, Delight, 23 December 1935
WATTS, Thomas H, Able Seaman, J 68490 (Po), Greenwich, 16 November 1918
WATTS, William J, Stoker Petty Officer, K 10280, Vivid, 10 February 1927
WAY, William E, Trimmer, RNR, TS 4137, Vera Grace, 1 December 1918

WEATHERLEY, Allan, Sick Berth Attendant, P/MX 50591, RN Hospital, Haslar, 13 May 1934
WEAVER, James, Able Seaman, 213937, Raleigh, 8 August 1922
WEAVING, Henry J, Marine, 22438 (Ply), Dunedin, 2 January 1928
WEAVING, William, Engine Room Artificer 1c, M 14169, Calcutta, 22 October 1929
WEBB, Albert, Able Seaman, P/J 111411, Victory, 11 March 1933
WEBB, Arthur A, Boy 1c, JX 132101, Repulse, 14 July 1930
WEBB, Charles S, Able Seaman, J 40368, Catspaw, 31 December 1919
WEBB, Edward W, Telegraphist, J 21648, Benbow, 25 January 1922
WEBB, Francis W, Boy 2c, J 102067, Impregnable, 5 June 1921
WEBB, Fred, Stoker Petty Officer, K 13071, Victory, 17 August 1929
WEBB, George T, Stoker 1c, K 13876, Pembroke, 1 September 1919
WEBB, Henry G, Boy 1c, JX 134334, Ganges, 3 March 1931
WEBB, James, Able Seaman, J 19636 (Ch), Fandango, 3 July 1919
WEBB, Oliver, Lance Corporal, RMLI, 11822 (Po), 1st RM Battalion, RND, 4 May 1919
WEBB, Thomas E, Coastguardsman 2c, 149238, HM Coast Guard Station Sheephaven, County Donegal, 17 October 1919
WEBB, Thomas P, Lieutenant Commander, RNR, Royal Naval Reserve, 19 July 1919
WEBB, W (initial only) R, Ordinary Seaman, RAN, 21363, Hobart (RAN), 1 November 1938
WEBB, William J H, Greaser, MMR, Glen Usk, 16 November 1918
WEBB, William, Stoker Petty Officer, 283774, Wildfire, 20 November 1918
WEBBER, Charles G, Act/Paymaster Commander, President, 6 February 1919
WEBBER, Frederick, Able Seaman, RNVR, R 1544, Hawke Battalion, RND, 1 December 1918
WEBBER, Frederick C, Leading Stoker, D/K 236616, Centurion, 19 June 1935
WEBBER, Frederick E, Leading Telegraphist, J 27488, Tamar, 6 June 1922
WEBBER, George J H, Stoker Petty Officer, K 3031, Vivid (ex-Walrus), 14 March 1920
WEBBER, James E C, Sub Lieutenant, Course at Portsmouth, 22 March 1931
WEBBER, Samuel C, Leading Stoker, 183706 (Dev), Kinross, 16 June 1919
WEBLEY, William T, Lieutenant, President, 15 May 1919
WEBSELL, Walter J, Stoker 1c, K 29291, Victory, 21 January 1924
WEBSTER, Albert E, Leading Seaman, J 92635, M.1, 12 November 1925
WEBSTER, Ernest J E, Paymaster Lieutenant (Rtd), Margaret and Andrew, steamship, 22 April 1919
WEBSTER, Harold, Able Seaman, J 76180, Carlisle, 11 May 1924
WEBSTER, John, Able Seaman, J 43078, Vivid, 7 February 1922
WEBSTER, Wilfred A, Gunner, Hermes, 6 June 1933
WEBSTER, William, Quartermaster Sergeant, RMLI, 8036 (Ply), RM Headquarters, 11 September 1919
WEBSTER, William C, Leading Deck Hand, RNR, SD 4685, ML.318, motor launch, 30 November 1918
WEEDON, Frank A W, Act/Sub Lieutenant, Britannia, RN College, Dartmouth, 21 July 1923
WEEDON, Thomas, Stoker 1c, SS 124187, Pembroke, 7 October 1919
WEEKLY, Charles R S, Stoker Petty Officer, P/K 57847, Ladybird, 5 December 1937
WEEKS, Albert E, Stoker 1c, D/K 23764, Caradoc, 1 April 1934
WEEKS, Ernest H, Leading Stoker, 305276 (Dev), Concord, 22 January 1920

WEEKS, George W S, Chief Petty Officer Mechanic 2c, F 54675, Pembroke, 10 February 1920
WEEKS, John R, Chief Engine Room Artificer 2c, 347574, Ambrose, 13 January 1924
WEEKS, Reginald J C, Marine, 23153 (Ch), Ramillies, 5 June 1928
WEEKS, William B, Boy 1c, JX 127358, Rodney, 11 September 1928
WEIGHILL, Ernest, Signalman, J 64055, Campbell, 27 March 1923
WEIGHTMAN, Leonard, Boy 2c, J 107275, Ganges, 4 June 1923
WEIR, Alexander, Stoker 1c, MC 913 (Ch), Gentian, 15 July 1919
WEIR, William Mc L, Able Seaman, J 41175, Malaya, 17 December 1918
WELBY, Richard M, Captain, Champion, 24 April 1930
WELCH, Charles, Able Seaman, RNVR, Sussex Z 198, Hawke Battalion, RND, 28 January 1919
WELCH, Douglas W R, Stoker 1c, P/KX 75178, Wallace, 10 July 1932
WELCH, G (initial only), Petty Officer, JX 158688, Campbell, 13 January 1939
WELCH, George J, Able Seaman, P/J 10850, Nelson, 5 January 1931
WELCH, James J, Private, RM, S 10383 (Deal), RM Labour Corps, 4 March 1921
WELCH, Richard G, Able Seaman, J 37574, Diomede, 20 November 1926
WELCH, William H M, Stoker 1c, K 18634, L.7, on books of Ambrose, 31 August 1920
WELDON, Bertram de W, Honorary Major, RM, Royal Marines, 7 October 1922
WELLER, Frederick, Able Seaman, J 76350, Cinceria, 19 February 1919
WELLER, William H L, Able Seaman, J 53045, Valerian, 22 October 1926
WELLINGS, Frederick J, Able Seaman, J72593, Pembroke, 7 May 1930
WELLINGTON, Frederick C, Able Seaman, J 49478, Warspite, 10 August 1920
WELLS, Charles T, Able Seaman, J 23612 (Po), L.55, 4 June 1919
WELLS, Edward, Ordinary Seaman, RNVR, London Z 8204, Penarth, 4 February 1919
WELLS, George A, Private, RMLI, 12308 (Ply), Colleen, 11 October 1921
WELLS, James T, Boy Servant, L 11475, Pembroke, 23 February 1919
WELLS, James W, Stoker Petty Officer, D/KX 81583, Thetis, 3 June 1939
WELLS, John A, Able Seaman, RNVR, R 5842, 63rd Divisional Depot Battalion, RND, 30 January 1919
WELLS, John J R, Marine, X 6 (Po), Nelson, 22 October 1928
WELLS, Stephen W, Private, RMLI, 13026 (Ch), Triad, 2 April 1919
WELLS, William A E, Stoker, RAN, 4633, Australia (RAN), 21 September 1919
WESS, Harry, Chief Baker, MMR, 946635, Eaglet, 24 February 1919
WEST, Albert, Able Seaman, J 69054, Revenge, 15 November 1920
WEST, Alexander G, Leading Seaman, D/JX 132508, Drake, 7 July 1937
WEST, Clement F, Leading Telegraphist, P/J 79168, Royal Sovereign, 1 January 1932
WEST, Dick, Petty Officer 2c (Pens), 139435, Royal Navy (demobilised), 21 August 1919
WEST, Frank, Leading Supply Assistant, M 37485, Scarab, 7 September 1928
WEST, Gilbert, Trimmer, RNR, TS 6399, Actaeon, 12 November 1918
WEST, James, Ty/Skipper, RNR, George A West, 13 November 1918

WEST, John G, Leading Telegraphist, P/J 53099, Royal Navy, 23 January 1939

WEST, John T E, Gunner, RMA, RMA 13942, Benbow, 24 September 1920

WEST, Lewis H, Stoker 1c, K 20832 (Po), K.5, 20 January 1921

WEST, Matthew, Deck Hand, RNR, DA 4714, Helmsdale II, 28 February 1919

WEST, Orlando, Petty Officer, J 133, Resolution, 21 September 1925

WEST, Robert H, Able Seaman, 234747, Queen Elizabeth, 13 January 1920

WESTALL, Robert C, Able Seaman, J 28978 (Ch), Erin's Isle, 7 February 1919

WESTBROOK, Cecil F, Officer's Steward 2c, L 6509, Rocket, 3 September 1919

WESTBROOK, William H, Marine, 18320 (Ch), Royal Marines HQ, 2 November 1930

WESTCOTT, Greenfield, Leading Seaman, K 1139 (Ch), L.55, 4 June 1919

WESTGATE, Joseph G, Deck Hand, RNR, DA 8152, Implacable, 2 December 1918

WESTLEY, John, Krooman, Lowestoft, 15 December 1919

WESTMACOTT, James H, Able Seaman, J 95664, Valerian, 22 October 1926

WESTON, Charles E S, Steward, P/L 14519, Nelson, 15 August 1936

WESTON, Sydney H J, Petty Officer, P/J 110315, Vernon, 8 March 1936

WESTWOOD, Albert, Sergeant, RM Police, RMP 80 (Ch), RM P, 20 November 1937

WESTWOOD, J (initial only) C, Leading Stoker, P/KX 80045, Hyperion, 6 November 1938

WESTWOOD, Ronald, Able Seaman, P/JX 145341, Osprey, 28 November 1937

WESTWOOD, Thomas H, Supply Petty Officer, D/M 6150, Caradoc, 10 February 1931

WETHERILL, Joseph W, Able Seaman, J 11196, Pembroke, 3 May 1929

WHALLEY, Albert, Senior Reserve Attendant, M 20518, Garth Castle, 12 November 1918

WHATFORD, Harry A, Able Seaman, J 25900, Vivid, 2 March 1929

WHAYMAN, George, Gunner, RMA, RMA 9052, RM Headquarters, 15 June 1921

WHEADON, John R, Stoker 1c, P/K 21435, Vernon, 1 September 1935

WHEATLAND, Reginald G, Able Seaman, J 18817, Victory I, 22 October 1922

WHEATLEY, Charlie, Ordinary Seaman, SS 9214, Shakespeare, 8 February 1921

WHEATLEY, John W, Engineman, RNR, ES 5070, Gunner, 20 December 1918

WHEATLEY, Thomas E, Stoker 1c, K 17736, Speedy, 23 September 1922

WHEATON, Harold, Bugler, RMLI, 19979 (Ch), Emile Nobel, 21 May 1919

WHEELDON, Harry, Ordnance Artificer, P/M 35305, Nelson, 8 August 1936

WHEELER, Frederic A J, Officer's Cook 3c, P/LX 20123, Winchester, 29 December 1935

WHEELER, Herbert, Telegraphist, P/JX 127710, Victory I, 20 November 1934

WHEELER, Horace A, Petty Officer, J 31616, L.12, 9 July 1929

WHEELER, William E, Leading Telegraphist, C/J 28333, Pembroke, 28 February 1938

WHELTON, John, Stoker 1c, D/KX 75209, Carlisle, 10 February 1934

WHENMEN, William F, Private, RMLI, 10368 (Ply) (RFR B 304), Plymouth Battalion, RND, 20 July 1919

WHIDDETT, Charles, Telegraphist, J 104990, Pembroke, 23 July 1927

WHIFFIN, Arthur C, Shipwright, C/MX 45374, Hawkins, 24 April 1938

WHITAKER, John R, Sergeant, RMLI, 15477 (Po), Portsmouth Division, RMLI, 5 April 1919

WHITBY, James H, Able Seaman, J 45294, Hermes, 26 December 1925

WHITE, Albert J G, Leading Stoker, K 27485, Sandhurst, 23 November 1919

WHITE, Alfred A, Lieutenant, RNVR, Royal Naval Volunteer Reserve, 5 February 1919

WHITE, Arthur G, Stoker 1c, K 18724, Victory, 15 November 1918

WHITE, Charles D, Stoker 1c, P/K 63977, Coventry, 7 November 1930

WHITE, Edmond H, Able Seaman, J 85394, Sepoy, 2 February 1929

WHITE, Edward H, Able Seaman, P/J 102222, Victory, 21 September 1935

WHITE, Ernest C, Quartermaster Sergeant, RM, E 24036 (Ch), Chatham, 29 July 1938

WHITE, Frederick R, Stoker Petty Officer, K 18594, Blake, 14 November 1920

WHITE, George E, Mechanician, P/M 66566, Hawkins, 21 April 1938

WHITE, Gibson J, Shipwright 1c, 342751, CMB.22B, coastal motor boat, 23 July 1919

WHITE, John B, Honorary Captain, RNR, Royal Naval Reserve, 6 January 1934

WHITE, Joseph, Chief Officer, HM Coast Guard, 23 July 1920

WHITE, Joseph F, Leading Stoker, K 16104, Cricket, 30 September 1925

WHITE, Richard F, Mechanician 1c, C/KX 78073, Cumberland, 21 November 1937

WHITE, Robert J, Assistant Steward, MMR, 882944, Hughli, Royal Fleet Auxiliary, 26 April 1919

WHITE, Thomas E, Trimmer, RNR, TS 5619, Idaho, 20 August 1919

WHITE, Victor J, Telegraphist, D/J 136249, Defiance, 13 February 1937

WHITEAR, Joseph H, Stoker 1c, D/K 64153, Ouse, 22 May 1933

WHITEFIELD, Edward, Armourers Crew, M 19227, Greenwich, 10 February 1919

WHITEHEAD, Charles A, Stoker 2c, K 55105, Pembroke, 2 December 1918

WHITEHEAD, Elliott E, Assistant Steward, MMR, 976082, Mariner, 10 March 1919

WHITEHEAD, John W, Signalman, J 31965, Ambrose, 21 February 1926

WHITELAW, Francis, Telegraphist, C/J 108874, Shoreham, 24 April 1934

WHITEWAY, Henry C, Cook, P/MX 47272, Effingham, 2 August 1930

WHITFIELD, George W, Stoker 1c, K 67000, Bruce, 27 March 1928

WHITFIELD, Henry, Deck Hand, RNR, DA 12109, Satellite, 14 November 1918

WHITFORD, Alfred W, Boy 2c, J 96633, Impregnable, 16 August 1920

WHITING, Francis C, Able Seaman, D/JX 127947, M.2, 29 January 1932

WHITING, Frederick J T, Able Seaman, C/JX 129841, L.26, 8 October 1933

WHITING, Walter, Private, RMLI, 118068 (Po), Renown, 5 January 1922

WHITLEY, William, Stoker 1c, C/K 60695, Poseidon, 9 June 1931

WHITMILL, William R, Stoker 1c, K 2651, Jessamine, 13 March 1919

WHITNEY, Edward H, Stoker 1c, K 64268, Gnat, 29 October 1926
WHITNEY, Willie, Able Seaman, C/J 22735, Pembroke, 30 January 1933
WHITTAKER, George, Rev, Chaplain, Capetown Dockyard, 22 June 1936
WHITTAKER, John E, Sub Lieutenant, RNR, Thermol, Royal Fleet Auxiliary, 26 May 1921
WHITTENHAM, Alfred J, Stoker Petty Officer, K 2099, Euraylus, 25 February 1920
WHITTINGTON, Herbert H, Supply Chief Petty Officer, C/M 26033, Pembroke, 22 June 1937
WHITTON, William R, Able Seaman, J 34371, Raleigh, 8 August 1922
WHITWORTH, Arthur, Able Seaman, RNVR, Tyneside Z 8389, Hawke Battalion, RND, 2 April 1919
WHY (no second name listed), Krooman, Dwarf, 27 January 1924
WHYMAN, Edward A, Private, RMLI, 14419 (Ply), RM, 8th Battalion, 2 December 1920
WHYMARK, Alfred, Petty Officer, 190755, Penguin, 15 July 1922

WIBNER, Lewis R, Paymaster Lieutenant Commander, Prince of Wales, 6 June 1920
WICKENDEN, Charles P, Corporal, RM, 20187 (Ply), Devonshire, 4 September 1929
WICKES, Henry T, Signalman, C/J 114687, Pembroke, 14 August 1938
WICKS, Richard W, Lieutenant, Royal Navy, 15 March 1937
WICKS, William C A, Able Seaman, J 14962 (Dev), Searcher, 20 January 1919
WIDGER, Frank, Able Seaman, 124641, Hannibal, 4 February 1919
WIDGER, Kenneth J, Able Seaman, D/SSX 20228, Revenge, 21 October 1938
WIGGETT, George J, Leading Stoker, C/KX 76332, Emerald, 5 November 1935
WIGGIN, John, Petty Officer, 239975, Ganges, 3 May 1926
WIGHT, Robert L, Lieutenant, Vindictive, 13 February 1927
WIGHTMAN, Charles, Ordinary Seaman, RNVR, Clyde Z 9146, James Hunniford, 14 November 1918
WIGHTMAN, William, Engine Room Artificer 1c, RNR, E D 214, Iron Duke, 29 October 1937
WILBY, Cecil F, Petty Officer Telegraphist, J 10920, Malabar, 14 November 1925
WILCOX, Herbert R, Stoker 1c, D/K 63698, Defiance, 6 May 1936
WILCOX, Norman D, Mersey Pilot, Thetis, 3 June 1939
WILD, Victor F, Private, RMLI, 16155 (Po), RM Headquarters, 11 May 1920
WILDER, William G, Stoker 1c, K 14837 (Ch), Dolphin, 23 January 1920
WILDING, Richard H, Able Seaman, D/J 114195, Berwick, 26 September 1931
WILDING, Thomas E, Stoker Petty Officer, K 16770, Catspaw, 31 December 1919
WILDISH, Charles B, Stoker 1c, K 32748, Grampus, 12 February 1919
WILDMAN, Roland S, Able Seaman, C/J 113186, Duchess, 8 December 1935
WILES, Henry C, Able Seaman, P/J 111134, Excellent, 18 April 1932
WILES, Stanley M, Petty Officer 2c, 155727, Research, 28 July 1919
WILKES, Albert H B, Stoker 1c, P/KX 79512, London, 2 April 1934
WILKES, Cyril P, Marine, 20317 (Ply), Cairo, 28 December 1924
WILKES, Stanley W, Lance Corporal, RMLI, 19792 (Ch), 3rd Battalion, RM, 18 May 1919
WILKIE, William J, Corporal, RMLI, 15709 (Po), RM HQ 8th RM Battalion, 15 April 1921
WILKIN, John, Leading Stoker, 226590, Montrose, 6 April 1924
WILKINS, Edward, Stoker 1c, K 23283, Dolphin, 29 April 1923
WILKINSON, Bertrand, Ty/Sub Lieutenant, RNVR, Royal Naval Volunteer Reserve, 11 March 1919
WILKINSON, Frederick C B, Able Seaman, 237559, Fisgard, 13 July 1926
WILKINSON, Harry, Chief Petty Officer, Tyneside Z 10666, Tarlair, 10 February 1919
WILKINSON, Robert, Able Seaman, RNVR, Tyneside Z 3717, Drake Battalion, RND, 9 January 1919
WILKINSON, Sidney, Stoker 1c, K 35069, Britannia, RN College, Dartmouth, 6 November 1926
WILKS, Albert H, Stoker 1c, K 22292, Tiger, 21 March 1920
WILKS, Frank, Petty Officer, J 7669 (Ch), L.55, 4 June 1919
WILLCOX, Norman R, Sergeant, RM, 215999 (Po), St Angelo, 25 August 1933
WILLCOX, Philip G, Leading Seaman, RNVR, Bristol 3/1036, Collingwood Battalion, RND, 28 November 1918
WILLDIGG, George J, Lieutenant Commander, RNR, Oriana, steamship, 23 March 1924
WILLEY, Harold, Private, RMLI, S 668 (Po), 2nd RM Battalion, RND, 6 February 1919
WILLGOSS, William J, Leading Stoker, D/KX 79835, Adventure, 14 June 1935
WILLIAM, George, Krooman, Flora, 21 November 1923
WILLIAMS, Albert E, Stoker Petty Officer, 295842, Victory (ex-Malaya), 13 March 1919
WILLIAMS, Albert J, Able Seaman, J 52287, Vivid, 17 February 1922
WILLIAMS, Archibald F, Signalman, J 10600, Revenge, 12 August 1925
WILLIAMS, Arthur W, Able Seaman, J 21611, Queen Elizabeth, 9 February 1925
WILLIAMS, Askett A, Chief Stoker, 167154, Victory, 5 April 1919
WILLIAMS, David, Leading Stoker, RNR, U 1955, Spiraea, 20 November 1918
WILLIAMS, David, Stoker 1c, D/KX 76557, Vivid, 17 April 1932
WILLIAMS, David J, Rigger, MMR, Hughli, Royal Fleet Auxiliary, 26 April 1919
WILLIAMS, Ernest, Leading Stoker, K 12089, Pembroke, 21 February 1919
WILLIAMS, Ernest, Private, RMLI, 15586 (Po), RM, 8th Battalion, 17 May 1921
WILLIAMS, Francis C J, Joiner 3c, M 13292, Prince Eugene, 18 November 1918
WILLIAMS, Frank, Marine, 16170 (Ply), Devonshire, 27 July 1929
WILLIAMS, Fred, Stoker Petty Officer, K 860, Shannon, 8 February 1919
WILLIAMS, Geoffrey H C, Act/Lieutenant, Catspaw, 31 December 1919
WILLIAMS, George, Able Seaman, 234521, Victory, 22 February 1919
WILLIAMS, George, Boatswain, Pembroke, 7 February 1922
WILLIAMS, George, Signalman, RNVR, London Z 1730, Pembroke, 3 March 1919
WILLIAMS, George S, Able Seaman, J 90464, Pembroke, 6 August 1921
WILLIAMS, Griffith, Leading Stoker, K 1591, Caesar, 22 February 1919
WILLIAMS, Harry C, Chief Engine Room Artificer 1c, P/M 6857, Windsor, 12 March 1934
WILLIAMS, Harvey L, Private, RMLI, 17130 (Po), Portsmouth Division, RMLI, 28 March 1919
WILLIAMS, Henry R, Stoker 1c, K 56132, M.1, 12 November 1925
WILLIAMS, James H, Sick Berth Petty Officer, D/M 24645, Tamar, 21 December 1926
WILLIAMS, James M, Assistant Steward, D/LX 21236, Harebell, 16 March 1932

WILLIAMS, James, Stoker 1c, D/KX 80559, Otway, 24 May 1933
WILLIAMS, John, Warrant Engineer, L.18, 9 February 1923
WILLIAMS, John T, Commissioned Boatswain, HM Dockyard Hong Kong, 21 December 1921
WILLIAMS, Jonathan, Commissioned Mechanician, Ulster Division, RNVR, 17 August 1926
WILLIAMS, Joseph, Private, RMLI, 20082 (Ply), 6th Battalion, RM, 1 January 1919
WILLIAMS, Keroo, Officer's Steward 2c, Dufferin (RIM), 3 May 1919
WILLIAMS, Leonard W, Engine Room Artificer 3c, D/M 36709, M.2, 29 January 1932
WILLIAMS, Nigel R, Sub Lieutenant, FAA Base Training Sqn, Gosport, 5 March 1935
WILLIAMS, Owen J, Deck Hand, RNR, SD 3696, Glendalough, sailing vessel, 16 November 1918
WILLIAMS, Percy M, Able Seaman, 162445, Victory, 23 June 1919
WILLIAMS, Richard A J, Chief Electrical Artificer 2c, D/M 36723, Drake, 14 March 1937
WILLIAMS, Robert, Stoker, RNR, S 2007, Victory, 2 March 1919
WILLIAMS, Thomas, Officer's Steward 4c, L 14619, Vivid, 18 March 1925
WILLIAMS, Trevor, Boy Artisan, M 24913, Indus, 12 February 1919
WILLIAMS, Wilfred T, Paymaster Lieutenant, RNR, Princess Margaret, 19 January 1919
WILLIAMS, William, Able Seaman, SS 2065, Pembroke, 15 February 1919
WILLIAMS, William, Warrant Engineer, Pembroke, 21 April 1920
WILLIAMS, Willam J P, Petty Officer Writer, P/M 26297, Vivid II, 14 December 1926
WILLIAMS, William A, Commander, RNR, President, 8 January 1919
WILLIAMS, William H, Petty Officer, 209267, Dolphin, 20 August 1923
WILLIAMS, William T, Able Seaman, J 63441, Royal Sovereign, 30 December 1918
WILLIAMSON, Donald, Blacksmith, MMR, 904140, City of Perth, 29 November 1918
WILLIAMSON, Frank, Deck Hand, RNR, DA 18345, Cambridge, 13 November 1918
WILLIAMSON, Frank, Signalman, RNVR, Mersey Z 3488, John Robert, 1 February 1919
WILLIAMSON, George E, Lieutenant, Hastings, 29 November 1937
WILLIAMSON, George F, Able Seaman, MMR, 882556, Burma, 3 October 1919
WILLIAMSON, Gilbert D, Telegraphist, J 102111, Clematis, 25 April 1926
WILLIAMSON, Harry, Able Seaman, RNVR, KP 224, Hawke Battalion, RND, 15 March 1919
WILLIAMSON, Henry, Ty/Skipper, RNR, T W Mould, 1 December 1918
WILLIAMSON, William L, Able Seaman, J 22510, Pembroke, 1 March 1920
WILLIE, John H, Stoker 1c, K 30108, Veronica, 17 March 1919
WILLIS, John T, Leading Stoker, K 2295, St Genny, 12 January 1930
WILLIS, John, Stoker 1c, D/KX 81887, Drake, 8 April 1936
WILLOUGHBY, Thomas J, Telegraphist, J 48094, St Genny, 12 January 1930
WILLS, Edward W, Deck Hand, RNR, DA 16496, Ivanhoe, 9 January 1919
WILLS, Gordon, Leading Seaman, SS 1368, Belgic, steamship, 27 April 1919
WILLS, Joseph G, Marine, X 1895 (Po), RM Portsmouth Division, 8 January 1937
WILLS, William H, Sailmaker, 200149, Rinaldo, 13 December 1918
WILLSON, Andrew C E C, Lieutenant, Royal Navy, 28 July 1922
WILLSON, George, Sergeant, RM, 16333 (Ply), Impregnable, 6 October 1926
WILSDON, Frederick P, Stoker 1c, K 39098, Tilbury, 1 March 1919
WILSON, Albert H, Chief Petty Officer Steward, P/L 14604, Hawkins, 12 April 1938
WILSON, Arthur, Sergeant, RM, A 16708, Royal Marines HQ, 8 October 1929
WILSON, Arthur, Trimmer Cook, RNR, TC 801, Pekin, 1 December 1918
WILSON, Charles L, Stoker 1c, K 8293 (Ch), Frostaxe, 29 April 1919
WILSON, Charles, Able Seaman, MMR, 870469, Nero, 29 January 1919
WILSON, Ernest C, Supply Petty Officer, M 12244, Delphinium, 2 July 1929
WILSON, Ernest G W, Telegraphist, C/J 113022, Pembroke, 13 January 1933
WILSON, George F, Deck Hand, RNR, DA 18637, Actaeon, 1 December 1918
WILSON, George J, Stoker Petty Officer, K 10090, Royalist, 11 August 1919
WILSON, Henry M, Sailmaker, P/J 92062, Victory, 2 September 1933
WILSON, Herbert, Deck Hand, RNR, DA 12292, Gunner, 27 April 1919
WILSON, James, Leading Deck Hand, RNR, DA 5204, Thalia, 4 March 1919
WILSON, James, Stoker Petty Officer, K 15592, Pembroke (ex-Blenheim), 21 May 1920
WILSON, John, Commissioned Engineer, Frobisher, 3 January 1929
WILSON, John, Petty Officer, J 71669, L.24, 10 January 1924
WILSON, John H, Petty Officer, P/96906, Warspite, 20 August 1938
WILSON, John L, Deck Hand, RNR, DA 20014, Reporto, 18 August 1919
WILSON, Philip L, Engineer Commander, Belfast, 1 November 1938
WILSON, Thomas, Able Seaman, C/JX 138072, Thetis, 3 June 1939
WILSON, Thomas M, Ordinary Seaman, J 76227 (Po), Windsor, 8 October 1919
WILSON, Thomas S, Leading Stoker, K 14988, Campanula, 14 March 1919
WILSON, William D C, Ordinary Seaman, D/SSX 16520, Drake, 24 November 1935
WILSON, William K, Engine Room Artificer 4c, M 14184 (Ch), Iolaire (Mistletoe, O/P), 1 January 1919
WILTSHIRE, Ernest J, Engine Room Artificer Apprentice, M 37334, Fisgard, 16 April 1921
WILTSHIRE, Richard, Signalman, J 31907 (Dev), K.5, 20 January 1921
WIMBER, Lewis R, Paymaster Lieutenant Commander, President, 6 June 1920
WINCH, William, Stoker 1c, C/KX 81018, Valiant, 12 March 1933
WINCHESTER, Alexander, Engineman, MMR, 975766, Ben Alder, 3 March 1919
WINCLES, Harry, Private, RMLI, S 1463 (Ch), 1st RM Battalion, RND, 7 January 1919
WINDEBANK, Charles, Stoker 1c, 310074, Wolsey, 3 May 1924
WINGFIELD, Harold, Able Seaman, C/JX 128093, M.2, 29 January 1932
WINSPEAR, Albert W, Petty Officer, P/J 92746, Revenge, 27 June 1933
WINSTANLEY, Alfred J G, Engine Room Artificer 3c, M 4807, Dolphin, 10 April 1922

WINSTANLEY, Thomas, Able Seaman, J 906997, Victory, 5 July 1924
WINSTANLEY, Willoughby A, Stoker 1c, K 38497, Pembroke, 25 February 1919
WINSTONE, Raymond, Stoker Petty Officer, 297951, Victory, 1 March 1919
WINTER, Albert, Able Seaman, 194988, Pembroke, 28 April 1922
WINTER, Albert R, Stoker 1c, P/K 65926, Poseidon, 9 June 1931
WINTER, George, Seaman, MMR, 931885, Europa, 29 November 1918
WINTER, Thomas J, Leading Stoker, K 8374, Cheltenham, 18 January 1920
WINZER, Edward A, Colour Sergeant, RM, G 20200 (Ply), Royal Marines HQ Plymouth, 22 March 1938
WISDOM, William J G, Armourers Mate, M 3732, Britomart, 6 May 1920
WISE, David G H, Midshipman, Barham, 3 February 1937
WISE, John D, Midshipman, Iron Duke, 19 November 1919
WISE, William H, Leading Telegraphist, J 30196, H.47, 9 July 1929
WISE, William J, Petty Officer, 239452, L.24, 10 January 1924
WISE, William M, Marine, 18219 (Pens), Royal Marines HQ, 2 January 1925
WISE, William, Leading Stoker, P/K 57961, Royal Sovereign, 29 May 1932
WISKER, William, Sailmakers Mate, 204376, Pembroke (ex-Wildfire), 21 January 1921
WITHERS, Albert W F, Able Seaman, J 98966, Vernon, 16 December 1924
WITHERS, George R, Ordinary Seaman, JX 125605, Eagle, 16 November 1928
WITNEY, Albert W, Able Seaman, RNVR, London Z 2073, Hawke Battalion, RND, 16 February 1919
WITT, Edward F, Private, RMLI, 8840 (Ply), Diana, 28 May 1919

WOOD, Arthur, Stoker 1c, K 46738, Bellerophon, 12 February 1919
WOOD, Charles W, Cook, M 15397, Constance, 31 January 1923
WOOD, Daniel E, Warrant Shipwright, Yarmouth, 3 December 1919
WOOD, Frank, Engine Room Artificer, P/MX 58815, Hood, 17 August 1939
WOOD, Frank L, Stoker 1c, SS 124877, Vivid, 22 January 1920
WOOD, George T, Stoker Petty Officer, K 3120, Repulse, 29 January 1924
WOOD, Harold D, Boy 1c, J 80652 (Dev), Resolution, 8 April 1919
WOOD, Harry H J, Ordnance Artificer 4c, M 36276, Cormorant, 13 March 1923
WOOD, Henry, Boy 2c, JX 161252, Caledonia, 21 June 1939
WOOD, Ira, Leading Cook, M 5872, Wistaria, 5 June 1929
WOOD, James E, 2nd Mate, MMR, St Issey, 23 February 1919
WOOD, Jim, Stoker 1c, P/K 63445, Cormorant, 30 April 1936
WOOD, John, Seaman, RNR, A 6905, Wellaston, steamship, 8 January 1919
WOOD, Joseph W, Able Seaman, J 20639, Columbine (ex-Tourmaline), 26 March 1920
WOOD, Leslie T, Boy Artisan, M 18356, Indus, 13 November 1919
WOOD, Leslie, Boy 1c, J 92369 (Dev), Vivid, 18 April 1921
WOOD, Syme, Stoker 1c, 276822, Victory, 13 December 1918
WOOD, Thomas (real name, but served as Thomas Hallam), Able Seaman, J 19500 (Po), Penarth, 4 February 1919
WOOD, Thomas, Private, RMLI, 18969 (Ch), 3rd Battalion, RM, 16 December 1918
WOOD, William B, Supply Assistant, D/MX 51179, Galatea, 27 January 1937
WOOD, William H, Lieutenant Commander, Hood, 29 June 1939
WOODARD, James, Stoker Petty Officer, 302926, Royal Sovereign, 28 May 1919
WOODBURY, Wilson J, Stoker Petty Officer, K 18627, Acorn, 4 August 1919
WOODCOCK, Frederick C, Able Seaman, J 21383, Ivy, 20 January 1920
WOODCOCK, John O, Ordinary Seaman, RNVR, Tyneside Z 11304, Margaret Ham, 13 November 1918
WOODHOUSE, Frank L, Stoker 1c, D/K 60100, M.2, 29 January 1932
WOODHOUSE, Frederick G H, Able Seaman, J 19535 (Dev), Suffolk, 28 February 1919
WOODLEY, Reginald E, Engine Room Artificer Apprentice, M 27006, Indus, 30 August 1920
WOODMAN, Thomas D, Stoker 1c, K 22098, Vivid, 21 April 1919
WOODROOFE, Robert, Lieutenant, RNR, Royal Naval Reserve, 18 September 1923
WOODRUFF, William H, Marine, 22484 (Ply), Diomede, 25 December 1927
WOODS, Albert, Leading Stoker, K 5318, L.3, 25 May 1928
WOODS, Arthur H, Sailmaker, C/J 43764, Caledonia, 24 September 1937
WOODS, Benjamin, Stoker 1c, K 5904, Victory, 26 November 1918
WOODS, John T, Musician, RMB, RMB 304, RM Eastney, 3 September 1919
WOODS, Roy W, Boy 2c, JX 142281, Ganges, 25 May 1935
WOODSIDE, David, Stoker 1c, K 19058, Hannibal, 30 December 1918
WOODWARD, Arthur H, Coastguardsman 2c, 166560, HM Coastguard Station Felixstowe, 4 June 1919
WOODWARD, Leslie S, Able Seaman, P/J 3739, Hood, 11 April 1931
WOODWARDS, Charles A, Stoker Petty Officer, 281765, Victoria & Albert, Royal Yacht, 17 November 1923
WOOLDRIDGE, Archibald D, Leading Stoker, K 20971, Lucia, 6 August 1920
WOOLLACOTT, Herbert C, Engine Room Artificer 4C, C/MX 47344, York, 5 July 1936
WOOLLARD, Edward R, Able Seaman, J 7042, Platypus, 23 October 1922
WOOLLARD, Edward S, Able Seaman, J 10309 (Po), Erin's Isle, 7 February 1919
WOOLNER, Frederick C, Able Seaman, J 96488, Valerian, 22 October 1926
WOOLNOUGH, James W, Deck Hand, RNR, TS 42, Refundo, 10 February 1919
WOOSTER, Hugh C, Boy 2c, JX 143216, Ganges, 26 April 1935
WOOTTON, William, Stoker Petty Officer, K 2665 (Ch), K.5, 20 January 1921
WORD, Cecil, Leading Stoker, P/K 56310, Malabar, 28 October 1930
WORROLL, Ernest H, Gunner, RMA, RMA 15055, Glory III, 3 May 1919
WORSNOP, Andrew, Able Seaman, RNVR, Mersey Z 1497, Hood Battalion, RND, 6 February 1919
WORTHINGTON, Bernard H, Leading Seaman, D/J 106822, Drake, 29 May 1935
WORTHINGTON, George R, Signalman, D/JX 141740, Drake, 28 April 1938
WOTTON, Arthur J, Electrical Artificer 2c, M 992, Caledon, 13 December 1918
WOTTON, Thomas, Able Seaman, J 5210, Vivid, 8 March 1919

WRAGG, William F, Petty Officer, C/J 12078, Pembroke, 18 August 1932
WRATHMALL, Charles (real name, but served as John Edward Wrathmall), Able Seaman, P/J 37310, M.2, 29 January 1932
WREN, Alfred W, Electrical Artificer 2c, M 7867, Dolphin, 8 July 1923
WREN, Richard E, Petty Officer Steward, P/L 12695, Iron Duke, 28 March 1938

WRIGHT, Albert A, Mechanician, P/K 46909, Resolution, 2 April 1935
WRIGHT, Charles E, Officer's Steward, L 12944, M.1, 12 November 1925
WRIGHT, Frederick C, Stoker 1c, C/K 55064, Sandhurst, 4 March 1932
WRIGHT, Frederick D, Able Seaman, D/J 108741, Furious, 1 August 1933
WRIGHT, Frederick G, Able Seaman, J 99863, M.1, 12 November 1925
WRIGHT, George, Able Seaman, J 33449, Pembroke, 25 October 1920
WRIGHT, Gerald C, Air Mechanic 1c, F 42421, President V, 10 February 1919
WRIGHT, Harold, Able Seaman, J 92721, Vivid, 18 May 1924
WRIGHT, Harry R, Able Seaman, C/JX 130068, Ganges, 19 January 1935
WRIGHT, Henry, Able Seaman, J 25323, Glowworm, 25 August 1919
WRIGHT, James, Signalman, JX 140212, Royal Oak, 23 August 1938
WRIGHT, John H, Stoker 1c, K 57263, Ramillies, 15 May 1920
WRIGHT, John R, Able Seaman, J 93615, Marlborough, 3 May 1922
WRIGHT, Joseph, Stoker 1c, K 11553, Greenwich, 8 August 1920
WRIGHT, Reginald H, Boy 2c, J 114301, Ganges, 16 November 1925
WRIGHT, Warren S, Paymaster Lieutenant, Malaya, 29 January 1926
WRIGHT, William S, Yeoman of Signals, J 31732, Pembroke, 18 June 1930
WRIGHTSON, Charles H, Shipwright 1c, 345525, Dublin, 16 June 1924

WYATT, Ernest S, Sick Berth Attendant, C/M 38908, RN Hospital, Chatham, 30 January 1932
WYATT, Herbert J, Chief Petty Officer Writer, D/M 7266, Greenwich, 7 February 1932
WYKES, Walter A, Able Seaman, P/J 111568, Repulse, 21 March 1937
WYLDBERE-SMITH, Hugh F, Captain (Rtd), Royal Navy, 8 May 1919
WYLIE, Thomas, Steward, MMR, 571796, Eaglet, 8 March 1919
WYNESS, Andrew, Fireman, MMR, Loch Rannock, 9 March 1919
WYNN, Albert, Stoker Petty Officer, K 2436, Valerian, 22 October 1926

Y

YABSLEY, Clarence J H, Joiner 1c, D/M 5726, Vivid, 24 November 1930
YALDEN, Percy W C, Marine, X 498 (Po), Egmont, 26 December 1932
YALLAND, Mark, Stoker 1c, D/KX 76010, Drake, 31 July 1934
YALLOP, Stanley, Able Seaman, C/JX 115315, Pembroke, 5 July 1936
YAPP, Frederick T, Leading Stoker, K 1672, Europa, 6 December 1918
YARLETT, Walter A, Able Seaman, J 52986, Benbow, 31 January 1929
YATES, Albert E, Stoker 1c, D/KX 81352, Thetis, 3 June 1939
YATES, Charles B, Corporal, RMLI, 19287 (Ch), RM, 8th Battalion, 24 July 1920
YATES, Frederick, Able Seaman, RNVR, Tyneside Z 4113, 63rd Machine Gun Battalion, RND, 2 December 1918
YATES, Herbert G, Joiner 1c, M 11871, Eagle, 19 April 1929
YATES, Lewis, Telegraphist, RNVR, Mersey Z 5191, Duchess of Richmond, 28 June 1919
YATES, Patrick, Leading Stoker, K 12972, Albury, 17 May 1927

YEARLING, Charles S, Master at Arms, 201729, Valiant, 21 November 1920
YEATES, Alfred, Private, RM, S 2147 (Deal), 188th Brigade HQ, RND, attached 63rd Divisional Train, 3 December 1918
YELLAND, Ernest J, Stoker 2c, D/KX 92149, Drake, 27 March 1938
YELLOP, Charles E, Petty Officer, J 36297, Ceres, 5 November 1928
YELVERTON, Brian J, Able Seaman, D/J 42355, Furious, 20 May 1935
YEO, Samuel, Officer's Steward 3c, P/L 12209, Victory, 6 April 1931
YEO, William, Leading Stoker, K 27880, Iron Duke, 28 June 1919
YEOMANS, Joseph R, Trimmer, RNR, TS 6030, Restless Wave, 1 January 1919

YORKE, Arthur L, Stoker 1c, K 22187, Moorhen, 20 April 1923
YOST, Edwin W, Signalman, J 28166, Victory, 2 December 1918
YOULES, Edward J, Act/Leading Stoker, D/KX 80198, Thetis, 3 June 1939
YOUNG, Alfred, Officer's Cook 2c, P/L 12499, Esk, 4 August 1938
YOUNG, Alfred H F, Honorary Captain, RNR, Royal Naval Reserve, 4 January 1936
YOUNG, Arthur W, Gunner, RMA, RMA 16509, Queen Elizabeth, 1 December 1920
YOUNG, Arthur W, Stoker, RNR, T 2123, Hyderabad, 7 February 1919
YOUNG, Charles, Coastguardsman 2c, 155620, HM Coastguard Station Costello Bay, 20 May 1920
YOUNG, Charles E, Sergeant, RM, 22052 (Po), Ramillies, 2 March 1939
YOUNG, Christopher, Able Seaman, P/J 94093, Cornflower, 28 September 1932
YOUNG, Edward C R, Engineer Sub Lieutenant, RNR, Teutonic, 29 December 1918
YOUNG, Edward J L, Paymaster Lieutenant Commander, RNR, Royal Naval Reserve, 29 January 1925
YOUNG, Edward V, Ordinary Seaman, RNVR, Bristol Z 10618, Victory, 12 November 1918
YOUNG, James, Civilian Contractor, Thetis, 3 June 1939
YOUNG, Percy, Leading Seaman, RNVR, London Z 553, Pembroke, 26 February 1919
YOUNG, Thomas, Stoker Petty Officer, 217754, Dolphin, 10 October 1923
YOUNG, Thomas E, Able Seaman, D/SSX 14264, Rodney, 19 May 1935
YOUNG, Thompson S, Stoker 1c, P/KX 83234, Royal Navy, 28 May 1938
YOUNG, Walter W, Able Seaman, RNVR, R 5604, Anson Battalion, RND, 21 November 1918
YOUNG, William H, Boatswain, RN College Dartmouth, 11 March 1921
YOUNG, William J, Artificer Apprentice, MX 47662, Fisgard, 3 June 1929
YOUNGS, Frederick W, Boy 2c, J 94152, Powerful, 27 February 1919
YOUSEF, Fareh, Seedie, Caesar, 23 March 1920
YOW, Kan, Able Seaman (Chinese), Tamar, 10 September 1926

YU, Chen C, Boat Boy (Chinese), Tern, 4 August 1932
YULE, David, Signal Boy, RNR, SB 1875, Implacable, 11 April 1919
YUSSUM, Mahamed, Deck Seedie, Hyacinth, 17 November 1918

Z

ZAMMIT, John, Officer's Cook 1c, L 5569, Royal Sovereign, 5 August 1927

ZAMMIT, John, Officer's Steward, E/LX 21659, St Angelo, 10 January 1935

ZAMMIT, Joseph, Petty Officer Steward, E/L 4707, Veteran, 3 April 1935

ROYAL NAVY ROLL OF HONOUR

Between the Wars

1918-1939

Part 2 - by DATE and SHIP

ships lost are in **bold**

1918

Monday, 11 November 1918 – Armistice Day

THE SPANISH INFLUENZA
The pandemic lasted from approximately July 1918 to April 1919 with a major peak in the UK between September 1918 and January 1919. It can be assumed that the vast majority of illness deaths in these periods were due to the Spanish flu.

Tuesday, 12 November 1918

Actaeon, Sheerness
 WEST, Gilbert, Trimmer, RNR, TS 6399, illness

Alert, hired drifter
 CLARK, Joseph, 2nd Hand, RNR, SA 346, illness

Barham, battleship
 COLLINS, Frederick S, Ordinary Seaman, J 82741, illness in UK

Ceto, Ramsgate
 WALKER, John, Able Seaman, RNVR, Clyde Z 6921, illness

Coronado, armed escort ship
 PARKER, William F, Able Seaman, J 254, illness

Crescent, Rosyth
 PENMAN, Andrew, Able Seaman, RNVR, Palace Z 2468, illness in hospital ship Garth Castle in UK

Eslem, Admiralty hired drifter
 MACLEOD, Norman, Deck Hand, RNR, A 7242, illness

Favorita, hired trawler
 PASS, Charles F, Telegraphist, RNVR, Bristol Z 10317, illness

Ganges, Shotley/Harwich
 PIGEON, Harold L, Boy 2c, J 93259, illness

Garth Castle, hospital ship
 WHALLEY, Albert, Senior Reserve Attendant, M 20518, illness

Girl May, hired drifter
 BARBER, Albert V, Deck Hand, RNR, DA 15004, illness

RUSSIAN INTERVENTION

Glory, battleship, Archangel, North Russia
 DEARLOVE, Reginald A, Private, RMLI, 17106 (Ply)

Lilac, sloop
 MASON, Peter, Stoker 1c, K 26961, illness

London, battleship
 AKERS, Henry C, Petty Officer, 206030, drowned

Magpie, depot ship, Yarmouth, IOW
 JORDAN, Richard, Stoker, RNR, S 4347, illness

ML.367, motor launch
 LOWCOCK, Alfred W B, Ty/Lieutenant, RNVR, illness

Pegasus, seaplane carrier
 SCREECH, William, Able Seaman, J 66673, illness

Pembroke, Chatham
 BECK, Sydney, Deck Hand, RNR, SD 2496, illness

Plumpton, paddle minesweeper, mined and beached 19 October 1918, later broken up
 McASKILL, John, Deck Hand, RNR, SD 4519, illness
 (presumably still on books)

President, London
 MOSS, James G, Engineer Lieutenant Commander, illness

RNAS Oldbury, Shropshire
 McKENNA, John, Aircraftsman 1c, F 36250, illness

RND, Anson Battalion, France
 SHORTER, Robert F, Able Seaman, RNVR, R 6001, DOW in UK

Sarpedon, Admiralty-hired trawler
 SNOWDEN, George I, Deck Hand, RNR, DA 12757, illness

Trebiskin, steamship, both drowned
 DOYLE, John, Seaman, RNR, B 5322
 SMITH, Edgar H, Leading Seaman, Newfoundland RNR, X 1204

Vesta, hired trawler
 McASKILL, Malcolm, Leading Seaman, RNR, A 2338, illness

Victor, destroyer
 BAKER, Alfred J, Chief Stoker, 281693, illness

Victory, Portsmouth
 WALTON, Albert, Able Seaman, J 29140, illness
 YOUNG, Edward V, Ordinary Seaman, RNVR, Bristol Z 10618, illness

Wednesday, 13 November 1918

Army, Command Depot, Aldershot
 HAVARD, William D, Able Seaman, RNVR, R 4209, illness in UK

Cambridge, paddle minesweeper
 WILLIAMSON, Frank, Deck Hand, RNR, DA 18345, illness

Charon, whaler, at Dar es Salaam, East Africa
 SPURR, David, Able Seaman, SS 4971, illness

Coningsby, hired trawler
 SLATER, Matthew W, Engineman, RNR, TS 2157, accident

Duchess of Fife, paddle minesweeper
 CLARKE, James C, Seaman, Newfoundland RNR, X 2327, illness

Flexin, steamship
 McLEOD, John, Seaman, RNR, D 2261, illness in Gibraltar

Ganges, Shotley/Harwich
 SMITH, Arthur A, Deck Hand, RNR, DA 5058, illness
 TIDMAN, Robert H, Signal Boy, RNR, SB 2477, illness

George A West, hired drifter
 WEST, James, Ty/Skipper, RNR, illness

Impregnable, Devonport
 ROBERTS, Henry C, Boy 2c, J 89707, illness

Margaret Ham, hired rescue tug
 WOODCOCK, John O, Ordinary Seaman, RNVR, Tyneside Z 11304, accident

P.40, patrol boat
 NASH, Albert, Telegraphist, RNVR, London Z 6563, illness

Peterel, destroyer
 HARDING, Frederick G, Stoker 1c, 304429, illness

RND, 1st RM Battalion
 HAWES, Cyril G, Private, RMLI, S 1619 (Po), German prisoner of war, illness

RND, 63rd Divisional Train
 McDONALD, Edward S, Private, RM, S 2518 (Deal), illness in RN Hospital Haslar

RND, Hood Battalion
 SANDS, William, Able Seaman, RNVR, Tyneside Z 4145, German prisoner of war, illness

Royal Oak, battleship
 ROBINSON, John S, Ty/Instructor Lieutenant, illness

Victor, destroyer
 EDMONDS, Frederick W J, Leading Signalman, J 5921, illness

Vivid, Devonport
 FAWCET, George H, Stoker 1c, K 38574, illness

Woolwich, destroyer depot ship
 EVANS, Robert, Able Seaman, J 28518, illness

Thursday, 14 November 1918

*Armoured cruiser **Cochrane** went aground in the River Mersey and declared total loss. There were no casualties (below, sister-ship Duke of Edinburgh)*

Barham, battleship
 STIRLING, William, Gunner, RMA, RMA 15137, illness in UK

Comrade, hired trawler
 HURR, James D, Deck Hand, RNR, DA 11974, illness

Europa, Mudros, Aegean
 MARKS, Alfred E, Wireless Telegraph Operator, RNR, WTS 375, illness

Ganges, Shotley/Harwich
 CAVE, Percy H E, Leading Seaman, 182484, illness
 HACKING, Harry V, Able Seaman, RNVR, Mersey Z 1786, illness

James Hunniford, Admiralty trawler
 WIGHTMAN, Charles, Ordinary Seaman, RNVR, Clyde Z 9146, illness

Joseph Burgin, Admiralty trawler
 MACAULAY, John, Deck Hand, RNR, DA 19586, illness

Pansy III, hired drifter
 MACLEOD, Murdo, Deck Hand, RNR, DA 12034, illness

Pembroke, Chatham
 LEE, Pierce, Deck Hand, RNR, DA 1420, illness

Petunia, sloop
 BAXTER, Joseph E, Leading Stoker, K 20414, illness

Philol, oiler, Royal Fleet Auxiliary
 COGGIN, Michael, Leading Stoker, MMR, 884479, illness

RM Labour Corps
 HOULIHAN, James, Private, RM, S 14804 (Deal), illness

RND, Collingwood Battalion
 BRUCE, John, Able Seaman, RNVR, Tyneside 2/169, interned in Holland, illness

Royal Arthur, ex-cruiser, submarine depot ship
 ELY, Charles, Stoker 1c, 291586, illness

Satellite, Tyne
 WHITFIELD, Henry, Deck Hand, RNR, DA 12109, illness

Seagull (RCN), Sydney, Cape Breton
 BALL, George B, Wireless Operator, RNCVR, VR 545, illness

Tarlair, Hawkscraig, Fife
 HODKINSON, Enoch D, Ty/Warrant Telegraphist, RNR, illness

Vernon, Portsmouth
 BENNETT, Clifton, Electrical Artificer 5c, M 30467, illness

Victory, Portsmouth
 TURNER, Robert C, Stoker 1c, K 21158, illness

Friday, 15 November 1918

Blake, ex-cruiser, destroyer depot ship
 STONE, John E, Stoker 1c, K 18080, illness

Cufie, steamship
 BEAN, George B, Seaman, RNR, A 7007, illness

Eaglet, Liverpool
 ORME, Joseph, Assistant Steward, MMR, 575280, illness

Ganges, Shotley/Harwich
 BUMFORD, John R, Boy 2c, J 91937, illness

Gibraltar, ex-cruiser, depot ship
 WARD, Cecil C, Signalman, RNVR, Bristol Z 10792, accident

Goissa, Admiralty hired yacht, mined and sunk in Dardanelles
 DONALDSON, William, Fireman, MMR, (no service number listed)
 HACKWORTH, John, 4th Engineer, MMR, (no service number listed)
 KING, Frederick, Greaser, MMR, (no service number listed)
 McCARTHY, James R, Telegraphist, RNVR, London Z 5486
 O'CONNOR, Denis, Trimmer, RNR, TS 7697

Grafton, 1st class cruiser
 ROUQUETTE, Arthur P H, Act/Paymaster Lieutenant Commander, illness

Lilac, sloop
 SCOTT, Edgar J, Leading Stoker, K 5724, illness

ML.73, motor launch
  MULLINS, Edward F, Deck Hand, RNR, DA 13045, illness

Pembroke, Chatham
  BROWN, William, Chief Stoker, 154094, illness

Petunia, sloop
  GRIMSHAW, Francis J, Able Seaman, J 6522, illness

President, London
  CHRISTIAN, Harold, Captain, accident

Prince Eugene, monitor
  CAREY, Michael (real name, but served as William Carter), Stoker 1c, 292476, illness
  MATSON, Charles L, Able Seaman, J 32394, illness

Racehorse, destroyer
  HARPER, James H, Officer's Steward 2c, L 7144, illness

RMA Battalion
  HEARNE, William R, Corporal, RMA, RMA 5030 (RFR B 220), discharged, illness in UK

RND, 63rd Sanitary Section, RM Medical Unit, France
  TATE, Thomas, Staff Sergeant, RM, S 3023 (Deal), illness

RND, Anson Battalion, France
  CRABTREE, George A, Able Seaman, RNVR, Tyneside Z 3348, DOW

RND, Anson Battalion
  SADLER, Frederick, Able Seaman, RNVR, KP 874, discharged, illness in UK

RND, Drake Battalion, France
  BERRY, Samuel, Able Seaman, RNVR, R 1921, DOW

Vaunter, tug
  MARTIN, Aubrey L, Telegraphist, RNVR, Bristol Z 6631, illness

Victory, Portsmouth
  WHITE, Arthur G, Stoker 1c, K 18724, illness

Vivid, Devonport
  JONES, James A, Chief Stoker, 300369, illness

Western Queen, paddle minesweeper
  GOURLAY, James, Deck Hand, RNR, DA 10283, illness

Women's Royal Naval Service
  COURT, Helen I, Steward, WRNS, G 2405, illness in UK

Saturday, 16 November 1918

Ceto, Ramsgate
  BARBER, Arthur, Deck Hand, RNR, DA 8163, illness

Clan Menzies, steamship
  CLARK, William, Seaman, RNR, A 2682, illness

Ganges II, Shotley
  BUTTERWORTH, Arthur, Able Seaman, RNVR, S 1992 (Palace), illness in UK

Glen Usk, paddle minesweeper
  WEBB, William J H, Greaser, MMR, (no service number listed), illness

Glendalough, sailing vessel, lost
  WILLIAMS, Owen J, Deck Hand, RNR, SD 3696

Greenwich, destroyer depot ship
  WATTS, Thomas H, Able Seaman, J 68490 (Po), drowned

Mollusc, mooring vessel
  DENNIS, John S C, Deck Hand, MMR, (no service number listed), illness

Powerful, ex-cruiser, accomodation ship, Portsmouth
  HEWITT, William J, Boy 2c, J 93486, illness

Princess Thyra, steamship
  ALLEN, George, Able Seaman, RNVR, Bristol Z 5190, illness

R R S, hired trawler
  GREY, Arthur T, Ty/Skipper, RNR, illness

RMLI, Chatham Division
  DUNSTAN, George A F, Private, RMLI, S 2745 (Ch), illness
  SNAPE, Edward, Private, RMLI, S 2258 (Ch), illness in UK

RN Depot, Crystal Palace
  BENNETT, Arthur, Ordinary Seaman, RNVR, Tyneside Z 12834, illness

RND, Hood Battalion
  PHILLIPS, George, Able Seaman, RNVR, R 1814, German prisoner of war, illness

Satellite, Tyne
  GELL, William G, Deck Hand, RNR, DA 16266, illness

Vivid, Devonport
  CONNOR, John, Deck Hand, RNR, SD 2647, illness
  DALY, Edward, Stoker 1c, K 54873, illness
  LOVERIDGE, Walter, Ordinary Seaman, J 43419, illness

Sunday, 17 November 1918

Avoca, armed merchant cruiser
  WATT, David, Seaman, RNR, C 1721, illness

Heather, believed decoy sloop (on books of Colleen, Queenstown)
  BULLOCK, Harry, Stoker 1c, K 32792, illness

Conway Castle, hired trawler
  PEARSON, Herbert W, Engineman, RNR, ES 1166, illness

Egmont, Malta
  HALES, Ernest E, Ordinary Seaman, RNVR, London Z 7424, illness

Everilda, steamship
  HARVEY, William J, Leading Seaman, RNR, A 4702, illness

Hecla II, Buncrana
  KELLY, John, Trimmer, RNR, ST 609, illness

Heugh, hired trawler
  EVANS, Richard W, Telegraphist, RNVR, Mersey Z 4039, illness

HM Coast Guard Station Skibbereen
  KERR, Thomas, Boatman, 294815, illness

Hyacinth, cruiser, East Africa Station
  YUSSUM, Mahamed, Deck Seedie, (no service number listed), illness

Kilfullert, patrol gunboat
 SPURGEON, Clement E, Stoker 1c, SS 112997, illness

Medina, destroyer
 LIMBRICK, Harold N, Stoker Petty Officer, 303473, illness

ML.43, motor launch
 FULLARTON, Kenneth, Ty/Lieutenant, RNVR, illness

Norsholt *(ship or establishment not identified)*
 BATES, John T G, Ty/Sub Lieutenant, RNVR, illness

Prince Eugene, monitor
 NEWING, William, Stoker Petty Officer, 280636, illness

RND, 149th (RN) Field Ambulance, RM Medical Unit
 GREENWOOD, Samuel, Private, RM, S 1550 (Deal), illness

RND, 2nd RM Battalion, both German prisoner of war, illness
 CORRIGAN, Patrick, Private, RMLI, S 673 (Po)
 LOVELL, Edgar W, Private, RMLI, S 1989 (Po)

RND, Anson Battalion
 JOHNSTON, William, Ty/Sub Lieutenant, RNVR, prisoner of war, illness

Royal Navy
 FINNIS, Frank, Admiral (ret), illness

Syringa, sloop
 EASON, William H W, Leading Seaman, J 14154, illness

Truculent, destroyer
 BARLOW, Charles E, Engine Room Artificer 3c, M 4609, illness

Western Queen, paddle minesweeper
 BAKER, William W J, Deck Hand, RNR, DA 3575, illness
 DAMMS, George L, Stoker, RNR, S 2046, illness

Wildfire, Sheerness
 LEE, Godfrey B, Stoker, RNR, S 2326, illness

Monday, 18 November 1918

Halcyon, Lowestoft
 BAXTER, George R, Deck Hand, RNR, DA 15977, illness

Lilac, sloop
 HARBOTT, Charles, Leading Stoker, K 13639, illness

Limpet, mooring vessel, Royal Fleet Auxiliary
 JONES, John, Cook, MMR, 898630, illness

Prince Eugene, monitor
 JAMES, Henry, Stoker 1c, K 44628, illness
 WILLIAMS, Francis C J, Joiner 3c, M 13292, illness

RM Engineers
 CLARK, Daniel, Private, RME, RME 8179, illness

RM Labour Corps
 FINNEMORE, George H, Private, RM, S 10853 (Deal), illness

RM, 3rd Battalion
 TRAVERSE, Stephen, Private, RMLI, 17697 (Ch), illness in Turkey

RNAS, 20th Armoured Car Squadron
 DUNN, Herbert O, Air Mechanic 1c, F 1231, illness

RND, 2nd RM Battalion
 THOMPSON, John, Private, RMLI, 15927 (Ply), discharged, illness in UK

RND, Regimental Depot, Aldershot
 MITCHELL, William, Able Seaman, RNVR, R 2702, illness in UK

Satellite, Tyne
 BEATTIE, Peter, Deck Hand, RNR, DA 6432, illness

Tartar, destroyer
 BURDON, John E, Engine Room Artificer 2c, M 11023, illness

Vivid, Devonport
 BIRCH, Fred, Leading Signalman, 236774, illness
 TOBIN, John F A, Trimmer, RNR, TS 8790, illness

WRNS, RAF Eastbourne
 HUNTER, Lucy A, Steward, WRNS, G 2508, illness

Tuesday, 19 November 1918

Barham, battleship
 LITTLE, Dugald C, Armourer's Crew, M 6574, illness in UK

Corfe Castle, steamship
 JONES, Elias, Leading Seaman, RNVR, Wales Z 250, illness

Fylde, hired tug
 MORGAN, Richard, Able Seaman, MMR, 757076, illness

Hawaker, steamship
 HUME, Walter J, Seaman, RNR, B 4017, illness

Hyndford, steamship
 BURRAGE, John, Seaman, Newfoundland RNR, Z 1789, illness

Kildysart, patrol gunboat
 DAVIES, Samuel W, Stoker 1c, K 10515, illness

Maggies, hired drifter
 SMITH, James R, Deck Hand, RNR, DA 6730, illness

Minerva, ex-cruiser, depot ship
 VINEY, Frederick C, Officer's Steward 1c, 365890, died

Peregrine, destroyer
 WALKER, Thomas, Chief Engine Room Artificer 1c, 269982 (Ch), drowned

President, London
 MORRIS, Percy F, Petty Officer 1c, Wales Z 1891, illness

Raven III, hired trawler
 TOMLINSON, William J, Trimmer, RNR, TS 5493, illness

RN Hospital Chatham
 PREVOST, Annette M, Nursing Sister, QARNNS, illness

Teutonic, armed merchant cruiser
 TAYLOR, William, Private, RMLI, 19297 (Ply), illness

Titania, submarine depot ship
 NEWTON, Isaac, Armourer, 342179, illness

Wednesday, 20 November 1918

Armoured Car Division, Russia
 HOWELL, David, Petty Officer Mechanic, F 2722, illness in Syria

Avoca, armed merchant cruiser
CARROLL, Albert E W, Fireman, MMR, 525049, illness

Ceto, Ramsgate
DIKE, Frederick J, Boatswain, 56437, illness

Colossus, battleship
HAYES, John F, Stoker Petty Officer, 303978, illness
JOHNSON, Arthur G, Shipwright 4c, M 31798, illness

Conqueror, battleship
GRANT, Thomas F, Chief Engine Room Artificer 2c, M 17547, accident

Cordelia, light cruiser
BIBBY, John, Able Seaman, J 50577 (Dev), drowned

Eaglet, Liverpool
HOWARD, John, Greaser, MMR, 927433, illness

Epic, hired rescue tug
FLANAGAN, William J, Assistant Cook, MMR, 881022, illness

Prince Eugene, monitor
AYRES, Arthur W, Leading Stoker, K 13360, illness

RND, 150th (RN) Field Ambulance, RM Medical Unit, France
DAVIES, James, Lance Corporal, RM, S 3477 (Deal), illness

RND, 1st RM Battalion, France
PALMER, Charles E, Private, RMLI, S 2690 (Ch), DOW

RND, 1st RM Battalion
ROLLIN, Herbert, Private, RMLI, S 1332 (Po), illness in UK

RND, 63rd Divisional Train
STRUTTON, William F, Private, RM, S 1795 (Deal), illness

Spiraea, fleet sweeping sloop
WILLIAMS, David, Leading Stoker, RNR, U 1955, illness

Sunland, steamship
LEMMEY, Harry, Able Seaman, RNVR, London Z 3010, illness

Valerian, fleet sweeping sloop
SAVORY, Ernest, Able Seaman, 213258, illness

Wildfire, Sheerness
WEBB, William, Stoker Petty Officer, 283774, illness

Thursday, 21 November 1918

Attentive II, Dover
BENTLEY, Joseph H, 2nd Hand, RNR, SA 2047, illness

Barham, battleship
BARNES, Frank V, Stoker 1c, K 5666, illness in UK

Ben Glas, hired trawler
LOADER, Arthur E, Deck Hand, RNR, DA 10563, illness

Conqueror, battleship
SMITH, Samuel E, Bandmaster 2c, RMB 1311, illness

Curacoa, light cruiser
ELLERBECK, George W, Boy 1c, J 79594, illness

J H F, hired drifter
DARNELL, George E, Engineman, RNR, ES 3694, illness

Kilfullert, patrol gunboat
LEY, Ernest A, Able Seaman, 221764, illness

Lilac, sloop
HOOLIHAN, Thomas, Stoker 1c, SS 115558, illness

Minotaur, armoured cruiser
KEELING, Thomas, Gunner, RMA, RMA 15740, illness in UK

Mollusc, mooring vessel, Royal Fleet Auxiliary
SAMUELS, Arthur, Able Seaman, 362723, illness

Patuca, kite balloon ship
GARRETT, Albert E, Private, RMLI, 11656 (Po), illness

Powerful, ex-cruiser, accomodation ship, Portsmouth
CHEESMAN, Donald A, Boy 2c, J 93372, illness

RND, Anson Battalion, France
YOUNG, Walter W, Able Seaman, RNVR, R 5604, illness

Sir John French, hired trawler
COULL, Andrew, 2nd Hand, RNR, SD 757, illness

TB.70, torpedo boat
HOBSON, William, Stoker 1c, 310797, drowned

Thalia, store hulk, Comarty
MARR, William, Engineman, RNR, ES 1290, illness

Undaunted, light cruiser
ABLETT, Joseph H, Sick Berth Steward, 351615, illness

Victory, Portsmouth
SPARROW, George E, 2nd Hand, RNR, DA 17406, illness

Vivid, Devonport
PEARCE, Charles H, Stoker Petty Officer, 308604, illness

Vixen, destroyer
BREDDY, Gilbert, Stoker Petty Officer, K 11187, illness
O'BRIEN, Cornelius, Stoker 1c, K 29524, illness

Friday, 22 November 1918

Army, Command Depot, Aldershot
MACKINNON, John, Able Seaman, RNVR, R 1187, illness in UK

Chelmer, destroyer
MURPHY, Christopher, Stoker 1c, K 26523, illness

Eaglet, Liverpool
O'CARROLL, Kevin, Fireman, MMR, 898499, illness

G.11, submarine, ran aground and wrecked on Northumberland coast *(below, sister-boats G.4 and G.10)*
BACK, George P, Telegraphist, J 40179 (Ch)
FOSTER, Pliny, Stoker 1c, SS 110928 (Dev)

Leonidas, destroyer
 TATHAM, Percival E, Officer's Steward 1c, L 6647, illness

Maidstone, submarine depot ship
 CRAIG, Thomas E, Able Seaman, J 46678 (Po), drowned

Niobe (RCN), ex-cruiser, harbour service, Halifax
 BROWN, John, Able Seaman, RNCVR, VR 3184, illness

Partridge, destroyer, sunk 12 November 1917
 RAPLEY, Horace, Stoker 1c, 223291, German prisoner of war, illness

Pembroke, Chatham
 WATSON, William, Petty Officer, J 7759, illness

Plasma, steamship
 SMITH, Albert, Able Seaman, RNVR, Mersey Z 1325, illness

Powerful, ex-cruiser, accomodation ship, Portsmouth
 FICKLING, Henry P, Boy 2c, J 93378, illness

Raymont, hired trawler
 SAUNDERS, Alfred E, Trimmer Cook, RNR, TE 725, illness

RMA, 526 Siege Battery, attached
 REYNOLDS, Arthur G, Private, RMLI, 16799 (Po), illness

RMLI, 2nd Reserve Battalion
 LLOYD, Daniel, Able Seaman, RNVR, Wales Z 693, illness in UK

RND, 1st RM Battalion, attached Nelson Battalion
 SMITH, Albert G, Able Seaman, RNVR, R 5695, German prisoner of war, illness

RND, 2nd Reserve Battalion
 ANDREWS, Henry G, Ty/Lieutenant Commander, RNVR, illness in UK

Themistocles, steamship
 GOULDING, Albert, Able Seaman, RNVR, Sussex 1/228, DEMS Gunner, on books of President III, illness

Tiger, battlecruiser
 BARTLETT, Leonard G, Able Seaman, J 10066, accident

Vivid, Devonport
 DEAKIN, James, Greaser, MMR, 496680, illness
 FAIRCHILD, Harry J, Chief Petty Officer, 157878, illness

Saturday, 23 November 1918

Abinsi, steamship
 PERRY, Frank W F, Seaman, RNR, A 8572, accident

Attentive, scout cruiser
 FLOOK, Harry, Signalman, RNVR, Wales Z 41, illness

Blake, ex-cruiser, destroyer depot ship
 BAILEY, Newman J, Engine Room Artificer 4c, M 14638, illness

Dianthus, fleet sweeping sloop
 FLYNN, James, Stoker 1c, K 34462, illness

G.11, submarine
 SANDFORD, Richard D, Lieutenant, illness

Ganges II, Shotley
 JONES, Thomas C, Boy 2c, J 92056, illness

RUSSIAN INTERVENTION

Glory, battleship, Archangel, North Russia
 GRAY, Ernest H, Private, RMLI, S 2547 (Ch), illness

Hecla II, Buncrana, Lough Swilly
 CORSTORPHINE, James W, Deck Hand, RNR, DA 10919, illness

Impregnable, Devonport
 COLLINS, Arthur L, Officer's Cook 2c, L 4293, illness

Oanfa, steamship
 TAYLOR, James, Able Seaman, RNVR, Clyde Z 5898, illness

Pembroke, Chatham
 GROVES, Albert E, Officer's Steward 3c, F 37525, illness

President, London
 BURNS, Frederick G, Ty/Lieutenant, RNVR, illness

President V, London
 HARVEY, Charles W, Able Seaman, RNVR, AA 2345, illness

RM, 3rd Battalion
 NETTLETON, George E H, Sergeant, RMLI, 15241 (Ch), illness in Lemnos

Shepherd Boy, hired drifter
 ROBINSON, Robert, Deck Hand, RNR, SD 3036, illness

Spider, hired trawler
 CLARKE, Hugh D, Able Seaman, RNVR, Bristol Z 9166, illness

Superb, battleship
 RUNNICLERS, Frederick J, Able Seaman, SS 5256 (Ch), drowned

Theseus, cruiser
 HORNSBY, Stanley H, Warrant Shipwright, illness

Valiant, battleship
 HIRE, Thomas J, Stoker 1c, 292159, illness

Vintage, hired drifter
 HUBBARD, Frederick, Deck Hand, RNR, DA 3032, illness

Vivid, Devonport
 NICHOLLS, Albert, Petty Officer 1c, 137402, illness

Vivien, destroyer
 DIXON, William H, Stoker Petty Officer, K 1625, illness

Women's Royal Naval Service
 DRYSDALE, Georgina, Telephonist, WRNS, G 668, illness

Sunday, 24 November 1918

Alaburn, hired drifter
 PATRICK, Fred, Telegraphist, RNVR, Tyneside Z 11598, illness

Blake, ex-cruiser, destroyer depot ship
 WALL, Horace, Leading Signalman, 220825, illness

Calypso, light cruiser
 MAULKIN, William H, Leading Seaman, J 7706, illness

Collingwood, battleship
 SIMPSON, Walter, Able Seaman, J 51382, illness

Europa, Mudros, Aegean
 STILL, Jasper, Stoker 1c, K 39625, illness

G.5, submarine
 ATTWOOD, Douglas R, Lieutenant, RNR, illness

Greyhound II, paddle minesweeper
 CHADDOCK, Richard, Chief Steward, MMR, 724836, illness

Hyacinth, 2nd class cruiser
 BAULSON, George, Chief Stoker, 304992, illness

Liberty IV, yacht serving as hospital ship
 SIBLEY, John R, Fireman, MMR, (no service number listed), illness

Maori, destroyer, sunk May 1915
 POPE, James, Seaman, RNR, A 4949, discharged, but service-related illness

Neptune, battleship
 PARKER, Henry, Stoker 1c, K 10078, illness

Pekin, Grimsby
 CUNDY, Thomas, Trimmer, RNR, ST 237, illness

Pembroke, Chatham
 FINDLAY, Charles, Able Seaman, RNVR, Clyde Z 6589, accident

President, London
 DAY, Sydney G, 3rd Writer, M 18560, illness
 PARKINSON, James F, Air Mechanic 1c, F 27459, illness

President IV, London
 SEPHTON, George, Telegraphist, RNVR, Mersey Z 3633, illness

RM Labour Corps
 WALSH, John, Private, RM, S 13001 (Deal), accident in Havre

RM School of Music
 COOPER, Henry, Bandmaster 1c, RMB 1073, illness

RMLI, Portsmouth Division
 SAUNDERS, John H, Private, RMLI, 12164 (Po), illness

RN Depot, Crystal Palace
 BAREHAM, Francis A, Ordinary Seaman, RNVR, London Z 9868, illness

RND, 1st RM Battalion, France
 BURDEN, Edward P, Private, RMLI, S 2503 (Po), illness

RND, Drake Battalion, France
 PHEASANT, Martin A, Able Seaman, RNVR, R 991, DOW

Serbol, oiler, Royal Fleet Auxiliary
 SEAR, William R T, Scullion, MMR, 877632, illness

Victory, Portsmouth
 COATES, Samuel, Ordinary Seaman, J 84904, illness

Women's Royal Naval Service
 CLARKE, Lucie E, Clerk, WRNS, G 6087, illness in UK

Monday, 25 November 1918

Brisk, destroyer
 JAMIESON, John, Stoker Petty Officer, 298536, illness

Colleen, Queenstown
 SHEPHERD, Edward N S, Deck Hand, RNR, DA 13423, illness

Ebenezer, hired drifter
 GORRY, Angus H, 2nd Hand, RNR, DA 12434, illness

Economy, hired drifter
 BREMNER, John, Leading Stoker, SS 101525, illness

George Robinson, hired screw tug
 DUNCAN, James C, Ty/Sub Lieutenant, RNVR, illness

Lily & Maggie, hired drifter
 McFADYEN, John, Engineman, RNR, ES 2563, illness

P.23, patrol boat
 ELLEN, Ernest G, Stoker 1c, K 4481, illness

Pactolus, submarine depot ship
 JENKINS, Albert J, Engineman, RNR, ES 2715, illness

Patuca, ex-armed merchant cruiser, kite balloon ship
 PARFITT, Bob, Private, RMLI, 8576 (Po), illness

Pembroke, Chatham
 FARRIMOND, Joseph, Senior Reserve Attendant, M 9918, illness

Powerful, ex-cruiser, accomodation ship, Portsmouth
 BRAY, William C, Boy 2c, J 87718, illness

Principal, hired drifter
 BRACKENBURY, Albert V, Deck Hand, RNR, DA 6940, illness

RM, 3rd Battalion
 THOMPSON, Edwin, Private, RMLI, 16580 (Ply), illness in Aegean

RMLI, Plymouth Division
 ALLEN, George, Private, RMLI, 14462 (Ply), illness

RND, 63rd Divisional Train, France
 COLE, George, Private, RM, S 2621 (Deal), illness

RND, Regimental HQ, attached to RAF
 DYSON, Henry R, Ty/Sub Lieutenant, RNVR, illness in UK

Royal Navy
 COLSTON, Charles S, Captain, illness

Venerable, battleship
 CAMPBELL, Guy, Act/Paymaster Lieutenant Commander, illness

Tuesday, 26 November 1918

Almanzora, armed merchant cruiser
 TAYLOR, George A, Signalman, RNVR, Tyneside Z 12241, illness

David Ogilvie, Admiralty trawler
 FROW, William, Trimmer, RNR, TS 524, accident

Fifinella, hired trawler
 SHIMMIN, Robert F, Deck Hand, RNR, DA 11025, illness

HM Coastguard Station Cahore, County Wexford, SE Ireland
 CORNICK, Percy J, Leading Boatman, HM Coast Guard, 202822, illness

King George V, battleship
 SPELMAN, John B, Private, RMLI, 15805 (Po), died in UK

Kingfisher, Yarmouth
  PEACH, Reginald H, Act/Ty/Paymaster Lieutenant, RNR, illness

Merlin II, hired trawler
  BRAND, James H, Leading Seaman, RNR, A 5859, illness

Quadrille, tunnel shallow-draught minesweeper
  COLLINS, Reginald C, Ty/Engineer Lieutenant, RNR, illness

Quintia, hired drifter
  MICKLEBOROUGH, William L, Ty/Skipper, RNR, illness

RND, 2nd RM Battalion
  LUCAS, John, Private, RMLI, S 1190 (Po), German prisoner of war, illness

RND, Hawke Battalion
  PLATT, Maurice C, Ty/Sub Lieutenant, RNVR, interned in Holland, illness

Sir John Moore, monitor
  PARKER, Tom, Sub Lieutenant, RNR, illness

Victory, Portsmouth
  WOODS, Benjamin, Stoker 1c, K 5904, illness

Vivid, Devonport
  CAMPKIN, Herbert C, Stoker 2c, K 53408, illness

Wednesday, 27 November 1918

Arrogant, ex-cruiser, submarine depot ship
  MILLS, Walter, Able Seaman, J 60799, illness

Belgol, oiler, Royal Fleet Auxiliary
  HALLETT, Fred, Leading Stoker, MMR, 589058, illness

Bronwen, steamship
  McDONALD, Angus, Leading Seaman, RNR, A 3091, illness

Clonmel, minesweeper
  CHAPLIN, William, Stoker 1c, K 266900, illness

Curacoa, light cruiser
  RIPLEY, John C C, Engine Room Artificer 3c, M 16984, illness

Europa, Mudros, Aegean
  SHUTE, William H, Deck Hand, RNR, DA 6805, illness

Kildysart, patrol gunboat
  EBSWORTH, William F, Stoker 1c, K 41588 (Ch), illness

Lorna, hired yacht
  TOTTENHAM, Charles L, Ty/Lieutenant, RNR, illness

Naval Anti Aircraft Corps, London
  SMITH, Lester H, Able Seaman, RNVR, AA 2752, died

Nugent, destroyer
  SMALLBONE, Alfred, Stoker 1c, K 39531 (Po), drowned

P.23, patrol boat
  FUDGE, John W, Stoker 1c, 308262, illness

P.67, patrol boat
  SUTTON, John, Stoker 1c, SS 112473, illness

President III, London
  TAYLOR, Charles W, Able Seaman, RNVR, Tyneside Z 8097, illness

Pride of Buckie, hired drifter
  STEWART, Charles, Deck Hand, RNR, DA 18072, illness

Prince Rupert, monitor
  PICKUP, William H, Surgeon Lieutenant, illness

Radstock, destroyer
  TICKNER, Stephen, Stoker 1c, K 35723, illness

Restless, destroyer
  DYER, William H, Stoker Petty Officer, K 18819, illness

RM Labour Corps
  LLOYD, John W, Corporal, RM, S 8245 (Deal), illness

RM, 3rd Battalion, all illness in Imbros
  CONBOY, Alexander, Private, RMLI, S 749 (Ply),
  HIGGS, Joseph, Gunner, RMA, RMA 2165
  PRISCOTT, Arthur, Colour Sergeant, RMLI, S 6711 (Po)
  SCOTCHER, Percy E, Gunner, RMA, RMA S 1967

RND, 149th (RN) Field Ambulance, RM Medical Unit, France
  HUDSON, Nathaniel, Private, RM, S 2344 (Deal), illness

Rob Roy, destroyer
  SUDELL, John W, Able Seaman, J 61819, illness

Romilly, hired trawler
  THOMPSON, George (real name, but served as James Casey), Trimmer, RNR, TS 5369, illness

Rugby, minesweeper
  MARTIN, Alexander, Seaman, RNR, A 3059, illness

Vortigern, destroyer
  ARNOLD, Frederick, Leading Telegraphist, J 34941, illness

Thursday, 28 November 1918

Attentive III, Dover
  ISAAC, David, Stoker, RNR, S 4910, illness

C.30, submarine
  STICKLY, Frederick, Petty Officer, 233420, illness in UK

Conflict, destroyer
  LE LION, Philip F, Stoker 1c, K 22356, illness

Dominion, battleship
  MERCER, Stuart W A, Stoker 2c, K 54268, illness

Eaglet, Liverpool
  FARRELL, Michael L, Storekeeper, MMR, 603603, illness

Gainsborough, minesweeper
  RICKETT, Reuben R, Able Seaman, 181006, illness

Ganges, Shotley/Harwich
  BROWN, Ralph, Signal Boy, J 89978, illness
  RHODES, Robert W, Boy 2c, J 93453, illness

Gazelle, hired screw minesweeper
  RANDALL, Albert, Stoker 1c, K 28336, illness

Iolaire, hired yacht
  STRINGLER, Albert, Chief Motor Mechanic, RNVR, MB 1316, illness

John Bradford, Admiralty trawler
  WALTON, Laverick, Trimmer, RNR, TS 788, illness

John Corwarder, Admiralty trawler
 JOHNSON, James, Ty/Skipper, RNR, illness

Loyal, destroyer
 LIPPIETT, Alfred H, Engine Room Artificer 1c, 271673, illness

M.27, monitor
 MOORE, Bertie M, Able Seaman, J 30231, illness

Oak, steamship
 HARVEY, William E, Leading Seaman, RNR, B 5151, illness

Pekin, Grimsby
 BRIGGS, Oscar C, 2nd Hand, RNR, DA 2576, illness

Pelargonium, convoy sloop
 THAIN, Charles, Shipwright 2c, 346319, illness

Pytchley, paddle minesweeper
 MACLEOD, Donald A, Stoker 1c, K 6317, died in UK

RND, Collingwood Battalion, both illness in UK
 MASON, Marcus B (real name, but served as James Biggs), Leading Seaman, 226435
 WILLCOX, Philip G, Leading Seaman, RNVR, Bristol 3/1036

RND, Hawke Battalion
 RAE, John, Able Seaman, RNVR, R 1247, discharged, illness in UK

Topaze, 3rd class cruiser
 REILLY, Trevor B, Ty/Lieutenant, RNR, illness

Friday, 29 November 1918

Actaeon, Sheerness
 ALLEN, Robert, Ty/Lieutenant, RNVR, illness

Almanzora, armed merchant cruiser
 BUCKLEY, Patrick J, Donkeyman, MMR, 600804, illness

Antilochus, steamship
 BLEWETT, Bertie, Able Seaman, RNVR, Bristol Z 1246, illness

Attentive, scout cruiser
 COULL, William, Deck Hand, RNR, DA 11369, illness

City of Perth, hired drifter
 WILLIAMSON, Donald, Blacksmith, MMR, 904140, illness

Colossus, battleship
 MACE, Sidney E, Painter 3c, M 13549, illness

Conflict, destroyer
 FOWKES, Charles W, Stoker 1c, K 12738, illness

Curacoa, light cruiser
 CROFTON, Harold M M, Act/Paymaster Sub Lieutenant, illness

Europa, Mudros, Aegean
 MILLS, Herbert G, Private, RMLI, 14270 (Ch), illness
 WINTER, George, Seaman, MMR, 931885, illness

Hazel, armed boarding steamer
 PLATT, Joseph, Greaser, MMR, 897131, illness

HM Coast Guard Station Swanage
 PAYNE, Tom G C, Signalman, RNVR, Palace Z 1312, illness

J.5, submarine
 TAYLOR, David, Engine Room Artificer 3c, M 5369, illness in UK

Orcoma, armed merchant cruiser
 McKIE, William, Able Seaman, RNVR, Clyde Z 5128, illness

Pembroke, Chatham
 McSHANE, Jeremiah, Leading Stoker, RNR, U 1510, died in UK

President IV, London
 HAVERSON, Frank, Leading Telegraphist, RNVR, London Z 6091, illness

Revenger, hired rescue tug
 McCORMACK, William G, Able Seaman, MMR, 600928, illness

RM Siege Battery
 BROWN, Walter M, Private, RMLI, 15988 (Ch), illness

RND, Hawke Battalion, France
 ROBERTS, Robert W, Able Seaman, RNVR, R 3417, DOW

Sea Sweeper, hired trawler
 FLETCHER, Thomas D, Engineman, RNR, ES 2932, illness

Tartar, destroyer
 EAGER, Albert J, Telegraphist, J 44662, illness

Ursa, destroyer
 BAKER, George W, Leading Seaman, 217831, illness
 FRASER, Henry J W, Officer's Steward 1c, L 4549, illness

Victory, Portsmouth
 McDONALD, Francis, Junior Reserve Attendant, M 34146, illness
 TURNER, Fred, Ordinary Seaman, RNVR, Tyneside Z 13092, illness

Vortigern, destroyer
 PARKER, Edward, Able Seaman, J 36614, illness

Women's Royal Naval Service
 KNOWLES, Alice, Telephonist, WRNS, G 6330, illness

Zaria, squadron supply ship, mercantile fleet auxiliary
 MAIN, Isaac, Engineman, RNR, ES 3260, illness

Saturday, 30 November 1918

Crescent, Rosyth
 CASPALL, William C, Junior Reserve Attendant, M 19971, illness in UK

Cresco, steamship
 REID, William J, Seaman, RNR, A 7833, illness

Ganges, Shotley/Harwich
 ADAMS, John T, Seaman, Newfoundland RNR, X 1516, illness

Ganges II, Shotley
 SMITH, George B, Trimmer, RNR, TS 5477, illness

Halcyon, Lowestoft
 ROWLEY, Arthur, Engine Room Artificer, RNR, EA 1271, illness

Hecla II, Buncrana
 REYNARD, Joseph, Trimmer, MMR, 947298, illness

Hercules, battleship
 JONES, John, Stoker 1c, K 40258, illness

Liberty, destroyer
 BLAKE, William K, Able Seaman, MMR, (no service number listed), illness

Marjoram, fleet sweeping sloop
 MAITLAND, Robert G, Able Seaman, J 70442, illness

ML.318, motor launch
 WEBSTER, William C, Leading Deck Hand, RNR, SD 4685, illness

Mollusc, mooring vessel, Royal Fleet Auxiliary
 GLANVILLE, Patrick, Able Seaman, MMR, 500659, illness

Neptune, battleship
 SELWAY, Upton, Petty Officer, 227897, illness

Parker, flotilla leader
 LAMB, Samuel G, Officer's Steward 2c, L 9093, illness

President, London
 FISHER, D'arcy G, Ty/Sub Lieutenant, RNVR, illness

President III, London
 STANTON, Richard H, Able Seaman, RNVR, London Z 6022, illness

Radstock, destroyer
 GARDNER, Frederick E W, Stoker 1c, K 42033, illness

RND, 1st RM Battalion
 FOWLER, Sidney F, Private, RMLI, S 1604 (Po), interned in Holland, illness

RND, Hawke Battalion
 JARVIS, James H, Able Seaman, RNVR, London Z 3110, illness in UK

Venerable, battleship
 HOOKEY, Samuel W, Stoker Petty Officer, 161337, illness

Victory, Portsmouth
 ALLEN, William T, Chief Sick Berth Steward, 150307, illness

Vivid, Devonport
 JONES, Harold, Signalman, RNVR, Mersey Z 3527, illness

Sunday, 1 December 1918

Actaeon, Sheerness
 WILSON, George F, Deck Hand, RNR, DA 18637, illness

Ambuscade, destroyer
 DAVIS, James, Able Seaman, J 12861 (Dev), drowned

Canada, battleship
 KENNY, Thomas M, Ordinary Seaman, J 86589, illness

Curacao, light cruiser
 SCOREY, Percival L, Warrant Shipwright, illness

MINED AND SUNK OFF THE TYNE

Ethelwulf, ex-hired trawler, returned to mercantile service January 1915
 JEFFERSON, Thomas, Deck Hand, RNR, DA 11417

 SANKEY, Edward F, Telegraphist, RNVR, Mersey Z 1965
 STEEDMAN, Robert, Ty/Skipper, RNR

T W Mould, fishing trawler LH.82, mined and sunk of the Tyne *(total of 10 crew died)*
 COLLIN, James, Deck Hand, RNR, DA 10993
 WILLIAMSON, Henry, Ty/Skipper, RNR

Konakry, steamship, collision
 DOWELL, William E, Gunner, RMA, RMA 11871
 RIDOUT, George W, Gunner, RMA, RMA 10438
 SIMS, Edward E, Gunner, RMA (RMR B 1259), RMA 9544, DEMS Gunner, on books of President III

Pekin, Grimsby
 WILSON, Arthur, Trimmer Cook, RNR, TC 801, illness

Pembroke, Chatham
 ONIONS, Horace F, Able Seaman, J 3176, illness

President III, London
 BAUM, Charles, Leading Seaman, RNVR, Bristol Z 5775, died in Gibraltar

Principal, hired drifter
 KNAGGS, Herbert, Deck Hand, RNR, DA 15743, illness

Queen Victoria, paddle netlayer
 JONES, Edward L, Ty/Lieutenant, RNR, illness

RM, 3rd Battalion
 HORTON, James A, Private, RMLI, 17932 (Ply), killed in accident
 RIDEOUT, Reginald J, Private, RMLI, S 1520 (Po), illness in Lemnos

RMLI, Chatham Division
 CLARKE, Frank, Lance Corporal, RMLI, S 1993 (Ch), illness

RND, Collingwood Battalion
 BARTER, Adrian E, Leading Seaman, RNVR, London 6/3568, ex-prisoner of war, illness in UK

RND, Hawke Battalion
 SHARP, Francis R G, Leading Seaman, RNVR, London Z 2833, illness in UK
 WEBBER, Frederick, Able Seaman, RNVR, R 1544, German prisoner of war, illness

Usk, destroyer
 PAFFEY, Rowland J, Stoker Petty Officer, K 10862, illness

Vera Grace, hired trawler
 WAY, William E, Trimmer, RNR, TS 4137, illness

Woolwich, destroyer depot ship
 GRAHAM, Samuel R, Stoker 1c, K 20381, drowned

Monday, 2 December 1918

Brisbane (RAN), 2nd class cruiser, both illness in Mudros
 CHITTS, Thomas J, Able Seaman, RAN, 2047
 GODIER, John F, Stoker 2c, RAN, 6546

Day Star or Daystar, motor drifter
 HEMPENSTALL, Daniel, Boatswain, MMR, 854217, illness

Implacable, battleship
 WATSON, Robert, Engineman, RNR, ES 651, illness

WESTGATE, Joseph G, Deck Hand, RNR, DA 8152, illness

Pekin, Grimsby
  McLEOD, Alexander, Deck Hand, RNR, DA 12625, illness

Pembroke, Chatham
  WHITEHEAD, Charles A, Stoker 2c, K 55105, illness

President III, London
  SWANTON, Francis J Y, Private, RMLI, 16677 (Ply), illness in UK

RM Labour Corps
  FOSTER, Edward, Private, RM, S 14979 (Deal), accident
  PRYOR, Charles J, Private, RM, S 11645 (Deal), illness

RM Submarine Miners
  PICKWORTH, Alfred N, Private, RMLI, S 2805 (Ch), illness in UK

RND, 63rd Machine Gun Battalion, France
  YATES, Frederick, Able Seaman, RNVR, Tyneside Z 4113, illness

RND, Hood Battalion, France
  GOCHER, Arthur W, Able Seaman, RNVR, R 1614, DOW

Vesper, destroyer
  SLEE, Frederick, Stoker Petty Officer, K 157, illness

Victory, Portsmouth
  THOMPSON, John, Stoker 1c, K 40926, illness
  YOST, Edwin W, Signalman, J 28166, illness

Wheatear, steamship
  HAM, George, Private, RMLI, 3707 (Ply), died in UK

Tuesday, 3 December 1918

CMB.52, coastal motor boat
  TYTE, Frederick C, Motor Mechanic, RNVR, MB 2586, illness

Curacoa, light cruiser
  HARPER, Edward J, Boy 1c, J 80072, illness

Daniel Henley, Admiralty trawler
  BELL, Edwin J, Telegraphist, RNVR, London Z 7057, illness

Dianthus, convoy sloop
  BROWN, Archibald Mc I, Stoker 1c, K 45315, illness

Egmont, Malta
  COX, Lionel W, Cook's Mate, M 20988, illness

Hazel, armed boarding steamer
  MATTHEWS, Edward, Signalman, RNVR, Bristol Z 1576, illness

Ipswich, hired trawler
  GLEESON, John W, Deck Hand, RNR, DA 12512, illness

Pembroke, Chatham
  CLAYTON, James, Reserve Wardmaster, M 9413, accident
  SMITH, William F, Leading Seaman, 211985, illness

Qui Sait, hired drifter
  KETT, Harry, Deck Hand, RNR, DA 8085, illness

RM, 3rd Battalion, both illness in Lemnos
  PLUMMER, John R, Private, RMLI, S 1508 (Ply)
  SKINNER, Robert R, Private, RMLI, 21403 (Ch)

RND, 188th Brigade HQ, attached 63rd Divisional Train, France
  YEATES, Alfred, Private, RM, S 2147 (Deal), illness

RND, 63rd Divisional Train, France
  DAVIES, Arthur H, Private, RM, S 2180 (Deal), illness

Victory, Portsmouth
  HILL, Charles T, Stoker 1c, SS 109647, illness

Vivid, Devonport
  HUNT, James, Seaman, Newfoundland RNR, X 1986, illness

Wednesday, 4 December 1918

Caledonian, steamship
  WATSON, Thomas T, Able Seaman, RNVR, Tyneside Z 6537, illness

County of Nairn, hired drifter
  PLUMMER, William J, Engineman, RNR, TS 6592, illness

Ganges, Shotley/Harwich
  STAFFORD, Herbert C C, Boy 2c, J 93277, illness

Glasgow, 2nd class cruiser
  ELLIOTT, John, Ordinary Seaman, J 78058, illness

Indomitable, battlecruiser
  JONES, Myrddin E, Surgeon Lieutenant, illness

Kildonan Castle, armed merchant cruiser
  LEWIS, Hugh, Ty/Engineer Sub Lieutenant, RNR, illness

Lavatera, hired drifter
  THOMPSON, Albert H, Deck Hand, RNR, DA 6839, illness

London, battleship
  BROOKS, Ernest E, Stoker 1c, K 49403, illness

M.25, monitor
  BYGRAVE, William, Able Seaman, J 22823, accident

Maori, destroyer, sunk May 1915
  RUDDOCK, William T, Stoker 1c, K 5670, German prisoner of war, illness

Miura, hired trawler
  TERRY, Albert E, Deck Hand, RNR, DA 14301, illness

Munster, destroyer
  FERRIS, Ernest J, Officer's Cook 1c, 365682, illness

President III, London
  HOWE, Thomas, Private, RMLI, S 6950 (Ch), illness

Ramillies, battleship
  GREENWOOD, Edward R, Ordinary Seaman, J 57143, illness

RM Labour Corps
  TAYLOR, James, Private, RM, S 14166 (Deal), illness

RM, 3rd Battalion
  CATELINET, John A, Private, RMLI, 19184 (Po), illness in Lemnos

Sceptre, destroyer
  CROSSLEY, James W, Able Seaman, J 53036 (Dev), drowned

William Carr, Admiralty trawler
  SPINKS, Ernest, Engineman, RNR, TS 240, illness

WRNS, London Division
PEARSON, Mabel C, Steward, WRNS, G 4229, illness in UK

Thursday, 5 December 1918

Balmoral, paddle minesweeper
JOHNSTON, John J, Deck Hand, RNR (Shetland Section), L 362, illness

RUSSIAN INTERVENTION

Cassandra, light cruiser, mined and sunk in Gulf of Finland, night of 4th/5th *(below, George Smith)*

EGGLESTON, Charles H, Stoker 1c, K 31712 (Dev)
GIDDY, Joseph, Stoker Petty Officer, 279642 (Dev)
GILHOOLY, John J, Stoker Petty Officer, 305788 (Dev)
KINGSBURY, Walter S, Stoker 2c, K 52659 (Dev)
McGILLVRAY, William, Stoker 1c, 309172 (Dev)
O'BRIEN, Daniel, Mechanician, 304458 (Dev)
PARTRIDGE, Richard H, Stoker 2c, K 43684 (Ch)
PERKINS, Cyril E, Stoker 1c, K 41030 (Dev)
REYNOLDS, Patrick, Stoker Petty Officer, 287229 (Dev)
RYDER, Thomas, Stoker Petty Officer, K 9251 (Dev)
SHRAPNELL, Arthur F, Able Seaman, J 26736 (Dev)

Freesia, hired trawler
CHALMERS, Andrew W, Seaman, RNR, A 8873, drowned

Halcyon II, Lowestoft
SHARMAN, Herbert V, Deck Hand, RNR, DA 18372, illness

Hebburn, steamship
WARD, Thomas, Able Seaman, RNVR, Mersey Z 3368, illness

Jabirn, steamship
PHILLIPS, Richard R, Able Seaman, RNVR, Mersey Z 2508, illness

Munster, destroyer
GAMBLE, Robert L, Able Seaman, J 30047, illness

Pembroke, Chatham
HALLAM, William, Chief Stoker, 284942, illness
LAMB, Charles W, Petty Officer Mechanic, F 2406, illness

RM, 3rd Battalion
LORENZ, Charles, Private, RMLI, S 354 (Ch), illness

RND, 150th (RN) Field Ambulance, RM Medical Unit, assigned Hood Battalion, France
AKED, George W, Able Seaman, RNVR, R 1308, illness

RND, Chatham Battalion
NEWMAN, Albert A, Private, RMLI, 7825 (Ch) (RFR B 800), discharged, illness in UK

RND, Hood Battalion
GUEST, Frank, Able Seaman, RNVR, Tyneside Z 4756, ex-prisoner of war, illness in Holland

Sligo, minesweeper
LAMKIN, John, Stoker 1c, K 31865, accident

RUSSIAN INTERVENTION

Suffolk, armoured cruiser, in Vladivostok
BREWER, Albert E J, Able Seaman, J 51017 (Dev)

Theseus, 1st class cruiser
KELLAND, William, Able Seaman, 214072, illness

Verdun II, paddle minesweeper
GARRIOCK, Andrew, Boatswain, MMR, 502401, illness

Friday, 6 December 1918

Egmont, Malta
MILNER, Frank, Able Seaman, RNVR, Tyneside Z 7991, illness

Europa, Mudros, Aegean
MACDONALD, Harry, Deck Hand, RNR, A 12209, illness
YAPP, Frederick T, Leading Stoker, K 1672, illness

Ganges, Shotley/Harwich
CLARK, Percy E, Boy 2c, J 92931, illness

Halcyon, Lowestoft
MILLER, Herbert, Act/Ty/Paymaster, RNR, illness

Halcyon II, Lowestoft
BECKMAN, Sidney C, Deck Hand, RNR, DA 4627, illness

Kildorrey, patrol gunboat
ALLEN, James H, Stoker 1c, K 29689, illness

ML.218, motor launch
FETHERSTON, John Mc D, Sub Lieutenant, RNVR, illness

Nero, steamship
SHANNON, William, Leading Seaman, RNR, B 5107, accident

Redgauntlet, destroyer
McKENZIE, Maurice, Leading Signalman, 233095, illness

Red Rose, miscellaneous small craft
CROMER, Ernest, Deck Hand, RNR, DA 11688, illness

RM Labour Corps
MONAGHAN, Edward, Private, RM, S 15116 (Deal), illness

RM, 3rd Battalion
BROWN, John W, Private, RMLI, S 236 (Ch), illness in Lemnos

RND, Hood Battalion, France
ROBSON, George, Petty Officer, RNVR, KX 459, illness

RND, Howe Battalion, both discharged, illness in UK
DEADMAN, Arthur, Able Seaman, RNVR, London Z 2788
STOBBS, John Y, Able Seaman, RNVR, Tyneside Z 2619

Victory, Portsmouth
 CHAPMAN, George W, Able Seaman, J 22107, illness

Vivid, Devonport
 HARRISON, Albert E, Signalman, RNVR, Mersey Z 3453, illness

Western Queen, paddle minesweeper
 O'DRISCOLL, Michael D, Ty/Lieutenant, RNR, illness

Saturday, 7 December 1918

Aden Command, attached to
 DE BURGH, Francis V, Commander, RIM, illness

Anthony Aslett, Admiralty trawler
 RHODES, Harry, Deck Hand, RNR, DA 12439, illness

Attentive II, hired drifter
 SKINNER, Benjamin, 1st Writer, 347122, died

Dorothy Rose, hired drifter
 MOYSE, Albert, Engineman, RNR, ES 3862, illness

Duchess of Kent, paddle minesweeper, both drowned
 McBURNEY, David, Trimmer, RNR, ST 3082
 STATTERS, Harold, Signalman, RNVR, Tyneside Z 8699

Halcyon, Lowestoft
 ADAMS, Randal J F, Deck Hand, RNR, SD 2629, illness

Leyland, hired trawler
 GRIFFIN, Edward, Deck Hand, RNR, DA 13903, illness

Lively, destroyer
 COPP, Richard H, Stoker Petty Officer, 295964, illness

Liverpool, 2nd class cruiser
 SELLICK, Leslie J, Able Seaman, J 49989, illness

Mollusc, mooring vessel, Royal Fleet Auxiliary
 PAWSEY, Henry, Fireman, MMR, (no service number listed), illness

Pembroke, Chatham
 TANDY, Frederick, Stoker 1c, 294401, illness

RM Deal
 HIBBERD, Lewis R, Private, RMLI, 21083 (Po), illness

St George, ex-cruiser, destroyer depot ship
 STEWART, William, Leading Seaman, 233149, illness

Stratchmaree, hired trawler
 THOMPSON, John E, Able Seaman, MMR, 934374, accident

Sunday, 8 December 1918

Blue Sky, Admiralty wood drifter
 McLEOD, John, Deck Hand, RNR, DA 3691, died in UK

Botha, destroyer
 BLACK, Benjamin, Stoker 1c, K 31201, illness

Crescent, Rosyth
 HOLT, Benjamin, Able Seaman, J 50716, illness

Hazel, armed boarding steamer
 TRESCOTHIE, Henry, Greaser, MMR, 960802, illness

ML.161, motor launch
 McLELLAN, Duncan, Deck Hand, RNR, SD 4759, illness

Pekin, Grimsby
 PATCHETT, John E, Leading Trimmer, RNR, TS 1312, illness

Pembroke, Chatham
 NASH, Arthur P, Stoker Petty Officer, K 7380, illness

President IV, London
 MAUNDER, Cecil E, Leading Telegraphist, RNVR, ZP 1028, illness

RM Labour Corps
 TORR, John, Private, RM, S 11616 (Deal), illness

RM, 3rd Battalion
 PEART, J R G, Private, RMLI, S 2037 (Ch), illness in Lemnos

Roxburgh, armoured cruiser
 ROBERTS, Roy M, Seaman, Newfoundland RNR, X 2538, illness

Superb, battleship
 STREVENS, Charles E, Boatswain, illness, buried at Sevastopol

TB.82, torpedo boat
 ALEXANDER, Henry, Able Seaman, SS 2011, illness

Tea Rose, hired drifter
 MITCHELL, Cecil C, Deck Hand, RNR, DA 21024, illness

Tigress, destroyer
 BAKER, Harry, Leading Seaman, J 20682, illness

Victory, Portsmouth
 JORDAN, Victor, Leading Stoker, K 22513, illness

Wallington, Immingham
 BARRATT, Walter, Deck Hand, RNR, DA 20489, illness in UK

Monday, 9 December 1918

Basuto, mercantile fleet auxiliary
 BUNTING, Francis, Engineman, MMR, (no service number listed), illness

Cornwall, armoured cruiser
 HAMILTON, James, Corporal, RMLI, 12453 (Ply), illness in Bermuda

Crescent, Rosyth
 MANNING, Frederick J, Able Seaman, MMR, 507186, illness

Lavatera, hired drifter
 GRIFFITHS, Frederick J, Deck Hand, RNR, DA 19120, illness

London, battleship
 BLACKMORE, Charles, Able Seaman, 185210, illness

Lord Nelson, battleship
 SATCHELL, George E, Leading Cook's Mate, M 8061, accident

Nairn, hired yacht
 GEDDES, James, Deck Hand, RNR, DA 5019, illness

Ottelie, hired trawler
 CLARK, George, Engineman, RNR, TS 6440, illness

Pembroke, Chatham
 SIMMONDS, Arthur H, Trimmer, RNR, TS 1966, illness

Peregrine, destroyer
  MEAKIN, William, Ty/Gunner, illness

Queen Elizabeth, battleship
  SUTTON, Wilfrid J, Act/Paymaster Sub Lieutenant, illness in UK

Royal Sovereign, battleship
  WATLING, Victor G, Able Seaman, J 47170, accident

Vernon, Portsmouth
  COMBES, Harry, Able Seaman, J 28776, illness

Tuesday, 10 December 1918

Boadicea II, hired yacht
  ALLSOP, Frederick W, Signalman, RNVR, London Z 5997, illness

Caldy, hired trawler
  SINNOT, William, Trimmer, RNR, TS 7316, illness

Challenger, 2nd class cruiser
  SHORTMAN, James H, Ordinary Seaman, J 77887, illness

Cinceria, hired drifter
  McINTOSH, James, Skipper, MMR, drowned

Colleen, Queenstown
  HARDING, Albert E, Ty/Paymaster Sub Lieutenant, RNR, illness

Earl of Peterborough, monitor
  BYRON, Charles G, Ty/Lieutenant, RNR, illness

Mollusc, mooring vessel, Royal Fleet Auxiliary
  BRYMNER, John, Linesman, MMR, (no service number listed), illness

Pekin, Grimsby
  BECKETT, Albert E, Leading Deck Hand, RNR, DA 7172, illness

Pembroke, Chatham
  BUCKIE, Herbert, Stoker 1c, 291863, illness
  NETTLETON, James W, Able Seaman, 215030, illness

RN Depot, Crystal Palace
  PREECE, Bernard A, Ordinary Seaman, RNVR, Bristol Z 11927, illness

RND, Collingwood Battalion
  FENTON, Samuel, Able Seaman, RNVR, KW 884, accident

Savage, destroyer
  WARD, Edward, Ordinary Seaman, J 73811, illness

Styx, Admiralty whaler
  STOTT, Fred, Ty/Engineer Sub Lieutenant, RNR, illness

Ugie Bank or Ugiebank, hired trawler
  CAMPBELL, Donald, Deck Hand, MMR, 973810, illness

Victory, Portsmouth
  McCLYMONT, John, Deck Hand, RNR, SD 3856, illness

Wallington, Immingham
  BRYANT, George, Engineman, RNR, ES 3152, illness

Woonda, hired rescue tug
  HARVEY, William C, Ordinary Seaman, MMR, 927496, illness

Wednesday, 11 December 1918

Admiralty, Ty/Assistant Inspector of Steel
  GOOCH, Thomas S, Commander, accident

Colleen, Queenstown
  KAYLL, Hugh O, Ty/Lieutenant, RNVR, illness

Egmont, Malta
  GREGSON, Frank, Sergeant, RMLI, 15775 (Po), illness

Gosforth, fleet messenger
  HOLTON, William, Able Seaman, MMR, 810230, illness

Honeysuckle, fleet sweeping sloop
  FORMBY, Henry J C, Ordinary Seaman, J 75191, illness

Marlow, minesweeper
  NELSON, Henry, Leading Stoker, RNR, V 466, illness

Pembroke, Chatham
  SWANSON, Angus S, Deck Hand, RNR, DA 19161, illness

RM Labour Corps
  SHERRY, William, Private, RM, S 11677 (Deal), illness

RM, 3rd Battalion
  FRENCH, William E A, Sergeant, RMLI, 15863 (Ply), illness in Lemnos

RNAS Armoured Cars
  JOHNSTON, James, Gunner, RMA, RMA 7527 (RFR B), discharged, illness in UK

Roxburgh, armoured cruiser
  SIMMONDS, William L, Stoker 1c, K 44781, illness

Sapphire, 3rd class cruiser
  JOHNSON, George F, Private, RMLI, 19362 (Ch), illness

St Vincent, Gosport
  LORAINE, John C, Private, RMLI, 19949 (Po), died in UK

Tobago, destroyer
  TROLLOPE, Douglas K, Lieutenant, illness

Vivid, Devonport
  BOURDEN, Harry H, Seaman, Newfoundland RNR, X 2793, illness

Wallington, Immingham
  McARTHUR, Archibald, Deck Hand, RNR, DA 13257, illness

Thursday, 12 December 1918

Challenger, 2nd class cruiser
  LOADER, Claude A E, Able Seaman, 238326, illness

Europa, Mudros, Aegean
  LINCOLN, Edward A, Stoker 1c, 174298, illness

HM Coastguard Station Whitburn
  LINFORD, Thomas, Leading Boatman, 174122, illness

Nairn, hired yacht
  DAVIDSON, William, Engineman, RNR, ES 2419, illness

P.42, patrol boat
  POLKINGHORNE, James, Stoker Petty Officer, K 1494, illness

Pembroke, Chatham
 BONHAM, William, Stoker 2c, K 54778, illness

RND, 149th (RN) Field Ambulance, RM Medical Unit, attached RND, 63rd Divisional Train
 McLAIN, John W, Private, RM, S 2086 (Deal), illness

Sapphire, 3rd class cruiser
 IZZARD, Thomas, Private, RMLI, 15267 (Ch), illness

St Vincent, Gosport
 SMITH, William, Private, RMLI, 19614 (Po), illness in UK

Superb, battleship
 BROCKS, Leslie B, Officer's Steward 3c, L 8946, illness, buried at Sevastopol

Friday, 13 December 1918

Botha, destroyer
 DISTIN, Alfred, Shipwright 2c, M 6749, illness

Caldy, hired trawler
 RALPH, George W, Able Seaman, RNVR, London Z 4410, illness

Caledon, light cruiser
 WOTTON, Arthur J, Electrical Artificer 2c, M 992, illness

Challenger, 2nd class cruiser
 GUNNINGHAM, Frank, Stoker Petty Officer, 287128, illness
 TUTT, William C E, Petty Officer, 155763, illness

Classin, Admiralty prize trawler
 BAXTER, George, Deck Hand, RNR, DA 1538, illness

Earl of Peterborough, monitor
 MEEHAN, Michael A, Surgeon Lieutenant, illness

Goissa, Admiralty hired yacht, mined and sunk in Dardanelles, 15 November 1918
 PERRY, John F S, Deck Hand, RNR, DA 17585, DOW

Hazel, armed boarding steamer
 BOOTH, Charles, Ty/Lieutenant, RNR, died in Greece

Iliona, hired yacht
 CAREY, William F H, Sergeant, RMA, RMA 7425, illness

Pekin, Grimsby
 FERGUSON, William J, Trimmer, RNR, TS 7543, illness

Princess Ena, fleet messenger
 SKINNER, George, Assistant Cook, MMR, 926367, died

Rinaldo, sloop
 WILLS, William H, Sailmaker, 200149, illness

RM Labour Corps
 MAY, Walter, Corporal, RM, S 11334 (Deal), illness

RN Engineering College Keyham
 VALLANCE, William R, Cadet, illness

Sapphire, 3rd class cruiser
 BROWN, James, Stoker Petty Officer, 288047, illness

Themistocles, steamship
 McDONALD, Angus, Seaman, RNR, A 4433, illness

Victory, Portsmouth
 CORDIER, Albert R, Able Seaman, 190947, illness
 WOOD, Syme, Stoker 1c, 276822, illness

Saturday, 14 December 1918

Adventure, scout cruiser
 LONGTHORPE, Percy, Able Seaman, J 10308, drowned

Botha, destroyer
 ROCHE, Michael H, Stoker 1c, K 6343, illness

Challenger, 2nd class cruiser
 HILL, Hubert, Stoker 1c, K 44813, illness
 MOORE, Frederick F, Painter 1c, M 2593, illness

Cumberland, armoured cruiser
 NOBLE, William, Stoker 1c, K 41261, illness

Egmont, Malta
 PALLETT, Frederick C, Sick Berth Attendant, M 4453, illness

Highland Glen, steamship
 MACKIN, Laurence, Leading Seaman, RNR, B 4800, illness

King Edward, hired drifter
 HARDY, George, Greaser, MMR, (no service number listed), drowned

Medusa II, hired yacht
 FRENCH, Percy, Deck Hand, MMR, (no service number listed), illness

RN Engineering College Keyham
 RITCHIE, Cyril H, Cadet, illness

Satyr, destroyer
 GILLHAM, Alfred, Able Seaman, 195805, accident

Susetta, fleet messenger
 APPLETON, George W, 2nd Officer, MMR, died Red Sea area

Victory, Portsmouth
 VASS, David A, Seaman, RNR, A 5309, illness

Vivid, Devonport
 MOUNTJOY, Robert E, Seaman, RNR, A 5650, illness

Women's Royal Naval Service
 HALL, Sarah A, Cook, WRNS, G 2676, illness

Sunday, 15 December 1918

Alston, steamship
 CARRICK, James A, Seaman, RNR, B 3519, illness

Britannia, battleship, lost 9 November 1918
 SEAMAN, Ernest, Artificer Engineer, DOW in UK

Challenger, 2nd class cruiser
 LANGFORD, Martyn H, Surgeon Lieutenant Commander, illness

Duke, patrol paddle vessel
 NUGENT, Charles R, Leading Telegraphist, J 35887, illness

Europa, Mudros, Aegean
 McPHEE, Neil, Deck Hand, RNR, SD 1715, illness

Grecian Prince, fishing trawler, mined and sunk near Fraserburgh *(seven crew lost in total)*
 SOUTER, John, Leading Deck Hand, RNR, DA 6963

Hermione, 2nd class cruiser
 BINNS, Alfred, Chief Motor Mechanic, RNVR, MB 918, illness
 STONE, Horace G, Ty/Lieutenant, RNVR, illness

Pembroke, Chatham
 MAYLE, George W H, Leading Seaman, 202701, illness

Monday, 16 December 1918

Berberis, fleet sweeping sloop
 BRINCAT, Carmelo, Officer's Cook 2c, L 10884, illness

Challenger, 2nd class cruiser
 MORRISON, Daniel J, Shipwright 1c, 342391, illness

Falstaff, hired trawler
 JENKINSON, George W, Deck Hand, RNR, DA 16193, illness

Hopeful, hired drifter
 PARKER, Reginald H, Deck Hand, RNR, DA 16937, illness

Lord Nelson, battleship
 COLLINS, James, Leading Seaman, J 24829, accident

Ocean Roamer, hired drifter
 WASS, Leonard, Signalman, RNVR, Tyneside Z 8792, illness

Pansy, fleet sweeping sloop
 HALLIGAN, Alexander, Leading Stoker, 288982, illness

Pembroke, Chatham
 PITT, Arthur, Petty Officer, J 838, accident

RM, 3rd Battalion, all illness in Lemnos
 MAHONY, George H, Private, RMLI, 19167 (Po)
 SIMPKIN, Joseph A, Sergeant, RMLI, 12439 (Ch)
 SMART, Percy, Private, RMLI, S 1946 (Po)
 WOOD, Thomas, Private, RMLI, 18969 (Ch)

Victory, Portsmouth
 HEMMING, Charles, Petty Officer, 217661, illness

Tuesday, 17 December 1918

Duke, patrol paddle vessel
 REYNOLDS, Hubert H, Signalman, RNVR, Bristol Z 6879, illness

Egmont, Malta
 BUTTIGIEG, Giovanni, Able Seaman, 228300, illness
 LEWIS, Charles A, Ty/Lieutenant, RNVR, illness

John Corwarder, Admiralty trawler
 MACCUISH, Roderick, Deck Hand, RNR, DA 18329, accident

Malaya, battleship
 WEIR, William Mc L, Able Seaman, J 41175, illness

Pavlova, hired trawler
 IZZARD, Henry W, Engineman, RNR, TS 623, illness

Pembroke, Chatham
 HOOPER, Albert E, Leading Cook's Mate, M 3531, illness

RM, 3rd Battalion, all illness in Lemnos
 ARBERRY, John, Private, RMLI, 19517 (Ply)
 JONES, Albert, Private, RMLI, 14534 (Ply)
 THOMAS, Albert H, Private, RMLI, 19176 (Po)

Vulcan, hired screw tug
 THOMPSON, Arthur, Signalman, RNVR, Tyneside Z 6967, illness

Wednesday, 18 December 1918

Eaglet, Liverpool
 STANSFIELD, Frederick, Trimmer Cook, RNR, TC 1123, illness

Falstaff, hired trawlers
 PITCHERS, Benjamin R, Engineman, RNR, TS 3444, illness

Fylde, hired tug
 DRISCOLL, James, Seaman, RNR, A 9300, illness

ML.486, motor launch
 ROBERTS, Charles F, Deck Hand, RNR, DA 14448, illness

Queen, hired tug
 SAYER, George S, Deck Hand, RNR, DA 18561, illness, buried at Taranto

RM Engineers
 TAYLOR, Henry F C, Private, RME, RME S 4885, illness in UK

RM, 3rd Battalion
 BISSON, John, Private, RMLI, 17006 (Po), illness in Imbros

Sapphire, 3rd class cruiser
 ALEXANDER, Frederick W, Stoker 1c, K 41772, illness

Vereker, 3-masted schooner Q-ship, also known as Viola and Violetta
 CORKE, Bernard A, Able Seaman, MMR, J 747559, drowned

Wireless Telegraph Station Ipswich
 BISHOP, Albert H, Leading Telegraphist, RNVR, London Z 2253, illness

Women's Royal Naval Service, both illness in UK
 BEARDSALL, Elizabeth, Section Leader Steward, WRNS, G 3243
 MACINTOSH, Evelyn M, Assistant Principal, WRNS

Thursday, 19 December 1918

Europa, Mudros, Aegean
 MABBITT, Thomas H W, Blacksmith 1c, M 5712, illness

Glasgow, 2nd class cruiser
 JOHNSTON, John, Chief Engine Room Artificer 2c, 271071, accident

President III, London
 BOYNE, John, Seaman, RNR, A 7628, illness
 THOMSON, James R, Leading Seaman, RNR, A 2202, illness

RM, 3rd Battalion
 MACKENZIE, Alexander S, Private, RMLI, S 2180 (Ply), illness in Mudros

RMLI, Portsmouth Division
 NICOLL, Kenneth C, Sergeant, RMLI, 11676 (Po), illness in UK

St Vincent, Gosport
 JORDAN, John A, Private, RMLI, 18411 (Po), illness in UK

Friday, 20 December 1918

Gitano, steamship, mined
  COOK, Thomas W, Seaman, RNR, A 3740
  CRESSWELL, Ernest, Leading Seaman, RNVR, Tyneside Z 7182
  HARDY, Hercules, Seaman, RNR, B 2981

Godetia, fleet sweeping sloop
  NEEDHAM, Louis, Lieutenant Paymaster, RNR, illness

Gunner, Admiralty trawler
  WHEATLEY, John W, Engineman, RNR, ES 5070, illness

Paxton, hired drifter
  BUGLER, Albert E, Ordinary Seaman, J 77855, illness

Pembroke, Chatham
  CROSSLEY, George, Leading Victualling Assistant, 101470, accident
  DAVIS, William J, Stoker 2c, K 49520, illness

RM Engineers
  BALL, Daniel, Private, RM, RMES 5670, illness

RM, 3rd Battalion
  MAGGINNIS, Richard E, Gunner, RMA, S 2208, illness in Italy

RMLI, Plymouth Division
  BINGHAM, John, Private, RMLI, 7622 (Ply), illness

Spear, destroyer
  HARVEY, Charles, Chief Armourer (Pens), 159077 (Dev), drowned

St Vincent, Gosport
  KING, Edgar W, Leading Seaman, 233441, illness in UK

TB.29, torpedo boat
  EVERETT, George A, Petty Officer, J 21596, illness

Teutonic, armed merchant cruiser
  BRIGGS, Ernest F, Paymaster Sub Lieutenant, RNR, illness

Victory, Portsmouth
  HANLON, John, Leading Seaman, C 3177, illness

Saturday, 21 December 1918

Pasley, destroyer
  TAYLOR, Edwin, Ordinary Seaman, J 50439, illness

President, London
  BAKER, Bertie N, Ty/Sub Lieutenant, RNVR, illness

RMA Eastney
  CATTELL, Charles V, Gunner, RMA, RMA 3102, illness

Vivid, Devonport
  ALMOND, William W, Stoker 1c, K 44070, illness

Warrior, hired yacht
  SYMONS, Thomas H, 3rd Writer, M 18229, illness, buried Arlington, USA

Sunday, 22 December 1918

Crescent, Rosyth
  MURDOCH, Peter, Able Seaman, J 50732, illness in UK

P.66, patrol boat
  PARNELL, Urban O, Able Seaman, J 27739, illness

RM Labour Corps
  COOK, Archibald, Private, RM, S 14426 (Deal), illness

RND, Hawke Battalion
  TAYLOR, Ivor E, Able Seaman, RNVR, Wales Z 634, discharged, illness in UK

Teutonic, armed merchant cruiser
  COWLING, John W, Midshipman, RNR, illness

Valverda, steamship
  HUGHSON, William, Seaman, RNR, B 4848, illness

Vivid, Devonport
  PEARMAIN, Charles, Able Seaman, RNVR, London Z 1281, illness in UK

Monday, 23 December 1918

Anemone, fleet sweeping sloop
  PEEK, Albert E, Yeoman of Signals, 230972, accident

Bryony, convoy sloop
  CROSBIE, Walter, Stoker 1c, K 28791, illness

Cuckoo, ex-gunboat, tender, Devonport
  HANCOCK, Thomas G, Petty Officer 1c, 132137, illness

Europa, Mudros, Aegean
  FRASER, Leonard J, Leading Signalman, 235685, illness

RND, 253rd Divisional Employment Company
  ALLEN, Walter, Able Seaman, RNVR, Tyneside Z 5681, discharged, illness in UK

RND, 2nd RM Battalion
  GOLDSTRAW, Ralph, Corporal, RMLI, 16513 (Po), illness in Germany

Teutonic, armed merchant cruiser
  HULSE, William, Boilermaker, MMR, 89596, illness

Tiger, battlecruiser
  RUSH, John, Stoker, RNR, V 457, illness

Vivid, Devonport
  TAMBLIN, Frederick T, Ordinary Seaman, J 53828, illness

Warrior, hired yacht
  SCHOFIELD, James, Private, RMLI, 11561 (Po), illness, buried Arlington, USA

Tuesday, 24 December 1918

Achilles, armoured cruiser
  JANES, Frederick, Ordinary Seaman, J 89461, illness

Agadir, hospital ship
  HARGREAVES, David, Senior Reserve Attendant, M 9843, illness

Badger, destroyer
  HARDY, William H, Lieutenant, illness

Caesar, battleship
  COLEMAN, James, Deck Hand, RNR, DA 16307, drowned

Courtfield, steamship
 PULMAN, Arthur, Leading Seaman, RNVR, London Z 2865, illness

Egmont, Malta
 RUCK-KEENE, Ernest L, Lieutenant, drowned

George Borthwick, Admiralty trawler
 GOSLIN, Joseph W, Deck Hand, RNR, DA 15349, illness

Queen, hired tug
 McLENNAN, Murdo, Deck Hand, RNR, DA 18784, illness, buried at Malta

RM Labour Corps
 PARSONS, William, Private, RM, S 11118 (Deal), illness

RND, Drake Battalion
 CREED, Beauford H, Able Seaman, RNVR, R 4944, illness in Germany

St Vincent, Gosport
 SAUNDERS, Ernest J, Stoker Petty Officer, K 11571, illness

Tyrant, destroyer
 BIGWOOD, George R, Stoker 1c, SS 112779, illness

Vernon, Portsmouth
 GRIFFITHS, Harold W J S, Electrical Artificer 5c, M 30408, illness

Victory, Portsmouth
 DAVIDSON, Alexander, Chief Shipwright 2c, 343859, illness

Zaria, squadron supply ship, mercantile fleet auxiliary
 NEAL, Henry, Trimmer, RNR, TS 2240, illness

Wednesday, 25 December 1918

Balmoral Castle, hired trawler
 MACKINNON, John, 2nd Hand, RNR, DA 10750, illness

Diana, 2nd class cruiser
 RUSTON, James W F, Private, RMLI, 19243 (Ch), illness

Doris, 2nd class cruiser
 CURTIS, Arthur, Petty Officer, 230628, illness

Egmont, Malta
 DUPEN, Arthur P L, Engineer Captain, accident, DOI

Gunner, Admiralty trawler
 PATTERSON, John, Trimmer, RNR, TS 5167, illness

Liverpool, 2nd class cruiser
 HILL, Ernest, Able Seaman, 148261, illness

Torch, destroyer
 SHEARER, Frederick, Able Seaman, J 30199 (Po), accident

Victory, Portsmouth
 BYCROFT, George E, Stoker Petty Officer, 310823, accident

Thursday, 26 December 1918

King George V, battleship
 HENRY, Robert, Private, RMLI, S 588 (Po), died in UK

Pembroke, Chatham
 COLLYER, Henry G, Leading Seaman, J 58, drowned

Saranac, steamship
 McHUGO, Henry E, Private, RMLI, 12125 (Ch), drowned

TB.17, torpedo boat
 MADDEN, Frank H, Leading Cook's Mate, M 3053, illness

TB.18, torpedo boat
 RANKIN, John, Leading Signalman, RNVR, Clyde Z 10, illness

Vivid, Devonport
 PERRY, Arthur W, Leading Stoker, K 21312, illness

Friday, 27 December 1918

Attentive III, hired trawler
 TATTON, Archibald, Engineman, RNR, ES 3728, illness

Cormorant, Gibraltar/Ascension Island
 CREBBIN, George, Private, RMLI, 13568 (Ply), accident in St Helena

Fanad Head, steamship
 BAIN, William, Seaman, RNR, A 9221, illness

Linmere, steamship
 MARKS, Nathan, Able Seaman, RNVR, London Z 5421, illness

Pembroke, Chatham
 EDGAR, Frederick W, Stoker 1c, 160092, illness

RM Labour Corps
 WAKEHAM, John, Private, RM, S 13624 (Deal), accident

Tyrant, destroyer
 THOMPSON, Joseph H, Able Seaman, J 46436, illness

Vernon, Portsmouth
 BULLEN, Albert T W, Electrical Artificer 5c, M 30451, illness

Victory, Portsmouth
 GREEN, Lawrence, Stoker 1c, K 48925, illness
 SPARROW, George R S, Chief Sick Berth Steward, 137897, illness

Saturday, 28 December 1918

Ark Royal, seaplane carrier
 MORTON, William M, Engineer Lieutenant, illness

Clinit, vessel not known, presumably miscellaneous small craft
 DOBSON, Herbert, Able Seaman, 223645, illness, buried at Accrington

Crescent, Rosyth
 WARREN, George A, Chief Yeoman of Signals, 160645, illness

Powerful, ex-cruiser, accommodation ship, Portsmouth
 EASTWOOD, Frank, Boy 2c, J 92268, illness
 SHIRLEY, Henry C, Boy 2c, J 93559, illness

RM Labour Corps
 STARKIE, Henry, Private, RM, S 11625 (Deal), illness

RMLI, Chatham Division
 GOODCHILD, Alfred E, Private, RMLI, 21889 (Ch), illness

Sunday, 29 December 1918

RUSSIAN INTERVENTION

Glory, battleship, Archangel, North Russia
  FAWCETT, Henry, Major, RMLI, accidently killed

———

Hazel, armed boarding steamer
  MAGEE, William, Greaser, MMR, 960901, illness

New Zealand, battlecruiser
  HUMPAGE, William T, Officer's Cook 1c, L 6176, illness

Robert Barton, Admiralty trawler
  HOLNESS, Thomas H, 2nd Hand, RNR, DA 16328, illness

RMA, 3rd Battery, Sevastopol
  PUPLET, Joseph R, Gunner, RMA, RMA S 1973, illness

RND, Plymouth Battalion
  HARDING, Kenneth G, Private, RMLI, 16409 (Ply), discharged, illness in UK

Teutonic, armed merchant cruiser
  YOUNG, Edward C R, Engineer Sub Lieutenant, RNR, illness

Vivid, Devonport
  LONG, Henry G, Stoker 2c, K 52822, illness

Monday, 30 December 1918

Ardgarvez, steamship
  MACLEOD, Donald, Leading Seaman, A 6994, illness

Conqueror, battleship
  HODGE, Harold, Petty Officer, J 1248, illness

Crescent, Rosyth
  JOHNSON, John E, Ordinary Seaman, MMR, 977324, drowned

Hannibal, battleship
  WOODSIDE, David, Stoker 1c, K 19058, accident

Kunishi, hired trawler
  MESSENGER, William G, Lieutenant, RNR, illness

New Zealand, battlecruiser
  ROWSE, Aaron C, Stoker 1c, 296287, illness

Osea, Clacton-on-Sea, Essex
  TAYLOR, Thomas W, Stoker 2c, SS 119041, illness

Pembroke, Chatham
  GRAHAM, Roderick, Seaman, RNR, C 1815, illness

Resolution, battleship
  BRACEGIRDLE, James E, Ordinary Seaman, J 76736, illness

RND, 63rd Divisional Train
  EVERETT, Walter H, Private, RM, S 2534 (Deal), illness in RN Hospital Haslar

Royal Sovereign, battleship
  WILLIAMS, William T, Able Seaman, J 63441, illness

William Bond, Admiralty trawler
  PATERSON, John, Trimmer, RNR, TS 3667, illness

Tuesday, 31 December 1918

Mersey, monitor
  MENDHAM, Edward, Private, RMLI, 12147 (Po), illness

ML.440, motor launch
  HEWES, Albert, Deck Hand, RNR, DA 13146, illness

Reclaim, hired drifter
  DORRELL, Alfred E, Ordinary Seaman, J 71751, drowned

RM Labour Corps
  GREGORY, Edward, Private, RM, S 9447 (Deal), illness

TB.18, torpedo boat
  BUXTON, James F, Able Seaman, J 78202, illness

1919

Wednesday, 1 January 1919

Abeille, miscellaneous small craft
 DIXON, Herbert, Able Seaman, J 11166, illness in Gibraltar

Cymric, auxiliary schooner Q-ship
 BARR, Walter, Cook, MMR, 821587, illness

Fox, 2nd class cruiser
 MATTHEWS, Ernest E, Stoker 1c, K 37610, illness

Iolaire, Admiralty yacht, struck Beasts of Holm rock outside Stornoway Harbour, Hebrides, lost *(below)*

BEATON, Alex, Able Seaman, MMR, 968068, (Rose II, O/P)
BROWN, Ernest A, Trimmer Cook, RNR, TC 902
BUCHANAN, Peter, Seaman, RNR, A 7700, (Pembroke, O/P)
CAMPBELL, Alexander, Deck Hand, RNR, DA 11999, (Venerable, O/P)
CAMPBELL, Alexander, Deck Hand, RNR, DA 13353, (Venerable, O/P)
CAMPBELL, Alexander, Leading Seaman, RNR, C 2999, (Victory, O/P)
CAMPBELL, Angus, Seaman, RNR, C 3590, (Excellent, O/P)
CAMPBELL, Donald, Leading Seaman, RNR, C 2058, (Pembroke, O/P)
CAMPBELL, Donald, Seaman, RNR, B 3356, (Victory, O/P)
CAMPBELL, Kenneth, Seaman, RNR, A 4804, (Galatea, O/P)
CAMPBELL, Murdo, Deck Hand, RNR, DA 20536, (Matthew Flynn, O/P)
COTTER, Leonard E, Lieutenant, RNR
CRICHTON, Angus, Seaman, RNR, B 2687, (Ganges II, O/P)
CRICHTON, Donald, Seaman, RNR, A 9066, (Pembroke, O/P)
DEWSBURY, Charles, Leading Deck Hand, MMR, (no service number listed)
FERGUSON, Murdo, Deck Hand, RNR, SD 258, (Morgan Jones, O/P)
GEORGE, Joseph W, Fireman, MMR, (no service number listed)
GILLIES, Angus, Seaman, RNR, A 4502, (Seahorse, O/P)
GILLIES, Donald W, Seaman, RNR, A 3309, (Pembroke, O/P)
HARRIS, Thomas E H, Greaser, MMR, (no service number listed)
HEAD, Herbert W, Private, RMLI, 11997 (Po)
HENLEY, Alfred, Cook, MMR, (no service number listed)
HUMPHREY, Frank, Steward, MMR, (no service number listed)
LEGGETT, Ernest, Deck Hand, MMR, (no service number listed)
MACARTHUR, Donald, Deck Hand, RNR, SD 4443, (Implacable, O/P)
MACASKILL, John, Seaman, RNR, A 3397, (Redoubtable, O/P)
MACASKILL, John, Deck Hand, RNR, 14567, (Sir John Fitzgerald, O/P)
MACASKILL, John, Leading Deck Hand, RNR, DA 9635
MACASKILL, John A, Signaller, RNVR, Clyde Z 8453, (Vivid, O/P)
MACAULAY, Donald, Deck Hand, RNR, A 2576, (Gunner, O/P)
MACAULAY, Donald, Deck Hand, RNR, SD 2658, (Max Pemberton, O/P)
MACAULAY, John, Seaman, RNR, C 1567, (Impericuse, O/P)
MACAULAY, Murdo, Deck Hand, RNR, SD 4004
MACDONALD, Alexander, 2nd Hand, RNR, DA 11708, (Pembroke, O/P)
MACDONALD, Angus, Seaman, RNR, D 1830, (Imperieuse, O/P)
MACDONALD, Angus, Seaman, RNR, A 4554, (Kent, O/P)
MACDONALD, Angus, Deck Hand, RNR, SD 2597, (Primrose, O/P)
MACDONALD, Donald, Leading Deck Hand, RNR, DA 12453, (Pembroke, O/P)
MACDONALD, Donald, Seaman, RNR, A 5296, (Vernon, O/P)
MACDONALD, Donald, Seaman, RNR, C 2373
MACDONALD, Ewen, Deck Hand, RNR, DA 19896, (John Gray, O/P)
MACDONALD, John, Leading Seaman, RNR, C 2443, (Arrogant, O/P)
MACDONALD, John, Leading Seaman, RNR, C 2554, (Arrogant, O/P)
MACDONALD, John, Deck Hand, RNR, DA 19654, (Boy George III, O/P)
MACDONALD, John, Seaman, RNR, B 3339, (Emperor of India, O/P)
MACDONALD, John, Deck Hand, RNR, DA 21078, (Genia, O/P)
MACDONALD, Malcolm, Seaman, RNR, C 1874, (Victory, O/P)
MACDONALD, Murdo, Deck Hand, RNR, DA 11997, (Aspire, O/P)
MACDONALD, Murdo, Seaman, RNR, A 9534, (Pembroke, O/P)
MACDONALD, Murdo, Deck Hand, RNR, DA 20516, (Venerable, O/P)
MACDONALD, William, Deck Hand, RNR, DA 1436, (Surf, O/P)
MACINNES, David, Deck Hand, RNR, DA 19531, (Daniel Henry, O/P)
MACIVER, Malcolm, Seaman, RNR, A 2778, (Victory, O/P)
MACIVER, Malcolm, Deck Hand, RNR, DA 10235
MACKAY, Angus, 2nd Hand, RNR, D 2258
MACKAY, Donald, Deck Hand, RNR, DA 12090
MACKAY, Malcolm, Seaman, RNR, A 7699, (Pembroke, O/P)
MACKAY, Murdo, Deck Hand, RNR, DA 16652, (Shikari II, O/P)
MACKAY, Murdo, Seaman, RNR, B 4511
MACKAY, Norman, Seaman, RNR, A 9494, (Pembroke, O/P)
MACKAY, William, Signalman, RNVR, Clyde Z 8218, (Vivid, O/P)
MACKENZIE, Alexander, Deck Hand, RNR, DA 12080, (Mary, O/P)
MACKENZIE, Alexander, Seaman, RNR, C 3360
MACKENZIE, Donald, Seaman, MMR, 967820, (Wickstead, O/P)
MACKENZIE, John, Seaman, RNR, C 2038, (Victory, O/P)
MACKENZIE, John, Seaman, RNR, A 5937, (Vivid III, ex-Albemarle, O/P)
MACKENZIE, Kenneth, Seaman, RNR, A 3046
MACKENZIE, Murdo, Seaman, RNR, C 2793, (President, O/P)
MACKENZIE, Norman, Deck Hand, RNR, DA 20072, (Victory, O/P)
MACKILLOP, Norman, Seaman, RNR, A 9522, (Pembroke, O/P)
MACKINNION, Murdo, Deck Hand, RNR, DA 21209, (Eddy, O/P)
MACLEAN, Donald, Seaman, RNR, B 2820, (Colleen, O/P)
MACLEAN, Kenneth, Deck Hand, RNR, DA 20994, (Venerable, O/P)
MACLEAN, Malcolm, Seaman, RNR, B 4280
MACLEAN, Murdo, Deck Hand, MMR, 947252, (Snipe, O/P)

MACLEOD, Alexander, Deck Hand, RNR, DA 17041, (Vivid, O/P)
MACLEOD, Alexander J, Deck Hand, RNR, DA 20422
MACLEOD, Allan, Seaman, RNR, A 4661, (President III, O/P)
MACLEOD, Donald, Deck Hand, RNR, SD 4125, (Beatrice, O/P)
MACLEOD, Donald, Ordinary Seaman, RNVR, Clyde Z 9964, (Crystal Palace, O/P)
MACLEOD, Donald, Seaman, RNR, A 3329, (Victory, O/P)
MACLEOD, Donald, Deck Hand, RNR, SD 3968, (Victory, O/P)
MACLEOD, Donald, Deck Hand, RNR, DA 4944
MACLEOD, Donald, Deck Hand, RNR, DA 6665
MACLEOD, John, Mate, MMR, (no service number listed), (Cornrig, O/P)
MACLEOD, John, Seaman, RNR, B 2736, (Excellent, O/P)
MACLEOD, John, Deck Hand, RNR, DA 19890, (Implacable, O/P)
MACLEOD, John, Deck Hand, RNR, SD 4435, (ML.502, O/P)
MACLEOD, M. (initial only), Leading Seaman, RNR, A 5478
MACLEOD, Malcolm, Able Seaman, MMR, 973832, (Agnes Nutten, O/P)
MACLEOD, Malcolm, Ordinary Seaman, J 65506 (Dev), (Maidstone, O/P)
MACLEOD, Malcolm, Leading Deck Hand, RNR, SD 4793, (ML.485, O/P)
MACLEOD, Malcolm, Deck Hand, RNR, DA 20774, (Sabreur, O/P)
MACLEOD, Murdo, Able Seaman, J 76479 (Dev), (Revenge, O/P)
MACLEOD, Norman, Trimmer Cook, RNR, TC 1186, (Venerable, O/P)
MACLEOD, Norman, Leading Seaman, RNR, A 4803
MACLEOD, Norman, Seaman, RNR, C 3343
MACLEOD, William, Deck Hand, RNR, DA 14603, (Dreel Castle, O/P)
MACPHAIL, Kenneth, Seaman, RNR, A 3320, (Pembroke, O/P)
MACPHAIL, Norman, Deck Hand, RNR, DA 14663, (Venerable, O/P)
MACRITCHIE, Donald, Cooper 4c, M 23885 (Ch), (Pembroke, O/P)
MACRITCHIE, Donald, Deck Hand, RNR, DA 13258, (Scarboro, O/P)
MARINER, Henry O, Deck Hand, MMR, 821982
MARTIN, Malcolm, Deck Hand, RNR, DA 12067, (Pembroke, O/P)
MARTIN, Norman, Seaman, RNR, C 3397, (Victory, O/P)
MASON, Reginald G W, Commander, RNR
MATHESON, Angus, Deck Hand, RNR, DA 18694, (Winner, O/P)
MATHESON, Malcolm, Deck Hand, RNR, DA 11907, drowned in Iceland, (O/P)
MATTHEWS, Albert R, Leading Victualling Assistant, M 15986
McASKILL, Donald, Deck Hand, RNR, DA 21143, (Gunner, O/P)
McASKILL, Donald, Seaman, RNR, A 7041, (Sigismund, O/P)
McAULAY, Donald, Seaman, RNR, C 2065, (Emperor of India, O/P)
McAULAY, Donald M, Deck Hand, RNR, SD 4363, (ML.372, O/P)
McCARTHY, Fred C, Carpenter, MMR, (no service number listed)
McDONALD, Alexander, Leading Seaman, C 2046, (Nairn, O/P)
McDONALD, David, Signal Boy, RNR, SB 1265
McDONALD, Donald, Leading Deck Hand, RNR, SD 3516, (Dreel Castle, O/P)
McDONALD, Donald, Leading Seaman, RNR, B 2688, (Ganges, O/P)
McDONALD, Donald, Deck Hand, RNR, DA 17809, (Santora, O/P)
McDONALD, Donald, Seaman, RNR, A 5351, (SS Mandala, O/P)
McDONALD, John, Seaman, RNR, A 3074, (Emperor of India, O/P)
McDONALD, John, Seaman, RNR, A 4490, (Seahorse, O/P)
McDONALD, John, Seaman, RNR, A 2558, (Venerable, O/P)
McDONALD, Roderick J, Seaman, RNR, A 2966, (Wallington, O/P)
McINNES, Malcolm, Seaman, RNR, A 8896, (Dublin, O/P)
McIVER, Alexander, Leading Seaman, C 1691
McIVER, Angus, Seaman, RNR, C 1855
McIVER, Donald, Deck Hand, RNR, DA 18720
McIVER, John, Seaman, RNR, A 2496, (Letterflourie, O/P)
McIVER, John, Seaman, RNR, C 2619, (Victory, O/P)
McIVER, John, Mate, MMR, (no service number listed)
McIVER, Murdo, Deck Hand, RNR, SD 775, (Zena Dare, O/P)
McKAY, Malcolm, Seaman, RNR, C 2613
McKENZIE, Alexander, Seaman, RNR, C 1663, (Roman Empire, O/P)
McKENZIE, Alexander, Seaman, RNR, B 3892
McKENZIE, John, Seaman, RNR, A 3274, (Emperor of India, O/P)
McKENZIE, Murdo, Seaman, RNR, B 3122, (Pembroke, O/P)
McKENZIE, Roderick, 2nd Hand, RNR, DA 7246, (Romilly, O/P)
McKINNON, Angus, Deck Hand, RNR, SD 2615, (Attentive III, O/P)
McLEAN, Malcolm, Seaman, RNR, C 2679, (Vernon, O/P)
McLEAN, Murdo, Deck Hand, MMR, 974252, (Snipe, O/P)
McLEAN, Murdo, Seaman, RNR, D 1903, (Victory, O/P)
McLEAY, Angus, Seaman, RNR, B 3689, (Emperor of India, O/P)
McLENNAN, Finlay, Deck Hand, RNR, DA 18771
McLEOD, Alexander, Seaman, RNR, A 2745, (Imperieuse, O/P)
McLEOD, Alexander A, Deck Hand, RNR, SD 3455, (Idaho, O/P)
McLEOD, Angus, Deck Hand, RNR, SD 4548, (Pembroke, O/P)
McLEOD, Angus, Deck Hand, RNR, DA 19972, (Resmilo, O/P)
McLEOD, Angus, Deck Hand, MMR, 973997, (Snipe, O/P)
McLEOD, Angus, Seaman, RNR, D 1920, (Vernon, O/P)
McLEOD, Angus, Seaman, RNR, C 2808
McLEOD, Donald, Deck Hand, RNR, SD 1427, (Dreel Castle, O/P)
McLEOD, Donald, Deck Hand, RNR, DA 10941, (Quercia, O/P)
McLEOD, Donald, Seaman, RNR, B 3553, (SS Saxonia, O/P)
McLEOD, John, Deck Hand, RNR, DA 15739, (Attentive III, O/P)
McLEOD, John, Deck Hand, RNR, SD 3607, (ML.411, O/P)
McLEOD, John, Able Seaman, MMR, 974908, (Rose, O/P)
McLEOD, John, Deck Hand, MMR, 968097, (Victor, O/P)
McLEOD, Malcolm, Deck Hand, RNR, DA 14384, (Idaho, O/P)
McLEOD, Malcolm, Deck Hand, RNR, DA 12081, (Wallington, O/P)
McLEOD, Murdo, Seaman, RNR, B 4219
McMILLAN, Malcolm, Seaman, RNR, D 1848, (Imperieuse, O/P)
McPHAIL, Donald, Seaman, RNR, D 2222, (Pembroke, O/P)
McRITCHIE, Angus, Deck Hand, RNR, DA 16522, (Hero, O/P)
MONTGOMERY, Angus, Deck Hand, RNR, SD 1445, (Unity, O/P)
MONTGOMERY, Norman, Seaman, RNR, C 3391, (Ariel II, O/P)
MOORE, Harold, Deck Hand, MMR, (no service number listed)
MORRISON, Angus, Leading Deck Hand, RNR, DA 14310, (Implacable, O/P)
MORRISON, Angus, Deck Hand, RNR, DA 12126, (St Ayles, O/P)
MORRISON, Donald, Deck Hand, RNR, DA 11859, (Sir Mark Sykes, O/P)
MORRISON, Farquhar, Seaman, RNR, B 3161, (Pembroke, O/P)
MORRISON, Finlay, Deck Hand, RNR, SD 4515, (ML.560, O/P)
MORRISON, George, Deck Hand, RNR, SD 3499, (ML.307, O/P)
MORRISON, John, Deck Hand, RNR, DA 21746, (David Conn, O/P)
MORRISON, John, Leading Seaman, RNR, C 3026, (SS Norwood, O/P)
MORRISON, John, Seaman, RNR, A 4645, (Venerable, O/P)
MORRISON, John, Petty Officer, A 5306, (Vivid, O/P)

MORRISON, Norman, Deck Hand, RNR, DA 12088, (Urka, O/P)
MORRISON, Roderick, Seaman, RNR, C 1750, (Ganges II, O/P)
MURRAY, Donald, Petty Officer, RNR, B 2811, (Imperiuese, O/P)
MURRAY, Donald, Deck Hand, RNR, DA 19804, (Joseph Burgen, O/P)
MURRAY, Evander, Seaman, RNR, DA 1829, (Thames, O/P)
MURRAY, John, Deck Hand, RNR, SD 4689, (ML.461, O/P)
MURRAY, John, Seaman, RNR, C 2061, (Pembroke, O/P)
MURRAY, Roderick, Ordinary Seaman, J 86329, (Roxburgh, O/P)
MURRAY, William, Seaman, RNR, A 6772, (Pembroke, O/P)
MURRAY, William J, Deck Hand, RNR, DA 11925, (Pactolus, O/P)
NICHOLSON, Donald, Deck Hand, RNR, DA 8955, (Calera, O/P)
NICOLSON, Malcolm, Seaman, RNR, A 5396, (Magpie, O/P)
NICOLSON, Murdo, Deck Hand, RNR, SD 4258, (ML.10, O/P)
PATERSON, Donald, Seaman, RNR, A 9521 (Pembroke, O/P)
RAMSAY, David, Seaman, RNR, D 1350
RANKIN, Charles, Engineer Sub Lieutenant, RNR
SMITH, Donald, Seaman, RNR, A 2971, (Emperor of India, O/P)
SMITH, Donald, Leading Seaman, RNR, A 4173
SMITH, John, Seaman, RNR, B 3516, (Duchess of Devonshire, O/P)
SMITH, John, Seaman, RNR, A 8055, (Pembroke, O/P)
SMITH, Kenneth, Seaman, RNR, C 1620, (Cove, O/P)
SMITH, Kenneth, Seaman, RNR, D 1958, (Pembroke, O/P)
STANLEY, William J J, Deck Hand, MMR, (no service number listed)
TAYLOR, Alfred S, Assistant Steward, MMR, (no service number listed)
THOMSON, Malcolm, Seaman, RNR, A 4557, (Redoubtable, O/P)
WILSON, William K, Engine Room Artificer 4c, M 14184 (Ch), (Mistletoe, O/P)

King George V, battleship
BEVIS, Albert J, Gunner, RMA, RMA 13514, illness

Landrail, destroyer
MARSHALL, Albert, Able Seaman, 208743, drowned (but not in Iolaire as in some sources)

Langton, hired screw tug
SAMUEL, Jack, Assistant Cook, MMR, (no service number listed), illness in Greece

Lobelia, fleet sweeping sloop
MURPHY, William D R, Lieutenant, RNR, died in Gibraltar

Mersey, monitor
BRIDLE, Sidney J, Telegraphist, J 32026, illness

Monarch, battleship
SWINHOE, Thomas W, Stoker 2c, K 50362, illness

Nerissa, destroyer
THOMAS, John J W, Able Seaman, J 64690, accident

Pembroke, Chatham
BROWN, Jack R, Deck Hand, RNR, DA 10376, illness

President III, London
BADCOCK, Frank, Seaman, RNR, C 3374, fishing accident off North Devon, drowned

Restless Wave, hired drifter
YEOMANS, Joseph R, Trimmer, RNR, TS 6030, accident

RM, 6th Battalion, Russia
WILLIAMS, Joseph, Private, RMLI, 20082 (Ply), illness

RND, 2nd RM Battalion
ROBERTSON, John A, Private, RMLI, 16607 (Ply), ex-prisoner of war, illness

William Bond, Admiralty trawler
NOBLE, Alexander, Trimmer, RNR, TS 1476, illness

Thursday, 2 January 1919

RUSSIAN INTERVENTION

Aspasia, hired trawler, Archangel
McWATTIE, John J H, Lieutenant, RNR, died

Mersey, monitor
BULLEN, Ernest, Petty Officer, 236107, illness

Friday, 3 January 1919

Ganges, Shotley/Harwich
NELSON, Walter J, Engineman, RNR, ST 1220, accident

L.11, submarine
GALE, Leonard F, Able Seaman, J 8830, accident in UK

Mersey, monitor
McLEAN, James, Leading Seaman, 237977, illness
SPRAY, William, Stoker 1c, 235034, illness

Pembroke, Chatham
SOLKHON, William G, Engine Room Artificer 1c, 268462, illness

RND, 1st RM Battalion
SERVANT, Harold D, Private, RMLI, S 458 (Ch), ex-prisoner of war, illness in Holland

Temeraire, battleship, Sevastopol
BLEWITT, Albert P, Ordinary Seaman, J 54766 (Dev), illness

Trewellard, steamship
MACKAY, George W, Seaman, RNR, A 5533, illness

Saturday, 4 January 1919

Excellent, Portsmouth
DENNIS, John, Petty Officer 1c, 175529, illness

Glenboyne, hired trawler, mined and sunk off Folkestone
ALLEN, Edward C, Stoker 2c, K 53025
BISSET, John D, Engineman, RNR, ES 2308

Macedonia, armed merchant cruiser
DURR, Henry, Trimmer, MMR, 863285, illness

RMLI, Chatham Division
RITCHIE, James, Private, RMLI, S 3310 (Ch), illness in UK

Strathgeldie, hired trawler
DURRANT, Arthur G, Deck Hand, RNR, DA 7872, illness

Trewta Y Tres, steamship
HOWELLS, Charles W, Seaman, RNR, A 2444, accident

Warspite, battleship
COUNIHAN, William J, Officer's Cook 1c, L 2813, illness

Sunday, 5 January 1919

Cormorant, Gibraltar/Ascension Island
DAY, Thomas E, Private, RMLI, 16844 (Ch), died in St Helena

Foresight, scout cruiser
SIMS, Frank, Telegraphist, J 34970, illness

President, London
LOVE, Robert, Chief Gunner, illness

RMA Battalion
PENWILL, William T, Gunner, RMA, RMA 2428 (RFR A), discharged, illness in UK

RND, 150th (RN) Field Ambulance, RM Medical Unit
STRICKLAND, John, Private, RM, S 4101 (Deal), discharged, illness in UK

Theseus II, Baku, Caspian Sea
PRENTICE, Charles L, Shipwright 4c, M 23950, illness

Warrior, hired yacht
PROWSE, Joseph, Deck Hand, MMR, (no service number listed), illness

Monday, 6 January 1919

Europa, Mudros, Aegean
McNAIR, George Mc F, Lieutenant, RNR, illness

Gloucester, 2nd class cruiser
OSWALD, Donald J S, Lieutenant Commander, illness

Lake Tanganika Flotilla
BRIGGS, James F, Stoker 1c, K 42368, illness

Mersey, monitor
GLOVER, Samuel J, Mate, illness

Musketeer, destroyer
BLAKE, William R, Able Seaman, J 3711, drowned

Myosotis, fleet sweeping sloop
CLUBB, Ernest C, Able Seaman, J 54346 (Ch), drowned
FREDERICKS, Arthur H, Ordinary Telegraphist, J 54669, drowned

RM, 3rd Battalion
FOSTER, Herbert C, Corporal, RMLI, 14061 (Ch), illness

RND, Anson Battalion, France
LISTER, William, Able Seaman, RNVR, Tyneside Z 1032, DOW

Sir John Moore, monitor
KELLY, John, Able Seaman, J 41061, illness

Warland, hired trawler
O'CONNELL, George, Engineman, RNR, TS 5876, drowned

Tuesday, 7 January 1919

RUSSIAN INTERVENTION

Glory, battleship, Archangel, North Russia
TAYLOR, James P, Private, RMLI, 21551 (Ch), illness

Ireland, hired paddle tug
IRVINE, James, Greaser, MMR, 886886, drowned

Ranmanika, trawler
ROGERS, Edward E, Ty/Skipper, RNR, drowned

RM, 3rd Battalion
PIPER, Alfred T, Private, RMLI, 19218 (Po), illness in Lemnos

RND, 1st RM Battalion
WINCLES, Harry, Private, RMLI, S 1463 (Ch), ex-prisoner of war, illness in Holland

Royal Naval Volunteer Reserve
FOX, Reginald W, Ty/Paymaster Sub Lieutenant, RNVR, illness

Wednesday, 8 January 1919

President, London
WILLIAMS, William A, Commander, RNR, illness

Tiger, battlecruiser
MARRAY, William, Yeoman of Signals, 207266, drowned

Wellaston, steamship
WOOD, John, Seaman, RNR, A 6905, illness

Westgate, steamship, ship lost
GRIBBIN, John, Able Seaman, RNVR, Tyneside Z 11042
RUNDLE, Joseph A M, Leading Seaman, RNR, B 4225
SHARP, James, Able Seaman, RNVR, Clyde Z 8330

Thursday, 9 January 1919

Blackburn, minesweeper
LAMBERT, James, Stoker 2c, K 53096, drowned

Ivanhoe, armed fishing smack, ship lost *(only one service number listed)*
BALLS, George W, Motor Driver, MMR
BROWN, George, Deck Hand, MMR
GOLDRING, Henry B, 3rd Hand, MMR
ROBINSON, Benjamin J, Mate, MMR,
TUCKER, John W J, Skipper, MMR
WILLS, Edward W, Deck Hand, RNR, DA 16496

Mitres, trawler
CARPENTER, Allan B, Deck Hand, RNR, DA 3818, illness, buried at Murmansk

Northumbria, steamship, mined and sunk in Tees Estuary *(a total of 21 merchant seamen were lost)*
BLYTHE, Claude R, Private, RMLI, 16620 (Ch)
POOLE, Thomas, Private, RMLI, 12274 (Ch)

RND, 2nd RM Battalion
FOSTER, Edwin J, Lance Corporal, RMLI, S 1582 (Ply), ex-prisoner of war, illness

RND, Drake Battalion
  WILKINSON, Robert, Able Seaman, RNVR, Tyneside Z 3717, ex-prisoner of war, illness in Holland

RND, Howe Battalion
  MORGAN, George, Able Seaman, RNVR, Bristol Z 322, illness

Transfer, hired paddle tug
  KELLY, John J, Able Seaman, MMR, 928448, accident

Westcott, destroyer
  HAMBLY, Richard B, Stoker Petty Officer, 172334, illness

Whirlwind, destroyer
  DINAN, Edward, Able Seaman, J 47798, illness

Friday, 10 January 1919

Excel, hired drifter
  MORRISON, Douglas, Deck Hand, RNR, DA 16315, illness

Marconi III, hired drifter
  MILLER, William J, Engineman, RNR, ES 5280, illness

Nairn, hired yacht
  KELLY, Francis G, Deck Hand, RNR, DA 10799, illness

RM Engineers
  VOSS, Ernest E, Private, RME, RME 346, illness

RMLI, Portsmouth Division
  STARES, James T, Private, RMLI, S 3122 (Po), illness

Thomas Booth, Admiralty trawler
  HILL, Herbert, Ordinary Seaman, RNVR, Tyneside Z 11526, illness

Warspite, battleship
  FUTCHER, William, Able Seaman, J 32378, illness

Saturday, 11 January 1919

Batsford, steamship
  MILLINER, Sydney S, Leading Seaman, RNR, C 1708, illness

Eaglet, Liverpool
  BACKWELL, George, Petty Officer 1c, 136192, illness

Leda, ex-torpedo gunboat, minesweeper
  RANSON, George A, Lieutenant, RNR, illness

Pembroke, Chatham
  McDIARMID, Peter C, Chief Engine Room Artificer 2c, M 17438, illness

RM Engineers
  CHAPPELL, Alfred L, Private, RME, RME 7895, illness

RMA, Howitzer Brigade
  REDWOOD, Arthur J, Gunner, RMA, RMA S 1645, illness

RND, 2nd RM Battalion
  SMITH, Arnold, Private, RMLI, S 40 (Ply), discharged, illness in UK

TB.30, torpedo boat
  BARTRAM, Stanley T, Stoker 1c, K 35202, illness

Sunday, 12 January 1919

Albatross, destroyer
  BROOKS, George, Stoker 2c, K 48680, illness

Canada, battleship
  LARNDER, Frederick J, Able Seaman, J 12675, died

Cyclops II, Scapa Flow
  NORRIS, Edward J, Private, RMLI, S 1048 (Ch), illness

RM Labour Corps
  GOODIER, George, Private, RM, S 11272 (Deal), illness

RMLI, Portsmouth Division
  HARDING, Thomas, Quartermaster Sergeant, 4300 (Po), died

Vivid, Devonport
  GREEN, Victor J, Leading Signalman, J 21033, illness

Monday, 13 January 1919

Astraea, 2nd class cruiser
  CHEETHAM, Sydney W, Able Seaman, J 69217 (Ch), drowned

Unattached List
  STRICK, James K, Honorary Major, RM, illness

Victory, Portsmouth
  ROSS, John Mc S, Trimmer, RNR, ST 2022, illness

Tuesday, 14 January 1919

Kildorrey, patrol gunboat
  HUTTON, John, Leading Stoker, 286939, illness

President, London
  CLAPTON, Thomas, Lieutenant, RNR, illness

RMLI, Chatham Division
  HOPKINS, Alec A, Private, RMLI, S 1853 (Ch), illness in UK

Tarlair, Hawkscraig, Fife
  HUMPHREYS, Ernest E, Lieutenant, RNVR, accident

Vivid, Devonport
  GRAINGER, Frederick S, Stoker 1c, K 39910, illness

Wednesday, 15 January 1919

Blenheim, ex-cruiser, destroyer depot ship
  LEFEAUX, Joseph H, Stoker 1c, K 31507 (Po), illness

Hannibal, battleship
  CHRISTIE, Thomas, Leading Trimmer, RNR, ST 693, illness

President VI, London
  HALEY, Thomas J, Petty Officer 1c, 163619, illness

Thursday, 16 January 1919

Benbow, battleship
  POOLE, Walter J, Able Seaman, J 66240, illness

Lydiard, destroyer
  DARGE, John, Engine Room Artificer 2c, 272208, illness

Pembroke, Chatham
DAVIES, Edwin G, 1st Writer, M 4566, illness

RND, Anson Battalion
CUSICK, John, Able Seaman, RNVR, Clyde Z 4373, accident in UK

Ruby Gem, hired drifter
MACLENNAN, John, Deck Hand, RNR, DA 19878, illness

Titania, submarine depot ship
MILLETT, Edward G, Artificer Engineer, illness

Vivid, Devonport
HOOPER, Robert, Stoker Petty Officer, 288183, illness

Friday, 17 January 1919

Gosforth, fleet messenger
McIVOR, Louis, Seaman, MMR, 669951, drowned

RMLI, Chatham Division
SLACK, John, Private, RMLI, 10043 (Ch), illness in UK

Stag, destroyer
BECKINGTON, Ernest A, Officer's Steward 2c, L 3458, illness

Vivid, Devonport
EVANS, John, Chief Stoker, 147793, illness
HASTIE, Robert, Stoker 1c, SS 110259, illness

Waltonhall, steamship
GEEVES, William C J, Leading Seaman, RNR, A 8052, illness

Saturday, 18 January 1919

Lobelia, fleet sweeping sloop
WALSH, Michael, Stoker 1c, K 31017, illness

Pontefract, paddle minesweeper
SAUNDERS, Leonard, Able Seaman, J 37056, illness

Powerful, ex-cruiser, training ship, Devonport
AUSTIN, Arthur G, Boy 2c, J 93548, illness

RM Labour Corps
CORNFORD, John E, Private, RM, S 8086 (Deal), illness

Sunday, 19 January 1919

Bellerophon, battleship
McCARTHY, Patrick, Leading Stoker, 304730, accident

Benbow, battleship
MORRIS, George, Able Seaman, J 50369, illness

Berwick, armoured cruiser
KITCHING, Cecil, Stoker 2c, K 54025 (Dev), drowned

Europa, Mudros, Aegean
BISHOP, John R, Deck Hand, RNR, DA 493, accident

John Cooper, Admiralty trawler
DOYLE, John, Ordinary Seaman, RNVR, Tyneside Z 12801, illness

Princess Margaret, minelayer
WILLIAMS, Wilfred T, Paymaster Lieutenant, RNR, illness

RND, Anson Battalion
SUTHERLAND, David L, Able Seaman, RNVR, Clyde 1/2611, discharged, illness in UK

RND, Hood Battalion
MADDISON, Robert, Able Seaman, RNVR, Tyneside Z 3456, illness in UK

Monday, 20 January 1919

Australia (RAN), battlecruiser
EVANS, Robert P, Leading Seaman, RAN, 2138, illness

Boadicea II, hired yacht
MACFARLANE, Donald, Deck Hand, RNR, SD 4113, illness

Leviathan, armoured cruiser
CALLOW, William, Private, RMLI, 16679 (Po), died in UK

RMLI, Portsmouth Division
INGRAM, Arthur J, Private, RMLI, 11964 (Po), illness

RND, Anson Battalion
GILLIES, Archie, Able Seaman, RNVR, R 855, illness in UK

Searcher, destroyer
WICKS, William C A, Able Seaman, J 14962 (Dev), drowned

Spiraea, convoy sloop
BLYTH, Joseph, Engine Room Artificer 3c, M 27519, drowned

Tiflis, oiler
GRAHAM, Albert E, Chief Engineer 1c, MMR, illness

Tuesday, 21 January 1919

Agincourt, battleship
HOW, Frank B, Private, RMLI, 9953 (Ch), died in UK

HM Coast Guard
GOLDFINCH, James R, Chief Officer, DOI

Orcoma, armed merchant cruiser
KINLEY, James, Seaman, RNR, C 2366, illness

RM Engineers, Bedenham
SMITH, Harry B, Private, RME, RME 5261, illness

RND, Hood Battalion, attached RM Medical Unit
DAVENPORT, George, Corporal, RM, S 3749 (Deal), discharged, illness in UK

Satellite, Tyne
PARK, Joh R, Deck Hand, RNR, DA 5522, illness

Silver King, hired drifter
CHALLIS, Charles E, Deck Hand, RNR, DA 10501, illness

St Vincent, Gosport
AYRES, James F, Private, RMLI, 18488 (Po), illness

Vivid, Devonport
ALLEN, Henry W, Officer's Steward 2c, 366101, illness

Wednesday, 22 January 1919

Goshawk, destroyer
MERSH, Frederick A, Stoker 1c, K 14089, illness

TB.36, torpedo boat
 MEAD, George W, Officer's Steward 2c, L 6193, illness

Thursday, 23 January 1919

Beacon Grange, steamship
 TIMMS, Arthur F, Leading Seaman, 228889, drowned

Gunner, Granton
 DAVIDSON, James, Chief Artificer Engineer, died

Victory, Portsmouth
 HADWICK, Frederick G, Stoker 1c, K 10413, illness

Vivid, Devonport
 WALKER, Frederick G, Able Seaman, RNVR, Bristol Z 3644, illness

Friday, 24 January 1919

Dolphin, Gosport
 BORNE, John, Stoker Petty Officer, 288252, died in UK

M.1, submarine
 FRY, Claude F, Stoker 1c, K 18575 (Ch), drowned

Queen Elizabeth, battleship
 HEATON-ELLIS, Michael, Sub Lieutenant, illness

Renown, battlecruiser
 SMITH, Percy E, Able Seaman, J 18802, illness

Saturday, 25 January 1919

Ocean Hope, hired drifter
 SCAIFE, John D, Stoker, RNR, T 2431, drowned

Pekin, Grimsby
 MILLER, George W G, Deck Hand, RNR, DA 19340, accident

Theseus, 1st class cruiser
 PHILLIPS, William G, Able Seaman, J 81964, drowned

Sunday, 26 January 1919

Bootle, minesweeper
 McSWEENEY, John, Stoker 1c, K 24837, illness

Europa, Mudros, Aegean
 AZZOPARDI, Eugenio, Officer's Cook 2c, 365058, illness

Nairana, seaplane carrier
 TYLEE, Errol T, Engineer Sub Lieutenant, RNR, illness

Neptune, battleship
 BECK, Robert H, Stoker 1c, K 12758, accident

P Fannon, hired trawler
 KING, Ernest, Engineman, RNR, ES 341, illness

President, London
 DE CARTERET, Harold R, Able Seaman, RNVR, AA 2787, died

Satellite, Tyne
 NICHOLSON, George A, Engine Room Artificer, RNR, EA 1923, illness

Taliesin, hired screw tug
 BENZIE, William R, Fireman, MMR, 897261, illness

Tintagel, destroyer, both drowned
 GREEN, James S, Petty Officer, 239935 (Ch)
 SLATTER, John I, Able Seaman, SS 4314

Vernon, Portsmouth
 STEPHENS, William, Petty Officer, 120024, illness

Victory, Portsmouth
 COWIE, Thomas, Fireman, MMR, 976119, illness

Monday, 27 January 1919

Eaglet, Liverpool
 JONES, Richard, Engineman, RNR, ES 1696, illness

Furious, aircraft carrier
 BURGESS, Harold, Mate, illness

John Cope, Admiralty trawler
 SMITH, Arthur, Skipper, RNR, illness

Leviathan, armoured cruiser
 DOWSON, John, Stoker 1c, K 32400, illness

Pembroke, Chatham
 PURVIS, Thomas, Engineman, RNR, ES 824, illness
 QUAINTON, Reginald J, Able Seaman, J 55896, illness

RM, 3rd Battalion
 KEMP, John F, Corporal, RMLI, 13262 (Ch), illness

Scour, Admiralty wood drifter
 RITCHIE, Alexander, Deck Hand, RNR, DA 21749, illness

Totnes, paddle minesweeper
 COATES, Fred, Trimmer, RNR, ST 1310, drowned

Vivid, Devonport
 HOOPER, Reginald J, Leading Seaman, 229738, illness

Wireless Signal Station Butt of Lewis
 MACAULAY, John, Leading Boatman, 198280, accident

Tuesday, 28 January 1919

Ganges II, Shotley
 EVANS, William T G, Boy 2c, J 92152, illness

HM Coast Guard Station Par
 JERVIS, William, Chief Petty Officer, 115760, illness

RM Labour Corps
 DAVIS, Walter, Private, RM, S 12416 (Deal), illness

RND, Drake Battalion
 BEDDOW, Enoch, Able Seaman, RNVR, Bristol Z 3659, illness in UK

RND, Hawke Battalion
 WELCH, Charles, Able Seaman, RNVR, Sussex-Z 198, discharged, illness in UK

Wednesday, 29 January 1919

Nero, hired rescue tug
 WILSON, Charles, Able Seaman, MMR, 870469

Pembroke, Chatham
 PINDER, Charles, Able Seaman, J 39932, illness

RM Labour Corps
 JONES, Thomas O, Private, RM, S 10412 (Deal), illness

Victory, Portsmouth
 STEWART, Donald, Deck Hand, RNR, DA 21701, illness

Vivid, Devonport
 PETERS, William, Petty Officer, 188315, illness

Thursday, 30 January 1919

Carnarvon, armoured cruiser
 ADDIS, Philip, Ordinary Seaman, J 89049, illness

Champion, light cruiser
 VENN, Samuel G, Able Seaman, J 45892, accident

Changuinola, armed merchant cruiser
 ISAAC, Frederick W, Chief Gunner, drowned

Eaglet, Liverpool
 HALL, Walter R, Trimmer, MMR, 867606, illness

Pembroke, Chatham
 DALES, William, Seaman, RNR, A 8406, illness

Renown, battlecruiser
 SCOTT, Arthur, Able Seaman, J 78912, illness

RM Engineers
 MILES, William G, Corporal, RME, RME S 1277, illness in UK

RMLI, Portsmouth Division
 PARSONS, William R, Private, RMLI, 16296 (Po), illness

RND, 63rd Divisional Depot Battalion
 WELLS, John A, Able Seaman, RNVR, R 5842, discharged, illness in UK

Sonia, hired rescue tug
 COLLINS, William, Fireman, MMR, 862678, accident

Vivid, Devonport
 GORDON, Alan, Leading Seaman, J 3435, drowned

Wallington, Immingham
 FORSHAW, Joseph A, Stoker Petty Officer, 311358, illness

Friday, 31 January 1919

Defiance, Devonport
 HESELTINE, John R, Able Seaman, J 39607, illness

ML.506, motor launch
 LAWRENCE, Robert R, Ty/Lieutenant, RNVR, illness

Pembroke, Chatham
 BEATON, George, Leading Deck Hand, RNR, DA 5012, illness

President III, London
 MUNRO, Torquil, Seaman, RNR, A 4517, illness

RM Engineers
 PEGGS, James, Private, RME, RME 5043, illness

RM Labour Corps
 HOLT, William E, Private, RM, S 15739 (Deal), illness

RND, Hawke Battalion, attached RM Medical Unit
 FOSTER, Joseph, Private, RM, S 3491 (Deal), discharged, illness in UK

Victory, Portsmouth
 ROWBOTHAM, Cyril S, Signalman, RNVR, Mersey Z 1403, illness

Saturday, 1 February 1919

Blake, ex-cruiser, destroyer depot ship
 LEWIS, Sidney J, Engine Room Artificer 3c, 272320, illness

Impregnable, Devonport
 LAMERTON, James H G, Master at Arms, 117580, illness

John Robert, hired drifter, went missing, presumed mined and sunk off SE Turkey
 BOWLES, John T, Engineman, RNR, DA 6507
 LEEMING, William L, 2nd Hand, RNR, DA 17145
 MACDONALD, George, Engineman, RNR, ES 1442
 MARTIN, Daniel C, Deck Hand, RNR, DA 18370
 McQUILLAN, James, Seaman, RNR, A 7602
 PATERSON, William, Deck Hand, RNR, DA 538
 STEPHEN, Alexander, Deck Hand, RNR, DA 7386
 STEWART, John, Ty/Skipper, RNR
 WILLIAMSON, Frank, Signalman, RNVR, Mersey Z 3488

Oak Branch, steamship
 MACLEOD, John, Seaman, RNR, A 5415, illness

President, London
 DOWNIE, David, Lieutenant, RNR, illness

RM Labour Corps
 BLACK, Thomas, Private, RM, S 13809 (Deal), illness

Saxifrage, convoy sloop
 DAY, John T, Stoker 1c, 312283, drowned

Sunflower, fleet sweeping sloop
 BROWN, Eric G, Able Seaman, J 45321, illness

Sydney (RAN), 2nd class cruiser
 McCLURE, John, Warrant Mechanician, RAN, illness

Tyne, destroyer depot ship
 CONNOLLEY, Peter, Stoker, RNR, T 2709, cause of death unknown

Valiant, battleship
 COWPER, William P, Surgeon, illness

Victory X, Portsmouth
 LARKIN, Arthur, Leading Seaman, RNVR, Sussex 6/55, illness

Sunday, 2 February 1919

Fisgard, Portsmouth
 ROGERS, Thomas G, Painter 1c, 341097, illness

Lively II, hired drifter
 BULLAMORE, Arthur, Deck Hand, RNR, SD 3177, drowned

Neptune, battleship
 HINES, Thomas H, Leading Stoker, K 30224, illness

Pembroke, Chatham
 NAPP, Ernest J, Able Seaman, J 30765, illness

Resolution, battleship
 FARRINGTON, George, Able Seaman, J 25501 (Dev), drowned

RM, 3rd Battalion
 BROWNLOW, John H, Gunner, RMA, RMA 2055, illness

RMLI, Portsmouth Division
 KENT, Edward, Private, RMLI, S 1540 (Po), illness

Monday, 3 February 1919

Colleen, Queenstown
 McKAY, David, Colour Sergeant, RMLI, 8618 (Ply), illness in UK

Indus, Devonport
 HUNT, Frederick, Able Seaman, RNVR, Bristol Z 74, illness in RN Plymouth

President, London
 FARMER, George, Able Seaman, RNVR, Bristol Z 5630, illness

Stelma, trawler
 TAYLOR, Thomas V, Skipper, RNR, illness

Vivid, Devonport
 MILLS, Samuel R, Chief Stoker, 145479, illness

Wallington, Immingham
 GILLIES, Henry N, Chief Engineman, RNR, ES 4606, illness

Tuesday, 4 February 1919

Bramble, 1st class gunboat, at Bombay
 FARAH, Yoosef, 2nd Seedie, (no service number listed), illness

Hannibal, battleship
 WIDGER, Frank, Able Seaman, 124641, illness

ML.72, motor launch
 MARNOCK, William, Leading Deck Hand, RNR, SD 1563, illness

Penarth, minesweeper, mined and sunk off the Tyne
 BAKER, Robert, Stoker 1c, 297161 (Po)
 BELLIS, Thomas, Stoker 1c, K 33651 (Po)
 BREINGAN, Henry H, Stoker 1c, SS 116567 (Po)
 BURTON, Victor L, Seaman, RNR, A 8845
 CLEMENTS, Harry, Stoker 1c, SS 104283
 DAVIS, Reginald W, Cook's Mate, M 25166 (Po)
 DAWES, George, Able Seaman (RFR B 1973), 166211 (Po)
 DENCH, Munro R, Leading Stoker, K 15254 (Po)
 DENNINGTON, James R, Able Seaman, 227476 (Po)
 GREEN, Charles, Leading Stoker, K 14964 (Po)
 GRUNDY, John W, Leading Stoker, K 17771 (Po)
 GUILLARD, Fred Mc L, Joiner 4c, M 18574 (Po)
 HARRISON, John A, Ordinary Seaman, RNVR, Mersey Z 4687
 HOMERSHAM, Cecil, Ordinary Seaman, RNVR, London Z 8019
 JONES, Elisha, Ordinary Seaman, J 78578 (Dev)
 JONES, William T, Stoker 1c, SS 111269 (Po)
 KELLAWAY, Frederick C, Signalman, J 24505 (Po)
 KENT, William J, Ordinary Telegraphist, J 75161 (Ch)
 KIRBY, George R S, Stoker 1c, K 2995 (Po)
 LEE, Thomas A, Stoker 1c, K 32961
 LEES, Andrew, Stoker 2c, SS 118635 (Po)
 MITCHELL, Tom, Engine Room Artificer 4c, M 25028 (Po)
 PETRIE, George, Officer's Steward 1c, L 8115 (Po)
 POND, Herbert G, Petty Officer, 201045
 ROBBINS, Arthur J, Stoker Petty Officer, 311639
 ROSIE, Alexander, Seaman, RNR, A 5290
 SLADE, John H, Stoker 1c, K 6773 (Po)
 STAPLES, Henry B G, Stoker 1c, K 13048 (Po)
 STOKES, John, Seaman, RNR, C 2602
 STURROCK, Peter A C, Lieutenant
 SUTTON, Sidney L, Leading Stoker, K 5326 (Po)
 TAYLOR, Thomas G, Officer's Steward 3c, L 8185
 TROTTER, Alfred, Artificer Engineer
 WELLS, Edward, Ordinary Seaman, RNVR, London Z 8204
 WOOD, Thomas (real name, but served as Thomas Hallam), Able Seaman, J 19500 (Po)

President III, London
 BAILEY, John, Able Seaman, RNVR, Z 3513 (Palace), illness

RM Labour Corps
 STEVENS, Richard, Private, RM, S 8440 (Deal), illness

TB.34, torpedo boat
 JONES, Samuel R, Able Seaman, J 24585, illness

Victory, Portsmouth
 PIPON, John R, Lieutenant, RNR, illness

Vivid, Devonport
 COOK, William H G, Officer's Steward 2c, L 5301, illness

Wednesday, 5 February 1919

Blake, ex-cruiser, destroyer depot ship
 BOOT, William, Engine Room Artificer 2c, M 12731, illness

Fresh Hope, 3-masted schooner Q-ship
 KING, Howard J, Chief Motor Mechanic, RNVR, MB 3058, illness

J A C, hired drifter
 McPHERSON, David R, Engineman, RNR, S 2477, illness

Loch Wasdale, hired trawler
 MAIN, Frederick A, 2nd Hand, RNR, DA 15511, illness

Pembroke, Chatham
 HAMMOND, Percy R, Deck Hand, RNR, DA 8759, illness
 KEOGH, John A, Surgeon Commander, illness

RMA Eastney
 HARPHAM, Cecil R, Gunner 2c, RMA, RMA 16286, illness
 POOLER, Cyril, Gunner, RMA, RMA 16754, illness in UK

RND, 2nd Reserve Battalion
 BOYLE, William, Able Seaman, RNVR, Tyneside Z 4517, illness in UK

Royal Naval Volunteer Reserve
 WHITE, Alfred A, Lieutenant, RNVR, illness

St Elvies, paddle minesweeper
 DICK, Andrew S, Assistant Steward, MMR, 943289, illness

Walpole, destroyer
 RYCE, Robert W, Stoker 1c, 221494, accident

Warspite, battleship
 GOODMAN, William L, Chief Stoker, 292767, illness

Thursday, 6 February 1919

Devonshire, armoured cruiser
 LEAR, Alfred J, Petty Officer, 239379, accident

Kilkeel, patrol gunboat
 BARTRAM, John E, Ordinary Seaman, J 78133, illness

ML.407, motor launch *(following, ML.369, Andy Hunter)*
 RANKIN, Edward H, Lieutenant, RNVR, accident

North Star II, hired yacht
 ABBOTT, William F C, Deck Hand, MMR, (no service number listed), illness

Pekin, Grimsby
 BARNETT, Harry P, Paymaster Lieutenant Commander, illness

Penarth, minesweeper, mined and sunk off the Tyne on 4th
 GUNDRY, George G, Engine Room Artificer 4c, M 30849 (Po), DOW
 PARKES, Henry W, Engine Room Artificer 4c, M 6248 (Po), DOW

President, London
 WEBBER, Charles G, Act/Paymaster Commander, illness

RM Eastney
 MILVERTON, Frederick W, Gunner, RMA, RMA 1859, illness

RM Engineers
 BARLEY, Hubert, Private, RM, RME 3152, illness

RMA Eastney
 BRADLEY, Samuel S, Gunner, RMA, RMA 15500, illness

RMLI, Chatham Division
 EVANS, Frederick R, Private, RMLI, 21797 (Ch), illness

RND, 1st RM Battalion, France
 DIGGLE, Edward, Quartermaster Sergeant, RMLI, 770 (Po), illness

RND, 2nd RM Battalion
 WILLEY, Harold, Private, RMLI, S 668 (Po), discharged, illness in UK

RND, Hood Battalion
 WORSNOP, Andrew, Able Seaman, RNVR, Mersey Z 1497, illness in UK

Sunflower, fleet sweeping sloop
 SEWARD, Ernest J, Able Seaman, RNVR, London Z 4121, illness

Vivid, Devonport
 LYNCH, William, Able Seaman, J 44937, accident

W S Bailey, hired trawler
 SUTHERLAND, James H, Seaman, RNR, B 3207, illness

Friday, 7 February 1919

Destiny, trawler
 JONES, Arthur E, Deck Hand, RNR, SD 5097, illness

Erin's Isle, paddle minesweeper, mined and sunk in Thames Estuary
 ALLAN, John, Ordinary Seaman, J 52387 (Ch)
 CLARK, Harold J, Able Seaman, J 22370 (Ch)
 CLARKE, William D, Able Seaman, J 45514 (Ch)
 COLLINS, Alfred G, Ordinary Telegraphist, J 49051 (Ch)
 CRAIG, George A, Cook's Mate, M 7668 (Po)
 CRAWFORD, Sidney E J, Ordinary Seaman, J 48129 (Ch)
 DARRACOTT, Harold T, Signalman, J 13633 (Dev)
 DICKESON, Arthur E, Signal Boy, RNR, SB 1555
 DUNKS, Frederick, Able Seaman, J 53176 (Po)
 FOWLOW, John, Seaman, Newfoundland RNR, X 688
 GARRINGTON, Alfred E, Signalman, RNVR, Bristol Z 4122
 GODLONTON, William C, Ordinary Seaman, J 58614 (Ch)
 GRAHAM, Christopher P, Stoker 1c, K 28796 (Po)
 LANE, William H, Officer's Steward 3c, L 8197 (Po)
 MAY, William P, Able Seaman, J 29283 (Po)
 McCANN, John (real name, but served as John Gallagher), Stoker 2c, K 54407 (Ch)
 MITCHELL, Charles A, Ordinary Seaman, SS 8741 (Ch)
 OSMAN, Arthur T, Stoker 2c, K 46992 (Po)
 POLLARD, John, Able Seaman, 229756 (Po)
 SUTTON, Herbert, Ordinary Seaman, SS 9330 (Po)
 TERREY, Henry C, Able Seaman, J 24742 (Ch)
 WESTALL, Robert C, Able Seaman, J 28978 (Ch)
 WOOLLARD, Edward S, Able Seaman, J 10309 (Po)

Hyderabad, purpose-built Q-ship
 YOUNG, Arthur W, Stoker, RNR, T 2123, drowned, buried in Ireland

Pembroke, Chatham
 SHRUBSALL, William W M, Chief Sick Berth Steward, 140885, illness

President, London
 WALKER, Frederick M, Captain (ret), illness

RM Labour Corps
 KELLY, James, Private, RM, S 15905 (Deal), illness

Soar, hired trawler
 BECKETT, John F, Deck Hand, RNR, DA 12692, accident

Suffolk, armoured cruiser
 ROBERTS, Bertie, Leading Stoker, SS 114049, illness in Singapore

Superb, battleship
 TURNER, Albert E, Able Seaman, SS 6856, drowned

Terrible, ex-1st class cruiser, harbour servie
 STEPHENS, Richard, Sub Lieutenant, RNR, illness

Victory, Portsmouth
 NEWHAM, Jesse, Armourers Crew, M 4485, illness

Saturday, 8 February 1919

Ocean Angler, hired drifter
 HARPER, Francis B, Deck Hand, RNR, DA 3925, illness

Ophir, armed merchant cruiser
 ARMSTRONG, Francis C, Cook, MMR, 846770, illness

President III, London
 PATRICK, Fred, Able Seaman, RNVR, Tyneside Z 9780, illness

RMLI, Chatham Division
 BURDEN, Norman W, Private, RMLI, 18317 (Ch), illness
 McCARTHY, Frank L, Colour Sergeant, RMLI, 11191 (Ch), illness

RND, 1st RM Battalion
 DOWDING, Norman P O, Sergeant, RMLI, 17082 (Ch), illness in UK

RND, Nelson Battalion
 HALE, Alfred G, Able Seaman, RNVR, Wales Z 1481, discharged, illness in UK

Royal Marine Light Infantry
 OGSTON, Alexander L, Captain, RM, illness

Shannon, armoured cruiser
 WILLIAMS, Fred, Stoker Petty Officer, K 860, illness

Vernon, Portsmouth
 PITT, George E, Stoker Petty Officer, 119896, illness

Vivid, Devonport
 HARVEY, Philip H, Stoker 1c, K 15306, illness

Sunday, 9 February 1919

Chama, steamship
 ECCLES, John, Able Seaman, RNVR, Mersey Z 1031, illness

Cheery, drifter
 THOMSON, George, Engineman, RNR, ES 3036, illness

Eaglet, Liverpool
 BASSINDALE, William H, Able Seaman, RNVR, Tyneside Z 4991, died in UK

Furious, aircraft carrier, both illness in UK
 CROSS, Stanley E, Private, RMLI, 19816 (Po)
 KING, Valentine E, Ordinary Seaman, J 68337

Ophir, armed merchant cruiser
 TAYLOR, Alexander, Engineer Sub Lieutenant, RNR, illness

Phaeton, light cruiser
 FOREMAN, Roland J, 2nd Writer, M 10383, illness

President III, London
 BESTOW, Leslie W, Able Seaman, RNVR, London Z 4773, illness

RMA Eastney
 SPEED, Harry, Gunner, RMA, RMA 10004, illness in UK

RMLI, Chatham Division
 JEFFERSON, Sydney, Private, RMLI, 16706 (Ch), illness

Victory, Portsmouth
 MACKENZIE, John, Engineman, RNR, ES 3071, illness

Monday, 10 February 1919

Ambitious, hired drifter
 JARMAN, Thomas W H, Company Sergeant Major, RMLI, 5372 (Ply), illness in UK

Bacchante, armoured cruiser
 CARNE, Robert R B, Stoker 2c, K 49920, illness

Bendigo, hired trawler
 ROSS, William, Cook, MMR, (no service number listed), illness

Britomart, 1st class gunboat
 AHMED, Gafar A S, Seedie Stoker 1c, 56258, illness

Devonshire, armoured cruiser
 BURKE, James A, Stoker 1c, 296276, died

Dolphin, Gosport
 SIMMONS, Ernest F, Able Seaman, J 27761, (ex-Arethusa), illness in UK

Douglas, flotilla leader
 NORTON, Charles, Leading Seaman, 171791 (Ch), illness

Flying Fish, hired paddle tug
 CONNOR, Albert W, Cook, MMR, 521605, illness

Greenwich, destroyer depot ship
 WHITEFIELD, Edward, Armourers Crew, M 19227, illness

Hyacinth, 2nd class cruiser
 REYNER, James F, Gunner, RMA, RMA S 2598, illness in UK

Island Prince, hired trawler
 ADAMS, Charles R, Deck Hand, RNR, D S 2867, illness

King George V, battleship
 PRETTY, Gerald H A, Gunner, illness

Pembroke, Chatham
 DAVIS, Charles A, Engine Room Artificer 3c, M 6102, illness

President, London
 BROOKE, Edward E, Lieutenant Commander, ex-Strongbow, illness

President V, London
 WRIGHT, Gerald C, Air Mechanic 1c, F 42421, illness

Refundo, hired trawler
 WOOLNOUGH, James W, Deck Hand, RNR, TS 42, illness

RMA Eastney
 MOORE, William E, Gunner, RMA, RMA 15359, illness in UK
 PETERS, John, Gunner, RMA, RMA S 2477, illness

RMLI, Chatham Division
 KNIGHT, Charles A, Private, RMLI, 21881 (Ch), illness

Tarlair, Hawkscraig, Fife
 WILKINSON, Harry, Chief Petty Officer, Tyneside Z 10666, illness

Victory, Portsmouth
 LEACH, Harry, Stoker 1, K 3202, illness

Vivid, Devonport
 LLEWELLYN, John W, Chief Petty Officer, 163981, illness

Vivid III, Devonport
 JONES, David A, Able Seaman, RNVR, Mersey 4/57, illness in UK

Wisby, steamship
 HALE, Alfred, Private, RMLI, 6935 (Ch), died in Savona

Tuesday, 11 February 1919

Attentive III, hired trawler
 POPLE, Frederick R, Stoker 2c, K 48782, illness

Greta, hired yacht
 MASSON, James, Chief Petty Officer, 147752, illness in UK

Impregnable, Devonport
 MILLS, Alfred J, Boy 2c, J 91628, illness

King George V, battleship
 KENNETT, John G, Petty Officer, J 13074, illness

Moorsom, destroyer
 CARNEY, Edward, Ordinary Seaman, J 65549, illness

Pembroke, Chatham
 HOOKER, David, Able Seaman, J 2030, illness

RM Labour Corps
 GRINDROD, John W, Private, RM, S 11717 (Deal), illness
 THOMPSON, William, Private, RM, S 11012 (Deal), illness in UK

RMA Eastney
 TANQUERAY-WILLAUME, Frederick G, Major, RMA, ex-Princess Royal, illness in UK

RND, 1st RM Battalion
 SIMS, Cecil F, Private, RMLI, S 2205 (Po), illness in UK

Strathlethen, hired trawler
 DAVIDSON, John H, Able Seaman, J 75864, illness

Victory, Portsmouth
 BASHFORD, Charles, Deck Hand, RNR, DA 12313, illness

Viscol, oiler, Royal Fleet Auxiliary
 RUSSUM, Sidney W, Engineer Sub Lieutenant, RNR, illness

Vivid, Devonport
 HAWORTH, Albert, Stoker 2c, K 26437, illness

Wednesday, 12 February 1919

Bellerophon, battleship
 WOOD, Arthur, Stoker 1c, K 46738, illness

Bootle, minesweeper
 PATEY, William P, Petty Officer 1c, 169866, died

Cyclops, fleet repair ship
 PYM, Frederick G, Telegraphist, RNVR, Bristol 1/1247, illness

Grampus, destroyer
 WILDISH, Charles B, Stoker 1c, K 32748, accident

Hecla, destroyer depot ship
 THOMSON, Michael W, Act/Warrant Schoolmaster, illness

HM Coastguard Station Ballycotten
 SPARLING, John, Petty Officer, 138852, illness

HM Coastguard Station Cleggan
 HUXFORD, Edward, Leading Boatman, 204643, illness

Idaho, hired yacht
 WALKER, George H, Signal Boy, RNR, SB 1944, illness

Implacable, battleship
 LAING, William, Stoker 1c, 298328, illness

Indus, Devonport
 WILLIAMS, Trevor, Boy Artisan, M 24913, illness

Iolanda, hired yacht
 DAVEY, Alfred, Assistant Cook, MMR, 851395, illness

K.10, submarine, both died in accident in UK
 BAKER, Sydney C, Able Seaman, J 21831 (Ch)
 NORMINGTON, Herbert H, Able Seaman, J 45712 (Dev)

Magic, destroyer
 WARD, Alfred E, Chief Artificer Engineer, illness

Marlborough, battleship
 LANE, Jeremiah, Boatswain, illness
 REILLY, Peter, Able Seaman, 231076, illness

Mikasa, hired trawler
 McALISTER, Donald, Lieutenant, RNR, illness

ML.62, motor launch
 SMITH, William, Chief Motor Mechanic, RNVR, MB 1383, illness

Pembroke, Chatham
 DEATON, John, Stoker, RNR, S 2220, illness

Phoebe, destroyer
 LEMARCHARD, Francis W, Surgeon Sub Lieutenant, RNVR, illness

President III, London
 SYKES, John, Able Seaman, RNVR, Tyneside Z 10849, illness

RMA, Howitzer Brigade
 MAY, Fredrick J, Gunner, RMA, RMA S 1042, illness

Satellite, Tyne
 REDDY, Nicholas L, Engineman, RNR, ES 924, illness

Velox, destroyer
 DEAN, Ernest J D, Able Seaman, J 3955, illness

Thursday, 13 February 1919

Bacchante, armoured cruiser
 CLARK, Gilbert J, Stoker Petty Officer, 307291, illness
 HAGON, Selonso, Stoker 1c, K 38860, illness

Classic, hospital ship
 BRACEWELL, Frank, Senior Reserve Attendant, M 10546, illness

Commonwealth, battleship
 TURNER, Henry W, Chief Petty Officer, 164104, illness

Conqueror, battleship
 MOTT, Alan B, Lieutenant, illness

Cyclops, fleet repair ship
 SAUNDERS, Sidney S, Officer's Chief Cook, L 686, illness

Eileen, hired yacht
 VINCENT, John, Gunner, RMA, RMA 14332, illness

RUSSIAN INTERVENTION

Glory, battleship, Archangel, North Russia
MEAD, Edward M L, Private, RMLI, S 2569 (Ch)

———

HM Coastguard Station Coverack
WARD, Edward, Petty Officer, 154371, accident

Melbourne (RAN), 2nd class cruiser
HOBBS, Roland A, Surgeon Lieutenant, RAN, illness

Passing, hired trawler
RENNIE, Thomas C, Lieutenant, RNR, illness

Pembroke, Chatham
PIKE, Charles A, Telegraphist, J 49161, illness
THOMAS, Henry J, Able Seaman, J 40178, illness

RMA, Portsmouth
DELL, Henry J, Gunner, RMA, RMA 1848, illness

RND, Anson Battalion
JONES, Benjamin J, Able Seaman, RNVR (Bugler), London Z 471, discharged, illness in UK

Stobo Castle, rescue tug, mercantile fleet auxiliary
HEATHERINGTON, Alexander, Chief Cook, MMR, 839736, illness

Vivid, Devonport
HERBERT, Herbert N F, Petty Officer, 158045, illness

Wildfire, Sheerness
KING, Edward, Stoker 1c, 281599, illness

Friday, 14 February 1919

Bacchante, armoured cruiser
EASTWOOD, Fred, Able Seaman, J 69111, illness
REED, John L, Stoker 1c, K 33083, illness

Balmoral, paddle minesweeper
CRONSHAW, James W, Trimmer, RNR, TS 4838, illness

Dolphin, Gosport
JOHNSON, Charles F, Chief Engine Room Artificer 2c, 270756, illness in UK

Inconstant, light cruiser
HANDLEY, George, Telegraphist, J 56327, illness

John Pender, cable ship
BENCKE, John A, Engineer Sub Lieutenant, RNR, illness

King George V, battleship
COLLINS, Alfred H, Yeoman of Signals, 225337, illness

Mallard, destroyer
BENNETT, William, Chief Stoker, 287559, illness

North Star, steamship
SMITH, David, Fireman, MMR, (no service number listed), illness

Pembroke, Chatham
CLARK, James C, Stoker 1c, K 43186, illness
COLLINS, Frank, Joiner 3c, M 8097, illness

Pembroke I, Chatham
COOK, Robert, Able Seaman, RNVR, Tyneside Z 5377, illness in UK

President, London
CAIN, John T, Able Seaman, RNVR, Clyde Z 7679, illness

President III, London
CUNNINGHAM, Joseph, Petty Officer, 187326, illness

RM Labour Corps
VANCE, William, Private, RM, S 8469 (Deal), illness

RMA Eastney
GARTLAND, Henry, Gunner, RMA, RMA 11590, illness

RMLI, Portsmouth Division
FLORY, John, Lance Corporal, RMLI, S 2260 (Po), illness

St Vincent, Gosport
GIBBONS, Thomas, Stoker, RNR, S 4936, illness

Warrego (RAN), destroyer
TAYLOR, John W, Act/Petty Officer, RAN, 7738, illness in UK

Saturday, 15 February 1919

Beluga, Admiralty whaler
HUNTER, George C, Leading Trimmer, RNR, ST 2555, illness

Cinceria, hired drifter
BARLOW, John R, Able Seaman, J 75456, illness

Courageous, light battlecruiser
METCALF, Walter, Chief Petty Officer, 154022, illness

Diligence, destroyer depot ship
MASTERS, George A, Leading Stoker, 312517, illness

Duthies, hired drifter
PATON, John, Trimmer, RNR, TS 2378, illness

Eaglet, Liverpool
BRAZIER, Robert, Trimmer, MMR, 864773, illness

Halcyon, Lowestoft
CRAIG, Thomas, Deck Hand, RNR, SD 2968, illness

Kurambra (RAN), oiler
RICHARDSON, William J M, Engineer Lieutenant, RNR, illness

Pembroke, Chatham
WILLIAMS, William, Able Seaman, SS 2065, illness

RMA Eastney
SMITH, John, Leading Bombardier, RMA, RMA 9643, illness

Velox, destroyer
SCOTT, George E D, Petty Officer, J 9020, illness

Victory, Portsmouth, all from illness
DREW, John A V, Senior Reserve Attendant, M 10514
MILES, William H, Junior Reserve Attendant, M 19708
SWANSON, Thomas N, Leading Deck Hand, RNR, DA 9751

Sunday, 16 February 1919

Attentive, scout cruiser
HAWKINS, Astley R, Lieutenant, RNR, illness

Australia (RAN), battlecruiser
  MOYLAN, Thomas J, Yeoman of Signals, RAN, 7619, illness

Bacchante, armoured cruiser
  BROOKER, Alfred W, Stoker 1c, K 37828, illness
  RUSSELL, Thomas, Blacksmith 1c, 341077, illness

Cambrian, light cruiser
  HUMPHREYS, Thomas H, Signalman, 221190, illness

George Fenwick, Admiralty trawler
  MATHESON, Donald, Trimmer, RNR, TS 2637, accident

Glasgow, 2nd class cruiser
  LAILLEY, Frank, Officer's Steward 2c, L 4930, illness

Hecla, destroyer depot ship
  HODDS, Thomas H, Shipwright 2c, M 13355, illness

Pembroke, Chatham
  LAPPIN, Albert, Leading Stoker, SS 109827, illness
  TOMLINSON, Thomas H, Seaman, RNR, A 7506, illness

Richard Welford, armed boarding steamer
  DONOHUE, James, Fireman, MMR, 891620, illness

RM Engineers
  PURDON, Alexander, Private, RME, RME 1899, illness

RM Labour Corps
  DUNCAN, William, Corporal, RM, S 10560 (Deal), illness
  SEYMOUR, Joseph C, Private, RM, S 12473 (Deal), illness

RND, Anson Battalion
  MOORE, Walter E, Able Seaman, RNVR, R 6241, illness in UK

RND, Hawke Battalion
  WITNEY, Albert W, Able Seaman, RNVR, London Z 2073, discharged, illness in UK

Rob Roy, destroyer
  BUCHAN, James, Stoker 1c, K 33821, illness

Velox, destroyer
  BILBIE, William, Leading Stoker, K 6939, illness

Vernon, Portsmouth
  OUTHOUSE, Ernest A, Deck Hand, RNR, DA 16561, illness

Victory, Portsmouth
  RAWLINGS, Percy, Able Seaman, RNVR, Bristol Z 9906, illness

Monday, 17 February 1919

Crescent, Rosyth
  ADKINS, Douglas C, 2nd Writer, M 15535, illness

Daisy, hired drifter
  DENNIS, William F, Petty Officer, 190208, illness

Diligence, destroyer depot ship
  MACPHERSON, Alan, 2nd Writer, M 15860, illness

Dolphin, Gosport
  REID, Horatius, Stoker 1c, 276385, illness in UK

Eaglet, Liverpool
  VIALES, Ernest J, Assistant Steward, MMR, 702625, illness

Pembroke, Chatham
  DAVIES, William H, Shipwright 2c, 346304, illness

President, London
  DOUGLAS, Archibald R, Sub Lieutenant, illness

President III, London
  BOWLER, Henry E, Leading Seaman, RNVR, Sussex 3/334, illness in RN Hospital Haslar

RMA Eastney
  BUCKLER, George A, Gunner, RMA, RMA 9792, illness

Sanfoin, fleet sweeping sloop
  MANN, John, Sub Lieutenant, RNVR, illness

Seabear, destroyer
  BANFIELD, George A V, Officer's Steward 1c, L 1033, illness

St Just, rescue tug
  ROSE, Robert G, Able Seaman, MMR, 877446, illness

Victory, Portsmouth, all illness
  CHAWNER, James, Able Seaman, RNVR, Bristol Z 4441
  JACKSON, John, Able Seaman, RNVR, Mersey Z 1564
  MIHELL, George V, Chief Engine Room Artificer 2c, M 1960

Viscol, oiler, Royal Fleet Auxiliary
  NORTH, William, Able Seaman, MMR, 614548, illness

Vivid, Devonport
  USHER, Robert, Seaman, RNR, A 5331, illness

Zaria, mercantile fleet auxiliary
  KEMP, William C, 2nd Hand, RNR, DA 7474, illness

Tuesday, 18 February 1919

Aiglon, paddle minesweeper
  CASTER, William, Trimmer, RNR, TS 6708, illness

Ambitious, Shetlands
  VEAL, John B G, Private, RMLI, S 1704 (Ch), illness in UK

Bacchante, armoured cruiser
  PRINGLE, Robert G, Able Seaman, J 71837, illness

Commonwealth, battleship
  FITZJOHN, George, Leading Seaman, 231743, illness

Conqueror, battleship
  SINCLAIR, Robert J, Gunner, illness

Crescent, Rosyth
  O'KEEFE, Sara, Steward, WRNS, G 4649, illness

Fisgard, Portsmouth
  HAYNES, Clarence F, Boy Artisan, M 22614, illness

Halcyon II, Lowestoft
  BAXTER, Gordon W, Engineman, RNR, TS 4759, illness

RUSSIAN INTERVENTION

Kent, armoured cruiser, at Vladivostok
  MANSON, Samuel, Stoker, RNR, S 3567, illness

Mantua, armed merchant cruiser
  SMITH, Frederick C, Petty Officer, 227488, illness in UK

Pembroke, Chatham
 JONES, William F, Stoker Petty Officer, K 3646, illness

Penelope, light cruiser
 MALTBY, Charles W, Able Seaman, 226206, illness

President III, London
 OATES, Thomas, Leading Seaman, RNVR, Clyde Z 6365, illness

Redoubtable, old battleship
 HOWARTH, Edward R A, Cook, MMR, 803012, illness

RM Labour Corps
 COOTE, John H, Private, RM, S 14085 (Deal), illness
 MATTHEWS, Patrick, Private, RM, S 14588 (Deal), illness

RMLI, HQ Chatham
 HART, George (real name, but served as George Routley), Private, RMLI, S 7304 (Ch), illness

RND, Hawke Battalion
 CLEMENTS, Harry M, Petty Officer, RNVR, Wales Z 373, discharged, illness in UK

Tiger, battlecruiser
 BACKHOUSE, John R, Engine Room Artificer 4c, M 33124, illness

Velox, destroyer
 MOORE, Arthur H, Able Seaman, J 38131, illness

Victory, Portsmouth
 DRIEU, Emile, Officer's Steward 3c, L 7071, illness

Wednesday, 19 February 1919

Bacchante, armoured cruiser
 HODGES, George H, Stoker 2c, K 49505, illness

Blake, ex-cruiser, destroyer depot ship
 CRICHTON, Thomas L, Able Seaman, J 31570, illness

Cinceria, hired drifter
 WELLER, Frederick, Able Seaman, J 76350, illness

Commonwealth, battleship
 BOYD, William A, Musician, RMB, RMB 1059, illness in UK

Eagle, aircraft carrier (below)
 ANDERSON, James, Quartermaster, MMR, 643978, illness

George Aunger, Admiralty trawler
 BANCONE, Francesco C, Deck Hand, RNR, DA 18798, illness

HM Coast Guard Station Staithes
 STEVENSON, James, Leading Signalman, RNVR, Clyde Z 3173, illness

Mastiff, destroyer
 BLAKEY, Andrew H, Lieutenant, RNR, illness

Monarch, battleship
 RICHES, George H, Musician, RMB, RMB 1187, illness in UK

P.16, patrol boat
 ELLIS, Percivial S, Engine Room Artificer 2c, 271960, illness

Pembroke, Chatham
 BANHAM, Karl F, Able Seaman, J 18609, illness

President, London
 BUCHANAN, William M, Lieutenant, RNR, illness
 DANIEL, Charles T, Lieutenant, RNR, illness

Research, depot ship, Portland
 PARKER, James H, Trimmer Cook, RNR, TC 603, illness
 TAYLOR, Albert W, Seaman, RNR, A 7279, illness

RM Labour Corps
 KENNEDY, Michael, Private, RM, S 12959 (Deal), illness

RMA Eastney
 RUSE, George E, Gunner, RMA, RMA 14218, illness

RMLI, Plymouth Division
 MANN, William H, Private, RMLI, 17185 (Ply), illness in UK

Royal Scot, armed boarding steamer
 DAVIDSON, Frank, Steward, 91507, illness

Vasco Da Gama, hired trawler
 HARRISON, Walter, Skipper (Warrant Officer), RNR, illness

Zaria, mercantile fleet auxiliary
 GEDDES, Alexander, Deck Hand, RNR, DA 4857, illness

Thursday, 20 February 1919

Aiglon, paddle minesweeper
 PETTETT, John T, Deck Hand, RNR, SD 3858, illness

Bacchante, armoured cruiser
 BASHFORD, William H, Stoker 1c, 312508, illness in UK
 GASKIN, Percy G, Petty Officer, 166544, illness

Benbow, battleship
 LEES, John R, Ordinary Seaman, J 85413, illness

Boadicea, scout cruiser
 ANDREWS, Albert, Able Seaman, J 7918, illness

Duke of Cornwall, armed boarding steamer
 THOMSON, Peter, Engineer Sub Lieutenant, RNR, illness

Halcyon II, Lowestoft
 CURTIS, Harold W, Engineman, RNR, ES 1999, illness

Kildangan, patrol gunboat
 DEGNIN, Francis, Stoker 1c, 282529, illness

Limol, oiler, Royal Fleet Auxiliary
 GIBBS, Henry P, Chief Petty Officer, MMR, 571460, illness

M.22, monitor
BOWLES, Gordon G, Private, RMLI, 16757 (Po), died

President III, London
LAMPKIN, Harry, Able Seaman, SS 2423, illness
SAUER, Frederick J, Leading Seaman, SS 1647, illness

Richard Welford, armed boarding steamer
SPENDER, Joseph G, Greaser, MMR, 601925, illness

RND, Benbow Battalion
THOMPSON, Hubert H, Chief Petty Officer (Quartermaster Sergeant), RNVR, London Z 485, discharged, illness in UK

Satellite, Tyne
NORRIS, Walter, Petty Officer, RNR, C 3585, illness

Savage, destroyer
MAY, Charles, Leading Stoker, K 23562, illness

Tanfield, steamship
WALTERS, Alfred C, Able Seaman, RNVR, Bristol Z 1811, illness

Victory, Portsmouth
McARA, William J, Electrical Artificer 3c, M 8402, illness

Wallington, Immingham
MARTINS, Reginald C K, Leading Seaman, 202519, illness

Friday, 21 February 1919

Bloemfontein, hired drifter
CRAWFORD, James F, Deck Hand, RNR, DA 8002, accident

Challenger, 2nd class cruiser
BOWMAN, Alfred, Stoker, RNR, U 1597, illness

Craigie, minesweeper
COGHILL, Thomas, Stoker 1c, 304353, died in Gibraltar

Cyclops, fleet repair ship
MORRIS, Thomas H, Ordinary Telegraphist, J 40837, illness

Dryad, Portsmouth
PAY, George E, Private, RMLI, S 1181 (Po), illness in UK

Emperor of India, battleship
MARCHANT, Thomas, Signal Boy, J 60737, illness

HM Coast Guard Plymouth
LUARD, Herbert Du C, Commander, illness

Kildimo, patrol gunboat
BARHAM, William, Leading Stoker, SS 114275, illness

Matador, steamship
McINNES, Gilbert, Leading Seaman, 234343, illness

Morning Star, hired trawler
KAY, William, Engineman, RNR, ES 2222, illness

Pembroke, Chatham, all illness
ATKINS, John, Stoker Petty Officer, K 7375
BRISTOW, Reginald, Stoker 1c, K 47221
WILLIAMS, Ernest, Leading Stoker, K 12089

Persian Empire
ASPINALL, Samuel, Leading Deck Hand, RNR, SD 1377, drowned

President, London
PRINCE, Herbert, Lieutenant, RNR, accident

Research
ECKETT, Urbain T M, Lieutenant, RNVR, illness

Royal Oak, battleship
BLACK-BARNES, Charles T, Lieutenant, illness

Victory, Portsmouth
DAYKIN, John R, Stoker 2c, SS 119164, illness

Vivid, Devonport, all illness
CHEW, Henry, Able Seaman, J 62026
DICKASON, Alfred C, Able Seaman, SS 849
JONES, Thomas H, Stoker 1c, K 7491

Waterhen, destroyer
COATES, Edward, Petty Officer, 239255, illness

Saturday, 22 February 1919

Archer, destroyer, both drowned
BURNS, Erasmus J, Gunner
FLETCHER, Henry A, Able Seaman, J 41003 (Ch)

Bacchante, armoured cruiser
CHEAL, Frederick J, Stoker Petty Officer, 286273, illness

Caesar, battleship
WILLIAMS, Griffith, Leading Stoker, K 1591, accident

Comus, light cruiser
MARTIN, William E, Chief Stoker, 276984, illness

Harden, mine carrier, mercantile fleet auxiliary
NEWMAN, Henry, Seaman, RNR, C 1744, illness

Harrow, minesweeper
NEWINGTON, James P, Stoker Petty Officer, 307026, illness

Hermione, 2nd class cruiser
POINTER, George H, Engineer Sub Lieutenant, RNR, illness

Kenilworth, paddle minesweeper
HART, Percy, Deck Hand, RNR, DA 16352, illness

Mallow, fleet sweeping sloop
BRASNETT, Archibald H, Stoker Petty Officer, K 5384 (Po), illness

Norseman, destroyer
HUGHES, William, Able Seaman, SS 3214, illness

Pembroke, Chatham
FULCHER, Frederick E, Stoker 1c, K 38413, illness
GOULDING, Michael J, Able Seaman, RNVR, London Z 7014, illness

RM Labour Corps
THOMAS, George E, Private, RM, S 14875 (Deal), illness

RM, 3rd Battalion
CLARK, Wilfred T De L, Major, RMLI, illness

RMA, Howitzer Brigade
HOLTON, Alfred E, Lieutenant, RMA, illness
POWELL, Gilbert G, Driver, RMA, RMA S 1272, illness

RND, Collingwood Battalion
 CAFFERY, William H, Stoker 1c, 283835, discharged, illness in UK

RND, Hood Battalion
 CROUCH, Horace, Able Seaman, RNVR, Bristol Z 4098, discharged, illness in UK
 HURST, Cecil C, Able Seaman, RNVR, Bristol Z 4594, illness in UK

Seadog, paddle tug
 BREHANT, John T, Able Seaman, MMR, 954203, illness

Snowdrop, fleet sweeping sloop
 MARTIN, Percy, Able Seaman, J 18000, illness

Vernon, Portsmouth
 GALLAGHER, Christopher, Deck Hand, RNR, SD 2591, illness

Victory, Portsmouth, all illness
 BRYANT, Edward, Deck Hand, RNR, SD 3121
 RAY, Francis E, Boy Servant, L 12053
 WILLIAMS, George, Able Seaman, 234521

Sunday, 23 February 1919

Ascania, hospital ship
 SIBLEY, Eric R, Signalman, RAN, 460, disappeared in Red Sea

Concord, light cruiser
 REED, William, Petty Officer, 235966, illness

Emperor of India, battleship
 OAKLEY, William T, Stoker 1c, K 3331, illness

Hero, hired trawler
 LIVINGSTONE, John A, Lieutenant, RNR, illness

Kingfisher, Yarmouth
 DAVIES, Ernest, Engine Room Artificer, RNR, EA 1792, illness

Macoris, steamship
 SMITH, William, Able Seaman, RNVR, Tyneside 5/216, illness in UK

Marlborough, battleship
 GILBERT, Edwin, Stoker Petty Officer, SS 109330, illness

P.62, patrol boat
 CURTIS, Walter W, Leading Signalman, J 14483, illness

Pembroke, Chatham
 WELLS, James T, Boy Servant, L 11475, illness

President, London
 HOULDSWORTH, Harold J, Sub Lieutenant, illness

Research
 GREENWELL, Evelyn E, Ty/Lieutenant, RNVR, illness

RND, 2nd Field Company, Divisional Engineers
 BROTHERHOOD, Richard H, Sapper, RM, S 845 (Deal), discharged, illness in UK

Sobo, torpedo sub-depot ship
 ROY, Peter A, Engineer Sub Lieutenant, RNR, illness

St Issey, rescue tug
 WOOD, James E, 2nd Mate, MMR, (no service number listed), drowned

Victory, Portsmouth
 CRADDICK, Frederick B, Deck Hand, RNR, DA 18779, illness
 SYMMS, Harry G, Petty Officer, 220122, illness

Vivid, Devonport
 WAKEHAM, Robert, Chief Petty Officer, 163258, illness

Monday, 24 February 1919

Auricula, convoy sloop
 HOUSE, Samuel J, Shipwright 2c, 344854, illness

Castor, light cruiser
 BEAL, Frederick, Petty Officer, 178228, illness

Comus, light cruiser
 DAVIES, John, Yeoman of Signals, 198789, illness

Eaglet, Liverpool
 WESS, Harry, Chief Baker, MMR, 946635, illness

Erin, battleship
 THOMAS, Clifford B, Stoker 1c, SS 16491, illness

Hermione, 2nd class cruiser
 BRETT, George F, Officer's Steward 3c, L 10024, illness

Impregnable, Devonport
 BOULTON, Robert W, Boy 2c, J 94034, illness

Ophir, armed merchant cruiser
 CROWSON, George E, Ordinary Seaman, J 77145, illness

Pembroke, Chatham
 CURTIS, Henry J, Cooper 1c, 343597, illness
 KILMARTIN, James, Stoker 1c, K 32248, illness

President III, London
 HALLIWELL, Jack, Able Seaman, RNVR, Tyneside Z 8924, illness

Royal Air Force
 THURSTAN, Denzil R, Paymaster Lieutenant Commander, illness

RND, 1st RM Battalion
 McNEIL, Allan, Ty/2nd Lieutenant, RMLI, illness in UK

Silanion, hired trawler
 McKENZIE, Murdo, Trimmer, RNR, TS 6842, illness

Sonia, hired rescue tug
 EVANS, David, Steward, MMR, 785375, illness

Tarlair, Hawkscraig, Fife
 CREETON, Cornelius, Leading Stoker, 291785, illness

Victory, Portsmouth
 CAMPBELL, Lawrence, Able Seaman, J 28822, illness
 VENABLES, George, Yeoman of Signals, 203160, illness

Vivid III, Devonport
 SCULLIN, John, Signalman, RNVR, Clyde 1/199, illness in UK

Wallington, Immingham
 BLIGH, William V, Stoker 1c, K 3614, illness

Tuesday, 25 February 1919

Ajax, battleship
 WARREN, Harold W, Leading Stoker, K 18826, illness

Benbow, battleship
 PEDLEY, William, Ordinary Seaman, J 85356, illness

Bon Accord, hired trawler
 MURRAY, Alexander, Deck Hand, RNR, DA 6787, died

Emperor of India, battleship
 CLIFFE, Wilfred C, Ordinary Seaman, J 83784, illness

Excellent, Portsmouth
 PERRY, Kenneth T, Armourers Crew, M 20684, illness

Impregnable, Devonport
 ALLEN, Richard J, Boy 2c, J 94070, illness
 SAWLE, Walter, Boy 2c, J 93962, illness

Mars, ex-battleship, depot ship, Invergordon
 MACDONALD, Donald, Seaman, RNR, A 3947, illness

ML.284, motor launch
 HOLLINGTON, Vernon, Ty/Lieutenant, RNVR, illness

ML.457, motor launch
 COLE, James, Leading Deck Hand, RNR, SD 4665, illness

Pembroke, Chatham, all illness
 KOHLER, Julius, Able Seaman, J 5647
 PANNETT, William J T, Able Seaman, J 69170
 SCOTT, George W, Ordinary Seaman, RNVR, London Z 6108
 WARDLEY, Edward, Armourers Mate, M 2872
 WINSTANLEY, Willoughby A, Stoker 1c, K 38497

Rene, hired drifter
 BROWN, George V, Trimmer, RNR, TS 3905, illness

Richard Welford, armed boarding steamer
 TAYLOR, John, Leading Signalman, RNVR, Bristol Z 748, illness

RND, 1st RM Battalion
 NETHERWAY, William P J, Private, RMLI, 11323 (Ch) (RFR B 1755), discharged, illness in UK

Rosabelle, hired yacht
 SPRINGETT, Percy, Assistant Steward, MMR, (no service number listed), illness

Royal Naval Reserve
 HEPWORTH, Campbell M W, Captain, RNR, illness

Victory, Portsmouth
 EASON, Jesse, Stoker 2c, SS 119490, illness
 GOULD, Alfred G, Petty Officer, 208490, illness

Vivid, Devonport
 HODGE, Harold R, Sick Berth Attendant, M 4418, illness
 STEER, William, Leading Cook's Mate, M 1850, illness

Wednesday, 26 February 1919

Actaeon, Sheerness
 FAST, Frank, Deck Hand, RNR, SD 3246, illness

Alsatian, armed merchant cruiser
 RILEY, William C, Fireman, MMR, 864152, illness

Arrogant, ex-cruiser, depot ship
 HEWETT, Joseph H, Lieutenant, RNVR, illness
 JENNINGS, Henry, Stoker, RNR, U 1672, illness

Courageous, light battlecruiser
 CLEMENTS, Nat F J, Able Seaman, J 39755, illness

Crescent, Rosyth
 GORDON, William E, Ordinary Seaman, MMR, (no service number listed), illness

Kilfinny, patrol gunboat
 CALLAGHAN, James, Stoker 1c, K 30260, illness

Pembroke, Chatham, all but one, illness
 CONNOLLY, Gerald S, Officer's Steward 3c, L 8710, drowned
 COTGROVE, Arthur T, Stoker 2c, K 50103
 DAVIES, William J, Shipwright 2c, 344865
 JOHNSTON, Harry, Stoker, RNR, S 5741
 SIMPSON, James, Engineman, RNR, TS 3336
 YOUNG, Percy, Leading Seaman, RNVR, London Z 553

Powerful, ex-cruiser, training ship
 HICKEY, Henry, Boy 2c, J 93862, illness

Renown, battlecruiser
 BLAKEY, John, Private, RMLI, S 1049 (Po), illness in RN Hospital Haslar

RM HQ Portsmouth
 ALLEN, William, Private, RMLI, 4347 (Po), illness

RMA Eastney
 JENKINSON, Harry, Gunner, RMA, RMA S 2216, illness

RMLI, 2nd Reserve Battalion
 CONN, David, Able Seaman, RNVR, Clyde Z 6845, discharged, illness in UK

Sagua, steamship
 MACIVER, Kenneth, Leading Seaman, A 5561, accident

Stobo Castle, paddle tug
 CONNOLLY, Joseph P, Ordinary Seaman, MMR, 907559, illness

Victory, Portsmouth
 BRIGGS, Harry, Telegraphist, J 52442, illness

Vivid, Devonport
 BERRY, Percival A, Stoker 2c, SS 119509, illness

Wallington, Immingham
 ALLOTT, Charles, Deck Hand, MMR, 975096, illness

Thursday, 27 February 1919

Actaeon, Sheerness
 LEA, Harold, Able Seaman, 170584, illness

Camito, commissioned escort ship
 HOUGHTON, Reginald R R, Engineer Lieutenant, RNR, illness

Lavatera, hired drifter
 KEITH, William, Stoker 1c, K 54636, drowned

Marchioness of Bute, paddle minesweeper
 HALFPENNY, John, Greaser, MMR, 587394, illness

Pembroke, Chatham
 SIMPSON, John, Able Seaman, J 2683, illness

Powerful, ex-cruiser, training ship
 STAGG, Sidney H, Boy 2c, J 94424, illness
 YOUNGS, Frederick W, Boy 2c, J 94152, illness

President III, London
 DYMOND, Hubert, Lance Corporal, RMLI, 15297 (Ch), died in UK

Renown, battlecruiser
 BERRY, William F, Engine Room Artificer 1c, 270639, illness

RM Headquarters
 SNAGG, Bertram C K, Captain, RM, illness

RM Labour Corps
 BRAZELL, William, Private, RM, S 14208 (Deal), accident

RMLI, Chatham Division
 MOULDEN, Robert B, Private, RMLI, 9312 (Ch), illness in UK

RMLI, Plymouth Division
 MONGER, William, Private, RMLI, 14136 (Ply), illness in UK

Vivid, Devonport
 JAMIESON, John, Able Seaman, J 24771, illness
 NOAD, Augustus J, Leading Signalman, J 26921, illness

Wallace, flotilla leader
 LOWDON, Sidney, Able Seaman, J 40777, illness

Wildfire, Sheerness
 STANDING, Thomas W, Able Seaman, RNVR, Palace Z 1772, discharged, illness in UK

Friday, 28 February 1919

Active, scout cruiser
 HARLAND, Sydney, Officer's Steward 3c, L 2612, illness

Agincourt, battleship
 GALLIGHAN, Alfred J, Private, RMLI, 10475 (Po), illness

Astral, Admiralty wood drifter
 LILLY, Robert, 2nd Hand, RNR, SA 279, illness

Colleen, Queenstown
 CORCORAN, John, Stoker 1c, 165758, illness

Colossus, battleship
 ELSON, Alfred, Stoker 1c, K 24549, illness

Eaglet, Liverpool
 ANDERSON, Charles H, Leading Fireman, MMR, 787481, illness

Helmsdale II, trawler
 WEST, Matthew, Deck Hand, RNR, DA 4714, drowned, buried in Istanbul

Impregnable, Devonport
 MEARS, Ivor W J, Boy 2c, J 94269, illness
 WAREHAM, Edward J, Boy 2c, J 94474, illness

Lucia, submarine depot ship
 MITCHELL, Harold, Petty Officer, 216864, illness

Macedonia, armed merchant cruiser (by now out of Admiralty service)
 PAYNE, Thomas A, Warrant Telegraphist, RNR, presumably discharged, illness

Ocean Retriever, hired drifter
 GREEN, George R, Deck Hand, RNR, DA 967, illness

Pembroke, Chatham
 HEADLAND, Ernest H, Stoker 1c, K 38404, illness

Pembroke, Chatham
 TAYLOR, Martin H, Leading Seaman, J 11405, illness

Richard Welford, armed boarding steamer
 HADDAWAY, Herbert, Quartermaster, MMR, 566173, illness

RND, 2nd Reserve Battalion
 ROBISON, Thomas I C, Ty/Sub Lieutenant, RNVR, illness

RND, Anson Battalion, France
 BOTTOMS, Arthur, Able Seaman, RNVR, KP 556, illness

Suffolk, armoured cruiser
 WOODHOUSE, Frederick G H, Able Seaman, J 19535 (Dev), illness in Hong Kong

Sydney (RAN), 2nd class cruiser
 HARDING, Fred A, Leading Stoker, RAN, 8476, illness

TB.55, torpedo boat
 HEALEY, Patrick, Stoker Petty Officer, 297395, illness

Vivid, Devonport
 DARCH, Herbert S, Chief Sick Berth Steward, 150397, illness

Saturday, 1 March 1919

Ambuscade, destroyer
 REED, Henry J, Chief Engine Room Artificer 1c, 269195, illness

Halcyon, Lowestoft
 HOWARD, Ernest, Deck Hand, RNR, SD 2125, illness

Jed, destroyer
 MILLER, George W, Leading Seaman, J 11912, illness

Leander, ex-cruiser, destroyer depot ship
 IRLAM, Wilfred, Able Seaman, SS 2770, illness

Lucia, submarine depot ship
 FISHER, Charles R, Officer's Steward 1c, 362953, illness

Morea, armed merchant cruiser
 ARNOLD, George, Trimmer, MMR, 971592, illness

Nerissa, destroyer
 MACDONALD, James W, Officer's Steward 2c, L 9730, illness

President, London
 DOBELL, John W, Lieutenant, illness

President III, London
 OSBORNE, George, Able Seaman, RNVR, Bristol Z 3912, illness
 SHERRIFF, John W, Able Seaman, RNVR, Bristol Z 5254, illness

RMLI, Chatham Division
 TEAHEN, Henry, Private, RMLI, 22323 (Ch), illness in UK

Tilbury, destroyer
 WILSDON, Frederick P, Stoker 1c, K 39098, drowned

Victory, Portsmouth
 WINSTONE, Raymond, Stoker Petty Officer, 297951, illness

Sunday, 2 March 1919

Commonwealth, battleship
  BEECH, Walter H, Officer's Steward 2c, L 9859, illness

Crescent, Rosyth
  BELCHER, Frederick E, Gunner, RMA, RMA S 2354, illness in UK

Eaglet, Liverpool
  CARDY, William H, Greaser, MMR, 915126, illness
  DALTON, Alexander, Fireman, MMR, 865477, illness

Europa, Mudros, Aegean
  EVANS, Bertram S, Captain, illness

Galatea, light cruiser
  FULLER, Henry R, Stoker 1c, SS 111647, illness

Impregnable, Devonport
  STANFORD, Ernest J, Boy 2c, J 93420, illness

Maidstone, submarine depot ship
  GORMAN, James, Stoker, RNR, S 3410, illness

Newbury, paddle minesweeper
  BUTCHER, William, Deck Hand, RNR, DA 19656, illness

Pembroke, Chatham
  LEWIS, David L, Surgeon Lieutenant, illness

President III, London
  DONOVAN, Cornelius, Leading Seaman, RNR, A 5639, drowned

RND, Collingwood Battalion
  COPELAND, Robert, Able Seaman, RNVR, Tyneside Z 718, discharged, illness in UK

Victory, Portsmouth
  WILLIAMS, Robert, Stoker, RNR, S 2007, illness

Monday, 3 March 1919

Ann Ford Melville, hired trawler
  CLARKE, William R, Skipper, RNR, illness

Ben Alder, hired trawler
  WINCHESTER, Alexander, Engineman, MMR, 975766, illness

Crescent, Rosyth
  RYAN, Albert J, Victualling Assistant, M 33103, illness

Egmont, Malta
  CALLAWAY, Frank Le M, Paymaster Lieutenant, illness

Impregnable, Devonport
  DAVEY, Joseph S, Boy 2c, J 93961, illness
  PEATY, William H, Boy 2c, J 93811, illness

Marlborough, battleship
  CARNOCHAN, Andrew, Able Seaman, J 32306, illness
  PRINGLE, Thomas E, Stoker 1c, SS 110615, illness

ML.205, motor launch
  HALL, Cecil, Chief Motor Mechanic, RNVR, MB 1307, illness

ML.240, motor launch
  BOSWELL, Walter O, Lieutenant, RNVR, illness

Pembroke, Chatham
  BEECH, Victor G, Officer's Steward 3c, L 12113, illness
  SMITH, Oliver, Leading Boatman, 290949, illness
  SMOOTHY, Harold T, Ordinary Seaman, J 73560, died
  WILLIAMS, George, Signalman, RNVR, London Z 1730, illness

RND, Hawke Battalion
  CHRISTIE, James, Able Seaman, RNVR, Clyde Z 7153, discharged, illness in UK

Sandringham, hired trawler
  BELTON, James, Stoker Petty Officer, 154822, illness

Victory, Portsmouth X
  MANSON, David, Deck Hand, RNR, DA 12388, illness

Tuesday, 4 March 1919

Anzac, flotilla leader
  BIGGS, William, Stoker 1c, SS 111180, illness

Boadicea, scout cruiser
  FRANKLIN, Percy, Stoker 1c, SS 112819, illness

Firefly, river gunboat
  KEAN, Cuthbert, Trimmer, RNR, TS 946, illness

Ganges, Shotley/Harwich
  SHORTER, Leonard W, Boy 2c, J 93796, illness

Jaboo II, hired trawler
  JEFFREY, Robert, Deck Hand, RNR, DA 5024, illness

Loch Rannoch, hired trawler
  CRAIGIE, James W, Deck Hand, MMR, (no service number listed), illness

Powerful, ex-cruiser, training ship
  SAXBY, Douglas A E, Boy 2c, J 94174, illness
  TITE, William E, Private, RMLI, 15412 (Ply), illness in UK

Thalia, store hulk, Cromarty
  WILSON, James, Leading Deck Hand, RNR, DA 5204, illness

Vivid, Devonport
  HALSTONE, Emly J, Ordinary Signalman, J 49378, accident

Wednesday, 5 March 1919

Excellent, Portsmouth
  HAMBLY, John R, Chief Gunner, illness

Fair Isle, hired trawler or drifter
  ATKINS, Thomas E, Engineman, RNR, ES 3859, illness

RMLI, Plymouth Division
  POTTER, Samuel, Private, RMLI, 10904 (Ply), illness in UK

RND, Collingwood Battalion
  JONES, George C, Able Seaman, RNVR, London Z 1211, discharged, illness in UK

Tomahawk, destroyer
  HONEYWELL, John H, Petty Officer, 218927, illness

Victory, Portsmouth
  BUCKLAND, Herbert, Chief Stoker, 308049, illness
  PENDLEBURY, Herbert, Petty Officer, 239381, illness

Thursday, 6 March 1919

Boadicea II, Kingstown, Co Dublin
　MARTIN, James F, 2nd Hand, RNR, SA 1122, accident

Greenwich, destroyer depot ship
　REYNOLDS, Ernest J, Ordinary Seaman, J 34880, illness

ML.360, motor launch
　TURNER, Edwin S, Lieutenant, RNVR, illness

Nigella, fleet sweeping sloop
　PARSON, Guy F, Lieutenant Commander, accident

Oriana, destroyer
　HODDER, Henry, Stoker Petty Officer, 293754, illness

Pembroke, Chatham
　ALLSOP, William B, Sub Lieutenant, RNR, illness

President, London
　ALLIN, Leslie J W, Lieutenant, illness

Ramillies, battleship
　BOULT, George W, Officer's Cook 1c, L 5921, illness

Superb, battleship
　GLENISTER, Henry, Officer's Cook 1c, 166000, accident

Wessex, destroyer
　MAIN, Sampson, Able Seaman, RNVR, Tyneside Z 9065, illness

Friday, 7 March 1919

Aspasia, hired trawler
　HEWETT, George R, Deck Hand, RNR, DA 3556, illness

Essex II, hired trawler
　MAY, James, Deck Hand, RNR, SD 4299, illness

James & Walter, steamship
　THORPE, William, Skipper, RNR, illness

Liverpool, 2nd class cruiser
　JOHN, Edwin, Stoker 1c, K 35290, illness

Pembroke, Chatham
　SPILLER, George C, Leading Signalman, J 5727, illness

Phaeton, light cruiser
　COOK, Albert E, Able Seaman, RNVR, London Z 4590, illness

RND, Drake Battalion
　MASON, Francis R, Able Seaman, RNVR, Clyde Z 4732, illness in UK

White Hill, drifter
　COWAP, John G, Trimmer, RNR, TS 4642, illness

Saturday, 8 March 1919

Caesar, battleship
　LOCK, Arnold V, Stoker 1c, 295899, illness

Colleen, Queenstown, Ireland
　HOUGHTON, James E, Deck Hand, RNR, SD 5090, illness

Crescent Moon, Admiralty steel drifter
　MOUGHTON, Arthur W, Deck Hand, RNR, DA 5260, illness

Duchess of Rothesay, paddle minesweeper
　BROWN, William G, Lieutenant, RNR, accident

E.11, submarine
　LAKE, William T, Engine Room Artificer 4c, M 8379, died in Malta

Eaglet, Liverpool
　WYLIE, Thomas, Steward, MMR, 571796, illness

Fox, 2nd class cruiser *(below, George Smith)*
　MILES, Harold A, Sick Berth Steward, 350984, illness, buried at Plymouth

Ganges, Shotley/Harwich
　PRESTON, Alec, Boy 2c, J 94569, illness

Kilcock, patrol gunboat
　DUNN, Arthur, Sub Lieutenant, RNR, illness

Pembroke, Chatham
　POTTER, Maurice W, Stoker 1c, K 38152, illness

President III, London
　ANSELL, Frederick L, Private, RMLI, 16646 (Po), illness
　CARTWRIGHT, Harry, Able Seaman, RNVR, Mersey Z 296, illness

RMA Eastney
　AYLWARD, Albert, Gunner, RMA, RMA 3358, illness in UK

Venus, 2nd class cruiser
　TAYLOR, Arthur, Petty Officer, 218813, illness

Victory, Portsmouth
　SPENCER, William, Stoker Petty Officer, 290271, illness

Vivid, Devonport
　WOTTON, Thomas, Able Seaman, J 5210, illness

Vulcan, submarine depot ship
　KEY, Frederick G, Officer's Steward 2c, L 3217, illness

Sunday, 9 March 1919

Ganges, Shotley/Harwich
　FUNNELL, Victor A, Boy 2c, J 93768, illness

Impregnable, Devonport
　SNELL, William E, Shipwright 1c, 104092, illness

Loch Rannoch, hired trawler
　WYNESS, Andrew, Fireman, MMR, (no service number listed), illness

Ramillies, battleship
　IRVINE, Walter R, Engine Room Artificer 4c, M 31608, illness

RMLI, Plymouth Division
 ALEXANDER, Charles E, Private, RMLI, S 5717 (Ply), illness
 PARRY, John, Private, RMLI, S 2368 (Ply), illness

Sabre, destroyer
 PENNINGTON, Archibald, Able Seaman, J 35931, illness

Undine, destroyer
 REDMAN, George L, Leading Seaman, 231081, illness

Victory, Portsmouth
 MILLAR, Thomas, Deck Hand, RNR, SD 3520, illness
 PICKLES, Albert E, Senior Reserve Attendant, M 15705, illness

Monday, 10 March 1919

Emmanuel Camelaire, Admiralty trawler, both drowned
 CUTHBERTSON, William, Deck Hand, RNR, DA 20407
 LEWIS, George, Trimmer Cook, RNR, TC 458

Ganges II, Shotley
 SANDEL, George W, Boy 2c, J 94638, illness

Kylemore, paddle minesweeper
 TREASURE, Douglas G, Lieutenant, RNVR, illness

Lucia, submarine depot ship
 KETTLE, Alfred, Shipwright 2c, 345932, illness

Mantua, armed merchant cruiser
 LEONARD, Thomas, Chief Carpenter, MMR, (no service number listed), illness in UK

Mariner, salvage vessel
 WHITEHEAD, Elliott E, Assistant Steward, MMR, 976082, illness

Pembroke, Chatham
 SMITH, Thomas B, Stoker Petty Officer, K 22271, illness

Petrel, hired drifter
 BUCK, James W, Deck Hand, RNR, DA 15469, illness

RND, 1st RM Battalion
 TATTON, Tom, Private, RMLI, S 1408 (Po), discharged, illness in UK

RND, Drake Battalion
 JOHNSTON, Andrew, Able Seaman, RNVR, Tyneside Z 6830, discharged, illness in UK

Sable, destroyer
 TREVELYAN, Percy, Sub Lieutenant, illness

Victory, Portsmouth
 POUNDS, Henry O J, Engine Room Artificer 4c, M 23085, illness

Tuesday, 11 March 1919

Concord, light cruiser
 MENHENITT, Arthur, Leading Cook's Mate, M 2827, illness

Coventry, light cruiser
 ELDERTON, Henry E, Stoker 1c, K 12072, illness

Dido, ex-cruiser, destroyer depot ship
 DANIEL, Horace S, Lieutenant, RNR, illness

HM Coast Guard Inchkeith
 WARRINGTON, Harry, Able Seaman, RNVR, Tyneside Z 9687, illness

HM Coast Guard Rosmoney
 LEMON, David, Leading Boatman, 168749, illness

RMA Battalion, South African Heavy Artillery
 HARVEY, Leonard, Sergeant, RMA, RMA 5973, discharged, illness

Royal Naval Reserve
 FINLAY, Thomas A, Lieutenant, RNR, illness

Royal Naval Volunteer Reserve
 WILKINSON, Bertrand, Ty/Sub Lieutenant, RNVR, illness

Victory, Portsmouth
 GAMBLE, John W, Ordinary Seaman, SS 8499, died

Vivid, Devonport
 ROGERS, Frederick, Able Seaman, 226638, illness

Wednesday, 12 March 1919

Bee, river gunboat
 COOK, William C, Stoker 1c, K 35042, illness

Ben Alder, hired trawler
 BROWN, Albert H, Able Seaman, J 76555, illness

Cleopatra, light cruiser
 PROWSE, Thomas C, Leading Signalman, J 6330, illness

Cyclops II, depot ship, White Sea, North Russia
 HARTNELL, Frank C, Gunner, RMA, RMA S 1827, contracted illness on active duty, died in UK

Pembroke, Chatham
 HARPER, Arthur G, Able Seaman, J 28006, illness
 MARSHALL, Thomas W, Ordinary Seaman, J 58619, illness

RM Deal
 COX, Joseph, Private, RMLI, 12939 (Deal), accident

Vivid, Devonport
 JOLLEY, John, Stoker Petty Officer, 126381, illness
 McCOMB, David, Chief Stoker, 299381, illness

Thursday, 13 March 1919

Cormorant, Gibraltar
 NEATE, John H D, Victualling Chief Petty Officer, 347341, illness

Humber, river monitor
 HIGH, Claude H, Able Seaman, J 18554, illness

Impregnable, Devonport
 TAYLOR, John W, Boy 2c, J 94284, illness

Jessamine, fleet sweeping sloop
 WHITMILL, William R, Stoker 1c, K 2651, illness

Pembroke, Chatham
 FIELD, William J, Chief Petty Officer Telegraphist, 213956, illness
 TOWNSEND, John, Chief Stoker, 296026, illness

Resolution, battleship
  BEALE, Harvey M, Ordinary Seaman, J 70671, illness

RND, Portsmouth Battalion
  BUSH, Joseph, Corporal, RMLI, 5112 (Po)(RFR A 833), discharged, illness in UK

Undine, destroyer
  DUVEY, Archibald F, Officer's Steward 2c, L 7203, illness

Victory, Portsmouth (ex-Malaya, battleship)
  WILLIAMS, Albert E, Stoker Petty Officer, 295842, illness

Friday, 14 March 1919

Attentive III, Dover
  LINKHORN, Walter R, Deck Hand, RNR, DA 5073, illness

Campanula, fleet sweeping sloop
  WILSON, Thomas S, Leading Stoker, K 14988, illness

Dolphin, Gosport
  LARDNER, Joseph J H, Chief Petty Officer, 169994, illness in UK

Hermione, 2nd class cruiser
  COOK, Harry S, Deck Hand, RNR, SD 4402, illness

Pembroke, Chatham, all illness
  HORSLEY, Ernest W, Leading Cook's Mate, M 7602
  HUNTER, Joseph, Stoker 1c, K 6497
  LAWRENCE, Frederick G, Stoker Petty Officer, K 4758
  SNELLING, Edward L, Stoker 1c, K 16304

President, London
  COCHRANE, Basil R, Lieutenant, illness
  PORT, Philip, Chief Engine Room Artificer 2c, 270423, died

RM Engineers
  HEAD, William A J, Private, RME, RME 859, illness

RMLI, Chatham Division
  BRANFILL, Richard B, Private, RMLI, 14189 (Ch), illness

Taurus, destroyer
  CUBBY, John, Signalman, J 3685, illness

Teakol, oiler
  DOUGLAS, Frederick T, Sub Lieutenant, RNR, train accident

Thisbe, destroyer
  RICHER, Douglas E, Able Seaman, 210449, illness

Saturday, 15 March 1919

Eaglet, Liverpool
  SPINDLEY, Alfred E, Engineman, MMR, (no service number listed), illness

President III, London
  WARBY, Joseph P, Able Seaman, RNVR, London Z 6251, illness

RND, Hawke Battalion
  WILLIAMSON, Harry, Able Seaman, RNVR, KP 224, discharged, illness in UK

Royal Navy
  LYON, Herbert, Admiral (ret), illness

Victory, Portsmouth
  DEAN, George, Engine Room Artificer 4c, M 11786, accident
  DOEL, Joseph, Officer's Steward 1c, 364987, illness

Women's Royal Naval Service
  HUNTER, Bessie S, Steward, WRNS, G 2066, illness in UK

Sunday, 16 March 1919

P.33, patrol boat
  CURTIS, Percy J, Leading Stoker, K 13430, accident

Pembroke, Chatham
  BOOTH, Henry L, Leading Signalman, 231204, ex-Commonwealth, illness

Ranger, destroyer
  CAVINEY, Martin, Stoker 1c, K 13925, illness

Revenge, battleship
  CRUMP, William G, Yeoman of Signals, 220097, illness

RM Engineers
  HARRISON, William, Private, RME, RME 2048, illness

RMLI, Plymouth Division
  FINDLAY, Wallace, Private, RMLI, 17626 (Ply), discharged, illness

TB.35, torpedo boat
  GUNFIELD, Ernest A, Ordinary Seaman, J 53761, illness

TB.63, torpedo boat
  HARDY, Charles A, Stoker Petty Officer, 309983, illness

Tingira (RAN), training ship, Sydney, all drowned
  BAMFORD, Herbert E, Boy 2c, RAN, 11130
  EARL, Leslie W H, Boy 2c, RAN, 6902
  FELLOWS, Charles W, Boy 2c, RAN, 6802
  McPHERSON, John E, Boy 2c, RAN, 11126
  PAGE, George W, Boy 2c, RAN, 6790

Welland, destroyer
  SCOTCHER, Cyril G, Sub Lieutenant, RNR, illness

Monday, 17 March 1919

RMLI, Chatham Division
  WALKER, John H, Private, RMLI, 20036 (Ch), illness

Veronica, fleet sweeping sloop
  WILLIE, John H, Stoker 1c, K 30108, illness

Victory, Portsmouth
  VATTER, George S W, Petty Officer Telegraphist, J 6164, illness

Tuesday, 18 March 1919

Fisgard, Portsmouth
  BROWN, Arthur H, Painter 3c, M 13869, illness

Indus, Devonport
  KENNY, Michael, Stoker 1c, 175623, illness

Inflexible, battlecruiser
  LARDNER, William G, Stoker Petty Officer, 312176, illness

Pembroke, Chatham
  HAZELL, Charles E, Able Seaman, J 32084, illness

Thalia, store hulk, Cromarty
 KITCHEN, William H, Petty Officer 1c, 97163, illness

Tiger, battlecruiser
 LEWER, Ernest, Stoker 1c, K 38640, illness

Victory, Portsmouth
 BRADLEY, William J, Able Seaman, J 78842, illness
 HODSON, George H, Deck Hand, RNR, DA 12217, illness

Vivid, Devonport
 CANNEL, James, Deck Hand, RNR, DA 18512, illness

Yarmouth, 2nd class cruiser
 HEAD, Albert H, Canteen Assistant, Admiralty civilian, illness

Wednesday, 19 March 1919

Duchess of Devonshire, armed boarding steamer
 NIGHTINGALE, Stanley J, Able Seaman, RNVR, Bristol Z 11066, illness

Egmont, Malta
 PASCOE, Nicholas, Deck Hand, RNR, DA 6592, illness

Gilia, convoy sloop
 GRANT, William J, Chief Stoker, 290035, illness

Pembroke, Chatham
 SMITH, Ernest S, Stoker 1c, K 25583, illness

Queen, battleship
 PONTING, Percy R, Lance Corporal, RMLI, 13786 (Ch), illness in Baku, Turkey

Rainstorm, Admiralty wood drifter
 TURNER, John G, 2nd Hand, RNR, SD 945, drowned

RMLI, Portsmouth Division
 COX, Thomas, Private, RMLI, 14931 (Po), illness

Thisbe, destroyer
 BROUGHTON, Frederick G, Stoker 1c, K 35876, illness

Victory, Portsmouth
 EARWICKER, Henry, Stoker Petty Officer, 119546, illness
 FODEN, James, Able Seaman, 215875, illness

Vindex, seaplane carrier
 HUGHES, William, Trimmer, MMR, 934705, illness

Walrus, destroyer
 GRIFFITHS, Willie, Able Seaman, J 47924, illness

Thursday, 20 March 1919

Abercrombie, monitor
 FRIEND, Frederick J, Private, RMLI, 14014 (Ch), illness

Centaur, light cruiser
 BURTON, James, Engine Room Artificer 4c, M 28432, illness

Glorious, light battlecruiser
 FLEMING, Ernest K, Engineer Lieutenant, illness

Valorous, destroyer
 PUTTOCK, Denys E, Sub Lieutenant, illness

Friday, 21 March 1919

Fisgard, Portsmouth
 MAPLESDEN, William J, Chief Stoker, 286221, accident

Galatea, light cruiser
 MINTER, Alfred E, Stoker 1c, 303046, drowned

Hannibal, battleship
 McCALMONT, Andrew, Ordinary Seaman, J 69697, illness

Pembroke, Chatham
 FORD, Frederick A, Stoker 1c, K 55403, illness

President, London
 RICHARDSON, RAYMOND De D., Lieutenant, illness

RMLI, Portsmouth Division
 STRUGNELL, Harold F H, Major, RMLI, illness in UK

Satellite, Tyne
 NOBLE, James, Deck Hand, RNR, DA 19967, accident

Vivid, Devonport
 WALDRON, Albury A, Officer's Steward 2c, L 5528, accident

Saturday, 22 March 1919

Caesar, battleship
 FROST, Bert, Trimmer, RNR, TS 3908, illness

Caledon, light cruiser
 FORMOSA, Vincenzo, Officer's Chief Cook, 359813, illness

Fisgard, Portsmouth
 PRISCOTT, Robert T, Stoker 1c, 116608, illness

Hyacinth, 2nd class cruiser
 BLESSINGTON, Thomas, Private, RMLI, 8085 (Ply), died in St Helena

President III, London
 MILLER, Arthur S, Private, RM, 15924 (Po), illness

Victory, Portsmouth
 BUGG, Rupert W, Leading Deck Hand, RNR, SD 5046, illness

Sunday, 23 March 1919

Bacchante, armoured cruiser
 JAMES, Albert, Armourers Crew, M 12815, illness

Boy Bob, hired drifter
 WALKER, Alexander, Engineman, RNR, ES 1292, illness

Caesar, battleship
 DAVIES, William J, Colour Sergeant, RMLI, 9303 (Ply), illness in Constantinople

Foresight, scout cruiser
 McCABE, William J, Private, RMLI, 15918 (Ply), died in Malta

Pembroke, Chatham
 MAY, William H, Lieutenant Commander, illness

RMLI, Plymouth Division
 SHIPLEY, Alexander W, Sergeant, RMLI, 9115 (Ply), illness in UK

RND, Anson Battalion
  MOLONEY, Stephen, Seaman, RNR, B 4558, discharged, illness in UK

Monday, 24 March 1919

Colleen, Queenstown, Ireland
  DEMELLWEEK, Joseph M, Seaman, RNR, B 3302, illness

Crescent, Rosyth
  McMANUS, William, Trimmer, MMR, (no service number listed), illness

Pembroke, Chatham
  LANGWORTHY, Charles H, Engine Room Artificer 4c, M 19324, illness
  SEAL, Jack, Ordinary Seaman, J 74031, died

RND, Drake Battalion
  SMITH, James H, Able Seaman, RNVR, Tyneside 6 131, discharged, illness in UK

Vigorous, depot ship, Larne
  COOPER, Albion, 2nd Hand, RNR, SA 1225, illness

Wahine, converted minelayer
  BELDHAM, Allen E, Assistant Steward, MMR, (no service number listed), illness

Tuesday, 25 March 1919

Aracari, hired trawler
  ROBERTS, David, Able Seaman, J 41628, illness

Hecla, destroyer depot ship
  STEVENS, Edmund, Chief Stoker, 299118, illness

Implacable, battleship
  ADAMS, William G A, Stoker 1c, K 25237, drowned

Maidstone, submarine depot ship
  McHUGH, Niel, Stoker, RNR, V 310, illness

President IV, London
  SILCOCK, Thomas R, Leading Signalman, RNVR, Wales Z 668, illness

RM Labour Corps, both accident in UK
  KNIGHT, George, Private, RM, S 9492 (Deal)
  SIMMONS, Joseph, Private, RM, S 8820 (Deal)

Wednesday, 26 March 1919

Fox, 2nd class cruiser
  LEAF, Alfred W, Warrant Shipwright, illness, buried at Gillingham

Ganges, Shotley/Harwich
  HILL, Victor A, Petty Officer Telegraphist, 223042, drowned

Gilia, convoy sloop
  BRAND, Frederick A, Stoker Petty Officer, 307776, illness

Nairn, hired patrol yacht
  PIRIE, George, Engineman, RNR, TS 3259, accident

Redpole, destroyer
  STRINGER, Frederick T, Lieutenant, illness

RND, Divisional Train Reserves
  ELLIOTT, Stanley, Private, RM, S 2540 (Deal), discharged, illness in UK

Sentinel, steamship
  COWELL, John R, Leading Seaman, RNR, B 4733, illness

Victory, Portsmouth
  GARDNER, Walter G, Electrical Artificer 4c, M 27779, illness
  JONES, Edward, Telegraphist, J 40462, illness

Vivid, Devonport
  DAVIES, David J, Officer's Cook 1c, L 9680, illness
  PERRING, William, Chief Stoker, 306472, illness

Thursday, 27 March 1919

Bombardier, Admiralty trawler, all drowned
  GRENYER, Alfred J, Engineman, RNR, ES 5076
  NICHOLS, William R, Ty/Skipper, RNR
  PORTER, Charles H, Trimmer Cook, RNR, TC 585
  PRIOR, George H, Leading Stoker, K 16131 (Dev)
  VANSTONE, Wilfred J, Leading Seaman, 232533 (Dev)

Columbine, Rosyth
  SAUNDERS, James, Able Seaman, J 34737, illness

Goeland II, hired trawler
  McGOWN, James, Seaman, RNR, A 6345, accident

King George V, battleship
  REEVES, Henry A, Musician, RMB, RMB 2037, illness in UK

Pembroke, Chatham
  PHILIP, Francis, Able Seaman, J 28184, illness

RND, Nelson Battalion
  DURHAM, Ernest R, Able Seaman, RNVR, London Z 198, discharged, illness in UK

Vivid, Devonport
  MORGAN, Frederick, Petty Officer 1c, 139526, illness

Friday, 28 March 1919

Arrogant, submarine depot ship
  POLE, Magnus, Seaman, RNR, B 3043, died

RMLI, Portsmouth Division
  WILLIAMS, Harvey L, Private, RMLI, 17130 (Po), illness

RND, Collingwood Battalion
  MARSHALL, Stanley, Able Seaman, RNVR, Tyneside Z 3/144, discharged, illness in UK

Victory, Portsmouth
  HALL, Frank E, Leading Seaman, 214858, illness

Saturday, 29 March 1919

Bonaventure, ex-cruiser, submarine depot ship
  PEARSON, William, Stoker 1c, K 16318, illness

Ceto, Ramsgate
  LEVERETT, William, Engineman, RNR, ES 1505, illness

Egmont, Malta
  CLARKE, Frederick, Deck Hand, RNR, DA 15332, illness

Gosforth, fleet messenger
 DOWNS, John P, Lieutenant, RNR, illness

Sunday, 30 March 1919

Cawdor Castle, steamship
 PACEY, James T, Skipper, MMR, illness

Impregnable, Devonport
 GRIFFIN, Arthur W B, Boy 2c, J 93638, illness

RND, 1st RM Battalion, France
 HOLT, Alfred, Private, RMLI, S 602 (Ply), DOW in UK

Victory, Portsmouth
 BOSWELL, James, Boy Servant, L 11998, illness
 O'CONNELL, Richard P, Fireman, MMR, (no service number listed), illness

Monday, 31 March 1919

Agamemnon, target ship
 BROOKS, Albert, Petty Officer 1c, 174789, illness

Egmont, Malta
 STEWART, William J, Engineman, RNR, TS 1376, illness

Ganges, Shotley/Harwich
 SCOTT, Percival G, Senior Reserve Attendant, M 10047, illness

Lion, battlecruiser
 GRAVES, George A, Leading Stoker, K 10914, illness

RM Engineers
 COOKMAN, Sidney G, Private, RME, RME 1168, illness

RMLI, Plymouth Division
 STRATFORD, Henry B, Private, RMLI, 13180 (Ply), illness in UK

TB.63, torpedo boat
 CUSSE, Francis N W, Chief Engine Room Artificer 2c, 271233, illness

Tuesday, 1 April 1919

Astraea, 2nd class cruiser
 GIBBS, James W, Leading Seaman, 234449 (Ch), drowned in Lagos

New Zealand, battlecruiser
 RENNIE, Andrew, Able Seaman, J 13182, accident

Pembroke, Chatham
 TOTTMAN, William, Able Seaman, 221957, illness

President III, London
 WALLACE, William, Leading Seaman, RNVR, Clyde Z 8667, illness

Prestol, oiler, mercantile fleet auxiliary
 MARTIN, Samuel A, Ordinary Seaman, MMR, 930305, illness

Talbot, 2nd class cruiser
 ATKINSON, George, Officer's Steward 1c, L 8058 (Po), illness

Wednesday, 2 April 1919

Glen Usk, paddle minesweeper
 CLAYTON, Edward W, Signalman, RNVR, London Z 3371, accident

Pembroke, Chatham
 CROWLEY, John M, Ordinary Telegraphist, J 25366, illness

RMLI, Portsmouth Division
 ELLIOTT, John G, Private, RMLI, 16932 (Po), died

RND, Hawke Battalion
 WHITWORTH, Arthur, Able Seaman, RNVR, Tyneside Z 8389, discharged, illness in UK

Triad, Admiralty Yacht, SNO, Persian Gulf
 WELLS, Stephen W, Private, RMLI, 13026 (Ch), illness in Taranto

Vivid, Devonport
 COLLINS, Fred, Yeoman of Signals, 210007, died

Thursday, 3 April 1919

Dove II, hired trawler
 BEAGARIE, Frederick B, 2nd Hand, RNR, DA 2197, illness

Pembroke, Chatham
 CHANDLER, Samuel, Stoker Petty Officer, 292046, illness

RND, Drake Battalion, France
 BRATBY, Kenneth K, Able Seaman, RNVR, R 6054, DOW in UK
 FILER, Ernest W, Able Seaman, RNVR, Bristol Z 1269, illness in UK

RND, Hood Battalion
 WASHINGTON, Harry G, Able Seaman, RNVR, R 2683, discharged, illness in UK

Royal Navy
 BOULTON, Robert, Lieutenant (ret), illness

Victory, Portsmouth
 CHILCRAFT, Albert, Leading Deck Hand, DA 12331, illness
 MUSTOE, Andrew, Able Seaman, 166669, illness

Friday, 4 April 1919

RND, 2nd Reserve Battalion
 FOORD, Harold R, Ty/Sub Lieutenant, RNVR, illness in UK

RND, Hawke Battalion, France
 LOWE, Frederick W, Able Seaman, RNVR, R 5539, illness

Vivid, Devonport
 MEAD, Frank, Chief Engine Room Artificer 1c, 268938, illness

Saturday, 5 April 1919

Fifinella, hired trawler
 SWANKIE, Robert, Deck Hand, RNR, SD 4601, accident

Impregnable, Devonport
 COOMBES, Alfred L, Boy 2c, J 94057, illness

New Zealand, battlecruiser
 FAWCUS, Victor C B, Midshipman, illness

RM Engineers, Chatham
DAVEY, Mark H, Private, RM, S 9613 (Ply), illness

RMLI, Chatham Division
HENDRY, John, Sergeant, RMLI, 15078 (Ch), illness

RMLI, Portsmouth Division
WHITAKER, John R, Sergeant, RMLI, 15477 (Po), illness

RND, Nelson Battalion
GODFREY, Charles J, Able Seaman, RNVR (Bugler), Bristol Z 474, discharged, illness in UK

Thunderer, battleship
DEARNELEY, Thomas, Boy 1c, J 82849, illness

Victory, Portsmouth
WILLIAMS, Askett A, Chief Stoker, 167154, illness

Sunday, 6 April 1919

Verdun, destroyer
MACKIE, Andrew, Leading Seaman, J 4237, accident

Monday, 7 April 1919

Acacia, fleet sweeping sloop
THORNTON, John, Chief Engine Room Artificer, RNR, EA 1025, accident

Cromorna, hired drifter
BROWNE, Ernest R, Skipper, RNR, illness

Eaglet, Liverpool
McFARLANE, Francis, Fireman, MMR, 904813, illness

Tuesday, 8 April 1919

Champion, light cruiser
HELPS, Walter J, Stoker 1c, K 3186, illness

Pembroke, Chatham
McCULLOCH, John D, Able Seaman, 216573, illness
TAYLOR, William H, Petty Officer, RNVR, Bristol Z 754, illness

President III, London
ROBERTSON, John, Seaman, RNR, B 4083, illness

Ramillies, battleship
WARREN, James W, Sergeant, RMA, RMA 10751, illness

Resolution, battleship
WOOD, Harold D, Boy 1c, J 80652 (Dev), drowned

RM Labour Corps
BARNES, John T, Private, RM, S 11945 (Deal), died

Wednesday, 9 April 1919

Bellerophon, battleship
GREEN, Joseph H, Signal Boy, J 81609, illness

Gloucester, light cruiser
BALFOUR, Robert S, Engine Room Artificer 3c, M 16479, illness in RN Plymouth

RND, Hood Battalion
MARSHALL, Robert, Able Seaman, RNVR, Mersey Z 1 149, discharged, illness in UK

Thistle, 1st class gunboat
FENN, Cecil H, Lieutenant, RNR, illness

Victory, Portsmouth
MILLSON, Henry B, Stoker 1c, SS 119660, illness

Vivid, Devonport
PINN, William H, Leading Seaman, 188778, died
WARD, Frederick J, Able Seaman, 181956, illness

Thursday, 10 April 1919

Emperor of India, battleship
FLINTHAM, Arthur E, Stoker 1c, K 52538, illness

RM Labour Corps
LANE, John, Private, RM, S 10971 (Deal), illness
O'RIORDON, Timothy, Private, RM, S 12860 (Deal), died in USA

RND, Drake Battalion
MITCHELL, Percy, Able Seaman, RNVR, ZW 752, discharged, illness in UK

Friday, 11 April 1919

Implacable, battleship
YULE, David, Signal Boy, RNR, SB 1875, drowned

Impregnable, Devonport
TOTTERDELL, Arthur E N, Boy 2c, J 94032, illness

RM Labour Corps
MARTIN, Edward W, Private, RM, S 14015 (Deal), illness

Spey, tender, Chatham
RATE, William R, Able Seaman, 196037, illness

Saturday, 12 April 1919

Marlborough, battleship
CAMM, Thomson, Ordinary Seaman, J 85434, illness

Sunday, 13 April 1919

Simpson, hired trawler
MOORE, Charles A, Ordinary Seaman, SS 8551, illness

TB.36, torpedo boat
JONES, Thomas I, Able Seaman, 237257, illness

Thomas Robins, Admiralty trawler
LEYSHON, Gomer T, Leading Telegraphist, RNVR, Wales Z 257, illness

Vivid, Devonport
LAWES, Thomas N E, Yeoman of Signals, 222699, illness

Monday, 14 April 1919

Acacia, fleet sweeping sloop
BEST, Frederick G, Able Seaman, J 17362, accident

Victory, Portsmouth
THOMAS, William H, Able Seaman, 129962, illness

Vivid, Devonport
THOMAS, John F, Petty Officer, 197274, illness

Tuesday, 15 April 1919

RND, 1st RM Battalion, attached Howe Battalion
BYRNE, John, Able Seaman, RNVR, R 3758, discharged, illness in UK

Sentinel, scout cruiser
BIRD, William, Ordinary Seaman, J 72647 (Ch), drowned

Wednesday, 16 April 1919

Caesar, battleship
CUTAJAR, Giovanni, Stoker 1c, K 55154, illness

Repulse, battlecruiser
ASHFORD, William J S, Boatswain, illness

RND, Deal Battalion
McGUIRE, William, Private, RMLI, 7315 (Ch) (RFR B 1213), discharged, illness in UK

Tiverton, minesweeper
WARREN, Thomas S, Stoker Petty Officer, K 4688, accident

Victory, Portsmouth
BLOOR, Edward W, Telegraphist, J 57992, illness

Thursday, 17 April 1919

Diana, 2nd class cruiser
TENNANT, Sidney, Able Seaman, J 37079, illness

Halcyon, Lowestoft
JACKSON, George, Engineman, RNR, ES 2287, illness

RMA Battalion
SIMPSON, Peter, Colour Sergeant, RMA, RMA 1985 (RFR A), discharged, illness in UK

Royal Naval Volunteer Reserve
COND, Frederick T P, Ty/Lieutenant, RNVR, illness

Friday, 18 April 1919

Mandala, steamship
MARTIN, Gilbert, Leading Seaman, RNVR, Clyde Z 6503, died

Pembroke, Chatham
BUCKLEE, Fred, Stoker Petty Officer, 297696, illness

RM Labour Corps
HODSON, Ernest, Private, RM, S 14332 (Deal), illness

Vivid, Devonport
LOVELL, Albert, Chief Petty Officer, 108631, illness

Saturday, 19 April 1919

Eaglet, Liverpool
HUBBARD, John E, Ordinary Seaman, MMR, 909321, illness

Impregnable, Devonport
STEVENS, Alfred W, Boy 2c, J 94136, illness

Offa II, hired trawler
COOK, Percy S, Skipper, RNR, illness

Pembroke, Chatham
COOK, Ivan, 1st Writer, M 5295, illness

Sunday, 20 April 1919

Crescent, Rosyth
GALYER, James M, Able Seaman, 187621, illness

Peter Lovett, Admiralty trawler
DAVIES, George S, Stoker Petty Officer, RNR, ES 1669, illness

Monday, 21 April 1919

Britomart, gunboat
MOOSSA, Almas, 2nd Seedie, (no service number listed), illness

RMLI, 1st Reserve Battalion
BRUEN, Charles J, Private, RMLI, 18554 (Po), discharged, illness in UK

RND, Anson Battalion
PANNETT, Hudson, Able Seaman, RNVR, KP 840, discharged, illness in UK

Vivid, Devonport
WOODMAN, Thomas D, Stoker 1c, K 22098, illness

Tuesday, 22 April 1919

Devonshire, armoured cruiser
HARRIES, William, Stoker 1c, K 35797, illness

Idaho, ex-hired yacht, tug
SWANSTON, John, Trimmer, RNR, TS 2918, illness

Margaret And Andrew, steamship
WEBSTER, Ernest J E, Paymaster Lieutenant (ret), illness

Royal Air Force, air crash
BATCHELOR, Thomas A, Paymaster Lieutenant

Wednesday, 23 April 1919

Endeavour, survey ship
EBBS, Sidney C, Able Seaman, J 39043, drowned

Melbourne (RAN), 2nd class cruiser
LAIDLAW, Robert S, Lieutenant (on loan to RAN), illness

ML.364, motor launch
SCOTT, William J, Sub Lieutenant, RNVR, illness

Pembroke, Chatham
EDWARDS, Arthur W, Stoker Petty Officer, K 370, died

Valiant, battleship
MOULTRIE, Lionel G F, Midshipman, illness

Victory, Portsmouth
ALBOROUGH, Sidney A, Boy 1c, J 57072, died

Westcott, destroyer
PETTIGREW, James R H, Able Seaman, J 21842, died

Thursday, 24 April 1919

Astraea, 2nd class cruiser
 MATHER, George, Stoker, RNR, S 5251, illness

HM Coastguard Station Charlestown
 CONDY, Edward J, Leading Boatman, HM Coast Guard, 205835, illness

Karavnos, tug
 TURNER, Harry W J, Stoker Petty Officer, 296381, illness

Lewis Pelley, launch, attached Inland Water Transport
 BELFIELD, James S, Engineer Sub Lieutenant, RIM, illness

Whitby Abbey, minesweeper
 LAWRENCE, Benjamin, Stoker, RNR, S 4627, illness

Friday, 25 April 1919

Danae, light cruiser
 HARNOTT, Joseph T, Able Seaman, 225207, illness

President V, London
 GREEN, George F, Paymaster Sub Lieutenant, RNR, illness
 RYAN, Patrick, 2nd Writer, M 7677, accident

RM Labour Corps, RM Depot Deal
 LEWIS, George, Private, RM, S 13220 (Deal), illness

Saturday, 26 April 1919

Cumberland, armoured cruiser
 THOMAS, Charles G, Leading Seaman, 188000, illness

Dreel Castle, hired drifter
 MOONEY, John, 2nd Hand, RNR, A 6297, illness

Hughli, salvage tug, Royal Fleet Auxiliary, carrying naval stores from Ostend to Dover, capsized in violent storm off Middlekerke, 11 survivors
 BROWN, Thomas W, Salvage Boatswain, MMR, (no service number listed)
 CAIN, John, Assistant Cook, MMR, 898718
 CAMERON, Simon, Salvage Shipwright, MMR, (no service number listed)
 DAVIES, Herbert E, Lieutenant, RNR
 DOBSON, John, Fireman, MMR, 918552
 DUNNE, Denis, Ship's Cook, MMR, 998261
 GILL, Thomas A, Engineer Lieutenant, RNR
 GORDON, Thomas, Sub Lieutenant, RNR
 HARRISON, Thomas, Fireman, MMR, 620629
 JOHNSON, Ernest E, Telegraphist, RNVR, Palace Z 1647
 McGLADDERY, William, Sub Lieutenant, RNVR
 McQUEEN, Andrew, Paymaster, RNR
 MEEK, Thomas, Foreman Rigger, MMR, 777136
 PATTERSON, William, Rigger, MMR, (no service number listed)
 ROSE, William, Assistant Steward, MMR, 981310
 TEBBETT, Thomas R C, Signalman, MMR, 977439
 WHITE, Robert J, Assistant Steward, MMR, 882944
 WILLIAMS, David J, Rigger, MMR, (no service number listed)

Sunday, 27 April 1919

Armadale Castle, armed merchant cruiser
 CHISHOLM, James, Engineer Commander, illness

Belgic, steamship
 WILLS, Gordon, Leading Seaman, SS 1368, accident

Excellent, Portsmouth
 LETLEY, Leonard W, Midshipman, RNR, drowned

Gunner, Granton
 WILSON, Herbert, Deck Hand, RNR, DA 12292, illness

Octavia, destroyer
 FEARNE, Sidney F, Stoker 1c, K 42233, illness

Ramillies, battleship
 CADD, William, Boy 1c, J 89738, illness

Severn, river monitor
 LUPTON, Richard, Able Seaman, J 59349, illness

Monday, 28 April 1919

Thalia, store hulk, Cromarty
 SUTHERLAND, Thomas, Engineman, RNR, S 2789, illness

Tuesday, 29 April 1919

Frostaxe, Admiralty trawler, sunk in collision with Greek steamship Epiros in English Channel off Newhaven, 11 survivors
 CHANNER, Frank, Stoker 1c, K 21141 (Ch)
 CLACKETT, William, Stoker 1c, 175961 (Ch)
 PARTRIDGE, John R, Ordinary Seaman, SS 7160 (Ch)
 PEARSON, Sidney J, Able Seaman, J 47400 (Ch)
 PRATT, Daniel J, Signalman, J 19619 (Ch)
 SHARMAN, John A, Telegraphist, J 38974 (Ch)
 SULLEY, Richard, Able Seaman, J 43778 (Ch)
 SUTTON, Leonard L, Engine Room Artificer 3c, M 8850 (Ch)
 WILSON, Charles L, Stoker 1c, K 8293 (Ch)

Implacable, battleship
 SOUTHWICK, John H, Engineman, RNR, ES 3236, illness

Wednesday, 30 April 1919

Bristol, 2nd class cruiser
 STEVENS, Albert E, Leading Stoker, 201785 (Po), illness

Thursday, 1 May 1919

Impregnable, Devonport
 RANSOME, Harry, Boy 2c, J 94107, illness

Lion, battlecruiser
 BERRIMAN, Wiiliam, Gunner, RMA, RMA 10689, illness in UK

RMLI, Portsmouth Division
 GODLEY, William, Private, RMLI, S 2313 (Po), illness

Victory, Portsmouth
 DOWLER, Bertie E, Cook's Mate 2c, M 34574, died

Friday, 2 May 1919

Doris, 2nd class cruiser
 ROBERTSON, Stewart, Painter 1c, 344870, illness

RND, Anson Battalion
 CAHALANE, Daniel, Seaman, RNR, A 5310, discharged, illness in UK

Sunhill, accommodation ship
 DALZIEL, William, Sub Lieutenant, RNR, illness (Heroic, armed boarding steamer)

Vindictive, cruiser/seaplane carrier
HAWKINS, Veines J, Leading Seaman, J 15592 (Po), drowned

Saturday, 3 May 1919

Dufferin (RIM), troopship
WILLIAMS, Keroo, Officer's Steward 2c, (no service number listed), illness

RUSSIAN INTERVENTION

Glory III, Archangel, North Russia
HITCHIN, Bertie T, Private, RMLI, 18521 (Ch), killed
WORROLL, Ernest H, Gunner, RMA, RMA 15055, killed

Venerable, battleship
DRISCOLL, Denis, Leading Stoker, 283113, illness

Sunday, 4 May 1919

*Destroyer **Tryphon** ran aground on Tenedos in the Aegean, salvaged but declared total loss, There were no casualties (below, S-class sister-ship Tenedos)*

Belgol, oiler, Royal Fleet Auxiliary
TENSON, Walter, Cook, MMR, 837360, illness

HM Coastguard Station Par Cornwall
BATES, George, Chief Officer, HM Coast Guard, illness in UK

PC.61, patrol boat
HEARNE, Charles W, Able Seaman, 238051, drowned
McDOWALL, Thomas, Able Seaman, J 18352, drowned

RND, 1st RM Battalion, France
WEBB, Oliver, Lance Corporal, RMLI, 11822 (Po), DOW in UK

Shincliffe, paddle minesweeper
LYNCH, Philip, Leading Trimmer, RNR, ST 1573, drowned

Monday, 5 May 1919

*Minesweeper **Cupar** mined and sunk in the North Sea off the Northumberland coast.*

President VI, London
ALUM, George, Stoker 1c, 98665, illness

Tuesday, 6 May 1919

Egmont, Malta
JARDINE, Peter G, Chief Motor Mechanic, RNVR, MB 1721, illness

Wireless Telegraph Station Seychelles
NORMAN, William, Stoker 1c, K 1223, illness

Wednesday, 7 May 1919

Alice, dockyard tug
WALLACE, Malcolm A, Sub Lieutenant, RNR, illness

Encounter (RAN), 2nd class cruiser
BIRD, Alfred L, Engine Room Artificer 3c, RAN, 3542, illness

Lord Nelson, battleship
BIRD, Stanley, Able Seaman, J 58513, illness

Thursday, 8 May 1919

Abercrombie, monitor
TILLING, John, Petty Officer, 202967, drowned

Actaeon, Sheerness
PERKINS, Arthur, Senior Reserve Attendant, M 10090, illness

Nairn, hired patrol yacht
McKINNION, Niel, Deck Hand, RNR, DA 14734, died in UK

Royal Navy
WYLDBERE-SMITH, Hugh F, Captain (ret), illness

Friday, 9 May 1919

Sydney (RAN), 2nd class cruiser
TAYLOR, Herbert S, Stoker, RAN, 335, illness

Saturday, 10 May 1919

Attentive II, Dover
TINLEY, Walter J, Chief Petty Officer, 155526, accident

RUSSIAN INTERVENTION

Glory, battleship, Murmansk
DRAKE-BROCKHAM, Lewis, Major, RMLI, killed

Idaho, ex-hired yacht, tug
JAY, George H, Trimmer, RNR, TS 7386, illness

New Zealand, battlecruiser
JACQUES, Frederick, Stoker 1c, 295765, illness

Sunday, 11 May 1919

Northolt, minesweeper
DAVIDSON, Adair, Deck Hand, RNR, SD 1601, accident

Pembroke, Chatham
LAMPORT, James E, Leading Stoker, SS 112469, illness

Speedy, destroyer
BOSLEY, Luther, Telegraphist, J 35185 (Po), illness

Monday, 12 May 1919

Bristol, 2nd class cruiser
ROBERTS, Albert S, Able Seaman, J 44650 (Ch), illness

Pembroke, Chatham
 HANKS, Cecil J, Able Seaman, J 61034, illness

Vigorous, depot ship, Larne
 FISHER, Edward G, Surgeon Lieutenant, accident

Vivid, Devonport
 NOBLE, Alexander, Leading Trimmer, RNR, TS 1513, illness

Tuesday, 13 May 1919

Bristol, 2nd class cruiser
 CRANER, Victor, Cook's Mate, M 10421 (Po), illness

Curacoa, light cruiser, mined
 PLUNKITT, George H, Ordinary Seaman, SS 9150 (Ch)

Elmol, oiler, Royal Fleet Auxiliary
 SANDERS, Arnold E, Cook, MMR, 550781, illness

Pembroke, Chatham
 SNAITH, Frederick, Stoker 1c, K 23857 (Ch), illness

President, London
 DAVIS, Frederick J, Lieutenant Commander, RNR (ret), illness

St Vincent, Gosport
 CURTIS, Charles E, Canteen Manager, Admiralty civilian, illness

Wednesday, 14 May 1919

Royal Navy
 HOOD, Martin A F, Lieutenant Commander, illness

Thursday, 15 May 1919

Lady Moyra, paddle minesweeper, accidental explosion, two killed, one died of injuries
 DAVIDSON, John D, Engineer T, RNR *(T abbreviation not known – perhaps Torpedo)*, DOI ashore
President, London
 BABBAGE, Sidney J, Lieutenant
 WEBLEY, William T, Lieutenant, killed ashore

Shincliffe, paddle minesweeper
 SWINDLE, Robert, Ordinary Seaman, J 76031 (Dev), drowned

St Aubin, rescue tug, all drowned
 CHARNOCK, Robert, Cook, MMR, 756501
 HARMAN, Robert, Able Seaman, MMR, 912591
 MAHONEY, Michael, Able Seaman, MMR, 997972

Friday, 16 May 1919

Thalia, store hulk, Cromarty
 MASSIE, Thomas, Deck Hand, RNR, DA 2549, accident

Victory, Portsmouth
 CHISHOLM, Joseph, Deck Hand, RNR, DA 10910, illness

Saturday, 17 May 1919

Cupar, minesweeper, sunk on 5 May
 STEPHEN, William C, Engine Room Artificer, RNR, EA 1810, killed *(listed in Ledger; reason for killed on this date is not known)*

HM Coastguard Station Sutton
 ANSELL, Alfred, Petty Officer 2c, 125583, illness

Pembroke, Chatham
 BOAL, James, Stoker Petty Officer, 287397, illness

Victory, Portsmouth
 IDE, Frederick, Chief Stoker, 276281, illness

Sunday, 18 May 1919

Assistance, repair ship
 BAILEY, Charles E, Stoker 1c, SS 116957, accident

Pearl III, hired drifter
 COCKING, John, Deck Hand, RNR, DA 15882, illness

RM, 3rd Battalion
 WILKES, Stanley W, Lance Corporal, RMLI, 19792 (Ch), illness in Lemnos

RND, Hawke Battalion
 HAMER, Harry, Able Seaman, RNVR, Mersey Z 607, discharged, illness in UK

Monday, 19 May 1919

Actaeon, Sheerness
 GREGG, Horace C, Leading Seaman, J 17905, drowned

Hannibal, battleship
 ALI, Ahmet, Seedie Stoker, (no service number listed), illness

Hood, battlecruiser, under construction, explosion on board
 McGREGOR, James, civilian engineer, killed
 MORTON, John, civilian engineer, killed

Ramillies, battleship
 LEGG, John T, Boy 1c, J 78784 (Dev), accident

Wednesday, 21 May 1919

Bird, drifter
 HEALEY, Timothy, Deck Hand, RNR, DA 18829, illness

RUSSIAN INTERVENTION

Emile Nobel, gunboat, ex-Russian tanker, Caspian Sea, in action off Alexandrovsk
 BESSANT, Frederick A, Stoker 1c, K 35840 (Po), DOW
 BURNETT, Oliver D, Stoker Petty Officer, 309917 (Ch), DOW
 COLLARD, William A, Able Seaman, J 36559 (Ch), KIA
 WHEATON, Harold, Bugler, RMLI, 19979 (Ch), KIA

Grafton, 1st class cruiser
 McMILLAN, John, Stoker, RNR, S 2753, drowned

Thursday, 22 May 1919

RUSSIAN INTERVENTION

Emile Nobel, gunboat, ex-Russian tanker, Caspian Sea, in action off Alexandrovsk
 DARKE, Herbert R, Chief Engine Room Artificer 2c, M 1 (Dev), DOW

Hydrangea, fleet sweeping sloop
  HORTON, Edwin, Chief Stoker, 299022 (Dev), illness in Hong Kong

Friday, 23 May 1919

Pontypool, minesweeper
  McALLISTER, George H, Lieutenant, RNR, accident

Saturday, 24 May 1919

Pembroke, Chatham
  WARREN, William, Stoker Petty Officer, K 3363, illness

Victory, Portsmouth
  BRADBURY, Henry A, Officer's Steward 2c, L 6249, illness

Sunday, 25 May 1919

Kent, armoured cruiser
  ASH, Charlie, Private, RMLI, 14771 (Po), illness in UK

RM Deal
  McMANUS, Thomas M, Private, RM, S 310 (Deal), illness

Vernon, Portsmouth
  FEDARB, Frederick, Surgeon Commander, illness

Monday, 26 May 1919

Defiance, Devonport
  LEARY, Timothy, Telegraphist, J 42012, illness

Victory, Portsmouth
  BRINDLE, Harold, Able Seaman, J 15930, illness

Tuesday, 27 May 1919

Cuckoo, ex-gunboat, tender, Devonport
  ROBINSON, John, Petty Officer, J 925, accident

Pembroke, Chatham
  BAKER, Robert, Stoker 1c, K 6474, died

RM Labour Corps
  MULLEN, John, Private, RM, S 14610 (Deal), illness

Wednesday, 28 May 1919

Diana, 2nd class cruiser
  WITT, Edward F, Private, RMLI, 8840 (Ply), killed in UK

RND, Anson Battalion
  DYE, Edgar E, Able Seaman, RNVR, R 744, illness in UK

Royal Sovereign, battleship
  WOODARD, James, Stoker Petty Officer, 302926, illness

Vivid, Devonport
  CARISS, Philip H, Victualling Chief Petty Officer, M 2636, accident

Friday, 30 May 1919

Vivid, Devonport
  WATSON, Alexander, Skipper, RNR, died

Sunday, 1 June 1919

Mimosa, fleet sweeping sloop
  TALBOT, Ernest T S, Stoker 1c, SS 102740, illness

RMA Eastney
  TAYLOR, William, Driver, RMA, RMA S 828, illness in UK

Monday, 2 June 1919

Ajax, battleship
  MOORE, Joseph G, Cooper 1c, 341717, died

RND, 2nd RM Battalion
  COOK, John W, Sergeant, RMLI, 7259 (Ply), discharged, illness in UK

RND, Anson Battalion
  SWEENEY, John, Petty Officer, RNVR, Clyde 3 509, discharged, illness in UK

Sunhill, accomodation ship
  OAKLEY, Alfred E, Engineer Sub Lieutenant, RNR, illness

Tuesday, 3 June 1919

Impregnable, Devonport
  BARRABLE, Harry G, Boy 2c, J 93977, illness

Wednesday, 4 June 1919

HM Coastguard Station Felixstowe
  WOODWARD, Arthur H, Coastguardsman 2c, 166560, illness

RUSSIAN INTERVENTION

L.55, submarine, probably mined after engagement with Soviet destroyers in Gulf of Finland, believed declared lost on 9 June. Bodies of the 42 crew returned to Britain after her salvage in 1928. *(below, L.5-class sister-boat L.52)*

ADAMS, Herbert J, Stoker 1c, K 24581 (Ch)
ANGUS, Donald M, Engine Room Artificer 3c, 272470 (Ch)
BARTON, William E, Leading Seaman, J 7512 (Dev)
BUTLER, Henry, Stoker 1c, K 15724 (Po)
CHAPMAN, Charles M S, Lieutenant
CLARKSON, Albert, Leading Seaman, J 28603
CLIFTON, Frederick, Stoker 1c, K 18374 (Po)
CROOK, Herbert, Petty Officer, J 4894 (Ch)
CRYSELL, Albert W, Able Seaman, J 15756 (Ch)
DAGG, Charles F, Petty Officer Telegraphist, J 3758 (Po)
DAVIES, Leonard F, Leading Signalman, J 7627 (Po)

EBLING, Francis J, Engine Room Artificer 3c, M 2182 (Ch)
FENN, William, Able Seaman, J 18493 (Po)
FINNIS, Jack F, Stoker 1c, K 16255 (Po)
FLODIN, Robert, Leading Stoker, K 8277 (Ch)
FRENCH, Henry G H, Boy Telegraphist, J 79157 (Dev)
GASCOYNE, Archibald T, Able Seaman, J 11344 (Po)
GISSING, Joseph, Able Seaman, J 8374 (Po)
GRIFFITHS, Clifford, Leading Stoker, K 12449
GUY, James, Chief Petty Officer, 226859
HAMMERSLEY, Rupert L, Leading Seaman, J 5015 (Ch)
HOWES, James, Stoker 1c, K 23105 (Ch)
JENNINGS, Harry C, Lieutenant
LEVEN, Bernard, Leading Stoker, K 11579 (Po)
LILLEY, Roger A, Electrical Artificer 4c, M 29898
O'CONNELL, Denis, Leading Stoker, K 9557 (Dev)
ORME, Louis, Able Seaman, J 22122 (Dev)
PARNELL, William, Act/Stoker Petty Officer, K 5042 (Ch)
POTTER, Cyril C N, Engine Room Artificer 2c, M 2722 (Ch)
POTTS, Bertram E, Able Seaman, J 1511 (Ch)
REID, John S G, Lieutenant, RNR
SHAW, William F, Engine Room Artificer 2c, 271948 (Po)
SOUTHWELL, Henry K M, Lieutenant
STAINES, John P, Stoker 1c, K 15531 (Ch)
TAYLOR, Thomas J C, Petty Officer, J 13653 (Po)
TRICKETT, Charles, Stoker 1c, K 14239 (Po)
TUNDERVARY, John H, Act/Leading Stoker, K 10680 (Po)
WAKELY, Alfred H, Artificer Engineer
WASH, Walter H, Able Seaman, J 12352 (Po)
WELLS, Charles T, Able Seaman, J 23612 (Po)
WESTCOTT, Greenfield, Leading Seaman, K 1139 (Ch)
WILKS, Frank, Petty Officer, J 7669 (Ch)

Pembroke, Chatham
STREET, Edward W L, Paymaster Captain, illness

Theseus, 1st class cruiser
PARNIS, Charles, Engineer Lieutenant, illness

Thursday, 5 June 1919

Excellent, Portsmouth
BAGGS, Albert G, Chief Gunner, illness

RND, Drake Battalion
RUSSELL, John R, Petty Officer 1c, 120983 (Po) (RFR A 1308), discharged, illness in UK

Rollicker, tug
SMITH, Joseph, Greaser, MMR, 410591, accident

Friday, 6 June 1919

Vivid, Devonport
WARD, Lawrence, Stoker 1c, SS 121004, illness

Sunday, 8 June 1919

RM Labour Corps
PATTERSON, John, Private, RM, S 14684 (Deal), illness in UK

Monday, 9 June 1919

Bullfinch, destroyer
NEWMAN, George, Stoker 1c, 295503, illness in UK

Larkspur, fleet sweeping sloop, all drowned
BEVEL, Ernest H, Stoker Petty Officer, 293392

BUTLER, James, Ordinary Seaman, RNVR, MC 922
HARMAN, Robert C, Petty Officer, 238099
MELDRUM, John, Ordinary Seaman, RNVR, MC 574
RENNIE, Robert D, Able Seaman, RNVR, MC 518
ROSS, John F, Ordinary Seaman, RNVR, MC 1644

Lion, battlecruiser
STARK, Albert E, Stoker 1c, K 37438, illness

RM, 3rd Battalion
MOORE, Frank, Gunner, RMA, RMA 14288, illness in Aegean

Wednesday, 11 June 1919

Caesar, battleship
GRIFFITHS, Arthur L, Officer's Steward 1c, 361492, drowned

Thursday, 12 June 1919

Benbow, battleship
MOBBS, William E, Ordinary Seaman, J 91196, accident

Cormorant, Gibraltar
RIMINGTON, Percy W, Commander, illness

Dolphin, Gosport
BLAKEMORE, John A, Leading Seaman, J 9300 (Ch), drowned

Hexham, paddle minesweeper
MADDEN, Edward, Leading Stoker, MC 688, accident

RND, Hawke Battalion
HAYES, Edwin, Leading Seaman, RNVR, KP 204, discharged, illness in UK

Friday, 13 June 1919

Gibraltar, ex-cruiser, depot ship
KILLIAN, Albert E, Shipwright 2c, 346954, drowned

Southampton, 2nd class cruiser
DAY, James J, Stoker 1c, K 43638 (Po), illness

Vivid, Devonport
SAUNDERS, Albert E, Petty Officer, 149374, illness

Saturday, 14 June 1919

Bilbrough, salvage vessel
TROUPIS, Demetrius, Donkeyman, MMR, (no service number listed), illness

RND, Drake Battalion
MACDONALD, John, Seaman, RNR, A 5812, discharged, presumed drowned on voyage to New York

Victory, Portsmouth
CRAWFORD, Thomas J, Able Seaman, MMR, 933204, illness

Sunday, 15 June 1919

Australia (RAN), battlecruiser
BENNETT, James, Leading Stoker, RAN, 8835, illness

Hyacinth, 2nd class cruiser
D'SOUZA, Raimundo C, Officer's Steward 1c, L 9101, illness

RM Labour Corps
 DUXFIELD, John, Private, RM, S 515 (Deal), died

Venus, 2nd class cruiser
 PHILLIPS, William, Private, RMLI, 13247 (Po), died in UK

Monday, 16 June 1919

Kinross, minesweeper, mined and sunk off Dardanelles
 BEAMES, John, Cook, M 7573
 BRACEWELL, Robinson, Chief Engine Room Artificer 1c, 270477
 BROOKS, Albert H, Stoker 1c, K 23341 (Dev)
 FLOOD, Arthur, Stoker Petty Officer, 292870 (Ch)
 JOYCE, Ralph, Stoker 1c, SS 118607 (Po)
 LETHBRIDGE, James A, Stoker 1c, K 14459 (Dev)
 MONTE, Emilio, Officer's Steward 2c, 122493
 OLIVER, William S, Able Seaman, J 11034 (Ch)
 RICHARDS, Edward A, Stoker 1c, K 14474 (Dev)
 STONE, Henry T, Stoker 1c, K 17232 (Dev)
 WEBBER, Samuel C, Leading Stoker, 183706 (Dev)

Tuesday, 17 June 1919

Kinross, minesweeper, mined and sunk on 16th
 McCORQUODALE, Duncan, Engine Room Artificer 4c, M 33412, DOW

Wednesday, 18 June 1919

Kingfisher, Great Yarmouth
 THURTIE, Herbert R, Engineman, RNR, DA 2994, accident

Royal Naval Reserve
 NORMAN, Horace O D, Lieutenant Commander, RNR (ret), illness

Thursday, 19 June 1919

Argus, aircraft carrier
 POWELL, Arthur F, Lieutenant Commander, illness

Hannibal, battleship
 UNWIN, William H, Stoker 1c, MC 1672, illness

RND, 1st RM Battalion
 BLACKFORD, George D, Private, RMLI, S 2411 (Ply), discharged, illness in UK

St Mallows, tug
 EVANS, Arthur W, Telegraphist, J 52560 (Po), drowned

Suffolk, armoured cruiser
 BENHAM, Edwin, Stoker 1c, K 39501, illness in UK

Friday, 20 June 1919

Assistance, fleet repair ship
 CRIPPS, Charles T, Ordinary Seaman, J 7827, illness

J.2, submarine
 LARKINS, Frank L, Sub Lieutenant, RAN, (Platypus, O/P)

Saturday, 21 June 1919

Seabear, destroyer
 HOWELL, William J, Chief Engine Room Artificer 1c, 269099, illness

Victory, Portsmouth
 DEAN, Edmund A, Stoker 1c, K 38050, illness

Sunday, 22 June 1919

Clan Graham, mercantile fleet auxiliary
 HANSON, Albert H, Able Seaman, J 64229, killed

Monday, 23 June 1919

Dragon, light cruiser
 RICHARDSON, Quinton H, Surgeon Lieutenant Commander, illness

Egmont, Malta
 FUSSELL, Bertram R, Chief Writer, 347127, accident

Victory, Portsmouth
 WILLIAMS, Percy M, Able Seaman, 162445, illness

Vivid, Devonport
 HORNE, Charles H, Leading Stoker, K 29221, drowned

Wireless Telegraph Station Aberdeen
 PERKINS, Norman G, Ordinary Telegraphist, RNVR, Bristol Z 7455, illness

Tuesday, 24 June 1919

Concord, light cruiser
 SCRIBBENS, Cecil W T, Leading Stoker, 304677, illness

ROSS, David D, Lieutenant Commander, RANR, illness

RUSSIAN INTERVENTION

Sword Dance, tunnel screw minesweeper, mined and sunk in Dvina River, North Russia *(below, George Smith)*
 HANSFORD, Archibald R, Leading Seaman, J 18293 (Po)

Vesper, destroyer
 MOODY, Charles J, Able Seaman, J 7839 (Dev), drowned

Wednesday, 25 June 1919

RND, 2nd RM Battalion
 JONES, Harry, Private, RMLI, S 74 (Ply), discharged, illness in UK

RND, Portsmouth Battalion
 NOBLE, George H, Private, RMLI, S 476 (Po), discharged, illness in UK

Friday, 27 June 1919

Hope, destroyer
SAVAGE, James T, Able Seaman, J 44609, died

Saturday, 28 June 1919

Charm, boarding tug
RICKWOOD, Alfred H, Telegraphist, J 47053, accident

Duchess Of Richmond, paddle minesweeper, mined and sunk off Dardanelles
HURST, George G, Stoker 2c, MC 956
YATES, Lewis, Telegraphist, RNVR, Mersey Z 5191

Iron Duke, battleship
YEO, William, Leading Stoker, K 27880, illness

Pembroke, Chatham
LAKE, Charles, Stoker Petty Officer, 310710, illness

RM Labour Corps
KEITH, John, Private, RM, S 1116 (Deal), illness

Monday, 30 June 1919

Geranium, fleet sweeping sloop
STANLEY, George T, Signalman, J 9099, illness

Tuesday, 1 July 1919

Egmont, Malta
HERRING, Arthur V, Able Seaman, J 34273, illness

Wednesday, 2 July 1919

Cuckoo, ex-gunboat, tender, Devonport
COOK, William J W, Signalman, 111469, illness

RUSSIAN INTERVENTION
(this is the same incident, but the relationship is not known)

Fox, 2nd class cruiser, Archangel base ship, mine explosion, North Russia
CHEESEBROUGH, Thomas M, Ordinary Seaman, J 85493, killed
SEXTON, John, Leading Seaman, J 24832 (Dev)

Glory, battleship, Murmansk base ship, mine explosion, North Russia
FITZHERBERT-BROCKHOLES, Roger H, Lieutenant, killed
POLLINGTON, Arthur B, Stoker 1c, SS 116444, DOW

M.24, monitor
CHILD, Archibald E, Able Seaman, J 31371, accident

RND, 188th Brigade Machine Gun Company
HUNT, Percy S, Private, RMLI, 18181 (Ch), discharged, accident in UK

Thursday, 3 July 1919

Egmont, Malta
WALTERS, Harold G, Stoker Petty Officer, K 30, illness

RUSSIAN INTERVENTION

Fandango, inshore tunnel minesweeper, mined in Dvina River, North Russia, lost *(sister-ship to Sword Dance, lost 24 June)*
ALEXANDER, Walter, Stoker 1c, 311118 (Ch)
BUSS, John W, Able Seaman, J 2144 (Ch)
DENNISON, William W, Engine Room Artificer 2c, 271982 (Ch)
EELS, Alfred H, Stoker 1c, K 4447 (Ch)
LIVESAY, James T, Gunner
NELSON, Charles W, Officer's Steward 2c, L 4055 (Ch)
WARREN, Christopher F, Mechanician, 308634 (Ch)
WEBB, James, Able Seaman, J 19636 (Ch)

Tryphon, destroyer, went aground on 4 May and later declared total loss
VASS, Jack, Able Seaman, 204902, still on books of Tryphon, illness

Vivid, Devonport
MAGUIRE, Thomas, Able Seaman, MMR, (no service number listed), illness

Friday, 4 July 1919

Victory, Portsmouth
JENKINS, John J, Stoker Petty Officer, U 898, illness

Saturday, 5 July 1919

Constance, light cruiser
SNOOK, Alfred J, Ordinary Seaman, J 55388, illness

Sunday, 6 July 1919

Dreadnought, battleship
REGAN, Daniel, Chief Gunner, died

Duchess of Richmond, paddle minesweeper
ROBINSON, James, Officer's Steward 2c, MC 1923, killed

President IV, London
NEILD, James H, Lieutenant Commander, accident

Monday, 7 July 1919

Juno, 2nd class cruiser
CAKEBREAD, Arthur, Lieutenant, RNVR, illness

Platypus (RAN), submarine depot ship
HAGGIS, Henry G, Stoker, RAN, 9536, died in Australia

Victory, Portsmouth
DICKINSON, Arthur, Lieutenant, RNR, illness

Tuesday, 8 July 1919

William Biggs, Admiralty trawler
FRASER, Gideon, Deck Hand, RNR, DA 19951, accident

Wednesday, 9 July 1919

RUSSIAN INTERVENTION

Glowworm, river gunboat, River Dvina, North Russia
HAMMOND, George R, Stoker 1c, SS 119282 (Dev), drowned

Mazurka, inshore tunnel minesweeper
 McMILLAN, John, Deck Hand, RNR, SD 4589, illness

ML.368, motor launch
 MACLEOD, Malcolm, Deck Hand, RNR, SD 4234, accident

Peter Pan, tug
 BUSTARD, Albert E, Able Seaman, MMR, 986733, accident

RND, Hawke Battalion, France
 PRATT, Frederick G, Able Seaman, RNVR, R 459, DOW in UK

Thursday, 10 July 1919

Egmont, Malta
 BRIFFA, Carmelo, Officer's Cook 3c, L 11138, illness

RND, Drake Battalion
 BAIRD, Alexander, Able Seaman, RNVR, Clyde Z 4043, discharged, DOW in UK

Victory, Portsmouth
 HALL, Edward H, Stoker Petty Officer, K 55279, illness

Watchman, destroyer
 LANG, William H, Leading Seaman, 220690, illness

Friday, 11 July 1919

Rigorous, destroyer
 TALL, John W H, Officer's Steward 2c, L 10807, accident

RND, 2nd RM Battalion
 GILFOY, Albert H, Private, RMLI, 16706 (Po), discharged, illness in UK

Zetland, minesweeper
 BARNFATHER, Norman, Able Seaman, 228236, died

Saturday, 12 July 1919

Delphinium, fleet sweeping sloop
 MUTTER, Ernest W, Able Seaman, SS 6441, accident

RUSSIAN INTERVENTION

Gentian, fleet sweeping sloop, Gulf of Finland
 HIRST, John, Able Seaman, RNVR, Tyneside Z 9031, drowned, buried at Tallinn

Victory, Portsmouth
 CONDON, Thomas J, Leading Deck Hand, RNR, SD 234, died

Monday, 14 July 1919

Alecto, submarine depot ship
 MORLEY, James W, Officer's Steward 2c, L 7828, illness

Eaglet, Liverpool
 STONE, Michael, Ordinary Seaman, MMR, 968726, illness

Tuesday, 15 July 1919

RUSSIAN INTERVENTION

Gentian, Arabis-class fleet sweeping sloop, paired with Myrtle *(following)*, mined in Gulf of Finland, lost
 BOYD, William, Stoker Petty Officer, 297448 (Po)
 FLOCKHART, William, Engine Room Artificer 4c, RNVR, MC 400
 HAIGH, Ernest, Able Seaman, J 44770 (Ch)
 McCREA, Robert L, Stoker Petty Officer, RNVR, MC 49 (Ch)
 McVEIGH, John M, Stoker 1c, RNVR, MC 433 (Ch)
 WEIR, Alexander, Stoker 1c, RNVR, MC 913 (Ch)

Myrtle, Azalea–class fleet sweeping sloop, mined in Gulf of Finland, lost
 AMEY, John E H, Stoker 1c, RNVR, MC 360 (Po)
 BIRCH, Alexander, Stoker 1c, RNVR, MC 375 (Po)
 GILLIES, James C, Engine Room Artificer 4c, RNVR, MC 410 (Po)
 JOHNSON, Robert, Shipwright 3c, M 13305 (Ch)
 PACKMAN, Thomas R, Chief Engine Room Artificer 2c, M 23475 (Po)
 PRIMMETT, Arthur, Leading Stoker, K 2814 (Po)

(below, Acacia-class, fleet sweeping sloop Acacia; similar to Arabis and Azalea-classes, CyberHeritage)

Indus, Devonport
 O'CONNELL, Thomas F, Petty Officer, 89851, illness

Victory, Portsmouth
 LOVELY, Ernest C, Ordinary Seaman, MMR, 938211, illness

Vivid, Devonport
 ANDERSON, John L, Petty Officer Telegraphist, 239158, illness

Wednesday, 16 July 1919

Jupiter, battleship
 ELLERY, Thomas, Stoker Petty Officer, 276591, accident

(The) King's Lancashire Military Convalescent Hospital, Blackpool, Assistant Instructor
 LAMB, Robert M, Ty/Lieutenant, RNVR, trench fever, died in UK

Thursday, 17 July 1919

Canada, battleship
 BELL, George, Stoker 1c, SS 120609, illness

Friday, 18 July 1919

Centaur, light cruiser
 ABBOT, Reginald F V, Able Seaman, J 31489, illness

Coronatia, hired trawler
 RODGER, James W, 2nd Hand, RNR, DA 11432, illness

Saturday, 19 July 1919

Royal Naval Reserve
  WEBB, Thomas P, Lieutenant Commander, RNR, illness

Tumult, destroyer
  PAYNE, Walter A, Stoker Petty Officer, 291029, died

Sunday, 20 July 1919

Pembroke, Chatham
  TOMLIN, Edwin, Ordinary Seaman, RNVR, Bristol Z 7436, illness

RND, Plymouth Battalion
  WHENMEN, William F, Private, RMLI, 10368 (Ply) (RFR B 304), discharged, illness in UK

Monday, 21 July 1919

Argo, store carrier
  GRAHAM, George R, Stoker 1c, 144440, illness

Tuesday, 22 July 1919

Dolphin, Gosport
  DOWLING, Frank, Shipwright 1c, 168832, illness

HM Coastguard Station Inch
  EVANS, Fred, Coastguardsman, 282409, illness

RUSSIAN INTERVENTION

Lobster, lighter/depot ship, White Sea, North Russia
  FITZGIBBONS, Frederick T, Able Seaman, MMR, 998936, drowned

---

Vivid, Devonport
  DINES, William S, Stoker Petty Officer, 306682, illness

Wednesday, 23 July 1919

CMB.22B, coastal motor boat
  WHITE, Gibson J, Shipwright 1c, 342751, illness

Thursday, 24 July 1919

Maidstone, submarine depot ship
  REEVE, Frederick C, Stoker 1c, K 39160, died

Friday, 25 July 1919

Royal Naval Reserve
  ROBERTS, W (initial only) C, Honorary Engineer Commander, RNR, illness

St Fagan, rescue tug
  MORGAN, John, Greaser, MMR, 997498, accident

Thalia, store hulk, Cromarty
  VICKERY, Samuel H, Surgeon Commander, illness

Saturday, 26 July 1919

Hecla II, hired drifter
  CURTIS, James, Stoker 1c, 291836, illness

Royal Oak, battleship
  SMITH, John E S, Midshipman, illness

Sunday, 27 July 1919

Haldon, paddle minesweeper
  COLEMAN, Thomas, Stoker 1c, SS 119415 (Po), drowned

Kruger, possibly miscellaneous harbour craft
  SIMS, Thomas J, Able Seaman, J 61241, accident, on Memorial, Haidar Pasha, Istanbul

Paladin, destroyer
  LAMBIRTH, Horace, Able Seaman, J 30941, accident

Monday, 28 July 1919

Research, depot ship
  WILES, Stanley M, Petty Officer 2c, 155727, illness

Tuesday, 29 July 1919

ML.368, motor launch
  LAWRENCE, Ernest S, Ordinary Seaman, J 53916, drowned

Morning Star, hired trawler, lost, no further information
  WALL, John T, 2nd Hand, RNR, DA 12571, drowned

Wednesday, 30 July 1919

Princess Margaret
  RAMPTON, Frederick G, Chief Petty Officer, 183835, drowned in Estonia

Tomahawk, destroyer
  FOWLER, Alick E, Signal Boy, J 67552, illness

Thursday, 31 July 1919

Assistance, repair ship
  SAUNDERS, Alfred J, Shipwright 3c, 345351, illness

HM Coast Guard Harwich
  HAYWARD, Frank, Chief Officer, HM Coast Guard, illness

London, battleship
  BROOKES, Reginald, Private, RMLI, 17630 (Ply), illness in UK

RMA Eastney
  SMITH, D (initial only) J, Gunner, RMA, RMA S 2588, illness in UK

Friday, 1 August 1919

RUSSIAN INTERVENTION

Pegasus, seaplane carrier, North Russia
  FAWDEN, William H, Officer's Steward 3c, L 10619, illness, buried at Archangel

---

Queen Elizabeth, battleship
  GREGORY, Arthur W, Corporal, RMLI, 16107 (Po), illness

Saturday, 2 August 1919

*Patrol paddle vessel **Princess Mary II** holed off Dardanelles, beached and abandoned. There were no casualties*

Excellent, Portsmouth
 HILL, Frederick C, Ty/Lieutenant, RNVR, illness in UK

Moorhen, river gunboat
 HAYWARD, William, Chief Engine Room Artificer 2c, 271630 (Dev), died in Hong Kong

Victory II, Portsmouth
 STONHAM, John G, Petty Officer, RNVR, Sussex 4/78, illness

Sunday, 3 August 1919

Walton Belle, paddle minesweeper
 BURFORD, Frederick W, Able Seaman, MMR, 100302, killed

Monday, 4 August 1919

Acorn, destroyer
 WOODBURY, Wilson J, Stoker Petty Officer, K 18627, died

RUSSIAN INTERVENTION

Nairana, seaplane carrier, North Russia
 TUCKER, Hubert F, Able Seaman, J 50198 (Po), drowned

Royal Sovereign, battleship
 DALE, William E, Petty Officer, 231041, illness

Saltburn, minesweeper
 JENKINS, Mortimer A, Ordinary Seaman, J 79190, accident

Victory, Portsmouth
 PATTERSON, Wiliam G, Able Seaman, 228491, illness

Tuesday, 5 August 1919

Britomart, gunboat
 VALLIS, William G, Able Seaman, J 12116, heat stroke

ship or unit not listed
 KEENAN, Daniel, Able Seaman, 230581, illness

Wednesday, 6 August 1919

Victory, Portsmouth
 ALBERT, Lancelot G A, Able Seaman, J 27242, illness

Thursday, 7 August 1919

Impregnable, Devonport
 MOFFATT, John, Colour Sergeant, RMLI, 12336 (Ply), illness in UK

Kent, armoured cruiser
 MAY, Charles H, Chief Petty Officer, 186585 (Ch), heat stroke in Hong Kong

Rosalind, destroyer
 ASMUSSON, William M, Leading Seaman, J 11351, drowned

Friday, 8 August 1919

Coventry, light cruiser
 JARMAN, Frederick J, Mechanician, 221248, illness

Heliotrope, fleet sweeping sloop
 SMITH, David, Petty Officer, J 10781, accident

Saturday, 9 August 1919

RM, 6th Battalion
 FAZAKERLEY, Walter E, Private, RMLI, 19580 (Ch), killed

Sunday, 10 August 1919

Doric, steamship
 NICKLEN, Thomas A, Able Seaman, RNVR, Bristol Z 1916, illness

Gainsborough, minesweeper
 PRICE, Frederick J, Seaman, Newfoundland RNR, X 1408, drowned

Monday, 11 August 1919

RUSSIAN INTERVENTION

Humber, river monitor, Archangel, accidental explosion
 McLAUGHLIN, Cyril E, Lieutenant

Royalist, light cruiser
 WILSON, George J, Stoker Petty Officer, K 10090, illness

Wednesday, 13 August 1919

Pembroke, Chatham
 CORBITT, Albert M, Seaman, RNR, C 3458, drowned

RMLI, Chatham Division
 JAMIESON, Andrew, Lieutenant, RMLI, illness

RN Hospital Capetown
 BARROW, Dick, Sick Berth Steward, 351003, illness

Thursday, 14 August 1919

Empress, seaplane carrier
 NICOLAIDI, Leonard F, Stoker 1c, SS 123040 (Ch), illness

Indus, Devonport
 BARRACK, Horace H, Able Seaman, 175021, illness

Pembroke, Chatham
 LEIGH, William R, Stoker Petty Officer, K 7600, accident

Friday, 15 August 1919

Fisgard, Portsmouth
 HALY, Charles V, Boy Artisan, M 33210, illness

Saturday, 16 August 1919

Holderness, minesweeper
 RODGERS, William J, Able Seaman, 186873, drowned

Sunday, 17 August 1919

Excellent, Portsmouth
 BUCKLE, Harry J, Engineer Lieutenant, illness

Pembroke, Chatham
 HARPER, William, Stoker 1c, SS 123134, illness

RM Headquarters
 HARWOOD, William T, Corporal, RMLI, 1300 (Ply), illness

Vivid, Devonport
 FARREN, Daniel, Chief Stoker, 172103, illness

Monday, 18 August 1919

RUSSIAN INTERVENTION
including Coastal Motor Boat Attack on Kronstadt Harbour, Gulf of Finland (the CMB's in this attack were 55-footers. Below, CMB's in the Dvina River, North Russia, also believed to be 55-footers, George Smith)

CMB.62BD, lost
 HOLMES, Sidney D, Leading Seaman, J 15841 (Po)
 MACLEAN, Hector F, Sub Lieutenant
 THATCHER, Francis L H, Chief Motor Mechanic, RNVR, MB 1974 (Po)

CMB.67A, lost
 BRADE, Frank T, Act/Lieutenant Commander, RNR

CMB.79A, lost
 SMITH, William G, Able Seaman, J 18754 (Ch)
 STEPHENS, Francis E, Chief Motor Mechanic, RNVR, MB 3005 (Po)
 USBORNE, Thomas R G, Sub Lieutenant

CMB.88BD, damaged
 DAYRELL-REED, Archibald, Lieutenant

Fox, 2nd class cruiser, explosion, Archangel, North Russia
 CHISMAN, Stanley, Able Seaman, J 20791

Egmont, Malta
 DALTON, James, Able Seaman, RNVR, London Z 3857, illness

Reporto, hired trawler
 WILSON, John L, Deck Hand, RNR, DA 20014, accident

Tuesday, 19 August 1919

Agamemnon, target ship
 ILES, Alexander J E, Boy Servant, L 12074, illness

Egmont, Malta
 WATSON-PAUL, Guy V, Lieutenant, RNR, illness

Wednesday, 20 August 1919

Idaho, ex-hired yacht, tug
 WHITE, Thomas E, Trimmer, RNR, TS 5619, illness

Thursday, 21 August 1919

Australia (RAN), battlecruiser
 EDWARDES, George M, Stoker, RAN, 5324, illness

Royal Navy
 WEST, Dick, Petty Officer 2c (Pens), 139435, demobilised, illness

Tamar, Hong Kong
 GRAHAM, John, Engine Room Artificer 1c, 270411, accident in Singapore

Vivid, Devonport
 JACKSON, Arthur T, Able Seaman, 230276, ex-Lord Nelson, illness

Friday, 22 August 1919

Emperor of India, battleship
 CLARK, Harry R, Corporal, RMA, RMA 9842, illness

Saturday, 23 August 1919

Attentive II, Dover
 CHAPMAN, William J, Deck Hand, RNR, DA 4071, drowned

Royal Sovereign, battleship
 HEWETSON, John C C, Act/Sub Lieutenant, illness

Yarmouth, 2nd class cruiser
 ASHDOWN, Henry, Ordinary Seaman, J 92539 (Ch), drowned

Sunday, 24 August 1919

Nairn, hired patrol yacht
 SWIFT, Lionel W, Engineer Commander, illness

RMLI, Plymouth Division
 AITKEN, Richard, Private, RMLI, 9868 (Ply), died

Victory, Portsmouth
 EVANS, Geraint M, Ordinary Telegraphist, J 45719, illness

Warspite, battleship
 JENKINS, Herbert, Private, RMLI, 14914 (Ply), illness

Monday, 25 August 1919

RUSSIAN INTERVENTION

Fox, 2nd class cruiser and Glowworm, river gunboat, explosion
 WAGANOFF, Walter G, Lieutenant (Russian Interpreter), killed

Glowworm, river gunboat, explosion of ammunition barge, River Dvina, North Russia
 AYRES, Joseph, Officer's Steward 2c, L 6251
 CASEY, Patrick, Yeoman of Signals, 227466

CLEVELAND, Robert G, Leading Seaman, J 16266
COASE, Edward H, Able Seaman, J 16309
DAWES, George, Leading Seaman, J 12434
FARMER, Thomas W, Signalman, J 33401
GLANVILLE, Leonard, Able Seaman, J 90427
HILL, Sidney, Able Seaman, SS 8798
KEITH, Alexander, Leading Seaman, 195605
LEADBETTER, William G, Able Seaman, J 20444
MACFARLANE, Thomas L, Lieutenant, RNVR
McCRAE, John, Stoker 1c, K 22922
MURRAY, Frederick, Able Seaman, J 44493 (Ch)
SMITH, Lancelot W H, Able Seaman, J 14515
SNELLGROVE, Ernest, Able Seaman, J 43244
SYKES, Harold, Armourers Crew, J 55280
THURSFIELD, Richard M R, Surgeon Lieutenant
WRIGHT, Henry, Able Seaman, J 25323

Sarepta, hired drifter
 SELWAY, Henry J, Chief Electrical Artificer 1c, 344628, illness

Tuesday, 26 August 1919

Attentive III, Dover
 TURNER, Walter, Stoker Petty Officer, 158282, illness
 VEAL, Frederick, Able Seaman, J 17299, illness

RUSSIAN INTERVENTION

Glowworm, river gunboat, explosion on 25th
 GREEN, Sebald W B, Commander, DOW
 McCOY, John R, Able Seaman, SS 7701, DOW

Lobster, lighter/depot ship, White Sea, North Russia, both drowned
 BOOTH, Edwin W, Ordinary Seaman, MMR, 998910
 CORK, Frederick T, Boatswain, MMR, 998921

Tribune, destroyer
 GLENDAY, Jan, Chief Engine Room Artificer 2c, 272152, illness

Wireless Telegraph Station, Falkland Islands
 FITZPATRICK, Robert, Stoker, RNR, V 760, exposure

Wednesday, 27 August 1919

Peyton, destroyer
 SPENCER, Thomas H, Officer's Steward 3c, L 9309, accident

RUSSIAN INTERVENTION

RM, 6th Battalion, all killed, buried at Archangel and Murmansk, North Russia
 BOOTHROYD, Richard, Private, RMLI, 18942 (Po)
 ELLIOTT, William B, Private, RMLI, 20278 (Po)
 MURRAY, Wallace, Private, RMLI, 20779 (Po)
 RENDALL, William G, Private, RMLI, 18931 (Ch)
 STOPFORD, Frederick L, Private, RMLI, 19449 (Po)

Tiger, battlecruiser
 BREWER, Arthur H, Able Seaman, J 36739, accident

Victory II, Portsmouth
 BECKWITH, Alfred, Chief Stoker, 281274, illness

Thursday, 28 August 1919

RUSSIAN INTERVENTION

Theseus II, Baku, Caspian Sea
 ANDERSON, William O, Able Seaman, J 25289, illness

Friday, 29 August 1919

Caesar, battleship
 GILROY, James, Stoker 1c, K 55462, illness

Hannibal, battleship
 FRANKLIN, Charles E, Signalman, J 52260, illness

K.15, submarine
 MARSHALL, Albert H, Leading Stoker, K 10007, drowned in UK

Sunday, 31 August 1919

RUSSIAN INTERVENTION

Vittoria, destroyer, torpedoed and sunk by Bolshevik submarine Pantera in Gulf of Finland, night of 31st/1st, sister-ship to Verulam lost four days later,
 BAMBRIDGE, Herbert K, Able Seaman, J 3947 (Ch)
 CLAREY, Albert W, Petty Officer, J 7631 (Ch)
 HARNESS, John D, Able Seaman, J 31257 (Ch)
 HUTCHINGS, Ernest, Able Seaman, J 41101 (Ch)
 MILES, Ernest A, Leading Seaman, J 8763 (Ch)
 OWERS, Leonard G, Able Seaman, J 36904 (Ch)
 PETTITT, John E, Able Seaman, J 48470 (Ch)
 SEARLES, Walter, Able Seaman, J 25694 (Ch)

Monday, 1 September 1919

E.42, submarine
 HIGGINSON, Nelson, Able Seaman, J 17064, drowned in UK

Pembroke, Chatham
 WEBB, George T, Stoker 1c, K 13876, illness

Tuesday, 2 September 1919

Lavatera, hired drifter
 BAIN, Alexander, Able Seaman, MMR, 973883, illness

Marlborough, battleship
 SHIRLEY, Donald M E, Ordinary Seaman, J 70973, illness

Sarepta, hired drifter
 HOY, Alfred J, Officer's Cook 1c, 363365, illness

Wednesday, 3 September 1919

Espiegle, sloop
 BARNARD, Walter F, Stoker 1c, 295020, illness

RM Eastney
 WOODS, John T, Musician, RMB, RMB 304, illness

Rocket, destroyer
 WESTBROOK, Cecil F, Officer's Steward 2c, L 6509, drowned

Thursday, 4 September 1919

Bramble, gunboat
  ABBAS, Sulman, Lascar Stoker 1c, (no service number listed), illness

Elf, tender
  COVE, James P, Engine Room Artificer 1c, 268543, drowned

RUSSIAN INTERVENTION

Verulam, destroyer, mined and sunk in Gulf of Finland *(below, Admiralty V-class sister-ship Venetia)*

ASHLEY, Alexis W, Midshipman
BOULTON, John, Able Seaman, J 45039 (Ch)
CLARK, Thomas J, Stoker 1c, SS 117078 (Ch)
COOKSON, Edgar C, Sub Lieutenant
EDGECOMBE, Arthur W, Midshipman
ELLIOTT, John, Stoker 1c, K 13388
HOUSE, Joseph, Engineer Lieutenant
JACKSON, Arthur F, Able Seaman, J 41800 (Ch)
JARVIS, Harold W, Leading Stoker, K 488 (Ch)
KING, William, Chief Stoker, 286715 (Ch)
LEES, Charles C D, Lieutenant
PARSONS, Randall R, Leading Seaman, 238893 (Ch)
PENDRILL, Reginald J, Able Seaman, J 38465 (Dev)
POLLEY, Frank A R, Able Seaman, J 32369 (Ch)
POWELL, Owen P, Sub Lieutenant
RUFFELL, William F, Ordinary Telegraphist, J 84918 (Ch)

Friday, 5 September 1919

Medway, destroyer
  GREY, John, Stoker, RNR, S 3001, illness

Royal Marine Light Infantry
  FRANKLIN, Charles, Major, RMLI, illness

Saturday, 6 September 1919

Vivid, Devonport
  JONES, Sidney, Able Seaman, J 653, illness

Sunday, 7 September 1919

Colleen, Queenstown, Ireland
  LANE, Maurice, Chief Stoker, 139625, illness

HM Coast Guard Cornwall
  MOORE, Henry, Chief Officer, HM Coast Guard, illness

RMLI, Portsmouth Division
  PETO, Frederick, Private, RMLI, 7940 (Po), illness in UK

Monday, 8 September 1919

Monarch, battleship
  OWEN, Fred, Stoker Petty Officer, 293326, illness

RUSSIAN INTERVENTION

RM, 6th Battalion, all killed in North Russia
  BURTON, Richard, Captain, RMLI
  DAVEY, Herbert, Private, RMLI, 17711 (Ch)
  HAWES, Thomas W, Private, RMLI, 22061 (Ch)
  JENKINS, Arthur, Private, RMLI, 17498 (Ch)

RMLI, Chatham Division
  TROLLOPE, Frank E, Private, RMLI, 19239 (Ch), ex-Superb, illness in UK

Tuesday, 9 September 1919

RUSSIAN INTERVENTION

Carlisle, light cruiser, Vladivostok
  REED, William H, Private, RMLI, 20028 (Po), illness

RM, 6th Battalion, all killed in North Russia
  GREEN, William S A, Private, RMLI, 19654 (Ch)
  NEALE, Arthur A, Sergeant, RMLI, 16383 (Ch)
  PIGGOTT, William C, Private, RMLI, 19459 (Ch)
  RAISTRICK, Charles, Private, RMLI, 17633 (Ch)

Wednesday, 10 September 1919

Cleethorpes, patrol paddle vessel
  MULLROY, Christopher, Petty Officer, 196715, accident

Sabrina, destroyer
  LAWRIE, Simon, Trimmer, RNR, TS 2252

Thursday, 11 September 1919

Britomart, gunboat
  ABDULLAH, Zariut, Seedie, (no service number listed), illness

Oakley, minesweeper
  HUNT, Richard H H, Officer's Steward 2c, L 5615, road accident

Pembroke, Chatham
  GOURLAY, Frank L, Petty Officer, 234705, illness

RM Headquarters
  WEBSTER, William, Quartermaster Sergeant, RMLI, 8036 (Ply), illness

Royal Naval Volunteer Reserve
  WATSON, Robert, Ty/Lieutenant, RNVR, illness

Friday, 12 September 1919

HM Coastguard Station Sunderland
  LAKE, James H, Chief Officer, HM Coast Guard, illness

Superb, battleship
  TYLER, Frederick P, Electrical Artificer 1c, 345114, illness

Saturday, 13 September 1919

Imperieuse, tug depot ship, Scapa Flow
 LEE, Thomas F, Sick Berth Steward, 133683, survivor from minesweeper Penarth, assigned to Imperieuse, illness

King George V, battleship
 HUSSEY, Percy, Boy Telegraphist, J 83490, illness

P.19, patrol boat
 DOMVILLE, Sir JAMES H, Lieutenant, died

TB.98, torpedo boat
 SANSOM, Harry, Able Seaman, 203674, illness

Monday, 15 September 1919

ML.229, motor launch, explosion
 LOCK, Frederick, Chief Motor Mechanic, RNVR, MB 761

Tuesday, 16 September 1919

Vivid, Devonport
 SANDERS, Thomas, Stoker Petty Officer, 300974, illness

Wednesday, 17 September 1919

Agincourt, battleship
 HOPWOOD, John, Stoker 1c, K 19441, drowned

Dragon, light cruiser
 TAYLOR, Hector R, Ordinary Seaman, J 46659, drowned

RUSSIAN INTERVENTION

Garth Castle, hospital ship, Archangel
 MILNER, Dermod R, Chaplain, accidental fall

Thursday, 18 September 1919

Barham, battleship
 FERGUSON, John W, Private, RMLI, 20051 (Po), drowned in UK

Britisher, screw tug
 MULLANEY, Frank, Trimmer, MMR, 949505, died

Salmon, destroyer
 FLYNN, Declan, Petty Officer, 198423, died

Friday, 19 September 1919

Attentive II, Dover
 BASS, Charles, Stoker Petty Officer, 298365, illness

Franklin (RAN), hired yacht, nominal vessel for RAN College, Jervis Bay
 ROLLE, Absolom R, Engineer Captain, RAN, illness

Satellite, Tyne
 McFETRIDGE, Robert, Trimmer, RNR, TS 8708, drowned

Saturday, 20 September 1919

Gannet, diving tender, Scapa Flow
 DES ROCHES, Philfras E, Ordinary Seaman, RNCVR, VR 3219, illness

ML.389, motor launch *(also shown as ML.365)*
 BROCKBANK, Harold G, Petty Officer, 234681, illness

Pekin, Grimsby
 FISHENDEN, James W, Gunner (ret), illness

Thistle III, hired drifter
 BAILEY, Joseph A, Engineman, RNR, TS 832, illness

Vivid, Devonport
 GLASHEEN, Patrick J, Able Seaman, 197086, illness

Sunday, 21 September 1919

Asteria, fleet messenger
 LAMONT, Archibald, Lieutenant, RNR, illness

Australia (RAN), battlecruiser
 WELLS, William A E, Stoker, RAN, 4633, illness

Fantome, ex-sloop, survey ship
 HOLMES, Bernard F, Chief Petty Officer Cook, RAN, 5054, illness

Heather, convoy sloop
 MACKENZIE, Donald, Stoker 1c, K 107944

Monday, 22 September 1919

RUSSIAN INTERVENTION

Caradoc, light cruiser
 NICKLEN, Reginald J, Able Seaman, J 45235 (Po), drowned in Yalta

---

Renown, battlecruiser
 TAYLOR, Cecil C, Boy Telegraphist, J 86916, illness

Tuesday, 23 September 1919

Daybreak, Admiralty steel drifter
 POTTER, William J, Petty Officer, RNR, C 3395, drowned

Wednesday, 24 September 1919

RUSSIAN INTERVENTION

Carlisle, light cruiser, Vladivostok
 SMITH, David J, Leading Stoker, 297225, accident

Pembroke, Chatham
 COULTER, Charles, Leading Signalman, J 12893, ex-Prince George, illness

Vivid, Devonport
 LAMB, Albert J, Chief Petty Officer, 139171, illness

Thursday, 25 September 1919

Actaeon, Sheerness
 FRATER, Thomas F, Stoker 1c, 303083, drowned

Pembroke, Chatham
 MACLEOD, Finlay, Deck Hand, RNR, SD 1449, died in UK

Spear, destroyer
 HYDE, Patrick, Stoker 1c, 300251, drowned

Tamar, Hong Kong
 LOVETT, Charles H, Private, RMLI, 9046 (Po), illness in Wei Hai Wei

Friday, 26 September 1919

Australia (RAN), battlecruiser
 EVANS, William J, Stoker Petty Officer, RAN, 8478 (RN K 8858), illness

Saturday, 27 September 1919

Phaeton, light cruiser
 BULLOCK, James W, Able Seaman, J 21915, drowned

Sunday, 28 September 1919

ex-Royal Marine Artillery
 FOGERTY, Harold E, Gunner, RMA, RMA 1756, illness

Pembroke, Chatham
 BANKS, Herbert L, Stoker 1c, SS 123889, illness

Monday, 29 September 1919

Huon (RAN), destroyer
 BRYDON, William E, Signalman, RAN, 4562, illness

Tuesday, 30 September 1919

Dauntless, light cruiser
 RIGGS, Sidney G, Leading Stoker, K 11704 (Dev), drowned

Platypus (RAN), submarine depot ship
 PAIGE, Henry P, Leading Seaman, RAN, 9340 (former J 9760), accident

Woodlark, river gunboat
 SIM, Ah, Stoker, (no service number listed), drowned

Wednesday, 1 October 1919

Pekin, Grimsby
 STEADMAN, Gilbert, Officer's Cook 2c, RNVR, MC 1654, ex-Cotswold, illness

Pembroke, Chatham
 TYNAN, Patrick, Stoker 1c, SS 121079, illness

Thursday, 2 October 1919

Abdiel, flotilla leader
 COWLES, Edward J, Leading Signalman, J 12334, illness

Erin, battleship
 DANDO, Wyndham G, Able Seaman, J 44115 (Dev), drowned

Ladybird, river gunboat
 HUNT, Edward W C, Ordinary Seaman, J 48744 (Po), drowned

Pembroke, Chatham
 BENNIE, James, Chief Engine Room Artificer 1c, 269188, illness

Friday, 3 October 1919

Burma, fuel ship
 WILLIAMSON, George F, Able Seaman, MMR, 882556, illness

Saturday, 4 October 1919

RUSSIAN INTERVENTION

Berbice, hospital ship, Archangel
 HANDEL, Thomas H, Sick Berth Attendant, M 7794, killed

Vivid, Devonport
 PYGRAM, Thomas, Leading Signalman, J 16583, accident

Sunday, 5 October 1919

Egmont, Malta
 GLOVER, George E, Stoker 1c, SS 118734, illness

Monday, 6 October 1919

RUSSIAN INTERVENTION

Lobster, lighter/depot ship, White Sea, North Russia
 MARTIN, John A, Lieutenant, RNR, drowned (listed as Murmansk)

Tuesday, 7 October 1919

Malaya, battleship
 SLATER, Reginald G, Boy 1c, J 93226, illness

Pembroke, Chatham
 WEEDON, Thomas, Stoker 1c, SS 124187, illness

Wednesday, 8 October 1919

Thunderer, battleship
 TRAVERS, William A, Stoker 1c, SS 116368, accident

Victory, Portsmouth
 SHARKEY, Walter, Signalman, J 39913, illness

Windsor, destroyer
 WILSON, Thomas M, Ordinary Seaman, J 76227 (Po), drowned

Friday, 10 October 1919

Caledon, light cruiser
 DOPSON, Thomas, Able Seaman, J 23419, illness

Fame, destroyer
 JOHNSTON, Joseph M, Able Seaman, J 2196 (Ch), illness in Hong Kong

Saturday, 11 October 1919

Espiegle, sloop
 O'HARA, Bernard P, Paymaster, illness

Hyacinth II, hired drifter
 DAWSON, John H, Able Seaman, J 35065, drowned

Sunday, 12 October 1919

Cottesmore, minesweeper
 MALONEY, John J, Stoker 1c, RNR, S 9288, drowned

Monday, 13 October 1919

Duke of Cornwall, armed boarding steamer
 HENRY, John T, Able Seaman, MMR, 586207, drowned

Tuesday, 14 October 1919

Frank, hired screw tug
 MARTIN, John, Deck Hand, MMR, 933879, illness

Wednesday, 15 October 1919

Pembroke, Chatham
 LIDSTONE, Frederick T, Able Seaman, 209638, illness

Thursday, 16 October 1919

Chelmsford, paddle minesweeper
 MOORE, Alfred, Petty Officer 1c, 144186 (Ch), drowned

Inflexible, battlecruiser
 CLEMENT, Sydney W, Sick Berth Steward, 351228, illness

Friday, 17 October 1919

Carnarvon, armoured cruiser
 WARBURTON, Herbert J, Engine Room Artificer 4c, M 13378, illness in Gibraltar

RUSSIAN INTERVENTION

Dragon, light cruiser, shore action, hit by coastal battery near Lett, Riga area *(below, NP/Paul Simpson)*

ALMOND, Percy J, Able Seaman, J 22758 (Ch)
BROAD, Charles W, Able Seaman, J 20915 (Ch)
GILLINGWATER, Lewis T E, Able Seaman, J 34181 (Ch)
LARN, William, Ordinary Seaman, J 84897 (Ch)
LOWE, George W, Able Seaman, J 38578 (Ch)
PAYNE, Alfred J, Boy 1c, J 90873 (Ch)
SLEATH, James W, Ordinary Seaman, SS 8121 (Ch)
STROUD, John S, Petty Officer, 204391 (Ch)
TRETT, William R H, Boy 1c, J 86811 (Ch)

Hawkins, cruiser
 TOWNSEND, Albert V, Boy 1c, J 70937, illness

HM Coast Guard Station Sheephaven, County Donegal
 WEBB, Thomas E, Coastguardsman 2c, 149238, illness

Saturday, 18 October 1919

*Submarine **H.41** alongside depot ship Vulcan at Blyth, holed by Vulcan's propellers during low speed trials, sank, but salvaged. There were no casualties*

Caesar, battleship
 HARDY, Joseph, Able Seaman, J 41148, illness

Sarepta, hired drifter
 PALMER, Ernest S, Leading Stoker, K 3790, exposure

Sunday, 19 October 1919

Calypso, light cruiser
 BARTER, Albert E (real name, but served as Frederick Brown), Stoker 1c, SS 117137, accident

Grenville, flotilla leader
 MILLER, Lawrence W, Leading Seaman, J 20680, ex-Skate, illness

Iron Duke, battleship
 FOREMAN, Esau, Ordinary Seaman, SS 8362, drowned

Tuesday, 21 October 1919

Caroline, light cruiser
 AYLWIN, Charlie, Chief Petty Officer Cook, 358237, illness

Wednesday, 22 October 1919

Ajax, battleship
 BARTOLO, Andrea, Officer's Cook 3c, L 8048, illness

RUSSIAN INTERVENTION

Carlisle, light cruiser, Vladivostok
 MARSH, Henry, Stoker Petty Officer, K 14716, shot in robbery

---

Rainbow (RCN), ex-cruiser, depot ship
 BRIDGEWATER, Harold E, Paymaster, RNCVR, illness in Esquimalt

RM Headquarters
 SNELL, Horace S, Warrant Officer 2c, illness

RMLI, Portsmouth Division
 SNELL, Horace S, Colour Sergeant Major, 7121 (Po), illness

Thursday, 23 October 1919

Gainsborough, minesweeper
 COX, Frank, Leading Seaman, SS 5817, illness

Pekin, Grimsby
 THOMSON, James R, Stoker Petty Officer, RNR, TS 561, drowned

Winchester, destroyer
 KING, Percival, Engineer Lieutenant Commander, illness

Friday, 24 October 1919

New Zealand, battlecruiser
 MURRAY, Archibald, Ordinary Seaman, J 82097 (Dev), drowned

Saturday, 25 October 1919

Marchioness of Bute, patrol paddle vessel
 BIRCH, Augustus H, Steward, MMR, 998218, accident

President, London
 McMAHON, Maurice, Lieutenant Commander, illness

Vivid, Devonport
 MARTYN, John L, Ty/Lieutenant, RNR, illness

Sunday, 26 October 1919

Pontefract, paddle minesweeper
 MORRISON, Donald, Deck Hand, RNR, DA 14665, illness

Tuesday, 28 October 1919

ML.236, motor launch
 WATNEY, Basil G, Lieutenant, RNVR, illness

Royal Air Force
 HOWARD, Andrew, Captain, RAF (ex-Assistant Paymaster, RNVR ex-Caribbean), illness

Wednesday, 29 October 1919

Royal Naval Reserve
 LIDDELL, Buchan M, Lieutenant, RNR, injured in Zanzibar 28 July 1918, DOI

Starfish, destroyer
 SHARP, Alfred E, Officer's Steward 1c, 359227 (Ch), drowned

Victory III, Portsmouth
 MARSHALL, William, Officer's Chief Cook, 364083, illness

Thursday, 30 October 1919

White Lilac, hired drifter
 CAMERON, Robert, Engineman, RNR, ES 2970, illness

Friday, 31 October 1919

Abingdon, minesweeper
 LINK, William, Petty Officer, 211675 (Dev), drowned

Emperor of India, battleship
 CORNES, William H, Able Seaman, J 94454, accident

Saturday, 1 November 1919

Pembroke, Chatham
 SAWYER, Lewis C, Able Seaman, J 8399, illness

Sunday, 2 November 1919

Crescent, Rosyth
 EASEY, John S, 2nd Hand, RNR, DA 3433, illness

Maidstone, submarine depot ship
 PETFORD, Ernest, Cook, M 10275, died

Pembroke, Chatham
 EDWARDS, Walter W, Ordinary Seaman, J 22025, ex-Powerful, illness

Superb, battleship
 HARVEY, William G A, Able Seaman, J 34108, illness

Vivid II, Devonport
 CLEMENTS, Edward F, Stoker 1c, K 16147, illness

Monday, 3 November 1919

Egmont, Malta
 SAUNDERS, Robert, Master at Arms, 196653, illness

Inland Water Transport
 MACKENZIE, Allan A, Captain, Royal Engineers (ex-Sub Lieutenant, RNR), illness

Victory, Portsmouth
 FRAZER, John, Chief Engine Room Artificer 2c, 269600, illness

Vivid, Devonport
 CROSS, William G N, Boy Shipwright, M 14328, illness

Tuesday, 4 November 1919

Caledon, light cruiser
 McEVELY, David A, Petty Officer 1c, 196906, accident

P.52, patrol boat
 DANIELS, John K, Commissioned Gunner, illness

Wednesday, 5 November 1919

Fisgard, Portsmouth
 CATHIE, Archibald, Boy Artisan, M 33270, illness

Lowestoft, 2nd class cruiser
 STUTTER, Alex-F, Stoker 1c, K 27428, drowned

Victory, Portsmouth
 TAYLOR, William, Stoker 1c, 286537, illness

Thursday, 6 November 1919

Actaeon, Sheerness
 SMITH, Thomas, Able Seaman, SS 7705, illness

Friday, 7 November 1919

RM Labour Corps
 TOLMIE, A (initial only), Private, RM, S 12516 (Deal), illness in UK

Saturday, 8 November 1919

Dolphin, Gosport
 HOLLOWAY, Sidney C, Able Seaman, J 18737, illness in UK

Victory, Portsmouth
 OSMOND, Charles W, Able Seaman, 226286, illness

Sunday, 9 November 1919

Danae, light cruiser
 HANNAN, Michael, Petty Officer, 217443 (Ch), drowned

Emperor of India, battleship
 HICKS, Albert E, Leading Seaman, J 18063, illness

Excellent, Portsmouth
 FITZSIMONS, William, Able Seaman, 195687, died

Frisky, rescue tug
 LAWDAY, William R, Able Seaman, MMR, 837044, drowned

Monday, 10 November 1919

Renown, battlecruiser
 FRANKLIN, Richard G, Leading Seaman, J 10734 (Po), drowned
 LIGHT, Reginald, Able Seaman, 236934 (Po), drowned

Vernon, Portsmouth
 PITCHER, James R, Chief Engine Room Artificer, 116531, died

Tuesday, 11 November 1919

Argus, aircraft carrier
 McCOY, Harold J, Able Seaman, J 23268, illness

Vernon, Portsmouth
 MOULD, Arthur L, Petty Officer 2c, 177745, illness

Thursday, 13 November 1919

Egmont, Malta
 PAYNE, James H, Able Seaman, 229737, accident

Indus, Devonport
 WOOD, Leslie T, Boy Artisan, M 18356, illness

Saturday, 15 November 1919

Theban, hired trawler
 BELLAIRS, George, Deck Hand, RNR, (no service number listed), illness

Sunday, 16 November 1919

Odin, sloop
 ALI, Yusef, Tindal, 130, illness

Monday, 17 November 1919

Resolution, battleship
 LANGDON, Reginald, Stoker 1c, SS 124415, illness

Victory, Portsmouth
 McGILL, William A, Petty Officer, 217484, illness

Tuesday, 18 November 1919

Eaglet, Liverpool
 MARSHALL, James, Fireman, MMR, 956807, drowned

Wednesday, 19 November 1919

Iron Duke, battleship
 WISE, John D, Midshipman, died in Constantinople

Pembroke, Chatham
 JENKINSON, James H, Stoker 1c, SS 120091, illness

Thursday, 20 November 1919

Splendid, destroyer
 DEXETER, Ernest, Ordinary Seaman, SS 8694, accident

Victory I, Portsmouth
 LUXTON, George J, Able Seaman, J 39970, illness

Vivid II, Devonport
 EDWARDS, John W, Chief Stoker, 277719, illness

Saturday, 22 November 1919

Royal Sovereign, battleship
 SHEPPARD, John W, Able Seaman, 179962 (Po), drowned

Sunday, 23 November 1919

Arctic Whale, Admiralty whaler
 WARREN, John T, Skipper, RNR, illness

Pembroke, Chatham
 SMITH, John A, Petty Officer Cook, M 18, accident

Platypus (RAN), submarine depot ship
 TRUDGEON, Frederick, Stoker Petty Officer, RAN, 9431, died

Sandhurst, destroyer depot ship
 WHITE, Albert J G, Leading Stoker, K 27485, illness

Monday, 24 November 1919

Cardiff, light cruiser
 SOANES, William F, Stoker 1c, SS 123994, illness

Danae, light cruiser
 SMITH, Harry, Yeoman of Signals, 226225, accident

HM Coast Guard Station Southsea
 WATTS, Edward, Coastguardsman 3c, 285179, illness

Inflexible, battlecruiser
 BLABEY, Robinette, Act/Officer's Chief Steward, 364034, illness

ML.434, motor launch
 CULLIMORE, Henry J, Able Seaman, J 28699, accident

Pembroke, Chatham
 LONG, Frederick, Stoker Petty Officer, 301101, illness

RMA Eastney
 BLAKEMAN, Alexander J, Sergeant, RMA, RMA 11551, accident

Victorious, battleship
 SABISTON, James, Trimmer, RNR, TS 6291, illness

Tuesday, 25 November 1919

Royal Oak, battleship
 FLATMAN, Alfred J, Stoker Petty Officer, 291902 (Ch), drowned

Thursday, 27 November 1919

Cleopatra, light cruiser
 ANSELL, Jesse, Stoker 1c, K 55316, illness

Fox, 2nd class cruiser
 BABBINGTON, Hugh, Lieutenant, illness, buried in Surrey

Friday, 28 November 1919

Attentive III, Dover
 RICHARDSON, Bertie, Petty Officer, 237493, ex-Gainsborough, illness

Comus, light cruiser
 LAWRENCE, Victor A, Victualling Chief Petty Officer, 342141, illness

Crescent, Rosyth
 KINGCROSS, George, Trimmer, RNR, TS 7876, drowned

Royal Naval Reserve
 CHAPMAN, Edward M H, Ty/Midshipman, RNR, illness

TB.36, torpedo boat
 OAKES, George, Artificer Engineer, illness

Saturday, 29 November 1919

Wildfire, Sheerness
 CARROLL, Henry, Stoker Petty Officer, 152362, illness

Sunday, 30 November 1919

HM Coastguard Station Withernsea
 WADE, Joseph J, Chief Officer, HM Coast Guard, illness

ML.378, motor launch, driven ashore in gale near Lands End, lost
 HERBERTSON, James D, Lieutenant, RNVR

Revenge, battleship
 HAMILL, Henry P, Able Seaman, SS 5674, illness

Silvio, fleet sweeping sloop, all drowned
 BRAY, William J, Stoker Petty Officer, K 11968
 COTTON, Alfred E, Stoker 1c, SS 120397
 DAVIS, David K, Stoker 1c, SS 120441
 GULLIFORD, Leonard H, Leading Seaman, K 18802
 THORPE, Clement G, Officer's Steward 3c, L 11661

Swindon, minesweeper
 CRONIN, Christopher, Stoker 1c, SS 122727, drowned

Monday, 1 December 1919

Galatea, light cruiser
 PETERS, Frederick W, Ordinary Seaman, J 80625, illness

Royal Naval Reserve
 MEEK, Leslie, Chief Warrant Engineer, RNR, drowned

Vivid, Devonport
 HARROWER, James, Ordinary Seaman, J 80387, illness

Wednesday, 3 December 1919

Catania, hired yacht, minelaying base ship, Taranto
 LAWS, Gilbert U, Lieutenant, RNVR, illness

Scimitar, destroyer
 HOLDEN, Thomas, Ordinary Signalman, J 85519, illness

Yarmouth, 2nd class cruiser
 WOOD, Daniel E, Warrant Shipwright, accident

Friday, 5 December 1919

Eaglet, Liverpool
 BILTON, Reginald E, Regulating Petty Officer, 224787, accident

New Zealand, battlecruiser
 HYNES, James F, Leading Seaman, J 26607, illness

Victory II, Portsmouth
 HUMM, William, Leading Stoker, 303310, illness

Saturday, 6 December 1919

HM Coast Guard
 PARKER, Edward C, Chief Officer, HM Coast Guard, died

Sydney (RAN), 2nd class cruiser
 BERRY, Thomas C J, Stoker 2c, RAN, 11260, drowned

Sunday, 7 December 1919

Cerberus, Williamston, Australia
 DANAFORD, Harold W, Chief Petty Officer, RAN, 8295, illness

Monday, 8 December 1919

Vivid, Devonport
 HOPPER, Edwin J, Able Seaman, 228745, drowned

Tuesday, 9 December 1919

Pembroke, Chatham
 LOVETT, Ernest J, Officer's Steward 3c, L 5980, illness

Wednesday, 10 December 1919

Royal Naval Volunteer Reserve
 GRANT, John F H, Ty/Sub Lieutenant, RNVR, illness

Thursday, 11 December 1919

Dragon, light cruiser
  RAXWORTHY, Henry F W, Able Seaman, J 34915, illness

Pembroke, Chatham
  MOSS, Herbert, Ordinary Seaman, J 89339, illness

Retort, rescue tug
  STEEL, John, Leading Fireman, MMR, 838261, drowned

Friday, 12 December 1919

Strathalva, hired trawler
  FLANNERY, Patrick, Skipper, RNR, illness

Stuart, flotilla leader
  BARTON, Robert, Leading Seaman, 238187, illness

Vivid, Devonport
  ROSE, Charles W, Petty Officer, J 531, illness

Saturday, 13 December 1919

Queen Elizabeth, battleship
  BENDELOW, James, Plumber 1c, M 622, accident

Sunday, 14 December 1919

Pomone, ex-cruiser, training ship
  BRAY, William J, Chief Stoker, 163063, illness

Monday, 15 December 1919

Lowestoft, 2nd class cruiser
  WESTLEY, John, Krooman, (no service number listed), illness

President, London
  HORSLER, Cyril G, Boy Servant, L 12399, illness

President III, London
  CURETON, Herbert R, Able Seaman, RNVR, Bristol Z 9862, illness

Theseus II, Baku, Caspian Sea
  JAGGER, Norman V, Engine Room Artificer 4c, M 7104, died

Tuesday, 16 December 1919

Tenedos, destroyer
  PALMER, Arthur S, Signalman, J 35450 (Ch), drowned

Victory, Portsmouth
  HODGE, Alfred L, Stoker Petty Officer, MC 1187, ex-Eaglet, illness

Wednesday, 17 December 1919

Chester, light cruiser
  HYAMS, Philip, Stoker 1c, SS 117451, illness

Lapwing, destroyer
  LEACH, Frederick S, Petty Officer, 208350 (Ch), drowned

RN Hospital Pembroke
  LAMBERT, Harry E, Warrant Wardmaster, illness

Tiger, battlecruiser
  MATTHEWS, Frederick W T, Regulating Petty Officer, 300592, drowned

Victory, Portsmouth
  MILLER, Alexander S, Chief Petty Officer, 171848, illness

Vivid, Devonport
  BRAITHWAITE, Charles, Stoker 1c, K 50409, accident

Friday, 19 December 1919

Europa, Mudros, Aegean
  SALIBA, Carmelo, Able Seaman, J 95744, illness

Victory, Portsmouth
  McILKENNON, Patrick, Deck Hand, RNR, DA 22775, drowned

Sunday, 21 December 1919

Pembroke VII, Grimsby
  SHIELDS, Robert, Petty Officer 1c, 137680, drowned

Monday, 22 December 1919

Impregnable, Devonport
  CHAMBERS, William F H, Boy 1c, J 94935, illness

Tuesday, 23 December 1919

Pembroke, Chatham
  PARADISE, Harris, Signalman, J 25052, illness

RM Eastney
  SIMPSON, Charles H, Gunner, RMA, RMA 15954, illness

Victorious, battleship
  LOCK, Christopher, Carpenter, MMR, 981391, illness

Wednesday, 24 December 1919

Birmingham, 2nd class cruiser
  MADDISON, Ernest, Leading Stoker, K 4355, illness

Niobe (RCN), ex-cruiser, harbour service
  LARGE, Charles A E, Leading Seaman, J 3485, illness

Royal Naval Volunteer Reserve
  EVANS, Evan, Lieutenant, RNVR, drowned

Thursday, 25 December 1919

Grenville, flotilla leader
  MARTIN, Richard, Ty/Surgeon Lieutenant, drowned

HM Coast Guard Station Pentewan
  SULLIVAN, Albert, Coastguardsman 2c, 142339, illness

Larkspur, fleet sweeping sloop
  SMITH, Waugh, Leading Signalman, 223412, exposure

Pembroke I
  JONES, George W, Leading Seaman, 206942, illness

RM Deal
  ROOS, Henry, Lance Corporal, RMLI, S 312 (Deal), illness

RM Headquarters
  ROOS, Henry, Lance Corporal, RMLI, D 312, illness

Friday, 26 December 1919

Furious, aircraft carrier
  BENNETT, Charles P, Gunner, illness

Oracle, destroyer
  GAUNT, George, Leading Stoker, K 18101, ex-Dido, illness

Saturday, 27 December 1919

Francol, oiler, Royal Fleet Auxiliary, boat accident, all drowned
  CAMPBELL, James, Able Seaman, J 20620 (Ch)
  RONAYNE, Patrick, Able Seaman, 101251
  SHEERAN, Charles, Greaser, MMR, 713819
  TYLER, John, Ordinary Seaman, MMR, 883964

Indomitable, battlecruiser
  PATTERSON, Francis W J, Artificer Engineer, drowned

Pembroke, Chatham
  LAWS, John, Trimmer, RNR, TS 7610, illness

Wistaria, fleet sweeping sloop, boat accident
  HOW, Alfred, Stoker Petty Officer, K 3435, drowned

Sunday, 28 December 1919

Victory, Portsmouth
  DAVIES, Thomas, Boy 1c, J 48302, illness

Monday, 29 December 1919

Erebus, monitor
  GLEN, George R, Signalman, J 48580 (Ch), drowned

Pembroke, Chatham
  LENNOX, William B, Able Seaman, SS 9172, illness

Tuesday, 30 December 1919

Blenheim, ex-cruiser, destroyer depot ship
  FARRUGIA, Giuseppe, Officer's Cook 2c, 365483, ex-Tobago, illness

Pembroke, Chatham
  ROBINS, James A, Stoker 1c, K 50283, ex-Euryalus, died

Resolution, battleship
  EDGECOMBE, Arthur, Leading Stoker, K 18083, died

Wednesday, 31 December 1919

Catspaw, Admiralty steel drifter, sailing Reval (Tallinn) for Copenhagen, lost in bad weather near Oland Island, no survivors, all members of crew buried in Kviberg Cemetery, Gothenburg, Sweden *(following, sister-ship Sheen, also steel-built, NP/Mark Teadham)*
  BENNETT, George H, Petty Officer, 191017
  BOWERMAN, Thomas J, Engine Room Artificer 5c, M 14502
  BREWER, Arthur B, Mechanician, 310926
  DINGLE, Edward H, Stoker 1c, K 24623
  JENKINS, David J, Stoker 1c, SS 120469

  JUSTIN, Thomas H, Able Seaman, J 20176
  LEADON, John, Able Seaman, SS 6815
  LEES, Arthur, Stoker 1c, K 55385
  MORCEL, Headby A, Ordinary Seaman, J 91014
  REYNOLDS, Rowland, Act/Lieutenant
  VALLINGS, Frederick F O, Sub Lieutenant
  WEBB, Charles S, Able Seaman, J 40368
  WILDING, Thomas E, Stoker Petty Officer, K 16770
  WILLIAMS, Geoffrey H C, Act/Lieutenant

1920

Thursday, 1 January 1920

Engadine, seaplane carrier
BLACKFORD, William J, Ty/Engineer Commander, illness

Friday, 2 January 1920

Caroline, light cruiser
HARE, Percy A, Leading Seaman, 213902, illness

Victory, Portsmouth
CHIPPENDALE, Albert H, Leading Seaman, J 2645, illness

Sunday, 4 January 1920

RM Headquarters
PAMPLIN, Arthur J, Corporal, RMLI, 17060 (Ch), illness

Monday, 5 January 1920

HM Coast Guard Station Tollesbury
HERBERT, George A, Coastguardsman 2c, 155129, died

Tuesday, 6 January 1920

Lion, battlecruiser
HARDING, Thomas, Yeoman of Signals, 234639, illness

Wednesday, 7 January 1920

Blake, ex-cruiser, destroyer depot ship
MILLIGAN, John D, Surgeon Lieutenant, illness

Victoria & Albert, Royal Yacht
HEATHER, Thomas, Petty Officer Rigger, 169382, illness

Vivid, Devonport
BACK, Charles, Stoker Petty Officer, K 6263, accident

Thursday, 8 January 1920

Australia (RAN), battlecruiser
MARRINER, Harold, Butcher 3c, RAN, 4908, accident
ROOTS, James, Able Seaman, RAN, 8510, illness

Eaglet, Liverpool
AITKEN, William, Fireman, MMR, (no service number listed), illness

Handy, dockyard tug
SMITH, George, Quartermaster, MMR, 588305, illness

Leonard, hired drifter, lost, circumstances not known
BRUCE, Henry, Trimmer, RNR, TS 5423
COLBY, Charles R, Trimmer, RNR, TS 7240
FISHER, Robert, Engineman, RNR, ES 4335
GILLIES, Roderick, Deck Hand, RNR, DA 20647
LAWSON, Thomas, Mate, MMR, (no service number listed)
MURRAY, John, Deck Hand, RNR, DA 22055

Saturday, 10 January 1920

Royal Naval Reserve
HUTCHINSON, Ernest H, Lieutenant, RNR, illness

Sunday, 11 January 1920

Excellent, Portsmouth
SCOTT, Henry T, Chief Petty Officer, 212649, died

Rigoletto, hired trawler
McHUGH, James, Engineman, RNR, ES 1133, illness

Royal Marines
TOOTELL, Edward, Major, RM, illness

Monday, 12 January 1920

Crescent, Rosyth
GOLDSWORTH, Albert E, Sergeant, RMA, RMA 12665, illness

Tuesday, 13 January 1920

Queen Elizabeth, battleship
WEST, Robert H, Able Seaman, 234747, illness

Wednesday, 14 January 1920

Royal Naval Volunteer Reserve
ATKINSON, Charles H F, Surgeon Lieutenant, RNVR, illness

Triad, Admiralty Yacht, SNO, Persian Gulf
BEVAN, George P, Captain, illness

Victory, Portsmouth
CALLEJA, Carmelo, Officer's Cook 1c, 167026, illness

Thursday, 15 January 1920

Royal Naval Volunteer Reserve
QUIGGAN, Edmund C, Ty/Lieutenant, RNVR, illness

Friday, 16 January 1920

Blake, ex-cruiser, destroyer depot ship
DIXON, William, Stoker Petty Officer, 298628 (Ch), drowned

Botha, destroyer
BLINCH, John R, Chief Petty Officer, 187787, accident

Excellent, Portsmouth
DALLIMORE, Arthur, Petty Officer, 236802, illness

Saturday, 17 January 1920

Vivid, Devonport
PICK, Henry T, Painter 1c, 145746, illness

Vivid II, Devonport
O'KEEFE, Daniel, Stoker Petty Officer, 305268, illness

Sunday, 18 January 1920

Cheltenham, paddle minesweeper
WINTER, Thomas J, Leading Stoker, K 8374, drowned

Monday, 19 January 1920

New Zealand, battlecruiser
  THORNE, Sydney R, Regulating Petty Officer, 216932, drowned

Tuesday, 20 January 1920

Ivy, convoy sloop, boat accident, all drowned
  CORBETT, George E, Ordinary Seaman, SS 9760
  MANN, Adam, Ordinary Seaman, J 79193
  WOODCOCK, Frederick C, Able Seaman, J 21383

Wednesday, 21 January 1920

Princess Margaret, minelayer
  CRICHTON, D (initial only), Engineer Lieutenant, RNR, illness

Thursday, 22 January 1920

RUSSIAN INTERVENTION

Concord, light cruiser, listed as Russia, so presumably in Black Sea
  WEEKS, Ernest H, Leading Stoker, 305276 (Dev), illness, buried near Instanbul

---

Tamar, Hong Kong
  LONG, Mok K, Stoker (Chinese), (no service number listed), illness

Vivid, Devonport
  WOOD, Frank L, Stoker 1c, SS 124877, illness

Friday, 23 January 1920

Dolphin, Gosport
  WILDER, William G, Stoker 1c, K 14837 (Ch), illness in UK

RND, Hood Battalion
  MARKEY, Charles A, Ty/Sub Lieutenant, RNVR, illness

Royal Naval Reserve
  MARSHALL, Robert N, Lieutenant, RNR, illness

Saturday, 24 January 1920

Ramillies, battleship
  MOUNCE, Harold, Engine Room Artificer 4c, M 6280, accident

Waterhen, destroyer
  ELLUL, Carmelo, Officer's Cook 2c, L 3784, illness

Sunday, 25 January 1920

RMLI, Portsmouth Division
  MORTEMORE, James A, Private, RMLI, 12302 (Po), died

Monday, 26 January 1920

Europa, Mudros, Aegean
  DOWNS, John M, Stoker 1c, K 56695, illness

Tuesday, 27 January 1920

Pembroke, Chatham
  GILLES, Walter A, Able Seaman, J 26257, ex-Whitshed, illness

Thursday, 29 January 1920

Phaeton, light cruiser
  LILLEY, James, Stoker 1c, K 11769, died

Friday, 30 January 1920

Royal Naval Volunteer Reserve
  MELVILL, James C D, Ty/Lieutenant, RNVR, illness
  STEADMAN, Lester, Ty/Lieutenant, RNVR, illness

Saturday, 31 January 1920

Vivid, Devonport
  FITZGERALD, John, Able Seaman, 184643, accident

Sunday, 1 February 1920

Caterham, minesweeper
  ALDRIDGE, Archibald P, Officer's Steward 2c, L 7061, drowned

Eaglet, Liverpool
  BRADY, Daniel, Quartermaster, MMR, 997437, illness

Monday, 2 February 1920

Eaglet, Liverpool
  HERON, Michael, Able Seaman, MMR, (no service number listed), illness

Wednesday, 4 February 1920

Caledon, light cruiser
  MANSFIELD, Francis D, Stoker 1c, SS 122132, illness

Caroline, light cruiser
  PALMER, Charles (real name, but served as Frederick C Durkin), Stoker Petty Officer, 308482, illness

Vivid, Devonport
  DAY, Charles S, Able Seaman, J 37762, illness

Thursday, 5 February 1920

Colleen, Queenstown, Ireland
  O'NEILL, Daniel, Stoker Petty Officer, 294586, illness

Marlborough, battleship
  ASH, Edward G, Chief Stoker, 294823, illness

Friday, 6 February 1920

Royal Navy
  MEARS, Arthur F, Act/Warrant Officer, illness

Triad, Admiralty Yacht, SNO, Persian Gulf
  BAKER, Henry, Petty Officer, J 2045, illness

Saturday, 7 February 1920

Resolution, battleship
  FARTHING, Frank C, Able Seaman, J 20334, drowned

Sunday, 8 February 1920

Eaglet, Liverpool
 HARBOARD, Ernest G, Engineman, RNR, ES 5151, illness

Monday, 9 February 1920

Ganges, Shotley/Harwich
 MILLER, Charles F, Chief Engine Room Artificer 2c, 271248, illness

Marguerite (RAN), fleet sweeping sloop
 HOBBS, Wilfred J, Stoker, RAN, 8566 (RN - K 19874), drowned

Victory, Portsmouth
 THOMAS, Charles F, Leading Cook, M 1724, illness

Vivid, Devonport
 KEOHANE, Daniel, Petty Officer, 211781, illness

Tuesday, 10 February 1920

Gardenia, convoy sloop
 CANNON, Andrew J, Chief Stoker, 294688, drowned

Pembroke, Chatham
 SUTTON, Charles, Armourers Mate, M 4207, died
 WEEKS, George W S, Chief Petty Officer Mechanic 2c, F 54675, illness

RMLI, Chatham Division
 BATTEN, Henry C, Private, RMLI, 14067 (Ch), illness

Vulcan, depot ship
 DUNKLING, George W, Private, RMLI, 21068 (Ch), illness

Wednesday, 11 February 1920

Senator, destroyer
 COLES, Arthur S, Stoker 1c, SS 124891, illness

Friday, 13 February 1920

Birmingham, 2nd class cruiser
 GEAREY, William G, Chief Petty Officer, 200304, illness

Julius, shore base, Constantinople
 MOORE, William E, Leading Seaman, 235944 (Po), illness, buried near Istanbul

Vernon, Portsmouth
 KING, William F, Petty Officer, 185277, illness

Saturday, 14 February 1920

Crescent, Rosyth
 TUCKER, Charles R, Chief Stoker, 305252 (Dev), illness in UK

Impregnable, Devonport
 BATCOCK, Frederick G, Boy 2c, J 96140, illness

Lucia, submarine depot ship
 TWITCHETT, Frederick G, Stoker 1c, K 31335, illness in UK

Sunday, 15 February 1920

Julius, shore base Constantinople
 OWEN, Harold W S, Paymaster Lieutenant, RNR, illness

Royal Naval Reserve
 ARMSTRONG, William L O, Sub Lieutenant, RNR, illness

Monday, 16 February 1920

Pembroke, Chatham
 ADAMS, John J, Able Seaman, J 52524, ex-Superb, illness

Veteran, destroyer
 SMITH, Sidney G, Able Seaman, J 23246, died

Thursday, 19 February 1920

Valiant, battleship
 SLADE, Harry, Able Seaman, 167464 (Dev), drowned

Friday, 20 February 1920

Pembroke, Chatham
 WALLIS, Henry (real name, but served as Henry Schwartz), Stoker 1c, K 6949, illness

Saturday, 21 February 1920

Bruce, flotilla leader
 THOMSON, Frederick W, Able Seaman, J 44418, illness

Sunday, 22 February 1920

Eaglet, Liverpool
 LYNCH, Michael J, 1st Writer, M 1928, illness

Vivid, Devonport
 COLEMAN, Herbert, Petty Officer, 222544, illness

Monday, 23 February 1920

Caledon, light cruiser
 GOULD, Harold P A, Officer's Stewart 1c, L 6443, illness

Centaur, light cruiser
 NORMAN, William H, Chief Engine Room Artificer 2c, M 2535, died

Pembroke, Chatham
 MUSKETT, Ernest W, Stoker Petty Officer, K 111, illness

Tuesday, 24 February 1920

Cormorant, Gibraltar
 BENCH, William J, Petty Officer, 192728, illness in Gibraltar

Minotaur, armoured cruiser
 BOND, John, Chief Warrant Engineer, RNR, illness

Vivid, Devonport
 CROWLEY, Albert, Stoker 1c, K 6200, illness

Wednesday, 25 February 1920

Euryalus, armoured cruiser
 WHITTENHAM, Alfred J, Stoker Petty Officer, K 2099, illness

Impregnable, Devonport
  FIELDER, Ernest B, Boy 1c, J 94861, illness

Women's Royal Naval Service
  DREWRY, Dorothy M, Telephonist, WRNS, G 2091, illness

Thursday, 26 February 1920

Pembroke, Chatham
  FULCHER, Herbert T, Stoker 1c, K 23502, illness

Friday, 27 February 1920

Sturdy, destroyer
  STARKS, Alfred, Stoker Petty Officer, K 11445, illness

unit not recorded
  GODWIN, James, Chief Stoker, 292626, illness

Vivid, Devonport
  FROST, Frank R, Boy Servant, L 13010, illness

Warspite, battleship
  DAVISON, William J, Paymaster Lieutenant Commander, illness

Saturday, 28 February 1920

Eaglet, Liverpool
  HOWELL, Thomas C S, Trimmer, RNR, TS 6651, illness

Hermione, 2nd class cruiser
  PURSE, Horace F, Officer's Steward 1c, L 4362, drowned

Pembroke, Chatham
  MANNING, Robert, Petty Officer, 229246, illness

Turbulent, destroyer
  AVES, Thomas, Leading Stoker, K 1919, illness

Sunday, 29 February 1920

Victory I, Portsmouth
  WALSH, Joseph A, Leading Telegraphist, J 41572, illness

Monday, 1 March 1920

Cordelia, light cruiser
  ADAMS, Percy, Gunner, died

Pembroke, Chatham
  WILLIAMSON, William L, Able Seaman, J 22510, illness

Tuesday, 2 March 1920

Iron Duke, battleship
  HEATON, James, Chief Engine Room Artificer 1c, 269745, illness

Vivid III, Devonport
  TOFTS, John R, Chief Writer, 347287, illness

Wednesday, 3 March 1920

Assistance, repair ship
  STEPHENSON, Robert W, Leading Stoker, K 1561, illness

HM Coastguard Station Craster
  CAMPBELL, George, Chief Officer, HM Coast Guard, illness

Vivid, Devonport
  MALES, William, Able Seaman, J 29834, illness

Thursday, 4 March 1920

Ceres, light cruiser
  HAY, William H, Leading Seaman, 208122, illness

Pembroke, Chatham
  COX, Walter J, Ordinary Seaman, J 44853, ex-Tamatrix, illness

Vivid, Devonport
  DOUGLAS, Arthur J, Boy Servant, L 13021, illness
  SPENDLOVE, Charles E, Engine Room Artificer 3c, M 2809, illness

Friday, 5 March 1920

Hecla, destroyer depot ship
  BROOKS, Albert W, Stoker 1c, K 12890, illness

Victory, Portsmouth
  DICKSON, Frederick, Engine Room Artificer 3c, M 549, illness

Vivid, Devonport
  GREEN, William C, Able Seaman, J 38408, illness

Saturday, 6 March 1920

Malabar, Bermuda
  EMMERSON, William G, Armourer, 342312, died

Vivid, Devonport
  LOVE, William, Stoker 1c, K 57930, illness

Sunday, 7 March 1920

Antrim, armoured cruiser
  BULLEN, Henry C, Stoker 1c, 302962, illness

Pembroke, Chatham
  SACKREE, Albert, Blacksmith 1c, 304140, accident

Monday, 8 March 1920

Ark Royal, seaplane carrier
  CALLAN, William D, Chief Gunner, illness

Ganges, Shotley/Harwich
  SANDY, Walter E, Stoker 1c, K 24214, illness

Tuesday, 9 March 1920

Indus, Devonport
  REYNOLDS, Francis C, Boy Artisan, M 35356, illness

President VI, London
  REED, William, Fireman, MMR, 917350, illness

Tenacious, destroyer
  DAVIES, Albert G, Able Seaman, J 11457, illness

Tiger, battlecruiser
STEVENS, Alfred S, Ordinary Seaman, J 64364 (Dev), drowned

Vivid, Devonport
POLMEAR, Harold A, Officer's Cook 3c, L 13090, illness

Wednesday, 10 March 1920

Carysfort, light cruiser
SWATRIDGE, Leslie W, Leading Signalman, J 23733, illness

Egmont, Malta
FARRER, Wilfred L, Ordinary Seaman, J 91781, illness

Victory, Portsmouth
HOSTLER, Thomas W, Officer's Steward 2c, L 3592, illness
SULLIVAN, Harold L, Leading Seaman, MC 1846, illness

Vivid, Devonport
URQUHART, Kenneth W, Engine Room Artificer 2c, M 3156, illness

Thursday, 11 March 1920

Assistance, repair ship
HILL, Edward, Leading Stoker, K 3475, illness

Eaglet III, Liverpool
DOYLE, Matthew, Trimmer, RNR, TS 8185, drowned

Poppy, fleet sweeping sloop, on books of Colleen, Queenstown, Ireland
BRUCE, James A, Leading Seaman, 193410, drowned

Resolution, battleship
TAYLOR, Thomas, Ordinary Seaman, J 86534 (Dev), drowned

RM Deal
DOWN, John, Private, RMLI, 20694 (Ply), illness

RMLI, Portsmouth Division
WILD, Victor F, Private, RMLI, 16155 (Po), illness

Victory, Portsmouth
DEARLING, Robert G, Leading Seaman, J 10528, illness

Victory II, RND Training Depot, Crystal Palace *(closed down 1919; either post discharge illness or Victory, Portsmouth)*
GENTRY, Frederick, Stoker 1c, K 46224, illness

Vivid, Devonport
SALISBURY, James, Gunner, illness

Friday, 12 March 1920

Vivid, Devonport
RIDDELL, Percivial B, Telegraphist, J 46220, illness

Saturday, 13 March 1920

Royal Marines
O'DWYER, Arthur, Lieutenant, RM, illness

Vivid, Devonport
CONNOR, John, Able Seaman, 203843, illness
O'FEE, Stewart, Naval Schoolmaster, illness

Vivid II, Devonport
SMITH, Charles, Stoker Petty Officer, 309543, illness

Sunday, 14 March 1920

Carol, oiler, Royal Fleet Auxiliary
FURLONG, Allan H, Lieutenant, RNR, illness

Queen Alexander's Royal Naval Nursing Service
BEARD, Eva G, Nursing Sister, illness (sometimes listed as Gladys Eva)

Veteran, destroyer
FRASER, John, Able Seaman, SS 5470, illness

Victory, Portsmouth
COOPER, Gilbert W, Stoker 1c, K 18140, illness

Vivid, Devonport
WEBBER, George J H, Stoker Petty Officer, K 3031, ex-Walrus, accident

Monday, 15 March 1920

HM Coast Guard Wireless Telegraph Station Rame Head
HARVEY, William, Chief Officer, HM Coast Guard, illness

Tuesday, 16 March 1920

Australia (RAN), battlecruiser
BRYANT, William W, Ordinary Seaman, RAN, 6171, illness

RMA Eastney
KWASNIEWSKI, Francis J, Gunner, RMA, RMA 8946, illness

Valiant, battleship
TAYLOR, Alfred G, Leading Stoker, K 18022, illness

Victory, Portsmouth
SUTTON, William S, Petty Officer, 213903, illness
VINCENT, Reginald G, Able Seaman, J 29249, illness

Wednesday, 17 March 1920

Dido, ex-cruiser, destroyer depot ship
MEAD, John D, Leading Cook, M 2042, illness

Thursday, 18 March 1920

P.54, patrol boat
MUDFORD, Edward S, Leading Seaman, J 26706, illness

RM Deal
SCHUBERT, Frederick W H, Private, RM, S 337 (Deal), illness

Royal Navy
DANVERS, Herbert, Surgeon, illness

Victory, Portsmouth
BARKER, Alfred, Stoker 1c, K 13516, illness
SYLVESTER, Sidney, Chief Artificer Engineer, illness

Woolwich, destroyer depot ship
CARNE, Thomas W, Stoker Petty Officer, 312380, ex-Garland, illness

Friday, 19 March 1920

Erebus, monitor
  MORETON, John A, Captain, illness

Espiegle, sloop
  EDWARDS, Albert E, Leading Signalman, 225965, illness

Lowestoft, 2nd class cruiser
  CURRYER, Henry, Private, RMLI, 17016 (Ch), drowned

Royal Navy
  MORTON, John A, Captain, illness

Sunday, 21 March 1920

Colleen, Queenstown, Ireland
  REES, Cedric W, Petty Officer, J 469, accident

Tiger, battlecruiser
  WILKS, Albert H, Stoker 1c, K 22292, illness

Victory, Portsmouth
  DAWSON, Alfred C, Officer's Cook 1c, 361164, illness

Monday, 22 March 1920

Eaglet, Liverpool
  McLEOD, John, Able Seaman, MMR, 109650, illness

Vernon, Portsmouth
  ROGERS, Harry L G, Petty Officer, 230176, illness

Victory, Portsmouth
  BRANDON, Edwin S, Petty Officer, 238874, illness

Tuesday, 23 March 1920

Caesar, battleship
  YOUSEF, Fareh, Seedie, (no service number listed), illness

Torch, destroyer
  TABONE, Guiseppe, Officer's Steward 2c, L 5320, accident

Vansittart, destroyer
  LOCKER, Philip C, Able Seaman, J 36999, illness

Victory, Portsmouth
  SORE, Charles E, Stoker Petty Officer, K 13050, illness

Wednesday, 24 March 1920

Renown, battlecruiser
  LUSH, William J, Gunner, RMA, RMA 15739, drowned

Royal Marines
  BRAYBROOKE, Charles W, Major, RM, illness

Victory, Portsmouth
  CLEAVER, Arthur, Petty Officer, J 10356, illness

Thursday, 25 March 1920

Blake, ex-cruiser, destroyer depot ship
  FORD, Victor, Boatswain, illness

Victory, Portsmouth
  PARKER, James E, Stoker 1c, K 55691, illness

Friday, 26 March 1920

Columbine, Rosyth
  WOOD, Joseph W, Able Seaman, J 20639 ex-Tourmaline, illness

Ganges, Shotley/Harwich
  LAWRENCE, Frederick T, Boy 2c, J 95478, illness

Lucia, submarine depot ship
  SLAYMAKER, William T, Signalman, J 12533, illness

Pembroke, Chatham
  ATCHESON, Robert Mc L, Fireman, MMR, 914382, died

Vivid II, Devonport
  O'MAHONEY, Patrick, Chief Stoker, 288189, illness

Saturday, 27 March 1920

Caledon, light cruiser
  RICHINGS, Reginald S, Private, RMLI, 19336 (Po), died

Sunday, 28 March 1920

RND, Hood Battalion
  BRUCE, George, Leading Seaman, RNVR, London Z 2817, wounded 4 Feb 1917, DOW

Monday, 29 March 1920

New Zealand, battlecruiser
  GRAY, Alexander, Gunner, RMA, RMA 13122, illness

Royal Navy
  SPARKS, John B, Captain, illness

Vivid, Devonport
  McDONALD, James, Able Seaman, J 36476, illness

Tuesday, 30 March 1920

Dianthus, convoy sloop
  RICE, Frank C, Victualling Petty Officer, 342743, illness

Strenuous, destroyer
  LAWLER, Edward A, Gunner, illness

Wednesday, 31 March 1920

Collingwood, battleship
  OLIVER, Charles W, Armourer, 342977, illness

Pembroke, Chatham
  WARD, Charles E, Able Seaman, J 1286, illness

Vivid, Devonport
  JAMES, Walter, Able Seaman, J 27900, illness

Friday, 2 April 1920

Pembroke, Chatham
  TREMERE, Albert, Petty Officer, 192669, illness

Vivid, Devonport
  LAWRENCE, Samuel L, Warrant Ordnance Officer, illness

Vulcan II, Portland
  COVENTRY, John H, Able Seaman, J 5773 (Ch), illness in UK

Saturday, 3 April 1920

Ascension Island, South Atlantic
  HARD, William, Krooman, (no service number listed), illness

Monday, 5 April 1920

Vivid, Devonport
  FINDLAY, James, Engine Room Artificer 3c, M 6587, illness

Tuesday, 6 April 1920

Victory, Portsmouth
  HAVILL, Harold E, Able Seaman, J 15241, illness

Wednesday, 7 April 1920

Australia (RAN), battlecruiser
  JOHNSON, George E, Ordinary Seaman, RAN, 6418, illness

Thursday, 8 April 1920

RM HQ
  HUTCHINSON, Thomas, Private, RMLI, 21149 (Po), illness

Vanity, destroyer
  KING, John L, Able Seaman, J 49364, illness

Friday, 9 April 1920

Victory II, RND Training Depot, Crystal Palace *(closed down 1919; either post discharge illness or Victory, Portsmouth)*
  CUDBY, Frederick, Chief Stoker, 288464, illness

Vivid, Devonport
  STEPHENS, Richard, Stoker Petty Officer, 174246, accident

Saturday, 10 April 1920

Victory, Portsmouth
  MILLETT, Thompson H, Paymaster Captain, accident

Sunday, 11 April 1920

Crescent, Rosyth
  PIGGOTT, Harold F F, Private, RMLI, 21096 (Ch), illness

Monday, 12 April 1920

Vivid, Devonport
  BURGESS, Robert O, Officer's Steward 2c, L 6606, illness

Tuesday, 13 April 1920

RMLI, Chatham Division
  BUSBY, Victor A H, Private, RMLI, 21231 (Ch), illness

Starfish, destroyer
  FEATHERSTONE, Henry V, Chief Engine Room Artificer 2c, 271283, accident

Wednesday, 14 April 1920

Pembroke, Chatham
  PLANT, Lewis N W, Stoker 1c, K 55480, illness

Friday, 16 April 1920

Mistley, minesweeper
  TWIGG, Charles, Stoker 1c, K 7163, drowned

RM HQ Portsmouth
  ALLEN, William, Private, RMLI, 15419 (Po), illness

Saturday, 17 April 1920

Magnolia, fleet sweeping sloop
  MAY, Harry, Stoker Petty Officer, 305369, illness

Sunday, 18 April 1920

Stonehenge, destroyer
  BIRD, John O, Leading Seaman, J 34198, accident

Tuesday, 20 April 1920

Victory, Portsmouth
  STOKOE, Frederick, Engine Room Artificer 3c, M 15821, illness

Wednesday, 21 April 1920

Pembroke, Chatham
  WILLIAMS, William, Warrant Engineer, illness

Thursday, 22 April 1920

Godetia, fleet sweeping sloop
  MUNN, James T, Stoker Petty Officer, K 2715, illness

RM Headquarters
  SALLEY, Cyril J, Private, RMLI, 16659 (Ply), accident

Friday, 23 April 1920

Badminton, minesweeper
  POTTER, Albert A, Stoker 1c, K 21548, illness

Sunday, 25 April 1920

Victory, Portsmouth
  LEVERSIDGE, Harry T, Leading Telegraphist, J 30404, illness

Monday, 26 April 1920

Royal Navy
  BENDELL, Albert, Lieutenant (ret), illness

Tuesday, 27 April 1920

Eaglet, Liverpool
 MORRIS, Thomas, Engineman, RNR, TS 1205, illness

Vivid, Devonport
 DEANE, Patrick, Regulating Petty Officer, 228541, drowned

Wild Swan, destroyer
 FREESTONE, Albert E, Able Seaman, J 2534, illness

Wednesday, 28 April 1920

Eaglet III, Liverpool
 BARRETT, Augustine, Stoker 1c, K 43568, illness

Friday, 30 April 1920

Conqueror, battleship
 ROWE, George M A, Commander, road accident

RM Labour Corps
 HAYES, Alfred G, Private, RM, S 8818 (Deal), illness

Victory, Portsmouth
 PRATT, George A M, Petty Officer, J 12015, illness

Saturday, 1 May 1920

RM Headquarters
 PLEASANTS, Andrew D, Private, RMLI, E 14646 (Ch), illness

RMLI, Chatham Division
 PLEASANTS, Andrew D, Private, RMLI, 14646 (Ch), illness

Royal Navy
 COOKE-HURLE, William A, Captain (ret), illness

Vivid, Devonport
 LINDSAY, William T, Able Seaman, J 7462, illness

Tuesday, 4 May 1920

Canterbury, light cruiser
 COWLEY, Alfred J, Able Seaman, J 30149, died

Colombo, light cruiser
 RUSBRIDGE, Percy M, Able Seaman, J 18638, died

Fisgard, Portsmouth
 HOLLANDS, Arthur J, Boy Artisan, M 35327, illness

Vivid, Devonport
 OGBORNE, Charles S, Stoker 1c, K 58212, illness

Wednesday, 5 May 1920

Benbow, battleship *(listed as Sevastopol, so presumably in Black Sea)*
 TREMLETT, Francis F, Petty Officer, 212980 (Dev), illness, buried near Instanbul

Crescent, Rosyth
 BLACKBURN, Ernest B, Gunner, RMA, RMA 13311, accident

Thursday, 6 May 1920

Britomart, gunboat
 WISDOM, William J G, Armourers Mate, M 3732, died

Hercules, battleship
 ADAM, William, Gunner, RMA, RMA 13580, died

Tuesday, 11 May 1920

Carlisle, light cruiser
 WEBSTER, Harold, Able Seaman, J 76180, drowned

Jumna, base ship, Bombay
 TYSON, Thomas J, Chief Engine Room Artificer 1c, 269749, illness

RM Headquarters
 WILD, Victor F, Private, RMLI, 6155 (Po), illness

Victory, Portsmouth
 PATIENCE, Charles G, Chief Petty Officer, 167749, illness

Wednesday, 12 May 1920

Emperor of India, battleship
 DRUMMOND-HAY, Edward de V, Lieutenant, illness

Thursday, 13 May 1920

Kempenfelt, flotilla leader
 SIMMONDS, Samuel, Officer's Steward 2c, L 2083, illness

Friday, 14 May 1920

Lucia, submarine depot ship
 ROBERTS, Richard S, Leading Seaman, J 26461, illness

Saturday, 15 May 1920

Ramillies, battleship
 WRIGHT, John H, Stoker 1c, K 57263, drowned

Resolution, battleship
 TOTHILL, Edwin J, Leading Stoker, K 22986 (Dev), drowned

Sunday, 16 May 1920

Crescent, Rosyth
 DIXIE, Albert E, Lieutenant Commander, illness

Ramillies, battleship
 MILES, Archie S, Regulating Petty Officer, K 14922, accident

RM Headquarters
 HOLLAND, Stanley L, Musician, RMLI, 16035 (Po), illness

Monday, 17 May 1920

Pembroke, Chatham
 GRAVER, William F, Boy 1c, J 91997, illness

Serene, destroyer, on books of Columbine, Rosyth
 BATEMAN, Herbert I, Able Seaman, J 22494, illness

Tring, minesweeper
 MORAM, James M, Stoker 1c, SS 121536, died

Tuesday, 18 May 1920

Ramillies, battleship, explosion
 CONNETT, Archibald, Engine Room Artificer 1c, 272114

Victory, Portsmouth
 BURN, John, Commander, RNR, illness

Wednesday, 19 May 1920

Ark Royal, seaplane carrier
 MATTISON, Cuthbert W, Chief Shipwright 2c, 343935, illness

Assistance, repair ship
 McKEON, John T, Leading Stoker, K 3417, illness

Blake, ex-cruiser, destroyer depot ship
 LEE, Douglas W, Stoker Petty Officer, K 19549, accident

Thursday, 20 May 1920

HM Coastguard Station Costello Bay
 YOUNG, Charles, Coastguardsman 2c, 155620, illness

Friday, 21 May 1920

Pembroke, Chatham
 WILSON, James, Stoker Petty Officer, K 15592, ex-Blenheim, illness

RM Artillery
 WACE, Stephen C, Lieutenant Colonel, RMA, illness

Vivid, Devonport
 CRIMMINS, Daniel, Ordinary Seaman, SS 9473 (Dev), illness

Monday, 24 May 1920

Delhi, light cruiser
 HAMER, Fred, Boy 1c, J 89948, drowned

Tuesday, 25 May 1920

Anzac (RAN), flotilla leader
 GREEN, Eric, Engine Room Artificer 3c, M 11777, illness

Tiger, battlecruiser
 BOWEN, Morris, Stoker 1c, K 11695, illness

Wednesday, 26 May 1920

Vanity, destroyer
 EASTON, Alfred, Able Seaman, J 35475, illness

Thursday, 27 May 1920

Tay, tender, Devonport
 BLATCHFORD, Albert, Petty Officer, 220400, illness

Victory, Portsmouth
 CRAWFORD, James A, Able Seaman, 213515, illness

Friday, 28 May 1920

Resolution, battleship
 TRETHEWEY, Walter A, Able Seaman, J 51871 (Po), drowned

Wildfire, Sheerness
 GOLDSMITH, Frederick W, Shipwright 1c, 91771, illness

Monday, 31 May 1920

Thisbe, destroyer
 DINMORE, Sidney A, Able Seaman, J 3412, illness

Tuesday, 1 June 1920

Australia (RAN), battlecruiser
 CAMPBELL, William, Able Seaman, RAN, 9073 (RN J 7936), drowned

Wednesday, 2 June 1920

Hecla, destroyer depot ship
 WALES, Michael, Leading Stoker, 303910, illness

Friday, 4 June 1920

Colleen, Queenstown, Ireland
 CONSTABLE, Frederick H, Stoker 1c, K 12620, illness

Victory, Portsmouth
 CURTIS, Owen S C, Leading Telegraphist, J 8621, accident

Saturday, 5 June 1920

Ark Royal, seaplane carrier
 SCOTT, Samuel, Warrant Engineer, illness

Sunday, 6 June 1920

Concord, light cruiser
 COLE, Charlie E, Victualling Chief Petty Officer, 361337 (Dev), illness

President, London
 WIMBER, Lewis R, Paymaster Lieutenant Commander, illness

Prince of Wales
 WIBNER, Lewis R, Paymaster Lieutenant Commander, illness

Tuesday, 8 June 1920

Malaya, battleship
 BARTER, Reginald W, Boy 1c, J 90112 (Dev), drowned

Thursday, 10 June 1920

Caroline, light cruiser
 HORTON, Bertie W J, Leading Victualling Assistant, M 4640, illness

Sunday, 13 June 1920

Tiger, battlecruiser
 SOPER, Sydney A, Stoker 1c, K 22972, accident

Tuesday, 15 June 1920

Ajax, battleship
  ARMSTRONG, Isaac, Regulating Petty Officer, 221060, drowned

Hood, battlecruiser
  HINGSTON, Sydney, Chief Stoker, 306670, illness

Friday, 18 June 1920

RMLI, Portsmouth Division
  PLESTED, William J, Private, RMLI, 8631 (Po), illness

Saturday, 19 June 1920

Lucia, submarine depot ship, boat accident, all drowned
  BARRETT, Ernest, Leading Seaman, J 8093 (Dev)
  DAND, William, Petty Officer, J 5946
  HART, Charles, Petty Officer, 218441 (Dev)
  PATTINSON, William, Petty Officer, J 11184 (Dev)
  SCRIVNER, Harold, Able Seaman, J 20222 (Dev)

RM Headquarters
  ADAMS, Vincent, Band Corporal, RMLI, 13528 (Ch), illness
  BUNTING, Henry J, Colour Sergeant, RMLI, 22760, illness, died of influenza

RMLI, Chatham Division
  ADAMS, Vincent, Corporal, RMLI, 13518 (Ch), illness

Monday, 21 June 1920

Victory, Portsmouth
  HARMS, Edward F, Able Seaman, 228812, died

Tuesday, 22 June 1920

Benbow, battleship
  MONKS, Henry G, Stoker 1c, K 16124, accident

Wednesday, 23 June 1920

Dido, ex-cruiser, destroyer depot ship
  CARTER, Edward W, Officer's Steward 2c, L 7528, drowned

Raider, destroyer
  MOSS, George T, Chief Stoker, 306064, illness

Friday, 25 June 1920

Glowworm, river gunboat
  ADSLEY, George W, Mechanician, 308309, illness

Marlborough, battleship
  PARKER, Reginald H, Midshipman, DOW

Saturday, 26 June 1920

Marlborough, battleship
  BROWN, John R S, Able Seaman, SS 7409, accident

Vivid, Devonport
  SCHOFIELD, Wilfred, Able Seaman, SS 9727, illness

Sunday, 27 June 1920

Julius, shore base Constantinople
  DOBSON, Frederick H J, Ordinary Seaman, J 93563, ex-Caradoc, illness

July 1920

RM Headquarters
  ENTWISTLE, William, Private, RMLI, 18459 (Ply), DOW, date not given in record

Thursday, 1 July 1920

RM, Adjutant General
  MERCER, David, Major General, RM, illness

RMLI, Plymouth Division
  ENTWHISLTE, William, Private, RMLI, 18059 (Ply), died

Tamar, Hong Kong
  TURNER, George D W, Lieutenant, illness

Friday, 2 July 1920

Caledon, light cruiser
  HARRIS, James A, Warrant Shipwright, illness

Cleopatra, light cruiser
  ALEXANDER, Frederick, Engineer Commander, illness

Vivid, Devonport
  JENKINS, John H, Stoker Petty Officer, 310627, illness

Saturday, 3 July 1920

Lucia, submarine depot ship
  DAVEY, William J, Petty Officer, 193429, illness

Sunday, 4 July 1920

Osborne, RN College, Ryde, Isle of Wight
  TALBOT, Henry F G, Captain, illness

Monday, 5 July 1920

Afrikander, Simonstown, South Africa
  HOSSEU, Said M, Officer's Cook 1c, (no service number listed), illness

RM Headquarters
  ROBSON, Stephen L, Private, RMLI, 12113 (Ply), illness

Tuesday, 6 July 1920

Royal Sovereign, battleship
  HUMPHREY, Fred, Able Seaman, J 23348 (Po), wounded on shore, DOW

Wednesday, 7 July 1920

Vivid, Devonport
  CRITCHLEY, David, Able Seaman, J 17823, drowned

Sunday, 11 July 1920

Ganges, Shotley/Harwich
 MARTIN, George E, Boy 2c, J 97437, illness

Vivid, Devonport
 DERBYSHIRE, William A, Signalman, J 19095 (Dev), drowned

Tuesday, 13 July 1920

Victory, Portsmouth
 BAYNE, John, Stoker 1c, KX 7858, illness

Wednesday, 14 July 1920

Veronica, fleet sweeping sloop
 FERGUSON, Alexander B, Sub Lieutenant, drowned

Saturday, 17 July 1920

Caradoc, light cruiser
 RAMSAY, Hubert L, Private, RMLI, 20471 (Ch), illness

Sunday, 18 July 1920

Ambrose, submarine depot ship
 COOKSON, Joseph, Able Seaman, J 62848, accident in Wei Hai Wei

Monday, 19 July 1920

Revenge, battleship
 WALLACE, Donald C, Able Seaman, J 69473, illness

Tuesday, 20 July 1920

Calypso, light cruiser
 CAME, John, Leading Telegraphist, J 808, drowned

Tempest, destroyer, both drowned
 EDWARDS, Frederick R, Ordinary Seaman, SS 9684 (Ch)
 LARKINS, Arthur T, Leading Seaman, J 14227 (Ch)

Wednesday, 21 July 1920

Titania, submarine depot ship *(below)*
 HOLMES, James, Warrant Engineer, drowned in Hong Kong

Friday, 23 July 1920

Ganges, Shotley/Harwich
 ADAMS, Albert A B, Boy 2c, J 96948, illness

HM Coast Guard
 WHITE, Joseph, Chief Officer, HM Coast Guard, illness

Malabar, Bermuda
 TREMLETT, Sidney W, Officer's Chief Steward, 359608, illness

Temeraire, battleship, explosion
 PARKER, Albert T, Stoker 1c, K 48040

Saturday, 24 July 1920

RM, 8th Battalion
 YATES, Charles B, Corporal, RMLI, 19287 (Ch), died

Sunday, 25 July 1920

HM Coastguard Station Ballygrovane, both killed by Irish Republican Army
 BROWN, Charles, Coastguardsman, 166914
 SNEWIN, Phillip W, Chief Officer, HM Coast Guard, 132104

Revenge, battleship
 O'NIELL, Arthur J, Private, RMLI, 13755 (Ply), died

Royal Arthur
 COLLINS, Gilbert P, Petty Officer, 223640, accident

Monday, 26 July 1920

Royal Arthur, ex-cruiser, depot ship
 FLORENCE, George W, Leading Cook, M 4585 (former L 45188), accident

Royal Oak, battleship
 SHARP, William, Chief Stoker, 291284, illness

Tuesday, 27 July 1920

Dauntless, light cruiser
 GUY, Francis, Officer's Steward 3c, L 11870 (Dev), drowned

Wednesday, 28 July 1920

Comus, light cruiser
 TUCKER, Alfred, Stoker Petty Officer, 302038, illness

Crescent, Rosyth
 SMITH, Charles E, Lieutenant, illness

Cricket, river gunboat
 HUGHES, Robert S P, Able Seaman, 216567, illness

Vampire, destroyer
 AYLING, Harry T, Leading Stoker, K 17614 (Po), drowned

Friday, 30 July 1920

Commander-in-Chief, North America Station
 NAPIER, Sir Trevylyan D W, Admiral, illness in Bermuda

Voyager, destroyer
 LARNER, Henry, Able Seaman, J 34741, illness

Monday, 2 August 1920

Columbine, Rosyth
 MILES, William S, Stoker Petty Officer, 307232, accident

Tuesday, 3 August 1920

Emperor of India, battleship
 CUMPSTEY, Harold, Gunner, RMA, RMA 16072, illness

Victory, Portsmouth
 ANDERSON, John A, Signalman, J 11253, illness

Friday, 6 August 1920

Lucia, submarine depot ship
 WOOLDRIDGE, Archibald D, Leading Stoker, K 20971, accident

Saturday, 7 August 1920

HM Coast Guard
 ACTON, Fitzmaurice, Commander, illness

Lucia, submarine depot ship
 ROWE, George, Petty Officer, 212126, died

Sunday, 8 August 1920

Greenwich, destroyer depot ship
 WRIGHT, Joseph, Stoker 1c, K 11553, drowned

Widgeon, river gunboat
 COOK, William R, Chief Petty Officer, 206122, illness

Monday, 9 August 1920

Odin, sloop
 MAHMOOD, Isman, Seedie Stoker, 140 (Aden), illness

Tuesday, 10 August 1920

Castor, light cruiser
 CRIBBEN, William S, Petty Officer, 191518, drowned

Jumna, base ship, Bombay
 BARGERY, David C, Commissioned Gunner, illness

Tamar, Hong Kong
 SUTTERS, Henry J, Sick Berth Steward, 351434 (Po), illness in Hong Kong

Warspite, battleship, both drowned
 HASKELL, Thomas W R H, Able Seaman, J 73410
 WELLINGTON, Frederick C, Able Seaman, J 49478

Wednesday, 11 August 1920

Caroline, light cruiser
 POOLE, Albert E, Blacksmith 1c, 345362 (Po), illness

RM Deal
 SOMNER, Arthur C, Armourer Quartermaster Sergeant, RM, S 351 (Deal), illness

Thursday, 12 August 1920

Ambrose, submarine depot ship
 MAHONEY, Henry C J, Cooper 1c, 344158, illness

Marlborough, battleship
 HOYLE, William, Shipwright 2c, M 7409, accident

Saturday, 14 August 1920

Dolphin, Gosport
 CROWDER, Robert J, Leading Telegraphist, J 40580, drowned in UK

Sunday, 15 August 1920

Moorhen, river gunboat
 SIMS, Henry T, Stoker 1c, K 22447 (Ch), illness in Hong Kong

Monday, 16 August 1920

Impregnable, Devonport
 WHITFORD, Alfred W, Boy 2c, J 96633, illness

Warspite, battleship
 HASKELL, Thomas R H, Able Seaman, J 73419, drowned

Tuesday, 17 August 1920

Tribune, destroyer
 CONROY, Walter, Stoker 1c, K 6865, illness

Wednesday, 18 August 1920

Barham, battleship
 SCHEPENS, Ferdinand, Private, RMLI, 12825 (Po), died

Friday, 20 August 1920

Victory, Portsmouth
 SAVILLE, Ernest R B, Chief Writer, 345591, illness

Wednesday, 25 August 1920

Lowestoft, 2nd class cruiser
 LEA, Frederick, Stoker 1c, K 23535, accident

Thursday, 26 August 1920

Cleopatra, light cruiser
 SMITH, Algie A, Stoker Petty Officer, 308836, illness

Monday, 30 August 1920

Gibraltar, ex-cruiser, depot ship
 COUSINS, William L, Able Seaman, J 43266, died

Indus, Devonport
 WOODLEY, Reginald E, Engine Room Artificer Apprentice, M 27006, illness

Tuesday, 31 August 1920

Caledon, light cruiser
 BURNELL, Arthur E, Private, RMLI, 19174 (Po), drowned

L.7, submarine, on books of Ambrose, submarine depot ship
 WELCH, William H M, Stoker 1c, K 18634, illness in Singapore

Wednesday, 1 September 1920

Valorous, destroyer
 CONNEELY, James, Stoker 1c, 300248, illness

Thursday, 2 September 1920

HM Coast Guard
 MURCH, John, Chief Officer, HM Coast Guard, illness

Pembroke, Chatham
 BRIGHT, George H, Engine Room Artificer 2c, M 1671, illness

Friday, 3 September 1920

Glowworm, river gunboat
 COYLE, Henry, Able Seaman, J 49359, drowned

RM Deal
 ANNING, John H, Private, RMLI, 20683 (Ply), illness

Royal Navy
 MARECAUX, Gerald C A, Vice Admiral, illness

Saturday, 4 September 1920

Cicala, river gunboat
 JOHNSON, John W, Shipwright 3c, 343852 (Ch), heat stroke in Hong Kong

Royal Oak, battleship
 SMITH, Alec, Musician, RMB, RMB 1910, illness

Spear, destroyer
 JOHNSON, Frank P, Telegraphist, J 50081, illness

Monday, 6 September 1920

Dartmouth, 2nd class cruiser
 PEEK, Albert G, Able Seaman, 237697, illness

L.17, submarine
 LINNINGTON, Albert E, Chief Engine Room Artificer 2c, M 1336, drowned in UK

Tuesday, 7 September 1920

Australia (RAN), battlecruiser
 SCULLY, James, Stoker, RAN, 5738, illness

Thursday, 9 September 1920

Renown, battlecruiser
 BARNES, Fred, Stoker 1c, K 7861 (Po), illness

Friday, 10 September 1920

Vivid, Devonport
 CAREY, Alfred, Able Seaman, J 9112, ex-Somme, illness

Saturday, 11 September 1920

RM Headquarters
 COLLINS, Cornelius R, Private, RMLI, 12030 (Po), died

Watchman, destroyer
 HATHERLY, Sidney W B, Able Seaman, J 49371, illness

Sunday, 12 September 1920

P.46, patrol boat
 GALE, William I, Stoker 1c, K 30752 (Po), illness

Platypus (RAN), submarine depot ship
 SHOEBRIDGE, Henry F, Engine Room Artificer 1c, 269037, illness

Pomone, ex-cruiser, training ship
 JOHNS, Richard, Leading Stoker, 305812, drowned

Saturday, 18 September 1920

Lucia, submarine depot ship
 KITT, Reginald S, Private, RMLI, 17996 (Ply), illness

Monday, 20 September 1920

Hawkins, cruiser
 HUMPHRYES, John, Able Seaman, J 25494, illness in Wei Hai Wei

Tuesday, 21 September 1920

Fisgard, Portsmouth
 NORRIS, William C, Commissioned Boatswain, illness

Wednesday, 22 September 1920

Rugby, minesweeper
 HUNT, John T, Warrant Engineer, illness

Thursday, 23 September 1920

Egmont, Malta
 BURY, George W, Lieutenant, RNVR, illness

Friday, 24 September 1920

Benbow, battleship
 WEST, John T E, Gunner, RMA, RMA 13942, illness

Pembroke, Chatham
 MITCHELL, Albert E, Chief Mechanician 2c, 289904, accident

Saturday, 25 September 1920

Brisbane (RAN), 2nd class cruiser
 EMSLIE, Alexander, Engine Room Artificer 3c, RAN, 2016, illness

Sunday, 26 September 1920

Actaeon, Sheerness
 LINTONBON, Henry J, Able Seaman, J 45654, road accident

Royal Sovereign, battleship
 STARES, John T, Private, RMLI, 16058 (Po), illness

Victory, Portsmouth
 McLEOD, John K, Lieutenant Commander, illness

Monday, 27 September 1920

Pembroke, Chatham
 ADAM, Herbert A, Captain, illness

Wednesday, 29 September 1920

Vivid, Devonport
 GOUGH, Charles H, Able Seaman, J 21314, died

Thursday, 30 September 1920

Cricket, river gunboat
 GOODFIELD, James, Able Seaman, J 8320, drowned

Royal Navy
 MILLAIS, Sir John E, Lieutenant Commander (ret), illness

Friday, 1 October 1920

Ramillies, battleship
 ISOM, Arthur W, Leading Seaman, J 8084, illness

Saturday, 2 October 1920

Badminton, minesweeper
 GOTT, Francis S, Sub Lieutenant, drowned

Blenheim, ex-cruiser, destroyer depot ship
 SPITERI, Angelo, Carpenters Mate, 343832, illness

Clematis, fleet sweeping sloop
 TIDDY, Richard J, Cook, M 7507, illness

Egmont, Malta, transferred from Clematis to hospital
 TINDALL, Noel S, Commander, illness

Monday, 4 October 1920

Mistley, minesweeper
 LIGHT, Robert, Leading Stoker, K 2544, illness

Tuesday, 5 October 1920

Northumbria, HM Transport
 FIRTH, Edward, Skipper, RNR, illness

Tiger, battlecruiser
 COTTAM, Charles H, Leading Stoker, K 9856, illness

Wednesday, 6 October 1920

Impregnable, Devonport
 MURPHY, Frederick L, Boy 2c, J 97898, illness

Thursday, 7 October 1920

Titania, submarine depot ship
 BROWNE, Louis C, Stoker 1c, SS 23159, illness in Wei Hai Wei

Friday, 8 October 1920

Lion, battlecruiser
 McLAUGHLIN, Charles, Plumber 1c, 344307, accident

Queen Elizabeth, battleship
 MILLS, Frederick W, Mechanician, 309822, drowned

Saturday, 9 October 1920

Ajax, battleship
 WATKIN, William R, Ordinary Seaman, J 94909, accident

Bryony, convoy sloop
 HAYDEN, Thomas (real name, but served as Thomas Helton), Chief Shipwright 2c, 343328, illness

Royal Naval Reserve
 HUTCHINSON, Henry, Captain, RNR, illness

Wednesday, 13 October 1920

Dunedin, light cruiser
 BUGGS, Harry, Stoker Petty Officer, K 4487, illness

Friday, 15 October 1920

Barham, battleship
 HENDRY, James S, Gunner, RMA, 9777, drowned

Saturday, 16 October 1920

Excellent, Portsmouth
 CRESSWELL, John, Act/Lieutenant, drowned

Sunday, 17 October 1920

Caledon, light cruiser
 TULLETT, James A, Leading Seaman, J 41685 (Po), drowned

Glowworm, river gunboat
 GADD, James, Able Seaman, 211709, drowned

Tuesday, 19 October 1920

Sylph, destroyer
 PHILLIPS, Charles J, Able Seaman, J 34124, accident

Wednesday, 20 October 1920

Venomous, destroyer
 EMERY, Charles J, Able Seaman, SS 6565, illness

Sunday, 24 October 1920

Cleopatra, light cruiser
 DEARNS, Edmund, Able Seaman, J 60545, drowned

Monday, 25 October 1920

Pembroke, Chatham
 WRIGHT, George, Able Seaman, J 33449, illness

Wednesday, 27 October 1920

HM Dockyard Pembroke
  PAGE, George F L L, Commander, illness

Thursday, 28 October 1920

Royal Naval Reserve
  BRISCOE, Robert F, Honorary Lieutenant, RNR, illness

Monday, 1 November 1920

Victory, Portsmouth
  BELCHER, Arthur, Able Seaman, 197362, illness in Gibraltar

Tuesday, 2 November 1920

Sabre, destroyer
  RAVEN, Frederick W, Leading Signalman, 225331, illness

Vampire, destroyer
  WARD, Frederick G, Able Seaman, J 4150, illness

Wednesday, 3 November 1920

Cleopatra, light cruiser, ship's boat lost in collision with Admiralty drifter Flat Calm
  BURGESS, Gilbert M, Able Seaman, J 40911
  COOPER, Russell, Ordinary Seaman, J 58364
  GEAR, Bert J J, Ordinary Seaman, J 77919
  KEEN, William G, Leading Seaman, J 18263
  STEELE, Frank C, Warrant Shipwright

Friday, 5 November 1920

Dwarf, 1st class gunboat
  TONNER, Charles, Chief Stoker, 302413 (Ch), drowned

Highflyer, 2nd class cruiser
  DE SOUZA, Pedro C, Officer's Cook 1c, 355326, illness

Vernon, Portsmouth
  FEBEN, Herbert E, Able Seaman, SS 7007, accident

Monday, 8 November 1920

Antrim, armoured cruiser
  KENYON, Walter, Stoker 1c, SS 117527, illness

RM Headquarters
  STARLING, Percy V, Gunner, RMA, RMA 13560, died

Royal Indian Marine, explosion
  HAWKEN, Alfred G, Leading Seaman, 238809

Vivid, Devonport
  THAIN, Alfred, Chief Shipwright 2c, 344427, ex-Malaya, illness

Tuesday, 9 November 1920

Victory, Portsmouth
  JOLLY, Frederick, Able Seaman, J 83696, train accident

Wednesday, 10 November 1920

Cambrian, light cruiser
  CLAY, William, Chief Plumber, 344151, illness

Carlisle, light cruiser
  HORNER, Frederick W, Chief Petty Officer, 199744, drowned

RM, 8th Battalion
  MUIR, Robert J, Corporal, RMLI, 11359 (Ply), killed

Victory, Portsmouth
  JACOBS, Thomas E G, Petty Officer, 205244, illness

Thursday, 11 November 1920

RMLI, Portsmouth Division
  BRADLEY, Thomas H J, Private, RMLI, 18070 (Po), accident

Vivid, Devonport
  EVEA, Ronald, Engine Room Artificer 2c, 271890, illness

Sunday, 14 November 1920

Blake, ex-cruiser, destroyer depot ship, fire
  WHITE, Frederick R, Stoker Petty Officer, K 18594

Monday, 15 November 1920

Revenge, battleship
  WEST, Albert, Able Seaman, J 69054, illness

Tuesday, 16 November 1920

Vivid, Devonport
  SMALE, Andrew C, Engine Room Artificer 2c, M 3152, illness

Wednesday, 17 November 1920

RM, 3rd Battalion
  JONES, Frank J, Private, RMLI, 16467 (Ply), killed

Thursday, 18 November 1920

Crescent, Rosyth, both drowned
  COOMBE, Frederick H, Able Seaman, J 52858 (Dev)
  HARRIS, Francis R, Able Seaman, J 80263 (Dev)

Friday, 19 November 1920

Birmingham, 2nd class cruiser
  BAGGLEY, Henry S, Leading Telegraphist, J 41284 (Po), drowned

Fantome, ex-sloop, survey ship
  KEYES, Arthur W, Officer's Cook 1c, L 10311, illness

Saturday, 20 November 1920

Iron Duke, battleship
  CHURCHER, Francis W G, Stoker 1c, K 5891, illness

Sunday, 21 November 1920

Greenwich, destroyer depot ship
 PERRETT, Warren, Chief Shipwright 2c, 346856, illness

Valiant, battleship
 YEARLING, Charles S, Master at Arms, 201729, drowned

Monday, 22 November 1920

Vivid, Devonport
 MOYES, Arthur J, Signal Lieutenant, accident

Tuesday, 23 November 1920

Royal Navy
 CALLAGHAN, Sir George A, Admiral of the Fleet, illness

Wednesday, 24 November 1920

Collingwood, battleship
 GLANVILLE, John J, Able Seaman, 222971, accident

Dunedin, light cruiser
 ALLISON, Eric W, Able Seaman, J 66121, illness

Pegasus, seaplane carrier
 GLANVILLE, John H, Chief Engine Room Artificer 1c, 269246, drowned

Friday, 26 November 1920

Cairo, light cruiser
 BIRCH, Steuart C, Ordinary Seaman, J 93587 (Dev), illness in Hong Kong

Sunday, 28 November 1920
(both men buried in same cemetery; presumably the same incident)

HM Coast Guard Station Sandgate
 McDERMOTT, James, Coastguardsman, 283038, mine explosion

HM Coastguard Station Deal
 WALKER, William E, Leading Boatman, 204453, mine explosion

Monday, 29 November 1920

RMLI, Adjutant General
 CAMPBELL, Gunning M, Major General, RM, illness

Wednesday, 1 December 1920

Queen Elizabeth, battleship, all drowned
 DUNN, Edward P, Gunner
 GROUT, Egbert W J, Petty Officer, 193771
 HEWITSON, Bertie, Able Seaman, J 6905 (Po)
 YOUNG, Arthur W, Gunner, RMA, RMA 16509

Thursday, 2 December 1920

Ramilles, battleship
 DREW, Benjamin, Leading Stoker, 300885, illness

RM, 8th Battalion
 WHYMAN, Edward A, Private, RMLI, 14419 (Ply), accident

Royal Naval Volunteer Reserve
 GREENWOOD, Charles, Paymaster Lieutenant Commander, RNVR, illness

Friday, 3 December 1920

Pembroke, Chatham
 BAILEY, Arthur J, Private, RMLI, 11767 (Ch), illness

Saturday, 4 December 1920

Tobago, destroyer
 ALESSANDRO, Antonio, Officer's Steward 1c, L 4825, accident

Sunday, 5 December 1920

Royal Sovereign, battleship
 STENNING, Frederick G, Musician, RMB, RMB 2185, illness

Wednesday, 8 December 1920

Ambrose, submarine depot ship
 CROZIER, William E, Telegraphist, J 57974, accident in Hong Kong

Walpole, destroyer
 FERRIS, William H, Able Seaman, J 8534

Thursday, 9 December 1920

Army, on loan to
 MONTGOMERY, Hugh F, Major & Brevet Lieutenant Colonel, illness

Jumna, base ship, Bombay
 NOAKES, Ernest S, Stoker 1c, K 18600, illness

Saturday, 11 December 1920

Venomous, destroyer
 PRICE, Alfred J, Leading Stoker, K 14102, illness

Victoria & Albert, Royal Yacht
 ANNETTS, Ivy, Private, RMLI, 8750 (Po), gun shot wound, died

Sunday, 12 December 1920

Ganges, Shotley/Harwich
 NEW, Herbert, Boy 2c, J 99722, illness

Monday, 13 December 1920

Pembroke, Chatham
 BRANSBY, Arthur, Able Seaman, 238417, illness

Tuesday, 14 December 1920

Pactolus, submarine depot ship
 HUTCHIESON, George P, Sub Lieutenant, RNVR, illness

Victory, Portsmouth
GODDEN, William, Coastguardsman, HM Coast Guard, 149623, illness, buried at Freshwater

Wednesday, 15 December 1920

RM Eastney
MILLER, John J, Musician, RMB, RMB 809, illness

Friday, 17 December 1920

Dragon, light cruiser
MARTIN, Thomas W, Private, RMLI, 12898 (Ch), illness

Pembroke, Chatham
BATES, Percival F, Leading Sick Berth Attendant, M 5509, illness

Monday, 20 December 1920

Wireless Telegraph Station Kingstown
JOHNS, William J V, Boatman, J 43841, illness

Tuesday, 21 December 1920

Senior Naval Officer Aberdeen
LAIRD, John K, Captain, illness

Friday, 24 December 1920

Warwick, destroyer
HAWKINS, Henry W, Able Seaman, 225264, drowned

Saturday, 25 December 1920

Heather, convoy sloop
GLAZEBROOK, Alfred, Leading Signalman, J 23547, accident

Sunday, 26 December 1920

Vivid, Devonport
READ, Harry C, Engineer Commander, illness

Monday, 27 December 1920

Assistance, repair ship
EMMERSON, John, Bugler, RMLI, 21014 (Po), illness

Tuesday, 28 December 1920

Emperor of India, battleship
ALMOND, Joseph A, Electrical Artificer 5c, M 33797, illness

Friday, 31 December 1920

Actaeon, Sheerness
PHILLIPS, Joseph L, Armourer, 295133, illness

1921

Saturday, 1 January 1921

HM Coast Guard Station Raffnay Head
KEARNEY, Thomas E, Leading Boatman, 218553, illness

Sunday, 2 January 1921

Aphis, river gunboat
McDERMOTT, Edward, Leading Seaman, 208984, accident

Tuesday, 4 January 1921

Royal Navy
GILLESPIE, Robert J, Engineer Lieutenant, illness in Canada

Thursday, 6 January 1921

Pembroke, Chatham
HINSELWOOD, George, Chief Petty Officer, 198586, died
TOLHURST, Frank, Leading Cook, M 7796, ex-Carnarvon, illness

Friday, 7 January 1921

Ganges, Shotley/Harwich
ELDRED, Leslie N, Boy 1c, J 96872, illness

Saturday, 8 January 1921

Carnarvon, armoured cruiser
LONGHURST, Gerald F, Commander, illness

Crescent, Rosyth
THOMAS, Charles E, Gunner, RMA, RMA 9404, illness

Highflyer, 2nd class cruiser
WARD, William R, Musician, RMB, RMB 2263, illness

Julius, shore base Constantinople
KEIGHLEY, Harold S, Sub Lieutenant, illness

Sunday, 9 January 1921

Laburnum, fleet sweeping sloop
PULLING, William J, Chief Petty Officer, 206709, illness

Monday, 10 January 1921

Kinsha, ex-river steamer, river gunboat
CLARKE, Ernest D, Able Seaman, J 443113, illness

Tuesday, 11 January 1921

Hibiscus, convoy sloop
PICKETT, Edward H, Leading Stoker, K 12218, illness

Saturday, 15 January 1921

Colleen, Queenstown, Ireland
GRIFFIN, John J, Gunner, illness

Sunday, 16 January 1921

Victory, Portsmouth
TEE, Alfred T, Chief Writer, 347262, illness

Tuesday, 18 January 1921

Queen Elizabeth, battleship
BELL, John H, Warrant Victualling Officer, illness

Thursday, 20 January 1921

Dunedin, light cruiser
BLAKELEY, Frederick J, Able Seaman, J 37779 (Ch), drowned

Greenwich, destroyer depot ship
FUNNELL, Thomas R, Chief Yeoman of Signals, 208436, illness

K.5, K-class fleet submarine, taking part in Atlantic Fleet exercises, disappeared off Scilly Isles, believed lost in diving accident, no survivors *(below, close sister-boat K.26 of K.26-class)*

ABURROW, Cecil F J, Able Seaman, J 4284 (Po)
ANDREWS, Herbert G, Petty Officer, J 5147 (Po)
BACKHOUSE, Albert E, Stoker 1c, K 21000 (Ch)
BAKER, George W, Engineer Lieutenant
BEAUMONT, George L, Chief Engine Room Artificer 2c, 272157 (Po)
BOWLES, Edward J, Engineer Lieutenant
BURNS, John, Stoker 1c, K 17609 (Po)
BUTLAND, Richard W H, Officer's Steward, L 9741 (Po)
CHARMAN, William H, Leading Telegraphist, J 31517 (Po)
CHASE, Frederick W, Leading Stoker, K 3799 (Po)
CLARKE, Benjamin J, Lieutenant
CLARKE, Cecil F, Able Seaman, J 32900 (Ch)
CLOWES, John H T, Able Seaman, J 25669 (Po)
CORNISH, Percy W, Able Seaman, J 11540 (Ch)
COX, John S, Telegraphist, J 49821 (Po)
CUDDEFORD, Frederick W F, Lieutenant
DONOVAN, Michael, Able Seaman, J 18322 (Po)
EDMONDS, Charles, Leading Seaman, J 2996 (Ch)
ELLIS, Charles A, Stoker 1c, SS 124701 (Ch)
EVANS, John H, Able Seaman, J 14734 (Dev)
FRENCH, Alfred F, Petty Officer, 214229 (Po)
GAIMES, John A, Lieutenant Commander
GEORGE, Walter, Able Seaman, J 17015 (Po)
GILLETT, Victor A, Able Seaman, J 24980 (Po)
HESTER, William J, Engine Room Artificer 3c, M 1516 (Po)
HICKLIN, William O, Leading Stoker, K 12306 (Ch)
HUTCHENCE, Harry, Stoker 1c, K 22154 (Po)
INIGHT, Walter, Leading Seaman, J 10959 (Po)
KENDALL, John G, Stoker 1c, K 24052 (Po)
LAMPARD, Thomas F, Leading Seaman, J 12698 (Po)
LAMPORT, Albert J, Leading Seaman, J 6059 (Po)
LASHMAR, Bertram A, Engine Room Artificer 2c, M 4306 (Po)

LAWRENCE, James G, Leading Seaman, J 26878 (Ch)
LAWRENCE, Stanfield, Stoker 1c, K 24155 (Po)
MACGREGOR, Robert S R, Stoker 1c, K 19376 (Po)
MALE, Bert E, Chief Stoker, 302183 (Po)
MANSFIELD, Richard A, Able Seaman, J 2617 (Ch)
METCALFE, Fred, Able Seaman, SS 8401 (Po)
MIDDLEMIST, Robert J M, Lieutenant
MOULD, William, Petty Officer, J 7392 (Po)
PAGE, Alfred G, Stoker Petty Officer, 229695 (Po)
PARR, Frederick, Stoker 1c, K 20815 (Po)
PARRY, James F, Stoker 1c, K 17768 (Po)
POLLARD, George, Engine Room Artificer 3c, M 10901 (Dev)
PURKIS, Frederick W, Stoker 1c, K 19579 (Ch)
RAGGETT, Alfred D, Stoker 1c, K 26671 (Po)
RILEY, Herbert, Engine Room Artificer 2c, M 4194 (Ch)
SEYMOUR, George, Stoker 1c, K 24204 (Ch)
SHEPPARD, William C, Petty Officer, J 5572 (Po)
SMITH, Frederick J, Stoker Petty Officer, 299134 (Po)
SMITH, William B, Stoker 1c, K 19915 (Po)
SMITH, William C, Able Seaman, J 6219 (Ch)
TANNER, William T, Signalman, J 21454 (Po)
WARD, Horace W, Able Seaman, SS 8464 (Ch)
WEST, Lewis H, Stoker 1c, K 20832 (Po)
WILTSHIRE, Richard, Signalman, J 31907 (Dev)
WOOTTON, William, Stoker Petty Officer, K 2665 (Ch)

Friday, 21 January 1921

Pembroke, Chatham
 WISKER, William, Sailmakers Mate, 204376 ex-Wildfire, died

Saturday, 22 January 1921

Resolution, battleship
 WARDER, Richard B G, Major, RMA, illness

Monday, 24 January 1921

Bluebell, fleet sweeping sloop
 FULLER, Walter T, Able Seaman, J 46176 (Ch), illness in Hong Kong

Columbine, Rosyth
 MITCHELL, Thomas P, Engine Room Artificer 4c, M 7080, died

Vivacious, destroyer
 SAVILLE, Samuel J, Able Seaman, SS 7258, illness

Tuesday, 25 January 1921

Vivid, Devonport
 PENNA, Richard J, Stoker 1c, K 56973, illness

Wednesday, 27 January 1921

Cardiff, light cruiser
 BOWER, Reginald T, Signalman, J 72840, illness

Friday, 28 January 1921

Carlisle, light cruiser
 HURN, Henry T, Engine Room Artificer 4c, M 11515 (Po), illness in Hong Kong

Resolution, battleship
 SLADE, Clifford S, Boy 1c, J 96081, illness

Saturday, 29 January 1921

Defiance, Devonport
 HILL, Henry T, Leading Seaman, J 58022, illness

Foxglove, fleet sweeping sloop
 TARRANT, Edward C, Stoker Petty Officer, 295348 (Po), illness

Pembroke, Chatham
 PYRKE, William H, Stoker 1c, 291189, illness

Monday, 31 January 1921

Iridescence, Admiralty wood drifter
 ATKINSON, Charles H, Stoker Petty Officer, 308044, drowned

Tuesday, 1 February 1921

Commonwealth, battleship
 THURNALL, William E V, 2nd Lieutenant, RMLI, illness

Victory, Portsmouth
 CROW, John W, Leading Stoker, K 18378, illness

Wednesday, 2 February 1921

Julius, shore base Constantinople
 MORRIS, James F, Act/Lieutenant, drowned

Thursday, 3 February 1921

RMLI Headquarters, Chatham Division
 BAIRD, James (real name, but served as James Manson), Sergeant, RMLI, 12258 (Ch), illness

Friday, 4 February 1921

Calypso, light cruiser
 UTTING, Frederick J, Stoker 1c, SS 124832, illness

Saturday, 5 February 1921

Vivid, Devonport
 LEEHANE, Charles, Leading Seaman, 193534, illness
 TRANTER, Thomas, Petty Officer, 220796, ex-Revenge, illness

Sunday, 6 February 1921

Birmingham, 2nd class cruiser
 SEALE, Henry, Officer's Steward 2c, South African, Y 5, illness

Royal Naval Reserve
 GRUBB, George H, Warrant Engineer, RNR, drowned

Turbulent, destroyer
 FISHER, Ernest E, Gunner, illness

Monday, 7 February 1921

Egmont, Malta
 CALLUS, Angelo, Petty Officer 1c, 235504, illness

Emperor of India, battleship
 BRADFORD, Samuel A, Gunner, RMA, RMA 10424, illness

Tuesday, 8 February 1921

Repulse, battlecruiser
 BERESFORD, Douglas R, Mechanician, 308090, accident

Shakespeare, flotilla leader
 WHEATLEY, Charlie, Ordinary Seaman, SS 9214, drowned

Thursday, 10 February 1921

Alacrity, hired yacht, sold 1919
 KWOK, Chun, Able Seaman, (no service number listed), post-discharge illness

Hawkins, cruiser
 AH, Nam, Officer's Steward 2c, (no service number listed), illness

Friday, 11 February 1921

Highflyer, 2nd class cruiser
 SAUNDERS, George W, Leading Seaman, 210574, illness

Vivid, Devonport
 COUPE, Frederick C, Boy 1c, J 99262, illness

Saturday, 12 February 1921

Tiger, battlecruiser
 FOX, Alfred F, Boatswain, illness

Sunday, 13 February 1921

Victory, Portsmouth
 PAXMAN, Percy, Chief Stoker, 293753, illness

Monday, 14 February 1921

Fisgard, Portsmouth
 DEACON, Charles J R, Engine Room Artificer Apprentice, M 36122, illness

Pembroke, Chatham
 HARDEN, Frederick S, Ordnance Artificer 2c, C/M 35988, illness

Venturous, destroyer
 VEREKER, Foley G P, Lieutenant, drowned

Whitley, destroyer
 OSBORNE, George R, Engineer Lieutenant, drowned

Tuesday, 15 February 1921

Malaya, battleship
 TILSON, Bertie W, Able Seaman, J 90737, drowned

Westcott, destroyer
 SIMONS, William, Stoker Petty Officer, 302622, illness

Thursday, 17 February 1921

Malaya, battleship
 MASON, Walter J, Chief Petty Officer Cook, 346978 (Po), illness

Friday, 18 February 1921

Vivid, Devonport
 MATTHIAS, Joseph, Stoker Petty Officer, 306237, illness

Saturday, 19 February 1921

Excellent, Portsmouth
 NOBES, Arthur J R, Leading Seaman, J 26386, accident

Sunday, 20 February 1921

Vivid, Devonport
 HANNAFORD, William G, Stoker 1c, K 1234, illness

Monday, 21 February 1921

Philomel, ex-cruiser, depot ship, New Zealand
 CRONIN, Michael, Stoker 1c, K 18115, drowned

Thursday, 24 February 1921

Highflyer, 2nd class cruiser
 GIMBLET, William J H, Chief Stoker, 305267, illness

Vulcan, depot ship
 STUDDY, Francis R B, Lieutenant, illness

Tuesday, 1 March 1921

Hawkins, cruiser
 DAVIES, John H, Petty Officer, 200545, illness, day not given

Wednesday, 2 March 1921

Victory, Portsmouth
 BUCKIE, Barry, Yeoman of Signals, 212183, accident

Wistaria, fleet sweeping sloop
 EDWARDS, William, Stoker Petty Officer, K 15468, accident

Friday, 4 March 1921

Ganges, Shotley/Harwich
 MACKINTOSH, Donald, Boy 2c, J 98326, illness

King George V, battleship
 BRADBURY, Arthur E, Leading Seaman, J 21068, road accident

RM Labour Corps
 WELCH, James J, Private, RM, S 10383 (Deal), illness

Monday, 7 March 1921

Royal Navy
 FORTIER, Richard L, Act/Commander, RNR, illness

Tuesday, 8 March 1921

Defiance, Torpedo School, with monitor M.31 for minelaying instruction
 QUICK, Richard H, Gunner, illness

Wednesday, 9 March 1921

Revenge, battleship
 NICHOLLS, Thomas A, Gunner, RMA, RMA 16203, illness

Friday, 11 March 1921

RN College Dartmouth
 YOUNG, William H, Boatswain, illness

Sunday, 13 March 1921

Victory II, RND Training Depot, Crystal Palace, but closed down 1919; either post discharge illness or Victory, Portsmouth
 MUNT, James, Stoker 2c, SS 125724, illness

Tuesday, 15 March 1921

Calypso, light cruiser
 CREW, Albert H, Able Seaman, J 74774, drowned

Wednesday, 16 March 1921

Hawkins, cruiser
 DUNN, William C, Stoker Petty Officer, 304436, illness

Sunday, 20 March 1921

Impregnable, Devonport
 LOWNDES, Alexander, Captain, illness

Whirlwind, destroyer
 SALMOND, William A C, Lieutenant Commander, illness

Wednesday, 23 March 1921

Royal Naval Volunteer Reserve
 CAIN, Percy E, Act/Lieutenant Commander, RNVR, illness

Friday, 25 March 1921

Hood, battlecruiser
 EDWARDS, Leonard T, Officer's Steward 2c, L 10673, illness

Vivid, Devonport
 SAMPSON, Archibald C, Officer's Steward 1c, 361436, ex-Valorous, illness

Saturday, 26 March 1921

Kellett, minesweeper completed as survey ship
 STONE, Sydney H, Victualling Chief Petty Officer, M 3052, died

Sunday, 27 March 1921

Impregnable, Devonport
 GRAY, Ernest C, Boy 2c, J 100801, illness

Wednesday, 30 March 1921

Vivid, Devonport
 GIBSON, William, Boy 1c, J 100938, illness

Thursday, 31 March 1921

Excellent, Portsmouth
 HAM, John B, Chief Gunner, illness

Friday, 1 April 1921

Bee, river gunboat
 ATKINS, Tom, Petty Officer, 217729 (Po), drowned

RMLI, Plymouth Division
 SANDERS, James, Private, RMLI, 14064 (Ply), illness

Tenedos, destroyer
 BROWN, Joseph, Able Seaman, J 15869, illness

Saturday, 2 April 1921

Birmingham, 2nd class cruiser
 MURRAY, John A, Telegraphist, J 54248, died

Rocket, destroyer
 LEACH, James, Stoker Petty Officer, K 11874, drowned

Scarab, river gunboat
 COX, John, Petty Officer, J 14302, accident

Tamar, Hong Kong
 HUTTON, Illtyd A R, Commander, illness

Monday, 4 April 1921

Victory, Portsmouth
 McDONAGH, John J, Stoker 1c, K 14409, illness

Vivid, Devonport
 LOCK, Alfred S, Victualling Chief Petty Officer, 341256, illness

Tuesday, 5 April 1921

Dunedin, light cruiser
 ANDREWS, Robert J, Leading Cook, M 3690, fall

Pembroke, Chatham
 SPITERI, Paolo, Officer's Cook 3c, 359710, illness

Royal Naval Reserve
 MACIVER, Henry, Honorary Captain, RNR, illness

Sunday, 10 April 1921

Tyrian, destroyer
 ROBINSON, Frederick, Gunner, illness

Monday, 11 April 1921

Victory, Portsmouth
 GROSSMITH, George H, Stoker 1c, K 3775, died

Tuesday, 12 April 1921

Vivid, Devonport
 AYERS, Harold, Master at Arms, 202816, illness

Wednesday, 13 April 1921

RMLI, Portsmouth Division
 DURDLE, Reginald H, Corporal, RMLI, 15940 (Po), died

Thursday, 14 April 1921

Cairo, light cruiser
 BOWEN, Thomas, Leading Stoker, 116939 (Dev), died in Hong Kong

Friday, 15 April 1921

RM HQ 8th RM Battalion
 WILKIE, William J, Corporal, RMLI, 15709 (Po), drowned

Sandhurst, destroyer depot ship
 REID, Herbert G, Shipwright 1c, 345752, illness

Tamar, Hong Kong
 BOWEN, Thomas, Leading Stoker, K 11639, illness

Vivid, Devonport
 SYMONS, Herbert, Able Seaman, 214508, illness

Saturday, 16 April 1921

Cambrian, light cruiser
 HEANEY, John, Private, RMLI, 11460 (Ply), drowned

Fisgard, Portsmouth
 WILTSHIRE, Ernest J, Engine Room Artificer Apprentice, M 37334, illness

Queen Elizabeth, battleship
 THOM, William S, Ordinary Seaman, J 81793, drowned

Wryneck, destroyer
 SMITH, Charles, Stoker 1c, SS 124290, illness

Sunday, 17 April 1921

Actaeon, Sheerness
 BARR, Lewis W, Stoker 1c, K 13350, illness

Pembroke, Chatham
 BOYD, Kenneth Mac C, Petty Officer, 217767, illness

Monday, 18 April 1921

Impregnable, Devonport
 BLAKE, William H, Py/Schoolmaster, illness

Vivid, Devonport
 WOOD, Leslie, Boy 1c, J 92369 (Dev), illness

Tuesday, 19 April 1921

Speedy, destroyer
 HOWE, Edward, Engine Room Artificer 3c, M 13672, illness

Wednesday, 21 April 1921

RMLI, Portsmouth Division
 ROWLANDS, Arthur, Private, RMLI, 19823 (Po), illness

Vivid I, Devonport
 STANSFIELD, George S E, Able Seaman, J 93754, illness

Wanderer, destroyer
 BOOTH, Major H, Able Seaman, J 26633, died

Sunday, 24 April 1921

Impregnable, Devonport
 POWELL, Cecil J, Boy 2c, J 98975, illness

Royal Naval Reserve
 POWELL, Warrington B, Honorary Lieutenant, RNR, illness

Tuesday, 26 April 1921

Caroline, light cruiser
 PELLET, Frank E, Ordinary Seaman, J 94860, illness

Hecla, destroyer depot ship
 HOLMES, Thomas W, Chief Electrical Artificer 1c, 345111, illness

RM Headquarters
 WATSON, Albert E, Private, RMLI, 19810 (Ch), illness

Valiant, battleship
 ROBINSON, Jack, Petty Officer, 230068, illness

Valkyrie, destroyer
 JEFFERY, Bertie, Able Seaman, J 11870, accident

Wednesday, 27 April 1921

Colleen, Queenstown, Ireland
 BRINSON, Alfred S, Coastguardsman 3c, 9763 (Ch), died

Wryneck, destroyer
 PLOWRIGHT, Edward, Able Seaman, J 27751, illness

Thursday, 28 April 1921

Valiant, battleship
 ANDREWS, Albert D, Private, RMLI, 14925 (Ply), killed

Sunday, 1 May 1921

Rear Admiral 1st Battle Squadron
 DOUGHTY, Henry M, Rear Admiral, illness

Monday, 2 May 1921

Fisgard, Portsmouth
 BAKER, Harry E, Engine Room Artificer Apprentice, M 35663, illness

Hawkins, cruiser
 MILLER, Herbert, Leading Seaman, J 13236, drowned

Thursday, 5 May 1921

Impregnable, Devonport
 SKINNER, William, Boy 2c, J 101626, illness

Friday, 6 May 1921

Chatham, 2nd class cruiser
 TAMBLING, Leonard J, Able Seaman, J 35268, accident
Sylph, destroyer
 TANNER, Thomas, Leading Stoker, K 7540, illness

Saturday, 7 May 1921

Vivid, Devonport
 PICKFORD, Harry, Stoker 1c, SS 112746, illness

Sunday, 8 May 1921

Cockchafer, river gunboat
 ENTWISTLE, Harold, Stoker 1c, K 9848, drowned

Tuesday, 10 May 1921

Philomel, ex-cruiser, depot ship, New Zealand
 EATON, William, Joiner 1c, 301045, accident

Wednesday, 11 May 1921

Pegasus, seaplane carrier
 REMFRY, Charles J, Commissioned Gunner, illness

Vivid, Devonport
 KITCHEN, Henry, Able Seaman, 222959, illness

Thursday, 12 May 1921

Ganges, Shotley/Harwich
 MATHER, Charles W, Boy 2c, J 101646, illness

Impregnable, Devonport
 GIBSON, Walter P, Boy 2c, J 101348, illness

Royal Naval Reserve
 LEWIS, Benjamin, Commissioned Engineer, RNR, illness

Friday, 13 May 1921

Concord, light cruiser
 EASTLEY, John, Mechanician, 358829, illness

Saturday, 14 May 1921

Repulse, battlecruiser
 ALLEN, John T, Warrant Engineer, illness

RM Headquarters
 FRANCIS, Bernard, Gunner, RMA, RMA 14710, killed
 PARKER, William, Gunner, RMA, RMA 14560, killed

Victoria & Albert, Royal Yacht
 BOLTON, Joseph E, Stoker Petty Officer, 278551, illness

Vivid, Devonport
 STEER, William J, Leading Seaman, 215835, illness

Sunday, 15 May 1921

Cambrian, light cruiser
 CORNER, John, Stoker 1c, K 31731, illness

Monday, 16 May 1921

ship or unit not listed
 SAVAGE, Arthur W, Engine Room Artificer 3c, M 3487, illness

Tuesday, 17 May 1921

RM, 8th Battalion
 WILLIAMS, Ernest, Private, RMLI, 15586 (Po), killed in Ireland

Thursday, 19 May 1921

Victory, Portsmouth
 MORRIS, Ernest J, Able Seaman, 202794, illness

Friday, 20 May 1921

Maidstone, submarine depot ship
 BEARN, Reginald Y R, Petty Officer, J 16630, drowned

Saturday, 21 May 1921

Indus, Devonport
 HINTON, Harry, Stoker Petty Officer, K 9766, illness

RM, 8th Battalion
 CHANDLER, Henry, Private, RMLI, 19831 (Ch), killed in Ireland

Sunday, 22 May 1921

Fisgard, Portsmouth
 McFARLANE, Henry, Chief Stoker, 292760, illness

Vivid, Devonport
 ASHLEY, Robert C, Leading Stoker, 297291, illness
 HAWKEY, Joseph, Able Seaman, J 25896, illness

Monday, 23 May 1921

Tyrian, destroyer
 ANSTREE, Edward C, Stoker 1c, K 10164, illness

Tuesday, 24 May 1921

RM Headquarters
 COUSINS, Frederick W, Gunner, RMA, RMA 10757, illness

Verdun, destroyer
 MOORE, Reginald, Able Seaman, J 34369, drowned

Wednesday, 25 May 1921

King George V, battleship
 RICE, John, Private, RMLI, 19099 (Ply), drowned

Warspite, battleship

NASH, Charles A, Ordinary Seaman, J 89843, drowned

Thursday, 26 May 1921

Gibraltar, ex-cruiser, depot ship
  ADAMS, Cecil F W, Private, RMLI, 20068 (Ch), illness
Thermol, Royal Fleet Auxiliary
  WHITTAKER, John E, Sub Lieutenant, RNR, illness

Saturday, 28 May 1921

Wallace, flotilla leader
  GORING, William H, Stoker 1c, K 25380, illness

Sunday, 29 May 1921

Vivid, Devonport
  HARRISON, John, Boy 1c, J 102159, died

Monday, 30 May 1921

Impregnable, Devonport
  CAWTE, Cecil F, Boy 2c, J 102033, illness

Mutine, ex-sloop, survey ship
  WARREN, Ernest P, Able Seaman, J 44287, illness

Victory, Portsmouth
  MOLES, Frank G F, Yeoman of Signals, 230523, illness

Vivid, Devonport
  CHAPMAN, Charles W, Boy 1c, J 102166, illness

Tuesday, 31 May 1921

Montrose, flotilla leader
  HEAD, Walter, Stoker Petty Officer, K 11511, illness

Wednesday, 1 June 1921

Blenheim, ex-cruiser, destroyer depot ship
  KENNEDY, Arthur F, Able Seaman, J 24122, illness

Hollyhock, fleet sweeping sloop
  ADAMS, Albert E, Engine Room Artificer 2c, M 122, illness

Woolwich, destroyer depot ship
  BAKER, Henry, Stoker 1c, K 14458, illness

Thursday, 2 June 1921

M.1, 12in-armed submarine monitor
  HUCKIN, Reginald A, Able Seaman, J 9676, drowned

Vivid, Devonport
  NEWCOMBE, William, Stoker 3c, K 59393, illness

Friday, 3 June 1921

Colleen, Queenstown, Ireland
  DIMENT, Percy J, Able Seaman, J 23290, illness

Saturday, 4 June 1921

Victory, Portsmouth
  HOLMES, Francis R, Petty Officer, J 16086, accident

Sunday, 5 June 1921

Fantome, ex-sloop, survey ship
  DELHI, Alfred J, Able Seaman, J 16934, died
Impregnable, Devonport
  WEBB, Francis W, Boy 2c, J 102067, illness

King George V, battleship
  STEER, Eli, Able Seaman, J 38492, illness

RM Headquarters
  JEFFERY, Ernest H, Private, RMLI, 7074, illness

Monday, 6 June 1921

RM Headquarters
  GARDNER, Alfred, Private, RMLI, 12268 (Po), illness

Wednesday, 8 June 1921

Pembroke, Chatham
  MILES, Albert E, Stoker Petty Officer, K 17884, illness

Tarantula, river gunboat
  FREEMAN, Ernest W, Petty Officer, M 6981, illness in Hong Kong

Thursday, 9 June 1921

Impregnable, Devonport
  HARRIS, Dermot, Boy 2c, J 101204, illness

Saturday, 11 June 1921

Blenheim, ex-cruiser, destroyer depot ship
  MAY, William T J, Boatswain, illness

Sunday, 12 June 1921

Colleen, Queenstown, Ireland
  KENNINGTON, William J, Coastguardsman 3c, 185133, killed

Hawkins, cruiser
  BROOKWAY, Henry T, Leading Signalman, J 19058, illness

Hood, battlecruiser
  NEWLAND, Frederick J, Leading Seaman, J 49071, cause unknown

Tomahawk, destroyer
  NOBES, George F, Able Seaman, J 27933, drowned

Wednesday, 15 June 1921

RM Headquarters
  WHAYMAN, George, Gunner, RMA, RMA 9052, illness

Friday, 17 June 1921

Royal Navy

VINES, Alfred E, Commissioned Gunner, illness

Monday, 20 June 1921

Victory, Portsmouth
CROOK, Frank W, Engine Room Artificer 2c, M 4908, accident

Saturday, 25 June 1921

Gibraltar, ex-cruiser, depot ship
HOWE, Arthur G, Petty Officer, 209255, ex-PC.72, illness

Monday, 27 June 1921

Valentine, destroyer
BALDWIN, Albert J, Able Seaman, J 55663, illness

Tuesday, 28 June 1921

Endeavour, survey ship
SLAUGHTER, Harry G, Stoker 1c, SS 124145, illness

Friday, 1 July 1921

Blenheim, ex-cruiser, destroyer depot ship
MARTIN, John, Leading Seaman, 230259, illness

Geranium (RAN), fleet sweeping sloop
LENTHALL, Frederick W, Stoker, RAN, 11026, drowned

Saturday, 2 July 1921

Indus, Devonport
PRYNN, Samuel H G, Able Seaman, 224200, drowned

RM Headquarters
CHILDS, William H, Private, RMLI, 19612 (Pensioner), illness

Sunday, 3 July 1921

RM Headquarters
CAMERON, John, Gunner, RMA, RMA 8752, killed by Irish Republican Army

Monday, 4 July 1921

HM Coast Guard Station St Agnes
HEARN, John, Coastguardsman 3c, 186260, illness

Malaya, battleship
LUMSDEN, James, Shipwright 2c, 345616, road accident

Thursday, 7 July 1921

Ascension Island
FRIDAY, Tom, Krooman, (no service number listed), illness

Merlin, ex-sloop, survey ship
MATTISON, Sidney, Stoker Petty Officer, K 375, illness

Friday, 8 July 1921

Assistance, repair ship
HOBBS, William R, Blacksmith 4c, M 32223, accident

Saturday, 9 July 1921

Hecla, destroyer depot ship, boat accident
GOOCH, Frederick W, Able Seaman, J 65665, drowned

Sunday, 10 July 1921

Impregnable, Devonport
RICHARDS, William H, Boy 1c, J 96325, illness

Wednesday, 13 July 1921

Comus, light cruiser
DOALEH, Ali, Seedie Stoker, 402, accident

Victory, Portsmouth
REED, John L, Ordinary Seaman, J 89773, illness

Thursday, 14 July 1921

Impregnable, Devonport
LANDLER, Charles H R, Boy 2c, J 102255, illness

Sunday, 17 July 1921

Emperor of India, battleship
MARSH, Eugene, Able Seaman, J 42309, died

Warspite, battleship
GIDLEY, Arthur T, Ordinary Seaman, J 89907, illness

Monday, 18 July 1921

Excellent, Portsmouth
STEVENS, Thomas H, Chief Petty Officer, 212326, illness

Royal Naval Reserve
RICHARDS, Guy W, Lieutenant, RNR, illness

Victory, Portsmouth
OLDERSHAW, Charles W, Boy 1c, J 97546, illness

Tuesday, 19 July 1921

Victory, Portsmouth
BOTTOMLEY, Frederick C, Lieutenant Commander, illness

Wednesday, 20 July 1921

Yarmouth, 2nd class cruiser
HAYWOOD, Arthur R, Warrant Shipwright, illness

Thursday, 21 July 1921

ex-New Zealand, battlecruiser
PRICE, Albert H, Stoker, (no service number given), illness

Iron Duke, battleship
BODDY, Walter M, Private, RMLI, 18767 (Po), drowned

Westcott, destroyer

BUNKER, Ronald O, Able Seaman, J 19911, drowned

Friday, 22 July 1921

Titania, submarine depot ship
 RODHAM, Thomas, Stoker 1c, K 22037, drowned

Saturday, 23 July 1921

Hercules, battleship
 CLARKE, Digby A P, Surgeon Lieutenant, accident

Victory, Portsmouth
 MUNRO, Alexander, Stoker 1c, 300999, illness

Sunday, 24 July 1921

Pembroke, Chatham
 FERGUSON, Peter, Able Seaman, J 7715, illness

Tuesday, 26 July 1921

Pembroke, Chatham
 COUGHLAN, William H, Petty Officer, J 4691, illness

Wednesday, 27 July 1921

Colleen, Queenstown, Ireland
 MINIHANE, Thomas, Coastguardsman 3c, 182289, illness

Comus, light cruiser
 LANGFORD, Alfred A, Able Seaman, 204179, illness

Royal Navy
 GREIG, Donald, Commander (ret), died in Mesopotamia

Sunday, 31 July 1921

RM Headquarters
 MASON, Henry G, Private, RMLI, 20517 (Po), illness

Sportive, destroyer
 OSMAN, Charles E, Able Seaman, J 41711, illness

Monday, 1 August 1921

Crocus, fleet sweeping sloop
 REEVES, Sidney G A, Officer's Steward 1c, 360506, heat stroke

Thruster, destroyer
 RELF, Benjamin O, Able Seaman, J 37822, drowned

Victory, Portsmouth
 LILLY, Reginald F, Able Seaman, J 35357, died, day not given in record

Tuesday, 2 August 1921

Tiger, battlecruiser
 BONE, Samuel T, Engine Room Artificer 5c, M 21995, drowned

Wednesday, 3 August 1921

Emperor of India, battleship

BEARD, Francis J, Stoker 1c, K 10768, illness

Saturday, 6 August 1921

Pembroke, Chatham
 WILLIAMS, George S, Able Seaman, J 90464, illness
Southampton, 2nd class cruiser
 JENNINGS, Harold, Electrical Artificer 2c, M 4843, drowned

Vivid II, Devonport
 FUGE, James S, Mechanician, 297278, illness

Sunday, 7 August 1921

President, London
 DAY, Thomas M, Lieutenant, RNR, illness

Monday, 8 August 1921

Spindrift, destroyer
 MANKEY, John, Engineer Lieutenant, illness

Tuesday, 9 August 1921

Ganges, Shotley/Harwich
 SMITH, Arthur H, Boy 2c, J 100100, illness

Royal Navy
 FENN, Cyril D, Lieutenant Commander, illness

Wednesday, 10 August 1921

Cairo, light cruiser
 COLLINS, Vincent H, Sergeant, 10298 (Ply), illness

Friday, 12 August 1921

Dee, destroyer
 RUSSELL, William H, Petty Officer, J 21098, died

Fantome, ex-sloop, survey ship
 SANDERS, Frederick J, Able Seaman, J 56750, illness

Iron Duke, battleship
 CRACKNELL, George N, Paymaster Lieutenant, illness

Saturday, 13 August 1921

Afrikander, Simonstown, South Africa *(below, light cruiser Durban in drydock, Simonstown, George Smith)*
 ANDERSON, Toby, Krooman, W 7, illness

Sunday, 14 August 1921

Excellent, Portsmouth
  BLACK, James, Chief Petty Officer, 191084, street accident

Tuesday, 16 August 1921

Cambrian, light cruiser
  HUXTABLE, William, Stoker Petty Officer, 217062, drowned

Saturday, 20 August 1921

Dolphin, Gosport
  DAWE, Samuel H, Painter 1c, 344039, illness

Monday, 22 August 1921

Ladybird, river gunboat
  CALEY, William, Able Seaman, J 83751, drowned

Tuesday, 23 August 1921

Afrikander, Simonstown, South Africa
  CROWLEY, Cornelius P, Telegraphist, J 46514, illness

Wednesday, 24 August 1921

Colleen, Queenstown, Ireland
  POWELL, John, Stoker Petty Officer, K 3347, illness

Saturday, 27 August 1921

Pembroke, Chatham
  RAMAGE, Arthur, Able Seaman, J 32546, illness

Sunday, 28 August 1921

Construction Inspector (ion) R. *(abbreviation only partly known)*
  CAMPBELL, O (initial only) M, Construction Worker, killed

Julius, shore base Constantinople
  LITTLE, William H, Leading Victualling Assistant, M 14267, drowned

Thursday, 1 September 1921

Victory III, Portsmouth
  HERITAGE, William H, Cook, M 11180, illness

Saturday, 3 September 1921

Clematis, fleet sweeping sloop
  MAGUIRE, Edward, Chief Stoker, 297375, illness

Monday, 5 September 1921

Diligence, Devonport, on books of Blenheim, ex-cruiser, destroyer depot ship
  DEACON, Henry S, Chief Stoker, 296535, died

Pembroke, Chatham
  BRAND, Frank H, Petty Officer, 239324, illness

Wednesday, 7 September 1921

Mutine, ex-sloop, survey ship
  JOHNSON, William, Stoker 1c, SS 123848, drowned

Friday, 9 September 1921

Raleigh, cruiser
  BENNETT, Francis T, Stoker 2c, K 59110, illness

Saturday, 10 September 1921

Vernon, Portsmouth
  LAYTON, Albert G, Able Seaman, SS 9191, illness

Monday, 12 September 1921

Iron Duke, battleship
  COMBEN, Horace S, Stoker 2c, K 59125, died

Tuesday, 13 September 1921

Leamington, minesweeper
  COOPER, Charles, Shipwright 3c, 346965, drowned

Thursday, 15 September 1921

Colombo, light cruiser
  HEATHER, Charles, Petty Officer, J 12617, illness

Seawolf, destroyer
  HOWE, Desmond J, Able Seaman, J 72191, illness

Friday, 16 September 1921

Dolphin, Gosport
  POWELL, Thomas, Engine Room Artificer 1c, 271798, illness

Saturday, 17 September 1921

Curacoa, light cruiser
  MITCHELL, Frederick C, Officer's Cook 1c, L 4508, drowned

Sunday, 18 September 1921

Canterbury, light cruiser
  LANE, Harry, Warrant Shipwright, illness

Wednesday, 21 September 1921

Royal Navy
 TINDAL-CARILL-WORSLEY, Charles N, Captain, illness

Saturday, 24 September 1921

Curacoa, light cruiser
 BILLINGHURST, Arthur, Stoker 1c, K 57348, drowned

Dolphin, Gosport
 TULLY, Ernest, Engine Room Artificer 4c, M 18353, accident

Julius, shore base Constantinople
 HENNESSY, John J, Able Seaman, J 23710, illness

Renown, battlecruiser
 SMALL, John E, Gunner, RMA, RMA 14079, illness

Monday, 26 September 1921

Short Course
 SOMERSET, John B, Sub Lieutenant, illness

Wednesday, 28 September 1921

Ganges, Shotley/Harwich
 GLINN, Samuel, Boy 2c, J 103059, illness

Friday, 30 September 1921

Lowestoft, 2nd class cruiser
 KEEHNEMUND, Edward (real name, but served as Edward Jarvis), Stoker 2c, SS 125807, illness

Veteran, destroyer
 DYSON, Alan W, Able Seaman, SS 9575, illness

Saturday, 1 October 1921

Fisgard, Portsmouth
 CONDY, Arthur, Boatswain, illness

Victory II, Portsmouth
 COBB, William, Chief Stoker, 296193, accident

Sunday, 2 October 1921

RM Headquarters
 SAMPHIER, Frank, Private, RMLI, 20648 (Po), illness

Tuesday, 4 October 1921

Hawkins, cruiser
 STUART, Colin S, Instructor Lieutenant, illness

Thursday, 6 October 1921

Renown, battlecruiser
 BAYLIS, Frederwick W, Able Seaman, J 5450, illness

Vancouver, destroyer
 STEELE, William R, Lieutenant, illness

Saturday, 8 October 1921

Fantome, ex-sloop, survey ship
 RUTHERFORD, Robert, Private, RMLI, 17872 (Ply), died

Gibraltar, ex-cruiser, depot ship
 FUNNELL, Henry G, Private, RMLI, 22734 (Ch), died

Sunday, 9 October 1921

Victory, Portsmouth
 COCK, William C, Coastguardsman 3c, 158101, illness

Monday, 10 October 1921

Royal Naval Reserve
 SONE, John D, Commissioned Engineer, illness

Tuesday, 11 October 1921

Caledon, light cruiser
 LANE, Herbert G, Able Seaman, J 6139, illness

Colleen, Queenstown, Ireland
 WELLS, George A, Private, RMLI, 12308 (Ply), illness

Impregnable, Devonport
 MAY, William, Chief Writer, 345195, illness

Wednesday, 12 October 1921

Spear, destroyer
 POWELL, William F, Chief Petty Officer, 239372, died

Thursday, 13 October 1921

Pembroke, Chatham
 TINGEY, Edward, Stoker 1c, SS 120405, illness

Vivid, Devonport
 CALLAGHAN, James, Coastguardsman 3c, 177301, illness

Friday, 14 October 1921

Valiant, battleship
 TRAVIS, Albert, Signalman, J 22463, drowned

Saturday, 15 October 1921

Gnat, river gunboat
 SUPPLE, George, Able Seaman, J 26315, illness

Sunday, 16 October 1921

Comus II, believed miscellaneous harbour craft, tender to Comus, light cruiser
 BAYLY, Richard W U, Lieutenant Commander, illness

RM Headquarters
 HOPKINSON, James A, RM Band, RMB 1103, illness

Tuesday, 18 October 1921

Indus, Devonport
  BULLEN, John F, Engine Room Artificer Apprentice, M 26915, illness

Thursday, 20 October 1921

Benbow, battleship
  CHANCE, Gilbert H T, Able Seaman, J 43099, illness

Friday, 21 October 1921

Vansittart, destroyer
  EDEY, George E, Leading Seaman, J 5173, drowned

Sunday, 23 October 1921

Pembroke, Chatham
  HUME, Frank, Telegraphist, J 28980, accident

Monday, 24 October 1921

Iron Duke, battleship, explosion
  SMITH, William J, Stoker 1c, SS 121644

Vivid, Devonport
  HENDERSON, William C, Chief Yeoman of Signals, 197526, illness

Wednesday, 26 October 1921

Antrim, armoured cruiser
  GULLIS, George, Stoker 1c, K 56738, illness

Victory, Portsmouth
  JOHNSTONE, John, Petty Officer, 200342, died

Thursday, 27 October 1921

Ganges, Shotley/Harwich
  NEWTON, George W, Boy 2c, J 102912, illness

Friday, 28 October 1921

Colombo, light cruiser
  MAXTED, Albert V, Petty Officer, 211613, illness

Ganges, Shotley/Harwich
  HOLMES, Walter, Boy 1c, J 100094, illness

Sunday, 30 October 1921

Pembroke, Chatham
  HOLLIDAY, Percy W, Stoker 1c, K 19040, illness

Monday, 31 October 1921

Barham, battleship
  BARR, Samuel A J, Boy 1c, J 97828, died

Royal Navy
  GARDNER, Henry R, Surgeon Commander, illness

Friday, 4 November 1921

Iron Duke, battleship
  BEAK, George H, Cadet Paymaster, illness

Pomone, ex-cruiser, training ship
  CLARK, Reginald H, Stoker 1c, K 30262, illness

Monday, 7 November 1921

Colossus, battleship
  BROCK, Edwin F, Boy 2c, J 104079, illness

Royal Navy
  KETCHLEY, Reginald E, Warrant Wardmaster, illness

Tuesday, 8 November 1921

Hawkins, cruiser
  DUFF, William, Stoker 1c, SS 125019, illness

Wednesday, 9 November 1921

Afrikander, Simonstown, South Africa
  IRWIN, Hugh, Able Seaman, 229237, illness

Fisgard, Portsmouth
  HORROCKS, Arthur R, Engine Room Artificer Apprentice, M 34515, illness

Vortigern, destroyer
  STONE, William H T, Able Seaman, SS 8782, drowned

Thursday, 10 November 1921

Calypso, light cruiser
  ALLEN, Robert, Stoker 1c, K 17094, accident

King George V, battleship
  SMALE, Richard G A, Boatswain, illness

Friday, 11 November 1921

Raleigh, cruiser
  BRENNAN, Joseph, Able Seaman, SS 5442, drowned

Vivid, Devonport
  PEPPER, Alexander J, Chief Engine Room Artificer 2c, 271368, illness

Sunday, 13 November 1921

Victory, Portsmouth
  PITHER, Henry, Able Seaman, J 34433, illness

Monday, 14 November 1921

Impregnable, Devonport
  GILES, Frederick, Boy 1c, J 100463, illness

Tumult, destroyer
  HARTLESS, Herbert W, Able Seaman, J 19492, illness

Tuesday, 15 November 1921

Southampton, 2nd class cruiser

JAMA, Mohamed, Seedie, Aden 411, illness

Saturday, 19 November 1921

Pembroke, Chatham
 GIDNEY, Francis W, Chief Stoker, 310023, illness

Sunday, 20 November 1921

Victory, Portsmouth
 BURDEN, Walter, Chief Mechanician 2c, 358236, illness

Wednesday, 23 November 1921

Titania, submarine depot ship
 NORMAN, William, Leading Stoker, 308772, illness

Thursday, 24 November 1921

Repulse, battlecruiser
 BENHAM, Arthur J A, Able Seaman, J 43246, illness

Sunday, 27 November 1921

Victory, Portsmouth
 HOYE, Albert C, Stoker 1c, SS 125865, drowned

Monday, 28 November 1921

Vernon, Portsmouth
 JONES, David R, Lieutenant, illness

Tuesday, 29 November 1921

Tiger, battlecruiser
 DIBLEY, Samuel F, Stoker 1c, SS 120419, illness

unit not recorded
 DIXON, Thomas, Leading Stoker, K 8572, illness

Thursday, 1 December 1921

Royal Naval Reserve
 SANDEMAN, John G, Honorary Lieutenant, RNR, illness

Sunday, 4 December 1921

Caradoc, light cruiser
 DUNBAR, Bernard C, Able Seaman, J 18422, drowned

Monday, 5 December 1921

Actaeon, Sheerness
 ORE, James, Commissioned Gunner, illness

Shakespeare, flotilla leader
 ARGENT, William E, Chief Petty Officer, 212349, illness

Tuesday, 6 December 1921

Vivid, Devonport
 RICHARDS, Ernest, Petty Officer, 237418, illness

Wednesday, 7 December 1921

Chrysanthemum, convoy sloop
 CLINCH, Arthur, Able Seaman, SS 4778, illness

Thursday, 8 December 1921

Victory, Portsmouth
 NEWBY, Alfred, Leading Boatman, 308779, illness

Friday, 9 December 1921

ML.358, motor launch
 PAGET, Alfred L, Lieutenant, illness
Venomous, destroyer
 EASTON, William S, Able Seaman, J 84915, drowned

Sunday, 11 December 1921

Pembroke, Chatham
 PEARKS, Donald W, Shipwright 4c, M 19193, illness

Monday, 12 December 1921

Blake, ex-cruiser, destroyer depot ship
 AYERS, Fred, Lieutenant Commander, illness

Resolution, battleship
 COUCH, Fred T, Shipwright 2c, M 7734, illness

Wednesday, 14 December 1921

Comus, light cruiser
 CROCKFORD, George, Ordinary Seaman, J 493499, drowned

Saturday, 17 December 1921

Merlin, ex-sloop, survey ship
 SPENCE, Archibald W, Stoker 1c, SS 122692, illness

Victory, Portsmouth
 HOPTON, Albert W, Stoker Petty Officer, 294505, illness
 LOVE, James, Stoker 1c, K 26166, died

Monday, 19 December 1921

Pembroke, Chatham
 REEVES, Ernest A, Stoker 1c, K 22764, illness

Wednesday, 21 December 1921

HM Dockyard Hong Kong
 WILLIAMS, John T, Commissioned Boatswain, illness

Thursday, 22 December 1921

Ganges, Shotley/Harwich

DAVEY, Sidney J, Boy 1c, J 98664, illness

Friday, 23 December 1921

Berwick Wireless Station
  GITTINS, George W, Coastguardsman 2c, 157060, illness

Ganges, Shotley/Harwich
  PUTNAM, Pelham W, Boy 2c, J 102647, illness

Monday, 26 December 1921

Calcutta, light cruiser
  TRICE, William J, Shipwright 2c, 342862, accident

Comus, light cruiser
  COMPTON, Alexander F, Able Seaman, J 43708, illness

ML.291, motor launch
  CADAGAN, Albert, Able Seaman, J 55263, drowned
  Seraph, destroyer, both drowned
  FORTLEY, William G, Able Seaman, J 36611
  VICKERY, William J, Able Seaman, 210467

Victory, Portsmouth
  BUDGEON, James, Stoker 1c, K 23665, illness

Tuesday, 27 December 1921

Afrikander, Simonstown, South Africa
  JENNER, Harold J, Able Seaman, J 8826, accident

Ganges, Shotley/Harwich
  HALL, John R, Boy 2c, J 105097, illness

Wednesday, 28 December 1921

Iron Duke, battleship
  PAIN, Philip T, Petty Officer, 233073, illness

Victory, Portsmouth
  JONES, Norman W B, Ordinary Seaman, SS 11859, illness

Friday, 30 December 1921

Collingwood, battleship
  COOK, William H, Stoker Petty Officer, K 27073, illness

Glorious, light battlecruiser
  LAKE, James C, Chief Petty Officer Telegraphist, 309546, illness

Marlborough, battleship
  SHANKLEY, Richard, Leading Seaman, J 7876, illness

1922

Tuesday, 3 January 1922

Valerian, fleet sweeping sloop
 COOPER, Herbert A S, Leading Seaman, J 2054, died

Wednesday, 4 January 1922

Tiger, battlecruiser
 BUTLER, Frank V, Able Seaman, J 31120, illness

Valerian, fleet sweeping sloop
 SAVILL, Jack H, Able Seaman, SS 9463, accidentally killed

Thursday, 5 January 1922

Curlew, light cruiser
 CHAPMAN, Ernest F, Engine Room Artificer 2c, M 7579, illness

Renown, battlecruiser
 WHITING, Walter, Private, RMLI, 118068 (Po), illness

Saturday, 7 January 1922

Victory, Portsmouth
 BELSEY, Percy T, Petty Officer, 207845, illness

Tuesday, 10 January 1922

Impregnable, Devonport
 BRAY, William J, Boy 2c, J 103439, illness

Malaya, battleship
 TREADWELL, Joseph T, Able Seaman, J 27654, illness

Wednesday, 11 January 1922

Blenheim, ex-cruiser, destroyer depot ship
 LAWRENCE, Edwin T, Petty Officer, J 15888, drowned

Wivern, destroyer
 HARRISON, George, Leading Seaman, J 19548, illness

Friday, 13 January 1922

Conqueror, battleship
 BEALE, Joseph, Officer's Chief Cook, L 743, illness

Glowworm, river gunboat
 HEADLY, William, Petty Officer, 233067, accidentally killed

Royal Oak, battleship
 BOUNDS, Francis C, Officer's Steward 1c, 357382, illness

Veteran, destroyer
 CURRAN, James J, Able Seaman, J 11215, illness

Saturday, 14 January 1922

Royal Naval Reserve
 KITSON, Roger W B, Midshipman, RNR, accidentally killed

Shakespeare, flotilla leader
 ROWELL, Leonard H, Stoker 1c, SS 124939, accidentally killed

Monday, 16 January 1922

HM Coast Guard
 PITCHER, Charles O, Chief Officer, HMCG, illness

Victory, Portsmouth
 MONKCOM, George W L, Commissioned Writer, illness

Tuesday, 17 January 1922

Vivid, Devonport
 BALDWIN, John R, Boy 1c, J 104052, illness

Wednesday, 18 January 1922

Vivid, Devonport
 LEWIS, Harry I, Able Seaman, J 79546, illness

Thursday, 19 January 1922

Veteran, destroyer
 HORSHAM, Sidney, Able Seaman, J 13230, illness

Wivern, destroyer
 SIDLEY, William, Able Seaman, J 10846, illness

Saturday, 21 January 1922

Vivid, Devonport
 HINGSTON, John, Able Seaman, 118541, illness

Sunday, 22 January 1922

Repulse, battlecruiser
 SPURDEN, Charles, Leading Stoker, K 15501, drowned

Vivid, Devonport
 GAME, George F, Regulating Petty Officer, M 36835, illness

Tuesday, 24 January 1922

Lion, battlecruiser
 STONE, Walter, Able Seaman, 183434, illness

Malaya, battleship
 KERSHAW, Cecil, Able Seaman, J 83717, drowned

Mantis, river gunboat
 HODNETT, Herbert, Able Seaman, 218089, illness

Wednesday, 25 January 1922

Benbow, battleship
 WEBB, Edward W, Telegraphist, J 21648, accidentally killed

President, London
 ANSELL, Walter, Boy Servant, L 14039, illness

Vivid, Devonport
 LESSLIE, David G, Leading Telegraphist, J 21679, illness

Thursday, 26 January 1922

Victory, Portsmouth
PEARSON, Magnus S, Seaman, RNR, A 9990, illness

Friday, 27 January 1922

Iron Duke, battleship
JONES, Leo F F, Able Seaman, J 17672, accidentally killed

Saturday, 28 January 1922

Vivid, Devonport
TOSH, James C, Boy 1c, J 104186, illness

Vivien, destroyer
DEIGHTON, Henry, Leading Stoker, 299695, illness

Walpole, destroyer
COLLINS, Richard H, Able Seaman, J 91136, drowned

Tuesday, 31 January 1922

Royal Oak, battleship
MAXEY, Lawrence S, Leading Seaman, J 12586, illness

Whitley, destroyer
DRING, Jack E, Gunner, illness

Wednesday, 1 February 1922

H.42, submarine
HILLIER, Horace J, Stoker 1c, K 55832, drowned

Vernon, Portsmouth
BONSOR, George, Chief Petty Officer, 200028, illness

Thursday, 2 February 1922

Caledon, light cruiser
CAWKWELL, George W, Able Seaman, J 36153, illness

Pandora, submarine depot ship
BISH, Harold T, Able Seaman, J 104725, drowned

Vivien, destroyer
PEACOCK, George B, Able Seaman, 215778, illness

Saturday, 4 February 1922

Royal Navy
FEGAN, Joseph, Commissioned Engineer, illness

Victory, Portsmouth
CHAPMAN, Charles W, Leading Seaman, 236737, illness

Sunday, 5 February 1922

Assistant Naval Attache to Italy, Greece, Rumania, Serb-Croatia-Slovenia
PEPLOE, Norman B F, Lieutenant, illness

Ganges, Shotley/Harwich
RILEY, Wilfred, Boy 2c, J 104129, illness

Pembroke, Chatham
GRIFFITHS, Frederick C E, Able Seaman, J 27007, illness

Tuesday, 7 February 1922

Pembroke, Chatham
WILLIAMS, George, Boatswain, illness

Vivid, Devonport
WEBSTER, John, Able Seaman, J 43078, illness

Wednesday, 8 February 1922

Ganges, Shotley/Harwich
GREEN, Ernest, Private, RMLI, 20866 (Ch), illness

Thursday, 9 February 1922

Emperor of India, battleship
PECK, Humphrey, Captain, RMA, illness

Monday, 13 February 1922

Valiant, battleship
CARN-DUFF, Herbert J, Lieutenant, drowned

Tuesday, 14 February 1922

Glorious, light battlecruiser
PHILLIPS, Bert G, Stoker 1c, K 18519, illness

Indus, Devonport
EDGINGTON, Frederick J, Ordnance Artificer Apprentice, M 35360, illness

Vivid, Devonport
SOLOMON, Walter H, Chief Petty Officer, 200412, illness

Wednesday, 15 February 1922

Endeavour, survey ship
THOMPSON, Stanley E, Engine Room Artificer 2c, M 4718, illness

Iron Duke, battleship
ALLEN, Herbert A, Yeoman of Signals, 221355, illness

Resolution, battleship
PRICE, Horace H, Ordinary Seaman, SS 10376, illness

Thursday, 16 February 1922

Ganges, Shotley/Harwich
JOHNSON, Ethelburt A, Chief Wardmaster, 346516, illness

Friday, 17 February 1922

Vivid, Devonport
WILLIAMS, Albert J, Able Seaman, J 52287, illness

Saturday, 18 February 1922

Blenheim, ex-cruiser, destroyer depot ship
HOLMES, Harold, Engine Room Artificer 1c, 270288, illness

Laburnum, fleet sweeping sloop
COWLING, James F, Stoker 1c, K 23934, drowned

Sunday, 19 February 1922

Dwarf, 1st class gunboat
ROWBOTHAM, Reginald, Private, RMLI, 17804 (Ch), drowned

Tuesday, 21 February 1922

Victory, Portsmouth
BARKER, William, Chief Petty Officer, 209391, illness

Wednesday, 22 February 1922

Excellent, Portsmouth
BOTWRIGHT, Tom W, Gunner, illness

Vivid, Devonport
NEWTON, William H, Petty Officer, J 30575, illness

Saturday, 25 February 1922

Emperor of India, battleship
BREWETON, Charles T, Stoker 1c, SS 124245, died

Monday, 27 February 1922

Vivid, Devonport
BURKE, Richard S, Chief Yeoman of Signals, 209562, illness

Tuesday, 28 February 1922

Ramillies, battleship
LAMB, Edward J, Stoker 1c, K 59104, illness

Friday, 3 March 1922

Vivid, Devonport
HALE, Hubert, Engine Room Artificer 1c, 270376, illness

Sunday, 5 March 1922

Verity, destroyer
KING, William J, Able Seaman, J 81400, illness

Wednesday, 8 March 1922

Victory, Portsmouth
SMITH, Charles W, Coastguardsman 3c, 279999, illness

Thursday, 9 March 1922

Erin, battleship
McELHERAN, George F, Boy 1c, J 100410, illness

Renown, battlecruiser
HUXLEY, Arthur G, Engine Room Artificer 1c, 271303, accidentally killed

Saturday, 11 March 1922

Pembroke, Chatham
PERRY, Sidney W, Able Seaman, J 70254, illness

Victory, Portsmouth
DAMEN, Arthur C, Able Seaman, SS 8331, illness

Tuesday, 14 March 1922

Royal Oak, battleship
McDONALD, Edward V J, Private, RMLI, 18042 (Ch), died

Scarab, river gunboat
ENTWISTLE, John G, Victualling Petty Officer, 341795, died

Thursday, 16 March 1922

Vivid, Devonport
BICKLEY, Frederick H, Engine Room Artificer 3c, M 15652, illness

Friday, 17 March 1922

Pembroke, Chatham
PRATT, Arthur C, Musician, RMB, RMB 1172, illness

Sunday, 19 March 1922

Impregnable, Devonport
BUNGEY, Stewart A, Boy 2c, J 103932, illness

Pembroke, Chatham
REEVE, Tom, Chief Stoker, 222003, illness

Victory, Portsmouth
GITTINGS, Arthur E, Stoker Petty Officer, 307391, illness

Monday, 20 March 1922

Colleen, Queenstown, Ireland
THOMAS, John E, Private, RMLI, 20396 (Ply), illness

Thursday, 23 March 1922

Curlew, light cruiser
DIXON, Joseph, Leading Telegraphist, J 22450, illness

H.42, submarine, surfacing and in collision with destroyer Versatile off Europa Point, Gibraltar, lost, no survivors *(below, H.21-class sister-boat H.34)*

ANDERSON, Herbert C, Leading Stoker, K 24252
BARNARD, George L, Stoker 1c, K 29260
BLACKWELL, Arthur W, Chief Engine Room Artificer, 272345
CANT, Athol H, Leading Telegraphist, J 34995

DALE, Samuel G, Boy 1c, J 98338
DAVIS, Montague E, Leading Telegraphist, J 85592
FOOKES, William, Stoker 1c, K 21909
FOWLER, Richard, Engine Room Artificer 2c, M 4712
GAMBLEN, Cyril, Leading Seaman, J 15398
HANSFORD, James G, Stoker Petty Officer, 308223
HARRIS, Walter G, Stoker 1c, J 18681
HARVEY, Edward J, Leading Signalman, J 10580
HAZELL, William J, Able Seaman, J 11956
HOOPER, Alwin S, Able Seaman, J 14872
KEARN, George J, Able Seaman, J 15564
McDONALD, Donald, Engine Room Artificer 4c, M 7995
OSWELL, Thomas M, Lieutenant
PARSONS, George W, Able Seaman, J 1878
PEARCE, William A, Able Seaman, J 17236
PENNY, Ernest, Petty Officer, J 9617
PORCH, Robert E, Petty Officer, J 12072
PORTER, Albert E, Ordinary Seaman, J 98344
PRICE, James C W, Lieutenant, DSC
RICKARD, George H, Able Seaman, J 13668
SEALY, Douglas C, Lieutenant
SMART, Henry J, Stoker 1c, K 18164

Titania, submarine depot ship
MORGAN, Harry, Leading Stoker, K 17310, illness

Sunday, 26 March 1922

Constance, light cruiser
JOHNS, Edward, Stoker 1c, K 56073, illness

Monday, 27 March 1922

Pembroke, Chatham
QUAYLE, Harold D, Able Seaman, J 83810, illness

Thursday, 30 March 1922

Columbine, Rosyth
RANN, Charles, Officer's Steward 2c, L 6011, illness

Sunday, 2 April 1922

Admiralty Department of Naval Ordnance
McKENZIE, Malcolm A, Lieutenant, illness

Wednesday, 5 April 1922

Crocus, fleet sweeping sloop
THORNTON, Arthur B, Stoker 1c, SS 122115, illness

Vivid, Devonport
KITLEY, John, Chief Stoker, 298539, illness

Thursday, 6 April 1922

Westcott, destroyer
COPKING, Frederick T, Engine Room Artificer 3c, M 32342, illness

Monday, 10 April 1922

Ajax, battleship
WARD, Arthur J, Stoker 1c, SS 122597, accidentally killed

Dolphin, Gosport
WINSTANLEY, Alfred J G, Engine Room Artificer 3c, M 4807, illness

Titania, submarine depot ship
ELLIOTT, John C, Able Seaman, J 2534, illness

Victory, Portsmouth
COLE, Ernest G, Able Seaman, J 37271, accidentally killed

Vivid, Devonport
DONOVAN, John J, Ordinary Seaman, J 102224, illness

Tuesday, 11 April 1922

Pembroke, Chatham
BLAKE, Frank M, Coastguardsman 3c, 178535, illness

Wednesday, 12 April 1922

Defiance, Devonport
GOSS, Herbert H, Leading Seaman, J 11484, drowned

Eagle, aircraft carrier
de CAEN, Raymond G F H, Lieutenant Commander, illness

Thursday, 13 April 1922

Royal Naval Reserve
BLAKELEY, Thomas, Paymaster Lieutenant, RNR, illness

Friday, 14 April 1922

Vivid, Devonport
BANNISTER, Frank D, Able Seaman, J 61094, illness
BURGE, Samuel, Able Seaman, J 12020, illness

Saturday, 15 April 1922

Cairo, light cruiser
ASTLEFORD, Samuel, Stoker 1c, SS 119889, illness

King George V, battleship
HOOPER, Samuel, Cook, M 34989, drowned
MATTHEWS, David O, Petty Officer Cook, M 97, drowned

Sunday, 16 April 1922

Colleen, Queenstown, Ireland
DALEY, John, Coastguardsman 2c, 147025, illness

President, London
GRIFFITHS, Albert J, Commissioned Shipwright, illness

Royal Oak, battleship
LONG, Alexander A, Leading Seaman, J 9853, died

Monday, 17 April 1922

Columbine, Rosyth
SCAIFE, Irving, Stoker 1c, SS 120477, illness

Thursday, 20 April 1922

Fitzroy, minesweeper completed as survey ship
VINEY, Rolf, Commander, illness

Friday, 21 April 1922

Ganges, Shotley/Harwich
 ALLAN, James L, Boy 2c, J 103807, illness

Victory, Portsmouth
 MOORE, George P, Blacksmith 2c, M 12644, illness

Vivid IV, Falmouth
 DODD, Charles, Petty Officer, 198415, illness

Saturday, 22 April 1922

Durban, light cruiser
 CONNELL, Thomas J, Supply Petty Officer, 310418, drowned

Sunday, 23 April 1922

Vivid, Devonport
 HARVEY, Henry, Coastguardsman 2c, 157954, illness

Monday, 24 April 1922

Erin, battleship
 SHERRY, Francis J, Boy 1c, J 100577, illness

Marlborough, battleship
 HOWELL, George, Boy 1c, J 99576, illness

Tamar, Hong Kong
 NIXON, John, Gunner, RMA, RMA 9841, illness

Tuesday, 25 April 1922

Southampton II, RN Base, Ceylon (Sri Lanka)
 TEE, Thomas G, Able Seaman, J 29582, illness

Wednesday, 26 April 1922

Pembroke, Chatham
 PAY, James A J, Leading Boatman, 202680, illness

Vivid, Devonport
 BEER, William A, Petty Officer, 208197, illness

Friday, 28 April 1922

Pembroke, Chatham
 WINTER, Albert, Able Seaman, 194988, illness

Monday, 1 May 1922

Excellent, Portsmouth
 GILBERT, Frederick J, Stoker Petty Officer, 305652, drowned

Royal Naval Reserve
 KELLY, Lionel M, Lieutenant, RNR, illness

Vernon, Portsmouth
 MILLER, John, Leading Seaman, J 13442, accidentally killed

Tuesday, 2 May 1922

Dolphin, Gosport
 HALL, Charles F, Stoker 1c, K 55015, illness

Pembroke, Chatham
 MAHONY, John, Blacksmith, 340008, illness

Wednesday, 3 May 1922

Marlborough, battleship
 WRIGHT, John R, Able Seaman, J 93615, accidentally killed

Friday, 5 May 1922

Ganges, Shotley/Harwich
 ATHROLL, Francis H, Boy 1c, J 101827, illness

Sunday, 7 May 1922

Caroline, light cruiser
 CAMPBELL, George H, Supply Petty Officer, 306297, died

Thursday, 11 May 1922

Tenacious, destroyer
 LIBBY, John F, Stoker 1c, K 46174, accidentally killed

Friday, 12 May 1922

Marlborough, battleship
 ROBINSON, Leonard, Ordinary Seaman, SS 10758, accidentally killed

Victory III, Portsmouth
 DENYER, Leonard G, Officer's Steward 2c, L 8260, died

Sunday, 14 May 1922

Victory, Portsmouth
 CHILTON, Thomas E, Stoker 1c, K 58237, illness

Tuesday, 16 May 1922

Victory, Portsmouth
 THRING, Harry L, Chief Engine Room Artificer 2c, M 849, accidentally killed

Thursday, 18 May 1922

Victory, Portsmouth
 SIMPKINS, Leslie C, Ordinary Seaman, J 74969, illness

Sunday, 21 May 1922

Victory, Portsmouth
 VALENTINE, Victor E D, Paymaster Lieutenant Commander, illness

Monday, 22 May 1922

Cairo, light cruiser
 MAHONY, Thomas S, Stoker 1c, K 22564, drowned

Tuesday, 23 May 1922

P.40, patrol boat
 TANNER, William H E, Able Seaman, 206524, illness

Tuesday, 30 May 1922

Victory, Portsmouth
BIGNELL, Alfred J, Able Seaman, J 27918, accidentally killed

Thursday, 1 June 1922

Egmont, Malta
MALLIA, Guiseppe, Able Seaman, J 81541, illness

Weymouth, 2nd class cruiser
HOWE, Ernest S R, Boy 1c, J 101273, illness

Saturday, June 3 1922

President, London
JOHNSON, Josephus, Boy Servant, L 13750, illness

Queen Elizabeth, battleship
FOWLER, Charles L, Able Seaman, J 21027, illness

Tuesday, 6 June 1922

Tamar, Hong Kong
WEBBER, Frederick E, Leading Telegraphist, J 27488, accidentally killed

Wednesday, 7 June 1922

Ganges, Shotley/Harwich
BLOOM, Reginald W, Boy 2c, J 105271, illness

Thursday, 8 June 1922

Royal Naval Reserve
BAIN, James, Honorary Engineer Commander, RNR, illness

Friday, 9 June 1922

Malaya, battleship
BARLOW, William, Plumber 1c, 345350, died

Pembroke, Chatham
BRAGG, Edward C, Sick Berth Attendant, M 35459, illness

Victory, Portsmouth
HEATH, Ernest S, Petty Officer, 239570, accidentally killed

Saturday, 10 June 1922

Queen Elizabeth, battleship
BUTLIN, Edward S R, Lieutenant, illness

Royal Navy
BUTLIN, Edward S R, Lieutenant, illness

Sunday, 11 June 1922

Ambrose, submarine depot ship
HUGHES, Robert, Ordinary Seaman, J 99237, illness

Benbow, battleship
HALL, Sidney R, Able Seaman, J 14076, illness

Carysfort, light cruiser
ROBINS, Leo V W, Ordinary Seaman, J 104408, drowned

Monday, 12 June 1922

Blue Sky, Admiralty wood drifter, tender to battleship Queen Elizabeth, foundered off Thames Estuary, lost (deaths recorded on the 13th) *(below, close sister-ship Sea Breeze, but steel construction, NP/Mark Teadham)*

BREWER, William E, Telegraphist, J 41903, died
CATOR, Richard B, Midshipman, died
DOWNS, George, Stoker 1c, SS 125714, died
DUNDAS, David, Midshipman, died
GAGE, Walter, Leading Stoker, K 10712, died
GILCREST, John, Stoker 1c, K 58766, died
GREGSON, John R, Assistant Mechanician, K 31502, died
HARROLD, Arthur S C, Able Seaman, J 65203, died
JENNINGS, Francis C H, Lieutenant, died
KIRK, Henry, Able Seaman, J 16149, died
LEECH, William D, Able Seaman, J 5899, died
NICHOLAS, Adolphus C J, Able Seaman, J 33795, died
SMITH, William, Stoker 1c, SS 125760, died
STEVENS, Frank R, Signalman, J 88422, died
WALKER, Robert H, Leading Seaman, 238522, died

Espiegle, sloop
MEREFIELD, William V, Able Seaman, 226574, illness

Impregnable, Devonport
BUTCHER, Henry J, Boy 2c, J 103454, drowned

Thursday, 15 June 1922

Vivid, Devonport
GOURD, William A, Leading Stoker, K 23868, illness

Monday, 19 June 1922

Maidstone, submarine depot ship
SKEA, Patrick, Stoker 1c, K 754, illness

Wednesday, 21 June 1922

Hong Kong Dockyard. illness
GREGORY, Reginald, Lieutenant Commander, illness

Friday, 23 June 1922

Ramillies, battleship
JAMES, Robert P, Officer's Steward 4c, L 13416, illness

Saturday, 24 June 1922

Iron Duke, battleship
FOSTER, Victor F, Signalman, J 71403, drowned

Pembroke, Chatham
BRYAN, Francis, Stoker 1c, K 37201, illness

Tuesday, 4 July 1922

ML.291, Rhine Patrol Flotilla
STEVENS, George H, Leading Stoker, K 19708, drowned

Wednesday, 5 July 1922

Columbine, Rosyth
TUSLER, Thomas, Petty Officer, J 24729, drowned

Foxglove, fleet sweeping sloop
KNIGHT, John A, Leading Stoker, K 20738, drowned

Thursday, 6 July 1922

Titania, submarine depot ship
REDGWELL, Harry, Stoker Petty Officer, K 13586, died from heat stroke

Friday, 7 July 1922

Widgeon, river gunboat
OUGH, George H, Able Seaman, 234417, drowned

Sunday, 9 July 1922

Excellent, Portsmouth
STONER, Archibald M, Petty Officer, J 14922, illness

Tuesday, 11 July 1922

L.8, submarine
PONSONBY, Patrick S J, Lieutenant, illness

Thursday, 13 July 1922

Vivid, Devonport
HARRIS, Arthur, Leading Stoker, K 15653, illness

Friday, 14 July 1922

Ganges, Shotley/Harwich
BRYAN, William C, Boy 1c, J 103997, illness

Saturday, 15 July 1922

Penguin, ex-cruiser, depot ship, Sydney, Australia
WHYMARK, Alfred, Petty Officer, 190755, illness

Sunday, 16 July 1922

Blenheim, ex-cruiser, destroyer depot ship
HAMMELL, Joseph, Petty Officer, 204818, illness

Monday, 17 July 1922

Renown, battlecruiser
AYTON, Alfred, Petty Officer, J 4029, illness

Tuesday, 18 July 1922

Diligence, Scapa Flow
FYSH, Alfred J, Gunner, illness

Wednesday, 19 July 1922

Impregnable, Devonport
WALLIS, James G, Surgeon Commander, illness

Vortigern, destroyer
ROBINSON, Hubert C, Able Seaman, J 32860, drowned

Thursday, 20 July 1922

Victory, Portsmouth
SMITH, Charles, Mechanician, 303360, illness

Saturday, 22 July 1922

Dido, ex-cruiser, destroyer depot ship
PIPER, Frederick, Able Seaman, J 27625, illness

Royal Navy
DUMARESQ, John S, Rear Admiral, illness

Victory, Portsmouth
SHEPPARD, Stanley H, 2nd Writer, M 27905, illness

Sunday, 23 July 1922

Iron Duke, battleship
MAYNARD, Gilbert J, Able Seaman, J 52901, drowned

Crocus, fleet sweeping sloop
DE SOUZA, Gaetano A, Officer's Steward 1c, 157258, drowned

Espiegle, sloop
FORD, Arthur J, Leading Stoker, K 973, illness

Sorceress, destroyer
HILLIARD, William G, Chief Stoker, 299354, illness

Wednesday, 26 July 1922

Repulse, battlecruiser
CHAPMAN, Ernest, Engine Room Artificer 2c, M 7355, illness

Thursday, 27 July 1922

Ganges, Shotley/Harwich
SYDENHAM, Ernest W, Boy 1c, J 104367, drowned

Friday, 28 July 1922

Royal Navy
WILLSON, Andrew C E C, Lieutenant, illness

Saturday, 29 July 1922

Defiance, Devonport
EDGECOMBE, Sydney W V, Able Seaman, J 5382, illness

Sunday, 30 July 1922

Cordelia, light cruiser
 BOARDMAN, Richard H, Leading Seaman, 217196, accidentally killed

Delhi, light cruiser
 FOSTER, Ernest C, Able Seaman, J 48676, illness

Pembroke, Chatham
 RIDGE, Samuel J, Boatman, J 42243, illness

Monday, 31 July 1922

Centurion, battleship
 HOWELL, George H, Able Seaman, J 11297, illness

Tuesday, 1 August 1922

Vindictive, cruiser/seaplane carrier
 HUDSON, John A, Engineer Commander, illness

Friday, 4 August 1922

Benbow, battleship
 DEACON, William, Able Seaman, SS 9734, illness

Vivid, Devonport
 DOUGLAS, Edward, Coastguardsman 3c, 181487, illness

Saturday, 5 August 1922

Tomahawk, destroyer
 IRVEN, Herbert, Chief Stoker, 308877, illness

Tuesday, 8 August 1922

Raleigh, cruiser, ran aground and wrecked, Point Amour, Fortreau Bay, Labrador, Canada, lost *(below, Nick Carter)*
 BASHFORD, Herbert, Stoker 1c, SS 123275
 EFFARD, Edward P, Stoker Petty Officer, 303078
 FIELD, Silas, Stoker 1c, K 59500
 FISHER, George, Stoker 1c, SS 120369
 LLOYD, John E, Stoker Petty Officer, 306551
 PETTET, Pat, Able Seaman, J 42323
 SOWDEN, William J, Leading Stoker, K 20564
 THORNHILL, George M, Stoker 1c, SS 122759
 TRIPP, Sydney G, Leading Stoker, K 14053
 TYLER, Reuben, Leading Stoker, K 18030
 WEAVER, James, Able Seaman, 213937
 WHITTON, William R, Able Seaman, J 34371

Thursday, 10 August 1922

Victory, Portsmouth
 SHAW, George W, Coastguardsman 3c, 278674, illness

Saturday, 12 August 1922

Centurion, battleship
 DASH, Percy D T, Chief Petty Officer Cook, 351548, illness

Dublin, 2nd class cruiser
 ANDERSON, James, Leading Stoker, K 9274, illness

Sunday, 13 August 1922

Marlborough, battleship
 TUNNICLIFF, Herbert, Able Seaman, J 32051, accidentally killed

Pembroke, Chatham
 McSHANE, James, Stoker 1c, K 55302, illness

Tuesday, 15 August 1922

Pembroke, Chatham
 ISAACS, George J, Officer's Cook 2c, L 5485, illness

Thursday, 17 August 1922

Pembroke, Chatham
 LUSCOMBE, James F, Coastguardsman 3c, 180480, illness

Tuesday, 22 August 1922

Argus, aircraft carrier
 GRUBB, Ernest G, Leading Seaman, 234683, illness

Durban, light cruiser
 MORLEY, Rowland C, Able Seaman, J 86911, illness

Hood, battlecruiser
 FIELD, Alfred G, Boy 1c, J 96703, drowned

Victory, Portsmouth
 DAVEY, Thomas G, Stoker Petty Officer, 302099, illness

Wednesday, 23 August 1922

Ambrose, submarine depot ship
 LEAH, George, Able Seaman, SS 8177, drowned

Thursday, 24 August 1922

Danae, light cruiser
 BOWELL, Ernest W, Leading Seaman, J 30334, illness

Monday, 28 August 1922

Durban, light cruiser
 HUGHES, Arthur F, Stoker 1c, K 56690, illness

Wednesday, 30 August 1922

Benbow, battleship
 BERRY, Robert E, Telegraphist, J 89337, illness

Tuesday, 5 September 1922

Vanquisher, destroyer
SERCOMBE, William H, Able Seaman, J 1271, illness

Wednesday, 6 September 1922

Tamar, Hong Kong
MAY, William C A, Chief Shipwright 2c, 342960, illness

Monday, 11 September 1922

Tamar, Hong Kong
PREECE, Richard P, Engine Room Artificer 2c, M 135, illness

Tuesday, 12 September 1922

Pembroke, Chatham
AYRES, Albert A, Ordinary Seaman, J 96319, illness

Wednesday, 13 September 1922

Barham, battleship
SPALDING, Leonard C, Boy 1c, J 101839, illness

Thursday, 14 September 1922

Victoria & Albert, Royal Yacht
BACON, William, Petty Officer, 219887, illness

Thursday, 21 September 1922

Capetown, light cruiser
LINEHAM, John J, Stoker 1c, K 20284, drowned

Saturday, 23 September 1922

Concord, light cruiser
COLLIER, Augustus H N, Leading Seaman, J 26855, accidentally killed

Indus, Devonport
HARMAN, George E, Engineer Lieutenant, killed

Sunday, 24 September 1922

Ceres, light cruiser
GARTON, Bert, Petty Officer, J 24317, drowned

Speedy, destroyer, in collision with Dutch tug Karabigha, Sea of Marmora, Turkey, lost, casualties drowned
BALLARD, George H, Able Seaman, J 68625
CROUCH, Ernest J, Stoker 1c, SS 122351
GRANT, Walter, Able Seaman, J 25919
HARMON, George E, Engineer Lieutenant
JORDAN, Frederick L A, Able Seaman, J 36608
JUDD, Alfred J, Stoker Petty Officer, K 1833
NEARY, Lawrence, Stoker 1c, K 33841
POVALL, William, Stoker 1c, K 14974
VIVIAN, Leslie T, Able Seaman, J 62748
WHEATLEY, Thomas E, Stoker 1c, K 17736

Monday, 25 September 1922

Royal Sovereign, battleship
HEMP, Bertie G T, Able Seaman, J 30557, accidentally killed

Thursday, 28 September 1922

Conquest, light cruiser
SMITH, Horace L, Stoker 1c, K 57944, illness

Impregnable, Devonport
HUGHES, Dick A, Petty Officer, J 11582, drowned

October 1922

Lucia, submarine depot ship, day not listed in record
SUTTON, Harold, Able Seaman, J 16325, drowned

Sunday, 1 October 1922

Pembroke, Chatham
PHILPOTT, James T, Petty Officer, 234270, illness

Monday, 2 October 1922

Ajax, battleship
VINCENT, William C, Leading Seaman, 219905, illness

Tuesday, 3 October 1922

Columbine, Rosyth
CROSS, Herbert, Yeoman of Signals, 232863, illness

Victory, Portsmouth
BATES, John E, Stoker 1c, SS 125141, illness

Wednesday, 4 October 1922

Victoria & Albert, Royal Yacht
SEYMOUR, Ralph F, Commander, illness

Saturday, 7 October 1922

Cricket, river gunboat
TAAFE, William H, Chief Petty Officer, 227963, illness

Royal Marines
WELDON, Bertram de W, Honorary Major, RM, illness

Sunday, 8 October 1922

Royal Navy
JONES, William J, Commissioned Engineer. ex-Marlborough, illness

Monday, 9 October 1922

Royal Marines HQ
JUDGE, William J, Corporal, RMLI, 17318 (Ch), ex-Vulcan, illness

Tuesday, 10 October 1922

Pembroke, Chatham
 MUNDAY, John W, Leading Boatman, 232149, illness

Victory, Portsmouth
 ADAMS, Henry C, Petty Officer, 213543, illness

Thursday, 12 October 1922

Revenge, battleship
 SOUTHALL, Lawrence E, Able Seaman, J 34682, drowned

Saturday, 14 October 1922

Pembroke, Chatham
 IZZARD, Cyril R, Telegraphist, J 44080, road accident, killed

Vivid, Devonport
 MANN, William G, Coastguardsman 3c, 9085 (Po), illness

Wednesday, 18 October 1922

Valiant, battleship
 HALLCHURCH, Frank D, Boy 1c, J 103137, illness

Saturday, 21 October 1922

Victory II, RND Training Depot, Crystal Palace, but closed down
 1919; either post discharge illness or Victory, Portsmouth
 BECHETT, Charlie, Stoker 1c, K 57475, illness

Sunday, 22 October 1922

Victory I
 WHEATLAND, Reginald G, Able Seaman, J 18817, illness in RN
 Hospital Haslar

Monday, 23 October 1922

Platypus (RAN), submarine depot ship
 WOOLLARD, Edward R, Able Seaman, J 7042, illness

Victory, Portsmouth
 ETHERINGTON, John A G, Officer's Cook 1c, 366011, died

Tuesday, 24 October 1922

Colombo, light cruiser
 PRATT, Stephen J, Stoker Petty Officer, 230458, illness

Victory, Portsmouth
 MAREHANT, Reginald W, Able Seaman, J 12395, illness

Wednesday, 25 October 1922

Hawkins, cruiser
 SPRINGETT, George W, Leading Cook, M 5990, illness

Thursday, 26 October 1922

Victory, Portsmouth
 CHARLWOOD, Frederick E, Master at Arms, 203311, illness

Friday, 27 October 1922

Ramillies, battleship
 CONDON, William J, Leading Seaman, J 17366, illness

Sunday, 29 October 1922

RM, 11th Battalion
 KING, Albert, Marine, 16262 (Ch), illness, 82nd General
 Hospital, Turkish National Area

Thursday, 2 November 1922

HM Coast Guard
 SAINSBURY, Walter H, Chief Officer, HMCG (cause of death
 not listed)

Friday, 3 November 1922

Venturous, destroyer
 ELSWORTHY, Frederick J, Officer's Steward 3c, L 9242, illness

Saturday, 4 November 1922

Clematis, fleet sweeping sloop
 CURTHOYS, Frederick A, Stoker Petty Officer, K 12943,
 accidentally killed

Monday, 6 November 1922

Clematis, fleet sweeping sloop
 HOLGATE, Harold R, Telegraphist, J 42659, illness

Pembroke, Chatham
 STONE, Ernest A, Able Seaman, J 36196, illness

Sunday, 12 November 1922

Lowestoft, 2nd class cruiser
 HENWOOD, Benjamin T, Chief Engine Room Artificer 1c,
 271162, accidentally killed

Tuesday, 14 November 1922

Restless, destroyer
 DONOVAN, Richard C, Stoker Petty Officer, K 12426, illness

Southampton II, RN Base, Ceylon *(Sri Lanka)*
 JANION, Arthur C A, Paymaster Lieutenant Commander,
 accidentally killed

Wednesday, 15 November 1922

Dublin, 2nd class cruiser
 COLLYER, Albert, Stoker Petty Officer, 311651, illness

Thursday, 16 November 1922

Ramillies, battleship
 HERBERT, Harry, Able Seaman, J 18644, illness

Saturday, 18 November 1922

Royal Navy
 LIVINGSTONE, Campbell W, Paymaster Lieutenant, ex-Southampton, illness

Tuesday, 21 November 1922

Victory, Portsmouth
 MILLER, Francis L, Stoker 2c, K 59873, illness

Wednesday, 22 November 1922

Crocus, fleet sweeping sloop
 BOXALL, Henry R, Engine Room Artificer 2c, M 12568, died

Thursday, 23 November 1922

Curacoa, light cruiser
 McCULLOCH, Robert, Telegraphist, J 90378, illness

Marlborough, battleship
 SEYBURN, David, Telegraphist, J 27892, stabbed and killed

Monday, 27 November 1922

Tumult, destroyer
 TURNER, Timothy, Lieutenant, accidentally killed

Tuesday, 28 November 1922

Dolphin, Gosport
 HOUFE, William L, Signalman, J 50197, illness

Pembroke, Chatham
 MORRIS, Sidney, Coastguardsman 2c, 154368, illness

Friday, 1 December 1922

Chatham, 2nd class cruiser
 DORAN, Hugh, Stoker 1c, K 57884, accidentally killed

Marlborough, battleship
 DUNNETT, Herbert C, Stoker 1c, SS 124104, drowned

Monday, 4 December 1922

Dolphin, Gosport
 THOMPSON, William G, Able Seaman, J 25667, illness

Pembroke, Chatham
 HILLMAN, Fred, 2nd Writer, M 25676, illness

Thursday, 7 December 1922

Chelmsford, paddle minesweeper
 MOORE, Ronald W, Stoker 1c, K 57902, drowned

Victory, Portsmouth
 BERRY, Arthur C, Able Seaman, J 45637, illness

Friday, 8 December 1922

Tamar, Hong Kong
 FIELD, Harry W, Private, RMLI, 15429 (Ply), died

Saturday, 9 December 1922

Courageous, light battlecruiser
 COOKE, Sidney E, Signalman, J 77474, drowned

Monday, 11 December 1922

Ambrose, submarine depot ship
 GUNN, Edwin H, Engine Room Artificer 1c, M 1547, illness

Vivid, Devonport
 BEAVIS, James T, Stoker 1c, K 19172, illness

Tuesday, 12 December 1922

Royal Marines HQ
 COLLINS, Albert A, Musician, RMLI, 21296 (Po), drowned

Wednesday, 13 December 1922

Exe, destroyer
 HEAD, William R, Boatswain, illness

Friday, 15 December 1922

Pembroke, Chatham
 NIGHTINGALE, Albert H, Able Seaman, J 93827, illness

Sunday, 17 December 1922

Capetown, light cruiser
 OSBORN, George F, Yeoman of Signals, 224043, accidentally killed

Wednesday, 20 December 1922

Iron Duke, battleship
 MITCHELL, Sam W, Electrical Artificer 4c, M 31010, illness

Saturday, 23 December 1922

Revenge, battleship
 SMITH, Reginald, Able Seaman, J 105873, illness

Monday, 25 December 1922

ML.249, motor launch
 JAMES, Arthur G, Stoker 1c, K 58470, died

1923

Tuesday, 2 January 1923

Hawkins, cruiser
 HOOPER, Geoffrey W W, Lieutenant Commander, illness

Pembroke, Chatham
 EARL, Ernest, Able Seaman, J 29063, died

Wednesday, 3 January 1923

Curacoa, light cruiser
 CRIBB, Sidney G, Able Seaman, J 91145, illness

Thursday, 4 January 1923

Barham, battleship
 BOND, Wilfred C, Leading Seaman, J 10428, illness

Wednesday, 10 January 1923

Vivid, Devonport
 CHAPMAN, Richard H, Stoker Petty Officer, 299203, accidentally killed

Friday, 12 January 1923

Tamar, Hong Kong
 KWOK, Kam, Able Seaman, (Chinese), illness

Tuesday, 16 January 1923

Pembroke, Chatham
 JARVIS, Clifford, Able Seaman, J 61069, accidentally killed

Wednesday, 17 January 1923

Clematis, fleet sweeping sloop
 MARDON, Arthur G, Able Seaman, J 41617, illness

Pandora, submarine depot ship
 MILLS, William H, Warrant Shipwright, illness

Saturday, 20 January 1923

Royal Naval Reserve
 GRAY, Robert E, Paymaster Commander, RNR, illness

Sunday, 21 January 1923

Royal Marines
 PARSONS, Cunliffe Mc N, Major General, RM, illness

Tuesday, 23 January 1923

Marlborough, battleship
 SHIELDS, John E, Stoker 1c, SS 118468, illness

Royal Marines HQ, on board Argus, aircraft carrier
 POSSEE, William C N, Corporal, RMLI, 13149 (Ch), illness

Vimiera, destroyer
 KING, Lexie W, Chief Stoker, 308406, illness

Friday, 26 January 1923

Victory, Portsmouth
 LILL, Joseph, Stoker 1c, K 30408, illness

Saturday, 27 January 1923

Charlestown Coast Guard Station, Cornwall
 LAMPSHIRE, James H, Coastguardsman 3c, 182845, illness

Danae, light cruiser
 HAMMOND, James, Leading Stoker, 300492, drowned

Tuesday, 30 January 1923

Royal Naval Reserve
 GREEN, Thomas F, Paymaster Lieutenant, RNR, illness

Wednesday, 31 January 1923

Constance, light cruiser
 WOOD, Charles W, Cook, M 15397, died

Hood, battlecruiser
 BROAD, Thomas M (real name, but served as Thomas Coombes), Petty Officer, 229152, illness

Sunday, 4 February 1923

Impregnable, Devonport
 FINAMORE, John S, Stoker Petty Officer, 308467, illness

Marlborough, battleship
 CUTMORE, William A, Gunner, RMA, RMA 13536, illness

Monday, 5 February 1923

Dublin, 2nd class cruiser
 TRY, Leonard C A, Able Seaman, J 94777, illness

Wednesday, 7 February 1923

Diomede, light cruiser
 SCHOLES, Henry P, Lieutenant, illness

Friday, 9 February 1923

L.18, submarine
 WILLIAMS, John, Warrant Engineer, illness

Vivid, Devonport
 BARTLETT, William H, Stoker 1c, K 19642, railway accident, killed

Saturday, 10 February 1923

Constance, light cruiser
 LEYSHON, Edward G, Paymaster Commander, illness

Monday, 12 February 1923

Malabar, Bermuda
  HARVEY, Harold E, Bugler, RMLI, 12169 (Ch), illness

Wednesday, 14 February 1923

Carlisle, light cruiser
  VESEY-FITZGERALD, William P D, Lieutenant, illness

Iroquois, fleet sweeping sloop
  NORRIS, Allan V, Able Seaman, J 88069, illness

Thursday, 15 February 1923

Tarantula, river gunboat
  TREMAYNE, John W L, Act/Sub Lieutenant, illness

Tourmaline, destroyer
  PINDER, Thomas H, Leading Seaman, J 25342, illness

Friday, 16 February 1923

Pembroke, Chatham
  HAMMOND, Thomas S, Coastguardsman 2c, 172058, illness

Royal Navy
  QUINE, William J A, Surgeon Lieutenant Commander, illness

Saturday, 17 February 1923

Belfast Coast Guard
  BLACKLER, George F, Leading Boatman, 215761, illness

Pembroke, Chatham
  LANE, Henry J, Chief Stoker, 298042, illness

Sunday, 18 February 1923

Pembroke, Chatham
  COX, Joseph, Chief Stoker, 308749, illness

Monday, 19 February 1923

Vernon, Portsmouth
  ROBINSON, Edward J, Electrical Artificer 4c, M 35224, illness

Tuesday, 20 February 1923

Royal Marines HQ
  CALLISTER, George, Sergeant, RMA, RMA 10298, illness

Friday, 23 February 1923

Chatham, 2nd class cruiser
  CHINNERY, Herbert C, Officer's Cook 1c, 363502, drowned

Saturday, 24 February 1923

Yarmouth, 2nd class cruiser
  PHILLIPS, Iver J, Stoker 1c, SS 118035, illness

Sunday, 25 February 1923

Capetown, light cruiser
  SUMNER, John A, Engine Room Artificer 3C, M 26727, illness

ML.291, motor launch
  HINE, William F, Leading Seaman, J 98680, accidentally killed

Tuesday, 27 February 1923

Marlborough, battleship
  CLAYDON, Walter, Chief Petty Officer, 222485, accidentally killed

Friday, 2 March 1923

Vivid, Devonport
  TUNBRIDGE, Harold W, Petty Officer, 209951, illness

Saturday, 3 March 1923

Vivid, Devonport
  GRAHAM, Edward E, Ordinary Seaman, J 98979, illness

Sunday, 4 March 1923

Diomede, light cruiser
  IVES, Sydney J, Leading Seaman, J 24083, illness

Warspite, battleship
  JANE, James H, Stoker 1c, K 56194, illness

Thursday, 8 March 1923

Coventry, light cruiser, at Gibraltar, torpedo explosion, both accidentally killed
  BURT, Fred H J, Chief Stoker, K 10238,
  JACKSON, Garibaldi, Engine Room Artificer 3c, M 33565

Saturday, 10 March 1923

Birmingham, 2nd class cruiser
  HUTCHINGS, Richard H, Chief Stoker, 302620, drowned

Pembroke, Chatham
  HARRIS, Stanley F, Chief Petty Officer Cook, 347299, illness

Monday, 12 March 1923

Defiance, Devonport
  EDWARDS, James, Stoker Petty Officer, 305412, illness

Tuesday, 13 March 1923

Cormorant, Gibraltar
  WOOD, Harry H J, Ordnance Artificer 4c, M 36276, accidentally killed

Wednesday, 14 March 1923

Wivern, destroyer
  SPENCER, Gerald, Able Seaman, J 69706, illness

Thursday, 15 March 1923

Cerberus, Williamston, Australia
 MEACHIN, Arthur, Stoker Petty Officer, 297045, illness

Egmont, Malta
 ESPOSITO, Joseph, Officer's Steward 2c, 360075, illness

Saturday, 17 March 1923

Vivid, Devonport
 SMITH, Albert, Stoker Petty Officer, K 331, illness

Tuesday, 20 March 1923

Ganges, Shotley/Harwich
 CRISPIN, Grenville, Boy 2c, J 105978, illness

Tuesday, 27 March 1923

Campbell, flotilla leader
 WEIGHILL, Ernest, Signalman, J 64055, train accident in Constantinople, killed

Wednesday, 28 March 1923

Barham, battleship
 KILVERT, Robert E, Major, RM, illness

Saturday, 31 March 1923

Southampton, 2nd class cruiser
 MITCHELL, David C, Chief Petty Officer Cook, 347257, illness

Sunday, 1 April 1923

Royal Marines HQ
 SNOWLING, Bert, Corporal, RMLI, (no service number listed), died

Victory, Portsmouth
 PARKER, George E, Able Seaman, SS 10980, accidentally killed

Monday, 2 April 1923

Excellent, Portsmouth
 ARNOLD, Charles H, Petty Officer, 236201, illness

Wednesday, 4 April 1923

Centurion, battleship
 LIGHT, Walter J, Stoker Petty Officer, 306662, illness

Sunday, 8 April 1923

Blenheim, ex-cruiser, destroyer depot ship
 McLEOD, John, Seaman, RNR, C 4847, illness

Tuesday, 10 April 1923

Titania, submarine depot ship
 SENNETT, George H C, Chief Engine Room Artificer 2c, 270992, illness

Thursday, 12 April 1923

Royal Marines HQ
 HOLNESS, Ernest R, Warrant Officer 2c, illness

Saturday, 14 April 1923

Centurion, battleship
 PEAT, Arnold, Ordinary Seaman, SS 11386, drowned

Tuesday, 17 April 1923

Violent, destroyer
 DUNROE, John, Able Seaman, 203394, illness

Wednesday, 18 April 1923

Vivid, Devonport
 HORNSSY, Frederick, Petty Officer, 116222, illness

Friday, 20 April 1923

Moorhen, river gunboat
 YORKE, Arthur L, Stoker 1c, K 22187, drowned

Saturday, 21 April 1923

Vivid, Devonport
 MATTHEWS, Arthur, Leading Cook, M 1634, illness

Thursday, 26 April 1923

Southampton, 2nd class cruiser
 LEWIN, William P, Stoker 1c, K 56891, heat stroke, died

Sunday, 29 April 1923

Dolphin, Gosport
 WILKINS, Edward, Stoker 1c, K 23283, illness

Monday, 30 April 1923

Centurion, battleship
 RAY, Bertram J, Ordinary Seaman, J 96458, illness

Wednesday, 2 May 1923

Pembroke, Chatham
 JONES, Frederick J, Officer's Steward 4c, L 13948, accidentally killed

Wednesday, 9 May 1923

Brisbane (RAN), 2nd class cruiser
 MARSHALL, George E, Able Seaman, J 99203, illness

Espiegle, sloop
 SCOTT, Charles, Stoker 1c, K 15386, illness

Tuesday, 15 May 1923

Lowestoft, 2nd class cruiser
 BEAMS, Percy T, Private, RMLI, 15826 (Ch), died

Vivid, Devonport
 GAVAN, William O, Petty Officer, J 4930, illness

Monday, 21 May 1923

RM, 11th Battalion
 COLE, Cyril J, Private, RMLI, 14909 (Po), illness

Tuesday, 22 May 1923

Vivid, Devonport
 RAWLINGS, Ernest W, Able Seaman, J 16094, drowned
 WATERS, Thomas J, Able Seaman, J 35067, killed

Wolfhound, destroyer
 FULLER, Arthur J, Leading Stoker, 307571, drowned

Friday, 25 May 1923

Gibraltar Dockyard
 BARTER, Frederick, Engineer Captain, illness

Saturday, 26 May 1923

Despatch, light cruiser
 CARTER, George H, Stoker 1c, K 56465, illness

Monday, 4 June 1923

Ganges, Shotley/Harwich
 WEIGHTMAN, Leonard, Boy 2c, J 107275, illness

Wednesday, 6 June 1923

Curacoa, light cruiser
 DODNEY, William E F, Private, RMLI, 19817 (Po), illness

Friday, 8 June 1923

Royal Naval Volunteer Reserve
 STEEGMAN, Edward J, Surgeon Commander, RNVR, illness

Sunday, 10 June 1923

Repulse, battlecruiser
 McBRIDE, John L, Engine Room Artificer 4c, RNVR, Mersey 5/102, illness

Warspite, battleship
 STACEY, George, Stoker Petty Officer, K 3037, illness

Tuesday, 12 June 1923

Diligence, Scapa Flow
 STAMPF, Charles W, Plumber, M 805, accidentally, killed

Wednesday, 13 June 1923

Pembroke, Chatham
 ALLISON, Kenneth, Boy 1c, J 103169, illness

Friday, 15 June 1923

Glorious, light battlecruiser
 WARE, John T, Gunner, illness

Sunday, 17 June 1923

Centurion, battleship
 COX, Thomas H, Stoker 1c, K 58473, burns, died

Centurion, battleship
 DILLON, Joseph, Stoker 1c, K 15795, accidentally killed

Monday, 18 June 1923

Centurion, battleship,
 RACE, George L, Stoker 1c, SS 122289, accidentally killed

Diomede, light cruiser
 DYER, George, Ordinary Seaman, J 95962, illness

Friday, 22 June 1923

Excellent, Portsmouth
 CALLAWAY, Albert A W, Leading Seaman, J 16817, illness

Royal Navy
 DICKSON, John H, Warrant Engineer, illness

Wednesday, 27 June 1923

President, London
 SAUNDERS, Charles, Chief Petty Officer Telegraphist, 201032, illness

Vivid, Devonport
 HARTLEY, Horace B, Chief Engine Room Artificer 1c, 270515, illness

Saturday, 30 June 1923

Comus, light cruiser
 PRESTON, James A, Stoker 1c, K 23631, illness

Tuesday, 3 July 1923

Wolverine, destroyer
 BAMSEY, Richard, Leading Stoker, K 1944, illness

Wednesday, 4 July 1923

Pembroke, Chatham
 COOK, Alfred W J, Stoker Petty Officer, K 15869, illness

Friday, 6 July 1923

Calcutta, light cruiser
 LEGG, Reginald G, Able Seaman, J 99300, drowned

Torch, destroyer
 McDONNELL, John, Stoker Petty Officer, K 9465, illness

Sunday, 8 July 1923

Dolphin, Gosport
  WREN, Alfred W, Electrical Artificer 2c, M 7867, illness

Pembroke, Chatham
  GREEN, Charles W, Stoker 2c, K 61453, illness

Sirdar, destroyer
  COWE, Thomas W, Stoker 1c, SS 119925, drowned

Tuesday, 10 July 1923

Victory, Portsmouth
  PAYNE, Albert, Able Seaman, 223540, illness

Wednesday, 11 July 1923

Ajax, battleship
  TEUMA, Albert, Officer's Steward 3c, 358428, illness

Saturday, 14 July 1923

Victory, Portsmouth
  MARSHALL, Henry G, Leading Seaman, J 23995, illness

Friday, 20 July 1923

Blenheim, ex-cruiser, destroyer depot ship
  BUTCHER, Edward M, Stoker 1c, 158337, illness

Saturday, 21 July 1923

Britannia, RN College, Dartmouth
  WEEDON, Frank A W, Act/Sub Lieutenant, illness

Sunday, 22 July 1923

Pembroke, Chatham
  BOXALL, Frederick A B, Sick Berth Attendant, M 30697, illness

Monday, 23 July 1923

Argus, aircraft carrier
  FRANCIS, William G, Bugler, RMLI, 21338 (Po), illness

Saturday, 28 July 1923

Barham, battleship
  SHEPHARD, Frederick E, Petty Officer Cook, 347798, illness

Wednesday, 1 August 1923

Bryony, convoy sloop
  McINTOSH, Harold, Stoker 1c, K 59805, died

Saturday, 4 August 1923

Iron Duke, battleship
  NICHOLLS, Douglas J, Boy 1c, J 103993, illness

King George V, battleship
  COPP, Ambrose, Stoker 1c, K 11976, drowned

Monday, 6 August 1923

Scarab, river gunboat
  ROWNTREE, James D, Able Seaman, J 43089, drowned

Friday, 10 August 1923

Velox destroyer
  PACKHAM, Charles R, Able Seaman, J 14619, illness

Sunday, 12 August 1923

Warwick, destroyer
  PRATT, Thomas, Stoker 1c, K 19474, illness

Wednesday, 15 August 1923

Vivid, Devonport
  BRANAGH, Henry, Master at Arms, M 7886, illness

Thursday, 16 August 1923

Royal Marines
  JONES, Walter T C, Lieutenant Colonel, RM, illness

Saturday, 18 August 1923

Carlisle, light cruiser
  HODKINSON, Frederick C, Able Seaman, J 99607, illness

Excellent, Portsmouth
  PEET, Frederick H, Gunner, illness

Hood, battlecuiser
  NICHOLS, Edgar, Marine, Ply/21303, illness

Sunday, 19 August 1923

Iron Duke, battleship
  FOSTER, Charles W, Stoker 1c, K 58245, illness

Monday, 20 August 1923

Dolphin, Gosport
  WILLIAMS, William H, Petty Officer, 209267, illness

Pembroke, Chatham
  THOMPSON, John, Chief Petty Officer, 214105, died

Thursday, 23 August 1923

Chatham, 2nd class cruiser
  READ, Cecil W, Petty Officer, 227245, illness

Monday, 27 August 1923

Carlisle, light cruiser
  SWANTON, Herbert F, Blacksmith, 346627, accidentally killed

Tuesday, 28 August 1923

Burslem, minesweeper
  FORD, Henry E, Stoker 1c, 310426, drowned

Castor, light cruiser
  BROWN, Eustace W, Engine Room Artificer 3c, M 34385, illness

Marlborough, battleship
  CLARK, Robert E, Master at Arms, 195657, illness

Wednesday, 29 August 1923

Ceres, light cruiser
  CORDING, Edward, Boy 1c, J 101694, drowned

Impregnable, Devonport
  BORGNET, Eric C J, Boy 2c, J 107596, illness

Thursday, 30 August 1923

Chrysanthemum, convoy sloop
  RIDDELL, Francis R C, Lieutenant, illness

Friday, 31 August 1923

Hawkins, cruiser
  PILE, Harry H, Leading Seaman, 235972, drowned

Sunday, 2 September 1923

Queen Elizabeth, battleship
  HOLLOWAY, John W B, Marine, 19800 (Po), died

Monday, 3 September 1923

Pembroke, Chatham
  NEVIN, John T, Regulating Petty Officer, M 36359, accidentally killed

Tuesday, 4 September 1923

Vivid, Devonport
  PARKER, Frederick W, Able Seaman, 217317, illness

Friday, 7 September 1923

RN Hospital, Haslar
  MARSH, Alex B, Surgeon Commander, illness

Sunday, 9 September 1923

Vanessa, destroyer
  KENNEDY, Alfred M, Able Seaman, J 10439, accidentally killed

Thursday, 13 September 1923

Pembroke, Chatham
  TURNER, Albert G, Able Seaman, J 83715, illness

Friday, 14 September 1923

Centurion, battleship
  MARSHALL, Charles A, Leading Stoker, 305171, illness

Constance, light cruiser
  SAUNDERS, Sydney, Marine, 13829 (Ch), road accident, killed

P.59, patrol boat
  RIGGS, Reginald O, Able Seaman, J 22629, illness

Pembroke, Chatham
  TUCKER, Robert H, Stoker 1c, K 47056, illness

Monday, 17 September 1923

Agamemnon, target ship
  CHIVERS, Horace W, Stoker 1c, K 14297, illness

Excellent, Portsmouth
  BURNS, Allan R, Able Seaman, J 24920, accidentally killed

Tuesday, 18 September 1923

Royal Naval Reserve
  WOODROOFE, Robert, Lieutenant, RNR, illness

Wednesday, 19 September 1923

Ceres, light cruiser
  VELLA, Raphaell, Officer's Steward 2c, 358722, illness

Friday, 21 September 1923

Victory, Portsmouth
  STUTCHBURY, Frederick N, Telegraphist, J 70431, illness

Sunday, 23 September 1923

Centaur, light cruiser
  POWELL, Bernard, Electrical Artificer 3c, M 33891, illness

Monday, 24 September 1923

P.47, patrol boat
  BOYD, Alfred, Engine Room Artificer 2c, M 18099, drowned

Wednesday, 26 September 1923

Vernon, Portsmouth
  BARKER, William A H, Commissioned Gunner, illness

Thursday, 27 September 1923

Pembroke, Chatham
  GREEN, John, Musician, RMB, RMB 2076, illness

Thursday, 4 October 1923

Vivid, Devonport
  TELFORD, William, Leading Stoker, K 10747, illness

Saturday, 6 October 1923

Fantome, ex-sloop, survey ship
  McDOUGAL, William J, Able Seaman, 233413, drowned

Warspite, battleship
 CAHILL, Joseph, Able Seaman, J 12725, illness

Tuesday, 9 October 1923

Seawolf, destroyer
 STOCKMAN, Frederick, Able Seaman, 203678, accidentally killed

Wednesday, 10 October 1923

Dolphin, Gosport
 YOUNG, Thomas, Stoker Petty Officer, 217754, illness

Saturday, 13 October 1923

Dolphin, Gosport
 JONES, Harold G, Petty Officer, J 7994, illness

Tuesday, 16 October 1923

Barham, battleship
 HUNTINGFORD, George T, Able Seaman, J 13272, illness

Comus, light cruiser
 PIDGEON, William J, Petty Officer, J 11337, drowned

Saturday, 20 October 1923

Philomel, ex-cruiser, depot ship, New Zealand *(below)*
 TICKELL, William G, Stoker Chief Petty Officer, M 618, accidentally killed

Sunday, 21 October 1923

Pembroke, Chatham
 KERR, William, Engine Room Artificer 2c, M 9383, illness

Monday, 22 October 1923

Pembroke, Chatham
 BIRD, Albert E, Sick Berth Attendant, M 33621, illness

Wednesday, 24 October 1923

Crocus, fleet sweeping sloop
 BOHO, Mordhammen, Seedie, (no service number listed), illness

Saturday, 27 October 1923

Delhi, light cruiser
 SMITH, James E, Engine Room Artificer 3c, M 14558, illness

Sunday, 28 October 1923

Vivid, Devonport
 JONES, Francis P, Stoker 1c, K 23368, illness

Monday, 29 October 1923

Ramillies, battleship
 CHURCHMAN, Henry E E, Petty Officer, J 12266, illness

Tuesday, 30 October 1923

Queen Elizabeth, battleship
 FAIRWEATHER, Frederick A, Able Seaman, J 7766, drowned

Walker, destroyer
 CLARK, Duncan, Able Seaman, J 95446, drowned

Thursday, 1 November 1923

Flora, Simonstown, South Africa
 SALAH, Abdullah B, Seedie, (no service number listed), illness

Friday, 2 November 1923

Pembroke, Chatham
 SCRAGG, William A, Regulating Petty Officer, M 37148, illness

Saturday, 3 November 1923

Royal Navy
 KNAPP, Christopher R, Warrant Mechanician, illness

Victory, Portsmouth
 EASTMENT, Walter J, Able Seaman, SS 5934, road accident, killed

Sunday, 4 November 1923

Tamar, Hong Kong
 RICHARDSON, Dudley J, Leading Stoker, K 21018, drowned

Thursday, 8 November 1923

Queen Elizabeth, battleship
 LOCOCK, Victor G, Able Seaman, J 58584, illness

Friday, 9 November 1923

Royal Marines HQ
 LUCAS, John J, Marine, RMLI, 14122 (Ch), died

Saturday, 10 November 1923

Columbine, Rosyth
 RAMSEY, Kenneth G, Lieutenant Commander, illness

Saturday, 17 November 1923

Victoria & Albert, Royal Yacht
 WOODWARDS, Charles A, Stoker Petty Officer, 281765, illness

Wednesday, 21 November 1923

Flora, Simonstown, South Africa
 WILLIAM, George, Krooman, (no service number listed), illness

Thursday, 22 November 1923

Tarantula, river gunboat
 SMITH, Patrick C, Lieutenant, illness

Friday, 23 November 1923

Enterprise, light cruiser
 TURNER, Percy, Commissioned Shipwright, illness

Saturday, 24 November 1923

Ajax, battleship
 LYONS, Edward J, Chief Stoker, 304685, illness

Defiance, Devonport
 BOLT, John G, Chief Engine Room Artificer 2c, M 1002, illness

Sunday, 25 November 1923

Hood, battlecruiser
 HORTON, James, Able Seaman, J 102952, drowned

Monday, 3 December 1923

Argus, aircraft carrier
 SMYTH, Sidney R, Shipwright 2c, 347216, illness

Tuesday, 4 December 1923

Vivid, Devonport
 EVANS, Harry, Sick Berth Petty Officer, M 3178, illness

Wednesday, 5 December 1923

L.11, submarine, fire onboard
 BEAL, George W (real name, but served as George W Brown),
  Leading Stoker, K 18357, killed

Saturday, 8 December 1923

Pembroke, Chatham
 DONNELLY, Thomas, Commissioned Gunner, illness

Sunday, 9 December 1923

Marazion, ex-minesweeper, submarine depot ship, Hong Kong
 LINGARD, Edward V, Leading Stoker, K 23637, illness

Thursday, 13 December 1923

Lucia, submarine depot ship
 EDWARDS, Garnet, Officer's Steward 1c, 360453, illness

Friday, 21 December 1923

Alecto, submarine depot ship
 TUCKER, Frederick J, Officer's Steward 3c, 363935, accidentally killed

Saturday, 22 December 1923

Royal Navy
 ROBERTSON, Frederick L, Engineer Commander, illness, date listed as 22nd/23rd

Thursday, 27 December 1923

Revenge, battleship
 DIPLOCK, Harry, Signalman Petty Officer, 311859, illness

Saturday, 29 December 1923

Birmingham, 2nd class cruiser
 BUXTON, Bernard, Commander, illness

Dolphin, Gosport
 O'BRIEN, Joseph, Stoker 1c, K 14645, died

Vivid, Devonport
 KEAST, Daniel C, Officer's Steward 3c, L 10802, illness

1924

Tuesday, 1 January 1924

HM Coast Guard, Dungeness, Kent
 COOK, Alfred C, Chief Officer, HMCG, illness

Friday, 4 January 1924

Durban, light cruiser
 JOHNSON, John N, Stoker Petty Officer, K 927, illness

Saturday, 5 January 1924

Rocket, destroyer
 BROOKES, Frederick R, Stoker 1c, K 43616, drowned

Sunday, 6 January 1924

Philomel, ex-cruiser, depot ship, New Zealand
 ANDERSON, Edward A, Lieutenant, illness

Victory, Portsmouth
 CLARK, Ernest A, Officer's Steward 4c, L 14378, illness

Monday, 7 January 1924

Magnolia, fleet sweeping sloop
 SIMPSON, Charles E, Regulating Petty Officer, 237028, illness

Vigorous, Larne, Ireland (but out of commission by 1919)
 FRY, James, Chief Petty Officer, 215283, died

Tuesday, 8 January 1924

Queen Elizabeth, battleship
 COOK, Fred, Marine, 15265 (Po), illness

Wednesday, 9 January 1924

Pembroke, Chatham
 LOVE, Herbert, Officer's Steward 4c, L 14804, illness

Thursday, 10 January 1924

L.24, submarine, submerged and in collision with battleship Resolution in English Channel off Portland Bill, Dorset, lost, no survivors *(below, L.9-class sister-boat L.12, NP/Mark Teadham)*

 BALLARD, Sidney R, Stoker 1c, J 22780
 BARTON, Donald H, Lieutenant
 BENNETT, Sidney F, Petty Officer, J 15947
 BUCK, Elijah F, Chief Petty Officer, 224883
 BULBECK, Harold J, Leading Seaman, J 27703
 BYRON, John, Warrant Engineer
 CANN, Headley, Leading Stoker, K 16998
 CHEVIS, Harry F, Leading Signalman, J 13882
 CRUMBIE, David W, Stoker 1c, K 55839
 DEMPSEY, William G, Leading Seaman, 215684
 DONALD, Hugh J, Able Seaman, 228142
 EDDIS, Paul L, Lieutenant Commander
 FLANAGAN, Bertie W, Stoker 1c, K 61053
 FLETCHER, David K, Engine Room Artificer 4c, M 21883
 FRANCE, Alfred J M, Able Seaman, J 20742
 GARRISH, William J, Able Seaman, J 16122
 GRAY, Donald N, Lieutenant
 GREEN, George W F, Stoker 1c, J 59790
 GRIGG, Alfred J, Stoker 1c, J 60726
 HILLMAN, Edward J, Stoker Petty Officer, K 15258
 JOHNSON, Edwin G, Act/Leading Stoker, K 20107
 JOHNSTONE, Edwin G, Leading Stoker, K 20107
 LANE, Percy, Engine Room Artificer 1c, M 3721
 LAWLEY, Arthur R, Able Seaman, J 76961
 LOUGH, Frederick C I, Able Seaman, J 11342
 LYONS, Edmond, Stoker 1c, K 17360
 MATTHEWS, Charles, Engine Room Artificer 2c, M 6689
 MITCHELL, James, Telegraphist, J 92053
 NEWING, Edward, Stoker 1c, K 22771
 PARKHURST, Thomas M J, Petty Officer Telegraphist, J 8157
 PHILLIPS, Sydney F, Stoker 1c, K 60396
 POUND, Ernest P V, Stoker 1c, K 24137
 QUANTOCK, Thomas H, Able Seaman, J 42358
 SMITH, Allan, Signalman, J 86413
 STAPLETON, Joseph B, Leading Seaman, J 7681
 STEDALL, Eric A, Sub Lieutenant
 STEWART, George W, Stoker 1c, K 56820
 TIPPEN, George J N, Leading Stoker, K 16549
 WALKER, William, Stoker 1c, K 22942
 WALLACE, Andrew C, Chief Engine Room Artificer 2c, M 1390
 WATERFIELD, George H, Able Seaman, J 32831
 WATKINSON, Donald J G, Lieutenant
 WILSON, John, Petty Officer, J 71669
 WISE, William J, Petty Officer, 239452

Saturday, 12 January 1924

Royal Australian Navy
 WALNE, Archibald F D, Signalman, RAN, 10030, drowned

Sunday, 13 January 1924

Ambrose, submarine depot ship
 WEEKS, John R, Chief Engine Room Artificer 2c, 347574, died

Royal Australian Navy
 CHAMBERS, Reuben H, Able Seaman, RAN, 9656 (former RN, J 17841), illness

Monday, 14 January 1924

Vancouver, destroyer
 CRITCHELL, Arthur W J, Stoker 1c, K 46631, illness

Wednesday, 16 January 1924

Scimitar, destroyer
 FOSTER, Frederick, Petty Officer, 219244, illness

Friday, 18 January 1924

Dunedin, light cruiser
 TELFER, John R, Able Seaman, J 91303, drowned

Eagle, aircraft carrier
 BURTON, George W, Leading Telegraphist, J 39729, air accident, killed

Glorious, ex-light battlecruiser, aircraft carrier
 SELLEY, Samuel G, Sailmaker's Mate, 149321, illness

Sunday, 20 January 1924

Constance, light cruiser
 FAIRWEATHER, Henry J, Stoker 1c, K 3600, illness

Monday, 21 January 1924

Victory, Portsmouth
 WEBSELL, Walter J, Stoker 1c, K 29291, illness

Tuesday, 22 January 1924

Ganges, Shotley/Harwich
 LODGE, Edgar, Boy 2c, J 106632, illness

Wednesday, 23 January 1924

Triad, Admiralty yacht, SNO, Persian Gulf
 ALI, Amhed, Seedie Stoker, Aden 460, illness

Vivid, Devonport
 LORAINE, Henry, Stoker 1c, 300767, illness

Thursday, 24 January 1924

Laburnum, fleet sweeping sloop
 COLLEY, William T, Sick Berth Attendant, M 18537, illness

Pembroke, Chatham
 SAMMONS, Frank, Petty Officer, 218503, illness

Friday, 25 January 1924

Birmingham, 2nd class cruiser
 KENDALL, Frederick G H, Ordinary Seaman, J 103519, illness

Vivid, Devonport
 STARKEY, Frank A, Able Seaman, J 87050, illness

Sunday, 27 January 1924

Admiralty, Plans Division
 NAYLOR, Charles G, Commander, illness

Dwarf, 1st class gunboat
 WHY, (no first name listed), Krooman, (no service number listed), drowned

Ganges, Shotley/Harwich
 MORTON, William J R, Boy 2c, J 108571, illness

Tuesday, 29 January 1924

Crocus, fleet sweeping sloop
 DOWLING, Frederick V, Able Seaman, J 14944, illness

Repulse, battlecruiser
 WOOD, George T, Stoker Petty Officer, K 3120 accidentally killed

Saturday, 2 February 1924

Vivid, Devonport
 GEARY, Maurice, Leading Seaman, J 17915, illness

Tuesday, 5 February 1924

Hood, battlecruiser
 BENGER, Walter F, Able Seaman, J 17941, illness

Wednesday, 6 February 1924

Ceres, light cruiser
 AVIS, William B, Private, RMLI, 19136 (Ch), illness

Vulcan, submarine depot ship
 SAUNDERS, Alexander F, Telegraphist, J 96342, illness

Thursday, 7 February 1924

Calypso, light cruiser
 GODDARD, Raymond H, Able Seaman, J 102209, illness

Sunday, 10 February 1924

Pembroke, Chatham
 OWEN, Alec, Stoker 2c, K 62705, illness

Vivid, Devonport
 RIGBY, Bertie, Able Seaman, J 12654, illness

Wednesday, 13 February 1924

Lucia, submarine depot ship
 WATSON, Bernard C, Gunner, illness

Saturday, 16 February 1924

Curlew, light cruiser
 TRUE, Henry L, Ordinary Seaman, J 102934, illness

Sunday, 17 February 1924

Delhi, light cruiser
 LAYFIELD, Henry, Marine, 18892 (Ply), accidentally killed

Diligence, formerly Scapa Flow, now Sheerness
 EDE, Sidney W G, Telegraphist, J 77429, illness

Resolution, battleship
 THOMAS, Hugh, Stoker 2c, K 61997, died

Monday, 18 February 1924

Dolphin, Gosport
 HILL, John H, Stoker Petty Officer, K 5328, illness

Teal, river gunboat
 NORTHCOTT, George T, Able Seaman, J 29731, drowned

Tuesday, 19 February 1924

Fisgard. Portsmouth
 HISCOCK, Reginald J, Able Seaman, J 93946, illness

Wednesday, 20 February 1924

Wolsey, destroyer
 HARVEY, William C, Ordinary Seaman, J 99015, accidentally killed

Thursday, 21 February 1924

Abdiel, flotilla leader
 MORROW, Carlton H, Chief Petty Officer, 215589, illness

Tamar, Hong Kong
 AN, Yow, Leading Stoker, (no service number listed), illness

Saturday, 23 February 1924

Glorious, light battlecruiser
 FRANKS, Alfred G, Stoker 1c, K 55851, illness

Senator, destroyer, motorcycle accident, both killed
 AUSTIN, William R, Leading Stoker, K 19479
 DICKENS, Walter, Stoker 1c, K 56538

Tamar, Hong Kong
 SHUE, Wah, Officer's Steward 3c, (no service number listed), illness

Wednesday, 27 February 1924

ML.473, motor launch
 ALFORD, Robert F, Able Seaman, 194808, illness

Pembroke, Chatham
 GOWER, John J, Commissioned Signal Boatswain, illness

Thursday, 28 February 1924

Vivid, Devonport
 WAREING, Percy, Stoker 2c, K 63504, illness

Friday, 29 February 1924

RN Hospital, Plymouth
 FENNELL, Walter J, Sick Berth Attendant, D/M 37262, illness

Saturday, 1 March 1924

Vivid, Devonport
 DAVIES, Morris, Stoker 1c, 234928, illness

Sunday, 2 March 1924

Victory, Portsmouth
 REID, William B F, Ordinary Seaman, P/SSX 14407, illness

Friday, 7 March 1924

Dolphin, Gosport
 BENNING, Charles S, Captain, illness

Saturday, 8 March 1924

Queen Elizabeth, battleship
 CHIVERS, Edward G, Officer's Steward 2c, L 3555, illness

Wednesday, 12 March 1924

Hecla, depot ship
 KENNEDY, Angus, Seaman, RNR, A 10014, illness

Truant, destroyer
 DRAKE, William P, Stoker 1C, SS 125649, illness

Friday, 14 March 1924

Royal Sovereign, battleship
 CHAPMAN, William H, Able Seaman, J 22830, illness

Tiger, battlecruiser
 SKINNER, John J, Marine, 216487 (Po), illness

Sunday, 16 March 1924

Barham, battleship
 PEEL, John W, Chief Engine Room Artificer 1c, 271103, illness

Ganges, Shotley/Harwich
 MATTHEWS, William B, Boy 1c, J 106576, illness

Tuesday, 18 March 1924

Blenheim, ex-cruiser, destroyer depot ship
 NANCARROW, Alfred G, Commissioned Engineer, illness

Constance, light cruiser
 RAINBIRD, Frank L, Signal Boy, J 103500, accidentally killed

Wednesday, 19 March 1924

Thunderer, battleship
 FOGERTY, James, Able Seaman, J 91673, shot by civilian, killed

Saturday, 22 March 1924

Royal Sovereign, battleship
 MELDRUM, Robert, Ordinary Seaman, RNVR, 14**66, illness

Victory, Portsmouth, both drowned
 McGRATH, Matthew, Stoker 2c, K 63398
 THOMAS, Leon A M, Stoker 2c, K 63496

Sunday, 23 March 1924

Oriana, steamship
 WILLDIGG, George J, Lieutenant Commander, RNR, illness

Monday, 24 March 1924

Orcades, steamship
 JACKSON, William S, Lieutenant Commander, RNR, illness

Tuesday, 25 March 1924

Devonport Dockyard
 BUDGE, John S, Engineer Commander, illness

Hood, battlecruiser
 PUNSHON, Alfred D, Commissioned Signal Boatswain, illness

Wednesday, 26 March 1924

Victory, Portsmouth
 STEPHENS, Frank H, Surgeon Commander, illness

Thursday, 27 March 1924

Benbow, battleship
 COLE, Leonard W, Able Seaman, J 89323, drowned

Friday, 28 March 1924

Valerian, fleet sweeping sloop
 ROSS, Alexander W, Surgeon Lieutenant, illness

Vivid, Devonport
 CRANE, Clarence C, Chief Yeoman of Signals, 223279, illness

Sunday, 30 March 1924

Ormonde, fleet sweeping sloop
 McGUINNESS, Richard A, Stoker Petty Officer, K 12851, illness

Victory, Portsmouth
 REVELL, William, Stoker Petty Officer, K 15419, illness

April 1924

Dauntless, light cruiser
 HARRHY, William J, Able Seaman, J 1625, drowned, day not listed in record

Wednesday, 2 April 1924

Fisgard, Portsmouth
 AYNSLEY, Thomas, Chief Engine Room Artificer 1c, 271623, illness

Saturday, 5 April 1924

Fisgard, Portsmouth
 DENNIS, Edward A, Leading Stoker, K 35336, illness

Sunday, 6 April 1924

Montrose, flotilla leader
 WILKIN, John, Leading Stoker, 226590, illness

Tuesday, 8 April 1924

Royal Sovereign, battleship
 RAYFIELD, Alfred A, Able Seaman, J 101799, illness

Triad, Admiralty yacht, SNO, Persian Gulf
 ABBAS, Habid B, Seedie Stoker, Aden 401, illness

Wednesday, 9 April 1924

Victory, Portsmouth
 SWAIN, Cecil E, Able Seaman, J 99183, illness

Friday, 11 April 1924

Britannia, RN College, Dartmouth
 SAYLE, James, Seaman, RNR, A 10182, illness

Wessex, destroyer
 DUFTON, Henry H, Stoker 1c, K 54540, illness

Sunday, 13 April 1924

Pembroke, Chatham
 THOMAS, David H, Shipwright Apprentice, M 35267, illness

Monday, 14 April 1924

Vivid, Devonport
 BANKS, John R, Shipwright 3c, M 11859, illness

Tuesday, 15 April 1924

Royal Navy
 EVERY, George E, Commissioned Engineer, illness

Royal Sovereign, battleship
 HERRINGTON, Frederick A, Stoker 2c, K 62089, illness

Wednesday, 16 April 1924

Pembroke, Chatham
 BRISK, William, Stoker Petty Officer, 304964, illness

Vernon, Portsmouth
 BAINES, John, Petty Officer, 239220, illness

Friday, 18 April 1924

Defiance, Devonport
 CONLIN, James, Able Seaman, J 96196, drowned

Saturday, 19 April 1924

Cormorant, Gibraltar
 BERNARD, William J, Signalman, J 76283, illness

Sunday, 20 April 1924

Pembroke, Chatham
  GOLDSMITH, Charles C, Able Seaman, J 20910, died

Royal Sovereign, battleship
  FINCHAM, Alfred S, Able Seaman, J 85499, illness

Monday, 21 April 1924

King George V, battleship
  EVANS, Richard, Stoker 1c, K 56091, road accident, killed

Saturday, 26 April 1924

Royal Sovereign, battleship
  STEVENS, Harry G, Ordinary Seaman, J 99539, illness

Sunday, 27 April 1924

Cyclops, repair ship
  MILLER, Robert O, Engine Room Artificer 1c, 272509, illness

Magnolia, fleet sweeping sloop
  ROBERTS, Michael, Commissioned Mechanician, illness

Tuesday, 29 April 1924

Victory, Portsmouth
  BRAY, Albert E, Chaplain, illness

Wednesday, 30 April 1924

Carysfort, light cruiser
  BASKERFIELD, Albert, Leading Seaman, J 22193, died

May 1924

Royal Naval Reserve
  CHAMBERLAYNE, Tankerville, Honorary Lieutenant, RNR, illness, day not given in Navy List

Saturday, 3 May 1924

Wolsey, destroyer
  WINDEBANK, Charles, Stoker 1c, 310074, accidentally killed

Monday, 5 May 1924

Queen Elizabeth, battleship
  BANISTER, George, Officer's Steward 3c, L 12419, illness

Ramillies, battleship
  PARKER, William, Stoker 1c, K 63846, died

Friday, 9 May 1924

Queen Elizabeth, battleship
  HARDY, Richard, Able Seaman, 228588, illness

Saturday, 10 May 1924

Emperor of India, battleship,
  PALMER, Victor M, Able Seaman, J 93436, accidentally killed

Sunday, 11 May 1924

Carlisle, light cruiser
  WEBSTER, Harold, Able Seaman, J 76180, drowned

L.33, submarine
  TREAGUS, James G, Leading Stoker, K 13717

Monday, 12 May 1924

Laconia, steamship
  PETERS, Vicary, Lieutenant Commander, RNR, illness

Wednesday, 14 May 1924

Vernon, Portsmouth
  BURN, Allen J, Able Seaman, J 49807, illness

Sunday, 18 May 1924

Hermes, aircraft carrier
  MARTIN, Reginald T, Officer's Steward 1c, L 3191, illness

Vivid, Devonport
  WRIGHT, Harold, Able Seaman, J 92721, illness

Monday, 19 May 1924

Emperor of India, battleship
  BOW, Robert W, Ordinary Seaman, J 101624, illness

Tuesday, 20 May 1924

K.2, submarine
  STONEMAN, Christopher J, Leading Stoker, K 11962, died

Wednesday, 21 May 1924

RN War College, Greenwich
  BUCKLE, Hugh C, Captain, illness

Thursday, 22 May 1924

Wolverine, destroyer
  THOMPSON, John M, Able Seaman, J 100923, illness

Sunday, 25 May 1924

Tiger, battlecruiser
  DALEY, Ernest, Stoker 1c, K 59298, accidentally killed

Tuesday, 27 May 1924

Royal Marines HQ
  STUART, Robert, Marine, 23587 (Ch), illness

Thursday, 29 May 1924

Royal Marines HQ
  MOORE, William P, Bandsman, 14997 (Po), illness

Friday, 30 May 1924

Defiance, Devonport
 BRYANT, Frederick A, Leading Seaman, J 11302, illness

June 1924

Royal Marines HQ
 MILLER, Roy L, Corporal, RM, 213488 (Po), accidentally killed, date not given in record

Wednesday, 4 June 1924

Pembroke, Chatham
 SMITH, Hugh C, Engine Room Artificer 2c, M 7333, died

Victoria & Albert, Royal Yacht
 FREER, Henry, Seaman Rigger, 227022, died

Thursday, 5 June 1924

Tamar, Hong Kong
 WATERWORTH, Frank R, Petty Officer, J 41623, illness

Friday, 6 June 1924

Royal Navy
 FINNEY, David, Warrant Mechanician, illness

Sunday, 8 June 1924

Registan, steamship
 LAWLOR, Leslie, Lieutenant Commander, RNR, illness

Warspite, battleship
 GREENWAY, William, Officer's Steward 2c, L 7403, illness

Friday, 13 June 1924

Vivid, Devonport
 RODEN, Walter, Able Seaman, 218464, illness

Saturday, 14 June 1924

Marlborough, battleship
 LINEY, James F T, Able Seaman, J 25576, illness

Monday, 16 June 1924

Dublin, light cruiser
 WRIGHTSON, Charles H, Shipwright 1c, 345525, illness

Wednesday, 18 June 1924

Shikari, destroyer
 HUNTER, Gordon, Leading Telegraphist, J 35039, illness

Tuesday, 24 June 1924

Centurion, battleship
 LISTER, Herbert, Ordinary Seaman, J 103458, illness

Monday, 30 June 1924

Southampton, light cruiser
 DEAN, Norman E, Paymaster Lieutenant, illness

Wednesday, 2 July 1924

Fisgard, Portsmouth
 PACKER, Thomas W, Chief Engine Room Artificer 1c, 270828, illness

Thursday, 3 July 1924

Tasmania (RAN), destroyer
 BACON, Edgar J, Petty Officer, J 23487, burns, died

Saturday, 5 July 1924

Marlborough, battleship
 WARD, Arthur R, Engine Room Artificer 3c, M 11360, illness

Sandhurst, destroyer depot ship
 GLINN, John H, Shipwright 2c, M 17053, illness

Victory, Portsmouth
 WINSTANLEY, Thomas, Able Seaman, J 906997, illness

Vivid, Devonport
 WATTS, Allan J N, Leading Seaman, J 10560, illness

Sunday, 6 July 1924

Maidstone, submarine depot ship
 HALE, Alfred J, Able Seaman, J 34121, drowned

Resolution, battleship
 LITHERLAND, Harold, Able Seaman, J 37340, illness

Sturgeon, destroyer
 HOOPER, George, Able Seaman, 219911, illness

Wednesday, 9 July 1924

Marlborough, battleship
 KYNVIN, Thomas C, Act/Gunner, illness

Sunday, 13 July 1924

Whitley, destroyer
 SHEPHERD, Moses, Leading Seaman, J 44339, drowned

Monday, 14 July 1924

X.1, submarine
 HILL, Geoffrey F K, Lieutenant, illness

Tuesday, 15 July 1924

Centurion, battleship
 KITCHENER, Walter, Able Seaman, 190701, illness

Friday, 18 July 1924

Victory, Portsmouth
 TAYLOR, William T, Leading Stoker, K 12468, illness

Saturday, 26 July 1924

Impregnable, Devonport
 ANDERSON, Gustave A M, Surgeon Lieutenant Commander, illness

Sunday, 27 July 1924

Victoria & Albert, Royal Yacht
 BUNDY, Walter W, Stoker 1c, K 10451, illness

Tuesday, 29 July 1924

Southampton, 2nd class cruiser
 FERNANDES, Louis C, Officer's Cook 2c, L 11047, died

Wednesday, 30 July 1924

Vivid, Devonport
 BOLTON, Cyril, Stoker 1c, K 19211, accidentally killed

Sunday, 3 August 1924

Iron Duke, battleship
 STEWARD, William F V, Corporal, RM, 213977 (Po), died

Tuesday, 5 August 1924

Teal, river gunboat
 HEWITT, Richard C, Able Seaman, J 99374, illness

Titania, submarine depot ship
 FRASER, James F, Warrant Engineer, illness

Thursday, 7 August 1924

Fisgard, Portsmouth
 GRIFFIN, Harold E M, Electrical Artificer Apprentice, M 37697, illness

Sunday, 10 August 1924

Repulse, battlecruiser
 HICKMAN, Leonard R, Chief Electrical Artificer 2c, M 2469, drowned

Tuesday, 12 August 1924

Dolphin, Gosport
 BENNETT, Edwin, Regulating Petty Officer, M 38034, died

Saturday, 16 August 1924

Weymouth, 2nd class cruiser
 HORGAN, William H, Chief Stoker, 308642, heat stroke, died

Sunday, 17 August 1924

Engineering Course
 JONES, Oswald O, Midshipman, illness

Friday, 22 August 1924

Engineering Course
 TOWER, Ernest C, Sub Lieutenant, illness

Tuesday, 26 August 1924

Vivid, Devonport
 JACKETT, Albert E, Stoker 2c, K 63160, illness

Wednesday, 27 August 1924

Royal Naval Reserve
 MAIN, James Mc C, Lieutenant Commander, RNR, illness

Wolfhound, destroyer
 GREEN, George W, Able Seaman, J 20759, illness

Monday, 1 September 1924

Curlew, light cruiser
 FAUX, James, Able Seaman, J 103187, illness

Fisgard, Portsmouth
 RUSSELL, Edward, Lieutenant, illness

Tuesday, 2 September 1924

Valentine, destroyer
 HARE, William G, Stoker Petty Officer, K 11033, illness

Wednesday, 3 September 1924

Royal Navy
 LOCK, Walter W, Engineer Commander, illness

Thursday, 4 September 1924

Resolution, battleship
 MADDEFORD, Frederick R, Engine Room Artificer 5c, M 35404, illness

Friday, 5 September 1924

Capetown, light cruiser
 SKINNER, Frederick, Signalman, J 68143, drowned

Tuesday, 9 September 1924

Benbow, battleship
 KENNEDY, William O, Chief Engine Room Artificer 1c, 271897, accidentally killed

Royal Naval Reserve
 THOMSON, Robert B, Commander, RNR, illness

Saturday, 13 September 1924

Thunderer, battleship
 BLAKEMAN, George E, Officer's Steward 3c, L 13338, illness

Sunday, 14 September 1924

Despatch, light cruiser
 NAUGHTON, Daniel, Stoker Petty Officer, 289258, drowned

Dragon, light cruiser
 MARTIN, Harold E, Able Seaman, SS 10737, illness

Dwarf, 1st class gunboat
 JACKSON, Ernest W, Leading Signalman, J 30788, illness

Titania, submarine depot ship
 NEWBOLD, Aubrey C, Lieutenant Commander, illness

Tuesday, 16 September 1924

Constance, light cruiser
 BURROWS, Edmund G, Lieutenant, accidentally killed

Constance, light cruiser
 O'CALLAGHAN, Denys P, Lieutenant Commander, accidentally killed

Thursday, 18 September 1924

Verity, destroyer
 PERRY, Laylard G, Engine Room Artificer 5c, M 34931, illness

Saturday, 20 September 1924

Diomede, light cruiser
 CLARK, Malcolm G, Stoker Petty Officer, K 3401, drowned

Revenge, battleship
 TITBALL, John, Stoker Petty Officer, K 5300, drowned

Monday, 22 September 1924

Curacoa, light cruiser
 MAGUIRE, William, Able Seaman, J 15873, accidentally killed

Fisgard, Portsmouth
 PAINE, Arthur F, Engine Room Artificer Apprentice, M 36100, illness

Tuesday, 23 September 1924

Vivid, Devonport
 RUSSELL, George E L, Leading Seaman, J 40716, illness

Thursday, 2 October 1924

Maidstone, submarine depot ship
 LAXTON, Percy A, Chief Petty Officer, 211099, accidentally killed

Friday, 3 October 1924

Gunnery Course
 CRAWFORD, William R, Engineer Captain, illness

Saturday, 4 October 1924

Fisgard, Portsmouth
 COX, Albert, Stoker Petty Officer, K 5970, illness

Tiger, battlecruiser
 POLING, Edward J, Leading Stoker, K 62218, illness

Sunday, 5 October 1924

Hawkins, cruiser
 NASH, Arthur J, Stoker 1c, K 25515, accidentally killed

Thursday, 9 October 1924

Vivid, Devonport
 TOMS, Ernest, Able Seaman, J 20076, illness

Saturday, 11 October 1924

Emperor of India, battleship
 WALDRON, Edward L, Ordinary Seaman, J 103545, illness

Sunday, 12 October 1924

Calliope, light cruiser
 FARMER, Stanley J, Ordinary Seaman, J 105755, drowned

Calliope, light cruiser
 PHILPIN, Thomas W, Able Seaman, J 30152, drowned

Wednesday, 15 October 1924

Macedonia, steamship
 MAXWELL, James, Lieutenant, RNR, illness

Pembroke, Chatham
 WALTER, Charles A, Petty Officer, J 1304, road accident, killed

Saturday, 18 October 1924

Queen Elizabeth, battleship
 ROBINSON, Henry, Stoker 1c, K 60966, died

Monday, 20 October 1924

HM Coast Guard
 THOMAS, William J, Station Officer, HMCG, illness

Titania, submarine depot ship
 WARD, Edward G, Shipwright 2c, M 6763, drowned

Victory, Portsmouth
 GORDON, John A, Able Seaman, J 42767, illness

Tuesday, 21 October 1924

Royal Australian Navy
 DENNER, Frederick, Petty Officer Telegraphist, RAN, 10827 (RN 236025), accidentally killed

Royal Naval Reserve
 MAIN, Frank M, Commander, RNR, illness

Royal Navy
 TACK, John P, Commissioned Gunner, illness

Wednesday, 22 October 1924

Coventry, light cruiser
 BAIRD, Sir George H, Rear Admiral, Rear Admiral Destroyers, illness

Danae, light cruiser
 HERSEY, Leslie E, Cook 1c, M 36876, illness

Thursday, 23 October 1924

Vivid, Devonport
 CLARKE, William H, Engineer Lieutenant Commander, illness

Friday, 24 October 1924

Badminton, minesweeper
 DAVIS, Edward C, Leading Seaman, J 10556, drowned

Saturday, 25 October 1924

Vivid, Devonport
 BARBER, William H, Chief Engine Room Artificer 1c, M 1545, illness

Thursday, 30 October 1924

Birmingham, 2nd class cruiser
 SAFE, (no first name listed), Seedie, X 53, illness

Friday, 31 October 1924

Crocus, fleet sweeping sloop
 SKINNER, John G, Armourer, M 5198, died

Saturday, 1 November 1924

Lucia, submarine depot ship
 McDONALD, Lionel E, Engineer Lieutenant, illness

Sunday, 2 November 1924

Calcutta, light cruiser
 FRENCH, George, Electrical Artificer 2c, M 6171, illness

Wednesday, 5 November 1924

Calcutta, light cruiser
 THOMAS, Charles H, Stoker 1c, K 58945, illness

Monday, 10 November 1924

Hood, battlecruiser
 ARNOTT, George, Stoker 1c, K 60731, illness

Pilot's Course, No.1, air crash
 CHANDLER, John M, Lieutenant, killed

Tuesday, 11 November 1924

Tamar, Hong Kong
 KAN, Dow, Officer's Steward 3c, (no service number listed), died

Saturday, 15 November 1924

Hood, battlecruiser *(below, Maritime Quest)*
 MACKEY, Michael, Officer's Steward 1c, L 6031, drowned

Wren, destroyer
 SPINKS, Thomas, Stoker Petty Officer, K 772, illness

Sunday, 16 November 1924

Hood, battlecruiser
 DAGLEISH, David, Able Seaman, J 41983, drowned day after accident

Monday, 17 November 1924

Argus, aircraft carrier
 BROWN, Alfred H, Leading Stoker, K 9126, accidentally killed

Birmingham, 2nd class cruiser, road accident, both killed
 COCKRILL, Francis T, Chief Petty Officer Telegraphist, 240069
 GARNER, William, Stoker Petty Officer, K 5490

Vivid, Devonport
 TAYLOR, Stephen, Mechanician, 307681, illness

Tuesday, 18 November 1924

Curlew, light cruiser
 EASEN, Henry J, Stoker 1c, K 60457, accidentally killed

Vimiera, destroyer
 KNIGHT, William, Able Seaman, 222481, illness

Friday, 21 November 1924

Marlborough, battleship
 DANN, William S, Able Seaman, J 43883, accidentally killed

Wednesday, 26 November 1924

Danae, light cruiser
 TREVETT, Arthur W, Master at Arms, 218878, illness

Thursday, 27 November 1924

Frobisher, cruiser
 BARNETT, William H, Marine, 13826 (Ply), illness

Friday, 28 November 1924

Ganges, Shotley/Harwich
 BURBRIDGE, Stanley H G, Boy 2c, J 112093, illness

Sunday, 30 November 1924

Impregnable, Devonport
 CARD, Ernest, Boy 2c, J 109656, illness

Monday, 1 December 1924

Royal Marines HQ
 STEADMAN, Joseph G, Marine, 17067 (Ch), accidentally killed

Tuesday, 2 December 1924

Dwarf, 1st class gunboat
 SMITH, Albert H, Able Seaman, J 22170, drowned

Thursday, 4 December 1924

Vimiera, destroyer
 USHER, David E, Ordinary Seaman, J 104705, accidentally killed

Saturday, 6 December 1924

Benbow, battleship
 CHAPPELL, Frederick J T, Leading Signalman, J 23743, illness

Egmont, Malta
 ROGERS, Robert, Telegraphist, J 87856, illness

Sunday, 7 December 1924

Chatham, 2nd class cruiser
 JEEMS, Herbert, Stoker 1c, K 57433, illness

Wednesday, 10 December 1924

Royal Marines HQ
 SILLENCE, Ernest, Bugler, 15575 (Ch), illness

Thursday, 11 December 1924

Argus, aircraft carrier
 HEATH, Maurice, Able Seaman, J 24409, illness

Tuesday, 16 December 1924

Vernon, Portsmouth
 WITHERS, Albert W F, Able Seaman, J 98966, illness

Thursday, 18 December 1924

Columbine, Rosyth
 HENDERSON, James T, Chief Stoker, 303510, illness

Sunday, 28 December 1924

Cairo, light cruiser
 WILKES, Cyril P, Marine, 20317 (Ply), illness

Tuesday, 30 December 1924

Revenge, battleship
 GOLDING, Richard F, Stoker 1c, K 61836, illness

Wednesday, 31 December 1924

Ganges, Shotley/Harwich
 COWDREY, William J, Musician, RMB, RMB 2559, illness

1925

Friday, 2 January 1925

Barham, battleship
ROWSELL, Raymond R, Boy 1c, J 107722, illness

Ramillies, battleship
COLE, James J, Petty Officer, 236546, drowned

Royal Marines HQ
WISE, William M, Marine, 18219 (Pens), died

Sunday, 4 January 1925

Argus, aircraft carrier
MURRAY, Lindley A, Petty Officer, J 57, illness

Tuesday, 6 January 1925

Emperor of India, battleship
CLEAR, John, Able Seaman, J 41724, illness

Thursday, 8 January 1925

Vivid, Devonport
EVANS, Leslie, Stoker 2c, K 65088, illness

Friday, 9 January 1925

Benbow, battleship
RENDELL, William J, Petty Officer, 233572, illness

Crocus, fleet sweeping sloop
CARNEIRO, Victor C, Officer's Steward 2c, L 8960, illness

Eagle, aircraft carrier,
NICHOLAS, Henry S, Musician, RMB, RMB 736, illness

Saturday, 10 January 1925

Cleopatra, light cruiser
HILL, Douglas, Engineer Commander, illness

Wednesday, 14 January 1925

Revenge, battleship
BARKER, George H, Able Seaman, 239724, illness

Saturday, 17 January 1925

Carysfort, light cruiser
HUME, Wellington B, Engineer Commander, illness

Sunday, 18 January 1925

Royal Naval Reserve
NOSWORTHY, Ernest P, Lieutenant Commander, RNR, illness

Victory, Portsmouth
LOVEJOY, Arthur T, Stoker 2c, K 65041, illness
MANCTON, Harry G, Stoker 2c, K 62882, illness

Thursday, 22 January 1925

Hood, battlecruiser
COLRIDGE, Bernard, Officer's Steward 3c, l 13377, drowned

Tuesday, 27 January 1925

Calliope, light cruiser
CARD, Frederick J, Stoker 2c, K 47579, illness

Thursday, 29 January 1925

Pembroke, Chatham
PORCH, George F, Yeoman of Signals, 226476, illness

Royal Naval Reserve
YOUNG, Edward J L, Paymaster Lieutenant Commander, RNR, illness

Sunday, 1 February 1925

RN Hospital, Bermuda
CHENERY, Rowland W, Leading Sick Berth Attendant, M 5510, illness

Vivid, Devonport
SHAW, Robert J, Able Seaman, 217865, illness

Thursday, 5 February 1925

Fisgard, Portsmouth
NEWELL, Alfred, Able Seaman, 198325, illness

Friday, 6 February 1925

Impregnable, Devonport
COOK, William H, Petty Officer, 220522, illness

Monday, 9 February 1925

M.29, ex-monitor, minelayer, later renamed Medusa
BAKER, George T H, Chief Engine Room Artificer 1c, M 695, died

Queen Elizabeth, battleship
WILLIAMS, Arthur W, Able Seaman, J 21611, illness

Thursday, 12 February 1925

Royal Naval Reserve
McNAB, John, Honorary Captain, RNR, illness

Tuesday, 17 February 1925

Royal Marines HQ
PRIESTLEY, William B, Marine, 11970 (Ply), illness

Thursday, 19 February 1925

Victory, Portsmouth
GOULD, William R, Ordinary Seaman, J 100332, illness

Saturday, 21 February 1925

Cornflower, fleet sweeping sloop
 ABDI, Ahmed, Seedie, (no service number listed), illness

Sunday, 22 February 1925

Ross, minesweeper
 DRUETT, Eldred W, Cook, M 36480, illness

Royal Naval Reserve
 SCHLOSSER, Robert E, Lieutenant Commander, RNR, illness

Monday, 23 February 1925

Tiger, battlecruiser
 SYMES, William C, Leading Seaman, J 8036, illness

Tuesday, 24 February 1925

Hood, battlecruiser
 LARCOMBE, Matthew F, Sick Berth Attendant, M 36018, drowned

Waterhen, destroyer
 BURREL, Thomas H, Chief Stoker, 307218, drowned

Friday, 27 February 1925

Tamar, Hong Kong
 AH, Yow, Leading Seaman, (no service number listed), illness

Vernon, Portsmouth
 FORD, Samuel H, Chief Engine Room Artificer 2c, M 2648, illness

Saturday, 28 February 1925

H.44, submarine
 BRADDICK, James W, Able Seaman, J 87229, road accident, killed

Tuesday, 3 March 1925

Repulse, battlecruiser
 STEVENS, Albert W, Stoker 1c, K 62923, accidentally killed

Wednesday, 4 March 1925

Royal Naval Reserve
 EVERETT, William B, Paymaster Commander, RNR, illness

Friday, 6 March 1925

Emperor of India, battleship
 EDWARDS, Alfred, Able Seaman, J 102259, illness

Wednesday, 11 March 1925

Royal Navy
 LESLIE, Maurice B, Lieutenant Commander, illness

Wednesday, 18 March 1925

Royal Naval Reserve
 MAGOWAN, Richard, Paymaster, Lieutenant Commander, RNR, illness

Vivid, Devonport
 WILLIAMS, Thomas, Officer's Steward 4c, L 14619, illness

Vortigern, destroyer
 STANLEY, Frank A, Ordinary Seaman, RNVR, Sussex 6/47, illness

Friday, 20 March 1925

Viceroy, destroyer
 GREEN, Alfred J, Able Seaman, J 38148, illness

Saturday, 21 March 1925

Windsor, destroyer
 DAGGER, William F, Stoker 2c, K 63988, illness

Wednesday, 25 March 1925

Vectis, destroyer
 FOX, Frederick C, Officer's Cook 2c, L 12270, illness

Tuesday, 31 March 1925

Fisgard, Portsmouth
 JAMES, John R, Chief Engine Room Artificer 1c, 272512, illness

Thursday, 2 April 1925

Royal Navy
 CULME-SEYMOUR, Sir Michael, Vice Admiral, illness

Saturday, 4 April 1925

Lupin, fleet sweeping sloop
 SULIMAN, Ali, Seedie, (no service number listed), illness

Monday, 6 April 1925

Woodcock, river gunboat
 READER, Ernest W, Able Seaman, J 103275, drowned

Tuesday, 7 April 1925

Royal Navy
 CLARKE, Christopher G, Lieutenant, illness

Tuesday, 14 April 1925

Bacchus, RFA, water distilling vessel and store-carrier, 11 men in motor-boat returning from leave, collided with motor-lighter just before midnight, six drowned in River Medway at Gillingham
 CHINN, Cyril, Able Seaman, RFA
 EDWARDS, Albert, Able Seaman, RFA
 RIDDLE, John, Stoker, RFA

STONEHOUSE, Cyril, Radio Officer, RFA
TUCKER, Edward, Stoker, RFA
WAKELEY, Victor Mortimer, 3rd Officer, RFA
(with thanks to Chris White, ex-RFA)

Friday, 17 April 1925

Conquest, light cruiser
 BOTTOMLEY, Joseph H, Stoker Petty Officer, K 22901, illness

Excellent, Portsmouth
 LINDEMANN, Frederick, Engine Room Artificer 2c, M 10835, illness

Saturday, 18 April 1925

Gnat, river gunboat
 STAFFORD, John J, Stoker 1c, K 21726, illness

Pembroke, Chatham
 MAYHEW, Bertie, Chief Stoker, 308183, illness

Sunday, 19 April 1925

Voyager, destroyer
 LESLIE, William D, Signalman, J 53447, drowned

Monday, 20 April 1925

Carysfort, light cruiser
 BACKLEY, John F, Telegraphist, J 48931, accidentally killed

Dido, destroyer depot ship
 COX, John, Stoker 1c, 303808, illness

Tuesday, 21 April 1925

Mackay, flotilla leader
 SUTTON, John W E, Signalman, J 69324, accidentally killed

Saturday, 25 April 1925

Tamar, Hong Kong
 OTHER, George W, Able Seaman, J 103925, accidentally killed

Whitehall, destroyer
 GILES, Thomas H, Stoker 1c, K 57320, illness

Sunday, 26 April 1925

Vivid, Devonport
 KEATE, Harry A D, Lieutenant Commander, illness

Wednesday, 29 April 1925

Pilot's Course
 DREDGE, Felix A St G, Lieutenant, illness

Royal Sovereign, battleship
 TAYLOR, Edgar H J, Marine, 23649 (Ch), illness

Thursday, April 30 1925

Portsmouth
 DONALDSON, Robert H, Lieutenant, RM, illness

Friday, May 1 1925

Pilot's Course, air crash
 ROSEVAERE, Harry L, Lieutenant, killed

Sunday, 3 May 1925

Victory, Portsmouth
 CLAY, Harold V, Able Seaman, J 92692, illness

Wanderer, destroyer
 COLLINS, Herbert P, Stoker Petty Officer, K 3290, died

Tuesday, 5 May 1925

Dolphin, Gosport
 SMITH, John, Mechanician, K 757, died

L.7, submarine
 TUKE, Samuel F G, Lieutenant, illness

Wednesday, 6 May 1925

FAA, 440 Flight, Hermes, aircraft carrier, aircraft accident at Malta
 DENISON, Christopher, Pilot Officer, RAF, pilot
 OLIVER, Carl L D, Telegraphist, J 48587, DOI
 RUST, Henry T, Lieutenant, DOI

Thursday, 7 May 1925

Royal Navy
 STURDEE, Sir Frederick C D, Admiral of the Fleet, illness

Friday, 8 May 1925

Ceres, light cruiser
 SAUNDERS, William, Mechanician, K 426, illness

Monday, 11 May 1925

Ajax, battleship
 SEXTON, Sidney W, Engine Room Artificer 3c, M 11523, illness

Tuesday, 12 May 1925

President, London
 FRANK, Harry, Chief Petty Officer, 199039, illness

Thursday, 14 May 1925

Pembroke, Chatham
 LEIGH, Alfred, Able Seaman, J 12317, illness

Friday, 15 May 1925

Impregnable, Devonport
 JESSOP, Charles J, Boy 2c, J 111087, illness

Pilot's Course
 MORGAN, David B, Lieutenant, illness

Victory, Portsmouth
 STARK, Maurice E, Sick Berth Attendant, M 38686, illness

Saturday, 16 May 1925

Blenheim, ex-cruiser, destroyer depot ship
 EGGLETON, William G, Stoker 1c, K 61596, died

Sunday, 17 May 1925

Defiance, Devonport
 HINDE, Joseph, Chief Petty Officer, J 1611, illness

Monday, 18 May 1925

Dublin, light cruiser
 BLANN, Frank A, Master at Arms, M 6580, illness

Impregnable, Devonport
 CROCKFORD, William, Able Seaman, J 104387, illness

Tuesday, 19 May 1925

Colombo, light cruiser
 HASSLIN, Elmi, Seedie Stoker, 2/123, illness

Wednesday, 20 May 1925

Diomede, light cruiser
 NORMANTON, Joe, Leading Seaman, J 78462, drowned
 SHEPHARD, Reginald S, Able Seaman, J 99766, drowned

Lowestoft, light cruiser
 NOAD, William S, Chief Stoker, 306741, illness

Friday, 22 May 1925

Teazer, destroyer
 POOTS, Albert, Able Seaman, J 9595, illness

Vivid, Devonport
 RAXWORTHY, Willie, Able Seaman, 211094, illness

Saturday, 23 May 1925

Eagle, aircraft carrier
 BIRMINGHAM, William, Supply Petty Officer, M 37350, illness

Sunday, 24 May 1925

Hollyhock, fleet sweeping sloop
 TAYLOR, Thomas W, Stoker 1c, K 63776, illness

Revenge, battleship
 FISHER, James L, Yeoman of Signals, J 4601, died

Monday, 25 May 1925

Royal Naval Reserve
 COOK, W (initial only), Paymaster Sub Lieutenant, RNR, illness

Royal Navy
 MURPHY, David, Commissioned Gunner, illness

Wednesday, 27 May 1925

Thanet, destroyer, all drowned
 BERESFORD, William C, Able Seaman, J 41740
 FRYATT, Frederick T, Leading Seaman, J 15046
 WARING, George H, Petty Officer, J 1411

Sunday, 31 May 1925

Vernon, Portsmouth
 JONES, Arthur, Able Seaman, J 30864, illness

Monday, 1 June 1925

Ganges, Shotley/Harwich
 CAKE, Percy L, Boy 2c, J 112646, illness

Tuesday, 9 June 1925

C.224, motor lighter
 RICHARDS, William, Deck Hand, RNR, (no service number listed), (cause of death not listed)

Thursday, 11 June 1925

Flinders, ex-minesweeper, survey ship
 LUCY, Richard H, Lieutenant, illness

Friday, 12 June 1925

Royal Naval Reserve
 PETERSEN, Sir William, Honorary Commander, RNR, illness

Saturday, 13 June 1925

Pembroke, Chatham
 LEECH, Charles W, Chief Steward, 307850, illness

Sunday, 14 June 1925

Tamar, Hong Kong
 BARTON, Albert, Able Seaman, J 104976, illness

Monday, 15 June 1925

Royal Naval Reserve
 COMPTON, Charles L, Honorary Paymaster Commander, RNR, illness

Tuesday, 16 June 1925

Stormcloud, destroyer
 RUNDLE, Ernest, Chief Petty Officer, 217987, illness

Wednesday, 17 June 1925

Hawkins, cruiser
 ROBINSON, George, Stoker Petty Officer, 216001, illness

Thursday, 18 June 1925

Queen Elizabeth, battleship
HICKLIN, Leslie J, Ordinary Signalman, J 106757, drowned

Saturday, 20 June 1925

Lucia, submarine depot ship
GREENLEES, Ean C C, Lieutenant, illness, died in HS Maine

Thursday, 25 June 1925

Ganges, Shotley/Harwich
JENNINGS, Frederick H, Boy 2c, J 113579, illness

Friday, 3 July 1925

Diomede, light cruiser, both accidentally killed
MARTIN, William G, Able Seaman, J 103840
NORLON, William G, Able Seaman, J 102840

Pembroke, Chatham
HARN, Cedric W, Able Seaman, J 98752, illness

Sunday, 5 July 1925

Cricket, river gunboat
MAYNARD, Sidney, Stoker 1c, K 57904, drowned

Valiant, battleship
MILLWARD, Edgar F, Electrical Artificer 3c, M 25784, train accident, killed

Saturday, 11 July 1925

Repulse, battlecruiser
HOSEY, Edward, Stoker 1c, K 64954, illness

Tuesday, 14 July 1925

Pilot's Course No.2
RYAN, John, Mate, air crash, killed

Wednesday, 15 July 1925

Hawkins, cruisers
ASHE, Harry, Private, RMLI, 20227 (Ch), drowned

Friday, 17 July 1925

Royal Naval Reserve
PEARCE, William F, Commander, RNR, illness

Wednesday, 22 July 1925

Dublin, light cruiser
GARFORTH, Holland, Stoker 1c, 307334, illness

Royal Marines HQ
CURTHOYS, George J, Quartermaster Sergeant, RM, 21804 (Ply), accidentally killed

Friday, 24 July 1925

M.3, submarine
FARMER, Dennis, Signalman, J 94295, illness

Pembroke, Chatham
PALMER, George F, Stoker Petty Officer, K 6993, illness

Saturday, 25 July 1925

Royal Sovereign, battleship
REDFERN, Richard J, Able Seaman, J 99353, accidentally killed

Tuesday, 28 July 1925

Effingham, cruiser
LEGG, Arthur F, Boy 1c, J 111100, illness

Saturday, 1 August 1925

Vivid, Devonport
BRENTON, Alfred, Chief Painter, 346970, illness

Wednesday, 5 August 1925

Cardiff, light cruiser
FITZSIMONS, Charles T, Marine, 21921 (Po), illness

Thursday, 6 August 1925

Scarab, river gunboat
ASKEW, George S, Stoker 1c, K 52144, illness

Sunday, 9 August 1925

Caradoc, light crusier
O'CALLAGHAN, Frederick G, Supply Chief Petty Officer, M 2767, illness

Wednesday, 12 August 1925

Clematis, fleet sweeping sloop
SULLIVAN, John, Leading Stoker, 306251, illness

Revenge, battleship
WILLIAMS, Archibald F, Signalman, J 10600, accidentally killed

Friday, 14 August 1925

Effingham, cruiser
LUCAS, Joseph A, Officer's Steward 2c, L 7454, died

Saturday, 15 August 1925

Centurion, battleship
BUTTLER, Sidney A, Marine, 18375 (Po), accidentally killed

Crocus, fleet sweeping sloop
HUTT, Ralph, Able Seaman, J 15181, heat stroke, died

RM, Portsmouth Division
BUTLER, Sidney A, Marine, 18375 (Po), road accident, Oxford

Monday, 17 August 1925

Benbow, battleship
  MILLER, Robert, Master at Arms, 233010, illness

Repulse, battlecruiser
  OLIVER, William F, Engine Room Artificer, M 34041, drowned

Wednesday, 19 August 1925

Tarantula, river gunboat
  AH, Wing, Stoker, (no service number listed), drowned

Victory, Portsmouth
  READ, Edward P, Able Seaman, J 79595, illness

Thursday, 20 August 1925

Carlisle, light cruiser
  MAY, George, Stoker Petty Officer, K 1615, drowned

Friday, 21 August 1925

Coventry, light cruiser
  BERRIMAN, George, Chief Petty Officer, 231083, illness

Sherborne, minesweeper
  GALLOP, Edward H, Stoker Petty Officer, 308006, illness

Monday, 24 August 1925

Vindictive, cruiser
  MARS, Walter P, Shipwright 1c, 345979, illness

Tuesday, 25 August 1925

Colombo, light cruiser
  ATTERBY, William, Able Seaman, 235767, illness

Wednesday, 26 August 1925

Bee, river gunboat
  LEE, John J, Engine Room Artificer 2c, M 3270, illness

Viscount, destroyer
  BISHOP, Alfred J, Gunner, illness

Thursday, 27 August 1925

Tamar, Hong Kong
  GAVIN, James J, Able Seaman, J 37572, drowned

Saturday, 29 August 1925

Vernon, Portsmouth
  PYCROFT, Cecil C, Petty Officer, J 535, illness

Sunday, 30 August 1925

Calliope, light cruiser
  ROBINSON, William G, Leading Telegraphist, J 27404, illness

Monday, 31 August 1925

Defiance, Devonport
  DUNN, William H, Able Seaman, J 94919, road accident, killed

Friday, 4 September 1925

Pembroke, Chatham
  SKELT, William P, Engine Room Artificer 4c, M 34508, illness

Revenge, battleship
  DELEMARE, Herbert A, Petty Officer, J 16376, illness

Saturday, 5 September 1925

Iron Duke, battleship
  STREET, Reginald C, Able Seaman, J 17962, illness

Tuesday, 8 September 1925

Royal Sovereign, battleship
  EDMONDS, Henry A, Able Seaman, J 46839, accidentally killed

Saturday, 12 September 1925

Constance, light cruiser
  WALTON, William D, Stoker 1c, K 24565, drowned

Wednesday, 16 September 1925

Royal Sovereign, battleship
  PLUCK, Thomas L, Ordinary Seaman, J 109702, illness

Monday, 21 September 1925

Resolution, battleship
  WEST, Orlando, Petty Officer, J 133, illness

Tuesday, 22 September 1925

Vernon, Portsmouth
  LADD, William, Able Seaman, J 96479, illness

Wednesday, 23 September 1925

Victory, Portsmouth
  PITT, Charles H, Leading Stoker, K 22939, illness

Thursday, 24 September 1925

Cricket, river gunboat
  WALTER, Arthur, Petty Officer, J 22770, illness

Friday, 25 September 1925

Vivid, Devonport
  CALDER, Robert, Telegraphist, J 82617, illness

Sunday, 27 September 1925

Tamar, Hong Kong
  KUM, You, Able Seaman, (Chinese), died

Monday, 28 September 1925

Victory, Portsmouth
 McCLURE, John S, Electrical Artificer 3c, M 30409, illness

Wednesday, 30 September 1925

Cricket, river gunboat
 WHITE, Joseph F, Leading Stoker, K 16104, drowned

Thursday, 1 October 1925

Vivid, Devonport
 POOLE, William W, Chief Stoker, K 309575, (cause of death not listed)

Friday, 2 October 1925

Barham, battleship
 BOWER, James, Petty Officer, J 572, illness

Wednesday, 7 October 1925

Adamant, submarine depot ship
 SAMMUT, Constantino, Officer's Steward 2c, L 14987, killed

Thursday, 8 October 1925

Titania, submarine depot ship
 LLOYD, Harry, Regulating Petty Officer, M 36479, drowned

Friday, 9 October 1925

Venomous, destroyer
 ROBINSON, Thomas W, Stoker 1c, K 58687, died

Saturday, 10 October 1925

Fisgard, Portsmouth
 JOWETT, Arthur R, Engine Room Artificer 1c, M 3910, illness

Sunday, 11 October 1925

Scarab, river gunboat
 PAMMENT, William F, Stoker 1c, K 41353, illness

Thursday, 15 October 1925

Iron Duke, battleship
 KING, George E, Boy 1c, J 109168, illness

Saturday, 17 October 1925

Repulse, battlecruiser
 BARRON, John L, Chief Stoker, 310664, illness

Wednesday, 21 October 1925

Assistance, fleet repair ship
 HOOPER, William, Stoker 1c, K 22357, drowned

Thursday, 22 October 1925

Wrestler, destroyer
 TOWNER, Arthur L A, Able Seaman, J 99640, drowned

Sunday, 25 October 1925

Vanquisher, destroyer
 LEGGETT, Frederick T, Leading Stoker, K 5166, illness

Monday, 26 October 1925

Revenge, battleship
 BERESFORD, James H, Stoker 2c, K 66152, accidentally killed

Wednesday, 28 October 1925

Ramillies, battleship
 HIGGIS, Harry C, Petty Officer, 238503, illness

Thursday, 29 October 1925

Pembroke, Chatham
 FAIRLEY, Albert V, Stoker Petty Officer, K 17442, illness

Monday, 2 November 1925

Royal Naval Reserve
 PEARSE, Cyril A, Lieutenant, RNR, illness

Thursday, 5 November 1925

Repulse, battlecruiser
 ALLEN, Sam O, Private, RMLI, 21338 (Ch), illness

Sunday, 8 November 1925

Repulse, battlecruiser
 HILL, Albert H, Leading Seaman, J 91934, illness

Monday, 9 November 1925

Royal Sovereign, battleship
 PACE, Edward W, Boy 1c, J 108006, illness

Tuesday, 10 November 1925

Carlisle, light cruiser
 HENRY, Donald Mc I, Able Seaman, J 55290, illness

Thursday, 12 November 1925

M.1, 12in-gunned submarine monitor, submerged, in collision with Swedish SS Vidar off Start Point, Devon, lost, no survivors *(over page)*
 ADAMS, Cecil P, Leading Seaman, J 52992
 ALEXANDER, Arthur H, Petty Officer, J 14439
 ALLEN, William C, Able Seaman, J 51425
 ANDREWS, Enoch J, Able Seaman, J 39562
 BABY, Ernest A, Able Seaman, J 71374
 BAKER, Edward C G, Stoker Petty Officer, K 12959

BALL, Harold, Able Seaman, J 39475
BALL, John S, Leading Stoker, K 35944
BELL, William MacD, Engine Room Artificer 3c, M 7020
BICKER, Roland, Chief Petty Officer, 224812
BUTTLE, James F, Able Seaman, J 22045
CARRIE, Alec M, Lieutenant Commander
CASEY, Robert C, Lieutenant, RAN
CLARK, Walter T, Able Seaman, J 98456
CLEAVER, Edward G, Stoker 1c, K 58802
CLOUGH, Nelson O, Signalman, J 39848
COWLING, Albert G, Act/Leading Stoker, K 18120
DEARING, Leonard A P, Able Seaman, J 48620
DENNIS, William, Electrical Artificer 2c, M 12651
DIXON, Reginald C, Petty Officer, 231628
DUGGAN, Albert F H, Leading Seaman, J 62085
EDDEN, Thomas H, Engine Room Artificer 3c, M 14514
ERSKINE, William, Act/Leading Stoker, K 63811
EVANS, Albert, Able Seaman, J 96694
FELTHAM, Frank, Stoker 1c, K 54863
FOLEY, John F, Able Seaman, J 48199
GARDNER, Charles, Chief Stoker, 233422
GAY, Albert A, Telegraphist, J 62961
GOOD, Cyril S, Warrant Engineer
GORE, Sidney J E, Engine Room Artificer 1c, M 4730
HARDING, Gordon G, Engine Room Artificer 2c, M 10953
HEWSON, Philip, Ordnance Artificer 3c, M 8641
HOBDAY, Albert E, Petty Officer, 236378
JEWELL, Henry G, Able Seaman, J 48749
JONES, Bertie, Petty Officer, J 20035
KEMBLE, George, Leading Stoker, K 10184
KENT, Arthur W, Leading Seaman, J 15182
KIDNEY, James, Leading Seaman, J 53085
LAW, John W, Able Seaman, J 65730
LITTELL, Robert C, Ordnance Artificer 3c, M 35596
LOVERING, Ernest T, Able Seaman, J 24879
MANNING, John, Able Seaman, J 103109
MANSELL, Cecil G C, Stoker 1c, K 60530
MARTIN, Charles J, Able Seaman, J 90561
MILLARD, Harold, Stoker 1c, K 62220
MORGAN, George P, Petty Officer, 239799
MORRISEY, James, Stoker 1c, K 62854
MOYSE, Victor C, Able Seaman, J 23751
NEIGHBOUR, Herbert E, Able Seaman, J 89919
NICHOLLS, David, Stoker 1c, K 57984
NICHOLSON, William F, Leading Seaman, J 19840
PEARSON, William A, Able Seaman, J 42464
PHILPOTT, Thomas W, Lieutenant
PRICE, William F, Leading Seaman, J 25784
SAYERS, Charles A, Able Seaman, J 31401
SMITH, Frederick W, Petty Officer Telegraphist, J 9944
SPRATLEY, Percival, Telegraphist, J 69385
STOREY, Charles C, Stoker 1c, K 58415
STYLES, Reginald P, Able Seaman, J 28159
TAMBLIN, William, Leading Seaman, J 94557
TAYLOR, Robert, Able Seaman, J 41914
THORPE, Charles A R, Lieutenant

TURNER, Walter I, Leading Signalman, J 36092
VAUGHAN, William C A, Leading Seaman, J 32281
WASHINGTON, Sidney W, Leading Seaman, J 24140
WEBSTER, Albert E, Leading Seaman, J 92635
WILLIAMS, Henry R, Stoker 1c, K 56132
WRIGHT, Charles E, Officer's Steward, L 12944
WRIGHT, Frederick G, Able Seaman, J 99863

Saturday, 14 November 1925

K.26, submarine
　DEACON, Donald C, Lieutenant, illness

Malabar, Bermuda
　WILBY, Cecil F, Petty Officer Telegraphist, J 10920, illness

Vivid, Devonport
　HARPER, Kenneth, Able Seaman, J 92090, illness
　LANGWORTHY, William H, Leading Stoker, K 6228, illness

Monday, 16 November 1925

Ganges, Shotley/Harwich
　WRIGHT, Reginald H, Boy 2c, J 114301, illness

Tuesday, 24 November 1925

Ramillies, battleship
　SADLE, Reginald C, Leading Seaman, J 29087, illness

Thursday, 26 November 1925

Hood, battlecruiser
　MATTIN, Nigel, Ordinary Seaman, J 106965, accidentally killed

Saturday, 28 November 1925

Royal Marines HQ
　POOLE, Jack, Marine, 24629 (Ch), illness

Monday, 30 November 1925

Harebell, fleet sweeping sloop
　PEARSE, Clarence E, Able Seaman, J 105084, accidentally killed

December 1925

Effingham, cruiser
　FROST, John E, Ordinary Seaman, J 110205, died, date approximate, day not given

Sunday, 6 December 1925

Excellent, Portsmouth
　SEARLE, Frederick, Able Seaman, J 91327, road accident, killed

Friday, 11 December 1925

Lupin, fleet sweeping sloop
　GUEST, John D, Chief Petty Officer, 221761, illness

Sunday, 13 December 1925

Victory, Portsmouth
 PECK, Francis W, Shipwright 1c, M 215827, illness

Monday, 14 December 1925

Diligence, destroyer depot ship
 HUGHES, William H, Corporal, RM, 17759 (Ply), illness

Tuesday, 15 December 1925

Victory, Portsmouth
 HUMPHREY, George, Petty Officer, J 7069, illness

Wednesday, 16 December 1925

Ajax, battleship
 CLARK, Percy H, Boy 1c, J 112873, illness

Victoria & Albert, Royal Yacht
 GARTRELL, Arthur E, Seaman Rigger, 219941, illness

Thursday, 17 December 1925

Cyclops, repair ship
 MARTIN, Percy, Shipwright 1c, 345735, illness

Verdun, destroyer
 EYRE, Harry, Stoker Petty Officer, K 23807, illness

Saturday, 19 December 1925

Ganges, Shotley/Harwich
 OUSLEY, Sydney J, Chief Joiner, M 2594, illness

Saturday, 26 December 1925

Hermes, aircraft carrier
 WHITBY, James H, Able Seaman, J 45294, accidentally killed

1926

Saturday, 2 January 1926

Hawkins, cruiser
  BATCHELOR, Edward E, Able Seaman, J 36735, accidentally killed

Sunday, 3 January 1926

Benbow, battleship
  SILCOCK, Frederick W S, Able Seaman, J 16490, died

Whirlwind, destroyer
  WALKER, Ernest, Able Seaman, J 90331, illness

Sunday, 10 January 1926

Durban, light cruiser
  ROBINSON, Frederick S, Sergeant, RM, 21853 (Ply), illness

Victory, Portsmouth
  SMALL, Ernest E, Petty Officer, 238010, illness

Tuesday, 12 January 1926

Ajax, battleship
  MACDONALD, Murdo, Seaman, RNR, A 9905, accidentally killed

Vernon, Portsmouth
  JACKSON, Cyrus E T, Leading Seaman, J 19496, died

Wednesday, 13 January 1926

Colombo. light cruiser
  WARWICK, Ralph D, Able Seaman, J 28845, illness

Ganges, Shotley/Harwich
  HOWLETT, Walter G, Boy 2c, J 113957, illness

Wolfhound, destroyer
  LANGSTAFF, Edward G, Lieutenant, drowned

Saturday, 16 January 1926

Pembroke, Chatham
  HAMMOND, Edward, Stoker 2c, K 66893, illness

Sunday, 17 January 1926

Resolution, battleship
  LYNCH, John P, Leading Seaman, J 94301, died

Thursday, 21 January 1926

Dragon, light cruiser
  STEPHENSON, Joseph H, Stoker 1c, K 59895, accidentally killed

RM Deal, Kent
  CONYBEARE, Charles B, Captain, RM, illness

Victory, Portsmouth
  BARTON, Ernest W, Able Seaman, J 16667, illness

Saturday, 23 January 1926

Victory, Portsmouth
  TAYLOR, Herbert C, Telegraphist, J 101213, accidentally killed

Tuesday, 26 January 1926

Ajax, battleship
  PAGE, George J, Able Seaman, J 105046, illness

Royal Marines HQ
  APPLEBY, James G, Marine, 211570 (Po), illness

Wednesday, 27 January 1926

Rocket, destroyer
  DUNN, Alfred G, Stoker Petty Officer, 306007, illness

Victory, Portsmouth
  GEORGE, Edgar R, Officer's Cook 1c, L 2734, illness

Friday, 29 January 1926

Malaya, battleship
  WRIGHT, Warren S, Paymaster Lieutenant, illness, died in Hospital Ship Maine

Sunday, 31 January 1926

Ganges, Shotley/Harwich
  McCUTCHEON, Richard, Boy 2c, J 113441, illness

Monday, 1 February 1926

Pembroke, Chatham
  CLARK, Roland A, Commander, illness

Wednesday, 3 February 1926

Douglas, flotilla leader
  CRAINES, Frederick C, Able Seaman, J 90335, illness

Thursday, 4 February 1926

Eagle, aircraft carrier
  BEARER, James H, Stoker 1c, K 26421, illness

Victory, Portsmouth
  HARBER, Rowland G, Able Seaman, SS 10831, illness

Vivid, Devonport
  ARSCOTT, Thomas H, Stoker Petty Officer, 310264, illness

Sunday, 7 February 1926

Burslem, minesweeper
  HOLSAN, William J, Leading Stoker, K 15620, illness

Monday, 8 February 1926

Vivid, Devonport
 LAWRY, Edwin S J, Sick Berth Attendant, M 38148, illness

Tuesday, 9 February 1926

Egmont, Malta
 MAGRI, Emmanuelle, Petty Officer, 236002, illness

Wednesday, 10 February 1926

FAA, 405 Flight, Eagle, aircraft carrier, air crash
 HANCOX, Henry R, Lieutenant, killed

Friday, 12 February 1926

Vivid, Devonport
 PEARSON, William B, Able Seaman, J 78869, died

Saturday, 13 February 1926

Shikari, destroyer
 PALMER, Reginald J, Able Seaman, J 64437, illness

Monday, 15 February 1926

Admiralty, Plans Division
 SANDFORD, Francis H, Captain, illness

Tuesday, 16 February 1926

Emerald, light cruiser
 FRIZZELL, Samuel, Able Seaman, J 55335, drowned

Wednesday, 17 February 1926

Montrose, flotilla leader
 FLAMARK, Joseph S, Able Seaman, J 8498, illness

Friday, 19 February 1926

Queen Elizabeth, battleship
 D'LOYDE, Phillip J, Marine, 18709 (Po), died

Sunday, 21 February 1926

Ambrose, submarine depot ship
 WHITEHEAD, John W, Signalman, J 31965, illness

Ganges, Shotley/Harwich
 BISHOP, John H, Boy 2c, JX 125927, illness

Vernon, Portsmouth
 HARRIS, Sidney R, Chief Petty Officer, 216991, illness

Tuesday, 23 February 1926

Calliope, light cruiser
 STEVENS, Stanley, Leading Supply Assistant, M 35208, illness

Wednesday, 24 February 1926

Barham, battleship, both accidentally killed
 SCOREY, Ernest J, Able Seaman, 231624
 STARKEY, Arthur E J, Able Seaman, 231624

Iron Duke, battleship
 SMITH, Bertie E, Officer's Steward 1c, 363090, illness

Thursday, 25 February 1926

Royal Marines HQ
 HEALEY, Norton G, Marine, 22408 (Po), illness

Friday, 26 February 1926

Vivid, Devonport
 JEFFERY, George H, Able Seaman, J 179, illness

Sunday, 28 February 1926

Ajax, battleship
 BAGDEN, Herbert T, Boy 1c, J 113865, illness

Monday, 1 March 1926

Lowestoft, light cruiser
 WATSON, John A, Stoker 1c, SS 125895, accidentally killed

Tuesday, 2 March 1926

Impregnable, Devonport
 CHARLESWORTH, Herbert, Boy 2c, J 115226, illness

Saturday, 6 March 1926

Royal Oak, battleship
 WATSON, James, Marine, 18380 (Ch), died

Sunday, 7 March 1926

Marlborough, battleship
 SAMPSHIRE, Thomas C, Stoker 1c, K 58448, illness

Monday, 8 March 1926

Defiance, Defiance
 PILLAR, Langmead C, Chief Engine Room Artificer 1c, 347832, illness

Friday, 12 March 1926

Ajax, battleship
 CHILVERS, George L, Boy 1c, J 113528, illness

Wednesday, 17 March 1926

Hermes, aircraft carrier
 SKITTLE, William F, Chief Stoker, 312059, illness

Saturday, 20 March 1926

Cockchafer, river gunboat
DALE, Ernest, Able Seaman, J 29304, drowned

Monday, 22 March 1926

Egmont, Malta
DE BONO, Emanuele, Officer's Cook 1c, 360394, illness

Venomous, destroyer
HATTON, Alfred, Chief Stoker, 309247, illness

Tuesday, 23 March 1926

Thunderer, battleship
HOURIHANE, Daniel, Stoker 1c, K 56500, illness

Friday, 26 March 1926

Fisgard, Portsmouth
ARROW, George, Stoker 1c, K 60201, illness

Medusa, ex-monitor, minelayer, tender to Egmont
SIMPSON, Gibson W, Lieutenant, illness

Tuesday, 30 March 1926

Egmont, Malta
BRYAN, Thomas L G, Lieutenant, RM, illness

Wednesday, 31 March 1926

Shikari, destroyer
CLAYTON, Harold E, Able Seaman, J 36354, illness

Vivid, Devonport
KITT, Walter J S, Chief Petty Officer Cook, 347577, illness

Friday, 2 April 1926

Protea (South African Naval Force), minesweeper, completed as survey vessel
SHEEHAN, Henry J, Stoker Petty Officer, K 13726, drowned

Sunday, 4 April 1926

Hollyhock, fleet sweeping sloop
PANTLING, Henry, Able Seaman, J 105596, illness

Friday, 9 April 1926

Pembroke, Chatham
WALE, William L K, Leading Stoker, K 59814, illness

Saturday, 10 April 1926

L.15, submarine
BERRIDGE, William L, Lieutenant, illness

Tuesday, 13 April 1926

Centurion, battleship
SWAYNE, Henry J, Warrant Writer, illness

Vernon, Portsmouth
BAVERSTOCK, Cecil G, Able Seaman, J 97768, illness

Tuesday, 20 April 1926

Danae, light cruiser
LILLYSTONE, Charles T, Able Seaman, J 37020, illness

Wednesday, 21 April 1926

Whitley, destroyer
MERCHANT, Henry P, Engineer Lieutenant, illness

Sunday, 25 April 1926

Clematis, fleet sweeping sloop
WILLIAMSON, Gilbert D, Telegraphist, J 102111, illness

Tuesday, 27 April 1926

Pembroke, Chatham
OSBORNE, Charles W, Officer's Cook 2c, L 12612, died

Friday, 30 April 1926

Columbine, Rosyth
STUBBINS, Herbert H, Ordinary Seaman, J 112647, illness

Pilot's Course
PORTAL, Nigel H, Lieutenant , air crash, killed

Monday, 3 May 1926

Endeavour, survey ship
CHITTENDEN, Arthur H J, Stoker 1c, K 5910, illness

Ganges, Shotley/Harwich
WIGGIN, John, Petty Officer, 239975, road accident, killed

Sunday, 9 May 1926

Ark Royal, seaplane carrier
COLLINS, Daniel, Able Seaman, J 26937, road accident, killed

Monday, 10 May 1926

Enterprise, light cruiser
WAITE, James H, Marine, 24396 (Ch), died

Tuesday, 11 May 1926

Dauntless, light cruiser
DEWING, Alfred P, Lieutenant, illness, died in HS Maine

Wednesday, 12 May 1926

Enterprise, light cruiser
EALES, Thomas B, Leading Signalman, J 25873, illness

Foxglove, fleet sweeping sloop
FINCH, Francis A, Stoker 1c, K 50279, drowned

Royal Marines HQ
HINE, William J, Marine, 19699 (Ply), illness

Vivid, Devonport
O'FLYNN, William, Leading Stoker, K 21706, illness

Monday, 17 May 1926

Queen Elizabeth, battleship
SIMPSON, Alfred, Blacksmith 4c, M 37793, accidentally killed

Tuesday, 18 May 1926

Teal, river gunboat
GILMAN, Francis E J, Sub Lieutenant, illness

Friday, 21 May 1926

unit not listed, flying Fairey Flycatcher
SMITH, Peter G, Lieutenant, air crash, killed

Saturday, 22 May 1926

Victory, Portsmouth
LOVELL, Frederick B R, Stoker 2c, KX 75657, illness

Warspite, battleship
BODY, William J, Chief Petty Officer Writer, M 7649, illness

Sunday, 23 May 1926

Furious, aircraft carrier
HOWARD, Albert J, Marine, 14972 (Po), illness

Royal Navy
BEWS, Samuel T, Commissioned Engineer, illness

Wednesday, 26 May 1926

Columbine, Rosyth
GILL, Sydney M, Able Seaman, J 162149, accidentally killed

Thursday, 27 May 1926

Pembroke, Chatham
WATKINS, Albert E, Able Seaman, J 101435, illness

Friday, 28 May 1926

Mackay, flotilla leader
McLUCKIE, John, Warrant Engineer, illness

Sunday, 30 May 1926

Royal Naval Reserve
TERNDRUP, John H, Lieutenant Commander, RNR, illness

Tuesday, 1 June 1926

Curlew, light cruiser
SALISBURY, William W, Able Seaman, J 97120, illness

Thursday, 3 June 1926

Vivid, Devonport
SNELL, Stanley W, Stoker 1c, 311447, illness

Saturday, 5 June 1926

Seabear, destroyer
HUMPHRIES, Morgan, Able Seaman, 204595, illness

Monday, 7 June 1926

Caroline, light cruiser
MARTIN, Ernest A, Chief Petty Officer, 211200, illness

Tuesday, 8 June 1926

Columbine, Rosyth
PIKE, Stanley J, Painter 4c, M 7895, illness

Wednesday, 9 June 1926

Royal Navy
BELL, Charles S, Engineer Commander, illness

Thursday, 10 June 1926

Victory, Portsmouth
SHEATH, Ernest K, Petty Officer, J 1828, illness

Sunday, 13 June 1926

Effingham, cruiser
HAWKINS, Arthur W, Leading Seaman, J 16167, illness

Ramillies, battleship
WALDRON, John, Midshipman, illness

Monday, 14 June 1926

Royal Naval Reserve
Earl of Dunraven, Honorary Captain, RNR, illness

Wednesday, 16 June 1926

Hood, battlecruiser
SIMS, Edward T, Electrical Artificer 3c, M 36225, illness

Thursday, 17 June 1926

Barham, battleship
BOOKER, Edward, Stoker Petty Officer, K 8774, illness

Saturday, 19 June 1926

Effingham, cruiser
ELSDON, Albert J, Musician, RMB, RMB 2802, illness

Sunday, 20 June 1926

Ambrose, submarine depot ship
LING, Cheung, Officer's Steward 3c, (no service number listed), drowned

Tuesday, 22 June 1926

Royal Marines HQ
 EDWARDS, John, Marine, 22605 (Ply), illness

Sunday, 27 June 1926

Impregnable, Devonport
 SAVILLE, Percy S, Stoker 1c, K 10730, accidentally killed

Wednesday, 30 June 1926

Pembroke, Chatham
 GAME, Neville L, Able Seaman, J 104373, road accident, killed

Friday, 2 July 1926

Curlew, light cruiser
 KITT, Herbert F, Able Seaman, J 106736, drowned

Wessex, destroyer
 CHEVES, Henry E, Able Seaman, J 78832, accidentally killed

Tuesday, 6 July 1926

Pembroke, Chatham
 CAZENAVE, Robert J, Petty Officer, J 936, illness

Sunday, 11 July 1926

Fisgard, Portsmouth
 REYNOLDS, Ernest, Leading Stoker, K 14221, illness

Tarantula, river gunboat
 BRANSFIELD, Michael J, Shipwright 1c, 346265, illness

Tuesday, 13 July 1926

Fisgard, Portsmouth
 WILKINSON, Frederick C B, Able Seaman, 237559, illness

Friday, 16 July 1926

Durban, light cruiser
 FAHEY, Michael T, Supply Chief Petty Officer, M 4604, illness

Royal Marines HQ
 BARROW, Alfred O, Marine, 22953 (Ch), died

Saturday, 17 July 1926

Clematis, fleet sweeping sloop
 MILFORD, Albert J, Commissioned Gunner, illness

Friday, 23 July 1926

RM Barracks
 FAWCKNER, William F S, Captain, RM, illness

Saturday, 24 July 1926

Vivid, Devonport
 MAHONEY, Francis J, Chief Petty Officer Cook, 347582, illness

Monday, 26 July 1926

Ramillies, battleship
 HUGHES, Ifor L, Lieutenant, RNR, illness

Wednesday, 28 July 1926

Effingham, cruiser
 FERHAN, Hassan, 2nd Tindal, Aden 503, illness

Ulster Division, RNVR
 ADAMS, E (initial only) T, Honorary Lieutenant, RNVR, illness

Vendetta, destroyer
 FOYLE, Frederick W, Telegraphist, J 87114, illness

Monday, 9 August 1926

H.29, submarine, accidentally flooded and sank alongside in
 Devonport Dockyard, one naval rating and five civilian workers
 killed *(below, H.21-class sister-boat H.28)*
 DALTON, Robert W, Chief Engine Room Artificer, 272358,
 ELLIOTT, George, Dockyard Fitter
 FLETCHER, John, Labourer
 HILL, Henry, Dockyard Fitter
 HOSKING, Edward, Chargeman Fitter
 TRUSCOTT, Arthur, Dockyard Fitter

Pembroke, Chatham
 ORRIN, Percival J, Ordinary Seaman, J 112929, illness

Tuesday, 10 August 1926

Hawkins, cruiser
 SIMMONS, Leonard, Stoker 1c, K 66047, accidentally killed

Wednesday, 11 August 1926

Bee, river gunboat
 SWEETLOVE, Lancelot D, Engineer Commander, illness

Thursday, 12 August 1926

Teal, river gunboat
 HIGGINS, Wilfred A, Lieutenant Commander, illness

Monday, 16 August 1926

Royal Naval Reserve
 SUTHERLAND, Bertram R U, Lieutenant Commander, RNR,
 illness

Tuesday, 17 August 1926

Royal Marines
 REES, John L L, Lieutenant, RAF Base Gosport, air crash

Ulster Division, RNVR
 WILLIAMS, Jonathan, Commissioned Mechanician, illness at home

Thursday, 19 August 1926

Fisgard, Portsmouth
 MILLS, Arthur J, Ordnance Artificer Apprentice, M 38432, illness

Friday, 20 August 1926

L.7, submarine
 CARLINE, Leonard, Leading Telegraphist, J 6437, illness

Royal Navy
 CHRISTIAN, Arthur H, Admiral, Rtd, died

Monday, 23 August 1926

Curlew, light cruiser
 McA'LEARY, Peter, Stoker 2c, K 66154, accidentally killed

Tuesday, 24 August 1926

Pembroke, Chatham
 DONALD, Edgar J, Officer's Cook 3c, L 14164, illness

Vulcan, ex-torpedo boat carrier, submarine depot ship
 THOM, Frederick C W, Chief Electrical Artificer 1c, M 1007, road accident, killed

Friday, 27 August 1926

Barham, battleship
 RANDALL, Norman L W, Marine, 21942 (Po), accidentally killed

Saturday, 28 August 1926

Royal Naval Reserve
 MACIVER, Charles, Honorary Captain, RNR, illness

Monday, 30 August 1926

Pembroke, Chatham
 GAMBRILL, Frank, Leading Seaman, J 101320, road accident, killed

Vivid, Devonport
 SALTER, Ernest J, Stoker 1c, K 24355, died

Tuesday, 3 August 1926

Tamar, Hong Kong
 CHU, Tsing, Officer's Steward 1c, (no service number listed), died

Wednesday, 1 September 1926

Gnat, river gunboat
 SKELTON, Charles T W, Able Seaman, J 12923, drowned

Thursday, 2 September 1926

Endeavour, survey ship
 PURSER, Arthur A, Able Seaman, J 96521, illness

Pembroke, Chatham
 BENNETT, John H, Stoker 1c, K 64918, illness

Sunday, 5 September 1926

WAHNSIEN INCIDENT, Yangtze River, China – recovery of seaman from two British merchant ships captured by Chinese troops

Cockchafer, river gunboat
 RIDGE, Christopher F, Sub Lieutenant, killed

Despatch, light cruiser, all killed *(below, NP/Mark Teadham)*
 DARLEY, Frederick C, Commander,
 FARMINER, Norman J, Able Seaman, J 108648
 HIGGINS, Alfred R, Lieutenant

Scarab, river gunboat, all killed
 FARROW, Frederick J, Able Seaman, J 91863
 HASLAM, Herbert, Leading Seaman, J 102105
 MARROTTE, William, Able Seaman, J 46224

Tamar, Hong Kong
 AH, Pong, Sailmaker, (no service number listed), died

Monday, 6 September 1926

FAA, 421 Sqn, Furious, aircraft carrier
 HADDOW, James W, Leading Telegraphist, J 48913, air crash, killed

Tuesday, 7 September 1926

Excellent, Portsmouth
 VASS, Reginald, Chief Petty Officer, 223858, died

Victory, Portsmouth
 LEARLY, Lionel F, Stoker 2c, KX 76175, illness

Wednesday, 8 September 1926

Royal Naval Reserve
 D'ARCY, Richard J, Paymaster Lieutenant, RNR, illness

Thursday, 9 September 1926

Royal Naval Reserve
 THOMAS, Evan, Paymaster Lieutenant Commander, RNR, illness

Friday, 10 September 1926

Tamar, Hong Kong
 WATTS, Alexander W, Stoker 1c, K 11139, illness
 YOW, Kan, Able Seaman, (Chinese), died

Tuesday, 14 September 1926

Emerald, light cruiser
  THOMAS, Lancelot J, Able Seaman, J 45533, illness

Wednesday, 15 September 1926

RN Hospital, Chatham
  CRUST, Harold S, Sick Berth Attendant, M 39264, illness

Saturday, 18 September 1926

Pembroke, Chatham
  ADAMS, Herbert A O, Engine Room Artificer Apprentice, M 37911, illness

Monday, 20 September 1926

Pembroke, Chatham
  STEVENS, Roland, Supply Assistant, M 37956, road accident, killed

Tuesday, 21 September 1926

Delhi, light cruiser
  BREMRIDGE, James P A, Lieutenant Commander, illness

Wednesday, 22 September 1926

Veronica, sweeping fleet sloop
  SWEENEY, William H, Officer's Steward 1, 363033, illness

Thursday, 23 September 1926

Moth, river gunboat
  HOLLOWAY, Harold L, Petty Officer, J 3262, illness

Sunday, 26 September 1926

Dunedin, light cruiser
  MILLER, Allan W, Able Seaman, J 51831, drowned

Thursday, 30 September 1926

Revenge, battleship
  BUTT, Ronald A F, Signal Boy, J 112249, accidentally killed

Friday, 1 October 1926

Royal Naval Reserve
  LIST, John, Honorary Engineer Commander, RNR, illness

Victory, Portsmouth
  SMITH, George H, Able Seaman, J 100920, road accident, killed

Sunday, 3 October 1926

Wild Swan, destroyer
  BEECH, George H, Able Seaman, J 104450, illness

Wednesday, 6 October 1926

Impregnable, Devonport
  WILLSON, George, Sergeant, RM, 16333 (Ply), road accident, killed

Thursday, 7 October 1926

Britannia, RN College, Dartmouth
  WATERS, Frederick W A, Stoker 1c, K 60872, illness

Royal Oak, battleship
  UDEN, Albert E, Able Seaman, J 81315, accidentally killed

Friday, 8 October 1926

Barham, battleship
  GRIFFITHS, Ernest, Chief Petty Officer Cook, 347943, illness

Monday, 11 October 1926

Engineering Course
  METCALFE, John F, Midshipman (E), illness

Tuesday, 12 October 1926

Victory, Portsmouth
  GUTTERIDGE, Sydney G W, Leading Seaman, J 32179, illness

Friday, 15 October 1926

Broke, flotilla leader
  KREIS, Percy H, Paymaster Lieutenant, illness

Sunday, 17 October 1926

Vivid, Devonport
  DOYLE, Martin, Leading Seaman, J 15434, illness

Monday, 18 October 1926

Resolution, battleship
  HIGGINS, William, Marine, 15909 (Po), road accident, killed

Thursday, 21 October 1926

Hermes, aircraft carrier, Avro Bison seaplane of 423 Flight, flying Gibraltar to Malta, crashed into the sea 5 1/2 miles from Valetta, all killed
  ANDERSON, Joseph E S, Lieutenant (Coventry)
  GIBBS, Robert W, Telegraphist, J 81144 (Egmont)
  CARSLAKE, Henry L, Lieutenant (Egmont I)
  LAY, Hugh N, Lieutenant (Hermes)

Friday, 22 October 1926

Valerian, fleet sweeping sloop, on passage to Bermuda, foundered in hurricane off there, 19 survivors rescued from carley float by light cruiser Curlew
  ALDRED, James, Stoker 1c, K 18460
  ALLAN, Alexander, Officer's Cook 2c, L 14118
  ARIS, Frederick J, Able Seaman, J 98858

ASQUITH, James W, Gunner
BAKER, Frederick, Stoker 1c, K 22941
BARNES, Jack N, Chief Petty Officer Writer, M 8494
BEECHAM, Gilbert H, Stoker 1c, K 16245
BELLIS, William H, Commissioned Engineer
BOYES, Jack, Stoker 1c, K 63216
BRAHAM, Harry G, Petty Officer, J 31109
BRIDGER, Arthur, Stoker Petty Officer, K 21764
BRIEN, Peter J, Stoker 1c, K 57245
BROCKHURST, Archibald, Leading Stoker, K 6755
BUGG, William H, Able Seaman, J 6759
BURBERRY, Bert, Leading Stoker, K 22945
BURGESS, William, Stoker 1c, K 47262
BURROWS, Alfred H S, Stoker 1c, K 57934
CHARLES, Harold, Chief Sick Berth Attendant, M 359
CLARKE, Ernest E, Stoker 1c, K 29851
COLTHERUP, Frederick C, Joiner 1c, M 8132
COOPER, Harold A, Stoker 1c, K 60045
CRAGG, Harold, Stoker 1c, K 58062
CROW, David, Stoker 1c, K 56426
DEW, George, Stoker 1c, K 12398
DICKINSON, Jesse, Chief Engine Room Artificer 1c, M 452
DONEGAN, Ernest G, Able Seaman, 223779
DUGGAN, Frederick C, Stoker Petty Officer, 233709
EDWARDS, Leonard, Leading Signalman, J 41856
FLAKE, Frederick C, Cook, M 7107
FULBROOK, Frank, Shipwright 1c, 347150
GOWER, Frederick J B, Stoker 1c, K 62483
GRAVESTOCK, Louis B, Stoker 1c, K 56743
GREENWOOD, Arthur G, Stoker 1c, K 59964
GRIFFIN, Leonard D, Stoker 1c, K 59339
HAY, William J, Leading Cook, M 4687
HAYNES, Henry C, Able Seaman, J 95694
HEYWOOD, Ernest E, Able Seaman, J 42399
HOLDEN, Ernest, Able Seaman, J 40164
HUDSON, Joseph, Ordinary Seaman, J 111510
JAMES, Arthur G, Leading Stoker, K 14152
JAMIE, Donald F, Able Seaman, J 52449
JOINER, Colin, Surgeon Lieutenant
LEVITT, Arthur, Leading Seaman, L 17145
LILLEY, George H, Leading Stoker, K 17175
LITTLEFIELD, Albert F, Canteen Manager, Admiralty civilian
LODDER, Sydney N, Telegraphist, J 90181
McGEORGE, Reginald H, Able Seaman, J 101426
MEADOWCROFT, Allan, Able Seaman, J 94841
MEAKER, Leonard S, Able Seaman, J 108162
MUGGLETON, Leonard H J, Chief Petty Officer, 224713
NEWMAN, Percival G, Chief Engine Room Artificer 2c, M 785
NORTON, Frank, Officer's Steward 1c, L 4709
NOYCE, Alfred G, Act/Yeoman of Signals, J 22520
PAINE, Alfred E, Able Seaman, 214039
PAINE, Horace S, Officer's Steward 3c, L 13079
PAINE, William C, Engine Room Artificer 2c, M 6252
PATTERSON, William F, Supply Petty Officer, M 31842
PEYTON (Pexton in Admiralty List), Dennis G W, Able Seaman, J 89272
PHILLIPS, Frank, Stoker 1c, K 57617
PIKE, Ernest C, Able Seaman, J 8633
PINK, William G, Stoker 1c, K 23787
POLING, Raymond G, Stoker 1c, K 60480
PRESTON, James, Stoker Petty Officer, 311643
READ, Edward, Stoker Petty Officer, K 11509
ROBILLIARD, Albert F, Leading Telegraphist, J 38478
ROCHESTER, James L, Engine Room Artificer 3c, M 14974
ROMERIL, Philip E, Able Seaman, J 62692
SIVITER, George, Stoker 1c, K 11842
SMITH, Charles H, Officer's Steward 2c, L 3554
SMITH, William G, Officer's Steward 2c, L 12593
SMITH, William S, Leading Stoker, 238460
SQUIRE, William, Chief Stoker, K 10540
SUMMERFORD, Ronald B, Sub Lieutenant

SYKES, George H, Able Seaman, J 80580
TAYLOR, Harold, Regulating Petty Officer, M 35731
THOMAS, Denis H, Leading Seaman, J 73983
THOMPSON, William H, Stoker Petty Officer, K 13914
THORNBACK, James J O, Officer's Steward 1c, L 3246
THORPE, George, Stoker 1c, K 64074
USHER, Charles J, Able Seaman, J 93569
WATSON, Robert D, Able Seaman, J 28030
WELLER, William H L, Able Seaman, J 53045
WESTMACOTT, James H, Able Seaman, J 95664
WOOLNER, Frederick C, Able Seaman, J 96488
WYNN, Albert, Stoker Petty Officer, K 2436

Saturday, 23 October 1926

Marlborough, battleship
HULSE, George T, Able Seaman, J 98409, accidentally killed

Victory, Portsmouth
MORRELL, Philip H, Leading Seaman, J 47854, illness

Sunday, 24 October 1926

Barham, battleship
PERRY, Cecil J, Marine, 216432 (Po), accidentally killed

Monday, 25 October 1926

Wallflower, fleet sweeping sloop
LOWER, Lewis C, Chief Petty Officer Writer, 347962, died

Tuesday, 26 October 1926

Frobisher, cruiser
BLACKMORE, Arthur E C, Supply Chief Petty Officer, M 4550, illness

Friday, 29 October 1926

Gnat, river gunboat
WHITNEY, Edward H, Stoker 1c, K 64268, illness

Royal Navy
GRAHAM, Francis C, Warrant Ordnance Officer, illness

Sunday, 31 October 1926

Admiralty Dockyard Department
ROBERTS, Ivor E S, Engineer Captain, illness

Monday, 1 November 1926

Dolphin, Gosport
SKILLERN, Reginald R, Engine Room Artificer 4c, M 35040, illness

Thursday, 4 November 1926

Ganges, Shotley/Harwich
HARTLAND, Edward G, Boy 2c, JX 127194, illness

Marlborough, battleship
SKEWS, Nathaniel R H, Leading Seaman, J 93752, illness

Saturday, 6 November 1926

Britannia, RN College, Dartmouth
 WILKINSON, Sidney, Stoker 1c, K 35069, illness

Wednesday, 17 November 1926

Dolphin, Gosport
 AUSTEN, Henry T, Petty Officer, 233645, illness

Ramillies, battleship
 COOPER, William G, Able Seaman, J 52280, accidentally killed

Thursday, 18 November 1926

Titania, submarine depot ship
 AH, Kay, Officer's Steward 3c, (no service number listed), illness

Saturday, 20 November 1926

Diomede, light cruiser
 WELCH, Richard G, Able Seaman, J 37574, illness

Monday, 22 November 1926

Ganges, Shotley/Harwich
 SPICER, Frank A, Boy 2c, JX 28249, illness

Wednesday, 24 November 1926

Royal Marines HQ
 SMITH, James W, Marine, 19397 (Ply), illness

Thursday, 25 November 1926

Centaur, light cruiser
 LEWINGTON, Leonard F, Officer's Steward 1c, 364140, illness

Friday, 26 November 1926

Resolution, battleship
 TURNER, Ernest G, Signalman, J 64645, illness

Saturday, 4 December 1926

Dauntless, light cruiser
 NARAN, Tomas, Officer's Steward 3c, LX 20237, illness

Malaya, battleship
 JOSSER, Sydney N, Boy 1c, J 112168, drowned

Monday, 6 December 1926

Capetown, light cruiser
 KILLHAM, Frederick, Steward 1c, L 3205 (served as Charles Frederick Hills)

Impregnable, Devonport
 SULLIVAN, David F, Boy 2c, JX 126379, illness

Friday, 10 December 1926

Caradoc, light cruiser
 BROAD, John R, Electrical Artificer 1c, 347604, illness

Comus, light cruiser
 FLEMING, Patrick, Ordinary Seaman, J 107373, died

Sunday, 12 December 1926

FAA, 401 Flight, Vindictive, cruiser, air crash
 MAUDE, Maurice A, Lieutenant, killed

Tuesday, 14 December 1926

Vivid II, Devonport
 WILLIAMS, Willam J P, Petty Officer Writer, P/M 26297, died

Wednesday, 15 December 1926

Royal Naval Volunteer Reserve
 DAY, Ernest F, Honorary Lieutenant Commander, RNVR, illness

Thursday, 16 December 1926

Victory, Portsmouth
 KETTLEY, Victor, Able Seaman, J 95438, illness

Sunday, 19 December 1926

Vivid, Devonport
 DENHAM, Ernest, Petty Officer, J 13071, road accident, killed

Monday, 20 December 1926

Cairo, light cruiser
 GEARY, William, Stoker Petty Officer, K 165, illness

Tamar, Hong Kong
 TOPP, John H, Lieutenant, drowned

Tuesday, 21 December 1926

Tamar, Hong Kong
 WILLIAMS, James H, Sick Berth Petty Officer, D/M 24645, illness

Saturday, 25 December 1926

Moth, river gunboat
 PILCHER, Richard L, Able Seaman, J 91388, drowned

Monday, 27 December 1926

Royal Marines HQ
 BEVAN, Winston, Marine, 22690 (Ply), road accident, killed

Tuesday, 28 December 1926

Emerald, light cruiser
 WARREN, Edwin N, Able Seaman, J 95403, illness

Excellent, Portsmouth
 PRITCHARD, Tom, Officer's Steward 1c, 363129, illness

Wednesday, 29 December 1926

President, London
 COLES, Edwin G, Warrant Writer, illness

Vivid, Devonport
 MAUNDERS, Harry L T, Stoker Petty Officer, K 58502, died

Thursday, 30 December 1926

Royal Marines HQ
 CUSWORTH, William R, Lance Sergeant, RM, 185644, illness

Friday, 31 December 1926

Emperor of India, battleship
 ROBERTSON, Sydney L, Leading Seaman, J 21332, accidentally killed

Pembroke, Chatham
 HUNT, Herbert, Leading Seaman, J 79164, illness

Vivid, Devonport
 KENEFICK, Edward, Chief Stoker, K 190, illness

1927

January 1927

Lupin, fleet sweeping sloop
 DERIA, Yueuf, Seedie, (no service number listed), died, day not listed in record

Saturday, 1 January 1927

Impregnable, Devonport
 HOSKIN, Albert L, Boy 2c, JX 126819, illness

Monday, 3 January 1927

Pembroke I, Chatham
 SHOOBRIDGE, Ernest A, Signalman, J 51841, road accident, killed

Witherington, destroyer
 JEFFES, Charles B, Sick Berth Attendant, M 36035, drowned

Tuesday, 4 January 1927

Dunedin, light cruiser
 BAKER, Sidney C A, Able Seaman, J 102919, illness

Thursday, 6 January 1927

Royal Naval Reserve
 DUNN, Arthur E, Captain, RNR, illness

Vindictive, cruiser
 FREEBORN, Richard, Stoker 1c, K 62300, illness

Tuesday, 11 January 1927

Royal Sovereign, battleship
 DICKENSON, James W E, Ordinary Seaman, J 112240, accidentally killed

Wednesday, 12 January 1927

Royal Sovereign, battleship
 MITCHELL, Henry H, Stoker 1c, K 21403, died

Thursday, 13 January 1927

Woodcock, river gunboat
 TREADWELL, Albert W, Chief Engine Room Artificer 1c, M 714, drowned

Friday, 14 January 1927

Impregnable, Devonport
 LIFTON, Gilbert D, Boy 2c, JX 127352, died

Victory, Portsmouth
 FAIRBANKS, James, Able Seaman, J 39862, illness

Sunday, 16 January 1927

Victory, Portsmouth
 MEATON, Charles H, Leading Stoker, K 21965, illness

Tuesday, 18 January 1927

FAA, 423 Sqn, Eagle, aircraft carrier, air crash, all killed
 BURTON, George W, Leading Telegraphist, J 39729
 CHAFE, Edwin, Lieutenant
 OWENS-JONES, Guy O, Lieutenant

Saturday, 22 January 1927

Victory, Portsmouth
 HILL, Leonard T, Sailmaker, 190552, illness

Sunday, 23 January 1927

Vivid, Devonport
 ENDACOTT, Ernest H, Able Seaman, J 44817, illness

Thursday, 27 January 1927

Emperor of India, battleship
 DOWNING, Edward E G, Boy 1c, JX 125064, illness

Sunday, 30 January 1927

Witherington, destroyer
 SNEDDON, John, Able Seaman, J 43079, drowned

Tuesday, 1 February 1927

FAA, 402 Flight, Eagle, aircraft carrier, air crash
 MILLS, John Y, Lieutenant, killed

Friday, 4 February 1927

Wolsey, destroyer
 STANLEY, Watson N, Signalman, J 87460, illness

Saturday, 5 February 1927

Ganges, Shotley/Harwich
 BEAUMONT, Owen D, Boy 2c, JX 128867, illness
 GERAGHTY, John P, Boy 1c, JX 126712, illness

Wednesday, 9 February 1927

Vivid, Devonport
 HODGE, Samuel C, Chief Engine Room Artificer 2c, M 1647, illness

Thursday, 10 February 1927

Vivid, Devonport
 WATTS, William J, Stoker Petty Officer, K 10280, illness

Sunday, 13 February 1927

Pembroke, Chatham
 GURNEY, Harold C, Sick Berth Attendant, MX 45765, illness

Renown, battlecruiser
BURNETT, John E, Bandmaster 1c, RMB 1467, illness

Vindictive, cruiser
WIGHT, Robert L, Lieutenant, missing

Tuesday, 15 February 1927

Columbine, Rosyth
CROOK, Arthur C, Officer's Steward 3c, L 12003, illness

Wednesday, 16 February 1927

Malaya, battleship
BORTHWICK, William J, Able Seaman, J 40070, accidentally killed

Thursday, 17 February 1927

Victory, Portsmouth
JAMES, Frederick D, Headmaster, illness

Sunday, 20 February 1927

Pembroke, Chatham
JOHNSON, Ernest H, Leading Seaman, J 97617, road accident, killed

Monday, 21 February 1927

Argus, aircraft carrier
DOBSON, Ernest, Stoker 1c, K 66560, illness

Wednesday, 23 February 1927

Royal Navy
MACLEOD, Kenneth, Captain, illness

Monday, 28 February 1927

Coventry, light cruiser
CRITTALL, Henry, Leading Seaman, J 48747, drowned

Victory, Portsmouth
SPENDER, Stanley G, Stoker 1c, K 57853, illness

Tuesday, 1 March 1927

Pembroke, Chatham
KING, William, Petty Officer, 240039, accidentally killed

Saturday, 5 March 1927

Carlisle, light cruiser
STEPHENS, Archibald A, Shipwright 4c, M 35260, illness

Monday, 7 March 1927

Ganges, Shotley/Harwich
MURPHY, Alexander, Schoolmaster (CWO), illness

Tuesday, 8 March 1927

Vivid, Devonport
BLACKHAND, Alfred, Ordinary Seaman, SSX 12573, illness

Thursday, 10 March 1927

Weymouth, light cruiser
GODDARD, Colin F, Leading Seaman, J 10907, drowned

Saturday, 12 March 1927

K.26, submarine
HALLS, Francis W G, Yeoman of Signals, 239838 (Cyclops), drowned

Petersfield, minesweeper
SPARGO, William H, Chief Engine Room Artificer 1c, M 1057, illness

Saturday, 19 March 1927

Caradoc, light cruiser
SMALE, Reginald F, Leading Seaman, J 43418, illness

Thursday, 24 March 1927

Emerald, light cruiser
KNOX, John, Able Seaman, J 98171, killed

Tuesday, 29 March 1927

Pembroke, Chatham
HORSPOOL, Leslie G, Chief Engine Room Artificer 2c, M 6613, illness

Vivid, Devonport
FRASER, James, Stoker Petty Officer, K 4534, illness

Friday, 1 April 1927

Pembroke, Chatham
GODFREY, Joseph, Leading Seaman, J 646, illness

Monday, 4 April 1927

Chrysanthemum, convoy sloop
BABBAGE, George, Stoker Petty Officer, K 6682, accidentally killed

Tuesday, 5 April 1927

Warspite, battleship
WARD, Thomas H, Ordinary Seaman, J 113840, drowned

Monday, 11 April 1927

Wessex, destroyer
BREACH, Mark E, Officer's Steward 1c, L 3459, accidentally killed

Wednesday, 13 April 1927

Argus, aircraft carrier
  PRESTON, James S, Ordinary Seaman, SSX 12239, drowned

Thursday, 14 April 1927

Vivid, Devonport
  HINDLEY, James T, Petty Officer, J 22852, illness

Saturday, 16 April 1927

Victory, Portsmouth
  GANDER, Harry, Supply Chief Petty Officer, 229146, illness

Friday, 22 April 1927

Sandhurst, destroyer depot ship
  BEDWELL, William B, Able Seaman, J 34857, died

Sunday, 24 April 1927

Titania, submarine depot ship
  BACON, Thomas S, Able Seaman, J 97017, illness

Wednesday, 27 April 1927

Repulse, battlecruiser
  SEAGRAVE, Percy G, Painter 1c, M 5138, illness

Friday, 29 April 1927

Sterling, destroyer
  BASSETT, Thomas, Petty Officer, J 4877, drowned

Sunday, 1 May 1927

Revenge, battleship
  MITCHELL, Benjamin, Stoker 1c, KX 75243, illness

Monday, 2 May 1927

Eagle, aircraft carrier
  CURTIN, Cornelius, Engine Room Artificer 1c, M 624, illness

Monday, 9 May 1927

Argus, aircraft carrier
  ABBILL, Rowland G, Able Seaman, J 34950, illness

Concord, light cruiser
  BURNETT, Reginald J, Ordinary Seaman, J 113249, illness

H.34, submarine
  GILBERT, George E, Stoker 1c, K 55719, road accident, killed

Tamar, Hong Kong
  AUBREY, George, Surgeon Lieutenant Commander, illness

Tuesday, 10 May 1927

Tyne Division RNVR
  LEEDS, The Duke Of, Honorary Captain, RNVR, illness

Victory, Portsmouth
  CROCKER, Frederick, Stoker 1c, K 66563, illness

Thursday, 12 May 1927

Benbow, battleship
  BUCKINGHAM, John, Petty Officer, J 395, illness

Friday, 13 May 1927

Ark Royal, seaplane carrier
  DRISCOLL, Walter J, Commissioned Gunner, illness

Mantis, river gunboat
  BEST, George, Supply Petty Officer, M 10303, illness

Sunday, 15 May 1927

Benbow, battleship
  PARROTT, Albert D, Boy 1c, JX 127320, illness

Cardiff, light cruiser
  TURRELL, Arthur T, Able Seaman, J 106497, illness

Tuesday, 17 May 1927

Albury, minesweeper
  YATES, Patrick, Leading Stoker, K 12972, accidentally killed

Thursday, 19 May 1927

Benbow, battleship
  PAINTER, William B, Boy 1c, JX 127608, illness

Saturday, 21 May 1927

Ganges, Shotley/Harwich
  RAVENSCROFT, Joseph W, Boy 2c, JX 129157, illness

Sunday, 22 May 1927

Hood, battlecruiser
  CANNIFFE, James, Able Seaman, 229493, illness

Wednesday, 25 May 1927

Benbow, battleship
  HOUGH, Harold J, Ordinary Seaman, J 115155, illness

Wednesday, 1 June 1927

Alresford, minesweeper
  SMITH, Albert, Stoker 1c, K 67118, illness

Birmingham, light cruiser
  GARRETT, Alfred L, Stoker 1c, KX 75052, illness

Despatch, light cruiser
  POMEROY, Arthur E, Shipwright 2c, 346236, illness

Thursday, 2 June 1927

Barham, battleship
  GAGO, John, Officer's Cook, L 33, illness

Eagle, aircraft carrier
 ASTLEY, Harold R, Ordinary Seaman, J 109902, accidentally killed

Portsmouth Dockyard
 IMMS, David H, Commissioned Boatswain, illness

Friday, 3 June 1927

Ganges, Shotley/Harwich
 CRUICKSHANK, David A, Boy 2c, JX 129600, illness

Sunday, 5 June 1927

Barham, battleship
 FRASER, Donald R H, Paymaster Cadet, illness

Thursday, 9 June 1927

Effingham, cruiser
 WATTS, Albert E, Stoker 1c, K 65436, accidentally killed

FAA, 402 Flight, Eagle, aircraft carrier, air crash
 FORBES, Haydon M S, Lieutenant Commander, killed

Friday, 10 June 1927

Tiger, battlecruiser
 ROBERTS, Thomas R, Stoker, (no service number listed), illness

Valkyrie, destroyer
 FIELD, Robert L E, Sub Lieutenant, illness

Vivid, Devonport
 BRAGG, Frederick E, Leading Seaman, J 98090, illness

Saturday, 11 June 1927

Excellent, Portsmouth
 COATES, Edwin J, Able Seaman, 232473, illness

Vivid, Devonport
 POPE, William C, Petty Officer, 236687, illness

Sunday, 12 June 1927

Lupin, fleet sweeping sloop
 CLIFTON, George E, Signalman, J 44897, illness

Tuesday, 14 June 1927

Hood, battlecruiser
 FOX, Samuel A, Petty Officer, J 8603, illness

Wednesday, 22 June 1927

RAF Training Base, Leuchars, Scotland
 SALMOND, Rawdon F G, Lieutenant, air crash, killed

Saturday, 25 June 1927

Tenacious, destroyer
 BUTLER, John, Stoker 1c, K 61542, died

Tuesday, 28 June 1927

Hawkins, cruiser
 BAILEY, Francis H, Able Seaman, J 99122, illness

Victory, Portsmouth
 TUCK, Arthur A, Petty Officer, 225535, illness

Saturday, 2 July 1927

Effingham, cruiser
 HILL, Henry C, Midshipman, illness

Sunday, 3 July 1927

Vivid, Devonport
 HARVEY, Thomas, Joiner 1c, M 14661, died

Monday, 4 July 1927

Barham, battleship
 GLANVILLE, Auston H, Able Seaman, J 105569, died

Sunday, 10 July 1927

Conquest, light cruiser
 McGOWAN, Patrick, Leading Stoker, K 60604, drowned

Vivid, Devonport
 CAUSER, Bert H, Leading Signalman, J 38389, illness

Tuesday, 12 July 1927

Hawkins, cruiser
 FAIRMAN, Richard Morgan (also known as Richard Morgan), Leading Stoker, K 48653, illness

Wednesday, 13 July 1927

Revenge, battleship
 IDLE, Richard, Stoker Petty Officer, K 59696, illness

Thursday, 14 July 1927

Titania, submarine depot ship
 CURTIS, George, Supply Chief Petty Officer, M 1459, illness

Vivid, Devonport
 JAGO, Frank, Supply Chief Petty Officer, M 4557, road accident, killed

Friday, 15 July 1927

Ramillies, battleship, both accidentally killed
 BARKER, Albert H, Boy 1c, JX 125176
 BRAID, Alexander C, Petty Officer, J 7272

Sunday, 17 July 1927

Triad, Admiralty yacht
 SMITH, Herbert W, Stoker 1c, K 63117, illness

Wednesday, 20 July 1927

Diomede, light cruiser
 FLUSKEY, Harry T, Signalman, J 33304, illness

Thursday, 21 July 1927

Excellent, Portsmouth
 CARTER, George A, Petty Officer, 218672, illness

Friday, 22 July 1927

Victory, Portsmouth
 NICHOLAS, Richard, Leading Seaman, J 94358, illness

Saturday, 23 July 1927

Pembroke, Chatham, road accident, both killed
 FRYER, Percy S, Leading Seaman, J 11258
 WHIDDETT, Charles, Telegraphist, J 104990

Sunday, 24 July 1927

President, London
 GLANVILLE, John W V, Chief Stoker, 293909, illness

Victory, Portsmouth
 STOCKS, Frederick A, Act/Cook, MX 46255, illness

Monday, 25 July 1927

Pembroke, Chatham
 BRAIN, Frederick J, Stoker Petty Officer, K 21058, illness

Thursday, 28 July 1927

Pembroke, Chatham
 BROWN, Francis, Leading Sick Berth Attendant, M 21645, illness

Saturday, 30 July 1927

Revenge, battleship
 MARTIN, Lawrence M, Cadet, illness

Vanoc, destroyer
 LOWER, James D, Petty Officer, J 6677, road accident, killed

Sunday, 31 July 1927

Royal Sovereign, battleship
 PHILIPS, Thomas C R, Midshipman, illness

Thursday, 4 August 1927

Emperor of India, battleship
 COLE, Walter, Marine, 21783 (Ply), ex-Hood, illness

Friday, 5 August 1927

Royal Sovereign, battleship
 ZAMMIT, John, Officer's Cook 1c, L 5569, illness

Sunday, 7 August 1927

Danae, light cruiser
 HILL, Charles H, Marine, 23280 (Ch), illness

Fisgard, Portsmouth
 TONKIN, Frederick, Electrical Artificer Apprentice, MX 45299, illness

Monday, 8 August 1927

Comus, light cruiser
 CLEMOTT, Thomas, Shipwright 1c, M 8518, drowned

Pembroke, Chatham
 THIRSK, Harold, Chief Engine Room Artificer 1c, M 1590, illness

Tuesday, 9 August 1927

Tetrarch, destroyer
 BLUNDY, Frank S, Leading Stoker, K 50717, illness

Victory, Portsmouth
 FRIBBANCE, George, Leading Stoker, K 43955, illness

Thursday, 11 August 1927

Victory, Portsmouth
 HOOD, George C, Engine Room Artificer 3c, M 37005, illness

Friday, 12 August 1927

Victory, Portsmouth
 SAINSBURY, Leonard J, Supply Assistant, M 38220, illness

Saturday, 13 August 1927

Danae, light cruiser
 McGARRY, John L, Able Seaman, J 97436, illness

Sunday, 14 August 1927

Barham, battleship
 BUTLER, Henry C, Petty Officer, 228827, illness

Monday, 15 August 1927

Vivid, Devonport
 NICKELS, Denis W G, Able Seaman, J 97780, illness

Wednesday, 17 August 1927

Delhi, light cruiser
 TULL, Alfred H, Corporal, RM, 14447 (Ply), heat stroke, died

Victory I, Portsmouth
 STORIER, Arthur, Able Seaman, 239943, illness

Thursday, 18 August 1927

Emerald, light cruiser
 RYAN, Michael J, Stoker 1c, K 64655, illness

Saturday, 20 August 1927

Valiant, battleship
 PLUMTRE, Montague W, Lieutenant, illness

Monday, 22 August 1927

Furious, aircraft carrier, boiler room accident, both killed
 COPELAND, Alfred G, Engine Room Artificer 5c, M 37093
 GEALER, Reginald W, Act/Warrant Engineer

Tuesday, 23 August 1927

Hawkins, cruiser
 AH, Ming, Officer's Steward 3c, (no service number listed), illness

Wednesday, 24 August 1927

Cardiff, light cruiser
 MURLEY, Edward J, Leading Stoker, K 12273, illness

Friday, 26 August 1927

Royal Naval Reserve
 HODGMAN, Edward J, Skipper, RNR, illness

Monday, 29 August 1927

Birmingham, light cruiser
 ANSELL, John A, Stoker 1c, KX 75156, illness

Egmont, Malta
 BOYLE, James C C, Surgeon Lieutenant (ex-Wolsey), illness

Kiawo, ex-river steamer, river gunboat
 JEFFREY, Archibald, Able Seaman, J 89758, drowned

Vivid, Devonport
 McMURRAY, Frederick L, Able Seaman, J 105537, illness

Tuesday, 30 August 1927

Whirlwind, destroyer
 LUBBOCK, Albert W, Able Seaman, J 109370, road accident, killed

Thursday, 1 September 1927

Amazon, destroyer
 LAMB, Clement J, Petty Officer, J 12104, illness

Tamar, Hong Kong
 MEN, Chuen, Officer's Steward 1c, (no service number listed), died

Thursday, 15 September 1927

Royal Navy
 SESSFORD, James H, Engineer Lieutenant, illness

Friday, 16 September 1927

Tamar, Hong Kong
 CHUNG, (no other name listed), Plumber's Mate, (Chinese), died

Saturday, 17 September 1927

Vernon, Portsmouth
 CRAWFORD, Robert E, Electrical Artificer 1c, M 616, illness

Wednesday, 21 September 1927

Benbow, battleship
 ADAMS, William J, Able Seaman, J 107355, accidentally killed

President II, London
 PACKARD, Max W, Petty Officer, 173121, illness

Friday, 23 September 1927

Benbow, battleship
 SHORE, William E, Leading Stoker, K 62747, died

Saturday, 24 September 1927

Sutton, minesweeper
 ANDREWS, Edward W T, Leading Seaman, J 41479, illness

Sunday, 2 October 1927

Ganges, Shotley/Harwich
 FOX, Frederick W R, Boy 2c, JX 129344, illness

Vivid, Devonport
 SIMKINS, Albert T, Stoker 1c, KX 76998, illness

Monday, 3 October 1927

Mantis, river gunboat
 McGOWAN, Joseph, Able Seaman, J 114296, drowned

Wednesday, 5 October 1927

Danae, light cruiser
 BARNES, William J, Chief Petty Officer Writer, 345816, illness

Friday, 7 October 1927

Royal Naval Reserve
 Earl Iveagh, Honorary Lieutenant, RNR, illness

Saturday, 8 October 1927

Ladybird, river gunboat
 HOWELL, Reginald, Stoker Petty Officer, K 18653, drowned

Monday, 10 October 1927

Emerald, light cruiser
 JEFFRY, Leonard N, Shipwright 3c, M 22076, illness

Wednesday, 12 October 1927

Portsmouth, training course
 PARRY, John L, Act/Sub Lieutenant, illness

Witherington, destroyer
ELDERTON, Charles, Able Seaman, J 43592, drowned

Thursday, 13 October 1927

Flora, Simonstown, South Africa
ALI BIN ISSA, Ailee, Seedie, X 118, died

Sunday, 16 October 1927

"Undergoing Short Course of Instruction"
REES, Frederick J, Act/Warrant Supply Officer, illness

Saturday, 22 October 1927

Defiance, Devonport
HIBBERD, James H, Cook, M 38486, illness

Sunday, 23 October 1927

Tiger, battlecruiser *(below, Maritime Quest)*
SOANES, Frederick G, Able Seaman, J 97395, drowned

Tuesday, 25 October 1927

Argus, aircraft carrier
TAYLOR, Robert J R, Ordinary Seaman, SSX 12204, drowned

Excellent, Portsmouth
WATKINS, Charles J, Able Seaman, J 98026, illness

Thursday, 27 October 1927

Curlew, light cruiser
HONEYWELL, Albert E, Engine Room Artificer 2c, M 7062, illness

Victory, Portsmouth
HUMPHREY, Wallace E, Telegraphist, J 60949, illness

Friday, 28 October 1927

Vivid, Devonport
SPRIDDELL, Nicholas J, Shipwright 1c, 347387, illness

Tuesday, 1 November 1927

Impregnable, Devonport
NORLEY, Percy G, Petty Officer, J 6568, illness

Tuesday, 8 November 1927

Barham, battleship
TILLETT, William, Stoker 1c, K 65323, illness

Wednesday, 9 November 1927

Queen Elizabeth, battleship
DAVIS, George E, Marine, 16163 (Ply), accidentally killed

Saturday, 12 November 1927

Marlborough, battleship
LAWSON, William, Chief Stoker, K 618, illness

Sunday, 13 November 1927

Restless, destroyer
BOOTH, Sidney G, Leading Stoker, K 22689, accidentally killed

Monday, 14 November 1927

Fisgard, Portsmouth
MATTHEWS, Henry J, Able Seaman, J 21664, illness

Friday, 18 November 1927

Lowestoft, light cruiser
REES, Elias, Stoker 1c, KX 76195, drowned

Monday, 21 November 1927

President, London
PALMER, George L, Leading Seaman, J 27459, died

Renown, battlecruiser
ROCHFORD, John, Ordnance Artificer 4c, MX 45752, illness

Thursday, 24 November 1927

Greenwich, destroyer depot ship
ELBOURNE, Henry J L, Gunner, illness

Friday, 25 November 1927

Kiawo, ex-river steamer, river gunboat
SPARROW, Edwin W, Telegraphist, J 94124, drowned

Saturday, 26 November 1927

Pembroke, Chatham
GARLINGE, Frederick J, Leading Stoker, K 21049, illness

Sunday, 27 November 1927

Victory, Portsmouth
POVEY, Charles A, Able Seaman, J 39684, accidentally killed

Wednesday, 30 November 1927

Emerald, light cruiser
WALL, Arthur W, Able Seaman, J 6916, illness

Thursday, 8 December 1927

Vivid, Devonport
 GILPIN, Frederick, Leading Stoker, K 9480, illness

Saturday, 10 December 1927

Excellent, Portsmouth
 DORMER, Archibald P, Engineer Lieutenant Commander, illness

Wednesday, 14 December 1927

Hong Kong Dockyard
 CARROLL, John J, Surgeon Lieutenant Commander, illness

Saturday, 17 December 1927

Lowestoft, light cruiser
 HOLTON, Cecil, Stoker 1c, K 57457, illness

Sunday, 18 December 1927

Ursula, destroyer
 DEAR, Ivo L, Able Seaman, J 94740, accidentally killed

Tuesday, 20 December 1927

Revenge, battleship
 VANSTONE, Jim, Commissioned Supply Officer, illness

Wednesday, 21 December 1927

Vernon, Portsmouth
 BRISTOW, John G, Plumber 2c, M 34887, street accident, killed

Thursday, 22 December 1927

Vindictive, cruiser
 PERKINS, James H, Chief Petty Officer, J 403, drowned

Friday, 23 December 1927

Philomel, ex-cruiser, depot ship, New Zealand
 HOUGHTON, Walter C, Engine Room Artificer 2c, M 14971, illness

Saturday, 24 December 1927

Vampire, destroyer
 HASARL, Frederick L, Chief Stoker, K 16139 (served as Frederick L Barnes), illness

Sunday, 25 December 1927

Diomede, light cruiser
 WOODRUFF, William H, Marine, 22484 (Ply), accidentally killed

Saturday, 31 December 1927

Rodney, battleship
 ALLEN, Thomas C, Stoker 1c, K 24703, illness

1928

Monday, 2 January 1928

Dunedin, light cruiser
 WEAVING, Henry J, Marine, 22438 (Ply), accidentally killed

Sandhurst, destroyer depot ship
 ALDIS, Charles W, Electrical Artificer 1c, M 9367, illness

Tuesday, 3 January 1928

Ramillies, battleship
 MUNNO, Charles J, Yeoman of Signals, 239367, illness

Thursday, 5 January 1928

Egmont, Malta
 GREEN, Frank, Commissioned Engineer, illness

Saturday, 7 January 1928

Lupin, fleet sweeping sloop
 STEVENS, Walter, Stoker Petty Officer, K 7821, illness

Verity, destroyer
 FOSTER, Walter, Able Seaman, J 105336, illness

Monday, 9 January 1928

Vindictive, cruiser
 MANTON, Walter H, Marine, 22513 (Ply), illness

Wednesday, 11 January 1928

Vernon, Portsmouth
 FUDGE, George, Commissioned Gunner, illness

Friday, 13 January 1928

Pangbourne, minesweeper
 O'SULLIVAN, John J, Stoker Petty Officer, K 62603, illness

Monday, 16 January 1928

Ramillies, battleship
 DRUGGAN, Thomas, Stoker 1c, KX 76889, illness

Tuesday, 17 January 1928

Pembroke, Chatham
 GOLEBY, Leonard E, Able Seaman, J 104429, road accident, killed

Friday, 20 January 1928

Royal Navy
 de ROBECK, Sir John M, Admiral of the Fleet, illness

Wednesday, 25 January 1928

Crocus, fleet sweeping sloop
 ABDULLAH, Ahmed, Seedie Stoker, (no service number listed), died

Verity, destroyer
 COOPER, Sidney F, Stoker 1c, KX 77402, illness

Saturday, 28 January 1928

Victory, Portsmouth
 JOHNSON, Leslie T, Telegraphist, J 94125, illness

Wednesday, 1 February 1928

Royal Naval Reserve
 BAILEY, Walter S, Honorary Lieutenant, RNR, illness

Thursday, 2 February 1928

Cyclops, repair ship
 COOK, Robert, Able Seaman, J 103562, illness

Vivid, Devonport
 DICKINSON, Cecil C, Lieutenant Commander, illness

Saturday, 4 February 1928

Tern, river gunboat
 ROWELL, Alfred C, Petty Officer, J 15045, illness

Vulcan, depot ship
 STEBBING, William F, Stoker 1c, K 61886, accidentally killed

Tuesday, 7 February 1928

Royal Naval Volunteer Reserve
 TINKER, Henry W C, Ty/Honorary Lieutenant Commander, RNVR, illness

Victory, Portsmouth
 TADD, Charles W, Stoker 2c, KX 78062, illness

Thursday, 9 February 1928

Cyclamen, fleet sweeping sloop
 BELA, Husif, Stoker Seedie, (no service number listed), illness

Enterprise, light cruiser
 DYER, Albert E, Able Seaman, J 103385, illness

Friday, 10 February 1928

Sirdar, destroyer
 SHAW, Fred, Stoker Petty Officer, K 7917, illness

Monday, 13 February 1928

Delhi, light cruiser
 CARPENTER, Henry L, Schoolmaster (ex-Curlew), illness

Tuesday, 14 February 1928

Diomede, light cruiser
 CARR, John G O, Telegraphist, J 51463, illness

Renown, battlecruiser
 SPENCER, Hon Cecil E R, Lieutenant Commander, illness

Saturday, 18 February 1928

Columbine, Rosyth
 ARNOT, David, Chief Yeoman of Signals, 233591, illness

Monday, 20 February 1928

Emperor of India, battleship
 HUGHES, Wilson, Marine, 17810 (Ply), illness

Tuesday, 21 February 1928

Wivern, destroyer
 KENNARD, Michael S, Able Seaman, J 10427, illness

Thursday, 23 February 1928

Vivid, Devonport
 NICHOLSON, Roland, Able Seaman, J 108665, illness

Saturday, 25 February 1928

St Vincent, Gosport
 COX, Frank, Leading Stoker, K 1162, illness

Sunday, 26 February 1928

Columbine, Rosyth
 MIDDLEDITCH, Frederick J, Able Seaman, J 98494, illness

Thursday, 1 March 1928

Pembroke, Chatham
 SPRINGETT, James E, Able Seaman, J 4305, illness

Monday, 5 March 1928

Titania, submarine depot ship
 GARRETT, Ernest W, Chief Engine Room Artificer 1c, M 3192, illness

Friday, 9 March 1928

Tamar, Hong Kong
 ROUGH, Ronald M, Able Seaman, J 103030, shot by local guards, killed

Sunday, 11 March 1928

Impregnable, Devonport
 CARR, George A, Boy 2c, JX 130747, illness

Marlborough, battleship
 GRIGSON, Frederick W, Leading Seaman, 240073, illness

Thursday, 15 March 1928

Windsor, destroyer
 BARLOW, Frederick W, Stoker Petty Officer, K 62738, illness

Friday, 16 March 1928

Impregnable, Devonport
 SISK, Richard, Boy 2c, JX 129690, illness

Saturday, 17 March 1928

Blanche, fishing trawler
 PIPE, William T, Skipper, RNR, illness

Sunday, 18 March 1928

Royal Navy
 CARTER, William E, Engineer Commander, illness

Tuesday, 20 March 1928

Vivid, Devonport
 TOMLINSON, William W, Stoker Petty Officer, K 485, illness

Thursday, 22 March 1928

Birmingham, 2nd class cruiser
 BRISTOW, Clifford L, Engine Room Artificer 4c, M 39528, died

Friday, 23 March 1928

Royal Naval Reserve
 COLLINS, Edward, Honorary Captain, RNR, illness

Royal Oak, battleship
 BURDY, Wallace J, Leading Signalman, J 37130, illness

Saturday, 24 March 1928

Royal Navy
 KENT, Henry E, Warrant Engineer, illness

Monday, 26 March 1928

Greenwich, destroyer depot ship
 GIBSON, William Mc L, Sick Berth Petty Officer, M 4131, illness

Tuesday, 27 March 1928

Bruce, flotilla leader
 WHITFIELD, George W, Stoker 1c, K 67000, accidentally killed

Wednesday, 28 March 1928

Fisgard, Portsmouth
 SHIRES, John E, Engine Room Artificer Apprentice, MX 45253, illness

Friday, 30 March 1928

Whirlwind, destroyer
 REDPATH, James F, Able Seaman, J 34210, died

Tuesday, 3 April 1928

FAA, 440 Flight, Hermes, aircraft carrier, air crash, both killed
 GRAHAM, John H P, Lieutenant
 JACKSON, Stanley, Telegraphist, J 77956

Thursday, 5 April 1928

Emerald, light cruiser
 PASCOE, John, Stoker Petty Officer, K 18892, illness

Sutton, minesweeper, road accident, both killed
 DAVIS, William F, Stoker Petty Officer, K 11817
 KING, Arthur J, Stoker Petty Officer, K 19344

Friday, 6 April 1928

Adventure, minelayer
 RULE, Samuel J, Leading Stoker, K 24541, drowned

Saturday, 7 April 1928

Pembroke, Chatham
 HEINSEN, Alfred W, Able Seaman, J 109121, illness

Tuesday, 10 April 1928

Pembroke, Chatham
 COOK, Edward, Signalman, J 107346, road accident, killed
 FRIEND, George J, Able Seaman, J 87667, road accident, killed
 PETTMAN, Herbert H, Stoker 1c, K 65730, illness

Wednesday, 11 April 1928

Waterhen, destroyer
 SMITH, Sidney I, Stoker 1c, K 62449, illness

Thursday, 12 April 1928

Petersfield, minesweeper
 LAI, Ying K, Stoker 2c, (no service number listed), died

Friday, 13 April 1928

Vivid, Devonport
 FAIRCLOUGH, Michael, Leading Seaman, 188414, illness

Saturday, 14 April 1928

Pembroke, Chatham
 KENNEDY, Thomas, Stoker 2c, KX 79070, illness

Royal Sovereign, battleship
 SCOTT, William H, Engine Room Artificer 1c, M 1655, accidentally killed

Sunday, 15 April 1928

Clematis, fleet sweeping sloop
 SHIRLEY, Gerald A, Stoker 1c, K 19504, died

Monday, 16 April 1928

Victory, Portsmouth
 TOMPKINS, Joseph G, Petty Officer, J 6002, illness

Vidette, destroyer
 LONG, Harold R, Leading Seaman, J 80028, died

Tuesday, 17 April 1928

Marshal Soult, monitor
 ASTON, Samuel, Leading Stoker, KX 75995, illness

Wednesday, 18 April 1928

Pembroke, Chatham
 DAVIES, David, Able Seaman, J 96644, illness

Queen Elizabeth, battleship
 CRIDLAND, Henry J, Stoker 1c, KX 76592, illness

Wednesday, 25 April 1928

Iron Duke, battleship
 WATKINS, James G, Warrant Engineer, illness

Thursday, 26 April 1928

Royal Navy
 BAKER, Henry J, Supply Petty Officer, M 35120, illness

Sunday, 29 April 1928

Dolphin, Gosport
 HURD, Edwin G, Officer's Cook 1c, L 411, illness

Royal Marines HQ
 DREW, Stanley W, Marine, G/X 318, illness

Monday, 30 April 1928

Dolphin, Gosport
 SHAW, William, Stoker 1c, K 18174, illness

Wednesday, 2 May 1928

Vivid, Devonport
 PARFITT, James H, Engine Room Artificer 2c, M 24132, illness

Friday, 4 May 1928

Effingham, cruiser
 BLAGG, George, Stoker 1c, K 61495, accidentally killed

Monday, 7 May 1928

Excellent, Portsmouth
 DOWNEY, Cyril F, Officer's Cook 1c, L 7085, died

Pembroke, Chatham
 BEALES, Henry A, Chief Petty Officer, 233857, accidentally killed

Tiger, battlecruiser
 NEALE, George, Able Seaman, J 99423, illness

Wednesday, 9 May 1928

Sandhurst, destroyer depot ship
 BOYD, William, Supply Petty Officer, M 3879, illness

Saturday, 12 May 1928

FAA, 446 Flight, Courageous, ex-battlecruiser, aircraft carrier
 CARTER, Percival R, Telegraphist, J 70337, aircraft accident, DOI

Monday, 14 May 1928

Victory, Portsmouth
 CADELL, Alexander R, Lieutenant, illness

Saturday, 19 May 1928

Dauntless, light cruiser
 POTTS, John E, Able Seaman, J 27413, died

Tuesday, 22 May 1928

H.24, submarine
 GOSWELL, Arthur F, Leading Seaman, J 31277, drowned

Wednesday, 23 May 1928

Hermes, aircraft carrier
 BOLAM, Thomas, Warrant Engineer, illness

Warspite, battleship
 WAKE, William G, Chief Stoker, K 16568, accidentally killed

Friday, 25 May 1928

L.3, submarine
 WOODS, Albert, Leading Stoker, K 5318, illness

Tuesday, 29 May 1928

Rodney, battleship
 INGOLDSBY, George, Able Seaman, J 100648, illness

June 1928

Royal Marines HQ,
 NORMAN, George T, Colour Sergeant, RM, B 15674, died, day not listed in record

Tuesday, 5 June 1928

Ramillies, battleship
 WEEKS, Reginald J C, Marine, 23153 (Ch), illness, died in RN Hospital Malta

Vernon, Portsmouth
 HORSWELL, Alfred R, Petty Officer, J 16410, illness

Thursday, 7 June 1928

Wishart, destroyer
 ESSAM, Charles A W, Gunner, illness

Friday, 8 June 1928

Veronica, fleet sweeping sloop
 BIGGS, Archibald A G, Able Seaman, J 43366, illness

Saturday, 9 June 1928

Ramillies, battleship
 HUMPHREYS, William G, Leading Seaman, J 53757, illness

Tuesday, 12 June 1928

Barham, battleship
 LEDWORD, Charles H, Marine, 215079 (Po), accidentally killed

Thursday, 14 June 1928

Yarmouth, light cruiser
 GILLMORE, Charles R, Ordinary Seaman, J 112780, illness

Saturday, 16 June 1928

Enterprise, light cruiser
 LOVEGROVE, John W, Mechanician, K 16698, illness
 FRANCIS, William, Stoker 1c, K 11660, illness

Cardiff, light cruiser
 NORTH, Percy B, Ordinary Seaman, JX 125329, illness

Tuesday, 19 June 1928

Rodney, battleship
 ROGERS, Arthur R, Officer's Steward 4c, LX 20362, illness

Wednesday, 20 June 1928

FAA, 403 Flight, Hermes, aircraft carrier
 ALDRIDGE, Raymond A, Lieutenant, air crash, air crash, killed

Ormonde, ex-sloop, survey ship *(below, Cyber Heritage)*
 CHAMBERLAIN, Henry, Able Seaman, J 7481, illness

Pembroke, Chatham
 BARLING, Charles F, Engine Room Artificer 3c, M 27333, illness

Thursday, 21 June 1928

Diomede, fleet sweeping sloop
 CARTER, Frank, Chief Electrical Artificer 1c, M 201, illness

Friday, 22 June 1928

Woodarra, steamship
 JONES, Derek H A, Py/Midshipman, RNR, illness

Saturday, 23 June 1928

Cumberland, heavy cruiser
 ENDERBY, Frederick, Ordinary Seaman, J 112342, illness

Monday, 25 June 1928

FAA, 463 Sqn, Courageous, ex-battlecruiser, aircraft carrier, air crash
 NICHOLSON, John, Lieutenant, killed

Thursday, 28 June 1928

Cyclamen, fleet sweeping sloop
 BARNES, William, Commissioned Engineer, illness

Saturday, 30 June 1928

Rodney, battleship
 REED, George H, Leading Seaman, J 2608, drowned

Monday, 2 July 1928

Pembroke, Chatham
 HURLEY, Joseph, Able Seaman, J 12837, illness

Viscount, destroyer
 HAWTHORN, George E, Leading Stoker, K 60245, illness

Wednesday, 4 July 1928

Impregnable, Devonport
 STUART, Robert J, Warrant Writer, illness

Kiawo, ex-river steamer, river gunboat
 RANDALL, William H, Leading Supply Assistant, M 38226, accidentally killed

Thursday, 5 July 1928

Centurion, target ship
 HATTON, Ronald F, Supply Petty Officer, M 32054, illness

Friday, 6 July 1928

Barham, battleship
 LLOYD, Joseph A, Leading Seaman, J 01118, illness

Sunday, 8 July 1928

Vivid, Devonport
 BAMPTON, Arthur, Able Seaman, J 108390, road accident, killed

Monday, 9 July 1928

Carlisle, light cruiser
 FAWCETT, Harry W, Marine, 21934 (Ch), illness

Wednesday, 11 July 1928

Pembroke, Chatham
 MITCHELL, Alfred D, Petty Officer, J 24827, illness

Saturday, 14 July 1928

Marlborough, battleship
 TAYLOR, William O' F, Boy 1c, JX 140419, accidentally killed

Sunday, 15 July 1928

Pembroke, Chatham
 DAWSON, Leslie T, Ordinary Seaman, J 112750, illness

Monday, 16 July 1928

Berwick, heavy cruiser
 BARTLETT, Harry L, Telegraphist, J 108182, illness

H.50, submarine
 BAKER, Charles F, Able Seaman, J 48065, road accident, killed

Tuesday, 17 July 1928

Pembroke, Chatham
 FAYER, Edward F, Leading Stoker, K 52364, drowned

Wednesday, 18 July 1928

Courageous, ex-battlecruiser, aircraft carrier
 FIDLER, Archibald F, Able Seaman, J 60983, accidentally killed

Saturday, 21 July 1928

Royal Naval Reserve
 CARROLL, George, Lieutenant Commander, RNR, illness

Wednesday, 25 July 1928

Berwick, heavy cruiser
 OSBORNE, Otto V (real name, but served as Otto Furneaux), Musician, RMB 1273 , illness

Vivid, Devonport
 BRAY, John, Chief Petty Officer Cook, 347534, illness

Friday, 3 August 1928

Cyclamen, fleet sweeping sloop
 BRADLEY, Robert G, Stoker 1c, K 21424, illness

Furious, aircraft carrier
　MOORE, Edmund L D, Lieutenant, killed

Monday, 6 August 1928

Lowestoft, light cruiser
　HOPLEY, Ernest, Stoker 1c, K 7532, illness

St Vincent, Gosport
　HAWKINS, Alfred J G, Boy 2c, JX 31987, illness

Tuesday, 7 August 1928

Flora, Simonstown, South Africa
　HASSAM, Suleiman B, Seedie, X 230, illness

Thursday, 9 August 1928

Sterling, destroyer
　WALSH, William, Stoker 1c, K 21647, illness

Wednesday, 15 August 1928

Columbine, Rosyth
　JOHNSON, William, Leading Seaman, J 63059, road accident, killed

Thursday, 23 August 1928

Cambrian, light cruiser
　TUMBER, John W, Engine Room Artificer 2c, M 7094, road accident, killed *(Mrs Tumber also died in the accident)*

Sunday, 26 August 1928

Ambrose, submarine depot ship
　BIDWELL, Norman R, Petty Officer, J 13512, died

Sunday, 26 August 1928

Lucia, submarine depot ship
　NEILSON, Stanley, Leading Stoker, K 6673, illness

Resolution, battleship
　COOK, George P, Leading Stoker, K 27636, drowned

Monday, 27 August 1928

Curlew, light cruiser
　HALLETT, Robert, Corporal, RM, 18527 (Ply), illness

Friday, 31 August 1928

Veronica, fleet sweeping sloop
　NICHOLS, Christopher H, Commissioned Engineer, illness

Tuesday, 4 September 1928

Despatch, light cruiser
　RICHARDS, William A, Electrical Artificer 2c, M 26877, road accident, killed

Thursday, 6 September 1928

FAA, 422 Sqn, Argus, aircraft carrier, air crash, all killed
　BOOTH, Charles S, Lieutenant
　GRIGSON, Edmond G B, Telegraphist, J 77760
　HALTON, Samuel, Pilot Officer RAF

Friday, 7 September 1928

Scarab, river gunboat
　WEST, Frank, Leading Supply Assistant, M 37485, illness

Sunday, 9 September 1928

Venomous, destroyer
　GREGG, Claude J M, Sub Lieutenant, illness

Victory, Portsmouth
　MORRIS, Frank, Electrical Artificer 4c, MX 47096, illness

Tuesday, 11 September 1928

Rodney, battleship
　WEEKS, William B, Boy 1c, JX 127358, accidentally killed

Monday, 17 September 1928

Emperor of India, battleship
　COLLETT, Leonard S, Marine, 21700 (Ply), illness

Royal Oak, battleship
　GILBERT, George W H, Leading Seaman, J 42464, accidentally killed

Thruster, destroyer
　REED, William J S, Able Seaman, J 62895, road accident, killed

Tuesday, 18 September 1928

Pembroke, Chatham
　BAKER, George C, Warrant Supply Officer, illness

Saturday, 22 September 1928

Frobisher, cruiser
　BORG, John, Officer's Steward 1c, LX 20438, illness

Sunday, 23 September 1928

Royal Naval Reserve
　KING, Samuel G, Chief Skipper, RNR, illness

Sunday, 30 September 1928

Tamar, Hong Kong
　BAMFORD, Edward, Major, RM, illness

Monday, 1 October 1928

Cornflower, fleet sweeping sloop
　COOKE, Reginald, Stoker 1c, K 5547, illness

Tuesday, 2 October 1928

Royal Navy
 MASTERS, Charles J, Chief Petty Officer, J 2296, died

Wednesday, 3 October 1928

Enterprise, light cruiser
 KELLY, John W, Marine, 24393 (Ch), illness

Saturday, 6 October 1928

Ganges, Shotley/Harwich
 HICKMAN, Alfred H J, Boy 2c, JX 132367, accidentally killed

Thursday, 11 October 1928

Pembroke, Chatham
 BATCHELOR, Frederick G H, Mechanician, K 1533, illness

Thursday, 18 October 1928

Barham, battleship
 ROBERTS, Arthur C, Ordinary Seaman, JX 127593, accidentally killed

Cockchafer, river gunboat
 CURSENS, Alfred H, Stoker 1c, K 63460, illness

Monday, 22 October 1928

Nelson, battleship *(below, Maritime Quest)*
 WELLS, John J R, Marine, X 6 (Po), illness

RN Hospital, Plymouth
 HORNE, Reginald J, Leading Sick Berth Attendant, D/M 19542, illness

Wednesday, 24 October 1928

Effingham, cruiser
 ROBBINS, George A, Able Seaman, J 105630, illness

Friday, 26 October 1928

Royal Marines HQ
 GOUGE, William A, Sergeant Major, 21832 (Deal), illness

Sunday, 28 October 1928

Centaur, light cruiser
 DAVISON, James R, Stoker 1c, K 56119, train accident, killed

Portsmouth Dockyard
 BIRD, Rev EDWARD G, Chaplain, illness

Monday, 29 October 1928

Royal Naval Volunteer Reserve
 MACINTYRE, John, Honorary Surgeon Commander, RNVR, illness

Tuesday, 30 October 1928

Voyager, destroyer
 SAMUEL, John, Chief Petty Officer, J 4791, torpedo accident, killed

Wednesday, 31 October 1928

Tamar, Hong Kong
 AH, Lum, Officer's Steward 3c, (no service number listed), died

Thursday, 1 November 1928

City of Harvard, steamship
 LARGE, Edwin R, Captain, RNR, illness

Vivid, Devonport
 HARWOOD, Ernest R, Leading Seaman, J 90941, illness

Friday, 2 November 1928

New Zealand Division of Royal Navy, on loan to
 TURNER, Stephen L, Warrant Engineer, illness

Monday, 5 November 1928

Carysfort, light cruiser
 ROSSITER, John, Commissioned Signal Boatswain, illness

Ceres, light cruiser
 YELLOP, Charles E, Petty Officer, J 36297, died

Terror, monitor
 NEWPORT, John, Stoker 1c, K 1189, died

Wednesday, 7 November 1928

Cornflower, fleet sweeping sloop
 FULLER, George B, Leading Telegraphist, J 48642, illness

Thursday, 8 November 1928

Furious, aircraft carrier
 GORDON, Robert W, Lieutenant, RM, illness

Friday, 9 November 1928

Kent, heavy cruiser
 COLLINS, Edgar G, Leading Stoker, K 23859, illness

Pembroke, Chatham
 KEEBLE, John E, Leading Supply Assistant, M 37378, illness

Victory, Portsmouth
  POLLARD, Henry W, Signalman, J 90130, illness

Saturday, 10 November 1928

RN Hospital, Chatham
  SMITH, Sydney J, Sick Berth Attendant, C/M 38532, illness

Sunday, 11 November 1928

Fitzroy, minesweeper, completed as survey ship
  BATE, John M I, Shipwright 3c, M 34326, accidentally killed

Pembroke, Chatham
  BROWN, Richard J, Engineer Commander, illness

Wednesday, 14 November 1928

Lupin, fleet sweeping sloop
  DE SOUZA, Joao V, Cook 2c, 356465, illness

Vega, destroyer
  HOWELL, Harry, Able Seaman, J 92392, illness

Thursday, 15 November 1928

Cornflower, fleet sweeping sloop
  LLOYD, George V, Able Seaman, J 112402, died
  O'HARA, Robert, Able Seaman, J 12732, died

Friday, 16 November 1928

Champion, light cruiser
  GARDNER, Hugh, Officer's Steward 3c, L 13534, illness

Eagle, aircraft carrier
  WITHERS, George R, Ordinary Seaman, JX 125605, drowned

Excellent, Portsmouth
  LAMBERT, Arthur, Ordnance Artificer 2c, M 11751, road accident, killed

Monday, 19 November 1928

Hood, battlecruiser
  SALES, Arthur J, Petty Officer, J 13923, illness

Royal Naval Reserve
  BOWMAN, Henry, Chief Skipper, RNR, illness

Thursday, 22 November 1928

RN Hospital, Plymouth
  EVES, William H, Paymaster Captain, illness

Sunday, 25 November 1928

Clyde Division RNVR
  HENRY, James A, Honorary Lieutenant, RNVR, illness

Peterel, river gunboat
  LANSDELL, William J, Stoker 1c, K 58445, drowned

Monday, 26 November 1928

Malabar, Bermuda
  FIGGETT, Arthur P, Able Seaman, J 102645, drowned

PC.74, patrol boat
  PASH, Sidney E, Petty Officer, J 99424, illness

Victory, Portsmouth
  GOODEY, Walter E, Leading Cook, M 5855, illness

Tuesday, 27 November 1928

Stuart, flotilla leader
  SULTANA, Joseph, Officer's Steward 3c, LX 20270, illness

Saturday, 1 December 1928

Pembroke, Chatham
  RUDGE, Anthony M, Stoker 1c, K 61362, illness

Saturday, 8 December 1928

Pembroke, Chatham
  TRUMBLY, Benjamin, Able Seaman, J 2192, illness

Wednesday, 12 December 1928

Furious, aircraft carrier
  FRANKS, George F, Telegraphist, J 100304, illness

Friday, 14 December 1928

Cricket, river gunboat
  SCOTT, Henry J, Surgeon Lieutenant, drowned

Monday, 17 December 1928

Pembroke, Chatham
  TREVELYN, Roger de T, Lieutenant, illness

Thursday, 20 December 1928

Witch, destroyer
  LEE, Frank, Able Seaman, J 103081, died

Saturday, 22 December 1928

Kent, heavy cruiser
  CHAUB, Edgar C, Leading Signalman, J 15794, drowned

Monday, 24 December 1928

Defiance, Devonport
  JONES, Herbert F, Petty Officer, J 36662, road accident, killed

Tuesday, 25 December 1928

Gnat, river gunboat
  RIED, Frederick T, Stoker Petty Officer, K 18667, illness

Friday, 28 December 1928

Douglas, flotilla leader
 HILDICK, James, Commissioned Gunner, illness

Saturday, 29 December 1928

Repulse, battlecruiser
 POWELL, Herbert, Stoker 1c, K 66627, drowned

Monday, 31 December 1928

Ganges, Shotley/Harwich
 BROWN, Leslie C F, Boy 2, SX 122166, illness

1929

Wednesday, 2 January 1929

Fisgard, Portsmouth
TURTLE, Arthur V, Stoker 1c, K 61242, died

Renown, battlecruiser
BAKER, Sydney W, Boy 2c, JX 128200, accidentally killed

Thursday, 3 January 1929

Egmont, Malta
BRACE, George W, Stoker Petty Officer, K 7108, (Wolsey), illness

Frobisher, cruiser
WILSON, John, Commissioned Engineer, illness

Saturday, 5 January 1929

Royal Marines HQ
BESTLEY, Oliver C, Marine, A 24365 (Ch), illness

Warspite, battleship
QUIN, Augustine W, Marine, 215839 (Po), illness

Sunday, 6 January 1929

Herald, ex-fleet sweeping sloop Merry Hampton, survey ship
NG, Fook, Officer's Cook 3c, (no service number listed), died

Monday, 7 January 1929

St Vincent, Gosport
ALLCOM, Eli F J, Boy 2c, JX 132417, illness

Tuesday, 8 January 1929

Renown, battlecruiser
STANFORD, Ernest E, Commissioned Gunner, illness

Thursday, 10 January 1929

Daffodil, fleet sweeping sloop
EDWARDS, Albert E, Able Seaman, J 32905, illness

Friday, 11 January 1929

Danae, light cruiser
JERVIS, Geoffrey, Boy 1c, JX 129450, illness

Victory, Portsmouth
ETHERINGTON, Harry T, Leading Stoker, K 12739, illness

Monday, 14 January 1929

Greenwich, destroyer depot ship
DUNCAN, Henry, Telegraphist, J 93280, illness

Pembroke, Chatham
FITZPATRICK, Charles A, Chief Stoker, K 15291, illness

Tuesday, 15 January 1929

Bee, river gunboat
LITTLEDALE, Bernard J, Commander (E), illness

Sunday, 20 January 1929

Pembroke, Chatham
TEMPLE, Harry P, Able Seaman, J 93647, drowned

Monday, 21 January 1929

H.33, submarine
NETTALL, Fred, Chief Engine Room Artificer 2c, M 7307, illness

Vivid, Devonport
NEEDHAM, Tom, Leading Seaman, J 7891, illness

Tuesday, 22 January 1929

Vivid, Devonport
MAXWELL, Henry S, Chief Petty Officer Writer, M 7313, illness

Wednesday, 23 January 1929

Royal Naval Reserve
DOWNINE, Alexander P, Paymaster Commander, RNR, illness

Friday, 25 January 1929

Castor, light cruiser
CHONG, Ah, Officer's Steward 1c, (no service number listed), died

Saturday, 26 January 1929

Pembroke, Chatham
SMITH, George J, Cook, M 36574, illness

Tuesday, 29 January 1929

Greenwich, destroyer depot ship
RANDALL, John M, Stoker 1c, K 55547, illness

Thursday, 31 January 1929

Benbow, battleship
YARLETT, Walter A, Able Seaman, J 52986, illness

London Division, RNVR
LOCKETT, Herbert A, Paymaster Commander, RNVR, illness

Friday, 1 February 1929

Warspite, battleship
FRANCIS, Arthur W, Ordinary Seaman, JX 126147, illness

Saturday, 2 February 1929

Gnat, river gunboat
TIMMS, Reginald A, Petty Officer, J 25827, illness

Sepoy, destroyer
  WHITE, Edmond H, Able Seaman, J 85394, illness

Monday, 4 February 1929

Furious, aircraft carrier
  BROWN, Harry G, Stoker 1c, K 8124, illness

Marlborough, battleship
  HUME, John H D, Able Seaman, J 16805, illness

Wednesday, 6 February 1929

FAA, 441 Flight, Argus, aircraft carrier, air crash
  CECIL, Richard F B, Lieutenant, killed
  GRANT, Heathcote A J, Lieutenant, DOI

Royal Marines HQ
  HARTWILL, William, Marine, E 16529, illness

Thursday, 7 February 1929

Courageous, ex-battlecruiser, aircraft carrier
  CHRISTIE, Charles P, Lieutenant Commander, illness

Vivid, Devonport
  FRY, Harry, Stoker Petty Officer, K 16115, illness

Monday, 11 February 1929

Defiance, Devonport
  COLE, Ernest, Petty Officer, J 7325, illness

Pembroke, Chatham
  STOREY, Edward C, Ordinary Seaman, SSX 13238, illness

Tuesday, 12 February 1929

Egmont, Malta
  HEARN, Francis M, Able Seaman, J 109767, illness

Saturday, 16 February 1929

Berwick, heavy cruiser
  KEMPSHALL, William A, Engine Room Artificer 2c, M 28880, drowned

Effingham, cruiser
  RINGSHAW, William, Electrical Artificer 1c, M 6026, illness

Monday, 18 February 1929

Victory, Portsmouth
  MERRYWEATHER, John C, Petty Officer, J 8602, illness

Monday, 25 February 1929

Pembroke, Chatham
  ALLEN, Alexander, Supply Chief Petty Officer, M 1029, illness

Victory, Portsmouth
  HARRISON, Edward H, Leading Seaman, 239613, illness

Tuesday, 26 February 1929

Excellent, Portsmouth
  JARVIS, Francis H, Officer's Cook, 360324, illness

Malaya, battleship
  JONES, David, Petty Officer, J 31300, illness

Friday, 1 March 1929

Eagle, aircraft carrier
  CORLETT, Douglas, Ordinary Seaman, J 113269, drowned

Saturday, 2 March 1929

Vivid, Devonport
  WHATFORD, Harry A, Able Seaman, J 25900, illness

Sunday, 3 March 1929

Castor, light cruiser
  ANDERSON, Frederick C, Stoker 1c, K 19512, illness

Monday, 4 March 1929

Royal Naval Reserve
  HIGNETT, Samuel M, Paymaster Lieutenant Commander, RNR, illness

Tuesday, 5 March 1929

St Vincent, Gosport
  HARFIELD, William L, Shipwright Lieutenant, illness

Saturday, 9 March 1929

Adventure, minelayer
  DURCAN, James, Stoker Petty Officer, K 2237, illness

Pembroke, Chatham
  EATON, Joseph S, Stoker Petty Officer, K 395, illness

Sunday, 10 March 1929

Enterprise, light cruiser
  COELLO, Vincent C, Officer's Steward 1c, L 11945, illness

Monday, 11 March 1929

Royal Navy
  KING, Albert E, Leading Stoker, K 60859, illness

Wednesday, 13 March 1929

Pembroke, Chatham
  STANLEY, Harry E, Able Seaman, J 102399, illness

Victory, Portsmouth
  AVIS, Alfred E, Stoker Petty Officer, K 18121, illness

Thursday, 14 March 1929

Vivid, Devonport
  POTTER, Douglas P, Electrical Artificer 4c, M 8032, illness

Friday, 15 March 1929

Victory, Portsmouth
 FUNNELL, Denis H, Stoker 2c, KX 79703, illness

Saturday, 16 March 1929

Pembroke, Chatham
 SMITH, John C, Able Seaman, J 107989, illness

Sunday, 17 March 1929

Pembroke, Chatham
 CARN, Francis C, Stoker 1c, K 58953, illness

Wednesday, 20 March 1929

Pembroke, Chatham
 HAYCOCK, Albert, Able Seaman, J 100477, illness

Thursday, 21 March 1929

Royal Sovereign, battleship
 BLACKLOCK, Percy R, Chief Engine Room Artificer 1c, M 1355, illness

Friday, 22 March 1929

Rodney, battleship
 DAVIES, David J, Stoker 1c, K 19673, illness

Vivid, Devonport, accident
 ALLEN, James A, Chief Petty Officer, J 1811, accidentally killed

Saturday, 23 March 1929

Caradoc, light cruiser
 BAKER, Arthur J, Able Seaman, J 96315, illness

President, RN College, Greenwich
 McCLINTOCK, John W L, Vice Admiral, illness

Tuesday, 26 March 1929

Hermes, aircraft carrier
 McDONALD, William H, Marine, 18423 (Ch), shot and killed (*no further information*)

Wednesday, 27 March 1929

Adventure, minelayer
 PENGILLEY, Edward G, Able Seaman, J 105021, illness

Saturday, 30 March 1929

Defiance, Devonport
 NEIL, Arthur C, Able Seaman, J 110537, accidentally killed

Sunday, 31 March 1929

Ladybird, river gunboat
 TUCKER, George W, Able Seaman, J 15265, drowned

Victory, Portsmouth
 SMITHERS, William A, Leading Seaman, J 31011, road accident, killed

Tuesday, 2 April 1929

Pembroke, Chatham
 EALES, Archibald I, Able Seaman, J 115552, illness

Wednesday, 3 April 1929

Royal Marines HQ
 THOMAS, Phillip, Marine, 21653 (Ply), illness

Wednesday, 10 April 1929

Victory, Portsmouth
 COLE, Ernest D, Stoker 1c, K 61253, illness

Thursday, 11 April 1929

St Vincent, Gosport
 HILL, George H, Boy 2c, JX 132042, illness

Friday, 12 April 1929

Magnolia, fleet sweeping sloop
 PITT, Herbert C, Stoker 1c, K 63750, died

Sunday, 14 April 1929

Egmont, Malta
 BALZAN, Frank, Officer's Steward 2c, 361116, illness

Victory, Portsmouth
 BAKER, William J L, Able Seaman, J 109467, illness

Monday, 15 April 1929

Dolphin, Gosport
 DAWSON, William, Engine Room Artificer 1c, M 4302, illness

Tuesday, 16 April 1929

Pembroke, Chatham
 HAYNES, Edwin A, Able Seaman, J 105458, illness

Thursday, 18 April 1929

Delphinium, fleet sweeping sloop
 MUNROE, Thomas D, Able Seaman, J 114228, illness

Friday, 19 April 1929

Eagle, aircraft carrier
 YATES, Herbert G, Joiner 1c, M 11871, accidentally killed

Tuesday, 23 April 1929

Caterham, minesweeper
 COOMBER, Ernest, Stoker 1c, K 55250, illness

Saturday, 27 April 1929

Delphinium, fleet sweeping sloop, both drowned
DANIELS, Thomas W, Stoker 1c, KX 77287
HELLIER, Frederick J J, Officer's Steward 1c, L 4490

Victory, Portsmouth
SHARPE, George E, Stoker 2c, KX 79754, illness

Sunday, 28 April 1929

Queen Elizabeth, battleship
SAVAGE, Robert, Leading Seaman, J 30724, illness

Monday, 29 April 1929

Vivid, Devonport
CARTER, Charles E, Stoker 1c, K 56694, illness

Tuesday, 30 April 1929

Engineering Course
PEEL, John, Midshipman (E), illness

Marazion, ex-minesweeper, submarine depot ship, Hong Kong
MILLARD, Thomas Mc G, Able Seaman, J 95327, accidentally killed

Friday, 3 May 1929

Pembroke, Chatham
WETHERILL, Joseph W, Able Seaman, J 11196, illness

Sunday, 5 May 1929

Tern, river gunboat
SNOW, Joseph B, Telegraphist, J 78013, killed

Tuesday, 7 May 1929

Hermes, aircraft carrier
EDWARDS, William, Stoker 1c, K 65969, illness

Friday, 10 May 1929

Vivid, Devonport
DEVEY, John, Able Seaman, J 110792, illness

Saturday, 11 May 1929

Britannia, RN College, Dartmouth
LAUGHTON, Reginald W, Lieutenant (E), illness

Nelson, battleship
TRILL, Charles F, Officer's Steward 3c, L 12662, illness

Tuesday, 14 May 1929

Vidette, destroyer
STEPHENS, Alec J F, Able Seaman, J 111312, illness

Saturday, 18 May 1929

Fisgard, Portsmouth
OSBORNE, Arthur G, Engine Room Artificer Apprentice, MX 46037, road accident, killed

Vivid, Devonport
HODGSON, Harold, Ordinary Seaman, SSX 13351, illness

Sunday, 19 May 1929

Pembroke, Chatham
WALKER, Edward C, Able Seaman, J 101332, illness

Tuesday, 21 May 1929

Sussex, heavy cruiser
BIRRELL, John, Stoker 1c, K 60709, illness

Wednesday, 22 May 1929

Iron Duke, battleship
GASSTOWN, Ernest W, Stoker Petty Officer, K 17657, illness

Thursday, 23 May 1929

Vivid, Devonport
HANNAM, Bertram W, Chief Yeoman of Signals, J 6510, illness

Friday, 24 May 1929

Eagle, aircraft carrier
SCARLETT, Bernard R, Able Seaman, J 104660, road accident, killed

Monday, 27 May 1929

Eagle, aircraft carrier
BARTER, Arthur T, Able Seaman, J 103212, illness

Saturday, 1 June 1929

Veronica, fleet sweeping sloop
DARKLEY, Albert E, Stoker 1c, K 60632, drowned

Monday, 3 June 1929

Fisgard, Portsmouth
YOUNG, William J, Artificer Apprentice, MX 47662, illness

Tuesday, 4 June 1929

Dolphin, Gosport
FAWCETT, Albert, Stoker 1c, KX 76083, illness

Effingham, cruiser
TURNBULL, Walter, Telegraphist Lieutenant, illness

Wednesday, 5 June 1929

Ceres, light cruiser
STANNARD, Richard G, Stoker Petty Officer, K 29220, illness

Vernon, Portsmouth
DENT, Edward S, Able Seaman, J 34711, illness

Wistaria, fleet sweeping sloop
WOOD, Ira, Leading Cook, M 5872, drowned

Friday, 7 June 1929

Royal Naval Volunteer Reserve
HARDING, Sir Charles O' B, Honorary Lieutenant Commander, RNVR, illness

Wednesday, 12 June 1929

Pembroke, Chatham
CLARKSON, Sydney W W, Able Seaman, J 58122, illness

Thursday, 13 June 1929

Dolphin, Gosport
SMART, Frederick T, Chief Petty Officer, 234844, died

Saturday, 15 June 1929

Greenwich, destroyer depot ship
HILL, Harold M, Surgeon Lieutenant (D), illness

Monday, 17 June 1929

Vivid, Devonport
ROBINSON, Hugh F R, Ordinary Seaman, P/JX 13354, illness

Tuesday, 18 June 1929

Effingham, cruiser
CREASY, Sydney E, Warrant Engineer, illness

Tamar, Hong Kong
ENGLAND, Maurice C, Sick Berth Attendant, M 27761, illness

Thursday, 20 June 1929

Cleopatra. light cruiser
WARREN, Thomas, Marine, 5994 (Ch), illness

Friday, 21 June 1929

Renown, battlecruiser
DODRIDGE, Arthur C, Musician, RMB, RMB 2051, illness

Saturday, 22 June 1929

Royal Sovereign, battleship
PRICE, Albert V, Able Seaman, J 110281, illness

Tuesday, 25 June 1929

Royal Naval Reserve
STOY, Albert F, Paymaster Commander, RNR, illness

Friday, 28 June 1929

Effingham, cruiser
BRYCE, Hugh, Stoker 1c, K 61869, illness

Philomel, ex-cruiser, depot ship, New Zealand
BAKER, William H, Marine, 20808 (Ply), illness

Tuesday, 2 July 1929

Delphinium, fleet sweeping sloop
WILSON, Ernest C, Supply Petty Officer, M 12244, illness

RN Hospital, Plymouth
NAUDE, Reginald C, Sick Berth Attendant, D/MX 47018, accidentally killed

Wednesday, 3 July 1929

Caradoc. light cruiser
GRIFFITHS, Philip G L, Boy 1c, JX 130149, illness

Saturday, 6 July 1929

Enterprise, cruiser
MANKELTOW, Joseph, Chief Shipwright, K 4494, illness

Titania, submarine depot ship
BAKER, Alfred R, Stoker 1c, KX 79349, illness

Sunday, 7 July 1929

Shakespeare, flotilla leader
SMART, Thomas W L, Able Seaman, JX 127578, illness

Wireless Telegraph Station Coulmer
ALLEN, Henry J, Petty Officer, 187212, died

Tuesday, 9 July 1929

H.47, submarine, in collision with submarine L.12 in St George's Channel off St David's Head, Wales, lost. There were three survivors *(below, H.21-class sister-boat H.49)*

AIN, David, Able Seaman, J 70878
BICKMORE, Noel A, Lieutenant
CREW, John, Stoker 1c, K 60475
CRIMMINS, Benjamin J, Stoker 1c, K 60910
DITCHER, John A, Engine Room Artificer 4c, M 37028
ELLIOTT, Edmund L V, Petty Officer, J 22587
GOODLET, Robert J N, Chief Engine Room Artificer 2c, 272329
HARRIS, Tom H, Leading Seaman, J 33023
HARTLAND, Sydney, Able Seaman, J 95907
HAWLEY, Frederick, Able Seaman, J 105790

HENDERSON, Clifford, Leading Stoker, J 44507
LEGG, Alfred A, Engine Room Artificer 4c, MX 46179
MACCABEE, Cyril T, Leading Stoker, K 62991
MANN, Cyril S, Leading Signalman, J 64425
McSWEENEY, John P, Leading Stoker, K 40797
PIKE, Edward L, Engine Room Artificer 1c, M 2667
ROBBINS, Percival H, Petty Officer, J 33626
SPENCER, Nathaniel, Leading Seaman, J 20156
STONE, Arthur C, Able Seaman, J 80084
TAYLOR, Alfred J H, Telegraphist, J 101888
WISE, William H, Leading Telegraphist, J 30196

L.12, in collision with H.47 above
 BULL, Charles E, Leading Signalman, J 40968
 SAMPSON, Arthur E R, Able Seaman, J 46212
 WHEELER, Horace A, Petty Officer, J 31616

Wednesday, 10 July 1929

Curlew, light cruiser
 EVANS, Frederick, Chief Petty Officer, 238216, drowned

Friday, 12 July 1929

Caradoc, light cruiser
 GREIG, Alexander S, Able Seaman, J 95524, illness

Shakespeare, flotilla leader, accidental fire at Gillingham
 NUTTON, John T, Officer's Steward 1c , L 3351
 and following members of the Sea Cadet Corps, a civilian youth organisation
 BRUNNING, David, Naval Cadet
 CHEESMAN, Eric, Naval Cadet
 SEARLES, Leonard, Naval Cadet
 SIDEN, Ivor, Naval Cadet

Wednesday, 17 July 1929

Curlew, light cruiser
 MELVIN, John, Engine Room Artificer 3c, M 35372, accidentally killed

Dunedin, light cruiser
 WATSON, Thomas B, Able Seaman, J 31885, illness

Thursday, 18 July 1929

Repulse, battlecruiser
 CRUSH, Edmond V, Signalman, J 87122, illness

Friday, 19 July 1929

Engineer in Chief's Department of Admiralty
 RUSSELL, Leslie S, Commander (E), illness

Monday, 22 July 1929

Wryneck, destroyer
 ROSS, Reginald W G, Able Seaman, J 16762, died

Tuesday, 23 July 1929

Vindictive, cruiser
 HUZZEY, Herbert C, Engine Room Artificer 2c, M 36944, accidentally killed

Thursday, 25 July 1929

Queen Elizabeth, battleship
 TUCKER, Hector J, Marine, 22594 (Ply), illness

Friday, 26 July 1929

Devonshire, heavy cruiser, explosion in 8in turret during gunnery firings in the Aegean *(below, NP/Mark Teadham)*

BACON, Edward, Corporal, RM 19230 (Po), killed
BATH, John A, Captain, RM, killed
BLACKMAN, James W R T, Marine, RM, 22306 (Ply), DOI in HS Maine
BRINDLE, Joseph S, Marine, RM, 222157 (Ply), DOI in HS Maine
GOLDSMITH, Samuel, Marine, 23034 (Ch), DOI in HS Maine
GRINDLE, Frank, Marine, 22763 (Ply), DOI in HS Maine
HARRIS, Edward C, Marine, X 315 (Ply), DOI in HS Maine
HOLE, William G, Marine, X 310 (Ply), DOI in Devonshire
LEVINS, James, Corporal, RM, 19038 (Ply), killed
McDONALD, Augustus A, Marine 19389 (Ply), DOI in Devonshire
OLD, John J, Marine, 14735 (Ply), DOI in HS Maine
SNELL, Walter E, Sergeant, RM, 21394 (Ply), killed
TAYLOR, Lionel R, Marine, 22343 (Ply), DOI in HS Maine

Saturday, 27 July 1929

Devonshire, heavy cruiser, explosion
 BARBER, Joseph, Marine, RM, 15639 (Ply), DOI in HS Maine
 EDWARDS, Arthur C, Ordnance Artificer 2c, M 6589, DOI in HS Maine
 HELLYER, William E, Marine, 2125 (Ply), DOI in HS Maine
 WILLIAMS, Frank, Marine, 16170 (Ply), DOI in HS Maine

Royal Marines HQ
 RIDDLE, Frederick C, Band Sergeant, RM, G 17069, illness

Sunday, 28 July 1929

Greenwich, destroyer depot ship
 RAWLINGS, Albert J B, Petty Officer, J 20014, road accident, killed

Monday, 29 July 1929

Flora, Simonstown, South Africa
 SHAMGAMA, Abuda, Seedie, X 252, illness

Wednesday, 31 July 1929

Resolution, battleship
 FEENSTRA, William M, Petty Officer, 237498, illness

August 1929

Effingham, cruiser
RICHARDSON, Thomas, Telegraphist, J 160468, date and cause not recorded

Thursday, 1 August 1929

St Vincent, Gosport
HAWKESWORTH, Cyril E, Cook, M 38529, illness

Vivid I, Devonport
STEEN, Joseph E, Able Seaman, J 100794, died

Friday, 2 August 1929

Greenwich, destroyer depot ship
TOOZE, Percy D, Leading Seaman, J 86905, road accident, killed

Sunday, 4 August 1929

Marshall Soult, monitor
IRONS, Harold R, Able Seaman, J 114442, illness

Thursday, 8 August 1929

Pembroke, Chatham
McCORMICK, Robert W J, Stoker 1c, KX 76884, illness

Saturday, 10 August 1929

Chatham, 2nd class cruiser
HORNE, John G, Lieutenant Colonel, RM, illness

Monday, 12 August 1929

Furious, aircraft carrier
QUICK, Ronald A, Telegraphist, J 87884, road accident, killed

Thursday, 15 August 1929

Victory, Portsmouth
LLOYD, Charles E, Stoker, K 57322, illness

Saturday, 17 August 1929

Victory, Portsmouth
WEBB, Fred, Stoker Petty Officer, K 13071, illness

Wednesday, 21 August 1929

Teazer, destroyer
SELBY, George L, Leading Seaman, J 90116, road accident, killed

Sunday, 25 August 1929

Marlborough, battleship
TURNER, Albert A C, Able Seaman, J 114047, road accident, killed

Pembroke, Chatham
TAIT, Henry, Petty Officer, J 1555, illness

Monday, 26 August 1929

Ambuscade, destroyer
BLAIR, Thomas M, Able Seaman, J 113613, illness

Tiger, battlecruiser
JOHNSON, Albert J, Stoker 1C, K 8490, illness

Tuesday, 27 August 1929

Victory, Portsmouth
OWEN, Samuel D, Officer's Steward 4c, LX 20778, illness

Friday, 30 August 1929

Rodney, battleship
FOSTER, Harry E, Painter 4c, M 30107, illness

Witherington, destroyer
SUTCLIFFE, Charles G, Stoker Petty Officer, K 29511, illness

Saturday, 31 August 1929

Pembroke, Chatham
TREVARTHEN, William H, Stoker 1c, K 60501, illness

Victory, Portsmouth
ISAACSON, Egerton W, Captain, illness

Sunday, 1 September 1929

Kent, heavy cruiser
HOLLOWAY, Henry E, Sick Berth Chief Petty Officer, M 1413, accidentally killed

Revenge, battleship
MATTHEWS, Leslie N, Ordnance Artificer 1C, M 5197, illness

Monday, 2 September 1929

Effingham, cruiser
CRAWFORD, John, Stoker 1c, K 63473, illness

Wednesday, 4 September 1929

Cicala, river gunboat
KEENAN, Louis Mc N, Supply Petty Officer, M 7655, illness

Devonshire, heavy cruiser
WICKENDEN, Charles P, Corporal, RM, 20187 (Ply), explosion on 27 July 1929, DOI

Endeavour, survey ship
SMITH, James, Able Seaman, J 86785, died

Hermes, aircraft carrier
ELLIOTT, Edward P R, Marine, 16223 (Ply), died

Monday, 9 September 1929

Pembroke, Chatham
HORSPOLE, John H, Able Seaman, J 108949, illness

Sunday, 15 September 1929

Calcutta, light cruiser
 SCRACE, Harold W, Able Seaman, J 97275, illness

Tuesday, 17 September 1929

Royal Naval Reserve
 RANALOW, William H, Paymaster Lieutenant Commander, RNR, illness

Valhalla, destroyer
 PHILLIPS, William L, Able Seaman, J 96198, illness

Friday, 20 September 1929

Flora, Simonstown, South Africa
 BAMBA, Abdia B, Seedie, X 146, illness

Saturday, 21 September 1929

H.33, submarine
 NUTTALL, Fred, Act/Chief Engine Room Artificer 2c, M 7304, illness

Wednesday, 25 September 1929

Vivid, Devonport
 HASLAND, Francis H, Able Seaman, J 9622, illness

Thursday, 26 September 1929

Pembroke, Chatham
 TOWNSLEY, William E, Stoker Petty Officer, K 1855, road accident, killed

Friday, 27 September 1929

Revenge, battleship
 FLETCHER, Ernest E, Leading Cook, M 5864, illness

Titania, submarine depot ship
 LITTLETON, Hugh, Paymaster Commander, illness

Saturday, 28 September 1929

Portsmouth
 KNOX, Thomas E N, Lieutenant, RM, illness

Vivid, Devonport
 SOLWAY, William E, Chief Petty Officer, 234593, illness
 VARCOE, Alfred, Stoker 1c, K 18051, illness

Saturday, 5 October 1929

Cicala, river gunboat
 CHENG, Chew, Able Seaman, (no service number listed), illness

Sunday, 6 October 1929

Warspite, battleship
 SMITH, John P de B, Lieutenant Commander, illness

Tuesday, 8 October 1929

Royal Marines HQ
 WILSON, Arthur, Sergeant, RM, A 16708, died

Wednesday, 9 October 1929

Argus, aircraft carrier
 MILLS, Herbert J, Able Seaman, J 33787, accidentally killed

Nelson, battleship
 SAWNEY, Ronald, Ordinary Seaman, JX 129209, drowned

Saturday, 12 October 1929

Royal Naval Volunteer Reserve
 TARDREW, Paul W, Lieutenant, RNVR, illness

Monday, 14 October 1929

Pembroke, Chatham
 FORD, Ernest L, Stoker 1c, K 65176, road accident, killed

Wednesday, 16 October 1929

Emerald, light cruiser
 ELSEY, Edwin, Able Seaman, J 109529, accidentally killed

Monday, 21 October 1929

Repulse, battlecruiser
 CROW, Andrew A, Electrical Artificer 4c, MX 46100, exposure, died

Tuesday, 22 October 1929

Calcutta, light cruiser
 WEAVING, William, Engine Room Artificer 1c, M 14169, illness

Monday, 28 October 1929

Revenge, battleship
 LEPPER, Edgar W, Master at Arms, M 35792, illness

Tarantula, river gunboat
 CORNWELL, George F, Stoker 1c, KX 77887, drowned

Thursday, 31 October 1929

Enterprise, light cruiser
 MARTIN, Ronald H, Marine, 23006 (Ch), illness

Pembroke, Chatham
 ABBOTT, Harry, Officer's Steward 3c, LX 20348, road accident, killed

Saturday, 2 November 1929

Greenwich, destroyer depot ship
 SLOAN, Hugh, Leading Stoker, K 24060, illness

Sunday, 3 November 1929

Pembroke, Chatham
 McCARTHY, Horace G, Leading Seaman, J 38359, illness

Friday, 8 November 1929

Fisgard, Portsmouth
 MORGAN, Harold H, Engine Room Artificer Apprentice, MX 46033, illness

Ramillies, battleship
 O'BRIEN, Terence R, Able Seaman, J 100437, illness

Saturday, 9 November 1929

Frobisher, cruiser
 LYNCH, James P, Leading Stoker, K 45626, drowned

Victory XI, Portland
 BAGULEY, Joseph W, Engineer Commander, illness

Tuesday, 19 November 1929

Walker, destroyer
 PEARSON, William, Able Seaman, J 91664, died

Saturday, 23 November 1929

Royal Oak, battleship
 MANN, Frank H, Able Seaman, J 29403, accidentally killed

Wednesday, 27 November 1929

Carlisle, light cruiser
 ROGERSON, John B, Able Seaman, J 11103, accidentally killed

Thursday, 28 November 1929

Fisgard, Portsmouth
 SMITHERS, Adrian H, Able Seaman, SSX 12728, drowned

Monday, 2 December 1929

Berwick, heavy cruiser
 SWALLOW, Reginald F, Corporal, RM, 21782 (Ply), illness

Enterprise, light cruiser
 BOTTOMLEY, William E, Petty Officer, J 41477, illness

Pembroke, Chatham
 COLLINS, William J, Able Seaman, J 85585, illness

Wednesday, 4 December 1929

Excellent, Portsmouth
 BISHOP, Frederick W J, Ordnance Artificer 2c, M 8918, illness
 SMITH, William C A, Chief Petty Officer, J 8688, illness

Friday, 6 December 1929

Pembroke, Chatham
 IDDON, Austin N, Telegraphist, J 112380, illness

Sunday, 8 December 1929

Walpole, destroyer
 BAILEY, Charles E, Ordnance Artificer 3c, M 37513, drowned
 FERDIS, William H, Able Seaman, J 108534, drowned

York, heavy cruiser
 COCKS, George, Engineer Commander, illness

Friday, 13 December 1929

Wallflower, fleet sweeping sloop
 HOWARD-CROCKETT, Edward W, Lieutenant, illness

Sunday, 15 December 1929

Curacoa, light cruiser
 DANEO, Santo, Officer's Cook 2c, L 11102, died

Monday, 16 December 1929

Marlborough, battleship
 PAGE, Mark W, Telegraphist, J 113114, illness

St Vincent, Gosport
 GASCOYNE, Alfred H R, Boy 2c, JX 133447, illness

Tuesday, 17 December 1929

Pembroke, Chatham
 LOCKWOOD, John G, Chief Petty Officer Writer, M 7785, illness

Saturday, 21 December 1929

Vivid, Devonport
 COLLINSON, Darlof J H, Stoker 2c, KX 79828, illness

Sunday, 22 December 1929

Warspite, battleship
 IGUANEY, Antonio, Officer's Cook 1c, 363966, illness

Monday, 23 December 1929

H.43, submarine
 DUCKWORTH, Thomas W, Engine Room Artificer 3c, M 34520, road accident, killed

Tuesday, 24 December 1929

Victory I, Portsmouth
 BARRETT, Charles A, Petty Officer Telegraphist, J 20177, illness

Friday, 27 December 1929

Eagle, aircraft carrier
 NEWMAN, James V, Able Seaman, J 43827, illness

Monday, 30 December 1929

Royal Naval Volunteer Reserve
 TAYLOR, Charles R R, Lieutenant Commander, RNVR, illness

1930

Thursday, 2 January 1930

M.2, submarine
 CHASE, Frederick W, Able Seaman, J 101278, illness

Sunday, 5 January 1930

Cairo, light cruiser
 MASON, Arthur J, Stoker 1C, KX 78370, illness

Friday, 10 January 1930

New Zealand Division of Royal Navy
 HODGES, Albert A, Schoolmaster, illness

Saturday, 11 January 1930

Campbell, flotilla leader
 MEASOM, Ernest, Able Seaman, JX 125478, illness

Sunday, 12 January 1930

St Genny, Admiralty rescue tug, foundered in English Channel approaches, off Ushant, France *(below, sister tug St Cyrus)*

BANKS, Harold, Able Seaman, J 32459
BURREN, Charles H B, Boatswain
CIVIL, Herbert G, Chief Engine Room Artificer 1c, M 804
COOMBES, Alfred E L, Stoker 1c, KX 76581
COTTEN, Richard R, Stoker 1c, K 62115
CROWTHER, James R, Stoker 1c, K 16109
FRAY, Thomas, Engine Room Artificer 2c, M 34649
GREEN, Leonard C, Stoker 1c, K 62435
HEBEL, Frederick J B, Leading Stoker, K 59712
HOWES, George A, Able Seaman, J 105307
KELLINGTON, Sydney R, Able Seaman, J 92220
KEMP, Claud W N, Officer's Steward 2c, L 12749
KNIGHT, Frederick A, Stoker 1c, K 65419
LEAN, Philip S, Commissioned Gunner
MAITLAND, Paul, Able Seaman, J 100943
PAUL, Charles F, Lieutenant
PEPLAR, William H, Engine Room Artificer 1c, M 14878
PINK, Frederick G, Leading Stoker, K 59106
PRIEST, Albert J, Officer's Steward 3c, L 14694
RAVEN, Henry A, Stoker 1c, K 58432
TITMUS, Sidney S, Able Seaman, J 106605
WILLIS, John T, Leading Stoker, K 2295
WILLOUGHBY, Thomas J, Telegraphist, J 48094

Vivid, Devonport
 SMITH, William C, Able Seaman, J 34717, illness

Monday, 13 January 1930

Valentine, destroyer
 AUSTIN, Ronald N, Able Seaman, J 109535, died

Vivid, Devonport
 HARRIS, William P, Boy 1c, JX 130253, illness

Tuesday, 14 January 1930

Glorious, ex-battlecruiser, aircraft carrier
 MITCHELL, Thomas, Able Seaman, JX 126137, killed

Friday, 17 January 1930

Victory, Portsmouth
 CHURCHER, Lionel S, Able Seaman, 200540, illness

Monday, 20 January 1930

Courageous, ex-battlecruiser, aircraft carrier
 POPE, Archibald F C, Marine, 22602 (Po), accidentally killed

Pembroke, Chatham
 SPINNER, James D, Engine Room Artificer Apprentice, MX 14605, illness

Thursday, 23 January 1930

Iron Duke, battleship
 SCARLETT, George J H, Corporal, RM, 16605 (Po), illness

Saturday, 25 January 1930

Jamaica, fishing trawler
 PALMER, Henry, Skipper, RNR, illness

Pembroke, Chatham
 HANDLEY, Herbert P, Sick Berth Petty Officer, M 294, illness

Monday, 27 January 1930

Victory, Portsmouth
 LISTER, William H, Petty Officer, J 24936, illness

Wednesday, 29 January 1930

Marlborough, battleship
 HODGSON, George C R, Able Seaman, J 115510, accidentally killed

Friday, 31 January 1930

Adventure, minelayer
 McDONALD, Donald G L L, Petty Officer Telegraphist, J 67471, illness

Laburnum, minesweeping sloop
 PENGELLY, Silvanus, Leading Stoker, K 55939, drowned

Saturday, 1 February 1930

Pembroke, Chatham
 BULL, Edward G, Leading Seaman, J 82644, illness

Sunday, 2 February 1930

Tamar, Hong Kong
  AH, Gon, Officer's Cook 1c, (no service number listed), died

Monday, 3 February 1930

Fisgard, Portsmouth
  McCALL, Robert, Stoker 1c, K 61736, illness

Thursday, 6 February 1930

Erebus, monitor
  HUNT, Francis, Marine, 15139 (Ply), died

Friday, 7 February 1930

Victory, Portsmouth
  TYLER, William T R, Stoker 1c, KX 78336, illness

Monday, 10 February 1930

Flora, Simonstown, South Africa
  MWINGE, Bin A, Seedie, X 222, illness

Thursday, 13 February 1930

Australia (RAN), heavy cruiser
  ROGERS, Harry E, Able Seaman, J 13661, accidentally killed

Greenwich, destroyer depot ship
  SMITH, John A, Commissioned Shipwright, illness

Sunday, 16 February 1930

Royal Navy
  ANDERSON-STUART, Archibald P, Surgeon Lieutenant Commander, illness

Monday, 17 February 1930

Vernon, Portsmouth
  McNAUGHT, Alexander, Able Seaman, J 104206, illness

Vivid, Devonport
  STEVENS, Ernest, Stoker 1c, K 19466, illness

Tuesday, 18 February 1930

Resource, fleet repair ship
  JEANS, George, Able Seaman, J 110233, illness

Wednesday, 19 February 1930

H.43, submarine
  CUMING-GIBSON-CRAIG, Robert J A, Lieutenant, illness

Medway, submarine depot ship
  ASHTON, Reginald W A, Paymaster Lieutenant Commander, illness

Queen Elizabeth, battleship
  MONAGHAN, Joseph, Able Seaman, JX 126384, illness

Friday, 21 February 1930

Pembroke, Chatham
  OADES, Arthur, Stoker 1c, K 9154, illness

Sunday, 23 February 1930

Royal Navy
  HENNESSY, Joseph, Lieutenant Commander, illness

Monday, 24 February 1930

Queen Elizabeth, battleship
  JONES, Ernest J, Able Seaman, J 105207, illness

Thursday, 27 February 1930

Courageous, ex-battlecruiser, aircraft carrier
  DAVEY, Martin J, Leading Stoker, P/K 60311, illness

Nelson, battleship
  DAY, Peter, Stoker Petty Officer, K 6063, accidentally killed

Monday, 3 March 1930

Senior Officers' War Course
  REDE, Roger L' E M, Captain, illness

Tuesday, 4 March 1930

Cornwall, heavy cruiser
  HEWINS, William, Stoker 1c, K 5131, illness

Wednesday, 5 March 1930

Lucia, submarine depot ship
  COLE, George V A, Able Seaman, J 112966, illness

Malcolm, flotilla leader
  COUSINS, Charles T, Able Seaman, J 96963, illness

Thursday, 6 March 1930

Victoria & Albert, Royal yacht
  SHAWYER, Frederick W, Marine, 18993 (Po), illness

Tuesday, 11 March 1930

Victory, Portsmouth
  FLEMING, William J, Able Seaman, J 80923, illness

Wednesday, 12 March 1930

Hood, battlecruiser
  BUCHAN, Charles, Marine, RM, Ply/18555, illness, after discharge

Saturday, 15 March 1930

Cornwall, heavy cruiser
  McMILLAN, John, Able Seaman, J 91891, illness

Sunday, 16 March 1930

Ramillies, battleship
 DONOVAN, Walter H, Boy 1c, JX 131171, illness

Steadfast, destroyer
 ALFORD, William H P, Stoker 1c, K 63582, illness

Monday, 17 March 1930

Excellent, Portsmouth
 CLARK, Frederick C, Able Seaman, J 96779, road accident, killed

Glorious, ex-battlecruiser, aircraft carrier
 CALLARD, William G, Leading Cook, M 5663, illness

Wednesday, 19 March 1930

FAA, 440 Flight, Adelaide (RAN)
 McGOWAN, Donald O, Leading Telegraphist, RAN, 13919, air crash, killed

Wednesday, 26 March 1930

Laburnum, minesweeping sloop
 LEONARD, Emmanuel, Chief Engine Room Artificer 1c, M 2238, illness

Royal Naval Reserve
 BRAY, George B, Lieutenant Commander, RNR, illness

Thursday, 27 March 1930

Royal Marines HQ
 CHILTON, Harry, Corporal, RM, E 17893, illness

Saturday, 29 March 1930

Nelson, battleship
 MARSHALL, Edwin J A, Ordinary Seaman, JX 130182, illness

Pembroke, Chatham
 ADAMS, William E, Engine Room Artificer Apprentice, MX 45990, illness

Sunday, 30 March 1930

Tiger, battlecruiser
 JACKSON, Joseph W, Leading Signalman, J 5922, accidentally killed

Warland, fishing trawler
 HAWKINS, James, Chief Skipper, RNR, illness

Friday, 4 April 1930

Ganges, Shotley/Harwich
 BARNSHAW, Sidney F, Boy 1c, JX 133237, illness

Saturday, 5 April 1930

Active, destroyer
 JAKEMAN, Edward V, Petty Officer, J 26111, road accident, killed

Monday, 7 April 1930

Terror, monitor
 GARDNER, Albert J, Commissioned Gunner, illness

Vivid, Devonport
 GERRARD, John W, Officer's Steward 3c, LX 20571, road accident, killed

Tuesday, 8 April 1930

Sepoy, destroyer, depth charge explosion *(below, N/P/Paul Simpson)*
 BELDERSON, William, Petty Officer, J 29333, killed
 DRAPER, William J A, Able Seaman, J 111460, DOW
 HEYWOOD, Robert W, Able Seaman, J 110561, DOW
 REDMOND-COOPER, James N, Able Seaman, J 109926, killed
 REED, Leslie G, Gunner, killed
 SMITH, Thomas E, Able Seaman, JX 125791, killed

Thursday, 10 April 1930

Victory, Portsmouth
 ARMISON, James R, Telegraphist, J 111484, accidentally killed

Saturday, 12 April 1930

Vivid, Devonport
 VEALE, Frederick L, Able Seaman, J 50203, illness

Friday, 18 April 1930

Revenge, battleship
 ELLIS, John A E, Marine, X 263 (Po), drowned

Tuesday, 22 April 1930

Castor, light cruiser
 LANG, James A, Cook, M 6160, illness

Thursday, 24 April 1930

Champion, light cruiser
 WELBY, Richard M, Captain, illness

Friday, 25 April 1930

Greenwich, destroyer depot ship
 CLARK, William H, Shipwright 1c, M 10278, accidentally killed

Vivid, Devonport
 BOWDEN, Albert H, Able Seaman, J 103863, illness

Sunday, 27 April 1930

Rodney, battleship
 BUTLER, Cecil, Telegraphist, J 89971, illness

Tuesday, 29 April 1930

Enterprise, light cruiser
 ATKINS, Walter J, Able Seaman, J 114309, illness

Wednesday, 30 April 1930

Vivid, Devonport
 CARTER, Horace W H, Signalman, 236058, illness

Saturday, 3 May 1930

Dunedin, light cruiser
 HALLIDAY, Albert J W, Leading Signalman, J 63052, road accident, killed

Sunday, 4 May 1930

Iroquois, survey ship
 WALSWORTH, Arthur N, Able Seaman, J 99609, drowned

Monday, 5 May 1930

Cumberland, heavy cruiser
 SMITH, Ronald J, Ordinary Seaman, JX 131188, illness

Tara, destroyer
 PHILLIPS, Frederick A, Chief Engine Room Artificer 1c, M 2019, accidentally killed

Wednesday, 7 May 1930

Pembroke, Chatham
 WELLINGS, Frederick J, Able Seaman, J72593, illness

Friday, 9 May 1930

Vivid, Devonport
 PEACOCK, Augustine P, Petty Officer, J 9709, illness

Sunday, 11 May 1930

Anthony, destroyer
 SPICER-SIMSON, Geoffrey E F, Lieutenant, illness

Thursday, 15 May 1930

Cumberland, heavy cruiser
 BUSHELL, Sidney, Stoker Petty Officer, K 22803, illness

Saturday, 17 May 1930

Adamant, submarine depot ship
 DERRICK, John H, Stoker 1c, KX 76591, illness

Victory, Portsmouth
 COX, John E, Petty Officer Writer, P/M 34948, illness

Sunday, 18 May 1930

Egmont, Malta
 GILBERT, William A, Sick Berth Attendant, M 38156, illness

Tuesday, 20 May 1930

Pembroke, Chatham
 GATES, William G, Leading Stoker, K 19883, illness

Friday, 30 May 1930

Royal Navy
 RAYNER, Frederick W, Able Seaman, J 104392, illness

Saturday, 31 May 1930

Tiger, battlecruiser
 CONNOR, John, Warrant Electrician, illness

Monday, 2 June 1930

Dolphin, Gosport
 DURANT, Arthur M, Stoker 1c, K 64431, accidentally killed

Friday, 6 June 1930

Kent, heavy cruiser
 TUSSLER, Henry, Able Seaman, 238070, drowned

Sunday, 15 June 1930

Revenge, battleship
 CHINNERY, Arthur, Mechanician, K 57977, drowned

Wednesday, 18 June 1930

Pembroke, Chatham
 WRIGHT, William S, Yeoman of Signals, J 31732, accidentally killed

Sunday, 22 June 1930

Wallflower, minesweeping sloop
 CARR, Arthur C, Leading Telegraphist, J 90634, illness

Monday, 23 June 1930

Ambrose, submarine depot ship
 CRADDOCK, William H, Commissioned Engineer, illness

Vivid, Devonport
 LATHAM, Arthur H, Stoker 1c, K 66009, road accident, killed

Wednesday, 25 June 1930

Shropshire, heavy cruiser
 TULBY, Victor E, Able Seaman, J 104682, illness

Suffolk, heavy cruiser
 AVIS, William T, Sick Berth Chief Petty Officer, M 1717, accidentally killed

Friday, 27 June 1930

Portsmouth, training course
 ACWORTH, Richard F, Act/Sub Lieutenant, illness

Saturday, 28 June 1930

Triad, Admiralty yacht, SNO Persian Gulf
 DEAN, Charles L, Leading Sick Berth Attendant, M 37776, illness

Sunday, 29 June 1930

Vivid, Devonport
 DONOVAN, Edward, Leading Stores Assistant, M 11680, illness

Tuesday, 1 July 1930

Egmont, Malta
 CARUANA, Salvatore, Able Seaman, JX 125615, illness

Revenge, battleship
 REYNOLDS, James A, Commissioned Gunner, drowned

Wednesday, 2 July 1930

Royal Sovereign, battleship
 HUMPHREYS, James W, Marine, 22085 (Ch), illness

Wakeful, destroyer
 DURRELL, Jack, Able Seaman, JX 126734, illness

Thursday, 3 July 1930

Wryneck, destroyer
 GIBSON, Albert, Able Seaman, J 9285, illness

Friday, 4 July 1930

Cornwall, heavy cruiser
 JONES, William H, Stoker 1c, K 6202, explosion, killed

Nelson, battleship
 BLEEK, John F, Able Seaman, J 75386, illness

Royal Naval Reserve
 SEDDALL, Harry V, Commander, RNR, illness

Saturday, 5 July 1930

Pandora, submarine
 DEWEY, Guy F J, Leading Cook, M 38718, drowned

X.1, experimental cruiser submarine
 COLMAN, George, Leading Seaman, J 91594, accidentally killed

Sunday, 6 July 1930

Nelson, battleship
 ROUSE, Eric J, Ordinary Seaman, JX 129090, illness

Monday, 7 July 1930

Delphinium, minesweeping sloop
 AKASSA, Emir, Krooman, W 250, drowned

Tuesday, 8 July 1930

RN Hospital, Bermuda
 SAUNDERS, Algernon H, Leading Sick Berth Attendant, M 2473, accidentally killed

Thursday, 10 July 1930

Cumberland, heavy cruiser
 PLATT, James, Stoker 1c, K 64537, illness

Royal Navy
 OLD, Ernest W, Leading Seaman, D/J 7357, accidentally killed

Saturday, 12 July 1930

Centaur, light cruiser
 JOHNSON, John, Stoker 1c, KX 78536, stabbed in Danzig, killed

Sunday, 13 July 1930

Courageous, ex-battlecruiser, aircraft carrier
 WATTS, Cecil G E, Able Seaman, SSX 12937, road accident, killed

Monday, 14 July 1930

Repulse, battlecruiser
 WEBB, Arthur A, Boy 1c, JX 132101, illness

Saturday, 19 July 1930

Castor, light cruiser
 DICKENS, Leslie A, Able Seaman, J 100803, illness

Sunday, 20 July 1930

M.3, minelaying submarine
 SPENCER, Samuel E H, Lieutenant, killed

Vivid, Devonport
 TAYLOR, Thomas T, Chief Shipwright 2c, M 6594, illness

Monday, 21 July 1930

Ulster Division, RNVR
 DUFFERIN and AVA, Marquess of, Captain, RNVR, killed

Tuesday, 22 July 1930

Iron Duke, battleship
 BATES, Arthur E, Supply Chief Petty Officer, M 37484, drowned

Rawalpindi, passenger liner
 PITTS, Thomas E, Commander, RNR, illness

Wednesday, 23 July 1930

Resolution, battleship
 CROCKER, Philip J B, Able Seaman, JX 127008, accidentally killed

Saturday, 26 July 1930

Royal Naval Reserve
 LEMMON, Frank E, Paymaster Lieutenant, RNR, illness

Sunday, 27 July 1930

Britannia, RN College, Dartmouth
 BUTLER-COLE, Thomas B, Lieutenant (E), illness

Monday, 28 July 1930

Arrow, destroyer
 KNIGHTLEY, Frederick J, Stoker Petty Officer, K 23803, illness

Pembroke, Chatham
 COOK, Frederick T, Assistant Cook, MX 48016, illness

Saturday, 2 August 1930

Effingham, cruiser
 WHITEWAY, Henry C, Cook, P/MX 47272, illness

Revenge, battleship
 DYSON, Sidney H, Electrical Artificer 4c, P/MX 46285, drowned

Monday, 4 August 1930

Queen Elizabeth, battleship
 SATTERFORD, Richard D, Chief Petty Officer Writer, D/M 19148, illness

Tuesday, 5 August 1930

Malaya, battleship
 PHILLIPS, William T E, Mechanician, D/K 58418, illness

Monday, 11 August 1930

Excellent, Portsmouth
 ROBERTSON, David J, Mechanician, P/K 59052, accidentally killed

Wednesday, 13 August 1930

Peterel, river gunboat
 O'BRIEN, Wilfred, Stoker 1c, P/K 66554, drowned

Saturday, 16 August 1930

Cumberland, heavy cruiser
 DALLISON, Stanley F, Able Seaman, C/J 115336, illness

Tuesday, 19 August 1930

Wessex, destroyer
 MUNDY, Thomas C G, Leading Seaman, C/J 41099, road accident, killed

Whirlwind, destroyer
 HALL, Frederick J, Able Seaman, C/J 87024, road accident, killed

Wednesday, 20 August 1930

Royal Naval Volunteer Reserve
 BRADLEY, Arthur R, Surgeon Captain, RNVR, illness
 KING, The Right Hon Henry D, Captain (Commodore 2c), RNVR, illness

Friday, 22 August 1930

Durban, light cruiser
 JERMY, John T, Signalman, J 111554, illness

Tuesday, 26 August 1930

Centurion, ex-battleship, target ship
 STONEHOUSE, William, Stoker 1c, K 56308, died

Wednesday, 27 August 1930

Dauntless, light cruiser, boat accident, boat from Vancouver (RCN), destroyer, both killed
 GREENWOOD, William J, Stoker 1c, P/KX 76929
 JOHNSON, Sidney, Able Seaman, P/SSX 12444

Thursday, 28 August 1930

Royal Oak, battleship
 MURRELL, Charles E, Petty Officer, C/J 57064, illness

Monday, 1 September 1930

Comus, light cruiser
 RIDHOLLS, Percy, Engine Room Artificer 1c, D/M 3860, illness

Friday, 5 September 1930

Dragon, light cruiser
 BEVAN, Louis H B, Captain, illness

Monday, 8 September 1930

York, heavy cruiser
 BILTON, Matthew W, Marine, 20945 (Ch), illness

Tuesday, 9 September 1930

Pembroke I, Chatham
 KNIGHT, Leonard J, Able Seaman, C/J 103068, road accident, killed

Wednesday, 10 September 1930

Cornwall, heavy cruiser
 BAKER, Arthur J, Chief Stoker, D/K 11977, illness

Saturday, 13 September 1930

Renown, battlecruiser
 GENGE, Reginald G R, Leading Telegraphist, D/J 43631, drowned

Sunday, 14 September 1930

Dryad, Portsmouth
 VICKERY, Richard H, Supply Chief Petty Officer, P/M 5347, accidentally killed

Tuesday, 16 September 1930

Centurion, ex-battleship, target ship
 TOWERS, Charles, Marine, X 210 (Ch), (ex-Hawkins), died

Wednesday, 17 September 1930

Victory, Portsmouth
 PUNNETT, George W, Petty Officer, P/238386, road accident, killed

Sunday, 21 September 1930

Pembroke, Chatham
 CAMPBELL, Alexander, Stoker 1c, C/K 63149, illness

Monday, 22 September 1930

Kent, heavy cruiser
 ELLIS, Charles W, Marine, 17747 (Ch), illness

Wednesday, 24 September 1930

Moth, river gunboat
 COLCLOUGH, George, Able Seaman, C/SSX 12913, illness

Saturday, 4 October 1930

Pembroke, Chatham
 HAYWARD, Ernest J, Officer's Chief Cook, C/L 3664, illness

Stuart, flotilla leader
 CAMPBELL, John, Stoker 1c, P/K 58712, drowned

Victory, Portsmouth
 DAY, Albert, Able Seaman, C/J 33641, illness

Sunday, 5 October 1930

Emperor of India, battleship
 BELLINGHAM, Cecil P, Telegraphist, P/J 110190, road accident, killed

Excellent, Portsmouth
 DELL, Reginald W, Chief Petty Officer, P/J 2002, killed

Monday, 6 October 1930

Engineer in Chief's Department
 BODDY, Robert H G, Engineer Commander, illness

Tuesday, 7 October 1930

Centaur, light cruiser
 DOWNER, Albert E, Stoker 1c, P/KX 77672, illness

Saturday, 11 October 1930

Tamar, Hong Kong
 SING, Yes H, Able Seaman, (no service number listed), illness

Monday, 13 October 1930

Delhi, light cruiser
 HARRIS, William T, Corporal, RM, 21436 (Ply), died

Wednesday, 15 October 1930

Glorious, ex-battlecruiser, aircraft carrier, air crash, both killed
 BARKER, Edward G, Leading Aircraftsman, RAF, 364505
 COWIN, Maurice T, Lieutenant

Friday, 17 October 1930

Constance, light cruiser
 PAYNE, Wilfred H, Officer's Steward 2c, P/L 12177, died

Wednesday, 22 October 1930

RN Hospital, Plymouth
 BENNETT, Charles C, Leading Sick Berth Attendant, D/M 24673, illness

Royal Naval Reserve
 DWYER, Robert M, Paymaster Lieutenant Commander, RNR, illness

Monday, 27 October 1930

Adventure, minelayer
 JONES, Henry, Commissioned Gunner, drowned

Courageous, ex-battlecruiser, aircraft carrier, deck accident
 SILLAR, David A C, Lieutenant, DOI

Tuesday, 28 October 1930

Malabar, Bermuda
 WORD, Cecil, Leading Stoker, P/K 56310, illness

Saturday, 1 November 1930

Cornwall, heavy cruiser
 CLEVERTON, Stanley, Stoker Petty Officer, D/K 5216, illness

Sunday, 2 November 1930

Royal Marines HQ
 WESTBROOK, William H, Marine, 18320 (Ch), illness

Tuesday, 4 November 1930

Carysfort, light cruiser
 JOHNSTON, William, Commissioned Gunner, illness

Wednesday, 5 November 1930

Iron Duke, battleship
 HUGHES, Cecil H, Stoker 1c, P/KX 79864, road accident, killed

Royal Naval Volunteer Reserve
 LLOYD, Thomas J, Surgeon Lieutenant, RNVR, illness

Tamar, Hong Kong
 ROURKE, John F, Chief Petty Officer Writer, D/M 5265, illness

Thursday, 6 November 1930

Royal Naval Reserve
 HUME-GOODIER, Robert S, Commander, RNR, illness

Friday, 7 November 1930

Coventry, light cruiser
 WHITE, Charles D, Stoker 1c, P/K 63977, drowned

Wednesday, 12 November 1930

Victory, Portsmouth
 MIDDLETON, Allan G T, Able Seaman, P/J 105859, illness

Thursday, 13 November 1930

Royal Naval Reserve
 ROBINSON, Alfred W C, Lieutenant Commander, RNR, illness

Saturday, 15 November 1930

Centurion, ex-battleship, target ship
 PINHORNE, Alfred S G, Able Seaman, P/J 113463, illness

Wednesday, 19 November 1930

Pembroke, Chatham
 HAMMOND, Thomas V, Signalman, C/J 87102, died

Vivid, Devonport
 BISS, Frederick J, Able Seaman, D/JX 125338, (ex-Malaya), illness

Monday, 24 November 1930

Vivid, Devonport
 YABSLEY, Clarence J H, Joiner 1c, D/M 5726, road accident, killed

Thursday, 27 November 1930

Carysfort, light cruiser
 BREWER, Herbert W, Regulating Petty Officer, D/M 38607, illness

Monday, 1 December 1930

Iroquois, survey ship
 HAWKINS, George, Leading Stoker, P/K 47313, illness

Wednesday, 3 December 1930

St Vincent, Gosport
 HALES, Victor R, Musician, RMB, RMB 1485, illness

Thursday, 4 December 1930

Defiance, Devonport
 ALFORD, Richard C, Petty Officer, D/J 21044, road accident, killed

Friday, 5 December 1930

Iron Duke, battleship
 BLAKE, Noah A G, Able Seaman, P/J 98067, road accident, killed

Wednesday, 10 December 1930

Defiance, Devonport
 DOYLE, Christopher, Stoker 1c, D/K 65333, illness

Thursday, 11 December 1930

Excellent, Portsmouth
 STREAMER, George W, Able Seaman, P/J 114782, accidentally killed

Monday, 15 December 1930

Pilot's Course No.17
 ASHEWANDEN, Cecil K, Lieutenant, illness

Tuesday, 16 December 1930

Delphinium, minesweeping sloop, both accidentally killed
 GORDON, Joseph T, Stoker 1c, P/K 62182
 McDONAGH, William, Stoker 1c, P/KX 78559

Friday, 19 December 1930

Kent, heavy cruiser
 VICE, Wilfred, Able Seaman, C/J 13006, accidentally killed

Monday, 22 December 1930

Cyclops, repair ship
 CROCKER, Albert, Leading Stoker, D/K 23313, died

Valiant, battleship
 MAY, Cyril, Stoker 1c, C/K 62438, illness

Thursday, 25 December 1930

Victory, Portsmouth
 LEGG, Edward, Commissioned Gunner, illness

Monday, 29 December 1930

Vivid, Devonport
 BEER, Reginald J, Chief Petty Officer Writer, D/M 6960, illness

Wednesday, 31 December 1930

Courageous, ex-battlecruiser, aircraft carrier
 COOKE, William C, Able Seaman, P/J 101384, accidentally killed

Egmont, Malta
 BRUNSDON, Richard T, Marine, 20456 (Po), illness

1931

Thursday, 1 January 1931

Dolphin, Gosport
 GIAMBELLI, John E, Leading Seaman, P/J 93139, illness
 LAWRENCE, William H, Writer, P/MX 46828, illness

Saturday, 3 January 1931

Vivid, Devonport
 GARLAND, Daniel, Stoker 1c, D/K 57373, illness

Sunday, 4 January 1931

Admiralty, Plans Division
 JEPSON, Charles F, Commander, illness

Monday, 5 January 1931

Nelson, battleship
 WELCH, George J, Able Seaman, P/J 10850, illness

Vivid, Devonport
 SUMMERS, Harry L, Able Seaman, D/SSX 12228, illness

Saturday, 10 January 1931

Delphinium, minesweeping sloop
 HUGGETT, William H, Stoker Petty Officer, P/K 62459, illness

Tuesday, 13 January 1931

Calypso, light cruiser
 BOREHAM, Wilfred M, Able Seaman, C/J 112917, drowned

Victory, Portsmouth
 BURNBY, Henry J, Chief Petty Officer, P/J 6397, died

Saturday, 17 January 1931

Effingham, cruiser
 MARSHMAN, Kenneth, Stoker 1c, P/KX 80136, accidentally killed

Tuesday, 20 January 1931

Egmont I, Malta
 HAMMOND, Albert V, Able Seaman, P/JX 126023, illness

Friday, 23 January 1931

Courageous, ex-battlecruiser, aircraft carrier
 HABENS, Eric C, Able Seaman, P/J 115394, drowned

Tuesday, 27 January 1931

Renown, battlecruiser
 COMSTOCK, William T, Corporal, RM, 21387 (Ply), illness

Specialised Torpedo "T" Course
 CARSTAIRS, Cyril R J, Lieutenant, illness

Wednesday, 28 January 1931

Victory, Portsmouth
 MARSH, Arthur E S, Able Seaman, P/J 90381, illness

Vivid, Devonport
 GEE, Cecil G, Able Seaman, D/J 27481, illness

Friday, 30 January 1931

Victory, Portsmouth
 MEECH, Stanley E, Able Seaman, P/J 98805, illness

Saturday, 31 January 1931

Champion, light cruiser
 BRISCOE, George, Stoker 1c, P/KX 78217, illness

Sunday, 1 February 1931

Vivid, Devonport
 HOUGHTON, Charles A H, Able Seaman, D/J 51607, illness

Tuesday, 3 February 1931

Vivid, Devonport
 GANDERTON, Charles F, Stoker 2c, D/KX 80593, illness

Saturday, 7 February 1931

RN Hospital, Haslar
 LEWTHWAITE, Cecil T M, Sick Berth Attendant, P/MX 47906, illness

Tuesday, 10 February 1931

Caradoc, light cruiser
 WESTWOOD, Thomas H, Supply Petty Officer, D/M 6150, illness

Marlborough, battleship
 KITSON, William T O, Boy Telegraphist, P/JX 133604, illness

Osiris, submarine
 HUMPHREY, Frank A, Leading Stoker, P/K 65561, illness

Thursday, 12 February 1931

Nelson, battleship
 SAUNDERS, George H, Able Seaman, P/JX 126228, illness

Royal Naval Reserve
 SHAW, Harold J, Paymaster Commander, RNR, illness

Monday, 16 February 1931

Mantis, river gunboat
 BULLER, Gordon, Able Seaman, C/J 111766, illness

Friday, 20 February 1931

Ormonde, ex-minesweeping sloop, survey vessel
 FARAH, Awali, Seaman Seedie, 2/360, illness

Sunday, 22 February 1931

Cairo, light cruiser
 HANDFORD, Isaac J, Chief Stoker, C/K 2154, illness

Sandwich, sloop
 GRAY, John J, Leading Cook, P/M 1242, illness

Tuesday, 3 March 1931

Ganges, Shotley/Harwich
 WEBB, Henry G, Boy 1c, JX 134334, illness

Sunday, 8 March 1931

Ganges, Shotley/Harwich
 PARSLEY, Ernest R, Officer's Steward 2c, C/L 14115, illness

Sunday, 15 March 1931

Dolphin, Gosport
 ELLIS, Albert H, Engine Room Artificer 1c, P/M 5868, illness

Tuesday, 17 March 1931

Courageous, ex-battlecruiser, aircraft carrier
 STOWELL, Ernest F, Leading Stoker, P/K 62320, illness

Wednesday, 18 March 1931

Folkestone, sloop
 ISMAIL, Abubakar, Seedie, 2/354, illness

Sunday, 22 March 1931

Portsmouth, training course
 WEBBER, James E C, Sub Lieutenant, illness

Monday, 23 March 1931

Pilot's Course, air accident
 McDOWELL, Alexander M, Lieutenant, DOI

Thursday, 26 March 1931

Victory, Portsmouth
 HULL, Herbert O, Leading Stoker, P/K 21458, accidentally killed

Saturday, 28 March 1931

Royal Naval Volunteer Reserve
 CAITHNESS, William, Surgeon Lieutenant Commander, RNVR, illness

Royal Navy
 CRUIKSHANK, George G, Surgeon Lieutenant Commander (D), illness

Sunday, 29 March 1931

Defiance, Devonport
 HUBBER, Frederick G, Electrical Artificer 3c, D/M 46203, illness

St Vincent, Gosport
 DE VOIL, Eric J, Gunner, illness

Tuesday, 31 March 1931

London, heavy cruiser
 KING, Thomas D, Leading Stoker, P/K 21104, accidentally killed

Wednesday, 1 April 1931

Glorious, ex-battlecruiser, aircraft carrier, collision
 BICKER, Ernest J, Ordinary Seaman, P/JX 132011, killed

Monday, 6 April 1931

Victory, Portsmouth
 YEO, Samuel, Officer's Steward 3c, P/L 12209, illness

Saturday, 11 April 1931

Hood, battlecruiser
 WOODWARD, Leslie S, Able Seaman, P/J 3739, illness

Sunday, 12 April 1931

Hood, battlecruiser
 BAVERIDGE, Albert C, Able Seaman, P/J 111587, road accident, killed

Monday, 13 April 1931

Valiant, battleship
 OATES, George, Marine, X 218 (Ch), illness

Tuesday, 14 April 1931

Ormonde, ex-minesweeping sloop, survey vessel
 STEPHENS, Reginald A, Lieutenant Commander, illness

Friday, 17 April 1931

Greenwich, destroyer depot ship
 LANDON, Arthur J, Captain, illness

Sunday, 19 April 1931

Lucia, submarine depot ship
 BRACE, Benjamin, Chief Engine Room Artificer 1c, D/M 1987, illness

Royal Naval Reserve, both accidentally killed
 CHAPMAN, Sydney, Lieutenant, RNR
 HARMAN, Charles G, Lieutenant, RNR

Tuesday, 21 April 1931

Pembroke, Chatham
 TUTT, Frederick E, Electrical Artificer Apprentice, C/MX 45652, illness

Wednesday, 22 April 1931

Valiant, battleship
 TWIDDY, Ernest F C, Stoker Petty Officer, C/K 65944, road accident, killed

Thursday, 23 April 1931

Repulse, battlecruiser
 DAVIES, Harry, Marine, 17756 (Ch), illness

Friday, 24 April 1931

Valiant, battleship
 BRENNAN, Albert, Stoker 1c, C/KX 80311, illness

Monday, 27 April 1931

Coventry, light cruiser
 BLACKMORE, Vernon J, Ordinary Seaman, P/JX 132096, illness

London, heavy cruiser
 MANNING, Alfred E, Leading Seaman, P/J 98935, accidentally killed

Saturday, 2 May 1931

Emerald, light cruiser
 HAMMETT, Leonard, Able Seaman, D/J 54919, illness

Sunday, 3 May 1931

Resolution, battleship
 GEACH, William D, Leading Cook, D/M 8597, illness

Monday, 4 May 1931

Pembroke, Chatham
 ARMITAGE, Stanley E, Leading Seaman, C/J 71497, road accident, killed

Wednesday, 6 May 1931

Adventure, minelayer
 HALL, Charles F, Stoker 2c, D/KX 80523, illness

Friday, 8 May 1931

Comus, light cruiser
 LEWIS, Harold, Able Seaman, D/J 108180, road accident, killed

Sunday, 10 May 1931

Pangbourne, minesweeper
 MAXWELL, John G, Leading Stoker, P/K 60408, road accident, killed

Monday, 11 May 1931

London Division, RNVR
 MARR, Henry G, Paymaster Lieutenant Commander, RNVR, illness

Sunday, 17 May 1931

Royal Oak, battleship
 ASHMORE, Eric H, Able Seaman, C/J 126869, illness

Monday, 18 May 1931

Stormcloud, destroyer
 MORGAN, Thomas D, Stoker 1c, D/KX 78737, illness

Tuesday, 19 May 1931

FAA, 446 Flight, Courageous, ex-battlecruiser, aircraft carrier, air crash, both killed
 COLQUHOUN, James A S, Lieutenant
 NANGLE, Henry N M, Lieutenant

Friday, 22 May 1931

Rodney, battleship
 JOHNSTONE, Edward J, Stoker 1c, D/K 17268, illness

Tuesday, 26 May 1931

Vivid, Devonport
 CLERRY, Cornelius, Stoker Petty Officer, D/K 55392, illness

Friday, 29 May 1931

Valiant, battleship
 EGGLETON, John H G, Able Seaman, C/JX 126702, illness

Saturday, 30 May 1931

Tamar, Hong Kong
 REED, William, Stoker 1c, P/K 27125, illness

Thursday, 4 June 1931

Flora, Simonstown, South Africa
 ROSS, William, Leading Stoker, D/K 10811, illness

Friday, 5 June 1931

Curlew, light cruiser
 VELLA, Guiseppe, Officer's Cook 1c, E/LX 20649, illness

Vivid, Devonport
 TUCKER, Frank P, Petty Officer, D/J 120, illness

Monday, 8 June 1931

Vivid, Devonport
 KIRBY, Francis H, Petty Officer, D/J 54543, illness

Tuesday, 9 June 1931

Poseidon, submarine, surfaced, in collision with Japanese SS Yuta in Yellow Sea area, 20 miles north of Wei Hai Wei, China, lost, there were some 34 survivors *(following, sister-boat Parthian)*
 BAGLEY, Arthur J, Stoker 1c, C/KX 75549
 BALSHAW, Robert, Stoker 1c, K 78864
 BEAUMONT, Charles J, Stoker 1c, D/KX 79220

BOWERS, Robert C, Able Seaman, C/J 104875
CLIFF, Harold, Leading Stoker, D/K 56978
COLLINGS, Amos D, Able Seaman, D/J 105478
DOWLING, Frank, Leading Seaman, C/J 106162
GAINES, Ernest G, Leading Stoker, P/K 26669
GRAY, Allan, Stoker 1c, P/K 76663
GRILLS, Thomas V, Petty Officer, P/J 23507
HEWS, George C, Able Seaman, D/J 93255
LOVOCK, Arthur H J, Able Seaman, C/J 100346
PAINE, Albert V, Engine Room Artificer 2c, P/M 15007
PIKE, William H H, Engine Room Artificer 3c, C/M 34932
POINTER, Frederick T A, Stoker 1c, C/K 48329
PYNE, William R, Stoker 1c, C/K 61364
SHERROCKS, Sydney, Leading Stoker, P/K 59646
TOLLIDAY, Frederick C H, Able Seaman, C/J 93958
WHITLEY, William, Stoker 1c, C/K 60695
WINTER, Albert R, Stoker 1c, P/K 65926

Wednesday, 10 June 1931

Comus, light cruiser
 ROWE, Thomas, Stoker 1c, D/K 75974, illness

Saturday, 13 June 1931

Victory, Portsmouth
 LANG, Arthur, Stoker Petty Officer, P/K 10159, illness

Thursday, 18 June 1931

Vivid, Devonport
 GREENWELL, Peter, Stoker 2c, D/KX 80514, illness

Friday, 19 June 1931

Nelson, battleship
 REES, Thomas E, Marine, 22314 (Po), drowned

Stuart, flotilla leader
 EVERSHED, Frederick W, Able Seaman, P/J 15722, illness

Sunday, 21 June 1931

RM Chatham Division
 CASELEY, Gordon T, Marine, 24303 (Ch), illness

Saturday, 27 June 1931

Champion, light cruiser
 LEACH, Albert G, Shipwright 1c, P/M 6688, illness

Sunday, 28 June 1931

Vivid, Devonport
 SYMONS, Samuel E, Stoker 1c, D/K 59472, road accident, killed

Tuesday, 7 July 1931

Folkestone, sloop
 SLASOR, Edward, Stoker 1c, P/K 66205, accidentally killed

Thursday, 9 July 1931

Singleton Abbey, Swansea, Wales
 ABBOTT, Henry N, Lieutenant, RNR, drowned

Friday, 10 July 1931

Kent, heavy cruiser
 TONG, Cyril F P, Writer, C/MX 46352, illness

Saturday, 18 July 1931

Senior Officer's War Course, Tactical Course
 EGERTON, Wilfred A, Rear Admiral, illness

Monday, 20 July 1931

Anthony, destroyer
 TRAVERS, Leonard G, Signalman, C/J 107114, illness

Wednesday, 22 July 1931

Vivid, Devonport
 THOMAS, Edward A, Petty Officer, D/J 13291, illness

Thursday, 23 July 1931

Shropshire, heavy cruiser
 SHAW, Norman, Stoker 1c, C/K 64933, accidentally killed

Vivid, Devonport
 BEER, Frank E, Able Seaman, D/JX 129720, road accident, killed

Friday, 24 July 1931

St Just, Admiralty rescue tug
 PHILLIPS, Charles F, Commissioned Gunner, illness

Thursday, 30 July 1931

Housatonic, passenger liner
 HAINES, Neville E, Midshipman, RNR, illness

Saturday, 1 August 1931

Curacoa, light cruiser
 GOODBAND, Charles W, Leading Seaman, P/J 81759, illness

Sunday, 2 August 1931

Canterbury, light cruiser
 RACKSTRAW, Frank, Blacksmith 2c, C/M 3669, illness

L.23, submarine
 HERRIDGE, William H P, Leading Seaman, P/J 99618, road accident, killed

Marshal Soult, monitor
 STRETTON, Albert E, Signalman, C/J 110814, road accident, killed

Tuesday, 4 August 1931

Cumberland, heavy cruiser
 DREW, Herbert G, Warrant Engineer, illness

Wednesday, 5 August 1931

Adventure, minelayer
 SHUTT, Edward P, Able Seaman, D/J 98403, accidentally killed

Campbell, flotilla leader
 RANDELL, Alfred, Stoker Petty Officer, P/K 29660, road accident, killed

Thursday, 6 August 1931

Fisgard, Portsmouth
 BEYER, Albert F, Petty Officer, P/J 15292, illness

Sunday, 9 August 1931

Pembroke, Chatham
 WALTON, Alfred R, Able Seaman, C/J 100300, died

Tuesday, 11 August 1931

Royal Navy
 HAMILTON, Rowan T, Lieutenant Commander, illness

Friday, 14 August 1931

Vivid, Devonport
 HANNAFORD, Alfred E, Chief Shipwright 2c, D/M 13711, illness

Saturday, 15 August 1931

Victory, Portsmouth
 KING, Frederick W, Commissioned Supply Officer, illness

Sunday, 16 August 1931

Scarborough, sloop
 CORNISH, John A, Able Seaman, C/J 17871, illness

Tuesday, 18 August 1931

RAF service, practicing for Schneider Trophy in experimental aircraft, air crash
 BRINTON, Gerald L, Lieutenant, killed

Friday, 21 August 1931

Dolphin, Gosport
 SAUNDERS, Henry, Yeoman of Signals, P/J 13571, illness

Saturday, 22 August 1931

Sturdy, destroyer
 TAYLOR, Alfred, Stoker Petty Officer, D/K 18808, illness

Friday, 28 August 1931

Courageous, ex-battlecruiser, aircraft carrier
 APPLETON, Wilfred G, Telegraphist, P/J 72284, died

Scarab, river gunboat
 HOOPER, Harold W, Leading Stoker, C/K 64549, drowned

Sunday, 30 August 1931

Chrysanthemum, convoy sloop
 HAKE, George, Able Seaman, D/J 16213, illness

Tuesday, 1 September 1931

Mantis, river gunboat
 LEE-DUNCAN, Harry, Surgeon Lieutenant, illness

Wednesday, 2 September 1931

Medway, submarine depot ship
 ROBERTSON, Alexander, Engine Room Artificer 1c, D/M 6286, illness

Friday, 4 September 1931

Pembroke, Chatham
 WARNES, William H, Able Seaman, C/J 108521, road accident, killed

Sunday, 6 September 1931

Pembroke, Chatham
 MILES, John G, Engine Room Artificer Apprentice, C/MX 46948, illness

Royal Naval Reserve
 MORRISON, Roderick, Honorary Engineer Commander, RNR, illness

Monday, 7 September 1931

Nelson, battleship
 McKAY, John, Seaman, RNR, B 7239, accidentally killed

Seraph, destroyer
 HALL, Archie, Able Seaman, D/J 114285, died

Wednesday, 9 September 1931

Waterhen, destroyer
 LANG, Ernest G, Leading Seaman, P/J 22361, illness

Thursday, 10 September 1931

Vimiera, destroyer
 AZZOPARDI, Giuseppe, Officer's Cook 2c, LX 20223 (on books of Egmont II, Malta), illness

Saturday, 12 September 1931

Enterprise, light cruiser
 GILLINGHAM, William H, Marine, 23040 (Ch), illness

Sunday, 13 September 1931

Cornwall, heavy cruiser
 JAMIESON, Robert, Able Seaman, P/J 102721, illness

Vesper, destroyer
 EVANS, Theophilius, Signalman, D/JX 128708, illness

Saturday, 19 September 1931

Vindictive, cruiser
 GREENE, William J, Engine Room Artificer 2c, C/M 38816, accidentally killed

Vivid, Devonport
 MEDWAY, Samuel W, Able Seaman, D/J 109647, road accident, killed

Monday, 21 September 1931

Dolphin, Gosport
 TOPPING, William J M, Leading Seaman, C/J 24196, illness

Wednesday, 23 September 1931

Calcutta, light cruiser
 NEWLAM, Frank, Petty Officer, C/J 5034, illness

Saturday, 26 September 1931

Berwick, heavy cruiser
 WILDING, Richard H, Able Seaman, D/J 114195, illness

Wednesday, 30 September 1931

Hastings, sloop
 ROBERTS, Henry D, Chief Stoker, D/K 15040, illness

Royal Navy
 DAWE, Reginald, Warrant Master at Arms, illness

Friday, 2 October 1931

FAA, 461 Flight, Glorious, ex-battlecruiser, aircraft carrier, air crash, both killed
 BENNEY, Frederick S, Lieutenant Commander
 ELLIOTT, Archibald G, Lieutenant Commander

Sussex, heavy cruiser
 LOVELESS, Albert E, Engine Room Artificer 4c, C/M 38821, road accident, killed

Saturday, 3 October 1931

Vivid, Devonport
 BEDFORD, Frederick C, Leading Seaman, D/J 77984, illness

Sunday, 4 October 1931

Walrus, destroyer
 GRIFFIN, Stephen, Stoker 1c, D/K 64428, accidentally killed

Tuesday, 6 October 1931

Ballarat, steamship
 MOONEY, James G N P, Chief Stoker, C/K 11764 (Vivid, O/P), drowned

RN Shore Signal Station, Beachy Head
 VENING, George, Signalman, J 21276, illness

Friday, 9 October 1931

Sussex, heavy cruiser
 GABRIEL, Charley, Marine, 23167 (Ch), road accident, killed

Monday, 12 October 1931

Boreas, destroyer
 O'LEARY, Patrick B, Able Seaman, P/J 87296, illness

Tuesday, 13 October 1931

RN Hospital, Malta
 MEHIGAN, Sidney L, Sick Berth Attendant, P/M 39307, died

Wednesday, 14 October 1931

L.53, submarine
 JONES, Albert E, Able Seaman, D/J 98728, drowned

Vivid, Devonport
 ALLEY, Cyril C, Petty Officer, D/J 62087, road accident, killed

Thursday, 15 October 1931

Coldsnap, drifter
 BARNETT, Fred, Marine, Ply X 515 (Exeter), onboard, drowned

Saturday, 17 October 1931

Revenge, battleship
 ROWE, Ernest T, Chief Engine Room Artificer 1c, P/M 2254, illness

Sunday, 18 October 1931

Queen Elizabeth, battleship
 DENHAM, William H, Regulating Petty Officer, D/M 39140, illness

Monday, 19 October 1931

Vidette, destroyer
 EMERY, Bertie G, Able Seaman, D/J 107505, drowned

Monday, 26 October 1931

Pembroke, Chatham
 CALDICOTT, Alfred G, Stoker Petty Officer, C/K 58055, road accident, killed

Tuesday, 27 October 1931

Cormorant, Gibraltar
 FREEMAN, Henry G, Telegraphist, P/J 105551, killed

Sunday, 1 November 1931

Royal Naval Reserve
 BROWN, Brian M, Sub Lieutenant, RNR, illness

Wednesday, 4 November 1931

Pangbourne, minesweeper
 HANCOCK, William G, Stoker Petty Officer, P/K 7725, illness

Monday, 9 November 1931

Hermes, aircraft carrier
 KIRBY, Frank, Supply Chief Petty Officer, C/M 11104, illness

Wednesday, 11 November 1931

*Minesweeper **Peterfield** grounded in South China Sea and wrecked. There were no casualties*

Thursday, 12 November 1931

Pembroke, Chatham
 DEAN, Arthur G, Ordnance Artificer Apprentice, C/MX 46517, illness

Saturday, 14 November 1931

Durban, light cruiser
 GRANT, Ernest H, Marine, X 140 (Po), killed in Brazil

Tuesday, 17 November 1931

Snapdragon, minesweeping sloop
 ELLIOTT, George H, Shipwright 2c, D/M 7213, illness

Sunday, 22 November 1931

Hermes, aircraft carrier
 COWSILL, Richard, Stoker 1c, C/K 60651, illness

Pembroke, Chatham
 DURRAN, James E, Stoker 1c, C/K 65768, illness

Thursday, 26 November 1931

Excellent, Portsmouth
 HOYLAND, Frederick A, Leading Seaman, P/J 108745, road accident, killed

Friday, 27 November 1931

Pembroke, Chatham
 DUNN, Joseph C J, Chief Engine Room Artificer 2c, C/M 2194, illness

Sunday, 29 November 1931

Ganges, Shotley/Harwich
 STEVENSON, Harry B P, Marine, 18767 (Ch), illness

Wednesday, 2 December 1931

Sandhurst, destroyer depot ship
 JONES, Leonard T, Leading Cook, C/M 38155, died

Shamrock, destroyer
 COLLYER, William A, Able Seaman, P/J 13580, drowned

Thursday, 3 December 1931

Iron Duke, gunnery training ship
 BROOKSMITH, Eldred S, Captain, illness

Friday, 4 December 1931

Valiant, battleship
 SNOWDEON, Leonard, Able Seaman, C/JX 125048, road accident, killed

Friday, 11 December 1931

Enterprise, light cruiser
 ALLEN, Harry A, Warrant Engineer, drowned

Tuesday, 15 December 1931

Queen Elizabeth, battleship
 SERVICE, John G, Ordinary Seaman, P/JX 132024, illness

Thursday, 17 December 1931

Pigmy, submarine depot ship, Gosport
 PRIDMORE, William R, Signalman, C/J 112576, road accident, killed

Friday, 18 December 1931

Pembroke, Chatham
 MARTIN, Henry T, Able Seaman, C/J 106200, illness

Saturday, 19 December 1931

Excellent, Portsmouth
 MERLE, Harold E, Leading Stoker, P/K 7140, illness

Royal Naval Reserve
 CALVERT, John J, Skipper, RNR, illness

Monday, 21 December 1931

FAA, 406 Flight, Emerald, light cruiser, air crash
 HEINEMANN, Peter D, Lieutenant, killed

Tuesday, 22 December 1931

M.2, seaplane-carrying submarine
 STILLMAN, Alfred H, Able Seaman, P/JX 128809, illness

Vernon, Portsmouth
 PRITCHARD, Thomas A, Petty Officer, P/J 32637, road accident, killed

Sunday, 27 December 1931

Wireless Telegraph Station, Aden
 POULTNEY, Albert D, Leading Telegraphist, C/82640, illness

Monday, 28 December 1931

Cyclamen
 HILLIARD, Harold, Stoker Petty Officer, C/K 21428, died

1932

Friday, 1 January 1932

Royal Sovereign, battleship
 WEST, Clement F, Leading Telegraphist, P/J 79168, illness

Saturday, 2 January 1932

Pembroke, Chatham
 TAYLOR, Walter J C, Stoker Petty Officer, C/K 34349, illness

Monday, 4 January 1932

Fisgard, Portsmouth
 HARRIS, Charlie, Petty Officer, P/J 7492, illness

Malaya, battleship
 MONK, William J, Able Seaman, D/J 113852, illness

Wednesday, 6 January 1932

Portsmouth
 GARDINER, Bernard C, Colonel, RM, illness

Queen Elizabeth, battleship
 BAIN, William A, Chief Petty Officer, D/M 3045, illness

Whirlwind, destroyer
 MURTON, James J, Able Seaman, C/JX 126051, shock after immersion, died

Saturday, 9 January 1932

Cumberland, heavy cruiser
 WARD, Patrick, Able Seaman, C/JX 131085, died

Emerald, light cruiser
 CONLON, Eugene, Stoker Petty Officer, D/K 22980, drowned

Monday, 11 January 1932

Cumberland, heavy cruiser
 TOTTMAN, Alfred G, Stoker 1c, C/K 59486, illness

Wednesday, 13 January 1932

Pembroke, Chatham
 KNIGHT, Albert W, Engine Room Artificer 5c, C/MX 46545, illness

Thursday, 14 January 1932

Campbell, flotilla leader
 ROBERTS, John D, Able Seaman, P/J 113282, accidentally killed

Royal Naval Reserve
 SINKINS, James, Chief Skipper, RNR, illness

Saturday, 16 January 1932

Cambrian, light cruiser
 NEWLAND, Harold E, Stoker 1c, C/K 67153, road accident on 15 December 1931, DOI

Monday, 18 January 1932

Pembroke, Chatham
 HOBMAN, Jack W, Master at Arms, C/M 35729, illness

Thursday, 21 January 1932

Resolution, battleship
 LEACH, John E, Able Seaman, D/J 106865, drowned

Friday, 22 January 1932

Pembroke, Chatham
 RALPH, Harry, Stoker Petty Officer, C/K 58194, illness

Saturday, 23 January 1932

Medway, submarine depot ship
 MUNSON, Cecil J, Able Seaman, C/J 110993, illness

Sunday, 24 January 1932

Royal Naval Reserve
 DAVISON, Anthony J, Honorary Engineer Commander, RNR, illness
 LESLIE, Norman, Lieutenant Commander, RNR, illness

Friday, 26 January 1932

M.2, seaplane-carrying submarine, diving accident in English Channel off Portland, lost. Crew declared dead on the 29th, there were no survivors *(below)*

ARBUTHNOT, Crofton K, Lieutenant Commander
BACK, Leonard S, Electrical Artificer 3c, D/M 37056
BANKS, Sydney W, Petty Officer, C/J 48971
BLAKE, Frederick J, Petty Officer, P/J 46983
BROWN, Dougal Mc P, Leading Steward, C/L 12605
BURRIDGE, Jack, Leading Telegraphist, P/J 60943
BUTCHER, Harold F, Able Seaman, C/J 91916
CHAPMAN, Cecil, Able Seaman, C/JX 126505
CLARKE, Allan, Petty Officer, D/J 43273
COLESHILL, Charles J, Able Seaman, P/J 102918
DRUMMOND, James, Stoker 1c, P/K 62886
EDWARDS, John H, Able Seaman, D/J 106978
ELLIS, Stanley G, Petty Officer Telegraphist, P/J 29040
ENGLAND, George, Able Seaman, C/J 58560
ESTCOURT, George, Act/Stoker Petty Officer, C/K 65495
FERGUSON, Douglas, Stoker 1c, P/KX 79049
GREGORY, Leslie, Leading Aircraftsman, RAF, 364018
HARDY, Charles P, Engine Room Artificer 1c, P/M 31105
HARMAN, Frank J, Leading Aircraftsman, RAF, 364868
HAYES, William A, Warrant Engineer
HEAD, Hamilton C W, Lieutenant

HORN, Stanley C A, Engine Room Artificer 1c, D/M 21453
JACKSON, Edward V, Engine Room Artificer 4c, C/M 39396
JACOBS, Albert E, Leading Seaman, C/J 96297
JARRETT, Sidney R W, Able Seaman, C/J 100140
KING, James, Act/Chief Petty Officer, C/J 18133
LAKIN, John W, Leading Stoker, P/K 59059
LEATHES, John D De M, Lieutenant Commander
LEAVY, Frederick W, Signalman, D/J 94973
LEWIS, John W J, Stoker 1c, D/K 63662
MACDONALD, Louis P, Stoker Petty Officer, P/K 16558
MACDONALD, Somerled, Lieutenant
MATTHEWS, Edward, Stoker 1c, P/K 64672
MORRIS, Thomas, Able Seaman, C/J 96156
O'DWYER, Albert A E, Able Seaman, C/J 102310
OLIVER, Frank H J, Leading Steward, C/L 12825
PEPLOW, William, Able Seaman, D/J 101056
POWELL, Henry, Act/Leading Stoker, P/K 60855
RAWLINGS, William H, Able Seaman, C/J 108253
READY, Frank, Able Seaman, P/J 25478
SHARPE, George, Leading Stoker, P/K 59370
SIMS, John H, Engine Room Artificer 3c, P/M 35324
SMALES, Joseph F, Yeoman of Signals, D/J 22885
SMITH, Reginald, Able Seaman, C/J 99442
SWEETLAND, Cecil S, Stoker 1c, D/KX 75588
THOMAS, Ernest J, Telegraphist, P/J 76817
THORNTON, Thomas, Able Seaman, C/JX 128413
THRELFALL, Charles H, Stoker 1c, P/KX 75873
TOPPIN, Henry C, Lieutenant (Pilot)
TOTTERDELL, James H F, Act/Leading Stoker, D/K 61154
TOWNSEND, Claud R, Lieutenant (Observer)
TREACY, Philip, Leading Seaman, C/J 105646
VINCENT, Arthur J, Able Seaman, C/J 24276
WALKER, Ralph, Stoker 1c, P/KX 78023
WATSON, William A, Stoker 1c, C/KX 67092
WHITING, Francis C, Able Seaman, D/JX 127947
WILLIAMS, Leonard W, Engine Room Artificer 3c, D/M 36709
WINGFIELD, Harold, Able Seaman, C/JX 128093
WOODHOUSE, Frank L, Stoker 1c, D/K 60100
WRATHMALL, Charles (real name, but served as John Edward Wrathmall), Able Seaman, P/J 37310

There were no more Royal Navy submarine losses until June 1939

Wednesday, 27 January 1932

Frobisher, cruiser
 BUSHELL, William J, Petty Officer, P/JX 126659, illness

Thursday, 28 January 1932

Constance, light cruiser
 EATON, George A, Chief Engine Room Artificer 2c, P/M 2114, died

Renown, battlecruiser
 HEATH, William H K, Leading Seaman, D/J 100045, accidentally killed

Saturday, 30 January 1932

RN Hospital, Chatham
 WYATT, Ernest S, Sick Berth Attendant, C/M 38908, road accident, killed

York, heavy cruiser
 HALLIMAN, Stanley H, Stoker 2c, C/KX 80885, illness

Sunday, 31 January 1932

Ganges, Shotley/Harwich
 HOLMES, Alfred J, Boy 1c, JX 136069, accidentally killed

Wednesday, 3 February 1932

Moth, river gunboat
 NORRIS, Leslie C, Leading Telegraphist, C/J 101627, illness

Victory, Portsmouth
 GULLIS, Harold V P, Ordinary Seaman, P/JX 133175, illness

Friday, 5 February 1932

Greenwich, destroyer depot ship
 FIGG, Bertram G E, Chief Engine Room Artificer 1c, P/M 559, illness

Sunday, 7 February 1932

Greenwich, destroyer depot ship
 WYATT, Herbert J, Chief Petty Officer Writer, D/M 7266, illness

Tuesday, 9 February 1932

Engineer Course
 HARVEY, Desmond, Act/Sub Lieutenant (E), illness

Otway, submarine
 BUCKLEY, John H, Lieutenant, illness, died in HS Maine

Thursday, 11 February 1932

Cornwall, heavy cruiser
 SKEET, Henry T, Stoker Petty Officer, P/K 59513, illness

Victory XI, Portland
 MUSSETT, Leslie A, Seaman, RNR, X 8198 B, illness

Saturday, 13 February 1932

Medway, submarine depot ship
 FELLOWS, John, Petty Officer, D/J 23876, illness

Wednesday, 17 February 1932

Courageous, ex-battlecruiser, aircraft carrier, aircraft crash at sea
 STANLEY, James, Able Seaman, P/SSX 12188, killed

Suffolk, heavy cruiser, Japanese shellfire at Shanghai *(below)*
 FRANCIS, Hubert A, Able Seaman, C/JX 132017, killed
 PRIOR, Herbert G, Leading Seaman, P/J 96430, DOW

Thursday, 18 February 1932

Pembroke, Chatham
 GOLDSWORTHY, Oliver W, Engine Room Artificer Apprentice, MX 47959, illness

Friday, 19 February 1932

Danae, light cruiser
 DAWE, William J T, Stoker Petty Officer, D/K 20268, died

Pembroke, Chatham
 LAMB, Albert C, Master at Arms, C/M 35500, illness

Tuesday, 23 February 1932

Resolution, battleship
 ATTARD, Joseph, Petty Officer Steward, E/L 7214, illness

Wednesday, 24 February 1932

Danae, light cruiser
 SMITH, Louis A, Supply Petty Officer, D/M 37351, illness

Thursday, 25 February 1932

FAA, 401 Flight, Courageous, ex-battlecruiser, aircraft carrier, air crash
 DITTON, Hugh, Lieutenant Commander, killed

Friday, 26 February 1932

Royal Naval Reserve
 SANDERSON, Harold A, Honorary Captain, RNR, illness

Sunday, 28 February 1932

Frobisher, cruiser
 MAUNSELL-SMYTH, George H, Commander (E), illness

Monday, 29 February 1932

Cambrian, light cruiser
 BENTHAM, James T, Able Seaman, CH/X 126569, illness

Tuesday, 1 March 1932

Cornwall, heavy cruiser
 KIRBY, George W, Leading Seaman, P/J 58367, accidentally killed

Thursday, 3 March 1932

Hastings, sloop
 AH, Mohamed, Seedie Seaman, Aden 2/386, illness

Royal Sovereign, battleship
 MAY, Percival C, Able Seaman, P/J 100631, illness

Friday, 4 March 1932

Sandhurst, destroyer depot ship
 WRIGHT, Frederick C, Stoker 1c, C/K 55064, illness

Vernon, Portsmouth
 BURNETT, John, Leading Telegraphist, P/J 26636, road accident, killed

Saturday, 5 March 1932

RN Hospital, Haslar
 WARBURTON, Llewellyn R, Surgeon Commander, illness

Monday, 7 March 1932

Excellent, Portsmouth
 ROWE, George, Able Seaman, P/J 105935, illness

York, heavy cruiser
 ADAMS, Alfred H, Stoker 1c, C/K 62450, road accident, killed

Friday, 11 March 1932

Exeter, heavy cruiser
 COLLINS, Thomas S, Act/Warrant Engineer, illness

Saturday, 12 March 1932

Cumberland, heavy cruiser
 CUNNINGTON, George E W, Telegraphist, C/JX 132330, illness

Kent, heavy cruiser
 RINTOUL, John G E, Corporal, RM, 19851 (Ch), illness

Zest, water carrier
 BOWIE, George N, Able Seaman, Dockyard Employee, drowned

Wednesday, 16 March 1932

Ganges, Shotley/Harwich
 AUSTIN, Thomas, Chief Petty Officer Telegraphist, J 2072, illness

Harebell, convoy sloop
 WILLIAMS, James M, Assistant Steward, D/LX 21236, illness

Thursday, 17 March 1932

Basilisk, alongside Bulldog, both destroyers
 BOARD, Thomas W, Able Seaman, D/J 115271, accidentally killed

Royal Australian Navy
 CURRY, Hugh F, Commander, illness

Friday, 18 March 1932

Olympus, submarine
 SPOONER, William H, Leading Signalman, D/J 25439, died

Monday, 21 March 1932

Dauntless, light cruiser
 ADLAM, Charles F, Able Seaman, P/JX 126050, illness

Wednesday, 23 March 1932

Diomede, light cruiser
 RIBBINS, Charles J (real name, but served as Charles J Rivvins), Able Seaman, C/J 30155, drowned

Saturday, 26 March 1932

Malaya, battleship
 ROBINSON, Robert H, Signal Boy, D/JX 134184, illness

Monday, 28 March 1932

Victory, Portsmouth
 ALLEN, Harold V, Supply Assistant, P/MX 45900, illness

Friday, 1 April 1932

Royal Naval Volunteer Reserve
 BEVIS, Restal R, Honorary Lieutenant, RNVR, illness

Sunday, 3 April 1932

Vernon, Portsmouth
 ORBELL, Charles T, Regulating Petty Officer, P/M 39588, illness

Vivid, Devonport
 RAINEY, Michael, Stoker 1c, D/K 6603, illness

Monday, 4 April 1932

Searcher, destroyer
 CHALCROFT, Ernest F, Leading Stoker, P/K 21165, drowned

Wednesday, 6 April 1932

Royal Naval Reserve
 BOTHERAS, William R, Lieutenant, RNR, illness

Thursday, 7 April 1932

Pembroke, Chatham
 CAST, William J, Engine Room Artificer Apprentice, MX 47799, road accident, killed

Sunday, 10 April 1932

Dragon, light cruiser
 TAYLOR, George R, Ordinary Seaman, C/JX 132968, drowned

Wednesday, 13 April 1932

Cormorant, Gibraltar
 KENNA, John, Stoker 1c, C/K 65940, illness

Friday, 15 April 1932

Danae, light cruiser
 ROBINSON, Wilfred J, Marine, 20953 (Ply), drowned

Sunday, 17 April 1932

Vivid, Devonport
 WILLIAMS, David, Stoker 1c, D/KX 76557, illness

Monday, 18 April 1932

Excellent, Portsmouth
 WILES, Henry C, Able Seaman, P/J 111134, road accident, killed

Tuesday, 19 April 1932

Victory, Portsmouth
 JOHNSTONE, Hope, Telegraphist Lieutenant, illness

Wednesday, 20 April 1932

Royal Navy
 DONOVAN, Alexander M, Lieutenant Commander, illness

Friday, 22 April 1932

Hermes, aircraft carrier
 BRUNNING, David J, Joiner 1c, C/M 4523, illness

Waterhen, destroyer
 GLINN, Ronald E, Able Seaman, D/J 110049, accidentally killed

Saturday, 23 April 1932

Vindictive, cruiser
 ALMOND, Amos, Engine Room Artificer 1c, C/M 2922, illness

Monday, 25 April 1932

FAA, 462 Sqn, Glorious, ex-battlecruiser, aircraft carrier, air crash
 IRVEN, Paul L H D, Lieutenant, killed
Resolution, battleship
 HAMILTON, Archibald, Midshipman, killed

Saturday, 30 April 1932

Royal Naval Reserve
 GRAINGER, Alfred A, Paymaster Commander, RNR, illness

Sunday, 1 May 1932

Cornwall, heavy cruiser
 BECKINGHAM, Frank W L, Ordinary Seaman, P/JX 133992, illness

Vivid, Devonport
 JEWELL, Courtney, Officer's Cook 2c, D/L 14669, illness

Tuesday, 3 May 1932

Orpheus, submarine
 TYRWHITT, Robert, Sub Lieutenant, illness

Thursday, 5 May 1932

Douglas, flotilla leader
 WALKER, James H, Sub Lieutenant, illness

Vernon, Portsmouth
 CONDLIFFE, William F G, Electrical Artificer 2c, P/M 35270, road accident, killed

Friday, 6 May 1932

Royal Naval Reserve
 TURNER, John, Chief Skipper, RNR, illness

Sunday, 8 May 1932

Portsmouth, training course
 TROTTER, Robert C W, Sub Lieutenant, illness

Renown, battlecruiser
 ALLEN, William E, Stoker 1c, D/K 65334, illness

Monday, 9 May 1932

Ladybird, river gunboat
 BOYD, Leonard F, Able Seaman, P/J 109533, drowned

Tuesday, 10 May 1932

Warspite, battleship
 DAGNELL, Arthur A, Stoker 1c, P/KX 80689, illness

Wednesday, 11 May 1932

Royal Naval Reserve
 SCHJONEMAN, Laurtiz P, Chief Skipper, RNR, illness

Royal Sovereign, battleship
 HEALING, John W M, Lieutenant Commander, illness

Thursday, 12 May 1932

Sussex, heavy cruiser
 CORDELL, Walter C E, Petty Officer, C/J 25139, accidentally killed

Saturday, 21 May 1932

Lucia, submarine depot ship
 FOX, Harold, Leading Stoker, D/K 21273, illness

Sunday, 22 May 1932

Malabar, Bermuda
 DAVIDSON, Robert G, Petty Officer, C/J 8339, accidentally killed

Monday, 23 May 1932

Parthian, submarine
 PETT, Ernest E, Stoker 1c, C/KX 79348, drowned

Royal Naval Reserve
 Earl of Inchcape, Honorary Captain, RNR, illness

Thursday, 26 May 1932

Vivid, Devonport
 MITCHELL, Richard C, Stoker 1c, D/K 64155, illness

Sunday, 29 May 1932

Royal Navy
 ROOKE, Robert L, Warrant Engineer, illness

Royal Sovereign, battleship
 WISE, William, Leading Stoker, P/K 57961, road accident, killed

Tuesday, 31 May 1932

Bruce, flotilla leader
 McDONALD, William G, Engineer Lieutenant Commander, illness

Victory
 CROCKFORD, Henry G, Stoker 1c, P/K 10170, illness

Thursday, 2 June 1932

Vivid, Devonport
 TUCKER, Victor E, Petty Officer, D/J 19624, illness

Monday, 6 June 1932

Pembroke, Chatham
 HILLS, Albert G, Stoker 1c, C/K 63453, illness

Wednesday, 8 June 1932

Endeavor, survey ship
 RICE, William V, Commander, illness

FAA, 466 Flight, Furious, aircraft carrier, air crash, both killed
 MARGETTS, Dennis J, Lieutenant
 NEWSHAM, James, Lieutenant

Thursday, 9 June 1932

Vivid, Devonport
 HISCOCK, William G, Telegraphist, D/J 41575, died

Friday, 10 June 1932

Scarab, river gunboat
 TURNBULL, Claude S B, Lieutenant, illness

Sunday, 12 June 1932

Courageous, ex-battlecruiser, aircraft carrier
 O'BRIEN, William, Chief Stoker, P/K 12324, illness

Thursday, 16 June 1932

H.24, submarine
 VOAK, William J, Able Seaman, P/J 109338, motorcycle accident, killed *(second man died the next day)*

Friday, 17 June 1932

H.24, submarine
 BRUCE, Alfred N, Leading Seaman, P/J 104004, motorcycle accident, DOI

Sunday, 19 June 1932

Constance, light cruiser
 LLOYD, George D, Commissioned Gunner, illness

Monday, 20 June 1932

Warspite, battleship
 GUY, Arthur T H, Able Seaman, P/J 113125, accidentally killed

Tuesday, 21 June 1932

RN Hospital, Plymouth
 GREET, William C, Paymaster Lieutenant, illness

Friday, 24 June 1932

Pembroke, Chatham
 SLATTERY, Ernest J, Stoker 1c, C/K 9976, illness

Sunday, 26 June 1932

Pembroke, Chatham
 AMOS, Edward W, Stoker 1c, C/K 66576, illness

Tuesday, 28 June 1932

Scimitar, destroyer
 BESWICK, Harry, Stoker 1c, C/K 65244, road accident, killed

Wednesday, 29 June 1932

Victory, Portsmouth
 AITKEN, Mark J, Surgeon Commander, illness

Thursday, 30 June 1932

Vivid, Devonport
 STRODE, John H, Supply Chief Petty Officer, D/M 985, illness

Saturday, 2 July 1932

Excellent, Portmouth
 CHERRY, George H, Able Seaman, P/J 49823, illness

Sunday, 3 July 1932

Vivid, Devonport
 COLLINS, Edwin T, Petty Officer, D/J 12991, illness

Wednesday, 6 July 1932

Cormorant, Gibraltar
 MILLS, Edward M, Telegraphist, P/J 101509 (served as Edward Haddock), road accident, killed

Thursday, 7 July 1932

Royal Naval Reserve
 FLETT, John R, Commissioned Engineer, RNR, illness

Sunday, 10 July 1932

Wallace, flotilla leader
 WELCH, Douglas W R, Stoker 1c, P/KX 75178, illness

Monday, 11 July 1932

Titania, submarine depot ship
 BEAUMONT, Harry, Able Seaman, C/JX 129191, road accident, killed

Friday, 15 July 1932

Malabar, Bermuda
 BELL, Raymond T, Leading Telegraphist, P/J 37637, illness

Monday, 18 July 1932

Royal Navy
 TURNER, Rev Archer, Chaplain, illness

Spey, ex-P.38, patrol boat
 STEEL, Richard W, Warrant Engineer, illness

Tuesday, 19 July 1932

Courageous, ex-battlecruiser, aircraft carrier
 EASTON, Sidney T, Able Seaman, P/J 18183, illness

Friday, 22 July 1932

Gannet, river gunboat
 ATKINSON, Eric, Able Seaman, D/J 97757, illness

Saturday, 23 July 1932

Royal Sovereign, battleship
 MILES, Claude L, Stoker 1c, P/K 59275, illness

Monday, 25 July 1932

Cornwall, heavy cruiser
 REES, John, Warrant Schoolmaster, illness

Tuesday, 2 August 1932

Calypso, light cruiser
 FIELD, Alfred, Commissioned Gunner, illness

Wednesday, 3 August 1932

Devonshire, heavy cruiser
 DAVEY, Frederick S, Stoker Petty Officer, D/K 59067, illness

Thursday, 4 August 1932

Tern, river gunboat
 YU, Chen C, Boat Boy, (Chinese), drowned

Saturday, 6 August 1932

Cornwall, heavy cruiser
 LEACH, Ernest, Cook, P/MX 48050, illness

Friday, 12 August 1932

L.27, submarine
 SMITH, Sidney N, Telegraphist, D/J 106613, road accident, killed

Sunday, 14 August 1932

RN Hospital, Plymouth
 JONES, James, Leading Sick Berth Attendant, D/M 35544, illness

Tuesday, 16 August 1932

Furious, aircraft carrier
 BAKER, Percy H, Able Seaman, D/J 81794, illness

Pilot's Course, air crash
 KAY, Andrew B, Lieutenant, killed

Thursday, 18 August 1932

Pembroke, Chatham
 WRAGG, William F, Petty Officer, C/J 12078, illness

Saturday, 20 August 1932

Victory, Portsmouth
 TRIGGS, Harry F, Able Seaman, P/JX 132275, road accident, killed

Sunday, 21 August 1932

Delhi, light cruiser
 TEMP, George, Chief Petty Officer, D/J 20729, illness

Whitshed, destroyer
 HALL, Henry J, Able Seaman, P/J 115344, illness

Monday, 22 August 1932

Vivien, destroyer
 LUCKHURST, Henry W, Stoker 1c, C/K 48734, road accident, killed

Wednesday, 24 August 1932

Challenger
 MUSSELL, Walter F, Steward, P/L 14878, illness

Royal Naval Reserve
 BRENNAN, Arthur P, Paymaster Lieutenant, RNR, illness

Vivid, Devonport
 BANBURY, Harry, Shipwright 1c, D/M 10283, illness

Thursday, 25 August 1932

Vivid, Devonport
 SMALE, Sydney C, Ordnance Artificer 4c, D/M 37937, illness

Saturday, 27 August 1932

Egmont, Malta
 SPEARING, John, Able Seaman, P J 6262, illness

Valiant, battleship
 BATES, Arthur R, Stoker 1c, C/K 63362, illness

Friday, 2 September 1932

Tarantula, river gunboat
 BISHOP, William W, Able Seaman, C/J 109403, illness

Tuesday, 6 September 1932

RN Hospital, Chatham
 GEE, John C, Colour Sergeant, RM, 17337 (Ch), illness

Thursday, 8 September 1932

Scout, destroyer
 CLEWORTH, William A, Stoker 1c, C/K 64940, illness

Friday, 9 September 1932

Malaya, battleship
 DEE, Paul, Able Seaman, D/JX 128356, died

Sunday, 11 September 1932

Gannet, river gunboat
 DAE, Min C, Officer's Steward 3c, (no service number listed), drowned

Monday, 12 September 1932

Rodney, battleship
 EALES, Joseph S, Supply Petty Officer, D/M 34126, illness

Tuesday, 13 September 1932

Pembroke, Chatham
 BOND, John D, Able Seaman, C/JX 128633, illness

Friday, 16 September 1932

Osprey, Portland
 HINTON, Alfred E, Able Seaman, D/JX 129414, road accident, killed

Monday, 19 September 1932

Victory, Portsmouth
 COOKSON, James W, Able Seaman, P/J 86453, illness

Vindictive, cruiser
 SHACKLEFORD, Harry E, Stoker 1c, P/K 63177, illness

Tuesday, 20 September 1932

Victory, Portsmouth
 NEWTON, Charles W, Able Seaman, P/J 91324, illness

Saturday, 24 September 1932

Cricket, river gunboat
 SEWARD, Reginald W J, Able Seaman, D/J 88015, illness

Sunday, 25 September 1932

Snapdragon, minesweeping sloop
 SMITH, Charles H H, Able Seaman, D/J 110664, drowned

Monday, 26 September 1932

Curacoa, light cruiser
  SCOVELL, Albert C, Stoker 1c, P/K 65231, illness

FAA, 401 Flight, Courageous, ex-battlecruiser, aircraft carrier, air crash
  KING, Henry M, Lieutenant, killed

Wednesday, 28 September 1932

Cornflower, minesweeping sloop
  YOUNG, Christopher, Able Seaman, P/J 94093, illness

Thursday, 29 September 1932

Concord, light cruiser
  ILIFF, Edward, Engineer Commander, illness

Saturday, 1 October 1932

Pilot's Course, air crash, both killed
  DICKSON, Robert D L, Lieutenant
  DOBSON, Vernon W, Sub Lieutenant

Tuesday, 4 October 1932

Devonshire, heavy cruiser
  LAKE, Percival G, Leading Signalman, D/J 48740, illness

Saturday, 8 October 1932

Cormorant, Gibraltar
  STUART, Alfred, Chief Stoker, P/K 11554, died

Sunday, 9 October 1932

Chatham
  BAKER, Hugh S, Lieutenant, RM, illness

Monday, 10 October 1932

Sussex, heavy cruiser
  GODBOLD, James, Able Seaman, C/JX 13236, illness

Thursday, 13 October 1932

Pembroke, Chatham
  GREGORY, Charles F, Stoker 1c, C/K 60527, illness

Sunday, 16 October 1932

Cyclops, repair ship
  VELLA, Joseph, Petty Officer Steward, E/LX 20354, illness

Monday, 17 October 1932

Delhi, light cruiser
  KELLY, Hugh, Marine, 18851 (Ply), drowned

Thursday, 27 October 1932

Vivid, Devonport
  PACKWOOD, William J, Stoker 1c, D/KX 80371, illness

Monday, 31 October 1932

St Vincent, Gosport
  PURTON, Leslie F, Boy 1c, P/JX 136155, illness

Tuesday, 1 November 1932

Vivid, Devonport
  HIGGINS, Arthur W, Stoker 1c, D/K 58913, illness

Wednesday, 2 November 1932

Vivid, Devonport
  PEARCE, Henry W, Chief Shipwright 2c, D/M 7407, illness

Friday, 4 November 1932

Ladybird, river gunboat
  HUNT, Frederick A, Chief Petty Officer, P/J 10673, illness

Saturday, 5 November 1932

Hermes, aircraft carrier
  FOWLER, William, Stoker Petty Officer, D/K 18396, illness

Sunday, 6 November 1932

Ganges, Shotley/Harwich
  SKINNER, Arthur, Stoker Petty Officer, C/K 18614, illness

Sunday, 13 November 1932

Victory, Portsmouth
  McMORRIS, Robert W, Stoker, RNR, V 1736, illness

Monday, 14 November 1932

RN Hospital, Chatham
  FEGAN, James, Sick Berth Attendant, C/MX 45757, illness

Tuesday, 15 November 1932

Portsmouth Dockyard
  PORTER, Alfred A, Commissioned Boatswain, illness

Friday, 18 November 1932

FAA, 405 Flight, Glorious, ex-battlecruiser, aircraft carrier
  DENNIS, Gerald W, Lieutenant, illness

Saturday, 19 November 1932

Effingham, cruiser
  REVANS, John C, Able Seaman, P/JX 126782, illness

Nelson, battleship
 BROWN, Sidney A, Shipwright 2c, P/M 33945, illness

Tuesday, 22 November 1932

Montrose, flotilla leader
 KENYON, Herbert L D, Petty Officer, D/J 89788, drowned

Thursday, 24 November 1932

London Division, RNVR
 BRISTOW, Geoffrey L, Lieutenant, RNVR, illness

Victoria & Albert, Royal Yacht
 HAMMOND, Samuel M, Keeper & Steward of Royal Cabins, illness

Friday, 25 November 1932

Vivid, Devonport
 GROCUTT, Richard, Able Seaman, D/J 14906, illness

Sunday, 27 November 1932

Cumberland, heavy cruiser
 TRIBBLE, Sidney L, Regulating Petty Officer, D/M 39274, illness

Wednesday, 30 November 1932

Thames, submarine
 BATCHELOR, Leonard J, Signalman, C/J 109536, drowned
 STUNNELL, Henry E, Able Seaman, J 95644, drowned

Monday, 5 December 1932

British Mariner, oil tanker
 DOWNES, Joseph L, Commissioned Engineer, RNR, illness

Ganges, Shotley/Harwich
 LARAMAN, Garfield H K, Boy 2c, JX 137684, illness

Wednesday, 7 December 1932

L.56, submarine
 REEMAN, Lancelot E, Stoker 1c, P/K 58359, road accident, killed

Tuesday, 13 December 1932

Dunedin, light cruiser
 PERRY, Walter F, Officer's Cook 2c, P/LX 20111, died

Fowey, sloop
 BARNFIELD, Frederick J, Signalman, P/J 113377, illness

Thursday, 15 December 1932

H.43, submarine
 HART, William H, Stoker 1c, C/KX 77685, road accident, killed

Pembroke, Chatham
 NESBITT, Samuel, Stoker 1c, C/K 65899, illness

Vernon, Portsmouth
 HUXLEY, Robert, Chief Petty Officer, P/J 14199, died

Friday, 16 December 1932

Queen Elizabeth, battleship
 CLAIF, Frank G, Able Seaman, D/J 93773, illness

Tuesday, 20 December 1932

Vivid, Devonport
 McRAE, Alexander, Seaman, RNR, X 6106 C, accidentally killed

Friday, 23 December 1932

Vivid, Devonport
 SHEARS, Reuben G, Commissioned Supply Officer, illness

Sunday, 25 December 1932

Cyclops, repair ship
 MAXWELL, George E, Stoker 1c, C/KX 75548, drowned

Monday, 26 December 1932

Egmont, Malta, both drowned
 NASON, George W P, Sergeant, RM, 15738 (Po)
 YALDEN, Percy W C, Marine, X 498 (Po)

Tuesday, 27 December 1932

Pembroke, Chatham
 MULFORD, Alfred, Stoker 1c, C/K 61933, illness

Veteran, destroyer
 STIRLING, Norman R, Petty Officer, C/J 22976, illness

Saturday, 31 December 1932

Sussex, heavy cruiser
 KNIGHT, Sidney J, Musician, RMB, RMB 2457, illness

Torpedo Depot of Admiralty
 SHARMAN, Laurence C, Commander, illness

1933

Sunday, 1 January 1933

Adventure, minelayer
 QUICK, Richard L, Shipwright 4c, D/MX 45721, illness

Wednesday, 4 January 1933

Cornwall, heavy cruiser
 HARDING, Thomas H, Able Seaman, P/J 12004, illness

Friday, 6 January 1933

Resolution, battleship
 SIMONS, James, Leading Stoker, D/K 21515, died

Saturday, 7 January 1933

Shoreham, sloop
 HARRISON, Lawrence R, Petty Officer, D/J 32191, illness

Tuesday, 10 January 1933

Royal Navy
 FOWLER, Lawrence P, Engineer Commander, illness

Wireless Telegraph Station, Matara, Ceylon *(Sri Lanka)*
 FULLER, Frank, Leading Telegraphist, C/J 108308, illness

Wednesday, 11 January 1933

Effingham, cruiser
 MILLAR, Hugh, Petty Officer, P/J 15505, illness

Thursday, 12 January 1933

RM Deal, Kent
 NICOLL, David I, Py/2nd Lieutenant, RM, illness

Friday, 13 January 1933

Pembroke, Chatham
 WILSON, Ernest G W, Telegraphist, C/J 113022, road accident, killed

Saturday, 14 January 1933

Vivid, Devonport
 JENKINS, William H, Engineman, RNR, E V 158, illness

Monday, 16 January 1933

Hastings, sloop
 BROWN, George J, Leading Stoker, D/KX 76521, drowned

Tuesday, 17 January 1933

Effingham, cruiser
 TOMPKINS, Albert J, Stoker 1c, P/KX 76068, illness

L.26, submarine
 McIVER, George A, Leading Stoker, C/K 58124, drowned

Wednesday, 18 January 1933

Queen Elizabeth, battleship
 McQUADE, William, Marine, 17376 (Ply), illness

Thursday, 19 January 1933

Shamrock, destroyer
 MORRIS, William J, Able Seaman, P/J 113074, killed

Saturday, 21 January 1933

Exeter, heavy cruiser
 BUSWELL, Leonard W, Able Seaman, D/J 109194, accidentally killed

Sunday, 22 January 1933

Valiant, battleship
 STOUT, Ernest C, Leading Stoker, C/K 11512, illness

Monday, 23 January 1933

Valiant, battleship
 SCOTT, Alfred W, Marine, 22359 (Ch), illness

Tuesday, 24 January 1933

Ganges, Shotley/Harwich
 CLARKE, Wilfred W, Boy 1c, JX 136868, illness

Pembroke, Chatham
 HIGGS, Jack D, Ordnance Artificer Apprentice, MX 47665, illness

Vivid, Devonport
 GRAVES, Clarence C, Able Seaman, D/J 6308, illness

Wednesday, 25 January 1933

Flora, Simonstown, South Africa
 SAID, Mohammed B, Steward, L 15173, illness

Hawkins, cruiser
 ROBINSON, James, Stoker 1c, P/KX 75510, drowned

Vivid, Devonport
 MOXHAM, Henry C, Able Seaman, D/JX 130512, illness

Friday, 27 January 1933

Vivid, Devonport
 HARDIE, Cyril N, Steward, D/LX 20573, illness

Sunday, 29 January 1933

Pembroke, Chatham
 EVANS, Reginald A, Petty Officer, C/J 6504, illness

Monday, 30 January 1933

Pembroke, Chatham
 WHITNEY, Willie, Able Seaman, C/J 22735, died

Victory, Portsmouth
 COLLINGWOOD, Joseph W, Petty Officer Telegraphist, P/J 8578, illness

Tuesday, 31 January 1933

Woolwich, destroyer depot ship
 JEFFERS, James, Stoker 1c, 295885, illness

Sunday, 5 February 1933

Courageous, ex-battlecruiser, aircraft carrier
 BOND, Walter C R, Able Seaman, P/J 11313, illness

Monday, 6 February 1933

Vernon, Portsmouth
 STRETTON, Thomas J, Able Seaman, P/J 34209, illness

Wednesday, 8 February 1933

Victory, Portsmouth
 PEPLOE, Charles R, Captain, illness

Friday, 10 February 1933

Victory, Portsmouth
 EDWARDS, Henry F, Lieutenant, illness

Saturday, 11 February 1933

Sandwich, sloop
 LANE, George H, Able Seaman, P/J 27327, accidentally killed

Monday, 13 February 1933

Pembroke, Chatham
 GILL, Thomas, Engine Room Artificer 1c, C/M 27234, illness

Friday, 24 February 1933

Royal Marines HQ, Portsmouth
 CHADWICK, Charles H, Marine, X 480 (Po), illness

Wednesday, 1 March 1933

Royal Sovereign, battleship
 ROBERTS, Peter H H, Lieutenant Commander, illness

Titania, submarine depot ship
 TALBOT, William F, Able Seaman, P/J 69605, road accident, killed

Saturday, 4 March 1933

Royal Navy
 LAURENCE, William G, Able Seaman, D/J 101904, illness

Tuesday, 7 March 1933

Bryony, convoy sloop
 FREWEN-LATON, Ivo W L, Commander, illness

Renown, battlecruiser
 DERRICK, David, Officer's Cook 1c, C/L 14247, illness

Friday, 10 March 1933

Devonshire, heavy cruiser
 VANNER, Eric G, Engine Room Artificer 1c, D/M 11315, died

Saturday, 11 March 1933

Victory, Portsmouth
 WEBB, Albert, Able Seaman, P/J 111411, road accident, killed

Sunday, 12 March 1933

Valiant, battleship
 WINCH, William, Stoker 1c, C/KX 81018, illness

Wednesday, 15 March 1933

Durban, light cruiser
 REEVE, Stanley E, Able Seaman, P/JX 128669, road accident, killed

Ganges, Shotley/Harwich
 BELSEY, Clifford N, Boy 2c, JX 137631, illness

Friday, 17 March 1933

RM Deal
 HUNTINGFORD, Walter L, Lieutenant Colonel, RM, illness

Wednesday, 22 March 1933

Cornwall, heavy cruiser
 BURNEY, James, Marine, 22256 (Po), drowned

Friday, 24 March 1933

Exeter, heavy cruiser, air crash, Arosa Bay, Spain, both killed
 ALTON, Barclay S F, Py/Lieutenant, RM
 CAREY, Thomas G, Lieutenant

RN Hospital, Plymouth
 SMITH, Duncan S, Sick Berth Attendant, D/M 36565, died

Tuesday, 28 March 1933

Durban, light cruiser
 LEEDS, Roland, Lieutenant Commander, illness

Saturday, 1 April 1933

Durban, light cruiser
 JOHNSON, William, Supply Petty Officer, P/M 38276, flying accident in Chilean aircraft, killed

Sunday, 2 April 1933

Berwick, heavy cruiser
 HOURIHANE, Patrick, Leading Stoker, D/K 22319, illness

Portland, RN Base, Captain In Charge
 LECKY, Arthur M, Captain, died

Vivid, Devonport
 HORNE, William J D, Painter 1c, D/M 5158, illness

Sunday, 9 April 1933

Tamar III, Hong Kong
 CARBERY, Patrick, Marine, 17700 (Ch), illness

Victory, Portsmouth
 HEATHCOTE, Charles F, Stoker 1c, P/K 57710, died

Tuesday, 11 April 1933

Cumberland, heavy cruiser
 MOOREY, Charles F, Stoker 1c, C/KX 77630, illness

Friday, 14 April 1933

Victoria & Albert, Royal Yacht
 GAVIN, Charles M, Paymaster Commander, illness

Tuesday, 18 April 1933

Royal Naval Reserve
 CUTSFORTH, Charles L, Commander, RNR, illness

Saturday, 22 April 1933

Victory, Portsmouth
 HOTSTON, Albert, Stoker Petty Officer, P/K 57765, illness

Thursday, 27 April 1933

Effingham, cruiser
 STUNDEN, George, Able Seaman, P/JX 126669, illness

Victory, Portsmouth
 BURRELL, Sykes S, Able Seaman, P/JX 132937, illness

Friday, 28 April 1933

Eagle, aircraft carrier, explosion
 STRATH, Harold E, Chief Electrical Artificer, D/M 10050, killed

Monday, 1 May 1933

Shoreham, sloop
 WALLER, Richard H, Stoker 1c, C/K 62005, illness

Monday, 8 May 1933

Excellent, Portsmouth
 COLE, Francis G, Chief Petty Officer, P/J 6566, illness

Thursday, 11 May 1933

Vivid, Devonport
 POLLARD, James W, Stoker 2c, D/KX 82183, illness

Tuesday, 16 May 1933

Royal Naval Reserve
 BEE, Robert W, Lieutenant Commander, RNR, illness

Thursday, 18 May 1933

Nelson, battleship
 ROLLINGS, Frederick G, Chief Mechanician 2c, P/K 13206, illness

Monday, 22 May 1933

Ouse, Admiralty trawler
 WHITEAR, Joseph H, Stoker 1c, D/K 64153, illness

Wednesday, 24 May 1933

Otway, submarine
 WILLIAMS, James, Stoker 1c, D/KX 80559, drowned

Wednesday, 31 May 1933

Cormorant, Gibraltar
 AMEY, William H, Stoker 1c, P/K 21194, illness

Danae, light cruiser
 HUGHES, Alfred S, Chief Engine Room Artificer 2c, D/M 12699, illness

Friday, 2 June 1933

Victory, Portsmouth
 HUNTER, William F, Supply Assistant, P/MX 46492, road accident, killed

Tuesday, 6 June 1933

Hermes, aircraft carrier
 WEBSTER, Wilfred A, Gunner, illness

Wednesday, 7 June 1933

Adventure, minelayer
 JAMES, Thomas D, Able Seaman, P/JX 132157, illness

Thursday, 8 June 1933

Caradoc, light cruiser
 BUNT, Frederick N, Leading Cook, D/M 39109, illness

Dunoon, minesweeper
 FIDLER, Fred, Stoker 1c, D/K 46727, illness

Glorious, ex-battlecruiser, aircraft carrier
 BARTLETT, William H, Supply Chief Petty Officer, D/M 1996, illness

Friday, 9 June 1933

Excellent, Portsmouth
 CALLINGHAM, Harry V, Able Seaman, P/JX 132669, road accident, killed

Sunday, 11 June 1933

Pembroke, Chatham
 CUTTER, Frederick J, Engine Room Artificer Apprentice, MX 49499, illness

Monday, 12 June 1933

Bryony, convoy sloop
 O'DRISCOLL, Denis, Stoker 1c, D/K 46480, illness

Tuesday, 13 June 1933

Vivid, Devonport
 CLEAVE, Robert H, Engine Room Artificer 1c, D/M 8936, illness

Thursday, 22 June 1933

Dundee, sloop
 SLACK, Frederick C, Chief Petty Officer, P/J 14245, illness

Monday, 26 June 1933

Devonshire, heavy cruiser
 PRICE, Philip E, Able Seaman, D/JX 126797, illness

Tuesday, 27 June 1933

Revenge, battleship
 WINSPEAR, Albert W, Petty Officer, P/J 92746, illness

Thursday, 29 June 1933

Hong Kong Dockyard
 LAWRIE, Edward Mc C W, Captain, illness

Friday, 30 June 1933

Vivid, Devonport
 FLOWER, William A, Blacksmith 3c, P/MX 46419, illness

Saturday, 1 July 1933

Ross, minesweeper
 RIGELSFORD, Joseph J, Stoker 1c, P/K 19044, illness

Monday, 3 July 1933

Adventure, minelayer
 BROOKS, Henry T, Petty Officer, D/J 33798, illness

Paymaster Director General of Admiralty
 MURRAY, Edward G, Paymaster Rear Admiral, illness

Pembroke, Chatham
 SECKER, Thomas J, Able Seaman, C/J 114050, road accident, killed

Thursday, 6 July 1933

Victory, Portsmouth
 FOREMAN, Ronald J, Leading Stoker, P/K 61778, illness

Friday, 7 July 1933

Greenwich, destroyer depot ship
 HOPE, John, Able Seaman, P/JX 130644, illness

Monday, 10 July 1933

Victoria & Albert, Royal Yacht *(below, Maritime Quest)*
 ANSELL, George, Commissioned Gunner (T), illness

Thursday, 13 July 1933

L.23, submarine
 BAKER, Henry W, Petty Officer Telegraphist, P/J 5700, illness

Saturday, 15 July 1933

Watchman, destroyer
 BELL, Robert Mc C, Able Seaman, D/JX 128282, accidentally killed

Monday, 17 July 1933

Cumberland, heavy cruiser
 MOFFAATT, Alfred, Able Seaman, C/JX 126876, illness

Royal Oak, battleship
 CRESSY, Alexander R, Stoker 1c, C/KX 81535, accidentally killed

Sunday, 23 July 1933

Cambrian, light cruiser
 LARGE, Ted S, Stoker 1c, C/KX 75999, illness

Wednesday, 26 July 1933

Royal Navy
 JAQUES, Frank, Engineer Commander, illness

Tuesday, 1 August 1933

Furious, aircraft carrier
 WRIGHT, Frederick D, Able Seaman, D/J 108741, road accident, killed

Wednesday, 9 August 1933

Duchess, destroyer
 ANDREWS, Benjamin H, Petty Officer, C/J 6697, illness

Frobisher, cruiser
 WALL, William J, Stoker 1c, C/KX 75909, illness

Pembroke, Chatham
 McCORMACK, Frederick S, Able Seaman, C/J 97004, road accident, killed

Tuesday, 15 August 1933

Challenger, survey ship
 BURROWS, William R, Able Seaman, P/J 113797, illness

Warspite, battleship
 TRANTER, John J S, Able Seaman, P/JX 127271, illness

Thursday, 17 August 1933

Hawkins, cruiser
 ACOURT, John J, Leading Signalman, P/J 26116, illness

Monday, 21 August 1933

Victory, Portsmouth
 VIGOUR, Cyril, Stoker 1c, P/KX 78095, died
 VIVIAN, Golfred R, Petty Officer, P/J 92875, road accident, killed

Tuesday, 22 August 1933

Norfolk, heavy cruiser
 BLAKE, Marcus, Paymaster Commander, illness

Friday, 25 August 1933

St Angelo, Malta
 WILLCOX, Norman R, Sergeant, RM, 215999 (Po), illness

Victory, Portsmouth
 KELLAND, Harold V, Electrical Artificer 1c, P/M 8185, illness

Monday, 28 August 1933

Pembroke, Chatham
 BRITTAIN, Harold J, Chief Shipwright 2c, C/M 2447, died

Saturday, 2 September 1933

Resolution, battleship
 STEPHENS, Alfred G, Sailmaker, D/J 21722, illness

Victory, Portsmouth
 WILSON, Henry M, Sailmaker, P/J 92062, illness

Tuesday, 5 September 1933

Caradoc, light cruiser
 HORBURY, Norman, Engine Room Artificer 1c, D/M 14530, illness

Rodney, battleship
 ALCORN, Charles F S, Able Seaman, D/J 23415, illness

Saturday, 9 September 1933

Victory, Portsmouth
 DALBY, Amos W, Telegraphist, P/JX 125356, road accident, killed

Monday, 11 September 1933

Duncan, destroyer
 FIELD, Percival C T, Petty Officer, P/J 22592, illness

Wednesday, 13 September 1933

Ganges, Shotley/Harwich
 MATTHEWS, Sydney H, Boy 1c, JX 137694, illness

Thursday, 14 September 1933

Furious, aircraft carrier
 BAILEY, John, Leading Stoker, D/KX 76248, accidentally killed

Saturday, 16 September 1933

Victory, Portsmouth
 HASSETT, Blenner C, Petty Officer, P/J 17282, illness

Monday, 18 September 1933

Proteus, submarine
 SELLS, Charles H, Petty Officer, D/J 21262, accidentally killed

Tuesday, 19 September 1933

St Vincent, Gosport
 ARNOLD, Robert A, Boy 2c, JX 139161, illness

Sunday, 24 September 1933

Acheron, destroyer
 KIRK, Herbert, Able Seaman, P/J 25950, illness

Wednesday, 27 September 1933

Victory, Portsmouth
 HONEYBUN, Francis C, Warrant Telegraphist, illness

Thursday, 28 September 1933

Dunoon, minesweeper
 NANGLE, James J, Able Seaman, D/J 27816, illness

Victory, Portsmouth
 BLOW, Charles H, Stoker 1c, P/K 22161, illness

Saturday, 30 September 1933

Rochester, sloop
 SCOTT, Thomas L, Engineer Commander, illness

Sunday, 1 October 1933

Engineer in Chief Department
FRENCH, Wilfred E, Engineer Commander, illness

Monday, 2 October 1933

FAA, 811 Sqn, Furious, aircraft carrier, air crash, both killed
BULLOCK, Osmund F L, Lieutenant
GOYNS, William F, Leading Telegraphist, P/J 41465

Tuesday, 3 October 1933

Pembroke, Chatham
MEAD, Albert J, Able Seaman, C/J 97731, illness

Sunday, 8 October 1933

L.26, submarine, battery explosion, both killed
RHODES, Leonard, Able Seaman, D/J 107566
WHITING, Frederick J T, Able Seaman, C/JX 129841

Tuesday, 10 October 1933

Royal Navy
MONEY, John P, Lieutenant Commander, illness

St Vincent, Gosport
TOLSON, Albert E S, Boy 2c, JX 138327, illness

Friday, 13 October 1933

Nelson, battleship
FIELD, William C, Able Seaman, P/J 24499, illness

Sunday, 15 October 1933

Ganges, Shotley/Harwich
GALLOWAY, Trevor A, Boy 2c, JX 138934, illness

Glorious, ex-battlecruiser, aircraft carrier
BUCK, Jack L W, Engine Room Artificer 5c, D/MX 47650, illness

Hood, battlecruiser
KEEGAN, Denis L, Stoker 1c, P/K 66573, drowned

Monday, 23 October 1933

Iron Duke, ex-battleship, gunnery training ship
BIRCH, Henry J M, Stoker 1c, P/K 57831, road accident, killed

Wednesday, 25 October 1933

Caradoc, light cruiser
BAKER, Norman S, Engine Room Artificer 3c, D/M 87009, illness

Saturday, 28 October 1933

Queen Elizabeth, battleship
HUDSON, John F, Leading Telegraphist, D/J 75323, illness

Sunday, 29 October 1933

Excellent, Portsmouth
SMITH, Alfred V, Writer, P/MX 47197, died

Ormonde, ex-minsweeping sloop, survey ship
MILLER, Arthur J, Leading Stoker, D/KX 75520, illness

Monday, 30 October 1933

Victory, Portsmouth
JORDAN, Albert C, Able Seaman, P/JX 126823, road accident, killed

Tuesday, 31 October 1933

L.56, submarine
FERGUSON, James, Able Seaman, D/JX 126620, road accident, killed

Thursday, 2 November 1933

Cornflower, minesweeping sloop
FURBER, Arthur J, Supply Chief Petty Officer, P/M 30215, illness

Despatch, light cruiser
BLACKBURN, John, Stoker 1c, P/KX 79634, accidentally killed

Sunday, 5 November 1933

Watchman, destroyer
GOSS, Sydney L, Signalman, D/JX 130532, accidentally killed

Monday, 6 November 1933

Caledon, light cruiser
SCANTLEBURY, Robert A, Leading Stoker, D/K 62794, illness

Dauntless, light cruiser
FAIRBURN, Arthur R, Leading Seaman, P/J 104894, illness

Victory, Portsmouth
DEAN, Lionel S K, Ordinary Seaman, P/SSX 14268, road accident, killed

Thursday, 9 November 1933

Laburnum, minesweeping sloop
HALL, Albert E, Able Seaman, D/J 38950, illness

Rochester, sloop
GARDNER, Herbert S, Able Seaman, C/J 109202, drowned

Tuesday, 14 November 1933

Danae, light cruiser
VESEY, Blakeman, Lieutenant, drowned

Wednesday, 15 November 1933

Defiance, Devonport
HOCKLEY, Charles C, Leading Seaman, D/J 105705, illness

Sunday, 19 November 1933

Admiralty, 2nd Sea Lord's Office
 ROBERTS, Ernest W, Engineer Rear Admiral, illness

Monday, 20 November 1933

Cornwall, heavy cruiser
 ADSHEAD, Alfred E, Commissioned Gunner, illness

Victory, Portsmouth
 RUNICLES, Charles N, Chief Petty Officer Writer, P/M 34998, illness

Tuesday, 21 November 1933

London, heavy cruiser
 PERING, Arthur W, Ordinary Seaman, P/JX 134915, died

Thursday, 23 November 1933

Blanche, destroyer
 ELEMENT, William H, Able Seaman, P/J 112399, illness

Pembroke, Chatham
 TOURLE, Cecil T, Leading Seaman, C/J 100904, illness

Friday, 24 November 1933

Vivid, Devonport
 LOWE, Ronald W, Steward, D/LX 21116, illness

Sunday, 26 November 1933

Shropshire, heavy cruiser
 CLARKE, George A, Ordinary Seaman, D/JX 135585, accidentally killed

Monday, 27 November 1933

Glorious, ex-battlecruiser, aircraft carrier
 CHAMBERLAIN, Frederick C S, Musician, RMB, RMB X 153, drowned

Thursday, 7 December 1933

Vivid, Devonport
 CLARK, Robert, Able Seaman, D/J 50353, illness

Friday, 8 December 1933

Renown, battlecruiser
 GORRING, Thomas W, Stoker 1c, C/KX 82296, illness

Friday, 15 December 1933

Herald, ex-minesweeping sloop, survey vessel
 CURTHOYS, Herbert W J, Able Seaman, D/JX 126453, illness

Wednesday, 20 December 1933

Dunoon, minesweeper
 BERRY, Richard, Leading Stoker, D/K 20193, illness

Friday, 22 December 1933

Brilliant, destroyer
 JUDGE, Harry W F, Able Seaman, C/J 107145, illness

Victory, Portsmouth
 PAFFORD, Gordon J, Electrical Artificer 1c, P/M 34357, illness

Monday, 25 December 1933

Effingham, cruiser
 JAMES, Robert, Able Seaman, P/JX 131872, illness

Tuesday, 26 December 1933

Tamar, Hong Kong
 SULLIVAN, John A, Signalman, D/J 30235, accidentally killed

Saturday, 30 December 1933

Royal Navy
 CROOKSHANK, Godfrey C C, Captain, illness

1934

Monday, 1 January 1934

Hood, battlecruiser
 NELSON, John L, Shipwright 1c, P/M 17302, illness

Wednesday, 3 January 1934

Revenge, battleship
 EARWICKER, William A, Telegraphist, P/JX 127484, illness

Saturday, 6 January 1934

Royal Naval Reserve
 WHITE, John B, Honorary Captain, RNR, illness

Sunday, 7 January 1934

Drake, Devonport
 JAMES, Harold, Petty Officer Steward, D/L 10647, illness

Royal Navy
 BONHAM-CARTER, Philip H, Lieutenant Commander, illness

Monday, 8 January 1934

RN Shore Signal Station, Spurn Point
 SHARMAN, George H, Signalman, SX 61, illness

Royal Naval Reserve
 DODD, James P, Paymaster Lieutenant Commander, RNR, illness

Tuesday, 9 January 1934

Dunedin, light cruiser
 LANGFORD, George E S, Chief Petty Officer Writer, C/M 37559, killed

Pembroke, Chatham
 PACKER, James A, Chief Engine Room Artificer 2c, C/M 4779, illness

RN Hospital, Haslar
 ABLETT, John G, Sick Berth Attendant, P/M 38616, illness

Friday, 12 January 1934

Osiris, submarine
 DUNN, Anthony, Petty Officer, D/J 20868, illness

Saturday, 13 January 1934

Resolution, battleship
 SIBLEY, Cyril V W, Able Seaman, P/J 19127, illness

Sunday, 14 January 1934

Exeter, heavy cruiser
 BOWER, Ivor, Chief Engine Room Artificer 2c, D/M 33637, illness

Wednesday, 17 January 1934

Calcutta, light cruiser
 ALLEN, Percival W, Engineer Commander, illness

Watchman, destroyer
 COURCEY, James, Ordinary Seaman, D/JX 135584, illness

Wednesday, 24 January 1934

Royal Oak, battleship
 ANDREWS, Leslie S, Leading Stoker, C/KX 76787, accidentally killed

Verity, destroyer
 GILLESPIE, Douglas E, Lieutenant, illness

Thursday, 25 January 1934

Gannet, river gunboat
 MATHESON, George Mc I, Stoker Petty Officer, D/K 60027, illness

Norfolk, heavy cruiser
 DIXON, Albert W, Stoker Petty Officer, D/K 61059, illness

Friday, 26 January 1934

Drake, Devonport
 ADDE, John W, Writer, D/MX 48532, illness

Sunday, 28 January 1934

Devonshire, heavy cruiser
 WALTERS, Maurice H, Midshipman, died

Nelson, battleship
 SMITH, William T, Ordnance Artificer, P M 35984, illness

RN Hospital, Malta
 WALTERS, Maurice H, Midshipman, illness

Saturday, 3 February 1934

Thanet, destroyer
 DODDRIDGE, Arthur H G, Stoker Petty Officer, D/K 33246, road accident, killed

Sunday, 4 February 1934

Victory, Portsmouth
 HALL, Thomas J, Stoker 2c, P/KX 80392, illness
 MOTTERAM, Roy, Leading Seaman, P/J 10964, illness

Wednesday, 7 February 1934

Adventure, minelayer
 AH, Chong, Officer's Cook 1c or Cook, (no service number listed), illness

Friday, 9 February 1934

Albury, minesweeping sloop
 RUTTER, John T, Leading Telegraphist, C/J 45926, illness

Saturday, 10 February 1934

Carlisle, light cruiser
 WHELTON, John, Stoker 1c, D/KX 75209, illness

Wednesday, 14 February 1934

Royal Naval Reserve
 HENDERSON, Algernon C F, Honorary Captain, RNR, illness

Friday, 16 February 1934

Vimy, destroyer
 COOK, Harry G, Stoker Petty Officer, P/K 58697, illness

Saturday, 17 February 1934

Drake, Devonport
 MULLETT, Loftus, Stoker 2c, D/KX 83457, illness

Pembroke, Chatham
 OWENS, Henry J, Stoker 1c, C/KX 78437, illness

Sunday, 18 February 1934

Devonshire, heavy cruiser
 POPPLESTONE, Horace, Chief Stoker, D/K 28493, accidentally killed

Whitshed, destroyer
 BAIN, Edward H, Able Seaman, P/J 80602, drowned

Monday, 19 February 1934

Arrow, destroyer
 DELLBRIDGE, Arthur F, Engineer Lieutenant Commander, illness

Wednesday, 21 February 1934

Sutton, minesweeping sloop
 HALLS, Frank, Leading Stoker, C/K 24861, illness

Saturday, 24 February 1934

RN Hospital, Haslar
 WALTON, Reginald F, Sick Berth Attendant, P/MX 49299, illness

Victory, Portsmouth
 JACOBS, Edward R, Stoker Petty Officer, P/K 63515, illness

Monday, 26 February 1934

Drake, Devonport
 DUGGAN, Patrick, Stoker 1c, D/K 65829, illness

Thursday, 1 March 1934

Royal Sovereign, battleship
 THORNTON-JONES, Horatio, Lieutenant Commander, illness

Thursday, 8 March 1934

Colombo, light cruiser
 FERNANDES, Domingo A, Officer's Cook 1c, G/LX 20874, illness

Ganges, Shotley/Harwich
 DALLIMORE, Kenneth J, Boy 2c, JX 140169, illness

Friday, 9 March 1934

Cumberland, heavy cruiser
 PEARSE, Hugh C B, Midshipman, illness

Monday, 12 March 1934

Windsor, destroyer
 WILLIAMS, Harry C, Chief Engine Room Artificer 1c, P/M 6857, drowned

Saturday, 17 March 1934

Royal Oak, battleship
 THOMAS, Louis A, Commissioned Shipwright, illness in HS Maine

Sunday, 18 March 1934

Cardiff, light cruiser
 LAWRENCE, Walter T, Able Seaman, C/JX 139708, illness

Saturday, 24 March 1934

Drake, Devonport
 JOHNSON, Arthur, Shipwright 1c, D/M 34810, illness

Wednesday, 28 March 1934

Ganges, Shotley/Harwich
 SIMMONDS, Albert, Boy 2c, JX 141179, illness

Saturday, 31 March 1934

Diomede, light cruiser
 CRAIGIE, Gideon, Petty Officer, C/J 17079, road accident, killed

Sunday, 1 April 1934

Caradoc, light cruiser
 WEEKS, Albert E, Stoker 1c, D/K 23764, illness

Monday, 2 April 1934

London, heavy cruiser
 WILKES, Albert H B, Stoker 1c, P/KX 79512, road accident, killed

Friday, 6 April 1934

Drake, Devonport
 TROUT, Alfred E, Master at Arms, D/M 37395, illness

Hawkins, cruiser
 PARRATT, Leonard W, Chief Stoker, P/K 58935, illness

Sunday, 8 April 1934

Medical Officer's Promotion Course
 BROWN, Annesley G L, Surgeon Lieutenant Commander, illness

Tuesday, 17 April 1934

RN Signal Shore Station, Needles, Isle of Wight
 GEORGE, Frank, Signalman, SX 49, illness

Friday, 20 April 1934

Victory, Portsmouth
 NEWLAND, William, Officer's Cook 2c, P/L 7505, illness

Sunday, 22 April 1934

Berwick, heavy cruiser
 GIDLEY, Reginald, Stoker Petty Officer, D/K 17999, drowned

Tuesday, 24 April 1934

Shoreham, sloop
 WHITELAW, Francis, Telegraphist, C/J 108874, illness

Wednesday, 25 April 1934

Ark Royal, seaplane carrier *(renamed Pegasus 21 December 1934)*
 EDWARDS, George A, Stoker Petty Officer, C/K 23225, accidentally killed

Dolphin, Gosport
 COVERDALE, Arthur M J, Engine Room Artificer 3c, P/M 38400, died

Saturday, 28 April 1934

Pembroke, Chatham
 REYNOLDS, John A, Able Seaman, C/J 103403, drowned

Monday, 30 April 1934

Durban, light cruiser
 GOODALL, Arthur E, Band Boy, RMB X 395, illness

Sunday, 6 May 1934

Glorious, ex-battlecruiser, aircraft carrier
 GRIMA, Paolo, Officer's Cook 3c, E/LX 20939, illness

Sunday, 13 May 1934

RN Hospital, Haslar
 WEATHERLEY, Allan, Sick Berth Attendant, P/MX 50591, illness

Monday, 21 May 1934

Victory, Portsmouth
 THOMAS, Moses, Stoker 1c, P/KX 76319, illness

Wednesday, 30 May 1934

Drake, Devonport
 BRADLEY, Charles A B, Chief Ordnance Artificer 1c, D/M 7379, road accident, killed

Thursday, 31 May 1934

Duncan, destroyer
 ABDILLA, Paul, Petty Officer Steward, E/LX 20219, illness

Sunday, 3 June 1934

Cyclops, submarine depot ship
 RYDER, Henry C, Electrical Artificer 3c, C/MX 48522, died

Monday, 4 June 1934

Royal Sovereign, battleship
 BANISTER, Charles, Supply Petty Officer, P/K 55412, illness

Friday, 8 June 1934

L.20, submarine
 SPARKS, William T, Warrant Engineer, illness

Saturday, 9 June 1934

St Vincent, Gosport
 TALBOT, Alfred R, Boy 2c, D/JX 141440, accidentally killed

Monday, 18 June 1934

St Vincent, Gosport
 TAYLOR, Thomas, Boy 2c, JX 140922, illness

Thursday, 21 June 1934

Courageous, ex-battlecruiser, aircraft carrier
 COATES, Arthur, Able Seaman, P/J 108548, accidentally killed

Sunday, 24 June 1934

Drake, Devonport
 HINGSTON, Edwin H, Chief Engine Room Artificer 2c, D/M 2662, illness

Monday, 25 June 1934

Ceres, light cruiser
 MARSH, Sydney H B, Stoker Petty Officer, C/K 61916, road accident, killed

Thursday, 28 June 1934

Mersey Division, RNVR
 CAMERON, George W L, Chief Petty Officer, D/J 5457, illness

Royal Navy
 ACHESON, Lon S, Commander (ex-Godetia), illness

Friday, 29 June 1934

Malabar, Bermuda
 PARTRIDGE, Frederick, Stoker 1c, D/KX 60320, illness

Pembroke, Chatham
 HARRISON, Robert, Stoker Petty Officer, C/K 20727, illness

Wednesday, 4 July 1934

Dryad, Portsmouth
 CANNON, Sidney R F C, Marine, 22080 (Po), illness

Friday, 13 July 1934

Brilliant, destroyer
 CORDELL, James H, Petty Officer, C/J 52070, drowned

Saturday, 14 July 1934

Bridgewater, sloop
 GRIFFITH, George, Able Seaman, D/JX 125757, illness

Monday, 16 July 1934

Devonshire, heavy cruiser
 ROBINSON, John W, Surgeon Lieutenant (D), accidentally shot, killed

Wednesday, 18 July 1934

Sussex, heavy cruiser
 RADWELL, Reginald L, Leading Stoker, C/K 63393, drowned

Friday, 20 July 1934

Cygnet, destroyer
 BENNETT, Francis E, Able Seaman, D/JX 127229, road accident, killed

Monday, 23 July 1934

Emerald, light cruiser
 COOPER, Thomas W, Able Seaman, C/JX 129289, accidentally killed

Wednesday, 25 July 1934

Nelson, battleship
 HAYNES, Hubert H, Cook, P/MX 48449, illness

Thursday, 26 July 1934

Ganges, Shotley/Harwich
 LEE, Douglas, Boy 2c, JX 140841, illness

Friday, 27 July 1934

Bee, river gunboat
 CRAVEN, George J, Stoker, P/KX 75188, illness

Colombo, light cruiser
 EDGE, Charles H, Marine, X 278 (Ch), illness

Tuesday, 31 July 1934

Drake, Devonport
 YALLAND, Mark, Stoker 1c, D/KX 76010, died

Saturday, 4 August 1934

Pembroke, Chatham
 POOLE, Arthur, Stoker Petty Officer, C/K 63929, illness

Monday, 6 August 1934

Codrington, flotilla leader
 JAMES, Richard B, Petty Officer, D/J 20826, illness

Marshall Soult, monitor
 DENNETT, Aubrey J D, Ordnance Artificer 2c, C/M 38740, road accident, killed

Tuesday, 7 August 1934

Victory, Portsmouth
 COLE, Albert H, Leading Telegraphist, P/J 45179, illness

Thursday, 16 August 1934

Wireless Telegraph Station, Flowerdown, near Winchester
 FULLSTONE, Frederick, Leading Telegraphist, P/J 27717, illness

Friday, 17 August 1934

Boreas, destroyer
 HENDLEY, Cyril, Able Seaman, P/J 98737, illness

Sunday, 19 August 1934

Greenwich, destroyer depot ship
 CURTIS, Charles, Leading Seaman, P/J 15863, died

Harebell, convoy sloop
 PARKER, Richard, Leading Seaman, D/J 103850, illness

Nelson, battleship
 LOAN, Reginald C, Able Seaman, P/J 64648, illness

Thursday, 23 August 1934

Royal Naval Volunteer Reserve
 Lord Bishop of Ripon, Honorary Chaplain, RNVR, illness

Stronghold, destroyer
 HUDSON, Herbert, Stoker Petty Officer, P/K 55909, road accident, killed

Friday, 24 August 1934

Ganges, Shotley/Harwich
 PHIPPS, Ronald, Boy 2c, JX 141713, illness

Royal Navy
 GOUGH, Ernest E, Commissioned Signal Boatswain, illness

Sunday, 26 August 1934

Royal Naval Reserve
 OULD, John H, Paymaster Lieutenant, RNR, illness

Friday, 31 August 1934

Terror, monitor
 McBEARTY, Henry, Petty Officer, D/J 25675, drowned

Sunday, 2 September 1934

Cornwall, heavy cruiser
 KILBURN, William A, Leading Stoker, P/KX 80210, died

Monday, 3 September 1934

Vernon, Portsmouth
 BUNDEY, Walter R T, Able Seaman, P/J 36942, illness

Tuesday, 4 September 1934

Whitshed, destroyer
 WALKER, Archibald R H, Lieutenant, illness

Wednesday, 5 September 1934

Drake, Devonport
 CREED, Ernest J, Able Seaman, D/J 113017, illness

Friday, 7 September 1934

Laburnum, sloop
 BROOKER, Alfred A, Supply Petty Officer, D/M 37366, illness

Saturday, 8 September 1934

Orpheus, submarine
 KNIGHTS, Edward, Petty Officer, P/J 69388, illness

Wednesday, 19 September 1934

Kent, heavy cruiser
 GODDING, Alexander, Musician, RMB, RMA X 151, illness

Thursday, 20 September 1934

Victory II, Portsmouth
 HELLIN, Hubert W, Stoker 2c, P/KX 84105, illness

Saturday, 22 September 1934

Lucia, submarine depot ship
 PRINCE, William A, Stoker 1c, D/KX 76072, accidentally killed

Monday, 24 September 1934

Pembroke, Chatham
 LATTER, Leonard H, Petty Officer, C/J 32329, illness

Thursday, 27 September 1934

Royal Navy
 SHARPLIN, George W, Warrant Engineer, illness

Sunday, 30 September 1934

Coventry, light cruiser
 REVELL, George W, Stoker 1c, P/K 61173, illness

Royal Naval Volunteer Reserve
 FARRELL, Alfred M, Lieutenant, RNVR, illness

Monday, 1 October 1934

Nelson, battleship
 COOPER, Stanley G, Engine Room Artificer 4c, RNR, E B X 891, illness

Monday, 8 October 1934

Laburnum, sloop
 TODD, William, Able Seaman, D/JX 131618, died

Tuesday, 9 October 1934

Royal Naval Reserve
 EYEIONS, Jack, Skipper, RNR, drowned

Monday, 15 October 1934

Victory, Portsmouth
 BUTLER, Charles W, Petty Officer Steward, P/L 4258, illness

Thursday, 18 October 1934

Eagle, aircraft carrier, flight deck accident
 RUSSELL, Edward G, Able Seaman, P/JX 126916, walked into propeller, killed

Sunday, 21 October 1934

Dainty, destroyer
 MURPHY, Robert J, Stoker Petty Officer, P/K 63070, died

Osprey, Portland
 RYAN, Jack, Able Seaman, D/JX 134116, road accident, killed

Wireless Telegraph Station, Matara, Ceylon (Sri Lanka)
 CARTER, Frederick A, Leading Telegraphist, C/J 39482, illness

Thursday, 1 November 1934

Drake, Devonport
 FENTON, William, Able Seaman, D/J 28811, illness

Monday, 5 November 1934

Hood, battlecruiser
 BINSTEAD, Charles E, Ordinary Telegraphist, P/JX 137172, illness

Monday, 12 November 1934

Escort, destroyer
 THOMPSON, Walter J, Able Seaman, C/J 110745, road accident, killed

Tuesday, 13 November 1934

Pembroke II, Chatham
 O'SHEA, Maurice M, Stoker 2c, C/KX 84431, illness

Tuesday, 20 November 1934

Victory I, Portsmouth
 WHEELER, Herbert, Telegraphist, P/JX 127710, road accident, killed

Saturday, 24 November 1934

St Vincent, Gosport
 HARFIELD, William S B, Boy 2c, JX 141612, illness

Monday, 26 November 1934

Pembroke, Chatham
 POOLE, Percy W, Petty Officer, C/J 46187, died

Wednesday, 28 November 1934

Royal Naval Volunteer Reserve
 DE JERSEY, Right Rev Norman S, Honorary Chaplain, RNVR, illness

Sunday, 2 December 1934

Danae, light cruiser
 LANGMAN, Harold, Petty Officer, D/J 13665, died

Tuesday, 4 December 1934

Drake, Devonport
 MILLER, William O, Stoker Petty Officer, D/K 65711, road accident, killed

Thursday, 6 December 1934

Capetown, light cruiser
 PATRICK, Ronald S, Ordinary Seaman, D/JX 139167, illness

Friday, 7 December 1934

Royal Navy
 BROWN, Albert G T, Lieutenant Commander, Rtd, illness

Saturday, 8 December 1934

Wolsey, destroyer
 WALKER, Charles G, Stoker 1c, C/KX 75281, died

Sunday, 9 December 1934

Royal Navy
 SAVAGE, Arthur, Able Seaman, C/J 100974, illness

Tuesday, 11 December 1934

Pembroke, Chatham
 NEWTON, Alfred N, Regulating Petty Officer, C/M 37819, illness

Thursday, 13 December 1934

Medical Officer's Post Graduate Course
 JOHNSTON, Stewart R, Surgeon Commander, illness

Saturday, 15 December 1934

Resource, fleet repair ship
 COLLINS, Arthur H, Warrant Electrician, illness, died in RN Hospital Malta

Monday, 17 December 1934

Royal Navy
 DALGLISH, Robin C, Rear Admiral, illness

Wednesday, 26 December 1934

RN Hospital, Haslar
 JONES, George S, Marine, X 93 (Po), illness

Thursday, 27 December 1934

Royal Navy
 NASH, Jack, Stoker Petty Officer, P/K 17438, illness

Sunday, 30 December 1934

Royal Naval Reserve
 MAINWARING, Sir Harry S, Honorary Commander, RNR, illness

Monday, 31 December 1934

Dorsetshire, heavy cruiser
 COWL, Edwin R, Marine, A 21171 (Ply), accidentally killed

1935

Tuesday, 1 January 1935

Sussex, heavy cruiser
 SPENCER, Leonard D, Able Seaman, C/J 113345, illness

Thursday, 3 January 1935

Keith, flotilla leader
 DAVIS, Charles A, Leading Signalman, C/J 73968, illness

Friday, 4 January 1935

Ganges, Shotley/Harwich
 BARRETT, Edward G, Boy 1c, JX 141391, illness

Thursday, 10 January 1935

St Angelo, Malta
 ZAMMIT, John, Officer's Steward, E/LX 21659, illness

Friday, 11 January 1935

Brazen, destroyer
 ELLUL, Lorenzo, Steward, E/LX 21107, died

RM Deal
 HYNE, Bernard S F, Marine, X 1498 (Po), illness

Wednesday, 16 January 1935

Ganges, Shotley/Harwich
 BUSHE, Thomas, Boy 2c, JX 142505, illness

Thursday, 17 January 1935

St Angelo, Malta
 DARMANIN, Carmelo, Leading Steward, E/LX 21227, illness

Saturday, 19 January 1935

Ganges, Shotley/Harwich
 WRIGHT, Harry R, Able Seaman, C/JX 130068, illness

Hood, battlecruiser
 BROWN, James M, Boy 1c, P/JX 141271, drowned

Marshall Soult, monitor
 DEGGAN, Hubert S, Chief Petty Officer, C/J 28977, killed

Suffolk, heavy cruiser
 BADHAM, Seymour W, Ordinary Seaman, P/JX 137592, illness

Tuesday, 22 January 1935

Adventure, minelayer
 HUGHES, Trevor H, Able Seaman, D/JX 130400, illness

Vambery, trawler
 JOHNSON, Fred A, Skipper, RNR, illness

Wednesday, 23 January 1935

Courageous, aircraft carrier
 HOOPER, Harry J, Chief Petty Officer Writer, P/M 7108, illness

Saturday, 26 January 1935

RM Barracks Chatham
 GURR, Hubert W J, Lance Corporal, RM, A 24453 (Ch), illness

Sunday, 27 January 1935

Esk, destroyer
 GUEST, George H, Leading Signalman, C/J 29344, illness

Monday, 28 January 1935

Colombo, light cruiser
 BAXTER, Frederick J, Stoker 1c, C/KX 77499, died

Tuesday, 29 January 1935

Dolphin, Gosport
 DOVE, Victor A, Able Seaman, P/J 104847, illness

Vesper, destroyer
 BEAL, Charles, Leading Stoker, C/KX 80601, illness

Thursday, 31 January 1935

Royal Navy
 COWELL, Edward W, Able Seaman, P/J 98346, illness

Saturday, 2 February 1935

Dauntless, light cruiser
 STEVENS, John M D, Leading Telegraphist, P/J 32661, electric shock, killed

Sunday, 3 February 1935

Berwick, heavy cruiser
 MAKIN, Herbert, Petty Officer, D/J 46697, died

Monday, 4 February 1935

Achilles, light cruiser
 JOLLEY, Leslie A, Writer, C/MX 30221, illness

Friday, 8 February 1935

Westcott, destroyer
 POPPELSTONE, William H, Able Seaman, D/J 25014, accidentally killed

Sunday, 10 February 1935

Hawkins, cruiser
 GOLDSMITH, Edward P, Paymaster Commander, illness

Hermes, aircraft carrier
 JOHNSON, William, Stoker 1c, D/KX 81784, illness

Tuesday, 12 February 1935

Emerald, light cruiser
  NAZARETH, John B, Officer's Chief Cook, G/LX 10888, illness

Wednesday, 13 February 1935

Drake, Devonport
  JEFFERY, Arthur S, Stoker Petty Officer, D/K 18457, illness

Thursday, 14 February 1935

Royal Navy
  NOONAN, John, Stoker 2c, P/KX 8456, illness

Friday, 15 February 1935

Terror, monitor
  MYATT, George, Stoker, D/K 20522, accidentally killed

Sunday, 17 February 1935

Malabar, Bermuda
  ARNOLD, Norman M, Boy 1c, C/JX 141016, illness

Wednesday, 20 February 1935

Valiant, battleship
  ABRAHAM, Arthur, Petty Officer, C/J 18810, drowned

Thursday, 21 February 1935

Marshal Soult, monitor
  LILLYWHITE, Charles H, Petty Officer, C/J 105965, illness

Wednesday, 27 February 1935

Pembroke, Chatham
  NICHOLSON, Basil E E, Petty Officer, C/J 90818, illness

Friday, 1 March 1935

Carlisle, light cruiser
  POSTLETHWAITE, John, Leading Stoker, D/KX 78237, road accident, killed

Osprey, Portland
  HEATHCOTE, Thomas, Able Seaman, D/J 106481, illness

Saturday, 2 March 1935

Royal Navy
  RIDDELL, Frederick, Able Seaman, P/JX (number not listed), illness

Tuesday, 5 March 1935

FAA, Base Training Sqn, Gosport, air crash
  WILLIAMS, Nigel R, Sub Lieutenant, killed

Wednesday, 6 March 1935

Specialist Physical and Recreational Training (PR/T) Course
  BRADSHAW, Robert H, Lieutenant, RM, illness

Friday, 8 March 1935

Cormorant, Gibraltar
  COLLINS, Francis J, Able Seaman, P/J 111235, illness

Tuesday, 12 March 1935

Victory, Portsmouth
  SMITH, Edgar J, Leading Seaman, P/J 109628, illness

Thursday, 21 March 1935

Hermes, aircraft carrier
  MARTIN, Wilfrid W G G, Musician, RMB, RMB X 532, illness

Sunday, 24 March 1935

Colombo, light cruiser
  PHIPPS, Sydney G, Leading Seaman, C/J 102377, illness

Valiant, battleship
  HARDY, Henry, Ordinary Seaman, RNVR, MDX 1683, illness

Sunday, 31 March 1935

Malabar, Bermuda
  ALLUM, Eric A F, Petty Officer Cook, C/M 10323, illness

Tuesday, 2 April 1935

Resolution, battleship
  WRIGHT, Albert A, Mechanician, P/K 46909, illness

Wednesday, 3 April 1935

Renown, battlecruiser
  PERKINS, Alan H, Marine, A 18530 (Ch), illness

Rodney, battleship
  GORDON, Willie, Chief Petty Officer, D/J 12581, died

Veteran, destroyer
  ZAMMIT, Joseph, Petty Officer Steward, E/L 4707, illness

Thursday, 4 April 1935

Royal Naval Volunteer Reserve
  CARTWRIGHT-TAYLOR, John W D, Paymaster Sub Lieutenant, RNVR, illness

Saturday, 6 April 1935

Courageous, aircraft carrier
  CASS, Arthur, Ordinary Seaman, P/SSX 14881, illness

Monday, 8 April 1935

Capetown, light cruiser
  COOK, Charles E C, Petty Officer, D/J 18194, illness

Queen Elizabeth, battleship
 HORTON, Horace W, Marine, X 560 (Ply), accidentally killed

Tuesday, 9 April 1935

Victory, Portsmouth
 PHALP, Arthur S, Leading Signalman, P/JX 127503, illness

Thursday, 11 April 1935

Royal Naval Reserve
 McLEOD, Murdo, Seaman, RNR, X 18132 A, illness

Friday, 12 April 1935

Scarborough, sloop
 SIMS, Edward, Stoker 1c, C/K 66438, died

Saturday, 13 April 1935

Royal Navy
 MARSHALL, John J, Stoker 2c, P/KX 85612, illness

Monday, 15 April 1935

Veteran, destroyer
 THROWER, John E, Leading Seaman, C/J 113794, died

Whitshed, destroyer
 ELLIS, Albert G, Petty Officer Cook, P/M 7670, illness

Thursday, 18 April 1935

Danae, light cruiser
 HALL, Wilfred E, Petty Officer, D/J 23775, accidentally killed

Norfolk, heavy cruiser
 NEWMAN, John W, Able Seaman, D/J 105864, illness

Friday, 19 April 1935

Pembroke, Chatham
 DAVIS, John G, Stoker 2c, C/KX 85637, illness

Saturday, 20 April 1935

Medway, submarine depot ship
 SLAYFORD, Ernest, Able Seaman, C/J 90496, illness

Monday, 22 April 1935

Bideford, sloop
 ADAN, Suleman, Somali Stoker, 2/259, illness

Friday, 26 April 1935

Ganges, Shotley/Harwich
 WOOSTER, Hugh C, Boy 2c, JX 143216, illness

Saturday, 27 April 1935

Leander, light cruiser
 POPE, Ernest W, Petty Officer Steward, D/L 12262, illness

Sunday, 28 April 1935

Colombo, light cruiser
 HOOPER, Eric C W, Supply Assistant, C/MX 47883, illness

Thursday, 2 May 1935

Barham, battleship
 CARTER, Walter W, Stoker 1c, D/KX 81328, accidentally killed

Pembroke, Chatham
 DUNN, Charles W, Able Seaman, C/J 96476, illness

Victory I, Portsmouth
 CAIN, James, Ordinary Seaman, P/SSX 14980, illness

Wednesday, 8 May 1935

Courageous, aircraft carrier, flight deck accident
 JAMIESON, William J M, Ordinary Seaman, P/SSX 15525, killed

Friday, 10 May 1935

Royal Naval Reserve
 ROLFE, Percy H, Honorary Commander, RNR, illness

Sunday, 12 May 1935

Pembroke, Chatham
 BRACE, Edward C, Leading Seaman, P/J 31814, illness

Thursday, 16 May 1935

Dolphin, Gosport
 JONES, Robert, Leading Stoker, C/KX 76100, illness

Drake, Devonport
 PERRING, William, Supply Chief Petty Officer, D/MX 52336, illness

Saturday, 18 May 1935

Calcutta, light cruiser
 NORTON, Reginald J, Stoker Petty Officer, D/K 23339, illness

Sunday, 19 May 1935

Diomede, light cruiser
 CUTTER, William H, Engine Room Artificer 4c, D/MX 46008, illness

Rodney, battleship
 YOUNG, Thomas E, Able Seaman, D/SSX 14264, drowned

Monday, 20 May 1935

Drake, Devonport
 DELLOW, Alfred J, Stoker Petty Officer, D/K 20937, illness

Furious, aircraft carrier
 YELVERTON, Brian J, Able Seaman, D/J 42355, illness

Grimsby, sloop
 WARD, Charles W, Stoker 1c, P/KX 79238, illness

Wednesday, 22 May 1935

Hood, battlecruiser
JOHNSON, William H, Stoker 1c, K 57511 (Po), illness

Saturday, 25 May 1935

Ganges, Shotley/Harwich
WOODS, Roy W, Boy 2c, JX 142281, illness

Monday, 27 May 1935

Drake, Devonport
DUNLOP, Frederick J, Corporal, RM, X 449 (Ch), died

RN Hospital, Malta
MANSELL, Robert, Leading Stoker, D/KX 56422, illness

Tuesday, 28 May 1935

Suffolk, heavy cruiser
HARRIS, Joseph E, Able Seaman, P/JX 132423, illness

Wednesday, 29 May 1935

Drake, Devonport
WORTHINGTON, Bernard H, Leading Seaman, D/J 106822, illness

Saturday, 1 June 1935

Royal Navy
CHAPMAN, Samuel C, Commissioned Gunner, illness

Wednesday, 5 June 1935

Drake, Devonport
DILBY, Robert J, Cook (S), D/MX 49645, illness

Saturday, 8 June 1935

Defiance, Devonport
HAMMETT, William A, Shipwright 1c, D/M 3415, illness

Monday, 10 June 1935

Dolphin, Gosport
MARSHALL, Harry H, Lieutenant (E), illness

RM Deal, Kent
MASON, Reginald, Marine, X 1685 (Po), struck by lightning, killed

Wednesday, 12 June 1935

Pembroke, Chatham
SHARMAN, John R, Stoker 1c, C/K 65522, died

Friday, 14 June 1935

Adventure, minelayer
WILLGOSS, William J, Leading Stoker, D/KX 79835, accidentally killed

Cornwall, heavy cruiser
EVES, Arthur, Commissioned Gunner, illness

Royal Navy
EVES, Arthur, Commissioned Gunner, illness

Saturday, 15 June 1935

St Angelo, Malta
BUSUTTIL, Guiseppe, Bandsman, E/M 4664, illness

Wednesday, 19 June 1935

Centurion, ex-battleship, target ship
WEBBER, Frederick C, Leading Stoker, D/K 236616, illness

Delhi, light cruiser
HILL, Thomas J E, Marine, 22672 (Ply), drowned

Tuesday, 25 June 1935

Royal Sovereign, battleship
CHAMPNESS, Richard A B, Shipwright 3c, P/M 39532, road accident, killed

Saturday, 29 June 1935

Furious, aircraft carrier
ROUTLEDGE, Richard F, Engine Room Artificer 3c, D/M 38825, illness

Sunday, 30 June 1935

Beaufort, survey ship
HIGGINSON, Charles W, Leading Telegraphist, D/J 16611, illness

Lupin, fleet sweeping sloop
TANNER, Frank S, Able Seaman, P/J 95659, illness

Friday, 5 July 1935

Boscawen, Portland
WALL, Leslie A, Cook, P/M 38483, illness

Saturday, 6 July 1935

Pembroke, Chatham
BEESON, Albert H, Able Seaman, C/J 107425, died

Friday, 12 July 1935

Royal Naval Reserve
RAMSAY, Charles T, Honorary Engineer Commander, RNR, illness

Tuesday, 16 July 1935

Royal Navy
HAYNES, John F, Surgeon Commander, illness

Thursday, 18 July 1935

Effingham, cruiser
 ASTLEY-RUSHTON, Edward A, Vice Admiral, Vice Admiral Reserve Fleet, illness

Sandwich, sloop
 SEVERS, Fred, Signalman, P/JX 133233, illness

Victory, Portsmouth
 STORIE, James, Stoker 2c, P/KX 84722, died

Saturday, 20 July 1935

Dryad, Portsmouth
 DUNCAN, George W D, Lieutenant Commander, illness

Monday, 29 July 1935

Pembroke, Chatham
 PHILLIPS, John M, Stoker 2c, KX 80386, accidentally killed

Wednesday, 31 July 1935

Drake, Devonport
 DAVIES, Richard F, Able Seaman, D/J 63005, illness

Friday, 2 August 1935

President II, London
 PARTRIDGE, Sydney G, Petty Officer, D/J 25481, illness

Sunday, 4 August 1935

Ganges, Shotley/Harwich
 COTTON, Albert J A, Boy 2c, JX 144440, illness

Tuesday, 6 August 1935

Curacoa, light cruiser
 HUMPHREYS, Arthur F, Paymaster Commander, illness

Wednesday, 7 August 1935

Drake, Devonport
 AGGETT, William H, Shipwright 3c, D/M 8077, illness

Saturday, 10 August 1935

RM Barracks Eastney
 CARTER, Frederick H, Marine, 24423 (Ch), died

Thursday, 15 August 1935

Queen Elizabeth, battleship
 NICHOLAS, Reginald D, Marine, 21667 (Ply), illness

St Angelo, Malta
 FARRELL, Joseph A, Commissioned Boatswain, illness, died in RN Hospital Malta

Friday, 16 August 1935

Kent, heavy cruiser
 AH, Po, Leading Steward, (no service number listed), illness

Saturday, 17 August 1935

Royal Navy
 SHEEHAN, Francis P O, Able Seaman, D/J 36681, illness

Sunday, 18 August 1935

Course at Portsmouth
 ANTHONY, George M, Sub Lieutenant, illness

Excellent, Portsmouth
 CALLOW, Cecil C, Musician, RMB X 259, road accident, killed

Friday, 23 August 1935

RM Portsmouth Division
 PEEL, James, Marine, 211377 (Po), illness

Wednesday, 28 August 1935

Delight, destroyer
 JENNER, Harry D, Commissioned Gunner, illness

Thursday, 29 August 1935

RN Hospital, Malta
 SOLLARS, Claude E, Ordinary Seaman, D/SSX 15764, illness

Sunday, 1 September 1935

Vernon, Portsmouth
 WHEADON, John R, Stoker 1c, P/K 21435, illness

Tuesday, 3 September 1935

Capetown, light cruiser
 KIDSTON, James, Able Seaman, D/JX 130799, died

Wednesday, 4 September 1935

Berwick, heavy cruiser
 MURRIE, James, Stoker 1c, D/KX 80608, drowned

Saturday, 7 September 1935

Titania, submarine depot ship
 CLARK, Charles L, Stoker 2c, C/KX 84988, illness

Sunday, 8 September 1935

Royal Navy
 PEARCE, Ernest A, Chief Engine Room Artificer, 12235, illness

Monday, 9 September 1935

Pembroke, Chatham
 WATERMAN, William, Chief Yeoman of Signals, C/J 13749, died

Tuesday, 10 September 1935

Royal Navy
 MURRAY, David, Midshipman, illness

Wednesday, 11 September 1935

Valiant, battleship
 GLADWIN, Frank H, Marine, 18254, illness

Thursday, 12 September 1935

L.71, submarine
 LODER, Hubert G, Act/Chief Engine Room Artificer 2c, P/M 6253, died from fall

Sunday, 15 September 1935

Harebell, sloop
 SADD, Charles W J, Commissioned Gunner, illness

Saturday, 21 September 1935

Nelson, battleship
 VINSON, Arthur W, Leading Cook, P/M 15326, died

Victory, Portsmouth
 WHITE, Edward H, Able Seaman, P/J 102222, illness

Sunday, 22 September 1935

Ganges, Shotley/Harwich
 GILLOW, Walter F P, Cook, C/M 36446, illness

Wednesday, 25 September 1935

Rochester, sloop
 PROOM, Joseph, Stoker 1c, C/KX 76957, illness

Saturday, 28 September 1935

Norfolk, heavy cruiser
 PEDDLE, Percy, Chief Mechanician 2c, D/K 55163, road accident, killed

Thursday, 3 October 1935

Montrose, flotilla leader
 SHERIDAY, John E, Chief Petty Officer Telegraphist, D/J 33153, illness

Friday, 4 October 1935

Drake, Devonport
 BROADRIBB, Walter F, Able Seaman, D/JX 127701, road accident, killed

Tuesday, 8 October 1935

Pembroke, Chatham
 McEMERY, Henry W, Regulating Petty Officer, C/M 39907, illness

RM Portsmouth Division
 JOHNSON, William W, Marine, 18124 (Po), illness

Thursday, 10 October 1935

Nelson, battleship
 BROWN, Robert A, Ordinary Seaman, P/JX 136366, illness

Friday, 11 October 1935

Engineer In Chief Department
 SMITH, Frederick W G, Engineer Captain, illness

Tuesday, 15 October 1935

Wild Swan, destroyer
 SYMES, Walter C, Ordinary Seaman, P/JX 136030, illness

Monday, 21 October 1935

Drake, Devonport
 CHAPMAN, Albert E, Able Seaman, D/J 29850, illness

Tuesday, 29 October 1935

Pembroke, Chatham
 CLARK, Ernest W, Chief Petty Officer Telegraphist, C/J 39039, illness

Thursday, 31 October 1935

Royal Navy
 BROOKS, William R, Petty Officer, P/J 23358, illness

Tuesday, 5 November 1935

Emerald, light cruiser
 WIGGETT, George J, Leading Stoker, C/KX 76332, illness

Pembroke, Chatham
 MATTHEWS, Francis V, Boy 2c, JX 144760, illness

Friday, 8 November 1935

Kent, heavy cruiser
 COBBETT, William, Marine, 20288 (Ch), illness

Saturday, 9 November 1935

Winchester, destroyer
 FRANKLIN, Herbert, Able Seaman, C/SSX 12843, illness

Monday, 11 November 1935

Ramillies, battleship
 BALDOCK, Thomas, Able Seaman, C/J 105047, died

Tuesday, 19 November 1935

Drake, Devonport
 TAVINOR, Harold L, Stoker 2c, D/KX 85466, illness

Rodney, battleship
 SMEE, Frederick J, Stoker 1c, D/KX 85130, illness

Sunday, 24 November 1935

Drake, Devonport
 WILSON, William D C, Ordinary Seaman, D/SSX 16520, illness

Wednesday, 27 November 1935

Victory, Portsmouth
 GILL, William, Musician, RMB, RMB X 146, died

Thursday, 28 November 1935

RM Chatham Division
 KERR, George, Marine, (no service number listed), died

Friday, 29 November 1935

Pembroke, Chatham
 LLEWELLYN, Griffith D, Schoolmaster, illness

Saturday, 30 November 1935

Excellent, Course, both accidentally killed
 JONES, Francis J, Lieutenant (E)
 NIXON, Ernest G, Lieutenant (E)

Sunday, 1 December 1935

Leith, sloop
 BRETT, Bertram H, Gunner, illness

Sunday, 8 December 1935

Duchess, destroyer
 WILDMAN, Roland S, Able Seaman, C/J 113186, illness

Saturday, 14 December 1935

Royal Navy
 ALLAM, Frank J, Ordinary Seaman, C/SSX 15858, illness

Sunday, 15 December 1935

Malta Dockyard
 VANHORN, Frederick, Constable, (no service number listed), illness

Monday, 16 December 1935

Cornwall, heavy cruiser
 GASK, Vivian D, Lieutenant, accidentally killed

Wednesday, 18 December 1935

Cameronia, passenger liner
 AVANT, John H, Stoker Petty Officer, P/K 63397, probably on passage, drowned

Friday, 20 December 1935

Effingham, cruiser
 PRIOR, Alfred, Leading Stoker, P/KX 78832, illness

Saturday, 21 December 1935

Selkirk, minesweeping sloop
 BRURTON, Harold, Leading Stoker, D/JX 77767, illness

Monday, 23 December 1935

Delight, destroyer
 WATTS, John C, Able Seaman, P/J 86158, illness

Wednesday, 25 December 1935

RM Plymouth Division
 CURLING, John E, Musician, RMB X 478, illness

Sunday, 29 December 1935

Winchester, destroyer
 WHEELER, Frederic A J, Officer's Cook 3c, P/LX 20123, illness

Tuesday, 31 December 1935

RM Deal
 BROWN, Arthur, Marine, X 1283 (Ch), illness

1936

Wednesday, 1 January 1936

Drake, Devonport
 LANGDON, Fernley J, Stoker 1c, D/K 66004, accidentally killed

Saturday, 4 January 1936

Royal Naval Reserve
 YOUNG, Alfred H F, Honorary Captain, RNR, illness

Sunday, 5 January 1936

Royal Naval Reserve
 GARDINER, William H, Chief Skipper, RNR, illness

Monday, 6 January 1936

Hermes, aircraft carrier
 FRIMSTON, George F, Able Seaman, D/JX 134542, illness

Tuesday, 7 January 1936

FAA, 822 Sqn, Furious, aircraft carrier, aircraft No.918, air crash
 HUNTER, John A, Telegraphist, P/J 112421, killed

Medea, ex-monitor M.22, coastal and instructional minelayer, Torpedo School, Portsmouth
 CLARKE, Wilbert, Able Seaman, P/J 80329, illness

Sunday, 19 January 1936

Kempenfelt, flotilla leader
 FIELDING, Thomas L, Able Seaman, D/JX 136957, accidentally killed

Tuesday, 21 January 1936

Royal Naval Reserve
 HUTCHISON, George S H, Lieutenant Commander, RNR, illness

Saturday, 25 January 1936

Curacoa, light cruiser
 JERRARD, James A, Leading Steward, P/L 8226, illness

Wednesday, 29 January 1936

Drake, Devonport
 FITZGERALD, John, Stoker 2c, D/KX 86011, illness

Friday, 31 January 1936

Ganges, Shotley/Harwich
 HOWLETT, Harold, Boy 2c, JX 145007, illness

Saturday, 1 February 1936

Victory, Portsmouth
 HARBIN, George E, Chief Engine Room Artificer 2c, P/M 27315, illness

Sunday, 2 February 1936

Nelson, battleship
 MARRIOTT, Edward, Able Seaman, P J 41822, illness

Monday, 3 February 1936

Victory, Portsmouth
 STEELE, Reginald J, Chief Stoker, P/K 64220 (O/P), accidentally killed in SS Rangitane

Saturday, 8 February 1936

Victory, Portsmouth
 POTTO, John E, Chief Petty Officer, P/J 27056, illness

Wolfhound, destroyer
 BARTLETT, Leslie, Able Seaman, C/J 107136, illness

Monday, 10 February 1936

Royal Marines
 SIBLEY, Walter, Marine, 124709, road accident, killed

Tuesday, 11 February 1936

Pembroke, Chatham
 CROUCH, William H, Leading Seaman, C/J 33828, illness

Wednesday, 12 February 1936

Pembroke, Chatham
 REBBECK, Thomas, Stoker 2c, C/KX 87887, illness

Speedwell, minesweeper
 PEARSON, James, Chief Petty Officer, P/J 22430, illness

Friday, 14 February 1936

Royal Sovereign, battleship
 BOOTH, Harry, Ordinary Seaman, D/JX 138752, accidentally killed

St Angelo, Malta
 GRIMMA, Guiseppe, Able Seaman, E/J 54000, illness

Saturday, 15 February 1936

Frobisher, cruiser
 OWEN, James E, Petty Officer, C/J 25504, illness

Sunday, 16 February 1936

Cairo, light cruiser
 CULVER, Ivor R, Ordinary Signalman, C/JX 141755, illness

Thursday, 20 February 1936

Pembroke, Chatham
 JAKEMAN, George A, Chief Engine Room Artificer 2c, C/M 28793, accidentally killed

Ramillies, battleship
HOGG, Audley A, Lieutenant Commander (E), illness

Wednesday, 26 February 1936

Defiance, Devonport
BUSH, Nathaniel, Able Seaman, D/JX 146057, illness

Excellent, Portsmouth
HILDRETH, Edward J, Petty Officer, P/J 21797, illness

Thursday, 27 February 1936

Orion, light cruiser
DANN, Arthur C, Seaman, RNR, A 16114, illness

Winchester, destroyer
STONE, Alec C, Able Seaman, P/J 96241, accidentally killed

Friday, 28 February 1936

Drake, Devonport
RILEY, John, Able Seaman, D/J 110869, illness

Excellent, Portsmouth
HOWARD, Atholl C, Schoolmaster (CWO), illness

Thursday, 5 March 1936

FAA, 822 Sqn, Furious, aircraft carrier, air crash
LAING, George A T, Lieutenant Commander, killed

Royal Sovereign, battleship
PUTT, Walter, Stoker 1c, D/K 28508, illness

Friday, 6 March 1936

Curlew, light cruiser
SELMAN, George J, Leading Seaman, C/J 114881, illness

Saturday, 7 March 1936

RN Hospital, Chatham
PRISTON, Julian L, Surgeon Commander, illness

Sunday, 8 March 1936

Vernon, Portsmouth
WESTON, Sydney H J, Petty Officer, P/J 110315, illness

Thursday, 12 March 1936

Drake, Devonport
BRADLEY, James G, Chief Engine Room Artificer 2c, D/M 10895, illness

Friday, 13 March 1936

Excellent, Portsmouth
MARSH, Thomas, Shipwright 1c, P/M 26662, illness

Pembroke, Chatham
BOWDEN, Sidney N, Leading Supply Assistant, C/MX 45468, illness

Sunday, 15 March 1936

Drake, Devonport
SHEPHEARD, William F H, Chief Petty Officer, D/JX 148414, accidentally killed

Royal Naval Reserve
MILLER, Alexander, Chief Skipper, RNR, illness

Monday, 16 March 1936

Barham, battleship
KELD, John R, Boy 1c, P/JX 140814, accidentally killed

Tuesday, 17 March 1936

Pembroke, Chatham
DOXSLEY, Richard J, Boy 1c, C/JX 142674, illness

Wednesday, 18 March 1936

Drake, Devonport
BRADLEY, Joseph A, Chief Stoker, P/K 55729, illness

Westcott, destroyer, explosion
BLACKMORE, Alfred E, Able Seaman, D/JX 126146, killed

Thursday, 19 March 1936

Drake, Devonport
STREET, Stanley, Officer's Cook 2c, D/L 13200, illness

Monday, 23 March 1936

Drake, Devonport
REYNOLDS, Leonard F, Stoker 1c, D/KX 82363, illness

Tuesday, 24 March 1936

Excellent, Plymouth
KENCHINGTON, Frederick W, Able Seaman, P/J 40267, illness

Wednesday, 1 April 1936

Bideford, sloop
HOLLAND, Frederick R, Stoker 1c, D/KX 80584, illness

Glasgow Recruiting Office
HALL, Matthew, Chief Yeoman of Signals, C/227218, illness

Thursday, 2 April 1936

Drake, Devonport
SMITH, Harold F, Armourer's Crew, D/M 10801, illness

Friday, 3 April 1936

Carlisle, light cruiser
HOOKINGS, James G, Leading Steward, D/L 14645, road accident, killed

Malta Dockyard
CARTER, Richard K D H, Lieutenant (E), illness

Sunday, 5 April 1936

St Angelo, Malta
 BENNETT, Thomas E, Marine, 21491 (Po), illness

Monday, 6 April 1936

Achilles, light cruiser
 PROBIN, David H, Able Seaman, P/J 113537, illness

RM Plymouth Division
 ATKINSON, Stephen B, Marine, X 1356 (Ply), illness

Wednesday, 8 April 1936

Drake, Devonport
 WILLIS, John, Stoker 1c, D/KX 81887, illness

Victory, Portsmouth
 READ, Thomas E, Stoker Petty Officer, P/K 57548, illness

Tuesday, 14 April 1936

Adventure, minelayer
 SIMM, Moses, Able Seaman, D/SSX 13487, illness

Escapade, destroyer
 FIST, Thomas, Able Seaman, D/JX 135210, illness

Wednesday, 15 April 1936

Royal Naval Reserve
 CAMPBELL, James, Skipper, RNR, illness

Monday, 20 April 1936

Crescent, destroyer
 FILMER, William E, Signalman, C/J 84441, illness

Friday, 24 April 1936

Hood, battlecruiser
 PUDDICK, Frank, Act/Engine Room Artificer 4c, P/MX 47971, illness

Monday, 27 April 1936

Pembroke, Chatham
 McMILLAN, Allan Mc R, Shipwright 2c, RNVR, CD/X 1275, illness

Thursday, 30 April 1936

Cormorant, Gibraltar
 WOOD, Jim, Stoker 1c, P/K 63445, illness

Victory, Portsmouth
 GROSE, Arthur E D, Stoker 2c, P/KX 87879, illness

Friday, 1 May 1936

Cygnet, destroyer
 CARTER, Francis A W, Able Seaman, D/J 100637, illness

Sunday, 3 May 1936

Hood, battlecruiser
 LYCETT, Harold, Chief Ordnance Artificer 2c, P/M 35424, illness

Monday, 4 May 1936

Victory, Portsmouth
 KEANS, Ernest H, Boy 1c, P/JX 143177, illness

Wednesday, 6 May 1936

Defiance, Devonport
 WILCOX, Herbert R, Stoker 1c, D/K 63698, illness

Thursday, 7 May 1936

Norfolk, heavy cruiser
 RENDELL, Walter J, Petty Officer, D/J 18076, accidentally killed

Friday, 8 May 1936

Royal Navy
 HOUSE, Samuel R, Chief Stoker, P/KX 88125, died

Sunday, 10 May 1936

Hood, battlecruiser
 NICHOLSON, Stanley G, Act/Leading Seaman, P/J 107109, illness

Monday, 11 May 1936

Cormorant, Gibraltar
 MACKERSY, William A N, Able Seaman, P/J 110194, illness

Pembroke, Chatham
 DEDMAN, James V, Electrical Artificer Apprentice, MX 58809, illness

Woolwich, destroyer depot ship
 BARTLETT, Charles W E, Sick Berth Attendant, C/MX 48842, illness

Wednesday, 13 May 1936

Medway, submarine depot ship
 MOULTON, Arthur W, Leading Signalman, C/J 113007, illness

Thursday, 14 May 1936

Barham, battleship
 HEMSTED, James E, Paymaster Commander, illness

Friday, 15 May 1936

Royal Naval Volunteer Reserve
 MINETT, Desmond R, Midshipman, RNVR, illness

Sunday, 17 May 1936

Barham, battleship
 LATHAM, William G, Boy 1c, P/JX 141609, illness

Monday, 18 May 1936

Neptune, light cruiser
  RICHARDS, Hugh le F, Lieutenant, illness

Tuesday, 19 May 1936

Drake, Devonport
  HARRIS, Charles, Stoker Petty Officer, D/K 59550, illness

Friday, 29 May 1936

Grimsby, sloop
  BROWN, Ernest E G, Able Seaman, D/JX 135452, illness

Sunday, 31 May 1936

Delhi, light cruiser
  THOMPSON, Victor E, Boy 1c, D/JX 143708, accidentally killed

FAA, 447 Flight, London, heavy cruiser, air crash on 22 May 1936
  HALE, John W, Lieutenant Commander, DOI

Pegasus, ex-Ark Royal, seaplane carrier
  STUBBINGS, Frederick E, Able Seaman, C/J 113783, illness

RAF, serving with
  HALL, John W, Lieutenant Commander, illness

Royal Sovereign, battleship
  HAY, Charles P, Midshipman, illness

Monday, 1 June 1936

Drake, Devonport
  HALL, Ewart E, Stoker Petty Officer, D/KX 79481, road accident, killed

Tuesday, 2 June 1936

Huntley, minesweeping sloop
  RADMORE, Edwin C, Engine Room Artificer 2c, D/M 36704, illness

Wednesday, 3 June 1936

Royal Naval Reserve
  BAIN, Ronald C, Engineer Lieutenant Commander, RNR, illness

Monday, 8 June 1936

Royal Navy
  HICKEY, Thomas E, Ordinary Telegraphist, P/JX 140554, accidentally killed

Sunday, 14 June 1936

Ganges, Shotley/Harwich
  CARVER, Eric A J, Boy 2c, JX 145536, illness

Pembroke, Chatham
  HALLETT, Edward J, Engine Room Artificer Apprentice, MX 49508, road accident, killed

Wednesday, 17 June 1936

Topaze, Admiralty trawler
  HIGHAM, Robert, Stoker Petty Officer, C/KX 87773, illness

Sunday, 21 June 1936

RN College Keyham
  MORRELL, George J, Midshipman (E), illness

Monday, 22 June 1936

Capetown Dockyard
  WHITTAKER, Rev Goerge, Chaplain, illness

Pearl, Admiralty trawler
  NICHOLAS, Eric, Able Seaman, D/JX 146070, died

Tuesday, 23 June 1936

Royal Navy
  PHIPPARD, Albert E, Stoker, P/K 56837, illness

Thursday, 25 June 1936

Ganges, Shotley/Harwich
  FRIEND, Norman E, Leading Cook, C/MX 49165, road accident, killed

Friday, 26 June 1936

Royal Navy
  PARRIS, Arthur C, Petty Officer Telegraphist, P/J 45264, illness

Saturday, 27 June 1936

Kent, heavy cruiser
  CROWTHER, George W, Petty Officer, C/J 39552, illness

Sunday, 28 June 1936

Royal Naval Reserve
  VAN DER VORD, Richard F, Paymaster Lieutenant Commander, RNR, illness

Sunday, 5 July 1936

Curlew, light cruiser
  JONES, Robert H, Able Seaman, C/JX 130702, accidentally killed

Pembroke, Chatham, aircraft accident
  YALLOP, Stanley, Able Seaman, C/JX 115315, killed

York, heavy cruiser
  WOOLLACOTT, Herbert C, Engine Room Artificer 4C, C/MX 47344, died

Monday, 6 July 1936

Cornwall, heavy cruiser
  KITCHIN, Reginald H, Paymaster Commander, illness

Thursday, 9 July 1936

Royal Navy
 ADAMS, Richard C H, Boy 2c, JX 148273, illness

Thursday, 16 July 1936

Norfolk, heavy cruiser
 ROSS, William D, Able Seaman, D/J 104953, illness

Friday, 17 July 1936

Drake, Devonport
 PATTENDEN, Reginald E, Able Seaman, D/J 103017, illness

Elfin, small miscellaneous vessel, on books of Alecto
 ARUNDELL, George, Telegraphist, C/J 102463 (Alecto), illness

Saturday, 18 July 1936

Syringa, Admiralty trawler
 STEPHENSON, Gerald, Chief Skipper, RNR, illness

Sunday, 19 July 1936

Venetia, destroyer
 HEMMETT, Albert G, Able Seaman, D/J 103913, illness

Monday, 20 July 1936

Frobisher, cruiser
 RADFORD, Victor G H, Sergeant, RM, 23203 (Ch), illness

Wednesday, 22 July 1936

St Angelo, Malta
 CHAMBERS, Alfred C, Able Seaman, D/JX 131754 (Fame), illness

Friday, 24 July 1936

Caledon, light cruiser
 HICKSON, James, Engine Room Artificer 1c, D/MX 52498, illness

Victory II, Portsmouth
 FUDGE, John E, Stoker Petty Officer, P/KX 64958, illness

Sunday, 26 July 1936

St Angelo, Malta
 MIFSUD, James, Petty Officer Steward, 362346, illness

Monday, 3 August 1936

Blackwater, Admiralty trawler
 ROBINS, Henry, Able Seaman, P/J 31591, drowned

Wednesday, 5 August 1936

President II, London
 JACQUES, James A, Leading Telegraphist, P/J 40558, died

Thursday, 6 August 1936

Amphion, light cruiser (*later HMAS Perth*)
 TINKLER, Basil I, Stoker 2c, D/KX 87942, illness

Saturday, 8 August 1936

Nelson, battleship
 WHEELDON, Harry, Ordnance Artificer, P/M 35305, illness

Sunday, 9 August 1936

Carlisle, light cruiser
 PARFITT, George V, Able Seaman, D/J 110652, died

Monday, 10 August 1936

Dainty, destroyer
 KNIGHT, Christopher H, Able Seaman, P/J 74225, died from fall

Wednesday, 12 August 1936

Fury, destroyer
 SELFE, Alfred T, Ordinary Seaman, P/SSX 16449, illness

Penelope, light cruiser,
 ROBERTSON, Gerald W T, Captain, road accident, killed
 Note: other passengers in the car, which was in collision with a lorry, were Lieutenant J H Unwin, Gunnery Officer and Lieutenant Commander K R Buckley, Torpedo Officer, all on route for HMS Penelope. They were too badly injured to join the ship for its commissioning.

Thursday, 13 August 1936

Exmouth, flotilla leader
 PLATT, Leonard, Able Seaman, P/SSX 1557, accidentally killed

Friday, 14 August 1936

Glorious, aircraft carrier
 DITES, Samuel, Leading Stoker, D/K 66002, illness

Saturday, 15 August 1936

Nelson, battleship
 WESTON, Charles E S, Steward, P/L 14519, illness

Tuesday, 25 August 1936

RM Chatham Division
 REDSHAW, George W, Sergeant, RM, 24483 (Ch), illness

Friday, 28 August 1936

Norfolk, heavy cruiser
 ARCHER, Richard, Able Seaman, D/JX 136245, illness

Friday, 28 August 1936

Valiant, battleship
 JOHNSON, Oliver W, Stoker 1c, C/KX 85597, on board drifter Moy, drowned

Tuesday, 1 September 1936

Royal Naval Reserve
 MACMAHON, Joseph, Commander, RNR, Rtd, illness

Thursday, 3 September 1936

Royal Marines
 HIRE, Ashton H, Major, RM, Rtd, Baronet, illness

Saturday, 5 September 1936

Royal Naval Reserve
 DAVIES, Harry R B, Commander, RNR, Rtd, illness

Wednesday, 9 September 1936

St Angelo, Malta
 BARLEY, Ronald L, Able Seaman, P/J 98175, illness

Thursday, 10 September 1936

Victoria & Albert, Royal Yacht
 HARWOOD, Archibald, Leading Stoker, P/KX 84801, road accident, killed

Sunday, 13 September 1936

Boscawen, Portland
 THOMPSON, Harold A, Paymaster Commander, illness

Rodney, battleship
 KING, Norman W, Electrical Artificer 3c, D/MX 46544, died

Wednesday, 16 September 1936

Despatch, light cruiser
 REES, Samuel G, Boy 1c, P/JX 142385, drowned

Saturday, 19 September 1936

Cormorant, Gibraltar
 SHEEN, Harold, Marine, 22355 (Ply), illness

Sunday, 20 September 1936

Delhi, light cruiser
 DRYDEN, Kenneth E, Engine Room Artificer 4c, D/MX 47900, illness

Norfolk III, RN Base, Aden
 LIVETT, Sidney G, Telegraphist, C/SSX 13943, illness

Ramillies, battleship
 EAGLES, George C, Leading Telegraphist, C/JX 130135, road accident, killed

Thursday, 24 September 1936

Furious, aircraft carrier
 HEITZMAN, Arthur J, Leading Telegraphist, D/J 111899, road accident, killed

Gipsy, destroyer
 CODROY, Harry, Able Seaman, D/J 111912, illness

Friday, 25 September 1936

Frobisher, cruiser
 STONE, Percy C, Marine, 23281 (Ch), illness

Sunday, 27 September 1936

Victory, Portsmouth
 PARTRIDGE, Thomas J, Able Seaman, P/JX 132377, road accident, killed

Friday, 2 October 1936

Royal Navy
 DAVIS, William, Stoker 1c, C/KX 76800, illness

Sunday, 4 October 1936

Drake, Devonport
 COLLINS, Walter J, Able Seaman, D/J 31104, illness
 LETHERBY, Arthur H, Stoker Petty Officer, D/KX 76197, accidentally killed

Tuesday, 6 October 1936

Enterprise, light cruiser
 PARFITT, Cyril N, Chief Engine Room Artificer 2c, P/MX 52062, illness

Thursday, 8 October 1936

Tarantula, river gunboat
 LINDLEY, Leslie F, Ordnance Artificer, C/M 39470, illness

Friday, 9 October 1936

Capetown, light cruiser
 HEROD, Adrian C, Petty Officer, D/J 111751, illness

Saturday, 10 October 1936

Pembroke, Chatham
 BURNS, Richard, Ordinary Seaman, C/SSX 18996, illness

Monday, 12 October 1936

Ganges, Shotley/Harwich
 HAYES, Daniel J, Boy 2c, JX 150083, illness

Thursday, 15 October 1936

Codrington, flotilla leader
 DICKENS, Gerald H C, Lieutenant, illness

Monday, 19 October 1936

Rodney, battleship
 HALL, Stanley P G, Petty Officer, D/J 64483, illness

Tuesday, 20 October 1936

Drake, Devonport
 MANN, Frederick A, Sick Berth Petty Officer, D/M 15592, illness

Woolwich, destroyer depot ship
 BEADELL, Cecil L G, Chief Electrical Artificer, C/M 35415, illness

Wednesday, 21 October 1936

Norfolk, heavy cruiser
 BLACKMORE, Joseph C, Mechanician, D/K 57495, illness

Plymouth Dockyard
 PRITCHARD, Henry G, Sergeant, RM Police, RMP X 98, illness

Monday, 26 October 1936

RN Hospital, Great Yarmouth
 COLLINS, Henry, Private, RMLI, (no service number listed, possibly pensioner), illness

Tuesday, 27 October 1936

Drake, Devonport
 WATSON, Henry C, Able Seaman, D/J 104432, illness

Royal Navy
 BLISS, Montagu H, Lieutenant, illness

Wednesday, 28 October 1936

Peshawur, passenger liner
 JENNINGS, Rodney P, Py/Midshipman, RNR, illness

Saturday, 31 October 1936

Barham, battleship
 ROSS, Alexander, Stoker 1c, P/K 62944, accidentally killed

Sunday, 1 November 1936

Ramillies, battleship
 MILLS, Harry H, Leading Seaman, C/JX 132693, illness

Wednesday, 4 November 1936

Drake, Devonport
 COLLINS, John, Stoker 1c, D/K 26399, illness

Royal Navy
 KELLY, Sir John D, Admiral of the Fleet, illness

Thursday, 5 November 1936

Cairo, light cruiser
 HUSKINSON, Herbert, Leading Stoker, C/KX 78924, illness

Tuesday, 10 November 1936

Drake, Devonport
 CURTISS, Ernest F, Petty Officer, D/JX 143378, illness

Victory I, Portsmouth
 CORNELIOUS, William F, Able Seaman, P/J 27450, illness

Thursday, 12 November 1936

Centurion, ex-battleship, target ship
 SWIFT, Albert E, Stoker 1c, D/K 29607, illness

Drake, Devonport
 BRAGG, Leslie P, Stoker 1c, D/KX 83226, accidentally killed

Saturday, 14 November 1936

Diomede, light cruiser
 HALL, Bertie S, Able Seaman, C/J 115638, illness

Sunday, 15 November 1936

Emerald, light cruiser
 GILLEN, Bernard, Able Seaman, C/SSX 15861, died

Rodney, battleship
 SPEDDING, Edgar C, Leading Signalman, D/J 110206, illness

Saturday, 21 November 1936

Devonport Dockyard
 PEYTON, Edward L, Lieutenant Commander, illness

Friday, 27 November 1936

Gnat, river gunboat
 OWENS, Harold T, Leading Seaman, P/J 110411, illness

Saturday, 28 November 1936

Victory, Portsmouth
 MURRAY, David, Telegraphist, P/JX 138913, road accident, killed

Monday, 30 November 1936

Pembroke, Chatham
 EMMS, Frederick G, Boy 1c, C/SSX 19089, illness

December 1936

Victory, Portsmouth
 SUTTON, Edward T, Supply Chief Petty Officer, P/M 37209, illness, day not listed in record

Tuesday, 1 December 1936

Kent, heavy cruiser
 FAIRBRASS, Percy J, Stoker 1c, C/KX 77149, accidentally killed

Thursday, 3 December 1936

Ganges, Shotley/Harwich
 FITZMAURICE, John, Marine, 24691 (Ch), road accident, killed

Medway, submarine depot ship
 HISLOP, Alexander, Able Seaman, P/JX 131909, died

Sunday, 13 December 1936

RM Barracks Chatham
 ATKINS, James S, Marine, X 392 (Ch), illness

Tuesday, 15 December 1936

Arethusa, light cruiser
 LAYZELL, Edward F, Stoker 1c, C/KX 85270, illness

Wednesday, 16 December 1936

Pembroke, Chatham
 OSWICK, Harold G, Stoker 1c, C/KX 79898, illness

Tuesday, 22 December 1936

Dorsetshire, heavy cruiser
 SMITH, Frederick G, Able Seaman, D/J 79452, illness

Saturday, 26 December 1936

Queen Elizabeth, battleship
 ENNION, Peter, Leading Seaman, D/J 39263, accidentally killed

Sunday, 27 December 1936

Victory, Portsmouth
 SAWYER, Reginald S, Able Seaman, P/JX 137877, illness

Monday, 28 December 1936

Gallant, destroyer
 DEADMAN, William D, Stoker 1c, C/K 60990, illness

Greenwich, destroyer depot ship
 LASHMAR, John M, Petty Officer, C/J 109212, illness

1937

Severn Division, RNVR
 PHILLIPS, Rev William T, Honorary Chaplain, RNVR, illness, day and month not given in Navy List

Saturday, 2 January 1937

St Vincent, Gosport
 LANE, David H, Boy 2c, JX 149128, road accident, killed

Sunday, 3 January 1937

Sussex, heavy cruiser
 CHALLEN, Charlie W, Musician, RMB, RMB X 13, died

Wednesday, 6 January 1937

Cardiff/Calcutta, light cruisers, in Reserve Fleet under Care and Maintenance (C & M)
 GANDER, Albert J, Leading Seaman, C/J 108661, road accident, killed
Note: when ships were in C & M, a man could be working on two or more ships of the Reserve Fleet

Milford, sloop
 DODSON, Alfred W, Able Seaman, P/J 104696, illness

Thursday, 7 January 1937

Cormorant, Gibraltar
 HALL, Frank, Stoker 2c, P/KX 87709, illness

St Vincent, Gosport
 HUTT, Victor S, Marine, X 1142 (Po), illness

Friday, 8 January 1937

RM Portsmouth Division
 WILLS, Joseph G, Marine, X 1895 (Po), illness

Saturday, 9 January 1937

Resource, fleet repair ship
 BOCKING, Andrew R, Able Seaman, P/JX 127652, drowned

Sunday, 10 January 1937

Pembroke, Chatham
 HOWARD, Ronald, Ordinary Seaman, C/SSX 18584, illness

Victory, Portsmouth
 EVERITT, Bertram A, Chief Petty Officer Writer, P/M 35463, illness

Monday, 11 January 1937

Ganges, Shotley/Harwich
 WADDLE, David, Boy 2c, JX 151631, illness

Greenwich, destroyer depot ship
 WALKER, Francis H G, Captain, illness

Tuesday, 12 January 1937

Comet, destroyer
 BRUNO, Oltemus, Wardroom Steward, L 390 (Maltese), illness

Woolston, destroyer
 WATSON, George, Engine Room Artificer 1c, C/MX 52472, died

Wednesday, 13 January 1937

Pembroke, Chatham
 WALLWORK, James, Stoker 2c, C/KX 89886, illness

Thursday, 14 January 1937

Drake, Devonport
 SARGENT, John, Stoker 2c, D/KX 90084, illness

Sunday, 17 January 1937

Ganges, Shotley/Harwich
 PATRICK, Kenneth C, Boy 2c, JX 150327, illness

Wednesday, 20 January 1937

Anthony, destroyer
 MAGEE, Richard D M, Act/Sub Lieutenant, illness

Friday, 22 January 1937

Hussar, minesweeper
 STEVENS, Robert J, Leading Stoker, C/K 26078, illness

Neptune, light cruiser
 LACEY, Leonard, Leading Seaman, P/JX 128212, drowned

RM Barracks Chatham
 ROBERTS, James W, Sergeant, RM, 24471 (Ch), illness

Saturday, 23 January 1937

Drake, Devonport
 TUCKER, Leslie J, Leading Seaman, D/J 95992, illness

Victory, Portsmouth
 GREEN, Samuel J, Stoker 1c, P/KX 81131, illness

Tuesday, 26 January 1937

Campbell, flotilla leader
 SPILSTED, William T, Engine Room Artificer, C/M 39546, illness

Speedwell, minesweeper
 ANDREWS, Clifford, Engine Room Artificer 3c, D/MX 50319, drowned

Wednesday, 27 January 1937

Brazen, destroyer
 EVANS, Robert W, Stoker Petty Officer, D/K 65280, drowned

Galatea, light cruiser
WOOD, William B, Supply Assistant, D/MX 51179, died from fall

Monday, 1 February 1937

Orion, light cruiser
BEDFORD, Arthur W F, Boy 1c, C/JX 144182, illness

Wednesday, 3 February 1937

Barham, battleship
WISE, David G H, Midshipman, illness

RM Depot Portsmouth
MILLER, Major H Mac D, Colour Sergeant, RM, 215819 (Po), illness

Thursday, 4 February 1937

Rainbow, submarine
BERLYN, Arthur C, Lieutenant (E), illness

Friday, 5 February 1937

FAA, 825 Sqn, Glorious, aircraft carrier, air crash at sea, both killed
OVERAL, Bert, Telegraphist, P/JX 129984
VARDON, Gerald A, Lieutenant

Royal Naval Reserve
PETTIT, Peter F, Chief Skipper, RNR, illness

Saturday, 6 February 1937

Devonport Dockyard
HIGGINSON, Edgar, Constable, RM Police, RMP X 266 (Ply), accidentally killed

Wednesday, 10 February 1937

Orion, light cruiser
BULLEN, John J, Marine, P/X 1484, illness

Friday, 12 February 1937

Drake, Devonport
THOMAS, Kenneth W, Engine Room Artificer 2c, D/M 34509, illness

Laconia, passenger liner
CONNELL, Ernest W, Lieutenant, RNR, illness

Pembroke, Chatham
BRADLEY, George F, Petty Officer, C/J 28505, illness

Royal Naval Reserve
MORGAN, John E, Skipper, RNR, illness

Saturday, 13 February 1937

Cairo, light cruiser
TURNER, John F, Able Seaman, P/J 92408, illness

Defiance, Devonport
WHITE, Victor J, Telegraphist, D/J 136249, road accident, killed

Drake, Devonport
McMAHON, Patrick, Leading Signalman, D/JX 133965, illness

Lucia, submarine depot ship
PROCTOR, John H, Stoker 1c, D/KX 83046, illness

Victoria & Albert, Royal Yacht
HOPKINS, Alex T, Colour Sergeant, RM, 214967 (Po), illness

Sunday, 14 February 1937

Nelson, battleship
GREEN, James, Leading Stoker, P/KX 87359, illness

RM Portsmouth Division
REYNOLDS, William H, Marine, X 2076 (Po), illness

Monday, 15 February 1937

Drake, Devonport
LEONARD, Hubert, Signalman, D/JX 134796, illness

FAA, 821 Sqn, Courageous, aircraft carrier, air crash, all killed
CURRIE, William H, Telegraphist, C/JX 133704
LAKE, George E, Sub Lieutenant
MACDONALD, Roderick W, Lieutenant

Tuesday, 16 February 1937

Ganges, Shotley/Harwich
DIXON, George E, Boy 2c, JX 150012, illness

Wednesday, 17 February 1937

Repulse, battlecruiser
GARRAWAY, Francis, Able Seaman, P/J 29054, illness

Monday, 22 February 1937

Royal Navy
EARLE, John C M, Cadet, accidentally killed

Tuesday, 23 February 1937

Drake, Devonport
HOPKINS, James H, Telegraphist, D/JX 138891, illness

Pembroke, Chatham
MEMORY, Stanley T, Electrical Artificer Apprentice, M 54069, illness

RN Barracks Portsmouth
RUMBELOW, Robert H, Stoker 1c, P/KX 83740, accidentally killed

Royal Navy
SWAYNE, Philip M, Cadet, accidentally killed

Victory, Portsmouth
GLADDIS, Albert O, Assistant Cook, P/MX 52136, illness

Wednesday, 24 February 1937

Boadicea, destroyer
  PARVEN, Walter J, Able Seaman, P/JX 138466, illness

Saturday, 27 February 1937

Resurce, fleet repair ship
  PEPPER, Frank V, Supply Chief Petty Officer, C/MX 53383, illness

Monday, 1 March 1937

Royal Navy
  APPLEYARD, Harold P L L, Paymaster Lieutenant, illness

Tuesday, 2 March 1937

Ganges, Shotley/Harwich
  BROUGH, George T, Boy 2c, JX 150358, illness

Thursday, 4 March 1937

Esk, destroyer
  DEACON, William H, Able Seaman, P/JX 149948, drowned

Saturday, 6 March 1937

Hood, battlecruiser, mooring accident
  SMITH, Douglas D, Ordinary Seaman, C/JX 141775, killed (*see also 8 March*)

Sunday, 7 March 1937

Greenwich, destroyer depot ship
  FRY, Harold J, Sailmaker, D/J 28639, illness

Monday, 8 March 1937

Hood, battlecruiser, mooring accident on 6th
  HAYWARD, Walter J, Corporal, RMLI, 217037 (Po), DOI

Thursday, 11 March 1937

Naval Ordnance Department of Admiralty
  MARSHALSEA, Percy G, Lieutenant, illness

Friday, 12 March 1937

Greenwich, destroyer depot ship
  LE HURAY, Donald L, Able Seaman, P/J 51936, illness

Sunday, 14 March 1937

Drake, Devonport
  WILLIAMS, Richard A J, Chief Electrical Artificer 2c, D/M 36723, illness

Monday, 15 March 1937

Royal Navy, air crash
  WICKS, Richard W, Lieutenant, killed

Tuesday, 16 March 1937

Rodney, battleship
  SMITH, Walter D, Painter, D/MX 50250, illness

Wednesday, 17 March 1937

Bulldog, destroyer
  BLOWFIELD, Robert, Telegraphist, C/UDX/604, illness

Pembroke, Chatham
  BANKS, Ernest A, Able Seaman, C/JX 135601, illness

Saturday, 20 March 1937

Royal Navy
  MOODY, George C, Stoker Petty Officer, P/K 59431, illness

Sunday, 21 March 1937

Impregnable, Devonport
  STAYTE, Joseph J, Able Seaman, D/J 114260, road accident, killed

Repulse, battlecruiser
  WYKES, Walter A, Able Seaman, P/J 111568, illness

Monday, 22 March 1937

FAA, 800 Sqn, Courageous, aircraft carrier
  JELF, Christopher B, Lieutenant, illness

Thursday, 25 March 1937

Courageous, aircraft carrier
  FARMER, Alfred A L, Marine, 21630 (Po), illness

Saturday, 27 March 1937

Royal Navy
  BYRNE, John, Boy 2c, JX 149054, illness

Sunday, 28 March 1937

Nelson, battleship
  MORRIS, Arthur S H, Commander, illness

Monday, 29 March 1937

Personnel Services, Department of Admiralty
  LILLEY, Austen G, Captain, illness

Wednesday, 31 March 1937

Royal Naval Reserve
  BARBER, William H, Chief Skipper, RNR, illness

Victory, Portsmouth
  GLOVER, Percy, Chief Stoker, P/K 59714, illness

Thursday, 1 April 1937

RM, Chatham Division
 HAIZELDEN, Alfred G, Colour Sergeant, RM, 10591 (Ch), 19937 (Pens), died

Sunday, 4 April 1937

Drake, Devonport
 PAGE, William J, Stoker 2c, D/KX 90844, illness

Monday, 5 April 1937

RM Barracks Chatham
 BENNETT, Edward, Marine, 19821 (Ch), illness

Wednesday, 7 April 1937

Royal Naval Reserve
 MOORE, Thomas W, Honorary Lieutenant, RNR, illness

Victory, Portsmouth
 ASHFORD, Thomas S, Shipwright 1c, P/M 33941, died

Sunday, 11 April 1937

Devonshire, heavy cruiser
 MALIA, Carmelo, Leading Steward, E/LX 20877, illness

Wednesday, 14 April 1937

RM Barracks Chatham
 HOME, Ian H, Marine, X 1655 (Ply), illness

Friday, 16 April 1937

Enterprise, light cruiser
 MACE, George W, Ordinary Seaman, P/SSX 17573, illness

Tuesday, 20 April 1937

Impregnable, Devonport
 STANIFORD, George F, Able Seaman, D/J 109508, accidentally killed

Sunday, 25 April 1937

Royal Naval Volunteer Reserve
 GRAY, George, Lieutenant Commander, RNVR, illness

Monday, 26 April 1937

Royal Naval Reserve
 MORGAN, John C V, Commander, RNR, illness

Tuesday, 27 April 1937

Royal Oak, battleship
 CAMPBELL, Patrick M, Boy 1c, JX 148593, died

Friday, 30 April 1937

Victory, Portsmouth
 DAVIES, Sydney, Chief Stoker, P/K 60052, illness

Saturday, 1 May 1937

Royal Sovereign, battleship
 ELSON, Dennis A R, Leading Seaman, D/JX 138407, illness

Sunday, 2 May 1937

Dorsetshire, heavy cruiser
 WALKER, Alfred J, Stoker Petty Officer, D/K 55148, illness

Royal Naval Volunteer Reserve
 LIVINGSTON, Charles, Honorary Commander, RNVR, illness

Monday, 3 May 1937

Cardiff, light cruiser
 BAKER, Reginald H, Marine, CH/X 1549, illness

Wednesday, 5 May 1937

Victory, Portsmouth
 SWATHERIDGE, Leonard F, Joiner 4c, P/MX 54253, road accident, killed

Monday, 10 May 1937

Drake, Devonport
 LEAHY, Herbert T, Supply Assistant, D/MX 52765, illness

Wanderer, destroyer
 HALL, Albert E, Able Seaman, C/J 102984, drowned

Tuesday, 11 May 1937

Drake, Devonport
 PERRYMAN, Dennis, Stoker Petty Officer, D/K 56057, illness

FAA, 821 Sqn, Courageous, aircraft carrier
 BAXTER, Frederick G, Telegraphist, D/JX 125974, accidentally killed

Thursday, 13 May 1937

Hunter, destroyer, mined in Mediterranean off Almeria during the Spanish Civil War, all killed (below)

BETTRIDGE, Arthur, Leading Seaman, D/JX 135096
CRAWFORD, George H, Ordinary Seaman, D/SSX 17152
GRIFFITHS, John H, Petty Officer Cook, D/MX 48073

HOUSE, Leslie V, Able Seaman, D/JX 135005
SWIGGS, Wilfrid R, Stoker Petty Officer, D/K 56346
TURNER, Bertie C, Petty Officer, D/J 72652
WAITES, Alfred, Stoker 1c, D/KX 86525
WATTERS, William, Leading Seaman, D/JX 130358

Tuesday, 18 May 1937

Victory I, Portsmouth
LOWMAN, Edgar M, Able Seaman, P/JX 128978, illness

Friday, 21 May 1937

Skipjack, minesweeper
INGRAM, Frederick, Stoker Petty Officer, C/K 59866, illness

Saturday, 22 May 1937

Dolphin, Gosport
SAWYER, Herbert J, Chief Petty Officer, C/JX 152928, illness

Tuesday, 25 May 1937

Pembroke, Chatham
BEARD, Sidney J, Leading Stoker, C/K 63616, illness

Monday, 31 May 1937

Queen Elizabeth, battleship
ST JOHN, Ralph G J, Act/Sub Lieutenant, illness

Tuesday, 1 June 1937

RM Plymouth Barracks
SMITH, Rodney B F, Lieutenant, RM, illness

Wednesday, 2 June 1937

Royal Naval Reserve
PLATTS, William, Chief Skipper, RNR, illness

Sunday, 6 June 1937

Berwick, heavy cruiser
DOWN, Eric F, Leading Stoker, D/KX 79932, illness

Thursday, 10 June 1937

RM Plymouth Division
SYMONS, Albert, Colour Sergeant, RM, 16662 (Ply), illness

Friday, 11 June 1937

Victory I, Portsmouth
FLICKER, John, Able Seaman, P/J 107300, illness

Saturday, 12 June 1937

Gipsy, destroyer
RANSOME, Philip C, Lieutenant Commander, illness

Monday, 14 June 1937

RM Portsmouth Division
HAYNES, Henry S J, Corporal, RM, 22744 (Po), died

Wednesday, 16 June 1937

RM Plymouth Division
HOLT, Ronald J, Marine, X 1440 (Ply), illness

Monday, 21 June 1937

Capetown, light cruiser
BOND, Alfred, Able Seaman, D/J 55438, illness

Devonshire, heavy cruiser
BRINDLEY, Thomas, Boy 1c, D/JX 148446, illness

Tuesday, 22 June 1937

Pembroke, Chatham
WHITTINGTON, Herbert H, Supply Chief Petty Officer, C/M 26033, illness

Thursday, 24 June 1937

Royal Naval Reserve
MAHONEY, Arthur M, Paymaster Sub Lieutenant, RNR, illness

Royal Navy
TITE, Luther V, Commissioned Gunner, illness

Victory, Portsmouth
FISHER, Sir William W, Admiral, illness

Friday, 25 June 1937

Suffolk, heavy cruiser
REDFERN, James, Stoker 2c, P/KX 89427, accidentally killed

Sunday, 27 June 1937

Dorsetshire, heavy cruiser
CAMERON, Stanley R, Ordinary Seaman, P/JX 140622, illness

Monday, 28 June 1937

Cumberland, heavy cruiser
BROOKE-SHORT, Cecil, Major, RM, illness

Tuesday, 29 June 1937

Douglas, flotilla leader
PAINTIN, Leslie A C, Able Seaman, P/JX 133896, illness

Wednesday, 30 June 1937

Glasgow, light cruiser
BROWNE, Charles A, Captain, illness

Friday, 2 July 1937

Ganges, Shotley/Harwich
DAVENPORT, Harry, Boy Telegraphist, D/JX 149205, accidentally killed

Saturday, 3 July 1937

RN Hospital, Haslar
RAYHILL, Frank, Sick Berth Chief Petty Officer, P/M 28992, illness

Sunday, 4 July 1937

Cormorant, Gibraltar
ADAMS, Clifford, Telegraphist, P/JX 136214, accidentally killed

Monday, 5 July 1937

Cardiff, light cruiser
HOWARD, Alfred J, Able Seaman, C/JX 126592, illness

Wednesday, 7 July 1937

Drake, Devonport
WEST, Alexander G, Leading Seaman, D/JX 132508, road accident, killed

Friday, 9 July 1937

On loan to Royal Australian Navy
LA TROBE, Ronald, Petty Officer, D/JX 25586, died

Wednesday, 14 July 1937

HM Coast Guard Southend, Essex
PHILLIPS, Walter, Chief Officer, HMCG, illness

Saturday, 17 July 1937

Vernon, Portsmouth
STAFFORD, George, Petty Officer, C/JX 127679, illness

Saturday, 24 July 1937

Pembroke, Chatham
THOMPSON, John J H, Stoker 2c, C/KX 91463, accidentally killed

Monday, 26 July 1937

Victory, Portsmouth
STEWART, Charles J, Stoker 1c, P/KX 77023, illness

Tuesday, 27 July 1937

Ganges, Shotley/Harwich
PRATT, Arthur W J, Boy 2c, JX 153704, illness

Saturday, 31 July 1937

RM Barracks Chatham
TAYLOR, Frank, Musician, RMB X 257 (Ch), died

Sunday, 1 August 1937

Rodney, battleship
FITZGERALD, Michael, Able Seaman, D/JX 110635, died

Thursday, 5 August 1937

Excellent, Portsmouth
EASTON, Arthur R, Ordnance Artificer 4c, P/MX 54557, road accident, died

Wishart, destroyer
CONNOLLY, William H, Able Seaman, C/JX 139213, drowned

Friday, 6 August 1937

Ramillies, battleship
SITWELL, Peter S L, Paymaster Midshipman, illness

Tuesday, 17 August 1937

FAA, 810 Sqn, Courageous, aircraft carrier, air crash
GOLDSMITH, John A, Lieutenant, killed

Thursday, 19 August 1937

Rodney, battleship
DAW, Walter E, Boy 1c, D/SSX 19193, accidentally killed

Friday, 20 August 1937

Cardiff, light cruiser
ALLEN, Herbert, Sick Berth Petty Officer, (service number not listed), died

Saturday, 21 August 1937

RN Hospital, Haslar
O'SHEA, William H, Leading Sick Berth Attendant, P/MX 47445, illness

Sunday, 22 August 1937

Royal Fleet Wing, Plymouth (as recorded, unit not known)
SAUNDERS, Arthur, Stoker, P/KX 76060, illness

Monday, 23 August 1937

Cardiff, light cruiser
MARKS, Albert E, Chief Stoker, P/K 28977, died

Thursday, 26 August 1937

Skipjack, minesweeper
PHILPOTT, Leonard G, Leading Steward, C/L 13487, died

Saturday, 28 August 1937

Drake, Devonport
KING, Walter E, Able Seaman, D/JX 127981, illness

Tuesday, 31 August 1937

RM Barracks Chatham
SCOTT, George H, Marine, 22916 (Ch), accidentally killed

Friday, 3 September 1937

FAA, 801 Sqn, Furious, aircraft carrier, air crash
KNOCKER, Charles A, Sub Lieutenant, killed

RN Hospital, Plymouth
MORSE, William C, Corporal, RM, G 17740 (Ply), bicycle accident, killed

Saturday, 4 September 1937

Furious, aircraft carrier
PHILP, Stephen R, Able Seaman, D/J 107388, illness

Tuesday, 7 September 1937

Eagle, aircraft carrier
BENNETT, Robert W, Petty Officer, D/JX 135100, accidentally killed

Wednesday, 8 September 1937

Ganges, Shotley/Harwich
ROSER, Herbert, Marine, 21-61 (Ch), illness

Grafton, destroyer
GRANT, Peter, Able Seaman, SSX 15583, died

RM Portsmouth Division
HOWE, James W, Marine, 215519 (Po), illness

Friday, 10 September 1937

Drake, Devonport
FORD, Frederick W, Petty Officer, D/J 110354, illness

Saturday, 11 September 1937

Drake, Devonport
APPLEBY, John R, Able Seaman, D/JX 152168, illness

Wednesday, 15 September 1937

Capetown, light cruiser
O'DRISCOLL, James A, Ordinary Seaman, D/SSX 17998, drowned

Victory, Portsmouth
SHIELS, George, Stoker 1c, P/KX 76611, illness

Thursday, 16 September 1937

Caroline, ex-cruiser, drill ship, Belfast
WARD, Charles H V, Chief Petty Officer, D/239383, illness

Monday, 20 September 1937

Vernon, Portsmouth
GILLHAM, Wilfred F, Electrical Artificer 5c, C/MX 54472, accidentally killed

Wednesday, 22 September 1937

Drake, Devonport
STANSBURY, William T, Chief Engine Room Artificer, D/M 7954, illness

Furious, aircraft carrier
HALL, William, Stoker 1c, D/KX 86583, illness

Thursday, 23 September 1937

Apollo, light cruiser (HMAS Hobart in 1938)
ROE, Thomas F, Able Seaman, D/JX 125986, drowned

Friday, 24 September 1937

Caledonia, Rosyth
WOODS, Arthur H, Sailmaker, C/J 43764, illness

Halcyon, minesweeper
MANNS, Albert A B, Leading Steward, P/LX 20008, died

Monday, 27 September 1937

Devonshire, heavy cruiser
QUINN, William, Boy 1c, D/JX 148364, heat stroke, died

Motor Torpedo Boat, MTB.6, accidental explosion
FARRANT, William H, Able Seaman, C/JX 134749, DOI in RN Hospital Malta

Thursday, 30 September 1937

Leander, light cruiser, both drowned
FORBES, William, Leading Seaman, D/JX 132031
PATERSON, Alexander M, Able Seaman, D/JX 142115

Weston, sloop
FRASER, William, Able Seaman, P/JX 151460, illness

Tuesday, 5 October 1937

Drake, Devonport
PHILLIPS, William H, Lieutenant, illness

Thursday, 7 October 1937

Royal Sovereign, battleship
FENNELL, Alfred E W, Officer's Cook 2c, D/L 9663, illness

Saturday, 9 October 1937

Royal Oak, battleship
EADES, Thomas E, Engine Room Artificer 4c, D/MX 53904, illness

Sunday, 10 October 1937

Wolfhound, destroyer
BRADLEY, Henry G N, Telegraphist, C/J 32678, illness

Monday, 11 October 1937

FAA, 801 Sqn, Furious, aircraft carrier, air crash
HARLEY, William R, Lieutenant, killed

Tuesday, 12 October 1937

Glasgow, light cruiser
JEFFERIES, Archibald J, Boy 1c, P/JX 150264, accidentally killed

Wednesday, 13 October 1937

Excellent, Portsmouth
DEUCHAR, William J, Gunner, illness

Monday, 18 October 1937

Cockchafer, river gunboat
HARDING, Dennis, Chief Petty Officer, D/JX 146583, illness

Drake, Devonport
COATES, Thomas P, Leading Telegraphist, D/J 39362, road accident, killed

Tuesday, 19 October 1937

Drake, Devonport
THOMAS, George H B, Able Seaman, D/J 108505, illness

Thursday, 21 October 1937

RN Hospital, Plymouth
TAYLOR, Alexander G, Surgeon Commander, illness

Vindictive, cruiser
LAY, Harold A, Leading Signalman, C/JX 130491, illness

Friday, 22 October 1937

Enterprise, light cruiser
PERRY, Percy W, Petty Officer, D/JX 147102, illness

Herald, survey ship
TREJIDJO, Frederick T, Leading Seaman, D/JX 126449, illness

Sunday, 24 October 1937

Neptune, light cruiser
ROEBUCK, George A, Ordinary Seaman, D/SSX 18227, drowned

Tuesday, 26 October 1937

Royal Naval Reserve
WARMAN, Edmund, Chief Skipper, RNR, illness

Friday, 29 October 1937

Iron Duke, gunnery training ship
WIGHTMAN, William, Engine Room Artificer 1c, RNR, E D 214, illness

Saturday, 30 October 1937

RN Barracks Portsmouth
MYERS, Charles, Able Seaman, C/JX 128824, illness

Monday, 1 November 1937

Nelson, battleship
CLARKE, William F, Officer's Cook 2c, P/L 14027, died

Tuesday, 2 November 1937

Apollo, light cruiser *(HMAS Hobart in 1938)*
SPICER, Hector C, Stoker Petty Officer, D/K 58974, illness

Wednesday, 3 November 1937

RM Engineers
LINGWOOD, George, Sapper, RME 1874332, illness

Vernon, Portsmouth
COOKE, Walter C, Senior Master, illness

Saturday, 6 November 1937

Defiance, Devonport
FROST, Robert G, Able Seaman, D/J 30105, illness

Sunday, 7 November 1937

Hostile, destroyer
MURRAY, Albert, Able Seaman, C/JX 148718, accidentally killed

RM Barracks Chatham
KIRKHAM, Alfred J, Corporal, RM, 21082 (Ch), accidentally killed

Friday, 12 November 1937

Fortune, destroyer
LEGGETT, Russell, Petty Officer, C/J 56608, illness

Saturday, 13 November 1937

Active, destroyer
SPERRING, Charles H, Lieutenant (E), illness, died in RN Hospital Malta

Dolphin, Gosport
TRELEASE, Ernest, Stoker 1c, P/K 58558, illness

Sunday, 14 November 1937

RN Barracks Portsmouth
HUGHES, John F, Ordinary Seaman, P/SSX 23092, died

Saturday, 20 November 1937

Royal Marine Police
WESTWOOD, Albert, Sergeant, RMP 80 (Ch), illness

Sunday, 21 November 1937

Cumberland, heavy cruiser
WHITE, Richard F, Mechanician 1c, C/KX 78073, illness

Resource, fleet repair ship
HUTTON, James, Able Seaman, P/JX 139667, accidentally killed

Saturday, 27 November 1937

York, heavy cruiser
LOVEDAY, George F, Shipwright, C/MX 47403, illness

Sunday, 28 November 1937

Ganges, Shotley/Harwich
 DUNHAM, Bernard W C, Boy 2c, JX 153295, illness

Osprey, Portland
 WESTWOOD, Ronald, Able Seaman, P/JX 145341, road crash, killed

Monday, 29 November 1937

Hastings, sloop
 WILLIAMSON, George E, Lieutenant, illness

Tuesday, 30 November 1937

Caledonia, Rosyth
 HAMILTON, Shaun R, Boy 2c, JX 158409, illness
 SHEPHERD, William K, Boy 2c, J 155466, illness

FAA, 711 Sqn, London, air crash, both killed
 BOOTH, Patrick A, Lieutenant
 BURNS, Norman S, Leading Aircraftsman, RAF, 590712

Wednesday, 1 December 1937

Basilisk, destroyer
 ERSKINE, Ralph J, Lieutenant, illness

Saturday, 4 December 1937

Pandora, submarine
 DALE, Frederick, Able Seaman, P/J 30004, illness

Sunday, 5 December 1937

Ladybird, river gunboat
 WEEKLY, Charles R S, Stoker Petty Officer, P/K 57847, drowned

Tuesday, 7 December 1937

Caledonia, Rosyth
 DOUGLAS, Gordon, Boy 2c, JX 154758, illness

Thursday, 9 December 1937

Barham, battleship
 HUDSON, John S, Ordinary Seaman, P/JX 141980, drowned

Thursday, 9 December 1937

Peterel, river gunboat
 HOLLOWAY, Frederick E, Leading Seaman, P/J 94303, died

Sunday, 12 December 1937

Hotspur, destroyer
 POTTS, Bertram D, Able Seaman, C/JX 141042, illness

Ladybird, river gunboat, Japanese shelling
 LONERGAN, Terrance N, Sick Berth Attendant, C/MX 50739, died

Wednesday, 15 December 1937

Royal Oak, battleship
 SKINGSLEY, Ronald S, Marine, X 899 (Ply), illness

Saturday, 18 December 1937

Capetown, light cruiser
 NICHOLL, Horace R, Cook, D/MX 51489, accidentally killed

Cardiff, light cruiser
 BROOMHAM, Charles, Chief Stoker, KX 75990, illness

Sunday, 19 December 1937

Victory, Portsmouth
 GILFILLAIN, Joseph E, Stoker 1c, D/KX 87920, illness

Wednesday, 22 December 1937

Drake, Devonport
 MITCHELL, George C, Marine, 19924 (Ply), illness

Friday, 24 December 1937

Folkestone, sloop
 CORNWELL, Arthur J, Supply Petty Officer, C/M 38229, illness

1938

Royal Navy
LEARY, John H, Act/Cook, MX 56971, illness, day and month not listed in record

Saturday, 1 January 1938

Sheffield, light cruiser
ASHDOWN, Harold H, Shipwright, C/M 19187, illness

Monday, 3 January 1938

Royal Navy
MOORE, Walter, Chief Stoker, P/K 28982, illness

Tuesday, 4 January 1938

Glasgow, light cruiser
McKENNAN, William D, Engine Room Artificer 4c, P/MX 52949, illness

Thursday, 6 January 1938

RM Plymouth Division
HOSKING, Norman V, Marine, X 1743 (Ply), illness

Friday, 14 January 1938

RM Deal
RICKARD, Thomas G, Marine, 16252 (Ply), illness

Saturday, 15 January 1938

Cardiff, light cruiser
DRIVER, Henry W, Leading Seaman, C/J 111730, road accident, killed

Ganges, Shotley/Harwich
ATKINSON, Horace W, Boy 2c, JX 152770, illness

Royal Naval Reserve
JOHNSON, William H, Chief Skipper, RNR, illness

Thursday, 20 January 1938

FAA, 716 Flight, Amphion, light cruiser (*HMAS Perth in 1939*), air crash, both killed
HAMMOND, Leslie V, Able Seaman, P/J 113195
PRICE, John C H, Lieutenant

Friday, 21 January 1938

Wolsey, destroyer
TAYLOR, Anthony, Able Seaman, D/JX 138966, illness

Sunday, 23 January 1938

Greenwich, destroyer depot ship
CORBEN, Percy M, Commissioned Gunner, illness

Salmon, submarine
SOLLITT, Daniel K, Signalman, P/JX 128638, illness

St Vincent, Gosport
HOTHAM, Robert, Boy 2c, JX 153869, accidentally killed

Monday, 24 January 1938

Nightingale, mining tender
FILLERY, Stanley E, Able Seaman, P/JX 140643, drowned

Tuesday, 25 January 1938

Victory, Portsmouth
SKINNER, Harry C, Ordinary Seaman, P/SSX 23413, illness

Friday, 28 January 1938

Royal Navy
DAVIS, Franklin H, Chief Engine Room Artificer, P/M 6236, illness

Saturday, 29 January 1938

Portsmouth
FIELD, Staunton A, Major, RM, illness

Royal Marines
SCOTT, S (initial only) A, Major, RM, illness
Note: Appears in the Navy List obituaries, but not in the active or retired name index, Perhaps Honorary rank

Wednesday, 2 February 1938

Pembroke, Chatham
HUBBLE, Walter J H, Able Seaman, C/J 62699, illness

Thursday, 3 February 1938

Caledonia, Rosyth
SIM, James, Stoker 1c, D/KX 80799, road accident, killed

Friday, 4 February 1938

Pembroke, Chatham
HARMER, Jack, Stoker 2c, C/KX 92050, illness

Sunday, 6 February 1938

Royal Navy
AH, Soo, Steward 2c, (no service number listed), illness

Sunday, 13 February 1938

York, heavy cruiser
GILBERT, Reginald R, Paymaster Lieutenant Commander, illness

Wednesday, 16 February 1938

Antelope, destroyer
SCOTT, Victor G, Lieutenant (E), illness

Monday, 28 February 1938

Pembroke, Chatham
 WHEELER, William E, Leading Telegraphist, C/J 28333, illness

Victory, Portsmouth
 WALL, Francis B, Petty Officer Cook, P/M 34657, illness

Friday, 4 March 1938

Revenge, battleship
 BELL, Sidney E, Signal Boy, D/JX 148885, accidentally killed

Victory, Portsmouth
 HALL, Thomas, Stoker 1c, C/KX 86083, illness

Saturday, 5 March 1938

Medway, submarine depot ship
 ABBOTT, Edgar G, Petty Officer, J 108344, died

Sunday, 6 March 1938

Boreas, destroyer, Spanish bombing
 LONG, George G, Able Seaman, P/JX 129165, DOW

Thursday, 10 March 1938

Royal Navy
 PEARN, Joseph, Chief Petty Officer (Pensioner), 118408, illness

Victory, Portsmouth
 O'SULLIVAN, Frederic D, Assistant Steward, P/LX 22363, accidentally killed

Friday, 11 March 1938

Emerald, cruiser
 McNEAL, John, Stoker 1c, C/KX 75275, illness

Monday, 14 March 1938

Royal Navy
 BRADY, Arthur C, Able Seaman, P/JX 141066, illness

Thursday, 17 March 1938

Drake, Devonport
 DARCH, George, Leading Steward, D/L 9398, accidentally killed

Saturday, 19 March 1938

Victory, Portsmouth
 CRICK, Alfred R, Chief Petty Officer Writer, P/M 35004, died

Sunday, 20 March 1938

Royal Navy
 HOUNSEL, Stephen J P, Able Seaman, P/JX 139937, illness

Tuesday, 22 March 1938

Royal Marines HQ Plymouth
 WINZER, Edward A, Colour Sergeant, RM, G 20200 (Ply), illness

Wednesday, 23 March 1938

Revenge, battleship
 BARKER, Allan, Able Seaman, D/J 98120, drowned

Thursday, 24 March 1938

Dorsetshire, heavy cruiser
 EVANS, Charles, Chief Engine Room Artificer 2c, D/MX 52413, illness

Pembroke, Chatham
 CLOVER, William G, Leading Signalman, C/J 77754, died

Sunday, 27 March 1938

Drake, Devonport
 YELLAND, Ernest J, Stoker 2c, D/KX 92149, illness

Monday, 28 March 1938

Iron Duke, gunnery training ship
 WREN, Richard E, Petty Officer Steward, P/L 12695, illness

Wednesday, 30 March 1938

Porpoise, submarine
 RICHARDSON, John J W, Stoker 1c, P/KX 80336, illness

Monday, 4 April 1938

Malaya, battleship
 BAINES, Michael H, Midshipman, illness

Pembroke, Chatham
 COLBURN, Henry N, Marine, X 2068 (Ply), illness

Thursday, 7 April 1938

Hastings, sloop
 FARRELL, James N, Stoker Petty Officer, C/K 65172, road accident, killed

Saturday, 9 April 1938

Victory, Portsmouth
 PESTELL, William C A, Petty Officer Steward, P/LX 21914, illness

Tuesday, 12 April 1938

Hawkins, cruiser
 WILSON, Albert H, Chief Petty Officer Steward, P/L 14604, illness

Thursday, 14 April 1938

Royal Navy
 HAMPER, William, Chief Blacksmith, P/M 27874, illness

Monday, 18 April 1938

Bee, river gunboat, Yangste River
 PEACOCK, Hubert W, Able Seaman, P/J 49260, drowned

Tuesday, 19 April 1938

Hastings, sloop
  RAY, Samuel H, Stoker Petty Officer, D/KX 86816, illness

Wednesday, 20 April 1938

Furious, aircraft carrier
  BURGESS, Ewart, Stoker, D/KX 90840, illness

Thursday, 21 April 1938

Hawkins, cruiser
  WHITE, George E, Mechanician, P/M 66566, illness

Friday, 22 April 1938

Braemar, drifter
  HENDERSON, Andrew, Chief Skipper, RNR, illness

Hawkins, cruiser
  WARREN, Frederick C, Able Seaman, P/J 48212, illness

Sunday, 24 April 1938

Hawkins, cruiser
  WHIFFIN, Arthur C, Shipwright, C/MX 45374, illness

Wednesday, 27 April 1938

Dorsetshire, heavy cruiser
  HALSALL, Frederick N, Act/Warrant Engineer, illness

Thursday, 28 April 1938

Drake, Devonport
  WORTHINGTON, George R, Signalman, D/JX 141740, road accident, killed

Sutton, SLOOP
  VERNON, John D, Petty Officer Steward, C/LX 20513, died

Friday, 29 April 1938

Pembroke, Chatham
  REDMAN, Douglas F, Chief Mechanician, C/K 58892, road accident, killed

RM Portsmouth Division
  HERRING, George, Marine, X 2103 (Po), illness

Saturday, 30 April 1938

RM Chatham Division
  STARKEY, Sydney W, Corporal, RM, X 537 (Ch), illness

Sunday, 1 May 1938

Royal Navy
  HIGGINS, Denis, Able Seaman, D/J 44452, illness

Wednesday, 4 May 1938

RN Hospital, Capetown
  STEPHENS, Wilfred, Sick Berth Petty Officer, D/M 39527, illness

Thursday, 5 May 1938

Proteus, submarine
  MOFFATT, Alaister S, Stoker 1c, P/KX 84091, drowned

RM Chatham Division
  GODFREY, Benjamin E, Marine, X 515 (Ch), illness

Sunday, 8 May 1938

Diana, destroyer
  BROWNLOW, Frederick, Able Seaman, C/SSX 17721, illness

RM Plymouth Barracks
  FORD, Peter H W, Captain, RM, illness

Tuesday, 10 May 1938

Royal Navy
  RADCLIFFE, John W, Leading Stoker, P/KX 54557, illness

Warspite, battleship
  AGIUS, Dominick, Leading Steward, E/L 4478, died

Wednesday, 11 May 1938

Wildfire, Sheerness
  CLARK, James W S, Boy 2c, C/SSX 23928, illness

Thursday, 12 May 1938

Robin, river gunboat
  TEMME, Francis B, Chief Petty Officer, C/JX 146573, illness

Saturday, 14 May 1938

Royal Navy
  SEABROOK, Archibald W, Commissioned Gunner, illness

Sunday, 15 May 1938

Centurion, target ship
  JENKINS, William J, Stoker 1c, D/K 64793, illness

Gloucester, light cruiser
  CURTAIN, Edgar C, Commissioned Gunner, illness

Tuesday, 17 May 1938

Drake, Devonport
  McELHINNEY, Richard J, Writer, D/MX 56415, illness

Monday, 23 May 1938

Boscawen, Portland
  CARTER, Alfred E, Chief Skipper, RNR, illness

Tuesday, 24 May 1938

Excellent, Portsmouth
 PRICE, John E, Petty Officer, P/J 109494, accidentally killed

Thursday, 26 May 1938

Ganges, Shotley/Harwich
 STRANGE, Philip A, Boy 2c, JX 157782, illness

RM Plymouth Division
 GRIFFITHS, Raymond O J, Marine, X 2215 (Ply), illness

Saturday, 28 May 1938

Royal Navy
 YOUNG, Thompson S, Stoker 1c, P/KX 83234, accidentally killed

June 1938

Royal Naval Reserve
 CARTER, P (initial only) W, Paymaster Lieutenant (Registrar Clerk), RNR, illness, date not given in Navy List

Friday, 3 June 1938

Drake, Devonport
 LUSCOMBE, John A G, Stoker 2c, D/KX 93424, illness

Royal Naval Reserve
 LLOYD, Stanley P, Act/Sub Lieutenant, RNR, illness

Saturday, 4 June 1938

Anthony, destroyer
 KENNARD, Alfred E, Stoker 1c, C/KX 78034, road accident, killed

Monday, 6 June 1938

Repulse, battlecruiser
 FARWELL, Frederick B, Stoker Petty Officer, P/K 60857, accidentally killed

Royal Navy
 MURTON, Willis, Boy 2c, JX 158216, illness

Friday, 10 June 1938

Royal Navy
 PROBERT, Thomas G, Leading Seaman, C/J 96331, illness

Sunday, 12 June 1938

Royal Navy
 DICKINSON, William A C, Leading Stoker, D/KX 78081, illness

Thursday, 16 June 1938

Keppel, flotilla leader
 HART, Thomas J, Petty Officer, C/JX 127585, accidentally killed

Rodney, battleship
 McINTOSH, Ronald C G, Ordinary Seaman, D/SSX 22241, accidentally killed

Friday, 17 June 1938

Repulse, battlecruiser
 MATTINGLEY, William J, Able Seaman, SSX 18955, accidentally killed

Saturday, 18 June 1938

Suffolk, heavy cruiser
 LYNCH, Herbert R, Chief Engine Room Artificer 2c, P M 347783, died

Monday, 20 June 1938

Defiance, Devonport
 LONEY, Edwin T, Petty Officer, D/J 92359, illness

Excellent, Portsmouth
 BALDWIN, Bertram W T, Petty Officer, P/JX 131302, road accident, killed

Moth, river gunboat
 TUCK, Arthur F, Able Seaman, C/JX 140107, accidentally killed

Tuesday, 21 June 1938

Enterprise, light cruiser
 COX, Albert C M, Engine Room Artificer 3c, P/MX 45610, illness

Wednesday, 22 June 1938

Caledonia, Rosyth
 SAMPSON, James, Boy 2c, JX 158483, illness

Courageous, aircraft carrier
 DUMMER, John W, Able Seaman, P/JX 149704, illness

Royal Navy
 DOUGLAS, Robert, Signalman, P/JX 125837, illness

Thursday, 23 June 1938

Pembroke, Chatham
 FIDLER, Richard, Ordinary Seaman, C/SSX 23693, illness

Saturday, 25 June 1938

Centurion, target ship
 RUSSELL, James W, Stoker 1c, D/KX 87097, illness

RM Barracks Chatham
 MOORE, Reginald, Marine Tailor, 22988 (Ch), illness

Monday, 27 June 1938

Barham, battleship
 EWENS, Arthur G, Electrical Artificer 2c, P/MX 4751, drowned

Thursday, 30 June 1938

Pembroke, Chatham
SMITH, Dennis L, Leading Signalman, C/JX 137083, illness

Friday, 1 July 1938

Medway, submarine depot ship
STICKELLS, Harry J, Able Seaman, C/J 90095, illness

Royal Navy
CALVERT, Thomas F P, Rear Admiral, illness

Saturday, 2 July 1938

Royal Navy
COOKE, Cecil H, Able Seaman, P/SSX 14152, illness

Tuesday, 5 July 1938

Curlew, light cruiser
KENDALL, Alfred P, Painter 1c, C/MX 46708, illness

Thursday, 7 July 1938

Resource, fleet repair ship
STEAD, Christopher D, Stoker 1c, KX 83701, illness

Sunday, 10 July 1938

Repulse, battlecruiser
RAPPE, Charles E, Colour Sergeant, RM, 14854 (Po), illness

Tuesday, 12 July 1938

Royal Navy
TAYLOR, Claude C R, Leading Stoker, P/KX 81948, illness

Wednesday, 20 July 1938

Express, destroyer
KNIGHT, Sidney H, Able Seaman, P/JX 140965, drowned

Sunday, 24 July 1938

Caledonia, Rosyth
LOCKERBIE, Bruce, Boy 2c, JX 158771, illness

Tuesday, 26 July 1938

Kent, heavy cruiser
MARSH, William A, Stoker 1c, C/K 63651, illness

Friday, 29 July 1938

Chatham
WHITE, Ernest C, Quartermaster Sergeant, RM, E 24036 (Ch), illness

Wednesday, 3 August 1938

Pembroke, Chatham
EVANS, William E, (rating), C/MX 389, illness

Thursday, 4 August 1938

Esk, destroyer
YOUNG, Alfred, Officer's Cook 2c, P/L 12499, road accident, killed

Saturday, 6 August 1938

St Vincent, Gosport
JARVIS, Thomas A, Boy 2c, JX 159123, illness

Sunday, 7 August 1938

Port Jackson, trawler
CHURCH, Colin J, Py/Midshipman, RNR, illness

Monday, 8 August 1938

Ladybird, river gunboat
SMITH, Frederick W, Stoker 1c, P/KX 64748, heat stroke, died

Westcott, destroyer
FIRTH, Cyril J, Commander, illness

Thursday, 11 August 1938

Devonshire, heavy cruiser
MITCHELL, Robert M, Ordinary Seaman, D/JX 146035, accidentally killed

Hawkins, cruiser
TAYLOR, William S, Stoker 1c, P/KX 84825, illness

Saturday, 13 August 1938

Tamar, Hong Kong
LO, Leung, Able Seaman, (Chinese), illness

Sunday, 14 August 1938

Pembroke, Chatham
WICKES, Henry T, Signalman, C/J 114687, road accident, killed

Monday, 15 August 1938

Iron Duke, gunnery training ship
SPEARS, Thomas, Leading Stoker, P/KX 7893, accidentally killed

Tuesday, 16 August 1938

Calcutta, light cruiser
THOMSON, Alexander P, Petty Officer, C/J 113357, illness

Saturday, 20 August 1938

Cardiff, light cruiser
ALLEN, Herbert, Sick Berth Petty Officer, D/M 39287, (cause of death not listed)

Warspite, battleship
WILSON, John H, Petty Officer, P/96906, illness

Monday, 22 August 1938

Stork, sloop
  MOHAMED, Ismail, 2nd Tindal, 357, illness

Tuesday, 23 August 1938

Royal Oak, battleship
  WRIGHT, James, Signalman, JX 140212, road accident, killed

Saturday, 27 August 1938

Folkestone, sloop
  BAKER, Alfred W, Telegraphist, C/JX 133942, shark attack, killed

Sunday, 28 August 1938

RN Hospital, Haslar
  JOHNSON, John S, Leading Supply Assistant, P/MX 47183, illness

Rodney, battleship
  MOCKRIDGE, Frederick J, Leading Cook, D/MX 50531, died

Thursday, 1 September 1938

Diomede, light cruiser
  JONES, John L, Chief Engine Room Artificer, D/MX 28769, died

Sunday, 4 September 1938

Furious, aircraft carrier
  DRUITT, Robert, Able Seaman, D/JX 143457, drowned

Saturday, 10 September 1938

Impregnable, Devonport
  OKE, Thomas W H, Boy 2c, JX 158150, illness

Malaya, battleship
  GAMBLIN, Reginald, Marine, X 1942 (Po), accidentally killed

Monday, 12 September 1938

Hood, battlecruiser
  VAIARELLA, Antonio, Steward, E/LX 21002, illness

Saturday, 24 September 1938

Deptford, sloop
  WAREHAM, Leslie, Leading Telegraphist, P/JX 134173, illness

Saturday, 1 October 1938

Pembroke, Chatham
  KING, Joseph W, Stoker, C/K 50749, road accident, killed

Sunday, 2 October 1938

Ganges, Shotley/Harwich
  BIRD, Edward F, Boy 2c, JX 156251, illness

Monday, 3 October 1938

Kent, heavy cruiser
  THOMPSON, Douglas P, Able Seaman, C/JX 141095, drowned

Tuesday, 4 October 1938

Victory, Portsmouth
  RAINES, Alec W, Shipwright 1c, P/M 19782, illness

Friday, 7 October 1938

Glasgow, light cruiser
  FARREN, Ernest R, Shipwright 3c, P/MX 45699, accidentally killed

Sunday, 9 October 1938

Pembroke, Chatham
  MUNRO, Henry, Stoker Petty Officer, C/308914, illness

Sheffield, light cruiser
  McCARRY, Daniel B, Blacksmith 3c, C/MX 51606, illness

Wednesday, 12 October 1938

FAA, 801 Sqn, Furious, aircraft carrier, air crash
  SNOW, John N, Lieutenant, RM, killed

Pembroke, Chatham
  BATEMAN, Frederick C, Stoker 1c, C/K 64805, illness

Friday, 14 October 1938

Aurora, light cruiser
  UPTON, Kenneth P, Stoker 1C, P/KX 91207, drowned

Sunday, 16 October 1938

Birmingham, light cruiser
  PITMAN, Frederick G, Chief Petty Officer, P/J 76252, died

Monday, 17 October 1938

Newcastle, light cruiser
  DUNSTAN, William J, Chief Ordnance Artificer, D/M 34953, illness

Royal Navy
  SCANLON, John, Able Seaman, SSX 17110, illness

Tuesday, 18 October 1938

Regent, submarine
  SANDERS, Herbert, Engine Room Artificer, D/MX 49136, illness

Wednesday, 19 October 1938

RN Hospital, Haslar
  SHORTER, Leonard F T, Supply Chief Petty Officer, P/M 37639, illness

Friday, 21 October 1938

Revenge, battleship
 WIDGER, Kenneth J, Able Seaman, D/SSX 20228, died

Saturday, 29 October 1938

RN Hospital, Haslar
 MORRIS, Nelson V, Petty Officer, P/216174, illness

Monday, 31 October 1938

Forth, submarine depot ship
 CURRY, John H, Chief Engine Room Artificer, MX 46717, accidentally killed

Tuesday, 1 November 1938

Belfast, light cruiser
 WILSON, Philip L, Engineer Commander, illness

Hobart (RAN), light cruiser
 WEBB, Walter R, Ordinary Seaman, RAN, 21363, died

Friday, 4 November 1938

Furious, aircraft carrier
 ROOKELL, George, Ordinary Seaman, D/SSX 21559, died

Royal Navy
 JEFFERSON, Ronald G, Engineering Commander, illness

Sunday, 6 November 1938

Cormorant, Gibraltar
 LEE-WHITE, Ronald, Paymaster Midshipman, illness

Hyperion, destroyer
 WESTWOOD, J (initial only) C, Leading Stoker, P/KX 80045, in France, killed in accident

Monday, 7 November 1938

Tamar, Hong Kong
 LEUNG, Sui, Leading Stoker, (Chinese), died

Sunday, 13 November 1938

Royal Navy
 McKNIGHT, William, Petty Officer Recruiter, C/188612, illness

Monday, 14 November 1938

Victory, Portsmouth
 KIRBY, John L, Ordinary Seaman, P/JX 148912, illness

Thursday, 17 November 1938

RN Hospital, Haslar
 GIBBS, Charles H, Stoker 1c, P/KX 80427, died

Friday, 18 November 1938

Cochrane, Rosyth
 AUSTEN, Frederick T L, Chief Engine Room Artificer 2c, C/M 31522, illness

Diamond, destroyer, sampan accident, all died
 CONNOR, John, Able Seaman, D/SSX 16501
 MUIR, George, Leading Stoker, D/KX 78208
 MULLIGAN, Patrick, Stoker 1c, D/KX 89328
 SHUTTLEWORTH, Stanley, Able Seaman, D/SSX 15187

Saturday, 26 November 1938

RN Engineering College, Keyham
 MORCOM, John E, Sub Lieutenant (E), illness

Friday, 2 December 1938

Drake, Devonport
 COSTELLO, Thomas, Able Seaman, D/SSX 17624, illness

Tuesday, 6 December 1938

RN Hospital, Plymouth
 PITTMAN, Francis R, Stoker 2c, D/KX 94065, illness

Wednesday, 7 December 1938

Ganges, Shotley/Harwich
 SLATER, Guy B S, Lieutenant, illness

Thursday, 8 December 1938

Hussar, minesweeper
 BRYANT, William C, Engine Room Artificer 4c, C/MX 48241, drowned

Friday, 9 December 1938

Drake, Devonport
 HINGSTON, Arthur E, Stoker, (no service number listed), illness

Royal Naval Reserve
 BOOTH, Charles, Honorary Captain, RNR, illness

Tamar II, Hong Kong
 KELLY, Phillip, Able Seaman, C/JX 134903, drowned

Sunday, 11 December 1938

RN Hospital, Plymouth
 BOZMAN, David, Stoker Petty Officer, D/K 64310, accidentally killed

Wednesday, 14 December 1938

Victory, Portsmouth
 PHYTHIAN, Richard, Stoker 1c, P/KX 76632, illness

Thursday, 15 December 1938

Camber (type not known)
 ARLAND, Gerald A T, Able Seaman, C/JX 145158, accidentally killed

London Division, RNVR
 BULL, William M, Surgeon Commander (D), RNVR, illness

Tuesday, 20 December 1938

Sabre, destroyer
 WARD, Thomas W, Officer's Cook 2c, C/LX 20162, illness

Wednesday, 21 December 1938

Suffolk, heavy cruiser
 POWELL, Joseph, Engine Room Artificer, P/MX 54699, died

Thursday, 22 December 1938

Norfolk, heavy cruiser
 MOIST, Leslie, Able Seaman, D/J 81175, illness

Friday, 23 December 1938

FAA, 714 Flight, Manchester, light cruiser, air crash, both killed
 BOXER, Peter N, Sub Lieutenant
 COLLIS, John F R, Sub Lieutenant (A)

Royal Navy
 HEARNE, Joseph, Regulating Petty Officer, D/M 39809, illness

Sunday, 25 December 1938

London Division, RNVR
 WATSON, Charles J T, Surgeon Lieutenant, RNVR, illness

Monday, 26 December 1938

Dainty, destroyer
 FARR, Derrick W, Able Seaman, P/JX 141054, accidentally killed

Thursday, 29 December 1938

Shropshire, heavy cruiser
 BAKER, Cyril H G, Able Seaman, C/JX 132107, illness

1939

January 1939

Decoy, destroyer
 TURK, Albert G, Able Seaman, D/JX 133320, illness, date not listed in record

Royal Navy
 RANDALL, Ernest J, Ordinary Seaman, C/JX 144652, died, day not listed in record

Wednesday, 4 January 1939

Malaya, battleship
 ROYSE, William J, Marine, 23164 (Ch), illness

Friday, 6 January 1939

Medway, submarine depot ship
 FAKELEY, Sidney J, Chief Stoker, C/K 56436, illness

Monday, 9 January 1939

Royal Navy
 McCARTHY, Charles J, Signalman, D/SX 86, illness

Suffolk, heavy cruiser
 LEGG, Walter J, Stoker 1c, P/KX 91808, illness

Tuesday, 10 January 1939

Maidstone, submarine depot ship
 PLATTS, Leonard H, Stoker 1c, P/KX 92289, illness

Wednesday, 11 January 1939

Drake, Devonport
 DUMINGHAM, James, Able Seaman, D/SSX 15375, illness

Thursday, 12 January 1939

Medway, submarine depot ship
 RAVEN, John I, Stoker Petty Officer, C/K 60365, illness

Friday, 13 January 1939

Campbell, flotilla leader
 WELCH, G (initial only), Petty Officer, JX 158688, illness

Sunday, 15 January 1939

Hussar, minesweeper
 MALONEY, James A, Leading Telegraphist, C/J 100558, boat accident, killed

Royal Navy
 DAWES, Arthur D, Electrical Artificer 5c, P/MX 58426, illness

Monday, 23 January 1939

Royal Navy
 WEST, John G, Leading Telegraphist, P/J 53099, illness

Friday, 27 January 1939

Royal Navy
 CLARKE, Nelson, Stoker 2c, C/KX 9543, illness

Tamar, Hong Kong
 PANG, Ping, Able Seaman, (no service number listed), illness

Saturday, 28 January 1939

Penelope, light cruiser
 BARFF, Edward M, Lieutenant (E), accidentally killed

Sunday, 29 January 1939

Caledonia, Rosyth
 BELL, Harper, Boy 2c, JX 158259, illness

Monday, 30 January 1939

Glorious, aircraft carrier, flying accident, both killed
 COUGHLIN, Bernard A, Leading Seaman, D/JX 137538
 PEERMAN, Robert H, Leading Signalman, D/JX 135816

Wednesday, 1 February 1939

Galatea, light cruiser
 DOHERTY, Henry E, Petty Officer, D/J 90806, drowned

Friday, 3 February 1939

Dunedin, light cruiser
 HYATT, Archibald A, Cook, P/M 38493, illness

RM Portsmouth Division
 SMITH, Charles H, Marine, X 3652 (Po), illness

Sheldrake, patrol vessel
 HORN, John E, Stoker Petty Officer, C/KX 88273, accidentally killed

Saturday, 4 February 1939

RN Hospital, Haslar
 MITCHELL, Dennis E, Able Seaman Air Mechanic, P/JX 154173, accidentally killed

Sunday, 5 February 1939

Marshal Soult, monitor
 EYRES, Frederick C, Stoker 1c, K 61309, illness

Monday, 6 February 1939

Ganges, Shotley/Harwich
 DABNOR, Frederick H, Boy 2c, JX 159907, illness

Thursday, 9 February 1939

Folkestone, sloop
  HOPKINS, Herbert A, Leading Seaman, C/JX 136803, died

Saturday, 11 February 1939

RN Hospital, Haslar
  PINE, Henry C, Chief Yeoman of Signals, P/JX 149535, illness

Wednesday, 15 February 1939

Pembroke, Chatham
  HARRIS, Richard C, Stoker 1c, C/KX 85030, road accident, killed

Thursday, 16 February 1939

Drake, Devonport
  ATKINS, Ernest F, Petty Officer, D/J 55586, illness

Saturday, 18 February 1939

RN Hospital, Capetown
  SANDERSON, David, Able Seaman, C/JX 148081, illness

Thursday, 23 February 1939

Drake, Devonport
  SHEEHAN, Edric W, Stoker Petty Officer, D/KX 79775, illness

Friday, 24 February 1939

Aurora, light cruiser
  CARTER, Joseph E, Stoker 1c, P/KX 82927, illness

Sheffield, light cruiser
  BROMLEY, James A E, Able Seaman, J 113690, died

Wednesday, 1 March 1939

Rorqual, submarine
  PURKINS, John H, Able Seaman, J 102141, accidentally killed

Royal Navy
  RANCE, Harry T, Chief Stoker, P/K 63059, illness

Thursday, 2 March 1939

Ramillies, battleship
  YOUNG, Charles E, Sergeant, RM, 22052 (Po), drowned

RM Plymouth Barracks
  TURNER, Alec T, Lieutenant, RM, illness

Friday, 3 March 1939

Caledonia, Rosyth, from motor boat
  CAIRNS, David C, Able Seaman, C/SSX 16483, died

Monday, 6 March 1939

Pandora, submarine
  MAYDELL, Stanley A, Stoker Petty Officer, C/KX 77914, illness

Thursday, 9 March 1939

Barham, battleship
  HOWELL, Aubrey W J, Stoker Petty Officer, P/K 58588, illness

St Delphine, steam trawler, collision, all killed
  HOSKINS, Alfred, Seaman, RNR, X 17783 A (Boscawen)
  MATHESON, Angus, Seaman, RNR, X 7434 (Boscawen)
  TUCKER, Oliver G, Skipper, RNR (Boscawen)

Friday, 10 March 1939

Dorsetshire, heavy cruiser
  CLEMENTSON, William E, Marine, X 1632 (Ply), died

Pembroke, Chatham
  HARTLAND, Frederick G, Leading Seaman, C/JX 134825, died

Royal Naval Reserve
  GROUND, Brian K U, Py/Sub Lieutenant, RNR, illness

Monday, 13 March 1939

Curlew, light cruiser
  BULL, Donald S, Boy 1c, C/J 156960, illness

Wednesday, 15 March 1939

Drake, Devonport
  JAMES, Sidney F, Act/Warrant Cook, illness

Saturday, 18 March 1939

Royal Navy
  FALKNER, Hubert E S, Act/Sub Lieutenant, illness

Sunday, 19 March 1939

Hermes, aircraft carrier
  LAMBERTH, Charles W, Stoker 1c, D/K 59731, illness

Penelope, light cruiser
  SOPP, Wilfred H, Marine, X 1136 (Po), drowned

Tuesday, 21 March 1939

Drake, Devonport
  CUMMINGS, Charles W, Ordinary Seaman, D/SSX 28928, illness

RAF Station Gosport, air crash
  O'BRIEN, Dermod D, Lieutenant, DOI

Friday, 24 March 1939

Neptune, light cruiser
  AFFON, Arthur Mc K, Petty Officer, D/J 62910, illness

Royal Navy
  FERGUSON, Robert E, Telegraphist, P/JX 134393, illness

Sunday, 26 March 1939

Pembroke, Chatham
  VAUDIN, George C, Ordnance Artificer Apprentice, C/MX 58919, illness

Tuesday, 28 March 1939

Woolwich, destroyer depot ship
 DREWERY, James E, Stoker 1c, C/KX 87003, illness

Thursday, 30 March 1939

Barham, battleship
 MURPHY, Sidney G, Able Seaman, P/JX 128569, illness

Friday, 31 March 1939

Pembroke, Chatham
 HIGGINS, Alfred G, Act/Cook, C/MX 57607, illness

Saturday, 1 April 1939

Medway, submarine depot ship
 COONEY, Joseph A, Stoker, P/KX 91806, illness

RN Hospital, Haslar
 KELLY, Charles E, Marine, 18486 (Po), illness

Monday, 3 April 1939

Birmingham, light cruiser
 BOXALL, Cyril H, Able Seaman, P/JX 135148, illness

Tuesday, 4 April 1939

Pembroke II, Chatham
 INGLIS, William H, Officer's Cook, C/MX 59002, illness

RM Chatham Division
 SMYTH, Arthur W, Marine, A 21265 (Ch), died

Sunday, 9 April 1939

Victory, Portsmouth
 FENN, Sidney, Chief Petty Officer Cook, P/M 38642, illness

Tuesday, 11 April 1939

Norfolk, heavy cruiser
 JOURDAIN, David C, Paymaster Midshipman, illness

Pembroke, Chatham
 MUIR, Robert W R, Chief Ordnance Artificer, C/MX 58260, accidentally killed

War Pathan, oiler, RFA
 CONNOR, John, Fireman, RNR, (no service number listed), illness

Thursday, 13 April 1939

Rodney, battleship
 PASCOE, Archibald J, Act/Cook, D/MX 55869, road accident, killed

Shropshire, heavy cruiser
 DANNAN, Kenneth P, Paymaster Midshipman, illness

Sunday, 16 April 1939

Royal Naval Reserve
 LAIDLAW, Henry M S, Captain, RNR, illness

Tuesday, 18 April 1939

Belfast, light cruiser
 PORTER, Thomas A, Commissioned Gunner, illness

Wednesday, 19 April 1939

Achilles, light cruiser
 LAMB, James G (rank not listed), New Zealand Division, 1430, illness

Thursday, 20 April 1939

Dwarf, submarine tender, Portsmouth
 BANKS, Jack S, Lieutenant, illness

Somali, destroyer
 BEARD, George A, Petty Officer, P/JX 127198, illness

Friday, 21 April 1939

York, heavy cruiser
 ADAMS, Frank D, Midshipman, illness

Saturday, 22 April 1939

Caledonia, Rosyth
 LEICESTER, Ian E, FAA Apprentice, FX 75561, illness

Sunday, 23 April 1939

Royal Navy
 BRICKNELL, Victor J, Able Seaman, P/J 86829, illness

Tuesday, 25 April 1939

RM HQ Chatham
 JONES, Denis J, Corporal, RM, X 765 (Ch), road accident, killed

Wednesday, 26 April 1939

Motor Torpedo Boat MTB.7
 HAYNES, William G, Able Seaman, P/J 103857, illness

Thursday, 27 April 1939

St Angelo, Malta
 ELLUL, Emmanuel, Able Seaman, E/JX 145940, accidentally killed

Friday, 28 April 1939

Merchant Navy Defence Instructional Officer, Cardiff, Wales
 DICKSON, Thomas H, Lieutenant Commander, illness

Tuesday, 2 May 1939

Royal Navy
 HENDERSON, Sir Reginald G H, Admiral, illness

Sunday, 7 May 1939

Mersey Division, RNVR
 McCULLOCH, John, Py/Midshipman, RNVR, illness

Tuesday, 9 May 1939

Protector, netlayer
 SMITH, Henry R J, Ordinary Seaman, P/JX 145036, illness

Friday, 12 May 1939

Devonport Dockyard
 CORNOCK, William C, Constable, RM Police, RMP X 355 (Ply), illness

Wednesday, 17 May 1939

Eskimo, destroyer
 PHIMINTER, Alexander, Able Seaman, C/SSX 10873, accidentally killed

Thursday, 18 May 1939

Berwick, heavy cruiser
 HALEY, James, Leading Stoker, P KX 79017, drowned

Friday, 19 May 1939

FAA, 802 Sqn, Glorious, aircraft carrier, air crash
 SYKES, William A, Sub Lieutenant (A), killed

Saturday, 20 May 1939

Glasgow, light cruiser
 GOY, Leslie N, Able Seaman, C/JX 138693, fell overboard, rescued, but suffered from exposure and shock, died

Hasty, destroyer
 HUTCHINSON, George M, Able Seaman, D/SSX 16796, illness

Monday, 22 May 1939

Tamar, Hong Kong
 MATTHEWS, Alfred W, Warrant Master at Arms, illness

Widgeon, patrol vessel
 MOREY, Reginald G, Petty Officer, P/J 113934, illness

Wednesday, 24 May 1939

Devonshire, heavy cruiser
 HOKINS, Llewellyn J, Stoker 2c, D/KX 95205, accidentally killed

Friday, 2 June 1939

751 Sqn, air crash
 ROBERTSON, Jack, Act/Sub Lieutenant (A), killed

Peregrine, Ford, Sussex, aircraft accident
 CHARTERIS, Hugh L, Midshipman (A), killed

Saturday, 3 June 1939

Naval Pilot's Course No.3
 THOM, James M W, Midshipman (A), road accident, killed

Pembroke, Chatham
 ROSS, Andrew, Able Seaman, C/J 115702, illness

Thetis, submarine, those on board included commanders of other submarines building at Cammell Laird, Admiralty officials, and civilian employees of Cammell Laird and Vickers Armstrong. Diving accident during final diving trials in Liverpool Bay on June 1, finally lost on the 3rd following rescue and salvage attempts. There were four survivors. Salvaged and renamed Thunderbolt, sunk in action 14 March 1943 *(below, sister-boat Thistle)*

ALLEN, William E, Leading Telegraphist, D/JX 135513
ANKERS, Thomas, Civilian Contractor
ARMSTRONG, James I, Civilian Contractor
ASLETT, William H, Admiralty Civilian
BAILEY, Frank, Admiralty Civilian
BATH, William G, Civilian Contractor
BATTEN, Francis B, Leading Signalman, D/JX 129058
BEATTY, William B, Civilian Contractor
BOLUS, Guy H, Lieutenant Commander
BRAMBRICK, Thomas, Stoker 1c, D/KX 86324
BRESNER, Frank R, Civilian Contractor
BROAD, Samuel, Civilian Contractor
BROOKE, Robert S, Leading Stoker, D/KX 81583
BROWN, William, Civilian Contractor
BYRNE, Alan W, Electrical Artificer 2c, P/MX 47269
CHAPMAN, Harold, Lieutenant
CHINN, Arnold G, Civilian Contractor
CORNISH, George P, Chief Petty Officer, C/J 71379
COSTLEY, James, Able Seaman, P/J 64330
CRAGG, Horace T, Civilian Contractor
CRAIG, James, Stoker 1c, D/KX 77855
CRAVEN, Archibald, Civilian Contractor
CREASEY, Jack C, Engine Room Artificer, D/MX 47691
CROMBLEHOME, Stanley, Able Seaman, D/SSX 14810
CROUT, Robert W, Civilian Contractor
CUNNINGHAM, David, Act/Leading Stoker, C/KX 80547
DILLON-SHALLAND, Harold J, Chief Stoker, P/K 58669
DOBELLS, Gilbert H, Civilian Contractor
DUNCAN, David N, Civilian Contractor
DUNN, Alfred H, Stoker 1c, D/KX 86322
ECCLESTON, Harold, Civilian Contractor
FENNEY, James S, Leading Stoker, C/KX 81255
FRENCH, Howard W E, Engine Room Artificer, D/MX 49582
GARNETT, Richard N, Lieutenant Commander (Taku)
GISBORNE, Edward, Admiralty Civilian
GLEN, Roy D, Commissioned Engineer
GOAD, Thomas T, Petty Officer, C/J 108935
GRAHAM, Graham T W, Telegraphist, P/J 112924
GREEN, Louis E, Stoker 1c, P/KX 80815
GRIFFITHS, John, Civilian Contractor
HAMBROOK, Walter L, Act/Leading Seaman, P/J 115289

HAMILTON, Clifford J S, Civilian Contractor
HARWOOD, George A, Act/Petty Officer, C/JX 134789
HAYTER, Reginald G B, Commander (Naval Engineering Department)
HENDERSON, Colin M H, Lieutenant (E), (Dolphin)
HILL, Albert A F, Admiralty Civilian
HILLS, Albert G, Stoker 1c, P/K 61207
HOLE, Wilfred T, Stoker 1c, D/KX 80876
HOMER, Richard, Civilian Contractor
HOPE, John A, Act/Petty Officer, D/J 81414
HORNE, Charles W, Admiralty Civilian
HORSMAN, Harry R, Admiralty Civilian
HOWELL, Harold G, Engine Room Artificer, D/MX 50785
HUGHES, Joseph C, Petty Officer Cook, P/MX 48198
HUNN, Leslie W, Admiralty Civilian
JACKSON, Peter F O, Act/Chief Engine Room Artificer, C/MX 46112
JACKSON, Stanley, Engineer Captain, (Dolphin)
JAMISON, Antony G, Lieutenant (E), (Trident)
KENDRICK, Edward A, Able Seaman, D/JX 157904
KENNEY, Thomas W, Leading Stoker, C/KX 82462
KIPLING, Robert, Civilian Contractor
LEWIS, Edward H, Civilian Contractor
LLOYD, Thomas C C, Lieutenant Commander (Trident)
LONGSTAFF, Norman, Able Seaman, P/JX 132478
LUCK, Walter A, Leading Seaman, C/JX 134188
MATTHEWS, William A, Stoker 1c, C/KX 87674
MITCHELL, Ernest, Petty Officer, P/J 102658
MORGANS, James A, Able Seaman, P/JX 132797
MORTIMER, Thomas W, Telegraphist, D/JX 138326
ORMES, William C, Chief Engine Room Artificer, C/M 14525
ORROCK, William, Stoker 1c, D/KX 85664
OWEN, Walter, Civilian Contractor
PAGE, James A, Civilian Contractor
PENNINGTON, Lionel G, Commander (E), (Engineer in Chief's Department)
POLAND, William A W, Lieutenant
QUINN, Philip L, Civilian Contractor
READ, John A, Leading Seaman, C/J 107220
ROBINSON, Arthur B, Civilian Contractor
ROGERS, Frank, Able Seaman, D/JX 135735
ROGERSON, Richard, Civilian Contractor
RYAN, Patrick E J, Lieutenant (Trident)
SCARTH, George L, Civilian Contractor
SMITH, Alfred H, Leading Seaman, D/J 80062
SMITH, Cornelius, Civilian Contractor
SMITH, William H, Civilian Contractor
SMITHERS, Cecil E, Act/Petty Officer, C/JX 129326
STEVENS, Stanley W G, Leading Seaman, P/JX 135921
STOCK, Francis H, Leading Steward, C/LX 21640
SUMMERS, George A, Civilian Contractor
TURNER, John H, Act/Leading Seaman, D/JX 134566
TYLER, Donald V, Civilian Contractor
WATKINSON, Arthur S, Civilian Contractor
WATTERSON, William, Civilian Contractor
WELLS, James W, Stoker Petty Officer, D/KX 81583
WILCOX, Norman D, Mersey Pilot
WILSON, Thomas, Able Seaman, C/JX 138072
YATES, Albert E, Stoker 1c, D/KX 81352
YOULES, Edward J, Act/Leading Stoker, D/KX 80198
YOUNG, James, Civilian Contractor

Tuesday, 6 June 1939

Petrobus, petrol carrier, RFA
 PRATT, John E, Ship's Steward, (neither service number nor cause of death listed)

Thursday, 15 June 1939

Naval Pilot's Course No.3, air crash
 REED, James V, Midshipman (A), killed

Friday, 16 June 1939

Penelope, light cruiser
 GARWOOD, Richard H, Paymaster Lieutenant, illness
 MEEKER, Stanley W, Stoker 1c, KX 91301, died

Saturday, 17 June 1939

Barham, battleship
 HOBBS, John B, Boy 1c, C/JX 154987, accidentally killed

Sunday, 18 June 1939

Caledon, light cruiser
 JOHNSON, Frederick R M, Captain, illness

Eskimo, destroyer
 DURRANT, Stanley R, Ordinary Seaman, C/JX 153427, illness

Wednesday, 21 June 1939

Caledonia, Rosyth
 WOOD, Henry, Boy 2c, JX 161252, illness

Sunday, 25 June 1939

Seal, minelaying submarine
 KIDD, Frederick J, Leading Steward, D/LX 21491, illness

Thursday, 29 June 1939

Hood, battlecruiser
 WOOD, William H, Lieutenant Commander, illness

July 1939

Royal Naval Reserves
 COWAP, Charles R, Captain, RNR, died, day not given in Navy List

Saturday, 1 July 1939

Codrington, destroyer leader
 MASON, Joseph H, Chief Petty Officer, D/JX 160909, illness

Pembroke, Chatham
 PALMER, Philip N, Leading Seaman, C/JX 133774, illness

Sunday, 2 July 1939

Ivanhoe, destroyer
 CARR, Robert W, Able Seaman, C/SSX 14782, accidentally killed

Monday, 3 July 1939

Dolphin, Gosport
 DRANSFIELD, Herbert, Able Seaman, D/JX 137532, road accident, killed

Tuesday, 4 July 1939

RN Hospital, Haslar
 TOWELL, Thomas, Marine, 216788 (Po), illness

Thursday, 6 July 1939

RN Hospital, Chatham
 BECK, James M, Sergeant, RM, RM Police, illness

Saturday, 8 July 1939

Javelin, destroyer
 CONNELL, James J, Stoker Petty Officer, K 63236, illness

Sunday, 9 July 1939

Afrikander, Simonstown, South Africa
 MALAFANE, Joseph, Bantie, Cape Station B 10, accidentally killed

RN Barracks Portsmouth
 JACKMAN, Maurice S, Shipwright Apprentice, MX 53959, illness

Tuesday, 11 July 1939

Kempenfelt, destroyer leader
 BAILEY, Reginald C, Stoker 1c, P/KX 91419, died

Saturday, 15 July 1939

Blanche, destroyer
 CAMERON, Robert F, Seaman, RNR, X 18393 A, road accident, killed

Monday, 17 July 1939

Londonderry, sloop
 KELLY, Ernest, Able Seaman, D/J 109116, accidentally killed

Wednesday, 19 July 1939

Matabele, destroyer
 BURCH, Ronald E, Leading Seaman, D/JX 130255, accidentally killed

Friday, 21 July 1939

Colombo, light cruiser
 LLOYD, David M, Lieutenant, illness

Tuesday, 25 July 1939

Glorious, aircraft carrier, flight deck accident
 LEE, Leonard, Ordinary Seaman, D/JX 153690, killed

Kent, heavy cruiser
 WALKER, Robert R, Able Seaman, C/JX 138078, illness

Victory II, Portsmouth
 GILLIES, Wilfred W, Stoker 1c, P/K 60825, illness

Wednesday, 26 July 1939

Medway, submarine depot ship
 BRUNDLE, Archie L, Able Seaman, C/JX 131734, accidentally killed

Thursday, 27 July 1939

Dainty, destroyer
 WATTS, Albert W L, Leading Stoker, P/KX 83422, illness

Saturday, 29 July 1939

Garland, destroyer
 SMITH, Benjamin, Able Seaman, J 109501, illness

Sunday, 30 July 1939

Pembroke, Chatham
 APPLETON, Ernest, Able Seaman, C/SSX 18858, illness

Monday, 31 July 1939

Pembroke, Chatham
 POULTER, William C, Act/Cook, C/MX 59324, accidentally killed

Wednesday, 2 August 1939

FAA, 800 Sqn, Ark Royal, aircraft carrier, air crash, both killed
 NORMAN, William H, Act/Leading Airman, FX 76326
 WATSON, Charles E, Sub Lieutenant (A)

Friday, 4 August 1939

Royal Navy
 DOYLE, Leslie R, Boy, SS 3007, illness

Monday, 7 August 1939

Raven, Eastleigh, Southampton
 ROWLAND, John W, Able Seaman, P/JX 132292, road accident, killed

Monday, 14 August 1939

Boadicea, destroyer
 NEW, John E, Able Seaman, C/J 92566, illness

Tuesday, 15 August 1939

Warspite, battleship
 BAILEY, Samuel G W, Leading Stoker, C/KX 75436, accidentally killed

Wednesday, 16 August 1939

Malaya, battleship
 SWIFT, Stanley, Ordinary Seaman, C/SSX 21825, illness

Thursday, 17 August 1939

Drake, Devonport
 EVISON, Alfred W, Ordinary Seaman, D/SSX 30581, illness

Hood, battlecruiser
 WOOD, Frank, Engine Room Artificer, P/MX 58815, illness

Monday, 21 August 1939

Hood, battlecruiser
 PROCTOR, Donald C, Ordinary Signalman, P/JX 156557, illness

Whitley, destroyer
 JENNINGS, Thomas J, Stoker 1c, P/KX 77678, drowned

Wednesday, 23 August 1939

Tedworth, minesweeper, diving on submarine Thetis
 PERDUE, Henry O, Petty Officer, P/J 104459, accidentally killed

Saturday, 26 August 1939

Drake, Devonport
 McCARTHY, William G, Commissioned Supply Officer, illness

FAA, 758 Sqn, Raven, Eastleigh, Southampton, air crash
 PEARCE, Henry W G, Act/Sub Lieutenant (A), killed

Royal Navy
 HUTT, Reuben J, Chief Yeoman of Signals, P/J 51430, road
  accident, killed

Sunday, 27 August 1939

Malaya, battleship
 KELLY, Richard R E U, Py/Lieutenant, RM, illness

Resolution, battleship
 PULLEN, George E W, Ordinary Seaman, C/JX 151891, died
  from fall

Tuesday, 29 August 1939

Jervis, destroyer
 HUDSON, Dudley J T, Leading Steward, C/LX 20555, died

Pembroke, Chatham
 DOWDE, Thomas, Stoker Petty Officer, C/K 3294, died from
  result of operation

Thursday, 31 August 1939

RN Hospital, Plymouth
 ROBINSON, William H, Able Seaman, 218742, illness

Voyager (RAN), destroyer
 MENEREAU, Cecil D, Gunner, illness

Friday, 1 September 1939

Victory I, Portsmouth
 LENNON, Peter, Ordinary Seaman, D/JX 150778, road accident,
  killed

Saturday, 2 September 1939

Cerberus (RAN), Williamston, Australia
 REILLY, Reginald S, Act/Plumber 4c, 19868 (RAN), illness

Sunday, 3 September 1939 – Declaration of War

NOTES

NOTES

NOTES

NOTES